S0-AIW-356

Household Spending

Household Spending

Who Spends How Much on What

BY THE EDITORS OF NEW STRATEGIST PUBLICATIONS

7th EDITION

New Strategist Publications, Inc.
Ithaca, New York

New Strategist Publications, Inc.

P.O. Box 242, Ithaca, New York 14851

800/848-0842

www.newstrategist.com

R
339.47
H 842

Copyright 2003. NEW STRATEGIST PUBLICATIONS, INC.

All rights reserved.

No part of this book may be reproduced, stored in a retrieval system, or transmitted in any form or by any means, electronic, mechanical, photocopying, microfilming, recording, or otherwise without written permission from the Publisher.

ISBN 1-885070-41-1

Printed in the United States of America

Contents

List of Tables

Introduction

Welcome to the seventh edition of *Household Spending: Who Spends How Much on What*. This edition is unique because it provides a comprehensive analysis of the spending of Americans in the year 2000, making it a vital archival record of the American way of life at this important moment in history.

Since we published the first edition of *Household Spending* in 1991, the economy has cycled through both good times and bad. The nation pulled out of a severe recession in the early 1990s, enjoyed a stunning economic recovery in the mid- to late-1990s, and entered another recession in 2000. Through it all, the average household held a surprisingly steady course. While spending grew strongly at the national level during the decade, it only inched up at the household level. This caution served Americans well, insulating their day-to-day lives from the economy's wild gyrations.

Between 1990 and 2000, consumer spending at the national level showed strong gains not only because of population and household growth but also because the baby-boom generation entered the peak-spending age groups. While spending at the aggregate level was soaring, spending by the average household rose only slightly and fell in many discretionary categories. In 2000, spending by the average household was only 2 percent greater than in 1990, after adjusting for inflation. The average household spent $38,045 in 2000, up from $37,393 in 1990—an increase of only $652, after adjusting for inflation, according to the Consumer Expenditure Survey,

So deep were the spending cuts made by individual households during the early 1990s that many industries still have not caught up. The average household spent 10 percent less on food away from home in 2000 than in 1990, after adjusting for inflation. It spent 10 percent less on housekeeping supplies, 4 percent less on furniture, 13 percent less on clothing, 28 percent less on reading material, and 10 percent less on gifts.

Clearly, Americans have tightened their belts over the past decade, perhaps explaining why inflation remained low despite the booming economy. Most businesses did not dare raise prices, knowing consumers were more than willing to shop around. Because consumers were so cautious during the boom times, they haven't had to cut their spending all that much during the current slowdown. This may be the reason consumer spending remained strong while business-to-business spending plummeted. The stability in consumer spending has kept the economy afloat.

Analyzing spending trends at the individual household level, as *Household Spending* does, provides deeper insight into the nation's economic ups and downs than any examination of aggregate figures. Unfortunately, the complexity of household spending statistics discourages many reporters from tackling the job of analyzing the data. It's much easier to analyze spending at the national level because it requires an examination of only two figures—today's and yesterday's. But analyzing trends in spending at the household level requires delving into the who, what, and why of spending—the mindset and motivations of individual consumers. The seventh edition of *Household Spending* is for those who want to know the who, what, and why. It's also for those who want, at their fingertips, a record of this important moment in American history.

Consumer spending is the result of a complex mix of wants and needs, hopes and fears. This mix determines the success of individual businesses and the health of our economy. Knowing how consumers spend their dollars is the key to understanding where our economy is headed, an insight of immense value as the nation copes with a period of turbulent change.

How to use this book

Household Spending is based on unpublished data collected by the Bureau of Labor Statistics' Consumer Expenditure Survey, an ongoing, nationwide survey of household spending. The New Strategist editors start with the average spending figures collected by the Bureau of Labor Statistics and analyze them in a variety of ways, calculating household spending indexes, per capita indexes, aggregate (or total) spending, and market shares. We do this for hundreds of spending categories by age of householder, household income, household type, race and Hispanic origin, and region.

The Bureau of Labor Statistics' Consumer Expenditure Survey is a complete accounting of household expenditures, including everything from big-ticket items such as homes and cars, to small purchases like laundry detergent and film. The survey does not include expenditures by government, business, or institutions. The lag time between data collection and publication is about two years. The data in this book are from the 2000 Consumer Expenditure Survey, unless otherwise noted.

The Consumer Expenditure Survey uses consumer units as its sampling unit. A "consumer unit" is defined by the Bureau of Labor Statistics as "a single person or group of persons in a sample household related by blood, marriage, adoption or other legal arrangement or who share responsibility for at least two out of three major types of expenses—food, housing, and other expenses." For convenience, consumer units are referred to as households in the text of this book. For more information about the Consumer Expenditure Survey and consumer units, see Appendix A.

Chapter 1 of *Household Spending* is devoted to summary household spending statistics. These are shown for the following consumer segments: age, income, age by income, household type, region, region by income, metros by region, race and Hispanic origin, education, household size, homeowners and renters, number of earners, and occupation.

Chapters 2 through 11 present detailed spending statistics organized by major product and service category (food, housing, transportation, and so on) and include all typical household expenditures. Within each chapter, spending statistics are shown by age of householder, household income, household type, race and Hispanic origin of householder, and region. For each of the demographic variables, tables show average spending, indexed spending, per capita indexed spending, total (or aggregate) spending, and share of spending.

How to use the data in this book

The data in *Household Spending* reveal how American households allocate their spending dollars. The starting point for all calculations in *Household Spending* are the unpublished detailed average household spending data collected by the Consumer Expenditure Survey. These are shown in the average spending tables in chapters 2 through 11. The remaining tables in each chapter were produced by New Strategist's statisticians and are based on the average figures. The indexed spending tables reveal whether spending by households in a given segment is above or below the average for all households (or for all households in that segment), and by how much. The indexed per capita spending tables adjust average spending for household size, revealing the individual consumers who spend the most on a particular product or service. The total (or aggregate) spending tables show the overall size of a particular market. The market share tables reveal how much spending in a market is accounted for by a household segment. These five types of tables are described in detail below.

Average Spending Tables The average spending tables report the average annual spending of households on each item or category of items in 2000. The Consumer Expenditure Survey produces average spending data for all households in a segment; i.e., all households with a householder aged 25 to 34, not just for those who purchased an item. When reviewing the spending data, it is important to remember that by including both purchasers and nonpurchasers in the calculation, the average is diluted, especially for infrequently purchased items. For example, the average household spent $208 on day care centers in 2000. Since only a small percentage of households spend money on day care, this figure greatly underestimates the amount spent on day care centers by those who make use of them. To get a more realistic idea of how much buyers spend on an item, Appendix C shows the percentage of households purchasing individual products and services during an average quarter of 2000, and the amount spent by purchasers per quarter. According to Appendix C, only 6.2 percent of households spent on day care centers during an average quarter of 2000. The purchasers spent an average of $840 per quarter, for an estimated annual cost of $3,360, a much more realistic figure than the average of $208 for all households.

For frequently purchased items such as milk, the average spending figures give a fairly accurate account of actual spending. But for most of the products and services examined in *Household Spending*, the average spending figures are less revealing than the indexes and market shares.

Average spending figures are useful in determining the market potential of a product or service in a local area. By multiplying the average amount married couples spend on children's clothing by the number of married couples in the Pittsburgh metropolitan area, for example, marketers can estimate the size of the market for children's clothing in Pittsburgh. The Pittsburgh media could show those figures to potential advertisers as evidence of the local demand for children's clothing.

Indexed Spending Tables The indexed spending tables compare the spending of each household segment with that of the average household. To compute the indexes, New Strategist's statisticians divided the average amount each household segment spends on a particular item by how much the average household spends on the item, then multiplied the resulting figure by 100.

An index of 100 is the average for all households. An index of 125 means the spending of a household segment is 25 percent above average (100 plus 25). An index of 75 indicates spending that is 25 percent below the average for all households (100 minus 25). Indexed spending figures identify the best customers for a product or service. Households with an index of 178 for outdoor furniture, for example, are a strong market for that product. Those with an index below 100 are either a weak or an underserved market.

Spending indexes can reveal hidden markets—household segments with a high propensity to buy a particular product or service, but which are overshadowed by larger household segments that account for a bigger share of the total market. Householders aged 55 to 64, for example, spend 52 percent more than the average household on gardening and lawn care services (with an index of 152). This is a higher index than that of any other age group, making householders aged 55 to 64 the best customers of this item. Householders aged 35 to 44 spend 21 percent less than average on gardening and lawn care services (with an index of 79), meaning they are a weaker or underserved market for this product.

Spending indexes reveal hidden markets—household segments with a high propensity to buy a particular product or service, but which may be overshadowed by larger household segments that account for a bigger share of the total market. For example, householders aged 55 to 64 spend 119 percent more than the average household on new cars, making them the best customers for this item. In contrast, householders aged 35 to 44 spend 2 percent less than average on new cars (with an index of 98). But the market share of 35-to-44-year-olds is much larger than that of 55-to-64-year-olds (22 versus 15 percent) because there are more households in the younger age group. Using the indexed spending tables, marketers can see that older householders are the bigger spenders on new cars and adjust their business strategy accordingly.

Indexed Per Capita Spending Tables The indexed per capita spending tables compare the spending of each household segment with the spending of the average household, after adjusting for household size. New Strategist statisticians adjusted for household size by dividing average household spending by the average number of people per household in a segment. While the indexed spending tables show which households are the biggest spenders, the indexed per capita spending tables show which people spend the most.

Households with the largest number of people (such as the middle-aged and married couples with children) typically spend more on food, for example, simply because there are more hungry people in the household. But after dividing average spending by the number of people in a household, larger households often turn out to spend less than average on a per capita basis. An index of 100 is the per capita average for all households. An index of 125 means that per capita spending by households in a segment is 25 percent greater than the per capita spending of the average household. An index of 75 means per capita spending by the segment is 25 percent below the per capita spending of the average household.

Per capita spending indexes reveal the best individual customers. The indexed spending tables, for example, show householders aged 35 to 44 spending 15 percent more than the average household on bakery products. But after dividing their bakery spending by 3.3 people (average household size for the age group), their per capita spending on bakery products falls to a below-average 87. In contrast, the spending index of householders aged 65 to 74 rises from 95 to 125, after adjusting for household size, making the older age group the best individual customers of bakery products. While the older age group does not account for the largest share of the bakery product market, it has the greatest propensity to buy bakery products. By knowing who their best customers are, businesses can target those most interested in their products.

Total Spending Tables To produce the total spending tables, New Strategist's statisticians multiplied average spending figures by the number of households in a segment. The result is the dollar size of the total household market and of each market segment. All totals are shown in thousands of dollars. To convert the numbers in the total spending tables to dollars, you must append "000" to the number. For example, households headed by people aged 45 to 54 spent approximately $9.1 billion ($9,117,739,000) on alcoholic beverages in 2000.

When comparing the total spending figures in *Household Spending* with total spending estimates from the Bureau of Economic Analysis, other government agencies, or trade associations, keep in mind that the Consumer Expenditure Survey includes only household spending, not spending by businesses or institutions. Sales data also will differ from household spending totals because sales figures for consumer products include the value of goods sold to industries, government, and foreign markets, which can be a significant proportion of sales.

Market Share Tables New Strategist's statisticians produced the market share tables by converting total spending data to percentages. To calculate the percentage of total spending on an item that is controlled by each demographic segment—i.e., its market share—each segment's total spending on an item was divided by aggregate household spending on the item.

Market shares reveal the biggest customers—the demographic segments that account for the largest share of spending on a particular product or service. In 2000, for example, married couples without children at home (most of them empty nesters) accounted for 42 percent of total household spending on ship fares. The cruise industry could reach an enormous share of its customers if it targeted only this demographic segment. Of course, by single-mindedly targeting the biggest customers, businesses cannot nurture potential growth markets. An additional danger of focusing only on the biggest customers is that businesses can end up ignoring their best customers. This is especially problematic because market shares are unstable, thanks to baby booms and busts over the past half century. Right now, the biggest customers of home maintenance and repair services, for example, are householders aged 35 to 44. They account for 25 percent of total household spending on this item because the age group is filled with the large baby-boom generation. But in fact the best customers of home maintenance and repair services are older householders. Those aged 55 or older have spending indexes ranging from 123 to 153 on this item, versus an index of only 113 for 35-to-44-year-olds. As the large baby-boom generation ages, the best customers of home maintenance and repair services will become the biggest customers as well. Marketers who ignore their best customers in favor of the biggest customers may end up with no customers.

For more information

The seventh edition of *Household Spending* offers researchers a detailed analysis of the voluminous and unpublished spending data collected by the Bureau of Labor Statistics. It provides a convenient way to compare and contrast spending on goods and services by demographic characteristic such as age of householder or household type. To purchase earlier editions of *Household Spending* or other New Strategist books, visit our web site at http://www.newstrategist.com.

1

Spending Overview

Between 1990 and 2000, spending by the average household grew a modest 2 percent to $38,045, after adjusting for inflation. The increase in spending was less than the 6 percent income growth during those years. While the media frequently claim consumers were on a spending spree as the economy boomed during the mid-to-late 1990s, in fact the substantial rise in spending at the national level was the result of demographic change. Faster than predicted population growth, coupled with the aging of the baby-boom generation into its peak earning and spending years, was the economic driver—not a shop-til-you-drop mentality.

Between 1990 and 2000, American households cut their spending on many discretionary items, even though they had more money at their disposal. Food away from home was just one of many discretionary categories in which spending fell between 1990 and 2000—down 10 percent, after adjusting for inflation. Spending on major appliances fell 2 percent during those years, spending on alcoholic beverages was down 4 percent, and spending on apparel dropped a substantial 13 percent. Spending on reading material plummeted 28 percent. Spending on fees and admissions to entertainment events was one of the few discretionary categories in which households boosted their spending. It grew 5 percent between 1990 and 2000, after adjusting for inflation. Also up 5 percent was spending on new cars and trucks.

Americans cut back on many of their discretionary purchases because their nondiscretionary expenses—the spending they cannot control—was on the rise. After adjusting for inflation, the average household spent 45 percent more on property taxes in 2000 than in 1990. Mortgage interest expenses were up 10 percent. Out-of-pocket spending on health insurance increased 28 percent and drug spending was up 25 percent. Spending on vehicle insurance rose 5 percent. Spending on water and other public services increased 16 percent, and telephone service spending was up 12 percent. Spending on education rose 18 percent. Spending on household personal services (mostly day care) rose 13 percent, after adjusting for inflation.

Americans are more cautious spenders than they once were, but spending patterns vary by demographic group. New spending patterns coupled with changing demographics will drive our economy in the 21st century.

Table 1.1 Spending Trends, 1990 to 2000

(average annual spending of consumer units (CU) by product and service category, 1990 and 2000; percent change 1990–2000; in 2000 dollars)

	2000	1990	percent change 1990—2000
Number of consumer units (in thousands, add 000)	109,367	96,968	12.8%
Average income before taxes	$44,649	$42,014	6.3
Average annual spending	38,045	37,393	1.7
FOOD	$5,158	$5,660	–8.9%
Food at home	3,021	3,274	–7.7
Cereals and bakery products	453	485	–6.6
Cereals and cereal products	156	170	–8.2
Bakery products	297	316	–6.1
Meats, poultry, fish, and eggs	795	880	–9.7
Beef	238	287	–17.1
Pork	167	174	–4.0
Other meats	101	130	–22.6
Poultry	145	142	1.9
Fish and seafood	110	108	1.8
Eggs	34	40	–14.0
Dairy products	325	389	–16.4
Fresh milk and cream	131	184	–29.0
Other dairy products	193	204	–5.5
Fruits and vegetables	521	538	–3.1
Fresh fruits	163	167	–2.6
Fresh vegetables	159	155	2.3
Processed fruits	115	123	–6.1
Processed vegetables	84	92	–8.9
Other food at home	927	983	–5.7
Sugar and other sweets	117	124	–5.5
Fats and oils	83	90	–7.4
Miscellaneous foods	437	443	–1.3
Nonalcoholic beverages	250	281	–10.9
Food prepared by CU on trips	40	46	–13.3
Food away from home	2,137	2,386	–10.4
ALCOHOLIC BEVERAGES	372	386	–3.6
HOUSING	12,319	11,466	7.4
Shelter	7,114	6,372	11.7
Owned dwellings	4,602	3,891	18.3
Mortgage interest and charges	2,639	2,394	10.2
Property taxes	1,139	787	44.8
Maintenance, repair, insurance, other expenses	825	711	16.0
Rented dwellings	2,034	2,020	0.7
Other lodging	478	460	4.0
Utilities, fuels, and public services	2,489	2,490	0.0
Natural gas	307	324	–5.3
Electricity	911	999	–8.8
Fuel oil and other fuels	97	132	–26.4
Telephone	877	780	12.4
Water and other public services	296	254	16.4

	2000	1990	percent change 1990–2000
Household services	**$684**	**$588**	**16.4%**
Personal services	326	289	13.0
Other household services	358	299	19.7
Housekeeping supplies	**482**	**535**	**−9.9**
Laundry and cleaning supplies	131	149	−12.0
Other household products	226	225	0.3
Postage and stationery	126	161	−21.6
Household furnishings and equipment	**1,549**	**1,482**	**4.5**
Household textiles	106	130	−18.7
Furniture	391	408	−4.3
Floor coverings	44	121	−63.7
Major appliances	189	194	−2.4
Small appliances, misc. housewares	87	99	−12.0
Miscellaneous household equipment	731	530	38.0
APPAREL AND RELATED SERVICES	**1,856**	**2,132**	**−12.9**
Men and boys	**440**	**518**	**−15.0**
Men, aged 16 or older	344	427	−19.4
Boys, aged 2 to 15	96	92	4.1
Women and girls	**725**	**887**	**−18.2**
Women, aged 16 or older	607	772	−21.4
Girls, aged 2 to 15	118	115	2.9
Children under age 2	**82**	**92**	**−11.1**
Footwear	**343**	**296**	**15.7**
Other apparel products and services	**266**	**340**	**−21.7**
TRANSPORTATION	**7,417**	**6,746**	**10.0**
Vehicle purchases	**3,418**	**2,805**	**21.9**
Cars and trucks, new	1,605	1,527	5.1
Cars and trucks, used	1,770	1,249	41.7
Other vehicles	43	29	48.4
Gasoline and motor oil	**1,291**	**1,379**	**−6.4**
Other vehicle expenses	**2,281**	**2,163**	**5.4**
Vehicle finance charges	328	395	−17.0
Maintenance and repairs	624	776	−19.6
Vehicle insurance	778	742	4.9
Vehicle rentals, leases, licenses, other charges	551	250	120.1
Public transportation	**427**	**398**	**7.3**
HEALTH CARE	**2,066**	**1,950**	**6.0**
Health insurance	983	765	28.4
Medical services	568	740	−23.3
Drugs	416	332	25.3
Medical supplies	99	112	−11.6
ENTERTAINMENT	**1,863**	**1,874**	**−0.6**
Fees and admissions	515	489	5.4
Television, radio, sound equipment	622	598	4.0
Pets, toys, and playground equipment	334	364	−8.1
Other entertainment products and services	393	423	−7.1

	2000	1990	percent change 1990–2000
PERSONAL CARE PRODUCTS, SERVICES	$564	$480	17.6%
READING	146	202	−27.6
EDUCATION	632	535	18.2
TOBACCO PRODUCTS, SMOKING SUPPLIES	319	361	−11.6
MISCELLANEOUS	776	1,109	−30.0
CASH CONTRIBUTIONS	1,192	1,075	10.9
PERSONAL INSURANCE AND PENSIONS	3,365	3,415	−1.5
Life and other personal insurance	399	455	−12.2
Pensions and Social Security	2,966	2,962	0.1
PERSONAL TAXES	3,117	3,889	−19.9
Federal income taxes	2,409	3,055	−21.2
State and local income taxes	562	735	−23.6
Other taxes	146	99	47.8
GIFTS	1,083	1,200	−9.8
Food	70	125	−44.1
Alcoholic beverages	14	–	–
Housing	291	306	−4.8
Housekeeping supplies	39	46	−15.4
Household textiles	13	18	−29.5
Appliances and misc. housewares	28	36	−21.3
Major appliances	8	9	−13.3
Small appliances and misc. housewares	21	26	−20.3
Miscellaneous household equipment	70	66	6.3
Other housing	140	141	−0.7
Apparel and services	244	311	−21.5
Males, aged 2 or older	68	80	−15.4
Females, aged 2 or older	85	125	−32.1
Children under age 2	41	41	0.4
Other apparel products and services	51	63	−19.4
Jewelry and watches	20	33	−39.3
All other apparel products and services	30	30	−1.0
Transportation	70	70	0.2
Health care	38	59	−35.9
Entertainment	94	87	8.1
Toys, games, hobbies, and tricycles	30	33	−8.9
Other entertainment	64	54	18.5
Personal care products and services	19	–	–
Reading	2	–	–
Education	151	126	19.4
All other gifts	89	116	−23.2

Note: Spending by category will not add to total spending because gift spending is also included in the preceding product and service categories and personal taxes are not included in the total. (–) means data not available.
Source: Bureau of Labor Statistics, 1990 and 2000 Consumer Expenditure Surveys, Internet site www.bls.gov/cex/; calculations by New Strategist

Spending Overview:
Spending by Age, 2000

The average household spent $38,045 in 2000, but some spent more while others spent less. Because spending rises with income, the most affluent householders spend the most. Householders aged 45 to 54 are in their peak earning years, which explains why they spent 21 percent more than the average household in 2000, the highest level of spending among all age groups.

Households headed by people under age 25 and householders aged 75 or older spend the least because their incomes are lowest. Householders under age 25 spend just 59 percent as much as the average household, while householders aged 75 or older spend 58 percent as much as the average.

Householders aged 45 to 54 spend more than other age groups on many products and services, including food at home, other lodging (a category that includes hotel and motel expenses as well as housing for children in college), men's and women's clothing, personal care products and services, transportation, education, and gifts.

Householders aged 35 to 44 spend the most on clothes for children aged 2 to 15, while householders aged 25 to 34 spend the most on infants' apparel. Spending on alcoholic beverages peaks in the 25-to-34 age group. Spending on medical services is highest in the 55-to-64 age group. Households headed by people aged 65 or older spend the most on drugs, 98 percent more than the average household.

As the early retirement trend comes to an end, the two-earner couples of the baby-boom generation should boost spending by householders aged 55 to 64 in the years ahead.

Table 1.2 Average spending by age of householder, 2000

(average annual spending of consumer units (CU) by product and service category and age of consumer unit reference person, 2000)

	total consumer units	under 25	25 to 34	35 to 44	45 to 54	55 to 64	aged 65 or older total	65 to 74	75 or older
Number of consumer units (in thousands, add 000)	109,367	8,306	18,887	23,983	21,874	14,161	22,155	11,538	10,617
Average number of persons per CU	2.5	1.9	2.9	3.3	2.7	2.1	1.7	1.9	1.5
Average income before taxes	$44,649	$19,744	$45,498	$56,500	$58,889	$48,108	$25,220	$29,349	$20,563
Average annual spending	38,045	22,543	38,945	45,149	46,160	39,340	26,533	30,782	21,908
FOOD	$5,158	$3,213	$5,260	$6,092	$6,295	$5,168	$3,652	$4,178	$3,077
Food at home	3,021	1,643	2,951	3,484	3,657	3,071	2,448	2,760	2,106
Cereals and bakery products	453	238	429	531	560	441	376	414	334
Cereals and cereal products	156	90	167	190	180	140	123	133	112
Bakery products	297	148	263	341	380	301	253	281	222
Meats, poultry, fish, and eggs	795	437	770	918	970	832	626	727	515
Beef	238	135	239	270	296	243	182	217	144
Pork	167	89	155	186	198	186	143	168	116
Other meats	101	55	98	120	121	99	79	86	70
Poultry	145	86	145	178	169	146	108	130	84
Fish and seafood	110	52	102	126	146	115	84	95	73
Eggs	34	21	30	37	40	43	30	32	28
Dairy products	325	175	317	383	377	321	275	310	236
Fresh milk and cream	131	73	134	157	146	126	112	118	104
Other dairy products	193	101	183	226	232	195	163	192	132
Fruits and vegetables	521	253	488	552	626	558	495	529	457
Fresh fruits	163	77	146	169	187	185	169	164	175
Fresh vegetables	159	74	148	164	201	173	146	162	128
Processed fruits	115	62	113	125	133	115	109	119	97
Processed vegetables	84	41	82	92	105	87	71	84	57
Other food at home	927	541	946	1,101	1,124	918	676	779	563
Sugar and other sweets	117	60	105	147	143	115	93	105	80
Fats and oils	83	42	77	90	102	90	74	87	60
Miscellaneous foods	437	271	485	518	528	398	304	348	256
Nonalcoholic beverages	250	147	247	300	300	263	176	199	151
Food prepared by CU on trips	40	19	31	46	52	52	29	40	17
Food away from home	2,137	1,569	2,309	2,607	2,638	2,097	1,205	1,418	971
ALCOHOLIC BEVERAGES	372	392	431	420	417	371	211	261	155
HOUSING	12,319	7,109	13,050	15,111	14,179	12,362	8,759	9,671	7,766
Shelter	7,114	4,574	7,905	8,930	8,297	6,587	4,597	5,114	4,034
Owned dwellings	4,602	634	4,142	6,433	5,964	4,780	3,043	3,619	2,418
Mortgage interest and charges	2,639	386	2,888	4,302	3,558	2,278	793	1,179	375
Property taxes	1,139	176	755	1,246	1,471	1,462	1,175	1,272	1,070
Maintenance, repair, insurance, other expenses	825	72	499	884	935	1,040	1,075	1,168	973
Rented dwellings	2,034	3,618	3,514	2,067	1,614	1,123	1,140	952	1,344
Other lodging	478	322	248	430	719	685	413	543	272
Utilities, fuels, and public services	2,489	1,248	2,341	2,810	2,857	2,756	2,198	2,438	1,937
Natural gas	307	102	273	350	344	341	310	318	301
Electricity	911	444	826	1,009	1,045	1,048	834	921	740
Fuel oil and other fuels	97	21	58	97	109	113	137	151	121
Telephone	877	589	950	1,018	1,007	909	620	720	511
Water and other public services	296	91	234	336	352	345	298	328	264

	total consumer units	under 25	25 to 34	35 to 44	45 to 54	55 to 64	aged 65 or older total	65 to 74	75 or older
Household services	**$684**	**$226**	**$871**	**$896**	**$583**	**$542**	**$661**	**$498**	**$839**
Personal services	326	154	641	542	147	93	215	99	340
Other household services	358	72	230	354	435	449	446	399	498
Housekeeping supplies	**482**	**194**	**437**	**570**	**532**	**585**	**421**	**511**	**322**
Laundry and cleaning supplies	131	55	125	157	137	184	95	110	79
Other household products	226	89	201	280	247	262	196	241	146
Postage and stationery	126	50	112	133	147	139	130	160	97
Household furnishings and equipment	**1,549**	**867**	**1,495**	**1,906**	**1,911**	**1,891**	**882**	**1,110**	**634**
Household textiles	106	35	120	124	125	125	73	101	43
Furniture	391	270	457	499	471	361	201	256	141
Floor coverings	44	6	42	53	51	56	38	40	36
Major appliances	189	77	181	212	223	221	160	196	122
Small appliances, misc. housewares	87	50	78	93	126	106	54	68	39
Miscellaneous household equipment	731	429	617	926	915	1,022	356	450	254
APPAREL AND RELATED SERVICES	**1,856**	**1,420**	**2,059**	**2,323**	**2,371**	**1,694**	**925**	**1,130**	**701**
Men and boys	**440**	**320**	**511**	**551**	**577**	**395**	**196**	**269**	**117**
Men, aged 16 or older	344	294	368	367	482	352	177	240	108
Boys, aged 2 to 15	96	26	143	184	95	42	19	29	9
Women and girls	**725**	**435**	**704**	**935**	**977**	**687**	**400**	**451**	**343**
Women, aged 16 or older	607	405	561	692	850	630	378	421	331
Girls, aged 2 to 15	118	31	144	242	126	57	22	31	12
Children under age 2	**82**	**101**	**165**	**105**	**54**	**53**	**20**	**31**	**8**
Footwear	**343**	**363**	**394**	**401**	**438**	**300**	**159**	**186**	**130**
Other apparel products and services	**266**	**201**	**285**	**331**	**325**	**259**	**150**	**192**	**103**
TRANSPORTATION	**7,417**	**5,189**	**8,357**	**8,702**	**8,827**	**7,842**	**4,397**	**5,797**	**2,875**
Vehicle purchases	**3,418**	**2,628**	**4,139**	**3,996**	**3,863**	**3,623**	**1,904**	**2,631**	**1,114**
Cars and trucks, new	1,605	1,061	1,845	1,724	1,690	2,097	1,076	1,447	673
Cars and trucks, used	1,770	1,547	2,217	2,198	2,128	1,508	823	1,173	441
Other vehicles	43	20	77	74	45	18	5	10	–
Gasoline and motor oil	**1,291**	**947**	**1,341**	**1,577**	**1,592**	**1,349**	**735**	**958**	**491**
Other vehicle expenses	**2,281**	**1,397**	**2,482**	**2,677**	**2,868**	**2,375**	**1,374**	**1,766**	**947**
Vehicle finance charges	328	228	436	406	391	349	115	182	43
Maintenance and repairs	624	442	570	708	801	672	441	558	314
Vehicle insurance	778	449	774	884	1,002	796	557	673	431
Vehicle rentals, leases, licenses, other charges	551	278	701	680	674	559	260	353	159
Public transportation	**427**	**216**	**395**	**451**	**505**	**495**	**385**	**442**	**322**
HEALTH CARE	**2,066**	**504**	**1,256**	**1,774**	**2,200**	**2,508**	**3,247**	**3,163**	**3,338**
Health insurance	983	211	640	850	976	1,132	1,619	1,608	1,631
Medical services	568	178	367	555	699	721	672	686	658
Drugs	416	81	181	284	407	538	822	744	908
Medical supplies	99	34	69	85	118	117	133	126	141
ENTERTAINMENT	**1,863**	**1,091**	**1,876**	**2,464**	**2,231**	**1,955**	**1,069**	**1,403**	**707**
Fees and admissions	515	271	460	715	637	509	319	416	214
Television, radio, sound equipment	622	473	680	789	696	581	399	468	325
Pets, toys, and playground equipment	334	173	351	451	384	358	187	262	104
Other entertainment products and services	393	175	385	509	514	507	164	257	63

	total consumer units	under 25	25 to 34	35 to 44	45 to 54	55 to 64	aged 65 or older		
							total	65 to 74	75 or older
PERSONAL CARE PRODUCTS AND SERVICES	$564	$345	$576	$644	$682	$569	$426	$479	$368
READING	146	57	118	151	178	179	148	166	128
EDUCATION	632	1,257	585	615	1,146	380	108	149	63
TOBACCO PRODUCTS AND SMOKING SUPPLIES	319	237	310	427	376	349	163	223	99
MISCELLANEOUS	776	322	804	852	927	824	661	761	553
CASH CONTRIBUTIONS	1,192	189	648	1,003	1,537	1,301	1,828	2,022	1,618
PERSONAL INSURANCE AND PENSIONS	3,365	1,216	3,614	4,570	4,795	3,838	939	1,379	460
Life and other personal insurance	399	54	242	412	549	587	378	514	230
Pensions and Social Security	2,966	1,162	3,373	4,158	4,246	3,252	561	865	231
PERSONAL TAXES	3,117	931	2,833	3,874	4,740	3,999	1,330	1,796	804
Federal income taxes	2,409	696	2,205	3,014	3,707	3,062	979	1,338	574
State and local income taxes	562	226	570	734	848	702	145	200	83
Other taxes	146	9	58	126	185	235	205	257	147
GIFTS	1,083	597	716	1,001	1,724	1,345	866	968	755
Food	70	11	32	67	137	121	29	29	29
Alcoholic beverages	14	6	27	18	17	10	5	3	6
Housing	291	143	215	274	428	335	268	268	269
Housekeeping supplies	39	27	36	46	43	45	31	37	24
Household textiles	13	3	8	12	21	23	9	12	5
Appliances and misc. housewares	28	10	19	26	42	38	25	31	18
Major appliances	8	1	4	4	16	9	9	11	6
Small appliances and misc. housewares	21	9	15	22	26	29	16	20	12
Miscellaneous household equipment	70	30	46	73	98	81	69	93	42
Other housing	140	73	106	117	224	147	134	94	178
Apparel and services	244	143	220	279	314	296	163	209	113
Males, aged 2 or older	68	33	57	65	90	107	45	53	37
Females, aged 2 or older	85	46	66	101	131	84	57	69	42
Children under age 2	41	23	50	53	43	48	18	27	7
Other apparel products and services	51	42	48	59	50	57	44	59	27
Jewelry and watches	20	11	18	18	17	29	25	35	14
All other apparel products and services	30	30	29	40	33	29	19	24	13
Transportation	70	166	32	44	93	122	40	57	21
Health care	38	1	9	13	40	45	98	108	87
Entertainment	94	32	81	102	106	124	86	113	57
Toys, games, hobbies, and tricycles	30	11	27	26	31	51	28	40	16
Other entertainment	64	21	54	77	76	73	58	73	41
Personal care products and services	19	12	16	32	21	25	5	7	2
Reading	2	0	1	1	2	3	3	4	3
Education	151	55	41	100	463	125	44	44	44
All other gifts	89	26	43	70	103	141	125	127	124

Note: Spending by category will not add to total spending because gift spending is also included in the preceding product and service categories and personal taxes are not included in the total. (–) means sample is too small to make a reliable estimate.
Source: Bureau of Labor Statistics, 2000 Consumer Expenditure Survey, Internet site www.bls.gov/cex/

Table 1.3 Indexed spending by age of householder, 2000

(indexed average annual spending of consumer units (CU) by product and service category and age of consumer unit reference person, 2000; index definition: an index of 100 is the average for all consumer units; an index of 132 means that spending by consumer units in that group is 32 percent above the average for all consumer units; an index of 68 indicates spending that is 32 percent below the average for all consumer units)

	total consumer units	under 25	25 to 34	35 to 44	45 to 54	55 to 64	aged 65 or older total	65 to 74	75 or older
Average spending of CU, total	$38,045	$22,543	$38,945	$45,149	$46,160	$39,340	$26,533	$30,782	$21,908
Average spending of CU, index	100	59	102	119	121	103	70	81	58
FOOD	**100**	**62**	**102**	**118**	**122**	**100**	**71**	**81**	**60**
Food at home	**100**	**54**	**98**	**115**	**121**	**102**	**81**	**91**	**70**
Cereals and bakery products	100	53	95	117	124	97	83	91	74
Cereals and cereal products	100	58	107	122	115	90	79	85	72
Bakery products	100	50	89	115	128	101	85	95	75
Meats, poultry, fish, and eggs	100	55	97	115	122	105	79	91	65
Beef	100	57	100	113	124	102	76	91	61
Pork	100	53	93	111	119	111	86	101	69
Other meats	100	54	97	119	120	98	78	85	69
Poultry	100	59	100	123	117	101	74	90	58
Fish and seafood	100	47	93	115	133	105	76	86	66
Eggs	100	62	88	109	118	126	88	94	82
Dairy products	100	54	98	118	116	99	85	95	73
Fresh milk and cream	100	56	102	120	111	96	85	90	79
Other dairy products	100	52	95	117	120	101	84	99	68
Fruits and vegetables	100	49	94	106	120	107	95	102	88
Fresh fruits	100	47	90	104	115	113	104	101	107
Fresh vegetables	100	47	93	103	126	109	92	102	81
Processed fruits	100	54	98	109	116	100	95	103	84
Processed vegetables	100	49	98	110	125	104	85	100	68
Other food at home	100	58	102	119	121	99	73	84	61
Sugar and other sweets	100	51	90	126	122	98	79	90	68
Fats and oils	100	51	93	108	123	108	89	105	72
Miscellaneous foods	100	62	111	119	121	91	70	80	59
Nonalcoholic beverages	100	59	99	120	120	105	70	80	60
Food prepared by CU on trips	100	48	78	115	130	130	73	100	43
Food away from home	**100**	**73**	**108**	**122**	**123**	**98**	**56**	**66**	**45**
ALCOHOLIC BEVERAGES	**100**	**105**	**116**	**113**	**112**	**100**	**57**	**70**	**42**
HOUSING	**100**	**58**	**106**	**123**	**115**	**100**	**71**	**79**	**63**
Shelter	**100**	**64**	**111**	**126**	**117**	**93**	**65**	**72**	**57**
Owned dwellings	100	14	90	140	130	104	66	79	53
Mortgage interest and charges	100	15	109	163	135	86	30	45	14
Property taxes	100	15	66	109	129	128	103	112	94
Maintenance, repair, insurance, other expenses	100	9	60	107	113	126	130	142	118
Rented dwellings	100	178	173	102	79	55	56	47	66
Other lodging	100	67	52	90	150	143	86	114	57
Utilities, fuels, and public services	**100**	**50**	**94**	**113**	**115**	**111**	**88**	**98**	**78**
Natural gas	100	33	89	114	112	111	101	104	98
Electricity	100	49	91	111	115	115	92	101	81
Fuel oil and other fuels	100	22	60	100	112	116	141	156	125
Telephone	100	67	108	116	115	104	71	82	58
Water and other public services	100	31	79	114	119	117	101	111	89

	total consumer units	under 25	25 to 34	35 to 44	45 to 54	55 to 64	aged 65 or older total	65 to 74	75 or older
Household services	100	33	127	131	85	79	97	73	123
Personal services	100	47	197	166	45	29	66	30	104
Other household services	100	20	64	99	122	125	125	111	139
Housekeeping supplies	100	40	91	118	110	121	87	106	67
Laundry and cleaning supplies	100	42	95	120	105	140	73	84	60
Other household products	100	39	89	124	109	116	87	107	65
Postage and stationery	100	40	89	106	117	110	103	127	77
Household furnishings and equipment	100	56	97	123	123	122	57	72	41
Household textiles	100	33	113	117	118	118	69	95	41
Furniture	100	69	117	128	120	92	51	65	36
Floor coverings	100	14	95	120	116	127	86	91	82
Major appliances	100	41	96	112	118	117	85	104	65
Small appliances, misc. housewares	100	57	90	107	145	122	62	78	45
Miscellaneous household equipment	100	59	84	127	125	140	49	62	35
APPAREL AND RELATED SERVICES	100	77	111	125	128	91	50	61	38
Men and boys	100	73	116	125	131	90	45	61	27
Men, aged 16 or older	100	85	107	107	140	102	51	70	31
Boys, aged 2 to 15	100	27	149	192	99	44	20	30	9
Women and girls	100	60	97	129	135	95	55	62	47
Women, aged 16 or older	100	67	92	114	140	104	62	69	55
Girls, aged 2 to 15	100	26	122	205	107	48	19	26	10
Children under age 2	100	123	201	128	66	65	24	38	10
Footwear	100	106	115	117	128	87	46	54	38
Other apparel products and services	100	76	107	124	122	97	56	72	39
TRANSPORTATION	100	70	113	117	119	106	59	78	39
Vehicle purchases	100	77	121	117	113	106	56	77	33
Cars and trucks, new	100	66	115	107	105	131	67	90	42
Cars and trucks, used	100	87	125	124	120	85	46	66	25
Other vehicles	100	47	179	172	105	42	12	23	–
Gasoline and motor oil	100	73	104	122	123	104	57	74	38
Other vehicle expenses	100	61	109	117	126	104	60	77	42
Vehicle finance charges	100	70	133	124	119	106	35	55	13
Maintenance and repairs	100	71	91	113	128	108	71	89	50
Vehicle insurance	100	58	99	114	129	102	72	87	55
Vehicle rentals, leases, licenses, other charges	100	50	127	123	122	101	47	64	29
Public transportation	100	51	93	106	118	116	90	104	75
HEALTH CARE	100	24	61	86	106	121	157	153	162
Health insurance	100	21	65	86	99	115	165	164	166
Medical services	100	31	65	98	123	127	118	121	116
Drugs	100	19	44	68	98	129	198	179	218
Medical supplies	100	34	70	86	119	118	134	127	142
ENTERTAINMENT	100	59	101	132	120	105	57	75	38
Fees and admissions	100	53	89	139	124	99	62	81	42
Television, radio, sound equipment	100	76	109	127	112	93	64	75	52
Pets, toys, and playground equipment	100	52	105	135	115	107	56	78	31
Other entertainment products and services	100	45	98	130	131	129	42	65	16

	total consumer units	under 25	25 to 34	35 to 44	45 to 54	55 to 64	aged 65 or older total	65 to 74	75 or older
PERSONAL CARE PRODUCTS AND SERVICES	100	61	102	114	121	101	76	85	65
READING	100	39	81	103	122	123	101	114	88
EDUCATION	100	199	93	97	181	60	17	24	10
TOBACCO PRODUCTS AND SMOKING SUPPLIES	100	74	97	134	118	109	51	70	31
MISCELLANEOUS	100	41	104	110	119	106	85	98	71
CASH CONTRIBUTIONS	100	16	54	84	129	109	153	170	136
PERSONAL INSURANCE AND PENSIONS	100	36	107	136	142	114	28	41	14
Life and other personal insurance	100	14	61	103	138	147	95	129	58
Pensions and Social Security	100	39	114	140	143	110	19	29	8
PERSONAL TAXES	100	30	91	124	152	128	43	58	26
Federal income taxes	100	29	92	125	154	127	41	56	24
State and local income taxes	100	40	101	131	151	125	26	36	15
Other taxes	100	6	40	86	127	161	140	176	101
GIFTS	100	55	66	92	159	124	80	89	70
Food	100	16	46	96	196	173	41	41	41
Alcoholic beverages	100	43	193	129	121	71	36	21	43
Housing	100	49	74	94	147	115	92	92	92
Housekeeping supplies	100	69	92	118	110	115	79	95	62
Household textiles	100	23	62	92	162	177	69	92	38
Appliances and misc. housewares	100	36	68	93	150	136	89	111	64
Major appliances	100	13	50	50	200	113	113	138	75
Small appliances and misc. housewares	100	43	71	105	124	138	76	95	57
Miscellaneous household equipment	100	43	66	104	140	116	99	133	60
Other housing	100	52	76	84	160	105	96	67	127
Apparel and services	100	59	90	114	129	121	67	86	46
Males, aged 2 or older	100	49	84	96	132	157	66	78	54
Females, aged 2 or older	100	54	78	119	154	99	67	81	49
Children under age 2	100	56	122	129	105	117	44	66	17
Other apparel products and services	100	82	94	116	98	112	86	116	53
Jewelry and watches	100	55	90	90	85	145	125	175	70
All other apparel products and services	100	100	97	133	110	97	63	80	43
Transportation	100	237	46	63	133	174	57	81	30
Health care	100	3	24	34	105	118	258	284	229
Entertainment	100	34	86	109	113	132	91	120	61
Toys, games, hobbies, and tricycles	100	37	90	87	103	170	93	133	53
Other entertainment	100	33	84	120	119	114	91	114	64
Personal care products and services	100	63	84	168	111	132	26	37	11
Reading	100	0	50	50	100	150	150	200	150
Education	100	36	27	66	307	83	29	29	29
All other gifts	100	29	48	79	116	158	140	143	139

Note: (–) means sample is too small to make a reliable estimate.
Source: Calculations by New Strategist based on the Bureau of Labor Statistics 2000 Consumer Expenditure Survey

Spending Overview:
Spending by Income, 2000

Among households reporting their incomes to Consumer Expenditure Survey interviewers, average spending was $40,238 in 2000. Not surprisingly, the most affluent households, those with incomes of $70,000 or more, spend the most—nearly twice as much as the average household. The highest income group spends the most on almost every product and service category, with a few exceptions such as rented dwellings and tobacco.

Households with incomes below $20,000 spend less than the average household on almost every category. One of the few exceptions is rent. Many low-income households spend more money than they make. The income they report to government interviewers is less than their reported expenditures. These households make up the difference through borrowing, use of savings, and unreported income.

Income makes a bigger difference in the purchasing of some products than others. Everyone has to buy food, but only those who can afford to do so will buy a new car. The most affluent households spend close to the average on such items as eggs, drugs, and tobacco. They spend well over twice what the average household spends on other lodging (a category that includes hotel and motel expenses as well as housing for children in college), mortgage interest, and fees and admissions to entertainment events.

Table 1.4 Average spending by household income, 2000

(average annual spending of consumer units (CU) by product and service category and before-tax income of consumer unit, 2000; complete income reporters only)

	complete income reporters	under $10,000	$10,000– $19,999	$20,000– $29,999	$30,000– $39,999	$40,000– $49,999	$50,000– $69,999	$70,000 or more
Number of consumer units in (in thousands, add 000s)	81,454	10,810	14,714	12,039	9,477	7,653	11,337	15,424
Average number of persons per CU	2.5	1.7	2.1	2.4	2.5	2.6	2.9	3.2
Average income before taxes	$44,649	$5,740	$14,586	$24,527	$34,422	$44,201	$58,561	$112,586
Average annual spending	40,238	16,456	22,620	29,852	35,609	42,323	49,245	75,964
FOOD	**$5,435**	**$2,517**	**$3,328**	**$4,507**	**$5,118**	**$6,228**	**$6,557**	**$8,665**
Food at home	**3,154**	**1,683**	**2,311**	**2,921**	**2,995**	**3,552**	**3,605**	**4,483**
Cereals and bakery products	474	245	344	449	460	510	542	679
Cereals and cereal products	163	92	117	176	159	177	183	213
Bakery products	312	153	226	273	301	333	359	466
Meats, poultry, fish, and eggs	817	446	633	800	803	938	898	1,095
Beef	243	125	194	230	244	278	268	329
Pork	171	109	141	181	169	193	188	202
Other meats	104	55	80	105	105	122	121	133
Poultry	150	82	110	145	151	174	160	206
Fish and seafood	114	51	76	103	90	134	128	184
Eggs	36	24	32	35	45	37	34	41
Dairy products	339	177	252	305	338	376	401	472
Fresh milk and cream	138	83	111	129	147	142	153	180
Other dairy products	201	94	140	176	192	233	248	292
Fruits and vegetables	544	305	410	519	508	595	580	785
Fresh fruits	170	92	131	168	159	182	172	248
Fresh vegetables	166	91	123	160	152	177	177	248
Processed fruits	120	75	86	110	113	128	134	175
Processed vegetables	87	48	69	81	85	107	97	114
Other food at home	980	510	673	848	886	1,133	1,185	1,451
Sugar and other sweets	125	58	85	107	109	146	147	193
Fats and oils	86	48	67	90	80	96	97	110
Miscellaneous foods	460	223	312	376	405	523	570	710
Nonalcoholic beverages	265	154	186	244	257	324	317	353
Food prepared by CU on trips	44	26	22	31	35	45	54	85
Food away from home	**2,280**	**834**	**1,017**	**1,586**	**2,122**	**2,676**	**2,952**	**4,182**
ALCOHOLIC BEVERAGES	**423**	**189**	**209**	**301**	**373**	**393**	**549**	**788**
HOUSING	**12,527**	**5,932**	**7,766**	**9,372**	**11,115**	**12,872**	**14914**	**22932**
Shelter	**7,134**	**3,447**	**4,343**	**5,209**	**6,562**	**7,371**	**8379**	**13202**
Owned dwellings	4,599	1,228	1,961	2,466	3,735	4,466	6,121	10,619
Mortgage interest and charges	2,673	462	664	1,096	2,030	2,756	3,871	6,841
Property taxes	1,084	446	659	717	924	920	1,302	2,244
Maintenance, repair, insurance, other expenses	842	320	638	654	781	791	948	1,533
Rented dwellings	2,062	1,945	2,208	2,475	2,530	2,567	1,742	1,381
Other lodging	473	273	174	268	297	337	516	1,203
Utilities, fuels, and public services	**2,487**	**1,528**	**1,973**	**2,224**	**2,444**	**2,596**	**2,873**	**3,543**
Natural gas	305	170	242	263	292	307	359	458
Electricity	897	576	764	859	883	930	1,018	1,184
Fuel oil and other fuels	95	81	92	87	85	95	98	121
Telephone	890	553	653	754	899	955	1,041	1,309
Water and other public services	300	150	223	261	285	308	357	472

	complete income reporters	under $10,000	$10,000–$19,999	$20,000–$29,999	$30,000–$39,999	$40,000–$49,999	$50,000–$69,999	$70,000 or more
Household services	**$708**	**$233**	**$368**	**$433**	**$412**	**$569**	**$844**	**$1,729**
Personal services	338	87	165	181	172	247	479	845
Other household services	370	145	202	252	240	322	365	885
Housekeeping supplies	**546**	**208**	**333**	**416**	**469**	**564**	**685**	**953**
Laundry and cleaning supplies	146	70	95	126	135	140	165	244
Other household products	258	91	150	176	235	256	356	448
Postage and stationery	142	47	88	114	99	168	164	262
Household furnishings and equipment	**1,652**	**516**	**749**	**1,089**	**1,228**	**1,772**	**2132**	**3504**
Household textiles	115	20	62	95	97	116	130	236
Furniture	413	135	187	248	301	378	437	1,021
Floor coverings	49	10	23	20	36	46	69	120
Major appliances	195	92	125	143	151	216	230	362
Small appliances, misc. housewares	95	38	42	61	77	118	129	177
Miscellaneous household equipment	784	221	311	523	565	898	1135	1588
APPAREL AND RELATED SERVICES	**2,004**	**868**	**978**	**1,391**	**1,686**	**1,986**	**2359**	**4004**
Men and boys	**483**	**174**	**228**	**347**	**398**	**398**	**578**	**1,022**
Men, aged 16 or older	382	131	175	266	309	309	461	824
Boys, aged 2 to 15	100	42	53	81	89	89	117	198
Women and girls	**769**	**317**	**349**	**490**	**622**	**861**	**921**	**1542**
Women, aged 16 or older	640	260	294	392	523	743	769	1274
Girls, aged 2 to 15	129	58	55	98	100	118	152	267
Children under age 2	**93**	**50**	**64**	**66**	**81**	**107**	**116**	**148**
Footwear	**374**	**212**	**200**	**302**	**369**	**392**	**443**	**609**
Other apparel products and services	**286**	**116**	**138**	**185**	**216**	**229**	**301**	**682**
TRANSPORTATION	**7,568**	**2,728**	**4,489**	**5,745**	**7,303**	**8,715**	**9656**	**13366**
Vehicle purchases	**3,466**	**1,101**	**2,199**	**2,545**	**3,380**	**4,261**	**4408**	**6015**
Cars and trucks, new	1,612	326	662	1,168	1,453	1,896	1986	3434
Cars and trucks, used	1,804	753	1,529	1,353	1,926	2,302	2317	2456
Other vehicles	50	–	–	–	–	62	105	126
Gasoline and motor oil	**1,316**	**597**	**829**	**1,088**	**1,340**	**1,484**	**1,729**	**2,059**
Other vehicle expenses	**2,345**	**836**	**1,232**	**1,812**	**2,223**	**2,605**	**3,029**	**4,313**
Vehicle finance charges	337	72	135	251	340	411	542	595
Maintenance and repairs	659	290	416	556	634	745	771	1115
Vehicle insurance	798	298	475	695	825	927	1,052	1,271
Vehicle rentals, leases, licenses, other charges	550	176	206	309	424	521	664	1,333
Public transportation	**441**	**194**	**229**	**300**	**360**	**366**	**489**	**978**
HEALTH CARE	**2,120**	**1,248**	**1,943**	**2,018**	**1,977**	**2,173**	**2320**	**2,882**
Health insurance	985	606	901	977	953	1,031	1,083	1,259
Medical services	583	283	423	474	529	605	679	984
Drugs	447	307	539	480	411	433	423	467
Medical supplies	105	52	80	88	83	104	134	172
ENTERTAINMENT	**1,958**	**763**	**957**	**1,399**	**1,658**	**1,982**	**2,507**	**3,912**
Fees and admissions	535	194	203	303	351	417	620	1,383
Television, radio, sound equipment	654	341	419	512	619	738	794	1,083
Pets, toys, and playground equipment	355	124	178	283	339	368	455	657
Other entertainment products and services	412	104	156	302	348	459	638	789

	complete income reporters	under $10,000	$10,000–$19,999	$20,000–$29,999	$30,000–$39,999	$40,000–$49,999	$50,000–$69,999	$70,000 or more
PERSONAL CARE PRODUCTS AND SERVICES	595	306	376	479	522	652	718	993
READING	156	69	86	127	138	151	191	294
EDUCATION	636	533	254	303	437	446	704	1,489
TOBACCO PRODUCTS AND SMOKING SUPPLIES	333	260	278	358	357	411	384	329
MISCELLANEOUS	832	386	491	692	804	1,006	1068	1328
CASH CONTRIBUTIONS	1,344	324	652	1,251	1,125	1,003	1269	3,151
PERSONAL INSURANCE AND PENSIONS	4,308	333	811	1,908	3,000	4,303	6051	11830
Life and other personal insurance	415	123	218	311	354	338	500	901
Pensions and Social Security	3,893	209	593	1,597	2,645	3,965	5551	10929
PERSONAL TAXES	3,117	310	151	861	1,702	2,703	4128	10008
Federal income taxes	2,409	227	33	578	1,236	2,024	3095	8045
State and local income taxes	562	48	39	179	336	511	847	1,673
Other taxes	146	35	80	104	131	168	186	290
GIFTS	1,163	527	625	770	891	1,026	1200	2577
Food	66	19	19	30	33	56	81	183
Alcoholic beverages	17	4	6	10	12	7	20	42
Housing	316	124	169	222	223	306	331	695
Housekeeping supplies	44	13	20	37	34	46	59	81
Household textiles	16	3	5	21	7	23	23	26
Appliances and misc. housewares	34	12	15	14	25	51	50	63
Major appliances	10	6	5	3	8	14	12	17
Small appliances and misc. housewares	24	5	9	11	17	37	38	46
Miscellaneous household equipment	78	22	51	59	77	63	83	154
Other housing	145	73	78	92	80	124	116	371
Apparel and services	276	154	169	180	226	281	299	527
Males, aged 2 or older	75	31	58	51	51	49	77	157
Females, aged 2 or older	97	55	51	55	83	103	98	199
Children under age 2	47	20	28	32	44	57	56	83
Other apparel products and services	57	48	32	43	48	72	67	88
Jewelry and watches	24	17	13	17	17	26	28	44
All other apparel products and services	34	31	19	26	31	46	39	45
Transportation	72	42	20	55	45	33	48	211
Health care	43	–	–	49	37	10	31	55
Entertainment	102	43	49	100	113	105	106	181
Toys, games, hobbies, and tricycles	32	12	21	34	33	36	35	49
Other entertainment	70	31	28	66	80	69	71	132
Personal care products and services	23	9	17	13	17	35	26	37
Reading	2	2	2	2	2	3	3	3
Education	149	47	43	19	92	87	151	486
All other gifts	98	73	54	90	92	101	104	160

Note: Spending by category will not add to total spending because gift spending is also included in the preceding product and service categories and personal taxes are not included in the total. (–) means sample is too small to make a reliable estimate.
Source: Bureau of Labor Statistics, 2000 Consumer Expenditure Survey, Internet site www.bls.gov/cex/; calculations by New Strategist

Table 1.5 Indexed spending by household income, 2000

(indexed average annual spending of consumer units (CU) by product and service category and before-tax income of consumer unit reference person, 2000; complete income reporters only; index definition: an index of 100 is the average for all consumer units; an index of 132 means that spending by consumer units in that group is 32 percent above the average for all consumer units; an index of 68 indicates spending that is 32 percent below the average for all consumer units)

	complete income reporters	under $10,000	$10,000– $19,999	$20,000– $29,999	$30,000– $39,999	$40,000– $49,999	$50,000– $69,999	$70,000 or more
Average spending of CU, total	$40,238	$16,456	$22,620	$29,852	$35,609	$42,323	$49,245	$75,964
Average spending of CU, index	100	41	56	74	88	105	122	189
FOOD	100	46	61	83	94	115	121	159
Food at home	100	53	73	93	95	113	114	142
Cereals and bakery products	100	52	73	95	97	108	114	143
Cereals and cereal products	100	56	72	108	98	109	112	131
Bakery products	100	49	73	88	96	107	115	149
Meats, poultry, fish, and eggs	100	55	77	98	98	115	110	134
Beef	100	51	80	95	100	114	110	135
Pork	100	64	82	106	99	113	110	118
Other meats	100	53	77	101	101	117	116	128
Poultry	100	55	73	97	101	116	107	137
Fish and seafood	100	45	66	90	79	118	112	161
Eggs	100	68	90	97	125	103	94	114
Dairy products	100	52	74	90	100	111	118	139
Fresh milk and cream	100	60	81	93	107	103	111	130
Other dairy products	100	47	70	88	96	116	123	145
Fruits and vegetables	100	56	75	95	93	109	107	144
Fresh fruits	100	54	77	99	94	107	101	146
Fresh vegetables	100	55	74	96	92	107	107	149
Processed fruits	100	63	72	92	94	107	112	146
Processed vegetables	100	56	80	93	98	123	111	131
Other food at home	100	52	69	87	90	116	121	148
Sugar and other sweets	100	47	68	86	87	117	118	154
Fats and oils	100	56	78	105	93	112	113	128
Miscellaneous foods	100	48	68	82	88	114	124	154
Nonalcoholic beverages	100	58	70	92	97	122	120	133
Food prepared by CU on trips	100	60	50	70	80	102	123	193
Food away from home	100	37	45	70	93	117	129	183
ALCOHOLIC BEVERAGES	100	45	49	71	88	93	130	186
HOUSING	100	47	62	75	89	103	119	183
Shelter	100	48	61	73	92	103	117	185
Owned dwellings	100	27	43	54	81	97	133	231
Mortgage interest and charges	100	17	25	41	76	103	145	256
Property taxes	100	41	61	66	85	85	120	207
Maintenance, repair, insurance, other expenses	100	38	76	78	93	94	113	182
Rented dwellings	100	94	107	120	123	124	84	67
Other lodging	100	58	37	57	63	71	109	254
Utilities, fuels, and public services	100	61	79	89	98	104	116	142
Natural gas	100	56	79	86	96	101	118	150
Electricity	100	64	85	96	98	104	113	132
Fuel oil and other fuels	100	85	97	92	89	100	103	127
Telephone	100	62	73	85	101	107	117	147
Water and other public services	100	50	74	87	95	103	119	157

	complete income reporters	under $10,000	$10,000–$19,999	$20,000–$29,999	$30,000–$39,999	$40,000–$49,999	$50,000–$69,999	$70,000 or more
Household services	100	33	52	61	58	80	119	244
Personal services	100	26	49	54	51	73	142	250
Other household services	100	39	55	68	65	87	99	239
Housekeeping supplies	100	38	61	76	86	103	125	175
Laundry and cleaning supplies	100	48	65	86	92	96	113	167
Other household products	100	35	58	68	91	99	138	174
Postage and stationery	100	33	62	80	70	118	115	185
Household furnishings and equipment	100	31	45	66	74	107	129	212
Household textiles	100	17	54	83	84	101	113	205
Furniture	100	33	45	60	73	92	106	247
Floor coverings	100	20	46	41	73	94	141	245
Major appliances	100	47	64	73	77	111	118	186
Small appliances, misc. housewares	100	40	45	64	81	124	136	186
Miscellaneous household equipment	100	28	40	67	72	115	145	203
APPAREL AND RELATED SERVICES	100	43	49	69	84	99	118	200
Men and boys	100	36	47	72	82	82	120	212
Men, aged 16 or older	100	34	46	70	81	81	121	216
Boys, aged 2 to 15	100	42	53	81	89	89	117	198
Women and girls	100	41	45	64	81	112	120	201
Women, aged 16 or older	100	41	46	61	82	116	120	199
Girls, aged 2 to 15	100	45	43	76	78	91	118	207
Children under age 2	100	53	69	71	87	115	125	159
Footwear	100	57	53	81	99	105	118	163
Other apparel products and services	100	40	48	65	76	80	105	238
TRANSPORTATION	100	36	59	76	96	115	128	177
Vehicle purchases	100	32	63	73	98	123	127	174
Cars and trucks, new	100	20	41	72	90	118	123	213
Cars and trucks, used	100	42	85	75	107	128	128	136
Other vehicles	100	–	–	–	–	124	210	252
Gasoline and motor oil	100	45	63	83	102	113	131	156
Other vehicle expenses	100	36	53	77	95	111	129	184
Vehicle finance charges	100	21	40	74	101	122	161	177
Maintenance and repairs	100	44	63	84	96	113	117	169
Vehicle insurance	100	37	60	87	103	116	132	159
Vehicle rentals, leases, licenses, other charges	100	32	37	56	77	95	121	242
Public transportation	100	44	52	68	82	83	111	222
HEALTH CARE	100	59	92	95	93	103	109	136
Health insurance	100	62	91	99	97	105	110	128
Medical services	100	49	73	81	91	104	116	169
Drugs	100	69	121	107	92	97	95	104
Medical supplies	100	49	76	84	79	99	128	164
ENTERTAINMENT	100	39	49	71	85	101	128	200
Fees and admissions	100	36	38	57	66	78	116	259
Television, radio, sound equipment	100	52	64	78	95	113	121	166
Pets, toys, and playground equipment	100	35	50	80	95	104	128	185
Other entertainment products and services	100	25	38	73	84	111	155	192

	complete income reporters	under $10,000	$10,000–$19,999	$20,000–$29,999	$30,000–$39,999	$40,000–$49,999	$50,000–$69,999	$70,000 or more
PERSONAL CARE PRODUCTS AND SERVICES	100	51	63	81	88	110	121	167
READING	100	44	55	81	88	97	122	188
EDUCATION	100	84	40	48	69	70	111	234
TOBACCO PRODUCTS AND SMOKING SUPPLIES	100	78	83	108	107	123	115	99
MISCELLANEOUS	100	46	59	83	97	121	128	160
CASH CONTRIBUTIONS	100	24	48	93	84	75	94	234
PERSONAL INSURANCE AND PENSIONS	100	8	19	44	70	100	140	275
Life and other personal insurance	100	30	53	75	85	81	120	217
Pensions and Social Security	100	5	15	41	68	102	143	281
PERSONAL TAXES	100	10	5	28	55	87	132	321
Federal income taxes	100	9	1	24	51	84	128	334
State and local income taxes	100	9	7	32	60	91	151	298
Other taxes	100	24	55	71	90	115	127	199
GIFTS	100	45	54	66	77	88	103	222
Food	100	28	29	45	50	85	123	277
Alcoholic beverages	100	25	36	59	71	41	118	247
Housing	100	39	54	70	71	97	105	220
Housekeeping supplies	100	30	45	84	77	105	134	184
Household textiles	100	21	32	131	44	144	144	163
Appliances and misc. housewares	100	34	44	41	74	150	147	185
Major appliances	100	60	51	30	80	140	120	170
Small appliances and misc. housewares	100	22	38	46	71	154	158	192
Miscellaneous household equipment	100	28	66	76	99	81	106	197
Other housing	100	50	54	63	55	86	80	256
Apparel and services	100	56	61	65	82	102	108	191
Males, aged 2 or older	100	41	78	68	68	65	103	209
Females, aged 2 or older	100	57	52	57	86	106	101	205
Children under age 2	100	43	61	68	94	121	119	177
Other apparel products and services	100	85	55	75	84	126	118	154
Jewelry and watches	100	71	54	71	71	108	117	183
All other apparel products and services	100	92	56	76	91	135	115	132
Transportation	100	58	27	76	63	46	67	293
Health care	100	–	–	114	86	23	72	128
Entertainment	100	42	48	98	111	103	104	177
Toys, games, hobbies, and tricycles	100	36	66	106	103	113	109	153
Other entertainment	100	44	40	94	114	99	101	189
Personal care products and services	100	39	72	57	74	152	113	161
Reading	100	83	77	100	100	150	150	150
Education	100	32	29	13	62	58	101	326
All other gifts	100	75	55	92	94	103	106	163

Note: (–) means sample is too small to make a reliable estimate.
Source: Calculations by New Strategist based on the Bureau of Labor Statistics 2000 Consumer Expenditure Survey

Spending Overview:
Spending by High-Income Households, 1999–2000

Among the nation's 82 million consumer units reporting their incomes in 1999–2000, 32 percent had an income of $50,000 or more. A more detailed look at the spending of high-income households reveals interesting patterns. Spending surges as income rises, in part because affluent households have more earners and more expenses than the average household. In 1999–2000, the average household had 1.4 earners, while households with incomes of $50,000 or more averaged close to two earners. Those with incomes of $90,000 or more had an average of 2.1 earners in the home.

The most affluent households, those with incomes of $90,000 or more, spend the most—more than twice as much as the average household ($88,442 versus $39,776 in 1999–2000). On many products, the most affluent consumer units spend more than three times the average. These items include "other lodging" (motels, hotels, vacation homes, college dorms), household services (much of which is day care), other apparel products and services (such as jewelry, watches, and drycleaning), fees and admissions to entertainment events, cash contributions, and gifts. The most affluent households spend more than four times the average on federal income taxes.

The most affluent households spend close to the average on items such as eggs and drugs. They spend less than average on rent and tobacco.

Table 1.6 Average spending of high-income households, 1999–2000

(average annual spending of consumer units (CU) by product and service category and before-tax income of consumer unit, 1999–2000; complete income reporters and consumer units with incomes of $50,000 or more only)

	complete income reporters	$50,000–$59,999	$60,000–$69,999	$70,000–$89,999	$90,000 or more
Number of consumer units in (in thousands, add 000s)	81,573	6,266	4,901	6,856	8,440
Average number of persons per CU	2.5	2.9	2.9	3.1	3.1
Average income before taxes	$44,299	$54,161	$64,087	$78,622	$140,940
Average annual spending	39,776	47,689	51,931	61,711	88,442
FOOD	**$5,325**	**$6,363**	**$6,777**	**$7,744**	**$9,450**
Food at home	**3,082**	**3,583**	**3,763**	**4,169**	**4,597**
Cereals and bakery products	467	546	579	624	712
Cereals and cereal products	163	184	195	205	223
Bakery products	305	362	385	419	489
Meats, poultry, fish, and eggs	788	899	913	1,027	1,087
Beef	231	267	277	317	320
Pork	164	187	188	191	198
Other meats	102	121	124	126	132
Poultry	145	161	165	192	212
Fish and seafood	111	130	122	162	185
Eggs	34	33	37	39	40
Dairy products	339	400	431	471	496
Fresh milk and cream	133	150	166	169	181
Other dairy products	206	250	265	303	315
Fruits and vegetables	529	568	615	699	825
Fresh fruits	164	170	180	217	265
Fresh vegetables	160	172	182	214	253
Processed fruits	118	135	140	158	186
Processed vegetables	88	91	112	111	121
Other food at home	959	1,170	1,225	1,347	1,477
Sugar and other sweets	122	150	156	160	195
Fats and oils	85	98	94	112	106
Miscellaneous foods	449	552	590	665	709
Nonalcoholic beverages	259	319	332	345	360
Food prepared by CU on trips	44	52	53	65	107
Food away from home	**2,243**	**2,780**	**3,014**	**3,575**	**4,853**
ALCOHOLIC BEVERAGES	**385**	**498**	**500**	**564**	**886**
HOUSING	**12,421**	**14,259**	**15,700**	**18,263**	**26,841**
Shelter	**7,098**	**7,892**	**8,921**	**10,544**	**15,522**
Owned dwellings	4,552	5,453	6,779	8,271	12,633
Mortgage interest and charges	2,595	3,346	4,274	5,320	7,811
Property taxes	1,082	1,162	1,491	1,704	2,754
Maintenance, repair, insurance, other expenses	875	944	1,014	1,248	2,067
Rented dwellings	2,071	1,988	1,549	1,446	1,278
Other lodging	474	451	593	826	1,611
Utilities, fuels, and public services	**2,428**	**2,756**	**2,934**	**3,147**	**3,747**
Natural gas	283	321	343	379	469
Electricity	893	1,016	1,049	1,100	1,268
Fuel oil and other fuels	86	82	94	101	124
Telephone	871	994	1,075	1,150	1,377
Water and other public services	295	343	373	418	508

	complete income reporters	$50,000–$59,999	$60,000–$69,999	$70,000–$89,999	$90,000 or more
Household services	**$713**	**$844**	**$796**	**$1,170**	**$2,337**
Personal services	347	514	392	684	1,055
Other household services	366	330	404	486	1,282
Housekeeping supplies	**547**	**697**	**778**	**855**	**1,023**
Laundry and cleaning supplies	139	148	190	204	221
Other household products	268	368	416	439	507
Postage and stationery	141	181	172	213	296
Household furnishings and equipment	**1,636**	**2,070**	**2,271**	**2,546**	**4,212**
Household textiles	120	114	194	182	279
Furniture	402	450	508	628	1,178
Floor coverings	48	50	73	97	126
Major appliances	193	183	283	246	440
Small appliances, misc. housewares	105	167	139	176	237
Miscellaneous household equipment	768	1,106	1,074	1,216	1,953
APPAREL AND RELATED SERVICES	**1,951**	**2,190**	**2,385**	**2,886**	**4,648**
Men and boys	**473**	**538**	**625**	**734**	**1,218**
Men, aged 16 or older	373	403	499	573	1,027
Boys, aged 2 to 15	100	135	127	161	190
Women and girls	**742**	**833**	**912**	**1,100**	**1,704**
Women, aged 16 or older	621	693	750	916	1,422
Girls, aged 2 to 15	121	140	162	184	282
Children under age 2	**88**	**112**	**114**	**129**	**153**
Footwear	**350**	**410**	**412**	**490**	**588**
Other apparel products and services	**298**	**297**	**322**	**431**	**986**
TRANSPORTATION	**7,394**	**9,243**	**9,874**	**11,735**	**14,687**
Vehicle purchases	**3,436**	**4,415**	**4,297**	**5,537**	**6,783**
Cars and trucks, new	1,614	1,923	1,837	2,809	4,246
Cars and trucks, used	1,780	2,407	2,411	2,652	2,416
Other vehicles	43	86	49	75	121
Gasoline and motor oil	**1,193**	**1,532**	**1,669**	**1,802**	**1,916**
Other vehicle expenses	**2,340**	**2,904**	**3,319**	**3,739**	**4,785**
Vehicle finance charges	333	519	561	594	587
Maintenance and repairs	685	768	886	977	1,300
Vehicle insurance	790	1,015	1,097	1,206	1,357
Vehicle rentals, leases, licenses, other charges	532	602	775	961	1,541
Public transportation	**425**	**393**	**588**	**658**	**1,203**
HEALTH CARE	**2,081**	**2,281**	**2,450**	**2,514**	**3,168**
Health insurance	965	1,058	1,095	1,162	1,303
Medical services	581	694	738	804	1,158
Drugs	422	376	479	402	512
Medical supplies	112	153	137	146	195
ENTERTAINMENT	**1,992**	**2,581**	**2,760**	**3,288**	**4,734**
Fees and admissions	530	573	751	878	1,726
Television, radio, sound equipment	643	807	852	1,013	1,087
Pets, toys, and playground equipment	361	484	490	603	746
Other entertainment products and services	458	717	667	793	1,175

	complete income reporters	$50,000–$59,999	$60,000–$69,999	$70,000–$89,999	$90,000 or more
PERSONAL CARE PRODUCTS AND SERVICES	$579	$696	$692	$845	$1,063
READING	163	183	220	250	363
EDUCATION	614	644	667	1,036	1,803
TOBACCO PRODUCTS AND SMOKING SUPPLIES	324	400	371	399	271
MISCELLANEOUS	884	985	1,210	1,121	2,046
CASH CONTRIBUTIONS	1,343	1,482	1,646	1,961	4,224
PERSONAL INSURANCE AND PENSIONS	4,320	5,884	6,680	9,107	14,257
Life and other personal insurance	411	459	572	698	1,128
Pensions and Social Security	3,909	5,425	6,108	8,408	13,129
PERSONAL TAXES	3,208	3,878	4,755	6,289	13,762
Federal income taxes	2,461	2,905	3,572	4,874	11,066
State and local income taxes	589	819	949	1,181	2,287
Other taxes	158	153	234	235	409
GIFTS	1,160	1,158	1,390	1,559	3,481
Food	76	61	102	127	318
Alcoholic beverages	17	13	33	31	44
Housing	311	338	353	401	917
Housekeeping supplies	45	65	71	66	99
Household textiles	17	19	21	25	37
Appliances and misc. housewares	34	40	53	67	76
Major appliances	9	13	6	18	10
Small appliances and misc. housewares	25	27	47	49	66
Miscellaneous household equipment	75	76	89	105	205
Other housing	139	138	118	138	500
Apparel and services	256	232	359	314	614
Males, aged 2 or older	67	47	101	89	177
Females, aged 2 or older	89	77	119	93	249
Children under age 2	45	48	63	68	93
Other apparel products and services	56	61	76	65	95
Jewelry and watches	26	33	33	42	37
All other apparel products and services	30	27	42	23	57
Transportation	70	73	60	94	238
Health care	44	36	29	47	88
Entertainment	110	125	142	128	294
Toys, games, hobbies, and tricycles	33	41	46	42	60
Other entertainment	77	84	95	87	235
Personal care products and services	22	29	18	32	32
Reading	2	2	3	2	5
Education	151	160	174	257	693
All other gifts	100	87	117	125	237

Note: Spending by category will not add to total spending because gift spending is also included in the preceding product and service categories and personal taxes are not included in the total.
Source: Bureau of Labor Statistics, 1999 and 2000 Consumer Expenditure Surveys, Internet site www.bls.gov/cex/

Table 1.7 Indexed spending of high-income households, 1999–2000

(indexed average annual spending of consumer units (CU) by product and service category and before-tax income of consumer unit reference person, 1999–2000; complete income reporters and consumer units with incomes of $50,000 or more only; index definition: an index of 100 is the average for all consumer units; an index of 132 means that spending by consumer units in that group is 32 percent above the average for all consumer units; an index of 68 indicates spending that is 32 percent below the average for all consumer units)

	complete income reporters	$50,000–$59,999	$60,000–$69,999	$70,000–$89,999	$90,000 or more
Average spending of CU, total	$39,776	$47,689	$51,931	$61,711	$88,442
Average spending of CU, index	100	120	131	155	222
FOOD	**100**	**119**	**127**	**145**	**177**
Food at home	**100**	**116**	**122**	**135**	**149**
Cereals and bakery products	100	117	124	134	152
Cereals and cereal products	100	113	120	126	137
Bakery products	100	119	126	137	160
Meats, poultry, fish, and eggs	100	114	116	130	138
Beef	100	116	120	137	139
Pork	100	114	115	116	121
Other meats	100	119	122	124	129
Poultry	100	111	114	132	146
Fish and seafood	100	117	110	146	167
Eggs	100	97	109	115	118
Dairy products	100	118	127	139	146
Fresh milk and cream	100	113	125	127	136
Other dairy products	100	121	129	147	153
Fruits and vegetables	100	107	116	132	156
Fresh fruits	100	104	110	132	162
Fresh vegetables	100	108	114	134	158
Processed fruits	100	114	119	134	158
Processed vegetables	100	103	127	126	138
Other food at home	100	122	128	140	154
Sugar and other sweets	100	123	128	131	160
Fats and oils	100	115	111	132	125
Miscellaneous foods	100	123	131	148	158
Nonalcoholic beverages	100	123	128	133	139
Food prepared by CU on trips	100	118	120	148	243
Food away from home	**100**	**124**	**134**	**159**	**216**
ALCOHOLIC BEVERAGES	**100**	**129**	**130**	**146**	**230**
HOUSING	**100**	**115**	**126**	**147**	**216**
Shelter	**100**	**111**	**126**	**149**	**219**
Owned dwellings	100	120	149	182	278
Mortgage interest and charges	100	129	165	205	301
Property taxes	100	107	138	157	255
Maintenance, repair, insurance, other expenses	100	108	116	143	236
Rented dwellings	100	96	75	70	62
Other lodging	100	95	125	174	340
Utilities, fuels, and public services	**100**	**114**	**121**	**130**	**154**
Natural gas	100	113	121	134	166
Electricity	100	114	117	123	142
Fuel oil and other fuels	100	95	109	117	144
Telephone	100	114	123	132	158
Water and other public services	100	116	126	142	172

	complete income reporters	$50,000–$59,999	$60,000–$69,999	$70,000–$89,999	$90,000 or more
Household services	100	118	112	164	328
Personal services	100	148	113	197	304
Other household services	100	90	110	133	350
Housekeeping supplies	100	127	142	156	187
Laundry and cleaning supplies	100	106	137	147	159
Other household products	100	137	155	164	189
Postage and stationery	100	128	122	151	210
Household furnishings and equipment	100	127	139	156	257
Household textiles	100	95	162	152	233
Furniture	100	112	126	156	293
Floor coverings	100	104	152	202	263
Major appliances	100	95	147	127	228
Small appliances, misc. housewares	100	159	132	168	226
Miscellaneous household equipment	100	144	140	158	254
APPAREL AND RELATED SERVICES	100	112	122	148	238
Men and boys	100	114	132	155	258
Men, aged 16 or older	100	108	134	154	275
Boys, aged 2 to 15	100	135	127	161	190
Women and girls	100	112	123	148	230
Women, aged 16 or older	100	112	121	148	229
Girls, aged 2 to 15	100	116	134	152	233
Children under age 2	100	127	130	147	174
Footwear	100	117	118	140	168
Other apparel products and services	100	100	108	145	331
TRANSPORTATION	100	125	134	159	199
Vehicle purchases	100	128	125	161	197
Cars and trucks, new	100	119	114	174	263
Cars and trucks, used	100	135	135	149	136
Other vehicles	100	200	114	174	281
Gasoline and motor oil	100	128	140	151	161
Other vehicle expenses	100	124	142	160	204
Vehicle finance charges	100	156	168	178	176
Maintenance and repairs	100	112	129	143	190
Vehicle insurance	100	128	139	153	172
Vehicle rentals, leases, licenses, other charges	100	113	146	181	290
Public transportation	100	92	138	155	283
HEALTH CARE	100	110	118	121	152
Health insurance	100	110	113	120	135
Medical services	100	119	127	138	199
Drugs	100	89	114	95	121
Medical supplies	100	137	122	130	174
ENTERTAINMENT	100	130	139	165	238
Fees and admissions	100	108	142	166	326
Television, radio, sound equipment	100	126	133	158	169
Pets, toys, and playground equipment	100	134	136	167	207
Other entertainment products and services	100	157	146	173	257

	complete income reporters	$50,000–$59,999	$60,000–$69,999	$70,000–$89,999	$90,000 or more
PERSONAL CARE PRODUCTS AND SERVICES	100	120	120	146	184
READING	100	112	135	153	223
EDUCATION	100	105	109	169	294
TOBACCO PRODUCTS AND SMOKING SUPPLIES	100	123	115	123	84
MISCELLANEOUS	100	111	137	127	231
CASH CONTRIBUTIONS	100	110	123	146	315
PERSONAL INSURANCE AND PENSIONS	100	136	155	211	330
Life and other personal insurance	100	112	139	170	274
Pensions and Social Security	100	139	156	215	336
PERSONAL TAXES	100	121	148	196	429
Federal income taxes	100	118	145	198	450
State and local income taxes	100	139	161	201	388
Other taxes	100	97	148	149	259
GIFTS	100	100	120	134	300
Food	100	80	134	167	418
Alcoholic beverages	100	76	194	182	259
Housing	100	109	114	129	295
Housekeeping supplies	100	144	158	147	220
Household textiles	100	112	124	147	218
Appliances and misc. housewares	100	118	156	197	224
Major appliances	100	144	67	200	111
Small appliances and misc. housewares	100	108	188	196	264
Miscellaneous household equipment	100	101	119	140	273
Other housing	100	99	85	99	360
Apparel and services	100	91	140	123	240
Males, aged 2 or older	100	70	151	133	264
Females, aged 2 or older	100	87	134	104	280
Children under age 2	100	107	140	151	207
Other apparel products and services	100	109	136	116	170
Jewelry and watches	100	127	127	162	142
All other apparel products and services	100	90	140	77	190
Transportation	100	104	86	134	340
Health care	100	82	66	107	200
Entertainment	100	114	129	116	267
Toys, games, hobbies, and tricycles	100	124	139	127	182
Other entertainment	100	109	123	113	305
Personal care products and services	100	132	82	145	145
Reading	100	100	150	100	250
Education	100	106	115	170	459
All other gifts	100	87	117	125	237

Source: Calculations by New Strategist based on the Bureau of Labor Statistics 1999 and 2000 Consumer Expenditure Surveys

Spending Overview:

Spending by Age and Income, 1999–2000

Within age groups, spending on most categories of products and services rises with income. There are some interesting exceptions, however. Among householders under age 25, those with incomes below $10,000 spend the most on education—fully $1,642 in 1999–2000. These young adults are attending college. Their incomes will rise when their schooling is complete and they embark on a career.

Only 5 percent of householders aged 65 or older have incomes of $70,000 or more. The proportion is a larger 22 percent among householders aged 55 to 64, and an even larger 31 percent among those aged 45 to 54.

Householders aged 65 or older with incomes of $70,000 or more spent the most in 1999–2000, fully $79,921. This age/income group spent $4,681 on apparel and $3,907 on entertainment (compared to the $1,951 and $1,992, respectively, the average household spent in 1999–2000). Close behind in spending are affluent householders aged 45 to 54 (spending $78,928 in 1999–2000) and 55 to 64 (spending $78,593). Affluent householders aged 55 to 64 spent slightly more on food away from home ($3,888) than on food at home ($3,834) in 1999–2000.

Table 1.8 Under age 25: Average spending by income, 1999–2000

(average annual spending of consumer units (CU) headed by people under age 25 by product and service category and before-tax income of consumer unit, 1999–2000; complete income reporters only)

	complete income reporters under 25	under $10,000	$10,000–$19,999	$20,000–$29,999	$30,000–$39,999	$40,000 or more
Number of consumer units in (in thousands, add 000s)	6,192	2,417	1,584	929	587	674
Average number of persons per CU	1.8	1.3	1.8	2.1	2.5	2.8
Average income before taxes	$19,018	$4,748	$14,238	$23,894	$34,222	$61,471
Average annual spending	23,146	13,297	20,029	28,009	33,285	48,220
FOOD	$3,303	$2,015	$3,052	$3,797	$4,262	$5,902
Food at home	1,689	981	1,698	1,814	2,051	3,143
Cereals and bakery products	247	140	261	251	287	480
Cereals and cereal products	93	55	93	99	111	173
Bakery products	155	85	168	152	176	306
Meats, poultry, fish, and eggs	431	224	425	472	481	898
Beef	131	56	145	132	158	285
Pork	86	55	84	83	79	179
Other meats	57	35	47	72	65	108
Poultry	83	38	82	94	99	176
Fish and seafood	54	30	47	69	57	113
Eggs	20	11	21	22	22	37
Dairy products	184	106	188	193	257	324
Fresh milk and cream	76	41	85	77	113	128
Other dairy products	108	66	103	116	144	195
Fruits and vegetables	261	150	249	293	310	500
Fresh fruits	78	43	76	91	95	144
Fresh vegetables	71	39	64	79	76	157
Processed fruits	68	39	71	81	74	120
Processed vegetables	44	30	38	42	65	79
Other food at home	566	360	576	605	717	940
Sugar and other sweets	66	47	78	62	73	96
Fats and oils	46	28	50	54	44	84
Miscellaneous foods	277	168	259	318	386	469
Nonalcoholic beverages	155	94	173	153	191	265
Food prepared by CU on trips	22	24	17	18	24	26
Food away from home	1,614	1,033	1,354	1,983	2,211	2,760
ALCOHOLIC BEVERAGES	421	302	337	512	565	674
HOUSING	6,931	4,123	6,283	8,511	9,484	13,862
Shelter	4,369	2,757	4,056	5,239	6,030	8,237
Owned dwellings	589	132	194	516	1,134	2,782
Mortgage interest and charges	352	24	99	284	769	1,859
Property taxes	149	88	65	96	195	599
Maintenance, repair, insurance, other expenses	87	20	30	136	170	324
Rented dwellings	3,500	2,182	3,658	4,605	4,728	5,258
Other lodging	280	443	204	118	168	198
Utilities, fuels, and public services	1,200	691	1,176	1,490	1,712	2,237
Natural gas	97	51	83	123	137	223
Electricity	424	232	432	545	625	754
Fuel oil and other fuels	17	5	12	25	46	35
Telephone	580	361	568	703	788	1,042
Water and other public services	82	42	80	93	116	183

	complete income reporters under 25	under $10,000	$10,000– $19,999	$20,000– $29,999	$30,000– $39,999	$40,000 or more
Household services	**$218**	**$76**	**$188**	**$353**	**$321**	**$519**
Personal services	149	41	126	283	197	359
Other household services	69	35	61	70	124	160
Housekeeping supplies	**221**	**108**	**177**	**283**	**259**	**493**
Laundry and cleaning supplies	58	38	61	73	60	89
Other household products	91	34	76	123	113	211
Postage and stationery	72	37	40	86	86	193
Household furnishings and equipment	**924**	**491**	**688**	**1,146**	**1,162**	**2,376**
Household textiles	39	22	34	73	20	67
Furniture	302	126	194	406	357	995
Floor coverings	7	3	4	8	14	21
Major appliances	93	33	62	64	191	310
Small appliances, misc. housewares	55	29	39	72	77	119
Miscellaneous household equipment	428	277	354	522	503	863
APPAREL AND RELATED SERVICES	**1,363**	**843**	**1,089**	**2,043**	**1,554**	**2,372**
Men and boys	**288**	**152**	**194**	**538**	**281**	**531**
Men, aged 16 or older	259	143	165	493	261	450
Boys, aged 2 to 15	29	9	28	45	21	81
Women and girls	**447**	**364**	**324**	**589**	**565**	**625**
Women, aged 16 or older	407	353	276	504	512	578
Girls, aged 2 to 15	40	10	48	85	53	47
Children under age 2	**111**	**56**	**128**	**131**	**155**	**185**
Footwear	**305**	**143**	**274**	**549**	**325**	**460**
Other apparel products and services	**212**	**128**	**169**	**238**	**227**	**571**
TRANSPORTATION	**5,375**	**2,352**	**4,739**	**6,756**	**8,761**	**12,840**
Vehicle purchases	**2,887**	**1,062**	**2,611**	**3,708**	**4,534**	**7,519**
Cars and trucks, new	1,091	396	751	1,244	1,558	3,765
Cars and trucks, used	1,780	666	1,859	2,425	2,976	3,660
Other vehicles	16	–	0	39	–	94
Gasoline and motor oil	**850**	**529**	**801**	**1,003**	**1,353**	**1,465**
Other vehicle expenses	**1,424**	**589**	**1,148**	**1,848**	**2,639**	**3,415**
Vehicle finance charges	230	55	153	320	473	706
Maintenance and repairs	462	258	451	607	803	716
Vehicle insurance	448	149	376	654	809	1,096
Vehicle rentals, leases, licenses, other charges	283	128	169	266	554	897
Public transportation	**214**	**173**	**178**	**196**	**234**	**442**
HEALTH CARE	**573**	**198**	**418**	**934**	**1,035**	**1,356**
Health insurance	238	62	185	331	511	629
Medical services	200	64	110	451	312	457
Drugs	95	51	101	106	141	166
Medical supplies	39	20	22	46	70	104
ENTERTAINMENT	**1,164**	**780**	**1,017**	**1,216**	**1,767**	**2,247**
Fees and admissions	287	253	235	255	377	499
Television, radio, sound equipment	493	332	486	530	640	921
Pets, toys, and playground equipment	177	86	145	243	263	376
Other entertainment products and services	207	109	150	188	486	451

	complete income reporters under 25	under $10,000	$10,000–$19,999	$20,000–$29,999	$30,000–$39,999	$40,000 or more
PERSONAL CARE PRODUCTS, SERVICES	$360	$239	$278	$465	$555	$601
READING	67	50	65	70	100	103
EDUCATION	1,294	1,642	1,023	810	1,082	1,526
TOBACCO PRODUCTS, SMOKING SUPPLIES	242	128	259	334	377	361
MISCELLANEOUS	344	182	308	446	428	794
CASH CONTRIBUTIONS	223	150	163	222	258	603
PERSONAL INSURANCE AND PENSIONS	1,486	293	999	1,893	3,057	4,979
Life and other personal insurance	54	13	28	75	134	162
Pensions and Social Security	1,432	280	970	1,818	2,923	4,817
PERSONAL TAXES	888	20	394	1,151	1,361	4,393
Federal income taxes	663	6	279	874	968	3,367
State and local income taxes	217	10	111	268	385	990
Other taxes	8	2	4	9	8	36
GIFTS	577	512	384	747	500	1,021
Food	15	21	13	8	1	17
Alcoholic beverages	9	5	6	10	23	11
Housing	139	128	94	218	126	149
Housekeeping supplies	20	13	11	35	34	21
Household textiles	2	4	–	2	6	1
Appliances and misc. housewares	8	5	9	13	6	15
Major appliances	2	1	2	–	–	8
Small appliances and misc. housewares	7	4	7	13	6	7
Miscellaneous household equipment	42	22	11	133	22	53
Other housing	66	84	65	35	57	58
Apparel and services	149	135	129	201	150	151
Males, aged 2 or older	29	36	7	53	13	30
Females, aged 2 or older	43	32	33	66	63	41
Children under age 2	30	27	26	36	36	35
Other apparel products and services	47	40	63	46	39	45
Jewelry and watches	18	24	13	28	7	8
All other apparel products and services	29	16	50	18	32	37
Transportation	122	82	13	200	24	502
Health care	3	1	0	5	11	7
Entertainment	37	32	41	34	31	54
Toys, games, hobbies, and tricycles	13	5	15	20	8	27
Other entertainment	24	27	26	15	23	27
Personal care products and services	20	7	15	40	35	26
Reading	–	–	–	–	–	–
Education	52	75	42	8	53	53
All other gifts	31	27	30	22	46	50

Note: Spending by category will not add to total spending because gift spending is also included in the preceding product and service categories and personal taxes are not included in the total. (–) means sample is too small to make a reliable estimate.
Source: Bureau of Labor Statistics, 1999 and 2000 Consumer Expenditure Surveys, Internet site www.bls.gov/cex/; calculations by New Strategist

Table 1.9 Under age 25: Indexed spending by income, 1999–2000

(indexed average annual spending of consumer units (CU) headed by people under age 25 by product and service category and before-tax income of consumer unit, 1999–2000; complete income reporters only; index definition: an index of 100 is the average for all consumer units; an index of 132 means that spending by consumer units in that group is 32 percent above the average for all consumer units; an index of 68 indicates spending that is 32 percent below the average for all consumer units)

	complete income reporters under 25	under $10,000	$10,000–$19,999	$20,000–$29,999	$30,000–$39,999	$40,000 or more
Average spending of CU, total	$23,146	$13,297	$20,029	$28,009	$33,285	$48,220
Average spending of CU, index	100	57	87	121	144	208
FOOD	**100**	**61**	**92**	**115**	**129**	**179**
Food at home	**100**	**58**	**101**	**107**	**121**	**186**
Cereals and bakery products	100	57	106	102	116	194
Cereals and cereal products	100	59	100	106	119	186
Bakery products	100	55	108	98	114	197
Meats, poultry, fish, and eggs	100	52	99	110	112	208
Beef	100	43	111	101	121	218
Pork	100	64	98	97	92	208
Other meats	100	61	83	126	114	189
Poultry	100	45	98	113	119	212
Fish and seafood	100	56	86	128	106	209
Eggs	100	53	104	110	110	185
Dairy products	100	57	102	105	140	176
Fresh milk and cream	100	53	112	101	149	168
Other dairy products	100	61	95	107	133	181
Fruits and vegetables	100	58	96	112	119	192
Fresh fruits	100	55	97	117	122	185
Fresh vegetables	100	54	91	111	107	221
Processed fruits	100	57	104	119	109	176
Processed vegetables	100	68	87	95	148	180
Other food at home	100	64	102	107	127	166
Sugar and other sweets	100	72	118	94	111	145
Fats and oils	100	60	109	117	96	183
Miscellaneous foods	100	61	93	115	139	169
Nonalcoholic beverages	100	61	111	99	123	171
Food prepared by CU on trips	100	110	75	82	109	118
Food away from home	**100**	**64**	**84**	**123**	**137**	**171**
ALCOHOLIC BEVERAGES	**100**	**72**	**80**	**122**	**134**	**160**
HOUSING	**100**	**59**	**91**	**123**	**137**	**200**
Shelter	**100**	**63**	**93**	**120**	**138**	**189**
Owned dwellings	100	22	33	88	193	472
Mortgage interest and charges	100	7	28	81	218	528
Property taxes	100	59	44	64	131	402
Maintenance, repair, insurance, other expenses	100	23	34	156	195	372
Rented dwellings	100	62	105	132	135	150
Other lodging	100	158	73	42	60	71
Utilities, fuels, and public services	**100**	**58**	**98**	**124**	**143**	**186**
Natural gas	100	52	85	127	141	230
Electricity	100	55	102	129	147	178
Fuel oil and other fuels	100	30	69	147	271	206
Telephone	100	62	98	121	136	180
Water and other public services	100	51	98	113	141	223

	complete income reporters under 25	under $10,000	$10,000–$19,999	$20,000–$29,999	$30,000–$39,999	$40,000 or more
Household services	100	35	86	162	147	238
Personal services	100	28	85	190	132	241
Other household services	100	51	88	101	180	232
Housekeeping supplies	100	49	80	128	117	223
Laundry and cleaning supplies	100	65	105	126	103	153
Other household products	100	38	84	135	124	232
Postage and stationery	100	51	56	119	119	268
Household furnishings and equipment	100	53	74	124	126	257
Household textiles	100	58	87	187	51	172
Furniture	100	42	64	134	118	329
Floor coverings	100	49	63	114	200	300
Major appliances	100	35	67	69	205	333
Small appliances, misc. housewares	100	53	71	131	140	216
Miscellaneous household equipment	100	65	83	122	118	202
APPAREL AND RELATED SERVICES	100	62	80	150	114	174
Men and boys	100	53	67	187	98	184
Men, aged 16 or older	100	55	64	190	101	174
Boys, aged 2 to 15	100	30	96	155	72	279
Women and girls	100	81	73	132	126	140
Women, aged 16 or older	100	87	68	124	126	142
Girls, aged 2 to 15	100	26	121	213	133	118
Children under age 2	100	50	115	118	140	167
Footwear	100	47	90	180	107	151
Other apparel products and services	100	61	80	112	107	269
TRANSPORTATION	100	44	88	126	163	239
Vehicle purchases	100	37	90	128	157	260
Cars and trucks, new	100	36	69	114	143	345
Cars and trucks, used	100	37	104	136	167	206
Other vehicles	100	–	3	244	–	588
Gasoline and motor oil	100	62	94	118	159	172
Other vehicle expenses	100	41	81	130	185	240
Vehicle finance charges	100	24	66	139	206	307
Maintenance and repairs	100	56	98	131	174	155
Vehicle insurance	100	33	84	146	181	245
Vehicle rentals, leases, licenses, other charges	100	45	60	94	196	317
Public transportation	100	81	83	92	109	207
HEALTH CARE	100	35	73	163	181	237
Health insurance	100	26	78	139	215	264
Medical services	100	32	55	226	156	229
Drugs	100	54	106	112	148	175
Medical supplies	100	51	57	118	179	267
ENTERTAINMENT	100	67	87	104	152	193
Fees and admissions	100	88	82	89	131	174
Television, radio, sound equipment	100	67	99	108	130	187
Pets, toys, and playground equipment	100	49	82	137	149	212
Other entertainment products and services	100	53	73	91	235	218

	complete income reporters under 25	under $10,000	$10,000– $19,999	$20,000– $29,999	$30,000– $39,999	$40,000 or more
PERSONAL CARE PRODUCTS, SERVICES	100	66	77	129	154	167
READING	100	74	97	104	149	154
EDUCATION	100	127	79	63	84	118
TOBACCO PRODUCTS, SMOKING SUPPLIES	100	53	107	138	156	149
MISCELLANEOUS	100	53	90	130	124	231
CASH CONTRIBUTIONS	100	67	73	100	116	270
PERSONAL INSURANCE AND PENSIONS	100	20	67	127	206	335
Life and other personal insurance	100	25	51	139	248	300
Pensions and Social Security	100	20	68	127	204	336
PERSONAL TAXES	100	2	44	130	153	495
Federal income taxes	100	1	42	132	146	508
State and local income taxes	100	5	51	124	177	456
Other taxes	100	26	55	113	100	450
GIFTS	100	89	67	129	87	177
Food	100	141	89	53	7	113
Alcoholic beverages	100	52	71	111	256	122
Housing	100	92	68	157	91	107
Housekeeping supplies	100	67	53	175	170	105
Household textiles	100	185	0	100	300	50
Appliances and misc. housewares	100	64	108	163	75	188
Major appliances	100	46	86	–	–	400
Small appliances and misc. housewares	100	53	98	186	86	100
Miscellaneous household equipment	100	52	27	317	52	126
Other housing	100	128	98	53	86	88
Apparel and services	100	90	86	135	101	101
Males, aged 2 or older	100	124	23	183	45	103
Females, aged 2 or older	100	75	78	153	147	95
Children under age 2	100	89	86	120	120	117
Other apparel products and services	100	84	134	98	83	96
Jewelry and watches	100	131	75	156	39	44
All other apparel products and services	100	54	171	62	110	128
Transportation	100	67	10	164	20	411
Health care	100	33	14	167	367	233
Entertainment	100	87	111	92	84	146
Toys, games, hobbies, and tricycles	100	42	119	154	62	208
Other entertainment	100	112	110	63	96	113
Personal care products and services	100	34	77	200	175	130
Reading	–	–	–	–	–	–
Education	100	144	80	15	102	102
All other gifts	100	86	96	71	148	161

Note: (–) means sample is too small to make a reliable estimate.
Source: Calculations by New Strategist based on the Bureau of Labor Statistics 1999 and 2000 Consumer Expenditure Surveys

Table 1.10 Aged 25 to 34: Average spending by income, 1999–2000

(average annual spending of consumer units (CU) headed by people aged 25 to 34 by product and service category and before-tax income of consumer unit, 1999–2000; complete income reporters only)

	complete income reporters aged 25–34	under $10,000	$10,000–$19,999	$20,000–$29,999	$30,000–$39,999	$40,000–$49,999	$50,000–$69,999	$70,000 or more
Number of consumer units in (in thousands, add 000s)	14,708	1,229	2,290	2,348	2,065	1,741	2,535	2,500
Average number of persons per CU	2.9	2.6	2.8	2.8	2.8	2.8	3.0	3.0
Average income before taxes	$43,966	$5,219	$14,747	$24,701	$34,330	$44,114	$58,061	$101,455
Average annual spending	40,001	18,835	23,598	28,765	34,615	41,641	48,023	70,199
FOOD	**$5,485**	**$3,501**	**$3,815**	**$4,673**	**$5,004**	**$5,780**	**$6,192**	**$7,762**
Food at home	**3,020**	**2,179**	**2,579**	**2,887**	**2,638**	**3,110**	**3,407**	**3,671**
Cereals and bakery products	444	301	360	431	387	480	506	537
Cereals and cereal products	174	128	147	192	164	186	188	180
Bakery products	271	174	212	238	224	295	318	357
Meats, poultry, fish, and eggs	782	583	750	780	720	745	834	905
Beef	239	166	249	208	264	257	242	249
Pork	154	97	153	182	128	134	176	165
Other meats	100	59	108	104	83	85	123	109
Poultry	151	135	127	157	133	132	154	195
Fish and seafood	105	85	81	99	81	109	105	154
Eggs	32	40	32	29	31	27	33	32
Dairy products	333	265	246	306	302	354	396	396
Fresh milk and cream	136	120	110	125	132	141	158	147
Other dairy products	197	145	136	181	170	213	237	250
Fruits and vegetables	490	406	438	459	411	463	527	639
Fresh fruits	145	127	133	130	124	113	157	199
Fresh vegetables	150	112	134	149	124	151	155	198
Processed fruits	111	100	86	101	95	107	130	141
Processed vegetables	84	67	85	79	68	92	85	101
Other food at home	971	624	785	911	818	1,068	1,145	1,193
Sugar and other sweets	106	78	68	102	94	118	135	124
Fats and oils	79	66	74	87	67	86	85	82
Miscellaneous foods	495	270	377	446	433	534	596	636
Nonalcoholic beverages	256	195	245	252	203	294	283	290
Food prepared by CU on trips	34	15	20	24	21	35	45	61
Food away from home	**2,466**	**1,323**	**1,236**	**1,786**	**2,365**	**2,670**	**2,785**	**4,091**
ALCOHOLIC BEVERAGES	**448**	**262**	**287**	**324**	**374**	**364**	**485**	**832**
HOUSING	**13,084**	**6,659**	**7,941**	**9,439**	**11,478**	**13,396**	**15,591**	**22,794**
Shelter	**7,822**	**4,023**	**4,738**	**5,583**	**7,005**	**8,184**	**9,118**	**13,730**
Owned dwellings	4,048	764	1,015	1,734	2,977	3,912	5,572	10,052
Mortgage interest and charges	2,813	395	569	1,149	2,016	2,961	3,913	7,062
Property taxes	742	223	274	300	500	587	974	1,915
Maintenance, repair, insurance, other expenses	493	146	174	284	462	364	684	1,076
Rented dwellings	3,525	3,120	3,629	3,729	3,871	4,095	3,280	3,004
Other lodging	249	139	94	121	157	177	266	674
Utilities, fuels, and public services	**2,295**	**1,523**	**1,843**	**1,997**	**2,199**	**2,323**	**2,635**	**3,087**
Natural gas	254	155	176	194	233	264	317	375
Electricity	810	604	742	772	761	787	913	959
Fuel oil and other fuels	53	26	44	44	45	67	51	80
Telephone	945	645	734	795	938	962	1,053	1,311
Water and other public services	234	94	147	191	221	242	301	362

	complete income reporters aged 25–34	under $10,000	$10,000– $19,999	$20,000– $29,999	$30,000– $39,999	$40,000– $49,999	$50,000– $69,999	$70,000 or more
Household services	**$867**	**$320**	**$414**	**$422**	**$488**	**$708**	**$1,145**	**$2,110**
Personal services	645	229	323	310	345	536	885	1,540
Other household services	222	91	92	112	143	172	259	571
Housekeeping supplies	**501**	**364**	**245**	**323**	**387**	**598**	**653**	**789**
Laundry and cleaning supplies	135	76	83	124	123	128	183	168
Other household products	237	246	112	137	174	267	318	369
Postage and stationery	129	42	50	62	90	203	152	252
Household furnishings and equipment	**1,599**	**429**	**702**	**1,115**	**1,398**	**1,583**	**2,041**	**3,078**
Household textiles	117	23	74	105	107	85	150	199
Furniture	481	174	177	331	331	503	609	1,030
Floor coverings	40	3	16	15	55	27	51	90
Major appliances	180	59	76	152	166	169	294	249
Small appliances, misc. housewares	89	29	31	63	106	93	112	140
Miscellaneous household equipment	691	141	328	449	635	707	824	1,371
APPAREL AND RELATED SERVICES	**2,217**	**1,413**	**1,392**	**1,727**	**2,146**	**1,971**	**2,398**	**3,663**
Men and boys	**566**	**392**	**306**	**409**	**601**	**468**	**552**	**1,013**
Men, aged 16 or older	421	212	161	274	478	351	384	862
Boys, aged 2 to 15	145	180	145	135	123	117	168	150
Women and girls	**757**	**420**	**518**	**549**	**688**	**707**	**807**	**1,311**
Women, aged 16 or older	615	299	406	396	548	607	656	1,128
Girls, aged 2 to 15	142	120	113	153	140	100	151	183
Children under age 2	**169**	**136**	**107**	**111**	**139**	**195**	**201**	**263**
Footwear	**414**	**289**	**276**	**423**	**456**	**316**	**500**	**481**
Other apparel products and services	**311**	**175**	**183**	**235**	**261**	**285**	**338**	**595**
TRANSPORTATION	**7,982**	**3,563**	**5,116**	**5,641**	**7,096**	**8,703**	**9,152**	**14,014**
Vehicle purchases	**3,919**	**1,787**	**2,747**	**2,582**	**3,381**	**4,401**	**4,077**	**7,243**
Cars and trucks, new	1,638	482	671	905	1,255	1,677	1,392	4,319
Cars and trucks, used	2,194	1,306	2,061	1,626	1,980	2,722	2,626	2,660
Other vehicles	86	–	15	51	146	2	59	264
Gasoline and motor oil	**1,229**	**553**	**890**	**1,049**	**1,165**	**1,275**	**1,548**	**1,738**
Other vehicle expenses	**2,445**	**1,040**	**1,301**	**1,770**	**2,225**	**2,643**	**3,092**	**4,193**
Vehicle finance charges	431	101	190	309	399	499	673	660
Maintenance and repairs	608	351	426	474	592	644	714	898
Vehicle insurance	764	278	446	636	774	867	967	1,128
Vehicle rentals, leases, licenses, other charges	642	311	237	351	459	633	738	1,507
Public transportation	**390**	**182**	**179**	**240**	**325**	**383**	**434**	**840**
HEALTH CARE	**1,265**	**410**	**819**	**1,068**	**1,128**	**1,431**	**1,734**	**1,789**
Health insurance	635	175	408	543	612	723	860	885
Medical services	372	124	224	343	292	427	515	537
Drugs	185	84	142	139	169	203	243	247
Medical supplies	73	26	44	44	55	77	116	120
ENTERTAINMENT	**1,959**	**816**	**1,110**	**1,344**	**1,504**	**2,106**	**2,536**	**3,528**
Fees and admissions	473	172	182	274	326	486	595	1,066
Television, radio, sound equipment	687	367	500	532	626	704	846	1,034
Pets, toys, and playground equipment	384	179	243	268	289	429	534	603
Other entertainment products and services	414	98	185	270	262	488	561	824

	complete income reporters aged 25–34	under $10,000	$10,000–$19,999	$20,000–$29,999	$30,000–$39,999	$40,000–$49,999	$50,000–$69,999	$70,000 or more
PERSONAL CARE PRODUCTS, SERVICES	$578	$347	$398	$423	$492	$673	$699	$861
READING	126	43	61	93	107	126	165	234
EDUCATION	544	713	438	421	318	658	518	802
TOBACCO PRODUCTS, SMOKING SUPPLIES	309	262	288	328	333	326	330	282
MISCELLANEOUS	834	349	398	682	907	950	1,112	1,198
CASH CONTRIBUTIONS	746	134	378	374	552	613	910	1,822
PERSONAL INSURANCE AND PENSIONS	4,423	362	1,158	2,227	3,177	4,544	6,199	10,618
Life and other personal insurance	239	98	86	155	151	196	366	503
Pensions and Social Security	4,183	264	1,073	2,072	3,026	4,348	5,833	10,115
PERSONAL TAXES	2,951	–149	–145	1,009	1,849	2,645	4,145	9,048
Federal income taxes	2,261	–155	–238	708	1,385	1,991	3,187	7,172
State and local income taxes	621	1	67	277	419	599	851	1,707
Other taxes	68	5	26	24	44	55	107	169
GIFTS	785	430	387	647	800	819	903	1,239
Food	42	43	10	36	26	64	55	59
Alcoholic beverages	28	9	5	14	15	17	37	75
Housing	241	111	153	195	202	189	325	394
Housekeeping supplies	44	20	13	24	34	40	67	81
Household textiles	8	–	5	6	4	6	13	16
Appliances and misc. housewares	23	2	9	5	26	20	41	38
Major appliances	4	1	2	3	1	3	13	2
Small appliances and misc. housewares	19	1	8	2	25	17	28	36
Miscellaneous household equipment	54	8	55	28	63	47	39	112
Other housing	112	81	70	132	74	76	166	146
Apparel and services	230	183	101	230	232	225	245	343
Males, aged 2 or older	54	43	28	52	41	63	43	101
Females, aged 2 or older	63	45	18	49	75	48	63	113
Children under age 2	50	46	23	35	58	65	54	71
Other apparel products and services	63	50	32	94	58	49	85	57
Jewelry and watches	36	22	18	61	42	25	49	27
All other apparel products and services	26	27	15	32	16	24	36	30
Transportation	28	12	13	12	50	25	26	47
Health care	8	–	7	8	6	11	11	13
Entertainment	84	26	38	74	84	74	104	143
Toys, games, hobbies, and tricycles	27	12	11	28	21	32	34	41
Other entertainment	57	14	27	46	63	41	70	101
Personal care products and services	19	6	2	20	17	47	22	20
Reading	1	1	–	1	1	2	2	1
Education	41	13	36	27	18	110	30	56
All other gifts	62	27	23	31	149	57	48	88

Note: Spending by category will not add to total spending because gift spending is also included in the preceding product and service categories and personal taxes are not included in the total. (–) means sample is too small to make a reliable estimate.
Source: Bureau of Labor Statistics, 1999 and 2000 Consumer Expenditure Surveys, Internet site www.bls.gov/cex/; calculations by New Strategist

Table 1.11 Aged 25 to 34: Indexed spending by income, 1999–2000

(indexed average annual spending of consumer units (CU) headed by people aged 25 to 34 by product and service category and before-tax income of consumer unit, 1999–2000; complete income reporters only; index definition: an index of 100 is the average for all consumer units; an index of 132 means that spending by consumer units in that group is 32 percent above the average for all consumer units; an index of 68 indicates spending that is 32 percent below the average for all consumer units)

	complete income reporters aged 25–34	under $10,000	$10,000–$19,999	$20,000–$29,999	$30,000–$39,999	$40,000–$49,999	$50,000–$69,999	$70,000 or more
Average spending of CU, total	$40,001	$18,835	$23,598	$28,765	$34,615	$41,641	$48,023	$70,199
Average spending of CU, index	100	47	59	72	87	104	120	175
FOOD	**100**	**64**	**70**	**85**	**91**	**105**	**113**	**142**
Food at home	**100**	**72**	**85**	**96**	**87**	**103**	**113**	**122**
Cereals and bakery products	100	68	81	97	87	108	114	121
Cereals and cereal products	100	73	85	110	94	107	108	103
Bakery products	100	64	78	88	83	109	117	132
Meats, poultry, fish, and eggs	100	74	96	100	92	95	107	116
Beef	100	70	104	87	110	108	101	104
Pork	100	63	100	118	83	87	114	107
Other meats	100	59	108	104	83	85	123	109
Poultry	100	89	84	104	88	87	102	129
Fish and seafood	100	81	77	94	77	104	100	147
Eggs	100	123	100	91	97	84	103	100
Dairy products	100	80	74	92	91	106	119	119
Fresh milk and cream	100	88	81	92	97	104	116	108
Other dairy products	100	74	69	92	86	108	120	127
Fruits and vegetables	100	83	89	94	84	94	108	130
Fresh fruits	100	88	92	90	86	78	108	137
Fresh vegetables	100	74	89	99	83	101	103	132
Processed fruits	100	90	77	91	86	96	117	127
Processed vegetables	100	80	101	94	81	110	101	120
Other food at home	100	64	81	94	84	110	118	123
Sugar and other sweets	100	73	64	96	89	111	127	117
Fats and oils	100	83	94	110	85	109	108	104
Miscellaneous foods	100	55	76	90	87	108	120	128
Nonalcoholic beverages	100	76	96	98	79	115	111	113
Food prepared by CU on trips	100	45	59	71	62	103	132	179
Food away from home	**100**	**54**	**50**	**72**	**96**	**108**	**113**	**166**
ALCOHOLIC BEVERAGES	**100**	**59**	**64**	**72**	**83**	**81**	**108**	**186**
HOUSING	**100**	**51**	**61**	**72**	**88**	**102**	**119**	**174**
Shelter	**100**	**51**	**61**	**71**	**90**	**105**	**117**	**176**
Owned dwellings	100	19	25	43	74	97	138	248
Mortgage interest and charges	100	14	20	41	72	105	139	251
Property taxes	100	30	37	40	67	79	131	258
Maintenance, repair, insurance, other expenses	100	30	35	58	94	74	139	218
Rented dwellings	100	89	103	106	110	116	93	85
Other lodging	100	56	38	49	63	71	107	271
Utilities, fuels, and public services	**100**	**66**	**80**	**87**	**96**	**101**	**115**	**135**
Natural gas	100	61	69	76	92	104	125	148
Electricity	100	75	92	95	94	97	113	118
Fuel oil and other fuels	100	48	83	83	85	126	96	151
Telephone	100	68	78	84	99	102	111	139
Water and other public services	100	40	63	82	94	103	129	155

	complete income reporters aged 25–34	under $10,000	$10,000– $19,999	$20,000– $29,999	$30,000– $39,999	$40,000– $49,999	$50,000– $69,999	$70,000 or more
Household services	100	37	48	49	56	82	132	243
Personal services	100	36	50	48	53	83	137	239
Other household services	100	41	41	50	64	77	117	257
Housekeeping supplies	100	73	49	64	77	119	130	157
Laundry and cleaning supplies	100	57	61	92	91	95	136	124
Other household products	100	104	47	58	73	113	134	156
Postage and stationery	100	33	39	48	70	157	118	195
Household furnishings and equipment	100	27	44	70	87	99	128	192
Household textiles	100	19	63	90	91	73	128	170
Furniture	100	36	37	69	69	105	127	214
Floor coverings	100	7	40	38	138	68	128	225
Major appliances	100	33	42	84	92	94	163	138
Small appliances, misc. housewares	100	33	34	71	119	104	126	157
Miscellaneous household equipment	100	20	47	65	92	102	119	198
APPAREL AND RELATED SERVICES	100	64	63	78	97	89	108	165
Men and boys	100	69	54	72	106	83	98	179
Men, aged 16 or older	100	50	38	65	114	83	91	205
Boys, aged 2 to 15	100	124	100	93	85	81	116	103
Women and girls	100	56	68	73	91	93	107	173
Women, aged 16 or older	100	49	66	64	89	99	107	183
Girls, aged 2 to 15	100	85	79	108	99	70	106	129
Children under age 2	100	80	64	66	82	115	119	156
Footwear	100	70	67	102	110	76	121	116
Other apparel products and services	100	56	59	76	84	92	109	191
TRANSPORTATION	100	45	64	71	89	109	115	176
Vehicle purchases	100	46	70	66	86	112	104	185
Cars and trucks, new	100	29	41	55	77	102	85	264
Cars and trucks, used	100	60	94	74	90	124	120	121
Other vehicles	100	–	17	59	170	2	69	307
Gasoline and motor oil	100	45	72	85	95	104	126	141
Other vehicle expenses	100	43	53	72	91	108	126	171
Vehicle finance charges	100	23	44	72	93	116	156	153
Maintenance and repairs	100	58	70	78	97	106	117	148
Vehicle insurance	100	36	58	83	101	113	127	148
Vehicle rentals, leases, licenses, other charges	100	48	37	55	71	99	115	235
Public transportation	100	47	46	62	83	98	111	215
HEALTH CARE	100	32	65	84	89	113	137	141
Health insurance	100	28	64	86	96	114	135	139
Medical services	100	33	60	92	78	115	138	144
Drugs	100	45	77	75	91	110	131	134
Medical supplies	100	36	60	60	75	105	159	164
ENTERTAINMENT	100	42	57	69	77	108	129	180
Fees and admissions	100	36	38	58	69	103	126	225
Television, radio, sound equipment	100	53	73	77	91	102	123	151
Pets, toys, and playground equipment	100	47	63	70	75	112	139	157
Other entertainment products and services	100	24	45	65	63	118	136	199

	complete income reporters aged 25–34	under $10,000	$10,000– $19,999	$20,000– $29,999	$30,000– $39,999	$40,000– $49,999	$50,000– $69,999	$70,000 or more
PERSONAL CARE PRODUCTS, SERVICES	100	60	69	73	85	116	121	149
READING	100	34	48	74	85	100	131	186
EDUCATION	100	131	80	77	58	121	95	147
TOBACCO PRODUCTS, SMOKING SUPPLIES	100	85	93	106	108	106	107	91
MISCELLANEOUS	100	42	48	82	109	114	133	144
CASH CONTRIBUTIONS	100	18	51	50	74	82	122	244
PERSONAL INSURANCE AND PENSIONS	100	8	26	50	72	103	140	240
Life and other personal insurance	100	41	36	65	63	82	153	210
Pensions and Social Security	100	6	26	50	72	104	139	242
PERSONAL TAXES	100	–5	–5	34	63	90	140	307
Federal income taxes	100	–7	–11	31	61	88	141	317
State and local income taxes	100	0	11	45	67	96	137	275
Other taxes	100	7	38	35	65	81	157	249
GIFTS	100	55	49	82	102	104	115	158
Food	100	103	23	86	62	152	131	140
Alcoholic beverages	100	32	16	50	54	61	132	268
Housing	100	46	64	81	84	78	135	163
Housekeeping supplies	100	46	30	55	77	91	152	184
Household textiles	100	–	57	75	50	75	163	200
Appliances and misc. housewares	100	10	39	22	113	87	178	165
Major appliances	100	20	–	75	25	75	325	50
Small appliances and misc. housewares	100	7	40	11	132	89	147	189
Miscellaneous household equipment	100	14	102	52	117	87	72	207
Other housing	100	72	63	118	66	68	148	130
Apparel and services	100	79	44	100	101	98	107	149
Males, aged 2 or older	100	79	51	96	76	117	80	187
Females, aged 2 or older	100	71	29	78	119	76	100	179
Children under age 2	100	93	45	70	116	130	108	142
Other apparel products and services	100	79	52	149	92	78	135	90
Jewelry and watches	100	61	50	169	117	69	136	75
All other apparel products and services	100	105	56	123	62	92	138	115
Transportation	100	42	48	43	179	89	93	168
Health care	100	0	88	100	75	138	138	163
Entertainment	100	31	45	88	100	88	124	170
Toys, games, hobbies, and tricycles	100	44	42	104	78	119	126	152
Other entertainment	100	25	47	81	111	72	123	177
Personal care products and services	100	33	8	105	89	247	116	105
Reading	100	59	0	100	100	200	200	100
Education	100	33	88	66	44	268	73	137
All other gifts	100	43	37	50	240	92	77	142

Note: (–) means sample is too small to make a reliable estimate.
Source: Calculations by New Strategist based on the Bureau of Labor Statistics 1999 and 2000 Consumer Expenditure Surveys

Table 1.12 Aged 35 to 44: Average spending by income, 1999–2000

(average annual spending of consumer units (CU) headed by people aged 35 to 44 by product and service category and before-tax income of consumer unit, 1999–2000; complete income reporters only)

	complete income reporters aged 35–44	under $10,000	$10,000–$19,999	$20,000–$29,999	$30,000–$39,999	$40,000–$49,999	$50,000–$69,999	$70,000 or more
Number of consumer units in (in thousands, add 000s)	18,103	1,325	1,903	2,320	2,256	2,048	3,398	4,853
Average number of persons per CU	3.2	2.5	3.0	3.1	3.0	3.0	3.3	3.6
Average income before taxes	$55,026	$5,034	$15,179	$24,570	$34,365	$44,233	$58,794	$110,392
Average annual spending	46,786	20,282	23,282	29,178	36,118	42,259	50,386	75,911
FOOD	$6,443	$4,030	$4,162	$4,408	$5,378	$6,653	$6,985	$8,959
Food at home	3,666	2,913	2,803	2,802	3,155	3,794	3,989	4,580
Cereals and bakery products	573	453	434	427	499	548	653	721
Cereals and cereal products	209	214	166	167	199	208	225	241
Bakery products	364	239	268	259	300	340	428	480
Meats, poultry, fish, and eggs	930	931	786	817	824	983	1,007	1,023
Beef	271	262	215	246	231	282	308	299
Pork	189	201	180	177	178	200	204	187
Other meats	125	106	110	108	116	140	134	137
Poultry	176	178	127	153	157	193	174	211
Fish and seafood	130	144	113	97	101	135	151	146
Eggs	39	40	40	37	41	34	35	43
Dairy products	418	298	303	306	371	413	486	525
Fresh milk and cream	166	133	131	126	172	150	187	196
Other dairy products	252	165	172	180	200	263	298	329
Fruits and vegetables	583	470	438	457	519	617	575	749
Fresh fruits	177	146	122	129	153	179	164	246
Fresh vegetables	171	148	128	140	159	172	169	214
Processed fruits	134	104	97	103	116	137	137	175
Processed vegetables	102	72	91	84	91	130	106	115
Other food at home	1,161	761	842	796	941	1,231	1,269	1,562
Sugar and other sweets	151	102	119	108	105	150	158	215
Fats and oils	95	66	81	84	83	105	100	110
Miscellaneous foods	544	317	390	341	418	589	610	755
Nonalcoholic beverages	318	251	232	232	297	335	352	390
Food prepared by CU on trips	52	25	21	31	38	52	49	92
Food away from home	2,777	1,116	1,359	1,606	2,223	2,859	2,996	4,378
ALCOHOLIC BEVERAGES	458	243	155	254	287	474	517	769
HOUSING	14,836	7,541	8,290	9,591	11,061	12,765	15,257	24,213
Shelter	8,701	4,455	4,922	5,629	6,606	7,646	8,912	14,081
Owned dwellings	6,212	1,597	1,972	2,657	3,833	4,933	6,864	12,024
Mortgage interest and charges	4,106	947	1,043	1,616	2,570	3,369	4,695	7,974
Property taxes	1,214	423	458	608	744	884	1,278	2,329
Maintenance, repair, insurance, other expenses	892	228	471	434	519	679	890	1,721
Rented dwellings	2,093	2,688	2,868	2,841	2,613	2,453	1,635	1,195
Other lodging	396	170	82	131	160	260	413	863
Utilities, fuels, and public services	2,700	1,858	2,041	2,254	2,412	2,553	2,853	3,490
Natural gas	310	193	218	222	280	278	347	422
Electricity	981	733	822	901	886	934	1,034	1,177
Fuel oil and other fuels	84	48	52	78	55	85	91	117
Telephone	992	706	738	816	929	951	1,015	1,285
Water and other public services	333	177	211	238	262	305	367	489

	complete income reporters aged 35–44	under $10,000	$10,000–$19,999	$20,000–$29,999	$30,000–$39,999	$40,000–$49,999	$50,000–$69,999	$70,000 or more
Household services	**$899**	**$275**	**$274**	**$278**	**$443**	**$540**	**$873**	**$1,994**
Personal services	554	179	158	143	269	289	526	1,272
Other household services	345	95	116	135	174	251	347	722
Housekeeping supplies	**655**	**302**	**347**	**389**	**515**	**547**	**805**	**999**
Laundry and cleaning supplies	165	139	144	128	140	164	154	215
Other household products	337	105	147	176	270	264	461	525
Postage and stationery	153	59	56	84	105	119	190	259
Household furnishings and equipment	**1,882**	**651**	**707**	**1,041**	**1,086**	**1,479**	**1,814**	**3,648**
Household textiles	124	45	56	53	83	135	94	240
Furniture	475	192	211	222	344	257	394	987
Floor coverings	47	16	7	16	24	23	67	92
Major appliances	212	82	109	135	123	171	194	389
Small appliances, misc. housewares	105	49	44	48	59	87	100	203
Miscellaneous household equipment	919	266	280	567	453	806	966	1,738
APPAREL AND RELATED SERVICES	**2,394**	**1,372**	**1,484**	**1,523**	**1,808**	**2,124**	**2,439**	**3,776**
Men and boys	**585**	**303**	**324**	**378**	**426**	**459**	**659**	**933**
Men, aged 16 or older	394	188	188	226	275	306	463	652
Boys, aged 2 to 15	191	116	136	152	151	152	196	281
Women and girls	**933**	**579**	**577**	**532**	**664**	**838**	**968**	**1,492**
Women, aged 16 or older	694	447	456	351	502	663	702	1,110
Girls, aged 2 to 15	238	132	121	181	162	175	266	382
Children under age 2	**110**	**79**	**79**	**58**	**75**	**124**	**106**	**168**
Footwear	**429**	**284**	**323**	**353**	**450**	**472**	**417**	**519**
Other apparel products and services	**337**	**127**	**182**	**202**	**193**	**232**	**289**	**665**
TRANSPORTATION	**8,671**	**2,969**	**4,273**	**6,084**	**7,788**	**8,529**	**9,472**	**13,096**
Vehicle purchases	**4,057**	**928**	**2,033**	**2,990**	**3,815**	**4,203**	**4,393**	**6,032**
Cars and trucks, new	1,797	62	473	825	1,341	1,545	2,043	3,401
Cars and trucks, used	2,208	866	1,560	2,152	2,435	2,559	2,282	2,552
Other vehicles	52	–	–	14	40	99	69	79
Gasoline and motor oil	**1,459**	**776**	**874**	**1,130**	**1,378**	**1,526**	**1,650**	**1,906**
Other vehicle expenses	**2,727**	**1,078**	**1,184**	**1,755**	**2,294**	**2,521**	**3,035**	**4,319**
Vehicle finance charges	414	143	159	248	346	374	545	623
Maintenance and repairs	780	357	413	535	651	799	865	1,147
Vehicle insurance	882	351	457	687	825	899	1,023	1,208
Vehicle rentals, leases, licenses, other charges	652	226	153	284	472	449	602	1,342
Public transportation	**427**	**187**	**182**	**209**	**301**	**278**	**394**	**838**
HEALTH CARE	**1,757**	**770**	**870**	**1,256**	**1,480**	**1,687**	**2,099**	**2,532**
Health insurance	803	312	372	611	698	844	940	1,135
Medical services	555	260	222	380	464	469	649	860
Drugs	297	172	210	207	260	288	379	372
Medical supplies	102	24	67	57	58	86	130	165
ENTERTAINMENT	**2,564**	**1,005**	**972**	**1,265**	**1,738**	**2,038**	**3,081**	**4,473**
Fees and admissions	685	202	193	252	366	453	719	1,439
Television, radio, sound equipment	799	414	442	566	661	701	899	1,190
Pets, toys, and playground equipment	487	222	210	287	382	503	540	769
Other entertainment products and services	594	167	127	159	330	381	923	1,075

	complete income reporters aged 35–44	under $10,000	$10,000–$19,999	$20,000–$29,999	$30,000–$39,999	$40,000–$49,999	$50,000–$69,999	$70,000 or more
PERSONAL CARE PRODUCTS, SERVICES	$670	$371	$363	$442	$545	$666	$706	$1,012
READING	165	62	55	104	114	129	191	287
EDUCATION	602	220	195	317	398	443	622	1,148
TOBACCO PRODUCTS, SMOKING SUPPLIES	424	530	487	436	432	479	443	324
MISCELLANEOUS	982	399	600	670	917	1,056	1,024	1,410
CASH CONTRIBUTIONS	1,040	321	284	381	784	518	1,130	2,125
PERSONAL INSURANCE AND PENSIONS	5,780	449	1,092	2,448	3,387	4,697	6,420	11,787
Life and other personal insurance	422	156	142	201	299	287	468	791
Pensions and Social Security	5,358	293	950	2,247	3,088	4,411	5,952	10,996
PERSONAL TAXES	**3,919**	**14**	**−120**	**715**	**1,675**	**2,451**	**4,133**	**9,615**
Federal income taxes	3,026	−53	−219	446	1,252	1,824	3,060	7,680
State and local income taxes	766	29	61	206	343	538	939	1,684
Other taxes	127	37	38	63	80	90	133	250
GIFTS	**1,084**	**522**	**577**	**510**	**761**	**968**	**1,054**	**1,925**
Food	**68**	**26**	**15**	**20**	**34**	**34**	**84**	**140**
Alcoholic beverages	**22**	**17**	**10**	**8**	**15**	**17**	**12**	**44**
Housing	**309**	**120**	**142**	**150**	**208**	**276**	**303**	**565**
Housekeeping supplies	56	20	19	42	26	33	72	98
Household textiles	15	11	1	3	14	41	12	18
Appliances and misc. housewares	30	3	3	14	16	23	32	62
Major appliances	6	–	–	3	12	6	13	4
Small appliances and misc. housewares	24	3	3	11	5	17	20	58
Miscellaneous household equipment	79	21	17	41	39	77	84	152
Other housing	130	65	102	50	112	102	102	236
Apparel and services	**260**	**242**	**222**	**131**	**151**	**346**	**226**	**379**
Males, aged 2 or older	55	45	90	14	18	37	46	92
Females, aged 2 or older	90	123	63	61	50	111	77	126
Children under age 2	59	17	38	31	39	58	56	102
Other apparel products and services	56	56	31	26	44	140	47	60
Jewelry and watches	24	2	6	11	12	66	19	33
All other apparel products and services	32	54	24	15	32	74	29	27
Transportation	**48**	**4**	**11**	**20**	**43**	**23**	**63**	**90**
Health care	**22**	**8**	**5**	**9**	**45**	**25**	**18**	**28**
Entertainment	**119**	**63**	**36**	**66**	**108**	**71**	**129**	**210**
Toys, games, hobbies, and tricycles	28	15	10	21	32	17	32	42
Other entertainment	91	49	26	45	76	54	97	169
Personal care products and services	**32**	**13**	**26**	**14**	**30**	**37**	**31**	**45**
Reading	**1**	**–**	**0**	**1**	**1**	**2**	**2**	**2**
Education	**108**	**10**	**19**	**14**	**42**	**57**	**84**	**282**
All other gifts	**97**	**18**	**91**	**77**	**85**	**80**	**102**	**139**

Note: Spending by category will not add to total spending because gift spending is also included in the preceding product and service categories and personal taxes are not included in the total. (–) means sample is too small to make a reliable estimate.
Source: Bureau of Labor Statistics, 1999 and 2000 Consumer Expenditure Surveys, Internet site www.bls.gov/cex/; calculations by New Strategist

Table 1.13 Aged 35 to 44: Indexed spending by income, 1999–2000

(indexed average annual spending of consumer units (CU) headed by people aged 35 to 44 by product and service category and before-tax income of consumer unit, 1999–2000; complete income reporters only; index definition: an index of 100 is the average for all consumer units; an index of 132 means that spending by consumer units in that group is 32 percent above the average for all consumer units; an index of 68 indicates spending that is 32 percent below the average for all consumer units)

	complete income reporters aged 35–44	under $10,000	$10,000–$19,999	$20,000–$29,999	$30,000–$39,999	$40,000–$49,999	$50,000–$69,999	$70,000 or more
Average spending of CU, total	$46,786	$20,282	$23,282	$29,178	$36,118	$42,259	$50,386	$75,911
Average spending of CU, index	**100**	**43**	**50**	**62**	**77**	**90**	**108**	**162**
FOOD	**100**	**63**	**65**	**68**	**83**	**103**	**108**	**139**
Food at home	**100**	**79**	**76**	**76**	**86**	**103**	**109**	**125**
Cereals and bakery products	100	79	76	75	87	96	114	126
Cereals and cereal products	100	103	79	80	95	100	108	115
Bakery products	100	66	74	71	82	93	118	132
Meats, poultry, fish, and eggs	100	100	84	88	89	106	108	110
Beef	100	97	80	91	85	104	114	110
Pork	100	106	95	94	94	106	108	99
Other meats	100	84	88	86	93	112	107	110
Poultry	100	101	72	87	89	110	99	120
Fish and seafood	100	111	87	75	78	104	116	112
Eggs	100	102	102	95	105	87	90	110
Dairy products	100	71	72	73	89	99	116	126
Fresh milk and cream	100	80	79	76	104	90	113	118
Other dairy products	100	65	68	71	79	104	118	131
Fruits and vegetables	100	81	75	78	89	106	99	128
Fresh fruits	100	83	69	73	86	101	93	139
Fresh vegetables	100	86	75	82	93	101	99	125
Processed fruits	100	77	72	77	87	102	102	131
Processed vegetables	100	70	89	82	89	127	104	113
Other food at home	100	66	73	69	81	106	109	135
Sugar and other sweets	100	68	79	72	70	99	105	142
Fats and oils	100	70	85	88	87	111	105	116
Miscellaneous foods	100	58	72	63	77	108	112	139
Nonalcoholic beverages	100	79	73	73	93	105	111	123
Food prepared by CU on trips	100	49	40	60	73	100	94	177
Food away from home	**100**	**40**	**49**	**58**	**80**	**103**	**108**	**158**
ALCOHOLIC BEVERAGES	**100**	**53**	**34**	**55**	**63**	**103**	**113**	**168**
HOUSING	**100**	**51**	**56**	**65**	**75**	**86**	**103**	**163**
Shelter	**100**	**51**	**57**	**65**	**76**	**88**	**102**	**162**
Owned dwellings	100	26	32	43	62	79	110	194
Mortgage interest and charges	100	23	25	39	63	82	114	194
Property taxes	100	35	38	50	61	73	105	192
Maintenance, repair, insurance, other expenses	100	26	53	49	58	76	100	193
Rented dwellings	100	128	137	136	125	117	78	57
Other lodging	100	43	21	33	40	66	104	218
Utilities, fuels, and public services	**100**	**69**	**76**	**83**	**89**	**95**	**106**	**129**
Natural gas	100	62	70	72	90	90	112	136
Electricity	100	75	84	92	90	95	105	120
Fuel oil and other fuels	100	57	62	93	65	101	108	139
Telephone	100	71	74	82	94	96	102	130
Water and other public services	100	53	63	71	79	92	110	147

	complete income reporters aged 35–44	under $10,000	$10,000– $19,999	$20,000– $29,999	$30,000– $39,999	$40,000– $49,999	$50,000– $69,999	$70,000 or more
Household services	**100**	**31**	**31**	**31**	**49**	**60**	**97**	**222**
Personal services	100	32	29	26	49	52	95	230
Other household services	100	28	33	39	50	73	101	209
Housekeeping supplies	**100**	**46**	**53**	**59**	**79**	**84**	**123**	**153**
Laundry and cleaning supplies	100	84	87	78	85	99	93	130
Other household products	100	31	44	52	80	78	137	156
Postage and stationery	100	38	37	55	69	78	124	169
Household furnishings and equipment	**100**	**35**	**38**	**55**	**58**	**79**	**96**	**194**
Household textiles	100	36	45	43	67	109	76	194
Furniture	100	40	44	47	72	54	83	208
Floor coverings	100	35	14	34	51	49	143	196
Major appliances	100	39	51	64	58	81	92	183
Small appliances, misc. housewares	100	47	42	46	56	83	95	193
Miscellaneous household equipment	100	29	30	62	49	88	105	189
APPAREL AND RELATED SERVICES	**100**	**57**	**62**	**64**	**76**	**89**	**102**	**158**
Men and boys	**100**	**52**	**55**	**65**	**73**	**78**	**113**	**159**
Men, aged 16 or older	100	48	48	57	70	78	118	165
Boys, aged 2 to 15	100	61	71	80	79	80	103	147
Women and girls	**100**	**62**	**62**	**57**	**71**	**90**	**104**	**160**
Women, aged 16 or older	100	64	66	51	72	96	101	160
Girls, aged 2 to 15	100	56	51	76	68	74	112	161
Children under age 2	**100**	**72**	**72**	**53**	**68**	**113**	**96**	**153**
Footwear	**100**	**66**	**75**	**82**	**105**	**110**	**97**	**121**
Other apparel products and services	**100**	**38**	**54**	**60**	**57**	**69**	**86**	**197**
TRANSPORTATION	**100**	**34**	**49**	**70**	**90**	**98**	**109**	**151**
Vehicle purchases	**100**	**23**	**50**	**74**	**94**	**104**	**108**	**149**
Cars and trucks, new	100	3	26	46	75	86	114	189
Cars and trucks, used	100	39	71	97	110	116	103	116
Other vehicles	100	–	–	27	77	190	133	152
Gasoline and motor oil	**100**	**53**	**60**	**77**	**94**	**105**	**113**	**131**
Other vehicle expenses	**100**	**40**	**43**	**64**	**84**	**92**	**111**	**158**
Vehicle finance charges	100	35	38	60	84	90	132	150
Maintenance and repairs	100	46	53	69	83	102	111	147
Vehicle insurance	100	40	52	78	94	102	116	137
Vehicle rentals, leases, licenses, other charges	100	35	24	44	72	69	92	206
Public transportation	**100**	**44**	**43**	**49**	**70**	**65**	**92**	**196**
HEALTH CARE	**100**	**44**	**50**	**71**	**84**	**96**	**119**	**144**
Health insurance	100	39	46	76	87	105	117	141
Medical services	100	47	40	68	84	85	117	155
Drugs	100	58	71	70	88	97	128	125
Medical supplies	100	24	66	56	57	84	127	162
ENTERTAINMENT	**100**	**39**	**38**	**49**	**68**	**79**	**120**	**174**
Fees and admissions	100	30	28	37	53	66	105	210
Television, radio, sound equipment	100	52	55	71	83	88	113	149
Pets, toys, and playground equipment	100	46	43	59	78	103	111	158
Other entertainment products and services	100	28	21	27	56	64	155	181

	complete income reporters aged 35–44	under $10,000	$10,000– $19,999	$20,000– $29,999	$30,000– $39,999	$40,000– $49,999	$50,000– $69,999	$70,000 or more
PERSONAL CARE PRODUCTS, SERVICES	100	55	54	66	81	99	105	151
READING	100	38	34	63	69	78	116	174
EDUCATION	100	37	32	53	66	74	103	191
TOBACCO PRODUCTS, SMOKING SUPPLIES	100	125	115	103	102	113	104	76
MISCELLANEOUS	100	41	61	68	93	108	104	144
CASH CONTRIBUTIONS	100	31	27	37	75	50	109	204
PERSONAL INSURANCE AND PENSIONS	100	8	19	42	59	81	111	204
Life and other personal insurance	100	37	34	48	71	68	111	187
Pensions and Social Security	100	5	18	42	58	82	111	205
PERSONAL TAXES	100	0	–3	18	43	63	105	245
Federal income taxes	100	–2	–7	15	41	60	101	254
State and local income taxes	100	4	8	27	45	70	123	220
Other taxes	100	29	30	50	63	71	105	197
GIFTS	100	48	53	47	70	89	97	178
Food	100	38	22	29	50	50	124	206
Alcoholic beverages	100	79	47	36	68	77	55	200
Housing	100	39	46	49	67	89	98	183
Housekeeping supplies	100	36	34	75	46	59	129	175
Household textiles	100	74	4	20	93	273	80	120
Appliances and misc. housewares	100	10	9	47	53	77	107	207
Major appliances	100	–	–	50	200	100	217	67
Small appliances and misc. housewares	100	13	11	46	21	71	83	242
Miscellaneous household equipment	100	27	22	52	49	97	106	192
Other housing	100	50	78	38	86	78	78	182
Apparel and services	100	93	85	50	58	133	87	146
Males, aged 2 or older	100	83	164	25	33	67	84	167
Females, aged 2 or older	100	136	70	68	56	123	86	140
Children under age 2	100	30	64	53	66	98	95	173
Other apparel products and services	100	101	56	46	79	250	84	107
Jewelry and watches	100	7	27	46	50	275	79	138
All other apparel products and services	100	170	76	47	100	231	91	84
Transportation	100	8	22	42	90	48	131	188
Health care	100	37	24	41	205	114	82	127
Entertainment	100	53	31	55	91	60	108	176
Toys, games, hobbies, and tricycles	100	53	36	75	114	61	114	150
Other entertainment	100	53	29	49	84	59	107	186
Personal care products and services	100	39	80	44	94	116	97	141
Reading	100	0	46	100	100	200	200	200
Education	100	9	17	13	39	53	78	261
All other gifts	100	19	94	79	88	82	105	143

Note: (–) means sample is too small to make a reliable estimate.
Source: Calculations by New Strategist based on the Bureau of Labor Statistics 1999 and 2000 Consumer Expenditure Surveys

Table 1.14 Aged 45 to 54: Average spending by income, 1999–2000

(average annual spending of consumer units (CU) headed by people aged 45 to 54 by product and service category and before-tax income of consumer unit, 1999–2000; complete income reporters only)

	complete income reporters aged 45–54	under $10,000	$10,000–$19,999	$20,000–$29,999	$30,000–$39,999	$40,000–$49,999	$50,000–$69,999	$70,000 or more
Number of consumer units in (in thousands, add 000s)	15,628	1,167	1,610	1,636	1,917	1,661	2,806	4,830
Average number of persons per CU	2.7	2.1	2.3	2.5	2.3	2.5	2.9	3.1
Average income before taxes	$59,351	$4,255	$14,640	$24,683	$34,388	$44,262	$58,467	$114,932
Average annual spending	49,411	19,761	23,099	30,706	36,874	42,819	49,327	78,928
FOOD	$6,440	$3,250	$3,536	$4,755	$5,134	$6,023	$6,715	$9,236
Food at home	3,718	2,319	2,461	3,268	3,183	3,673	3,756	4,814
Cereals and bakery products	568	353	359	478	464	547	566	765
Cereals and cereal products	185	137	142	159	144	186	182	237
Bakery products	383	215	217	319	320	361	384	528
Meats, poultry, fish, and eggs	956	659	676	941	831	978	918	1,180
Beef	281	197	185	293	214	280	255	367
Pork	198	158	152	209	199	208	186	219
Other meats	121	76	98	128	104	115	131	140
Poultry	172	106	128	159	155	188	185	202
Fish and seafood	146	91	75	107	122	149	127	212
Eggs	38	31	38	46	36	39	33	40
Dairy products	391	254	256	340	344	376	383	513
Fresh milk and cream	149	105	111	138	145	146	144	181
Other dairy products	242	149	145	202	199	230	239	332
Fruits and vegetables	632	382	432	554	539	625	619	827
Fresh fruits	190	100	130	172	164	188	176	255
Fresh vegetables	195	111	128	174	174	201	186	254
Processed fruits	140	87	103	112	114	125	148	186
Processed vegetables	107	84	72	95	86	110	110	132
Other food at home	1,171	672	737	955	1,005	1,148	1,269	1,530
Sugar and other sweets	149	84	105	121	133	138	167	189
Fats and oils	102	72	68	98	90	114	101	122
Miscellaneous foods	542	293	347	414	435	524	574	742
Nonalcoholic beverages	324	196	198	287	313	330	375	386
Food prepared by CU on trips	54	27	18	35	34	42	52	92
Food away from home	2,722	931	1,075	1,487	1,951	2,351	2,959	4,421
ALCOHOLIC BEVERAGES	412	167	224	252	349	291	352	689
HOUSING	14,662	7,521	7,929	9,687	11,691	13,124	14,044	22,380
Shelter	8,513	4,414	4,454	5,594	6,915	7,711	7,813	13,162
Owned dwellings	6,117	1,945	1,733	2,977	4,409	5,211	6,122	10,637
Mortgage interest and charges	3,663	1,131	787	1,568	2,428	3,334	3,717	6,515
Property taxes	1,378	519	496	778	1,124	1,060	1,410	2,274
Maintenance, repair, insurance, other expenses	1,076	294	451	631	857	816	995	1,848
Rented dwellings	1,658	2,306	2,550	2,424	2,239	2,095	1,114	880
Other lodging	738	164	171	193	266	406	576	1,645
Utilities, fuels, and public services	2,826	1,813	2,091	2,275	2,491	2,710	2,990	3,580
Natural gas	321	161	229	273	278	281	339	427
Electricity	1,036	750	821	847	894	988	1,109	1,272
Fuel oil and other fuels	99	63	90	77	94	86	102	124
Telephone	1,020	682	731	802	943	1,013	1,063	1,279
Water and other public services	350	156	219	276	281	343	378	478

	complete income reporters aged 45–54	under $10,000	$10,000–$19,999	$20,000–$29,999	$30,000–$39,999	$40,000–$49,999	$50,000–$69,999	$70,000 or more
Household services	**$613**	**$210**	**$216**	**$302**	**$284**	**$508**	**$501**	**$1,179**
Personal services	151	60	70	96	84	143	141	252
Other household services	462	151	145	206	200	365	360	927
Housekeeping supplies	**633**	**288**	**294**	**484**	**588**	**575**	**690**	**888**
Laundry and cleaning supplies	153	125	86	137	125	152	185	183
Other household products	313	115	152	222	314	277	339	446
Postage and stationery	167	49	56	125	150	147	167	259
Household furnishings and equipment	**2,078**	**796**	**875**	**1,032**	**1,413**	**1,619**	**2,050**	**3,571**
Household textiles	169	67	61	127	100	98	217	270
Furniture	495	165	257	184	391	264	427	919
Floor coverings	58	21	14	9	35	72	49	107
Major appliances	237	146	144	120	155	217	183	397
Small appliances, misc. housewares	145	84	50	74	90	107	117	262
Miscellaneous household equipment	973	313	347	518	642	861	1,058	1,615
APPAREL AND RELATED SERVICES	**2,391**	**834**	**1,170**	**1,848**	**1,943**	**1,845**	**2,146**	**3,849**
Men and boys	**608**	**151**	**221**	**442**	**442**	**514**	**576**	**1,016**
Men, aged 16 or older	509	97	162	376	358	436	504	855
Boys, aged 2 to 15	99	54	58	66	84	78	73	161
Women and girls	**965**	**322**	**485**	**798**	**793**	**731**	**886**	**1,521**
Women, aged 16 or older	826	262	337	686	714	639	787	1,297
Girls, aged 2 to 15	138	60	148	113	79	92	98	224
Children under age 2	**59**	**43**	**40**	**35**	**65**	**64**	**60**	**74**
Footwear	**413**	**195**	**270**	**384**	**393**	**324**	**381**	**575**
Other apparel products and services	**346**	**124**	**153**	**188**	**250**	**212**	**242**	**663**
TRANSPORTATION	**9,090**	**3,204**	**4,572**	**6,070**	**7,223**	**8,668**	**9,814**	**13,505**
Vehicle purchases	**4,082**	**1,265**	**2,033**	**2,797**	**3,328**	**4,124**	**4,574**	**5,879**
Cars and trucks, new	1,827	310	185	1,043	1,650	1,727	2,007	3,005
Cars and trucks, used	2,199	943	1,826	1,732	1,675	2,324	2,464	2,795
Other vehicles	56	12	22	22	4	73	103	79
Gasoline and motor oil	**1,489**	**652**	**914**	**1,103**	**1,278**	**1,424**	**1,687**	**2,004**
Other vehicle expenses	**3,044**	**1,139**	**1,445**	**1,925**	**2,333**	**2,846**	**3,173**	**4,689**
Vehicle finance charges	428	111	165	255	385	453	494	620
Maintenance and repairs	883	373	481	644	668	825	853	1,343
Vehicle insurance	1,049	479	550	735	906	976	1,175	1,467
Vehicle rentals, leases, licenses, other charges	684	176	249	291	375	592	650	1,259
Public transportation	**476**	**148**	**180**	**245**	**283**	**274**	**380**	**932**
HEALTH CARE	**2,231**	**1,136**	**1,303**	**1,505**	**1,831**	**2,250**	**2,337**	**3,143**
Health insurance	947	496	522	642	790	1,061	1,064	1,255
Medical services	741	310	289	399	548	702	685	1,234
Drugs	422	293	440	372	411	396	434	471
Medical supplies	121	36	53	93	82	92	154	182
ENTERTAINMENT	**2,378**	**845**	**970**	**1,277**	**1,855**	**1,702**	**2,631**	**3,891**
Fees and admissions	661	166	168	205	273	422	586	1,379
Television, radio, sound equipment	751	348	464	550	598	709	843	1,034
Pets, toys, and playground equipment	425	199	149	288	309	341	472	663
Other entertainment products and services	541	131	188	234	675	230	729	815

	complete income reporters aged 45–54	under $10,000	$10,000–$19,999	$20,000–$29,999	$30,000–$39,999	$40,000–$49,999	$50,000–$69,999	$70,000 or more
PERSONAL CARE PRODUCTS, SERVICES	$688	$420	$354	$596	$508	$621	$662	$996
READING	203	73	71	111	145	170	207	343
EDUCATION	1,083	348	207	398	560	441	974	2,276
TOBACCO PRODUCTS, SMOKING SUPPLIES	403	404	464	453	394	423	404	362
MISCELLANEOUS	1,130	669	497	643	804	1,018	1,088	1,799
CASH CONTRIBUTIONS	1,670	435	463	630	855	1,036	1,267	3,498
PERSONAL INSURANCE AND PENSIONS	6,631	456	1,341	2,481	3,582	5,206	6,686	12,962
Life and other personal insurance	594	164	255	259	326	399	515	1,144
Pensions and Social Security	6,037	292	1,086	2,222	3,255	4,806	6,171	11,817
PERSONAL TAXES	5,048	136	335	820	2,211	3,182	4,537	11,305
Federal income taxes	3,940	57	184	562	1,655	2,405	3,397	9,025
State and local income taxes	901	25	65	183	457	604	932	1,895
Other taxes	207	54	86	75	99	172	208	384
GIFTS	1,796	601	694	897	1,101	1,005	1,555	3,442
Food	162	15	26	59	60	66	89	394
Alcoholic beverages	17	9	10	7	24	11	11	26
Housing	440	117	161	216	274	295	401	824
Housekeeping supplies	53	14	19	39	56	38	67	76
Household textiles	30	7	8	22	10	7	42	54
Appliances and misc. housewares	54	12	3	19	34	73	43	98
Major appliances	16	2	–	4	8	42	5	27
Small appliances and misc. housewares	38	11	3	15	26	30	37	70
Miscellaneous household equipment	89	22	47	52	68	53	67	166
Other housing	214	61	84	84	107	124	182	431
Apparel and services	351	122	277	179	294	242	312	571
Males, aged 2 or older	95	23	54	66	99	71	89	148
Females, aged 2 or older	147	33	119	65	98	82	117	272
Children under age 2	46	24	37	25	38	51	48	63
Other apparel products and services	61	42	67	23	58	39	59	88
Jewelry and watches	20	3	14	8	20	16	21	31
All other apparel products and services	41	39	53	16	38	23	38	57
Transportation	93	14	20	125	27	42	110	157
Health care	47	24	5	16	11	13	33	110
Entertainment	119	45	40	83	94	123	125	182
Toys, games, hobbies, and tricycles	38	18	20	40	36	48	44	41
Other entertainment	81	27	21	43	58	75	81	140
Personal care products and services	22	22	32	26	11	24	13	24
Reading	3	1	–	1	1	2	3	5
Education	429	112	90	110	220	112	377	950
All other gifts	114	121	30	76	84	75	80	198

Note: Spending by category will not add to total spending because gift spending is also included in the preceding product and service categories and personal taxes are not included in the total. (–) means sample is too small to make a reliable estimate.
Source: Bureau of Labor Statistics, 1999 and 2000 Consumer Expenditure Surveys, Internet site www.bls.gov/cex/; calculations by New Strategist

Table 1.15 Aged 45 to 54: Indexed spending by income, 1999–2000

(indexed average annual spending of consumer units (CU) headed by people aged 45 to 54 by product and service category and before-tax income of consumer unit, 1999–2000; complete income reporters only; index definition: an index of 100 is the average for all consumer units; an index of 132 means that spending by consumer units in that group is 32 percent above the average for all consumer units; an index of 68 indicates spending that is 32 percent below the average for all consumer units)

	complete income reporters aged 45–54	under $10,000	$10,000–$19,999	$20,000–$29,999	$30,000–$39,999	$40,000–$49,999	$50,000–$69,999	$70,000 or more
Average spending of CU, total	$49,411	$19,761	$23,099	$30,706	$36,874	$42,819	$49,327	$78,928
Average spending of CU, index	100	40	47	62	75	87	100	160
FOOD	**100**	**50**	**55**	**74**	**80**	**94**	**104**	**143**
Food at home	**100**	**62**	**66**	**88**	**86**	**99**	**101**	**129**
Cereals and bakery products	100	62	63	84	82	96	100	135
Cereals and cereal products	100	74	77	86	78	101	98	128
Bakery products	100	56	57	83	84	94	100	138
Meats, poultry, fish, and eggs	100	69	71	98	87	102	96	123
Beef	100	70	66	104	76	100	91	131
Pork	100	80	77	106	101	105	94	111
Other meats	100	63	81	106	86	95	108	116
Poultry	100	62	75	92	90	109	108	117
Fish and seafood	100	62	51	73	84	102	87	145
Eggs	100	81	99	121	95	103	87	105
Dairy products	100	65	65	87	88	96	98	131
Fresh milk and cream	100	70	75	93	97	98	97	121
Other dairy products	100	61	60	83	82	95	99	137
Fruits and vegetables	100	60	68	88	85	99	98	131
Fresh fruits	100	53	69	91	86	99	93	134
Fresh vegetables	100	57	65	89	89	103	95	130
Processed fruits	100	62	73	80	81	89	106	133
Processed vegetables	100	79	67	89	80	103	103	123
Other food at home	100	57	63	82	86	98	108	131
Sugar and other sweets	100	56	70	81	89	93	112	127
Fats and oils	100	70	67	96	88	112	99	120
Miscellaneous foods	100	54	64	76	80	97	106	137
Nonalcoholic beverages	100	61	61	89	97	102	116	119
Food prepared by CU on trips	100	49	34	65	63	78	96	170
Food away from home	**100**	**34**	**39**	**55**	**72**	**86**	**109**	**162**
ALCOHOLIC BEVERAGES	**100**	**40**	**54**	**61**	**85**	**71**	**85**	**167**
HOUSING	**100**	**51**	**54**	**66**	**80**	**90**	**96**	**153**
Shelter	**100**	**52**	**52**	**66**	**81**	**91**	**92**	**155**
Owned dwellings	100	32	28	49	72	85	100	174
Mortgage interest and charges	100	31	21	43	66	91	101	178
Property taxes	100	38	36	56	82	77	102	165
Maintenance, repair, insurance, other expenses	100	27	42	59	80	76	92	172
Rented dwellings	100	139	154	146	135	126	67	53
Other lodging	100	22	23	26	36	55	78	223
Utilities, fuels, and public services	**100**	**64**	**74**	**81**	**88**	**96**	**106**	**127**
Natural gas	100	50	71	85	87	88	106	133
Electricity	100	72	79	82	86	95	107	123
Fuel oil and other fuels	100	64	91	78	95	87	103	125
Telephone	100	67	72	79	92	99	104	125
Water and other public services	100	45	63	79	80	98	108	137

	complete income reporters aged 45–54	under $10,000	$10,000– $19,999	$20,000– $29,999	$30,000– $39,999	$40,000– $49,999	$50,000– $69,999	$70,000 or more
Household services	100	34	35	49	46	83	82	192
Personal services	100	39	47	64	56	95	93	167
Other household services	100	33	31	45	43	79	78	201
Housekeeping supplies	100	46	46	76	93	91	109	140
Laundry and cleaning supplies	100	81	56	90	82	99	121	120
Other household products	100	37	48	71	100	88	108	142
Postage and stationery	100	29	33	75	90	88	100	155
Household furnishings and equipment	100	38	42	50	68	78	99	172
Household textiles	100	40	36	75	59	58	128	160
Furniture	100	33	52	37	79	53	86	186
Floor coverings	100	37	25	16	60	124	84	184
Major appliances	100	61	61	51	65	92	77	168
Small appliances, misc. housewares	100	58	35	51	62	74	81	181
Miscellaneous household equipment	100	32	36	53	66	88	109	166
APPAREL AND RELATED SERVICES	100	35	49	77	81	77	90	161
Men and boys	100	25	36	73	73	85	95	167
Men, aged 16 or older	100	19	32	74	70	86	99	168
Boys, aged 2 to 15	100	54	59	67	85	79	74	163
Women and girls	100	33	50	83	82	76	92	158
Women, aged 16 or older	100	32	41	83	86	77	95	157
Girls, aged 2 to 15	100	43	107	82	57	67	71	162
Children under age 2	100	73	68	59	110	108	102	125
Footwear	100	47	65	93	95	78	92	139
Other apparel products and services	100	36	44	54	72	61	70	192
TRANSPORTATION	100	35	50	67	79	95	108	149
Vehicle purchases	100	31	50	69	82	101	112	144
Cars and trucks, new	100	17	10	57	90	95	110	164
Cars and trucks, used	100	43	83	79	76	106	112	127
Other vehicles	100	21	39	39	7	130	184	141
Gasoline and motor oil	100	44	61	74	86	96	113	135
Other vehicle expenses	100	37	47	63	77	93	104	154
Vehicle finance charges	100	26	38	60	90	106	115	145
Maintenance and repairs	100	42	54	73	76	93	97	152
Vehicle insurance	100	46	52	70	86	93	112	140
Vehicle rentals, leases, licenses, other charges	100	26	36	43	55	87	95	184
Public transportation	100	31	38	51	59	58	80	196
HEALTH CARE	100	51	58	67	82	101	105	141
Health insurance	100	52	55	68	83	112	112	133
Medical services	100	42	39	54	74	95	92	167
Drugs	100	69	104	88	97	94	103	112
Medical supplies	100	30	44	77	68	76	127	150
ENTERTAINMENT	100	36	41	54	78	72	111	164
Fees and admissions	100	25	25	31	41	64	89	209
Television, radio, sound equipment	100	46	62	73	80	94	112	138
Pets, toys, and playground equipment	100	47	35	68	73	80	111	156
Other entertainment products and services	100	24	35	43	125	43	135	151

	complete income reporters aged 45–54	under $10,000	$10,000–$19,999	$20,000–$29,999	$30,000–$39,999	$40,000–$49,999	$50,000–$69,999	$70,000 or more
PERSONAL CARE PRODUCTS, SERVICES	100	61	51	87	74	90	96	145
READING	100	36	35	55	71	84	102	169
EDUCATION	100	32	19	37	52	41	90	210
TOBACCO PRODUCTS, SMOKING SUPPLIES	100	100	115	112	98	105	100	90
MISCELLANEOUS	100	59	44	57	71	90	96	159
CASH CONTRIBUTIONS	100	26	28	38	51	62	76	209
PERSONAL INSURANCE AND PENSIONS	100	7	20	37	54	79	101	195
Life and other personal insurance	100	28	43	44	55	67	87	193
Pensions and Social Security	100	5	18	37	54	80	102	196
PERSONAL TAXES	100	3	7	16	44	63	90	224
Federal income taxes	100	1	5	14	42	61	86	229
State and local income taxes	100	3	7	20	51	67	103	210
Other taxes	100	26	42	36	48	83	100	186
GIFTS	100	33	39	50	61	56	87	192
Food	100	9	16	36	37	41	55	243
Alcoholic beverages	100	52	60	41	141	65	65	153
Housing	100	27	37	49	62	67	91	187
Housekeeping supplies	100	27	36	74	106	72	126	143
Household textiles	100	25	27	73	33	23	140	180
Appliances and misc. housewares	100	23	6	35	63	135	80	181
Major appliances	100	10	–	25	50	263	31	169
Small appliances and misc. housewares	100	29	9	39	68	79	97	184
Miscellaneous household equipment	100	25	52	58	76	60	75	187
Other housing	100	28	39	39	50	58	85	201
Apparel and services	100	35	79	51	84	69	89	163
Males, aged 2 or older	100	25	57	69	104	75	94	156
Females, aged 2 or older	100	22	81	44	67	56	80	185
Children under age 2	100	53	80	54	83	111	104	137
Other apparel products and services	100	69	109	38	95	64	97	144
Jewelry and watches	100	13	69	40	100	80	105	155
All other apparel products and services	100	96	128	39	93	56	93	139
Transportation	100	15	22	134	29	45	118	169
Health care	100	50	10	34	23	28	70	234
Entertainment	100	38	34	70	79	103	105	153
Toys, games, hobbies, and tricycles	100	48	51	105	95	126	116	108
Other entertainment	100	33	26	53	72	93	100	173
Personal care products and services	100	99	148	118	50	109	59	109
Reading	100	21	0	33	33	67	100	167
Education	100	26	21	26	51	26	88	221
All other gifts	100	106	26	67	74	66	70	174

Note: (–) means sample is too small to make a reliable estimate.
Source: Calculations by New Strategist based on the Bureau of Labor Statistics 1999 and 2000 Consumer Expenditure Surveys

Table 1.16 Aged 55 to 64: Average spending by income, 1999–2000

(average annual spending of consumer units (CU) headed by people aged 55 to 64 by product and service category and before-tax income of consumer unit, 1999–2000; complete income reporters only)

	complete income reporters aged 55–64	under $10,000	$10,000–$19,999	$20,000–$29,999	$30,000–$39,999	$40,000–$49,999	$50,000–$69,999	$70,000 or more
Number of consumer units in (in thousands, add 000s)	9,959	1,310	1,626	1,488	1,078	961	1,330	2,166
Average number of persons per CU	2.1	1.7	2.0	2.0	2.1	2.1	2.3	2.5
Average income before taxes	$48,764	$5,623	$14,575	$24,593	$34,323	$44,477	$59,096	$119,876
Average annual spending	42,213	19,148	22,611	30,028	35,630	40,540	49,559	78,593
FOOD	**$5,355**	**$2,633**	**$3,293**	**$4,741**	**$4,833**	**$5,844**	**$6,267**	**$8,387**
Food at home	**3,151**	**1,845**	**2,273**	**3,230**	**2,987**	**3,612**	**3,457**	**4,221**
Cereals and bakery products	453	280	331	476	461	498	490	582
Cereals and cereal products	143	84	110	173	145	163	141	177
Bakery products	309	196	221	303	316	335	349	405
Meats, poultry, fish, and eggs	822	490	633	859	794	984	806	1,087
Beef	238	137	174	230	222	292	238	334
Pork	181	124	149	212	155	241	186	201
Other meats	99	53	81	120	103	112	101	113
Poultry	145	87	117	137	138	171	127	212
Fish and seafood	117	59	78	123	102	121	115	186
Eggs	42	29	33	37	74	47	39	40
Dairy products	332	176	238	318	331	386	370	451
Fresh milk and cream	124	79	98	129	133	133	133	151
Other dairy products	208	97	140	188	198	253	237	300
Fruits and vegetables	579	333	390	576	502	649	665	832
Fresh fruits	186	114	114	184	155	244	211	262
Fresh vegetables	185	105	123	191	150	171	223	279
Processed fruits	119	61	83	115	106	136	121	179
Processed vegetables	90	53	70	86	90	98	109	112
Other food at home	965	567	682	1,001	898	1,095	1,125	1,269
Sugar and other sweets	125	68	74	127	113	160	167	158
Fats and oils	92	52	68	104	104	102	102	108
Miscellaneous foods	423	242	299	439	387	462	484	580
Nonalcoholic beverages	268	167	199	301	254	311	305	322
Food prepared by CU on trips	57	37	42	31	40	59	67	102
Food away from home	**2,204**	**788**	**1,020**	**1,511**	**1,846**	**2,232**	**2,810**	**4,166**
ALCOHOLIC BEVERAGES	**375**	**117**	**185**	**264**	**227**	**264**	**651**	**698**
HOUSING	**12,689**	**7,208**	**7,775**	**9,451**	**11,189**	**11,890**	**15,063**	**21,495**
Shelter	**6,826**	**3,845**	**4,173**	**4,740**	**6,332**	**6,029**	**7,685**	**12,125**
Owned dwellings	4,877	1,945	2,260	3,244	4,918	4,078	5,756	9,529
Mortgage interest and charges	2,361	692	884	1,184	2,380	1,879	2,840	5,199
Property taxes	1,408	707	773	1,106	1,358	1,102	1,687	2,506
Maintenance, repair, insurance, other expenses	1,107	545	603	954	1,180	1,097	1,230	1,824
Rented dwellings	1,216	1,663	1,669	1,113	1,006	1,530	963	799
Other lodging	733	236	244	383	408	421	965	1,798
Utilities, fuels, and public services	**2,669**	**1,862**	**2,159**	**2,329**	**2,598**	**2,715**	**2,859**	**3,670**
Natural gas	323	238	262	249	294	320	327	483
Electricity	1,005	716	860	937	1,030	1,031	1,058	1,281
Fuel oil and other fuels	98	80	76	115	83	95	100	122
Telephone	898	615	684	738	849	913	1,010	1,287
Water and other public services	345	213	276	289	340	357	364	498

	complete income reporters aged 55–64	under $10,000	$10,000–$19,999	$20,000–$29,999	$30,000–$39,999	$40,000–$49,999	$50,000–$69,999	$70,000 or more
Household services	**$540**	**$324**	**$241**	**$386**	**$356**	**$379**	**$467**	**$1,212**
Personal services	89	8	46	79	53	46	62	232
Other household services	450	316	195	306	304	333	404	980
Housekeeping supplies	**658**	**318**	**410**	**574**	**585**	**581**	**741**	**1,134**
Laundry and cleaning supplies	182	74	120	163	163	125	172	356
Other household products	321	155	176	288	298	288	422	517
Postage and stationery	155	88	114	123	124	168	148	262
Household furnishings and equipment	**1,997**	**859**	**792**	**1,423**	**1,319**	**2,185**	**3,311**	**3,352**
Household textiles	136	36	58	205	99	194	132	204
Furniture	386	230	141	267	263	400	460	756
Floor coverings	88	89	21	39	23	75	106	197
Major appliances	206	110	127	199	182	257	258	279
Small appliances, misc. housewares	136	48	46	116	108	142	244	211
Miscellaneous household equipment	1,046	346	400	596	644	1,117	2,112	1,705
APPAREL AND RELATED SERVICES	**1,874**	**717**	**797**	**1,175**	**1,575**	**1,449**	**2,101**	**4,093**
Men and boys	**452**	**102**	**155**	**215**	**401**	**282**	**469**	**1,147**
Men, aged 16 or older	405	75	119	172	338	256	404	1,087
Boys, aged 2 to 15	47	27	36	43	63	26	65	60
Women and girls	**725**	**283**	**354**	**458**	**599**	**632**	**831**	**1,503**
Women, aged 16 or older	666	249	302	394	569	577	791	1,396
Girls, aged 2 to 15	59	34	51	64	30	55	40	106
Children under age 2	**66**	**38**	**24**	**60**	**51**	**45**	**94**	**120**
Footwear	**333**	**125**	**140**	**285**	**339**	**290**	**303**	**680**
Other apparel products and services	**299**	**169**	**125**	**158**	**186**	**200**	**404**	**644**
TRANSPORTATION	**7,635**	**3,494**	**4,284**	**5,311**	**6,995**	**8,036**	**9,057**	**13,507**
Vehicle purchases	**3,412**	**1,495**	**1,762**	**2,070**	**3,223**	**3,828**	**3,809**	**6,396**
Cars and trucks, new	1,844	799	759	1,194	1,550	1,703	1,241	4,315
Cars and trucks, used	1,545	696	1,003	874	1,673	2,119	2,489	2,028
Other vehicles	23	–	–	2	–	5	78	53
Gasoline and motor oil	**1,256**	**687**	**867**	**1,053**	**1,287**	**1,296**	**1,573**	**1,803**
Other vehicle expenses	**2,421**	**1,076**	**1,452**	**1,935**	**2,117**	**2,501**	**2,971**	**4,063**
Vehicle finance charges	329	103	175	287	382	392	421	501
Maintenance and repairs	751	361	562	658	533	890	842	1,169
Vehicle insurance	818	416	534	732	708	795	964	1,309
Vehicle rentals, leases, licenses, other charges	523	197	180	259	494	424	744	1,084
Public transportation	**546**	**235**	**203**	**252**	**368**	**412**	**704**	**1,244**
HEALTH CARE	**2,572**	**1,622**	**1,917**	**2,477**	**2,519**	**2,630**	**2,998**	**3,434**
Health insurance	1,094	658	796	1,140	1,122	1,199	1,310	1,356
Medical services	783	606	483	626	744	683	926	1,200
Drugs	552	294	548	591	524	563	584	662
Medical supplies	143	64	88	120	129	185	178	216
ENTERTAINMENT	**2,288**	**1,068**	**1,294**	**1,929**	**1,720**	**2,109**	**2,311**	**4,342**
Fees and admissions	576	199	185	330	414	453	589	1,392
Television, radio, sound equipment	600	394	405	481	536	638	697	904
Pets, toys, and playground equipment	384	170	238	353	332	388	403	651
Other entertainment products and services	728	304	465	764	437	629	622	1,396

	complete income reporters aged 55–64	under $10,000	$10,000– $19,999	$20,000– $29,999	$30,000– $39,999	$40,000– $49,999	$50,000– $69,999	$70,000 or more
PERSONAL CARE PRODUCTS, SERVICES	$597	$306	$398	$537	$566	$554	$697	938
READING	201	100	95	147	181	193	238	369
EDUCATION	425	155	194	130	157	243	368	1,206
TOBACCO PRODUCTS, SMOKING SUPPLIES	362	336	315	354	378	461	398	345
MISCELLANEOUS	959	545	402	867	939	925	1,179	1,579
CASH CONTRIBUTIONS	1,811	353	636	634	1,005	1,500	1,910	4,863
PERSONAL INSURANCE AND PENSIONS	5,068	495	1,023	2,010	3,346	4,443	6,320	13,338
Life and other personal insurance	622	172	346	405	567	505	781	1,233
Pensions and Social Security	4,446	322	678	1,605	2,779	3,938	5,539	12,105
PERSONAL TAXES	4,120	1,637	315	1,372	2,047	3,153	4,674	11,488
Federal income taxes	3,186	1,376	179	934	1,504	2,282	3,460	9,155
State and local income taxes	696	175	12	229	340	604	907	1,935
Other taxes	238	86	125	208	202	267	307	399
GIFTS	1,578	617	678	1,159	923	1,010	1,761	3,582
Food	111	18	23	52	56	56	124	319
Alcoholic beverages	14	3	1	5	15	4	44	21
Housing	388	146	132	276	284	388	437	823
Housekeeping supplies	55	17	36	48	48	56	74	88
Household textiles	29	11	9	74	12	50	24	32
Appliances and misc. housewares	49	4	10	41	56	78	94	63
Major appliances	9	–	5	–	1	43	10	12
Small appliances and misc. housewares	40	3	4	41	55	35	84	52
Miscellaneous household equipment	105	34	19	69	97	67	170	216
Other housing	150	80	58	44	71	136	74	424
Apparel and services	350	143	200	177	318	188	510	692
Males, aged 2 or older	118	20	66	49	92	61	148	287
Females, aged 2 or older	104	32	58	48	111	71	165	187
Children under age 2	59	29	23	58	49	42	80	107
Other apparel products and services	69	62	51	21	66	14	117	111
Jewelry and watches	33	43	12	14	25	13	78	42
All other apparel products and services	35	19	38	8	42	1	39	70
Transportation	137	32	27	161	14	55	70	407
Health care	53	7	31	147	13	10	25	91
Entertainment	152	66	125	114	89	138	180	269
Toys, games, hobbies, and tricycles	56	24	33	53	40	68	63	91
Other entertainment	96	42	92	61	49	69	117	178
Personal care products and services	29	12	5	61	39	5	29	45
Reading	3	2	2	2	2	5	4	5
Education	173	57	67	39	23	47	142	564
All other gifts	166	129	64	126	68	115	195	345

Note: Spending by category will not add to total spending because gift spending is also included in the preceding product and service categories and personal taxes are not included in the total. (–) means sample is too small to make a reliable estimate.
Source: Bureau of Labor Statistics, 1999 and 2000 Consumer Expenditure Surveys, Internet site www.bls.gov/cex/; calculations by New Strategist

Table 1.17 Aged 55 to 64: Indexed spending by income, 1999–2000

(indexed average annual spending of consumer units (CU) headed by people aged 55 to 64 by product and service category and before-tax income of consumer unit, 1999–2000; complete income reporters only; index definition: an index of 100 is the average for all consumer units; an index of 132 means that spending by consumer units in that group is 32 percent above the average for all consumer units; an index of 68 indicates spending that is 32 percent below the average for all consumer units)

	complete income reporters aged 55–64	under $10,000	$10,000–$19,999	$20,000–$29,999	$30,000–$39,999	$40,000–$49,999	$50,000–$69,999	$70,000 or more
Average spending of CU, total	$42,213	$19,148	$22,611	$30,028	$35,630	$40,540	$49,559	$78,593
Average spending of CU, index	100	45	54	71	84	96	117	186
FOOD	100	49	61	89	90	109	117	157
Food at home	100	59	72	103	95	115	110	134
Cereals and bakery products	100	62	73	105	102	110	108	128
Cereals and cereal products	100	59	77	121	101	114	99	124
Bakery products	100	64	71	98	102	108	113	131
Meats, poultry, fish, and eggs	100	60	77	105	97	120	98	132
Beef	100	58	73	97	93	123	100	140
Pork	100	68	82	117	86	133	103	111
Other meats	100	53	82	121	104	113	102	114
Poultry	100	60	81	94	95	118	88	146
Fish and seafood	100	51	67	105	87	103	98	159
Eggs	100	70	79	88	176	112	93	95
Dairy products	100	53	72	96	100	116	111	136
Fresh milk and cream	100	64	79	104	107	107	107	122
Other dairy products	100	47	67	90	95	122	114	144
Fruits and vegetables	100	57	67	99	87	112	115	144
Fresh fruits	100	61	61	99	83	131	113	141
Fresh vegetables	100	57	66	103	81	92	121	151
Processed fruits	100	51	70	97	89	114	102	150
Processed vegetables	100	59	78	96	100	109	121	124
Other food at home	100	59	71	104	93	113	117	132
Sugar and other sweets	100	55	59	102	90	128	134	126
Fats and oils	100	57	74	113	113	111	111	117
Miscellaneous foods	100	57	71	104	91	109	114	137
Nonalcoholic beverages	100	62	74	112	95	116	114	120
Food prepared by CU on trips	100	65	73	54	70	104	118	179
Food away from home	100	36	46	69	84	101	127	189
ALCOHOLIC BEVERAGES	100	31	49	70	61	70	174	186
HOUSING	100	57	61	74	88	94	119	169
Shelter	100	56	61	69	93	88	113	178
Owned dwellings	100	40	46	67	101	84	118	195
Mortgage interest and charges	100	29	37	50	101	80	120	220
Property taxes	100	50	55	79	96	78	120	178
Maintenance, repair, insurance, other expenses	100	49	55	86	107	99	111	165
Rented dwellings	100	137	137	92	83	126	79	66
Other lodging	100	32	33	52	56	57	132	245
Utilities, fuels, and public services	100	70	81	87	97	102	107	138
Natural gas	100	74	81	77	91	99	101	150
Electricity	100	71	86	93	102	103	105	127
Fuel oil and other fuels	100	81	77	117	85	97	102	124
Telephone	100	69	76	82	95	102	112	143
Water and other public services	100	62	80	84	99	103	106	144

	complete income reporters aged 55–64	under $10,000	$10,000–$19,999	$20,000–$29,999	$30,000–$39,999	$40,000–$49,999	$50,000–$69,999	$70,000 or more
Household services	**100**	**60**	**45**	**71**	**66**	**70**	**86**	**224**
Personal services	100	9	51	89	60	52	70	261
Other household services	100	70	43	68	68	74	90	218
Housekeeping supplies	**100**	**48**	**62**	**87**	**89**	**88**	**113**	**172**
Laundry and cleaning supplies	100	41	66	90	90	69	95	196
Other household products	100	48	55	90	93	90	131	161
Postage and stationery	100	57	73	79	80	108	95	169
Household furnishings and equipment	**100**	**43**	**40**	**71**	**66**	**109**	**166**	**168**
Household textiles	100	26	43	151	73	143	97	150
Furniture	100	60	36	69	68	104	119	196
Floor coverings	100	102	24	44	26	85	120	224
Major appliances	100	54	62	97	88	125	125	135
Small appliances, misc. housewares	100	35	34	85	79	104	179	155
Miscellaneous household equipment	100	33	38	57	62	107	202	163
APPAREL AND RELATED SERVICES	**100**	**38**	**43**	**63**	**84**	**77**	**112**	**218**
Men and boys	**100**	**23**	**34**	**48**	**89**	**62**	**104**	**254**
Men, aged 16 or older	100	19	29	42	83	63	100	268
Boys, aged 2 to 15	100	58	77	91	134	55	138	128
Women and girls	**100**	**39**	**49**	**63**	**83**	**87**	**115**	**207**
Women, aged 16 or older	100	37	45	59	85	87	119	210
Girls, aged 2 to 15	100	58	87	108	51	93	68	180
Children under age 2	**100**	**58**	**36**	**91**	**77**	**68**	**142**	**182**
Footwear	**100**	**38**	**42**	**86**	**102**	**87**	**91**	**204**
Other apparel products and services	**100**	**57**	**42**	**53**	**62**	**67**	**135**	**215**
TRANSPORTATION	**100**	**46**	**56**	**70**	**92**	**105**	**119**	**177**
Vehicle purchases	**100**	**44**	**52**	**61**	**94**	**112**	**112**	**187**
Cars and trucks, new	100	43	41	65	84	92	67	234
Cars and trucks, used	100	45	65	57	108	137	161	131
Other vehicles	100	–	–	9	–	22	339	230
Gasoline and motor oil	**100**	**55**	**69**	**84**	**102**	**103**	**125**	**144**
Other vehicle expenses	**100**	**44**	**60**	**80**	**87**	**103**	**123**	**168**
Vehicle finance charges	100	31	53	87	116	119	128	152
Maintenance and repairs	100	48	75	88	71	119	112	156
Vehicle insurance	100	51	65	89	87	97	118	160
Vehicle rentals, leases, licenses, other charges	100	38	34	50	94	81	142	207
Public transportation	**100**	**43**	**37**	**46**	**67**	**75**	**129**	**228**
HEALTH CARE	**100**	**63**	**75**	**96**	**98**	**102**	**117**	**134**
Health insurance	100	60	73	104	103	110	120	124
Medical services	100	77	62	80	95	87	118	153
Drugs	100	53	99	107	95	102	106	120
Medical supplies	100	45	62	84	90	129	124	151
ENTERTAINMENT	**100**	**47**	**57**	**84**	**75**	**92**	**101**	**190**
Fees and admissions	100	35	32	57	72	79	102	242
Television, radio, sound equipment	100	66	68	80	89	106	116	151
Pets, toys, and playground equipment	100	44	62	92	86	101	105	170
Other entertainment products and services	100	42	64	105	60	86	85	192

	complete income reporters aged 55–64	under $10,000	$10,000– $19,999	$20,000– $29,999	$30,000– $39,999	$40,000– $49,999	$50,000– $69,999	$70,000 or more
PERSONAL CARE PRODUCTS, SERVICES	**100**	**51**	**67**	**90**	**95**	**93**	**117**	**157**
READING	**100**	**50**	**48**	**73**	**90**	**96**	**118**	**184**
EDUCATION	**100**	**36**	**46**	**31**	**37**	**57**	**87**	**284**
TOBACCO PRODUCTS, SMOKING SUPPLIES	**100**	**93**	**87**	**98**	**104**	**127**	**110**	**95**
MISCELLANEOUS	**100**	**57**	**42**	**90**	**98**	**96**	**123**	**165**
CASH CONTRIBUTIONS	**100**	**19**	**35**	**35**	**55**	**83**	**105**	**269**
PERSONAL INSURANCE AND PENSIONS	**100**	**10**	**20**	**40**	**66**	**88**	**125**	**263**
Life and other personal insurance	100	28	56	65	91	81	126	198
Pensions and Social Security	100	7	15	36	63	89	125	272
PERSONAL TAXES	**100**	**40**	**8**	**33**	**50**	**77**	**113**	**279**
Federal income taxes	100	43	6	29	47	72	109	287
State and local income taxes	100	25	2	33	49	87	130	278
Other taxes	100	36	52	87	85	112	129	168
GIFTS	**100**	**39**	**43**	**73**	**58**	**64**	**112**	**227**
Food	**100**	**16**	**21**	**47**	**50**	**50**	**112**	**287**
Alcoholic beverages	**100**	**24**	**10**	**36**	**107**	**29**	**314**	**150**
Housing	**100**	**38**	**34**	**71**	**73**	**100**	**113**	**212**
Housekeeping supplies	100	31	65	87	87	102	135	160
Household textiles	100	39	32	255	41	172	83	110
Appliances and misc. housewares	100	7	19	84	114	159	192	129
Major appliances	100	0	54	–	11	478	111	133
Small appliances and misc. housewares	100	8	10	103	138	88	210	130
Miscellaneous household equipment	100	32	18	66	92	64	162	206
Other housing	100	53	39	29	47	91	49	283
Apparel and services	**100**	**41**	**57**	**51**	**91**	**54**	**146**	**198**
Males, aged 2 or older	100	17	56	42	78	52	125	243
Females, aged 2 or older	100	30	56	46	107	68	159	180
Children under age 2	100	49	39	98	83	71	136	181
Other apparel products and services	100	89	74	30	96	20	170	161
Jewelry and watches	100	129	38	42	76	39	236	127
All other apparel products and services	100	54	109	23	120	3	111	200
Transportation	**100**	**24**	**19**	**118**	**10**	**40**	**51**	**297**
Health care	**100**	**14**	**58**	**277**	**25**	**19**	**47**	**172**
Entertainment	**100**	**44**	**82**	**75**	**59**	**91**	**118**	**177**
Toys, games, hobbies, and tricycles	100	43	59	95	71	121	113	163
Other entertainment	100	44	96	64	51	72	122	185
Personal care products and services	**100**	**43**	**18**	**210**	**134**	**17**	**100**	**155**
Reading	**100**	**78**	**74**	**67**	**67**	**167**	**133**	**167**
Education	**100**	**33**	**39**	**23**	**13**	**27**	**82**	**326**
All other gifts	**100**	**78**	**39**	**76**	**41**	**69**	**117**	**208**

Note: (–) means sample is too small to make a reliable estimate.
Source: Calculations by New Strategist based on the Bureau of Labor Statistics 1999 and 2000 Consumer Expenditure Surveys

Table 1.18 Aged 65 or older: Average spending by income, 1999–2000

(average annual spending of consumer units (CU) headed by people aged 65 or older by product and service category and before-tax income of consumer unit, 1999–2000; complete income reporters only)

	complete income reporters aged 65+	under $10,000	$10,000–$19,999	$20,000–$29,999	$30,000–$39,999	$40,000–$49,999	$50,000–$69,999	$70,000 or more
Number of consumer units in (in thousands, add 000s)	16,983	3,704	6,162	3,077	1,561	807	839	833
Average number of persons per CU	1.7	1.3	1.5	1.9	2.0	1.9	2.1	2.4
Average income before taxes	$25,903	$7,094	$14,393	$24,325	$34,602	$44,512	$58,529	$133,355
Average annual spending	27,925	13,897	21,785	29,721	34,193	41,539	51,569	79,921
FOOD	**$3,715**	**$2,086**	**$2,940**	**$4,117**	**$5,244**	**$5,755**	**$6,391**	**$7,722**
Food at home	**2,427**	**1,586**	**2,098**	**2,696**	**3,304**	**3,442**	**3,703**	**3,834**
Cereals and bakery products	376	263	329	423	530	490	558	521
Cereals and cereal products	120	86	106	138	171	159	168	146
Bakery products	256	177	222	284	359	332	390	375
Meats, poultry, fish, and eggs	605	409	534	642	826	760	929	990
Beef	171	111	150	161	216	229	317	336
Pork	136	90	116	168	201	176	184	179
Other meats	81	59	72	90	105	104	107	119
Poultry	103	80	89	111	138	116	151	161
Fish and seafood	84	46	80	81	128	103	136	156
Eggs	30	24	28	32	38	33	34	38
Dairy products	273	165	243	304	367	393	426	431
Fresh milk and cream	108	81	100	118	133	125	149	153
Other dairy products	165	84	143	187	234	268	277	278
Fruits and vegetables	488	311	416	563	656	737	706	784
Fresh fruits	162	97	137	201	210	259	234	248
Fresh vegetables	144	94	125	157	190	203	192	264
Processed fruits	108	71	89	122	149	157	175	175
Processed vegetables	74	49	65	83	107	118	105	96
Other food at home	684	438	576	763	926	1,061	1,085	1,110
Sugar and other sweets	99	60	84	117	139	133	154	150
Fats and oils	75	51	67	84	109	100	106	107
Miscellaneous foods	302	189	255	328	410	485	490	499
Nonalcoholic beverages	175	124	153	199	214	243	263	258
Food prepared by CU on trips	33	14	16	36	53	100	72	96
Food away from home	**1,288**	**500**	**842**	**1,422**	**1,939**	**2,312**	**2,688**	**3,888**
ALCOHOLIC BEVERAGES	**216**	**49**	**154**	**217**	**306**	**388**	**578**	**661**
HOUSING	**9,067**	**5,425**	**7,726**	**9,347**	**9,854**	**12,194**	**13,948**	**24,472**
Shelter	**4,614**	**2,945**	**4,020**	**4,799**	**5,114**	**6,160**	**6,652**	**11,257**
Owned dwellings	3,034	1,455	2,551	3,346	3,389	4,106	5,205	8,592
Mortgage interest and charges	766	265	537	823	794	955	1,560	3,440
Property taxes	1,113	597	1,007	1,183	1,251	1,478	1,713	2,731
Maintenance, repair, insurance, other expenses	1,155	593	1,008	1,340	1,343	1,673	1,932	2,421
Rented dwellings	1,151	1,357	1,254	955	1,035	1,257	597	864
Other lodging	429	133	215	497	691	797	850	1,801
Utilities, fuels, and public services	**2,192**	**1,614**	**2,006**	**2,398**	**2,482**	**2,717**	**2,960**	**3,544**
Natural gas	290	192	277	333	305	386	320	513
Electricity	843	622	774	922	953	1,063	1,148	1,323
Fuel oil and other fuels	123	111	115	117	188	135	125	127
Telephone	630	491	573	671	677	735	923	1,033
Water and other public services	305	198	266	355	360	397	444	548

	complete income reporters aged 65+	under $10,000	$10,000–$19,999	$20,000–$29,999	$30,000–$39,999	$40,000–$49,999	$50,000–$69,999	$70,000 or more
Household services	**$756**	**$271**	**$493**	**$574**	**$413**	**$994**	**$1,389**	**$5,197**
Personal services	274	104	185	144	–	450	633	2,147
Other household services	482	168	308	431	411	545	755	3,050
Housekeeping supplies	**454**	**215**	**360**	**530**	**541**	**681**	**859**	**1,070**
Laundry and cleaning supplies	106	63	94	136	113	142	143	178
Other household products	215	97	156	227	253	361	501	592
Postage and stationery	133	55	111	167	175	178	216	301
Household furnishings and equipment	**1,052**	**379**	**847**	**1,046**	**1,305**	**1,642**	**2,088**	**3,403**
Household textiles	95	27	81	101	163	104	209	238
Furniture	216	77	189	216	286	221	352	755
Floor coverings	37	7	40	26	41	102	28	134
Major appliances	174	95	156	214	146	271	221	412
Small appliances, misc. housewares	83	24	50	68	73	163	461	177
Miscellaneous household equipment	447	149	331	421	596	781	817	1,688
APPAREL AND RELATED SERVICES	**1,105**	**478**	**849**	**915**	**1,298**	**1,655**	**1,910**	**4,681**
Men and boys	**229**	**69**	**153**	**196**	**354**	**262**	**527**	**1,004**
Men, aged 16 or older	209	60	138	171	332	238	470	959
Boys, aged 2 to 15	20	10	14	25	22	24	56	45
Women and girls	**443**	**208**	**425**	**375**	**501**	**872**	**727**	**1,021**
Women, aged 16 or older	418	190	411	339	475	816	657	992
Girls, aged 2 to 15	25	18	14	35	26	56	70	29
Children under age 2	**23**	**10**	**23**	**21**	**14**	**47**	**41**	**55**
Footwear	**177**	**123**	**144**	**138**	**275**	**264**	**275**	**423**
Other apparel products and services	**234**	**67**	**104**	**186**	**153**	**210**	**340**	**2,178**
TRANSPORTATION	**4,559**	**1,894**	**3,783**	**4,816**	**5,653**	**8,253**	**8,667**	**11,449**
Vehicle purchases	**1,977**	**796**	**1,768**	**1,841**	**2,061**	**4,251**	**3,341**	**5,545**
Cars and trucks, new	1,256	394	1,058	1,335	874	3,027	2,327	4,188
Cars and trucks, used	717	402	702	507	1,176	1,224	1,014	1,357
Other vehicles	–	–	–	–	–	–	–	–
Gasoline and motor oil	**696**	**343**	**556**	**820**	**969**	**1,124**	**1,255**	**1,362**
Other vehicle expenses	**1,475**	**590**	**1,188**	**1,701**	**2,142**	**2,255**	**3,105**	**3,080**
Vehicle finance charges	116	43	76	142	178	198	326	241
Maintenance and repairs	512	209	444	562	866	766	880	912
Vehicle insurance	582	255	479	687	799	897	1,103	1,182
Vehicle rentals, leases, licenses, other charges	265	84	189	310	299	394	796	746
Public transportation	**410**	**165**	**272**	**454**	**481**	**623**	**966**	**1,461**
HEALTH CARE	**3,259**	**2,033**	**3,031**	**3,710**	**3,981**	**3,982**	**4,592**	**5,336**
Health insurance	1,629	1,085	1,481	1,863	2,060	2,025	2,091	2,624
Medical services	664	323	582	699	915	763	1,360	1,390
Drugs	809	530	825	979	809	877	923	1,111
Medical supplies	158	94	145	168	197	317	217	211
ENTERTAINMENT	**1,184**	**489**	**826**	**1,316**	**1,559**	**1,861**	**2,294**	**3,907**
Fees and admissions	354	109	210	381	427	676	938	1,386
Television, radio, sound equipment	421	252	370	443	592	553	647	797
Pets, toys, and playground equipment	202	81	158	233	266	254	377	595
Other entertainment products and services	206	47	88	260	275	378	331	1,129

	complete income reporters aged 65+	under $10,000	$10,000–$19,999	$20,000–$29,999	$30,000–$39,999	$40,000–$49,999	$50,000–$69,999	$70,000 or more
PERSONAL CARE PRODUCTS, SERVICES	$453	$260	$383	$504	$570	$652	$754	$914
READING	167	80	134	196	217	256	288	391
EDUCATION	121	44	47	92	181	94	450	705
TOBACCO PRODUCTS, SMOKING SUPPLIES	166	138	150	180	148	224	230	264
MISCELLANEOUS	753	339	530	761	766	1,018	1,117	3,573
CASH CONTRIBUTIONS	2,014	362	918	2,754	2,910	3,178	5,920	7,984
PERSONAL INSURANCE AND PENSIONS	1,145	220	313	797	1,506	2,031	4,429	7,863
Life and other personal insurance	388	167	234	477	634	573	760	1,184
Pensions and Social Security	757	53	80	320	873	1,459	3,670	6,678
PERSONAL TAXES	1,293	129	340	769	1,396	2,835	3,769	11,266
Federal income taxes	903	52	173	436	886	2,042	2,865	8,760
State and local income taxes	157	10	31	67	139	305	455	1,670
Other taxes	233	68	136	265	371	488	449	836
GIFTS	955	444	737	914	1,198	1,253	1,621	3,469
Food	38	14	21	21	103	68	54	151
Alcoholic beverages	8	4	8	12	6	17	11	7
Housing	274	130	225	280	286	264	291	1,159
Housekeeping supplies	32	10	24	47	50	41	61	58
Household textiles	15	5	17	10	30	8	12	49
Appliances and misc. housewares	32	11	28	31	33	63	51	110
Major appliances	12	9	16	11	9	4	9	25
Small appliances and misc. housewares	20	2	12	20	24	59	42	85
Miscellaneous household equipment	71	23	64	83	111	62	96	201
Other housing	124	81	92	108	61	90	71	741
Apparel and services	175	78	141	203	189	242	295	547
Males, aged 2 or older	47	15	38	58	46	82	98	122
Females, aged 2 or older	69	33	62	81	74	55	101	207
Children under age 2	20	9	20	18	12	34	37	52
Other apparel products and services	39	22	20	47	57	70	59	166
Jewelry and watches	22	7	15	24	10	21	22	159
All other apparel products and services	17	15	6	23	47	50	37	7
Transportation	52	50	39	34	55	87	81	156
Health care	107	49	138	87	124	1	182	205
Entertainment	116	27	58	130	138	237	199	604
Toys, games, hobbies, and tricycles	33	10	23	37	36	50	89	107
Other entertainment	84	17	35	93	102	187	110	497
Personal care products and services	9	2	9	17	11	2	20	4
Reading	5	2	3	7	5	7	6	10
Education	59	24	20	30	107	32	294	321
All other gifts	111	64	73	93	172	297	188	305

Note: Spending by category will not add to total spending because gift spending is also included in the preceding product and service categories and personal taxes are not included in the total. (–) means sample is too small to make a reliable estimate.
Source: Bureau of Labor Statistics, 1999 and 2000 Consumer Expenditure Surveys, Internet site www.bls.gov/cex/; calculations by New Strategist

Table 1.19 Aged 65 or older: Indexed spending by income, 1999–2000

(indexed average annual spending of consumer units (CU) headed by people aged 65 or older by product and service category and before-tax income of consumer unit, 1999–2000; index definition: an index of 100 is the average for all consumer units; an index of 132 means that spending by consumer units in that group is 32 percent above the average for all consumer units; an index of 68 indicates spending that is 32 percent below the average for all consumer units)

	complete income reporters aged 65+	under $10,000	$10,000–$19,999	$20,000–$29,999	$30,000–$39,999	$40,000–$49,999	$50,000–$69,999	$70,000 or more
Average spending of CU, total	$27,925	$13,897	$21,785	$29,721	$34,193	$41,539	$51,569	$79,921
Average spending of CU, index	100	50	78	106	122	149	185	286
FOOD	100	56	79	111	141	155	172	208
Food at home	100	65	86	111	136	142	153	158
Cereals and bakery products	100	70	87	113	141	130	148	139
Cereals and cereal products	100	72	88	115	143	133	140	122
Bakery products	100	69	87	111	140	130	152	146
Meats, poultry, fish, and eggs	100	68	88	106	137	126	154	164
Beef	100	65	88	94	126	134	185	196
Pork	100	66	85	124	148	129	135	132
Other meats	100	72	89	111	130	128	132	147
Poultry	100	77	87	108	134	113	147	156
Fish and seafood	100	54	95	96	152	123	162	186
Eggs	100	79	95	107	127	110	113	127
Dairy products	100	60	89	111	134	144	156	158
Fresh milk and cream	100	75	93	109	123	116	138	142
Other dairy products	100	51	87	113	142	162	168	168
Fruits and vegetables	100	64	85	115	134	151	145	161
Fresh fruits	100	60	85	124	130	160	144	153
Fresh vegetables	100	65	86	109	132	141	133	183
Processed fruits	100	65	82	113	138	145	162	162
Processed vegetables	100	67	87	112	145	159	142	130
Other food at home	100	64	84	112	135	155	159	162
Sugar and other sweets	100	60	85	118	140	134	156	152
Fats and oils	100	68	89	112	145	133	141	143
Miscellaneous foods	100	63	85	109	136	161	162	165
Nonalcoholic beverages	100	71	88	114	122	139	150	147
Food prepared by CU on trips	100	42	49	109	161	303	218	291
Food away from home	100	39	65	110	151	180	209	302
ALCOHOLIC BEVERAGES	100	23	71	100	142	180	268	306
HOUSING	100	60	85	103	109	134	154	270
Shelter	100	64	87	104	111	134	144	244
Owned dwellings	100	48	84	110	112	135	172	283
Mortgage interest and charges	100	35	70	107	104	125	204	449
Property taxes	100	54	90	106	112	133	154	245
Maintenance, repair, insurance, other expenses	100	51	87	116	116	145	167	210
Rented dwellings	100	118	109	83	90	109	52	75
Other lodging	100	31	50	116	161	186	198	420
Utilities, fuels, and public services	100	74	92	109	113	124	135	162
Natural gas	100	66	96	115	105	133	110	177
Electricity	100	74	92	109	113	126	136	157
Fuel oil and other fuels	100	90	94	95	153	110	102	103
Telephone	100	78	91	107	107	117	147	164
Water and other public services	100	65	87	116	118	130	146	180

	complete income reporters aged 65+	under $10,000	$10,000– $19,999	$20,000– $29,999	$30,000– $39,999	$40,000– $49,999	$50,000– $69,999	$70,000 or more
Household services	100	36	65	76	55	131	184	687
Personal services	100	38	67	53	–	164	231	784
Other household services	100	35	64	89	85	113	157	633
Housekeeping supplies	100	47	79	117	119	150	189	236
Laundry and cleaning supplies	100	60	89	128	107	134	135	168
Other household products	100	45	72	106	118	168	233	275
Postage and stationery	100	41	83	126	132	134	162	226
Household furnishings and equipment	100	36	80	99	124	156	198	323
Household textiles	100	28	85	106	172	109	220	251
Furniture	100	36	88	100	132	102	163	350
Floor coverings	100	18	107	70	111	276	76	362
Major appliances	100	55	90	123	84	156	127	237
Small appliances, misc. housewares	100	29	61	82	88	196	555	213
Miscellaneous household equipment	100	33	74	94	133	175	183	378
APPAREL AND RELATED SERVICES	100	43	77	83	117	150	173	424
Men and boys	100	30	67	86	155	114	230	438
Men, aged 16 or older	100	29	66	82	159	114	225	459
Boys, aged 2 to 15	100	49	71	125	110	120	280	225
Women and girls	100	47	96	85	113	197	164	230
Women, aged 16 or older	100	46	98	81	114	195	157	237
Girls, aged 2 to 15	100	70	58	140	104	224	280	116
Children under age 2	100	44	100	91	61	204	178	239
Footwear	100	70	81	78	155	149	155	239
Other apparel products and services	100	29	44	79	65	90	145	931
TRANSPORTATION	100	42	83	106	124	181	190	251
Vehicle purchases	100	40	89	93	104	215	169	280
Cars and trucks, new	100	31	84	106	70	241	185	333
Cars and trucks, used	100	56	98	71	164	171	141	189
Other vehicles	–	–	–	–	–	–	–	–
Gasoline and motor oil	100	49	80	118	139	161	180	196
Other vehicle expenses	100	40	81	115	145	153	211	209
Vehicle finance charges	100	37	65	122	153	171	281	208
Maintenance and repairs	100	41	87	110	169	150	172	178
Vehicle insurance	100	44	82	118	137	154	190	203
Vehicle rentals, leases, licenses, other charges	100	32	71	117	113	149	300	282
Public transportation	100	40	66	111	117	152	236	356
HEALTH CARE	100	62	93	114	122	122	141	164
Health insurance	100	67	91	114	126	124	128	161
Medical services	100	49	88	105	138	115	205	209
Drugs	100	66	102	121	100	108	114	137
Medical supplies	100	59	92	106	125	201	137	134
ENTERTAINMENT	100	41	70	111	132	157	194	330
Fees and admissions	100	31	59	108	121	191	265	392
Television, radio, sound equipment	100	60	88	105	141	131	154	189
Pets, toys, and playground equipment	100	40	78	115	132	126	187	295
Other entertainment products and services	100	23	43	126	133	183	161	548

	complete income reporters aged 65+	under $10,000	$10,000– $19,999	$20,000– $29,999	$30,000– $39,999	$40,000– $49,999	$50,000– $69,999	$70,000 or more
PERSONAL CARE PRODUCTS, SERVICES	**100**	**57**	**85**	**111**	**126**	**144**	**166**	**202**
READING	**100**	**48**	**80**	**117**	**130**	**153**	**172**	**234**
EDUCATION	**100**	**36**	**39**	**76**	**150**	**78**	**372**	**583**
TOBACCO PRODUCTS, SMOKING SUPPLIES	**100**	**83**	**91**	**108**	**89**	**135**	**139**	**159**
MISCELLANEOUS	**100**	**45**	**70**	**101**	**102**	**135**	**148**	**475**
CASH CONTRIBUTIONS	**100**	**18**	**46**	**137**	**144**	**158**	**294**	**396**
PERSONAL INSURANCE AND PENSIONS	**100**	**19**	**27**	**70**	**132**	**177**	**387**	**687**
Life and other personal insurance	100	43	60	123	163	148	196	305
Pensions and Social Security	100	7	11	42	115	193	485	882
PERSONAL TAXES	**100**	**10**	**26**	**59**	**108**	**219**	**291**	**871**
Federal income taxes	100	6	19	48	98	226	317	970
State and local income taxes	100	6	20	43	89	194	290	1,064
Other taxes	100	29	58	114	159	209	193	359
GIFTS	**100**	**47**	**77**	**96**	**125**	**131**	**170**	**363**
Food	**100**	**38**	**56**	**55**	**271**	**179**	**142**	**397**
Alcoholic beverages	**100**	**53**	**101**	**150**	**75**	**213**	**138**	**88**
Housing	**100**	**48**	**82**	**102**	**104**	**96**	**106**	**423**
Housekeeping supplies	100	32	75	147	156	128	191	181
Household textiles	100	34	114	67	200	53	80	327
Appliances and misc. housewares	100	34	86	97	103	197	159	344
Major appliances	100	71	133	92	75	33	75	208
Small appliances and misc. housewares	100	12	58	100	120	295	210	425
Miscellaneous household equipment	100	32	90	117	156	87	135	283
Other housing	100	65	75	87	49	73	57	598
Apparel and services	**100**	**45**	**81**	**116**	**108**	**138**	**169**	**313**
Males, aged 2 or older	100	31	81	123	98	174	209	260
Females, aged 2 or older	100	48	89	117	107	80	146	300
Children under age 2	100	43	101	90	60	170	185	260
Other apparel products and services	100	57	52	121	146	179	151	426
Jewelry and watches	100	30	67	109	45	95	100	723
All other apparel products and services	100	91	33	135	276	294	218	41
Transportation	**100**	**96**	**75**	**65**	**106**	**167**	**156**	**300**
Health care	**100**	**46**	**129**	**81**	**116**	**1**	**170**	**192**
Entertainment	**100**	**23**	**50**	**112**	**119**	**204**	**172**	**521**
Toys, games, hobbies, and tricycles	100	30	71	112	109	152	270	324
Other entertainment	100	20	42	111	121	223	131	592
Personal care products and services	**100**	**24**	**96**	**189**	**122**	**22**	**222**	**44**
Reading	**100**	**37**	**68**	**140**	**100**	**140**	**120**	**200**
Education	**100**	**40**	**34**	**51**	**181**	**54**	**498**	**544**
All other gifts	**100**	**57**	**66**	**84**	**155**	**268**	**169**	**275**

Note: (–) means sample is too small to make a reliable estimate.
Source: Calculations by New Strategist based on the Bureau of Labor Statistics 1999 and 2000 Consumer Expenditure Surveys

Spending Overview:
Spending by Household Type, 2000

Married couples spent 28 percent more than the average household in 2000. Among married couples, those with children aged 18 or older living at home spend the most—$54,550 in 2000. Behind the higher spending of married couples are their higher incomes, primarily a function of the greater number of earners in the household. Most married couples have at least two earners today, and couples with adult children at home often have three earners in the household. The more earners the greater the spending, particularly on products and services needed by workers such as food away from home, men's and women's clothes, and transportation.

Married couples with younger children at home also have distinct spending patterns. Couples with school-aged children spend 42 percent more than the average household overall. They spend 48 percent more than the average household on food at home ($4,458 in 2000). They spend more than other household types on children's clothes, and on fees and admissions to entertainment events. The biggest spenders on household services (mostly day care) are married couples with preschoolers, while couples without children at home spend the most on public transportation (i.e., airfare).

Single-parents spend less than the average household on most items. Some of the exceptions are rent, household personal services (mostly day care), and clothes.

Table 1.20 Average spending by household type, 2000

(average annual spending of consumer units (CU) by product and service category and type of consumer unit, 2000)

	total married couples	married couples, no children	married couples with children total	oldest child under 6	oldest child 6 to 17	oldest child 18 or older	single parent, at least one child <18	single person
Number of consumer units (in thousands, add 000s)	56,287	22,805	28,777	5,291	15,396	8,090	6,132	32,323
Average number of persons per CU	3.2	2.0	3.9	3.5	4.1	3.8	2.9	1.0
Average income before taxes	$60,588	$53,232	$66,913	$62,928	$69,472	$64,725	$25,095	$24,977
Average annual spending	48,619	42,196	53,586	50,756	54,170	54,550	28,923	23,059
FOOD	$6,575	$5,575	$7,251	$5,817	$7,508	$7,858	$4,255	$2,825
Food at home	3,892	3,155	4,357	3,659	4,458	4,724	2,647	1,477
Cereals and bakery products	590	456	680	542	702	749	388	221
Cereals and cereal products	203	149	240	186	256	251	153	69
Bakery products	387	307	440	356	445	497	234	151
Meats, poultry, fish, and eggs	1,018	846	1,113	819	1,155	1,271	754	352
Beef	307	251	335	245	345	391	223	100
Pork	213	189	226	151	236	268	159	71
Other meats	129	100	148	108	153	170	91	47
Poultry	183	143	207	171	210	230	153	68
Fish and seafood	144	126	153	109	168	156	93	50
Eggs	43	37	44	33	44	56	33	18
Dairy products	420	335	481	415	497	505	279	162
Fresh milk and cream	169	121	201	176	209	206	117	65
Other dairy products	252	214	280	239	288	299	162	98
Fruits and vegetables	665	578	710	619	717	771	408	279
Fresh fruits	206	180	216	188	215	241	114	93
Fresh vegetables	204	183	211	184	213	229	117	86
Processed fruits	147	123	164	152	169	163	105	60
Processed vegetables	108	91	119	94	120	138	72	40
Other food at home	1,199	940	1,373	1,265	1,388	1,428	818	462
Sugar and other sweets	156	123	172	127	176	202	107	56
Fats and oils	106	94	113	74	118	135	78	39
Miscellaneous foods	566	413	677	733	678	628	359	221
Nonalcoholic beverages	316	252	356	286	357	413	241	125
Food prepared by CU on trips	55	58	54	45	59	50	32	22
Food away from home	2,683	2,420	2,894	2,158	3,050	3,134	1,608	1,348
ALCOHOLIC BEVERAGES	420	461	396	375	365	477	187	325
HOUSING	15,204	12,832	17,132	18,702	17,433	15,537	10,732	8,189
Shelter	8,536	7,153	9,693	10,398	10,035	8,581	6,331	5,054
Owned dwellings	6,505	5,234	7,587	7,864	7,937	6,743	2,797	2,332
Mortgage interest and charges	3,922	2,692	4,940	5,485	5,280	3,938	1,694	1,005
Property taxes	1,534	1,460	1,618	1,504	1,604	1,719	646	723
Maintenance, repair, insurance, other expenses	1,050	1,082	1,029	874	1,053	1,086	457	604
Rented dwellings	1,355	1,121	1,502	2,162	1,543	993	3,315	2,435
Other lodging	675	798	604	372	556	845	219	287
Utilities, fuels, and public services	3,006	2,689	3,180	2,804	3,193	3,401	2,335	1,628
Natural gas	368	318	396	360	397	418	306	208
Electricity	1,116	1,022	1,161	956	1,170	1,277	863	569
Fuel oil and other fuels	120	129	120	114	118	130	43	68
Telephone	1,016	871	1,097	1,045	1,096	1,133	893	607
Water and other public services	386	348	405	329	412	443	230	175

	total married couples	married couples, no children	married couples with children				single parent, at least one child <18	single person
			total	oldest child under 6	oldest child 6 to 17	oldest child 18 or older		
Household services	$911	$533	$1,221	$2,380	$1,183	$534	$786	$387
Personal services	444	54	750	1,990	661	107	586	124
Other household services	467	478	471	390	523	427	200	264
Housekeeping supplies	647	573	703	618	724	730	368	224
Laundry and cleaning supplies	173	134	203	150	226	200	151	53
Other household products	317	286	338	302	345	353	140	102
Postage and stationery	156	154	162	166	153	177	77	69
Household furnishings and equipment	2,103	1,884	2,336	2,502	2,297	2,291	912	895
Household textiles	144	129	162	179	157	163	60	63
Furniture	521	437	608	722	635	484	272	226
Floor coverings	65	61	71	46	60	108	22	20
Major appliances	258	218	290	265	274	342	104	104
Small appliances, misc. housewares	117	110	122	125	120	124	36	49
Miscellaneous household equipment	999	929	1,082	1,165	1,052	1,071	417	433
APPAREL AND RELATED SERVICES	2,312	1,725	2,749	2,590	2,838	2,698	1,921	1,028
Men and boys	565	424	683	538	717	727	406	223
Men, aged 16 or older	434	400	467	390	421	620	148	211
Boys, aged 2 to 15	131	25	216	148	296	107	259	12
Women and girls	906	691	1,052	777	1,094	1,190	812	414
Women, aged 16 or older	736	657	778	623	695	1,079	532	397
Girls, aged 2 to 15	170	34	274	154	400	111	279	16
Children under age 2	118	38	173	498	102	63	111	17
Footwear	406	298	480	449	537	387	411	191
Other apparel products and services	316	274	361	328	388	331	180	183
TRANSPORTATION	9,910	8,309	11,088	10,745	10,644	12,158	5,017	3,732
Vehicle purchases	4,709	3,824	5,365	5,594	5,102	5,716	2,338	1,456
Cars and trucks, new	2,277	2,113	2,478	2,640	2,379	2,559	524	797
Cars and trucks, used	2,379	1,685	2,817	2,816	2,658	3,119	1,810	628
Other vehicles	53	26	70	137	65	38	4	32
Gasoline and motor oil	1,697	1,411	1,879	1,594	1,866	2,092	894	682
Other vehicle expenses	2,984	2,493	3,352	3,150	3,192	3,793	1,518	1,272
Vehicle finance charges	457	350	534	551	517	556	217	129
Maintenance and repairs	776	673	851	712	827	988	470	396
Vehicle insurance	994	837	1,097	957	982	1,408	554	437
Vehicle rentals, leases, licenses, other charges	757	633	871	929	866	841	276	310
Public transportation	520	581	491	407	485	558	267	322
HEALTH CARE	2,640	3,044	2,306	1,897	2,251	2,681	1,014	1,488
Health insurance	1,288	1,479	1,131	1,025	1,078	1,303	453	657
Medical services	717	738	698	548	731	732	363	418
Drugs	504	671	361	241	327	509	145	351
Medical supplies	132	157	116	84	115	138	54	62
ENTERTAINMENT	2,454	1,968	2,864	2,191	3,250	2,586	1,433	1,026
Fees and admissions	714	595	850	486	1,049	708	404	281
Television, radio, sound equipment	735	570	854	717	917	825	591	429
Pets, toys, and playground equipment	444	388	498	481	547	423	255	177
Other entertainment products and services	561	414	662	506	736	629	182	139

	total married couples	married couples, no children	married couples with children				single parent, at least one child <18	single person
			total	oldest child under 6	oldest child 6 to 17	oldest child 18 or older		
PERSONAL CARE PRODUCTS AND SERVICES	$700	$611	$769	$649	$774	$845	$569	$338
READING	182	197	176	174	174	181	76	113
EDUCATION	811	447	1,126	420	1,032	1,769	395	407
TOBACCO PRODUCTS AND SMOKING SUPPLIES	343	286	358	275	336	455	299	203
MISCELLANEOUS	908	878	893	687	960	909	784	561
CASH CONTRIBUTIONS	1,512	1,915	1,220	848	1,270	1,370	407	1,047
PERSONAL INSURANCE AND PENSIONS	4,648	3,949	5,257	5,388	5,334	5,027	1,834	1,778
Life and other personal insurance	608	613	601	482	590	702	150	155
Pensions and Social Security	4,039	3,335	4,656	4,906	4,744	4,325	1,683	1,623
PERSONAL TAXES	4,308	4,358	4,457	4,164	4,734	4,120	597	2,090
Federal income taxes	3,361	3,396	3,467	3,260	3,646	3,261	353	1,621
State and local income taxes	752	726	816	756	906	678	203	360
Other taxes	195	236	175	147	182	181	41	109
GIFTS	1,355	1,477	1,266	918	1,147	1,728	683	807
Food	109	101	116	58	87	213	30	31
Alcoholic beverages	19	14	24	45	14	27	8	10
Housing	379	417	358	345	324	436	214	192
Housekeeping supplies	50	50	52	49	45	69	23	25
Household textiles	19	14	24	10	15	53	5	8
Appliances and misc. housewares	35	44	27	35	23	28	8	19
Major appliances	10	11	6	2	7	5	3	5
Small appliances and misc. housewares	25	33	21	34	16	23	5	14
Miscellaneous household equipment	85	87	83	70	66	122	50	64
Other housing	190	221	172	181	174	164	128	77
Apparel and services	280	301	261	270	221	334	203	187
Males, aged 2 or older	74	87	68	59	45	124	47	51
Females, aged 2 or older	100	122	82	65	79	100	74	60
Children under age 2	57	38	65	105	51	60	39	17
Other apparel products and services	48	54	46	41	46	50	43	59
Jewelry and watches	14	17	13	16	8	19	7	36
All other apparel products and services	35	38	33	25	38	31	36	23
Transportation	72	101	57	15	61	75	19	58
Health care	28	29	14	3	14	21	8	62
Entertainment	112	123	96	100	92	102	51	73
Toys, games, hobbies, and tricycles	36	47	27	34	24	29	13	24
Other entertainment	76	76	69	67	68	73	38	49
Personal care products and services	23	15	29	26	31	28	29	14
Reading	2	3	2	2	1	2	0	2
Education	237	271	229	19	234	355	67	72
All other gifts	94	102	81	35	67	136	54	105

Note: Spending by category will not add to total spending because gift spending is also included in the preceding product and service categories and personal taxes are not included in the total.
Source: Bureau of Labor Statistics, 2000 Consumer Expenditure Survey, Internet site www.bls.gov/cex/; calculations by New Strategist

Table 1.21 Indexed spending by household type, 2000

(indexed average annual spending of consumer units (CU) by product and service category and type of consumer unit, 2000; index definition: an index of 100 is the average for all consumer units; an index of 132 means that spending by consumer units in that group is 32 percent above the average for all consumer units; an index of 68 indicates spending that is 32 percent below the average for all consumer units)

	total married couples	married couples, no children	married couples with children — total	oldest child under 6	oldest child 6 to 17	oldest child 18 or older	single parent, at least one child <18	single person
Average spending of CU, total	$48,619	$42,196	$53,586	$50,756	$54,170	$54,550	$28,923	$23,059
Average spending of CU, index	128	111	141	133	142	143	76	61
FOOD	127	108	141	113	146	152	82	55
Food at home	129	104	144	121	148	156	88	49
Cereals and bakery products	130	101	150	120	155	165	86	49
Cereals and cereal products	130	96	154	119	164	161	98	44
Bakery products	130	103	148	120	150	167	79	51
Meats, poultry, fish, and eggs	128	106	140	103	145	160	95	44
Beef	129	105	141	103	145	164	94	42
Pork	128	113	135	90	141	160	95	43
Other meats	128	99	147	107	151	168	90	47
Poultry	126	99	143	118	145	159	106	47
Fish and seafood	131	115	139	99	153	142	85	45
Eggs	126	109	129	97	129	165	97	53
Dairy products	129	103	148	128	153	155	86	50
Fresh milk and cream	129	92	153	134	160	157	89	50
Other dairy products	131	111	145	124	149	155	84	51
Fruits and vegetables	128	111	136	119	138	148	78	54
Fresh fruits	126	110	133	115	132	148	70	57
Fresh vegetables	128	115	133	116	134	144	74	54
Processed fruits	128	107	143	132	147	142	91	52
Processed vegetables	129	108	142	112	143	164	86	48
Other food at home	129	101	148	136	150	154	88	50
Sugar and other sweets	133	105	147	109	150	173	91	48
Fats and oils	128	113	136	89	142	163	94	47
Miscellaneous foods	130	95	155	168	155	144	82	51
Nonalcoholic beverages	126	101	142	114	143	165	96	50
Food prepared by CU on trips	138	145	135	113	148	125	80	55
Food away from home	126	113	135	101	143	147	75	63
ALCOHOLIC BEVERAGES	113	124	106	101	98	128	50	87
HOUSING	123	104	139	152	142	126	87	66
Shelter	120	101	136	146	141	121	89	71
Owned dwellings	141	114	165	171	172	147	61	51
Mortgage interest and charges	149	102	187	208	200	149	64	38
Property taxes	135	128	142	132	141	151	57	63
Maintenance, repair, insurance, other expenses	127	131	125	106	128	132	55	73
Rented dwellings	67	55	74	106	76	49	163	120
Other lodging	141	167	126	78	116	177	46	60
Utilities, fuels, and public services	121	108	128	113	128	137	94	65
Natural gas	120	104	129	117	129	136	100	68
Electricity	123	112	127	105	128	140	95	62
Fuel oil and other fuels	124	133	124	118	122	134	44	70
Telephone	116	99	125	119	125	129	102	69
Water and other public services	130	118	137	111	139	150	78	59

	total married couples	married couples, no children	married couples with children				single parent, at least one child <18	single person
			total	oldest child under 6	oldest child 6 to 17	oldest child 18 or older		
Household services	**133**	**78**	**179**	**348**	**173**	**78**	**115**	**57**
Personal services	136	17	230	610	203	33	180	38
Other household services	130	134	132	109	146	119	56	74
Housekeeping supplies	**134**	**119**	**146**	**128**	**150**	**151**	**76**	**46**
Laundry and cleaning supplies	132	102	155	115	173	153	115	40
Other household products	140	127	150	134	153	156	62	45
Postage and stationery	124	122	129	132	121	140	61	55
Household furnishings and equipment	**136**	**122**	**151**	**162**	**148**	**148**	**59**	**58**
Household textiles	136	122	153	169	148	154	57	59
Furniture	133	112	155	185	162	124	70	58
Floor coverings	148	139	161	105	136	245	50	45
Major appliances	137	115	153	140	145	181	55	55
Small appliances, misc. housewares	134	126	140	144	138	143	41	56
Miscellaneous household equipment	137	127	148	159	144	147	57	59
APPAREL AND RELATED SERVICES	**125**	**93**	**148**	**140**	**153**	**145**	**104**	**55**
Men and boys	**128**	**96**	**155**	**122**	**163**	**165**	**92**	**51**
Men, aged 16 or older	126	116	136	113	122	180	43	61
Boys, aged 2 to 15	136	26	225	154	308	111	270	13
Women and girls	**125**	**95**	**145**	**107**	**151**	**164**	**112**	**57**
Women, aged 16 or older	121	108	128	103	114	178	88	65
Girls, aged 2 to 15	144	29	232	131	339	94	236	14
Children under age 2	**144**	**46**	**211**	**607**	**124**	**77**	**135**	**21**
Footwear	**118**	**87**	**140**	**131**	**157**	**113**	**120**	**56**
Other apparel products and services	**119**	**103**	**136**	**123**	**146**	**124**	**68**	**69**
TRANSPORTATION	**134**	**112**	**149**	**145**	**144**	**164**	**68**	**50**
Vehicle purchases	**138**	**112**	**157**	**164**	**149**	**167**	**68**	**43**
Cars and trucks, new	142	132	154	164	148	159	33	50
Cars and trucks, used	134	95	159	159	150	176	102	35
Other vehicles	123	60	163	319	151	88	9	74
Gasoline and motor oil	**131**	**109**	**146**	**123**	**145**	**162**	**69**	**53**
Other vehicle expenses	**131**	**109**	**147**	**138**	**140**	**166**	**67**	**56**
Vehicle finance charges	139	107	163	168	158	170	66	39
Maintenance and repairs	124	108	136	114	133	158	75	63
Vehicle insurance	128	108	141	123	126	181	71	56
Vehicle rentals, leases, licenses, other charges	137	115	158	169	157	153	50	56
Public transportation	**122**	**136**	**115**	**95**	**114**	**131**	**63**	**75**
HEALTH CARE	**128**	**147**	**112**	**92**	**109**	**130**	**49**	**72**
Health insurance	131	150	115	104	110	133	46	67
Medical services	126	130	123	96	129	129	64	74
Drugs	121	161	87	58	79	122	35	84
Medical supplies	133	159	117	85	116	139	55	63
ENTERTAINMENT	**132**	**106**	**154**	**118**	**174**	**139**	**77**	**55**
Fees and admissions	139	116	165	94	204	137	78	55
Television, radio, sound equipment	118	92	137	115	147	133	95	69
Pets, toys, and playground equipment	133	116	149	144	164	127	76	53
Other entertainment products and services	143	105	168	129	187	160	46	35

	total married couples	married couples, no children	married couples with children			single parent, at least one child <18	single person
			total	oldest child under 6	oldest child 6 to 17	oldest child 18 or older		
PERSONAL CARE PRODUCTS AND SERVICES	124	108	136	115	137	150	101	60
READING	125	135	121	119	119	124	52	77
EDUCATION	128	71	178	66	163	280	63	64
TOBACCO PRODUCTS AND SMOKING SUPPLIES	108	90	112	86	105	143	94	64
MISCELLANEOUS	117	113	115	89	124	117	101	72
CASH CONTRIBUTIONS	127	161	102	71	107	115	34	88
PERSONAL INSURANCE AND PENSIONS	138	117	156	160	159	149	55	53
Life and other personal insurance	152	154	151	121	148	176	38	39
Pensions and Social Security	136	112	157	165	160	146	57	55
PERSONAL TAXES	138	140	143	134	152	132	19	67
Federal income taxes	140	141	144	135	151	135	15	67
State and local income taxes	134	129	145	135	161	121	36	64
Other taxes	134	162	120	101	125	124	28	75
GIFTS	125	136	117	85	106	160	63	75
Food	156	144	166	83	124	304	43	44
Alcoholic beverages	136	100	171	321	100	193	57	71
Housing	130	143	123	119	111	150	74	66
Housekeeping supplies	128	128	133	126	115	177	59	64
Household textiles	146	108	185	77	115	408	38	62
Appliances and misc. housewares	125	157	96	125	82	100	29	68
Major appliances	125	138	75	25	88	63	38	63
Small appliances and misc. housewares	119	157	100	162	76	110	24	67
Miscellaneous household equipment	121	124	119	100	94	174	71	91
Other housing	136	158	123	129	124	117	91	55
Apparel and services	115	123	107	111	91	137	83	77
Males, aged 2 or older	109	128	100	87	66	182	69	75
Females, aged 2 or older	118	144	96	76	93	118	87	71
Children under age 2	139	93	159	256	124	146	95	41
Other apparel products and services	94	106	90	80	90	98	84	116
Jewelry and watches	70	85	65	80	40	95	35	180
All other apparel products and services	117	127	110	83	127	103	120	77
Transportation	103	144	81	21	87	107	27	83
Health care	74	76	37	8	37	55	21	163
Entertainment	119	131	102	106	98	109	54	78
Toys, games, hobbies, and tricycles	120	157	90	113	80	97	43	80
Other entertainment	119	119	108	105	106	114	59	77
Personal care products and services	121	79	153	137	163	147	153	74
Reading	100	150	100	100	50	100	0	100
Education	157	179	152	13	155	235	44	48
All other gifts	106	115	91	39	75	153	61	118

Note: Spending index for total consumer units is 100.
Source: Calculations by New Strategist based on the Bureau of Labor Statistics 2000 Consumer Expenditure Survey

Spending Overview:
Spending by Household Type and Age, 1999–2000

On average, women who live alone spent an annual average of $21,269 in 1999–2000, only 57 percent of the $37,622 the average household spent during that time period. Forty-three percent of women who live alone are aged 65 or older, many of them elderly widows with low incomes.

Among women who live alone, spending peaks in the 25-to-54 age group at more than $26,000 in 1999–2000. Women under age 25 spend much more than the average household on education, with an index of 238. Despite their small household size, women aged 25 to 34 spend fully 84 percent more than average on women's clothes, more than almost any other household type. Women aged 65 or older spend less than their middle-aged counterparts, an average of $18,204 in 1999–2000. But they spend more than the average household on household services, health care, and cash contributions.

On average, men who live alone spent an annual average of $24,760 in 1999–2000, only 66 percent of what the average household spent during the time period. Among men who live alone, those under age 25 spend much more than the average household on education, with an index of 252. They spent $650 on alcoholic beverages in 1999–2000, more than any other household type. Men aged 25 to 34 who live alone spend 12 percent more than the average household on food away from home despite their smaller household size. They spend 66 percent more than average on men's clothes, more than almost any other household type. They spend eight times the average on gifts of jewelry and watches. Men aged 65 or older who live alone spend less than their middle-aged counterparts, an average of $20,287 in 1999–2000. They spend more than the average household on health care and cash contributions.

Table 1.22 Average spending of single-person consumer units headed by women, by age, 1999–2000

(average annual spending of single-person consumer units headed by women by product and service category and age, 1999–2000)

	total single-person consumer units headed by women	under 25	25 to 34	35 to 44	45 to 54	55 to 64	65 or older
Number of consumer units (in thousands, add 000s)	18,270	2,202	1,712	1,699	2,473	2,383	7,800
Average income before taxes	$21,948	$10,925	$29,545	$36,655	$30,716	$23,762	$16,701
Average annual spending	21,269	14,739	27,907	26,010	26,480	23,470	18,204
FOOD	**$2,475**	**$2,006**	**$3,000**	**$2,889**	**$3,212**	**$2,636**	**$2,084**
Food at home	**1,525**	**871**	**1,454**	**1,573**	**1,823**	**1,714**	**1,545**
Cereals and bakery products	237	134	205	228	259	265	257
Cereals and cereal products	74	51	68	78	70	85	79
Bakery products	162	83	137	151	190	179	178
Meats, poultry, fish, and eggs	346	176	317	362	433	400	349
Beef	94	47	82	95	133	100	96
Pork	68	35	67	81	73	81	68
Other meats	45	26	40	52	52	41	49
Poultry	69	36	58	73	79	97	67
Fish and seafood	52	24	56	42	78	59	51
Eggs	17	8	14	17	19	22	19
Dairy products	168	98	151	177	175	195	176
Fresh milk and cream	64	34	52	62	58	72	76
Other dairy products	103	65	99	115	117	123	101
Fruits and vegetables	298	148	265	267	361	337	321
Fresh fruits	101	48	84	93	119	114	112
Fresh vegetables	91	38	83	80	118	99	98
Processed fruits	63	36	59	53	69	72	68
Processed vegetables	43	25	38	41	55	52	43
Other food at home	476	315	516	538	594	518	443
Sugar and other sweets	63	44	64	76	66	67	63
Fats and oils	44	29	34	45	47	55	47
Miscellaneous foods	228	147	269	230	304	230	214
Nonalcoholic beverages	122	74	125	164	157	142	107
Food prepared by CU on trips	18	21	24	24	21	25	12
Food away from home	**951**	**1,136**	**1,546**	**1,316**	**1,390**	**922**	**538**
ALCOHOLIC BEVERAGES	**157**	**238**	**337**	**216**	**203**	**125**	**72**
HOUSING	**8,190**	**4,747**	**10,077**	**10,425**	**10,153**	**8,607**	**7494**
Shelter	**4,870**	**3,220**	**6,807**	**6,824**	**6,519**	**5,064**	**3903**
Owned dwellings	2,349	200	1,856	3,380	3,767	3,132	2,149
Mortgage interest and charges	894	86	1,238	2,080	2,012	1,234	330
Property taxes	787	92	397	719	973	1,005	958
Maintenance, repair, insurance, other expenses	668	23	221	581	782	892	862
Rented dwellings	2,279	2,697	4,688	3,161	2,523	1,698	1541
Other lodging	242	323	263	282	228	234	212
Utilities, fuels, and public services	**1,664**	**736**	**1,627**	**1,836**	**1,896**	**1,947**	**1,737**
Natural gas	212	45	145	201	240	257	254
Electricity	592	225	499	624	637	705	660
Fuel oil and other fuels	61	9	23	42	64	61	87
Telephone	610	419	857	795	749	685	502
Water and other public services	189	37	104	173	206	239	234

	total single-person consumer units headed by women	under 25	25 to 34	35 to 44	45 to 54	55 to 64	65 or older
Household services	**$536**	**$41**	**$177**	**$328**	**$286**	**$323**	**$944**
Personal services	225	–	–	75	33	–	499
Other household services	311	41	173	252	253	322	445
Housekeeping supplies	**274**	**143**	**235**	**333**	**316**	**319**	**276**
Laundry and cleaning supplies	60	25	64	70	68	73	60
Other household products	117	51	86	161	143	134	119
Postage and stationery	96	67	85	102	105	112	97
Household furnishings and equipment	**847**	**606**	**1,231**	**1,105**	**1,136**	**954**	**635**
Household textiles	85	24	145	73	99	107	77
Furniture	212	191	279	411	284	236	131
Floor coverings	28	6	33	38	44	40	23
Major appliances	117	33	224	129	82	116	122
Small appliances, misc. housewares	60	37	82	54	120	65	41
Miscellaneous household equipment	344	315	468	400	507	390	242
APPAREL AND RELATED SERVICES	**1,108**	**1,114**	**1,618**	**1,454**	**1,312**	**1,074**	**849**
Men and boys	**49**	**36**	**75**	**85**	**63**	**45**	**34**
Men, aged 16 or older	36	34	60	78	48	23	22
Boys, aged 2 to 15	12	2	15	7	14	22	12
Women and girls	**641**	**724**	**1,081**	**848**	**892**	**602**	**394**
Women, aged 16 or older	627	724	1,073	830	876	580	380
Girls, aged 2 to 15	14	1	8	18	16	22	14
Children under age 2	**21**	**8**	**18**	**36**	**23**	**45**	**14**
Footwear	**172**	**217**	**219**	**217**	**156**	**178**	**140**
Other apparel products and services	**226**	**129**	**225**	**269**	**178**	**205**	**266**
TRANSPORTATION	**2,935**	**2,632**	**5,290**	**3,387**	**3,969**	**3,564**	**1881**
Vehicle purchases	**1,093**	**1,197**	**2,564**	**746**	**1,571**	**1,414**	**567**
Cars and trucks, new	636	650	1,534	239	849	975	349
Cars and trucks, used	457	547	1,030	507	721	439	218
Other vehicles	–	–	–	–	–	–	–
Gasoline and motor oil	**495**	**506**	**668**	**701**	**667**	**636**	**312**
Other vehicle expenses	**1,065**	**742**	**1,619**	**1,594**	**1,432**	**1,246**	**745**
Vehicle finance charges	106	91	230	203	149	127	42
Maintenance and repairs	325	242	354	447	405	436	252
Vehicle insurance	391	229	537	494	488	443	336
Vehicle rentals, leases, licenses, other charges	244	179	498	450	390	240	115
Public transportation	**282**	**188**	**440**	**347**	**300**	**269**	**257**
HEALTH CARE	**1,632**	**297**	**902**	**1,159**	**1,330**	**1,593**	**2378**
Health insurance	747	119	404	462	490	614	1183
Medical services	389	82	284	372	441	478	459
Drugs	416	66	163	258	322	402	637
Medical supplies	81	30	51	67	77	99	100
ENTERTAINMENT	**884**	**687**	**1,148**	**1,339**	**1,109**	**1,180**	**617**
Fees and admissions	244	255	366	408	288	274	156
Television, radio, sound equipment	346	244	432	460	396	393	302
Pets, toys, and playground equipment	197	91	209	324	327	290	125
Other entertainment products and services	96	96	142	147	98	224	34

	total single-person consumer units headed by women	under 25	25 to 34	35 to 44	45 to 54	55 to 64	65 or older
PERSONAL CARE PRODUCTS AND SERVICES	$417	$307	$550	$485	$563	$428	$350
READING	126	60	131	130	175	144	121
EDUCATION	348	1,505	762	220	287	144	41
TOBACCO PRODUCTS AND SMOKING SUPPLIES	140	91	145	231	230	194	87
MISCELLANEOUS	593	264	781	551	618	570	647
CASH CONTRIBUTIONS	940	156	617	430	473	1,446	1336
PERSONAL INSURANCE, PENSIONS	1,323	635	2,549	3,095	2,846	1,765	245
Life and other personal insurance	128	27	71	137	177	198	130
Pensions and Social Security	1,195	608	2,478	2,958	2,670	1,567	115
PERSONAL TAXES	1,618	576	2,341	3,837	2,446	2,052	868
Federal income taxes	1,188	461	1,779	2,993	1,927	1,503	535
State and local income taxes	306	113	532	800	428	394	137
Other taxes	123	–	29	44	91	155	196
GIFTS	753	374	670	957	902	989	706
Food	40	10	38	34	49	84	32
Alcoholic beverages	8	6	19	16	10	5	4
Housing	212	151	178	236	238	233	216
Housekeeping supplies	34	26	35	65	41	41	25
Household textiles	22	2	20	8	31	35	22
Appliances and misc. housewares	23	3	20	17	20	17	32
Major appliances	9	–	3	3	3	1	18
Small appliances and misc. housewares	14	3	16	14	17	16	15
Miscellaneous household equipment	58	45	50	66	68	71	55
Other housing	75	75	53	79	78	69	81
Apparel and services	169	97	156	359	196	206	130
Males, aged 2 or older	48	29	75	85	63	45	34
Females, aged 2 or older	64	35	50	149	78	67	51
Children under age 2	21	8	18	36	23	45	14
Other apparel products and services	36	24	13	90	32	49	31
Jewelry and watches	18	9	13	38	16	33	13
All other apparel products and services	19	15	0	52	17	16	19
Transportation	48	10	78	33	59	116	31
Health care	48	1	34	11	18	12	92
Entertainment	69	31	75	66	89	119	54
Toys, games, hobbies, and tricycles	24	8	24	21	34	43	19
Other entertainment	45	23	51	45	55	76	35
Personal care products and services	17	10	26	32	34	15	8
Reading	3	0	2	2	3	3	4
Education	54	41	29	79	119	84	28
All other gifts	85	16	33	89	85	113	107

Note: Spending by category will not add to total spending because gift spending is also included in the preceding product and service categories and personal taxes are not included in the total. (–) means sample is too small to make a reliable estimate.
Source: Bureau of Labor Statistics, 1999 and 2000 Consumer Expenditure Surveys, Internet site www.bls.gov/cex/

Table 1.23 Indexed spending of single-person consumer units headed by women, by age, 1999–2000

(indexed average annual spending of single-person consumer units headed by women by product and service category and age, 1999–2000; index definition: an index of 100 is the average for all consumer units; an index of 132 means that spending by consumer units in that group is 32 percent above the average for all consumer units; an index of 68 indicates spending that is 32 percent below the average for all consumer units)

	total single-person consumer units headed by women	under 25	25 to 34	35 to 44	45 to 54	55 to 64	65 or older
Average spending of CU, total	$21,269	$14,739	$27,907	$26,010	$26,480	$23,470	$18,204
Average spending of CU, index	57	39	74	69	70	62	48
FOOD	49	39	59	57	63	52	41
Food at home	51	29	49	53	61	58	52
Cereals and bakery products	53	30	45	51	57	59	57
Cereals and cereal products	47	32	43	49	44	54	50
Bakery products	55	28	47	52	65	61	61
Meats, poultry, fish, and eggs	45	23	41	47	56	52	45
Beef	41	21	36	41	58	44	42
Pork	42	22	41	50	45	50	42
Other meats	45	26	40	53	53	41	49
Poultry	49	26	41	52	56	69	48
Fish and seafood	48	22	52	39	72	55	47
Eggs	52	24	42	52	58	67	58
Dairy products	52	30	47	55	54	60	54
Fresh milk and cream	50	27	41	49	46	57	60
Other dairy products	52	33	50	58	59	62	51
Fruits and vegetables	58	29	52	52	71	66	63
Fresh fruits	64	30	53	59	75	72	71
Fresh vegetables	59	25	54	52	77	64	64
Processed fruits	55	32	52	46	61	63	60
Processed vegetables	51	29	45	48	65	61	51
Other food at home	52	35	57	59	65	57	49
Sugar and other sweets	55	39	56	67	58	59	55
Fats and oils	53	35	41	54	57	66	57
Miscellaneous foods	53	34	63	54	71	54	50
Nonalcoholic beverages	50	30	51	67	64	58	43
Food prepared by CU on trips	45	53	60	60	53	63	30
Food away from home	45	53	73	62	65	43	25
ALCOHOLIC BEVERAGES	46	69	98	63	59	36	21
HOUSING	67	39	83	86	83	71	61
Shelter	69	46	96	97	92	72	55
Owned dwellings	51	4	41	74	83	69	47
Mortgage interest and charges	34	3	48	80	78	48	13
Property taxes	70	8	35	64	86	89	85
Maintenance, repair, insurance, other expenses	80	3	26	69	93	106	103
Rented dwellings	112	133	231	156	124	84	76
Other lodging	51	69	56	60	48	50	45
Utilities, fuels, and public services	68	30	67	75	78	80	71
Natural gas	73	16	50	70	83	89	88
Electricity	65	25	55	69	70	78	73
Fuel oil and other fuels	71	10	27	49	74	71	101
Telephone	71	49	99	92	87	79	58
Water and other public services	65	13	36	59	71	82	80

	total single-person consumer units headed by women	under 25	25 to 34	35 to 44	45 to 54	55 to 64	65 or older
Household services	79	6	26	49	42	48	140
Personal services	69	–	–	23	10	–	154
Other household services	89	12	49	72	72	92	127
Housekeeping supplies	56	29	48	68	64	65	56
Laundry and cleaning supplies	48	20	51	56	54	58	48
Other household products	49	21	36	68	60	56	50
Postage and stationery	76	53	67	81	83	89	77
Household furnishings and equipment	56	40	81	73	75	63	42
Household textiles	77	22	132	66	90	97	70
Furniture	56	51	74	109	75	62	35
Floor coverings	64	14	75	86	100	91	52
Major appliances	63	18	120	69	44	62	66
Small appliances, misc. housewares	64	39	87	57	128	69	44
Miscellaneous household equipment	48	44	66	56	71	55	34
APPAREL AND RELATED SERVICES	61	61	89	80	72	59	47
Men and boys	11	8	17	19	14	10	8
Men, aged 16 or older	10	10	17	23	14	7	6
Boys, aged 2 to 15	13	2	16	7	15	23	13
Women and girls	92	104	156	122	128	87	57
Women, aged 16 or older	108	124	184	143	151	100	65
Girls, aged 2 to 15	12	1	7	16	14	19	12
Children under age 2	26	10	23	45	29	56	18
Footwear	53	67	68	67	48	55	43
Other apparel products and services	80	46	80	96	63	73	95
TRANSPORTATION	41	36	73	47	55	49	26
Vehicle purchases	33	36	76	22	47	42	17
Cars and trucks, new	39	40	95	15	53	60	22
Cars and trucks, used	27	32	60	30	42	26	13
Other vehicles	–	–	–	–	–	–	–
Gasoline and motor oil	42	43	57	60	57	54	27
Other vehicle expenses	47	33	71	70	63	55	33
Vehicle finance charges	33	28	71	63	46	39	13
Maintenance and repairs	50	38	55	69	63	68	39
Vehicle insurance	51	30	70	64	64	58	44
Vehicle rentals, leases, licenses, other charges	46	34	94	85	73	45	22
Public transportation	68	46	107	84	73	65	62
HEALTH CARE	81	15	45	58	66	79	118
Health insurance	78	12	42	48	51	64	124
Medical services	69	15	50	66	78	85	82
Drugs	106	17	41	66	82	102	162
Medical supplies	78	29	49	64	74	95	96
ENTERTAINMENT	46	36	60	70	58	62	32
Fees and admissions	48	50	72	80	57	54	31
Television, radio, sound equipment	56	40	70	75	64	64	49
Pets, toys, and playground equipment	58	27	62	96	96	86	37
Other entertainment products and services	22	22	32	33	22	51	8

	total single-person consumer units headed by women	under 25	25 to 34	35 to 44	45 to 54	55 to 64	65 or older
PERSONAL CARE PRODUCTS AND SERVICES	76	56	100	88	102	78	63
READING	82	39	86	85	114	94	79
EDUCATION	55	238	120	35	45	23	6
TOBACCO PRODUCTS AND SMOKING SUPPLIES	45	29	47	75	74	63	28
MISCELLANEOUS	72	32	95	67	75	69	79
CASH CONTRIBUTIONS	79	13	52	36	40	122	113
PERSONAL INSURANCE, PENSIONS	39	19	75	91	84	52	7
Life and other personal insurance	32	7	18	35	45	50	33
Pensions and Social Security	40	20	83	99	89	52	4
PERSONAL TAXES	50	18	73	120	76	64	27
Federal income taxes	48	19	72	122	78	61	22
State and local income taxes	52	19	90	136	73	67	23
Other taxes	78	–	18	28	58	98	124
GIFTS	69	34	61	88	83	91	65
Food	53	13	50	45	64	111	42
Alcoholic beverages	53	40	127	107	67	33	27
Housing	73	52	61	81	82	80	74
Housekeeping supplies	85	65	88	163	103	103	63
Household textiles	147	13	133	53	207	233	147
Appliances and misc. housewares	77	10	67	57	67	57	107
Major appliances	113	–	38	38	38	13	225
Small appliances and misc. housewares	64	14	73	64	77	73	68
Miscellaneous household equipment	85	66	74	97	100	104	81
Other housing	54	54	38	57	57	50	59
Apparel and services	73	42	68	155	85	89	56
Males, aged 2 or older	79	48	123	139	103	74	56
Females, aged 2 or older	82	45	64	191	100	86	65
Children under age 2	53	20	45	90	58	113	35
Other apparel products and services	71	47	25	176	63	96	61
Jewelry and watches	78	39	57	165	70	143	57
All other apparel products and services	68	54	0	186	61	57	68
Transportation	72	15	116	49	88	173	46
Health care	123	3	87	28	46	31	236
Entertainment	68	31	74	65	88	118	53
Toys, games, hobbies, and tricycles	77	26	77	68	110	139	61
Other entertainment	64	33	73	64	79	109	50
Personal care products and services	89	53	137	168	179	79	42
Reading	150	0	100	100	150	150	200
Education	34	26	18	50	75	53	18
All other gifts	94	18	37	99	94	126	119

Note: Spending index for total consumer units is 100. (–) means sample is too small to make a reliable estimate.
Source: Calculations by New Strategist based on the Bureau of Labor Statistics 1999 and 2000 Consumer Expenditure Surveys

Table 1.24 Average spending of single-person consumer units headed by men, by age, 1999–2000

(average annual spending of single-person consumer units headed by men by product and service category and age, 1999–2000)

	total single-person consumer units headed by men	under 25	25 to 34	35 to 44	45 to 54	55 to 64	65 or older
Number of consumer units (in thousands, add 000s)	13,667	2,199	2,725	2,485	2,220	1,470	2,569
Average income before taxes	$29,267	$11,561	$36,007	$35,005	$39,313	$33,318	$21,439
Average annual spending	24,760	16,039	28,147	28,863	27,648	28,139	20,287
FOOD	**$3,110**	**$2,190**	**$3,716**	**$3,615**	**$3,269**	**$3,439**	**$2,447**
Food at home	**1,386**	**820**	**1,325**	**1,510**	**1,552**	**1,700**	**1,433**
Cereals and bakery products	202	116	189	207	237	241	224
Cereals and cereal products	67	37	68	71	73	73	80
Bakery products	135	79	121	136	164	168	144
Meats, poultry, fish, and eggs	346	183	308	412	415	448	326
Beef	97	57	81	115	116	135	87
Pork	70	28	58	85	83	90	76
Other meats	50	27	43	55	57	68	52
Poultry	61	34	56	78	75	69	51
Fish and seafood	52	27	55	60	67	63	43
Eggs	17	10	14	19	18	22	18
Dairy products	147	86	135	157	164	180	164
Fresh milk and cream	57	32	44	57	68	62	75
Other dairy products	91	54	91	100	95	118	89
Fruits and vegetables	238	117	214	243	257	295	296
Fresh fruits	74	32	66	70	71	107	99
Fresh vegetables	69	38	62	70	85	84	78
Processed fruits	56	30	51	59	55	61	74
Processed vegetables	39	17	35	44	46	43	44
Other food at home	452	317	479	491	479	536	423
Sugar and other sweets	47	35	46	50	50	50	51
Fats and oils	36	22	34	40	37	40	40
Miscellaneous foods	212	135	222	222	241	245	210
Nonalcoholic beverages	133	105	145	149	133	167	108
Food prepared by CU on trips	25	20	32	31	18	35	15
Food away from home	**1,724**	**1,370**	**2,391**	**2,105**	**1,717**	**1,739**	**1,013**
ALCOHOLIC BEVERAGES	**493**	**650**	**577**	**628**	**361**	**495**	**281**
HOUSING	**8,210**	**4,416**	**9,310**	**9,544**	**9,573**	**9,335**	**7,148**
Shelter	**5,401**	**3,172**	**6,407**	**6,546**	**6,375**	**5,744**	**4,095**
Owned dwellings	2,281	292	1,993	3,206	2,873	3,477	2,198
Mortgage interest and charges	1,152	130	1,350	2,002	1,617	1,625	321
Property taxes	647	133	367	688	794	1,087	964
Maintenance, repair, insurance, other expenses	482	28	276	516	462	765	913
Rented dwellings	2,738	2,453	4,119	3,020	2,793	1,920	1,663
Other lodging	382	427	295	319	709	346	234
Utilities, fuels, and public services	**1,491**	**682**	**1,560**	**1,684**	**1,632**	**1,684**	**1,693**
Natural gas	174	48	152	176	199	229	251
Electricity	536	227	532	606	582	642	637
Fuel oil and other fuels	51	7	29	43	48	53	121
Telephone	585	356	736	711	642	563	464
Water and other public services	145	44	111	148	160	197	219

	total single-person consumer units headed by men	under 25	25 to 34	35 to 44	45 to 54	55 to 64	65 or older
Household services	$283	$51	$207	$211	$339	$408	$510
Personal services	68	5	41	22	75	5	224
Other household services	215	46	166	189	264	402	285
Housekeeping supplies	178	67	154	192	198	207	233
Laundry and cleaning supplies	47	20	46	58	58	50	46
Other household products	87	27	66	88	88	104	137
Postage and stationery	44	20	42	46	52	54	49
Household furnishings and equipment	857	444	982	911	1,028	1,292	618
Household textiles	41	10	40	73	65	43	17
Furniture	212	102	342	223	230	244	122
Floor coverings	10	2	16	9	2	8	18
Major appliances	92	24	82	104	101	132	112
Small appliances, misc. housewares	58	17	31	35	72	49	129
Miscellaneous household equipment	445	289	472	466	558	816	219
APPAREL AND RELATED SERVICES	836	769	1,246	1,003	833	725	408
Men and boys	396	395	582	512	381	295	185
Men, aged 16 or older	387	391	568	497	371	284	180
Boys, aged 2 to 15	10	3	14	15	10	11	5
Women and girls	46	31	57	58	71	59	10
Women, aged 16 or older	35	23	28	46	64	53	5
Girls, aged 2 to 15	11	8	29	13	6	6	4
Children under age 2	9	19	15	6	8	7	3
Footwear	152	170	221	132	197	121	74
Other apparel products and services	233	154	372	294	177	242	137
TRANSPORTATION	4,571	3,679	4,946	5,755	4,411	5,455	3,428
Vehicle purchases	2,000	1,934	1,753	2,706	1,647	2,534	1,635
Cars and trucks, new	962	684	887	1,405	769	1,115	930
Cars and trucks, used	972	1,242	738	1,213	783	1,371	688
Other vehicles	67	8	128	88	96	47	16
Gasoline and motor oil	796	629	916	969	851	807	592
Other vehicle expenses	1,482	881	1,871	1,710	1,703	1,773	1,009
Vehicle finance charges	150	102	217	182	158	187	63
Maintenance and repairs	475	338	491	583	521	589	366
Vehicle insurance	489	259	557	571	568	535	439
Vehicle rentals, leases, licenses, other charges	368	182	606	375	455	463	141
Public transportation	292	234	406	370	210	342	193
HEALTH CARE	1,121	323	640	818	1,196	1,466	2,336
Health insurance	488	108	319	405	441	584	1,056
Medical services	374	147	192	252	475	568	681
Drugs	211	49	90	135	232	264	496
Medical supplies	48	20	38	25	48	49	103
ENTERTAINMENT	1,244	1,003	1,610	1,488	1,129	1,293	905
Fees and admissions	341	308	481	390	285	341	221
Television, radio, sound equipment	522	467	642	579	530	551	369
Pets, toys, and playground equipment	159	73	163	231	179	197	117
Other entertainment products and services	222	155	324	289	135	203	199

	total single-person consumer units headed by men	under 25	25 to 34	35 to 44	45 to 54	55 to 64	65 or older
PERSONAL CARE PRODUCTS AND SERVICES	$226	$147	$258	$290	$254	$210	$178
READING	108	62	108	105	140	127	109
EDUCATION	502	1,597	616	154	313	253	87
TOBACCO PRODUCTS AND SMOKING SUPPLIES	271	159	226	375	402	321	172
MISCELLANEOUS	636	162	757	886	639	776	592
CASH CONTRIBUTIONS	1,151	178	1,211	1,161	1,425	1,435	1,510
PERSONAL INSURANCE, PENSIONS	2,282	704	2,928	3,041	3,704	2,809	684
Life and other personal insurance	166	34	109	156	236	255	236
Pensions and Social Security	2,117	670	2,819	2,885	3,468	2,554	448
PERSONAL TAXES	2,858	679	3,597	3,080	4,284	4,934	1,422
Federal income taxes	2,256	527	2,888	2,392	3,373	3,996	1,069
State and local income taxes	497	148	668	608	784	731	149
Other taxes	104	4	41	79	126	207	203
GIFTS	883	565	934	949	994	902	928
Food	30	29	26	16	81	29	7
Alcoholic beverages	11	11	15	19	6	14	4
Housing	174	129	166	147	215	196	199
Housekeeping supplies	13	6	13	17	16	14	9
Household textiles	4	–	4	8	7	4	0
Appliances and misc. housewares	12	5	7	10	11	35	12
Major appliances	4	1	2	6	2	9	6
Small appliances and misc. housewares	8	4	5	5	9	26	6
Miscellaneous household equipment	52	38	59	43	56	57	57
Other housing	94	80	83	69	124	86	120
Apparel and services	182	142	299	205	156	189	92
Males, aged 2 or older	28	16	22	44	31	36	19
Females, aged 2 or older	45	31	57	58	71	47	9
Children under age 2	9	19	15	6	8	7	3
Other apparel products and services	100	76	206	97	47	100	61
Jewelry and watches	79	39	189	70	29	68	56
All other apparel products and services	21	37	16	28	18	31	5
Transportation	59	102	47	43	89	48	32
Health care	80	4	12	38	38	73	297
Entertainment	93	26	99	159	68	76	104
Toys, games, hobbies, and tricycles	22	5	30	32	18	28	22
Other entertainment	70	21	69	127	50	47	83
Personal care products and services	11	1	9	35	7	8	1
Reading	1	1	1	1	1	1	2
Education	110	82	103	73	225	150	58
All other gifts	131	38	156	213	109	119	133

Note: Spending by category will not add to total spending because gift spending is also included in the preceding product and service categories and personal taxes are not included in the total. (–) means sample is too small to make a reliable estimate.
Source: Bureau of Labor Statistics, 1999 and 2000 Consumer Expenditure Surveys, Internet site www.bls.gov/cex/

Table 1.25 Indexed spending of single-person consumer units headed by men, by age, 1999–2000

(indexed average annual spending of single-person consumer units headed by men by product and service category and age, 1999–2000; index definition: an index of 100 is the average for all consumer units; an index of 132 means that spending by consumer units in that group is 32 percent above the average for all consumer units; an index of 68 indicates spending that is 32 percent below the average for all consumer units)

	total single-person consumer units headed by men	under 25	25 to 34	35 to 44	45 to 54	55 to 64	65 or older
Average spending of CU, total	$24,760	$16,039	$28,147	$28,863	$27,648	$28,139	$20,287
Average spending of CU, index	66	43	75	77	73	75	54
FOOD	**61**	**43**	**73**	**71**	**64**	**68**	**48**
Food at home	**47**	**28**	**45**	**51**	**52**	**57**	**48**
Cereals and bakery products	45	26	42	46	53	53	50
Cereals and cereal products	42	23	43	45	46	46	51
Bakery products	46	27	41	46	56	57	49
Meats, poultry, fish, and eggs	45	24	40	53	54	58	42
Beef	42	25	35	50	51	59	38
Pork	43	17	36	52	51	56	47
Other meats	51	27	43	56	58	69	53
Poultry	43	24	40	55	53	49	36
Fish and seafood	48	25	51	56	62	58	40
Eggs	52	30	42	58	55	67	55
Dairy products	46	27	42	49	51	56	51
Fresh milk and cream	45	25	35	45	54	49	59
Other dairy products	46	27	46	51	48	60	45
Fruits and vegetables	47	23	42	48	50	58	58
Fresh fruits	47	20	42	44	45	68	63
Fresh vegetables	45	25	40	45	55	55	51
Processed fruits	49	26	45	52	48	54	65
Processed vegetables	46	20	41	52	54	51	52
Other food at home	50	35	53	54	53	59	46
Sugar and other sweets	41	31	40	44	44	44	45
Fats and oils	43	27	41	48	45	48	48
Miscellaneous foods	50	32	52	52	56	57	49
Nonalcoholic beverages	54	43	59	61	54	68	44
Food prepared by CU on trips	63	50	80	78	45	88	38
Food away from home	**81**	**64**	**112**	**99**	**81**	**82**	**48**
ALCOHOLIC BEVERAGES	**143**	**188**	**167**	**182**	**105**	**143**	**81**
HOUSING	**67**	**36**	**76**	**78**	**79**	**77**	**59**
Shelter	**76**	**45**	**91**	**93**	**90**	**81**	**58**
Owned dwellings	50	6	44	70	63	76	48
Mortgage interest and charges	44	5	52	77	62	63	12
Property taxes	57	12	32	61	70	96	85
Maintenance, repair, insurance, other expenses	57	3	33	62	55	91	109
Rented dwellings	135	121	203	149	138	95	82
Other lodging	81	91	63	68	151	73	50
Utilities, fuels, and public services	**61**	**28**	**64**	**69**	**67**	**69**	**70**
Natural gas	60	17	53	61	69	79	87
Electricity	59	25	59	67	64	71	70
Fuel oil and other fuels	59	8	34	50	56	62	141
Telephone	68	41	85	82	74	65	54
Water and other public services	50	15	38	51	55	68	75

	total single-person consumer units headed by men	under 25	25 to 34	35 to 44	45 to 54	55 to 64	65 or older
Household services	42	8	31	31	50	60	76
Personal services	21	2	13	7	23	2	69
Other household services	61	13	47	54	75	115	81
Housekeeping supplies	36	14	31	39	40	42	48
Laundry and cleaning supplies	37	16	37	46	46	40	37
Other household products	37	11	28	37	37	44	58
Postage and stationery	35	16	33	37	41	43	39
Household furnishings and equipment	56	29	64	60	67	85	41
Household textiles	37	9	36	66	59	39	15
Furniture	56	27	90	59	61	65	32
Floor coverings	23	5	36	20	5	18	41
Major appliances	49	13	44	56	54	71	60
Small appliances, misc. housewares	62	18	33	37	77	52	137
Miscellaneous household equipment	63	41	66	66	78	115	31
APPAREL AND RELATED SERVICES	46	42	69	55	46	40	22
Men and boys	90	90	133	117	87	67	42
Men, aged 16 or older	113	114	166	145	108	83	52
Boys, aged 2 to 15	11	3	15	16	11	12	5
Women and girls	7	4	8	8	10	8	1
Women, aged 16 or older	6	4	5	8	11	9	1
Girls, aged 2 to 15	10	7	26	12	5	5	4
Children under age 2	11	24	19	8	10	9	4
Footwear	47	53	68	41	61	37	23
Other apparel products and services	83	55	132	105	63	86	49
TRANSPORTATION	63	51	69	80	61	76	48
Vehicle purchases	59	58	52	80	49	75	49
Cars and trucks, new	60	42	55	87	48	69	58
Cars and trucks, used	57	73	43	71	46	80	40
Other vehicles	168	20	320	220	240	118	40
Gasoline and motor oil	68	54	78	83	73	69	50
Other vehicle expenses	65	39	82	75	75	78	44
Vehicle finance charges	46	31	67	56	49	58	19
Maintenance and repairs	74	52	76	91	81	91	57
Vehicle insurance	64	34	73	74	74	70	57
Vehicle rentals, leases, licenses, other charges	69	34	114	70	86	87	27
Public transportation	71	57	99	90	51	83	47
HEALTH CARE	56	16	32	41	59	73	116
Health insurance	51	11	33	42	46	61	111
Medical services	66	26	34	45	84	101	121
Drugs	54	12	23	34	59	67	126
Medical supplies	46	19	37	24	46	47	99
ENTERTAINMENT	65	53	85	78	59	68	48
Fees and admissions	67	61	94	77	56	67	43
Television, radio, sound equipment	85	76	104	94	86	90	60
Pets, toys, and playground equipment	47	22	48	68	53	58	35
Other entertainment products and services	51	35	74	66	31	46	45

	total single-person consumer units headed by men	under 25	25 to 34	35 to 44	45 to 54	55 to 64	65 or older
PERSONAL CARE PRODUCTS AND SERVICES	41	27	47	53	46	38	32
READING	71	41	71	69	92	83	71
EDUCATION	79	252	97	24	49	40	14
TOBACCO PRODUCTS AND SMOKING SUPPLIES	88	51	73	121	130	104	56
MISCELLANEOUS	77	20	92	108	78	95	72
CASH CONTRIBUTIONS	97	15	102	98	120	121	127
PERSONAL INSURANCE AND PENSIONS	67	21	86	90	109	83	20
Life and other personal insurance	42	9	27	39	59	64	59
Pensions and Social Security	71	22	94	96	116	85	15
PERSONAL TAXES	89	21	112	96	134	154	44
Federal income taxes	92	21	117	97	137	162	43
State and local income taxes	84	25	113	103	133	124	25
Other taxes	66	3	26	50	80	131	128
GIFTS	81	52	86	87	91	83	85
Food	39	38	34	21	107	38	9
Alcoholic beverages	73	73	100	127	40	93	27
Housing	60	44	57	51	74	67	68
Housekeeping supplies	33	15	33	43	40	35	23
Household textiles	27	–	27	53	47	27	0
Appliances and misc. housewares	40	17	23	33	37	117	40
Major appliances	50	13	25	75	25	113	75
Small appliances and misc. housewares	36	18	23	23	41	118	27
Miscellaneous household equipment	76	56	87	63	82	84	84
Other housing	68	58	60	50	90	62	87
Apparel and services	79	61	129	89	68	82	40
Males, aged 2 or older	46	26	36	72	51	59	31
Females, aged 2 or older	58	40	73	74	91	60	12
Children under age 2	23	48	38	15	20	18	8
Other apparel products and services	196	149	404	190	92	196	120
Jewelry and watches	343	170	822	304	126	296	243
All other apparel products and services	75	132	57	100	64	111	18
Transportation	88	152	70	64	133	72	48
Health care	205	10	31	97	97	187	762
Entertainment	92	26	98	157	67	75	103
Toys, games, hobbies, and tricycles	71	16	97	103	58	90	71
Other entertainment	100	30	99	181	71	67	119
Personal care products and services	58	5	47	184	37	42	5
Reading	50	50	50	50	50	50	100
Education	69	52	65	46	142	94	36
All other gifts	146	42	173	237	121	132	148

Note: Spending index for total consumer units is 100. (–) means sample is too small to make a reliable estimate.
Source: Calculations by New Strategist based on the Bureau of Labor Statistics 1999 and 2000 Consumer Expenditure Surveys

Spending Overview:
Spending by Region, 2000

Households in the Northeast have the highest incomes, but those in the West spend the most. With an average before-tax income of $46,670, Western households spent an average of $41,328 in 2000, 9 percent more than the average household. Households in the Northeast had even higher incomes, but they spent only $38,902 in 2000—just 2 percent more than the average household. Households in the South had the lowest incomes and spent 9 percent less than average, just $34,707 in 2000.

Households in the Northeast and West spend more than average on most products and services. Those in the Midwest spend close to the average while households in the South spend less than average on most items. Households in the Northeast spend the most on apparel and property taxes. Those in the West spend the most on alcoholic beverages and mortgage interest. Households in the Midwest spend the most on food away from home, but they spend 29 percent less than average on fish and seafood. Households in the South spend 18 percent less than average on alcoholic beverages.

The biggest consumers of natural gas are households in the Midwest, spending 40 percent more than the average household on this item. The South spends the most on electricity, while the Northeast spends the most on fuel oil. Western households spend 19 percent more than average on water and other public services.

Western households spend the most on new cars and trucks, while those in the Midwest spend the most on used vehicles. Households in the South spend the most on vehicle finance charges. Public transportation spending is highest in the Northeast and West. Households in the Midwest spend 10 percent more than average on entertainment, while those in the South spend 13 percent less. Spending on tobacco is 13 percent above average in the Midwest.

Table 1.26 Average spending by region, 2000

(average annual spending of consumer units (CU) by product and service category and region of residence, 2000)

	total	Northeast	Midwest	South	West
Number of consumer units (in thousands, add 000s)	109,367	20,994	25,717	38,245	24,410
Average number of persons per CU	2.5	2.5	2.5	2.5	2.6
Average income before taxes	$44,649	$47,439	$44,377	$41,984	$46,670
Average annual spending	38,045	38,902	39,213	34,707	41,328
FOOD	**$5,158**	**$5,377**	**$5,255**	**$4,724**	**$5,554**
Food at home	**3,021**	**3,202**	**2,933**	**2,823**	**3,269**
Cereals and bakery products	453	491	444	422	480
Cereals and cereal products	156	164	152	148	167
Bakery products	297	326	292	274	313
Meats, poultry, fish, and eggs	795	883	721	779	821
Beef	238	248	226	230	255
Pork	167	162	160	176	164
Other meats	101	116	103	94	94
Poultry	145	174	125	142	146
Fish and seafood	110	149	78	100	124
Eggs	34	35	28	36	38
Dairy products	325	354	330	286	356
Fresh milk and cream	131	132	132	122	145
Other dairy products	193	222	197	164	211
Fruits and vegetables	521	579	482	470	592
Fresh fruits	163	181	151	141	196
Fresh vegetables	159	184	137	139	190
Processed fruits	115	131	113	103	123
Processed vegetables	84	83	81	86	84
Other food at home	927	895	957	867	1,021
Sugar and other sweets	117	126	124	107	117
Fats and oils	83	89	75	82	87
Miscellaneous foods	437	398	468	410	484
Nonalcoholic beverages	250	240	249	238	277
Food prepared by CU on trips	40	41	41	29	55
Food away from home	**2,137**	**2,175**	**2,322**	**1,901**	**2,285**
ALCOHOLIC BEVERAGES	**372**	**390**	**388**	**304**	**449**
HOUSING	**12,319**	**13,505**	**11,961**	**10,855**	**13,972**
Shelter	**7,114**	**8,222**	**6,633**	**5,839**	**8,667**
Owned dwellings	4,602	5,229	4,599	3,803	5,320
Mortgage interest and charges	2,639	2,574	2,471	2,238	3,498
Property taxes	1,139	1,780	1,224	825	987
Maintenance, repair, insurance, other expenses	825	874	903	739	834
Rented dwellings	2,034	2,434	1,531	1,643	2,832
Other lodging	478	559	503	393	515
Utilities, fuels, and public services	**2,489**	**2,570**	**2,513**	**2,596**	**2,226**
Natural gas	307	413	430	190	272
Electricity	911	816	834	1,148	704
Fuel oil and other fuels	97	271	73	57	35
Telephone	877	856	884	891	864
Water and other public services	296	214	291	311	351

	total	Northeast	Midwest	South	West
Household services	**$684**	**$643**	**$670**	**$645**	**$796**
Personal services	326	312	369	284	360
Other household services	358	331	301	361	436
Housekeeping supplies	**482**	**530**	**514**	**440**	**472**
Laundry and cleaning supplies	131	146	133	126	122
Other household products	226	245	238	213	216
Postage and stationery	126	139	143	101	135
Household furnishings and equipment	**1,549**	**1,540**	**1,631**	**1,334**	**1,811**
Household textiles	106	134	117	85	106
Furniture	391	388	378	338	489
Floor coverings	44	47	54	41	37
Major appliances	189	179	198	168	221
Small appliances, misc. housewares	87	91	103	72	93
Miscellaneous household equipment	731	702	782	630	865
APPAREL AND RELATED SERVICES	**1,856**	**2,115**	**1,917**	**1,617**	**1,945**
Men and boys	**440**	**484**	**489**	**382**	**445**
Men, aged 16 or older	344	374	386	295	354
Boys, aged 2 to 15	96	110	103	87	91
Women and girls	**725**	**849**	**771**	**612**	**746**
Women, aged 16 or older	607	705	646	499	652
Girls, aged 2 to 15	118	144	125	113	95
Children under age 2	**82**	**82**	**88**	**82**	**75**
Footwear	**343**	**382**	**324**	**303**	**391**
Other apparel products and services	**266**	**318**	**245**	**238**	**288**
TRANSPORTATION	**7,417**	**6,664**	**7,841**	**7,211**	**7,943**
Vehicle purchases	**3,418**	**2,719**	**3,759**	**3,566**	**3,430**
Cars and trucks, new	1,605	1,456	1,540	1,632	1,759
Cars and trucks, used	1,770	1,246	2,132	1,909	1,620
Other vehicles	43	17	86	24	51
Gasoline and motor oil	**1,291**	**1,094**	**1,352**	**1,290**	**1,400**
Other vehicle expenses	**2,281**	**2,251**	**2,327**	**2,073**	**2,586**
Vehicle finance charges	328	228	353	366	329
Maintenance and repairs	624	570	610	584	749
Vehicle insurance	778	808	750	747	831
Vehicle rentals, leases, licenses, other charges	551	646	615	376	677
Public transportation	**427**	**600**	**403**	**283**	**527**
HEALTH CARE	**2,066**	**1,862**	**2,172**	**2,147**	**2,001**
Health insurance	983	908	1,047	1,063	853
Medical services	568	504	575	533	669
Drugs	416	349	439	470	368
Medical supplies	99	101	111	82	111
ENTERTAINMENT	**1,863**	**1,915**	**2,040**	**1,617**	**2,021**
Fees and admissions	515	577	566	395	595
Television, radio, sound equipment	622	627	665	574	648
Pets, toys, and playground equipment	334	316	360	313	355
Other entertainment products and services	393	395	449	335	423

	total	Northeast	Midwest	South	West
PERSONAL CARE PRODUCTS AND SERVICES	**$564**	**$578**	**$544**	**$550**	**$594**
READING	**146**	**172**	**164**	**114**	**158**
EDUCATION	**632**	**823**	**667**	**477**	**674**
TOBACCO PRODUCTS AND SMOKING SUPPLIES	**319**	**326**	**360**	**334**	**245**
MISCELLANEOUS	**776**	**738**	**798**	**729**	**859**
CASH CONTRIBUTIONS	**1,192**	**1,064**	**1,615**	**953**	**1,233**
PERSONAL INSURANCE AND PENSIONS	**3,365**	**3,371**	**3,490**	**3,077**	**3,679**
Life and other personal insurance	399	423	429	407	333
Pensions and Social Security	2,966	2,948	3,061	2,670	3,346
PERSONAL TAXES	**3,117**	**2,983**	**3,667**	**2,516**	**3,582**
Federal income taxes	2,409	2,196	2,699	2,053	2,827
State and local income taxes	562	633	815	321	614
Other taxes	146	154	153	142	140
GIFTS	**1,083**	**1,096**	**1,291**	**908**	**1,131**
Food	**70**	**66**	**103**	**49**	**72**
Alcoholic beverages	**14**	**13**	**19**	**13**	**13**
Housing	**291**	**277**	**349**	**270**	**276**
Housekeeping supplies	39	49	44	28	42
Household textiles	13	19	14	9	13
Appliances and misc. housewares	28	25	41	26	21
Major appliances	8	5	10	10	5
Small appliances and misc. housewares	21	20	31	17	16
Miscellaneous household equipment	70	63	95	56	73
Other housing	140	121	154	150	127
Apparel and services	**244**	**269**	**258**	**206**	**269**
Males, aged 2 or older	68	69	77	49	86
Females, aged 2 or older	85	103	86	72	90
Children under age 2	41	49	42	37	37
Other apparel products and services	51	47	52	48	57
Jewelry and watches	20	25	19	17	23
All other apparel products and services	30	23	34	31	34
Transportation	**70**	**60**	**74**	**49**	**109**
Health care	**38**	**17**	**69**	**40**	**20**
Entertainment	**94**	**88**	**109**	**85**	**97**
Toys, games, hobbies, and tricycles	30	32	39	23	27
Other entertainment	64	56	70	61	69
Personal care products and services	**19**	**14**	**24**	**15**	**25**
Reading	**2**	**2**	**2**	**1**	**2**
Education	**151**	**193**	**183**	**117**	**135**
All other gifts	**89**	**96**	**100**	**63**	**112**

Note: Spending by category will not add to total spending because gift spending is also included in the preceding product and service categories and personal taxes are not included in the total.
Source: Bureau of Labor Statistics, 2000 Consumer Expenditure Survey, Internet site www.bls.gov/cex/

Table 1.27 Indexed spending by region, 2000

(indexed average annual spending of consumer units (CU) by product and service category and region of residence, 2000; index definition: an index of 100 is the average for all consumer units; an index of 132 means that spending by consumer units in that group is 32 percent above the average for all consumer units; an index of 68 indicates spending that is 32 percent below the average for all consumer units)

	total	Northeast	Midwest	South	West
Average spending of CU, total	$38,045	$38,902	$39,213	$34,707	$41,328
Average spending of CU, index	100	102	103	91	109
FOOD	100	104	102	92	108
Food at home	100	106	97	93	108
Cereals and bakery products	100	108	98	93	106
Cereals and cereal products	100	105	97	95	107
Bakery products	100	110	98	92	105
Meats, poultry, fish, and eggs	100	111	91	98	103
Beef	100	104	95	97	107
Pork	100	97	96	105	98
Other meats	100	115	102	93	93
Poultry	100	120	86	98	101
Fish and seafood	100	135	71	91	113
Eggs	100	103	82	106	112
Dairy products	100	109	102	88	110
Fresh milk and cream	100	101	101	93	111
Other dairy products	100	115	102	85	109
Fruits and vegetables	100	111	93	90	114
Fresh fruits	100	111	93	87	120
Fresh vegetables	100	116	86	87	119
Processed fruits	100	114	98	90	107
Processed vegetables	100	99	96	102	100
Other food at home	100	97	103	94	110
Sugar and other sweets	100	108	106	91	100
Fats and oils	100	107	90	99	105
Miscellaneous foods	100	91	107	94	111
Nonalcoholic beverages	100	96	100	95	111
Food prepared by CU on trips	100	103	103	73	138
Food away from home	100	102	109	89	107
ALCOHOLIC BEVERAGES	100	105	104	82	121
HOUSING	100	110	97	88	113
Shelter	100	116	93	82	122
Owned dwellings	100	114	100	83	116
Mortgage interest and charges	100	98	94	85	133
Property taxes	100	156	107	72	87
Maintenance, repair, insurance, other expenses	100	106	109	90	101
Rented dwellings	100	120	75	81	139
Other lodging	100	117	105	82	108
Utilities, fuels, and public services	100	103	101	104	89
Natural gas	100	135	140	62	89
Electricity	100	90	92	126	77
Fuel oil and other fuels	100	279	75	59	36
Telephone	100	98	101	102	99
Water and other public services	100	72	98	105	119

	total	Northeast	Midwest	South	West
Household services	**100**	**94**	**98**	**94**	**116**
Personal services	100	96	113	87	110
Other household services	100	92	84	101	122
Housekeeping supplies	**100**	**110**	**107**	**91**	**98**
Laundry and cleaning supplies	100	111	102	96	93
Other household products	100	108	105	94	96
Postage and stationery	100	110	113	80	107
Household furnishings and equipment	**100**	**99**	**105**	**86**	**117**
Household textiles	100	126	110	80	100
Furniture	100	99	97	86	125
Floor coverings	100	107	123	93	84
Major appliances	100	95	105	89	117
Small appliances, misc. housewares	100	105	118	83	107
Miscellaneous household equipment	100	96	107	86	118
APPAREL AND RELATED SERVICES	**100**	**114**	**103**	**87**	**105**
Men and boys	**100**	**110**	**111**	**87**	**101**
Men, aged 16 or older	100	109	112	86	103
Boys, aged 2 to 15	100	115	107	91	95
Women and girls	**100**	**117**	**106**	**84**	**103**
Women, aged 16 or older	100	116	106	82	107
Girls, aged 2 to 15	100	122	106	96	81
Children under age 2	**100**	**100**	**107**	**100**	**91**
Footwear	**100**	**111**	**94**	**88**	**114**
Other apparel products and services	**100**	**120**	**92**	**89**	**108**
TRANSPORTATION	**100**	**90**	**106**	**97**	**107**
Vehicle purchases	**100**	**80**	**110**	**104**	**100**
Cars and trucks, new	100	91	96	102	110
Cars and trucks, used	100	70	120	108	92
Other vehicles	100	40	200	56	119
Gasoline and motor oil	**100**	**85**	**105**	**100**	**108**
Other vehicle expenses	**100**	**99**	**102**	**91**	**113**
Vehicle finance charges	100	70	108	112	100
Maintenance and repairs	100	91	98	94	120
Vehicle insurance	100	104	96	96	107
Vehicle rentals, leases, licenses, other charges	100	117	112	68	123
Public transportation	**100**	**141**	**94**	**66**	**123**
HEALTH CARE	**100**	**90**	**105**	**104**	**97**
Health insurance	100	92	107	108	87
Medical services	100	89	101	94	118
Drugs	100	84	106	113	88
Medical supplies	100	102	112	83	112
ENTERTAINMENT	**100**	**103**	**110**	**87**	**108**
Fees and admissions	100	112	110	77	116
Television, radio, sound equipment	100	101	107	92	104
Pets, toys, and playground equipment	100	95	108	94	106
Other entertainment products and services	100	101	114	85	108

	total	Northeast	Midwest	South	West
PERSONAL CARE PRODUCTS AND SERVICES	100	102	96	98	105
READING	100	118	112	78	108
EDUCATION	100	130	106	75	107
TOBACCO PRODUCTS AND SMOKING SUPPLIES	100	102	113	105	77
MISCELLANEOUS	100	95	103	94	111
CASH CONTRIBUTIONS	100	89	135	80	103
PERSONAL INSURANCE AND PENSIONS	100	100	104	91	109
Life and other personal insurance	100	106	108	102	83
Pensions and Social Security	100	99	103	90	113
PERSONAL TAXES	100	96	118	81	115
Federal income taxes	100	91	112	85	117
State and local income taxes	100	113	145	57	109
Other taxes	100	105	105	97	96
GIFTS	100	101	119	84	104
Food	100	94	147	70	103
Alcoholic beverages	100	93	136	93	93
Housing	100	95	120	93	95
Housekeeping supplies	100	126	113	72	108
Household textiles	100	146	108	69	100
Appliances and misc. housewares	100	89	146	93	75
Major appliances	100	63	125	125	63
Small appliances and misc. housewares	100	95	148	81	76
Miscellaneous household equipment	100	90	136	80	104
Other housing	100	86	110	107	91
Apparel and services	100	110	106	84	110
Males, aged 2 or older	100	101	113	72	126
Females, aged 2 or older	100	121	101	85	106
Children under age 2	100	120	102	90	90
Other apparel products and services	100	92	102	94	112
Jewelry and watches	100	125	95	85	115
All other apparel products and services	100	77	113	103	113
Transportation	100	86	106	70	156
Health care	100	45	182	105	53
Entertainment	100	94	116	90	103
Toys, games, hobbies, and tricycles	100	107	130	77	90
Other entertainment	100	88	109	95	108
Personal care products and services	100	74	126	79	132
Reading	100	100	100	50	100
Education	100	128	121	77	89
All other gifts	100	108	112	71	126

Source: Calculations by New Strategist based on the Bureau of Labor Statistics 2000 Consumer Expenditure Survey

Spending Overview:

Spending by Region and Income, 1999–2000

Households with incomes of $70,000 or more are most commonly found in the Northeast and West, where they account for 21 percent of households. In the Midwest, 19 percent of households have incomes of at least $70,000, while in the South the proportion is a smaller 16 percent.

In every region, spending rises with income. The most affluent households in the Northeast spend 87 percent more than the average northeastern household, $76,222 versus $40,819 for complete income reporters in 1999–2000. The spending gap is greatest for items such as mortgage interest, other lodging (a category that includes vacation homes and hotels and motels on out-of-town trips), household services, men's clothes, fees and admissions to entertainment events, and education.

In the Midwest, the most affluent households spent $73,735 in 1999–2000, or 85 percent more than the $39,870 the average Midwestern household spent. Households with incomes of $70,000 or more in the Midwest spend more than twice the average on public transportation and fees and admissions to entertainment events.

The most affluent Southern households spend twice as much as the average southern household, $73,491 versus $36,561 in 1999–2000. The richest households in the South spend more than three times the average on other lodging. They spend less than some of the low- and middle-income households on tobacco.

The most affluent households in the West spend nearly twice as much as the average Western household, $82,707 versus $43,598 in 1999–2000. The gap is greatest for items such as other lodging, furniture, and new cars and trucks.

Table 1.28 Average spending in the Northeast by income, 1999–2000

(average annual spending of consumer units (CU) in the Northeast by product and service category and before-tax income of consumer unit, 1999–2000; complete income reporters only)

	complete income reporters in the Northeast	under $10,000	$10,000– $19,999	$20,000– $29,999	$30,000– $39,999	$40,000– $49,999	$50,000– $69,999	$70,000 or more
Number of consumer units (in thousands, add 000s)	15,359	2,010	2,732	2,046	1,691	1,455	2,216	3,209
Average number of persons per CU	2.4	1.8	1.9	2.3	2.4	2.4	2.8	3.1
Average income before taxes	$47,876	$5,541	$14,631	$24,387	$34,354	$44,064	$58,647	$119,080
Average annual spending	40,819	17,255	22,438	28,925	35,673	40,025	48,534	76,222
FOOD	$5,776	$2,930	$3,629	$4,399	$5,244	$6,582	$6,917	$9,233
Food at home	3,367	1,920	2,480	2,978	2,930	3,896	4,097	4,692
Cereals and bakery products	525	312	394	459	501	600	612	716
Cereals and cereal products	179	113	134	168	178	226	209	222
Bakery products	346	200	260	292	323	374	404	494
Meats, poultry, fish, and eggs	905	563	688	845	780	1,025	1,070	1,230
Beef	249	153	178	236	195	281	307	349
Pork	166	95	139	161	135	192	212	205
Other meats	121	71	101	110	114	129	140	160
Poultry	178	113	115	169	167	190	206	255
Fish and seafood	154	102	121	130	136	193	161	217
Eggs	38	30	34	39	33	40	44	44
Dairy products	384	202	291	320	365	443	481	520
Fresh milk and cream	144	89	128	120	154	149	177	172
Other dairy products	240	113	163	200	211	294	304	348
Fruits and vegetables	611	346	455	582	512	690	722	853
Fresh fruits	191	119	141	182	165	241	206	262
Fresh vegetables	191	102	143	180	166	194	227	275
Processed fruits	142	78	102	146	114	151	173	200
Processed vegetables	87	47	68	74	68	105	117	116
Other food at home	942	496	652	772	772	1,137	1,212	1,374
Sugar and other sweets	132	59	88	99	103	152	185	205
Fats and oils	92	53	76	84	77	113	116	115
Miscellaneous foods	421	200	288	351	342	509	539	626
Nonalcoholic beverages	254	163	183	211	217	306	316	347
Food prepared by CU on trips	43	22	17	27	32	56	56	81
Food away from home	2,409	1,011	1,149	1,421	2,314	2,687	2,820	4,541
ALCOHOLIC BEVERAGES	429	226	235	315	391	418	504	758
HOUSING	13,575	6,485	8,653	10,094	11,522	13,077	14,915	24,755
Shelter	8,177	4,043	5,172	5,938	7,037	8,055	9,017	14,829
Owned dwellings	5,251	1,440	2,454	2,851	3,971	4,459	6,356	11,819
Mortgage interest and charges	2,626	454	691	1,023	1,707	2,312	3,492	6,682
Property taxes	1,781	645	1,126	1,221	1,505	1,399	2,122	3,488
Maintenance, repair, insurance, other expenses	845	342	636	607	759	749	742	1,649
Rented dwellings	2,434	2,407	2,535	2,785	2,757	3,221	2,110	1,837
Other lodging	493	195	183	302	309	375	550	1,173
Utilities, fuels, and public services	2,503	1,427	1,960	2,221	2,396	2,472	2,830	3,662
Natural gas	385	200	337	370	399	367	421	528
Electricity	812	444	631	724	770	834	950	1,168
Fuel oil and other fuels	236	123	212	222	217	211	245	349
Telephone	855	570	628	724	796	858	963	1,266
Water and other public services	215	90	152	181	215	202	251	350

	complete income reporters in the Northeast	under $10,000	$10,000–$19,999	$20,000–$29,999	$30,000–$39,999	$40,000–$49,999	$50,000–$69,999	$70,000 or more
Household services	$666	$232	$303	$360	$370	$461	$606	$1,733
Personal services	318	94	100	152	183	233	333	846
Other household services	349	138	202	207	187	228	273	887
Housekeeping supplies	599	197	367	489	476	549	728	1,091
Laundry and cleaning supplies	148	64	85	126	111	116	159	287
Other household products	294	87	151	225	244	234	418	543
Postage and stationery	157	45	132	138	121	200	151	261
Household furnishings and equipment	1,629	586	850	1,087	1,242	1,540	1,734	3,440
Household textiles	132	60	73	116	126	91	146	243
Furniture	405	189	150	188	279	334	398	998
Floor coverings	49	7	51	33	32	18	27	123
Major appliances	187	77	135	199	190	175	177	298
Small appliances, misc. housewares	108	44	45	54	76	78	154	234
Miscellaneous household equipment	748	210	396	497	539	843	832	1,543
APPAREL AND RELATED SERVICES	2,207	1,051	1,176	1,215	1,865	1,848	2,765	4,352
Men and boys	518	247	168	267	485	384	671	1,104
Men, aged 16 or older	411	169	121	205	383	305	540	899
Boys, aged 2 to 15	107	78	46	62	102	79	131	206
Women and girls	875	397	607	435	645	819	1,150	1,627
Women, aged 16 or older	745	338	543	367	541	749	961	1,357
Girls, aged 2 to 15	130	59	63	68	105	70	188	270
Children under age 2	93	61	54	56	72	102	115	162
Footwear	382	218	212	204	391	257	512	687
Other apparel products and services	339	128	136	253	272	285	318	772
TRANSPORTATION	6,611	2,351	3,536	4,899	7,372	7,076	8,323	11,184
Vehicle purchases	2,719	877	1,569	1,910	3,720	3,217	3,473	4,094
Cars and trucks, new	1,404	309	699	860	2,069	1,489	1,871	2,326
Cars and trucks, used	1,302	567	862	1,049	1,651	1,728	1,582	1,727
Other vehicles	13	–	9	1	–	–	20	41
Gasoline and motor oil	1,007	397	515	811	1,028	1,096	1,394	1,613
Other vehicle expenses	2,299	780	1,087	1,738	2,084	2,257	2,911	4,344
Vehicle finance charges	237	43	77	154	245	323	393	396
Maintenance and repairs	639	260	394	552	538	617	731	1,134
Vehicle insurance	828	300	445	680	836	833	1,071	1,405
Vehicle rentals, leases, licenses, other charges	595	177	171	352	464	484	717	1,409
Public transportation	586	297	364	439	540	506	546	1,134
HEALTH CARE	1,890	929	1,691	1,974	1,789	1,631	1,974	2,710
Health insurance	875	528	900	993	852	773	869	1,059
Medical services	558	177	276	494	503	472	640	1,091
Drugs	346	178	414	392	338	294	332	395
Medical supplies	110	46	100	96	96	92	134	165
ENTERTAINMENT	1,957	799	984	1,308	1,615	1,752	2,473	3,823
Fees and admissions	588	208	219	294	383	461	633	1,463
Television, radio, sound equipment	674	370	459	524	586	726	820	1,066
Pets, toys, and playground equipment	342	139	176	272	304	315	477	584
Other entertainment products and services	353	82	130	218	341	251	543	711

	complete income reporters in the Northeast	under $10,000	$10,000– $19,999	$20,000– $29,999	$30,000– $39,999	$40,000– $49,999	$50,000– $69,999	$70,000 or more
PERSONAL CARE PRODUCTS AND SERVICES	$598	$295	$369	$495	$548	$645	$719	$956
READING	194	89	111	147	166	181	216	365
EDUCATION	776	726	173	421	543	334	682	1,930
TOBACCO PRODUCTS AND SMOKING SUPPLIES	341	240	251	354	408	331	395	403
MISCELLANEOUS	827	497	342	593	734	716	1,173	1,447
CASH CONTRIBUTIONS	1,258	297	595	730	690	1,307	1,572	2,819
PERSONAL INSURANCE AND PENSIONS	4,381	339	693	1,980	2,788	4,126	5,904	11,487
Life and other personal insurance	414	109	170	228	287	280	422	1,054
Pensions and Social Security	3,967	231	523	1,752	2,501	3,846	5,482	10,433
PERSONAL TAXES	3,404	297	263	1,220	1,808	2,777	3,899	10,201
Federal income taxes	2,533	240	93	735	1,202	1,914	2,787	7,997
State and local income taxes	666	–4	26	255	399	655	893	1,882
Other taxes	205	61	144	230	207	208	218	322
GIFTS	1,241	531	547	748	1,095	985	1,270	2,745
Food	97	23	13	17	101	52	50	315
Alcoholic beverages	18	12	6	12	23	21	25	25
Housing	315	123	154	240	295	239	347	632
Housekeeping supplies	47	11	19	32	35	70	66	84
Household textiles	21	12	5	43	24	17	17	29
Appliances and misc. housewares	41	8	32	22	21	26	66	81
Major appliances	12	1	27	13	6	9	7	12
Small appliances and misc. housewares	29	7	5	9	15	17	59	70
Miscellaneous household equipment	74	10	31	50	98	41	77	161
Other housing	131	82	67	94	117	84	121	277
Apparel and services	297	94	139	191	250	347	367	573
Males, aged 2 or older	71	21	34	27	72	77	93	143
Females, aged 2 or older	107	21	38	60	59	164	142	225
Children under age 2	55	26	37	40	45	47	67	95
Other apparel products and services	64	27	30	63	74	58	64	110
Jewelry and watches	36	9	15	63	36	26	35	58
All other apparel products and services	28	18	15	1	38	32	29	52
Transportation	67	28	26	18	55	25	41	202
Health care	21	2	19	45	18	5	10	35
Entertainment	102	28	90	88	78	94	121	170
Toys, games, hobbies, and tricycles	37	12	26	39	32	41	50	52
Other entertainment	65	15	65	49	46	53	71	118
Personal care products and services	17	4	14	8	6	8	33	32
Reading	3	2	3	2	1	3	3	3
Education	211	103	36	44	157	121	165	637
All other gifts	93	112	48	81	111	70	110	119

Note: Spending by category will not add to total spending because gift spending is also included in the preceding product and service categories and personal taxes are not included in the total. (–) means sample is too small to make a reliable estimate.
Source: Bureau of Labor Statistics, 1999 and 2000 Consumer Expenditure Surveys, Internet site www.bls.gov/cex/; calculations by New Strategist

Table 1.29 Indexed spending in the Northeast by income, 1999–2000

(indexed average annual spending of consumer units (CU) in the Northeast by product and service category and before-tax income of consumer unit, 1999–2000; complete income reporters only; index definition: an index of 100 is the average for all consumer units; an index of 132 means that spending by consumer units in that group is 32 percent above the average for all consumer units; an index of 68 indicates spending that is 32 percent below the average for all consumer units)

	complete income reporters in the Northeast	under $10,000	$10,000–$19,999	$20,000–$29,999	$30,000–$39,999	$40,000–$49,999	$50,000–$69,999	$70,000 or more
Average spending of CU, total	$40,819	$17,255	$22,438	$28,925	$35,673	$40,025	$48,534	$76,222
Average spending of CU, index	100	42	55	71	87	98	119	187
FOOD	100	51	63	76	91	114	120	160
Food at home	100	57	74	88	87	116	122	139
Cereals and bakery products	100	59	75	87	95	114	117	136
Cereals and cereal products	100	63	75	94	99	126	117	124
Bakery products	100	58	75	84	93	108	117	143
Meats, poultry, fish, and eggs	100	62	76	93	86	113	118	136
Beef	100	62	71	95	78	113	123	140
Pork	100	57	84	97	81	116	128	123
Other meats	100	58	84	91	94	107	116	132
Poultry	100	63	65	95	94	107	116	143
Fish and seafood	100	66	78	84	88	125	105	141
Eggs	100	79	89	103	87	105	116	116
Dairy products	100	53	76	83	95	115	125	135
Fresh milk and cream	100	62	89	83	107	103	123	119
Other dairy products	100	47	68	83	88	123	127	145
Fruits and vegetables	100	57	75	95	84	113	118	140
Fresh fruits	100	62	74	95	86	126	108	137
Fresh vegetables	100	53	75	94	87	102	119	144
Processed fruits	100	55	72	103	80	106	122	141
Processed vegetables	100	54	79	85	78	121	134	133
Other food at home	100	53	69	82	82	121	129	146
Sugar and other sweets	100	44	67	75	78	115	140	155
Fats and oils	100	58	83	91	84	123	126	125
Miscellaneous foods	100	47	68	83	81	121	128	149
Nonalcoholic beverages	100	64	72	83	85	120	124	137
Food prepared by CU on trips	100	50	39	63	74	130	130	188
Food away from home	100	42	48	59	96	112	117	189
ALCOHOLIC BEVERAGES	100	53	55	73	91	97	117	177
HOUSING	100	48	64	74	85	96	110	182
Shelter	100	49	63	73	86	99	110	181
Owned dwellings	100	27	47	54	76	85	121	225
Mortgage interest and charges	100	17	26	39	65	88	133	254
Property taxes	100	36	63	69	85	79	119	196
Maintenance, repair, insurance, other expenses	100	40	75	72	90	89	88	195
Rented dwellings	100	99	104	114	113	132	87	75
Other lodging	100	40	37	61	63	76	112	238
Utilities, fuels, and public services	100	57	78	89	96	99	113	146
Natural gas	100	52	88	96	104	95	109	137
Electricity	100	55	78	89	95	103	117	144
Fuel oil and other fuels	100	52	90	94	92	89	104	148
Telephone	100	67	73	85	93	100	113	148
Water and other public services	100	42	71	84	100	94	117	163

	complete income reporters in the Northeast	under $10,000	$10,000–$19,999	$20,000–$29,999	$30,000–$39,999	$40,000–$49,999	$50,000–$69,999	$70,000 or more
Household services	100	35	45	54	56	69	91	260
Personal services	100	29	31	48	58	73	105	266
Other household services	100	40	58	59	54	65	78	254
Housekeeping supplies	100	33	61	82	79	92	122	182
Laundry and cleaning supplies	100	43	57	85	75	78	107	194
Other household products	100	30	52	77	83	80	142	185
Postage and stationery	100	29	84	88	77	127	96	166
Household furnishings and equipment	100	36	52	67	76	95	106	211
Household textiles	100	45	56	88	95	69	111	184
Furniture	100	47	37	46	69	82	98	246
Floor coverings	100	14	103	67	65	37	55	251
Major appliances	100	41	72	106	102	94	95	159
Small appliances, misc. housewares	100	40	42	50	70	72	143	217
Miscellaneous household equipment	100	28	53	66	72	113	111	206
APPAREL AND RELATED SERVICES	100	48	53	55	85	84	125	197
Men and boys	100	48	32	52	94	74	130	213
Men, aged 16 or older	100	41	30	50	93	74	131	219
Boys, aged 2 to 15	100	73	43	58	95	74	122	193
Women and girls	100	45	69	50	74	94	131	186
Women, aged 16 or older	100	45	73	49	73	101	129	182
Girls, aged 2 to 15	100	45	49	52	81	54	145	208
Children under age 2	100	66	58	60	77	110	124	174
Footwear	100	57	55	53	102	67	134	180
Other apparel products and services	100	38	40	75	80	84	94	228
TRANSPORTATION	100	36	53	74	112	107	126	169
Vehicle purchases	100	32	58	70	137	118	128	151
Cars and trucks, new	100	22	50	61	147	106	133	166
Cars and trucks, used	100	44	66	81	127	133	122	133
Other vehicles	100	–	67	8	–	–	154	315
Gasoline and motor oil	100	39	51	81	102	109	138	160
Other vehicle expenses	100	34	47	76	91	98	127	189
Vehicle finance charges	100	18	33	65	103	136	166	167
Maintenance and repairs	100	41	62	86	84	97	114	177
Vehicle insurance	100	36	54	82	101	101	129	170
Vehicle rentals, leases, licenses, other charges	100	30	29	59	78	81	121	237
Public transportation	100	51	62	75	92	86	93	194
HEALTH CARE	100	49	89	104	95	86	104	143
Health insurance	100	60	103	113	97	88	99	121
Medical services	100	32	49	89	90	85	115	196
Drugs	100	51	120	113	98	85	96	114
Medical supplies	100	42	91	87	87	84	122	150
ENTERTAINMENT	100	41	50	67	83	90	126	195
Fees and admissions	100	35	37	50	65	78	108	249
Television, radio, sound equipment	100	55	68	78	87	108	122	158
Pets, toys, and playground equipment	100	41	51	80	89	92	139	171
Other entertainment products and services	100	23	37	62	97	71	154	201

	complete income reporters in the Northeast	under $10,000	$10,000– $19,999	$20,000– $29,999	$30,000– $39,999	$40,000– $49,999	$50,000– $69,999	$70,000 or more
PERSONAL CARE PRODUCTS AND SERVICES	100	49	62	83	92	108	120	160
READING	100	46	57	76	86	93	111	188
EDUCATION	100	94	22	54	70	43	88	249
TOBACCO PRODUCTS AND SMOKING SUPPLIES	100	71	74	104	120	97	116	118
MISCELLANEOUS	100	60	41	72	89	87	142	175
CASH CONTRIBUTIONS	100	24	47	58	55	104	125	224
PERSONAL INSURANCE AND PENSIONS	100	8	16	45	64	94	135	262
Life and other personal insurance	100	26	41	55	69	68	102	255
Pensions and Social Security	100	6	13	44	63	97	138	263
PERSONAL TAXES	100	9	8	36	53	82	115	300
Federal income taxes	100	9	4	29	47	76	110	316
State and local income taxes	100	–1	4	38	60	98	134	283
Other taxes	100	30	70	112	101	101	106	157
GIFTS	100	43	44	60	88	79	102	221
Food	100	23	13	18	104	54	52	325
Alcoholic beverages	100	65	31	67	128	117	139	139
Housing	100	39	49	76	94	76	110	201
Housekeeping supplies	100	23	39	68	74	149	140	179
Household textiles	100	58	25	205	114	81	81	138
Appliances and misc. housewares	100	20	79	54	51	63	161	198
Major appliances	100	5	227	108	50	75	58	100
Small appliances and misc. housewares	100	26	17	31	52	59	203	241
Miscellaneous household equipment	100	13	42	68	132	55	104	218
Other housing	100	63	51	72	89	64	92	211
Apparel and services	100	32	47	64	84	117	124	193
Males, aged 2 or older	100	29	47	38	101	108	131	201
Females, aged 2 or older	100	20	36	56	55	153	133	210
Children under age 2	100	47	67	73	82	85	122	173
Other apparel products and services	100	42	47	98	116	91	100	172
Jewelry and watches	100	24	42	175	100	72	97	161
All other apparel products and services	100	64	54	4	136	114	104	186
Transportation	100	42	38	27	82	37	61	301
Health care	100	10	91	214	86	24	48	167
Entertainment	100	27	88	86	76	92	119	167
Toys, games, hobbies, and tricycles	100	33	70	105	86	111	135	141
Other entertainment	100	23	99	75	71	82	109	182
Personal care products and services	100	25	85	47	35	47	194	188
Reading	100	64	88	67	33	100	100	100
Education	100	49	17	21	74	57	78	302
All other gifts	100	120	52	87	119	75	118	128

Note: (–) means sample is too small to make a reliable estimate.
Source: Calculations by New Strategist based on the Bureau of Labor Statistics 1999 and 2000 Consumer Expenditure Surveys

Table 1.30 Average spending in the Midwest by income, 1999–2000

(average annual spending of consumer units (CU) in the Midwest by product and service category and before-tax income of consumer unit, 1999–2000; complete income reporters only)

	complete income reporters in the Midwest	under $10,000	$10,000– $19,999	$20,000– $29,999	$30,000– $39,999	$40,000– $49,999	$50,000– $69,999	$70,000 or more
Number of consumer units (in thousands, add 000s)	18,930	2,447	3,391	2,798	2,269	1,718	2,769	3,539
Average number of persons per CU	2.4	1.7	1.8	2.3	2.3	2.5	3.0	3.2
Average income before taxes	$43,171	$5,823	$14,404	$24,525	$34,418	$44,014	$58,847	$104,241
Average annual spending	39,870	15,930	22,287	30,614	35,305	40,275	51,049	73,735
FOOD	**$5,245**	**$2,489**	**$3,021**	**$4,286**	**$4,861**	**$5,717**	**$6,741**	**$8,431**
Food at home	**2,921**	**1,624**	**1,928**	**2,577**	**2,743**	**3,271**	**3,550**	**4,263**
Cereals and bakery products	447	268	305	390	400	464	548	661
Cereals and cereal products	151	90	99	135	140	159	179	225
Bakery products	296	178	206	255	260	305	368	435
Meats, poultry, fish, and eggs	688	415	454	620	652	792	848	949
Beef	219	127	134	180	252	228	277	304
Pork	154	97	113	158	130	206	189	178
Other meats	100	58	71	101	97	101	132	123
Poultry	116	72	73	100	96	141	133	179
Fish and seafood	74	42	42	57	51	91	88	129
Eggs	26	19	20	24	26	25	27	35
Dairy products	333	177	218	284	316	382	412	486
Fresh milk and cream	134	84	90	114	142	141	158	188
Other dairy products	199	93	128	171	175	241	254	299
Fruits and vegetables	463	262	343	418	426	525	493	694
Fresh fruits	142	71	111	131	130	166	132	225
Fresh vegetables	131	73	100	122	114	148	141	196
Processed fruits	107	64	77	87	89	115	123	167
Processed vegetables	83	54	56	77	93	96	98	106
Other food at home	991	501	607	865	949	1,109	1,250	1,473
Sugar and other sweets	126	67	87	115	100	137	144	202
Fats and oils	76	40	56	79	72	88	93	96
Miscellaneous foods	483	217	280	397	473	551	612	754
Nonalcoholic beverages	262	157	161	239	264	298	350	335
Food prepared by CU on trips	43	20	24	35	41	34	50	85
Food away from home	**2,323**	**865**	**1,093**	**1,709**	**2,118**	**2,446**	**3,192**	**4,168**
ALCOHOLIC BEVERAGES	**383**	**167**	**180**	**300**	**346**	**339**	**463**	**748**
HOUSING	**11,828**	**5,657**	**7,435**	**8,939**	**10,239**	**12,148**	**14,609**	**21,152**
Shelter	**6,497**	**3,100**	**4,006**	**4,776**	**5,796**	**6,582**	**8,053**	**11,783**
Owned dwellings	4,438	1,169	1,868	2,588	3,605	4,537	6,206	9,724
Mortgage interest and charges	2,368	423	429	973	1,826	2,594	3,830	5,767
Property taxes	1,133	466	749	824	889	1,030	1,307	2,274
Maintenance, repair, insurance, other expenses	937	279	690	791	890	913	1,068	1,683
Rented dwellings	1,579	1,738	1,927	1,874	1,916	1,693	1,278	869
Other lodging	480	192	211	314	275	352	570	1,190
Utilities, fuels, and public services	**2,433**	**1,477**	**1,922**	**2,219**	**2,365**	**2,525**	**2,833**	**3,439**
Natural gas	391	236	322	352	351	406	447	568
Electricity	821	529	678	802	802	857	938	1,075
Fuel oil and other fuels	69	47	66	71	98	69	67	69
Telephone	867	535	643	724	862	891	1,029	1,291
Water and other public services	285	130	213	270	252	301	351	436

	complete income reporters in the Midwest	under $10,000	$10,000– $19,999	$20,000– $29,999	$30,000– $39,999	$40,000– $49,999	$50,000– $69,999	$70,000 or more
Household services	**$661**	**$340**	**$347**	**$386**	**$286**	**$576**	**$800**	**$1,574**
Personal services	384	201	188	176	116	290	506	983
Other household services	277	139	159	209	170	286	294	591
Housekeeping supplies	**577**	**237**	**336**	**451**	**473**	**597**	**783**	**978**
Laundry and cleaning supplies	143	66	103	133	109	143	181	224
Other household products	279	96	151	191	236	315	419	462
Postage and stationery	155	75	83	126	128	139	183	292
Household furnishings and equipment	**1,660**	**504**	**824**	**1,107**	**1,320**	**1,868**	**2,140**	**3,378**
Household textiles	128	27	62	89	73	123	192	265
Furniture	373	104	180	258	318	366	479	789
Floor coverings	51	21	18	32	28	57	115	78
Major appliances	195	85	107	165	177	302	202	331
Small appliances, misc. housewares	109	37	58	71	98	123	127	215
Miscellaneous household equipment	805	230	398	492	627	897	1,025	1,700
APPAREL AND RELATED SERVICES	**1,837**	**736**	**885**	**1,376**	**1,734**	**1,673**	**2,155**	**3,638**
Men and boys	**509**	**181**	**204**	**348**	**553**	**379**	**591**	**1,084**
Men, aged 16 or older	402	104	162	252	475	280	451	887
Boys, aged 2 to 15	107	76	41	95	78	100	140	197
Women and girls	**685**	**275**	**347**	**497**	**594**	**700**	**792**	**1,351**
Women, aged 16 or older	557	237	301	385	506	598	639	1,062
Girls, aged 2 to 15	127	38	46	112	89	102	153	289
Children under age 2	**86**	**28**	**43**	**50**	**92**	**124**	**111**	**146**
Footwear	**309**	**143**	**171**	**291**	**297**	**254**	**378**	**524**
Other apparel products and services	**248**	**109**	**119**	**190**	**199**	**216**	**283**	**532**
TRANSPORTATION	**7,522**	**2,853**	**4,409**	**5,920**	**7,051**	**8,272**	**10,015**	**12,983**
Vehicle purchases	**3,596**	**1,393**	**2,220**	**2,882**	**3,234**	**3,933**	**4,903**	**6,050**
Cars and trucks, new	1,431	567	910	1,260	902	1,399	1,540	2,935
Cars and trucks, used	2,109	826	1,308	1,567	2,304	2,498	3,304	2,944
Other vehicles	56	–	3	56	28	36	60	171
Gasoline and motor oil	**1,216**	**538**	**751**	**1,010**	**1,203**	**1,381**	**1,635**	**1,894**
Other vehicle expenses	**2,322**	**809**	**1,216**	**1,723**	**2,316**	**2,624**	**3,040**	**4,195**
Vehicle finance charges	349	94	143	231	376	410	547	613
Maintenance and repairs	632	306	382	491	596	730	839	1,018
Vehicle insurance	772	255	481	663	776	865	1,023	1,252
Vehicle rentals, leases, licenses, other charges	569	154	209	338	568	619	631	1,312
Public transportation	**387**	**113**	**222**	**305**	**297**	**335**	**436**	**844**
HEALTH CARE	**2,218**	**1,277**	**2,247**	**2,373**	**2,107**	**2,225**	**2,370**	**2,657**
Health insurance	1,062	624	1,054	1,175	1,040	1,138	1,122	1,211
Medical services	591	275	522	603	544	543	683	850
Drugs	445	325	558	506	403	432	428	410
Medical supplies	120	53	112	89	120	112	137	187
ENTERTAINMENT	**2,156**	**704**	**919**	**1,525**	**2,016**	**2,229**	**3,091**	**4,119**
Fees and admissions	557	169	204	366	338	505	712	1,358
Television, radio, sound equipment	659	312	395	470	642	649	868	1,147
Pets, toys, and playground equipment	384	121	212	289	346	497	528	643
Other entertainment products and services	557	101	109	400	689	577	982	972

	complete income reporters in the Midwest	under $10,000	$10,000–$19,999	$20,000–$29,999	$30,000–$39,999	$40,000–$49,999	$50,000–$69,999	$70,000 or more
PERSONAL CARE PRODUCTS AND SERVICES	$553	$281	$373	$490	$488	$556	$649	$906
READING	178	81	118	152	148	167	224	312
EDUCATION	611	458	228	178	415	362	839	1,491
TOBACCO PRODUCTS AND SMOKING SUPPLIES	366	294	276	365	409	466	430	375
MISCELLANEOUS	885	297	566	667	881	867	1,228	1,508
CASH CONTRIBUTIONS	1,616	311	918	2,286	1,259	770	1,383	3,481
PERSONAL INSURANCE AND PENSIONS	4,471	326	713	1,756	3,351	4,483	6,853	11,934
Life and other personal insurance	420	144	178	227	402	371	623	873
Pensions and Social Security	4,051	181	535	1,529	2,948	4,113	6,230	11,061
PERSONAL TAXES	3,407	96	362	1,020	1,994	2,915	4,742	10,601
Federal income taxes	2,495	22	168	618	1,400	2,074	3,375	8,138
State and local income taxes	765	25	83	273	489	708	1,193	2,189
Other taxes	147	50	113	130	105	134	175	273
GIFTS	1,247	507	780	837	996	846	1,454	2,688
Food	88	19	20	24	36	66	139	252
Alcoholic beverages	16	11	5	12	14	15	13	37
Housing	335	153	240	228	256	271	361	686
Housekeeping supplies	50	25	29	46	51	35	60	85
Household textiles	18	1	13	18	15	20	25	28
Appliances and misc. housewares	40	14	15	20	49	59	35	84
Major appliances	8	12	3	4	7	24	10	7
Small appliances and misc. housewares	32	2	12	16	42	35	25	77
Miscellaneous household equipment	95	38	81	81	69	66	99	186
Other housing	131	73	100	64	72	90	142	304
Apparel and services	241	132	182	194	205	220	270	407
Males, aged 2 or older	77	49	77	70	56	57	69	130
Females, aged 2 or older	73	24	47	53	66	71	87	135
Children under age 2	44	13	26	25	46	51	52	81
Other apparel products and services	47	46	31	46	37	41	61	61
Jewelry and watches	22	11	19	21	19	21	20	39
All other apparel products and services	25	35	12	26	18	20	41	22
Transportation	65	47	28	28	33	30	66	180
Health care	65	19	149	108	44	12	22	53
Entertainment	117	38	42	79	152	115	142	226
Toys, games, hobbies, and tricycles	38	12	19	40	40	55	49	53
Other entertainment	79	27	24	40	111	60	93	172
Personal care products and services	26	9	14	40	17	29	25	40
Reading	2	1	2	3	3	3	2	3
Education	178	47	32	18	52	27	308	587
All other gifts	115	32	66	102	184	59	106	216

Note: Spending by category will not add to total spending because gift spending is also included in the preceding product and service categories and personal taxes are not included in the total. (–) means sample is too small to make a reliable estimate.
Source: Bureau of Labor Statistics, 1999 and 2000 Consumer Expenditure Surveys, Internet site www.bls.gov/cex/; calculations by New Strategist

Table 1.31 Indexed spending in the Midwest by income, 1999–2000

(indexed average annual spending of consumer units (CU) in the Midwest by product and service category and before-tax income of consumer unit, 1999–2000; complete income reporters only; index definition: an index of 100 is the average for all consumer units; an index of 132 means that spending by consumer units in that group is 32 percent above the average for all consumer units; an index of 68 indicates spending that is 32 percent below the average for all consumer units)

	complete income reporters in the Midwest	under $10,000	$10,000–$19,999	$20,000–$29,999	$30,000–$39,999	$40,000–$49,999	$50,000–$69,999	$70,000 or more
Average spending of CU, total	$39,870	$15,930	$22,287	$30,614	$35,305	$40,275	$51,049	$73,735
Average spending of CU, index	100	40	56	77	89	101	128	185
FOOD	100	47	58	82	93	109	129	161
Food at home	100	56	66	88	94	112	122	146
Cereals and bakery products	100	60	68	87	89	104	123	148
Cereals and cereal products	100	60	66	89	93	105	119	149
Bakery products	100	60	70	86	88	103	124	147
Meats, poultry, fish, and eggs	100	60	66	90	95	115	123	138
Beef	100	58	61	82	115	104	126	139
Pork	100	63	73	103	84	134	123	116
Other meats	100	58	71	101	97	101	132	123
Poultry	100	62	63	86	83	122	115	154
Fish and seafood	100	56	56	77	69	123	119	174
Eggs	100	74	76	92	100	96	104	135
Dairy products	100	53	65	85	95	115	124	146
Fresh milk and cream	100	63	67	85	106	105	118	140
Other dairy products	100	47	65	86	88	121	128	150
Fruits and vegetables	100	57	74	90	92	113	106	150
Fresh fruits	100	50	78	92	92	117	93	158
Fresh vegetables	100	55	77	93	87	113	108	150
Processed fruits	100	60	72	81	83	107	115	156
Processed vegetables	100	65	67	93	112	116	118	128
Other food at home	100	51	61	87	96	112	126	149
Sugar and other sweets	100	53	69	91	79	109	114	160
Fats and oils	100	53	73	104	95	116	122	126
Miscellaneous foods	100	45	58	82	98	114	127	156
Nonalcoholic beverages	100	60	62	91	101	114	134	128
Food prepared by CU on trips	100	48	55	81	95	79	116	198
Food away from home	100	37	47	74	91	105	137	179
ALCOHOLIC BEVERAGES	100	44	47	78	90	89	121	195
HOUSING	100	48	63	76	87	103	124	179
Shelter	100	48	62	74	89	101	124	181
Owned dwellings	100	26	42	58	81	102	140	219
Mortgage interest and charges	100	18	18	41	77	110	162	244
Property taxes	100	41	66	73	78	91	115	201
Maintenance, repair, insurance, other expenses	100	30	74	84	95	97	114	180
Rented dwellings	100	110	122	119	121	107	81	55
Other lodging	100	40	44	65	57	73	119	248
Utilities, fuels, and public services	100	61	79	91	97	104	116	141
Natural gas	100	60	82	90	90	104	114	145
Electricity	100	64	83	98	98	104	114	131
Fuel oil and other fuels	100	68	95	103	142	100	97	100
Telephone	100	62	74	84	99	103	119	149
Water and other public services	100	46	75	95	88	106	123	153

	complete income reporters in the Midwest	under $10,000	$10,000– $19,999	$20,000– $29,999	$30,000– $39,999	$40,000– $49,999	$50,000– $69,999	$70,000 or more
Household services	100	51	52	58	43	87	121	238
Personal services	100	52	49	46	30	76	132	256
Other household services	100	50	57	75	61	103	106	213
Housekeeping supplies	100	41	58	78	82	103	136	169
Laundry and cleaning supplies	100	46	72	93	76	100	127	157
Other household products	100	34	54	68	85	113	150	166
Postage and stationery	100	48	53	81	83	90	118	188
Household furnishings and equipment	100	30	50	67	80	113	129	203
Household textiles	100	21	49	70	57	96	150	207
Furniture	100	28	48	69	85	98	128	212
Floor coverings	100	41	36	63	55	112	225	153
Major appliances	100	43	55	85	91	155	104	170
Small appliances, misc. housewares	100	34	53	65	90	113	117	197
Miscellaneous household equipment	100	29	49	61	78	111	127	211
APPAREL AND RELATED SERVICES	100	40	48	75	94	91	117	198
Men and boys	100	36	40	68	109	74	116	213
Men, aged 16 or older	100	26	40	63	118	70	112	221
Boys, aged 2 to 15	100	71	39	89	73	93	131	184
Women and girls	100	40	51	73	87	102	116	197
Women, aged 16 or older	100	43	54	69	91	107	115	191
Girls, aged 2 to 15	100	30	36	88	70	80	120	228
Children under age 2	100	33	50	58	107	144	129	170
Footwear	100	46	55	94	96	82	122	170
Other apparel products and services	100	44	48	77	80	87	114	215
TRANSPORTATION	100	38	59	79	94	110	133	173
Vehicle purchases	100	39	62	80	90	109	136	168
Cars and trucks, new	100	40	64	88	63	98	108	205
Cars and trucks, used	100	39	62	74	109	118	157	140
Other vehicles	100	–	6	100	50	64	107	305
Gasoline and motor oil	100	44	62	83	99	114	134	156
Other vehicle expenses	100	35	52	74	100	113	131	181
Vehicle finance charges	100	27	41	66	108	117	157	176
Maintenance and repairs	100	48	60	78	94	116	133	161
Vehicle insurance	100	33	62	86	101	112	133	162
Vehicle rentals, leases, licenses, other charges	100	27	37	59	100	109	111	231
Public transportation	100	29	57	79	77	87	113	218
HEALTH CARE	100	58	101	107	95	100	107	120
Health insurance	100	59	99	111	98	107	106	114
Medical services	100	47	88	102	92	92	116	144
Drugs	100	73	125	114	91	97	96	92
Medical supplies	100	44	94	74	100	93	114	156
ENTERTAINMENT	100	33	43	71	94	103	143	191
Fees and admissions	100	30	37	66	61	91	128	244
Television, radio, sound equipment	100	47	60	71	97	98	132	174
Pets, toys, and playground equipment	100	32	55	75	90	129	138	167
Other entertainment products and services	100	18	20	72	124	104	176	175

	complete income reporters in the Midwest	under $10,000	$10,000– $19,999	$20,000– $29,999	$30,000– $39,999	$40,000– $49,999	$50,000– $69,999	$70,000 or more
PERSONAL CARE PRODUCTS AND SERVICES	100	51	67	89	88	101	117	164
READING	100	45	66	85	83	94	126	175
EDUCATION	100	75	37	29	68	59	137	244
TOBACCO PRODUCTS AND SMOKING SUPPLIES	100	80	75	100	112	127	117	102
MISCELLANEOUS	100	34	64	75	100	98	139	170
CASH CONTRIBUTIONS	100	19	57	141	78	48	86	215
PERSONAL INSURANCE AND PENSIONS	100	7	16	39	75	100	153	267
Life and other personal insurance	100	34	42	54	96	88	148	208
Pensions and Social Security	100	4	13	38	73	102	154	273
PERSONAL TAXES	100	3	11	30	59	86	139	311
Federal income taxes	100	1	7	25	56	83	135	326
State and local income taxes	100	3	11	36	64	93	156	286
Other taxes	100	34	77	88	71	91	119	186
GIFTS	100	41	63	67	80	68	117	216
Food	100	21	23	27	41	75	158	286
Alcoholic beverages	100	69	30	75	88	94	81	231
Housing	100	46	72	68	76	81	108	205
Housekeeping supplies	100	50	59	92	102	70	120	170
Household textiles	100	7	74	100	83	111	139	156
Appliances and misc. housewares	100	36	38	50	123	148	88	210
Major appliances	100	150	38	50	88	300	125	88
Small appliances and misc. housewares	100	7	37	50	131	109	78	241
Miscellaneous household equipment	100	40	85	85	73	69	104	196
Other housing	100	56	76	49	55	69	108	232
Apparel and services	100	55	75	80	85	91	112	169
Males, aged 2 or older	100	64	101	91	73	74	90	169
Females, aged 2 or older	100	33	64	73	90	97	119	185
Children under age 2	100	29	59	57	105	116	118	184
Other apparel products and services	100	98	65	98	79	87	130	130
Jewelry and watches	100	49	85	95	86	95	91	177
All other apparel products and services	100	142	47	104	72	80	164	88
Transportation	100	72	44	43	51	46	102	277
Health care	100	29	229	166	68	18	34	82
Entertainment	100	33	36	68	130	98	121	193
Toys, games, hobbies, and tricycles	100	32	49	105	105	145	129	139
Other entertainment	100	34	30	51	141	76	118	218
Personal care products and services	100	33	54	154	65	112	96	154
Reading	100	33	78	150	150	150	100	150
Education	100	26	18	10	29	15	173	330
All other gifts	100	28	57	89	160	51	92	188

Note: (–) means sample is too small to make a reliable estimate.
Source: Calculations by New Strategist based on the Bureau of Labor Statistics 1999 and 2000 Consumer Expenditure Surveys

Table 1.32 Average spending in the South by income, 1999–2000

(average annual spending of consumer units (CU) in the South by product and service category and before-tax income of consumer unit, 1999–2000; complete income reporters only)

	complete income reporters in the South	under $10,000	$10,000–$19,999	$20,000–$29,999	$30,000–$39,999	$40,000–$49,999	$50,000–$69,999	$70,000 or more
Number of consumer units (in thousands, add 000s)	28,069	4,333	5,524	4,354	3,136	2,451	3,686	4,585
Average number of persons per CU	2.5	1.7	2.2	2.5	2.6	2.7	2.9	3.1
Average income before taxes	$41,196	$6,049	$14,560	$24,509	$34,249	$44,369	$58,212	$111,730
Average annual spending	36,561	14,981	20,944	28,261	34,335	41,040	48,036	73,491
FOOD	**$4,934**	**$2,432**	**$3,177**	**$4,367**	**$5,247**	**$6,033**	**$6,143**	**$8,136**
Food at home	**2,900**	**1,726**	**2,239**	**2,797**	**3,084**	**3,420**	**3,467**	**4,019**
Cereals and bakery products	438	269	333	424	455	504	541	604
Cereals and cereal products	157	110	125	164	165	186	183	192
Bakery products	281	159	208	260	290	319	358	411
Meats, poultry, fish, and eggs	787	504	637	787	903	923	917	978
Beef	226	131	184	213	242	282	262	303
Pork	178	132	147	197	217	211	193	188
Other meats	98	60	80	107	100	129	120	111
Poultry	145	92	122	148	163	166	162	186
Fish and seafood	104	64	70	87	126	96	146	156
Eggs	36	24	34	36	55	39	34	34
Dairy products	301	172	234	288	313	333	368	435
Fresh milk and cream	121	79	100	115	132	127	148	161
Other dairy products	180	92	135	173	181	206	219	274
Fruits and vegetables	482	290	375	471	505	544	539	703
Fresh fruits	141	80	108	146	142	150	161	215
Fresh vegetables	142	88	105	134	150	162	155	215
Processed fruits	107	66	85	101	119	111	126	153
Processed vegetables	92	57	78	91	94	122	98	120
Other food at home	891	491	660	826	908	1,115	1,103	1,299
Sugar and other sweets	112	66	86	107	116	140	139	151
Fats and oils	86	57	71	87	98	105	93	103
Miscellaneous foods	413	209	305	375	400	506	525	637
Nonalcoholic beverages	247	143	186	238	266	321	304	327
Food prepared by CU on trips	34	15	12	19	28	43	41	82
Food away from home	**2,035**	**706**	**938**	**1,570**	**2,163**	**2,613**	**2,677**	**4,118**
ALCOHOLIC BEVERAGES	**316**	**105**	**153**	**246**	**320**	**336**	**499**	**622**
HOUSING	**10,964**	**5,427**	**6,863**	**8,873**	**10,174**	**11,449**	**13,876**	**21,067**
Shelter	**5,811**	**2,906**	**3,517**	**4,592**	**5,364**	**6,037**	**7,094**	**11,630**
Owned dwellings	3,704	1,131	1,611	2,345	2,969	3,556	5,110	9,401
Mortgage interest and charges	2,141	438	636	1,182	1,662	2,153	3,143	5,989
Property taxes	769	352	441	558	611	660	985	1,751
Maintenance, repair, insurance, other expenses	794	341	534	604	696	743	982	1,661
Rented dwellings	1,711	1,651	1,788	2,037	2,072	2,152	1,532	1,027
Other lodging	395	124	117	210	322	328	452	1,202
Utilities, fuels, and public services	**2,534**	**1,652**	**2,062**	**2,357**	**2,505**	**2,742**	**2,992**	**3,647**
Natural gas	171	113	137	146	151	181	198	279
Electricity	1,109	753	960	1,072	1,109	1,168	1,295	1,480
Fuel oil and other fuels	49	57	50	48	39	46	44	55
Telephone	896	546	672	810	917	1,016	1,091	1,345
Water and other public services	308	182	243	282	289	331	364	488

	complete income reporters in the South	under $10,000	$10,000– $19,999	$20,000– $29,999	$30,000– $39,999	$40,000– $49,999	$50,000– $69,999	$70,000 or more
Household services	**$668**	**$186**	**$306**	**$406**	**$478**	**$545**	**$958**	**$1,767**
Personal services	304	68	130	178	233	264	553	725
Other household services	364	118	177	228	245	281	405	1,042
Housekeeping supplies	**499**	**232**	**283**	**411**	**514**	**559**	**716**	**878**
Laundry and cleaning supplies	131	81	92	141	136	159	164	175
Other household products	259	110	131	186	273	265	380	510
Postage and stationery	109	41	59	84	104	135	172	193
Household furnishings and equipment	**1,453**	**451**	**695**	**1,106**	**1,313**	**1,567**	**2,116**	**3,144**
Household textiles	101	22	54	92	133	121	115	196
Furniture	372	116	181	282	345	336	551	823
Floor coverings	46	12	18	12	47	67	43	132
Major appliances	186	82	130	168	122	201	287	323
Small appliances, misc. housewares	89	24	32	54	88	108	198	159
Miscellaneous household equipment	660	194	280	499	578	734	921	1,512
APPAREL AND RELATED SERVICES	**1,772**	**715**	**1,035**	**1,502**	**1,752**	**1,897**	**2,144**	**3,545**
Men and boys	**401**	**128**	**212**	**335**	**389**	**436**	**477**	**865**
Men, aged 16 or older	307	95	146	265	298	338	332	702
Boys, aged 2 to 15	94	33	66	70	92	98	145	163
Women and girls	**682**	**294**	**407**	**574**	**644**	**690**	**827**	**1,379**
Women, aged 16 or older	560	253	330	439	533	581	678	1,141
Girls, aged 2 to 15	123	41	78	135	110	108	148	238
Children under age 2	**89**	**62**	**59**	**72**	**86**	**99**	**115**	**143**
Footwear	**337**	**144**	**225**	**352**	**441**	**450**	**409**	**450**
Other apparel products and services	**264**	**87**	**131**	**168**	**192**	**223**	**316**	**708**
TRANSPORTATION	**7,299**	**2,567**	**4,379**	**5,559**	**6,994**	**9,076**	**10,308**	**13,777**
Vehicle purchases	**3,640**	**1,169**	**2,234**	**2,546**	**3,265**	**4,734**	**5,254**	**7,083**
Cars and trucks, new	1,747	419	736	985	1,347	2,071	2,655	4,314
Cars and trucks, used	1,856	750	1,492	1,561	1,821	2,614	2,528	2,701
Other vehicles	37	–	6	–	97	50	72	69
Gasoline and motor oil	**1,206**	**547**	**797**	**1,058**	**1,318**	**1,480**	**1,622**	**1,901**
Other vehicle expenses	**2,156**	**744**	**1,238**	**1,748**	**2,204**	**2,599**	**3,042**	**3,997**
Vehicle finance charges	378	90	162	298	397	470	638	714
Maintenance and repairs	647	256	445	534	726	823	783	1,105
Vehicle insurance	752	304	470	688	812	948	1,033	1,205
Vehicle rentals, leases, licenses, other charges	379	94	162	228	269	359	588	972
Public transportation	**297**	**107**	**109**	**207**	**207**	**263**	**390**	**795**
HEALTH CARE	**2,144**	**1,267**	**1,732**	**1,959**	**2,108**	**2,342**	**2,567**	**3,224**
Health insurance	1,011	595	810	923	1,086	1,202	1,208	1,415
Medical services	559	275	317	411	535	607	747	1,097
Drugs	477	346	546	528	407	410	489	544
Medical supplies	98	50	59	96	79	124	124	168
ENTERTAINMENT	**1,744**	**614**	**919**	**1,223**	**1,464**	**1,711**	**2,413**	**3,979**
Fees and admissions	428	117	146	213	301	406	533	1,283
Television, radio, sound equipment	601	305	406	546	603	690	782	975
Pets, toys, and playground equipment	339	125	179	262	286	345	451	747
Other entertainment products and services	376	66	188	201	274	269	647	974

	complete income reporters in the South	under $10,000	$10,000– $19,999	$20,000– $29,999	$30,000– $39,999	$40,000– $49,999	$50,000– $69,999	$70,000 or more
PERSONAL CARE PRODUCTS AND SERVICES	$570	$294	$362	$505	$542	$674	$726	$983
READING	124	49	66	105	118	126	155	263
EDUCATION	473	295	236	275	312	324	569	1,226
TOBACCO PRODUCTS AND SMOKING SUPPLIES	340	249	320	348	337	460	408	328
MISCELLANEOUS	815	349	444	723	813	1,123	847	1,587
CASH CONTRIBUTIONS	1,175	284	377	632	1,085	1,091	1,692	3,182
PERSONAL INSURANCE AND PENSIONS	3,890	332	881	1,945	3,070	4,398	5,689	11,571
Life and other personal insurance	434	152	237	388	428	373	490	972
Pensions and Social Security	3,457	180	644	1,556	2,642	4,025	5,199	10,599
PERSONAL TAXES	2,500	(21)	15	689	1,423	2,458	3,726	9,370
Federal income taxes	2,009	(68)	(90)	466	1,098	1,883	2,962	7,892
State and local income taxes	341	3	38	113	201	400	581	1,113
Other taxes	150	44	67	110	125	175	184	364
GIFTS	998	416	556	697	798	998	1,066	2,434
Food	52	15	17	35	34	35	26	183
Alcoholic beverages	15	5	7	6	16	7	33	32
Housing	285	115	169	179	208	293	309	709
Housekeeping supplies	34	8	17	24	32	22	72	67
Household textiles	13	9	5	5	8	35	9	30
Appliances and misc. housewares	29	2	9	11	28	56	45	69
Major appliances	10	0	1	2	8	27	13	24
Small appliances and misc. housewares	20	1	8	10	20	29	32	45
Miscellaneous household equipment	61	14	41	53	63	71	62	129
Other housing	147	82	98	86	77	109	121	414
Apparel and services	237	116	175	191	230	237	259	448
Males, aged 2 or older	49	26	35	43	41	43	36	113
Females, aged 2 or older	91	40	74	76	100	62	95	178
Children under age 2	44	30	23	32	36	48	49	90
Other apparel products and services	53	21	43	41	52	84	79	67
Jewelry and watches	20	9	11	14	11	32	41	30
All other apparel products and services	33	12	32	27	41	52	38	37
Transportation	54	47	12	62	29	39	70	117
Health care	49	38	48	26	36	22	62	93
Entertainment	97	30	46	103	90	104	124	197
Toys, games, hobbies, and tricycles	27	13	15	31	25	27	34	50
Other entertainment	70	18	31	72	65	77	90	147
Personal care products and services	19	6	6	20	23	38	18	33
Reading	2	0	1	2	2	2	2	2
Education	105	27	25	21	82	66	89	402
All other gifts	84	17	50	52	48	153	73	217

Note: Spending by category will not add to total spending because gift spending is also included in the preceding product and service categories and personal taxes are not included in the total. (–) means sample is too small to make a reliable estimate.
Source: Bureau of Labor Statistics, 1999 and 2000 Consumer Expenditure Surveys, Internet site www.bls.gov/cex/; calculations by New Strategist

Table 1.33 Indexed spending in the South by income, 1999–2000

(indexed average annual spending of consumer units (CU) in the South by product and service category and before-tax income of consumer unit, 1999–2000; complete income reporters only; index definition: an index of 100 is the average for all consumer units; an index of 132 means that spending by consumer units in that group is 32 percent above the average for all consumer units; an index of 68 indicates spending that is 32 percent below the average for all consumer units)

	complete income reporters in the South	under $10,000	$10,000–$19,999	$20,000–$29,999	$30,000–$39,999	$40,000–$49,999	$50,000–$69,999	$70,000 or more
Average spending of CU, total	$36,561	$14,981	$20,944	$28,261	$34,335	$41,040	$48,036	$73,491
Average spending of CU, index	100	41	57	77	94	112	131	201
FOOD	**100**	**49**	**64**	**89**	**106**	**122**	**125**	**165**
Food at home	**100**	**60**	**77**	**96**	**106**	**118**	**120**	**139**
Cereals and bakery products	100	62	76	97	104	115	124	138
Cereals and cereal products	100	70	80	104	105	118	117	122
Bakery products	100	57	74	93	103	114	127	146
Meats, poultry, fish, and eggs	100	64	81	100	115	117	117	124
Beef	100	58	81	94	107	125	116	134
Pork	100	74	83	111	122	119	108	106
Other meats	100	61	81	109	102	132	122	113
Poultry	100	63	84	102	112	114	112	128
Fish and seafood	100	61	68	84	121	92	140	150
Eggs	100	67	94	100	153	108	94	94
Dairy products	100	57	78	96	104	111	122	145
Fresh milk and cream	100	66	83	95	109	105	122	133
Other dairy products	100	51	75	96	101	114	122	152
Fruits and vegetables	100	60	78	98	105	113	112	146
Fresh fruits	100	57	76	104	101	106	114	152
Fresh vegetables	100	62	74	94	106	114	109	151
Processed fruits	100	62	79	94	111	104	118	143
Processed vegetables	100	62	85	99	102	133	107	130
Other food at home	100	55	74	93	102	125	124	146
Sugar and other sweets	100	59	76	96	104	125	124	135
Fats and oils	100	67	82	101	114	122	108	120
Miscellaneous foods	100	51	74	91	97	123	127	154
Nonalcoholic beverages	100	58	75	96	108	130	123	132
Food prepared by CU on trips	100	45	36	56	82	126	121	241
Food away from home	**100**	**35**	**46**	**77**	**106**	**128**	**132**	**202**
ALCOHOLIC BEVERAGES	**100**	**33**	**48**	**78**	**101**	**106**	**158**	**197**
HOUSING	**100**	**50**	**63**	**81**	**93**	**104**	**127**	**192**
Shelter	**100**	**50**	**61**	**79**	**92**	**104**	**122**	**200**
Owned dwellings	100	31	43	63	80	96	138	254
Mortgage interest and charges	100	20	30	55	78	101	147	280
Property taxes	100	46	57	73	79	86	128	228
Maintenance, repair, insurance, other expenses	100	43	67	76	88	94	124	209
Rented dwellings	100	97	105	119	121	126	90	60
Other lodging	100	31	30	53	82	83	114	304
Utilities, fuels, and public services	**100**	**65**	**81**	**93**	**99**	**108**	**118**	**144**
Natural gas	100	66	80	85	88	106	116	163
Electricity	100	68	87	97	100	105	117	133
Fuel oil and other fuels	100	116	103	98	80	94	90	112
Telephone	100	61	75	90	102	113	122	150
Water and other public services	100	59	79	92	94	107	118	158

	complete income reporters in the South	under $10,000	$10,000–$19,999	$20,000–$29,999	$30,000–$39,999	$40,000–$49,999	$50,000–$69,999	$70,000 or more
Household services	**100**	**28**	**46**	**61**	**72**	**82**	**143**	**265**
Personal services	100	22	43	59	77	87	182	238
Other household services	100	32	49	63	67	77	111	286
Housekeeping supplies	**100**	**46**	**57**	**82**	**103**	**112**	**143**	**176**
Laundry and cleaning supplies	100	62	70	108	104	121	125	134
Other household products	100	42	51	72	105	102	147	197
Postage and stationery	100	38	54	77	95	124	158	177
Household furnishings and equipment	**100**	**31**	**48**	**76**	**90**	**108**	**146**	**216**
Household textiles	100	22	53	91	132	120	114	194
Furniture	100	31	49	76	93	90	148	221
Floor coverings	100	26	39	26	102	146	93	287
Major appliances	100	44	70	90	66	108	154	174
Small appliances, misc. housewares	100	27	36	61	99	121	222	179
Miscellaneous household equipment	100	29	42	76	88	111	140	229
APPAREL AND RELATED SERVICES	**100**	**40**	**58**	**85**	**99**	**107**	**121**	**200**
Men and boys	**100**	**32**	**53**	**84**	**97**	**109**	**119**	**216**
Men, aged 16 or older	100	31	47	86	97	110	108	229
Boys, aged 2 to 15	100	35	70	74	98	104	154	173
Women and girls	**100**	**43**	**60**	**84**	**94**	**101**	**121**	**202**
Women, aged 16 or older	100	45	59	78	95	104	121	204
Girls, aged 2 to 15	100	33	63	110	89	88	120	193
Children under age 2	**100**	**69**	**67**	**81**	**97**	**111**	**129**	**161**
Footwear	**100**	**43**	**67**	**104**	**131**	**134**	**121**	**134**
Other apparel products and services	**100**	**33**	**50**	**64**	**73**	**84**	**120**	**268**
TRANSPORTATION	**100**	**35**	**60**	**76**	**96**	**124**	**141**	**189**
Vehicle purchases	**100**	**32**	**61**	**70**	**90**	**130**	**144**	**195**
Cars and trucks, new	100	24	42	56	77	119	152	247
Cars and trucks, used	100	40	80	84	98	141	136	146
Other vehicles	100	–	16	–	262	135	195	186
Gasoline and motor oil	**100**	**45**	**66**	**88**	**109**	**123**	**134**	**158**
Other vehicle expenses	**100**	**35**	**57**	**81**	**102**	**121**	**141**	**185**
Vehicle finance charges	100	24	43	79	105	124	169	189
Maintenance and repairs	100	40	69	83	112	127	121	171
Vehicle insurance	100	40	63	91	108	126	137	160
Vehicle rentals, leases, licenses, other charges	100	25	43	60	71	95	155	256
Public transportation	**100**	**36**	**37**	**70**	**70**	**89**	**131**	**268**
HEALTH CARE	**100**	**59**	**81**	**91**	**98**	**109**	**120**	**150**
Health insurance	100	59	80	91	107	119	119	140
Medical services	100	49	57	74	96	109	134	196
Drugs	100	73	114	111	85	86	103	114
Medical supplies	100	51	60	98	81	127	127	171
ENTERTAINMENT	**100**	**35**	**53**	**70**	**84**	**98**	**138**	**228**
Fees and admissions	100	27	34	50	70	95	125	300
Television, radio, sound equipment	100	51	67	91	100	115	130	162
Pets, toys, and playground equipment	100	37	53	77	84	102	133	220
Other entertainment products and services	100	18	50	53	73	72	172	259

	complete income reporters in the South	under $10,000	$10,000– $19,999	$20,000– $29,999	$30,000– $39,999	$40,000– $49,999	$50,000– $69,999	$70,000 or more
PERSONAL CARE PRODUCTS AND SERVICES	100	52	63	89	95	118	127	172
READING	100	40	53	85	95	102	125	212
EDUCATION	100	62	50	58	66	68	120	259
TOBACCO PRODUCTS AND SMOKING SUPPLIES	100	73	94	102	99	135	120	96
MISCELLANEOUS	100	43	55	89	100	138	104	195
CASH CONTRIBUTIONS	100	24	32	54	92	93	144	271
PERSONAL INSURANCE AND PENSIONS	100	9	23	50	79	113	146	297
Life and other personal insurance	100	35	55	89	99	86	113	224
Pensions and Social Security	100	5	19	45	76	116	150	307
PERSONAL TAXES	100	–1	1	28	57	98	149	375
Federal income taxes	100	–3	–4	23	55	94	147	393
State and local income taxes	100	1	11	33	59	117	170	326
Other taxes	100	29	44	73	83	117	123	243
GIFTS	100	42	56	70	80	100	107	244
Food	100	29	33	67	65	67	50	352
Alcoholic beverages	100	33	44	40	107	47	220	213
Housing	100	40	59	63	73	103	108	249
Housekeeping supplies	100	25	50	71	94	65	212	197
Household textiles	100	70	36	38	62	269	69	231
Appliances and misc. housewares	100	8	32	38	97	193	155	238
Major appliances	100	3	10	20	80	270	130	240
Small appliances and misc. housewares	100	5	38	50	100	145	160	225
Miscellaneous household equipment	100	22	67	87	103	116	102	211
Other housing	100	55	67	59	52	74	82	282
Apparel and services	100	49	74	81	97	100	109	189
Males, aged 2 or older	100	54	71	88	84	88	73	231
Females, aged 2 or older	100	44	82	84	110	68	104	196
Children under age 2	100	68	52	73	82	109	111	205
Other apparel products and services	100	39	81	77	98	158	149	126
Jewelry and watches	100	43	53	70	55	160	205	150
All other apparel products and services	100	37	98	82	124	158	115	112
Transportation	100	88	22	115	54	72	130	217
Health care	100	77	98	53	73	45	127	190
Entertainment	100	31	48	106	93	107	128	203
Toys, games, hobbies, and tricycles	100	46	55	115	93	100	126	185
Other entertainment	100	26	44	103	93	110	129	210
Personal care products and services	100	31	31	105	121	200	95	174
Reading	100	15	27	100	100	100	100	100
Education	100	26	24	20	78	63	85	383
All other gifts	100	20	60	62	57	182	87	258

Note: (–) means sample is too small to make a reliable estimate.
Source: Calculations by New Strategist based on the Bureau of Labor Statistics 1999 and 2000 Consumer Expenditure Surveys

Table 1.34 Average spending in the West by income, 1999–2000

(average annual spending of consumer units (CU) in the West by product and service category and before-tax income of consumer unit, 1999–2000; complete income reporters only)

	complete income reporters in the West	under $10,000	$10,000– $19,999	$20,000– $29,999	$30,000– $39,999	$40,000– $49,999	$50,000– $69,999	$70,000 or more
Number of consumer units (in thousands, add 000s)	19,215	2,362	3,528	2,602	2,370	1,894	2,496	3,963
Average number of persons per CU	2.6	1.7	2.2	2.5	2.7	2.7	2.9	3.1
Average income before taxes	$47,086	$4,894	$14,718	$24,535	$34,564	$44,493	$58,489	$117,404
Average annual spending	43,598	18,096	24,312	30,621	36,673	45,254	51,042	82,707
FOOD	**$5,633**	**$2,796**	**$3,677**	**$4,642**	**$5,002**	**$5,929**	**$6,530**	**$9,171**
Food at home	**3,298**	**1,808**	**2,507**	**2,941**	**3,063**	**3,581**	**3,693**	**4,778**
Cereals and bakery products	487	241	357	423	457	516	559	733
Cereals and cereal products	171	94	131	166	180	179	191	227
Bakery products	317	147	226	257	277	337	367	507
Meats, poultry, fish, and eggs	797	424	661	777	729	872	808	1,126
Beef	238	122	210	221	210	288	240	328
Pork	152	75	122	171	152	138	152	212
Other meats	94	52	83	95	88	90	95	131
Poultry	147	88	103	134	145	175	165	202
Fish and seafood	127	57	108	119	91	144	119	205
Eggs	39	30	35	37	43	38	37	48
Dairy products	364	211	259	322	365	394	421	515
Fresh milk and cream	141	84	110	138	151	152	150	185
Other dairy products	223	128	150	184	214	243	270	330
Fruits and vegetables	607	365	477	543	558	665	671	852
Fresh fruits	199	125	162	176	177	202	227	280
Fresh vegetables	193	110	153	183	180	207	212	268
Processed fruits	129	81	94	111	121	151	141	183
Processed vegetables	86	50	69	74	79	104	91	123
Other food at home	1,043	567	753	876	953	1,135	1,235	1,552
Sugar and other sweets	123	71	89	112	123	122	153	172
Fats and oils	88	49	70	93	84	100	85	121
Miscellaneous foods	491	266	341	380	447	547	600	746
Nonalcoholic beverages	281	145	221	245	257	296	329	410
Food prepared by CU on trips	59	36	33	46	42	71	67	104
Food away from home	**2,335**	**987**	**1,170**	**1,701**	**1,939**	**2,347**	**2,837**	**4,393**
ALCOHOLIC BEVERAGES	**457**	**261**	**279**	**302**	**280**	**417**	**549**	**875**
HOUSING	**14,215**	**6,764**	**8,558**	**10,216**	**12,394**	**14,764**	**16,750**	**25,482**
Shelter	**8,707**	**4,363**	**5,167**	**6,345**	**8,065**	**9,353**	**9,914**	**15,313**
Owned dwellings	5,345	1,237	1,882	2,855	4,349	5,408	6,925	12,084
Mortgage interest and charges	3,457	490	738	1,388	2,799	3,875	4,803	8,350
Property taxes	932	349	512	587	811	808	1,055	1,932
Maintenance, repair, insurance, other expenses	957	398	632	880	739	725	1,067	1,801
Rented dwellings	2,793	2,677	3,052	3,221	3,440	3,604	2,479	1,773
Other lodging	569	449	234	270	276	341	510	1,456
Utilities, fuels, and public services	**2,206**	**1,226**	**1,683**	**1,865**	**2,180**	**2,362**	**2,607**	**3,169**
Natural gas	259	132	194	210	244	262	318	395
Electricity	713	397	598	630	697	747	813	987
Fuel oil and other fuels	37	37	35	39	41	56	33	30
Telephone	849	508	622	714	886	929	1,000	1,188
Water and other public services	348	152	234	272	312	369	443	568

	complete income reporters in the West	under $10,000	$10,000–$19,999	$20,000–$29,999	$30,000–$39,999	$40,000–$49,999	$50,000–$69,999	$70,000 or more
Household services	**$867**	**$216**	**$525**	**$465**	**$422**	**$784**	**$841**	**$2,148**
Personal services	399	44	267	177	149	404	387	1,027
Other household services	469	171	258	288	273	380	454	1,121
Housekeeping supplies	**544**	**255**	**345**	**406**	**497**	**570**	**687**	**889**
Laundry and cleaning supplies	137	80	117	109	152	133	157	188
Other household products	245	116	142	186	216	272	329	395
Postage and stationery	162	59	85	111	129	165	201	307
Household furnishings and equipment	**1,891**	**703**	**839**	**1,136**	**1,230**	**1,695**	**2,701**	**3,962**
Household textiles	131	40	86	133	68	122	142	251
Furniture	472	175	256	269	369	334	431	1,130
Floor coverings	47	34	16	10	27	44	52	114
Major appliances	206	88	121	107	147	179	219	455
Small appliances, misc. housewares	122	61	57	105	74	113	129	245
Miscellaneous household equipment	913	306	303	513	546	903	1,729	1,767
APPAREL AND RELATED SERVICES	**2,130**	**965**	**1,174**	**1,698**	**1,881**	**2,009**	**2,164**	**4,054**
Men and boys	**507**	**153**	**245**	**411**	**373**	**480**	**615**	**1,012**
Men, aged 16 or older	412	132	175	310	267	399	515	858
Boys, aged 2 to 15	95	22	70	101	106	82	100	153
Women and girls	**783**	**392**	**460**	**569**	**754**	**784**	**762**	**1,434**
Women, aged 16 or older	681	335	406	482	671	649	653	1,266
Girls, aged 2 to 15	102	57	55	87	83	135	109	168
Children under age 2	**84**	**30**	**56**	**67**	**77**	**123**	**111**	**122**
Footwear	**389**	**220**	**235**	**433**	**462**	**367**	**361**	**560**
Other apparel products and services	**367**	**171**	**179**	**218**	**215**	**256**	**315**	**925**
TRANSPORTATION	**8,036**	**2,753**	**4,599**	**5,956**	**7,240**	**9,211**	**8,870**	**14,997**
Vehicle purchases	**3,553**	**907**	**2,030**	**2,580**	**3,148**	**4,507**	**3,239**	**7,111**
Cars and trucks, new	1,766	285	741	1,237	1,250	2,186	1,144	4,406
Cars and trucks, used	1,727	615	1,276	1,318	1,879	2,209	1,974	2,583
Other vehicles	61	6	12	25	20	111	121	123
Gasoline and motor oil	**1,303**	**606**	**828**	**1,084**	**1,291**	**1,417**	**1,676**	**2,000**
Other vehicle expenses	**2,661**	**969**	**1,462**	**2,002**	**2,404**	**2,878**	**3,357**	**4,777**
Vehicle finance charges	330	68	116	239	337	409	507	582
Maintenance and repairs	833	353	599	709	760	891	931	1,359
Vehicle insurance	831	283	496	714	828	919	1,091	1,327
Vehicle rentals, leases, licenses, other charges	668	264	250	340	479	659	828	1,508
Public transportation	**519**	**272**	**279**	**290**	**397**	**409**	**597**	**1,108**
HEALTH CARE	**2,008**	**1,055**	**1,790**	**1,772**	**1,798**	**2,043**	**2,362**	**2,805**
Health insurance	874	452	761	822	790	913	1,007	1,210
Medical services	622	333	472	520	572	598	763	946
Drugs	383	207	445	331	356	384	392	474
Medical supplies	129	63	113	99	80	148	200	175
ENTERTAINMENT	**2,222**	**1,021**	**1,094**	**1,514**	**1,699**	**2,202**	**2,697**	**4,402**
Fees and admissions	605	258	262	350	421	554	773	1,313
Television, radio, sound equipment	665	351	456	490	622	679	852	1,054
Pets, toys, and playground equipment	386	144	178	272	333	439	496	722
Other entertainment products and services	566	267	199	402	324	530	577	1,313

	complete income reporters in the West	under $10,000	$10,000– $19,999	$20,000– $29,999	$30,000– $39,999	$40,000– $49,999	$50,000– $69,999	$70,000 or more
PERSONAL CARE PRODUCTS AND SERVICES	$607	$329	$386	$461	$568	$636	$682	$1,011
READING	179	75	107	133	153	176	224	327
EDUCATION	696	867	388	403	369	738	552	1,322
TOBACCO PRODUCTS AND SMOKING SUPPLIES	247	201	228	252	256	293	302	227
MISCELLANEOUS	1,030	373	566	769	904	1,114	1,195	1,948
CASH CONTRIBUTIONS	1,386	284	647	682	1,224	1,091	1,524	3,316
PERSONAL INSURANCE AND PENSIONS	4,751	351	817	1,822	2,905	4,630	6,642	12,772
Life and other personal insurance	368	69	153	233	234	328	485	852
Pensions and Social Security	4,383	282	663	1,590	2,672	4,303	6,157	11,920
PERSONAL TAXES	3,891	815	335	960	2,100	3,185	4,846	11,623
Federal income taxes	3,031	666	228	731	1,596	2,504	3,713	9,126
State and local income taxes	716	126	56	173	384	544	947	2,148
Other taxes	144	24	50	56	120	136	186	350
GIFTS	1,247	630	598	943	830	967	1,314	2,694
Food	83	32	24	43	41	67	115	204
Alcoholic beverages	22	3	12	13	12	17	15	59
Housing	320	124	126	265	188	246	377	707
Housekeeping supplies	56	16	24	61	42	43	75	104
Household textiles	18	1	17	7	4	7	33	41
Appliances and misc. housewares	29	8	9	32	13	25	44	56
Major appliances	6	2	4	3	4	5	10	9
Small appliances and misc. housewares	23	6	5	29	9	20	34	47
Miscellaneous household equipment	75	30	20	68	38	49	90	174
Other housing	141	70	55	97	91	121	136	331
Apparel and services	269	195	143	176	207	235	276	518
Males, aged 2 or older	78	17	43	46	39	65	105	172
Females, aged 2 or older	88	88	51	59	72	30	61	189
Children under age 2	40	11	18	29	39	63	53	63
Other apparel products and services	63	79	31	40	57	77	57	94
Jewelry and watches	29	38	13	21	26	45	35	35
All other apparel products and services	33	40	18	19	31	32	22	59
Transportation	100	35	43	163	48	56	88	209
Health care	37	10	31	18	45	10	22	86
Entertainment	129	62	59	80	73	125	144	286
Toys, games, hobbies, and tricycles	32	11	24	24	28	36	46	51
Other entertainment	97	51	35	56	45	90	99	234
Personal care products and services	25	15	22	31	43	18	24	22
Reading	4	1	3	4	1	4	4	6
Education	144	28	64	76	57	97	124	416
All other gifts	115	125	70	75	113	92	125	181

Note: Spending by category will not add to total spending because gift spending is also included in the preceding product and service categories and personal taxes are not included in the total.
Source: Bureau of Labor Statistics, 1999 and 2000 Consumer Expenditure Surveys, Internet site www.bls.gov/cex/; calculations by New Strategist

Table 1.35 Indexed spending in the West by income, 1999–2000

(indexed average annual spending of consumer units (CU) in the West by product and service category and before-tax income of consumer unit, 1999–2000; complete income reporters only; index definition: an index of 100 is the average for all consumer units; an index of 132 means that spending by consumer units in that group is 32 percent above the average for all consumer units; an index of 68 indicates spending that is 32 percent below the average for all consumer units)

	complete income reporters in the West	under $10,000	$10,000– $19,999	$20,000– $29,999	$30,000– $39,999	$40,000– $49,999	$50,000– $69,999	$70,000 or more
Average spending of CU, total	$43,598	$18,096	$24,312	$30,621	$36,673	$45,254	$51,042	$82,707
Average spending of CU, index	100	42	56	70	84	104	117	190
FOOD	100	50	65	82	89	105	116	163
Food at home	100	55	76	89	93	109	112	145
Cereals and bakery products	100	49	73	87	94	106	115	151
Cereals and cereal products	100	55	76	97	105	105	112	133
Bakery products	100	46	71	81	87	106	116	160
Meats, poultry, fish, and eggs	100	53	83	97	91	109	101	141
Beef	100	51	88	93	88	121	101	138
Pork	100	49	80	113	100	91	100	139
Other meats	100	55	88	101	94	96	101	139
Poultry	100	60	70	91	99	119	112	137
Fish and seafood	100	45	85	94	72	113	94	161
Eggs	100	77	90	95	110	97	95	123
Dairy products	100	58	71	88	100	108	116	141
Fresh milk and cream	100	59	78	98	107	108	106	131
Other dairy products	100	57	67	83	96	109	121	148
Fruits and vegetables	100	60	79	89	92	110	111	140
Fresh fruits	100	63	81	88	89	102	114	141
Fresh vegetables	100	57	79	95	93	107	110	139
Processed fruits	100	63	73	86	94	117	109	142
Processed vegetables	100	58	80	86	92	121	106	143
Other food at home	100	54	72	84	91	109	118	149
Sugar and other sweets	100	57	73	91	100	99	124	140
Fats and oils	100	55	80	106	95	114	97	138
Miscellaneous foods	100	54	70	77	91	111	122	152
Nonalcoholic beverages	100	52	78	87	91	105	117	146
Food prepared by CU on trips	100	60	55	78	71	120	114	176
Food away from home	100	42	50	73	83	101	121	188
ALCOHOLIC BEVERAGES	100	57	61	66	61	91	120	191
HOUSING	100	48	60	72	87	104	118	179
Shelter	100	50	59	73	93	107	114	176
Owned dwellings	100	23	35	53	81	101	130	226
Mortgage interest and charges	100	14	21	40	81	112	139	242
Property taxes	100	37	55	63	87	87	113	207
Maintenance, repair, insurance, other expenses	100	42	66	92	77	76	111	188
Rented dwellings	100	96	109	115	123	129	89	63
Other lodging	100	79	41	47	49	60	90	256
Utilities, fuels, and public services	100	56	76	85	99	107	118	144
Natural gas	100	51	75	81	94	101	123	153
Electricity	100	56	84	88	98	105	114	138
Fuel oil and other fuels	100	101	94	105	111	151	89	81
Telephone	100	60	73	84	104	109	118	140
Water and other public services	100	44	67	78	90	106	127	163

	complete income reporters in the West	under $10,000	$10,000–$19,999	$20,000–$29,999	$30,000–$39,999	$40,000–$49,999	$50,000–$69,999	$70,000 or more
Household services	**100**	**25**	**61**	**54**	**49**	**90**	**97**	**248**
Personal services	100	11	67	44	37	101	97	257
Other household services	100	36	55	61	58	81	97	239
Housekeeping supplies	**100**	**47**	**63**	**75**	**91**	**105**	**126**	**163**
Laundry and cleaning supplies	100	58	86	80	111	97	115	137
Other household products	100	47	58	76	88	111	134	161
Postage and stationery	100	36	53	69	80	102	124	190
Household furnishings and equipment	**100**	**37**	**44**	**60**	**65**	**90**	**143**	**210**
Household textiles	100	30	66	102	52	93	108	192
Furniture	100	37	54	57	78	71	91	239
Floor coverings	100	73	34	21	57	94	111	243
Major appliances	100	43	59	52	71	87	106	221
Small appliances, misc. housewares	100	50	47	86	61	93	106	201
Miscellaneous household equipment	100	33	33	56	60	99	189	194
APPAREL AND RELATED SERVICES	**100**	**45**	**55**	**80**	**88**	**94**	**102**	**190**
Men and boys	**100**	**30**	**48**	**81**	**74**	**95**	**121**	**200**
Men, aged 16 or older	100	32	42	75	65	97	125	208
Boys, aged 2 to 15	100	23	74	106	112	86	105	161
Women and girls	**100**	**50**	**59**	**73**	**96**	**100**	**97**	**183**
Women, aged 16 or older	100	49	60	71	99	95	96	186
Girls, aged 2 to 15	100	55	53	85	81	132	107	165
Children under age 2	**100**	**36**	**66**	**80**	**92**	**146**	**132**	**145**
Footwear	**100**	**57**	**60**	**111**	**119**	**94**	**93**	**144**
Other apparel products and services	**100**	**47**	**49**	**59**	**59**	**70**	**86**	**252**
TRANSPORTATION	**100**	**34**	**57**	**74**	**90**	**115**	**110**	**187**
Vehicle purchases	**100**	**26**	**57**	**73**	**89**	**127**	**91**	**200**
Cars and trucks, new	100	16	42	70	71	124	65	249
Cars and trucks, used	100	36	74	76	109	128	114	150
Other vehicles	100	10	20	41	33	182	198	202
Gasoline and motor oil	**100**	**46**	**64**	**83**	**99**	**109**	**129**	**153**
Other vehicle expenses	**100**	**36**	**55**	**75**	**90**	**108**	**126**	**180**
Vehicle finance charges	100	21	35	72	102	124	154	176
Maintenance and repairs	100	42	72	85	91	107	112	163
Vehicle insurance	100	34	60	86	100	111	131	160
Vehicle rentals, leases, licenses, other charges	100	40	37	51	72	99	124	226
Public transportation	**100**	**52**	**54**	**56**	**76**	**79**	**115**	**213**
HEALTH CARE	**100**	**53**	**89**	**88**	**90**	**102**	**118**	**140**
Health insurance	100	52	87	94	90	104	115	138
Medical services	100	54	76	84	92	96	123	152
Drugs	100	54	116	86	93	100	102	124
Medical supplies	100	49	88	77	62	115	155	136
ENTERTAINMENT	**100**	**46**	**49**	**68**	**76**	**99**	**121**	**198**
Fees and admissions	100	43	43	58	70	92	128	217
Television, radio, sound equipment	100	53	69	74	94	102	128	158
Pets, toys, and playground equipment	100	37	46	70	86	114	128	187
Other entertainment products and services	100	47	35	71	57	94	102	232

	complete income reporters in the West	under $10,000	$10,000–$19,999	$20,000–$29,999	$30,000–$39,999	$40,000–$49,999	$50,000–$69,999	$70,000 or more
PERSONAL CARE PRODUCTS AND SERVICES	100	54	64	76	94	105	112	167
READING	100	42	60	74	85	98	125	183
EDUCATION	100	125	56	58	53	106	79	190
TOBACCO PRODUCTS AND SMOKING SUPPLIES	100	81	92	102	104	119	122	92
MISCELLANEOUS	100	36	55	75	88	108	116	189
CASH CONTRIBUTIONS	100	21	47	49	88	79	110	239
PERSONAL INSURANCE AND PENSIONS	100	7	17	38	61	97	140	269
Life and other personal insurance	100	19	42	63	64	89	132	232
Pensions and Social Security	100	6	15	36	61	98	140	272
PERSONAL TAXES	100	21	9	25	54	82	125	299
Federal income taxes	100	22	8	24	53	83	123	301
State and local income taxes	100	18	8	24	54	76	132	300
Other taxes	100	16	35	39	83	94	129	243
GIFTS	100	51	48	76	67	78	105	216
Food	100	39	29	52	49	81	139	246
Alcoholic beverages	100	13	56	59	55	77	68	268
Housing	100	39	39	83	59	77	118	221
Housekeeping supplies	100	28	44	109	75	77	134	186
Household textiles	100	3	95	39	22	39	183	228
Appliances and misc. housewares	100	26	32	110	45	86	152	193
Major appliances	100	33	65	50	67	83	167	150
Small appliances and misc. housewares	100	25	21	126	39	87	148	204
Miscellaneous household equipment	100	40	26	91	51	65	120	232
Other housing	100	49	39	69	65	86	96	235
Apparel and services	100	72	53	65	77	87	103	193
Males, aged 2 or older	100	21	55	59	50	83	135	221
Females, aged 2 or older	100	100	58	67	82	34	69	215
Children under age 2	100	26	46	73	98	158	133	158
Other apparel products and services	100	125	49	63	90	122	90	149
Jewelry and watches	100	131	46	72	90	155	121	121
All other apparel products and services	100	121	54	58	94	97	67	179
Transportation	100	35	43	163	48	56	88	209
Health care	100	27	83	49	122	27	59	232
Entertainment	100	48	46	62	57	97	112	222
Toys, games, hobbies, and tricycles	100	36	74	75	88	113	144	159
Other entertainment	100	53	36	58	46	93	102	241
Personal care products and services	100	59	87	124	172	72	96	88
Reading	100	31	73	100	25	100	100	150
Education	100	20	45	53	40	67	86	289
All other gifts	100	109	61	65	98	80	109	157

Source: Calculations by New Strategist based on the Bureau of Labor Statistics 1999 and 2000 Consumer Expenditure Surveys

Spending Overview:
Spending by Metropolitan Area, 1999–2000

Within regions, spending levels vary considerably by metropolitan area. Among the four Northeastern metropolitan areas examined by the Consumer Expenditure Survey, spending ranged from $35,526 in Pittsburgh to $46,277 in New York in 1999–2000. In the Midwest, spending ranged from $37,647 in Kansas City to $49,893 in Minneapolis-St. Paul. Among selected metropolitan areas in the South, spending was greatest in Washington, D.C. ($47,894) and least in Tampa ($35,404). San Francisco had the highest spending ($55,040), not only for the Western region, but among all the metropolitan areas included in the survey. Among Western metropolitan areas, household spending was lowest in Honolulu ($41,972).

Spending levels by metropolitan area vary significantly by product and service category. Households in Pittsburgh spend much more on housekeeping supplies than the average household in Boston, New York, or Philadelphia, although overall household spending in the other metro areas is far greater than in Pittsburgh. Households in Pittsburgh also spend more than those in the other metropolitan areas on tobacco and cash contributions.

Households in Minneapolis-St. Paul spend more than twice as much as households in Kansas City on alcoholic beverages. But Kansas City and Minneapolis-St. Paul residents spend about the same amount on food at home.

In the South, households in Miami spend significantly more than those in Washington, D.C., on meats, poultry, fish, and eggs. Households in Houston spend 37 percent more than the average southern household on vehicle purchases.

In the West, spending on tobacco is 15 percent below average in Los Angeles, but 96 percent above average in Anchorage. Spending on owned dwellings is 8 percent below the Western average in Phoenix.

Table 1.36 Average spending in selected Northeastern metros, 1999–2000

(average annual spending of consumer units in selected Northeastern metropolitan areas by product and service category, 1999–2000)

	total consumer units in the Northeast	Boston	New York	Philadelphia	Pittsburgh
Number of consumer units (in thousands, add 000s)	20,987	2,512	7,483	2,074	1,010
Average number of persons per consumer unit	2.5	2.4	2.6	2.6	2.3
Average income before taxes	$47,876	$49,557	$57,063	$49,932	$41,371
Average annual spending	38,763	37,727	46,277	39,666	35,526
FOOD	**$5,429**	**$4,924**	**$6,416**	**$5,408**	**$5,032**
Food at home	**3,144**	**2,596**	**3,611**	**3,062**	**2,682**
Cereals and bakery products	489	400	555	464	444
Meats, poultry, fish, and eggs	857	702	1,049	855	702
Dairy products	357	298	392	347	323
Fruits and vegetables	572	506	695	571	433
Other food at home	869	689	920	824	780
Food away from home	**2,285**	**2,328**	**2,805**	**2,346**	**2,350**
ALCOHOLIC BEVERAGES	**379**	**457**	**422**	**360**	**356**
HOUSING	**13,431**	**13,362**	**16,838**	**14,235**	**10,451**
Shelter	**8,239**	**8,633**	**10,962**	**8,455**	**5,293**
Owned dwellings	5,271	5,455	6,634	6,107	3,420
Rented dwellings	2,429	2,636	3,697	1,688	1,421
Other lodging	539	543	630	660	452
Utilities, fuels, public services	**2,512**	**2,362**	**2,687**	**2,864**	**2,490**
Household services	**650**	**667**	**915**	**616**	**383**
Housekeeping supplies	**516**	**384**	**544**	**533**	**675**
Household furnishings and equipment	**1,513**	**1,315**	**1,731**	**1,767**	**1,610**
APPAREL AND RELATED SERVICES	**1,998**	**1,805**	**2,832**	**1,826**	**1,995**
TRANSPORTATION	**6,565**	**6,587**	**7,003**	**6,872**	**6,359**
Vehicle purchases	2,713	2,808	2,607	2,879	2,505
Gasoline and motor oil	1,000	965	982	931	1,026
Other vehicle expenses	2,283	2,214	2,513	2,576	2,465
Public transportation	569	599	900	487	363
HEALTH CARE	**1,833**	**1,740**	**1,960**	**1,779**	**2,073**
ENTERTAINMENT	**1,915**	**1,939**	**2,229**	**1,667**	**1,840**
PERSONAL CARE PRODUCTS AND SERVICES	**569**	**522**	**712**	**597**	**562**
READING	**184**	**202**	**214**	**167**	**159**
EDUCATION	**881**	**1,031**	**1,119**	**1,135**	**495**
TOBACCO PRODUCTS AND SMOKING SUPPLIES	**322**	**319**	**325**	**306**	**388**
MISCELLANEOUS	**782**	**598**	**902**	**854**	**935**
CASH CONTRIBUTIONS	**1,082**	**854**	**1,299**	**1,146**	**1,458**
PERSONAL INSURANCE AND PENSIONS	**3,396**	**3,388**	**4,006**	**3,313**	**3,424**
Life and other personal insurance	413	387	526	459	463
Pensions and Social Security	2,983	3,002	3,480	2,853	2,962

Source: Bureau of Labor Statistics, 1999 and 2000 Consumer Expenditure Surveys, Internet site www.bls.gov/cex/

Table 1.37 Indexed spending in selected Northeastern metros, 1999–2000

(indexed average annual spending of consumer units in selected Northeastern metropolitan areas by product and service category, 1999–2000; index definition: an index of 100 is the average for all consumer units; an index of 132 means that spending by consumer units in that group is 32 percent above the average for all consumer units; an index of 68 indicates spending that is 32 percent below the average for all consumer units)

	total consumer units in the Northeast	Boston	New York	Philadelphia	Pittsburgh
Average spending of consumer unit, total	$38,763	$37,727	$46,277	$39,666	$35,526
Average spending of consumer unit, index	100	97	119	102	92
FOOD	100	91	118	100	93
Food at home	100	83	115	97	85
Cereals and bakery products	100	82	113	95	91
Meats, poultry, fish, and eggs	100	82	122	100	82
Dairy products	100	83	110	97	90
Fruits and vegetables	100	88	122	100	76
Other food at home	100	79	106	95	90
Food away from home	100	102	123	103	103
ALCOHOLIC BEVERAGES	100	121	111	95	94
HOUSING	100	99	125	106	78
Shelter	100	105	133	103	64
Owned dwellings	100	103	126	116	65
Rented dwellings	100	109	152	69	59
Other lodging	100	101	117	122	84
Utilities, fuels, public services	100	94	107	114	99
Household services	100	103	141	95	59
Housekeeping supplies	100	74	105	103	131
Household furnishings and equipment	100	87	114	117	106
APPAREL AND RELATED SERVICES	100	90	142	91	100
TRANSPORTATION	100	100	107	105	97
Vehicle purchases	100	104	96	106	92
Gasoline and motor oil	100	97	98	93	103
Other vehicle expenses	100	97	110	113	108
Public transportation	100	105	158	86	64
HEALTH CARE	100	95	107	97	113
ENTERTAINMENT	100	101	116	87	96
PERSONAL CARE PRODUCTS AND SERVICES	100	92	125	105	99
READING	100	110	116	91	86
EDUCATION	100	117	127	129	56
TOBACCO PRODUCTS AND SMOKING SUPPLIES	100	99	101	95	120
MISCELLANEOUS	100	76	115	109	120
CASH CONTRIBUTIONS	100	79	120	106	135
PERSONAL INSURANCE AND PENSIONS	100	100	118	98	101
Life and other personal insurance	100	94	127	111	112
Pensions and Social Security	100	101	117	96	99

Source: Calculations by New Strategist based on the Bureau of Labor Statistics 1999 and 2000 Consumer Expenditure Surveys

Table 1.38   Average spending in selected Midwestern metros, 1999–2000

(average annual spending of consumer units (CU) in selected Midwestern metropolitan areas by product and service category, 1999–2000)

	total consumer units in the Midwest	Chicago	Cincinnati	Cleveland	Detroit	Kansas City	Milwaukee	Minneapolis–St. Paul	St. Louis
Number of consumer units (in thousands, add 000s)	25,741	2,979	895	1,180	2,065	776	699	1,331	1,006
Average number of persons per CU	2.5	2.7	2.3	2.4	2.7	2.5	2.6	2.4	2.5
Average income before taxes	$43,171	$51,332	$45,737	$48,578	$49,041	$51,298	$43,161	$60,574	$45,251
Average annual spending	37,848	43,437	39,772	38,834	41,360	37,647	38,877	49,893	38,935
FOOD	$5,059	$5,452	$5,492	$5,274	$6,040	$5,302	$4,627	$5,794	$5,619
Food at home	2,836	2,936	2,813	3,107	3,295	3,030	2,716	3,133	3,338
Cereals and bakery products	436	443	412	462	516	449	414	464	514
Meats, poultry, fish, and eggs	688	770	642	796	869	771	632	653	972
Dairy products	318	307	341	326	326	349	289	384	328
Fruits and vegetables	460	494	432	549	562	544	470	550	526
Other food at home	934	922	987	973	1,022	917	911	1,083	997
Food away from home	2,223	2,516	2,678	2,167	2,745	2,272	1,911	2,661	2,281
ALCOHOLIC BEVERAGES	355	422	369	315	428	274	518	663	324
HOUSING	11,744	15,322	12,749	12,567	13,845	11,513	13,313	15,637	11,557
Shelter	6,562	9,396	7,410	7,156	7,704	6,606	8,332	9,285	6,411
Owned dwellings	4,525	6,330	4,620	5,247	5,608	4,603	5,378	6,425	4,627
Rented dwellings	1,565	2,239	2,292	1,435	1,618	1,683	2,541	2,121	1,412
Other lodging	472	827	497	474	478	320	414	739	373
Utilities, fuels, public services	2,457	2,796	2,411	2,584	2,637	2,645	2,271	2,414	2,668
Household services	629	762	796	463	697	549	686	1,041	795
Housekeeping supplies	528	535	587	570	651	454	491	670	388
Household furnishings and equipment	1,569	1,833	1,545	1,795	2,157	1,259	1,533	2,226	1,294
APPAREL AND RELATED SERVICES	1,772	2,095	1,802	1,815	2,498	1,722	1,862	2,266	1,944
TRANSPORTATION	7,389	7,418	7,911	8,277	7,635	7,889	7,017	8,303	7,950
Vehicle purchases	3,570	3,374	3,872	4,253	2,871	3,824	3,369	3,312	4,345
Gasoline and motor oil	1,195	1,120	1,117	1,073	1,268	1,341	1,129	1,348	1,105
Other vehicle expenses	2,248	2,193	2,601	2,506	3,093	2,403	2,081	2,906	2,038
Public transportation	376	731	320	445	403	321	438	736	462
HEALTH CARE	2,130	2,033	1,882	1,770	1,638	1,931	2,283	2,334	2,133
ENTERTAINMENT	2,070	2,054	1,961	1,861	2,071	1,864	1,927	2,959	1,877
PERSONAL CARE PRODUCTS AND SERVICES	531	644	519	584	638	524	562	656	535
READING	165	157	165	172	173	144	187	267	127
EDUCATION	617	1,022	681	535	602	562	726	634	687
TOBACCO PRODUCTS AND SMOKING SUPPLIES	353	289	378	332	463	339	427	384	241
MISCELLANEOUS	826	757	909	1,203	972	743	905	1,185	870
CASH CONTRIBUTIONS	1,383	2,414	1,616	953	1,236	968	1,347	1,509	1,472
PERSONAL INSURANCE AND PENSIONS	3,454	3,358	3,339	3,176	3,122	3,873	3,176	7,302	3,599
Life and other personal insurance	403	354	398	357	376	449	364	491	429
Pensions and Social Security	3,051	3,003	2,940	2,818	2,746	3,424	2,812	6,811	3,170

Source: Bureau of Labor Statistics, 1999 and 2000 Consumer Expenditure Surveys, Internet site www.bls.gov/cex/

Table 1.39 Indexed spending in selected Midwestern metros, 1999–2000

(indexed average annual spending of consumer units (CU) in selected Midwestern metropolitan areas by product and service category, 1999–2000; index definition: an index of 100 is the average for all consumer units; an index of 132 means that spending by consumer units in that group is 32 percent above the average for all consumer units; an index of 68 indicates spending that is 32 percent below the average for all consumer units)

	total consumer units in the Midwest	Chicago	Cincinnati	Cleveland	Detroit	Kansas City	Milwaukee	Minneapolis– St. Paul	St. Louis
Average spending of CU, total	$37,848	$43,437	$39,772	$38,834	$41,360	$37,647	$38,877	$49,893	$38,935
Average spending of CU, index	100	115	105	103	109	99	103	132	103
FOOD	100	108	109	104	119	105	91	115	111
Food at home	100	104	99	110	116	107	96	110	118
Cereals and bakery products	100	102	94	106	118	103	95	106	118
Meats, poultry, fish, and eggs	100	112	93	116	126	112	92	95	141
Dairy products	100	97	107	103	103	110	91	121	103
Fruits and vegetables	100	107	94	119	122	118	102	120	114
Other food at home	100	99	106	104	109	98	98	116	107
Food away from home	100	113	120	97	123	102	86	120	103
ALCOHOLIC BEVERAGES	100	119	104	89	121	77	146	187	91
HOUSING	100	130	109	107	118	98	113	133	98
Shelter	100	143	113	109	117	101	127	141	98
Owned dwellings	100	140	102	116	124	102	119	142	102
Rented dwellings	100	143	146	92	103	108	162	136	90
Other lodging	100	175	105	100	101	68	88	157	79
Utilities, fuels, public services	100	114	98	105	107	108	92	98	109
Household services	100	121	127	74	111	87	109	166	126
Housekeeping supplies	100	101	111	108	123	86	93	127	73
Household furnishings and equipment	100	117	98	114	137	80	98	142	82
APPAREL AND RELATED SERVICES	100	118	102	102	141	97	105	128	110
TRANSPORTATION	100	100	107	112	103	107	95	112	108
Vehicle purchases	100	95	108	119	80	107	94	93	122
Gasoline and motor oil	100	94	93	90	106	112	94	113	92
Other vehicle expenses	100	98	116	111	138	107	93	129	91
Public transportation	100	194	85	118	107	85	116	196	123
HEALTH CARE	100	95	88	83	77	91	107	110	100
ENTERTAINMENT	100	99	95	90	100	90	93	143	91
PERSONAL CARE PRODUCTS AND SERVICES	100	121	98	110	120	99	106	124	101
READING	100	95	100	104	105	87	113	162	77
EDUCATION	100	166	110	87	98	91	118	103	111
TOBACCO PRODUCTS AND SMOKING SUPPLIES	100	82	107	94	131	96	121	109	68
MISCELLANEOUS	100	92	110	146	118	90	110	143	105
CASH CONTRIBUTIONS	100	175	117	69	89	70	97	109	106
PERSONAL INSURANCE AND PENSIONS	100	97	97	92	90	112	92	211	104
Life and other personal insurance	100	88	99	89	93	111	90	122	106
Pensions and Social Security	100	98	96	92	90	112	92	223	104

Source: Calculations by New Strategist based on the Bureau of Labor Statistics 1999 and 2000 Consumer Expenditure Surveys

Table 1.40 Average spending in selected Southern metros, 1999–2000

(average annual spending of consumer units in selected Southern metropolitan areas by product and service category, 1999–2000)

	total consumer units in the South	Atlanta	Baltimore	Dallas–Fort Worth	Houston	Miami	Tampa	Washington, D.C.
Number of consumer units (in thousands, add 000s)	38,030	1,734	1,007	1,966	1,733	1,504	1,125	1,890
Average number of persons per consumer unit	2.5	2.6	2.7	2.5	2.9	2.7	2.5	2.5
Average income before taxes	$41,196	$53,936	$50,813	$56,046	$54,733	$46,034	$45,116	$69,331
Average annual spending	34,102	37,624	41,725	46,600	46,299	39,773	35,404	47,894
FOOD	**$4,670**	**$4,689**	**$5,531**	**$6,865**	**$6,080**	**$5,560**	**$4,589**	**$5,705**
Food at home	**2,776**	**2,629**	**3,175**	**3,888**	**3,174**	**3,425**	**2,628**	**3,013**
Cereals and bakery products	419	387	478	539	473	501	370	472
Meats, poultry, fish, and eggs	759	779	869	1,084	813	1,089	727	705
Dairy products	288	265	328	376	336	384	264	303
Fruits and vegetables	460	433	537	658	559	610	510	609
Other food at home	850	766	963	1,231	992	841	757	925
Food away from home	**1,894**	**2,060**	**2,356**	**2,977**	**2,906**	**2,134**	**1,961**	**2,692**
ALCOHOLIC BEVERAGES	**280**	**322**	**334**	**326**	**609**	**427**	**326**	**470**
HOUSING	**10,598**	**13,663**	**13,779**	**14,339**	**13,870**	**14,535**	**11,258**	**16,978**
Shelter	**5,691**	**8,254**	**8,323**	**8,087**	**7,337**	**8,787**	**6,281**	**10,698**
Owned dwellings	3,673	5,722	6,133	4,873	4,397	5,817	4,042	6,779
Rented dwellings	1,644	2,143	1,558	2,855	2,446	2,654	1,761	2,918
Other lodging	374	390	632	359	494	315	478	1,001
Utilities, fuels, public services	**2,521**	**3,055**	**2,483**	**3,041**	**2,929**	**2,768**	**2,576**	**2,639**
Household services	**601**	**803**	**610**	**962**	**1,005**	**1,009**	**714**	**969**
Housekeeping supplies	**449**	**364**	**699**	**559**	**597**	**454**	**436**	**516**
Household furnishings and equipment	**1,337**	**1,188**	**1,664**	**1,690**	**2,002**	**1,516**	**1,250**	**2,157**
APPAREL AND RELATED SERVICES	**1,617**	**1,873**	**1,894**	**2,429**	**2,376**	**1,950**	**1,101**	**2,059**
TRANSPORTATION	**7,038**	**7,056**	**7,185**	**8,948**	**9,722**	**7,463**	**7,752**	**7,813**
Vehicle purchases	3,516	3,194	3,214	4,441	4,813	3,023	4,130	3,222
Gasoline and motor oil	1,180	1,128	1,172	1,469	1,442	1,250	1,102	1,195
Other vehicle expenses	2,058	2,426	2,285	2,624	2,988	2,756	2,140	2,526
Public transportation	284	309	513	415	478	433	379	871
HEALTH CARE	**2,052**	**1,910**	**1,843**	**1,963**	**2,195**	**1,746**	**2,388**	**2,222**
ENTERTAINMENT	**1,604**	**1,551**	**2,013**	**2,180**	**2,225**	**1,483**	**1,568**	**2,535**
PERSONAL CARE PRODUCTS AND SERVICES	**538**	**579**	**632**	**639**	**858**	**676**	**432**	**677**
READING	**115**	**140**	**135**	**164**	**131**	**73**	**102**	**242**
EDUCATION	**465**	**342**	**798**	**617**	**460**	**505**	**427**	**724**
TOBACCO PRODUCTS AND SMOKING SUPPLIES	**318**	**241**	**324**	**276**	**307**	**203**	**359**	**216**
MISCELLANEOUS	**753**	**812**	**2,000**	**652**	**1,001**	**804**	**598**	**931**
CASH CONTRIBUTIONS	**1,042**	**1,164**	**1,084**	**1,868**	**1,442**	**1,035**	**1,209**	**1,707**
PERSONAL INSURANCE AND PENSIONS	**3,012**	**3,281**	**4,173**	**5,333**	**5,023**	**3,314**	**3,294**	**5,614**
Life and other personal insurance	409	423	444	475	459	308	643	716
Pensions and Social Security	2,603	2,858	3,730	4,858	4,564	3,006	2,651	4,898

Source: Bureau of Labor Statistics, 1999 and 2000 Consumer Expenditure Surveys, Internet site www.bls.gov/cex/

Table 1.41 Indexed spending in selected Southern metros, 1999–2000

(indexed average annual spending of consumer units (CU) in selected Southern metropolitan areas by product and service category, 1999–2000; index definition: an index of 100 is the average for all consumer units; an index of 132 means that spending by consumer units in that group is 32 percent above the average for all consumer units; an index of 68 indicates spending that is 32 percent below the average for all consumer units)

	total consumer units in the South	Atlanta	Baltimore	Dallas–Fort Worth	Houston	Miami	Tampa	Washington, D.C.
Average spending of CU, total	$34,102	$37,624	$41,725	$46,600	$46,299	$39,773	$35,404	$47,894
Average spending of CU, index	100	110	122	137	136	117	104	140
FOOD	100	100	118	147	130	119	98	122
Food at home	100	95	114	140	114	123	95	109
Cereals and bakery products	100	92	114	129	113	120	88	113
Meats, poultry, fish, and eggs	100	103	114	143	107	143	96	93
Dairy products	100	92	114	131	117	133	92	105
Fruits and vegetables	100	94	117	143	122	133	111	132
Other food at home	100	90	113	145	117	99	89	109
Food away from home	100	109	124	157	153	113	104	142
ALCOHOLIC BEVERAGES	100	115	119	116	218	153	116	168
HOUSING	100	129	130	135	131	137	106	160
Shelter	100	145	146	142	129	154	110	188
Owned dwellings	100	156	167	133	120	158	110	185
Rented dwellings	100	130	95	174	149	161	107	177
Other lodging	100	104	169	96	132	84	128	268
Utilities, fuels, public services	100	121	98	121	116	110	102	105
Household services	100	134	101	160	167	168	119	161
Housekeeping supplies	100	81	156	124	133	101	97	115
Household furnishings and equipment	100	89	124	126	150	113	93	161
APPAREL AND RELATED SERVICES	100	116	117	150	147	121	68	127
TRANSPORTATION	100	100	102	127	138	106	110	111
Vehicle purchases	100	91	91	126	137	86	117	92
Gasoline and motor oil	100	96	99	124	122	106	93	101
Other vehicle expenses	100	118	111	128	145	134	104	123
Public transportation	100	109	181	146	168	152	133	307
HEALTH CARE	100	93	90	96	107	85	116	108
ENTERTAINMENT	100	97	125	136	139	92	98	158
PERSONAL CARE PRODUCTS AND SERVICES	100	108	117	119	159	126	80	126
READING	100	122	117	143	114	63	89	210
EDUCATION	100	74	172	133	99	109	92	156
TOBACCO PRODUCTS AND SMOKING SUPPLIES	100	76	102	87	97	64	113	68
MISCELLANEOUS	100	108	266	87	133	107	79	124
CASH CONTRIBUTIONS	100	112	104	179	138	99	116	164
PERSONAL INSURANCE AND PENSIONS	100	109	139	177	167	110	109	186
Life and other personal insurance	100	103	109	116	112	75	157	175
Pensions and Social Security	100	110	143	187	175	115	102	188

Source: Calculations by New Strategist based on the Bureau of Labor Statistics 1999 and 2000 Consumer Expenditure Surveys

Table 1.42 Average spending in selected Western metros, 1999–2000

(average annual spending of consumer units (CU) in selected Western metropolitan areas by product and service category, 1999–2000)

	total consumer units in the West	Anchorage	Denver	Honolulu	Los Angeles	Phoenix	Portland	San Diego	San Francisco	Seattle
Number of consumer units (in thousands, add 000s)	24,158	101	1,106	294	5,377	1,223	1,044	878	2,757	1,430
Average number of persons per CU	2.6	2.6	2.5	2.7	2.8	2.5	2.5	2.6	2.5	2.4
Average income before taxes	$47,086	$54,506	$55,168	$51,906	$52,776	$47,492	$49,035	$52,898	$64,818	$51,292
Average annual spending	41,933	53,028	46,002	41,972	44,748	41,991	44,331	47,338	55,040	43,602
FOOD	$5,508	$6,964	$5,676	$5,771	$5,490	$5,486	$5,655	$5,243	$7,442	$6,543
Food at home	3,257	4,466	3,279	3,278	3,187	2,895	3,362	2,725	4,355	3,839
Cereals and bakery products	482	604	489	485	455	453	527	422	681	573
Meats, poultry, fish, and eggs	807	1,044	808	828	870	628	750	650	1,106	902
Dairy products	355	466	347	308	342	348	378	286	420	409
Fruits and vegetables	588	794	561	649	604	520	568	496	800	741
Other food at home	1,025	1,557	1,073	1,009	917	946	1,139	871	1,349	1,213
Food away from home	2,250	2,498	2,397	2,493	2,303	2,591	2,293	2,518	3,086	2,703
ALCOHOLIC BEVERAGES	407	591	621	409	337	467	519	406	781	427
HOUSING	14,086	17,504	15,773	14,084	16,550	13,123	14,654	17,011	19,682	14,644
Shelter	8,746	10,720	10,110	9,717	10,293	7,793	9,095	10,996	12,963	9,489
Owned dwellings	5,393	6,360	5,910	5,704	5,958	4,974	6,100	6,423	8,266	5,781
Rented dwellings	2,788	3,264	2,916	3,404	3,828	2,341	2,359	4,102	3,963	2,896
Other lodging	565	1,096	1,284	610	507	478	636	471	734	812
Utilities, fuels, public services	2,202	2,485	2,311	2,113	2,290	2,599	2,344	2,104	2,226	2,225
Household services	864	900	794	630	1,429	577	812	1,013	1,477	660
Housekeeping supplies	492	738	473	497	481	538	451	479	595	636
Household furnishings and equipment	1,781	2,661	2,084	1,127	2,056	1,616	1,953	2,419	2,421	1,634
APPAREL AND RELATED SERVICES	2,021	2,490	2,178	1,974	2,450	1,979	1,517	2,020	3,137	1,917
TRANSPORTATION	7,873	9,812	8,340	5,775	7,701	8,858	7,800	9,982	9,726	7,401
Vehicle purchases	3,462	4,276	3,257	1,553	2,933	4,223	3,304	5,323	4,409	2,766
Gasoline and motor oil	1,291	1,334	1,196	1,071	1,383	1,118	1,248	1,349	1,424	1,300
Other vehicle expenses	2,605	3,172	3,141	2,101	2,924	2,965	2,658	2,684	2,992	2,657
Public transportation	515	1,030	746	1,050	461	552	590	625	900	679
HEALTH CARE	1,982	2,530	2,045	2,211	1,833	2,168	1,984	1,927	2,030	2,514
ENTERTAINMENT	2,181	3,392	2,548	1,997	1,962	2,042	2,718	2,888	2,290	2,301
PERSONAL CARE PRODUCTS AND SERVICES	582	710	599	702	674	627	485	669	692	579
READING	173	274	193	182	148	181	215	210	230	209
EDUCATION	701	701	617	906	695	562	824	575	967	609
TOBACCO PRODUCTS AND SMOKING SUPPLIES	239	468	324	230	204	261	239	249	222	366
MISCELLANEOUS	957	1,297	1,075	978	1,220	883	832	768	1,023	930
CASH CONTRIBUTIONS	1,297	1,837	1,103	1,926	1,447	1,584	2,265	810	904	1,061
PERSONAL INSURANCE AND PENSIONS	3,927	4,459	4,909	4,826	4,038	3,770	4,623	4,580	5,915	4,100
Life and other personal insurance	356	496	524	655	370	364	378	545	354	421
Pensions and Social Security	3,571	3,963	4,385	4,171	3,668	3,406	4,245	4,035	5,561	3,679

Source: Bureau of Labor Statistics, 1999 and 2000 Consumer Expenditure Surveys, Internet site www.bls.gov/cex/

Table 1.43 Indexed spending in selected Western metros, 1999–2000

(indexed average annual spending of consumer units (CU) in selected Western metropolitan areas by product and service category, 1999–2000; index definition: an index of 100 is the average for all consumer units; an index of 132 means that spending by consumer units in that group is 32 percent above the average for all consumer units; an index of 68 indicates spending that is 32 percent below the average for all consumer units)

	total consumer units in the West	Anchorage	Denver	Honolulu	Los Angeles	Phoenix	Portland	San Diego	San Francisco	Seattle
Average spending of CU, total	$41,933	$53,028	$46,002	$41,972	$44,748	$41,991	$44,331	$47,338	$55,040	$43,602
Average spending of CU, index	100	126	110	100	107	100	106	113	131	104
FOOD	100	126	103	105	100	100	103	95	135	119
Food at home	100	137	101	101	98	89	103	84	134	118
Cereals and bakery products	100	125	101	101	94	94	109	88	141	119
Meats, poultry, fish, and eggs	100	129	100	103	108	78	93	81	137	112
Dairy products	100	131	98	87	96	98	106	81	118	115
Fruits and vegetables	100	135	95	110	103	88	97	84	136	126
Other food at home	100	152	105	98	89	92	111	85	132	118
Food away from home	100	111	107	111	102	115	102	112	137	120
ALCOHOLIC BEVERAGES	100	145	153	100	83	115	128	100	192	105
HOUSING	100	124	112	100	117	93	104	121	140	104
Shelter	100	123	116	111	118	89	104	126	148	108
Owned dwellings	100	118	110	106	110	92	113	119	153	107
Rented dwellings	100	117	105	122	137	84	85	147	142	104
Other lodging	100	194	227	108	90	85	113	83	130	144
Utilities, fuels, public services	100	113	105	96	104	118	106	96	101	101
Household services	100	104	92	73	165	67	94	117	171	76
Housekeeping supplies	100	150	96	101	98	109	92	97	121	129
Household furnishings and equipment	100	149	117	63	115	91	110	136	136	92
APPAREL AND RELATED SERVICES	100	123	108	98	121	98	75	100	155	95
TRANSPORTATION	100	125	106	73	98	113	99	127	124	94
Vehicle purchases	100	124	94	45	85	122	95	154	127	80
Gasoline and motor oil	100	103	93	83	107	87	97	104	110	101
Other vehicle expenses	100	122	121	81	112	114	102	103	115	102
Public transportation	100	200	145	204	90	107	115	121	175	132
HEALTH CARE	100	128	103	112	92	109	100	97	102	127
ENTERTAINMENT	100	156	117	92	90	94	125	132	105	106
PERSONAL CARE PRODUCTS AND SERVICES	100	122	103	121	116	108	83	115	119	99
READING	100	158	112	105	86	105	124	121	133	121
EDUCATION	100	100	88	129	99	80	118	82	138	87
TOBACCO PRODUCTS AND SMOKING SUPPLIES	100	196	136	96	85	109	100	104	93	153
MISCELLANEOUS	100	136	112	102	127	92	87	80	107	97
CASH CONTRIBUTIONS	100	142	85	148	112	122	175	62	70	82
PERSONAL INSURANCE AND PENSIONS	100	114	125	123	103	96	118	117	151	104
Life and other personal insurance	100	139	147	184	104	102	106	153	99	118
Pensions and Social Security	100	111	123	117	103	95	119	113	156	103

Source: Calculations by New Strategist based on the Bureau of Labor Statistics 1999 and 2000 Consumer Expenditure Surveys

Spending Overview:
Spending by Race and Ethnicity, 2000

Hispanics and blacks spend less overall than non-Hispanic whites because their incomes are considerably lower. In 2000, whites and others (this category includes Asians, Pacific Islanders, and American Indians) spent an average of $39,406 versus the $28,152 blacks spent. Non-Hispanics spent $38,549 versus the $32,735 spent by Hispanics.

Despite lower overall spending, Hispanic and black spending exceeds that of the average household in many categories. Because of their larger families, Hispanic households spend 16 percent more than average on food at home. They spend 30 percent more on meats, poultry, fish, and eggs, and 40 to 43 percent more on fresh fruits and vegetables. Hispanics spend 31 percent more than non-Hispanics on laundry and cleaning supplies and 12 percent more on apparel.

Blacks spend 26 percent more than the average household on fish and seafood. They spend 12 percent more on telephone services, 51 percent more on boys' clothes, and 11 percent more on personal care products and services.

Table 1.44 Average spending by race and Hispanic origin, 2000

(average annual spending of consumer units (CU) by product and service category and by race and Hispanic origin of consumer unit reference person, 2000)

	total consumer units	race black	race white and other	Hispanic origin Hispanic	Hispanic origin non-Hispanic
Number of consumer units (in thousands, add 000s)	109,367	13,230	96,137	9,473	99,894
Average number of persons per CU	2.5	2.7	2.5	3.4	2.4
Average income before taxes	$44,649	$32,657	$46,260	$34,891	$45,669
Average annual spending	38,045	28,152	39,406	32,735	38,549
FOOD	**$5,158**	**$4,095**	**$5,304**	**$5,362**	**$5,139**
Food at home	**3,021**	**2,691**	**3,066**	**3,496**	**2,977**
Cereals and bakery products	453	393	462	491	450
Cereals and cereal products	156	159	156	201	152
Bakery products	297	234	306	290	298
Meats, poultry, fish, and eggs	795	909	780	1,036	773
Beef	238	236	239	326	230
Pork	167	199	163	213	163
Other meats	101	106	100	116	99
Poultry	145	185	140	190	141
Fish and seafood	110	139	106	136	108
Eggs	34	43	33	55	33
Dairy products	325	245	336	359	321
Fresh milk and cream	131	102	135	170	128
Other dairy products	193	143	200	189	194
Fruits and vegetables	521	454	530	670	507
Fresh fruits	163	131	168	228	157
Fresh vegetables	159	129	163	228	152
Processed fruits	115	118	115	125	114
Processed vegetables	84	76	85	89	83
Other food at home	927	691	959	940	926
Sugar and other sweets	117	89	121	110	118
Fats and oils	83	83	83	100	82
Miscellaneous foods	437	316	454	405	440
Nonalcoholic beverages	250	186	258	292	246
Food prepared by CU on trips	40	17	43	34	40
Food away from home	**2,137**	**1,404**	**2,238**	**1,865**	**2,162**
ALCOHOLIC BEVERAGES	**372**	**211**	**394**	**285**	**380**
HOUSING	**12,319**	**9,906**	**12,651**	**10,850**	**12,458**
Shelter	**7,114**	**5,678**	**7,312**	**6,437**	**7,178**
Owned dwellings	4,602	2,607	4,877	2,949	4,759
Mortgage interest and charges	2,639	1,574	2,785	1,751	2,723
Property taxes	1,139	640	1,207	665	1,183
Maintenance, repair, insurance, other expenses	825	393	884	533	853
Rented dwellings	2,034	2,843	1,923	3,307	1,913
Other lodging	478	227	512	181	506
Utilities, fuels, and public services	**2,489**	**2,571**	**2,478**	**2,170**	**2,519**
Natural gas	307	342	303	242	313
Electricity	911	938	908	749	927
Fuel oil and other fuels	97	43	104	30	103
Telephone	877	986	862	889	876
Water and other public services	296	261	301	259	300

	total consumer units	race		Hispanic origin	
		black	white and other	Hispanic	non-Hispanic
Household services	**$684**	**$468**	**$714**	**$465**	**$705**
Personal services	326	292	331	255	333
Other household services	358	176	383	211	372
Housekeeping supplies	**482**	**303**	**507**	**474**	**483**
Laundry and cleaning supplies	131	126	131	172	127
Other household products	226	126	240	227	226
Postage and stationery	126	51	136	76	130
Household furnishings and equipment	**1,549**	**887**	**1,640**	**1,303**	**1,572**
Household textiles	106	57	113	89	108
Furniture	391	283	405	447	385
Floor coverings	44	25	47	27	46
Major appliances	189	108	200	166	191
Small appliances, misc. housewares	87	36	94	66	89
Miscellaneous household equipment	731	377	779	508	752
APPAREL AND RELATED SERVICES	**1,856**	**1,695**	**1,878**	**2,076**	**1,836**
Men and boys	**440**	**390**	**447**	**483**	**436**
Men, aged 16 or older	344	245	358	359	343
Boys, aged 2 to 15	96	145	89	124	93
Women and girls	**725**	**604**	**742**	**691**	**728**
Women, aged 16 or older	607	473	626	540	613
Girls, aged 2 to 15	118	131	116	150	115
Children under age 2	**82**	**89**	**81**	**137**	**77**
Footwear	**343**	**352**	**342**	**516**	**327**
Other apparel products and services	**266**	**260**	**267**	**249**	**267**
TRANSPORTATION	**7,417**	**5,214**	**7,721**	**6,719**	**7,484**
Vehicle purchases	**3,418**	**2,285**	**3,574**	**3,146**	**3,444**
Cars and trucks, new	1,605	869	1,706	1,079	1,655
Cars and trucks, used	1,770	1,414	1,819	2,058	1,743
Other vehicles	43	2	49	9	47
Gasoline and motor oil	**1,291**	**956**	**1,337**	**1,244**	**1,296**
Other vehicle expenses	**2,281**	**1,705**	**2,361**	**1,945**	**2,313**
Vehicle finance charges	328	290	334	274	333
Maintenance and repairs	624	452	647	546	631
Vehicle insurance	778	634	798	696	786
Vehicle rentals, leases, licenses, other charges	551	330	582	428	563
Public transportation	**427**	**268**	**448**	**385**	**431**
HEALTH CARE	**2,066**	**1,107**	**2,198**	**1,243**	**2,144**
Health insurance	983	639	1,030	600	1,019
Medical services	568	191	620	364	587
Drugs	416	235	441	211	436
Medical supplies	99	41	107	69	102
ENTERTAINMENT	**1,863**	**1,014**	**1,980**	**1,186**	**1,928**
Fees and admissions	515	181	561	262	539
Television, radio, sound equipment	622	567	629	545	629
Pets, toys, and playground equipment	334	159	358	218	345
Other entertainment products and services	393	107	433	162	415

	total consumer units	race		Hispanic origin	
		black	white and other	Hispanic	non-Hispanic
PERSONAL CARE PRODUCTS AND SERVICES	$564	$627	$555	$564	$564
READING	146	72	157	59	155
EDUCATION	632	383	666	363	657
TOBACCO PRODUCTS AND SMOKING SUPPLIES	319	243	329	173	332
MISCELLANEOUS	776	572	804	602	792
CASH CONTRIBUTIONS	1,192	700	1,260	645	1,244
PERSONAL INSURANCE AND PENSIONS	3,365	2,313	3,510	2,608	3,437
Life and other personal insurance	399	358	404	189	419
Pensions and Social Security	2,966	1,955	3,105	2,420	3,018
PERSONAL TAXES	3,117	1,626	3,318	1,581	3,278
Federal income taxes	2,409	1,240	2,566	1,258	2,530
State and local income taxes	562	338	592	271	592
Other taxes	146	48	159	52	156
GIFTS	1,083	571	1,154	825	1,108
Food	70	26	76	44	73
Alcoholic beverages	14	10	15	11	15
Housing	291	133	313	208	299
Housekeeping supplies	39	14	43	36	39
Household textiles	13	3	15	13	13
Appliances and misc. housewares	28	6	31	12	30
Major appliances	8	2	8	8	8
Small appliances and misc. housewares	21	3	23	4	22
Miscellaneous household equipment	70	19	77	35	74
Other housing	140	92	147	111	143
Apparel and services	244	194	251	291	240
Males, aged 2 or older	68	38	72	65	68
Females, aged 2 or older	85	87	85	96	84
Children under age 2	41	34	42	61	39
Other apparel products and services	51	35	53	70	49
Jewelry and watches	20	8	22	11	21
All other apparel products and services	30	27	31	59	28
Transportation	70	23	77	26	75
Health care	38	6	43	12	41
Entertainment	94	43	101	69	96
Toys, games, hobbies, and tricycles	30	17	31	23	30
Other entertainment	64	26	69	46	66
Personal care products and services	19	10	20	31	18
Reading	2	–	2	1	2
Education	151	39	166	71	159
All other gifts	89	87	89	62	91

Note: Spending by category will not add to total spending because gift spending is also included in the preceding product and service categories and personal taxes are not included in the total. (–) means sample is too small to make a reliable estimate. Other races include Asians, Native Americans, and Pacific Islanders.
Source: Bureau of Labor Statistics, 2000 Consumer Expenditure Survey, Internet site www.bls.gov/cex/

Table 1.45 Indexed spending by race and Hispanic origin, 2000

(indexed average annual spending of consumer units (CU) by product and service category and by race and Hispanic origin of consumer unit reference person, 2000; index definition: an index of 100 is the average for all consumer units; an index of 132 means that spending by consumer units in that group is 32 percent above the average for all consumer units; an index of 68 indicates spending that is 32 percent below the average for all consumer units)

	total consumer units	race black	race white and other	Hispanic origin Hispanic	Hispanic origin non-Hispanic
Average spending of CU, total	$38,045	$28,152	$39,406	$32,735	$38,549
Average spending of CU, index	100	74	104	86	101
FOOD	100	79	103	104	100
Food at home	100	89	101	116	99
Cereals and bakery products	100	87	102	108	99
Cereals and cereal products	100	102	100	129	97
Bakery products	100	79	103	98	100
Meats, poultry, fish, and eggs	100	114	98	130	97
Beef	100	99	100	137	97
Pork	100	119	98	128	98
Other meats	100	105	99	115	98
Poultry	100	128	97	131	97
Fish and seafood	100	126	96	124	98
Eggs	100	126	97	162	97
Dairy products	100	75	103	110	99
Fresh milk and cream	100	78	103	130	98
Other dairy products	100	74	104	98	101
Fruits and vegetables	100	87	102	129	97
Fresh fruits	100	80	103	140	96
Fresh vegetables	100	81	103	143	96
Processed fruits	100	103	100	109	99
Processed vegetables	100	90	101	106	99
Other food at home	100	75	103	101	100
Sugar and other sweets	100	76	103	94	101
Fats and oils	100	100	100	120	99
Miscellaneous foods	100	72	104	93	101
Nonalcoholic beverages	100	74	103	117	98
Food prepared by CU on trips	100	43	108	85	100
Food away from home	100	66	105	87	101
ALCOHOLIC BEVERAGES	100	57	106	77	102
HOUSING	100	80	103	88	101
Shelter	100	80	103	90	101
Owned dwellings	100	57	106	64	103
Mortgage interest and charges	100	60	106	66	103
Property taxes	100	56	106	58	104
Maintenance, repair, insurance, other expenses	100	48	107	65	103
Rented dwellings	100	140	95	163	94
Other lodging	100	47	107	38	106
Utilities, fuels, and public services	100	103	100	87	101
Natural gas	100	111	99	79	102
Electricity	100	103	100	82	102
Fuel oil and other fuels	100	44	107	31	106
Telephone	100	112	98	101	100
Water and other public services	100	88	102	88	101

	total consumer units	race		Hispanic origin	
		black	white and other	Hispanic	non-Hispanic
Household services	100	68	104	68	103
Personal services	100	90	102	78	102
Other household services	100	49	107	59	104
Housekeeping supplies	100	63	105	98	100
Laundry and cleaning supplies	100	96	100	131	97
Other household products	100	56	106	100	100
Postage and stationery	100	40	108	60	103
Household furnishings and equipment	100	57	106	84	101
Household textiles	100	54	107	84	102
Furniture	100	72	104	114	98
Floor coverings	100	57	107	61	105
Major appliances	100	57	106	88	101
Small appliances, misc. housewares	100	41	108	76	102
Miscellaneous household equipment	100	52	107	69	103
APPAREL AND RELATED SERVICES	100	91	101	112	99
Men and boys	100	89	102	110	99
Men, aged 16 or older	100	71	104	104	100
Boys, aged 2 to 15	100	151	93	129	97
Women and girls	100	83	102	95	100
Women, aged 16 or older	100	78	103	89	101
Girls, aged 2 to 15	100	111	98	127	97
Children under age 2	100	109	99	167	94
Footwear	100	103	100	150	95
Other apparel products and services	100	98	100	94	100
TRANSPORTATION	100	70	104	91	101
Vehicle purchases	100	67	105	92	101
Cars and trucks, new	100	54	106	67	103
Cars and trucks, used	100	80	103	116	98
Other vehicles	100	5	114	21	109
Gasoline and motor oil	100	74	104	96	100
Other vehicle expenses	100	75	104	85	101
Vehicle finance charges	100	88	102	84	102
Maintenance and repairs	100	72	104	88	101
Vehicle insurance	100	81	103	89	101
Vehicle rentals, leases, licenses, other charges	100	60	106	78	102
Public transportation	100	63	105	90	101
HEALTH CARE	100	54	106	60	104
Health insurance	100	65	105	61	104
Medical services	100	34	109	64	103
Drugs	100	56	106	51	105
Medical supplies	100	41	108	70	103
ENTERTAINMENT	100	54	106	64	103
Fees and admissions	100	35	109	51	105
Television, radio, sound equipment	100	91	101	88	101
Pets, toys, and playground equipment	100	48	107	65	103
Other entertainment products and services	100	27	110	41	106

	total consumer units	race		Hispanic origin	
		black	white and other	Hispanic	non-Hispanic
PERSONAL CARE PRODUCTS AND SERVICES	100	111	98	100	100
READING	100	49	108	40	106
EDUCATION	100	61	105	57	104
TOBACCO PRODUCTS AND SMOKING SUPPLIES	100	76	103	54	104
MISCELLANEOUS	100	74	104	78	102
CASH CONTRIBUTIONS	100	59	106	54	104
PERSONAL INSURANCE AND PENSIONS	100	69	104	78	102
Life and other personal insurance	100	90	101	47	105
Pensions and Social Security	100	66	105	82	102
PERSONAL TAXES	100	52	106	51	105
Federal income taxes	100	51	107	52	105
State and local income taxes	100	60	105	48	105
Other taxes	100	33	109	36	107
GIFTS	100	53	107	76	102
Food	100	37	109	63	104
Alcoholic beverages	100	71	107	79	107
Housing	100	46	108	71	103
Housekeeping supplies	100	36	110	92	100
Household textiles	100	23	115	100	100
Appliances and misc. housewares	100	21	111	43	107
Major appliances	100	25	100	100	100
Small appliances and misc. housewares	100	14	110	19	105
Miscellaneous household equipment	100	27	110	50	106
Other housing	100	66	105	79	102
Apparel and services	100	80	103	119	98
Males, aged 2 or older	100	56	106	96	100
Females, aged 2 or older	100	102	100	113	99
Children under age 2	100	83	102	149	95
Other apparel products and services	100	69	104	137	96
Jewelry and watches	100	40	110	55	105
All other apparel products and services	100	90	103	197	93
Transportation	100	33	110	37	107
Health care	100	16	113	32	108
Entertainment	100	46	107	73	102
Toys, games, hobbies, and tricycles	100	57	103	77	100
Other entertainment	100	41	108	72	103
Personal care products and services	100	53	105	163	95
Reading	100	0	100	50	100
Education	100	26	110	47	105
All other gifts	100	98	100	70	102

Note: (–) means sample is too small to make a reliable estimate. Other races include Asians, Native Americans, and Pacific Islanders.
Source: Calculations by New Strategist based on the Bureau of Labor Statistics 2000 Consumer Expenditure Survey

Spending Overview:
Spending by Education, 2000

Because college graduates have the highest incomes, their spending is well above average. The average household headed by a college graduate spent $54,176 in 2000, or 42 percent more than the average household. In contrast, households headed by people who did not graduate from high school spent only $23,386 in 2000, 39 percent less than average.

Many people who did not graduate from high school are elderly. Consequently, the spending of the least-educated is average or above average for products and services consumed heavily by older Americans. These include meats, poultry, fish, eggs, and drugs.

High school graduates form the largest household segment by education, accounting for 29 percent of all householders. They spent $32,447 in 2000, or 15 percent less than the average household. Their spending is below average in most categories with some exceptions such as meats, fuel oil, used cars and trucks, and tobacco.

Combined, householders with some college and college graduates account for 54 percent of all households. Those with some college spend close to the average on most products and services. College graduates outspend others on most items, particularly those favored by the affluent. These include food away from home, alcoholic beverages, other lodging (which includes vacation homes and hotel and motel expenses), new cars and trucks, public transportation (which includes airline fares), fees and admissions to entertainment events, and education.

Table 1.46 Average spending by education, 2000

(average annual spending of consumer units (CU) by product and service category and educational attainment of consumer unit reference person, 2000)

	total consumer units	not a high school graduate	high school graduate	some college or associate's degree	college degree or more
Number of consumer units (in thousands, add 000s)	109,367	17,991	31,900	31,416	28,059
Average number of persons per CU	2.5	2.6	2.6	2.5	2.4
Average income before taxes	$44,649	$23,329	$36,134	$42,021	$71,140
Average annual spending	38,045	23,386	32,447	37,584	54,176
FOOD	**$5,158**	**$4,048**	**$4,713**	**$5,052**	**$6,428**
Food at home	**3,021**	**2,901**	**2,902**	**2,888**	**3,359**
Cereals and bakery products	453	436	436	437	500
Cereals and cereal products	156	166	148	149	167
Bakery products	297	270	287	289	332
Meats, poultry, fish, and eggs	795	871	813	740	789
Beef	238	258	255	223	223
Pork	167	203	182	150	147
Other meats	101	104	103	96	101
Poultry	145	153	143	140	148
Fish and seafood	110	104	97	101	139
Eggs	34	50	33	30	31
Dairy products	325	293	318	307	369
Fresh milk and cream	131	139	132	121	137
Other dairy products	193	154	186	187	232
Fruits and vegetables	521	499	475	474	634
Fresh fruits	163	163	143	144	206
Fresh vegetables	159	160	143	143	192
Processed fruits	115	97	104	107	146
Processed vegetables	84	79	84	81	89
Other food at home	927	802	861	929	1,067
Sugar and other sweets	117	110	109	117	130
Fats and oils	83	86	83	79	86
Miscellaneous foods	437	342	401	440	527
Nonalcoholic beverages	250	243	241	253	258
Food prepared by CU on trips	40	22	27	40	67
Food away from home	**2,137**	**1,146**	**1,811**	**2,164**	**3,069**
ALCOHOLIC BEVERAGES	**372**	**145**	**283**	**386**	**595**
HOUSING	**12,319**	**7,670**	**10,317**	**11,887**	**18,029**
Shelter	**7,114**	**4,236**	**5,793**	**6,887**	**10,716**
Owned dwellings	4,602	2,090	3,693	4,357	7,521
Mortgage interest and charges	2,639	962	1,963	2,600	4,526
Property taxes	1,139	629	992	1,031	1,752
Maintenance, repair, insurance, other expenses	825	499	738	726	1,243
Rented dwellings	2,034	2,028	1,797	2,110	2,221
Other lodging	478	118	303	419	974
Utilities, fuels, and public services	**2,489**	**2,087**	**2,414**	**2,433**	**2,894**
Natural gas	307	243	296	303	365
Electricity	911	831	926	892	968
Fuel oil and other fuels	97	106	113	72	102
Telephone	877	683	802	876	1,087
Water and other public services	296	224	277	291	372

	total consumer units	not a high school graduate	high school graduate	some college or associate's degree	college degree or more
Household services	**$684**	**$262**	**$435**	**$661**	**$1,266**
Personal services	326	135	228	326	561
Other household services	358	126	207	336	706
Housekeeping supplies	**482**	**360**	**417**	**447**	**665**
Laundry and cleaning supplies	131	133	120	124	149
Other household products	226	151	200	208	319
Postage and stationery	126	76	97	116	197
Household furnishings and equipment	**1,549**	**726**	**1,258**	**1,458**	**2,487**
Household textiles	106	45	89	101	168
Furniture	391	214	241	381	684
Floor coverings	44	16	49	30	74
Major appliances	189	122	173	192	245
Small appliances, misc. housewares	87	32	68	82	149
Miscellaneous household equipment	731	297	638	673	1,167
APPAREL AND RELATED SERVICES	**1,856**	**1,177**	**1,501**	**1,844**	**2,683**
Men and boys	**440**	**268**	**381**	**449**	**601**
Men, aged 16 or older	344	191	284	356	491
Boys, aged 2 to 15	96	78	97	92	110
Women and girls	**725**	**405**	**563**	**725**	**1,099**
Women, aged 16 or older	607	319	462	601	950
Girls, aged 2 to 15	118	86	101	124	149
Children under age 2	**82**	**66**	**76**	**73**	**109**
Footwear	**343**	**301**	**296**	**351**	**412**
Other apparel products and services	**266**	**137**	**185**	**246**	**463**
TRANSPORTATION	**7,417**	**4,512**	**7,000**	**7,887**	**9,227**
Vehicle purchases	**3,418**	**2,166**	**3,419**	**3,762**	**3,836**
Cars and trucks, new	1,605	644	1,354	1,875	2,204
Cars and trucks, used	1,770	1,506	2,007	1,844	1,586
Other vehicles	43	15	58	42	46
Gasoline and motor oil	**1,291**	**898**	**1,278**	**1,374**	**1,466**
Other vehicle expenses	**2,281**	**1,284**	**2,056**	**2,370**	**3,076**
Vehicle finance charges	328	180	350	363	361
Maintenance and repairs	624	379	548	648	838
Vehicle insurance	778	506	778	793	936
Vehicle rentals, leases, licenses, other charges	551	219	380	566	941
Public transportation	**427**	**164**	**247**	**382**	**850**
HEALTH CARE	**2,066**	**1,672**	**1,896**	**1,929**	**2,660**
Health insurance	983	827	976	918	1,162
Medical services	568	324	423	535	926
Drugs	416	463	413	379	430
Medical supplies	99	59	84	98	142
ENTERTAINMENT	**1,863**	**896**	**1,519**	**1,872**	**2,860**
Fees and admissions	515	132	298	464	1,064
Television, radio, sound equipment	622	418	566	639	797
Pets, toys, and playground equipment	334	192	303	327	464
Other entertainment products and services	393	154	351	442	536

	total consumer units	not a high school graduate	high school graduate	some college or associate's degree	college degree or more
PERSONAL CARE PRODUCTS AND SERVICES	$564	$365	$496	$572	$755
READING	146	59	105	136	261
EDUCATION	632	128	310	715	1,226
TOBACCO PRODUCTS AND SMOKING SUPPLIES	319	373	408	331	168
MISCELLANEOUS	776	515	652	794	1,063
CASH CONTRIBUTIONS	1,192	507	697	976	2,438
PERSONAL INSURANCE AND PENSIONS	3,365	1,318	2,551	3,202	5,785
Life and other personal insurance	399	225	355	340	625
Pensions and Social Security	2,966	1,093	2,196	2,863	5,159
PERSONAL TAXES	3,117	650	1,884	2,859	6,401
Federal income taxes	2,409	476	1,377	2,192	5,072
State and local income taxes	562	118	368	528	1,109
Other taxes	146	57	140	139	221
GIFTS	1,083	475	749	963	1,975
Food	70	22	33	69	143
Alcoholic beverages	14	4	8	10	32
Housing	291	135	224	260	499
Housekeeping supplies	39	21	34	36	59
Household textiles	13	2	11	10	25
Appliances and misc. housewares	28	5	25	24	51
Major appliances	8	3	12	7	7
Small appliances and misc. housewares	21	2	13	17	44
Miscellaneous household equipment	70	17	57	59	130
Other housing	140	89	97	130	236
Apparel and services	244	139	213	228	360
Males, aged 2 or older	68	30	72	58	95
Females, aged 2 or older	85	41	71	80	133
Children under age 2	41	31	38	38	53
Other apparel products and services	51	37	32	53	79
Jewelry and watches	20	6	13	20	37
All other apparel products and services	30	30	19	33	41
Transportation	70	34	33	41	169
Health care	38	14	18	28	87
Entertainment	94	36	86	102	130
Toys, games, hobbies, and tricycles	30	18	31	29	37
Other entertainment	64	18	56	73	92
Personal care products and services	19	16	14	21	25
Reading	2	1	2	1	4
Education	151	29	58	105	386
All other gifts	89	45	60	98	140

Note: Spending by category will not add to total spending because gift spending is also included in the preceding product and service categories and personal taxes are not included in the total.
Source: Bureau of Labor Statistics, 2000 Consumer Expenditure Survey, Internet site www.bls.gov/cex/

Table 1.47 Indexed spending by education, 2000

(indexed average annual spending of consumer units (CU) by product and service category and educational attainment of consumer unit reference person, 2000; index definition: an index of 100 is the average for all consumer units; an index of 132 means that spending by consumer units in that group is 32 percent above the average for all consumer units; an index of 68 indicates spending that is 32 percent below the average for all consumer units)

	total consumer units	not a high school graduate	high school graduate	some college or associate's degree	college degree or more
Average spending of CU, total	$38,045	$23,386	$32,447	$37,584	$54,176
Average spending of CU, index	100	61	85	99	142
FOOD	100	78	91	98	125
Food at home	100	96	96	96	111
Cereals and bakery products	100	96	96	97	110
Cereals and cereal products	100	106	95	95	107
Bakery products	100	91	97	97	112
Meats, poultry, fish, and eggs	100	110	102	93	99
Beef	100	108	107	94	94
Pork	100	122	109	90	88
Other meats	100	103	102	95	100
Poultry	100	106	99	97	102
Fish and seafood	100	95	88	92	126
Eggs	100	147	97	87	91
Dairy products	100	90	98	94	114
Fresh milk and cream	100	106	101	92	105
Other dairy products	100	80	96	97	120
Fruits and vegetables	100	96	91	91	122
Fresh fruits	100	100	88	88	126
Fresh vegetables	100	101	90	90	121
Processed fruits	100	84	90	93	127
Processed vegetables	100	94	100	97	106
Other food at home	100	87	93	100	115
Sugar and other sweets	100	94	93	100	111
Fats and oils	100	104	100	95	104
Miscellaneous foods	100	78	92	101	121
Nonalcoholic beverages	100	97	96	101	103
Food prepared by CU on trips	100	55	68	99	168
Food away from home	100	54	85	101	144
ALCOHOLIC BEVERAGES	100	39	76	104	160
HOUSING	100	62	84	96	146
Shelter	100	60	81	97	151
Owned dwellings	100	45	80	95	163
Mortgage interest and charges	100	36	74	99	172
Property taxes	100	55	87	90	154
Maintenance, repair, insurance, other expenses	100	60	89	88	151
Rented dwellings	100	100	88	104	109
Other lodging	100	25	63	88	204
Utilities, fuels, and public services	100	84	97	98	116
Natural gas	100	79	96	99	119
Electricity	100	91	102	98	106
Fuel oil and other fuels	100	109	116	74	105
Telephone	100	78	91	100	124
Water and other public services	100	76	94	98	126

	total consumer units	not a high school graduate	high school graduate	some college or associate's degree	college degree or more
Household services	100	38	64	97	185
Personal services	100	41	70	100	172
Other household services	100	35	58	94	197
Housekeeping supplies	100	75	87	93	138
Laundry and cleaning supplies	100	102	92	94	114
Other household products	100	67	88	92	141
Postage and stationery	100	60	77	92	156
Household furnishings and equipment	100	47	81	94	161
Household textiles	100	42	84	95	158
Furniture	100	55	62	97	175
Floor coverings	100	36	111	69	168
Major appliances	100	65	92	102	130
Small appliances, misc. housewares	100	37	78	94	171
Miscellaneous household equipment	100	41	87	92	160
APPAREL AND RELATED SERVICES	100	63	81	99	145
Men and boys	100	61	87	102	137
Men, aged 16 or older	100	56	83	104	143
Boys, aged 2 to 15	100	81	101	96	115
Women and girls	100	56	78	100	152
Women, aged 16 or older	100	53	76	99	157
Girls, aged 2 to 15	100	73	86	105	126
Children under age 2	100	80	93	89	133
Footwear	100	88	86	102	120
Other apparel products and services	100	52	70	93	174
TRANSPORTATION	100	61	94	106	124
Vehicle purchases	100	63	100	110	112
Cars and trucks, new	100	40	84	117	137
Cars and trucks, used	100	85	113	104	90
Other vehicles	100	35	135	97	107
Gasoline and motor oil	100	70	99	106	114
Other vehicle expenses	100	56	90	104	135
Vehicle finance charges	100	55	107	111	110
Maintenance and repairs	100	61	88	104	134
Vehicle insurance	100	65	100	102	120
Vehicle rentals, leases, licenses, other charges	100	40	69	103	171
Public transportation	100	38	58	89	199
HEALTH CARE	100	81	92	93	129
Health insurance	100	84	99	93	118
Medical services	100	57	74	94	163
Drugs	100	111	99	91	103
Medical supplies	100	60	85	99	143
ENTERTAINMENT	100	48	82	100	154
Fees and admissions	100	26	58	90	207
Television, radio, sound equipment	100	67	91	103	128
Pets, toys, and playground equipment	100	57	91	98	139
Other entertainment products and services	100	39	89	112	136

	total consumer units	not a high school graduate	high school graduate	some college or associate's degree	college degree or more
PERSONAL CARE PRODUCTS AND SERVICES	100	65	88	101	134
READING	100	40	72	93	179
EDUCATION	100	20	49	113	194
TOBACCO PRODUCTS AND SMOKING SUPPLIES	100	117	128	104	53
MISCELLANEOUS	100	66	84	102	137
CASH CONTRIBUTIONS	100	43	58	82	205
PERSONAL INSURANCE AND PENSIONS	100	39	76	95	172
Life and other personal insurance	100	56	89	85	157
Pensions and Social Security	100	37	74	97	174
PERSONAL TAXES	100	21	60	92	205
Federal income taxes	100	20	57	91	211
State and local income taxes	100	21	65	94	197
Other taxes	100	39	96	95	151
GIFTS	100	44	69	89	182
Food	100	31	47	98	204
Alcoholic beverages	100	29	57	72	229
Housing	100	46	77	89	171
Housekeeping supplies	100	54	87	93	151
Household textiles	100	15	85	79	192
Appliances and misc. housewares	100	18	89	86	182
Major appliances	100	38	150	82	88
Small appliances and misc. housewares	100	10	62	80	210
Miscellaneous household equipment	100	24	81	84	186
Other housing	100	64	69	93	169
Apparel and services	100	57	87	94	148
Males, aged 2 or older	100	44	106	86	140
Females, aged 2 or older	100	48	84	94	156
Children under age 2	100	76	93	92	129
Other apparel products and services	100	73	63	103	155
Jewelry and watches	100	30	65	101	185
All other apparel products and services	100	100	63	109	137
Transportation	100	49	47	59	241
Health care	100	37	47	73	229
Entertainment	100	38	91	108	138
Toys, games, hobbies, and tricycles	100	60	103	96	123
Other entertainment	100	28	88	114	144
Personal care products and services	100	84	74	110	132
Reading	100	50	100	64	200
Education	100	19	38	70	256
All other gifts	100	51	67	110	157

Source: Calculations by New Strategist based on the Bureau of Labor Statistics 2000 Consumer Expenditure Survey

Spending Overview:

Spending by Household Size, 2000

Spending tends to increase with household size because larger households usually have more earners. Incomes peak for households with four people, at $63,959 in 2000. Spending is highest for this household size as well, at $52,032—37 percent above average. Only 14 percent of the nation's households are home to four people, however.

Two-person households are most common, accounting for 30 percent of the total. They spent an average of $38,627 in 2000, just 2 percent more than the average household. Households with two people (many of them older empty-nesters) spend the most on alcoholic beverages, other lodging (primarily hotel and motel expenses on trips), public transportation (such as airline fares), reading material, and cash contributions.

Households with five or more people have slightly lower incomes and spending than those with just four people. They spend more than four-person households on many nondiscretionary items, however, such as food at home, laundry and cleaning supplies, telephone service, electricity, water, and children's clothing.

Single-person households are almost as numerous as two-person households, accounting for slightly less than 30 percent of households in 2000. Single-person households spend less than the average household on almost every item.

Table 1.48 Average spending by household size, 2000

(average annual spending of consumer units (CU) by product and service category, by number of people in consumer unit, 2000)

	total consumer units	one person	two or more people				
			total	two people	three people	four people	five or more people
Number of consumer units							
(in thousands, add 000s)	109,367	32,323	77,044	33,312	16,840	15,836	11,056
Average number of persons per CU	2.5	1.0	3.1	2.0	3.0	4.0	5.6
Average income before taxes	$44,649	$24,977	$53,314	$47,121	$54,600	$63,959	$54,746
Average annual spending	38,045	23,059	44,251	38,627	45,156	52,032	49,100
FOOD	**$5,158**	**$2,825**	**$6,088**	**$5,104**	**$6,093**	**$7,122**	**$7,833**
Food at home	**3,021**	**1,477**	**3,634**	**2,894**	**3,687**	**4,247**	**5,111**
Cereals and bakery products	453	221	546	421	550	647	805
Cereals and cereal products	156	69	191	138	185	229	318
Bakery products	297	151	355	282	365	419	487
Meats, poultry, fish, and eggs	795	352	971	774	1,007	1,109	1,366
Beef	238	100	293	228	317	342	399
Pork	167	71	205	171	216	218	282
Other meats	101	47	122	91	121	142	195
Poultry	145	68	176	137	176	212	252
Fish and seafood	110	50	134	112	135	154	175
Eggs	34	18	41	34	41	40	63
Dairy products	325	162	389	306	395	449	566
Fresh milk and cream	131	65	158	114	165	183	253
Other dairy products	193	98	231	193	230	266	313
Fruits and vegetables	521	279	617	522	611	695	826
Fresh fruits	163	93	191	166	182	213	258
Fresh vegetables	159	86	187	160	183	206	258
Processed fruits	115	60	137	113	139	163	176
Processed vegetables	84	40	101	83	108	114	134
Other food at home	927	462	1,111	872	1,124	1,346	1,549
Sugar and other sweets	117	56	142	109	136	163	226
Fats and oils	83	39	101	86	99	107	140
Miscellaneous foods	437	221	523	391	539	661	736
Nonalcoholic beverages	250	125	299	237	310	363	395
Food prepared by CU on trips	40	22	47	48	39	52	51
Food away from home	**2,137**	**1,348**	**2,454**	**2,210**	**2,407**	**2,875**	**2,722**
ALCOHOLIC BEVERAGES	**372**	**325**	**390**	**429**	**411**	**329**	**318**
HOUSING	**12,319**	**8,189**	**14,040**	**12,096**	**14,193**	**16,921**	**15,585**
Shelter	**7,114**	**5,054**	**7,979**	**6,936**	**8,023**	**9,510**	**8,862**
Owned dwellings	4,602	2,332	5,555	4,535	5,338	7,351	6,385
Mortgage interest and charges	2,639	1,005	3,324	2,356	3,292	4,810	4,164
Property taxes	1,139	723	1,313	1,248	1,191	1,557	1,346
Maintenance, repair, insurance, other expenses	825	604	918	931	855	984	876
Rented dwellings	2,034	2,435	1,866	1,765	2,160	1,665	2,009
Other lodging	478	287	558	636	525	494	467
Utilities, fuels, and public services	**2,489**	**1,628**	**2,850**	**2,545**	**2,839**	**3,156**	**3,348**
Natural gas	307	208	349	301	336	396	446
Electricity	911	569	1,055	952	1,044	1,158	1,233
Fuel oil and other fuels	97	68	109	118	96	106	107
Telephone	877	607	990	865	1,031	1,108	1,136
Water and other public services	296	175	347	309	332	389	425

	total consumer units	one person	two or more people				
			total	two people	three people	four people	five or more people
Household services	$684	$387	$809	$501	$921	$1,308	$846
Personal services	326	124	411	102	524	862	526
Other household services	358	264	398	400	398	446	320
Housekeeping supplies	482	224	585	515	553	663	755
Laundry and cleaning supplies	131	53	161	122	148	170	299
Other household products	226	102	275	239	268	340	315
Postage and stationery	126	69	148	154	137	153	141
Household furnishings and equipment	1,549	895	1,818	1,600	1,857	2,283	1,775
Household textiles	106	63	124	109	132	163	105
Furniture	391	226	460	391	521	578	407
Floor coverings	44	20	55	49	57	63	58
Major appliances	189	104	224	186	215	260	303
Small appliances, misc. housewares	87	49	103	97	99	120	105
Miscellaneous household equipment	731	433	852	769	832	1,100	798
APPAREL AND RELATED SERVICES	1,856	1,028	2,191	1,679	2,259	2,729	2,946
Men and boys	440	223	528	408	543	660	687
Men, aged 16 or older	344	211	398	376	427	425	380
Boys, aged 2 to 15	96	12	130	32	116	234	307
Women and girls	725	414	850	665	843	1,062	1,155
Women, aged 16 or older	607	397	691	615	700	775	803
Girls, aged 2 to 15	118	16	160	49	143	286	352
Children under age 2	82	17	108	39	142	165	196
Footwear	343	191	404	295	421	482	619
Other apparel products and services	266	183	301	272	310	360	289
TRANSPORTATION	7,417	3,732	8,963	7,529	9,721	10,711	9,629
Vehicle purchases	3,418	1,456	4,241	3,397	4,805	5,282	4,435
Cars and trucks, new	1,605	797	1,944	1,767	2,493	2,072	1,458
Cars and trucks, used	1,770	628	2,249	1,606	2,275	3,093	2,937
Other vehicles	43	32	48	24	37	117	39
Gasoline and motor oil	1,291	682	1,547	1,307	1,572	1,813	1,850
Other vehicle expenses	2,281	1,272	2,704	2,324	2,879	3,146	2,955
Vehicle finance charges	328	129	412	327	476	477	474
Maintenance and repairs	624	396	719	646	700	823	825
Vehicle insurance	778	437	921	804	1,000	1,022	1,009
Vehicle rentals, leases, licenses, other charges	551	310	652	546	703	824	647
Public transportation	427	322	471	501	465	469	389
HEALTH CARE	2,066	1,488	2,307	2,596	2,080	2,143	2,018
Health insurance	983	657	1,119	1,241	1,031	1,062	970
Medical services	568	418	631	663	575	651	588
Drugs	416	351	443	560	377	325	359
Medical supplies	99	62	114	132	97	104	101
ENTERTAINMENT	1,863	1,026	2,212	1,821	2,192	2,797	2,598
Fees and admissions	515	281	613	520	514	856	695
Television, radio, sound equipment	622	429	703	572	723	898	790
Pets, toys, and playground equipment	334	177	398	348	387	472	463
Other entertainment products and services	393	139	498	382	568	571	649

	total consumer units	one person	two or more people				
			total	two people	three people	four people	five or more people
PERSONAL CARE PRODUCTS AND SERVICES	$564	$338	$656	$575	$693	$736	$738
READING	146	113	160	173	145	168	134
EDUCATION	632	407	726	476	841	952	986
TOBACCO PRODUCTS AND SMOKING SUPPLIES	319	203	367	318	399	389	436
MISCELLANEOUS	776	561	866	855	794	990	831
CASH CONTRIBUTIONS	1,192	1,047	1,254	1,497	1,144	1,116	887
PERSONAL INSURANCE AND PENSIONS	3,365	1,778	4,031	3,480	4,191	4,930	4,160
Life and other personal insurance	399	155	501	484	480	560	499
Pensions and Social Security	2,966	1,623	3,530	2,996	3,711	4,370	3,661
PERSONAL TAXES	3,117	2,090	3,570	3,604	3,437	4,275	2,687
Federal income taxes	2,409	1,621	2,756	2,773	2,686	3,335	2,008
State and local income taxes	562	360	651	635	620	774	574
Other taxes	146	109	163	197	131	166	106
GIFTS	1,083	807	1,196	1,282	1,324	1,097	883
Food	70	31	86	77	114	80	80
Alcoholic beverages	14	10	16	13	24	14	19
Housing	291	192	332	350	338	335	263
Housekeeping supplies	39	25	45	43	45	45	50
Household textiles	13	8	15	11	25	19	9
Appliances and misc. housewares	28	19	32	38	22	28	34
Major appliances	8	5	8	8	8	5	17
Small appliances and misc. housewares	21	14	23	30	14	23	17
Miscellaneous household equipment	70	64	73	74	71	88	53
Other housing	140	77	167	183	175	156	117
Apparel and services	244	187	267	295	266	242	214
Males, aged 2 or older	68	51	74	91	77	46	54
Females, aged 2 or older	85	60	95	119	81	81	62
Children under age 2	41	17	50	34	64	66	61
Other apparel products and services	51	59	47	52	44	49	37
Jewelry and watches	20	36	14	18	13	11	7
All other apparel products and services	30	23	33	34	31	38	29
Transportation	70	58	75	104	73	42	39
Health care	38	62	28	35	25	32	6
Entertainment	94	73	102	107	110	95	87
Toys, games, hobbies, and tricycles	30	24	32	41	29	24	19
Other entertainment	64	49	70	66	81	71	67
Personal care products and services	19	14	21	15	27	28	21
Reading	2	2	2	3	2	1	1
Education	151	72	184	199	239	160	90
All other gifts	89	105	82	84	107	66	64

Note: Spending by category will not add to total spending because gift spending is also included in the preceding product and service categories and personal taxes are not included in the total.
Source: Bureau of Labor Statistics, 2000 Consumer Expenditure Survey, Internet site www.bls.gov/cex/

Table 1.49 Indexed spending by size of household, 2000

(indexed annual spending of consumer units (CU) by product and service category and by number of people in consumer unit, 2000; index definition: an index of 100 is the average for all consumer units; an index of 132 means that spending by consumer units in that group is 32 percent above the average for all consumer units; an index of 68 indicates spending that is 32 percent below the average for all consumer units)

	total consumer units	one person	two or more people				
			total	two people	three people	four people	five or more people
Average spending of CU, total	$38,045	$23,059	$44,251	$38,627	$45,156	$52,032	$49,100
Average spending of CU, index	100	61	116	102	119	137	129
FOOD	100	55	118	99	118	138	152
Food at home	100	49	120	96	122	141	169
Cereals and bakery products	100	49	121	93	121	143	178
Cereals and cereal products	100	44	122	88	119	147	204
Bakery products	100	51	120	95	123	141	164
Meats, poultry, fish, and eggs	100	44	122	97	127	139	172
Beef	100	42	123	96	133	144	168
Pork	100	43	123	102	129	131	169
Other meats	100	47	121	90	120	141	193
Poultry	100	47	121	94	121	146	174
Fish and seafood	100	45	122	102	123	140	159
Eggs	100	53	121	100	121	118	185
Dairy products	100	50	120	94	122	138	174
Fresh milk and cream	100	50	121	87	126	140	193
Other dairy products	100	51	120	100	119	138	162
Fruits and vegetables	100	54	118	100	117	133	159
Fresh fruits	100	57	117	102	112	131	158
Fresh vegetables	100	54	118	101	115	130	162
Processed fruits	100	52	119	98	121	142	153
Processed vegetables	100	48	120	99	129	136	160
Other food at home	100	50	120	94	121	145	167
Sugar and other sweets	100	48	121	93	116	139	193
Fats and oils	100	47	122	104	119	129	169
Miscellaneous foods	100	51	120	89	123	151	168
Nonalcoholic beverages	100	50	120	95	124	145	158
Food prepared by CU on trips	100	55	118	120	98	130	128
Food away from home	100	63	115	103	113	135	127
ALCOHOLIC BEVERAGES	100	87	105	115	110	88	85
HOUSING	100	66	114	98	115	137	127
Shelter	100	71	112	97	113	134	125
Owned dwellings	100	51	121	99	116	160	139
Mortgage interest and charges	100	38	126	89	125	182	158
Property taxes	100	63	115	110	105	137	118
Maintenance, repair, insurance, other expenses	100	73	111	113	104	119	106
Rented dwellings	100	120	92	87	106	82	99
Other lodging	100	60	117	133	110	103	98
Utilities, fuels, and public services	100	65	115	102	114	127	135
Natural gas	100	68	114	98	109	129	145
Electricity	100	62	116	105	115	127	135
Fuel oil and other fuels	100	70	112	122	99	109	110
Telephone	100	69	113	99	118	126	130
Water and other public services	100	59	117	104	112	131	144

	total consumer units	one person	two or more people				
			total	two people	three people	four people	five or more people
Household services	100	57	118	73	135	191	124
Personal services	100	38	126	31	161	264	161
Other household services	100	74	111	112	111	125	89
Housekeeping supplies	100	46	121	107	115	138	157
Laundry and cleaning supplies	100	40	123	93	113	130	228
Other household products	100	45	122	106	119	150	139
Postage and stationery	100	55	117	122	109	121	112
Household furnishings and equipment	100	58	117	103	120	147	115
Household textiles	100	59	117	103	125	154	99
Furniture	100	58	118	100	133	148	104
Floor coverings	100	45	125	111	130	143	132
Major appliances	100	55	119	98	114	138	160
Small appliances, misc. housewares	100	56	118	111	114	138	121
Miscellaneous household equipment	100	59	117	105	114	150	109
APPAREL AND RELATED SERVICES	100	55	118	90	122	147	159
Men and boys	100	51	120	93	123	150	156
Men, aged 16 or older	100	61	116	109	124	124	110
Boys, aged 2 to 15	100	13	135	33	121	244	320
Women and girls	100	57	117	92	116	146	159
Women, aged 16 or older	100	65	114	101	115	128	132
Girls, aged 2 to 15	100	14	136	42	121	242	298
Children under age 2	100	21	132	48	173	201	239
Footwear	100	56	118	86	123	141	180
Other apparel products and services	100	69	113	102	117	135	109
TRANSPORTATION	100	50	121	102	131	144	130
Vehicle purchases	100	43	124	99	141	155	130
Cars and trucks, new	100	50	121	110	155	129	91
Cars and trucks, used	100	35	127	91	129	175	166
Other vehicles	100	74	112	56	86	272	91
Gasoline and motor oil	100	53	120	101	122	140	143
Other vehicle expenses	100	56	119	102	126	138	130
Vehicle finance charges	100	39	126	100	145	145	145
Maintenance and repairs	100	63	115	104	112	132	132
Vehicle insurance	100	56	118	103	129	131	130
Vehicle rentals, leases, licenses, other charges	100	56	118	99	128	150	117
Public transportation	100	75	110	117	109	110	91
HEALTH CARE	100	72	112	126	101	104	98
Health insurance	100	67	114	126	105	108	99
Medical services	100	74	111	117	101	115	104
Drugs	100	84	106	135	91	78	86
Medical supplies	100	63	115	133	98	105	102
ENTERTAINMENT	100	55	119	98	118	150	139
Fees and admissions	100	55	119	101	100	166	135
Television, radio, sound equipment	100	69	113	92	116	144	127
Pets, toys, and playground equipment	100	53	119	104	116	141	139
Other entertainment products and services	100	35	127	97	145	145	165

	total consumer units	one person	two or more people				
			total	two people	three people	four people	five or more people
PERSONAL CARE PRODUCTS AND SERVICES	100	60	116	102	123	130	131
READING	100	77	110	118	99	115	92
EDUCATION	100	64	115	75	133	151	156
TOBACCO PRODUCTS AND SMOKING SUPPLIES	100	64	115	100	125	122	137
MISCELLANEOUS	100	72	112	110	102	128	107
CASH CONTRIBUTIONS	100	88	105	126	96	94	74
PERSONAL INSURANCE AND PENSIONS	100	53	120	103	125	147	124
Life and other personal insurance	100	39	126	121	120	140	125
Pensions and Social Security	100	55	119	101	125	147	123
PERSONAL TAXES	100	67	115	116	110	137	86
Federal income taxes	100	67	114	115	111	138	83
State and local income taxes	100	64	116	113	110	138	102
Other taxes	100	75	112	135	90	114	73
GIFTS	100	75	110	118	122	101	82
Food	100	44	123	110	163	114	114
Alcoholic beverages	100	71	114	93	171	100	136
Housing	100	66	114	120	116	115	90
Housekeeping supplies	100	64	115	110	115	115	128
Household textiles	100	62	115	85	192	146	69
Appliances and misc. housewares	100	68	114	136	79	100	121
Major appliances	100	63	100	100	100	63	213
Small appliances and misc. housewares	100	67	110	143	67	110	81
Miscellaneous household equipment	100	91	104	106	101	126	76
Other housing	100	55	119	131	125	111	84
Apparel and services	100	77	109	121	109	99	88
Males, aged 2 or older	100	75	109	134	113	68	79
Females, aged 2 or older	100	71	112	140	95	95	73
Children under age 2	100	41	122	83	156	161	149
Other apparel products and services	100	116	92	102	86	96	73
Jewelry and watches	100	180	70	90	65	55	35
All other apparel products and services	100	77	110	113	103	127	97
Transportation	100	83	107	149	104	60	56
Health care	100	163	74	92	66	84	16
Entertainment	100	78	109	114	117	101	93
Toys, games, hobbies, and tricycles	100	80	107	137	97	80	63
Other entertainment	100	77	109	103	127	111	105
Personal care products and services	100	74	111	79	142	147	111
Reading	100	100	100	150	100	50	50
Education	100	48	122	132	158	106	60
All other gifts	100	118	92	94	120	74	72

Source: Calculations by New Strategist based on the Bureau of Labor Statistics 2000 Consumer Expenditure Survey

Spending Overview:

Spending by Homeowners and Renters, 2000

Homeowners spend far more than renters because their incomes are higher and they have more money to spend. Homeowners had an average income of $53,447 in 2000, and they spent $43,603—15 percent more than the average household. In contrast, the average income of renters was just $28,448 and they spent $27,406—28 percent less than average.

Renters spend less than homeowners on nearly every product and service category. The spending of renters is close to the average for some foods, such as fish and eggs. They spend 2 percent more than average on infants' clothes and 5 percent more than average on tobacco.

Table 1.50 Average spending by homeowners and renters, 2000

(average annual spending of consumer units (CU) by product and service category and by homeownership status, 2000)

	total consumer units	homeowners	renters
Number of consumer units (in thousands, add 000s)	109,367	71,834	37,532
Average number of persons per CU	2.5	2.6	2.3
Average income before taxes	$44,649	$53,447	$28,448
Average annual spending	38,045	43,603	27,406
FOOD	$5,158	$5,698	$4,124
Food at home	3,021	3,326	2,436
Cereals and bakery products	453	503	358
Cereals and cereal products	156	167	137
Bakery products	297	337	221
Meats, poultry, fish, and eggs	795	856	679
Beef	238	259	199
Pork	167	182	138
Other meats	101	110	83
Poultry	145	154	129
Fish and seafood	110	116	99
Eggs	34	36	31
Dairy products	325	364	250
Fresh milk and cream	131	144	107
Other dairy products	193	220	142
Fruits and vegetables	521	569	428
Fresh fruits	163	181	129
Fresh vegetables	159	170	138
Processed fruits	115	126	93
Processed vegetables	84	92	68
Other food at home	927	1,034	722
Sugar and other sweets	117	136	81
Fats and oils	83	92	67
Miscellaneous foods	437	489	338
Nonalcoholic beverages	250	270	210
Food prepared by CU on trips	40	47	26
Food away from home	2,137	2,371	1,688
ALCOHOLIC BEVERAGES	372	393	331
HOUSING	12,319	13,874	9,341
Shelter	7,114	7,627	6,133
Owned dwellings	4,602	6,976	59
Mortgage interest and charges	2,639	4,007	19
Property taxes	1,139	1,723	19
Maintenance, repair, insurance, other expenses	825	1,245	20
Rented dwellings	2,034	47	5,836
Other lodging	478	603	238
Utilities, fuels, and public services	2,489	2,917	1,669
Natural gas	307	378	172
Electricity	911	1,074	600
Fuel oil and other fuels	97	130	33
Telephone	877	939	758
Water and other public services	296	396	106

	total consumer units	homeowners	renters
Household services	**$684**	**$852**	**$364**
Personal services	326	378	228
Other household services	358	474	137
Housekeeping supplies	**482**	**579**	**297**
Laundry and cleaning supplies	131	147	99
Other household products	226	281	120
Postage and stationery	126	151	78
Household furnishings and equipment	**1,549**	**1,899**	**878**
Household textiles	106	134	54
Furniture	391	467	244
Floor coverings	44	63	10
Major appliances	189	240	92
Small appliances, misc. housewares	87	106	53
Miscellaneous household equipment	731	890	426
APPAREL AND RELATED SERVICES	**1,856**	**2,052**	**1,482**
Men and boys	**440**	**497**	**331**
Men, aged 16 or older	344	394	248
Boys, aged 2 to 15	96	103	82
Women and girls	**725**	**827**	**531**
Women, aged 16 or older	607	688	452
Girls, aged 2 to 15	118	139	79
Children under age 2	**82**	**81**	**84**
Footwear	**343**	**359**	**313**
Other apparel products and services	**266**	**288**	**224**
TRANSPORTATION	**7,417**	**8,530**	**5,289**
Vehicle purchases	**3,418**	**3,916**	**2,465**
Cars and trucks, new	1,605	1,959	927
Cars and trucks, used	1,770	1,904	1,513
Other vehicles	43	53	25
Gasoline and motor oil	**1,291**	**1,475**	**939**
Other vehicle expenses	**2,281**	**2,653**	**1,570**
Vehicle finance charges	328	385	220
Maintenance and repairs	624	706	466
Vehicle insurance	778	899	546
Vehicle rentals, leases, licenses, other charges	551	663	338
Public transportation	**427**	**485**	**314**
HEALTH CARE	**2,066**	**2,561**	**1,117**
Health insurance	983	1,227	516
Medical services	568	702	311
Drugs	416	512	233
Medical supplies	99	120	57
ENTERTAINMENT	**1,863**	**2,229**	**1,163**
Fees and admissions	515	640	275
Television, radio, sound equipment	622	680	511
Pets, toys, and playground equipment	334	404	200
Other entertainment products and services	393	505	178

	total consumer units	homeowners	renters
PERSONAL CARE PRODUCTS AND SERVICES	$564	$628	$441
READING	146	173	95
EDUCATION	632	645	607
TOBACCO PRODUCTS AND SMOKING SUPPLIES	319	311	334
MISCELLANEOUS	776	917	505
CASH CONTRIBUTIONS	1,192	1,505	593
PERSONAL INSURANCE AND PENSIONS	3,365	4,087	1,983
Life and other personal insurance	399	527	153
Pensions and Social Security	2,966	3,560	1,830
PERSONAL TAXES	3,117	3,917	1,645
Federal income taxes	2,409	3,013	1,297
State and local income taxes	562	681	342
Other taxes	146	223	6
GIFTS	1,083	1,306	656
Food	70	89	33
Alcoholic beverages	14	13	17
Housing	291	350	179
Housekeeping supplies	39	45	28
Household textiles	13	18	4
Appliances and misc. housewares	28	35	14
Major appliances	8	10	4
Small appliances and misc. housewares	21	26	10
Miscellaneous household equipment	70	88	36
Other housing	140	163	97
Apparel and services	244	284	168
Males, aged 2 or older	68	81	43
Females, aged 2 or older	85	102	53
Children under age 2	41	45	32
Other apparel products and services	51	56	40
Jewelry and watches	20	23	15
All other apparel products and services	30	33	25
Transportation	70	77	58
Health care	38	52	12
Entertainment	94	110	62
Toys, games, hobbies, and tricycles	30	35	19
Other entertainment	64	75	43
Personal care products and services	19	23	13
Reading	2	3	1
Education	151	197	63
All other gifts	89	110	50

Note: Spending by category will not add to total spending because gift spending is also included in the preceding product and service categories and personal taxes are not included in the total.
Source: Bureau of Labor Statistics, 2000 Consumer Expenditure Survey, Internet site www.bls.gov/cex/

Table 1.51 Indexed spending by homeowners and renters, 2000

(indexed annual spending of consumer units (CU) by product and service category and by home-ownership status, 2000; index definition: an index of 100 is the average for all consumer units; an index of 132 means that spending by consumer units in that group is 32 percent above the average for all consumer units; an index of 68 indicates spending that is 32 percent below the average for all consumer units)

	total consumer units	homeowners	renters
Average spending of CU, total	$38,045	$43,603	$27,406
Average spending of CU, index	100	115	72
FOOD	100	110	80
Food at home	100	110	81
Cereals and bakery products	100	111	79
Cereals and cereal products	100	107	88
Bakery products	100	113	74
Meats, poultry, fish, and eggs	100	108	85
Beef	100	109	84
Pork	100	109	83
Other meats	100	109	82
Poultry	100	106	89
Fish and seafood	100	105	90
Eggs	100	106	91
Dairy products	100	112	77
Fresh milk and cream	100	110	82
Other dairy products	100	114	74
Fruits and vegetables	100	109	82
Fresh fruits	100	111	79
Fresh vegetables	100	107	87
Processed fruits	100	110	81
Processed vegetables	100	110	81
Other food at home	100	112	78
Sugar and other sweets	100	116	69
Fats and oils	100	111	81
Miscellaneous foods	100	112	77
Nonalcoholic beverages	100	108	84
Food prepared by CU on trips	100	118	65
Food away from home	100	111	79
ALCOHOLIC BEVERAGES	100	106	89
HOUSING	100	113	76
Shelter	100	107	86
Owned dwellings	100	152	1
Mortgage interest and charges	100	152	1
Property taxes	100	151	2
Maintenance, repair, insurance, other expenses	100	151	2
Rented dwellings	100	2	287
Other lodging	100	126	50
Utilities, fuels, and public services	100	117	67
Natural gas	100	123	56
Electricity	100	118	66
Fuel oil and other fuels	100	134	34
Telephone	100	107	86
Water and other public services	100	134	36

	total consumer units	homeowners	renters
Household services	**100**	**125**	**53**
Personal services	100	116	70
Other household services	100	132	38
Housekeeping supplies	**100**	**120**	**62**
Laundry and cleaning supplies	100	112	76
Other household products	100	124	53
Postage and stationery	100	120	62
Household furnishings and equipment	**100**	**123**	**57**
Household textiles	100	126	51
Furniture	100	119	62
Floor coverings	100	143	23
Major appliances	100	127	49
Small appliances, misc. housewares	100	122	61
Miscellaneous household equipment	100	122	58
APPAREL AND RELATED SERVICES	**100**	**111**	**80**
Men and boys	**100**	**113**	**75**
Men, aged 16 or older	100	115	72
Boys, aged 2 to 15	100	107	85
Women and girls	**100**	**114**	**73**
Women, aged 16 or older	100	113	74
Girls, aged 2 to 15	100	118	67
Children under age 2	**100**	**99**	**102**
Footwear	**100**	**105**	**91**
Other apparel products and services	**100**	**108**	**84**
TRANSPORTATION	**100**	**115**	**71**
Vehicle purchases	**100**	**115**	**72**
Cars and trucks, new	100	122	58
Cars and trucks, used	100	108	85
Other vehicles	100	123	58
Gasoline and motor oil	**100**	**114**	**73**
Other vehicle expenses	**100**	**116**	**69**
Vehicle finance charges	100	117	67
Maintenance and repairs	100	113	75
Vehicle insurance	100	116	70
Vehicle rentals, leases, licenses, other charges	100	120	61
Public transportation	**100**	**114**	**74**
HEALTH CARE	**100**	**124**	**54**
Health insurance	100	125	52
Medical services	100	124	55
Drugs	100	123	56
Medical supplies	100	121	58
ENTERTAINMENT	**100**	**120**	**62**
Fees and admissions	100	124	53
Television, radio, sound equipment	100	109	82
Pets, toys, and playground equipment	100	121	60
Other entertainment products and services	100	128	45

	total consumer units	homeowners	renters
PERSONAL CARE PRODUCTS AND SERVICES	100	111	78
READING	100	118	65
EDUCATION	100	102	96
TOBACCO PRODUCTS AND SMOKING SUPPLIES	100	97	105
MISCELLANEOUS	100	118	65
CASH CONTRIBUTIONS	100	126	50
PERSONAL INSURANCE AND PENSIONS	100	121	59
Life and other personal insurance	100	132	38
Pensions and Social Security	100	120	62
PERSONAL TAXES	100	126	53
Federal income taxes	100	125	54
State and local income taxes	100	121	61
Other taxes	100	153	4
GIFTS	100	121	61
Food	100	127	47
Alcoholic beverages	100	93	121
Housing	100	120	62
Housekeeping supplies	100	115	72
Household textiles	100	138	31
Appliances and misc. housewares	100	125	50
Major appliances	100	125	50
Small appliances and misc. housewares	100	124	48
Miscellaneous household equipment	100	126	51
Other housing	100	116	69
Apparel and services	100	116	69
Males, aged 2 or older	100	119	63
Females, aged 2 or older	100	120	62
Children under age 2	100	110	78
Other apparel products and services	100	110	78
Jewelry and watches	100	115	75
All other apparel products and services	100	110	83
Transportation	100	110	83
Health care	100	137	32
Entertainment	100	117	66
Toys, games, hobbies, and tricycles	100	117	63
Other entertainment	100	117	67
Personal care products and services	100	121	68
Reading	100	150	50
Education	100	130	42
All other gifts	100	124	56

Source: Calculations by New Strategist based on the Bureau of Labor Statistics 2000 Consumer Expenditure Survey

Spending Overview:
Spending by Number of Earners in Household, 2000

Behind the growing affluence of the United States are dual-earner households. Accounting for 33 percent of all households, dual-earners outspend the average household by 29 percent. In 2000, the average dual-income household spent $48,923. Households with three or more earners spend even more ($55,810), but they account for a much smaller share of households—just under 10 percent in 2000.

By category, spending does not always rise with the number of earners in a household. Single-person households with one earner (many of them young adults) spend more than other households on rent. Two-person households with no earners (many of them elderly) spend more than other households on drugs. Two-earner households spend more on mortgage interest than three-earner households. In general, however, three-earner households outspend the others on most products and services because they are the largest households, averaging 4.4 people.

The needs of two-earner households are readily apparent in these tables. This household type spends 31 percent more than the average household on food away from home, 79 percent more than average on personal household services (primarily day care), 40 percent more on pets, toys, and playground equipment, 36 percent more on new vehicles, and 40 percent more on used cars and trucks.

Table 1.52 Average spending by number of earners in household, 2000

(average annual spending of consumer units (CU) by product and service category, by CU size and number of earners in CU, 2000)

| | total consumer units | single-person CUs | | CUs with two or more people | | | |
		no earner	one earner	no earner	one earner	two earners	three+ earners
Number of consumer units (in thousands, add 000s)	109,367	12,527	19,796	9,430	20,782	36,285	10,546
Average number of persons per CU	2.5	1.0	1.0	2.3	3.0	3.1	4.4
Average income before taxes	$44,649	$13,847	$31,246	$22,208	$42,133	$62,951	$68,931
Average annual spending	38,045	17,273	26,657	27,644	37,924	48,923	55,810
FOOD	$5,158	$2,184	$3,201	$4,340	$5,328	$6,430	$8,151
Food at home	3,021	1,507	1,460	2,956	3,379	3,640	4,825
Cereals and bakery products	453	237	211	444	514	541	731
Cereals and cereal products	156	77	65	150	186	189	248
Bakery products	297	160	146	294	328	352	483
Meats, poultry, fish, and eggs	795	366	344	790	907	965	1,311
Beef	238	99	100	227	269	296	401
Pork	167	76	68	192	189	200	272
Other meats	101	51	44	99	105	125	170
Poultry	145	70	66	126	176	175	227
Fish and seafood	110	48	51	111	129	130	185
Eggs	34	21	16	35	40	40	56
Dairy products	325	170	158	328	365	392	490
Fresh milk and cream	131	76	58	130	148	160	198
Other dairy products	193	94	100	198	217	233	292
Fruits and vegetables	521	305	265	571	579	601	801
Fresh fruits	163	105	86	186	179	185	244
Fresh vegetables	159	95	81	165	180	179	255
Processed fruits	115	66	56	136	127	135	166
Processed vegetables	84	38	41	85	93	101	136
Other food at home	927	429	482	823	1,015	1,141	1,493
Sugar and other sweets	117	56	55	123	116	145	201
Fats and oils	83	44	36	91	95	98	132
Miscellaneous foods	437	203	232	350	482	544	702
Nonalcoholic beverages	250	112	132	219	276	305	405
Food prepared by CU on trips	40	14	27	39	45	49	53
Food away from home	2,137	678	1,741	1,385	1,949	2,790	3,326
ALCOHOLIC BEVERAGES	372	173	415	242	274	458	535
HOUSING	12,319	6,835	9,041	8,981	12,840	15,570	15,691
Shelter	7,114	3,793	5,851	4,495	7,344	9,007	8,808
Owned dwellings	4,602	1,895	2,609	2,876	4,732	6,436	6,540
Mortgage interest and charges	2,639	320	1,438	824	2,677	4,136	4,045
Property taxes	1,139	831	655	1,109	1,190	1,384	1,493
Maintenance, repair, insurance, other expenses	825	744	516	943	865	916	1,002
Rented dwellings	2,034	1,705	2,897	1,140	2,121	1,981	1,617
Other lodging	478	194	345	478	491	590	651
Utilities, fuels, and public services	2,489	1,621	1,633	2,369	2,702	2,899	3,402
Natural gas	307	234	192	310	316	357	422
Electricity	911	609	545	949	1,028	1,050	1,218
Fuel oil and other fuels	97	88	56	130	111	97	125
Telephone	877	490	681	670	929	1,046	1,205
Water and other public services	296	200	160	310	317	349	432

	total consumer units	single-person CUs		CUs with two or more people			
		no earner	one earner	no earner	one earner	two earners	three+ earners
Household services	**$684**	**$607**	**$249**	**$438**	**$702**	**$1,030**	**$588**
Personal services	326	299	13	110	334	582	246
Other household services	358	308	236	329	369	449	341
Housekeeping supplies	**482**	**220**	**227**	**495**	**534**	**609**	**691**
Laundry and cleaning supplies	131	54	53	119	153	169	194
Other household products	226	104	101	208	251	292	332
Postage and stationery	126	63	73	168	130	149	165
Household furnishings and equipment	**1,549**	**593**	**1,082**	**1,184**	**1,558**	**2,025**	**2,201**
Household textiles	106	43	76	73	116	137	144
Furniture	391	118	294	217	408	547	478
Floor coverings	44	16	22	30	46	55	91
Major appliances	189	112	99	182	194	233	293
Small appliances, misc. housewares	87	34	58	84	73	117	131
Miscellaneous household equipment	731	271	533	598	721	935	1,065
APPAREL AND RELATED SERVICES	**1,856**	**612**	**1,275**	**952**	**1,922**	**2,456**	**2,981**
Men and boys	**440**	**96**	**298**	**204**	**439**	**588**	**807**
Men, aged 16 or older	344	85	285	168	296	443	671
Boys, aged 2 to 15	96	12	13	35	143	145	136
Women and girls	**725**	**259**	**504**	**428**	**713**	**949**	**1,190**
Women, aged 16 or older	607	241	489	369	537	768	1,050
Girls, aged 2 to 15	118	18	15	59	176	182	140
Children under age 2	**82**	**14**	**19**	**31**	**139**	**112**	**101**
Footwear	**343**	**128**	**227**	**167**	**378**	**441**	**550**
Other apparel products and services	**266**	**114**	**227**	**122**	**252**	**366**	**332**
TRANSPORTATION	**7,417**	**2,178**	**4,715**	**4,980**	**7,148**	**9,948**	**12,716**
Vehicle purchases	**3,418**	**806**	**1,868**	**2,240**	**3,291**	**4,727**	**6,234**
Cars and trucks, new	1,605	471	1,003	1,161	1,501	2,186	2,687
Cars and trucks, used	1,770	335	814	1,079	1,745	2,479	3,497
Other vehicles	43	–	52	–	45	62	50
Gasoline and motor oil	**1,291**	**403**	**859**	**880**	**1,292**	**1,680**	**2,187**
Other vehicle expenses	**2,281**	**731**	**1,614**	**1,488**	**2,178**	**3,015**	**3,764**
Vehicle finance charges	328	45	183	123	302	500	581
Maintenance and repairs	624	237	495	485	607	772	970
Vehicle insurance	778	329	505	587	782	957	1,374
Vehicle rentals, leases, licenses, other charges	551	121	430	293	487	786	839
Public transportation	**427**	**238**	**374**	**372**	**388**	**526**	**531**
HEALTH CARE	**2,066**	**2,172**	**1,056**	**3,413**	**2,136**	**2,129**	**2,273**
Health insurance	983	1,009	435	1,652	1,041	1,029	1,108
Medical services	568	508	361	696	585	637	641
Drugs	416	578	209	902	417	353	399
Medical supplies	99	77	52	164	93	110	125
ENTERTAINMENT	**1,863**	**663**	**1,253**	**1,145**	**1,958**	**2,498**	**2,697**
Fees and admissions	515	170	351	367	544	694	691
Television, radio, sound equipment	622	306	505	417	619	773	881
Pets, toys, and playground equipment	334	115	215	183	371	466	414
Other entertainment products and services	393	71	182	179	424	564	711

	total consumer units	single-person CUs		CUs with two or more people			
		no earner	one earner	no earner	one earner	two earners	three+ earners
PERSONAL CARE PRODUCTS AND SERVICES	**$564**	**$277**	**$375**	**$478**	**$572**	**$700**	**$837**
READING	**146**	**96**	**124**	**141**	**139**	**176**	**168**
EDUCATION	**632**	**163**	**561**	**121**	**640**	**755**	**1,337**
TOBACCO PRODUCTS AND SMOKING SUPPLIES	**319**	**166**	**226**	**228**	**335**	**383**	**503**
MISCELLANEOUS	**776**	**409**	**656**	**611**	**741**	**963**	**1,005**
CASH CONTRIBUTIONS	**1,192**	**1,189**	**956**	**1,606**	**1,096**	**1,225**	**1,347**
PERSONAL INSURANCE AND PENSIONS	**3,365**	**156**	**2,803**	**406**	**2,795**	**5,233**	**5,571**
Life and other personal insurance	399	135	167	380	488	502	632
Pensions and Social Security	2,966	21	2,636	26	2,307	4,732	4,939
PERSONAL TAXES	**3,117**	**530**	**2,969**	**552**	**2,541**	**4,629**	**4,543**
Federal income taxes	2,409	307	2,362	348	1,938	3,600	3,536
State and local income taxes	562	56	531	33	455	868	820
Other taxes	146	167	77	171	148	161	188
GIFTS	**1,083**	**716**	**861**	**685**	**1,058**	**1,341**	**1,437**
Food	**70**	**14**	**41**	**47**	**50**	**99**	**153**
Alcoholic beverages	**14**	**3**	**13**	**5**	**11**	**22**	**19**
Housing	**291**	**178**	**201**	**206**	**272**	**395**	**346**
Housekeeping supplies	39	20	28	30	36	48	66
Household textiles	13	5	9	6	19	13	24
Appliances and misc. housewares	28	21	18	25	21	41	26
Major appliances	8	8	4	3	8	12	4
Small appliances and misc. housewares	21	13	14	22	14	30	22
Miscellaneous household equipment	70	53	70	41	55	91	77
Other housing	140	79	76	103	141	202	153
Apparel and services	**244**	**138**	**216**	**165**	**246**	**292**	**316**
Males, aged 2 or older	68	38	59	38	61	86	95
Females, aged 2 or older	85	39	72	84	87	99	112
Children under age 2	41	14	19	19	57	51	64
Other apparel products and services	51	48	66	24	42	57	45
Jewelry and watches	20	30	39	8	10	17	15
All other apparel products and services	30	18	27	16	31	40	30
Transportation	**70**	**31**	**75**	**26**	**72**	**84**	**95**
Health care	**38**	**137**	**15**	**53**	**32**	**23**	**16**
Entertainment	**94**	**52**	**87**	**71**	**99**	**112**	**104**
Toys, games, hobbies, and tricycles	30	17	29	25	33	35	26
Other entertainment	64	35	58	46	66	77	78
Personal care products and services	**19**	**4**	**21**	**8**	**21**	**22**	**30**
Reading	**2**	**2**	**2**	**4**	**2**	**2**	**2**
Education	**151**	**46**	**89**	**24**	**176**	**203**	**277**
All other gifts	**89**	**112**	**100**	**76**	**76**	**89**	**79**

Note: Spending by category will not add to total spending because gift spending is also included in the preceding product and service categories and personal taxes are not included in the total. (–) means sample is too small to make a reliable estimate.
Source: Bureau of Labor Statistics, 2000 Consumer Expenditure Surveys, Internet site www.bls.gov/cex/

Table 1.53 Indexed spending by number of earners in household, 2000

(indexed average annual spending of consumer units (CU) by product and service category, CU size, and number of earners in CU, 2000; index definition: an index of 100 is the average for all consumer units; an index of 132 means that spending by consumer units in that group is 32 percent above the average for all consumer units; an index of 68 indicates spending that is 32 percent below the average for all consumer units)

	total consumer units	single-person CUs		CUs with two or more people			
		no earner	one earner	no earner	one earner	two earners	three+ earners
Average spending of CU, total	$38,045	$17,273	$26,657	$27,644	$37,924	$48,923	$55,810
Average spending of CU, index	100	45	70	73	100	129	147
FOOD	100	42	62	84	103	125	158
Food at home	100	50	48	98	112	120	160
Cereals and bakery products	100	52	47	98	113	119	161
Cereals and cereal products	100	49	42	96	119	121	159
Bakery products	100	54	49	99	110	119	163
Meats, poultry, fish, and eggs	100	46	43	99	114	121	165
Beef	100	42	42	95	113	124	168
Pork	100	46	41	115	113	120	163
Other meats	100	50	44	98	104	124	168
Poultry	100	48	46	87	121	121	157
Fish and seafood	100	44	46	101	117	118	168
Eggs	100	62	47	103	118	118	165
Dairy products	100	52	49	101	112	121	151
Fresh milk and cream	100	58	44	99	113	122	151
Other dairy products	100	49	52	103	112	121	151
Fruits and vegetables	100	59	51	110	111	115	154
Fresh fruits	100	64	53	114	110	113	150
Fresh vegetables	100	60	51	104	113	113	160
Processed fruits	100	57	49	118	110	117	144
Processed vegetables	100	45	49	101	111	120	162
Other food at home	100	46	52	89	109	123	161
Sugar and other sweets	100	48	47	105	99	124	172
Fats and oils	100	53	43	110	114	118	159
Miscellaneous foods	100	46	53	80	110	124	161
Nonalcoholic beverages	100	45	53	88	110	122	162
Food prepared by CU on trips	100	35	68	98	113	123	133
Food away from home	100	32	81	65	91	131	156
ALCOHOLIC BEVERAGES	100	47	112	65	74	123	144
HOUSING	100	55	73	73	104	126	127
Shelter	100	53	82	63	103	127	124
Owned dwellings	100	41	57	62	103	140	142
Mortgage interest and charges	100	12	54	31	101	157	153
Property taxes	100	73	58	97	104	122	131
Maintenance, repair, insurance, other expenses	100	90	63	114	105	111	121
Rented dwellings	100	84	142	56	104	97	79
Other lodging	100	41	72	100	103	123	136
Utilities, fuels, and public services	100	65	66	95	109	116	137
Natural gas	100	76	63	101	103	116	137
Electricity	100	67	60	104	113	115	134
Fuel oil and other fuels	100	91	58	134	114	100	129
Telephone	100	56	78	76	106	119	137
Water and other public services	100	68	54	105	107	118	146

	total consumer units	single-person CUs		CUs with two or more people			
		no earner	one earner	no earner	one earner	two earners	three+ earners
Household services	100	**89**	**36**	**64**	**103**	**151**	**86**
Personal services	100	92	4	34	102	179	75
Other household services	100	86	66	92	103	125	95
Housekeeping supplies	100	**46**	**47**	**103**	**111**	**126**	**143**
Laundry and cleaning supplies	100	41	40	91	117	129	148
Other household products	100	46	45	92	111	129	147
Postage and stationery	100	50	58	133	103	118	131
Household furnishings and equipment	100	**38**	**70**	**76**	**101**	**131**	**142**
Household textiles	100	41	72	69	109	129	136
Furniture	100	30	75	55	104	140	122
Floor coverings	100	36	50	68	105	125	207
Major appliances	100	59	52	96	103	123	155
Small appliances, misc. housewares	100	39	67	97	84	134	151
Miscellaneous household equipment	100	37	73	82	99	128	146
APPAREL AND RELATED SERVICES	100	**33**	**69**	**51**	**104**	**132**	**161**
Men and boys	100	**22**	**68**	**46**	**100**	**134**	**183**
Men, aged 16 or older	100	25	83	49	86	129	195
Boys, aged 2 to 15	100	13	14	36	149	151	142
Women and girls	100	**36**	**70**	**59**	**98**	**131**	**164**
Women, aged 16 or older	100	40	81	61	88	127	173
Girls, aged 2 to 15	100	15	13	50	149	154	119
Children under age 2	100	**17**	**23**	**38**	**170**	**137**	**123**
Footwear	100	**37**	**66**	**49**	**110**	**129**	**160**
Other apparel products and services	100	**43**	**85**	**46**	**95**	**138**	**125**
TRANSPORTATION	100	**29**	**64**	**67**	**96**	**134**	**171**
Vehicle purchases	100	**24**	**55**	**66**	**96**	**138**	**182**
Cars and trucks, new	100	29	62	72	94	136	167
Cars and trucks, used	100	19	46	61	99	140	198
Other vehicles	100	–	121	–	105	144	116
Gasoline and motor oil	100	**31**	**67**	**68**	**100**	**130**	**169**
Other vehicle expenses	100	**32**	**71**	**65**	**95**	**132**	**165**
Vehicle finance charges	100	14	56	38	92	152	177
Maintenance and repairs	100	38	79	78	97	124	155
Vehicle insurance	100	42	65	75	101	123	177
Vehicle rentals, leases, licenses, other charges	100	22	78	53	88	143	152
Public transportation	100	**56**	**88**	**87**	**91**	**123**	**124**
HEALTH CARE	100	**105**	**51**	**165**	**103**	**103**	**110**
Health insurance	100	103	44	168	106	105	113
Medical services	100	89	64	123	103	112	113
Drugs	100	139	50	217	100	85	96
Medical supplies	100	78	53	166	94	111	126
ENTERTAINMENT	100	**36**	**67**	**61**	**105**	**134**	**145**
Fees and admissions	100	33	68	71	106	135	134
Television, radio, sound equipment	100	49	81	67	100	124	142
Pets, toys, and playground equipment	100	34	64	55	111	140	124
Other entertainment products and services	100	18	46	46	108	144	181

	total consumer units	single-person CUs		CUs with two or more people			
		no earner	one earner	no earner	one earner	two earners	three+ earners
PERSONAL CARE PRODUCTS AND SERVICES	100	49	66	85	101	124	148
READING	100	66	85	97	95	121	115
EDUCATION	100	26	89	19	101	119	212
TOBACCO PRODUCTS AND SMOKING SUPPLIES	100	52	71	71	105	120	158
MISCELLANEOUS	100	53	85	79	95	124	130
CASH CONTRIBUTIONS	100	100	80	135	92	103	113
PERSONAL INSURANCE AND PENSIONS	100	5	83	12	83	156	166
Life and other personal insurance	100	34	42	95	122	126	158
Pensions and Social Security	100	1	89	1	78	160	167
PERSONAL TAXES	100	17	95	18	82	149	146
Federal income taxes	100	13	98	14	80	149	147
State and local income taxes	100	10	94	6	81	154	146
Other taxes	100	114	53	117	101	110	129
GIFTS	100	66	80	63	98	124	133
Food	100	20	59	67	71	141	219
Alcoholic beverages	100	21	93	36	79	157	136
Housing	100	61	69	71	93	136	119
Housekeeping supplies	100	51	72	77	92	123	169
Household textiles	100	38	69	46	146	100	185
Appliances and misc. housewares	100	75	64	89	75	146	93
Major appliances	100	100	50	38	100	150	50
Small appliances and misc. housewares	100	62	67	105	67	143	105
Miscellaneous household equipment	100	76	100	59	79	130	110
Other housing	100	56	54	74	101	144	109
Apparel and services	100	57	89	68	101	120	130
Males, aged 2 or older	100	56	87	56	90	126	140
Females, aged 2 or older	100	46	85	99	102	116	132
Children under age 2	100	34	46	46	139	124	156
Other apparel products and services	100	94	129	47	82	112	88
Jewelry and watches	100	150	195	40	50	85	75
All other apparel products and services	100	60	90	53	103	133	100
Transportation	100	44	107	37	103	120	136
Health care	100	361	39	139	84	61	42
Entertainment	100	55	93	76	105	119	111
Toys, games, hobbies, and tricycles	100	57	97	83	110	117	87
Other entertainment	100	55	91	72	103	120	122
Personal care products and services	100	21	111	42	111	116	158
Reading	100	100	100	200	100	100	100
Education	100	30	59	16	117	134	183
All other gifts	100	126	112	85	85	100	89

Note: (–) means sample is too small to make a reliable estimate.
Source: Calculations by New Strategist based on the Bureau of Labor Statistics 2000 Consumer Expenditure Survey

Spending Overview:
Spending by Occupation of Householder, 2000

Households headed by managers and professionals spent $54,185 in 2000, 42 percent more than the average household. Behind the higher level of spending is their higher incomes, averaging $73,811 in 2000. Among wage and salary workers, average household income was $51,905. Their spending was only 10 percent above average. Households headed by retirees spend 32 percent less than average, while the self-employed spend 29 percent more than average.

Households headed by managers and professionals spend more than average on many of the products and services associated with the income elite. They spend 45 percent more than the average household on food away from home, 54 percent more on alcoholic beverages, 75 percent more on other lodging (which includes vacation homes and hotel and motel expenses), 48 percent more on men's clothes, 53 percent more on women's clothes, 58 percent more on new cars and trucks; 83 percent more on fees and admissions to entertainment events, and 64 percent more on gifts.

The self-employed are the biggest spenders on products and services needed by people who are likely to work at home. They spend more than managers and professionals on electricity, fuel oil, and health insurance. Their spending is below that of managers and professionals on household personal services (mostly day care) and men's and women's clothes.

The retired spend more than average on maintenance and repairs for owned dwellings, fuel oil, health care, and cash contributions.

Table 1.54 Average spending by occupation of householder, 2000

(average annual spending of consumer units (CU) by product and service category and by selected occupation of consumer unit reference person, 2000)

	total consumer units	self-employed	wage and salary workers total	managers and professionals	technical, sales, admin. support	retired
Number of consumer units (in thousands, add 000s)	109,367	5,736	72,083	25,361	20,832	19,499
Average number of persons per CU	2.5	2.5	2.7	2.6	2.6	1.7
Average income before taxes	$44,649	$58,847	$51,905	$73,811	$43,489	$22,306
Average annual spending	38,045	48,986	41,875	54,185	37,354	25,938
FOOD	**$5,158**	**$6,131**	**$5,562**	**$6,487**	**$5,102**	**$3,686**
Food at home	**3,021**	**3,424**	**3,127**	**3,397**	**2,866**	**2,453**
Cereals and bakery products	453	512	465	511	428	374
Cereals and cereal products	156	169	160	171	148	120
Bakery products	297	343	305	341	280	254
Meats, poultry, fish, and eggs	795	862	824	826	757	636
Beef	238	259	252	242	235	185
Pork	167	190	167	157	150	145
Other meats	101	109	104	105	96	79
Poultry	145	144	152	155	143	108
Fish and seafood	110	121	114	136	102	87
Eggs	34	38	35	32	31	31
Dairy products	325	369	332	364	310	277
Fresh milk and cream	131	156	132	132	126	113
Other dairy products	193	213	200	232	184	164
Fruits and vegetables	521	642	519	592	465	487
Fresh fruits	163	204	159	187	141	163
Fresh vegetables	159	199	159	181	139	146
Processed fruits	115	140	114	134	104	107
Processed vegetables	84	99	87	90	82	69
Other food at home	927	1,039	986	1,103	906	680
Sugar and other sweets	117	130	122	143	109	96
Fats and oils	83	101	84	86	76	73
Miscellaneous foods	437	477	472	540	439	303
Nonalcoholic beverages	250	279	266	270	246	177
Food prepared by CU on trips	40	53	43	64	36	30
Food away from home	**2,137**	**2,707**	**2,434**	**3,090**	**2,235**	**1,233**
ALCOHOLIC BEVERAGES	**372**	**430**	**428**	**572**	**377**	**226**
HOUSING	**12,319**	**15,223**	**13,418**	**17,877**	**12,026**	**8,663**
Shelter	**7,114**	**8,551**	**7,936**	**10,603**	**7,126**	**4,413**
Owned dwellings	4,602	6,233	5,138	7,627	4,147	2,937
Mortgage interest and charges	2,639	3,589	3,198	4,766	2,652	754
Property taxes	1,139	1,442	1,158	1,691	921	1,136
Maintenance, repair, insurance, other expenses	825	1,202	781	1,170	574	1,047
Rented dwellings	2,034	1,510	2,293	2,139	2,587	1,098
Other lodging	478	808	505	837	392	379
Utilities, fuels, and public services	**2,489**	**3,000**	**2,564**	**2,934**	**2,445**	**2,179**
Natural gas	307	310	314	367	290	309
Electricity	911	1,138	918	1,005	884	835
Fuel oil and other fuels	97	151	85	93	83	124
Telephone	877	1,042	948	1,105	906	613
Water and other public services	296	359	299	363	281	297

	total consumer units	self-employed	wage and salary workers			retired
			total	managers and professionals	technical, sales, admin. support	
Household services	$684	$950	$727	$1,172	$618	$574
Personal services	326	316	383	560	362	194
Other household services	358	635	344	612	256	380
Housekeeping supplies	482	584	499	642	443	436
Laundry and cleaning supplies	131	121	141	162	119	98
Other household products	226	295	233	300	211	199
Postage and stationery	126	168	125	180	114	139
Household furnishings and equipment	1,549	2,138	1,692	2,525	1,394	1,060
Household textiles	106	162	114	159	91	81
Furniture	391	398	452	720	360	204
Floor coverings	44	38	51	82	50	33
Major appliances	189	236	190	228	191	177
Small appliances, misc. housewares	87	125	94	133	87	57
Miscellaneous household equipment	731	1,180	790	1,202	616	508
APPAREL AND RELATED SERVICES	1,856	1,999	2,137	2,742	1,919	926
Men and boys	440	480	521	642	443	180
Men, aged 16 or older	344	392	402	510	341	161
Boys, aged 2 to 15	96	88	119	132	102	19
Women and girls	725	732	819	1,089	772	433
Women, aged 16 or older	607	628	679	931	632	402
Girls, aged 2 to 15	118	104	140	158	140	30
Children under age 2	82	89	96	100	89	23
Footwear	343	355	392	444	365	158
Other apparel products and services	266	342	310	467	249	132
TRANSPORTATION	7,417	8,729	8,497	10,073	7,782	4,399
Vehicle purchases	3,418	3,901	3,985	4,497	3,686	1,866
Cars and trucks, new	1,605	2,145	1,833	2,528	1,606	982
Cars and trucks, used	1,770	1,718	2,099	1,913	2,046	884
Other vehicles	43	38	53	56	34	–
Gasoline and motor oil	1,291	1,569	1,457	1,586	1,355	761
Other vehicle expenses	2,281	2,711	2,600	3,259	2,369	1,404
Vehicle finance charges	328	329	401	437	398	130
Maintenance and repairs	624	783	685	826	612	452
Vehicle insurance	778	842	858	974	824	573
Vehicle rentals, leases, licenses, other charges	551	756	656	1,022	535	249
Public transportation	427	548	455	731	372	368
HEALTH CARE	2,066	3,020	1,737	2,199	1,562	3,172
Health insurance	983	1,529	819	1,002	744	1,580
Medical services	568	822	528	729	459	668
Drugs	416	547	298	344	277	793
Medical supplies	99	123	92	124	83	130
ENTERTAINMENT	1,863	2,424	2,105	2,826	1,835	1,105
Fees and admissions	515	737	573	943	460	340
Television, radio, sound equipment	622	716	691	842	648	398
Pets, toys, and playground equipment	334	499	372	467	322	191
Other entertainment products and services	393	472	469	574	406	176

	total consumer units	self-employed	wage and salary workers			retired
			total	managers and professionals	technical, sales, admin. support	
PERSONAL CARE PRODUCTS AND SERVICES	$564	$626	$616	$751	$585	$427
READING	146	193	152	234	134	142
EDUCATION	632	598	773	1,152	755	123
TOBACCO PRODUCTS AND SMOKING SUPPLIES	319	325	344	231	341	179
MISCELLANEOUS	776	1,343	806	959	742	609
CASH CONTRIBUTIONS	1,192	2,079	1,074	1,775	796	1,681
PERSONAL INSURANCE AND PENSIONS	3,365	5,867	4,226	6,307	3,399	600
Life and other personal insurance	399	683	408	606	324	338
Pensions and Social Security	2,966	5,184	3,819	5,701	3,075	262
PERSONAL TAXES	3,117	4,093	3,911	6,891	2,658	885
Federal income taxes	2,409	3,308	3,042	5,482	2,034	577
State and local income taxes	562	548	736	1,208	525	98
Other taxes	146	237	133	201	99	209
GIFTS	1,083	1,405	1,182	1,781	1,027	801
Food	70	111	80	130	74	30
Alcoholic beverages	14	28	17	21	17	6
Housing	291	359	321	508	254	208
Housekeeping supplies	39	38	43	54	42	32
Household textiles	13	24	13	16	14	15
Appliances and misc. housewares	28	22	31	49	28	25
Major appliances	8	6	8	6	9	7
Small appliances and misc. housewares	21	16	23	42	19	18
Miscellaneous household equipment	70	94	78	132	57	58
Other housing	140	180	155	258	112	78
Apparel and services	244	250	275	320	280	164
Males, aged 2 or older	68	68	76	84	84	49
Females, aged 2 or older	85	77	94	113	100	57
Children under age 2	41	59	46	52	42	20
Other apparel products and services	51	45	59	71	53	39
Jewelry and watches	20	18	22	30	20	23
All other apparel products and services	30	27	37	41	34	15
Transportation	70	113	84	163	51	33
Health care	38	26	22	35	15	115
Entertainment	94	189	97	131	93	66
Toys, games, hobbies, and tricycles	30	37	31	42	27	27
Other entertainment	64	152	67	89	66	39
Personal care products and services	19	12	24	21	25	6
Reading	2	4	2	3	1	3
Education	151	135	181	347	138	49
All other gifts	89	179	79	101	78	121

Note: Spending by category will not add to total spending because gift spending is also included in the preceding product and service categories and personal taxes are not included in the total. Note: (–) means sample is too small to make a reliable estimate.
Source: Bureau of Labor Statistics, 2000 Consumer Expenditure Surveys, Internet site www.bls.gov/cex/

Table 1.55 Indexed spending by occupation of householder, 2000

(indexed average annual spending of consumer units (CU) by product and service category and selected occupation of consumer unit reference person, 2000; index definition: an index of 100 is the average for all consumer units; an index of 132 means that spending by consumer units in that group is 32 percent above the average for all consumer units; an index of 68 indicates spending that is 32 percent below the average for all consumer units)

	total consumer units	self-employed	wage and salary workers total	wage and salary workers managers and professionals	wage and salary workers technical, sales, admin. support	retired
Average spending of CU, total	$38,045	$48,986	$41,875	$54,185	$37,354	$25,938
Average spending of CU, index	100	129	110	142	98	68
FOOD	100	119	108	126	99	71
Food at home	100	113	104	112	95	81
Cereals and bakery products	100	113	103	113	94	83
Cereals and cereal products	100	108	103	110	95	77
Bakery products	100	115	103	115	94	86
Meats, poultry, fish, and eggs	100	108	104	104	95	80
Beef	100	109	106	102	99	78
Pork	100	114	100	94	90	87
Other meats	100	108	103	104	95	78
Poultry	100	99	105	107	99	74
Fish and seafood	100	110	104	124	93	79
Eggs	100	112	103	94	91	91
Dairy products	100	114	102	112	95	85
Fresh milk and cream	100	119	101	101	96	86
Other dairy products	100	110	104	120	95	85
Fruits and vegetables	100	123	100	114	89	93
Fresh fruits	100	125	98	115	87	100
Fresh vegetables	100	125	100	114	87	92
Processed fruits	100	122	99	117	90	93
Processed vegetables	100	118	104	107	98	82
Other food at home	100	112	106	119	98	73
Sugar and other sweets	100	111	104	122	93	82
Fats and oils	100	122	101	104	92	88
Miscellaneous foods	100	109	108	124	100	69
Nonalcoholic beverages	100	112	106	108	98	71
Food prepared by CU on trips	100	133	108	160	90	75
Food away from home	100	127	114	145	105	58
ALCOHOLIC BEVERAGES	100	116	115	154	101	61
HOUSING	100	124	109	145	98	70
Shelter	100	120	112	149	100	62
Owned dwellings	100	135	112	166	90	64
Mortgage interest and charges	100	136	121	181	100	29
Property taxes	100	127	102	148	81	100
Maintenance, repair, insurance, other expenses	100	146	95	142	70	127
Rented dwellings	100	74	113	105	127	54
Other lodging	100	169	106	175	82	79
Utilities, fuels, and public services	100	121	103	118	98	88
Natural gas	100	101	102	120	94	101
Electricity	100	125	101	110	97	92
Fuel oil and other fuels	100	156	88	96	86	128
Telephone	100	119	108	126	103	70
Water and other public services	100	121	101	123	95	100

	total consumer units	self-employed	wage and salary workers			retired
			total	managers and professionals	technical, sales, admin. support	
Household services	100	139	106	171	90	84
Personal services	100	97	117	172	111	60
Other household services	100	177	96	171	72	106
Housekeeping supplies	100	121	104	133	92	90
Laundry and cleaning supplies	100	92	108	124	91	75
Other household products	100	131	103	133	93	88
Postage and stationery	100	133	99	143	90	110
Household furnishings and equipment	100	138	109	163	90	68
Household textiles	100	153	108	150	86	76
Furniture	100	102	116	184	92	52
Floor coverings	100	86	116	186	114	75
Major appliances	100	125	101	121	101	94
Small appliances, misc. housewares	100	144	108	153	100	66
Miscellaneous household equipment	100	161	108	164	84	69
APPAREL AND RELATED SERVICES	100	108	115	148	103	50
Men and boys	100	109	118	146	101	41
Men, aged 16 or older	100	114	117	148	99	47
Boys, aged 2 to 15	100	92	124	138	106	20
Women and girls	100	101	113	150	106	60
Women, aged 16 or older	100	103	112	153	104	66
Girls, aged 2 to 15	100	88	119	134	119	25
Children under age 2	100	109	117	122	109	28
Footwear	100	103	114	129	106	46
Other apparel products and services	100	129	117	176	94	50
TRANSPORTATION	100	118	115	136	105	59
Vehicle purchases	100	114	117	132	108	55
Cars and trucks, new	100	134	114	158	100	61
Cars and trucks, used	100	97	119	108	116	50
Other vehicles	100	88	123	130	79	–
Gasoline and motor oil	100	122	113	123	105	59
Other vehicle expenses	100	119	114	143	104	62
Vehicle finance charges	100	100	122	133	121	40
Maintenance and repairs	100	125	110	132	98	72
Vehicle insurance	100	108	110	125	106	74
Vehicle rentals, leases, licenses, other charges	100	137	119	185	97	45
Public transportation	100	128	107	171	87	86
HEALTH CARE	100	146	84	106	76	154
Health insurance	100	156	83	102	76	161
Medical services	100	145	93	128	81	118
Drugs	100	131	72	83	67	191
Medical supplies	100	124	93	125	84	131
ENTERTAINMENT	100	130	113	152	98	59
Fees and admissions	100	143	111	183	89	66
Television, radio, sound equipment	100	115	111	135	104	64
Pets, toys, and playground equipment	100	149	111	140	96	57
Other entertainment products and services	100	120	119	146	103	45

	total consumer units	self-employed	wage and salary workers			retired
			total	managers and professionals	technical, sales, admin. support	
PERSONAL CARE PRODUCTS AND SERVICES	100	111	109	133	104	76
READING	100	132	104	160	92	97
EDUCATION	100	95	122	182	119	19
TOBACCO PRODUCTS AND SMOKING SUPPLIES	100	102	108	72	107	56
MISCELLANEOUS	100	173	104	124	96	78
CASH CONTRIBUTIONS	100	174	90	149	67	141
PERSONAL INSURANCE AND PENSIONS	100	174	126	187	101	18
Life and other personal insurance	100	171	102	152	81	85
Pensions and Social Security	100	175	129	192	104	9
PERSONAL TAXES	100	131	125	221	85	28
Federal income taxes	100	137	126	228	84	24
State and local income taxes	100	98	131	215	93	17
Other taxes	100	162	91	138	68	143
GIFTS	100	130	109	164	95	74
Food	100	159	114	186	106	43
Alcoholic beverages	100	200	121	150	121	43
Housing	100	123	110	175	87	71
Housekeeping supplies	100	97	110	138	108	82
Household textiles	100	185	100	123	108	115
Appliances and misc. housewares	100	79	111	175	100	89
Major appliances	100	75	100	75	113	88
Small appliances and misc. housewares	100	76	110	200	90	86
Miscellaneous household equipment	100	134	111	189	81	83
Other housing	100	129	111	184	80	56
Apparel and services	100	102	113	131	115	67
Males, aged 2 or older	100	100	112	124	124	72
Females, aged 2 or older	100	91	111	133	118	67
Children under age 2	100	144	112	127	102	49
Other apparel products and services	100	88	116	139	104	76
Jewelry and watches	100	90	110	150	100	115
All other apparel products and services	100	90	123	137	113	50
Transportation	100	161	120	233	73	47
Health care	100	68	58	92	39	303
Entertainment	100	201	103	139	99	70
Toys, games, hobbies, and tricycles	100	123	103	140	90	90
Other entertainment	100	238	105	139	103	61
Personal care products and services	100	63	126	111	132	32
Reading	100	200	100	150	50	150
Education	100	89	120	230	91	32
All other gifts	100	201	89	113	88	136

Note: (–) means sample is too small to make a reliable estimate.
Source: Calculations by New Strategist based on the Bureau of Labor Statistics 2000 Consumer Expenditure Survey

CHAPTER

2

Spending on Apparel, 2000

Americans spend less on apparel than they once did. In 2000, the average household spent 13 percent less on apparel than in 1990, after adjusting for inflation. Overall, Americans devoted 4.9 percent of their spending dollars to clothes, shoes, and related products and services in 2000, down from 5.7 percent in 1990.

Households headed by people aged 35 to 54 spend the most on apparel, more than $2,300 in 2000. Those aged 35 to 44 spend the most on boys' and girls' apparel. Those aged 45 to 54 spend the most on men's and women's clothes.

Affluent households spend much more on apparel, accessories, and related services than the average household. Households with incomes of $70,000 or more spent an average of more than $4,000 on clothes in 2000, cumulatively accounting for 38 percent of the market. Affluent households are particularly important consumers of men's suits (56 percent of the market), watches (54 percent), jewelry (52 percent), and professional dry cleaning (54 percent).

Married couples with school-aged children spend more on clothes and related products than any other household type, $2,838 in 2000. In part, this is because these households are larger than average. After adjusting for household size, single-person households and married couples without children at home spend the most on apparel.

On apparel, blacks spend almost as much as whites, and Hispanics outspend non-Hispanics. Black households spent 8 percent less than the average household on apparel in 2000, while Hispanics spent 12 percent more. Blacks are the biggest spenders on men's suits, boys' clothes, and professional laundry and dry cleaning. Hispanics are the biggest spenders on girls' clothes and infants' apparel. They are also the biggest spenders on footwear.

Spending on apparel is greatest in the Northeast, where households spend an average of $2,115 on clothes in 2000—14 percent more than the average household. Apparel spending is 13 percent below average in the South. Not surprisingly, spending on coats and jackets is much higher in the Northeast than in the South. Spending on uniforms is well above average in the South.

Table 2.1 Apparel: Average spending by age, 2000

(average annual spending of consumer units (CU) on apparel, accessories, and related services, by age of consumer unit reference person, 2000)

	total consumer units	under 25	25 to 34	35 to 44	45 to 54	55 to 64	65 to 74	75+
Number of consumer units								
(in thousands, add 000)	109,367	8,306	18,887	23,983	21,874	14,161	11,538	10,617
Average number of persons per CU	2.5	1.9	2.9	3.3	2.7	2.1	1.9	1.5
Average before-tax income of CU	$44,649.00	$19,744.00	$45,498.00	$56,500.00	$58,889.00	$48,108.00	$29,349.00	$20,563.00
Average spending of CU, total	38,044.67	22,543.18	38,945.27	45,149.37	46,160.28	39,340.03	30,781.81	21,908.04
Apparel, average spending	1,856.16	1,420.27	2,059.39	2,323.09	2,370.78	1,693.67	1,129.73	700.91
MEN'S APPAREL	**$344.29**	**$293.54**	**$368.17**	**$367.18**	**$482.26**	**$352.42**	**$240.01**	**$107.68**
Suits	33.23	15.97	36.01	43.25	49.50	23.73	24.13	8.25
Sport coats and tailored jackets	11.31	6.47	7.72	13.80	17.08	11.75	12.39	2.19
Coats and jackets	34.76	50.50	31.89	30.84	47.31	32.19	41.26	6.99
Underwear	17.45	21.07	14.45	17.46	26.87	14.80	13.21	8.95
Hosiery	11.50	10.29	13.12	11.98	17.32	9.96	5.79	4.83
Nightwear	3.34	1.84	2.78	4.47	4.19	3.72	2.82	1.30
Accessories	23.29	15.64	34.24	21.51	31.02	24.84	10.26	10.07
Sweaters and vests	15.96	15.94	14.66	18.52	21.62	16.05	11.99	5.07
Active sportswear	16.11	9.75	16.31	16.92	27.96	20.67	3.25	2.63
Shirts	85.47	66.57	97.84	87.01	105.17	106.48	62.63	30.16
Pants	68.65	60.98	73.28	76.22	99.11	67.93	37.75	20.62
Shorts and shorts sets	13.64	12.01	16.10	14.59	21.15	11.50	6.79	3.22
Uniforms	5.52	4.17	6.68	6.21	9.19	3.89	2.26	1.16
Costumes	4.06	2.33	3.08	4.42	4.79	4.91	5.48	2.23
BOYS' (AGED 2 TO 15) APPAREL	**95.76**	**26.43**	**143.11**	**183.97**	**94.51**	**42.49**	**28.80**	**9.17**
Coats and jackets	7.84	2.32	9.42	15.48	10.09	2.72	2.25	0.39
Sweaters	3.56	0.64	3.31	7.17	4.42	1.98	1.99	0.14
Shirts	20.84	3.98	41.25	33.56	18.36	9.55	6.46	2.78
Underwear	5.09	0.95	8.55	8.63	4.81	2.85	0.53	2.29
Nightwear	2.95	3.56	5.37	2.78	3.37	2.42	1.30	–
Hosiery	4.30	2.88	7.12	8.16	3.42	1.44	0.81	0.49
Accessories	4.40	0.84	6.47	9.32	4.12	1.41	0.68	0.44
Suits, sport coats, and vests	3.64	0.32	3.34	7.57	4.53	1.70	2.29	0.09
Pants	23.39	4.79	32.91	50.63	21.84	8.60	6.01	1.32
Shorts and shorts sets	8.95	4.11	13.47	18.51	6.88	4.55	2.13	0.65
Uniforms	3.66	0.35	3.48	7.75	4.37	2.52	0.96	0.30
Active sportswear	3.81	0.13	3.73	8.65	3.91	1.83	2.12	0.15
Costumes	3.33	1.57	4.69	5.76	4.38	0.92	1.26	0.12
WOMEN'S APPAREL	**607.11**	**404.61**	**560.52**	**692.30**	**850.16**	**629.95**	**420.95**	**330.73**
Coats and jackets	43.26	10.79	43.32	53.55	60.57	35.94	16.78	49.45
Dresses	86.74	64.35	66.32	78.35	138.60	91.48	73.53	65.83
Sport coats and tailored jackets	8.33	3.64	7.48	7.86	12.08	13.09	5.74	3.29
Sweaters and vests	49.27	45.14	43.83	57.79	62.41	48.78	35.14	31.36
Shirts, blouses, and tops	99.26	64.51	102.91	114.39	136.22	109.86	64.95	32.28
Skirts	12.76	11.15	11.07	11.77	21.13	17.17	6.87	2.80
Pants	85.55	67.05	89.55	100.09	119.09	86.21	41.50	37.04
Shorts and shorts sets	20.40	14.89	24.60	26.37	26.67	20.28	4.73	7.19
Active sportswear	27.78	17.07	25.65	30.17	45.39	24.81	14.44	17.73

	total consumer units	under 25	25 to 34	35 to 44	45 to 54	55 to 64	65 to 74	75+
Nightwear	$32.21	$27.88	$27.31	$28.82	$42.04	$39.67	$41.52	$12.57
Undergarments	32.20	23.08	30.68	41.03	39.33	29.02	30.25	13.23
Hosiery	20.95	12.70	19.37	23.32	30.40	21.66	16.94	9.13
Suits	33.80	15.84	26.30	34.51	49.74	37.38	34.74	20.94
Accessories	39.29	15.01	27.79	65.15	44.90	40.10	22.28	24.25
Uniforms	8.69	7.89	8.21	10.28	13.53	7.95	5.12	1.45
Costumes	6.63	3.60	6.14	8.86	8.06	6.55	6.43	2.20
GIRLS' (AGED 2 TO 15) APPAREL	**118.09**	**30.82**	**143.73**	**242.44**	**126.45**	**56.67**	**30.55**	**12.16**
Coats and jackets	6.95	2.88	8.67	13.11	6.82	4.76	2.89	0.81
Dresses and suits	18.19	1.01	24.56	44.64	12.80	6.85	1.63	1.52
Shirts, blouses, and sweaters	28.79	5.46	30.73	55.88	34.03	19.59	7.97	3.85
Skirts and pants	21.75	7.89	27.72	44.73	22.07	8.87	7.86	1.72
Shorts and shorts sets	8.35	3.33	12.65	16.17	8.11	3.39	2.02	0.92
Active sportswear	8.97	5.18	10.65	16.33	12.62	2.97	0.42	1.38
Underwear and nightwear	7.40	1.99	9.39	14.51	8.48	3.76	2.10	0.46
Hosiery	4.92	0.97	6.22	9.85	5.17	0.98	3.21	0.66
Accessories	4.98	0.43	5.18	9.64	6.79	3.01	1.01	0.53
Uniforms	3.90	1.17	4.38	8.80	4.86	0.46	0.62	0.30
Costumes	3.87	0.50	3.57	8.78	4.70	2.03	0.82	–
CHILDREN UNDER AGE 2	**81.92**	**100.54**	**165.19**	**105.33**	**54.36**	**53.40**	**31.41**	**7.78**
Coats, jackets, and snowsuits	2.70	2.68	4.55	3.16	2.32	2.60	1.41	0.69
Outerwear including dresses	22.97	22.39	39.68	23.36	21.13	25.79	12.52	4.18
Underwear	44.65	59.83	101.12	60.63	23.92	18.58	12.95	1.46
Nightwear and loungewear	3.99	4.54	6.51	4.27	3.97	3.63	2.08	1.02
Accessories	7.61	11.10	13.33	13.90	3.03	2.81	2.45	0.44
FOOTWEAR	**343.09**	**362.97**	**393.88**	**400.66**	**437.65**	**300.03**	**185.57**	**130.47**
Men's	117.55	152.94	145.79	114.60	158.85	107.11	55.94	39.68
Boys'	37.26	14.80	55.90	75.24	28.70	23.28	4.59	1.91
Women's	155.95	182.18	151.04	148.92	214.36	156.86	114.58	84.37
Girls'	32.33	13.04	41.15	61.90	35.74	12.78	10.46	4.51
OTHER APPAREL PRODUCTS AND SERVICES	**265.90**	**201.36**	**284.78**	**331.21**	**325.39**	**258.70**	**192.44**	**102.91**
Material for making clothes	4.75	0.35	4.08	4.81	6.51	4.20	8.30	2.89
Sewing patterns and notions	4.69	0.48	2.11	4.98	7.24	6.01	8.45	1.19
Watches	22.63	21.22	20.53	27.97	26.19	27.70	7.64	17.60
Jewelry	107.32	69.53	105.79	142.69	138.34	95.02	84.05	37.50
Shoe repair and other shoe services	1.83	0.45	1.32	2.23	2.75	2.21	1.72	0.60
Coin-operated apparel laundry and dry cleaning	37.93	75.02	67.14	39.38	29.56	20.38	18.75	15.15
Apparel alteration, repair, and tailoring services	5.70	2.36	5.78	5.22	8.14	5.29	5.63	4.81
Clothing rental	3.37	1.82	3.30	5.82	2.80	5.17	1.28	0.27
Watch and jewelry repair	4.74	1.93	2.55	4.39	6.29	6.88	7.61	2.42
Professional laundry, dry cleaning	72.40	27.83	71.51	93.38	96.58	85.42	48.50	20.20
Clothing storage	0.55	0.37	0.67	0.34	0.98	0.42	0.51	0.28

Note: (–) means sample is too small to make a reliable estimate.
Source: Bureau of Labor Statistics, unpublished data from the 2000 Consumer Expenditure Survey

Table 2.2 Apparel: Indexed spending by age, 2000

(indexed average annual spending of consumer units (CU) on apparel, accessories, and related services, by age of consumer unit reference person, 2000; index definition: an index of 100 is the average for all consumer units; an index of 132 means that spending by consumer units in that group is 32 percent above the average for all consumer units; an index of 68 indicates spending that is 32 percent below the average for all consumer units)

	total consumer units	under 25	25 to 34	35 to 44	45 to 54	55 to 64	65 to 74	75+
Average spending of CU, total	$38,045	$22,543	$38,945	$45,149	$46,160	$39,340	$30,782	$21,908
Average spending of CU, index	100	59	102	119	121	103	81	58
Apparel, spending index	100	77	111	125	128	91	61	38
MEN'S APPAREL	100	85	107	107	140	102	70	31
Suits	100	48	108	130	149	71	73	25
Sport coats and tailored jackets	100	57	68	122	151	104	110	19
Coats and jackets	100	145	92	89	136	93	119	20
Underwear	100	121	83	100	154	85	76	51
Hosiery	100	89	114	104	151	87	50	42
Nightwear	100	55	83	134	125	111	84	39
Accessories	100	67	147	92	133	107	44	43
Sweaters and vests	100	100	92	116	135	101	75	32
Active sportswear	100	61	101	105	174	128	20	16
Shirts	100	78	114	102	123	125	73	35
Pants	100	89	107	111	144	99	55	30
Shorts and shorts sets	100	88	118	107	155	84	50	24
Uniforms	100	76	121	113	166	70	41	21
Costumes	100	57	76	109	118	121	135	55
BOYS' (AGED 2 TO 15) APPAREL	100	28	149	192	99	44	30	10
Coats and jackets	100	30	120	197	129	35	29	5
Sweaters	100	18	93	201	124	56	56	4
Shirts	100	19	198	161	88	46	31	13
Underwear	100	19	168	170	94	56	10	45
Nightwear	100	121	182	94	114	82	44	–
Hosiery	100	67	166	190	80	33	19	11
Accessories	100	19	147	212	94	32	15	10
Suits, sport coats, and vests	100	9	92	208	124	47	63	2
Pants	100	20	141	216	93	37	26	6
Shorts and shorts sets	100	46	151	207	77	51	24	7
Uniforms	100	10	95	212	119	69	26	8
Active sportswear	100	3	98	227	103	48	56	4
Costumes	100	47	141	173	132	28	38	4
WOMEN'S APPAREL	100	67	92	114	140	104	69	54
Coats and jackets	100	25	100	124	140	83	39	114
Dresses	100	74	76	90	160	105	85	76
Sport coats and tailored jackets	100	44	90	94	145	157	69	39
Sweaters and vests	100	92	89	117	127	99	71	64
Shirts, blouses, and tops	100	65	104	115	137	111	65	33
Skirts	100	87	87	92	166	135	54	22
Pants	100	78	105	117	139	101	49	43
Shorts and shorts sets	100	73	121	129	131	99	23	35
Active sportswear	100	61	92	109	163	89	52	64

	total consumer units	under 25	25 to 34	35 to 44	45 to 54	55 to 64	65 to 74	75+
Nightwear	100	87	85	89	131	123	129	39
Undergarments	100	72	95	127	122	90	94	41
Hosiery	100	61	92	111	145	103	81	44
Suits	100	47	78	102	147	111	103	62
Accessories	100	38	71	166	114	102	57	62
Uniforms	100	91	94	118	156	91	59	17
Costumes	100	54	93	134	122	99	97	33
GIRLS' (AGED 2 TO 15) APPAREL	**100**	**26**	**122**	**205**	**107**	**48**	**26**	**10**
Coats and jackets	100	41	125	189	98	68	42	12
Dresses and suits	100	6	135	245	70	38	9	8
Shirts, blouses, and sweaters	100	19	107	194	118	68	28	13
Skirts and pants	100	36	127	206	101	41	36	8
Shorts and shorts sets	100	40	151	194	97	41	24	11
Active sportswear	100	58	119	182	141	33	5	15
Underwear and nightwear	100	27	127	196	115	51	28	6
Hosiery	100	20	126	200	105	20	65	13
Accessories	100	9	104	194	136	60	20	11
Uniforms	100	30	112	226	125	12	16	8
Costumes	100	13	92	227	121	52	21	–
CHILDREN UNDER AGE 2	**100**	**123**	**202**	**129**	**66**	**65**	**38**	**9**
Coats, jackets, and snowsuits	100	99	169	117	86	96	52	26
Outerwear including dresses	100	97	173	102	92	112	55	18
Underwear	100	134	226	136	54	42	29	3
Nightwear and loungewear	100	114	163	107	99	91	52	26
Accessories	100	146	175	183	40	37	32	6
FOOTWEAR	**100**	**106**	**115**	**117**	**128**	**87**	**54**	**38**
Men's	100	130	124	97	135	91	48	34
Boys'	100	40	150	202	77	62	12	5
Women's	100	117	97	95	137	101	73	54
Girls'	100	40	127	191	111	40	32	14
OTHER APPAREL PRODUCTS AND SERVICES	**100**	**76**	**107**	**125**	**122**	**97**	**72**	**39**
Material for making clothes	100	7	86	101	137	88	175	61
Sewing patterns and notions	100	10	45	106	154	128	180	25
Watches	100	94	91	124	116	122	34	78
Jewelry	100	65	99	133	129	89	78	35
Shoe repair and other shoe services	100	25	72	122	150	121	94	33
Coin-operated apparel laundry and dry cleaning	100	198	177	104	78	54	49	40
Apparel alteration, repair, and tailoring services	100	41	101	92	143	93	99	84
Clothing rental	100	54	98	173	83	153	38	8
Watch and jewelry repair	100	41	54	93	133	145	161	51
Professional laundry, dry cleaning	100	38	99	129	133	118	67	28
Clothing storage	100	67	122	62	178	76	93	51

Note: (–) means sample is too small to make a reliable estimate.
Source: Calculations by New Strategist based on the 2000 Consumer Expenditure Survey

Table 2.3 Apparel: Indexed per capita spending by age, 2000

(indexed average annual per capita spending of consumer units (CU) on apparel, accessories, and related services, by age of consumer unit reference person, 2000; index definition: an index of 100 is the average for all consumer units; an index of 132 means that spending by consumer units in that group is 32 percent above the average for all consumer units; an index of 68 indicates spending that is 32 percent below the average for all consumer units)

	total consumer units	under 25	25 to 34	35 to 44	45 to 54	55 to 64	65 to 74	75+
Per capita spending of CU, total	$15,218	$11,865	$13,429	$13,682	$17,096	$18,733	$16,201	$14,605
Per capita spending of CU, index	100	78	88	90	112	123	106	96
Apparel, per capita spending index	100	101	96	95	118	109	80	63
MEN'S APPAREL	**100**	**112**	**92**	**81**	**130**	**122**	**92**	**52**
Suits	100	63	93	99	138	85	96	41
Sport coats and tailored jackets	100	75	59	92	140	124	144	32
Coats and jackets	100	191	79	67	126	110	156	34
Underwear	100	159	71	76	143	101	100	85
Hosiery	100	118	98	79	139	103	66	70
Nightwear	100	72	72	101	116	133	111	65
Accessories	100	88	127	70	123	127	58	72
Sweaters and vests	100	131	79	88	125	120	99	53
Active sportswear	100	80	87	80	161	153	27	27
Shirts	100	102	99	77	114	148	96	59
Pants	100	117	92	84	134	118	72	50
Shorts and shorts sets	100	116	102	81	144	100	66	39
Uniforms	100	99	104	85	154	84	54	35
Costumes	100	76	65	82	109	144	178	92
BOYS' (AGED 2 TO 15) APPAREL	**100**	**36**	**129**	**146**	**91**	**53**	**40**	**16**
Coats and jackets	100	39	104	150	119	41	38	8
Sweaters	100	24	80	153	115	66	74	7
Shirts	100	25	171	122	82	55	41	22
Underwear	100	25	145	128	87	67	14	75
Nightwear	100	159	157	71	106	98	58	–
Hosiery	100	88	143	144	74	40	25	19
Accessories	100	25	127	160	87	38	20	17
Suits, sport coats, and vests	100	12	79	158	115	56	83	4
Pants	100	27	121	164	86	44	34	9
Shorts and shorts sets	100	60	130	157	71	61	31	12
Uniforms	100	13	82	160	111	82	35	14
Active sportswear	100	4	84	172	95	57	73	7
Costumes	100	62	121	131	122	33	50	6
WOMEN'S APPAREL	**100**	**88**	**80**	**86**	**130**	**124**	**91**	**91**
Coats and jackets	100	33	86	94	130	99	51	191
Dresses	100	98	66	68	148	126	112	126
Sport coats and tailored jackets	100	57	77	71	134	187	91	66
Sweaters and vests	100	121	77	89	117	118	94	106
Shirts, blouses, and tops	100	86	89	87	127	132	86	54
Skirts	100	115	75	70	153	160	71	37
Pants	100	103	90	89	129	120	64	72
Shorts and shorts sets	100	96	104	98	121	118	31	59
Active sportswear	100	81	80	82	151	106	68	106

	total consumer units	under 25	25 to 34	35 to 44	45 to 54	55 to 64	65 to 74	75+
Nightwear	100	114	73	68	121	147	170	65
Undergarments	100	94	82	97	113	107	124	68
Hosiery	100	80	80	84	134	123	106	73
Suits	100	62	67	77	136	132	135	103
Accessories	100	50	61	126	106	122	75	103
Uniforms	100	119	81	90	144	109	78	28
Costumes	100	71	80	101	113	118	128	55
GIRLS' (AGED 2 TO 15) APPAREL	**100**	**34**	**105**	**156**	**99**	**57**	**34**	**17**
Coats and jackets	100	55	108	143	91	82	55	19
Dresses and suits	100	7	116	186	65	45	12	14
Shirts, blouses, and sweaters	100	25	92	147	109	81	36	22
Skirts and pants	100	48	110	156	94	49	48	13
Shorts and shorts sets	100	52	131	147	90	48	32	18
Active sportswear	100	76	102	138	130	39	6	26
Underwear and nightwear	100	35	109	149	106	60	37	10
Hosiery	100	26	109	152	97	24	86	22
Accessories	100	11	90	147	126	72	27	18
Uniforms	100	39	97	171	115	14	21	13
Costumes	100	17	80	172	112	62	28	–
CHILDREN UNDER AGE 2	**100**	**161**	**174**	**97**	**61**	**78**	**50**	**16**
Coats, jackets, and snowsuits	100	131	145	89	80	115	69	43
Outerwear including dresses	100	128	149	77	85	134	72	30
Underwear	100	176	195	103	50	50	38	5
Nightwear and loungewear	100	150	141	81	92	108	69	43
Accessories	100	192	151	138	37	44	42	10
FOOTWEAR	**100**	**139**	**99**	**88**	**118**	**104**	**71**	**63**
Men's	100	171	107	74	125	108	63	56
Boys'	100	52	129	153	71	74	16	9
Women's	100	154	83	72	127	120	97	90
Girls'	100	53	110	145	102	47	43	23
OTHER APPAREL PRODUCTS AND SERVICES	**100**	**100**	**92**	**94**	**113**	**116**	**95**	**65**
Material for making clothes	100	10	74	77	127	105	230	101
Sewing patterns and notions	100	13	39	80	143	153	237	42
Watches	100	123	78	94	107	146	44	130
Jewelry	100	85	85	101	119	105	103	58
Shoe repair and other shoe services	100	32	62	92	139	144	124	55
Coin-operated apparel laundry and dry cleaning	100	260	153	79	72	64	65	67
Apparel alteration, repair, and tailoring services	100	54	87	69	132	110	130	141
Clothing rental	100	71	84	131	77	183	50	13
Watch and jewelry repair	100	54	46	70	123	173	211	85
Professional laundry, dry cleaning	100	51	85	98	124	140	88	47
Clothing storage	100	89	105	47	165	91	122	85

Note: Per capita indexes account for household size and show how much each person in a particular household demographic segment spends relative to a person in the average household. (–) means sample is too small to make a reliable estimate.
Source: Calculations by New Strategist based on the 2000 Consumer Expenditure Survey

Table 2.4 Apparel: Total spending by age, 2000

(total annual spending on apparel, accessories, and related services, by consumer unit (CU) age group, 2000; numbers in thousands)

	total consumer units	under 25	25 to 34	35 to 44	45 to 54	55 to 64	65 to 74	75+
Number of consumer units	109,367	8,306	18,887	23,983	21,874	14,161	11,538	10,617
Total spending of all CUs	$4,160,831,424	$187,243,653	$735,559,314	$1,082,817,341	$1,009,709,965	$557,094,165	$355,160,524	$232,597,661
Apparel, total spending	203,002,651	11,796,763	38,895,699	55,714,667	51,858,442	23,984,061	13,034,825	7,441,561
MEN'S APPAREL	**$37,653,964**	**$2,438,143**	**$6,953,627**	**$8,806,078**	**$10,548,955**	**$4,990,620**	**$2,769,235**	**$1,143,239**
Suits	3,634,265	132,647	680,121	1,037,265	1,082,763	336,041	278,412	87,590
Sport coats and tailored jackets	1,236,941	53,740	145,808	330,965	373,608	166,392	142,956	23,251
Coats and jackets	3,801,597	419,453	602,306	739,636	1,034,859	455,843	476,058	74,213
Underwear	1,908,454	175,007	272,917	418,743	587,754	209,583	152,417	95,022
Hosiery	1,257,721	85,469	247,797	287,316	378,858	141,044	66,805	51,280
Nightwear	365,286	15,283	52,506	107,204	91,652	52,679	32,537	13,802
Accessories	2,547,157	129,906	646,691	515,874	678,531	351,759	118,380	106,913
Sweaters and vests	1,745,497	132,398	276,883	444,165	472,916	227,284	138,341	53,828
Active sportswear	1,761,902	80,984	308,047	405,792	611,597	292,708	37,499	27,923
Shirts	9,347,597	552,930	1,847,904	2,086,761	2,300,489	1,507,863	722,625	320,209
Pants	7,508,045	506,500	1,384,039	1,827,984	2,167,932	961,957	435,560	218,923
Shorts and shorts sets	1,491,766	99,755	304,081	349,912	462,635	162,852	78,343	34,187
Uniforms	603,706	34,636	126,165	148,934	201,022	55,086	26,076	12,316
Costumes	444,030	19,353	58,172	106,005	104,776	69,531	63,228	23,676
BOYS' (AGED 2 TO 15) APPAREL	**10,472,984**	**219,528**	**2,702,919**	**4,412,153**	**2,067,312**	**601,701**	**332,294**	**97,358**
Coats and jackets	857,437	19,270	177,916	371,257	220,709	38,518	25,961	4,141
Sweaters	389,347	5,316	62,516	171,958	96,683	28,039	22,961	1,486
Shirts	2,279,208	33,058	779,089	804,869	401,607	135,238	74,535	29,515
Underwear	556,678	7,891	161,484	206,973	105,214	40,359	6,115	24,313
Nightwear	322,633	29,569	101,423	66,673	73,715	34,270	14,999	–
Hosiery	470,278	23,921	134,475	195,701	74,809	20,392	9,346	5,202
Accessories	481,215	6,977	122,199	223,522	90,121	19,967	7,846	4,671
Suits, sport coats, and vests	398,096	2,658	63,083	181,551	99,089	24,074	26,422	956
Pants	2,558,094	39,786	621,571	1,214,259	477,728	121,785	69,343	14,014
Shorts and shorts sets	978,835	34,138	254,408	443,925	150,493	64,433	24,576	6,901
Uniforms	400,283	2,907	65,727	185,868	95,589	35,686	11,076	3,185
Active sportswear	416,688	1,080	70,449	207,453	85,527	25,915	24,461	1,593
Costumes	364,192	13,040	88,580	138,142	95,808	13,028	14,538	1,274
WOMEN'S APPAREL	**66,397,799**	**3,360,691**	**10,586,541**	**16,603,431**	**18,596,400**	**8,920,722**	**4,856,921**	**3,511,360**
Coats and jackets	4,731,216	89,622	818,185	1,284,290	1,324,908	508,946	193,608	525,011
Dresses	9,486,494	534,491	1,252,586	1,879,068	3,031,736	1,295,448	848,389	698,917
Sport coats and tailored jackets	911,027	30,234	141,275	188,506	264,238	185,367	66,228	34,930
Sweaters and vests	5,388,512	374,933	827,817	1,385,978	1,365,156	690,774	405,445	332,949
Shirts, blouses, and tops	10,855,768	535,820	1,943,661	2,743,415	2,979,676	1,555,727	749,393	342,717
Skirts	1,395,523	92,612	209,079	282,280	462,198	243,144	79,266	29,728
Pants	9,356,347	556,917	1,691,331	2,400,458	2,604,975	1,220,820	478,827	393,254
Shorts and shorts sets	2,231,087	123,676	464,620	632,432	583,380	287,185	54,575	76,336
Active sportswear	3,038,215	141,783	484,452	723,567	992,861	351,334	166,609	188,239

	total consumer units	under 25	25 to 34	35 to 44	45 to 54	55 to 64	65 to 74	75+
Nightwear	$3,522,711	$231,571	$515,804	$691,190	$919,583	$561,767	$479,058	$133,456
Undergarments	3,521,617	191,702	579,453	984,022	860,304	410,952	349,025	140,463
Hosiery	2,291,239	105,486	365,841	559,284	664,970	306,727	195,454	96,933
Suits	3,696,605	131,567	496,728	827,653	1,088,013	529,338	400,830	222,320
Accessories	4,297,029	124,673	524,870	1,562,492	982,143	567,856	257,067	257,462
Uniforms	950,399	65,534	155,062	246,545	295,955	112,580	59,075	15,395
Costumes	725,103	29,902	115,966	212,489	176,304	92,755	74,189	23,357
GIRLS' (AGED 2 TO 15) APPAREL	**12,915,149**	**255,991**	**2,714,629**	**5,814,439**	**2,765,967**	**802,504**	**352,486**	**129,103**
Coats and jackets	760,101	23,921	163,750	314,417	149,181	67,406	33,345	8,600
Dresses and suits	1,989,386	8,389	463,865	1,070,601	279,987	97,003	18,807	16,138
Shirts, blouses, and sweaters	3,148,676	45,351	580,398	1,340,170	744,372	277,414	91,958	40,875
Skirts and pants	2,378,732	65,534	523,548	1,072,760	482,759	125,608	90,689	18,261
Shorts and shorts sets	913,214	27,659	238,921	387,805	177,398	48,006	23,307	9,768
Active sportswear	981,022	43,025	201,147	391,642	276,050	42,058	4,846	14,651
Underwear and nightwear	809,316	16,529	177,349	347,993	185,492	53,245	24,230	4,884
Hosiery	538,086	8,057	117,477	236,233	113,089	13,878	37,037	7,007
Accessories	544,648	3,572	97,835	231,196	148,524	42,625	11,653	5,627
Uniforms	426,531	9,718	82,725	211,050	106,308	6,514	7,154	3,185
Costumes	423,250	4,153	67,427	210,571	102,808	28,747	9,461	–
CHILDREN UNDER AGE 2	**8,959,345**	**835,085**	**3,119,944**	**2,526,129**	**1,189,071**	**756,197**	**362,409**	**82,600**
Coats, jackets, and snowsuits	295,291	22,260	85,936	75,786	50,748	36,819	16,269	7,326
Outerwear including dresses	2,512,160	185,971	749,436	560,243	462,198	365,212	144,456	44,379
Underwear	4,883,237	496,948	1,909,853	1,454,089	523,226	263,111	149,417	15,501
Nightwear and loungewear	436,374	37,709	122,954	102,407	86,840	51,404	23,999	10,829
Accessories	832,283	92,197	251,764	333,364	66,278	39,792	28,268	4,671
FOOTWEAR	**37,522,724**	**3,014,829**	**7,439,212**	**9,609,029**	**9,573,156**	**4,248,725**	**2,141,107**	**1,385,200**
Men's	12,856,091	1,270,320	2,753,536	2,748,452	3,474,685	1,516,785	645,436	421,283
Boys'	4,075,014	122,929	1,055,783	1,804,481	627,784	329,668	52,959	20,278
Women's	17,055,784	1,513,187	2,852,692	3,571,548	4,688,911	2,221,294	1,322,024	895,756
Girls'	3,535,835	108,310	777,200	1,484,548	781,777	180,978	120,687	47,883
OTHER APPAREL PRODUCTS AND SERVICES	**29,080,685**	**1,672,496**	**5,378,640**	**7,943,409**	**7,117,581**	**3,663,451**	**2,220,373**	**1,092,595**
Material for making clothes	519,493	2,907	77,059	115,358	142,400	59,476	95,765	30,683
Sewing patterns and notions	512,931	3,987	39,852	119,435	158,368	85,108	97,496	12,634
Watches	2,474,975	176,253	387,750	670,805	572,880	392,260	88,150	186,859
Jewelry	11,737,266	577,516	1,998,056	3,422,134	3,026,049	1,345,578	969,769	398,138
Shoe repair and other shoe services	200,142	3,738	24,931	53,482	60,154	31,296	19,845	6,370
Coin-operated apparel laundry and dry cleaning	4,148,290	623,116	1,268,073	944,451	646,595	288,601	216,338	160,848
Apparel alteration, repair, and tailoring services	623,392	19,602	109,167	125,191	178,054	74,912	64,959	51,068
Clothing rental	368,567	15,117	62,327	139,581	61,247	73,212	14,769	2,867
Watch and jewelry repair	518,400	16,031	48,162	105,285	137,587	97,428	87,804	25,693
Professional laundry, dry cleaning	7,918,171	231,156	1,350,609	2,239,533	2,112,591	1,209,633	559,593	214,463
Clothing storage	60,152	3,073	12,654	8,154	21,437	5,948	5,884	2,973

Note: Numbers may not add to total because of rounding. (–) means sample is too small to make a reliable estimate.
Source: Calculations by New Strategist based on the 2000 Consumer Expenditure Survey

Table 2.5 Apparel: Market shares by age, 2000

(percentage of total annual spending on apparel, accessories, and related services accounted for by consumer unit age groups, 2000)

	total consumer units	under 25	25 to 34	35 to 44	45 to 54	55 to 64	65 to 74	75+
Share of total consumer units	100.0%	7.6%	17.3%	21.9%	20.0%	12.9%	10.5%	9.7%
Share of total before-tax income	100.0	3.4	17.6	27.7	26.4	14.0	6.9	4.5
Share of total spending	100.0	4.5	17.7	26.0	24.3	13.4	8.5	5.6
Share of apparel spending	100.0	5.8	19.2	27.4	25.5	11.8	6.4	3.7
MEN'S APPAREL	**100.0%**	**6.5%**	**18.5%**	**23.4%**	**28.0%**	**13.3%**	**7.4%**	**3.0%**
Suits	100.0	3.6	18.7	28.5	29.8	9.2	7.7	2.4
Sport coats and tailored jackets	100.0	4.3	11.8	26.8	30.2	13.5	11.6	1.9
Coats and jackets	100.0	11.0	15.8	19.5	27.2	12.0	12.5	2.0
Underwear	100.0	9.2	14.3	21.9	30.8	11.0	8.0	5.0
Hosiery	100.0	6.8	19.7	22.8	30.1	11.2	5.3	4.1
Nightwear	100.0	4.2	14.4	29.3	25.1	14.4	8.9	3.8
Accessories	100.0	5.1	25.4	20.3	26.6	13.8	4.6	4.2
Sweaters and vests	100.0	7.6	15.9	25.4	27.1	13.0	7.9	3.1
Active sportswear	100.0	4.6	17.5	23.0	34.7	16.6	2.1	1.6
Shirts	100.0	5.9	19.8	22.3	24.6	16.1	7.7	3.4
Pants	100.0	6.7	18.4	24.3	28.9	12.8	5.8	2.9
Shorts and shorts sets	100.0	6.7	20.4	23.5	31.0	10.9	5.3	2.3
Uniforms	100.0	5.7	20.9	24.7	33.3	9.1	4.3	2.0
Costumes	100.0	4.4	13.1	23.9	23.6	15.7	14.2	5.3
BOYS' (AGED 2 TO 15) APPAREL	**100.0**	**2.1**	**25.8**	**42.1**	**19.7**	**5.7**	**3.2**	**0.9**
Coats and jackets	100.0	2.2	20.7	43.3	25.7	4.5	3.0	0.5
Sweaters	100.0	1.4	16.1	44.2	24.8	7.2	5.9	0.4
Shirts	100.0	1.5	34.2	35.3	17.6	5.9	3.3	1.3
Underwear	100.0	1.4	29.0	37.2	18.9	7.2	1.1	4.4
Nightwear	100.0	9.2	31.4	20.7	22.8	10.6	4.6	–
Hosiery	100.0	5.1	28.6	41.6	15.9	4.3	2.0	1.1
Accessories	100.0	1.4	25.4	46.4	18.7	4.1	1.6	1.0
Suits, sport coats, and vests	100.0	0.7	15.8	45.6	24.9	6.0	6.6	0.2
Pants	100.0	1.6	24.3	47.5	18.7	4.8	2.7	0.5
Shorts and shorts sets	100.0	3.5	26.0	45.4	15.4	6.6	2.5	0.7
Uniforms	100.0	0.7	16.4	46.4	23.9	8.9	2.8	0.8
Active sportswear	100.0	0.3	16.9	49.8	20.5	6.2	5.9	0.4
Costumes	100.0	3.6	24.3	37.9	26.3	3.6	4.0	0.3
WOMEN'S APPAREL	**100.0**	**5.1**	**15.9**	**25.0**	**28.0**	**13.4**	**7.3**	**5.3**
Coats and jackets	100.0	1.9	17.3	27.1	28.0	10.8	4.1	11.1
Dresses	100.0	5.6	13.2	19.8	32.0	13.7	8.9	7.4
Sport coats and tailored jackets	100.0	3.3	15.5	20.7	29.0	20.3	7.3	3.8
Sweaters and vests	100.0	7.0	15.4	25.7	25.3	12.8	7.5	6.2
Shirts, blouses, and tops	100.0	4.9	17.9	25.3	27.4	14.3	6.9	3.2
Skirts	100.0	6.6	15.0	20.2	33.1	17.4	5.7	2.1
Pants	100.0	6.0	18.1	25.7	27.8	13.0	5.1	4.2
Shorts and shorts sets	100.0	5.5	20.8	28.3	26.1	12.9	2.4	3.4
Active sportswear	100.0	4.7	15.9	23.8	32.7	11.6	5.5	6.2

	total consumer units	under 25	25 to 34	35 to 44	45 to 54	55 to 64	65 to 74	75+
Nightwear	100.0%	6.6%	14.6%	19.6%	26.1%	15.9%	13.6%	3.8%
Undergarments	100.0	5.4	16.5	27.9	24.4	11.7	9.9	4.0
Hosiery	100.0	4.6	16.0	24.4	29.0	13.4	8.5	4.2
Suits	100.0	3.6	13.4	22.4	29.4	14.3	10.8	6.0
Accessories	100.0	2.9	12.2	36.4	22.9	13.2	6.0	6.0
Uniforms	100.0	6.9	16.3	25.9	31.1	11.8	6.2	1.6
Costumes	100.0	4.1	16.0	29.3	24.3	12.8	10.2	3.2
GIRLS' (AGED 2 TO 15) APPAREL	**100.0**	**2.0**	**21.0**	**45.0**	**21.4**	**6.2**	**2.7**	**1.0**
Coats and jackets	100.0	3.1	21.5	41.4	19.6	8.9	4.4	1.1
Dresses and suits	100.0	0.4	23.3	53.8	14.1	4.9	0.9	0.8
Shirts, blouses, and sweaters	100.0	1.4	18.4	42.6	23.6	8.8	2.9	1.3
Skirts and pants	100.0	2.8	22.0	45.1	20.3	5.3	3.8	0.8
Shorts and shorts sets	100.0	3.0	26.2	42.5	19.4	5.3	2.6	1.1
Active sportswear	100.0	4.4	20.5	39.9	28.1	4.3	0.5	1.5
Underwear and nightwear	100.0	2.0	21.9	43.0	22.9	6.6	3.0	0.6
Hosiery	100.0	1.5	21.8	43.9	21.0	2.6	6.9	1.3
Accessories	100.0	0.7	18.0	42.4	27.3	7.8	2.1	1.0
Uniforms	100.0	2.3	19.4	49.5	24.9	1.5	1.7	0.7
Costumes	100.0	1.0	15.9	49.8	24.3	6.8	2.2	–
CHILDREN UNDER AGE 2	**100.0**	**9.3**	**34.8**	**28.2**	**13.3**	**8.4**	**4.0**	**0.9**
Coats, jackets, and snowsuits	100.0	7.5	29.1	25.7	17.2	12.5	5.5	2.5
Outerwear including dresses	100.0	7.4	29.8	22.3	18.4	14.5	5.8	1.8
Underwear	100.0	10.2	39.1	29.8	10.7	5.4	3.1	0.3
Nightwear and loungewear	100.0	8.6	28.2	23.5	19.9	11.8	5.5	2.5
Accessories	100.0	11.1	30.2	40.1	8.0	4.8	3.4	0.6
FOOTWEAR	**100.0**	**8.0**	**19.8**	**25.6**	**25.5**	**11.3**	**5.7**	**3.7**
Men's	100.0	9.9	21.4	21.4	27.0	11.8	5.0	3.3
Boys'	100.0	3.0	25.9	44.3	15.4	8.1	1.3	0.5
Women's	100.0	8.9	16.7	20.9	27.5	13.0	7.8	5.3
Girls'	100.0	3.1	22.0	42.0	22.1	5.1	3.4	1.4
OTHER APPAREL PRODUCTS AND SERVICES	**100.0**	**5.8**	**18.5**	**27.3**	**24.5**	**12.6**	**7.6**	**3.8**
Material for making clothes	100.0	0.6	14.8	22.2	27.4	11.4	18.4	5.9
Sewing patterns and notions	100.0	0.8	7.8	23.3	30.9	16.6	19.0	2.5
Watches	100.0	7.1	15.7	27.1	23.1	15.8	3.6	7.5
Jewelry	100.0	4.9	17.0	29.2	25.8	11.5	8.3	3.4
Shoe repair and other shoe services	100.0	1.9	12.5	26.7	30.1	15.6	9.9	3.2
Coin-operated apparel laundry and dry cleaning	100.0	15.0	30.6	22.8	15.6	7.0	5.2	3.9
Apparel alteration, repair, and tailoring services	100.0	3.1	17.5	20.1	28.6	12.0	10.4	8.2
Clothing rental	100.0	4.1	16.9	37.9	16.6	19.9	4.0	0.8
Watch and jewelry repair	100.0	3.1	9.3	20.3	26.5	18.8	16.9	5.0
Professional laundry, dry cleaning	100.0	2.9	17.1	28.3	26.7	15.3	7.1	2.7
Clothing storage	100.0	5.1	21.0	13.6	35.6	9.9	9.8	4.9

Note: Numbers may not add to total because of rounding. (–) means sample is too small to make a reliable estimate.
Source: Calculations by New Strategist based on the 2000 Consumer Expenditure Survey

Table 2.6   Apparel: Average spending by income, 2000

(average annual spending on apparel, accessories, and related services, by before-tax income of consumer unit (CU), 2000; complete income reporters only)

	complete income reporters	under $10,000	$10,000– $19,999	$20,000– $29,999	$30,000– $39,999	$40,000– $49,999	$50,000– $69,999	$70,000 or more
Number of consumer units (in thousands, add 000)	81,454	10,810	14,714	12,039	9,477	7,653	11,337	15,424
Average number of persons per CU	2.5	1.7	2.1	2.4	2.5	2.6	2.9	3.2
Average before-tax income of CU	$44,649.00	$5,739.61	$14,586.29	$24,527.00	$34,422.00	$44,201.00	$58,561.00	$112,586.00
Average spending of CU, total	40,238.44	16,455.72	22,620.20	29,851.59	35,609.24	42,323.03	49,245.37	75,963.85
Apparel, average spending	2,003.79	867.55	978.91	1,390.56	1,685.91	1,986.15	2,359.11	4,003.96
MEN'S APPAREL	**$382.42**	**$131.57**	**$174.76**	**$266.15**	**$309.23**	**$308.61**	**$461.02**	**$824.48**
Suits	35.23	11.32	10.56	15.29	18.83	27.16	37.67	103.36
Sport coats and tailored jackets	10.99	1.90	3.33	5.92	6.27	10.13	14.47	29.40
Coats and jackets	41.24	17.76	4.50	15.53	35.86	23.27	67.23	97.39
Underwear	18.86	10.80	7.15	15.91	15.01	22.67	23.09	33.33
Hosiery	12.91	4.95	6.16	11.35	13.09	10.36	14.67	24.19
Nightwear	3.65	1.25	2.77	1.90	2.34	5.90	3.71	7.19
Accessories	26.01	14.03	10.42	15.76	30.82	16.28	28.04	53.94
Sweaters and vests	14.33	4.79	5.91	10.20	12.75	13.57	17.82	31.03
Active sportswear	18.57	1.19	5.20	8.29	32.21	11.49	11.78	47.24
Shirts	96.74	32.18	53.83	65.36	77.65	78.64	116.12	199.42
Pants	78.68	25.75	55.29	81.40	48.51	62.05	90.92	145.21
Shorts and shorts sets	15.61	2.28	5.98	9.13	9.80	15.02	27.07	31.76
Uniforms	6.06	1.66	1.09	8.06	4.07	8.52	5.07	13.07
Costumes	3.54	1.72	2.56	2.05	2.01	3.56	3.35	7.95
BOYS' (AGED 2 TO 15) APPAREL	**100.32**	**41.74**	**52.68**	**80.64**	**88.52**	**88.99**	**117.01**	**197.63**
Coats and jackets	7.70	2.55	3.87	5.40	7.28	6.24	8.68	17.01
Sweaters	3.28	1.28	2.23	1.64	3.03	2.52	3.74	7.15
Shirts	23.26	16.42	15.51	13.42	16.91	27.79	27.38	40.01
Underwear	5.84	1.73	2.09	3.92	9.43	2.43	6.79	11.52
Nightwear	3.18	0.32	1.14	2.45	2.20	2.17	4.23	7.46
Hosiery	5.15	0.32	1.99	5.50	4.05	3.03	6.27	11.31
Accessories	4.82	1.59	1.88	2.26	2.05	2.29	4.78	13.95
Suits, sport coats, and vests	3.58	0.69	1.78	2.43	3.08	1.83	4.19	8.94
Pants	24.13	9.85	14.72	27.84	22.92	24.58	27.37	38.35
Shorts and shorts sets	9.31	3.86	4.13	8.72	8.21	8.82	11.09	18.11
Uniforms	3.37	0.79	0.93	2.31	3.20	2.50	4.72	7.89
Active sportswear	3.90	1.29	1.80	2.92	3.82	3.13	4.48	8.48
Costumes	2.82	1.02	0.62	1.84	2.33	1.67	3.29	7.46
WOMEN'S APPAREL	**640.44**	**259.48**	**293.73**	**391.67**	**522.55**	**742.58**	**768.79**	**1,274.42**
Coats and jackets	45.81	23.92	21.25	26.80	16.47	75.83	66.36	82.18
Dresses	90.70	35.83	32.54	72.02	79.36	82.26	73.75	208.38
Sport coats and tailored jackets	6.81	1.92	3.70	2.78	5.37	6.78	5.50	18.18
Sweaters and vests	50.71	18.86	21.06	26.15	49.19	48.73	56.24	109.71
Shirts, blouses, and tops	108.65	40.92	60.64	56.00	104.26	126.82	134.26	201.91
Skirts	14.36	6.09	3.88	7.60	10.49	22.75	17.97	28.67
Pants	91.71	35.87	42.36	66.30	82.90	101.13	110.37	171.60
Shorts and shorts sets	23.09	11.02	9.23	9.22	23.01	33.16	30.68	41.61
Active sportswear	30.92	8.06	10.96	17.66	13.38	51.36	35.14	68.81

	complete income reporters	under $10,000	$10,000– $19,999	$20,000– $29,999	$30,000– $39,999	$40,000– $49,999	$50,000– $69,999	$70,000 or more
Nightwear	$33.20	$19.32	$20.09	$25.39	$17.90	$31.89	$51.70	$54.97
Undergarments	34.07	14.61	14.30	24.30	33.05	28.23	54.05	58.12
Hosiery	21.99	11.01	13.59	16.83	16.54	32.04	26.32	34.61
Suits	33.76	15.51	14.73	16.60	30.22	32.53	43.11	74.00
Accessories	40.30	10.49	20.54	17.73	27.92	54.41	43.04	89.39
Uniforms	8.84	3.45	3.21	4.68	8.75	10.05	11.93	18.43
Costumes	5.54	2.61	1.65	1.61	3.75	4.61	8.37	13.83
GIRLS' (AGED 2 TO 15) APPAREL	**128.71**	**57.76**	**55.17**	**98.49**	**99.61**	**118.30**	**152.33**	**267.42**
Coats and jackets	7.02	3.00	4.41	5.06	5.24	7.96	8.06	13.72
Dresses and suits	22.15	8.69	3.77	19.74	23.65	20.84	24.24	45.67
Shirts, blouses, and sweaters	31.56	23.86	11.43	17.60	15.30	29.87	38.61	69.25
Skirts and pants	21.98	6.38	13.35	17.96	20.42	26.64	26.46	39.61
Shorts and shorts sets	8.56	3.12	5.32	6.32	6.34	7.86	11.31	16.90
Active sportswear	10.57	2.60	3.21	10.04	7.66	2.93	12.37	25.92
Underwear and nightwear	7.85	2.45	3.95	6.82	6.35	7.94	10.08	15.43
Hosiery	5.57	2.87	2.84	4.57	2.46	4.37	5.16	12.99
Accessories	5.42	1.33	2.67	5.21	6.07	4.40	7.29	8.99
Uniforms	4.15	1.56	3.11	3.00	3.76	3.14	5.04	7.96
Costumes	3.86	1.90	1.11	2.17	2.36	2.36	3.70	10.98
CHILDREN UNDER AGE 2	**92.71**	**49.70**	**64.11**	**66.45**	**81.34**	**106.70**	**115.75**	**148.37**
Coats, jackets, and snowsuits	2.89	1.28	1.72	1.81	3.13	2.65	4.79	4.58
Outerwear including dresses	24.74	8.63	13.11	23.62	20.02	23.31	37.64	42.12
Underwear	51.73	29.42	40.97	33.18	48.04	62.36	56.15	81.22
Nightwear and loungewear	4.20	2.03	2.69	3.37	2.92	5.62	6.07	6.53
Accessories	9.14	8.34	5.62	4.47	7.24	12.76	11.09	13.92
FOOTWEAR	**373.57**	**211.87**	**200.01**	**302.17**	**368.95**	**392.24**	**443.29**	**609.47**
Men's	126.64	44.73	80.54	89.67	133.33	116.59	154.33	219.80
Boys'	37.72	28.90	15.98	35.58	30.91	47.10	43.71	58.56
Women's	170.32	98.16	92.37	141.07	172.19	197.85	200.11	263.69
Girls'	38.88	40.08	11.11	35.85	32.53	30.70	45.13	67.43
OTHER APPAREL PRODUCTS AND SERVICES	**285.62**	**115.44**	**138.46**	**184.98**	**215.72**	**228.73**	**300.92**	**682.16**
Material for making clothes	5.93	0.61	3.75	5.69	3.04	2.87	8.71	12.31
Sewing patterns and notions	5.45	0.97	3.98	3.21	8.40	6.68	8.78	6.11
Watches	26.26	14.42	9.73	10.30	15.66	16.71	25.93	74.30
Jewelry	116.00	25.32	37.19	65.38	77.95	88.99	130.50	320.39
Shoe repair and other shoe services	2.10	1.26	0.55	1.43	1.43	0.95	2.45	5.44
Coin-operated apparel laundry and dry cleaning	40.93	49.92	51.59	55.62	44.54	43.73	27.12	19.53
Apparel alteration, repair, and tailoring services	6.10	1.68	3.30	4.01	3.84	5.38	7.21	14.45
Clothing rental	3.77	0.42	1.98	1.22	2.22	3.69	6.50	8.80
Watch and jewelry repair	5.37	2.49	4.25	3.33	3.26	6.11	4.78	11.43
Professional laundry, dry cleaning	73.07	18.34	21.71	34.57	54.69	53.64	78.77	207.24
Clothing storage	0.62	–	0.43	0.23	0.70	–	0.16	2.16

Note: (–) means sample is too small to make a reliable estimate.
Source: Bureau of Labor Statistics, unpublished data from the 2000 Consumer Expenditure Survey; calculations by New Strategist

Table 2.7 Apparel: Indexed spending by income, 2000

(indexed average annual spending of consumer units (CU) on apparel, accessories, and related services, by before-tax income of consumer unit, 2000; complete income reporters only; index definition: an index of 100 is the average for all consumer units; an index of 132 means that spending by consumer units in that group is 32 percent above the average for all consumer units; an index of 68 indicates spending that is 32 percent below the average for all consumer units)

	complete income reporters	under $10,000	$10,000– $19,999	$20,000– $29,999	$30,000– $39,999	$40,000– $49,999	$50,000– $69,999	$70,000 or more
Average spending of CU, total	$40,238	$16,456	$22,620	$29,852	$35,609	$42,323	$49,245	$75,964
Average spending of CU, index	100	41	56	74	88	105	122	189
Apparel, spending index	100	43	49	69	84	99	118	200
MEN'S APPAREL	**100**	**34**	**46**	**70**	**81**	**81**	**121**	**216**
Suits	100	32	30	43	53	77	107	293
Sport coats and tailored jackets	100	17	30	54	57	92	132	268
Coats and jackets	100	43	11	38	87	56	163	236
Underwear	100	57	38	84	80	120	122	177
Hosiery	100	38	48	88	101	80	114	187
Nightwear	100	34	76	52	64	162	102	197
Accessories	100	54	40	61	118	63	108	207
Sweaters and vests	100	33	41	71	89	95	124	217
Active sportswear	100	6	28	45	173	62	63	254
Shirts	100	33	56	68	80	81	120	206
Pants	100	33	70	103	62	79	116	185
Shorts and shorts sets	100	15	38	58	63	96	173	203
Uniforms	100	27	18	133	67	141	84	216
Costumes	100	49	72	58	57	101	95	225
BOYS' (AGED 2 TO 15) APPAREL	**100**	**42**	**53**	**80**	**88**	**89**	**117**	**197**
Coats and jackets	100	33	50	70	95	81	113	221
Sweaters	100	39	68	50	92	77	114	218
Shirts	100	71	67	58	73	119	118	172
Underwear	100	30	36	67	161	42	116	197
Nightwear	100	10	36	77	69	68	133	235
Hosiery	100	6	39	107	79	59	122	220
Accessories	100	33	39	47	43	48	99	289
Suits, sport coats, and vests	100	19	50	68	86	51	117	250
Pants	100	41	61	115	95	102	113	159
Shorts and shorts sets	100	41	44	94	88	95	119	195
Uniforms	100	24	28	69	95	74	140	234
Active sportswear	100	33	46	75	98	80	115	217
Costumes	100	36	22	65	83	59	117	265
WOMEN'S APPAREL	**100**	**41**	**46**	**61**	**82**	**116**	**120**	**199**
Coats and jackets	100	52	46	59	36	166	145	179
Dresses	100	40	36	79	87	91	81	230
Sport coats and tailored jackets	100	28	54	41	79	100	81	267
Sweaters and vests	100	37	42	52	97	96	111	216
Shirts, blouses, and tops	100	38	56	52	96	117	124	186
Skirts	100	42	27	53	73	158	125	200
Pants	100	39	46	72	90	110	120	187
Shorts and shorts sets	100	48	40	40	100	144	133	180
Active sportswear	100	26	35	57	43	166	114	223

	complete income reporters	under $10,000	$10,000– $19,999	$20,000– $29,999	$30,000– $39,999	$40,000– $49,999	$50,000– $69,999	$70,000 or more
Nightwear	100	58	60	76	54	96	156	166
Undergarments	100	43	42	71	97	83	159	171
Hosiery	100	50	62	77	75	146	120	157
Suits	100	46	44	49	90	96	128	219
Accessories	100	26	51	44	69	135	107	222
Uniforms	100	39	36	53	99	114	135	208
Costumes	100	47	30	29	68	83	151	250
GIRLS' (AGED 2 TO 15) APPAREL	**100**	**45**	**43**	**77**	**77**	**92**	**118**	**208**
Coats and jackets	100	43	63	72	75	113	115	195
Dresses and suits	100	39	17	89	107	94	109	206
Shirts, blouses, and sweaters	100	76	36	56	48	95	122	219
Skirts and pants	100	29	61	82	93	121	120	180
Shorts and shorts sets	100	36	62	74	74	92	132	197
Active sportswear	100	25	30	95	72	28	117	245
Underwear and nightwear	100	31	50	87	81	101	128	197
Hosiery	100	51	51	82	44	78	93	233
Accessories	100	25	49	96	112	81	135	166
Uniforms	100	38	75	72	91	76	121	192
Costumes	100	49	29	56	61	61	96	284
CHILDREN UNDER AGE 2	**100**	**54**	**69**	**72**	**88**	**115**	**125**	**160**
Coats, jackets, and snowsuits	100	44	59	63	108	92	166	158
Outerwear including dresses	100	35	53	95	81	94	152	170
Underwear	100	57	79	64	93	121	109	157
Nightwear and loungewear	100	48	64	80	70	134	145	155
Accessories	100	91	61	49	79	140	121	152
FOOTWEAR	**100**	**57**	**54**	**81**	**99**	**105**	**119**	**163**
Men's	100	35	64	71	105	92	122	174
Boys'	100	77	42	94	82	125	116	155
Women's	100	58	54	83	101	116	117	155
Girls'	100	103	29	92	84	79	116	173
OTHER APPAREL PRODUCTS AND SERVICES	**100**	**40**	**48**	**65**	**76**	**80**	**105**	**239**
Material for making clothes	100	10	63	96	51	48	147	208
Sewing patterns and notions	100	18	73	59	154	123	161	112
Watches	100	55	37	39	60	64	99	283
Jewelry	100	22	32	56	67	77	113	276
Shoe repair and other shoe services	100	60	26	68	68	45	117	259
Coin-operated apparel laundry and dry cleaning	100	122	126	136	109	107	66	48
Apparel alteration, repair, and tailoring services	100	28	54	66	63	88	118	237
Clothing rental	100	11	52	32	59	98	172	233
Watch and jewelry repair	100	46	79	62	61	114	89	213
Professional laundry, dry cleaning	100	25	30	47	75	73	108	284
Clothing storage	100	–	69	37	113	–	26	348

Note: (–) means sample is too small to make a reliable estimate.
Source: Calculations by New Strategist based on the 2000 Consumer Expenditure Survey

Table 2.8 Apparel: Indexed per capita spending by income, 2000

(indexed average annual per capita spending of consumer units (CU) on apparel, accessories, and related services, by before-tax income of consumer unit, 2000; complete income reporters only; index definition: an index of 100 is the average for all consumer units; an index of 132 means that spending by consumer units in that group is 32 percent above the average for all consumer units; an index of 68 indicates spending that is 32 percent below the average for all consumer units)

	complete income reporters	under $10,000	$10,000– $19,999	$20,000– $29,999	$30,000– $39,999	$40,000– $49,999	$50,000– $69,999	$70,000 or more
Per capita spending of CU, total	$16,095	$9,492	$10,819	$12,438	$14,244	$16,278	$16,981	$23,739
Per capita spending of CU, index	100	59	67	77	88	101	106	147
Apparel, per capita spending index	100	62	58	72	84	95	101	156
MEN'S APPAREL	**100**	**50**	**55**	**72**	**81**	**78**	**104**	**168**
Suits	100	46	36	45	53	74	92	229
Sport coats and tailored jackets	100	25	36	56	57	89	114	209
Coats and jackets	100	62	13	39	87	54	141	184
Underwear	100	83	45	88	80	116	106	138
Hosiery	100	55	57	92	101	77	98	146
Nightwear	100	49	91	54	64	155	88	154
Accessories	100	78	48	63	118	60	93	162
Sweaters and vests	100	48	49	74	89	91	107	169
Active sportswear	100	9	33	47	173	59	55	199
Shirts	100	48	67	70	80	78	103	161
Pants	100	47	84	108	62	76	100	144
Shorts and shorts sets	100	21	46	61	63	93	149	159
Uniforms	100	39	22	139	67	135	72	168
Costumes	100	70	87	60	57	97	82	175
BOYS' (AGED 2 TO 15) APPAREL	**100**	**60**	**63**	**84**	**88**	**85**	**101**	**154**
Coats and jackets	100	48	60	73	95	78	97	173
Sweaters	100	56	81	52	92	74	98	170
Shirts	100	102	80	60	73	115	101	134
Underwear	100	43	43	70	161	40	100	154
Nightwear	100	15	43	80	69	66	115	183
Hosiery	100	9	46	111	79	57	105	172
Accessories	100	48	47	49	43	46	85	226
Suits, sport coats, and vests	100	28	59	71	86	49	101	195
Pants	100	59	73	120	95	98	98	124
Shorts and shorts sets	100	60	53	98	88	91	103	152
Uniforms	100	34	33	71	95	71	121	183
Active sportswear	100	48	55	78	98	77	99	170
Costumes	100	52	26	68	83	57	101	207
WOMEN'S APPAREL	**100**	**58**	**55**	**64**	**82**	**111**	**103**	**155**
Coats and jackets	100	75	55	61	36	159	125	140
Dresses	100	57	43	83	87	87	70	179
Sport coats and tailored jackets	100	41	65	43	79	96	70	209
Sweaters and vests	100	54	50	54	97	92	96	169
Shirts, blouses, and tops	100	54	67	54	96	112	107	145
Skirts	100	61	32	55	73	152	108	156
Pants	100	56	55	75	90	106	104	146
Shorts and shorts sets	100	69	48	42	100	138	115	141
Active sportswear	100	38	42	59	43	160	98	174

	complete income reporters	under $10,000	$10,000–$19,999	$20,000–$29,999	$30,000–$39,999	$40,000–$49,999	$50,000–$69,999	$70,000 or more
Nightwear	100	84	72	80	54	92	134	129
Undergarments	100	62	50	74	97	80	137	133
Hosiery	100	72	74	80	75	140	103	123
Suits	100	66	52	51	90	93	110	171
Accessories	100	38	61	46	69	130	92	173
Uniforms	100	56	43	55	99	109	116	163
Costumes	100	68	36	30	68	80	130	195
GIRLS' (AGED 2 TO 15) APPAREL	**100**	**65**	**51**	**80**	**77**	**88**	**102**	**162**
Coats and jackets	100	62	75	75	75	109	99	153
Dresses and suits	100	57	20	93	107	90	94	161
Shirts, blouses, and sweaters	100	109	43	58	48	91	105	171
Skirts and pants	100	42	73	85	93	117	104	141
Shorts and shorts sets	100	53	74	77	74	88	114	154
Active sportswear	100	35	36	99	72	27	101	192
Underwear and nightwear	100	45	60	90	81	97	111	154
Hosiery	100	74	61	85	44	75	80	182
Accessories	100	35	59	100	112	78	116	130
Uniforms	100	54	90	75	91	73	105	150
Costumes	100	71	35	59	61	59	83	222
CHILDREN UNDER AGE 2	**100**	**77**	**83**	**75**	**88**	**111**	**108**	**125**
Coats, jackets, and snowsuits	100	64	71	65	108	88	143	124
Outerwear including dresses	100	50	63	99	81	91	131	133
Underwear	100	82	95	67	93	116	94	123
Nightwear and loungewear	100	70	77	84	70	129	125	121
Accessories	100	132	73	51	79	134	105	119
FOOTWEAR	**100**	**82**	**64**	**84**	**99**	**101**	**102**	**127**
Men's	100	51	76	74	105	89	105	136
Boys'	100	110	51	98	82	120	100	121
Women's	100	83	65	86	101	112	101	121
Girls'	100	149	34	96	84	76	100	135
OTHER APPAREL PRODUCTS AND SERVICES	**100**	**58**	**58**	**67**	**76**	**77**	**91**	**187**
Material for making clothes	100	15	76	100	51	47	127	162
Sewing patterns and notions	100	26	87	61	154	118	139	88
Watches	100	79	44	41	60	61	85	221
Jewelry	100	31	38	59	67	74	97	216
Shoe repair and other shoe services	100	86	31	71	68	43	101	202
Coin-operated apparel laundry and dry cleaning	100	176	151	142	109	103	57	37
Apparel alteration, repair, and tailoring services	100	40	65	68	63	85	102	185
Clothing rental	100	16	63	34	59	94	149	182
Watch and jewelry repair	100	67	95	65	61	109	77	166
Professional laundry, dry cleaning	100	36	36	49	75	71	93	222
Clothing storage	100	–	83	39	113	–	22	272

Note: Per capita indexes account for household size and show how much each person in a particular household demographic segment spends relative to a person in the average household. (–) means sample is too small to make a reliable estimate.
Source: Calculations by New Strategist based on the 2000 Consumer Expenditure Survey

Table 2.9 Apparel: Total spending by income, 2000

(total annual spending on apparel, accessories, and related services, by before-tax income group of consumer units (CU), 2000; complete income reporters only; numbers in thousands)

	complete income reporters	under $10,000	$10,000– $19,999	$20,000– $29,999	$30,000– $39,999	$40,000– $49,999	$50,000– $69,999	$70,000 or more
Number of consumer units	81,454	10,810	14,714	12,039	9,477	7,653	11,337	15,424
Total spending of all CUs	$3,277,581,892	$177,886,368	$332,833,656	$359,383,292	$337,468,767	$323,898,149	$558,294,760	$1,171,666,422
Apparel, total spending	163,216,711	9,378,214	14,403,731	16,740,952	15,977,369	15,200,006	26,745,230	61,757,079
MEN'S APPAREL	**$31,149,639**	**$1,422,286**	**$2,571,471**	**$3,204,180**	**$2,930,573**	**$2,361,792**	**$5,226,584**	**$12,716,780**
Suits	2,869,624	122,359	155,316	184,076	178,452	207,855	427,065	1,594,225
Sport coats and tailored jackets	895,179	20,498	48,983	71,271	59,421	77,525	164,046	453,466
Coats and jackets	3,359,163	192,002	66,224	186,966	339,845	178,085	762,187	1,502,143
Underwear	1,536,222	116,702	105,269	191,540	142,250	173,494	261,771	514,082
Hosiery	1,051,571	53,557	90,673	136,643	124,054	79,285	166,314	373,107
Nightwear	297,307	13,526	40,711	22,874	22,176	45,153	42,060	110,899
Accessories	2,118,619	151,657	153,250	189,735	292,081	124,591	317,889	831,971
Sweaters and vests	1,167,236	51,788	86,988	122,798	120,832	103,851	202,025	478,607
Active sportswear	1,512,601	12,858	76,461	99,803	305,254	87,933	133,550	728,630
Shirts	7,879,860	347,837	792,119	786,869	735,889	601,832	1,316,452	3,075,854
Pants	6,408,801	278,376	813,557	979,975	459,729	474,869	1,030,760	2,239,719
Shorts and shorts sets	1,271,497	24,689	88,032	109,916	92,875	114,948	306,893	489,866
Uniforms	493,611	17,903	16,073	97,034	38,571	65,204	57,479	201,592
Costumes	288,347	18,570	37,735	24,680	19,049	27,245	37,979	122,621
BOYS' (AGED 2 TO 15) APPAREL	**8,171,465**	**451,161**	**775,071**	**970,825**	**838,904**	**681,040**	**1,326,542**	**3,048,245**
Coats and jackets	627,196	27,553	56,877	65,011	68,993	47,755	98,405	262,362
Sweaters	267,169	13,891	32,802	19,744	28,715	19,286	42,400	110,282
Shirts	1,894,620	177,477	228,151	161,563	160,256	212,677	310,407	617,114
Underwear	475,691	18,733	30,766	47,193	89,368	18,597	76,978	177,684
Nightwear	259,024	3,482	16,728	29,496	20,849	16,607	47,956	115,063
Hosiery	419,488	3,448	29,212	66,215	38,382	23,189	71,083	174,445
Accessories	392,608	17,166	27,657	27,208	19,428	17,525	54,191	215,165
Suits, sport coats, and vests	291,605	7,448	26,150	29,255	29,189	14,005	47,502	137,891
Pants	1,965,485	106,513	216,641	335,166	217,213	188,111	310,294	591,510
Shorts and shorts sets	758,337	41,738	60,775	104,980	77,806	67,499	125,727	279,329
Uniforms	274,500	8,576	13,690	27,810	30,326	19,133	53,511	121,695
Active sportswear	317,671	13,998	26,536	35,154	36,202	23,954	50,790	130,796
Costumes	229,700	11,068	9,152	22,152	22,081	12,781	37,299	115,063
WOMEN'S APPAREL	**52,166,400**	**2,804,994**	**4,321,981**	**4,715,315**	**4,952,206**	**5,682,965**	**8,715,772**	**19,656,654**
Coats and jackets	3,731,408	258,585	312,677	322,645	156,086	580,327	752,323	1,267,544
Dresses	7,387,878	387,311	478,844	867,049	752,095	629,536	836,104	3,214,053
Sport coats and tailored jackets	554,702	20,711	54,479	33,468	50,891	51,887	62,354	280,408
Sweaters and vests	4,130,532	203,860	309,819	314,820	466,174	372,931	637,593	1,692,167
Shirts, blouses, and tops	8,849,977	442,372	892,292	674,184	988,072	970,553	1,522,106	3,114,260
Skirts	1,169,679	65,781	57,021	91,496	99,414	174,106	203,726	442,206
Pants	7,470,146	387,791	623,261	798,186	785,643	773,948	1,251,265	2,646,758
Shorts and shorts sets	1,880,773	119,092	135,757	111,000	218,066	253,773	347,819	641,793
Active sportswear	2,518,558	87,156	161,275	212,609	126,802	393,058	398,382	1,061,325

	complete income reporters	under $10,000	$10,000–$19,999	$20,000–$29,999	$30,000–$39,999	$40,000–$49,999	$50,000–$69,999	$70,000 or more
Nightwear	$2,704,273	$208,886	$295,531	$305,670	$169,638	$244,054	$586,123	$847,857
Undergarments	2,775,138	157,981	210,448	292,548	313,215	216,044	612,765	896,443
Hosiery	1,791,173	119,068	199,969	202,616	156,750	245,202	298,390	533,825
Suits	2,749,887	167,647	216,690	199,847	286,395	248,952	488,738	1,141,376
Accessories	3,282,596	113,398	302,152	213,451	264,598	416,400	487,944	1,378,751
Uniforms	720,053	37,292	47,275	56,343	82,924	76,913	135,250	284,264
Costumes	451,255	28,207	24,250	19,383	35,539	35,280	94,891	213,314
GIRLS' (AGED 2 TO 15) APPAREL	**10,483,944**	**624,339**	**811,733**	**1,185,721**	**944,004**	**905,350**	**1,726,965**	**4,124,686**
Coats and jackets	571,807	32,427	64,958	60,917	49,659	60,918	91,376	211,617
Dresses and suits	1,804,206	93,958	55,493	237,650	224,131	159,489	274,809	704,414
Shirts, blouses, and sweaters	2,570,688	257,950	168,246	211,886	144,998	228,595	437,722	1,068,112
Skirts and pants	1,790,359	68,929	196,440	216,220	193,520	203,876	299,977	610,945
Shorts and shorts sets	697,246	33,748	78,259	76,086	60,084	60,153	128,221	260,666
Active sportswear	860,969	28,086	47,271	120,872	72,594	22,423	140,239	399,790
Underwear and nightwear	639,414	26,468	58,131	82,106	60,179	60,765	114,277	237,992
Hosiery	453,699	31,007	41,725	55,018	23,313	33,444	58,499	200,358
Accessories	441,481	14,366	39,214	62,723	57,525	33,673	82,647	138,662
Uniforms	338,034	16,890	45,747	36,117	35,634	24,030	57,138	122,775
Costumes	314,412	20,511	16,396	26,125	22,366	18,061	41,947	169,356
CHILDREN UNDER AGE 2	**7,551,600**	**537,288**	**943,274**	**799,992**	**770,859**	**816,575**	**1,312,258**	**2,288,459**
Coats, jackets, and snowsuits	235,402	13,860	25,262	21,791	29,663	20,280	54,304	70,642
Outerwear including dresses	2,015,172	93,338	192,944	284,361	189,730	178,391	426,725	649,659
Underwear	4,213,615	318,003	602,762	399,454	455,275	477,241	636,573	1,252,737
Nightwear and loungewear	342,107	21,933	39,640	40,571	27,673	43,010	68,816	100,719
Accessories	744,490	90,153	82,666	53,814	68,613	97,652	125,727	214,702
FOOTWEAR	**30,428,771**	**2,290,261**	**2,942,915**	**3,637,825**	**3,496,539**	**3,001,813**	**5,025,579**	**9,400,465**
Men's	10,315,335	483,542	1,184,998	1,079,537	1,263,568	892,263	1,749,639	3,390,195
Boys'	3,072,445	312,406	235,109	428,348	292,934	360,456	495,540	903,229
Women's	13,873,245	1,061,069	1,359,184	1,698,342	1,631,845	1,514,146	2,268,647	4,067,155
Girls'	3,166,932	433,244	163,477	431,598	308,287	234,947	511,639	1,040,040
OTHER APPAREL PRODUCTS AND SERVICES	**23,264,891**	**1,247,884**	**2,037,367**	**2,226,974**	**2,044,378**	**1,750,471**	**3,411,530**	**10,521,636**
Material for making clothes	483,022	6,608	55,131	68,502	28,810	21,964	98,745	189,869
Sewing patterns and notions	443,924	10,487	58,588	38,645	79,607	51,122	99,539	94,241
Watches	2,138,982	155,922	143,208	124,002	148,410	127,882	293,968	1,146,003
Jewelry	9,448,664	273,666	547,251	787,110	738,732	681,040	1,479,479	4,941,695
Shoe repair and other shoe services	171,053	13,614	8,026	17,216	13,552	7,270	27,776	83,907
Coin-operated apparel laundry and dry cleaning	3,333,912	539,677	759,119	669,609	422,106	334,666	307,459	301,231
Apparel alteration, repair, and tailoring services	496,869	18,168	48,542	48,276	36,392	41,173	81,740	222,877
Clothing rental	307,082	4,530	29,109	14,688	21,039	28,240	73,691	135,731
Watch and jewelry repair	437,408	26,896	62,523	40,090	30,895	46,760	54,191	176,296
Professional laundry, dry cleaning	5,951,844	198,279	319,466	416,188	518,297	410,507	893,015	3,196,470
Clothing storage	50,501	–	6,323	2,769	6,634	–	1,814	33,316

Note: Numbers may not add to total because of rounding. (–) means sample is too small to make a reliable estimate.
Source: Calculations by New Strategist based on the 2000 Consumer Expenditure Survey

Table 2.10   Apparel: Market shares by income, 2000

(percentage of total annual spending on apparel, accessories, and related services accounted for by before-tax income group of consumer units, 2000; complete income reporters only)

	complete income reporters	under $10,000	$10,000– $19,999	$20,000– $29,999	$30,000– $39,999	$40,000– $49,999	$50,000– $69,999	$70,000 or more
Share of total consumer units	100.0%	13.3%	18.1%	14.8%	11.6%	9.4%	13.9%	18.9%
Share of total before-tax income	100.0	1.7	5.9	8.1	9.0	9.3	18.3	47.7
Share of total spending	100.0	5.4	10.2	11.0	10.3	9.9	17.0	35.7
Share of apparel spending	100.0	5.7	8.8	10.3	9.8	9.3	16.4	37.8
MEN'S APPAREL	**100.0%**	**4.6%**	**8.3%**	**10.3%**	**9.4%**	**7.6%**	**16.8%**	**40.8%**
Suits	100.0	4.3	5.4	6.4	6.2	7.2	14.9	55.6
Sport coats and tailored jackets	100.0	2.3	5.5	8.0	6.6	8.7	18.3	50.7
Coats and jackets	100.0	5.7	2.0	5.6	10.1	5.3	22.7	44.7
Underwear	100.0	7.6	6.9	12.5	9.3	11.3	17.0	33.5
Hosiery	100.0	5.1	8.6	13.0	11.8	7.5	15.8	35.5
Nightwear	100.0	4.5	13.7	7.7	7.5	15.2	14.1	37.3
Accessories	100.0	7.2	7.2	9.0	13.8	5.9	15.0	39.3
Sweaters and vests	100.0	4.4	7.5	10.5	10.4	8.9	17.3	41.0
Active sportswear	100.0	0.9	5.1	6.6	20.2	5.8	8.8	48.2
Shirts	100.0	4.4	10.1	10.0	9.3	7.6	16.7	39.0
Pants	100.0	4.3	12.7	15.3	7.2	7.4	16.1	34.9
Shorts and shorts sets	100.0	1.9	6.9	8.6	7.3	9.0	24.1	38.5
Uniforms	100.0	3.6	3.3	19.7	7.8	13.2	11.6	40.8
Costumes	100.0	6.4	13.1	8.6	6.6	9.4	13.2	42.5
BOYS' (AGED 2 TO 15) APPAREL	**100.0**	**5.5**	**9.5**	**11.9**	**10.3**	**8.3**	**16.2**	**37.3**
Coats and jackets	100.0	4.4	9.1	10.4	11.0	7.6	15.7	41.8
Sweaters	100.0	5.2	12.3	7.4	10.7	7.2	15.9	41.3
Shirts	100.0	9.4	12.0	8.5	8.5	11.2	16.4	32.6
Underwear	100.0	3.9	6.5	9.9	18.8	3.9	16.2	37.4
Nightwear	100.0	1.3	6.5	11.4	8.0	6.4	18.5	44.4
Hosiery	100.0	0.8	7.0	15.8	9.1	5.5	16.9	41.6
Accessories	100.0	4.4	7.0	6.9	4.9	4.5	13.8	54.8
Suits, sport coats, and vests	100.0	2.6	9.0	10.0	10.0	4.8	16.3	47.3
Pants	100.0	5.4	11.0	17.1	11.1	9.6	15.8	30.1
Shorts and shorts sets	100.0	5.5	8.0	13.8	10.3	8.9	16.6	36.8
Uniforms	100.0	3.1	5.0	10.1	11.0	7.0	19.5	44.3
Active sportswear	100.0	4.4	8.4	11.1	11.4	7.5	16.0	41.2
Costumes	100.0	4.8	4.0	9.6	9.6	5.6	16.2	50.1
WOMEN'S APPAREL	**100.0**	**5.4**	**8.3**	**9.0**	**9.5**	**10.9**	**16.7**	**37.7**
Coats and jackets	100.0	6.9	8.4	8.6	4.2	15.6	20.2	34.0
Dresses	100.0	5.2	6.5	11.7	10.2	8.5	11.3	43.5
Sport coats and tailored jackets	100.0	3.7	9.8	6.0	9.2	9.4	11.2	50.6
Sweaters and vests	100.0	4.9	7.5	7.6	11.3	9.0	15.4	41.0
Shirts, blouses, and tops	100.0	5.0	10.1	7.6	11.2	11.0	17.2	35.2
Skirts	100.0	5.6	4.9	7.8	8.5	14.9	17.4	37.8
Pants	100.0	5.2	8.3	10.7	10.5	10.4	16.8	35.4
Shorts and shorts sets	100.0	6.3	7.2	5.9	11.6	13.5	18.5	34.1
Active sportswear	100.0	3.5	6.4	8.4	5.0	15.6	15.8	42.1

	complete income reporters	under $10,000	$10,000–$19,999	$20,000–$29,999	$30,000–$39,999	$40,000–$49,999	$50,000–$69,999	$70,000 or more
Nightwear	100.0%	7.7%	10.9%	11.3%	6.3%	9.0%	21.7%	31.4%
Undergarments	100.0	5.7	7.6	10.5	11.3	7.8	22.1	32.3
Hosiery	100.0	6.6	11.2	11.3	8.8	13.7	16.7	29.8
Suits	100.0	6.1	7.9	7.3	10.4	9.1	17.8	41.5
Accessories	100.0	3.5	9.2	6.5	8.1	12.7	14.9	42.0
Uniforms	100.0	5.2	6.6	7.8	11.5	10.7	18.8	39.5
Costumes	100.0	6.3	5.4	4.3	7.9	7.8	21.0	47.3
GIRLS' (AGED 2 TO 15) APPAREL	**100.0**	**6.0**	**7.7**	**11.3**	**9.0**	**8.6**	**16.5**	**39.3**
Coats and jackets	100.0	5.7	11.4	10.7	8.7	10.7	16.0	37.0
Dresses and suits	100.0	5.2	3.1	13.2	12.4	8.8	15.2	39.0
Shirts, blouses, and sweaters	100.0	10.0	6.5	8.2	5.6	8.9	17.0	41.5
Skirts and pants	100.0	3.9	11.0	12.1	10.8	11.4	16.8	34.1
Shorts and shorts sets	100.0	4.8	11.2	10.9	8.6	8.6	18.4	37.4
Active sportswear	100.0	3.3	5.5	14.0	8.4	2.6	16.3	46.4
Underwear and nightwear	100.0	4.1	9.1	12.8	9.4	9.5	17.9	37.2
Hosiery	100.0	6.8	9.2	12.1	5.1	7.4	12.9	44.2
Accessories	100.0	3.3	8.9	14.2	13.0	7.6	18.7	31.4
Uniforms	100.0	5.0	13.5	10.7	10.5	7.1	16.9	36.3
Costumes	100.0	6.5	5.2	8.3	7.1	5.7	13.3	53.9
CHILDREN UNDER AGE 2	**100.0**	**7.1**	**12.5**	**10.6**	**10.2**	**10.8**	**17.4**	**30.3**
Coats, jackets, and snowsuits	100.0	5.9	10.7	9.3	12.6	8.6	23.1	30.0
Outerwear including dresses	100.0	4.6	9.6	14.1	9.4	8.9	21.2	32.2
Underwear	100.0	7.5	14.3	9.5	10.8	11.3	15.1	29.7
Nightwear and loungewear	100.0	6.4	11.6	11.9	8.1	12.6	20.1	29.4
Accessories	100.0	12.1	11.1	7.2	9.2	13.1	16.9	28.8
FOOTWEAR	**100.0**	**7.5**	**9.7**	**12.0**	**11.5**	**9.9**	**16.5**	**30.9**
Men's	100.0	4.7	11.5	10.5	12.2	8.6	17.0	32.9
Boys'	100.0	10.2	7.7	13.9	9.5	11.7	16.1	29.4
Women's	100.0	7.6	9.8	12.2	11.8	10.9	16.4	29.3
Girls'	100.0	13.7	5.2	13.6	9.7	7.4	16.2	32.8
OTHER APPAREL PRODUCTS AND SERVICES	**100.0**	**5.4**	**8.8**	**9.6**	**8.8**	**7.5**	**14.7**	**45.2**
Material for making clothes	100.0	1.4	11.4	14.2	6.0	4.5	20.4	39.3
Sewing patterns and notions	100.0	2.4	13.2	8.7	17.9	11.5	22.4	21.2
Watches	100.0	7.3	6.7	5.8	6.9	6.0	13.7	53.6
Jewelry	100.0	2.9	5.8	8.3	7.8	7.2	15.7	52.3
Shoe repair and other shoe services	100.0	8.0	4.7	10.1	7.9	4.3	16.2	49.1
Coin-operated apparel laundry and dry cleaning	100.0	16.2	22.8	20.1	12.7	10.0	9.2	9.0
Apparel alteration, repair, and tailoring services	100.0	3.7	9.8	9.7	7.3	8.3	16.5	44.9
Clothing rental	100.0	1.5	9.5	4.8	6.9	9.2	24.0	44.2
Watch and jewelry repair	100.0	6.1	14.3	9.2	7.1	10.7	12.4	40.3
Professional laundry, dry cleaning	100.0	3.3	5.4	7.0	8.7	6.9	15.0	53.7
Clothing storage	100.0	–	12.5	5.5	13.1	–	3.6	66.0

Note: Numbers may not add to total because of rounding. (–) means sample is too small to make a reliable estimate.
Source: Calculations by New Strategist based on the 2000 Consumer Expenditure Survey

Table 2.11 Apparel: Average spending by household type, 2000

(average annual spending of consumer units (CU) on apparel, accessories, and related services, by type of consumer unit, 2000)

	total married couples	married couples, no children	married couples with children				single parent, at least one child <18	single person
			total	oldest child under 6	oldest child 6 to 17	oldest child 18 or older		
Number of consumer units (in thousands, add 000)	56,287	22,805	28,777	5,291	15,396	8,090	6,132	32,323
Average number of persons per CU	3.2	2.0	3.9	3.5	4.1	3.8	2.9	1.0
Average before-tax income of CU	$60,588.00	$53,232.00	$66,913.00	$62,928.00	$69,472.00	$64,725.00	$25,095.00	$24,977.00
Average spending of CU, total	48,619.37	42,195.54	53,585.53	50,755.90	54,170.40	54,550.20	28,923.25	23,059.00
Apparel, average spending	2,311.71	1,725.35	2,748.84	2,589.69	2,838.41	2,697.50	1,920.54	1,027.66
MEN'S APPAREL	**$434.44**	**$399.56**	**$466.58**	**$390.15**	**$421.13**	**$620.21**	**$147.64**	**$210.92**
Suits	46.46	37.51	53.74	40.11	58.48	53.64	7.43	16.73
Sport coats and tailored jackets	16.72	14.60	18.58	10.11	17.51	26.17	1.36	4.80
Coats and jackets	49.34	50.85	51.01	48.56	46.64	62.32	6.45	16.44
Underwear	22.46	18.05	24.14	12.02	23.25	36.11	8.50	11.01
Hosiery	15.04	15.05	14.95	17.94	12.49	17.67	0.62	7.56
Nightwear	4.52	4.09	4.97	3.77	5.38	4.97	2.19	1.40
Accessories	30.85	31.49	29.90	32.39	22.99	42.43	15.21	14.92
Sweaters and vests	20.15	18.15	22.16	15.53	19.65	31.28	5.17	11.47
Active sportswear	22.83	25.81	20.65	11.91	22.91	23.16	7.36	7.44
Shirts	95.85	84.19	107.00	92.16	87.81	159.98	50.05	58.05
Pants	77.50	72.02	82.71	79.98	66.90	118.47	36.62	50.39
Shorts and shorts sets	18.90	19.40	18.80	13.57	20.01	20.59	4.79	6.81
Uniforms	8.11	4.32	10.60	8.11	9.26	14.77	1.61	1.53
Costumes	5.71	4.02	7.36	3.98	7.85	8.63	0.31	2.37
BOYS' (AGED 2 TO 15) APPAREL	**131.01**	**24.54**	**216.41**	**147.54**	**296.20**	**107.18**	**258.79**	**12.14**
Coats and jackets	11.43	1.74	19.07	10.75	27.77	7.96	17.60	0.57
Sweaters	5.10	1.31	8.13	4.06	12.19	3.06	6.45	0.68
Shirts	26.40	6.52	43.06	37.99	52.63	27.03	72.57	3.58
Underwear	7.29	1.40	12.24	12.09	13.78	9.11	10.93	0.54
Nightwear	3.71	2.54	5.01	7.78	4.68	3.40	6.61	0.41
Hosiery	5.36	1.65	7.78	6.71	9.65	4.71	15.36	0.17
Accessories	6.94	1.13	12.05	12.72	13.19	9.07	4.05	0.59
Suits, sport coats, and vests	4.99	0.54	8.48	4.76	11.99	4.25	8.10	0.73
Pants	31.38	3.73	52.81	21.64	79.51	22.40	72.50	2.31
Shorts and shorts sets	12.09	1.63	20.49	14.04	29.62	7.35	25.40	1.04
Uniforms	5.44	1.10	8.78	5.68	12.74	3.27	6.32	0.60
Active sportswear	5.54	0.83	9.00	3.26	14.31	2.65	8.73	0.34
Costumes	5.35	0.42	9.51	6.04	14.16	2.91	4.17	0.57
WOMEN'S APPAREL	**735.85**	**657.10**	**778.24**	**622.85**	**694.77**	**1,079.12**	**532.39**	**397.44**
Coats and jackets	52.56	51.66	49.61	33.07	45.60	71.89	53.00	29.86
Dresses	103.30	75.38	124.03	79.26	98.49	215.42	56.84	65.63
Sport coats and tailored jackets	9.73	8.35	10.71	4.48	11.23	13.80	6.67	7.24
Sweaters and vests	62.32	59.93	63.55	58.99	57.11	80.98	36.79	27.66
Shirts, blouses, and tops	118.66	106.18	130.67	106.40	115.17	183.72	86.01	74.20
Skirts	13.96	12.88	15.66	11.68	11.17	28.49	7.91	10.56
Pants	101.14	89.44	106.66	98.55	87.69	153.58	83.04	48.44
Shorts and shorts sets	26.23	23.07	30.12	25.21	28.99	36.60	20.53	10.03
Active sportswear	34.39	37.82	28.99	27.65	27.82	32.57	24.32	18.37

	total married couples	married couples, no children	married couples with children				single parent, at least one child <18	single person
			total	oldest child under 6	oldest child 6 to 17	oldest child 18 or older		
Nightwear	$39.72	$37.91	$39.69	$32.79	$39.54	$45.76	$21.11	$17.39
Undergarments	38.43	30.32	45.38	48.91	41.62	50.40	49.19	17.80
Hosiery	23.77	19.20	25.80	20.82	24.74	32.19	20.88	13.20
Suits	38.71	43.14	36.11	26.62	30.98	52.06	24.03	25.94
Accessories	53.00	45.29	48.13	36.50	49.43	55.07	29.98	23.53
Uniforms	10.71	8.60	12.12	4.19	12.57	16.45	7.90	4.70
Costumes	9.20	7.93	11.02	7.75	12.60	10.16	4.18	2.91
GIRLS' (AGED 2 TO 15) APPAREL	**170.27**	**34.21**	**273.67**	**154.18**	**399.59**	**110.71**	**279.46**	**16.25**
Coats and jackets	9.46	2.19	14.83	9.98	21.17	5.94	19.15	0.88
Dresses and suits	25.05	5.19	39.94	22.90	60.15	11.39	58.28	2.64
Shirts, blouses, and sweaters	45.42	9.71	73.55	37.52	104.55	38.01	44.91	3.46
Skirts and pants	29.56	4.28	49.23	25.55	73.62	18.29	61.03	2.60
Shorts and shorts sets	11.52	1.89	18.57	15.12	26.26	6.21	23.79	0.86
Active sportswear	14.16	3.76	21.98	7.81	32.87	10.75	10.41	2.54
Underwear and nightwear	10.39	1.55	17.03	13.37	23.81	6.52	20.91	0.75
Hosiery	6.70	1.58	9.85	7.78	13.07	4.76	12.29	0.77
Accessories	6.59	3.15	9.53	4.22	14.16	4.17	10.84	1.13
Uniforms	5.32	0.57	8.35	5.16	12.56	2.41	12.41	0.21
Costumes	6.10	0.34	10.80	4.77	17.37	2.26	5.43	0.41
CHILDREN UNDER AGE 2	**118.31**	**38.32**	**172.59**	**497.84**	**101.77**	**62.76**	**110.93**	**17.27**
Coats, jackets, and snowsuits	3.75	2.14	4.74	16.19	1.86	2.72	3.29	0.88
Outerwear including dresses	32.82	23.08	39.49	106.86	23.73	25.42	24.99	6.57
Underwear	65.72	7.02	106.11	319.39	62.11	21.28	63.39	6.45
Nightwear and loungewear	5.43	3.19	6.78	17.16	4.57	4.21	5.11	1.33
Accessories	10.59	2.89	15.48	38.24	9.51	9.13	14.16	2.04
FOOTWEAR	**405.93**	**298.01**	**480.34**	**449.29**	**536.77**	**386.84**	**411.03**	**190.66**
Men's	142.23	122.12	155.70	184.48	142.97	158.62	40.05	76.10
Boys'	46.67	10.78	71.51	60.99	102.16	15.44	104.67	1.46
Women's	173.91	161.72	179.57	157.82	181.67	193.26	181.38	107.90
Girls'	43.13	3.40	73.57	46.01	109.96	19.53	84.93	5.21
OTHER APPAREL PRODUCTS AND SERVICES	**315.90**	**273.60**	**361.01**	**327.84**	**388.19**	**330.68**	**180.29**	**182.97**
Material for making clothes	6.12	4.96	7.18	8.16	8.51	3.54	3.40	2.17
Sewing patterns and notions	5.96	5.78	6.04	3.89	7.08	5.65	5.77	3.40
Watches	30.06	27.11	34.99	29.37	33.93	40.67	9.48	15.06
Jewelry	131.96	112.23	156.98	123.57	187.12	121.48	40.73	67.74
Shoe repair and other shoe services	2.36	2.10	2.84	2.14	2.99	3.00	1.30	1.18
Coin-operated apparel laundry and dry cleaning	25.81	17.52	28.73	41.79	29.31	19.10	72.80	37.89
Apparel alteration, repair, and tailoring services	7.09	7.37	7.20	5.00	6.58	9.82	2.20	4.34
Clothing rental	4.89	4.67	5.21	1.35	3.98	10.07	0.94	0.61
Watch and jewelry repair	6.12	6.46	6.09	5.70	6.42	5.72	1.94	2.62
Professional laundry, dry cleaning	94.75	84.57	105.04	105.84	101.42	111.42	41.48	47.66
Clothing storage	0.78	0.84	0.70	1.03	0.84	0.21	0.25	0.31

Note: Average spending figures for total consumer units can be found on Average Spending by Age and Average Spending by Region tables.
Source: Bureau of Labor Statistics, unpublished data from the 2000 Consumer Expenditure Survey

Table 2.12 Apparel: Indexed spending by household type, 2000

(indexed average annual spending of consumer units (CU) on apparel, accessories, and related services, by type of consumer unit, 2000; index definition: an index of 100 is the average for all consumer units; an index of 132 means that spending by consumer units in that group is 32 percent above the average for all consumer units; an index of 68 indicates spending that is 32 percent below the average for all consumer units)

	total married couples	married couples, no children	married couples with children				single parent, at least one child <18	single person
			total	oldest child under 6	oldest child 6 to 17	oldest child 18 or older		
Average spending of CU, total	$48,619	$42,196	$53,586	$50,756	$54,170	$54,550	$28,923	$23,059
Average spending of CU, index	128	111	141	133	142	143	76	61
Apparel, spending index	125	93	148	140	153	145	103	55
MEN'S APPAREL	**126**	**116**	**136**	**113**	**122**	**180**	**43**	**61**
Suits	140	113	162	121	176	161	22	50
Sport coats and tailored jackets	148	129	164	89	155	231	12	42
Coats and jackets	142	146	147	140	134	179	19	47
Underwear	129	103	138	69	133	207	49	63
Hosiery	131	131	130	156	109	154	5	66
Nightwear	135	122	149	113	161	149	66	42
Accessories	132	135	128	139	99	182	65	64
Sweaters and vests	126	114	139	97	123	196	32	72
Active sportswear	142	160	128	74	142	144	46	46
Shirts	112	99	125	108	103	187	59	68
Pants	113	105	120	117	97	173	53	73
Shorts and shorts sets	139	142	138	99	147	151	35	50
Uniforms	147	78	192	147	168	268	29	28
Costumes	141	99	181	98	193	213	8	58
BOYS' (AGED 2 TO 15) APPAREL	**137**	**26**	**226**	**154**	**309**	**112**	**270**	**13**
Coats and jackets	146	22	243	137	354	102	224	7
Sweaters	143	37	228	114	342	86	181	19
Shirts	127	31	207	182	253	130	348	17
Underwear	143	28	240	238	271	179	215	11
Nightwear	126	86	170	264	159	115	224	14
Hosiery	125	38	181	156	224	110	357	4
Accessories	158	26	274	289	300	206	92	13
Suits, sport coats, and vests	137	15	233	131	329	117	223	20
Pants	134	16	226	93	340	96	310	10
Shorts and shorts sets	135	18	229	157	331	82	284	12
Uniforms	149	30	240	155	348	89	173	16
Active sportswear	145	22	236	86	376	70	229	9
Costumes	161	13	286	181	425	87	125	17
WOMEN'S APPAREL	**121**	**108**	**128**	**103**	**114**	**178**	**88**	**65**
Coats and jackets	121	119	115	76	105	166	123	69
Dresses	119	87	143	91	114	248	66	76
Sport coats and tailored jackets	117	100	129	54	135	166	80	87
Sweaters and vests	126	122	129	120	116	164	75	56
Shirts, blouses, and tops	120	107	132	107	116	185	87	75
Skirts	109	101	123	92	88	223	62	83
Pants	118	105	125	115	103	180	97	57
Shorts and shorts sets	129	113	148	124	142	179	101	49
Active sportswear	124	136	104	100	100	117	88	66

	total married couples	married couples, no children	married couples with children				single parent, at least one child <18	single person
			total	oldest child under 6	oldest child 6 to 17	oldest child 18 or older		
Nightwear	123	118	123	102	123	142	66	54
Undergarments	119	94	141	152	129	157	153	55
Hosiery	113	92	123	99	118	154	100	63
Suits	115	128	107	79	92	154	71	77
Accessories	135	115	122	93	126	140	76	60
Uniforms	123	99	139	48	145	189	91	54
Costumes	139	120	166	117	190	153	63	44
GIRLS' (AGED 2 TO 15) APPAREL	**144**	**29**	**232**	**131**	**338**	**94**	**237**	**14**
Coats and jackets	136	32	213	144	305	85	276	13
Dresses and suits	138	29	220	126	331	63	320	15
Shirts, blouses, and sweaters	158	34	255	130	363	132	156	12
Skirts and pants	136	20	226	117	338	84	281	12
Shorts and shorts sets	138	23	222	181	314	74	285	10
Active sportswear	158	42	245	87	366	120	116	28
Underwear and nightwear	140	21	230	181	322	88	283	10
Hosiery	136	32	200	158	266	97	250	16
Accessories	132	63	191	85	284	84	218	23
Uniforms	136	15	214	132	322	62	318	5
Costumes	158	9	279	123	449	58	140	11
CHILDREN UNDER AGE 2	**144**	**47**	**211**	**608**	**124**	**77**	**135**	**21**
Coats, jackets, and snowsuits	139	79	176	600	69	101	122	33
Outerwear including dresses	143	100	172	465	103	111	109	29
Underwear	147	16	238	715	139	48	142	14
Nightwear and loungewear	136	80	170	430	115	106	128	33
Accessories	139	38	203	502	125	120	186	27
FOOTWEAR	**118**	**87**	**140**	**131**	**156**	**113**	**120**	**56**
Men's	121	104	132	157	122	135	34	65
Boys'	125	29	192	164	274	41	281	4
Women's	112	104	115	101	116	124	116	69
Girls'	133	11	228	142	340	60	263	16
OTHER APPAREL PRODUCTS AND SERVICES	**119**	**103**	**136**	**123**	**146**	**124**	**68**	**69**
Material for making clothes	129	104	151	172	179	75	72	46
Sewing patterns and notions	127	123	129	83	151	120	123	72
Watches	133	120	155	130	150	180	42	67
Jewelry	123	105	146	115	174	113	38	63
Shoe repair and other shoe services	129	115	155	117	163	164	71	64
Coin-operated apparel laundry and dry cleaning	68	46	76	110	77	50	192	100
Apparel alteration, repair, and tailoring services	124	129	126	88	115	172	39	76
Clothing rental	145	139	155	40	118	299	28	18
Watch and jewelry repair	129	136	128	120	135	121	41	55
Professional laundry, dry cleaning	131	117	145	146	140	154	57	66
Clothing storage	142	153	127	187	153	38	45	56

Note: Spending index for total consumer units is 100.
Source: Calculations by New Strategist based on the 2000 Consumer Expenditure Survey

Table 2.13 Apparel: Indexed per capita spending by household type, 2000

(indexed average annual per capita spending of consumer units (CU) on apparel, accessories, and related services, by type of consumer unit, 2000; index definition: an index of 100 is the average for all consumer units; an index of 132 means that spending by consumer units in that group is 32 percent above the average for all consumer units; an index of 68 indicates spending that is 32 percent below the average for all consumer units)

	total married couples	married couples, no children	married couples with children				single parent, at least one child <18	single person
			total	oldest child under 6	oldest child 6 to 17	oldest child 18 or older		
Per capita spending of CU, total	$15,194	$21,098	$13,740	$14,502	$13,212	$14,355	$9,974	$23,059
Per capita spending of CU, index	100	139	90	95	87	94	66	152
Apparel, per capita spending index	97	116	95	100	93	96	89	138
MEN'S APPAREL	**99**	**145**	**87**	**81**	**75**	**119**	**37**	**153**
Suits	109	141	104	86	107	106	19	126
Sport coats and tailored jackets	115	161	105	64	94	152	10	106
Coats and jackets	111	183	94	100	82	118	16	118
Underwear	101	129	89	49	81	136	42	158
Hosiery	102	164	83	111	66	101	5	164
Nightwear	106	153	95	81	98	98	57	105
Accessories	103	169	82	99	60	120	56	160
Sweaters and vests	99	142	89	70	75	129	28	180
Active sportswear	111	200	82	53	87	95	39	115
Shirts	88	123	80	77	63	123	50	170
Pants	88	131	77	83	59	114	46	184
Shorts and shorts sets	108	178	88	71	89	99	30	125
Uniforms	115	98	123	105	102	176	25	69
Costumes	110	124	116	70	118	140	7	146
BOYS' (AGED 2 TO 15) APPAREL	**107**	**32**	**145**	**110**	**189**	**74**	**233**	**32**
Coats and jackets	114	28	156	98	216	67	194	18
Sweaters	112	46	146	81	209	57	156	48
Shirts	99	39	132	130	154	85	300	43
Underwear	112	34	154	170	165	118	185	27
Nightwear	98	108	109	188	97	76	193	35
Hosiery	97	48	116	111	137	72	308	10
Accessories	123	32	176	206	183	136	79	34
Suits, sport coats, and vests	107	19	149	93	201	77	192	50
Pants	105	20	145	66	207	63	267	25
Shorts and shorts sets	106	23	147	112	202	54	245	29
Uniforms	116	38	154	111	212	59	149	41
Active sportswear	114	27	151	61	229	46	198	22
Costumes	126	16	183	130	259	57	108	43
WOMEN'S APPAREL	**95**	**135**	**82**	**73**	**70**	**117**	**76**	**164**
Coats and jackets	95	149	74	55	64	109	106	173
Dresses	93	109	92	65	69	163	56	189
Sport coats and tailored jackets	91	125	82	38	82	109	69	217
Sweaters and vests	99	152	83	86	71	108	64	140
Shirts, blouses, and tops	93	134	84	77	71	122	75	187
Skirts	85	126	79	65	53	147	53	207
Pants	92	131	80	82	63	118	84	142
Shorts and shorts sets	100	141	95	88	87	118	87	123
Active sportswear	97	170	67	71	61	77	75	165

	total married couples	married couples, no children	married couples with children				single parent, at least one child <18	single person
			total	oldest child under 6	oldest child 6 to 17	oldest child 18 or older		
Nightwear	96	147	79	73	75	93	56	135
Undergarments	93	118	90	108	79	103	132	138
Hosiery	89	115	79	71	72	101	86	158
Suits	89	160	68	56	56	101	61	192
Accessories	105	144	79	66	77	92	66	150
Uniforms	96	124	89	34	88	125	78	135
Costumes	108	150	107	83	116	101	54	110
GIRLS' (AGED 2 TO 15) APPAREL	**113**	**36**	**149**	**93**	**206**	**62**	**204**	**34**
Coats and jackets	106	39	137	103	186	56	238	32
Dresses and suits	108	36	141	90	202	41	276	36
Shirts, blouses, and sweaters	123	42	164	93	221	87	134	30
Skirts and pants	106	25	145	84	206	55	242	30
Shorts and shorts sets	108	28	143	129	192	49	246	26
Active sportswear	123	52	157	62	223	79	100	71
Underwear and nightwear	110	26	148	129	196	58	244	25
Hosiery	106	40	128	113	162	64	215	39
Accessories	103	79	123	61	173	55	188	57
Uniforms	107	18	137	95	196	41	274	13
Costumes	123	11	179	88	274	38	121	26
CHILDREN UNDER AGE 2	**113**	**58**	**135**	**434**	**76**	**50**	**117**	**53**
Coats, jackets, and snowsuits	109	99	113	428	42	66	105	81
Outerwear including dresses	112	126	110	332	63	73	94	72
Underwear	115	20	152	511	85	31	122	36
Nightwear and loungewear	106	100	109	307	70	69	110	83
Accessories	109	47	130	359	76	79	160	67
FOOTWEAR	**92**	**109**	**90**	**94**	**95**	**74**	**103**	**139**
Men's	95	130	85	112	74	89	29	162
Boys'	98	36	123	117	167	27	242	10
Women's	87	130	74	72	71	82	100	173
Girls'	104	13	146	102	207	40	226	40
OTHER APPAREL PRODUCTS AND SERVICES	**93**	**129**	**87**	**88**	**89**	**82**	**58**	**172**
Material for making clothes	101	131	97	123	109	49	62	114
Sewing patterns and notions	99	154	83	59	92	79	106	181
Watches	104	150	99	93	91	118	36	166
Jewelry	96	131	94	82	106	74	33	158
Shoe repair and other shoe services	101	143	99	84	100	108	61	161
Coin-operated apparel laundry and dry cleaning	53	58	49	79	47	33	165	250
Apparel alteration, repair, and tailoring services	97	162	81	63	70	113	33	190
Clothing rental	113	173	99	29	72	197	24	45
Watch and jewelry repair	101	170	82	86	83	79	35	138
Professional laundry, dry cleaning	102	146	93	104	85	101	49	165
Clothing storage	111	191	82	134	93	25	39	141

Note: Per capita indexes account for household size and show how much each person in a particular household demographic segment spends relative to a person in the average household. Spending index for total consumer units is 100.
Source: Calculations by New Strategist based on the 2000 Consumer Expenditure Survey

Table 2.14 Apparel: Total spending by household type, 2000

(total annual spending on apparel, accessories, and related services, by consumer unit (CU) type, 2000; numbers in thousands)

	total married couples	married couples, no children	married couples with children				single parent, at least one child <18	single person
			total	oldest child under 6	oldest child 6 to 17	oldest child 18 or older		
Number of consumer units	56,287	22,805	28,777	5,291	15,396	8,090	6,132	32,323
Total spending of all CUs	$2,736,638,479	$962,269,290	$1,542,030,797	$268,549,467	$834,007,478	$441,311,118	$177,357,369	$745,336,057
Apparel, total spending	130,119,221	39,346,607	79,103,369	13,702,050	43,700,160	21,822,775	11,776,751	33,217,054
MEN'S APPAREL	**$24,453,324**	**$9,111,966**	**$13,426,773**	**$2,064,284**	**$6,483,717**	**$5,017,499**	**$905,328**	**$6,817,567**
Suits	2,615,094	855,416	1,546,476	212,222	900,358	433,948	45,561	540,764
Sport coats and tailored jackets	941,119	332,953	534,677	53,492	269,584	211,715	8,340	155,150
Coats and jackets	2,777,201	1,159,634	1,467,915	256,931	718,069	504,169	39,551	531,390
Underwear	1,264,206	411,630	694,677	63,598	357,957	292,130	52,122	355,876
Hosiery	846,556	343,215	430,216	94,921	192,296	142,950	3,802	244,362
Nightwear	254,417	93,272	143,022	19,947	82,830	40,207	13,429	45,252
Accessories	1,736,454	718,129	860,432	171,375	353,954	343,259	93,268	482,259
Sweaters and vests	1,134,183	413,911	637,698	82,169	302,531	253,055	31,702	370,745
Active sportswear	1,285,032	588,597	594,245	63,016	352,722	187,364	45,132	240,483
Shirts	5,395,109	1,919,953	3,079,139	487,619	1,351,923	1,294,238	306,907	1,876,350
Pants	4,362,243	1,642,416	2,380,146	423,174	1,029,992	958,422	224,554	1,628,756
Shorts and shorts sets	1,063,824	442,417	541,008	71,799	308,074	166,573	29,372	220,120
Uniforms	456,488	98,518	305,036	42,910	142,567	119,489	9,873	49,454
Costumes	321,399	91,676	211,799	21,058	120,859	69,817	1,901	76,606
BOYS' (AGED 2 TO 15) APPAREL	**7,374,160**	**559,635**	**6,227,631**	**780,634**	**4,560,295**	**867,086**	**1,586,900**	**392,401**
Coats and jackets	643,360	39,681	548,777	56,878	427,547	64,396	107,923	18,424
Sweaters	287,064	29,875	233,957	21,481	187,677	24,755	39,551	21,980
Shirts	1,485,977	148,689	1,239,138	201,005	810,291	218,673	444,999	115,716
Underwear	410,332	31,927	352,230	63,968	212,157	73,700	67,023	17,454
Nightwear	208,825	57,925	144,173	41,164	72,053	27,506	40,533	13,252
Hosiery	301,698	37,628	223,885	35,503	148,571	38,104	94,188	5,495
Accessories	390,632	25,770	346,763	67,302	203,073	73,376	24,835	19,071
Suits, sport coats, and vests	280,872	12,315	244,029	25,185	184,598	34,383	49,669	23,596
Pants	1,766,286	85,063	1,519,713	114,497	1,224,136	181,216	444,570	74,666
Shorts and shorts sets	680,510	37,172	589,641	74,286	456,030	59,462	155,753	33,616
Uniforms	306,201	25,086	252,662	30,053	196,145	26,454	38,754	19,394
Active sportswear	311,830	18,928	258,993	17,249	220,317	21,439	53,532	10,990
Costumes	301,135	9,578	273,669	31,958	218,007	23,542	25,570	18,424
WOMEN'S APPAREL	**41,418,789**	**14,985,166**	**22,395,412**	**3,295,499**	**10,696,679**	**8,730,081**	**3,264,615**	**12,846,453**
Coats and jackets	2,958,445	1,178,106	1,427,627	174,973	702,058	581,590	324,996	965,165
Dresses	5,814,447	1,719,041	3,569,211	419,365	1,516,352	1,742,748	348,543	2,121,358
Sport coats and tailored jackets	547,673	190,422	308,202	23,704	172,897	111,642	40,900	234,019
Sweaters and vests	3,507,806	1,366,704	1,828,778	312,116	879,266	655,128	225,596	894,054
Shirts, blouses, and tops	6,679,015	2,421,435	3,760,291	562,962	1,773,157	1,486,295	527,413	2,398,367
Skirts	785,767	293,728	450,648	61,799	171,973	230,484	48,504	341,331
Pants	5,692,867	2,039,679	3,069,355	521,428	1,350,075	1,242,462	509,201	1,565,726
Shorts and shorts sets	1,476,408	526,111	866,763	133,386	446,330	296,094	125,890	324,200
Active sportswear	1,935,710	862,485	834,245	146,296	428,317	263,491	149,130	593,774

	total married couples	married couples, no children	married couples with children			single parent, at least one child <18	single person
			total	oldest child under 6	oldest child 6 to 17	oldest child 18 or older		
Nightwear	$2,235,720	$864,538	$1,142,159	$173,492	$608,758	$370,198	$129,447	$562,097
Undergarments	2,163,109	691,448	1,305,900	258,783	640,782	407,736	301,633	575,349
Hosiery	1,337,942	437,856	742,447	110,159	380,897	260,417	128,036	426,664
Suits	2,178,870	983,808	1,039,137	140,846	476,968	421,165	147,352	838,459
Accessories	2,983,211	1,032,838	1,385,037	193,122	761,024	445,516	183,837	760,560
Uniforms	602,834	196,123	348,777	22,169	193,528	133,081	48,443	151,918
Costumes	517,840	180,844	317,123	41,005	193,990	82,194	25,632	94,060
GIRLS' (AGED 2 TO 15) APPAREL	**9,583,987**	**780,159**	**7,875,402**	**815,766**	**6,152,088**	**895,644**	**1,713,649**	**525,249**
Coats and jackets	532,475	49,943	426,763	52,804	325,933	48,055	117,428	28,444
Dresses and suits	1,409,989	118,358	1,149,353	121,164	926,069	92,145	357,373	85,333
Shirts, blouses, and sweaters	2,556,556	221,437	2,116,548	198,518	1,609,652	307,501	275,388	111,838
Skirts and pants	1,663,844	97,605	1,416,692	135,185	1,133,454	147,966	374,236	84,040
Shorts and shorts sets	648,426	43,101	534,389	80,000	404,299	50,239	145,880	27,798
Active sportswear	797,024	85,747	632,518	41,323	506,067	86,968	63,834	82,100
Underwear and nightwear	584,822	35,348	490,072	70,741	366,579	52,747	128,220	24,242
Hosiery	377,123	36,032	283,453	41,164	201,226	38,508	75,362	24,889
Accessories	370,931	71,836	274,245	22,328	218,007	33,735	66,471	36,525
Uniforms	299,447	12,999	240,288	27,302	193,374	19,497	76,098	6,788
Costumes	343,351	7,754	310,792	25,238	267,429	18,283	33,297	13,252
CHILDREN UNDER AGE 2	**6,659,315**	**873,888**	**4,966,622**	**2,634,071**	**1,566,851**	**507,728**	**680,223**	**558,218**
Coats, jackets, and snowsuits	211,076	48,803	136,403	85,661	28,637	22,005	20,174	28,444
Outerwear including dresses	1,847,339	526,339	1,136,404	565,396	365,347	205,648	153,239	212,362
Underwear	3,699,182	160,091	3,053,527	1,689,892	956,246	172,155	388,707	208,483
Nightwear and loungewear	305,638	72,748	195,108	90,794	70,360	34,059	31,335	42,990
Accessories	596,079	65,906	445,468	202,328	146,416	73,862	86,829	65,939
FOOTWEAR	**22,848,582**	**6,796,118**	**13,822,744**	**2,377,193**	**8,264,111**	**3,129,536**	**2,520,436**	**6,162,703**
Men's	8,005,700	2,784,947	4,480,579	976,084	2,201,166	1,283,236	245,587	2,459,780
Boys'	2,626,914	245,838	2,057,843	322,698	1,572,855	124,910	641,836	47,192
Women's	9,788,872	3,688,025	5,167,486	835,026	2,796,991	1,563,473	1,112,222	3,487,652
Girls'	2,427,658	77,537	2,117,124	243,439	1,692,944	157,998	520,791	168,403
OTHER APPAREL PRODUCTS AND SERVICES	**17,781,063**	**6,239,448**	**10,388,785**	**1,734,601**	**5,976,573**	**2,675,201**	**1,105,538**	**5,914,139**
Material for making clothes	344,476	113,113	206,619	43,175	131,020	28,639	20,849	70,141
Sewing patterns and notions	335,471	131,813	173,813	20,582	109,004	45,709	35,382	109,898
Watches	1,691,987	618,244	1,006,907	155,397	522,386	329,020	58,131	486,784
Jewelry	7,427,633	2,559,405	4,517,413	653,809	2,880,900	982,773	249,756	2,189,560
Shoe repair and other shoe services	132,837	47,891	81,727	11,323	46,034	24,270	7,972	38,141
Coin-operated apparel laundry and dry cleaning	1,452,767	399,544	826,763	221,111	451,257	154,519	446,410	1,224,718
Apparel alteration, repair, and tailoring services	399,075	168,073	207,194	26,455	101,306	79,444	13,490	140,282
Clothing rental	275,243	106,499	149,928	7,143	61,276	81,466	5,764	19,717
Watch and jewelry repair	344,476	147,320	175,252	30,159	98,842	46,275	11,896	84,686
Professional laundry, dry cleaning	5,333,193	1,928,619	3,022,736	559,999	1,561,462	901,388	254,355	1,540,514
Clothing storage	43,904	19,156	20,144	5,450	12,933	1,699	1,533	10,020

Note: Total spending figures for total consumer units can be found on Total Spending by Age and Total Spending by Region tables. Spending by type of consumer unit will not add to total because not all types of consumer units are shown.
Source: Calculations by New Strategist based on the 2000 Consumer Expenditure Survey

Table 2.15 Apparel: Market shares by household type, 2000

(percentage of total annual spending on apparel, accessories, and related services accounted for by types of consumer units, 2000)

	total married couples	married couples, no children	married couples with children				single parent, at least one child <18	single person
			total	oldest child under 6	oldest child 6 to 17	oldest child 18 or older		
Share of total consumer units	51.5%	20.9%	26.3%	4.8%	14.1%	7.4%	5.6%	29.6%
Share of total before-tax income	69.8	24.9	39.4	6.8	21.9	10.7	3.2	16.5
Share of total spending	65.8	23.1	37.1	6.5	20.0	10.6	4.3	17.9
Share of apparel spending	64.1	19.4	39.0	6.7	21.5	10.7	5.8	16.4
MEN'S APPAREL	**64.9%**	**24.2%**	**35.7%**	**5.5%**	**17.2%**	**13.3%**	**2.4%**	**18.1%**
Suits	72.0	23.5	42.6	5.8	24.8	11.9	1.3	14.9
Sport coats and tailored jackets	76.1	26.9	43.2	4.3	21.8	17.1	0.7	12.5
Coats and jackets	73.1	30.5	38.6	6.8	18.9	13.3	1.0	14.0
Underwear	66.2	21.6	36.4	3.3	18.8	15.3	2.7	18.6
Hosiery	67.3	27.3	34.2	7.5	15.3	11.4	0.3	19.4
Nightwear	69.6	25.5	39.2	5.5	22.7	11.0	3.7	12.4
Accessories	68.2	28.2	33.8	6.7	13.9	13.5	3.7	18.9
Sweaters and vests	65.0	23.7	36.5	4.7	17.3	14.5	1.8	21.2
Active sportswear	72.9	33.4	33.7	3.6	20.0	10.6	2.6	13.6
Shirts	57.7	20.5	32.9	5.2	14.5	13.8	3.3	20.1
Pants	58.1	21.9	31.7	5.6	13.7	12.8	3.0	21.7
Shorts and shorts sets	71.3	29.7	36.3	4.8	20.7	11.2	2.0	14.8
Uniforms	75.6	16.3	50.5	7.1	23.6	19.8	1.6	8.2
Costumes	72.4	20.6	47.7	4.7	27.2	15.7	0.4	17.3
BOYS' (AGED 2 TO 15) APPAREL	**70.4**	**5.3**	**59.5**	**7.5**	**43.5**	**8.3**	**15.2**	**3.7**
Coats and jackets	75.0	4.6	64.0	6.6	49.9	7.5	12.6	2.1
Sweaters	73.7	7.7	60.1	5.5	48.2	6.4	10.2	5.6
Shirts	65.2	6.5	54.4	8.8	35.6	9.6	19.5	5.1
Underwear	73.7	5.7	63.3	11.5	38.1	13.2	12.0	3.1
Nightwear	64.7	18.0	44.7	12.8	22.3	8.5	12.6	4.1
Hosiery	64.2	8.0	47.6	7.5	31.6	8.1	20.0	1.2
Accessories	81.2	5.4	72.1	14.0	42.2	15.2	5.2	4.0
Suits, sport coats, and vests	70.6	3.1	61.3	6.3	46.4	8.6	12.5	5.9
Pants	69.0	3.3	59.4	4.5	47.9	7.1	17.4	2.9
Shorts and shorts sets	69.5	3.8	60.2	7.6	46.6	6.1	15.9	3.4
Uniforms	76.5	6.3	63.1	7.5	49.0	6.6	9.7	4.8
Active sportswear	74.8	4.5	62.2	4.1	52.9	5.1	12.8	2.6
Costumes	82.7	2.6	75.1	8.8	59.9	6.5	7.0	5.1
WOMEN'S APPAREL	**62.4**	**22.6**	**33.7**	**5.0**	**16.1**	**13.1**	**4.9**	**19.3**
Coats and jackets	62.5	24.9	30.2	3.7	14.8	12.3	6.9	20.4
Dresses	61.3	18.1	37.6	4.4	16.0	18.4	3.7	22.4
Sport coats and tailored jackets	60.1	20.9	33.8	2.6	19.0	12.3	4.5	25.7
Sweaters and vests	65.1	25.4	33.9	5.8	16.3	12.2	4.2	16.6
Shirts, blouses, and tops	61.5	22.3	34.6	5.2	16.3	13.7	4.9	22.1
Skirts	56.3	21.0	32.3	4.4	12.3	16.5	3.5	24.5
Pants	60.8	21.8	32.8	5.6	14.4	13.3	5.4	16.7
Shorts and shorts sets	66.2	23.6	38.8	6.0	20.0	13.3	5.6	14.5
Active sportswear	63.7	28.4	27.5	4.8	14.1	8.7	4.9	19.5

	total married couples	married couples, no children	married couples with children			single parent, at least one child <18	single person
			total	oldest child under 6	oldest child 6 to 17	oldest child 18 or older	
Nightwear	63.5%	24.5%	32.4%	4.9%	17.3%	10.5%	3.7%	16.0%
Undergarments	61.4	19.6	37.1	7.3	18.2	11.6	8.6	16.3
Hosiery	58.4	19.1	32.4	4.8	16.6	11.4	5.6	18.6
Suits	58.9	26.6	28.1	3.8	12.9	11.4	4.0	22.7
Accessories	69.4	24.0	32.2	4.5	17.7	10.4	4.3	17.7
Uniforms	63.4	20.6	36.7	2.3	20.4	14.0	5.1	16.0
Costumes	71.4	24.9	43.7	5.7	26.8	11.3	3.5	13.0
GIRLS' (AGED 2 TO 15) APPAREL	**74.2**	**6.0**	**61.0**	**6.3**	**47.6**	**6.9**	**13.3**	**4.1**
Coats and jackets	70.1	6.6	56.1	6.9	42.9	6.3	15.4	3.7
Dresses and suits	70.9	5.9	57.8	6.1	46.6	4.6	18.0	4.3
Shirts, blouses, and sweaters	81.2	7.0	67.2	6.3	51.1	9.8	8.7	3.6
Skirts and pants	69.9	4.1	59.6	5.7	47.6	6.2	15.7	3.5
Shorts and shorts sets	71.0	4.7	58.5	8.8	44.3	5.5	16.0	3.0
Active sportswear	81.2	8.7	64.5	4.2	51.6	8.9	6.5	8.4
Underwear and nightwear	72.3	4.4	60.6	8.7	45.3	6.5	15.8	3.0
Hosiery	70.1	6.7	52.7	7.7	37.4	7.2	14.0	4.6
Accessories	68.1	13.2	50.4	4.1	40.0	6.2	12.2	6.7
Uniforms	70.2	3.0	56.3	6.4	45.3	4.6	17.8	1.6
Costumes	81.1	1.8	73.4	6.0	63.2	4.3	7.9	3.1
CHILDREN UNDER AGE 2	**74.3**	**9.8**	**55.4**	**29.4**	**17.5**	**5.7**	**7.6**	**6.2**
Coats, jackets, and snowsuits	71.5	16.5	46.2	29.0	9.7	7.5	6.8	9.6
Outerwear including dresses	73.5	21.0	45.2	22.5	14.5	8.2	6.1	8.5
Underwear	75.8	3.3	62.5	34.6	19.6	3.5	8.0	4.3
Nightwear and loungewear	70.0	16.7	44.7	20.8	16.1	7.8	7.2	9.9
Accessories	71.6	7.9	53.5	24.3	17.6	8.9	10.4	7.9
FOOTWEAR	**60.9**	**18.1**	**36.8**	**6.3**	**22.0**	**8.3**	**6.7**	**16.4**
Men's	62.3	21.7	34.9	7.6	17.1	10.0	1.9	19.1
Boys'	64.5	6.0	50.5	7.9	38.6	3.1	15.8	1.2
Women's	57.4	21.6	30.3	4.9	16.4	9.2	6.5	20.4
Girls'	68.7	2.2	59.9	6.9	47.9	4.5	14.7	4.8
OTHER APPAREL PRODUCTS AND SERVICES	**61.1**	**21.5**	**35.7**	**6.0**	**20.6**	**9.2**	**3.8**	**20.3**
Material for making clothes	66.3	21.8	39.8	8.3	25.2	5.5	4.0	13.5
Sewing patterns and notions	65.4	25.7	33.9	4.0	21.3	8.9	6.9	21.4
Watches	68.4	25.0	40.7	6.3	21.1	13.3	2.3	19.7
Jewelry	63.3	21.8	38.5	5.6	24.5	8.4	2.1	18.7
Shoe repair and other shoe services	66.4	23.9	40.8	5.7	23.0	12.1	4.0	19.1
Coin-operated apparel laundry and dry cleaning	35.0	9.6	19.9	5.3	10.9	3.7	10.8	29.5
Apparel alteration, repair, and tailoring services	64.0	27.0	33.2	4.2	16.3	12.7	2.2	22.5
Clothing rental	74.7	28.9	40.7	1.9	16.6	22.1	1.6	5.3
Watch and jewelry repair	66.4	28.4	33.8	5.8	19.1	8.9	2.3	16.3
Professional laundry, dry cleaning	67.4	24.4	38.2	7.1	19.7	11.4	3.2	19.5
Clothing storage	73.0	31.8	33.5	9.1	21.5	2.8	2.5	16.7

Note: Market share for total consumer units is 100.0%. Market shares by type of consumer unit will not add to total because not all types of consumer units are shown.

Source: Calculations by New Strategist based on the 2000 Consumer Expenditure Survey

Table 2.16   Apparel: Average spending by race and Hispanic origin, 2000

(average annual spending of consumer units (CU) on apparel, accessories, and related services, by race and Hispanic origin of consumer unit reference person, 2000)

	total consumer units	race		Hispanic origin	
		black	white and other	Hispanic	non-Hispanic
Number of consumer units (in thousands, add 000)	109,367	13,230	96,137	9,473	99,894
Average number of persons per CU	2.5	2.7	2.5	3.4	2.4
Average before-tax income of CU	$44,649.00	$32,657.00	$46,260.00	$34,891.00	$45,669.00
Average spending of CU, total	38,044.67	28,152.24	39,406.20	32,734.95	38,548.91
Apparel, average spending	1,856.16	1,695.20	1,878.33	2,075.58	1,835.82
MEN'S APPAREL	**$344.29**	**$245.29**	**$357.93**	**$359.08**	**$342.97**
Suits	33.23	36.72	32.75	21.16	34.38
Sport coats and tailored jackets	11.31	6.71	11.94	5.21	11.89
Coats and jackets	34.76	31.53	35.20	28.96	35.29
Underwear	17.45	10.44	18.42	22.78	16.95
Hosiery	11.50	7.67	12.02	16.96	10.99
Nightwear	3.34	2.73	3.43	1.79	3.49
Accessories	23.29	11.81	24.87	29.83	22.68
Sweaters and vests	15.96	10.92	16.66	12.54	16.29
Active sportswear	16.11	9.76	16.99	10.05	16.67
Shirts	85.47	46.48	90.83	90.44	85.00
Pants	68.65	55.86	70.41	96.85	66.03
Shorts and shorts sets	13.64	5.74	14.73	13.56	13.65
Uniforms	5.52	5.59	5.52	6.12	5.47
Costumes	4.06	3.33	4.17	2.83	4.18
BOYS' (AGED 2 TO 15) APPAREL	**95.76**	**144.64**	**89.04**	**123.51**	**93.15**
Coats and jackets	7.84	14.86	6.88	8.49	7.78
Sweaters	3.56	4.08	3.48	4.35	3.48
Shirts	20.84	40.84	18.08	23.17	20.62
Underwear	5.09	10.33	4.37	5.73	5.04
Nightwear	2.95	3.97	2.81	3.24	2.92
Hosiery	4.30	6.31	4.03	5.43	4.20
Accessories	4.40	2.50	4.67	6.29	4.23
Suits, sport coats, and vests	3.64	4.43	3.53	5.81	3.43
Pants	23.39	33.23	22.04	36.53	22.15
Shorts and shorts sets	8.95	12.36	8.48	9.80	8.87
Uniforms	3.66	3.41	3.69	3.82	3.64
Active sportswear	3.81	5.66	3.55	7.74	3.44
Costumes	3.33	2.66	3.42	3.12	3.35
WOMEN'S APPAREL	**607.11**	**473.20**	**625.55**	**540.33**	**613.37**
Coats and jackets	43.26	36.67	44.17	39.59	43.60
Dresses	86.74	80.24	87.64	95.74	85.90
Sport coats and tailored jackets	8.33	4.01	8.92	4.44	8.70
Sweaters and vests	49.27	24.63	52.66	30.31	51.03
Shirts, blouses, and tops	99.26	67.04	103.70	98.13	99.37
Skirts	12.76	7.86	13.43	10.40	12.97
Pants	85.55	63.44	88.59	94.66	84.70
Shorts and shorts sets	20.40	7.55	22.16	23.56	20.10
Active sportswear	27.78	19.49	28.92	15.54	28.92

	total consumer units	race		Hispanic origin	
		black	white and other	Hispanic	non-Hispanic
Nightwear	$32.21	$23.48	$33.42	$26.65	$32.73
Undergarments	32.20	40.93	31.00	36.88	31.77
Hosiery	20.95	23.27	20.63	15.90	21.42
Suits	33.80	41.78	32.70	16.33	35.46
Accessories	39.29	20.71	41.85	21.67	40.93
Uniforms	8.69	9.41	8.59	4.94	9.04
Costumes	6.63	2.69	7.17	5.59	6.73
GIRLS' (AGED 2 TO 15) APPAREL	**118.09**	**131.07**	**116.30**	**150.31**	**115.07**
Coats and jackets	6.95	13.53	6.05	8.26	6.83
Dresses and suits	18.19	16.46	18.43	27.18	17.36
Shirts, blouses, and sweaters	28.79	25.75	29.21	33.50	28.35
Skirts and pants	21.75	32.48	20.28	26.52	21.30
Shorts and shorts sets	8.35	12.13	7.83	8.96	8.29
Active sportswear	8.97	3.42	9.73	15.34	8.38
Underwear and nightwear	7.40	9.28	7.14	8.51	7.30
Hosiery	4.92	5.85	4.79	6.33	4.79
Accessories	4.98	1.71	5.44	5.95	4.89
Uniforms	3.90	8.13	3.32	6.21	3.68
Costumes	3.87	2.33	4.08	3.54	3.90
CHILDREN UNDER AGE 2	**81.92**	**89.04**	**80.94**	**136.90**	**76.80**
Coats, jackets, and snowsuits	2.70	3.45	2.60	3.35	2.64
Outerwear including dresses	22.97	28.26	22.24	27.71	22.52
Underwear	44.65	39.50	45.36	88.14	40.61
Nightwear and loungewear	3.99	4.60	3.91	4.77	3.92
Accessories	7.61	13.25	6.84	12.93	7.12
FOOTWEAR	**343.09**	**351.99**	**341.86**	**516.37**	**326.99**
Men's	117.55	91.42	121.14	211.29	108.84
Boys'	37.26	58.51	34.33	53.71	35.73
Women's	155.95	157.76	155.70	196.46	152.19
Girls'	32.33	44.30	30.69	54.92	30.24
OTHER APPAREL PRODUCTS AND SERVICES	**265.90**	**259.96**	**266.72**	**249.09**	**267.49**
Material for making clothes	4.75	0.88	5.28	0.63	5.13
Sewing patterns and notions	4.69	1.82	5.09	2.29	4.92
Watches	22.63	24.15	22.42	23.86	22.51
Jewelry	107.32	63.13	113.40	58.23	111.98
Shoe repair and other shoe services	1.83	0.95	1.95	1.08	1.90
Coin-operated apparel laundry and dry cleaning	37.93	66.76	33.96	106.48	31.43
Apparel alteration, repair, and tailoring services	5.70	3.54	5.99	2.84	5.97
Clothing rental	3.37	3.10	3.41	1.54	3.55
Watch and jewelry repair	4.74	1.81	5.14	6.50	4.57
Professional laundry, dry cleaning	72.40	93.62	69.48	45.64	74.93
Clothing storage	0.55	0.20	0.60	–	0.60

Note: Other races include American Indians, Asians, and Pacific Islanders. (–) means sample is too small to make a reliable estimate.
Source: Bureau of Labor Statistics, unpublished data from the 2000 Consumer Expenditure Survey

Table 2.17 Apparel: Indexed spending by race and Hispanic origin, 2000

(indexed average annual spending of consumer units (CU) on apparel, accessories, and related services, by race and Hispanic origin of consumer unit reference person, 2000; index definition: an index of 100 is the average for all consumer units; an index of 132 means that spending by consumer units in that group is 32 percent above the average for all consumer units; an index of 68 indicates spending that is 32 percent below the average for all consumer units)

	total consumer units	race black	race white and other	Hispanic origin Hispanic	Hispanic origin non-Hispanic
Average spending of CU, total	$38,045	$28,152	$39,406	$32,735	$38,549
Average spending of CU, index	100	74	104	86	101
Apparel, spending index	100	91	101	112	99
MEN'S APPAREL	100	71	104	104	100
Suits	100	111	99	64	103
Sport coats and tailored jackets	100	59	106	46	105
Coats and jackets	100	91	101	83	102
Underwear	100	60	106	131	97
Hosiery	100	67	105	147	96
Nightwear	100	82	103	54	104
Accessories	100	51	107	128	97
Sweaters and vests	100	68	104	79	102
Active sportswear	100	61	105	62	103
Shirts	100	54	106	106	99
Pants	100	81	103	141	96
Shorts and shorts sets	100	42	108	99	100
Uniforms	100	101	100	111	99
Costumes	100	82	103	70	103
BOYS' (AGED 2 TO 15) APPAREL	100	151	93	129	97
Coats and jackets	100	190	88	108	99
Sweaters	100	115	98	122	98
Shirts	100	196	87	111	99
Underwear	100	203	86	113	99
Nightwear	100	135	95	110	99
Hosiery	100	147	94	126	98
Accessories	100	57	106	143	96
Suits, sport coats, and vests	100	122	97	160	94
Pants	100	142	94	156	95
Shorts and shorts sets	100	138	95	109	99
Uniforms	100	93	101	104	99
Active sportswear	100	149	93	203	90
Costumes	100	80	103	94	101
WOMEN'S APPAREL	100	78	103	89	101
Coats and jackets	100	85	102	92	101
Dresses	100	93	101	110	99
Sport coats and tailored jackets	100	48	107	53	104
Sweaters and vests	100	50	107	62	104
Shirts, blouses, and tops	100	68	104	99	100
Skirts	100	62	105	82	102
Pants	100	74	104	111	99
Shorts and shorts sets	100	37	109	115	99
Active sportswear	100	70	104	56	104

		race		Hispanic origin	
	total consumer units	black	white and other	Hispanic	non-Hispanic
Nightwear	100	73	104	83	102
Undergarments	100	127	96	115	99
Hosiery	100	111	98	76	102
Suits	100	124	97	48	105
Accessories	100	53	107	55	104
Uniforms	100	108	99	57	104
Costumes	100	41	108	84	102
GIRLS' (AGED 2 TO 15) APPAREL	**100**	**111**	**98**	**127**	**97**
Coats and jackets	100	195	87	119	98
Dresses and suits	100	90	101	149	95
Shirts, blouses, and sweaters	100	89	101	116	98
Skirts and pants	100	149	93	122	98
Shorts and shorts sets	100	145	94	107	99
Active sportswear	100	38	108	171	93
Underwear and nightwear	100	125	96	115	99
Hosiery	100	119	97	129	97
Accessories	100	34	109	119	98
Uniforms	100	208	85	159	94
Costumes	100	60	105	91	101
CHILDREN UNDER AGE 2	**100**	**109**	**99**	**167**	**94**
Coats, jackets, and snowsuits	100	128	96	124	98
Outerwear including dresses	100	123	97	121	98
Underwear	100	88	102	197	91
Nightwear and loungewear	100	115	98	120	98
Accessories	100	174	90	170	94
FOOTWEAR	**100**	**103**	**100**	**151**	**95**
Men's	100	78	103	180	93
Boys'	100	157	92	144	96
Women's	100	101	100	126	98
Girls'	100	137	95	170	94
OTHER APPAREL PRODUCTS AND SERVICES	**100**	**98**	**100**	**94**	**101**
Material for making clothes	100	19	111	13	108
Sewing patterns and notions	100	39	109	49	105
Watches	100	107	99	105	99
Jewelry	100	59	106	54	104
Shoe repair and other shoe services	100	52	107	59	104
Coin-operated apparel laundry and dry cleaning	100	176	90	281	83
Apparel alteration, repair, and tailoring services	100	62	105	50	105
Clothing rental	100	92	101	46	105
Watch and jewelry repair	100	38	108	137	96
Professional laundry, dry cleaning	100	129	96	63	103
Clothing storage	100	36	109	–	109

Note: Other races include American Indians, Asians, and Pacific Islanders. (–) means sample is too small to make a reliable estimate.
Source: Calculations by New Strategist based on the 2000 Consumer Expenditure Survey

Table 2.18 Apparel: Indexed per capita spending by race and Hispanic origin, 2000

(indexed average annual per capita spending of consumer units (CU) on apparel, accessories, and related services, by race and Hispanic origin of consumer unit reference person, 2000; index definition: an index of 100 is the average for all consumer units; an index of 132 means that spending by consumer units in that group is 32 percent above the average for all consumer units; an index of 68 indicates spending that is 32 percent below the average for all consumer units)

	total consumer units	race		Hispanic origin	
		black	white and other	Hispanic	non-Hispanic
Per capita spending of CU, total	$15,218	$10,427	$15,762	$9,628	$16,062
Per capita spending of CU, index	100	69	104	63	106
Apparel, per capita spending index	100	85	101	82	103
MEN'S APPAREL	**100**	**66**	**104**	**77**	**104**
Suits	100	102	99	47	108
Sport coats and tailored jackets	100	55	106	34	110
Coats and jackets	100	84	101	61	106
Underwear	100	55	106	96	101
Hosiery	100	62	105	108	100
Nightwear	100	76	103	39	109
Accessories	100	47	107	94	101
Sweaters and vests	100	63	104	58	106
Active sportswear	100	56	105	46	108
Shirts	100	50	106	78	104
Pants	100	75	103	104	100
Shorts and shorts sets	100	39	108	73	104
Uniforms	100	94	100	82	103
Costumes	100	76	103	51	107
BOYS' (AGED 2 TO 15) APPAREL	**100**	**140**	**93**	**95**	**101**
Coats and jackets	100	176	88	80	103
Sweaters	100	106	98	90	102
Shirts	100	181	87	82	103
Underwear	100	188	86	83	103
Nightwear	100	125	95	81	103
Hosiery	100	136	94	93	102
Accessories	100	53	106	105	100
Suits, sport coats, and vests	100	113	97	117	98
Pants	100	132	94	115	99
Shorts and shorts sets	100	128	95	81	103
Uniforms	100	86	101	77	104
Active sportswear	100	138	93	149	94
Costumes	100	74	103	69	105
WOMEN'S APPAREL	**100**	**72**	**103**	**65**	**105**
Coats and jackets	100	78	102	67	105
Dresses	100	86	101	81	103
Sport coats and tailored jackets	100	45	107	39	109
Sweaters and vests	100	46	107	45	108
Shirts, blouses, and tops	100	63	104	73	104
Skirts	100	57	105	60	106
Pants	100	69	104	81	103
Shorts and shorts sets	100	34	109	85	103
Active sportswear	100	65	104	41	108

	total consumer units	race		Hispanic origin	
		black	white and other	Hispanic	non-Hispanic
Nightwear	100	67	104	61	106
Undergarments	100	118	96	84	103
Hosiery	100	103	98	56	107
Suits	100	114	97	36	109
Accessories	100	49	107	41	109
Uniforms	100	100	99	42	108
Costumes	100	38	108	62	106
GIRLS' (AGED 2 TO 15) APPAREL	**100**	**103**	**98**	**94**	**102**
Coats and jackets	100	180	87	87	102
Dresses and suits	100	84	101	110	99
Shirts, blouses, and sweaters	100	83	101	86	103
Skirts and pants	100	138	93	90	102
Shorts and shorts sets	100	135	94	79	103
Active sportswear	100	35	108	126	97
Underwear and nightwear	100	116	96	85	103
Hosiery	100	110	97	95	101
Accessories	100	32	109	88	102
Uniforms	100	193	85	117	98
Costumes	100	56	105	67	105
CHILDREN UNDER AGE 2	**100**	**101**	**99**	**123**	**98**
Coats, jackets, and snowsuits	100	118	96	91	102
Outerwear including dresses	100	114	97	89	102
Underwear	100	82	102	145	95
Nightwear and loungewear	100	107	98	88	102
Accessories	100	161	90	125	97
FOOTWEAR	**100**	**95**	**100**	**111**	**99**
Men's	100	72	103	132	96
Boys'	100	145	92	106	100
Women's	100	94	100	93	102
Girls'	100	127	95	125	97
OTHER APPAREL PRODUCTS AND SERVICES	**100**	**91**	**100**	**69**	**105**
Material for making clothes	100	17	111	10	113
Sewing patterns and notions	100	36	109	36	109
Watches	100	99	99	78	104
Jewelry	100	54	106	40	109
Shoe repair and other shoe services	100	48	107	43	108
Coin-operated apparel laundry and dry cleaning	100	163	90	206	86
Apparel alteration, repair, and tailoring services	100	58	105	37	109
Clothing rental	100	85	101	34	110
Watch and jewelry repair	100	35	108	101	100
Professional laundry, dry cleaning	100	120	96	46	108
Clothing storage	100	34	109	–	114

Note: Per capita indexes account for household size and show how much each person in a particular household demographic segment spends relative to a person in the average household. Other races include Asians, Native Americans, and Pacific Islanders. (–) means sample is too small to make a reliable estimate.
Source: Calculations by New Strategist based on the 2000 Consumer Expenditure Survey

Table 2.19 Apparel: Total spending by race and Hispanic origin, 2000

(total annual spending on apparel, accessories, and related services, by race and Hispanic origin groups, 2000; numbers in thousands)

	total consumer units	race black	race white and other	Hispanic origin Hispanic	Hispanic origin non-Hispanic
Number of consumer units	109,367	13,230	96,137	9,473	99,894
Total spending of all consumer units	$4,160,831,424	$372,454,135	$3,788,393,849	$310,098,181	$3,850,804,816
Apparel, total spending	203,002,651	22,427,496	180,577,011	19,661,969	183,387,403
MEN'S APPAREL	**$37,653,964**	**$3,245,187**	**$34,410,316**	**$3,401,565**	**$34,260,645**
Suits	3,634,265	485,806	3,148,487	200,449	3,434,356
Sport coats and tailored jackets	1,236,941	88,773	1,147,876	49,354	1,187,740
Coats and jackets	3,801,597	417,142	3,384,022	274,338	3,525,259
Underwear	1,908,454	138,121	1,770,844	215,795	1,693,203
Hosiery	1,257,721	101,474	1,155,567	160,662	1,097,835
Nightwear	365,286	36,118	329,750	16,957	348,630
Accessories	2,547,157	156,246	2,390,927	282,580	2,265,596
Sweaters and vests	1,745,497	144,472	1,601,642	118,791	1,627,273
Active sportswear	1,761,902	129,125	1,633,368	95,204	1,665,233
Shirts	9,347,597	614,930	8,732,124	856,738	8,490,990
Pants	7,508,045	739,028	6,769,006	917,460	6,596,001
Shorts and shorts sets	1,491,766	75,940	1,416,098	128,454	1,363,553
Uniforms	603,706	73,956	530,676	57,975	546,420
Costumes	444,030	44,056	400,891	26,809	417,557
BOYS' (AGED 2 TO 15) APPAREL	**10,472,984**	**1,913,587**	**8,560,038**	**1,170,010**	**9,305,126**
Coats and jackets	857,437	196,598	661,423	80,426	777,175
Sweaters	389,347	53,978	334,557	41,208	347,631
Shirts	2,279,208	540,313	1,738,157	219,489	2,059,814
Underwear	556,678	136,666	420,119	54,280	503,466
Nightwear	322,633	52,523	270,145	30,693	291,690
Hosiery	470,278	83,481	387,432	51,438	419,555
Accessories	481,215	33,075	448,960	59,585	422,552
Suits, sport coats, and vests	398,096	58,609	339,364	55,038	342,636
Pants	2,558,094	439,633	2,118,859	346,049	2,212,652
Shorts and shorts sets	978,835	163,523	815,242	92,835	886,060
Uniforms	400,283	45,114	354,746	36,187	363,614
Active sportswear	416,688	74,882	341,286	73,321	343,635
Costumes	364,192	35,192	328,789	29,556	334,645
WOMEN'S APPAREL	**66,397,799**	**6,260,436**	**60,138,500**	**5,118,546**	**61,271,983**
Coats and jackets	4,731,216	485,144	4,246,371	375,036	4,355,378
Dresses	9,486,494	1,061,575	8,425,447	906,945	8,580,895
Sport coats and tailored jackets	911,027	53,052	857,542	42,060	869,078
Sweaters and vests	5,388,512	325,855	5,062,574	287,127	5,097,591
Shirts, blouses, and tops	10,855,768	886,939	9,969,407	929,585	9,926,467
Skirts	1,395,523	103,988	1,291,120	98,519	1,295,625
Pants	9,356,347	839,311	8,516,777	896,714	8,461,022
Shorts and shorts sets	2,231,087	99,887	2,130,396	223,184	2,007,869
Active sportswear	3,038,215	257,853	2,780,282	147,210	2,888,934

	total consumer units	race		Hispanic origin	
		black	white and other	Hispanic	non-Hispanic
Nightwear	$3,522,711	$310,640	$3,212,899	$252,455	$3,269,531
Undergarments	3,521,617	541,504	2,980,247	349,364	3,173,632
Hosiery	2,291,239	307,862	1,983,306	150,621	2,139,729
Suits	3,696,605	552,749	3,143,680	154,694	3,542,241
Accessories	4,297,029	273,993	4,023,333	205,280	4,088,661
Uniforms	950,399	124,494	825,817	46,797	903,042
Costumes	725,103	35,589	689,302	52,954	672,287
GIRLS' (AGED 2 TO 15) APPAREL	**12,915,149**	**1,734,056**	**11,180,733**	**1,423,887**	**11,494,803**
Coats and jackets	760,101	179,002	581,629	78,247	682,276
Dresses and suits	1,989,386	217,766	1,771,805	257,476	1,734,160
Shirts, blouses, and sweaters	3,148,676	340,673	2,808,162	317,346	2,831,995
Skirts and pants	2,378,732	429,710	1,949,658	251,224	2,127,742
Shorts and shorts sets	913,214	160,480	752,753	84,878	828,121
Active sportswear	981,022	45,247	935,413	145,316	837,112
Underwear and nightwear	809,316	122,774	686,418	80,615	729,226
Hosiery	538,086	77,396	460,496	59,964	478,492
Accessories	544,648	22,623	522,985	56,364	488,482
Uniforms	426,531	107,560	319,175	58,827	367,610
Costumes	423,250	30,826	392,239	33,534	389,587
CHILDREN UNDER AGE 2	**8,959,345**	**1,177,999**	**7,781,329**	**1,296,854**	**7,671,859**
Coats, jackets, and snowsuits	295,291	45,644	249,956	31,735	263,720
Outerwear including dresses	2,512,160	373,880	2,138,087	262,497	2,249,613
Underwear	4,883,237	522,585	4,360,774	834,950	4,056,695
Nightwear and loungewear	436,374	60,858	375,896	45,186	391,584
Accessories	832,283	175,298	657,577	122,486	711,245
FOOTWEAR	**37,522,724**	**4,656,828**	**32,865,395**	**4,891,573**	**32,664,339**
Men's	12,856,091	1,209,487	11,646,036	2,001,550	10,872,463
Boys'	4,075,014	774,087	3,300,383	508,795	3,569,213
Women's	17,055,784	2,087,165	14,968,531	1,861,066	15,202,868
Girls'	3,535,835	586,089	2,950,445	520,257	3,020,795
OTHER APPAREL PRODUCTS AND SERVICES	**29,080,685**	**3,439,271**	**25,641,661**	**2,359,630**	**26,720,646**
Material for making clothes	519,493	11,642	507,603	5,968	512,456
Sewing patterns and notions	512,931	24,079	489,337	21,693	491,478
Watches	2,474,975	319,505	2,155,392	226,026	2,248,614
Jewelry	11,737,266	835,210	10,901,936	551,613	11,186,130
Shoe repair and other shoe services	200,142	12,569	187,467	10,231	189,799
Coin-operated apparel laundry and dry cleaning	4,148,290	883,235	3,264,813	1,008,685	3,139,668
Apparel alteration, repair, and tailoring services	623,392	46,834	575,861	26,903	596,367
Clothing rental	368,567	41,013	327,827	14,588	354,624
Watch and jewelry repair	518,400	23,946	494,144	61,575	456,516
Professional laundry, dry cleaning	7,918,171	1,238,593	6,679,599	432,348	7,485,057
Clothing storage	60,152	2,646	57,682	–	59,936

Note: Other races include American Indians, Asians, and Pacific Islanders. Numbers may not add to total because of rounding. (–) means sample is too small to make a reliable estimate.
Source: Calculations by New Strategist based on the 2000 Consumer Expenditure Survey

Table 2.20   Apparel: Market shares by race and Hispanic origin, 2000

(percentage of total annual spending on apparel, accessories, and related services accounted for by race and Hispanic origin groups, 2000)

	total consumer units	race		Hispanic origin	
		black	white and other	Hispanic	non-Hispanic
Share of total consumer units	100.0%	12.1%	87.9%	8.7%	91.3%
Share of total before-tax income	100.0	8.8	91.1	6.8	93.4
Share of total spending	100.0	9.0	91.0	7.5	92.5
Share of apparel spending	100.0	11.0	89.0	9.7	90.3
MEN'S APPAREL	**100.0%**	**8.6%**	**91.4%**	**9.0%**	**91.0%**
Suits	100.0	13.4	86.6	5.5	94.5
Sport coats and tailored jackets	100.0	7.2	92.8	4.0	96.0
Coats and jackets	100.0	11.0	89.0	7.2	92.7
Underwear	100.0	7.2	92.8	11.3	88.7
Hosiery	100.0	8.1	91.9	12.8	87.3
Nightwear	100.0	9.9	90.3	4.6	95.4
Accessories	100.0	6.1	93.9	11.1	88.9
Sweaters and vests	100.0	8.3	91.8	6.8	93.2
Active sportswear	100.0	7.3	92.7	5.4	94.5
Shirts	100.0	6.6	93.4	9.2	90.8
Pants	100.0	9.8	90.2	12.2	87.9
Shorts and shorts sets	100.0	5.1	94.9	8.6	91.4
Uniforms	100.0	12.3	87.9	9.6	90.5
Costumes	100.0	9.9	90.3	6.0	94.0
BOYS' (AGED 2 TO 15) APPAREL	**100.0**	**18.3**	**81.7**	**11.2**	**88.8**
Coats and jackets	100.0	22.9	77.1	9.4	90.6
Sweaters	100.0	13.9	85.9	10.6	89.3
Shirts	100.0	23.7	76.3	9.6	90.4
Underwear	100.0	24.6	75.5	9.8	90.4
Nightwear	100.0	16.3	83.7	9.5	90.4
Hosiery	100.0	17.8	82.4	10.9	89.2
Accessories	100.0	6.9	93.3	12.4	87.8
Suits, sport coats, and vests	100.0	14.7	85.2	13.8	86.1
Pants	100.0	17.2	82.8	13.5	86.5
Shorts and shorts sets	100.0	16.7	83.3	9.5	90.5
Uniforms	100.0	11.3	88.6	9.0	90.8
Active sportswear	100.0	18.0	81.9	17.6	82.5
Costumes	100.0	9.7	90.3	8.1	91.9
WOMEN'S APPAREL	**100.0**	**9.4**	**90.6**	**7.7**	**92.3**
Coats and jackets	100.0	10.3	89.8	7.9	92.1
Dresses	100.0	11.2	88.8	9.6	90.5
Sport coats and tailored jackets	100.0	5.8	94.1	4.6	95.4
Sweaters and vests	100.0	6.0	94.0	5.3	94.6
Shirts, blouses, and tops	100.0	8.2	91.8	8.6	91.4
Skirts	100.0	7.5	92.5	7.1	92.8
Pants	100.0	9.0	91.0	9.6	90.4
Shorts and shorts sets	100.0	4.5	95.5	10.0	90.0
Active sportswear	100.0	8.5	91.5	4.8	95.1

	total consumer units	race		Hispanic origin	
		black	white and other	Hispanic	non-Hispanic
Nightwear	100.0%	8.8%	91.2%	7.2%	92.8%
Undergarments	100.0	15.4	84.6	9.9	90.1
Hosiery	100.0	13.4	86.6	6.6	93.4
Suits	100.0	15.0	85.0	4.2	95.8
Accessories	100.0	6.4	93.6	4.8	95.2
Uniforms	100.0	13.1	86.9	4.9	95.0
Costumes	100.0	4.9	95.1	7.3	92.7
GIRLS' (AGED 2 TO 15) APPAREL	**100.0**	**13.4**	**86.6**	**11.0**	**89.0**
Coats and jackets	100.0	23.5	76.5	10.3	89.8
Dresses and suits	100.0	10.9	89.1	12.9	87.2
Shirts, blouses, and sweaters	100.0	10.8	89.2	10.1	89.9
Skirts and pants	100.0	18.1	82.0	10.6	89.4
Shorts and shorts sets	100.0	17.6	82.4	9.3	90.7
Active sportswear	100.0	4.6	95.4	14.8	85.3
Underwear and nightwear	100.0	15.2	84.8	10.0	90.1
Hosiery	100.0	14.4	85.6	11.1	88.9
Accessories	100.0	4.2	96.0	10.3	89.7
Uniforms	100.0	25.2	74.8	13.8	86.2
Costumes	100.0	7.3	92.7	7.9	92.0
CHILDREN UNDER AGE 2	**100.0**	**13.1**	**86.9**	**14.5**	**85.6**
Coats, jackets, and snowsuits	100.0	15.5	84.6	10.7	89.3
Outerwear including dresses	100.0	14.9	85.1	10.4	89.5
Underwear	100.0	10.7	89.3	17.1	83.1
Nightwear and loungewear	100.0	13.9	86.1	10.4	89.7
Accessories	100.0	21.1	79.0	14.7	85.5
FOOTWEAR	**100.0**	**12.4**	**87.6**	**13.0**	**87.1**
Men's	100.0	9.4	90.6	15.6	84.6
Boys'	100.0	19.0	81.0	12.5	87.6
Women's	100.0	12.2	87.8	10.9	89.1
Girls'	100.0	16.6	83.4	14.7	85.4
OTHER APPAREL PRODUCTS AND SERVICES	**100.0**	**11.8**	**88.2**	**8.1**	**91.9**
Material for making clothes	100.0	2.2	97.7	1.1	98.6
Sewing patterns and notions	100.0	4.7	95.4	4.2	95.8
Watches	100.0	12.9	87.1	9.1	90.9
Jewelry	100.0	7.1	92.9	4.7	95.3
Shoe repair and other shoe services	100.0	6.3	93.7	5.1	94.8
Coin-operated apparel laundry and dry cleaning	100.0	21.3	78.7	24.3	75.7
Apparel alteration, repair, and tailoring services	100.0	7.5	92.4	4.3	95.7
Clothing rental	100.0	11.1	88.9	4.0	96.2
Watch and jewelry repair	100.0	4.6	95.3	11.9	88.1
Professional laundry, dry cleaning	100.0	15.6	84.4	5.5	94.5
Clothing storage	100.0	4.4	95.9	–	99.6

Note: Other races include American Indians, Asians, and Pacific Islanders. Numbers may not add to total because of rounding. (–) means sample is too small to make a reliable estimate.
Source: Calculations by New Strategist based on the 2000 Consumer Expenditure Survey

Table 2.21 Apparel: Average spending by region, 2000

(average annual spending of consumer units (CU) on apparel, accessories, and related services, by region in which consumer unit lives, 2000)

	total consumer units	Northeast	Midwest	South	West
Number of consumer units (in thousands, add 000)	109,367	20,994	25,717	38,245	24,410
Average number of persons per CU	2.5	2.5	2.5	2.5	2.6
Average before-tax income of CU	$44,649.00	$47,439.00	$44,377.00	$41,984.00	$46,670.00
Average spending of CU, total	38,044.67	38,901.91	39,212.70	34,707.07	41,328.19
Apparel, average spending	1,856.16	2,115.34	1,917.30	1,616.86	1,945.35
MEN'S APPAREL	**$344.29**	**$374.21**	**$386.07**	**$294.96**	**$353.64**
Suits	33.23	43.56	26.43	31.46	34.30
Sport coats and tailored jackets	11.31	18.49	11.72	9.33	7.80
Coats and jackets	34.76	50.95	48.55	21.31	26.95
Underwear	17.45	15.69	18.37	16.62	19.46
Hosiery	11.50	10.67	13.85	9.69	12.68
Nightwear	3.34	4.36	4.58	2.33	2.77
Accessories	23.29	20.91	27.24	20.82	25.28
Sweaters and vests	15.96	24.18	17.37	11.76	14.00
Active sportswear	16.11	19.41	17.98	12.92	16.25
Shirts	85.47	71.97	92.31	78.83	101.41
Pants	68.65	71.72	81.26	58.14	69.46
Shorts and shorts sets	13.64	9.55	17.75	11.79	16.02
Uniforms	5.52	7.97	3.22	6.81	3.83
Costumes	4.06	4.77	5.43	3.16	3.43
BOYS' (AGED 2 TO 15) APPAREL	**95.76**	**109.53**	**102.73**	**86.56**	**91.12**
Coats and jackets	7.84	10.74	10.00	6.73	4.83
Sweaters	3.56	5.46	3.00	3.36	2.80
Shirts	20.84	23.28	23.45	17.67	20.95
Underwear	5.09	7.89	5.89	2.78	5.41
Nightwear	2.95	3.22	3.76	2.67	2.28
Hosiery	4.30	2.73	4.64	3.94	5.98
Accessories	4.40	5.24	4.51	2.65	6.37
Suits, sport coats, and vests	3.64	7.28	2.58	2.66	3.14
Pants	23.39	22.18	24.52	23.22	23.53
Shorts and shorts sets	8.95	8.44	8.98	10.48	6.95
Uniforms	3.66	5.56	4.26	2.51	3.19
Active sportswear	3.81	2.35	2.34	5.91	3.32
Costumes	3.33	5.17	4.79	1.96	2.37
WOMEN'S APPAREL	**607.11**	**704.58**	**646.46**	**498.79**	**651.54**
Coats and jackets	43.26	60.16	59.81	23.45	42.23
Dresses	86.74	110.23	86.48	68.58	94.89
Sport coats and tailored jackets	8.33	9.45	7.76	5.38	12.59
Sweaters and vests	49.27	57.88	64.41	33.61	50.63
Shirts, blouses, and tops	99.26	93.54	113.52	82.49	116.61
Skirts	12.76	18.28	11.88	9.95	13.15
Pants	85.55	98.11	82.76	75.45	93.36
Shorts and shorts sets	20.40	19.98	25.41	16.98	20.98
Active sportswear	27.78	30.99	25.93	27.98	26.48

	total consumer units	Northeast	Midwest	South	West
Nightwear	$32.21	$38.24	$32.06	$26.88	$35.48
Undergarments	32.20	39.00	34.16	28.40	30.02
Hosiery	20.95	22.02	23.17	17.71	22.85
Suits	33.80	32.91	27.40	36.90	36.44
Accessories	39.29	55.48	37.25	28.29	44.41
Uniforms	8.69	8.37	6.77	11.61	6.41
Costumes	6.63	9.95	7.69	5.12	5.02
GIRLS' (AGED 2 TO 15) APPAREL	**118.09**	**144.10**	**124.90**	**113.46**	**94.72**
Coats and jackets	6.95	8.93	7.62	6.83	4.74
Dresses and suits	18.19	17.66	18.70	22.47	11.19
Shirts, blouses, and sweaters	28.79	38.62	33.54	24.52	21.58
Skirts and pants	21.75	21.87	19.73	22.96	21.90
Shorts and shorts sets	8.35	8.24	8.26	9.44	6.81
Active sportswear	8.97	16.58	12.39	5.09	4.61
Underwear and nightwear	7.40	8.91	7.56	6.43	7.47
Hosiery	4.92	5.93	3.81	4.87	5.24
Accessories	4.98	7.55	5.69	3.28	4.63
Uniforms	3.90	2.97	2.03	5.95	3.47
Costumes	3.87	6.84	5.55	1.62	3.07
CHILDREN UNDER AGE 2	**81.92**	**82.16**	**87.86**	**82.03**	**75.39**
Coats, jackets, and snowsuits	2.70	4.86	2.42	1.96	2.29
Outerwear including dresses	22.97	24.90	25.65	23.07	18.32
Underwear	44.65	40.07	47.65	46.30	42.99
Nightwear and loungewear	3.99	4.68	4.56	2.72	4.78
Accessories	7.61	7.65	7.59	7.99	7.00
FOOTWEAR	**343.09**	**382.33**	**324.27**	**303.50**	**391.35**
Men's	117.55	108.98	120.24	98.09	154.24
Boys'	37.26	36.93	41.33	35.35	36.32
Women's	155.95	197.37	138.54	136.52	167.92
Girls'	32.33	39.05	24.16	33.55	32.88
OTHER APPAREL PRODUCTS AND SERVICES	**265.90**	**318.42**	**245.01**	**237.56**	**287.60**
Material for making clothes	4.75	1.42	8.54	2.33	7.73
Sewing patterns and notions	4.69	3.73	7.15	3.03	5.67
Watches	22.63	20.98	23.97	21.00	25.19
Jewelry	107.32	140.17	101.75	91.01	110.49
Shoe repair and other shoe services	1.83	1.89	1.02	1.77	2.71
Coin-operated apparel laundry and dry cleaning	37.93	49.52	35.18	26.13	49.33
Apparel alteration, repair, and tailoring services	5.70	7.45	6.09	4.44	5.75
Clothing rental	3.37	4.00	3.90	2.74	3.28
Watch and jewelry repair	4.74	5.65	3.85	3.61	6.64
Professional laundry, dry cleaning	72.40	82.48	53.18	81.14	70.26
Clothing storage	0.55	1.13	0.37	0.34	0.56

Source: Bureau of Labor Statistics, unpublished data from the 2000 Consumer Expenditure Survey

Table 2.22 Apparel: Indexed spending by region, 2000

(indexed average annual spending of consumer units (CU) on apparel, accessories, and related services, by region in which consumer unit lives, 2000; index definition: an index of 100 is the average for all consumer units; an index of 132 means that spending by consumer units in that group is 32 percent above the average for all consumer units; an index of 68 indicates spending that is 32 percent below the average for all consumer units)

	total consumer units	Northeast	Midwest	South	West
Average spending of CU, total	**$38,045**	**$38,902**	**$39,213**	**$34,707**	**$41,328**
Average spending of CU, index	**100**	**102**	**103**	**91**	**109**
Apparel, spending index	**100**	**114**	**103**	**87**	**105**
MEN'S APPAREL	**100**	**109**	**112**	**86**	**103**
Suits	100	131	80	95	103
Sport coats and tailored jackets	100	163	104	82	69
Coats and jackets	100	147	140	61	78
Underwear	100	90	105	95	112
Hosiery	100	93	120	84	110
Nightwear	100	131	137	70	83
Accessories	100	90	117	89	109
Sweaters and vests	100	152	109	74	88
Active sportswear	100	120	112	80	101
Shirts	100	84	108	92	119
Pants	100	104	118	85	101
Shorts and shorts sets	100	70	130	86	117
Uniforms	100	144	58	123	69
Costumes	100	117	134	78	84
BOYS' (AGED 2 TO 15) APPAREL	**100**	**114**	**107**	**90**	**95**
Coats and jackets	100	137	128	86	62
Sweaters	100	153	84	94	79
Shirts	100	112	113	85	101
Underwear	100	155	116	55	106
Nightwear	100	109	127	91	77
Hosiery	100	63	108	92	139
Accessories	100	119	103	60	145
Suits, sport coats, and vests	100	200	71	73	86
Pants	100	95	105	99	101
Shorts and shorts sets	100	94	100	117	78
Uniforms	100	152	116	69	87
Active sportswear	100	62	61	155	87
Costumes	100	155	144	59	71
WOMEN'S APPAREL	**100**	**116**	**106**	**82**	**107**
Coats and jackets	100	139	138	54	98
Dresses	100	127	100	79	109
Sport coats and tailored jackets	100	113	93	65	151
Sweaters and vests	100	117	131	68	103
Shirts, blouses, and tops	100	94	114	83	117
Skirts	100	143	93	78	103
Pants	100	115	97	88	109
Shorts and shorts sets	100	98	125	83	103
Active sportswear	100	112	93	101	95

	total consumer units	Northeast	Midwest	South	West
Nightwear	100	119	100	83	110
Undergarments	100	121	106	88	93
Hosiery	100	105	111	85	109
Suits	100	97	81	109	108
Accessories	100	141	95	72	113
Uniforms	100	96	78	134	74
Costumes	100	150	116	77	76
GIRLS' (AGED 2 TO 15) APPAREL	**100**	**122**	**106**	**96**	**80**
Coats and jackets	100	128	110	98	68
Dresses and suits	100	97	103	124	62
Shirts, blouses, and sweaters	100	134	116	85	75
Skirts and pants	100	101	91	106	101
Shorts and shorts sets	100	99	99	113	82
Active sportswear	100	185	138	57	51
Underwear and nightwear	100	120	102	87	101
Hosiery	100	121	77	99	107
Accessories	100	152	114	66	93
Uniforms	100	76	52	153	89
Costumes	100	177	143	42	79
CHILDREN UNDER AGE 2	**100**	**100**	**107**	**100**	**92**
Coats, jackets, and snowsuits	100	180	90	73	85
Outerwear including dresses	100	108	112	100	80
Underwear	100	90	107	104	96
Nightwear and loungewear	100	117	114	68	120
Accessories	100	101	100	105	92
FOOTWEAR	**100**	**111**	**95**	**88**	**114**
Men's	100	93	102	83	131
Boys'	100	99	111	95	97
Women's	100	127	89	88	108
Girls'	100	121	75	104	102
OTHER APPAREL PRODUCTS AND SERVICES	**100**	**120**	**92**	**89**	**108**
Material for making clothes	100	30	180	49	163
Sewing patterns and notions	100	80	152	65	121
Watches	100	93	106	93	111
Jewelry	100	131	95	85	103
Shoe repair and other shoe services	100	103	56	97	148
Coin-operated apparel laundry and dry cleaning	100	131	93	69	130
Apparel alteration, repair, and tailoring services	100	131	107	78	101
Clothing rental	100	119	116	81	97
Watch and jewelry repair	100	119	81	76	140
Professional laundry, dry cleaning	100	114	73	112	97
Clothing storage	100	205	67	62	102

Source: Calculations by New Strategist based on the 2000 Consumer Expenditure Survey

Table 2.23 Apparel: Indexed per capita spending by region, 2000

(indexed average annual per capita spending of consumer units (CU) on apparel, accessories, and related services, by region in which consumer unit lives, 2000; index definition: an index of 100 is the average for all consumer units; an index of 132 means that spending by consumer units in that group is 32 percent above the average for all consumer units; an index of 68 indicates spending that is 32 percent below the average for all consumer units)

	total consumer units	Northeast	Midwest	South	West
Per capita spending of CU, total	**$15,218**	**$15,561**	**$15,685**	**$13,883**	**$15,895**
Per capita spending of CU, index	**100**	**102**	**103**	**91**	**104**
Apparel, per capita spending index	**100**	**114**	**103**	**87**	**101**
MEN'S APPAREL	**100**	**109**	**112**	**86**	**99**
Suits	100	131	80	95	99
Sport coats and tailored jackets	100	163	104	82	66
Coats and jackets	100	147	140	61	75
Underwear	100	90	105	95	107
Hosiery	100	93	120	84	106
Nightwear	100	131	137	70	80
Accessories	100	90	117	89	104
Sweaters and vests	100	152	109	74	84
Active sportswear	100	120	112	80	97
Shirts	100	84	108	92	114
Pants	100	104	118	85	97
Shorts and shorts sets	100	70	130	86	113
Uniforms	100	144	58	123	67
Costumes	100	117	134	78	81
BOYS' (AGED 2 TO 15) APPAREL	**100**	**114**	**107**	**90**	**91**
Coats and jackets	100	137	128	86	59
Sweaters	100	153	84	94	76
Shirts	100	112	113	85	97
Underwear	100	155	116	55	102
Nightwear	100	109	127	91	74
Hosiery	100	63	108	92	134
Accessories	100	119	103	60	139
Suits, sport coats, and vests	100	200	71	73	83
Pants	100	95	105	99	97
Shorts and shorts sets	100	94	100	117	75
Uniforms	100	152	116	69	84
Active sportswear	100	62	61	155	84
Costumes	100	155	144	59	68
WOMEN'S APPAREL	**100**	**116**	**106**	**82**	**103**
Coats and jackets	100	139	138	54	94
Dresses	100	127	100	79	105
Sport coats and tailored jackets	100	113	93	65	145
Sweaters and vests	100	117	131	68	99
Shirts, blouses, and tops	100	94	114	83	113
Skirts	100	143	93	78	99
Pants	100	115	97	88	105
Shorts and shorts sets	100	98	125	83	99
Active sportswear	100	112	93	101	92

	total consumer units	Northeast	Midwest	South	West
Nightwear	100	119	100	83	106
Undergarments	100	121	106	88	90
Hosiery	100	105	111	85	105
Suits	100	97	81	109	104
Accessories	100	141	95	72	109
Uniforms	100	96	78	134	71
Costumes	100	150	116	77	73
GIRLS' (AGED 2 TO 15) APPAREL	**100**	**122**	**106**	**96**	**77**
Coats and jackets	100	128	110	98	66
Dresses and suits	100	97	103	124	59
Shirts, blouses, and sweaters	100	134	116	85	72
Skirts and pants	100	101	91	106	97
Shorts and shorts sets	100	99	99	113	78
Active sportswear	100	185	138	57	49
Underwear and nightwear	100	120	102	87	97
Hosiery	100	121	77	99	102
Accessories	100	152	114	66	89
Uniforms	100	76	52	153	86
Costumes	100	177	143	42	76
CHILDREN UNDER AGE 2	**100**	**100**	**107**	**100**	**88**
Coats, jackets, and snowsuits	100	180	90	73	82
Outerwear including dresses	100	108	112	100	77
Underwear	100	90	107	104	93
Nightwear and loungewear	100	117	114	68	115
Accessories	100	101	100	105	88
FOOTWEAR	**100**	**111**	**95**	**88**	**110**
Men's	100	93	102	83	126
Boys'	100	99	111	95	94
Women's	100	127	89	88	104
Girls'	100	121	75	104	98
OTHER APPAREL PRODUCTS AND SERVICES	**100**	**120**	**92**	**89**	**104**
Material for making clothes	100	30	180	49	156
Sewing patterns and notions	100	80	152	65	116
Watches	100	93	106	93	107
Jewelry	100	131	95	85	99
Shoe repair and other shoe services	100	103	56	97	142
Coin-operated apparel laundry and dry cleaning	100	131	93	69	125
Apparel alteration, repair, and tailoring services	100	131	107	78	97
Clothing rental	100	119	116	81	94
Watch and jewelry repair	100	119	81	76	135
Professional laundry, dry cleaning	100	114	73	112	93
Clothing storage	100	205	67	62	98

Note: Per capita indexes account for household size and show how much each person in a particular household demographic segment spends relative to a person in the average household.
Source: Calculations by New Strategist based on the 2000 Consumer Expenditure Survey

Table 2.24 Apparel: Total spending by region, 2000

(total annual spending on apparel, accessories, and related services, by region in which consumer units live, 2000; numbers in thousands)

	total consumer units	Northeast	Midwest	South	West
Number of consumer units	109,367	20,994	25,717	38,245	24,410
Total spending of all consumer units	$4,160,831,424	$816,706,699	$1,008,433,006	$1,327,371,892	$1,008,821,118
Apparel, total spending	203,002,651	44,409,448	49,307,204	61,836,811	47,485,994
MEN'S APPAREL	**$37,653,964**	**$7,856,165**	**$9,928,562**	**$11,280,745**	**$8,632,352**
Suits	3,634,265	914,499	679,700	1,203,188	837,263
Sport coats and tailored jackets	1,236,941	388,179	301,403	356,826	190,398
Coats and jackets	3,801,597	1,069,644	1,248,560	815,001	657,850
Underwear	1,908,454	329,396	472,421	635,632	475,019
Hosiery	1,257,721	224,006	356,180	370,594	309,519
Nightwear	365,286	91,534	117,784	89,111	67,616
Accessories	2,547,157	438,985	700,531	796,261	617,085
Sweaters and vests	1,745,497	507,635	446,704	449,761	341,740
Active sportswear	1,761,902	407,494	462,392	494,125	396,663
Shirts	9,347,597	1,510,938	2,373,936	3,014,853	2,475,418
Pants	7,508,045	1,505,690	2,089,763	2,223,564	1,695,519
Shorts and shorts sets	1,491,766	200,493	456,477	450,909	391,048
Uniforms	603,706	167,322	82,809	260,448	93,490
Costumes	444,030	100,141	139,643	120,854	83,726
BOYS' (AGED 2 TO 15) APPAREL	**10,472,984**	**2,299,473**	**2,641,907**	**3,310,487**	**2,224,239**
Coats and jackets	857,437	225,476	257,170	257,389	117,900
Sweaters	389,347	114,627	77,151	128,503	68,348
Shirts	2,279,208	488,740	603,064	675,789	511,390
Underwear	556,678	165,643	151,473	106,321	132,058
Nightwear	322,633	67,601	96,696	102,114	55,655
Hosiery	470,278	57,314	119,327	150,685	145,972
Accessories	481,215	110,009	115,984	101,349	155,492
Suits, sport coats, and vests	398,096	152,836	66,350	101,732	76,647
Pants	2,558,094	465,647	630,581	888,049	574,367
Shorts and shorts sets	978,835	177,189	230,939	400,808	169,650
Uniforms	400,283	116,727	109,554	95,995	77,868
Active sportswear	416,688	49,336	60,178	226,028	81,041
Costumes	364,192	108,539	123,184	74,960	57,852
WOMEN'S APPAREL	**66,397,799**	**14,791,953**	**16,625,012**	**19,076,224**	**15,904,091**
Coats and jackets	4,731,216	1,262,999	1,538,134	896,845	1,030,834
Dresses	9,486,494	2,314,169	2,224,006	2,622,842	2,316,265
Sport coats and tailored jackets	911,027	198,393	199,564	205,758	307,322
Sweaters and vests	5,388,512	1,215,133	1,656,432	1,285,414	1,235,878
Shirts, blouses, and tops	10,855,768	1,963,779	2,919,394	3,154,830	2,846,450
Skirts	1,395,523	383,770	305,518	380,538	320,992
Pants	9,356,347	2,059,721	2,128,339	2,885,585	2,278,918
Shorts and shorts sets	2,231,087	419,460	653,469	649,400	512,122
Active sportswear	3,038,215	650,604	666,842	1,070,095	646,377

	total consumer units	Northeast	Midwest	South	West
Nightwear	$3,522,711	$802,811	$824,487	$1,028,026	$866,067
Undergarments	3,521,617	818,766	878,493	1,086,158	732,788
Hosiery	2,291,239	462,288	595,863	677,319	557,769
Suits	3,696,605	690,913	704,646	1,411,241	889,500
Accessories	4,297,029	1,164,747	957,958	1,081,951	1,084,048
Uniforms	950,399	175,720	174,104	444,024	156,468
Costumes	725,103	208,890	197,764	195,814	122,538
GIRLS' (AGED 2 TO 15) APPAREL	**12,915,149**	**3,025,235**	**3,212,053**	**4,339,278**	**2,312,115**
Coats and jackets	760,101	187,476	195,964	261,213	115,703
Dresses and suits	1,989,386	370,754	480,908	859,365	273,148
Shirts, blouses, and sweaters	3,148,676	810,788	862,548	937,767	526,768
Skirts and pants	2,378,732	459,139	507,396	878,105	534,579
Shorts and shorts sets	913,214	172,991	212,422	361,033	166,232
Active sportswear	981,022	348,081	318,634	194,667	112,530
Underwear and nightwear	809,316	187,057	194,421	245,915	182,343
Hosiery	538,086	124,494	97,982	186,253	127,908
Accessories	544,648	158,505	146,330	125,444	113,018
Uniforms	426,531	62,352	52,206	227,558	84,703
Costumes	423,250	143,599	142,729	61,957	74,939
CHILDREN UNDER AGE 2	**8,959,345**	**1,724,867**	**2,259,496**	**3,137,237**	**1,840,270**
Coats, jackets, and snowsuits	295,291	102,031	62,235	74,960	55,899
Outerwear including dresses	2,512,160	522,751	659,641	882,312	447,191
Underwear	4,883,237	841,230	1,225,415	1,770,744	1,049,386
Nightwear and loungewear	436,374	98,252	117,270	104,026	116,680
Accessories	832,283	160,604	195,192	305,578	170,870
FOOTWEAR	**37,522,724**	**8,026,636**	**8,339,252**	**11,607,358**	**9,552,854**
Men's	12,856,091	2,287,926	3,092,212	3,751,452	3,764,998
Boys'	4,075,014	775,308	1,062,884	1,351,961	886,571
Women's	17,055,784	4,143,586	3,562,833	5,221,207	4,098,927
Girls'	3,535,835	819,816	621,323	1,283,120	802,601
OTHER APPAREL PRODUCTS AND SERVICES	**29,080,685**	**6,684,909**	**6,300,922**	**9,085,482**	**7,020,316**
Material for making clothes	519,493	29,811	219,623	89,111	188,689
Sewing patterns and notions	512,931	78,308	183,877	115,882	138,405
Watches	2,474,975	440,454	616,436	803,145	614,888
Jewelry	11,737,266	2,942,729	2,616,705	3,480,677	2,697,061
Shoe repair and other shoe services	200,142	39,679	26,231	67,694	66,151
Coin-operated apparel laundry and dry cleaning	4,148,290	1,039,623	904,724	999,342	1,204,145
Apparel alteration, repair, and tailoring services	623,392	156,405	156,617	169,808	140,358
Clothing rental	368,567	83,976	100,296	104,791	80,065
Watch and jewelry repair	518,400	118,616	99,010	138,064	162,082
Professional laundry, dry cleaning	7,918,171	1,731,585	1,367,630	3,103,199	1,715,047
Clothing storage	60,152	23,723	9,515	13,003	13,670

Note: Numbers may not add to total because of rounding.
Source: Calculations by New Strategist based on the 2000 Consumer Expenditure Survey

Table 2.25 Apparel: Market shares by region, 2000

(percentage of total annual spending on apparel, accessories, and related services accounted for by consumer units by region, 2000)

	total consumer units	Northeast	Midwest	South	West
Share of total consumer units	100.0%	19.2%	23.5%	35.0%	22.3%
Share of total before-tax income	100.0	20.4	23.4	32.9	23.3
Share of total spending	100.0	19.6	24.2	31.9	24.2
Share of apparel spending	100.0	21.9	24.3	30.5	23.4
MEN'S APPAREL	**100.0%**	**20.9%**	**26.4%**	**30.0%**	**22.9%**
Suits	100.0	25.2	18.7	33.1	23.0
Sport coats and tailored jackets	100.0	31.4	24.4	28.8	15.4
Coats and jackets	100.0	28.1	32.8	21.4	17.3
Underwear	100.0	17.3	24.8	33.3	24.9
Hosiery	100.0	17.8	28.3	29.5	24.6
Nightwear	100.0	25.1	32.2	24.4	18.5
Accessories	100.0	17.2	27.5	31.3	24.2
Sweaters and vests	100.0	29.1	25.6	25.8	19.6
Active sportswear	100.0	23.1	26.2	28.0	22.5
Shirts	100.0	16.2	25.4	32.3	26.5
Pants	100.0	20.1	27.8	29.6	22.6
Shorts and shorts sets	100.0	13.4	30.6	30.2	26.2
Uniforms	100.0	27.7	13.7	43.1	15.5
Costumes	100.0	22.6	31.4	27.2	18.9
BOYS' (AGED 2 TO 15) APPAREL	**100.0**	**22.0**	**25.2**	**31.6**	**21.2**
Coats and jackets	100.0	26.3	30.0	30.0	13.8
Sweaters	100.0	29.4	19.8	33.0	17.6
Shirts	100.0	21.4	26.5	29.7	22.4
Underwear	100.0	29.8	27.2	19.1	23.7
Nightwear	100.0	21.0	30.0	31.7	17.3
Hosiery	100.0	12.2	25.4	32.0	31.0
Accessories	100.0	22.9	24.1	21.1	32.3
Suits, sport coats, and vests	100.0	38.4	16.7	25.6	19.3
Pants	100.0	18.2	24.7	34.7	22.5
Shorts and shorts sets	100.0	18.1	23.6	40.9	17.3
Uniforms	100.0	29.2	27.4	24.0	19.5
Active sportswear	100.0	11.8	14.4	54.2	19.4
Costumes	100.0	29.8	33.8	20.6	15.9
WOMEN'S APPAREL	**100.0**	**22.3**	**25.0**	**28.7**	**24.0**
Coats and jackets	100.0	26.7	32.5	19.0	21.8
Dresses	100.0	24.4	23.4	27.6	24.4
Sport coats and tailored jackets	100.0	21.8	21.9	22.6	33.7
Sweaters and vests	100.0	22.6	30.7	23.9	22.9
Shirts, blouses, and tops	100.0	18.1	26.9	29.1	26.2
Skirts	100.0	27.5	21.9	27.3	23.0
Pants	100.0	22.0	22.7	30.8	24.4
Shorts and shorts sets	100.0	18.8	29.3	29.1	23.0
Active sportswear	100.0	21.4	21.9	35.2	21.3

	total consumer units	Northeast	Midwest	South	West
Nightwear	100.0%	22.8%	23.4%	29.2%	24.6%
Undergarments	100.0	23.2	24.9	30.8	20.8
Hosiery	100.0	20.2	26.0	29.6	24.3
Suits	100.0	18.7	19.1	38.2	24.1
Accessories	100.0	27.1	22.3	25.2	25.2
Uniforms	100.0	18.5	18.3	46.7	16.5
Costumes	100.0	28.8	27.3	27.0	16.9
GIRLS' (AGED 2 TO 15) APPAREL	**100.0**	**23.4**	**24.9**	**33.6**	**17.9**
Coats and jackets	100.0	24.7	25.8	34.4	15.2
Dresses and suits	100.0	18.6	24.2	43.2	13.7
Shirts, blouses, and sweaters	100.0	25.8	27.4	29.8	16.7
Skirts and pants	100.0	19.3	21.3	36.9	22.5
Shorts and shorts sets	100.0	18.9	23.3	39.5	18.2
Active sportswear	100.0	35.5	32.5	19.8	11.5
Underwear and nightwear	100.0	23.1	24.0	30.4	22.5
Hosiery	100.0	23.1	18.2	34.6	23.8
Accessories	100.0	29.1	26.9	23.0	20.8
Uniforms	100.0	14.6	12.2	53.4	19.9
Costumes	100.0	33.9	33.7	14.6	17.7
CHILDREN UNDER AGE 2	**100.0**	**19.3**	**25.2**	**35.0**	**20.5**
Coats, jackets, and snowsuits	100.0	34.6	21.1	25.4	18.9
Outerwear including dresses	100.0	20.8	26.3	35.1	17.8
Underwear	100.0	17.2	25.1	36.3	21.5
Nightwear and loungewear	100.0	22.5	26.9	23.8	26.7
Accessories	100.0	19.3	23.5	36.7	20.5
FOOTWEAR	**100.0**	**21.4**	**22.2**	**30.9**	**25.5**
Men's	100.0	17.8	24.1	29.2	29.3
Boys'	100.0	19.0	26.1	33.2	21.8
Women's	100.0	24.3	20.9	30.6	24.0
Girls'	100.0	23.2	17.6	36.3	22.7
OTHER APPAREL PRODUCTS AND SERVICES	**100.0**	**23.0**	**21.7**	**31.2**	**24.1**
Material for making clothes	100.0	5.7	42.3	17.2	36.3
Sewing patterns and notions	100.0	15.3	35.8	22.6	27.0
Watches	100.0	17.8	24.9	32.5	24.8
Jewelry	100.0	25.1	22.3	29.7	23.0
Shoe repair and other shoe services	100.0	19.8	13.1	33.8	33.1
Coin-operated apparel laundry and dry cleaning	100.0	25.1	21.8	24.1	29.0
Apparel alteration, repair, and tailoring services	100.0	25.1	25.1	27.2	22.5
Clothing rental	100.0	22.8	27.2	28.4	21.7
Watch and jewelry repair	100.0	22.9	19.1	26.6	31.3
Professional laundry, dry cleaning	100.0	21.9	17.3	39.2	21.7
Clothing storage	100.0	39.4	15.8	21.6	22.7

Note: Numbers may not add to total because of rounding.
Source: Calculations by New Strategist based on the 2000 Consumer Expenditure Survey

Spending on Entertainment, 2000

Entertainment spending held steady during the 1990s. The average household spent $1,863 on entertainment in 2000, down slightly from $1,874 in 1990, after adjusting for inflation. Overall, Americans devoted 4.9 percent of their spending dollars to entertainment in 2000, down from 5.0 percent a decade earlier. The average American household now spends a bit more on entertainment than on clothes.

Households headed by people aged 35 to 44 spend the most on entertainment, averaging $2,464 in 2000, or 32 percent more than the average household. Households headed by the youngest and the oldest adults spend far less than average on entertainment. When adjusted for household size, however, the entertainment spending of householders aged 55 to 64 is greater than that of any other age group—25 percent above average. The per capita entertainment spending of 65-to-74-year-olds is about average and exceeds that of householders under age 35.

Households with incomes of $70,000 or more spent $3,912 on entertainment in 2000, twice the average. These affluent households spend far more than average on nearly every entertainment category. They account for 38 percent of all entertainment spending, and for fully 61 percent of spending on fees for recreational lessons.

Married couples with school-aged children at home spend the most on entertainment among household types—74 percent more than the average household. They are especially big spenders on fees for recreational lessons, spending more than four times as much as the average household. On a per capita basis, married couples without children at home and single-person households spend the most on entertainment, 32 and 38 percent above what the average person spends, respectively.

Black and Hispanic households spend much less on entertainment than the average household. In some categories, however, they spend more. Hispanics spend 41 percent more than average on portable color TVs, for example. Blacks spend more than twice the average on tape recorders and players.

Households in the South spend 13 percent less on entertainment than the average household, but they are the biggest spenders on satellite dishes and motorboats. Western households account for 33 percent of spending on bicycles.

Table 3.1 Entertainment: Average spending by age, 2000

(average annual spending of consumer units (CU) on entertainment, by age of consumer unit reference person, 2000)

	total consumer units	under 25	25 to 34	35 to 44	45 to 54	55 to 64	65 to 74	75+
Number of consumer units (in thousands, add 000)	109,367	8,306	18,887	23,983	21,874	14,161	11,538	10,617
Average number of persons per CU	2.5	1.9	2.9	3.3	2.7	2.1	1.9	1.5
Average before-tax income of CU	$44,649.00	$19,744.00	$45,498.00	$56,500.00	$58,889.00	$48,108.00	$29,349.00	$20,563.00
Average spending of CU, total	38,044.67	22,543.18	38,945.27	45,149.37	46,160.28	39,340.03	30,781.81	21,908.04
Entertainment, average spending	1,863.50	1,091.22	1,876.33	2,464.36	2,231.28	1,955.31	1,403.00	706.51
FEES AND ADMISSIONS	**$514.85**	**$270.78**	**$460.45**	**$714.75**	**$637.35**	**$508.98**	**$415.74**	**$214.20**
Recreation expenses on trips	25.49	13.87	23.51	30.97	28.98	30.15	26.98	10.69
Social, recreation, civic club membership	98.18	37.33	83.92	117.57	119.05	109.88	109.84	56.12
Fees for participant sports	71.49	31.52	59.49	100.51	81.07	67.22	74.23	41.54
Participant sports on trips	35.05	19.35	30.25	43.21	42.32	41.46	30.13	19.27
Movie, theater, opera, ballet	89.16	84.58	93.49	107.33	110.98	84.00	63.83	33.45
Movie, other admissions on trips	44.94	23.89	42.47	56.26	48.03	58.55	40.26	20.75
Admission to sports events	35.33	19.78	30.91	51.56	52.84	32.18	17.07	6.71
Admission to sports events on trips	14.98	7.96	14.16	18.75	16.01	19.52	13.42	6.92
Fees for recreational lessons	74.74	18.62	58.73	157.63	109.09	35.86	13.01	8.06
Other entertainment services on trips	25.49	13.87	23.51	30.97	28.98	30.15	26.98	10.69
TELEVISION, RADIO, SOUND EQUIPMENT	**621.82**	**473.20**	**680.47**	**789.36**	**695.93**	**580.74**	**468.08**	**324.55**
Television	**453.53**	**302.72**	**479.56**	**527.14**	**495.38**	**475.90**	**416.49**	**283.13**
Cable service and community antenna	321.18	170.76	317.14	348.04	364.50	361.04	321.96	242.10
Black-and-white TV	0.77	0.27	1.23	1.25	0.85	0.07	0.70	0.13
Color TV, console	30.19	25.44	39.81	45.62	20.25	33.25	22.36	6.84
Color TV, portable, table model	34.35	45.96	34.71	36.09	34.85	32.58	35.32	20.95
VCRs and video disc players	23.80	21.00	31.75	34.52	26.54	15.51	13.49	4.28
Video cassettes, tapes, and discs	20.80	26.50	28.53	24.80	22.35	18.19	11.59	3.83
Video game hardware and software	18.72	11.17	23.17	33.12	21.60	10.92	6.57	1.83
Repair of TV, radio, and sound equipment	3.23	0.31	2.77	2.82	4.03	4.11	4.46	3.16
Rental of television sets	0.49	1.31	0.45	0.89	0.42	0.24	0.05	–
Radio and sound equipment	**168.29**	**170.49**	**200.91**	**262.21**	**200.55**	**104.85**	**51.59**	**41.43**
Radios	10.44	12.42	8.77	12.65	14.10	13.29	4.62	1.42
Tape recorders and players	4.39	2.77	4.13	3.89	10.06	4.90	–	–
Sound components and component systems	23.16	23.00	30.74	32.78	28.63	13.98	7.51	6.07
Miscellaneous sound equipment	0.42	–	0.96	0.62	0.45	0.18	0.02	–
Sound equipment accessories	4.04	0.47	5.95	3.84	7.56	1.87	2.00	2.05
Satellite dishes	2.70	2.68	2.51	3.61	2.05	3.19	2.01	2.49
Compact disc, tape, record, video mail order clubs	8.52	7.40	9.51	10.56	9.33	9.45	5.95	2.94
Records, CDs, audio tapes, needles	39.46	60.13	50.15	54.78	45.27	24.90	13.03	5.90
Rental of VCR, radio, sound equipment	0.54	0.73	0.26	0.34	1.44	0.22	0.41	–
Musical instruments and accessories	31.70	11.31	28.10	74.94	32.05	7.11	5.06	17.46
Rental and repair of musical instruments	1.34	0.10	0.54	3.21	1.47	1.61	0.32	0.00
Rental of video cassettes, tapes, discs, films	41.56	49.49	59.31	61.00	48.15	24.16	10.66	3.09

	total consumer units	under 25	25 to 34	35 to 44	45 to 54	55 to 64	65 to 74	75+
PETS, TOYS, PLAYGROUND EQUIPMENT	$333.71	$172.63	$350.83	$451.05	$383.98	$358.35	$262.24	$104.28
Pets	209.43	98.68	171.17	264.02	281.43	241.53	184.78	75.32
Pet food	85.97	40.57	71.17	103.96	107.95	108.75	83.72	33.89
Pet purchase, supplies, and medicines	38.10	32.74	33.55	50.10	53.66	36.62	23.82	7.67
Pet services	19.36	7.08	11.29	23.79	27.93	24.79	21.79	5.77
Veterinarian services	66.00	18.28	55.17	86.17	91.90	71.37	55.44	27.99
Toys, games, hobbies, and tricycles	120.96	73.84	170.92	180.97	101.60	115.92	75.88	28.96
Playground equipment	3.32	0.12	8.73	6.06	0.95	0.89	1.58	0.01
OTHER ENTERTAINMENT SUPPLIES, EQUIPMENT, SERVICES	393.12	174.60	384.58	509.20	514.01	507.23	256.94	63.47
Unmotored recreational vehicles	48.06	–	32.45	59.98	71.54	105.02	11.19	2.22
Boat without motor and boat trailers	15.87	–	14.95	19.52	5.88	55.98	3.49	2.22
Trailer and other attachable campers	32.19	–	17.50	40.46	65.66	49.04	7.70	–
Motorized recreational vehicles	81.96	37.81	30.45	102.26	101.29	162.17	96.19	–
Motorized camper	21.35	–	–	2.88	20.63	108.74	23.78	–
Other vehicle	21.74	37.81	10.48	35.18	15.79	23.63	29.63	–
Motorboats	38.87	–	19.97	64.19	64.87	29.80	42.77	–
Rental of recreational vehicles	2.79	0.65	5.99	2.69	3.66	1.15	1.89	0.37
Boat and trailer rental on trips	0.59	0.42	0.23	1.31	1.03	0.08	0.13	–
Rental of campers on trips	0.61	–	2.05	–	1.12	0.27	–	–
Rental of other vehicles on trips	1.40	0.22	3.25	1.29	1.51	0.62	1.19	0.37
Rental of other RVs	0.03	–	0.17	–	–	0.04	–	–
Outboard motors	3.58	–	0.88	0.39	2.78	12.26	5.02	6.86
Docking and landing fees	8.17	0.19	7.69	9.46	7.43	9.38	13.13	6.87
Sports, recreation, exercise equipment	143.58	60.50	181.89	191.04	200.70	117.94	73.22	26.92
Athletic gear, game tables, exercise equipment	58.64	11.95	69.14	75.21	74.67	54.23	50.83	20.30
Bicycles	11.73	12.31	18.36	18.23	10.22	7.56	4.48	1.33
Camping equipment	17.02	11.06	13.86	19.31	44.85	5.29	0.32	–
Hunting and fishing equipment	25.85	6.03	44.44	31.29	34.90	22.67	6.05	2.49
Winter sports equipment	5.84	8.56	7.01	11.29	6.57	0.84	0.72	–
Water sports equipment	8.24	0.45	6.43	8.78	15.21	15.27	1.27	0.18
Other sports equipment	14.25	8.56	19.90	24.61	11.62	11.04	7.55	2.20
Rental and repair of misc. sports equipment	2.02	1.59	2.74	2.32	2.66	1.05	2.00	0.43
Photographic equipment and supplies	94.91	73.06	113.61	123.37	116.83	91.37	53.17	19.53
Film	21.40	15.81	24.10	28.01	24.39	23.65	13.70	5.21
Other photographic supplies	1.44	1.22	–	1.69	3.92	0.97	0.44	0.35
Film processing	31.43	24.07	36.85	41.16	36.52	32.26	19.66	6.77
Repair and rental of photographic equipment	0.27	–	0.34	0.43	0.19	0.19	0.46	0.02
Photographic equipment	20.21	11.41	23.30	20.32	30.97	23.19	12.05	4.06
Photographer fees	20.17	20.55	29.03	31.76	20.84	11.11	6.85	3.12
Fireworks	1.18	–	1.76	1.98	0.69	1.07	1.50	–
Souvenirs	2.00	0.19	0.04	4.27	2.27	3.52	1.04	–
Visual goods	1.09	–	1.83	1.72	0.61	1.90	0.19	–
Pinball, electronic video games	5.80	2.20	7.98	12.03	6.22	1.44	0.41	0.70

Note: (–) means sample is too small to make a reliable estimate.
Source: Bureau of Labor Statistics, unpublished data from the 2000 Consumer Expenditure Survey

Table 3.2 Entertainment: Indexed spending by age, 2000

(indexed average annual spending of consumer units (CU) on entertainment by age of consumer unit reference person, 2000; index definition: an index of 100 is the average for all consumer units; an index of 132 means that spending by consumer units in that group is 32 percent above the average for all consumer units; an index of 68 indicates spending that is 32 percent below the average for all consumer units)

	total consumer units	under 25	25 to 34	35 to 44	45 to 54	55 to 64	65 to 74	75+
Average spending of CU, total	$38,045	$22,543	$38,945	$45,149	$46,160	$39,340	$30,782	$21,908
Average spending of CU, index	100	59	102	119	121	103	81	58
Entertainment, spending index	100	59	101	132	120	105	75	38
FEES AND ADMISSIONS	100	53	89	139	124	99	81	42
Recreation expenses on trips	100	54	92	121	114	118	106	42
Social, recreation, civic club membership	100	38	85	120	121	112	112	57
Fees for participant sports	100	44	83	141	113	94	104	58
Participant sports on trips	100	55	86	123	121	118	86	55
Movie, theater, opera, ballet	100	95	105	120	124	94	72	38
Movie, other admissions on trips	100	53	95	125	107	130	90	46
Admission to sports events	100	56	87	146	150	91	48	19
Admission to sports events on trips	100	53	95	125	107	130	90	46
Fees for recreational lessons	100	25	79	211	146	48	17	11
Other entertainment services on trips	100	54	92	121	114	118	106	42
TELEVISION, RADIO, SOUND EQUIPMENT	100	76	109	127	112	93	75	52
Television	100	67	106	116	109	105	92	62
Cable service and community antenna	100	53	99	108	113	112	100	75
Black-and-white TV	100	35	160	162	110	9	91	17
Color TV, console	100	84	132	151	67	110	74	23
Color TV, portable, table model	100	134	101	105	101	95	103	61
VCRs and video disc players	100	88	133	145	112	65	57	18
Video cassettes, tapes, and discs	100	127	137	119	107	87	56	18
Video game hardware and software	100	60	124	177	115	58	35	10
Repair of TV, radio, and sound equipment	100	10	86	87	125	127	138	98
Rental of television sets	100	267	92	182	86	49	10	–
Radio and sound equipment	100	101	119	156	119	62	31	25
Radios	100	119	84	121	135	127	44	14
Tape recorders and players	100	63	94	89	229	112	–	–
Sound components and component systems	100	99	133	142	124	60	32	26
Miscellaneous sound equipment	100	–	229	148	107	43	5	–
Sound equipment accessories	100	12	147	95	187	46	50	51
Satellite dishes	100	99	93	134	76	118	74	92
Compact disc, tape, record, video mail order clubs	100	87	112	124	110	111	70	35
Records, CDs, audio tapes, needles	100	152	127	139	115	63	33	15
Rental of VCR, radio, sound equipment	100	135	48	63	267	41	76	–
Musical instruments and accessories	100	36	89	236	101	22	16	55
Rental and repair of musical instruments	100	7	40	240	110	120	24	0
Rental of video cassettes, tapes, discs, films	100	119	143	147	116	58	26	7

	total consumer units	under 25	25 to 34	35 to 44	45 to 54	55 to 64	65 to 74	75+
PETS, TOYS, PLAYGROUND EQUIPMENT	**100**	**52**	**105**	**135**	**115**	**107**	**79**	**31**
Pets	**100**	**47**	**82**	**126**	**134**	**115**	**88**	**36**
Pet food	100	47	83	121	126	126	97	39
Pet purchase, supplies, and medicines	100	86	88	131	141	96	63	20
Pet services	100	37	58	123	144	128	113	30
Veterinarian services	100	28	84	131	139	108	84	42
Toys, games, hobbies, and tricycles	**100**	**61**	**141**	**150**	**84**	**96**	**63**	**24**
Playground equipment	**100**	**4**	**263**	**183**	**29**	**27**	**48**	**0**
OTHER ENTERTAINMENT SUPPLIES, EQUIPMENT, SERVICES	**100**	**44**	**98**	**130**	**131**	**129**	**65**	**16**
Unmotored recreational vehicles	**100**	**–**	**68**	**125**	**149**	**219**	**23**	**5**
Boat without motor and boat trailers	100	–	94	123	37	353	22	14
Trailer and other attachable campers	100	–	54	126	204	152	24	–
Motorized recreational vehicles	**100**	**46**	**37**	**125**	**124**	**198**	**117**	**–**
Motorized camper	100	–	–	13	97	509	111	–
Other vehicle	100	174	48	162	73	109	136	–
Motorboats	100	–	51	165	167	77	110	–
Rental of recreational vehicles	**100**	**23**	**215**	**96**	**131**	**41**	**68**	**13**
Boat and trailer rental on trips	100	71	39	222	175	14	22	–
Rental of campers on trips	100	–	336	–	184	44	–	–
Rental of other vehicles on trips	100	16	232	92	108	44	85	26
Rental of other RVs	100	–	567	–	–	133	–	–
Outboard motors	**100**	**–**	**25**	**11**	**78**	**342**	**140**	**192**
Docking and landing fees	**100**	**2**	**94**	**116**	**91**	**115**	**161**	**84**
Sports, recreation, exercise equipment	**100**	**42**	**127**	**133**	**140**	**82**	**51**	**19**
Athletic gear, game tables, exercise equipment	100	20	118	128	127	92	87	35
Bicycles	100	105	157	155	87	64	38	11
Camping equipment	100	65	81	113	264	31	2	–
Hunting and fishing equipment	100	23	172	121	135	88	23	10
Winter sports equipment	100	147	120	193	113	14	12	–
Water sports equipment	100	5	78	107	185	185	15	2
Other sports equipment	100	60	140	173	82	77	53	15
Rental and repair of miscellaneous sports equipment	100	79	136	115	132	52	99	21
Photographic equipment and supplies	**100**	**77**	**120**	**130**	**123**	**96**	**56**	**21**
Film	100	74	113	131	114	111	64	24
Other photographic supplies	100	85	–	117	272	67	31	24
Film processing	100	77	117	131	116	103	63	22
Repair and rental of photographic equipment	100	–	126	159	70	70	170	7
Photographic equipment	100	56	115	101	153	115	60	20
Photographer fees	100	102	144	157	103	55	34	15
Fireworks	**100**	**–**	**149**	**168**	**58**	**91**	**127**	**–**
Souvenirs	**100**	**10**	**2**	**214**	**114**	**176**	**52**	**–**
Visual goods	**100**	**–**	**168**	**158**	**56**	**174**	**17**	**–**
Pinball, electronic video games	**100**	**38**	**138**	**207**	**107**	**25**	**7**	**12**

Note: (–) means sample is too small to make a reliable estimate.
Source: Calculations by New Strategist based on the 2000 Consumer Expenditure Survey

Table 3.3 Entertainment: Indexed per capita spending by age, 2000

(indexed average annual per capita spending of consumer units (CU) on entertainment by age of consumer unit reference person, 2000; index definition: an index of 100 is the average for all consumer units; an index of 132 means that spending by consumer units in that group is 32 percent above the average for all consumer units; an index of 68 indicates spending that is 32 percent below the average for all consumer units)

	total consumer units	under 25	25 to 34	35 to 44	45 to 54	55 to 64	65 to 74	75+
Per capita spending of CU, total	$15,218	$11,865	$13,429	$13,682	$17,096	$18,733	$16,201	$14,605
Per capita spending of CU, index	100	78	88	90	112	123	106	96
Entertainment, per capita spending index	100	77	87	100	111	125	99	63
FEES AND ADMISSIONS	100	69	77	105	115	118	106	69
Recreation expenses on trips	100	72	80	92	105	141	139	70
Social, recreation, civic club membership	100	50	74	91	112	133	147	95
Fees for participant sports	100	58	72	107	105	112	137	97
Participant sports on trips	100	73	74	93	112	141	113	92
Movie, theater, opera, ballet	100	125	90	91	115	112	94	63
Movie, other admissions on trips	100	70	81	95	99	155	118	77
Admission to sports events	100	74	75	111	138	108	64	32
Admission to sports events on trips	100	70	81	95	99	155	118	77
Fees for recreational lessons	100	33	68	160	135	57	23	18
Other entertainment services on trips	100	72	80	92	105	141	139	70
TELEVISION, RADIO, SOUND EQUIPMENT	100	100	94	96	104	111	99	87
Television	100	88	91	88	101	125	121	104
Cable service and community antenna	100	70	85	82	105	134	132	126
Black-and-white TV	100	46	138	123	102	11	120	28
Color TV, console	100	111	114	114	62	131	97	38
Color TV, portable, table model	100	176	87	80	94	113	135	102
VCRs and video disc players	100	116	115	110	103	78	75	30
Video cassettes, tapes, and discs	100	168	118	90	99	104	73	31
Video game hardware and software	100	79	107	134	107	69	46	16
Repair of TV, radio, and sound equipment	100	13	74	66	116	151	182	163
Rental of television sets	100	352	79	138	79	58	13	–
Radio and sound equipment	100	133	103	118	110	74	40	41
Radios	100	157	72	92	125	152	58	23
Tape recorders and players	100	83	81	67	212	133	–	–
Sound components and component systems	100	131	114	107	114	72	43	44
Miscellaneous sound equipment	100	–	197	112	99	51	6	–
Sound equipment accessories	100	15	127	72	173	55	65	85
Satellite dishes	100	131	80	101	70	141	98	154
Compact disc, tape, record, video mail order clubs	100	114	96	94	101	132	92	58
Records, CDs, audio tapes, needles	100	201	110	105	106	75	43	25
Rental of VCR, radio, sound equipment	100	178	42	48	247	49	100	–
Musical instruments and accessories	100	47	76	179	94	27	21	92
Rental and repair of musical instruments	100	10	35	181	102	143	31	0
Rental of video cassettes, tapes, discs, films	100	157	123	111	107	69	34	12

	total consumer units	under 25	25 to 34	35 to 44	45 to 54	55 to 64	65 to 74	75+
PETS, TOYS, PLAYGROUND EQUIPMENT	**100**	**68**	**91**	**102**	**107**	**128**	**103**	**52**
Pets	**100**	**62**	**70**	**96**	**124**	**137**	**116**	**60**
Pet food	100	62	71	92	116	151	128	66
Pet purchase, supplies, and medicines	100	113	76	100	130	114	82	34
Pet services	100	48	50	93	134	152	148	50
Veterinarian services	100	36	72	99	129	129	111	71
Toys, games, hobbies, and tricycles	**100**	**80**	**122**	**113**	**78**	**114**	**83**	**40**
Playground equipment	**100**	**5**	**227**	**138**	**26**	**32**	**63**	**1**
OTHER ENTERTAINMENT SUPPLIES, EQUIPMENT, SERVICES	**100**	**58**	**84**	**98**	**121**	**154**	**86**	**27**
Unmotored recreational vehicles	**100**	**–**	**58**	**95**	**138**	**260**	**31**	**8**
Boat without motor and boat trailers	100	–	81	93	34	420	29	23
Trailer and other attachable campers	100	–	47	95	189	181	31	–
Motorized recreational vehicles	**100**	**61**	**32**	**95**	**114**	**236**	**154**	**–**
Motorized camper	100	–	–	10	89	606	147	–
Other vehicle	100	229	42	123	67	129	179	–
Motorboats	100	–	44	125	155	91	145	–
Rental of recreational vehicles	**100**	**31**	**185**	**73**	**121**	**49**	**89**	**22**
Boat and trailer rental on trips	100	94	34	168	162	16	29	–
Rental of campers on trips	100	–	290	–	170	53	–	–
Rental of other vehicles on trips	100	21	200	70	100	53	112	44
Rental of other RVs	100	–	489	–	–	159	–	–
Outboard motors	**100**	**–**	**21**	**8**	**72**	**408**	**185**	**319**
Docking and landing fees	**100**	**3**	**81**	**88**	**84**	**137**	**211**	**140**
Sports, recreation, exercise equipment	**100**	**55**	**109**	**101**	**129**	**98**	**67**	**31**
Athletic gear, game tables, exercise equipment	100	27	102	97	118	110	114	58
Bicycles	100	138	135	118	81	77	50	19
Camping equipment	100	86	70	86	244	37	2	–
Hunting and fishing equipment	100	31	148	92	125	104	31	16
Winter sports equipment	100	193	103	146	104	17	16	–
Water sports equipment	100	7	67	81	171	221	20	4
Other sports equipment	100	79	120	131	76	92	70	26
Rental and repair of miscellaneous sports equipment	100	104	117	87	122	62	130	35
Photographic equipment and supplies	**100**	**101**	**103**	**98**	**114**	**115**	**74**	**34**
Film	100	97	97	99	106	132	84	41
Other photographic supplies	100	111	–	89	252	80	40	41
Film processing	100	101	101	99	108	122	82	36
Repair and rental of photographic equipment	100	–	109	121	65	84	224	12
Photographic equipment	100	74	99	76	142	137	78	33
Photographer fees	100	134	124	119	96	66	45	26
Fireworks	**100**	**–**	**129**	**127**	**54**	**108**	**167**	**–**
Souvenirs	**100**	**13**	**2**	**162**	**105**	**210**	**68**	**–**
Visual goods	**100**	**–**	**145**	**120**	**52**	**208**	**23**	**–**
Pinball, electronic video games	**100**	**50**	**119**	**157**	**99**	**30**	**9**	**20**

Note: Per capita indexes account for household size and show how much each person in a particular household demographic segment spends relative to a person in the average household. (–) means sample is too small to make a reliable estimate.
Source: Calculations by New Strategist based on the 2000 Consumer Expenditure Survey

Table 3.4 Entertainment: Total spending by age, 2000

(total annual spending on entertainment, by consumer unit (CU) age group, 2000; numbers in thousands)

	total consumer units	under 25	25 to 34	35 to 44	45 to 54	55 to 64	65 to 74	75+
Number of consumer units	109,367	8,306	18,887	23,983	21,874	14,161	11,538	10,617
Total spending of all CUs	$4,160,831,424	$187,243,653	$735,559,314	$1,082,817,341	$1,009,709,965	$557,094,165	$355,160,524	$232,597,661
Entertainment, total spending	203,805,405	9,063,673	35,438,245	59,102,746	48,807,019	27,689,145	16,187,814	7,501,017
FEES AND ADMISSIONS	**$56,307,600**	**$2,249,099**	**$8,696,519**	**$17,141,849**	**$13,941,394**	**$7,207,666**	**$4,796,808**	**$2,274,161**
Recreation expenses on trips	2,787,765	115,204	444,033	742,754	633,909	426,954	311,295	113,496
Social, recreation, civic club membership	10,737,652	310,063	1,584,997	2,819,681	2,604,100	1,556,011	1,267,334	595,826
Fees for participant sports	7,818,647	261,805	1,123,588	2,410,531	1,773,325	951,902	856,466	441,030
Participant sports on trips	3,833,313	160,721	571,332	1,036,305	925,708	587,115	347,640	204,590
Movie, theater, opera, ballet	9,751,162	702,521	1,765,746	2,574,095	2,427,577	1,189,524	736,471	355,139
Movie, other admissions on trips	4,914,953	198,430	802,131	1,349,284	1,050,608	829,127	464,520	220,303
Admission to sports events	3,863,936	164,293	583,797	1,236,563	1,155,822	455,701	196,954	71,240
Admission to sports events on trips	1,638,318	66,116	267,440	449,681	350,203	276,423	154,840	73,470
Fees for recreational lessons	8,174,090	154,658	1,109,234	3,780,440	2,386,235	507,813	150,109	85,573
Other entertainment services on trips	2,787,765	115,204	444,033	742,754	633,909	426,954	311,295	113,496
TELEVISION, RADIO, SOUND EQUIPMENT	**68,006,588**	**3,930,399**	**12,852,037**	**18,931,221**	**15,222,773**	**8,223,859**	**5,400,707**	**3,445,747**
Television	**49,601,216**	**2,514,392**	**9,057,450**	**12,642,399**	**10,835,942**	**6,739,220**	**4,805,462**	**3,005,991**
Cable service and community antenna	35,126,493	1,418,333	5,989,823	8,347,043	7,973,073	5,112,687	3,714,774	2,570,376
Black-and-white TV	84,213	2,243	23,231	29,979	18,593	991	8,077	1,380
Color TV, console	3,301,790	211,305	751,891	1,094,104	442,949	470,853	257,990	72,620
Color TV, portable, table model	3,756,756	381,744	655,568	865,546	762,309	461,365	407,522	222,426
VCRs and video disc players	2,602,935	174,426	599,662	827,893	580,536	219,637	155,648	45,441
Video cassettes, tapes, and discs	2,274,834	220,109	538,846	594,778	488,884	257,589	133,725	40,663
Video game hardware and software	2,047,350	92,778	437,612	794,317	472,478	154,638	75,805	19,429
Repair of TV, radio, and sound equipment	353,255	2,575	52,317	67,632	88,152	58,202	51,459	33,550
Rental of television sets	53,590	10,881	8,499	21,345	9,187	3,399	577	–
Radio and sound equipment	**18,405,372**	**1,416,090**	**3,794,587**	**6,288,582**	**4,386,831**	**1,484,781**	**595,245**	**439,862**
Radios	1,141,791	103,161	165,639	303,385	308,423	188,200	53,306	15,076
Tape recorders and players	480,121	23,008	78,003	93,294	220,052	69,389	–	–
Sound components and component systems	2,532,940	191,038	580,586	786,163	626,253	197,971	86,650	64,445
Miscellaneous sound equipment	45,934	–	18,132	14,869	9,843	2,549	231	–
Sound equipment accessories	441,843	3,904	112,378	92,095	165,367	26,481	23,076	21,765
Satellite dishes	295,291	22,260	47,406	86,579	44,842	45,174	23,191	26,436
Compact disc, tape, record, video mail order clubs	931,807	61,464	179,615	253,260	204,084	133,821	68,651	31,214
Records, CDs, audio tapes, needles	4,315,622	499,440	947,183	1,313,789	990,236	352,609	150,340	62,640
Rental of VCR, radio, sound equipment	59,058	6,063	4,911	8,154	31,499	3,115	4,731	–
Musical instruments and accessories	3,466,934	93,941	530,725	1,797,286	701,062	100,685	58,382	185,373
Rental and repair of musical instruments	146,552	831	10,199	76,985	32,155	22,799	3,692	0
Rental of video cassettes, tapes, discs, films	4,545,293	411,064	1,120,188	1,462,963	1,053,233	342,130	122,995	32,807

	total consumer units	under 25	25 to 34	35 to 44	45 to 54	55 to 64	65 to 74	75+
PETS, TOYS, PLAYGROUND EQUIPMENT	**$36,496,862**	**$1,433,865**	**$6,626,126**	**$10,817,532**	**$8,399,179**	**$5,074,594**	**$3,025,725**	**$1,107,141**
Pets	**22,904,731**	**819,636**	**3,232,888**	**6,331,992**	**6,156,000**	**3,420,306**	**2,131,992**	**799,672**
Pet food	9,402,281	336,974	1,344,188	2,493,273	2,361,298	1,540,009	965,961	359,810
Pet purchase, supplies, and medicines	4,166,883	271,938	633,659	1,201,548	1,173,759	518,576	274,835	81,432
Pet services	2,117,345	58,806	213,234	570,556	610,941	351,051	251,413	61,260
Veterinarian services	7,218,222	151,834	1,041,996	2,066,615	2,010,221	1,010,671	639,667	297,170
Toys, games, hobbies, and tricycles	**13,229,032**	**613,315**	**3,228,166**	**4,340,204**	**2,222,398**	**1,641,543**	**875,503**	**307,468**
Playground equipment	**363,098**	**997**	**164,884**	**145,337**	**20,780**	**12,603**	**18,230**	**106**
OTHER ENTERTAINMENT SUPPLIES, EQUIPMENT, SERVICES	**42,994,355**	**1,450,228**	**7,263,562**	**12,212,144**	**11,243,455**	**7,182,884**	**2,964,574**	**673,861**
Unmotored recreational vehicles	**5,256,178**	**–**	**612,883**	**1,438,500**	**1,564,866**	**1,487,188**	**129,110**	**23,570**
Boat without motor and boat trailers	1,735,654	–	282,361	468,148	128,619	792,733	40,268	23,570
Trailer and other attachable campers	3,520,524	–	330,523	970,352	1,436,247	694,455	88,843	–
Motorized recreational vehicles	**8,963,719**	**314,050**	**575,109**	**2,452,502**	**2,215,617**	**2,296,489**	**1,109,840**	**–**
Motorized camper	2,334,985	–	–	69,071	451,261	1,539,867	274,374	–
Other vehicle	2,377,639	314,050	197,936	843,722	345,390	334,624	341,871	–
Motorboats	4,251,095	–	377,173	1,539,469	1,418,966	421,998	493,480	–
Rental of recreational vehicles	**305,134**	**5,399**	**113,133**	**64,514**	**80,059**	**16,285**	**21,807**	**3,928**
Boat and trailer rental on trips	64,527	3,489	4,344	31,418	22,530	1,133	1,500	–
Rental of campers on trips	66,714	–	38,718	–	24,499	3,823	–	–
Rental of other vehicles on trips	153,114	1,827	61,383	30,938	33,030	8,780	13,730	3,928
Rental of other RVs	3,281	–	3,211	–	–	566	–	–
Outboard motors	**391,534**	**–**	**16,621**	**9,353**	**60,810**	**173,614**	**57,921**	**72,833**
Docking and landing fees	**893,528**	**1,578**	**145,241**	**226,879**	**162,524**	**132,830**	**151,494**	**72,939**
Sports, recreation, exercise equipment	**15,702,914**	**502,513**	**3,435,356**	**4,581,712**	**4,390,112**	**1,670,148**	**844,812**	**285,810**
Athletic gear, game tables, exercise equip.	6,413,281	99,257	1,305,847	1,803,761	1,633,332	767,951	586,477	215,525
Bicycles	1,282,875	102,247	346,765	437,210	223,552	107,057	51,690	14,121
Camping equipment	1,861,426	91,864	261,774	463,112	981,049	74,912	3,692	–
Hunting and fishing equipment	2,827,137	50,085	839,338	750,428	763,403	321,030	69,805	26,436
Winter sports equipment	638,703	71,099	132,398	270,768	143,712	11,895	8,307	–
Water sports equipment	901,184	3,738	121,443	210,571	332,704	216,238	14,653	1,911
Other sports equipment	1,558,480	71,099	375,851	590,222	254,176	156,337	87,112	23,357
Rental and repair of misc. sports equipment	220,921	13,207	51,750	55,641	58,185	14,869	23,076	4,565
Photographic equipment and supplies	**10,380,022**	**606,836**	**2,145,752**	**2,958,783**	**2,555,539**	**1,293,891**	**613,475**	**207,350**
Film	2,340,454	131,318	455,177	671,764	533,507	334,908	158,071	55,315
Other photographic supplies	157,488	10,133	–	40,531	85,746	13,736	5,077	3,716
Film processing	3,437,405	199,925	695,986	987,140	798,838	456,834	226,837	71,877
Repair and rental of photographic equipment	29,529	–	6,422	10,313	4,156	2,691	5,307	212
Photographic equipment	2,210,307	94,771	440,067	487,335	677,438	328,394	139,033	43,105
Photographer fees	2,205,932	170,688	548,290	761,700	455,854	157,329	79,035	33,125
Fireworks	**129,053**	**–**	**33,241**	**47,486**	**15,093**	**15,152**	**17,307**	**–**
Souvenirs	**218,734**	**1,578**	**755**	**102,407**	**49,654**	**49,847**	**12,000**	**–**
Visual goods	**119,210**	**–**	**34,563**	**41,251**	**13,343**	**26,906**	**2,192**	**–**
Pinball, electronic video games	**634,329**	**18,273**	**150,718**	**288,515**	**136,056**	**20,392**	**4,731**	**7,432**

Note: Numbers may not add to total because of rounding. (–) means sample is too small to make a reliable estimate.
Source: Calculations by New Strategist based on the 2000 Consumer Expenditure Survey

Table 3.5 Entertainment: Market shares by age, 2000

(percentage of total annual spending on entertainment accounted for by consumer unit age groups, 2000)

	total consumer units	under 25	25 to 34	35 to 44	45 to 54	55 to 64	65 to 74	75+
Share of total consumer units	100.0%	7.6%	17.3%	21.9%	20.0%	12.9%	10.5%	9.7%
Share of total before-tax income	100.0	3.4	17.6	27.7	26.4	14.0	6.9	4.5
Share of total spending	100.0	4.5	17.7	26.0	24.3	13.4	8.5	5.6
Share of entertainment spending	100.0	4.4	17.4	29.0	23.9	13.6	7.9	3.7
FEES AND ADMISSIONS	100.0%	4.0%	15.4%	30.4%	24.8%	12.8%	8.5%	4.0%
Recreation expenses on trips	100.0	4.1	15.9	26.6	22.7	15.3	11.2	4.1
Social, recreation, civic club membership	100.0	2.9	14.8	26.3	24.3	14.5	11.8	5.5
Fees for participant sports	100.0	3.3	14.4	30.8	22.7	12.2	11.0	5.6
Participant sports on trips	100.0	4.2	14.9	27.0	24.1	15.3	9.1	5.3
Movie, theater, opera, ballet	100.0	7.2	18.1	26.4	24.9	12.2	7.6	3.6
Movie, other admissions on trips	100.0	4.0	16.3	27.5	21.4	16.9	9.5	4.5
Admission to sports events	100.0	4.3	15.1	32.0	29.9	11.8	5.1	1.8
Admission to sports events on trips	100.0	4.0	16.3	27.4	21.4	16.9	9.5	4.5
Fees for recreational lessons	100.0	1.9	13.6	46.2	29.2	6.2	1.8	1.0
Other entertainment services on trips	100.0	4.1	15.9	26.6	22.7	15.3	11.2	4.1
TELEVISION, RADIO, SOUND EQUIPMENT	100.0	5.8	18.9	27.8	22.4	12.1	7.9	5.1
Television	100.0	5.1	18.3	25.5	21.8	13.6	9.7	6.1
Cable service and community antenna	100.0	4.0	17.1	23.8	22.7	14.6	10.6	7.3
Black-and-white TV	100.0	2.7	27.6	35.6	22.1	1.2	9.6	1.6
Color TV, console	100.0	6.4	22.8	33.1	13.4	14.3	7.8	2.2
Color TV, portable, table model	100.0	10.2	17.5	23.0	20.3	12.3	10.8	5.9
VCRs and video disc players	100.0	6.7	23.0	31.8	22.3	8.4	6.0	1.7
Video cassettes, tapes, and discs	100.0	9.7	23.7	26.1	21.5	11.3	5.9	1.8
Video game hardware and software	100.0	4.5	21.4	38.8	23.1	7.6	3.7	0.9
Repair of TV, radio, and sound equipment	100.0	0.7	14.8	19.1	25.0	16.5	14.6	9.5
Rental of television sets	100.0	20.3	15.9	39.8	17.1	6.3	1.1	–
Radio and sound equipment	100.0	7.7	20.6	34.2	23.8	8.1	3.2	2.4
Radios	100.0	9.0	14.5	26.6	27.0	16.5	4.7	1.3
Tape recorders and players	100.0	4.8	16.2	19.4	45.8	14.5	–	–
Sound components and component systems	100.0	7.5	22.9	31.0	24.7	7.8	3.4	2.5
Miscellaneous sound equipment	100.0	–	39.5	32.4	21.4	5.5	0.5	–
Sound equipment accessories	100.0	0.9	25.4	20.8	37.4	6.0	5.2	4.9
Satellite dishes	100.0	7.5	16.1	29.3	15.2	15.3	7.9	9.0
Compact disc, tape, record, video mail order clubs	100.0	6.6	19.3	27.2	21.9	14.4	7.4	3.3
Records, CDs, audio tapes, needles	100.0	11.6	21.9	30.4	22.9	8.2	3.5	1.5
Rental of VCR, radio, sound equipment	100.0	10.3	8.3	13.8	53.3	5.3	8.0	–
Musical instruments and accessories	100.0	2.7	15.3	51.8	20.2	2.9	1.7	5.3
Rental and repair of musical instruments	100.0	0.6	7.0	52.5	21.9	15.6	2.5	0.0
Rental of video cassettes, tapes, discs, films	100.0	9.0	24.6	32.2	23.2	7.5	2.7	0.7

	total consumer units	under 25	25 to 34	35 to 44	45 to 54	55 to 64	65 to 74	75+
PETS, TOYS, PLAYGROUND EQUIPMENT	**100.0%**	**3.9%**	**18.2%**	**29.6%**	**23.0%**	**13.9%**	**8.3%**	**3.0%**
Pets	**100.0**	**3.6**	**14.1**	**27.6**	**26.9**	**14.9**	**9.3**	**3.5**
Pet food	100.0	3.6	14.3	26.5	25.1	16.4	10.3	3.8
Pet purchase, supplies, and medicines	100.0	6.5	15.2	28.8	28.2	12.4	6.6	2.0
Pet services	100.0	2.8	10.1	26.9	28.9	16.6	11.9	2.9
Veterinarian services	100.0	2.1	14.4	28.6	27.8	14.0	8.9	4.1
Toys, games, hobbies, and tricycles	**100.0**	**4.6**	**24.4**	**32.8**	**16.8**	**12.4**	**6.6**	**2.3**
Playground equipment	**100.0**	**0.3**	**45.4**	**40.0**	**5.7**	**3.5**	**5.0**	**0.0**
OTHER ENTERTAINMENT SUPPLIES, EQUIPMENT, SERVICES	**100.0**	**3.4**	**16.9**	**28.4**	**26.2**	**16.7**	**6.9**	**1.6**
Unmotored recreational vehicles	**100.0**	**–**	**11.7**	**27.4**	**29.8**	**28.3**	**2.5**	**0.4**
Boat without motor and boat trailers	100.0	–	16.3	27.0	7.4	45.7	2.3	1.4
Trailer and other attachable campers	100.0	–	9.4	27.6	40.8	19.7	2.5	–
Motorized recreational vehicles	**100.0**	**3.5**	**6.4**	**27.4**	**24.7**	**25.6**	**12.4**	**–**
Motorized camper	100.0	–	–	3.0	19.3	65.9	11.8	–
Other vehicle	100.0	13.2	8.3	35.5	14.5	14.1	14.4	–
Motorboats	100.0	–	8.9	36.2	33.4	9.9	11.6	–
Rental of recreational vehicles	100.0	1.8	37.1	21.1	26.2	5.3	7.1	1.3
Boat and trailer rental on trips	100.0	5.4	6.7	48.7	34.9	1.8	2.3	–
Rental of campers on trips	**100.0**	**–**	**58.0**	**–**	**36.7**	**5.7**	**–**	**–**
Rental of other vehicles on trips	100.0	1.2	40.1	20.2	21.6	5.7	9.0	2.6
Rental of other RVs	100.0	–	97.9	–	–	17.3	–	–
Outboard motors	**100.0**	**–**	**4.2**	**2.4**	**15.5**	**44.3**	**14.8**	**18.6**
Docking and landing fees	**100.0**	**0.2**	**16.3**	**25.4**	**18.2**	**14.9**	**17.0**	**8.2**
Sports, recreation, exercise equipment	**100.0**	**3.2**	**21.9**	**29.2**	**28.0**	**10.6**	**5.4**	**1.8**
Athletic gear, game tables, exercise equipment	100.0	1.5	20.4	28.1	25.5	12.0	9.1	3.4
Bicycles	100.0	8.0	27.0	34.1	17.4	8.3	4.0	1.1
Camping equipment	100.0	4.9	14.1	24.9	52.7	4.0	0.2	–
Hunting and fishing equipment	100.0	1.8	29.7	26.5	27.0	11.4	2.5	0.9
Winter sports equipment	100.0	11.1	20.7	42.4	22.5	1.9	1.3	–
Water sports equipment	100.0	0.4	13.5	23.4	36.9	24.0	1.6	0.2
Other sports equipment	100.0	4.6	24.1	37.9	16.3	10.0	5.6	1.5
Rental and repair of misc. sports equipment	100.0	6.0	23.4	25.2	26.3	6.7	10.4	2.1
Photographic equipment and supplies	**100.0**	**5.8**	**20.7**	**28.5**	**24.6**	**12.5**	**5.9**	**2.0**
Film	100.0	5.6	19.4	28.7	22.8	14.3	6.8	2.4
Other photographic supplies	100.0	6.4	–	25.7	54.4	8.7	3.2	2.4
Film processing	100.0	5.8	20.2	28.7	23.2	13.3	6.6	2.1
Repair and rental of photographic equipment	100.0	–	21.7	34.9	14.1	9.1	18.0	0.7
Photographic equipment	100.0	4.3	19.9	22.0	30.6	14.9	6.3	2.0
Photographer fees	100.0	7.7	24.9	34.5	20.7	7.1	3.6	1.5
Fireworks	**100.0**	**–**	**25.8**	**36.8**	**11.7**	**11.7**	**13.4**	**–**
Souvenirs	**100.0**	**0.7**	**0.3**	**46.8**	**22.7**	**22.8**	**5.5**	**–**
Visual goods	**100.0**	**–**	**29.0**	**34.6**	**11.2**	**22.6**	**1.8**	**–**
Pinball, electronic video games	**100.0**	**2.9**	**23.8**	**45.5**	**21.4**	**3.2**	**0.7**	**1.2**

Note: Numbers may not add to total because of rounding. (–) means sample is too small to make a reliable estimate.
Source: Calculations by New Strategist based on the 2000 Consumer Expenditure Survey

Table 3.6 Entertainment: Average spending by income, 2000

(average annual spending on entertainment, by before-tax income of consumer units (CU), 2000; complete income reporters only)

	complete income reporters	under $10,000	$10,000–19,999	$20,000–29,999	$30,000–39,999	$40,000–49,999	$50,000–69,999	$70,000 or more
Number of consumer units (in thousands, add 000)	81,454	10,810	14,714	12,039	9,477	7,653	11,337	15,424
Average number of persons per CU	2.5	1.7	2.1	2.4	2.5	2.6	2.9	3.2
Average before-tax income of CU	$44,649.00	$5,739.61	$14,586.29	$24,527.00	$34,422.00	$44,201.00	$58,561.00	$112,586.00
Average spending of CU, total	40,238.44	16,455.72	22,620.20	29,851.59	35,609.24	42,323.03	49,245.37	75,963.85
Entertainment, average spending	1,957.63	763.25	956.82	1,399.42	1,657.52	1,982.16	2,507.40	3,912.42
FEES AND ADMISSIONS	**$535.44**	**$193.26**	**$203.46**	**$302.69**	**$350.83**	**$417.01**	**$620.42**	**$1,383.39**
Recreation expenses on trips	27.35	12.04	13.33	21.44	18.26	21.83	34.13	59.39
Social, recreation, civic club membership	101.63	38.35	42.68	46.22	58.15	51.36	108.95	291.76
Fees for participant sports	75.37	22.71	32.79	47.73	55.81	61.46	92.07	181.13
Participant sports on trips	36.16	12.59	12.20	26.34	27.29	24.59	35.26	95.04
Movie, theater, opera, ballet	92.48	44.35	42.64	62.42	77.26	90.53	106.12	197.54
Movie, other admissions on trips	44.84	14.86	16.95	28.24	34.08	39.56	59.19	104.09
Admission to sports events	35.74	11.67	6.32	15.88	18.25	27.35	47.16	102.71
Admission to sports events on trips	14.94	4.95	5.65	9.41	11.36	13.18	19.72	34.69
Fees for recreational lessons	79.58	19.69	17.57	23.56	32.11	65.32	83.69	257.65
Other entertainment services on trips	27.35	12.04	13.33	21.44	18.26	21.83	34.13	59.39
TELEVISION, RADIO, SOUND EQUIPMENT	**654.37**	**341.51**	**419.57**	**511.93**	**619.44**	**738.45**	**794.03**	**1,083.38**
Television	**464.88**	**265.76**	**330.72**	**397.02**	**444.50**	**509.32**	**575.41**	**694.64**
Cable service and community antenna	324.11	201.12	251.13	293.21	323.63	339.24	386.69	450.84
Black-and-white TV	0.83	0.65	0.31	0.34	0.86	1.07	1.62	1.11
Color TV, console	29.14	10.95	11.39	12.96	27.88	35.90	44.00	57.95
Color TV, portable, table model	37.51	26.70	25.84	30.39	36.95	48.00	41.06	54.31
VCRs and video disc players	26.71	8.69	15.75	23.49	19.02	32.33	33.55	49.23
Video cassettes, tapes, and discs	22.53	9.12	12.50	19.01	20.96	26.91	33.82	34.74
Video game hardware and software	20.26	6.27	9.56	13.61	13.14	22.12	30.50	41.39
Repair of TV, radio, and sound equipment	3.25	1.80	2.66	3.16	2.01	3.64	3.86	5.04
Rental of television sets	0.54	0.46	1.59	0.85	0.05	0.10	0.29	0.04
Radio and sound equipment	**189.48**	**75.75**	**88.86**	**114.90**	**174.93**	**229.12**	**218.62**	**388.74**
Radios	12.26	11.10	6.55	2.39	18.22	20.21	14.77	15.86
Tape recorders and players	5.50	3.69	1.74	8.24	–	4.99	6.62	10.56
Sound components and component systems	24.70	7.21	10.79	13.93	19.83	29.95	37.39	49.72
Miscellaneous sound equipment	0.56	–	–	0.09	–	1.14	0.23	1.98
Sound equipment accessories	4.96	–	1.81	2.35	3.91	9.23	3.90	11.75
Satellite dishes	3.12	1.07	1.87	0.42	3.85	3.49	4.46	6.26
Compact disc, tape, record, video mail order clubs	9.75	4.69	6.82	7.03	9.62	14.35	12.72	13.80
Records, CDs, audio tapes, needles	43.38	20.38	20.71	35.93	42.22	49.07	57.22	74.66
Rental of VCR, radio, sound equipment	0.67	0.17	0.49	0.66	1.55	0.55	–	1.20
Musical instruments and accessories	38.77	5.45	13.79	7.51	31.49	45.89	21.80	123.75
Rental and repair of musical instruments	1.58	0.49	0.35	0.50	0.93	1.71	2.38	4.09
Rental of video cassettes, tapes, discs, films	44.25	21.48	23.96	35.84	43.30	48.56	57.13	75.11

	complete income reporters	under $10,000	$10,000– 19,999	$20,000– 29,999	$30,000– 39,999	$40,000– 49,999	$50,000– 69,999	$70,000 or more
PETS, TOYS, PLAYGROUND EQUIPMENT	**$355.35**	**$124.08**	**$177.92**	**$283.01**	**$339.44**	**$367.69**	**$455.21**	**$656.65**
Pets	**225.94**	**82.91**	**109.39**	**170.31**	**228.58**	**241.10**	**275.02**	**418.78**
Pet food	93.97	38.96	63.45	75.56	103.24	108.06	112.27	139.50
Pet purchase, supplies, and medicines	40.78	13.23	12.07	34.48	43.14	34.32	47.69	82.69
Pet services	21.03	6.17	6.94	10.03	20.71	12.72	26.20	54.00
Veterinarian services	70.15	24.54	26.93	50.24	61.50	86.00	88.86	142.61
Toys, games, hobbies, and tricycles	**126.37**	**40.24**	**67.47**	**109.60**	**109.66**	**124.24**	**175.93**	**230.91**
Playground equipment	**3.04**	**0.92**	**1.06**	**3.09**	**1.20**	**2.35**	**4.26**	**6.96**
OTHER ENTERTAINMENT SUPPLIES, EQUIPMENT, SERVICES	**412.46**	**104.41**	**155.86**	**301.80**	**347.81**	**459.02**	**637.74**	**789.00**
Unmotored recreational vehicles	**47.60**	**1.51**	**0.67**	**88.46**	**22.84**	**70.64**	**72.73**	**78.06**
Boat without motor and boat trailers	19.13	1.51	0.45	48.29	19.84	21.00	6.89	34.16
Trailer and other attachable campers	28.47	–	0.22	40.17	3.00	49.65	65.83	43.91
Motorized recreational vehicles	**79.16**	**17.20**	**60.75**	**49.56**	**55.57**	**123.41**	**93.38**	**145.31**
Motorized camper	22.33	2.57	60.67	–	–	84.55	22.18	–
Other vehicle	20.41	3.02	0.08	25.89	41.98	4.99	22.01	40.95
Motorboats	36.41	11.62	–	23.67	13.60	33.86	49.19	104.36
Rental of recreational vehicles	**3.48**	**0.89**	**0.55**	**2.19**	**2.20**	**2.20**	**6.37**	**8.39**
Boat and trailer rental on trips	0.74	0.10	0.18	0.33	1.53	0.57	0.79	1.58
Rental of campers on trips	0.82	–	0.22	–	–	–	4.67	0.67
Rental of other vehicles on trips	1.68	0.71	0.12	1.83	0.06	1.58	0.72	5.47
Rental of other RVs	0.05	–	0.03	0.03	–	0.05	–	0.16
Outboard motors	**4.58**	**0.79**	**1.92**	**10.91**	**12.22**	**–**	**1.68**	**4.56**
Docking and landing fees	**8.28**	**0.47**	**2.59**	**4.58**	**0.68**	**7.13**	**21.82**	**17.37**
Sports, recreation, exercise equipment	**153.44**	**45.62**	**43.32**	**75.85**	**169.72**	**146.74**	**261.20**	**289.75**
Athletic gear, game tables, exercise equipment	69.17	13.08	18.37	43.48	61.19	73.68	105.23	140.52
Bicycles	12.88	3.91	5.53	10.20	8.56	7.17	19.97	28.56
Camping equipment	10.10	8.69	7.66	0.57	13.50	8.88	24.84	7.92
Hunting and fishing equipment	27.66	11.04	4.29	2.95	70.16	4.56	65.37	32.79
Winter sports equipment	6.10	2.16	1.60	2.83	2.65	5.91	5.77	18.16
Water sports equipment	9.44	1.64	0.95	5.57	1.89	18.64	15.26	21.84
Other sports equipment	16.08	3.45	3.92	9.16	9.64	26.62	21.70	36.52
Rental and repair of misc. sports equipment	2.00	1.66	1.00	1.08	2.12	1.28	3.06	3.42
Photographic equipment and supplies	**103.31**	**36.31**	**42.01**	**63.06**	**69.39**	**96.61**	**156.37**	**225.13**
Film	22.28	10.83	9.09	15.18	18.24	21.63	31.38	44.55
Other photographic supplies	1.77	1.41	0.36	1.31	–	3.83	0.41	4.59
Film processing	33.51	11.62	13.54	19.57	26.06	30.90	49.48	72.94
Repair and rental of photographic equipment	0.34	0.23	–	0.08	0.32	0.30	0.38	0.92
Photographic equipment	23.46	6.53	12.62	12.16	13.33	20.32	37.59	51.88
Photographer fees	21.95	5.69	6.40	14.75	11.43	19.63	37.12	50.25
Fireworks	**1.47**	**1.02**	**–**	**2.74**	**5.64**	**0.71**	**0.53**	**0.56**
Souvenirs	**2.49**	**–**	**0.15**	**0.27**	**0.84**	**2.93**	**1.76**	**8.86**
Visual goods	**1.52**	**–**	**–**	**1.27**	**0.23**	**–**	**8.31**	**0.51**
Pinball, electronic video games	**7.14**	**0.61**	**3.90**	**2.90**	**8.49**	**8.64**	**13.58**	**10.51**

Note: (–) means sample is too small to make a reliable estimate.
Source: Bureau of Labor Statistics, unpublished data from the 2000 Consumer Expenditure Survey; calculations by New Strategist

Table 3.7 Entertainment: Indexed spending by income, 2000

(indexed average annual spending of consumer units (CU) on entertainment by before-tax income of consumer unit, 2000; complete income reporters only; index definition: an index of 100 is the average for all consumer units; an index of 132 means that spending by consumer units in that group is 32 percent above the average for all consumer units; an index of 68 indicates spending that is 32 percent below the average for all consumer units)

	complete income reporters	under $10,000	$10,000–19,999	$20,000–29,999	$30,000–39,999	$40,000–49,999	$50,000–69,999	$70,000 or more
Average spending of CU, total	$40,238	$16,456	$22,620	$29,852	$35,609	$42,323	$49,245	$75,964
Average spending of CU, index	100	41	56	74	88	105	122	189
Entertainment, spending index	100	39	49	71	85	101	128	200
FEES AND ADMISSIONS	100	36	38	57	66	78	116	258
Recreation expenses on trips	100	44	49	78	67	80	125	217
Social, recreation, civic club membership	100	38	42	45	57	51	107	287
Fees for participant sports	100	30	44	63	74	82	122	240
Participant sports on trips	100	35	34	73	75	68	98	263
Movie, theater, opera, ballet	100	48	46	67	84	98	115	214
Movie, other admissions on trips	100	33	38	63	76	88	132	232
Admission to sports events	100	33	18	44	51	77	132	287
Admission to sports events on trips	100	33	38	63	76	88	132	232
Fees for recreational lessons	100	25	22	30	40	82	105	324
Other entertainment services on trips	100	44	49	78	67	80	125	217
TELEVISION, RADIO, SOUND EQUIPMENT	100	52	64	78	95	113	121	166
Television	100	57	71	85	96	110	124	149
Cable service and community antenna	100	62	77	90	100	105	119	139
Black-and-white TV	100	79	38	41	104	129	195	134
Color TV, console	100	38	39	44	96	123	151	199
Color TV, portable, table model	100	71	69	81	99	128	109	145
VCRs and video disc players	100	33	59	88	71	121	126	184
Video cassettes, tapes, and discs	100	40	55	84	93	119	150	154
Video game hardware and software	100	31	47	67	65	109	151	204
Repair of TV, radio, and sound equipment	100	55	82	97	62	112	119	155
Rental of television sets	100	84	294	157	9	19	54	7
Radio and sound equipment	100	40	47	61	92	121	115	205
Radios	100	91	53	19	149	165	120	129
Tape recorders and players	100	67	32	150	–	91	120	192
Sound components and component systems	100	29	44	56	80	121	151	201
Miscellaneous sound equipment	100	–	–	16	–	204	41	354
Sound equipment accessories	100	–	36	47	79	186	79	237
Satellite dishes	100	34	60	13	123	112	143	201
Compact disc, tape, record, video mail order clubs	100	48	70	72	99	147	130	142
Records, CDs, audio tapes, needles	100	47	48	83	97	113	132	172
Rental of VCR, radio, sound equipment	100	25	73	99	231	82	–	179
Musical instruments and accessories	100	14	36	19	81	118	56	319
Rental and repair of musical instruments	100	31	22	32	59	108	151	259
Rental of video cassettes, tapes, discs, films	100	49	54	81	98	110	129	170

	complete income reporters	under $10,000	$10,000–19,999	$20,000–29,999	$30,000–39,999	$40,000–49,999	$50,000–69,999	$70,000 or more
PETS, TOYS, PLAYGROUND EQUIPMENT	**100**	**35**	**50**	**80**	**96**	**103**	**128**	**185**
Pets	**100**	**37**	**48**	**75**	**101**	**107**	**122**	**185**
Pet food	100	41	68	80	110	115	119	148
Pet purchase, supplies, and medicines	100	32	30	85	106	84	117	203
Pet services	100	29	33	48	98	60	125	257
Veterinarian services	100	35	38	72	88	123	127	203
Toys, games, hobbies, and tricycles	**100**	**32**	**53**	**87**	**87**	**98**	**139**	**183**
Playground equipment	**100**	**30**	**35**	**102**	**39**	**77**	**140**	**229**
OTHER ENTERTAINMENT SUPPLIES, EQUIPMENT, SERVICES	**100**	**25**	**38**	**73**	**84**	**111**	**155**	**191**
Unmotored recreational vehicles	**100**	**3**	**1**	**186**	**48**	**148**	**153**	**164**
Boat without motor and boat trailers	100	8	2	252	104	110	36	179
Trailer and other attachable campers	100	–	1	141	11	174	231	154
Motorized recreational vehicles	**100**	**22**	**77**	**63**	**70**	**156**	**118**	**184**
Motorized camper	100	11	272	–	–	379	99	–
Other vehicle	100	15	0	127	206	24	108	201
Motorboats	100	32	–	65	37	93	135	287
Rental of recreational vehicles	**100**	**25**	**16**	**63**	**63**	**63**	**183**	**241**
Boat and trailer rental on trips	100	13	24	45	207	77	107	214
Rental of campers on trips	100	–	27	–	–	–	570	82
Rental of other vehicles on trips	100	42	7	109	4	94	43	326
Rental of other RVs	100	–	66	60	–	100	–	320
Outboard motors	**100**	**17**	**42**	**238**	**267**	**–**	**37**	**100**
Docking and landing fees	**100**	**6**	**31**	**55**	**8**	**86**	**264**	**210**
Sports, recreation, exercise equipment	**100**	**30**	**28**	**49**	**111**	**96**	**170**	**189**
Athletic gear, game tables, exercise equipment	100	19	27	63	88	107	152	203
Bicycles	100	30	43	79	66	56	155	222
Camping equipment	100	86	76	6	134	88	246	78
Hunting and fishing equipment	100	40	16	11	254	16	236	119
Winter sports equipment	100	35	26	46	43	97	95	298
Water sports equipment	100	17	10	59	20	197	162	231
Other sports equipment	100	21	24	57	60	166	135	227
Rental and repair of misc. sports equipment	100	83	50	54	106	64	153	171
Photographic equipment and supplies	**100**	**35**	**41**	**61**	**67**	**94**	**151**	**218**
Film	100	49	41	68	82	97	141	200
Other photographic supplies	100	80	21	74	–	216	23	259
Film processing	100	35	40	58	78	92	148	218
Repair and rental of photographic equipment	100	68	–	24	94	88	112	271
Photographic equipment	100	28	54	52	57	87	160	221
Photographer fees	100	26	29	67	52	89	169	229
Fireworks	**100**	**70**	**–**	**186**	**384**	**48**	**36**	**38**
Souvenirs	**100**	**–**	**6**	**11**	**34**	**118**	**71**	**356**
Visual goods	**100**	**–**	**–**	**84**	**15**	**–**	**547**	**34**
Pinball, electronic video games	**100**	**9**	**55**	**41**	**119**	**121**	**190**	**147**

Note: (–) means sample is too small to make a reliable estimate.
Source: Calculations by New Strategist based on the 2000 Consumer Expenditure Survey

Table 3.8 Entertainment: Indexed per capita spending by income, 2000

(indexed average annual per capita spending of consumer units (CU) on entertainment by before-tax income of consumer unit, 2000; complete income reporters only; index definition: an index of 100 is the average for all consumer units; an index of 132 means that spending by consumer units in that group is 32 percent above the average for all consumer units; an index of 68 indicates spending that is 32 percent below the average for all consumer units)

	complete income reporters	under $10,000	$10,000– 19,999	$20,000– 29,999	$30,000– 39,999	$40,000– 49,999	$50,000– 69,999	$70,000 or more
Per capita spending of CU, total	$16,095	$9,492	$10,819	$12,438	$14,244	$16,278	$16,981	$23,739
Per capita spending of CU, index	100	59	67	77	88	101	106	147
Entertainment, per capita spending index	100	56	58	74	85	97	110	156
FEES AND ADMISSIONS	**100**	**52**	**45**	**59**	**66**	**75**	**100**	**202**
Recreation expenses on trips	100	63	58	82	67	77	108	170
Social, recreation, civic club membership	100	54	50	47	57	49	92	224
Fees for participant sports	100	43	52	66	74	78	105	188
Participant sports on trips	100	50	40	76	75	65	84	205
Movie, theater, opera, ballet	100	69	55	70	84	94	99	167
Movie, other admissions on trips	100	48	45	66	76	85	114	181
Admission to sports events	100	47	21	46	51	74	114	225
Admission to sports events on trips	100	48	45	66	76	85	114	181
Fees for recreational lessons	100	36	26	31	40	79	91	253
Other entertainment services on trips	100	63	58	82	67	77	108	170
TELEVISION, RADIO, SOUND EQUIPMENT	**100**	**75**	**77**	**81**	**95**	**109**	**105**	**129**
Television	**100**	**82**	**85**	**89**	**96**	**105**	**107**	**117**
Cable service and community antenna	100	89	93	94	100	101	103	109
Black-and-white TV	100	114	45	43	104	124	168	104
Color TV, console	100	54	47	46	96	118	130	155
Color TV, portable, table model	100	103	82	84	99	123	94	113
VCRs and video disc players	100	47	71	92	71	116	108	144
Video cassettes, tapes, and discs	100	58	66	88	93	115	129	120
Video game hardware and software	100	45	56	70	65	105	130	160
Repair of TV, radio, and sound equipment	100	80	98	101	62	108	102	121
Rental of television sets	100	122	352	164	9	18	46	6
Radio and sound equipment	**100**	**58**	**56**	**63**	**92**	**116**	**99**	**160**
Radios	100	131	64	20	149	159	104	101
Tape recorders and players	100	97	38	156	–	87	104	150
Sound components and component systems	100	42	52	59	80	117	130	157
Miscellaneous sound equipment	100	–	–	17	–	196	35	276
Sound equipment accessories	100	–	44	49	79	179	68	185
Satellite dishes	100	50	72	14	123	108	123	157
Compact disc, tape, record, video mail order clubs	100	69	84	75	99	142	112	111
Records, CDs, audio tapes, needles	100	68	57	86	97	109	114	134
Rental of VCR, radio, sound equipment	100	36	87	103	231	79	–	140
Musical instruments and accessories	100	20	43	20	81	114	48	249
Rental and repair of musical instruments	100	45	26	33	59	104	130	202
Rental of video cassettes, tapes, discs, films	100	70	65	84	98	106	111	133

	complete income reporters	under $10,000	$10,000– 19,999	$20,000– 29,999	$30,000– 39,999	$40,000– 49,999	$50,000– 69,999	$70,000 or more
PETS, TOYS, PLAYGROUND EQUIPMENT	**100**	**50**	**60**	**83**	**96**	**99**	**110**	**144**
Pets	**100**	**53**	**58**	**79**	**101**	**103**	**105**	**145**
Pet food	100	60	81	84	110	111	103	116
Pet purchase, supplies, and medicines	100	47	35	88	106	81	101	158
Pet services	100	42	39	50	98	58	107	201
Veterinarian services	100	50	46	75	88	118	109	159
Toys, games, hobbies, and tricycles	**100**	**46**	**64**	**90**	**87**	**95**	**120**	**143**
Playground equipment	**100**	**44**	**42**	**106**	**39**	**74**	**121**	**179**
OTHER ENTERTAINMENT SUPPLIES, EQUIPMENT, SERVICES	**100**	**37**	**45**	**76**	**84**	**107**	**133**	**149**
Unmotored recreational vehicles	**100**	**5**	**2**	**194**	**48**	**143**	**132**	**128**
Boat without motor and boat trailers	100	–	3	263	104	106	31	140
Trailer and other attachable campers	100	–	1	147	11	168	199	120
Motorized recreational vehicles	**100**	**31**	**92**	**65**	**70**	**150**	**102**	**143**
Motorized camper	100	17	325	–	–	364	86	–
Other vehicle	100	21	0	132	206	24	93	157
Motorboats	100	46	–	68	37	89	116	224
Rental of recreational vehicles	**100**	**37**	**19**	**66**	**63**	**61**	**158**	**188**
Boat and trailer rental on trips	100	19	29	46	207	74	92	167
Rental of campers on trips	100	–	32	–	–	–	491	64
Rental of other vehicles on trips	100	61	9	113	4	90	37	254
Rental of other RVs	100	–	78	63	–	96	–	250
Outboard motors	**100**	**25**	**50**	**248**	**267**	**–**	**32**	**78**
Docking and landing fees	**100**	**8**	**37**	**58**	**8**	**83**	**227**	**164**
Sports, recreation, exercise equipment	**100**	**43**	**34**	**51**	**111**	**92**	**147**	**148**
Athletic gear, game tables, exercise equipment	100	27	32	65	88	102	131	159
Bicycles	100	44	51	82	66	54	134	173
Camping equipment	100	124	91	6	134	85	212	61
Hunting and fishing equipment	100	58	19	11	254	16	204	93
Winter sports equipment	100	51	31	48	43	93	82	233
Water sports equipment	100	25	12	61	20	190	139	181
Other sports equipment	100	31	29	59	60	159	116	177
Rental and repair of misc. sports equipment	100	120	60	56	106	62	132	134
Photographic equipment and supplies	**100**	**51**	**49**	**64**	**67**	**90**	**130**	**170**
Film	100	70	49	71	82	93	121	156
Other photographic supplies	100	115	25	77	–	208	20	203
Film processing	100	50	48	61	78	89	127	170
Repair and rental of photographic equipment	100	99	–	25	94	85	96	211
Photographic equipment	100	40	64	54	57	83	138	173
Photographer fees	100	37	35	70	52	86	146	179
Fireworks	**100**	**100**	**–**	**194**	**384**	**46**	**31**	**30**
Souvenirs	**100**	**–**	**7**	**11**	**34**	**113**	**61**	**278**
Visual goods	**100**	**–**	**–**	**87**	**15**	**–**	**471**	**26**
Pinball, electronic video games	**100**	**12**	**65**	**42**	**119**	**116**	**164**	**115**

Note: Per capita indexes account for household size and show how much each person in a particular household demographic segment spends relative to a person in the average household. (–) means sample is too small to make a reliable estimate.
Source: Calculations by New Strategist based on the 2000 Consumer Expenditure Survey

Table 3.9 Entertainment: Total spending by income, 2000

(total annual spending on entertainment, by before-tax income group of consumer units (CU), 2000; complete income reporters only; numbers in thousands)

	complete income reporters	under $10,000	$10,000– 19,999	$20,000– 29,999	$30,000– 39,999	$40,000– 49,999	$50,000– 69,999	$70,000 or more
Number of consumer units	81,454	10,810	14,714	12,039	9,477	7,653	11,337	15,424
Total spending of all CUs	$3,277,581,892	$177,886,368	$332,833,656	$359,383,292	$337,468,767	$323,898,149	$558,294,760	$1,171,666,422
Entertainment, total spending	159,456,794	8,250,679	14,078,602	16,847,617	15,708,317	15,169,470	28,426,394	60,345,166
FEES AND ADMISSIONS	**$43,613,730**	**$2,089,095**	**$2,993,728**	**$3,644,085**	**$3,324,816**	**$3,191,378**	**$7,033,702**	**$21,337,407**
Recreation expenses on trips	2,227,767	130,151	196,107	258,116	173,050	167,065	386,932	916,031
Social, recreation, civic club membership	8,278,170	414,554	627,961	556,443	551,088	393,058	1,235,166	4,500,106
Fees for participant sports	6,139,188	245,444	482,486	574,621	528,911	470,353	1,043,798	2,793,749
Participant sports on trips	2,945,377	136,134	179,570	317,107	258,627	188,187	399,743	1,465,897
Movie, theater, opera, ballet	7,532,866	479,391	627,461	751,474	732,193	692,826	1,203,082	3,046,857
Movie, other admissions on trips	3,652,397	160,624	249,379	339,981	322,976	302,753	671,037	1,605,484
Admission to sports events	2,911,166	126,165	92,996	191,179	172,955	209,310	534,653	1,584,199
Admission to sports events on trips	1,216,923	53,517	83,100	113,287	107,659	100,867	223,566	535,059
Fees for recreational lessons	6,482,109	212,856	258,561	283,639	304,306	499,894	948,794	3,973,994
Other entertainment services on trips	2,227,767	130,151	196,107	258,116	173,050	167,065	386,932	916,031
TELEVISION, RADIO, SOUND EQUIPMENT	**53,301,054**	**3,691,734**	**6,173,515**	**6,163,125**	**5,870,433**	**5,651,358**	**9,001,918**	**16,710,053**
Television	**37,866,336**	**2,872,871**	**4,866,163**	**4,779,724**	**4,212,527**	**3,897,826**	**6,523,423**	**10,714,127**
Cable service and community antenna	26,400,056	2,174,118	3,695,073	3,529,955	3,067,042	2,596,204	4,383,905	6,953,756
Black-and-white TV	67,607	7,076	4,581	4,093	8,150	8,189	18,366	17,121
Color TV, console	2,373,570	118,353	167,584	156,025	264,219	274,743	498,828	893,821
Color TV, portable, table model	3,055,340	288,623	380,229	365,865	350,175	367,344	465,497	837,677
VCRs and video disc players	2,175,636	93,963	231,797	282,796	180,253	247,421	380,356	759,324
Video cassettes, tapes, and discs	1,835,159	98,585	183,913	228,861	198,638	205,942	383,417	535,830
Video game hardware and software	1,650,258	67,828	140,633	163,851	124,528	169,284	345,779	638,399
Repair of TV, radio, and sound equipment	264,726	19,437	39,102	38,043	19,049	27,857	43,761	77,737
Rental of television sets	43,985	4,924	23,399	10,233	474	765	3,288	617
Radio and sound equipment	**15,433,904**	**818,863**	**1,307,432**	**1,383,281**	**1,657,812**	**1,753,455**	**2,478,495**	**5,995,926**
Radios	998,626	120,039	96,307	28,773	172,671	154,667	167,447	244,625
Tape recorders and players	447,997	39,866	25,573	99,201	–	38,188	75,051	162,877
Sound components and component systems	2,011,914	77,897	158,766	167,703	187,929	229,207	423,890	766,881
Miscellaneous sound equipment	45,614	–	–	1,084	–	8,724	2,608	30,540
Sound equipment accessories	404,012	–	26,616	28,292	37,055	70,637	44,214	181,232
Satellite dishes	254,136	11,611	27,453	5,056	36,486	26,709	50,563	96,554
Compact disc, tape, record, video mail order clubs	794,177	50,741	100,332	84,634	91,169	109,821	144,207	212,851
Records, CDs, audio tapes, needles	3,533,475	220,314	304,675	432,561	400,119	375,533	648,703	1,151,556
Rental of VCR, radio, sound equipment	54,574	1,796	7,153	7,946	14,689	4,209	–	18,509
Musical instruments and accessories	3,157,972	58,949	202,924	90,413	298,431	351,196	247,147	1,908,720
Rental and repair of musical instruments	128,697	5,349	5,139	6,020	8,814	13,087	26,982	63,084
Rental of video cassettes, tapes, discs, films	3,604,340	232,230	352,493	431,478	410,354	371,630	647,683	1,158,497

	complete income reporters	under $10,000	$10,000– 19,999	$20,000– 29,999	$30,000– 39,999	$40,000– 49,999	$50,000– 69,999	$70,000 or more
PETS, TOYS, PLAYGROUND EQUIPMENT	**$28,944,679**	**$1,341,255**	**$2,617,947**	**$3,407,157**	**$3,216,873**	**$2,813,932**	**$5,160,716**	**$10,128,170**
Pets	18,403,717	896,293	1,609,578	2,050,362	2,166,253	1,845,138	3,117,902	6,459,263
Pet food	7,654,232	421,206	933,615	909,667	978,405	826,983	1,272,805	2,151,648
Pet purchase, supplies, and medicines	3,321,694	143,062	177,578	415,105	408,838	262,651	540,662	1,275,411
Pet services	1,712,978	66,707	102,176	120,751	196,269	97,346	297,029	832,896
Veterinarian services	5,713,998	265,319	396,209	604,839	582,836	658,158	1,007,406	2,199,617
Toys, games, hobbies, and tricycles	10,293,342	434,953	992,783	1,319,474	1,039,248	950,809	1,994,518	3,561,556
Playground equipment	247,620	9,937	15,586	37,201	11,372	17,985	48,296	107,351
OTHER ENTERTAINMENT SUPPLIES, EQUIPMENT, SERVICES	33,596,517	1,128,703	2,293,332	3,633,370	3,296,195	3,512,880	7,230,058	12,169,536
Unmotored recreational vehicles	**3,877,210**	**16,285**	**9,862**	**1,064,970**	**216,455**	**540,608**	**824,540**	**1,203,997**
Boat without motor and boat trailers	1,558,215	16,285	6,590	581,363	188,024	160,713	78,112	526,884
Trailer and other attachable campers	2,318,995	–	3,272	483,607	28,431	379,971	746,315	677,268
Motorized recreational vehicles	**6,447,899**	**185,920**	**893,875**	**596,653**	**526,637**	**944,457**	**1,058,649**	**2,241,261**
Motorized camper	1,818,868	27,747	892,750	–	–	647,061	251,455	–
Other vehicle	1,662,476	32,607	1,125	311,690	397,844	38,188	249,527	631,613
Motorboats	2,965,740	125,567	–	284,963	128,887	259,131	557,667	1,609,649
Rental of recreational vehicles	**283,460**	**9,586**	**8,152**	**26,365**	**20,849**	**16,837**	**72,217**	**129,407**
Boat and trailer rental on trips	60,276	1,080	2,652	3,973	14,500	4,362	8,956	24,370
Rental of campers on trips	66,792	–	3,215	–	–	–	52,944	10,334
Rental of other vehicles on trips	136,843	7,716	1,803	22,031	569	12,092	8,163	84,369
Rental of other RVs	4,073	–	482	361	–	383	–	2,468
Outboard motors	**373,059**	**8,495**	**28,234**	**131,345**	**115,809**	**–**	**19,046**	**70,333**
Docking and landing fees	**674,439**	**5,071**	**38,111**	**55,139**	**6,444**	**54,566**	**247,373**	**267,915**
Sports, recreation, exercise equipment	**12,498,302**	**493,161**	**637,467**	**913,158**	**1,608,436**	**1,123,001**	**2,961,224**	**4,469,104**
Athletic gear, game tables, exercise equip.	5,634,173	141,441	270,307	523,456	579,898	563,873	1,192,993	2,167,380
Bicycles	1,049,128	42,261	81,403	122,798	81,123	54,872	226,400	440,509
Camping equipment	822,685	93,902	112,676	6,862	127,940	67,959	281,611	122,158
Hunting and fishing equipment	2,253,018	119,309	63,087	35,515	664,906	34,898	741,100	505,753
Winter sports equipment	496,869	23,303	23,549	34,070	25,114	45,229	65,414	280,100
Water sports equipment	768,926	17,743	13,924	67,057	17,912	142,652	173,003	336,860
Other sports equipment	1,309,780	37,322	57,733	110,277	91,358	203,723	246,013	563,284
Rental and repair of misc. sports equipment	162,908	17,951	14,787	13,002	20,091	9,796	34,691	52,750
Photographic equipment and supplies	**8,415,013**	**392,521**	**618,192**	**759,179**	**657,609**	**739,356**	**1,772,767**	**3,472,405**
Film	1,814,795	117,047	133,779	182,752	172,860	165,534	355,755	687,139
Other photographic supplies	144,174	15,293	5,342	15,771	–	29,311	4,648	70,796
Film processing	2,729,524	125,629	199,178	235,603	246,971	236,478	560,955	1,125,027
Repair and rental of photographic equipment	27,694	2,516	–	963	3,033	2,296	4,308	14,190
Photographic equipment	1,910,911	70,569	185,656	146,394	126,328	155,509	426,158	800,197
Photographer fees	1,787,915	61,467	94,156	177,575	108,322	150,228	420,829	775,056
Fireworks	**119,737**	**11,062**	**–**	**32,987**	**53,450**	**5,434**	**6,009**	**8,637**
Souvenirs	**202,820**	**–**	**2,203**	**3,251**	**7,961**	**22,423**	**19,953**	**136,657**
Visual goods	**123,810**	**–**	**–**	**15,290**	**2,180**	**–**	**94,210**	**7,866**
Pinball, electronic video games	**581,582**	**6,637**	**57,331**	**34,913**	**80,460**	**66,122**	**153,956**	**162,106**

Note: Numbers may not add to total because of rounding. (–) means sample is too small to make a reliable estimate.
Source: Calculations by New Strategist based on the 2000 Consumer Expenditure Survey

Table 3.10 Entertainment: Market shares by income, 2000

(percentage of total annual spending on entertainment accounted for by before-tax income group of consumer units, 2000; complete income reporters only)

	complete income reporters	under $10,000	$10,000–19,999	$20,000–29,999	$30,000–39,999	$40,000–49,999	$50,000–69,999	$70,000 or more
Share of total consumer units	100.0%	13.3%	18.1%	14.8%	11.6%	9.4%	13.9%	18.9%
Share of total before-tax income	100.0	1.7	5.9	8.1	9.0	9.3	18.3	47.7
Share of total spending	100.0	5.4	10.2	11.0	10.3	9.9	17.0	35.7
Share of entertainment spending	100.0	5.2	8.8	10.6	9.9	9.5	17.8	37.8
FEES AND ADMISSIONS	100.0%	4.8%	6.9%	8.4%	7.6%	7.3%	16.1%	48.9%
Recreation expenses on trips	100.0	5.8	8.8	11.6	7.8	7.5	17.4	41.1
Social, recreation, civic club membership	100.0	5.0	7.6	6.7	6.7	4.7	14.9	54.4
Fees for participant sports	100.0	4.0	7.9	9.4	8.6	7.7	17.0	45.5
Participant sports on trips	100.0	4.6	6.1	10.8	8.8	6.4	13.6	49.8
Movie, theater, opera, ballet	100.0	6.4	8.3	10.0	9.7	9.2	16.0	40.4
Movie, other admissions on trips	100.0	4.4	6.8	9.3	8.8	8.3	18.4	44.0
Admission to sports events	100.0	4.3	3.2	6.6	5.9	7.2	18.4	54.4
Admission to sports events on trips	100.0	4.4	6.8	9.3	8.8	8.3	18.4	44.0
Fees for recreational lessons	100.0	3.3	4.0	4.4	4.7	7.7	14.6	61.3
Other entertainment services on trips	100.0	5.8	8.8	11.6	7.8	7.5	17.4	41.1
TELEVISION, RADIO, SOUND EQUIPMENT	100.0	6.9	11.6	11.6	11.0	10.6	16.9	31.4
Television	100.0	7.6	12.9	12.6	11.1	10.3	17.2	28.3
Cable service and community antenna	100.0	8.2	14.0	13.4	11.6	9.8	16.6	26.3
Black-and-white TV	100.0	10.5	6.8	6.1	12.1	12.1	27.2	25.3
Color TV, console	100.0	5.0	7.1	6.6	11.1	11.6	21.0	37.7
Color TV, portable, table model	100.0	9.4	12.4	12.0	11.5	12.0	15.2	27.4
VCRs and video disc players	100.0	4.3	10.7	13.0	8.3	11.4	17.5	34.9
Video cassettes, tapes, and discs	100.0	5.4	10.0	12.5	10.8	11.2	20.9	29.2
Video game hardware and software	100.0	4.1	8.5	9.9	7.5	10.3	21.0	38.7
Repair of TV, radio, and sound equipment	100.0	7.3	14.8	14.4	7.2	10.5	16.5	29.4
Rental of television sets	100.0	11.2	53.2	23.3	1.1	1.7	7.5	1.4
Radio and sound equipment	100.0	5.3	8.5	9.0	10.7	11.4	16.1	38.8
Radios	100.0	12.0	9.6	2.9	17.3	15.5	16.8	24.5
Tape recorders and players	100.0	8.9	5.7	22.1	–	8.5	16.8	36.4
Sound components and component systems	100.0	3.9	7.9	8.3	9.3	11.4	21.1	38.1
Miscellaneous sound equipment	100.0	–	–	2.4	–	19.1	5.7	67.0
Sound equipment accessories	100.0	–	6.6	7.0	9.2	17.5	10.9	44.9
Satellite dishes	100.0	4.6	10.8	2.0	14.4	10.5	19.9	38.0
Compact disc, tape, record, video mail order clubs	100.0	6.4	12.6	10.7	11.5	13.8	18.2	26.8
Records, CDs, audio tapes, needles	100.0	6.2	8.6	12.2	11.3	10.6	18.4	32.6
Rental of VCR, radio, sound equipment	100.0	3.3	13.1	14.6	26.9	7.7	–	33.9
Musical instruments and accessories	100.0	1.9	6.4	2.9	9.5	11.1	7.8	60.4
Rental and repair of musical instruments	100.0	4.2	4.0	4.7	6.8	10.2	21.0	49.0
Rental of video cassettes, tapes, discs, films	100.0	6.4	9.8	12.0	11.4	10.3	18.0	32.1

	complete income reporters	under $10,000	$10,000–19,999	$20,000–29,999	$30,000–39,999	$40,000–49,999	$50,000–69,999	$70,000 or more
PETS, TOYS, PLAYGROUND EQUIPMENT	100.0%	4.6%	9.0%	11.8%	11.1%	9.7%	17.8%	35.0%
Pets	100.0	4.9	8.7	11.1	11.8	10.0	16.9	35.1
Pet food	100.0	5.5	12.2	11.9	12.8	10.8	16.6	28.1
Pet purchase, supplies, and medicines	100.0	4.3	5.3	12.5	12.3	7.9	16.3	38.4
Pet services	100.0	3.9	6.0	7.0	11.5	5.7	17.3	48.6
Veterinarian services	100.0	4.6	6.9	10.6	10.2	11.5	17.6	38.5
Toys, games, hobbies, and tricycles	100.0	4.2	9.6	12.8	10.1	9.2	19.4	34.6
Playground equipment	100.0	4.0	6.3	15.0	4.6	7.3	19.5	43.4
OTHER ENTERTAINMENT SUPPLIES, EQUIPMENT, SERVICES	100.0	3.4	6.8	10.8	9.8	10.5	21.5	36.2
Unmotored recreational vehicles	100.0	0.4	0.3	27.5	5.6	13.9	21.3	31.1
Boat without motor and boat trailers	100.0	1.0	0.4	37.3	12.1	10.3	5.0	33.8
Trailer and other attachable campers	100.0	–	0.1	20.9	1.2	16.4	32.2	29.2
Motorized recreational vehicles	100.0	2.9	13.9	9.3	8.2	14.6	16.4	34.8
Motorized camper	100.0	1.5	49.1	–	–	35.6	13.8	–
Other vehicle	100.0	2.0	0.1	18.7	23.9	2.3	15.0	38.0
Motorboats	100.0	4.2	–	9.6	4.3	8.7	18.8	54.3
Rental of recreational vehicles	100.0	3.4	2.9	9.3	7.4	5.9	25.5	45.7
Boat and trailer rental on trips	100.0	1.8	4.4	6.6	24.1	7.2	14.9	40.4
Rental of campers on trips	100.0	–	4.8	–	–	–	79.3	15.5
Rental of other vehicles on trips	100.0	5.6	1.3	16.1	0.4	8.8	6.0	61.7
Rental of other RVs	100.0	–	11.8	8.9	–	9.4	–	60.6
Outboard motors	100.0	2.3	7.6	35.2	31.0	–	5.1	18.9
Docking and landing fees	100.0	0.8	5.7	8.2	1.0	8.1	36.7	39.7
Sports, recreation, exercise equipment	100.0	3.9	5.1	7.3	12.9	9.0	23.7	35.8
Athletic gear, game tables, exercise equipment	100.0	2.5	4.8	9.3	10.3	10.0	21.2	38.5
Bicycles	100.0	4.0	7.8	11.7	7.7	5.2	21.6	42.0
Camping equipment	100.0	11.4	13.7	0.8	15.6	8.3	34.2	14.8
Hunting and fishing equipment	100.0	5.3	2.8	1.6	29.5	1.5	32.9	22.4
Winter sports equipment	100.0	4.7	4.7	6.9	5.1	9.1	13.2	56.4
Water sports equipment	100.0	2.3	1.8	8.7	2.3	18.6	22.5	43.8
Other sports equipment	100.0	2.8	4.4	8.4	7.0	15.6	18.8	43.0
Rental and repair of misc. sports equipment	100.0	11.0	9.1	8.0	12.3	6.0	21.3	32.4
Photographic equipment and supplies	100.0	4.7	7.3	9.0	7.8	8.8	21.1	41.3
Film	100.0	6.4	7.4	10.1	9.5	9.1	19.6	37.9
Other photographic supplies	100.0	10.6	3.7	10.9	–	20.3	3.2	49.1
Film processing	100.0	4.6	7.3	8.6	9.0	8.7	20.6	41.2
Repair and rental of photographic equipment	100.0	9.1	–	3.5	11.0	8.3	15.6	51.2
Photographic equipment	100.0	3.7	9.7	7.7	6.6	8.1	22.3	41.9
Photographer fees	100.0	3.4	5.3	9.9	6.1	8.4	23.5	43.3
Fireworks	100.0	9.2	–	27.5	44.6	4.5	5.0	7.2
Souvenirs	100.0	–	1.1	1.6	3.9	11.1	9.8	67.4
Visual goods	100.0	–	–	12.3	1.8	–	76.1	6.4
Pinball, electronic video games	100.0	1.1	9.9	6.0	13.8	11.4	26.5	27.9

Note: Numbers may not add to total because of rounding. (–) means sample is too small to make a reliable estimate.
Source: Calculations by New Strategist based on the 2000 Consumer Expenditure Survey

Table 3.11 Entertainment: Average spending by household type, 2000

(average annual spending of consumer units (CU) on entertainment, by type of consumer unit, 2000)

	total married couples	married couples, no children	married couples with children				single parent, at least one child <18	single person
			total	oldest child under 6	oldest child 6 to 17	oldest child 18 or older		
Number of consumer units (in thousands, add 000)	56,287	22,805	28,777	5,291	15,396	8,090	6,132	32,323
Average number of persons per CU	3.2	2.0	3.9	3.5	4.1	3.8	2.9	1.0
Average before-tax income of CU	$60,588.00	$53,232.00	$66,913.00	$62,928.00	$69,472.00	$64,725.00	$25,095.00	$24,977.00
Average spending of CU, total	48,619.37	42,195.54	53,585.53	50,755.90	54,170.40	54,550.20	28,923.25	23,059.00
Entertainment, average spending	2,454.48	1,967.68	2,864.09	2,191.04	3,249.80	2,585.73	1,433.02	1,026.22
FEES AND ADMISSIONS	**$713.76**	**$595.13**	**$849.86**	**$486.15**	**$1,049.16**	**$708.45**	**$403.92**	**$281.25**
Recreation expenses on trips	33.65	33.55	34.25	21.92	36.04	38.91	21.60	15.65
Social, recreation, civic club membership	142.27	161.18	142.52	79.16	175.00	122.14	58.08	55.84
Fees for participant sports	98.87	92.91	109.09	74.68	126.07	99.31	52.34	41.27
Participant sports on trips	49.49	55.26	48.22	31.32	57.44	41.72	18.35	21.25
Movie, theater, opera, ballet	105.76	86.73	124.37	81.80	138.38	125.55	82.85	66.15
Movie, other admissions on trips	60.97	53.36	68.50	56.37	71.73	70.28	30.20	24.35
Admission to sports events	48.98	36.71	63.03	35.76	73.82	60.34	23.76	18.93
Admission to sports events on trips	20.32	17.78	22.83	18.79	23.90	23.42	10.06	8.12
Fees for recreational lessons	119.81	24.08	202.81	64.44	310.75	87.87	85.06	14.04
Other entertainment services on trips	33.65	33.55	34.25	21.92	36.04	38.91	21.60	15.65
TELEVISION, RADIO, SOUND EQUIPMENT	**735.18**	**569.99**	**853.97**	**717.47**	**917.05**	**824.96**	**591.39**	**428.64**
Television	**533.43**	**465.24**	**575.39**	**533.01**	**583.38**	**587.91**	**416.36**	**316.76**
Cable service and community antenna	370.61	354.44	378.85	350.61	369.50	415.14	300.43	237.53
Black-and-white TV	0.82	0.53	0.82	1.34	0.99	0.15	0.60	0.62
Color TV, console	39.35	25.79	46.98	43.11	50.30	43.19	10.23	15.39
Color TV, portable, table model	38.66	35.13	37.39	42.29	37.35	34.26	40.30	22.61
VCRs and video disc players	31.41	21.26	39.87	33.03	41.65	40.98	14.92	14.51
Video cassettes, tapes, and discs	23.66	16.64	28.49	32.85	29.17	24.33	20.30	15.36
Video game hardware and software	24.54	7.76	37.66	26.04	48.99	23.71	26.41	7.93
Repair of TV, radio, and sound equipment	3.93	3.70	4.43	2.01	5.21	4.53	2.80	2.44
Rental of television sets	0.45	–	0.89	1.73	0.22	1.61	0.37	0.37
Radio and sound equipment	**201.75**	**104.74**	**278.58**	**184.46**	**333.67**	**237.05**	**175.03**	**111.88**
Radios	9.06	3.75	12.55	10.32	8.01	24.03	17.36	9.61
Tape recorders and players	5.42	2.82	6.32	2.12	7.97	6.31	–	3.76
Sound components and component systems	26.02	17.75	30.69	28.96	34.30	24.94	27.69	16.44
Miscellaneous sound equipment	0.76	0.16	1.19	0.68	1.69	0.55	–	0.03
Sound equipment accessories	5.13	2.94	6.92	7.85	6.14	7.79	0.67	3.64
Satellite dishes	3.45	3.33	3.58	3.07	3.25	4.56	0.65	2.07
Compact disc, tape, record, video mail order clubs	9.32	9.09	9.33	7.07	9.83	9.85	6.49	7.20
Records, CDs, audio tapes, needles	42.96	29.09	54.21	39.98	59.60	53.26	42.30	32.27
Rental of VCR, radio, sound equipment	0.18	0.04	0.31	0.64	0.33	0.04	0.46	0.73
Musical instruments and accessories	47.70	9.46	82.81	23.97	122.56	45.65	16.65	15.13
Rental and repair of musical instruments	1.95	1.00	2.79	0.14	4.47	1.32	3.04	0.39
Rental of video cassettes, tapes, discs, films	49.79	25.30	67.89	59.67	75.52	58.74	59.71	20.61

	total married couples	married couples, no children	married couples with children				single parent, at least one child <18	single person
			total	oldest child under 6	oldest child 6 to 17	oldest child 18 or older		
PETS, TOYS, PLAYGROUND EQUIPMENT	**$444.46**	**$388.25**	**$498.00**	**$481.49**	**$547.46**	**$422.84**	**$255.37**	**$176.89**
Pets	**273.13**	**284.40**	**274.89**	**163.02**	**295.64**	**316.74**	**119.07**	**127.10**
Pet food	110.48	110.04	114.16	77.59	116.04	140.68	50.28	52.19
Pet purchase, supplies, and medicines	47.75	51.03	46.44	20.83	58.76	41.73	27.58	24.67
Pet services	27.33	29.35	28.83	15.29	34.02	27.80	9.40	11.11
Veterinarian services	87.56	93.99	85.47	49.32	86.82	106.54	31.81	39.14
Toys, games, hobbies, and tricycles	**165.69**	**103.17**	**213.67**	**281.50**	**247.28**	**105.35**	**132.96**	**49.41**
Playground equipment	**5.63**	**0.67**	**9.43**	**36.97**	**4.54**	**0.75**	**3.33**	**0.38**
OTHER ENTERTAINMENT SUPPLIES, EQUIPMENT, SERVICES	**561.08**	**414.31**	**662.26**	**505.93**	**736.13**	**629.48**	**182.34**	**139.43**
Unmotored recreational vehicles	**71.59**	**42.28**	**78.36**	**66.19**	**96.78**	**51.26**	**0.87**	**9.98**
Boat without motor and boat trailers	28.30	12.30	17.43	1.47	28.68	6.48	–	3.00
Trailer and other attachable campers	43.29	29.98	60.93	64.73	68.10	44.78	0.87	6.98
Motorized recreational vehicles	**136.38**	**121.83**	**140.73**	**35.39**	**158.36**	**176.06**	**2.77**	**9.91**
Motorized camper	38.24	79.56	10.79	–	20.16	–	–	–
Other vehicle	36.24	24.32	34.89	35.39	39.10	26.54	2.77	3.18
Motorboats	61.90	17.95	95.05	–	99.10	149.52	–	6.73
Rental of recreational vehicles	**3.69**	**3.79**	**3.42**	**4.66**	**4.03**	**1.46**	**1.09**	**1.31**
Boat and trailer rental on trips	0.47	0.18	0.30	–	0.18	0.74	1.09	0.34
Rental of campers on trips	0.98	2.28	–	–	–	–	–	–
Rental of other vehicles on trips	2.04	1.17	3.07	4.66	3.81	0.62	–	0.93
Rental of other RVs	0.01	–	0.03	–	0.05	–	–	0.03
Outboard motors	**5.11**	**4.11**	**2.65**	**–**	**2.35**	**4.97**	**–**	**2.92**
Docking and landing fees	**9.10**	**11.35**	**8.03**	**5.09**	**9.05**	**8.02**	**0.14**	**8.38**
Sports, recreation, exercise equipment	**188.44**	**119.15**	**252.35**	**176.50**	**292.75**	**230.83**	**105.65**	**60.15**
Athletic gear, game tables, exercise equipment	77.66	63.84	91.24	52.64	104.86	94.62	22.24	23.18
Bicycles	14.54	9.26	19.10	17.81	24.48	9.72	20.49	5.31
Camping equipment	15.80	2.23	27.50	4.39	33.87	33.30	22.38	4.85
Hunting and fishing equipment	38.70	17.77	60.00	58.10	66.75	47.32	8.78	11.27
Winter sports equipment	7.59	2.67	11.55	4.91	16.50	6.45	2.71	4.59
Water sports equipment	12.80	9.60	15.46	13.33	14.04	19.57	0.81	4.07
Other sports equipment	18.66	12.41	23.59	23.37	27.39	16.50	26.10	5.86
Rental and repair of misc. sports equipment	2.68	1.37	3.90	1.95	4.86	3.35	2.14	1.01
Photographic equipment and supplies	**131.37**	**105.18**	**155.64**	**199.82**	**147.79**	**141.83**	**65.26**	**43.57**
Film	29.58	22.38	35.43	47.14	34.39	29.74	16.77	10.26
Other photographic supplies	1.41	1.82	1.16	–	1.45	1.51	1.14	0.09
Film processing	43.11	33.57	51.82	71.19	48.95	44.62	23.87	16.31
Repair and rental of photographic equipment	0.39	0.18	0.60	0.91	0.41	0.75	0.09	0.17
Photographic equipment	27.84	23.56	32.02	30.47	29.19	38.42	6.24	11.42
Photographer fees	29.04	23.68	34.60	50.10	33.39	26.78	17.15	5.32
Fireworks	**2.12**	**1.09**	**2.72**	**–**	**5.09**	**–**	**–**	**0.30**
Souvenirs	**3.34**	**1.34**	**2.77**	**0.23**	**2.97**	**4.49**	**–**	**0.11**
Visual goods	**1.25**	**1.24**	**1.43**	**6.25**	**–**	**0.45**	**0.69**	**1.11**
Pinball, electronic video games	**8.68**	**2.96**	**14.14**	**11.81**	**16.97**	**10.10**	**5.87**	**1.69**

Note: Average spending figures for total consumer units can be found on Average Spending by Age and Average Spending by Region tables. (–) means sample is too small to make a reliable estimate.
Source: Bureau of Labor Statistics, unpublished data from the 2000 Consumer Expenditure Survey

Table 3.12 Entertainment: Indexed spending by household type, 2000

(indexed average annual spending of consumer units (CU) on entertainment by type of consumer unit, 2000; index definition: an index of 100 is the average for all consumer units; an index of 132 means that spending by consumer units in that group is 32 percent above the average for all consumer units; an index of 68 indicates spending that is 32 percent below the average for all consumer units)

	total married couples	married couples, no children	married couples with children				single parent, at least one child <18	single person
			total	oldest child under 6	oldest child 6 to 17	oldest child 18 or older		
Average spending of CU, total	$48,619	$42,196	$53,586	$50,756	$54,170	$54,550	$28,923	$23,059
Average spending of CU, index	128	111	141	133	142	143	76	61
Entertainment, spending index	132	106	154	118	174	139	77	55
FEES AND ADMISSIONS	**139**	**116**	**165**	**94**	**204**	**138**	**78**	**55**
Recreation expenses on trips	132	132	134	86	141	153	85	61
Social, recreation, civic club membership	145	164	145	81	178	124	59	57
Fees for participant sports	138	130	153	104	176	139	73	58
Participant sports on trips	141	158	138	89	164	119	52	61
Movie, theater, opera, ballet	119	97	139	92	155	141	93	74
Movie, other admissions on trips	136	119	152	125	160	156	67	54
Admission to sports events	139	104	178	101	209	171	67	54
Admission to sports events on trips	136	119	152	125	160	156	67	54
Fees for recreational lessons	160	32	271	86	416	118	114	19
Other entertainment services on trips	132	132	134	86	141	153	85	61
TELEVISION, RADIO, SOUND EQUIPMENT	**118**	**92**	**137**	**115**	**147**	**133**	**95**	**69**
Television	**118**	**103**	**127**	**118**	**129**	**130**	**92**	**70**
Cable service and community antenna	115	110	118	109	115	129	94	74
Black-and-white TV	106	69	106	174	129	19	78	81
Color TV, console	130	85	156	143	167	143	34	51
Color TV, portable, table model	113	102	109	123	109	100	117	66
VCRs and video disc players	132	89	168	139	175	172	63	61
Video cassettes, tapes, and discs	114	80	137	158	140	117	98	74
Video game hardware and software	131	41	201	139	262	127	141	42
Repair of TV, radio, and sound equipment	122	115	137	62	161	140	87	76
Rental of television sets	92	–	182	353	45	329	76	76
Radio and sound equipment	**120**	**62**	**166**	**110**	**198**	**141**	**104**	**66**
Radios	87	36	120	99	77	230	166	92
Tape recorders and players	123	64	144	48	182	144	–	86
Sound components and component systems	112	77	133	125	148	108	120	71
Miscellaneous sound equipment	181	38	283	162	402	131	–	7
Sound equipment accessories	127	73	171	194	152	193	17	90
Satellite dishes	128	123	133	114	120	169	24	77
Compact disc, tape, record, video mail order clubs	109	107	110	83	115	116	76	85
Records, CDs, audio tapes, needles	109	74	137	101	151	135	107	82
Rental of VCR, radio, sound equipment	33	7	57	119	61	7	85	135
Musical instruments and accessories	150	30	261	76	387	144	53	48
Rental and repair of musical instruments	146	75	208	10	334	99	227	29
Rental of video cassettes, tapes, discs, films	120	61	163	144	182	141	144	50

	total married couples	married couples, no children	married couples with children				single parent, at least one child <18	single person
			total	oldest child under 6	oldest child 6 to 17	oldest child 18 or older		
PETS, TOYS, PLAYGROUND EQUIPMENT	**133**	**116**	**149**	**144**	**164**	**127**	**77**	**53**
Pets	**130**	**136**	**131**	**78**	**141**	**151**	**57**	**61**
Pet food	129	128	133	90	135	164	58	61
Pet purchase, supplies, and medicines	125	134	122	55	154	110	72	65
Pet services	141	152	149	79	176	144	49	57
Veterinarian services	133	142	130	75	132	161	48	59
Toys, games, hobbies, and tricycles	**137**	**85**	**177**	**233**	**204**	**87**	**110**	**41**
Playground equipment	**170**	**20**	**284**	**1,114**	**137**	**23**	**100**	**11**
OTHER ENTERTAINMENT SUPPLIES, EQUIPMENT, SERVICES	**143**	**105**	**168**	**129**	**187**	**160**	**46**	**35**
Unmotored recreational vehicles	**149**	**88**	**163**	**138**	**201**	**107**	**2**	**21**
Boat without motor and boat trailers	178	78	110	9	181	41	–	19
Trailer and other attachable campers	134	93	189	201	212	139	3	22
Motorized recreational vehicles	**166**	**149**	**172**	**43**	**193**	**215**	**3**	**12**
Motorized camper	179	373	51	–	94	–	–	–
Other vehicle	167	112	160	163	180	122	13	15
Motorboats	159	46	245	–	255	385	–	17
Rental of recreational vehicles	**132**	**136**	**123**	**167**	**144**	**52**	**39**	**47**
Boat and trailer rental on trips	80	31	51	–	31	125	185	58
Rental of campers on trips	161	374	–	–	–	–	–	–
Rental of other vehicles on trips	146	84	219	333	272	44	–	66
Rental of other RVs	33	–	100	–	167	–	–	100
Outboard motors	**143**	**115**	**74**	**–**	**66**	**139**	**–**	**82**
Docking and landing fees	**111**	**139**	**98**	**62**	**111**	**98**	**2**	**103**
Sports, recreation, exercise equipment	**131**	**83**	**176**	**123**	**204**	**161**	**74**	**42**
Athletic gear, game tables, exercise equipment	132	109	156	90	179	161	38	40
Bicycles	124	79	163	152	209	83	175	45
Camping equipment	93	13	162	26	199	196	131	28
Hunting and fishing equipment	150	69	232	225	258	183	34	44
Winter sports equipment	130	46	198	84	283	110	46	79
Water sports equipment	155	117	188	162	170	238	10	49
Other sports equipment	131	87	166	164	192	116	183	41
Rental and repair of misc. sports equipment	133	68	193	97	241	166	106	50
Photographic equipment and supplies	**138**	**111**	**164**	**211**	**156**	**149**	**69**	**46**
Film	138	105	166	220	161	139	78	48
Other photographic supplies	98	126	81	–	101	105	79	6
Film processing	137	107	165	227	156	142	76	52
Repair and rental of photographic equipment	144	67	222	337	152	278	33	63
Photographic equipment	138	117	158	151	144	190	31	57
Photographer fees	144	117	172	248	166	133	85	26
Fireworks	**180**	**92**	**231**	**–**	**431**	**–**	**–**	**25**
Souvenirs	**167**	**67**	**139**	**12**	**149**	**225**	**–**	**6**
Visual goods	**115**	**114**	**131**	**573**	**–**	**41**	**63**	**102**
Pinball, electronic video games	**150**	**51**	**244**	**204**	**293**	**174**	**101**	**29**

Note: Spending index for total consumer units is 100. (–) means sample is too small to make a reliable estimate.
Source: Calculations by New Strategist based on the 2000 Consumer Expenditure Survey

Table 3.13 Entertainment: Indexed per capita spending by household type, 2000

(indexed average annual per capita spending of consumer units (CU) on entertainment by type of consumer unit, 2000; index definition: an index of 100 is the average for all consumer units; an index of 132 means that spending by consumer units in that group is 32 percent above the average for all consumer units; an index of 68 indicates spending that is 32 percent below the average for all consumer units)

	total married couples	married couples, no children	married couples with children				single parent, at least one child <18	single person
			total	oldest child under 6	oldest child 6 to 17	oldest child 18 or older		
Per capita spending of CU, total	$15,194	$21,098	$13,740	$14,502	$13,212	$14,355	$9,974	$23,059
Per capita spending of CU, index	100	139	90	95	87	94	66	152
Entertainment, per capita spending index	103	132	99	84	106	91	66	138
FEES AND ADMISSIONS	**108**	**144**	**106**	**67**	**124**	**91**	**68**	**137**
Recreation expenses on trips	103	165	86	61	86	100	73	153
Social, recreation, civic club membership	113	205	93	58	109	82	51	142
Fees for participant sports	108	162	98	75	108	91	63	144
Participant sports on trips	110	197	88	64	100	78	45	152
Movie, theater, opera, ballet	93	122	89	66	95	93	80	185
Movie, other admissions on trips	106	148	98	90	97	103	58	135
Admission to sports events	108	130	114	72	127	112	58	134
Admission to sports events on trips	106	148	98	90	97	103	58	136
Fees for recreational lessons	125	40	174	62	254	77	98	47
Other entertainment services on trips	103	165	86	61	86	100	73	153
TELEVISION, RADIO, SOUND EQUIPMENT	**92**	**115**	**88**	**82**	**90**	**87**	**82**	**172**
Television	**92**	**128**	**81**	**84**	**78**	**85**	**79**	**175**
Cable service and community antenna	90	138	76	78	70	85	81	185
Black-and-white TV	83	86	68	124	78	13	67	201
Color TV, console	102	107	100	102	102	94	29	127
Color TV, portable, table model	88	128	70	88	66	66	101	165
VCRs and video disc players	103	112	107	99	107	113	54	152
Video cassettes, tapes, and discs	89	100	88	113	86	77	84	185
Video game hardware and software	102	52	129	99	160	83	122	106
Repair of TV, radio, and sound equipment	95	143	88	44	98	92	75	189
Rental of television sets	72	–	116	252	27	216	65	189
Radio and sound equipment	**94**	**78**	**106**	**78**	**121**	**93**	**90**	**166**
Radios	68	45	77	71	47	151	143	230
Tape recorders and players	96	80	92	34	111	95	–	214
Sound components and component systems	88	96	85	89	90	71	103	177
Miscellaneous sound equipment	141	48	182	116	245	86	–	18
Sound equipment accessories	99	91	110	139	93	127	14	225
Satellite dishes	100	154	85	81	73	111	21	192
Compact disc, tape, record, video mail order clubs	85	133	70	59	70	76	66	211
Records, CDs, audio tapes, needles	85	92	88	72	92	89	92	204
Rental of VCR, radio, sound equipment	26	9	37	85	37	5	73	338
Musical instruments and accessories	118	37	167	54	236	95	45	119
Rental and repair of musical instruments	114	93	133	7	203	65	196	73
Rental of video cassettes, tapes, discs, films	94	76	105	103	111	93	124	124

	total married couples	married couples, no children	married couples with children				single parent, at least one child <18	single person
			total	oldest child under 6	oldest child 6 to 17	oldest child 18 or older		
PETS, TOYS, PLAYGROUND EQUIPMENT	**104**	**145**	**96**	**103**	**100**	**83**	**66**	**133**
Pets	**102**	**170**	**84**	**56**	**86**	**99**	**49**	**152**
Pet food	100	160	85	64	82	108	50	152
Pet purchase, supplies, and medicines	98	167	78	39	94	72	62	162
Pet services	110	190	95	56	107	94	42	143
Veterinarian services	104	178	83	53	80	106	42	148
Toys, games, hobbies, and tricycles	**107**	**107**	**113**	**166**	**125**	**57**	**95**	**102**
Playground equipment	**132**	**25**	**182**	**795**	**83**	**15**	**86**	**29**
OTHER ENTERTAINMENT SUPPLIES, EQUIPMENT, SERVICES	**112**	**132**	**108**	**92**	**114**	**105**	**40**	**89**
Unmotored recreational vehicles	**116**	**110**	**105**	**98**	**123**	**70**	**2**	**52**
Boat without motor and boat trailers	139	97	70	7	110	27	–	47
Trailer and other attachable campers	105	116	121	144	129	92	2	54
Motorized recreational vehicles	**130**	**186**	**110**	**31**	**118**	**141**	**3**	**30**
Motorized camper	140	466	32	–	58	–	–	–
Other vehicle	130	140	103	116	110	80	11	37
Motorboats	124	58	157	–	155	253	–	43
Rental of recreational vehicles	**103**	**170**	**79**	**119**	**88**	**34**	**34**	**117**
Boat and trailer rental on trips	62	38	33	–	19	83	159	144
Rental of campers on trips	126	467	–	–	–	–	–	–
Rental of other vehicles on trips	114	104	141	238	166	29	–	166
Rental of other RVs	26	–	64	–	102	–	–	250
Outboard motors	**112**	**144**	**47**	**–**	**40**	**91**	**–**	**204**
Docking and landing fees	**87**	**174**	**63**	**45**	**68**	**65**	**1**	**256**
Sports, recreation, exercise equipment	**103**	**104**	**113**	**88**	**124**	**106**	**63**	**105**
Athletic gear, game tables, exercise equipment	103	136	100	64	109	106	33	99
Bicycles	97	99	104	108	127	55	151	113
Camping equipment	73	16	104	18	121	129	113	71
Hunting and fishing equipment	117	86	149	161	157	120	29	109
Winter sports equipment	102	57	127	60	172	73	40	196
Water sports equipment	121	146	120	116	104	156	8	123
Other sports equipment	102	109	106	117	117	76	158	103
Rental and repair of misc. sports equipment	104	85	124	69	147	109	91	125
Photographic equipment and supplies	**108**	**139**	**105**	**150**	**95**	**98**	**59**	**115**
Film	108	131	106	157	98	91	68	120
Other photographic supplies	76	158	52	–	61	69	68	16
Film processing	107	134	106	162	95	93	65	130
Repair and rental of photographic equipment	113	83	142	241	93	183	29	157
Photographic equipment	108	146	102	108	88	125	27	141
Photographer fees	112	147	110	177	101	87	73	66
Fireworks	**140**	**115**	**148**	**–**	**263**	**–**	**–**	**64**
Souvenirs	**130**	**84**	**89**	**8**	**91**	**148**	**–**	**14**
Visual goods	**90**	**142**	**84**	**410**	**–**	**27**	**55**	**255**
Pinball, electronic video games	**117**	**64**	**156**	**145**	**178**	**115**	**87**	**73**

Note: Per capita indexes account for household size and show how much each person in a particular household demographic segment spends relative to a person in the average household. Spending index for total consumer units is 100. (–) means sample is too small to make a reliable estimate.
Source: Calculations by New Strategist based on the 2000 Consumer Expenditure Survey

Table 3.14 Entertainment: Total spending by household type, 2000

(total annual spending on entertainment, by consumer unit (CU) type, 2000; numbers in thousands)

	total married couples	married couples, no children	married couples with children				single parent, at least one child <18	single person
			total	oldest child under 6	oldest child 6 to 17	oldest child 18 or older		
Number of consumer units	56,287	22,805	28,777	5,291	15,396	8,090	6,132	32,323
Total spending of all CUs	$2,736,638,479	$962,269,290	$1,542,030,797	$268,549,467	$834,007,478	$441,311,118	$177,357,369	$745,336,057
Entertainment, total spending	138,155,316	44,872,942	82,419,918	11,592,793	50,033,921	20,918,556	8,787,279	33,170,509
FEES AND ADMISSIONS	**$40,175,409**	**$13,571,940**	**$24,456,421**	**$2,572,220**	**$16,152,867**	**$5,731,361**	**$2,476,837**	**$9,090,844**
Recreation expenses on trips	1,894,058	765,108	985,612	115,979	554,872	314,782	132,451	505,855
Social, recreation, civic club membership	8,007,951	3,675,710	4,101,298	418,836	2,694,300	988,113	356,147	1,804,916
Fees for participant sports	5,565,096	2,118,813	3,139,283	395,132	1,940,974	803,418	320,949	1,333,970
Participant sports on trips	2,785,644	1,260,204	1,387,627	165,714	884,346	337,515	112,522	686,864
Movie, theater, opera, ballet	5,952,913	1,977,878	3,578,995	432,804	2,130,498	1,015,700	508,036	2,138,166
Movie, other admissions on trips	3,431,818	1,216,875	1,971,225	298,254	1,104,355	568,565	185,186	787,065
Admission to sports events	2,756,937	837,172	1,813,814	189,206	1,136,533	488,151	145,696	611,874
Admission to sports events on trips	1,143,752	405,473	656,979	99,418	367,964	189,468	61,688	262,463
Fees for recreational lessons	6,743,745	549,144	5,836,263	340,952	4,784,307	710,868	521,588	453,815
Other entertainment services on trips	1,894,058	765,108	985,612	115,979	554,872	314,782	132,451	505,855
TELEVISION, RADIO, SOUND EQUIPMENT	**41,381,077**	**12,998,622**	**24,574,695**	**3,796,134**	**14,118,902**	**6,673,926**	**3,626,403**	**13,854,931**
Television	**30,025,174**	**10,609,798**	**16,557,998**	**2,820,156**	**8,981,718**	**4,756,192**	**2,553,120**	**10,238,633**
Cable service and community antenna	20,860,525	8,083,004	10,902,166	1,855,078	5,688,822	3,358,483	1,842,237	7,677,682
Black-and-white TV	46,155	12,087	23,597	7,090	15,242	1,214	3,679	20,040
Color TV, console	2,214,893	588,141	1,351,943	228,095	774,419	349,407	62,730	497,451
Color TV, portable, table model	2,176,055	801,140	1,075,972	223,756	575,041	277,163	247,120	730,823
VCRs and video disc players	1,767,975	484,834	1,147,339	174,762	641,243	331,528	91,489	469,007
Video cassettes, tapes, and discs	1,331,750	379,475	819,857	173,809	449,101	196,830	124,480	496,481
Video game hardware and software	1,381,283	176,967	1,083,742	137,778	754,250	191,814	161,946	256,321
Repair of TV, radio, and sound equipment	221,208	84,379	127,482	10,635	80,213	36,648	17,170	78,868
Rental of television sets	25,329	–	25,612	9,153	3,387	13,025	2,269	11,960
Radio and sound equipment	**11,355,902**	**2,388,596**	**8,016,697**	**975,978**	**5,137,183**	**1,917,735**	**1,073,284**	**3,616,297**
Radios	509,960	85,519	361,151	54,603	123,322	194,403	106,452	310,624
Tape recorders and players	305,076	64,310	181,871	11,217	122,706	51,048	–	121,534
Sound components and component systems	1,464,588	404,789	883,166	153,227	528,083	201,765	169,795	531,390
Miscellaneous sound equipment	42,778	3,649	34,245	3,598	26,019	4,450	–	970
Sound equipment accessories	288,752	67,047	199,137	41,534	94,531	63,021	4,108	117,656
Satellite dishes	194,190	75,941	103,022	16,243	50,037	36,890	3,986	66,909
Compact disc, tape, record, video mail order clubs	524,595	207,297	268,489	37,407	151,343	79,687	39,797	232,726
Records, CDs, audio tapes, needles	2,418,090	663,397	1,560,001	211,534	917,602	430,873	259,384	1,043,063
Rental of VCR, radio, sound equipment	10,132	912	8,921	3,386	5,081	324	2,821	23,596
Musical instruments and accessories	2,684,890	215,735	2,383,023	126,825	1,886,934	369,309	102,098	489,047
Rental and repair of musical instruments	109,760	22,805	80,288	741	68,820	10,679	18,641	12,606
Rental of video cassettes, tapes, discs, films	2,802,530	576,967	1,953,671	315,714	1,162,706	475,207	366,142	666,177

	total married couples	married couples, no children	married couples with children			single parent, at least one child <18	single person
			total	oldest child under 6	oldest child 6 to 17	oldest child 18 or older		
PETS, TOYS, PLAYGROUND EQUIPMENT	$25,017,320	$8,854,041	$14,330,946	$2,547,564	$8,428,694	$3,420,776	$1,565,929	$5,717,615
Pets	15,373,668	6,485,742	7,910,510	862,539	4,551,673	2,562,427	730,137	4,108,253
Pet food	6,218,588	2,509,462	3,285,182	410,529	1,786,552	1,138,101	308,317	1,686,937
Pet purchase, supplies, and medicines	2,687,704	1,163,739	1,336,404	110,212	904,669	337,596	169,121	797,408
Pet services	1,538,324	669,327	829,641	80,899	523,772	224,902	57,641	359,109
Veterinarian services	4,928,490	2,143,442	2,459,570	260,952	1,336,681	861,909	195,059	1,265,122
Toys, games, hobbies, and tricycles	9,326,193	2,352,792	6,148,782	1,489,417	3,807,123	852,282	815,311	1,597,079
Playground equipment	316,896	15,279	271,367	195,608	69,898	6,068	20,420	12,283
OTHER ENTERTAINMENT SUPPLIES, EQUIPMENT, SERVICES	31,581,510	9,448,340	19,057,856	2,676,876	11,333,457	5,092,493	1,118,109	4,506,796
Unmotored recreational vehicles	4,029,586	964,195	2,254,966	350,211	1,490,025	414,693	5,335	322,584
Boat without motor and boat trailers	1,592,922	280,502	501,583	7,778	441,557	52,423	–	96,969
Trailer and other attachable campers	2,436,664	683,694	1,753,383	342,486	1,048,468	362,270	5,335	225,615
Motorized recreational vehicles	7,676,421	2,778,333	4,049,787	187,248	2,438,111	1,424,325	16,986	320,321
Motorized camper	2,152,415	1,814,366	310,504	–	310,383	–	–	–
Other vehicle	2,039,841	554,618	1,004,030	187,248	601,984	214,709	16,986	102,787
Motorboats	3,484,165	409,350	2,735,254	–	1,525,744	1,209,617	–	217,534
Rental of recreational vehicles	207,699	86,431	98,417	24,656	62,046	11,811	6,684	42,343
Boat and trailer rental on trips	26,455	4,105	8,633	–	2,771	5,987	6,684	10,990
Rental of campers on trips	55,161	51,995	–	–	–	–	–	–
Rental of other vehicles on trips	114,825	26,682	88,345	24,656	58,659	5,016	–	30,060
Rental of other RVs	563	–	863	–	770	–	–	970
Outboard motors	287,627	93,729	76,259	–	36,181	40,207	–	94,383
Docking and landing fees	512,212	258,837	231,079	26,931	139,334	64,882	858	270,867
Sports, recreation, exercise equipment	10,606,722	2,717,216	7,261,876	933,862	4,507,179	1,867,415	647,846	1,944,228
Athletic gear, game tables, exercise equip.	4,371,248	1,455,871	2,625,613	278,518	1,614,425	765,476	136,376	749,247
Bicycles	818,413	211,174	549,641	94,233	376,894	78,635	125,645	171,635
Camping equipment	889,335	50,855	791,368	23,227	521,463	269,397	137,234	156,767
Hunting and fishing equipment	2,178,307	405,245	1,726,620	307,407	1,027,683	382,819	53,839	364,280
Winter sports equipment	427,218	60,889	332,374	25,979	254,034	52,181	16,618	148,363
Water sports equipment	720,474	218,928	444,892	70,529	216,160	158,321	4,967	131,555
Other sports equipment	1,050,315	283,010	678,849	123,651	421,696	133,485	160,045	189,413
Rental and repair of misc. sports equipment	150,849	31,243	112,230	10,317	74,825	27,102	13,122	32,646
Photographic equipment and supplies	7,394,423	2,398,630	4,478,852	1,057,248	2,275,375	1,147,405	400,174	1,408,313
Film	1,664,969	510,376	1,019,569	249,418	529,468	240,597	102,834	331,634
Other photographic supplies	79,365	41,505	33,381	–	22,324	12,216	6,990	2,909
Film processing	2,426,533	765,564	1,491,224	376,666	753,634	360,976	146,371	527,188
Repair and rental of photographic equipment	21,952	4,105	17,266	4,815	6,312	6,068	552	5,495
Photographic equipment	1,567,030	537,286	921,440	161,217	449,409	310,818	38,264	369,129
Photographer fees	1,634,574	540,022	995,684	265,079	514,072	216,650	105,164	171,958
Fireworks	119,328	24,857	78,273	–	78,366	–	–	9,697
Souvenirs	187,999	30,559	79,712	1,217	45,726	36,324	–	3,556
Visual goods	70,359	28,278	41,151	33,069	–	3,641	4,231	35,879
Pinball, electronic video games	488,571	67,503	406,907	62,487	261,270	81,709	35,995	54,626

Note: Total spending figures for total consumer units can be found on Total Spending by Age and Total Spending by Region tables. Spending by type of consumer unit will not add to total because not all types of consumer units are shown. (–) means sample is too small to make a reliable estimate.
Source: Calculations by New Strategist based on the 2000 Consumer Expenditure Survey

Table 3.15 Entertainment: Market shares by household type, 2000

(percentage of total annual spending on entertainment accounted for by types of consumer units, 2000)

	total married couples	married couples, no children	married couples with children				single parent, at least one child <18	single person
			total	oldest child under 6	oldest child 6 to 17	oldest child 18 or older		
Share of total consumer units	51.5%	20.9%	26.3%	4.8%	14.1%	7.4%	5.6%	29.6%
Share of total before-tax income	69.8	24.9	39.4	6.8	21.9	10.7	3.2	16.5
Share of total spending	65.8	23.1	37.1	6.5	20.0	10.6	4.3	17.9
Share of entertainment spending	67.8	22.0	40.4	5.7	24.5	10.3	4.3	16.3
FEES AND ADMISSIONS	**71.3%**	**24.1%**	**43.4%**	**4.6%**	**28.7%**	**10.2%**	**4.4%**	**16.1%**
Recreation expenses on trips	67.9	27.4	35.4	4.2	19.9	11.3	4.8	18.1
Social, recreation, civic club membership	74.6	34.2	38.2	3.9	25.1	9.2	3.3	16.8
Fees for participant sports	71.2	27.1	40.2	5.1	24.8	10.3	4.1	17.1
Participant sports on trips	72.7	32.9	36.2	4.3	23.1	8.8	2.9	17.9
Movie, theater, opera, ballet	61.0	20.3	36.7	4.4	21.8	10.4	5.2	21.9
Movie, other admissions on trips	69.8	24.8	40.1	6.1	22.5	11.6	3.8	16.0
Admission to sports events	71.4	21.7	46.9	4.9	29.4	12.6	3.8	15.8
Admission to sports events on trips	69.8	24.7	40.1	6.1	22.5	11.6	3.8	16.0
Fees for recreational lessons	82.5	6.7	71.4	4.2	58.5	8.7	6.4	5.6
Other entertainment services on trips	67.9	27.4	35.4	4.2	19.9	11.3	4.8	18.1
TELEVISION, RADIO, SOUND EQUIPMENT	**60.8**	**19.1**	**36.1**	**5.6**	**20.8**	**9.8**	**5.3**	**20.4**
Television	**60.5**	**21.4**	**33.4**	**5.7**	**18.1**	**9.6**	**5.1**	**20.6**
Cable service and community antenna	59.4	23.0	31.0	5.3	16.2	9.6	5.2	21.9
Black-and-white TV	54.8	14.4	28.0	8.4	18.1	1.4	4.4	23.8
Color TV, console	67.1	17.8	40.9	6.9	23.5	10.6	1.9	15.1
Color TV, portable, table model	57.9	21.3	28.6	6.0	15.3	7.4	6.6	19.5
VCRs and video disc players	67.9	18.6	44.1	6.7	24.6	12.7	3.5	18.0
Video cassettes, tapes, and discs	58.5	16.7	36.0	7.6	19.7	8.7	5.5	21.8
Video game hardware and software	67.5	8.6	52.9	6.7	36.8	9.4	7.9	12.5
Repair of TV, radio, and sound equipment	62.6	23.9	36.1	3.0	22.7	10.4	4.9	22.3
Rental of television sets	47.3	–	47.8	17.1	6.3	24.3	4.2	22.3
Radio and sound equipment	**61.7**	**13.0**	**43.6**	**5.3**	**27.9**	**10.4**	**5.8**	**19.6**
Radios	44.7	7.5	31.6	4.8	10.8	17.0	9.3	27.2
Tape recorders and players	63.5	13.4	37.9	2.3	25.6	10.6	–	25.3
Sound components and component systems	57.8	16.0	34.9	6.0	20.8	8.0	6.7	21.0
Miscellaneous sound equipment	93.1	7.9	74.6	7.8	56.6	9.7	–	2.1
Sound equipment accessories	65.4	15.2	45.1	9.4	21.4	14.3	0.9	26.6
Satellite dishes	65.8	25.7	34.9	5.5	16.9	12.5	1.3	22.7
Compact disc, tape, record, video mail order clubs	56.3	22.2	28.8	4.0	16.2	8.6	4.3	25.0
Records, CDs, audio tapes, needles	56.0	15.4	36.1	4.9	21.3	10.0	6.0	24.2
Rental of VCR, radio, sound equipment	17.2	1.5	15.1	5.7	8.6	0.5	4.8	40.0
Musical instruments and accessories	77.4	6.2	68.7	3.7	54.4	10.7	2.9	14.1
Rental and repair of musical instruments	74.9	15.6	54.8	0.5	47.0	7.3	12.7	8.6
Rental of video cassettes, tapes, discs, films	61.7	12.7	43.0	6.9	25.6	10.5	8.1	14.7

	total married couples	married couples, no children	married couples with children				single parent, at least one child <18	single person
			total	oldest child under 6	oldest child 6 to 17	oldest child 18 or older		
PETS, TOYS, PLAYGROUND EQUIPMENT	**68.5%**	**24.3%**	**39.3%**	**7.0%**	**23.1%**	**9.4%**	**4.3%**	**15.7%**
Pets	**67.1**	**28.3**	**34.5**	**3.8**	**19.9**	**11.2**	**3.2**	**17.9**
Pet food	66.1	26.7	34.9	4.4	19.0	12.1	3.3	17.9
Pet purchase, supplies, and medicines	64.5	27.9	32.1	2.6	21.7	8.1	4.1	19.1
Pet services	72.7	31.6	39.2	3.8	24.7	10.6	2.7	17.0
Veterinarian services	68.3	29.7	34.1	3.6	18.5	11.9	2.7	17.5
Toys, games, hobbies, and tricycles	**70.5**	**17.8**	**46.5**	**11.3**	**28.8**	**6.4**	**6.2**	**12.1**
Playground equipment	**87.3**	**4.2**	**74.7**	**53.9**	**19.3**	**1.7**	**5.6**	**3.4**
OTHER ENTERTAINMENT SUPPLIES, EQUIPMENT, SERVICES	**73.5**	**22.0**	**44.3**	**6.2**	**26.4**	**11.8**	**2.6**	**10.5**
Unmotored recreational vehicles	**76.7**	**18.3**	**42.9**	**6.7**	**28.3**	**7.9**	**0.1**	**6.1**
Boat without motor and boat trailers	91.8	16.2	28.9	0.4	25.4	3.0	–	5.6
Trailer and other attachable campers	69.2	19.4	49.8	9.7	29.8	10.3	0.2	6.4
Motorized recreational vehicles	**85.6**	**31.0**	**45.2**	**2.1**	**27.2**	**15.9**	**0.2**	**3.6**
Motorized camper	92.2	77.7	13.3	–	13.3	–	–	–
Other vehicle	85.8	23.3	42.2	7.9	25.3	9.0	0.7	4.3
Motorboats	82.0	9.6	64.3	–	35.9	28.5	–	5.1
Rental of recreational vehicles	**68.1**	**28.3**	**32.3**	**8.1**	**20.3**	**3.9**	**2.2**	**13.9**
Boat and trailer rental on trips	41.0	6.4	13.4	–	4.3	9.3	10.4	17.0
Rental of campers on trips	82.7	77.9	–	–	–	–	–	–
Rental of other vehicles on trips	75.0	17.4	57.7	16.1	38.3	3.3	–	19.6
Rental of other RVs	17.2	–	26.3	–	23.5	–	–	29.6
Outboard motors	**73.5**	**23.9**	**19.5**	–	**9.2**	**10.3**	–	**24.1**
Docking and landing fees	**57.3**	**29.0**	**25.9**	**3.0**	**15.6**	**7.3**	**0.1**	**30.3**
Sports, recreation, exercise equipment	**67.5**	**17.3**	**46.2**	**5.9**	**28.7**	**11.9**	**4.1**	**12.4**
Athletic gear, game tables, exercise equipment	68.2	22.7	40.9	4.3	25.2	11.9	2.1	11.7
Bicycles	63.8	16.5	42.8	7.3	29.4	6.1	9.8	13.4
Camping equipment	47.8	2.7	42.5	1.2	28.0	14.5	7.4	8.4
Hunting and fishing equipment	77.0	14.3	61.1	10.9	36.4	13.5	1.9	12.9
Winter sports equipment	66.9	9.5	52.0	4.1	39.8	8.2	2.6	23.2
Water sports equipment	79.9	24.3	49.4	7.8	24.0	17.6	0.6	14.6
Other sports equipment	67.4	18.2	43.6	7.9	27.1	8.6	10.3	12.2
Rental and repair of misc. sports equipment	68.3	14.1	50.8	4.7	33.9	12.3	5.9	14.8
Photographic equipment and supplies	**71.2**	**23.1**	**43.1**	**10.2**	**21.9**	**11.1**	**3.9**	**13.6**
Film	71.1	21.8	43.6	10.7	22.6	10.3	4.4	14.2
Other photographic supplies	50.4	26.4	21.2	–	14.2	7.8	4.4	1.8
Film processing	70.6	22.3	43.4	11.0	21.9	10.5	4.3	15.3
Repair and rental of photographic equipment	74.3	13.9	58.5	16.3	21.4	20.5	1.9	18.6
Photographic equipment	70.9	24.3	41.7	7.3	20.3	14.1	1.7	16.7
Photographer fees	74.1	24.5	45.1	12.0	23.3	9.8	4.8	7.8
Fireworks	**92.5**	**19.3**	**60.7**	–	**60.7**	–	–	**7.5**
Souvenirs	**85.9**	**14.0**	**36.4**	**0.6**	**20.9**	**16.6**	–	**1.6**
Visual goods	**59.0**	**23.7**	**34.5**	**27.7**	–	**3.1**	**3.5**	**30.1**
Pinball, electronic video games	**77.0**	**10.6**	**64.1**	**9.9**	**41.2**	**12.9**	**5.7**	**8.6**

Note: Market share for total consumer units is 100.0%. Market shares by type of consumer unit will not add to total because not all types of consumer units are shown. (–) means sample is too small to make a reliable estimate.
Source: Calculations by New Strategist based on the 2000 Consumer Expenditure Survey

Table 3.16 Entertainment: Average spending by race and Hispanic origin, 2000

(average annual spending of consumer units (CU) on entertainment, by race and Hispanic origin of consumer unit reference person, 2000)

	total consumer units	race — black	race — white and other	Hispanic origin — Hispanic	Hispanic origin — non-Hispanic
Number of consumer units (in thousands, add 000)	109,367	13,230	96,137	9,473	99,894
Average number of persons per CU	2.5	2.7	2.5	3.4	2.4
Average before-tax income of CU	$44,649.00	$32,657.00	$46,260.00	$34,891.00	$45,669.00
Average spending of CU, total	38,044.67	28,152.24	39,406.20	32,734.95	38,548.91
Entertainment, average spending	1,863.50	1,014.12	1,980.40	1,186.30	1,927.55
FEES AND ADMISSIONS	**$514.85**	**$180.63**	**$560.85**	**$262.39**	**$538.79**
Recreation expenses on trips	25.49	10.58	27.54	16.90	26.30
Social, recreation, civic club membership	98.18	26.31	108.08	33.15	104.35
Fees for participant sports	71.49	22.17	78.28	28.23	75.59
Participant sports on trips	35.05	8.11	38.76	14.91	36.96
Movie, theater, opera, ballet	89.16	46.35	95.05	71.21	90.86
Movie, other admissions on trips	44.94	17.24	48.75	26.71	46.66
Admission to sports events	35.33	11.60	38.60	11.19	37.62
Admission to sports events on trips	14.98	5.74	16.25	8.90	15.55
Fees for recreational lessons	74.74	21.95	82.01	34.28	78.58
Other entertainment services on trips	25.49	10.58	27.54	16.90	26.30
TELEVISION, RADIO, SOUND EQUIPMENT	**621.82**	**567.33**	**629.32**	**544.58**	**629.14**
Television	**453.53**	**461.11**	**452.49**	**390.02**	**459.55**
Cable service and community antenna	321.18	342.52	318.24	251.74	327.76
Black-and-white TV	0.77	1.24	0.71	1.05	0.74
Color TV, console	30.19	29.28	30.31	29.37	30.27
Color TV, portable, table model	34.35	33.38	34.48	48.47	33.01
VCRs and video disc players	23.80	18.81	24.49	27.96	23.41
Video cassettes, tapes, and discs	20.80	15.72	21.50	14.58	21.39
Video game hardware and software	18.72	16.72	18.99	12.25	19.33
Repair of TV, radio, and sound equipment	3.23	2.02	3.40	3.16	3.24
Rental of television sets	0.49	1.43	0.36	1.45	0.40
Radio and sound equipment	**168.29**	**106.22**	**176.83**	**154.56**	**169.59**
Radios	10.44	4.48	11.26	10.91	10.40
Tape recorders and players	4.39	9.96	3.63	2.81	4.54
Sound components and component systems	23.16	19.17	23.71	31.64	22.36
Miscellaneous sound equipment	0.42	–	0.48	0.09	0.45
Sound equipment accessories	4.04	0.45	4.53	5.28	3.92
Satellite dishes	2.70	1.02	2.94	6.32	2.36
Compact disc, tape, record, video mail order clubs	8.52	5.14	8.99	7.03	8.67
Records, CDs, audio tapes, needles	39.46	30.19	40.74	35.87	39.80
Rental of VCR, radio, sound equipment	0.54	0.52	0.54	0.35	0.55
Musical instruments and accessories	31.70	4.33	35.47	14.57	33.33
Rental and repair of musical instruments	1.34	0.30	1.48	1.30	1.35
Rental of video cassettes, tapes, discs, films	41.56	30.67	43.06	38.40	41.86

	total consumer units	race black	race white and other	Hispanic origin Hispanic	Hispanic origin non-Hispanic
PETS, TOYS, PLAYGROUND EQUIPMENT	**$333.71**	**$159.24**	**$357.72**	**$217.72**	**$344.64**
Pets	**209.43**	**69.16**	**228.74**	**123.34**	**217.52**
Pet food	85.97	30.05	93.67	66.58	87.77
Pet purchase, supplies, and medicines	38.10	21.49	40.38	22.18	39.58
Pet services	19.36	5.04	21.33	5.22	20.70
Veterinarian services	66.00	12.58	73.35	29.36	69.47
Toys, games, hobbies, and tricycles	**120.96**	**88.43**	**125.43**	**91.96**	**123.71**
Playground equipment	**3.32**	**1.64**	**3.55**	**2.42**	**3.41**
OTHER ENTERTAINMENT SUPPLIES, EQUIPMENT, SERVICES	**393.12**	**106.92**	**432.51**	**161.61**	**414.98**
Unmotored recreational vehicles	**48.06**	**6.82**	**53.73**	**2.34**	**52.39**
Boat without motor and boat trailers	15.87	–	18.05	2.34	17.15
Trailer and other attachable campers	32.19	6.82	35.68	–	35.24
Motorized recreational vehicles	**81.96**	**17.18**	**90.87**	**–**	**89.73**
Motorized camper	21.35	13.78	22.39	–	23.37
Other vehicle	21.74	0.08	24.72	–	23.80
Motorboats	38.87	3.32	43.76	–	42.56
Rental of recreational vehicles	**2.79**	**0.98**	**3.04**	**0.95**	**2.97**
Boat and trailer rental on trips	0.59	–	0.67	0.56	0.59
Rental of campers on trips	0.61	–	0.70	0.34	0.64
Rental of other vehicles on trips	1.40	0.93	1.47	–	1.54
Rental of other RVs	0.03	–	0.04	0.05	0.03
Outboard motors	**3.58**	**–**	**4.07**	**–**	**3.92**
Docking and landing fees	**8.17**	**0.40**	**9.24**	**3.44**	**8.62**
Sports, recreation, exercise equipment	**143.58**	**41.49**	**157.64**	**89.54**	**148.62**
Athletic gear, game tables, exercise equipment	58.64	23.62	63.46	28.19	61.47
Bicycles	11.73	6.77	12.41	15.71	11.35
Camping equipment	17.02	5.24	18.64	10.95	17.58
Hunting and fishing equipment	25.85	2.18	29.11	17.08	26.66
Winter sports equipment	5.84	0.37	6.59	1.41	6.26
Water sports equipment	8.24	0.09	9.36	1.88	8.84
Other sports equipment	14.25	2.39	15.88	13.66	14.30
Rental and repair of miscellaneous sports equipment	2.02	0.83	2.19	0.66	2.15
Photographic equipment and supplies	**94.91**	**37.52**	**102.81**	**57.98**	**98.41**
Film	21.40	9.55	23.03	15.64	21.94
Other photographic supplies	1.44	1.90	1.37	–	1.57
Film processing	31.43	10.75	34.28	18.44	32.66
Repair and rental of photographic equipment	0.27	0.11	0.29	0.27	0.27
Photographic equipment	20.21	7.03	22.02	10.68	21.11
Photographer fees	20.17	8.17	21.82	12.94	20.86
Fireworks	**1.18**	**–**	**1.35**	**1.25**	**1.18**
Souvenirs	**2.00**	**0.19**	**2.25**	**–**	**2.18**
Visual goods	**1.09**	**–**	**1.24**	**–**	**1.20**
Pinball, electronic video games	**5.80**	**2.34**	**6.27**	**6.11**	**5.77**

Note: Other races include Asians, Native Americans, and Pacific Islanders. (–) means sample is too small to make a reliable estimate.
Source: Bureau of Labor Statistics, unpublished data from the 2000 Consumer Expenditure Survey

Table 3.17 Entertainment: Indexed spending by race and Hispanic origin, 2000

(indexed average annual spending of consumer units (CU) on entertainment by race and Hispanic origin of consumer unit reference person, 2000; index definition: an index of 100 is the average for all consumer units; an index of 132 means that spending by consumer units in that group is 32 percent above the average for all consumer units; an index of 68 indicates spending that is 32 percent below the average for all consumer units)

	total consumer units	race black	race white and other	Hispanic origin Hispanic	Hispanic origin non-Hispanic
Average spending of CU, total	$38,045	$28,152	$39,406	$32,735	$38,549
Average spending of CU, index	100	74	104	86	101
Entertainment, spending index	100	54	106	64	103
FEES AND ADMISSIONS	100	35	109	51	105
Recreation expenses on trips	100	42	108	66	103
Social, recreation, civic club membership	100	27	110	34	106
Fees for participant sports	100	31	109	39	106
Participant sports on trips	100	23	111	43	105
Movie, theater, opera, ballet	100	52	107	80	102
Movie, other admissions on trips	100	38	108	59	104
Admission to sports events	100	33	109	32	106
Admission to sports events on trips	100	38	108	59	104
Fees for recreational lessons	100	29	110	46	105
Other entertainment services on trips	100	42	108	66	103
TELEVISION, RADIO, SOUND EQUIPMENT	100	91	101	88	101
Television	100	102	100	86	101
Cable service and community antenna	100	107	99	78	102
Black-and-white TV	100	161	92	136	96
Color TV, console	100	97	100	97	100
Color TV, portable, table model	100	97	100	141	96
VCRs and video disc players	100	79	103	117	98
Video cassettes, tapes, and discs	100	76	103	70	103
Video game hardware and software	100	89	101	65	103
Repair of TV, radio, and sound equipment	100	63	105	98	100
Rental of television sets	100	292	73	296	82
Radio and sound equipment	100	63	105	92	101
Radios	100	43	108	105	100
Tape recorders and players	100	227	83	64	103
Sound components and component systems	100	83	102	137	97
Miscellaneous sound equipment	100	–	114	21	107
Sound equipment accessories	100	11	112	131	97
Satellite dishes	100	38	109	234	87
Compact disc, tape, record, video mail order clubs	100	60	106	83	102
Records, CDs, audio tapes, needles	100	77	103	91	101
Rental of VCR, radio, sound equipment	100	96	100	65	102
Musical instruments and accessories	100	14	112	46	105
Rental and repair of musical instruments	100	22	110	97	101
Rental of video cassettes, tapes, discs, films	100	74	104	92	101

	total consumer units	race		Hispanic origin	
		black	white and other	Hispanic	non-Hispanic
PETS, TOYS, PLAYGROUND EQUIPMENT	**100**	**48**	**107**	**65**	**103**
Pets	**100**	**33**	**109**	**59**	**104**
Pet food	100	35	109	77	102
Pet purchase, supplies, and medicines	100	56	106	58	104
Pet services	100	26	110	27	107
Veterinarian services	100	19	111	44	105
Toys, games, hobbies, and tricycles	**100**	**73**	**104**	**76**	**102**
Playground equipment	**100**	**49**	**107**	**73**	**103**
OTHER ENTERTAINMENT SUPPLIES, EQUIPMENT, SERVICES	**100**	**27**	**110**	**41**	**106**
Unmotored recreational vehicles	**100**	**14**	**112**	**5**	**109**
Boat without motor and boat trailers	100	–	114	15	108
Trailer and other attachable campers	100	21	111	–	109
Motorized recreational vehicles	**100**	**21**	**111**	**–**	**109**
Motorized camper	100	65	105	–	109
Other vehicle	100	0	114	–	109
Motorboats	100	9	113	–	109
Rental of recreational vehicles	**100**	**35**	**109**	**34**	**106**
Boat and trailer rental on trips	100	–	114	95	100
Rental of campers on trips	100	–	115	56	105
Rental of other vehicles on trips	100	66	105	–	110
Rental of other RVs	100	–	133	167	100
Outboard motors	**100**	**–**	**114**	**–**	**109**
Docking and landing fees	**100**	**5**	**113**	**42**	**106**
Sports, recreation, exercise equipment	**100**	**29**	**110**	**62**	**104**
Athletic gear, game tables, exercise equipment	100	40	108	48	105
Bicycles	100	58	106	134	97
Camping equipment	100	31	110	64	103
Hunting and fishing equipment	100	8	113	66	103
Winter sports equipment	100	6	113	24	107
Water sports equipment	100	1	114	23	107
Other sports equipment	100	17	111	96	100
Rental and repair of miscellaneous sports equipment	100	41	108	33	106
Photographic equipment and supplies	**100**	**40**	**108**	**61**	**104**
Film	100	45	108	73	103
Other photographic supplies	100	132	95	–	109
Film processing	100	34	109	59	104
Repair and rental of photographic equipment	100	41	107	100	100
Photographic equipment	100	35	109	53	104
Photographer fees	100	41	108	64	103
Fireworks	**100**	**–**	**114**	**106**	**100**
Souvenirs	**100**	**10**	**113**	**–**	**109**
Visual goods	**100**	**–**	**114**	**–**	**110**
Pinball, electronic video games	**100**	**40**	**108**	**105**	**99**

Note: Other races include Asians, Native Americans, and Pacific Islanders. (–) means sample is too small to make a reliable estimate.
Source: Calculations by New Strategist based on the 2000 Consumer Expenditure Survey

Table 3.18 Entertainment: Indexed per capita spending by race and Hispanic origin, 2000

(indexed average annual per capita spending of consumer units (CU) on entertainment by race and Hispanic origin of consumer unit reference person, 2000; index definition: an index of 100 is the average for all consumer units; an index of 132 means that spending by consumer units in that group is 32 percent above the average for all consumer units; an index of 68 indicates spending that is 32 percent below the average for all consumer units)

	total consumer units	race — black	race — white and other	Hispanic origin — Hispanic	Hispanic origin — non-Hispanic
Per capita spending of CU, total	$15,218	$10,427	$15,762	$9,628	$16,062
Per capita spending of CU, index	100	69	104	63	106
Entertainment, per capita spending index	100	50	106	47	108
FEES AND ADMISSIONS	100	32	109	37	109
Recreation expenses on trips	100	38	108	49	107
Social, recreation, civic club membership	100	25	110	25	111
Fees for participant sports	100	29	109	29	110
Participant sports on trips	100	21	111	31	110
Movie, theater, opera, ballet	100	48	107	59	106
Movie, other admissions on trips	100	36	108	44	108
Admission to sports events	100	30	109	23	111
Admission to sports events on trips	100	35	108	44	108
Fees for recreational lessons	100	27	110	34	110
Other entertainment services on trips	100	38	108	49	107
TELEVISION, RADIO, SOUND EQUIPMENT	100	84	101	64	105
Television	100	94	100	63	106
Cable service and community antenna	100	99	99	58	106
Black-and-white TV	100	149	92	100	100
Color TV, console	100	90	100	72	104
Color TV, portable, table model	100	90	100	104	100
VCRs and video disc players	100	73	103	86	102
Video cassettes, tapes, and discs	100	70	103	52	107
Video game hardware and software	100	83	101	48	108
Repair of TV, radio, and sound equipment	100	58	105	72	104
Rental of television sets	100	270	73	218	85
Radio and sound equipment	100	58	105	68	105
Radios	100	40	108	77	104
Tape recorders and players	100	210	83	47	108
Sound components and component systems	100	77	102	100	101
Miscellaneous sound equipment	100	–	114	16	112
Sound equipment accessories	100	10	112	96	101
Satellite dishes	100	35	109	172	91
Compact disc, tape, record, video mail order clubs	100	56	106	61	106
Records, CDs, audio tapes, needles	100	71	103	67	105
Rental of VCR, radio, sound equipment	100	89	100	48	106
Musical instruments and accessories	100	13	112	34	110
Rental and repair of musical instruments	100	21	110	71	105
Rental of video cassettes, tapes, discs, films	100	68	104	68	105

	total consumer units	race		Hispanic origin	
		black	white and other	Hispanic	non-Hispanic
PETS, TOYS, PLAYGROUND EQUIPMENT	100	44	107	48	108
Pets	100	31	109	43	108
Pet food	100	32	109	57	106
Pet purchase, supplies, and medicines	100	52	106	43	108
Pet services	100	24	110	20	111
Veterinarian services	100	18	111	33	110
Toys, games, hobbies, and tricycles	100	68	104	56	107
Playground equipment	100	46	107	54	107
OTHER ENTERTAINMENT SUPPLIES, EQUIPMENT, SERVICES	100	25	110	30	110
Unmotored recreational vehicles	100	13	112	4	114
Boat without motor and boat trailers	100	–	114	11	113
Trailer and other attachable campers	100	20	111	–	114
Motorized recreational vehicles	100	19	111	–	114
Motorized camper	100	60	105	–	114
Other vehicle	100	0	114	–	114
Motorboats	100	8	113	–	114
Rental of recreational vehicles	100	33	109	25	111
Boat and trailer rental on trips	100	–	114	70	104
Rental of campers on trips	100	–	115	41	109
Rental of other vehicles on trips	100	62	105	–	115
Rental of other RVs	100	–	133	123	104
Outboard motors	100	–	114	–	114
Docking and landing fees	100	5	113	31	110
Sports, recreation, exercise equipment	100	27	110	46	108
Athletic gear, game tables, exercise equipment	100	37	108	35	109
Bicycles	100	53	106	98	101
Camping equipment	100	29	110	47	108
Hunting and fishing equipment	100	8	113	49	107
Winter sports equipment	100	6	113	18	112
Water sports equipment	100	1	114	17	112
Other sports equipment	100	16	111	70	105
Rental and repair of miscellaneous sports equipment	100	38	108	24	111
Photographic equipment and supplies	100	37	108	45	108
Film	100	41	108	54	107
Other photographic supplies	100	122	95	–	114
Film processing	100	32	109	43	108
Repair and rental of photographic equipment	100	38	107	74	104
Photographic equipment	100	32	109	39	109
Photographer fees	100	38	108	47	108
Fireworks	100	–	114	78	104
Souvenirs	100	9	113	–	114
Visual goods	100	–	114	–	115
Pinball, electronic video games	100	37	108	77	104

Note: Per capita indexes account for household size and show how much each person in a particular household demographic segment spends relative to a person in the average household. Other races include Asians, Native Americans, and Pacific Islanders. (–) means sample is too small to make a reliable estimate.
Source: Calculations by New Strategist based on the 2000 Consumer Expenditure Survey

Table 3.19 Entertainment: Total spending by race and Hispanic origin, 2000

(total annual spending on entertainment, by consumer unit race and Hispanic origin groups, 2000; numbers in thousands)

	total consumer units	race		Hispanic origin	
		black	white and other	Hispanic	non-Hispanic
Total spending of all consumer units	$4,160,831,424	$372,454,135	$3,788,393,849	$310,098,181	$3,850,804,816
Entertainment, total spending	203,805,405	13,416,808	190,389,715	11,237,820	192,550,680
FEES AND ADMISSIONS	$56,307,600	$2,389,735	$53,918,436	$2,485,620	$53,821,888
Recreation expenses on trips	2,787,765	139,973	2,647,613	160,094	2,627,212
Social, recreation, civic club membership	10,737,652	348,081	10,390,487	314,030	10,423,939
Fees for participant sports	7,818,647	293,309	7,525,604	267,423	7,550,987
Participant sports on trips	3,833,313	107,295	3,726,270	141,242	3,692,082
Movie, theater, opera, ballet	9,751,162	613,211	9,137,822	674,572	9,076,369
Movie, other admissions on trips	4,914,953	228,085	4,686,679	253,024	4,661,054
Admission to sports events	3,863,936	153,468	3,710,888	106,003	3,758,012
Admission to sports events on trips	1,638,318	75,940	1,562,226	84,310	1,553,352
Fees for recreational lessons	8,174,090	290,399	7,884,195	324,734	7,849,671
Other entertainment services on trips	2,787,765	139,973	2,647,613	160,094	2,627,212
TELEVISION, RADIO, SOUND EQUIPMENT	68,006,588	7,505,776	60,500,937	5,158,806	62,847,311
Television	49,601,216	6,100,485	43,501,031	3,694,659	45,906,288
Cable service and community antenna	35,126,493	4,531,540	30,594,639	2,384,733	32,741,257
Black-and-white TV	84,213	16,405	68,257	9,947	73,922
Color TV, console	3,301,790	387,374	2,913,912	278,222	3,023,791
Color TV, portable, table model	3,756,756	441,617	3,314,804	459,156	3,297,501
VCRs and video disc players	2,602,935	248,856	2,354,395	264,865	2,338,519
Video cassettes, tapes, and discs	2,274,834	207,976	2,066,946	138,116	2,136,733
Video game hardware and software	2,047,350	221,206	1,825,642	116,044	1,930,951
Repair of TV, radio, and sound equipment	353,255	26,725	326,866	29,935	323,657
Rental of television sets	53,590	18,919	34,609	13,736	39,958
Radio and sound equipment	18,405,372	1,405,291	16,999,906	1,464,147	16,941,023
Radios	1,141,791	59,270	1,082,503	103,350	1,038,898
Tape recorders and players	480,121	131,771	348,977	26,619	453,519
Sound components and component systems	2,532,940	253,619	2,279,408	299,726	2,233,630
Miscellaneous sound equipment	45,934	–	46,146	853	44,952
Sound equipment accessories	441,843	5,954	435,501	50,017	391,584
Satellite dishes	295,291	13,495	282,643	59,869	235,750
Compact disc, tape, record, video mail order clubs	931,807	68,002	864,272	66,595	866,081
Records, CDs, audio tapes, needles	4,315,622	399,414	3,916,621	339,797	3,975,781
Rental of VCR, radio, sound equipment	59,058	6,880	51,914	3,316	54,942
Musical instruments and accessories	3,466,934	57,286	3,409,979	138,022	3,329,467
Rental and repair of musical instruments	146,552	3,969	142,283	12,315	134,857
Rental of video cassettes, tapes, discs, films	4,545,293	405,764	4,139,659	363,763	4,181,563

	total consumer units	race		Hispanic origin	
		black	white and other	Hispanic	non-Hispanic
PETS, TOYS, PLAYGROUND EQUIPMENT	$36,496,862	$2,106,745	$34,390,128	$2,062,462	$34,427,468
Pets	22,904,731	914,987	21,990,377	1,168,400	21,728,943
Pet food	9,402,281	397,562	9,005,153	630,712	8,767,696
Pet purchase, supplies, and medicines	4,166,883	284,313	3,882,012	210,111	3,953,805
Pet services	2,117,345	66,679	2,050,602	49,449	2,067,806
Veterinarian services	7,218,222	166,433	7,051,649	278,127	6,939,636
Toys, games, hobbies, and tricycles	13,229,032	1,169,929	12,058,464	871,137	12,357,887
Playground equipment	363,098	21,697	341,286	22,925	340,639
OTHER ENTERTAINMENT SUPPLIES, EQUIPMENT, SERVICES	42,994,355	1,414,552	41,580,214	1,530,932	41,454,012
Unmotored recreational vehicles	5,256,178	90,229	5,165,441	22,167	5,233,447
Boat without motor and boat trailers	1,735,654	–	1,735,273	22,167	1,713,182
Trailer and other attachable campers	3,520,524	90,229	3,430,168	–	3,520,265
Motorized recreational vehicles	8,963,719	227,291	8,735,969	–	8,963,489
Motorized camper	2,334,985	182,309	2,152,507	–	2,334,523
Other vehicle	2,377,639	1,058	2,376,507	–	2,377,477
Motorboats	4,251,095	43,924	4,206,955	–	4,251,489
Rental of recreational vehicles	305,134	12,965	292,256	8,999	296,685
Boat and trailer rental on trips	64,527	–	64,412	5,305	58,937
Rental of campers on trips	66,714	–	67,296	3,221	63,932
Rental of other vehicles on trips	153,114	12,304	141,321	–	153,837
Rental of other RVs	3,281	–	3,845	474	2,997
Outboard motors	391,534	–	391,278	–	391,584
Docking and landing fees	893,528	5,292	888,306	32,587	861,086
Sports, recreation, exercise equipment	15,702,914	548,913	15,155,037	848,212	14,846,246
Athletic gear, game tables, exercise equipment	6,413,281	312,493	6,100,854	267,044	6,140,484
Bicycles	1,282,875	89,567	1,193,060	148,821	1,133,797
Camping equipment	1,861,426	69,325	1,791,994	103,729	1,756,137
Hunting and fishing equipment	2,827,137	28,841	2,798,548	161,799	2,663,174
Winter sports equipment	638,703	4,895	633,543	13,357	625,336
Water sports equipment	901,184	1,191	899,842	17,809	883,063
Other sports equipment	1,558,480	31,620	1,526,656	129,401	1,428,484
Rental and repair of miscellaneous sports equipment	220,921	10,981	210,540	6,252	214,772
Photographic equipment and supplies	10,380,022	496,390	9,883,845	549,245	9,830,569
Film	2,340,454	126,347	2,214,035	148,158	2,191,674
Other photographic supplies	157,488	25,137	131,708	–	156,834
Film processing	3,437,405	142,223	3,295,576	174,682	3,262,538
Repair and rental of photographic equipment	29,529	1,455	27,880	2,558	26,971
Photographic equipment	2,210,307	93,007	2,116,937	101,172	2,108,762
Photographer fees	2,205,932	108,089	2,097,709	122,581	2,083,789
Fireworks	129,053	–	129,785	11,841	117,875
Souvenirs	218,734	2,514	216,308	–	217,769
Visual goods	119,210	–	119,210	–	119,873
Pinball, electronic video games	634,329	30,958	602,779	57,880	576,388

Note: Other races include Asians, Native Americans, and Pacific Islanders. Numbers may not add to total because of rounding. (–) means sample is too small to make a reliable estimate.
Source: Calculations by New Strategist based on the 2000 Consumer Expenditure Survey

Table 3.20 Entertainment: Market shares by race and Hispanic origin, 2000

(percentage of total annual spending on entertainment accounted for by consumer unit race and Hispanic origin groups, 2000)

	total consumer units	race		Hispanic origin	
		black	white and other	Hispanic	non-Hispanic
Share of total consumer units	100.0%	12.1%	87.9%	8.7%	91.3%
Share of total before-tax income	100.0	8.8	91.1	6.8	93.4
Share of total spending	100.0	9.0	91.0	7.5	92.5
Share of entertainment spending	100.0	6.6	93.4	5.5	94.5
FEES AND ADMISSIONS	**100.0%**	**4.2%**	**95.8%**	**4.4%**	**95.6%**
Recreation expenses on trips	100.0	5.0	95.0	5.7	94.2
Social, recreation, civic club membership	100.0	3.2	96.8	2.9	97.1
Fees for participant sports	100.0	3.8	96.3	3.4	96.6
Participant sports on trips	100.0	2.8	97.2	3.7	96.3
Movie, theater, opera, ballet	100.0	6.3	93.7	6.9	93.1
Movie, other admissions on trips	100.0	4.6	95.4	5.1	94.8
Admission to sports events	100.0	4.0	96.0	2.7	97.3
Admission to sports events on trips	100.0	4.6	95.4	5.1	94.8
Fees for recreational lessons	100.0	3.6	96.5	4.0	96.0
Other entertainment services on trips	100.0	5.0	95.0	5.7	94.2
TELEVISION, RADIO, SOUND EQUIPMENT	**100.0**	**11.0**	**89.0**	**7.6**	**92.4**
Television	**100.0**	**12.3**	**87.7**	**7.4**	**92.6**
Cable service and community antenna	100.0	12.9	87.1	6.8	93.2
Black-and-white TV	100.0	19.5	81.1	11.8	87.8
Color TV, console	100.0	11.7	88.3	8.4	91.6
Color TV, portable, table model	100.0	11.8	88.2	12.2	87.8
VCRs and video disc players	100.0	9.6	90.5	10.2	89.8
Video cassettes, tapes, and discs	100.0	9.1	90.9	6.1	93.9
Video game hardware and software	100.0	10.8	89.2	5.7	94.3
Repair of TV, radio, and sound equipment	100.0	7.6	92.5	8.5	91.6
Rental of television sets	100.0	35.3	64.6	25.6	74.6
Radio and sound equipment	**100.0**	**7.6**	**92.4**	**8.0**	**92.0**
Radios	100.0	5.2	94.8	9.1	91.0
Tape recorders and players	100.0	27.4	72.7	5.5	94.5
Sound components and component systems	100.0	10.0	90.0	11.8	88.2
Miscellaneous sound equipment	100.0	–	100.0	1.9	97.9
Sound equipment accessories	100.0	1.3	98.6	11.3	88.6
Satellite dishes	100.0	4.6	95.7	20.3	79.8
Compact disc, tape, record, video mail order clubs	100.0	7.3	92.8	7.1	92.9
Records, CDs, audio tapes, needles	100.0	9.3	90.8	7.9	92.1
Rental of VCR, radio, sound equipment	100.0	11.6	87.9	5.6	93.0
Musical instruments and accessories	100.0	1.7	98.4	4.0	96.0
Rental and repair of musical instruments	100.0	2.7	97.1	8.4	92.0
Rental of video cassettes, tapes, discs, films	100.0	8.9	91.1	8.0	92.0

	total consumer units	race		Hispanic origin	
		black	white and other	Hispanic	non-Hispanic
PETS, TOYS, PLAYGROUND EQUIPMENT	**100.0%**	**5.8%**	**94.2%**	**5.7%**	**94.3%**
Pets	**100.0**	**4.0**	**96.0**	**5.1**	**94.9**
Pet food	100.0	4.2	95.8	6.7	93.3
Pet purchase, supplies, and medicines	100.0	6.8	93.2	5.0	94.9
Pet services	100.0	3.1	96.8	2.3	97.7
Veterinarian services	100.0	2.3	97.7	3.9	96.1
Toys, games, hobbies, and tricycles	**100.0**	**8.8**	**91.2**	**6.6**	**93.4**
Playground equipment	**100.0**	**6.0**	**94.0**	**6.3**	**93.8**
OTHER ENTERTAINMENT SUPPLIES, EQUIPMENT, SERVICES	**100.0**	**3.3**	**96.7**	**3.6**	**96.4**
Unmotored recreational vehicles	**100.0**	**1.7**	**98.3**	**0.4**	**99.6**
Boat without motor and boat trailers	100.0	–	100.0	1.3	98.7
Trailer and other attachable campers	100.0	2.6	97.4	–	100.0
Motorized recreational vehicles	**100.0**	**2.5**	**97.5**	**–**	**100.0**
Motorized camper	100.0	7.8	92.2	–	100.0
Other vehicle	100.0	–	100.0	–	100.0
Motorboats	100.0	1.0	99.0	–	100.0
Rental of recreational vehicles	**100.0**	**4.2**	**95.8**	**2.9**	**97.2**
Boat and trailer rental on trips	100.0	–	99.8	8.2	91.3
Rental of campers on trips	100.0	–	100.0	4.8	95.8
Rental of other vehicles on trips	100.0	8.0	92.3	–	100.0
Rental of other RVs	100.0	–	100.0	14.4	91.3
Outboard motors	**100.0**	**–**	**99.9**	**–**	**100.0**
Docking and landing fees	**100.0**	**0.6**	**99.4**	**3.6**	**96.4**
Sports, recreation, exercise equipment	**100.0**	**3.5**	**96.5**	**5.4**	**94.5**
Athletic gear, game tables, exercise equipment	100.0	4.9	95.1	4.2	95.7
Bicycles	100.0	7.0	93.0	11.6	88.4
Camping equipment	100.0	3.7	96.3	5.6	94.3
Hunting and fishing equipment	100.0	1.0	99.0	5.7	94.2
Winter sports equipment	100.0	0.8	99.2	2.1	97.9
Water sports equipment	100.0	0.1	99.9	2.0	98.0
Other sports equipment	100.0	2.0	98.0	8.3	91.7
Rental and repair of miscellaneous sports equipment	100.0	5.0	95.3	2.8	97.2
Photographic equipment and supplies	**100.0**	**4.8**	**95.2**	**5.3**	**94.7**
Film	100.0	5.4	94.6	6.3	93.6
Other photographic supplies	100.0	16.0	83.6	–	99.6
Film processing	100.0	4.1	95.9	5.1	94.9
Repair and rental of photographic equipment	100.0	4.9	94.4	8.7	91.3
Photographic equipment	100.0	4.2	95.8	4.6	95.4
Photographer fees	100.0	4.9	95.1	5.6	94.5
Fireworks	**100.0**	**–**	**100.0**	**9.2**	**91.3**
Souvenirs	**100.0**	**1.1**	**98.9**	**–**	**99.6**
Visual goods	**100.0**	**–**	**100.0**	**–**	**100.0**
Pinball, electronic video games	**100.0**	**4.9**	**95.0**	**9.1**	**90.9**

Note: Other races include Asians, Native Americans, and Pacific Islanders. Numbers may not add to total because of rounding. (–) means sample is too small to make a reliable estimate.
Source: Calculations by New Strategist based on the 2000 Consumer Expenditure Survey

Table 3.21   Entertainment: Average spending by region, 2000

(average annual spending of consumer units (CU) on entertainment, by region in which consumer unit lives, 2000)

	total consumer units	Northeast	Midwest	South	West
Number of consumer units (in thousands, add 000)	109,367	20,994	25,717	38,245	24,410
Average number of persons per CU	2.5	2.5	2.5	2.5	2.6
Average before-tax income of CU	$44,649.00	$47,439.00	$44,377.00	$41,984.00	$46,670.00
Average spending of CU, total	38,044.67	38,901.91	39,212.70	34,707.07	41,328.19
Entertainment, average spending	1,863.50	1,915.01	2,040.03	1,616.59	2,021.16
FEES AND ADMISSIONS	**$514.85**	**$576.95**	**$566.11**	**$394.88**	**$595.41**
Recreation expenses on trips	25.49	27.51	27.58	17.73	33.70
Social, recreation, civic club membership	98.18	104.94	110.45	86.08	98.42
Fees for participant sports	71.49	64.45	85.19	60.22	80.78
Participant sports on trips	35.05	32.98	37.79	26.09	47.99
Movie, theater, opera, ballet	89.16	104.70	93.81	61.53	114.19
Movie, other admissions on trips	44.94	53.28	49.69	30.27	55.74
Admission to sports events	35.33	38.52	39.88	30.81	34.88
Admission to sports events on trips	14.98	17.76	16.56	10.09	18.58
Fees for recreational lessons	74.74	105.29	77.58	54.34	77.44
Other entertainment services on trips	25.49	27.51	27.58	17.73	33.70
TELEVISION, RADIO, SOUND EQUIPMENT	**621.82**	**626.80**	**664.54**	**574.13**	**647.86**
Television	**453.53**	**475.25**	**451.70**	**442.68**	**453.78**
Cable service and community antenna	321.18	362.72	315.17	321.58	291.16
Black-and-white TV	0.77	0.42	0.39	1.30	0.65
Color TV, console	30.19	21.18	28.66	32.51	35.92
Color TV, portable, table model	34.35	33.18	31.82	30.30	44.36
VCRs and video disc players	23.80	18.46	26.60	19.83	31.68
Video cassettes, tapes, and discs	20.80	17.44	22.51	16.91	27.96
Video game hardware and software	18.72	19.28	22.95	15.84	18.29
Repair of TV, radio, and sound equipment	3.23	2.57	3.28	3.63	3.13
Rental of television sets	0.49	0.01	0.31	0.79	0.63
Radio and sound equipment	**168.29**	**151.55**	**212.84**	**131.46**	**194.08**
Radios	10.44	4.54	15.55	9.02	12.75
Tape recorders and players	4.39	2.65	3.74	4.87	5.94
Sound components and component systems	23.16	27.71	23.99	18.25	26.07
Miscellaneous sound equipment	0.42	–	0.27	0.58	0.70
Sound equipment accessories	4.04	2.74	3.56	3.29	6.96
Satellite dishes	2.70	1.37	1.92	3.56	3.34
Compact disc, tape, record, video mail order clubs	8.52	9.39	8.63	6.61	10.66
Records, CDs, audio tapes, needles	39.46	36.86	43.84	31.85	49.02
Rental of VCR, radio, sound equipment	0.54	0.31	0.30	1.02	0.21
Musical instruments and accessories	31.70	26.96	66.19	14.61	26.24
Rental and repair of musical instruments	1.34	1.38	1.52	0.77	2.01
Rental of video cassettes, tapes, discs, films	41.56	37.65	43.31	37.03	50.18

	total consumer units	Northeast	Midwest	South	West
PETS, TOYS, PLAYGROUND EQUIPMENT	**$333.71**	**$316.17**	**$360.22**	**$312.67**	**$354.86**
Pets	**209.43**	**200.24**	**209.02**	**198.47**	**235.98**
Pet food	85.97	80.08	90.00	84.71	89.18
Pet purchase, supplies, and medicines	38.10	31.18	39.88	34.08	49.12
Pet services	19.36	18.09	15.92	17.26	27.37
Veterinarian services	66.00	70.90	63.22	62.42	70.31
Toys, games, hobbies, and tricycles	**120.96**	**114.74**	**143.46**	**112.04**	**116.57**
Playground equipment	**3.32**	**1.19**	**7.74**	**2.16**	**2.31**
OTHER ENTERTAINMENT SUPPLIES, EQUIPMENT, SERVICES	**393.12**	**395.10**	**449.17**	**334.90**	**423.03**
Unmotored recreational vehicles	**48.06**	**58.10**	**65.80**	**25.15**	**56.63**
Boat without motor and boat trailers	15.87	7.86	40.31	5.92	12.61
Trailer and other attachable campers	32.19	50.24	25.49	19.23	44.02
Motorized recreational vehicles	**81.96**	**47.99**	**98.80**	**101.28**	**63.16**
Motorized camper	21.35	–	36.00	28.00	13.85
Other vehicle	21.74	11.94	41.84	24.33	4.93
Motorboats	38.87	36.05	20.96	48.95	44.38
Rental of recreational vehicles	**2.79**	**3.93**	**4.14**	**1.03**	**3.15**
Boat and trailer rental on trips	0.59	0.46	1.16	0.11	0.85
Rental of campers on trips	0.61	1.35	0.46	–	1.10
Rental of other vehicles on trips	1.40	1.85	2.41	0.72	1.03
Rental of other RVs	0.03	–	–	0.02	0.12
Outboard motors	**3.58**	**0.22**	**10.30**	**1.36**	**2.86**
Docking and landing fees	**8.17**	**12.37**	**7.67**	**6.01**	**8.47**
Sports, recreation, exercise equipment	**143.58**	**164.01**	**143.93**	**116.36**	**167.67**
Athletic gear, game tables, exercise equipment	58.64	67.41	59.13	48.76	66.10
Bicycles	11.73	11.58	13.46	7.09	17.31
Camping equipment	17.02	44.18	7.24	6.93	18.79
Hunting and fishing equipment	25.85	16.99	31.90	28.50	23.27
Winter sports equipment	5.84	8.57	6.41	1.32	9.96
Water sports equipment	8.24	1.54	10.18	9.48	10.02
Other sports equipment	14.25	11.81	12.73	13.30	19.41
Rental and repair of miscellaneous sports equipment	2.02	1.95	2.90	0.98	2.80
Photographic equipment and supplies	**94.91**	**98.73**	**106.65**	**73.24**	**113.30**
Film	21.40	22.50	23.45	17.96	23.67
Other photographic supplies	1.44	0.72	0.24	1.12	3.90
Film processing	31.43	32.24	34.84	25.36	36.65
Repair and rental of photographic equipment	0.27	0.09	0.54	0.26	0.15
Photographic equipment	20.21	22.03	23.27	14.07	25.03
Photographer fees	20.17	21.16	24.31	14.47	23.90
Fireworks	**1.18**	**–**	**2.82**	**0.90**	**0.99**
Souvenirs	**2.00**	**4.03**	**0.91**	**2.38**	**0.66**
Visual goods	**1.09**	**1.15**	**1.76**	**0.98**	**0.52**
Pinball, electronic video games	**5.80**	**4.57**	**6.39**	**6.21**	**5.61**

Note: (–) means sample is too small to make a reliable estimate.
Source: Bureau of Labor Statistics, unpublished data from the 2000 Consumer Expenditure Survey

Table 3.22 Entertainment: Indexed spending by region, 2000

(indexed average annual spending of consumer units (CU) on entertainment by region in which consumer unit lives, 2000; index definition: an index of 100 is the average for all consumer units; an index of 132 means that spending by consumer units in that group is 32 percent above the average for all consumer units; an index of 68 indicates spending that is 32 percent below the average for all consumer units)

	total consumer units	Northeast	Midwest	South	West
Average spending of CU, total	$38,045	$38,902	$39,213	$34,707	$41,328
Average spending of CU, index	100	102	103	91	109
Entertainment, spending index	100	103	109	87	108
FEES AND ADMISSIONS	100	112	110	77	116
Recreation expenses on trips	100	108	108	70	132
Social, recreation, civic club membership	100	107	112	88	100
Fees for participant sports	100	90	119	84	113
Participant sports on trips	100	94	108	74	137
Movie, theater, opera, ballet	100	117	105	69	128
Movie, other admissions on trips	100	119	111	67	124
Admission to sports events	100	109	113	87	99
Admission to sports events on trips	100	119	111	67	124
Fees for recreational lessons	100	141	104	73	104
Other entertainment services on trips	100	108	108	70	132
TELEVISION, RADIO, SOUND EQUIPMENT	100	101	107	92	104
Television	100	105	100	98	100
Cable service and community antenna	100	113	98	100	91
Black-and-white TV	100	55	51	169	84
Color TV, console	100	70	95	108	119
Color TV, portable, table model	100	97	93	88	129
VCRs and video disc players	100	78	112	83	133
Video cassettes, tapes, and discs	100	84	108	81	134
Video game hardware and software	100	103	123	85	98
Repair of TV, radio, and sound equipment	100	80	102	112	97
Rental of television sets	100	2	63	161	129
Radio and sound equipment	100	90	126	78	115
Radios	100	43	149	86	122
Tape recorders and players	100	60	85	111	135
Sound components and component systems	100	120	104	79	113
Miscellaneous sound equipment	100	–	64	138	167
Sound equipment accessories	100	68	88	81	172
Satellite dishes	100	51	71	132	124
Compact disc, tape, record, video mail order clubs	100	110	101	78	125
Records, CDs, audio tapes, needles	100	93	111	81	124
Rental of VCR, radio, sound equipment	100	57	56	189	39
Musical instruments and accessories	100	85	209	46	83
Rental and repair of musical instruments	100	103	113	57	150
Rental of video cassettes, tapes, discs, films	100	91	104	89	121

	total consumer units	Northeast	Midwest	South	West
PETS, TOYS, PLAYGROUND EQUIPMENT	**100**	**95**	**108**	**94**	**106**
Pets	**100**	**96**	**100**	**95**	**113**
Pet food	100	93	105	99	104
Pet purchase, supplies, and medicines	100	82	105	89	129
Pet services	100	93	82	89	141
Veterinarian services	100	107	96	95	107
Toys, games, hobbies, and tricycles	**100**	**95**	**119**	**93**	**96**
Playground equipment	**100**	**36**	**233**	**65**	**70**
OTHER ENTERTAINMENT SUPPLIES, EQUIPMENT, SERVICES	**100**	**101**	**114**	**85**	**108**
Unmotored recreational vehicles	**100**	**121**	**137**	**52**	**118**
Boat without motor and boat trailers	100	50	254	37	79
Trailer and other attachable campers	100	156	79	60	137
Motorized recreational vehicles	**100**	**59**	**121**	**124**	**77**
Motorized camper	100	–	169	131	65
Other vehicle	100	55	192	112	23
Motorboats	100	93	54	126	114
Rental of recreational vehicles	**100**	**141**	**148**	**37**	**113**
Boat and trailer rental on trips	100	78	197	19	144
Rental of campers on trips	100	221	75	–	180
Rental of other vehicles on trips	100	132	172	51	74
Rental of other RVs	100	–	–	67	400
Outboard motors	**100**	**6**	**288**	**38**	**80**
Docking and landing fees	**100**	**151**	**94**	**74**	**104**
Sports, recreation, exercise equipment	**100**	**114**	**100**	**81**	**117**
Athletic gear, game tables, exercise equipment	100	115	101	83	113
Bicycles	100	99	115	60	148
Camping equipment	100	260	43	41	110
Hunting and fishing equipment	100	66	123	110	90
Winter sports equipment	100	147	110	23	171
Water sports equipment	100	19	124	115	122
Other sports equipment	100	83	89	93	136
Rental and repair of miscellaneous sports equipment	100	97	144	49	139
Photographic equipment and supplies	**100**	**104**	**112**	**77**	**119**
Film	100	105	110	84	111
Other photographic supplies	100	50	17	78	271
Film processing	100	103	111	81	117
Repair and rental of photographic equipment	100	33	200	96	56
Photographic equipment	100	109	115	70	124
Photographer fees	100	105	121	72	118
Fireworks	**100**	**–**	**239**	**76**	**84**
Souvenirs	**100**	**202**	**46**	**119**	**33**
Visual goods	**100**	**106**	**161**	**90**	**48**
Pinball, electronic video games	**100**	**79**	**110**	**107**	**97**

Note: (–) means sample is too small to make a reliable estimate.
Source: Calculations by New Strategist based on the 2000 Consumer Expenditure Survey

Table 3.23 Entertainment: Indexed per capita spending by region, 2000

(indexed average annual per capita spending of consumer units (CU) on entertainment by region in which consumer unit lives, 2000; index definition: an index of 100 is the average for all consumer units; an index of 132 means that spending by consumer units in that group is 32 percent above the average for all consumer units; an index of 68 indicates spending that is 32 percent below the average for all consumer units)

	total consumer units	Northeast	Midwest	South	West
Per capita spending of CU, total	$15,218	$15,561	$15,685	$13,883	$15,895
Per capita spending of CU, index	100	102	103	91	104
Entertainment, per capita spending index	100	103	109	87	104
FEES AND ADMISSIONS	**100**	**112**	**110**	**77**	**111**
Recreation expenses on trips	100	108	108	70	127
Social, recreation, civic club membership	100	107	112	88	96
Fees for participant sports	100	90	119	84	109
Participant sports on trips	100	94	108	74	132
Movie, theater, opera, ballet	100	117	105	69	123
Movie, other admissions on trips	100	119	111	67	119
Admission to sports events	100	109	113	87	95
Admission to sports events on trips	100	119	111	67	119
Fees for recreational lessons	100	141	104	73	100
Other entertainment services on trips	100	108	108	70	127
TELEVISION, RADIO, SOUND EQUIPMENT	**100**	**101**	**107**	**92**	**100**
Television	**100**	**105**	**100**	**98**	**96**
Cable service and community antenna	100	113	98	100	87
Black-and-white TV	100	55	51	169	81
Color TV, console	100	70	95	108	114
Color TV, portable, table model	100	97	93	88	124
VCRs and video disc players	100	78	112	83	128
Video cassettes, tapes, and discs	100	84	108	81	129
Video game hardware and software	100	103	123	85	94
Repair of TV, radio, and sound equipment	100	80	102	112	93
Rental of television sets	100	2	63	161	124
Radio and sound equipment	**100**	**90**	**126**	**78**	**111**
Radios	100	43	149	86	117
Tape recorders and players	100	60	85	111	130
Sound components and component systems	100	120	104	79	108
Miscellaneous sound equipment	100	–	64	138	160
Sound equipment accessories	100	68	88	81	166
Satellite dishes	100	51	71	132	119
Compact disc, tape, record, video mail order clubs	100	110	101	78	120
Records, CDs, audio tapes, needles	100	93	111	81	119
Rental of VCR, radio, sound equipment	100	57	56	189	37
Musical instruments and accessories	100	85	209	46	80
Rental and repair of musical instruments	100	103	113	57	144
Rental of video cassettes, tapes, discs, films	100	91	104	89	116

	total consumer units	Northeast	Midwest	South	West
PETS, TOYS, PLAYGROUND EQUIPMENT	**100**	**95**	**108**	**94**	**102**
Pets	**100**	**96**	**100**	**95**	**108**
Pet food	100	93	105	99	100
Pet purchase, supplies, and medicines	100	82	105	89	124
Pet services	100	93	82	89	136
Veterinarian services	100	107	96	95	102
Toys, games, hobbies, and tricycles	**100**	**95**	**119**	**93**	**93**
Playground equipment	**100**	**36**	**233**	**65**	**67**
OTHER ENTERTAINMENT SUPPLIES, EQUIPMENT, SERVICES	**100**	**101**	**114**	**85**	**103**
Unmotored recreational vehicles	**100**	**121**	**137**	**52**	**113**
Boat without motor and boat trailers	100	50	254	37	76
Trailer and other attachable campers	100	156	79	60	131
Motorized recreational vehicles	**100**	**59**	**121**	**124**	**74**
Motorized camper	100	–	169	131	62
Other vehicle	100	55	192	112	22
Motorboats	100	93	54	126	110
Rental of recreational vehicles	**100**	**141**	**148**	**37**	**109**
Boat and trailer rental on trips	100	78	197	19	139
Rental of campers on trips	100	221	75	–	173
Rental of other vehicles on trips	100	132	172	51	71
Rental of other RVs	100	–	–	67	385
Outboard motors	**100**	**6**	**288**	**38**	**77**
Docking and landing fees	**100**	**151**	**94**	**74**	**100**
Sports, recreation, exercise equipment	**100**	**114**	**100**	**81**	**112**
Athletic gear, game tables, exercise equipment	100	115	101	83	108
Bicycles	100	99	115	60	142
Camping equipment	100	260	43	41	106
Hunting and fishing equipment	100	66	123	110	87
Winter sports equipment	100	147	110	23	164
Water sports equipment	100	19	124	115	117
Other sports equipment	100	83	89	93	131
Rental and repair of miscellaneous sports equipment	100	97	144	49	133
Photographic equipment and supplies	**100**	**104**	**112**	**77**	**115**
Film	100	105	110	84	106
Other photographic supplies	100	50	17	78	260
Film processing	100	103	111	81	112
Repair and rental of photographic equipment	100	33	200	96	53
Photographic equipment	100	109	115	70	119
Photographer fees	100	105	121	72	114
Fireworks	**100**	**–**	**239**	**76**	**81**
Souvenirs	**100**	**202**	**46**	**119**	**32**
Visual goods	**100**	**106**	**161**	**90**	**46**
Pinball, electronic video games	**100**	**79**	**110**	**107**	**93**

Note: Per capita indexes account for household size and show how much each person in a particular household demographic segment spends relative to a person in the average household. (–) means sample is too small to make a reliable estimate.
Source: Calculations by New Strategist based on the 2000 Consumer Expenditure Survey

Table 3.24 Entertainment: Total spending by region, 2000

(total annual spending on entertainment, by region in which consumer units live, 2000; numbers in thousands)

	total consumer units	Northeast	Midwest	South	West
Number of consumer units	109,367	20,994	25,717	38,245	24,410
Total spending of all consumer units	$4,160,831,424	$816,706,699	$1,008,433,006	$1,327,371,892	$1,008,821,118
Entertainment, total spending	203,805,405	40,203,720	52,463,452	61,826,485	49,336,516
FEES AND ADMISSIONS	**$56,307,600**	**$12,112,488**	**$14,558,651**	**$15,102,186**	**$14,533,958**
Recreation expenses on trips	2,787,765	577,545	709,275	678,084	822,617
Social, recreation, civic club membership	10,737,652	2,203,110	2,840,443	3,292,130	2,402,432
Fees for participant sports	7,818,647	1,353,063	2,190,831	2,303,114	1,971,840
Participant sports on trips	3,833,313	692,382	971,845	997,812	1,171,436
Movie, theater, opera, ballet	9,751,162	2,198,072	2,412,512	2,353,215	2,787,378
Movie, other admissions on trips	4,914,953	1,118,560	1,277,878	1,157,676	1,360,613
Admission to sports events	3,863,936	808,689	1,025,594	1,178,328	851,421
Admission to sports events on trips	1,638,318	372,853	425,874	385,892	453,538
Fees for recreational lessons	8,174,090	2,210,458	1,995,125	2,078,233	1,890,310
Other entertainment services on trips	2,787,765	577,545	709,275	678,084	822,617
TELEVISION, RADIO, SOUND EQUIPMENT	**68,006,588**	**13,159,039**	**17,089,975**	**21,957,602**	**15,814,263**
Television	**49,601,216**	**9,977,399**	**11,616,369**	**16,930,297**	**11,076,770**
Cable service and community antenna	35,126,493	7,614,944	8,105,227	12,298,827	7,107,216
Black-and-white TV	84,213	8,817	10,030	49,719	15,867
Color TV, console	3,301,790	444,653	737,049	1,243,345	876,807
Color TV, portable, table model	3,756,756	696,581	818,315	1,158,824	1,082,828
VCRs and video disc players	2,602,935	387,549	684,072	758,398	773,309
Video cassettes, tapes, and discs	2,274,834	366,135	578,890	646,723	682,504
Video game hardware and software	2,047,350	404,764	590,205	605,801	446,459
Repair of TV, radio, and sound equipment	353,255	53,955	84,352	138,829	76,403
Rental of television sets	53,590	210	7,972	30,214	15,378
Radio and sound equipment	**18,405,372**	**3,181,641**	**5,473,606**	**5,027,688**	**4,737,493**
Radios	1,141,791	95,313	399,899	344,970	311,228
Tape recorders and players	480,121	55,634	96,182	186,253	144,995
Sound components and component systems	2,532,940	581,744	616,951	697,971	636,369
Miscellaneous sound equipment	45,934	–	6,944	22,182	17,087
Sound equipment accessories	441,843	57,524	91,553	125,826	169,894
Satellite dishes	295,291	28,762	49,377	136,152	81,529
Compact disc, tape, record, video mail order clubs	931,807	197,134	221,938	252,799	260,211
Records, CDs, audio tapes, needles	4,315,622	773,839	1,127,433	1,218,103	1,196,578
Rental of VCR, radio, sound equipment	59,058	6,508	7,715	39,010	5,126
Musical instruments and accessories	3,466,934	565,998	1,702,208	558,759	640,518
Rental and repair of musical instruments	146,552	28,972	39,090	29,449	49,064
Rental of video cassettes, tapes, discs, films	4,545,293	790,424	1,113,803	1,416,212	1,224,894

	total consumer units	Northeast	Midwest	South	West
PETS, TOYS, PLAYGROUND EQUIPMENT	$36,496,862	$6,637,673	$9,263,778	$11,958,064	$8,662,133
Pets	22,904,731	4,203,839	5,375,367	7,590,485	5,760,272
Pet food	9,402,281	1,681,200	2,314,530	3,239,734	2,176,884
Pet purchase, supplies, and medicines	4,166,883	654,593	1,025,594	1,303,390	1,199,019
Pet services	2,117,345	379,781	409,415	660,109	668,102
Veterinarian services	7,218,222	1,488,475	1,625,829	2,387,253	1,716,267
Toys, games, hobbies, and tricycles	13,229,032	2,408,852	3,689,361	4,284,970	2,845,474
Playground equipment	363,098	24,983	199,050	82,609	56,387
OTHER ENTERTAINMENT SUPPLIES, EQUIPMENT, SERVICES	42,994,355	8,294,729	11,551,305	12,808,251	10,326,162
Unmotored recreational vehicles	5,256,178	1,219,751	1,692,179	961,862	1,382,338
Boat without motor and boat trailers	1,735,654	165,013	1,036,652	226,410	307,810
Trailer and other attachable campers	3,520,524	1,054,739	655,526	735,451	1,074,528
Motorized recreational vehicles	8,963,719	1,007,502	2,540,840	3,873,454	1,541,736
Motorized camper	2,334,985	–	925,812	1,070,860	338,079
Other vehicle	2,377,639	250,668	1,075,999	930,501	120,341
Motorboats	4,251,095	756,834	539,028	1,872,093	1,083,316
Rental of recreational vehicles	305,134	82,506	106,468	39,392	76,892
Boat and trailer rental on trips	64,527	9,657	29,832	4,207	20,749
Rental of campers on trips	66,714	28,342	11,830	–	26,851
Rental of other vehicles on trips	153,114	38,839	61,978	27,536	25,142
Rental of other RVs	3,281	–	–	765	2,929
Outboard motors	391,534	4,619	264,885	52,013	69,813
Docking and landing fees	893,528	259,696	197,249	229,852	206,753
Sports, recreation, exercise equipment	15,702,914	3,443,226	3,701,448	4,450,188	4,092,825
Athletic gear, game tables, exercise equipment	6,413,281	1,415,206	1,520,646	1,864,826	1,613,501
Bicycles	1,282,875	243,111	346,151	271,157	422,537
Camping equipment	1,861,426	927,515	186,191	265,038	458,664
Hunting and fishing equipment	2,827,137	356,688	820,372	1,089,983	568,021
Winter sports equipment	638,703	179,919	164,846	50,483	243,124
Water sports equipment	901,184	32,331	261,799	362,563	244,588
Other sports equipment	1,558,480	247,939	327,377	508,659	473,798
Rental and repair of miscellaneous sports equipment	220,921	40,938	74,579	37,480	68,348
Photographic equipment and supplies	10,380,022	2,072,738	2,742,718	2,801,064	2,765,653
Film	2,340,454	472,365	603,064	686,880	577,785
Other photographic supplies	157,488	15,116	6,172	42,834	95,199
Film processing	3,437,405	676,847	895,980	969,893	894,627
Repair and rental of photographic equipment	29,529	1,889	13,887	9,944	3,662
Photographic equipment	2,210,307	462,498	598,435	538,107	610,982
Photographer fees	2,205,932	444,233	625,180	553,405	583,399
Fireworks	129,053	–	72,522	34,421	24,166
Souvenirs	218,734	84,606	23,402	91,023	16,111
Visual goods	119,210	24,143	45,262	37,480	12,693
Pinball, electronic video games	634,329	95,943	164,332	237,501	136,940

Note: Numbers may not add to total because of rounding. (–) means sample is too small to make a reliable estimate.
Source: Calculations by New Strategist based on the 2000 Consumer Expenditure Survey

Table 3.25 Entertainment: Market shares by region, 2000

(percentage of total annual spending on entertainment accounted for by consumer units by region, 2000)

	total consumer units	Northeast	Midwest	South	West
Share of total consumer units	100.0%	19.2%	23.5%	35.0%	22.3%
Share of total before-tax income	100.0	20.4	23.4	32.9	23.3
Share of total spending	100.0	19.6	24.2	31.9	24.2
Share of entertainment spending	100.0	19.7	25.7	30.3	24.2
FEES AND ADMISSIONS	**100.0%**	**21.5%**	**25.9%**	**26.8%**	**25.8%**
Recreation expenses on trips	100.0	20.7	25.4	24.3	29.5
Social, recreation, civic club membership	100.0	20.5	26.5	30.7	22.4
Fees for participant sports	100.0	17.3	28.0	29.5	25.2
Participant sports on trips	100.0	18.1	25.4	26.0	30.6
Movie, theater, opera, ballet	100.0	22.5	24.7	24.1	28.6
Movie, other admissions on trips	100.0	22.8	26.0	23.6	27.7
Admission to sports events	100.0	20.9	26.5	30.5	22.0
Admission to sports events on trips	100.0	22.8	26.0	23.6	27.7
Fees for recreational lessons	100.0	27.0	24.4	25.4	23.1
Other entertainment services on trips	100.0	20.7	25.4	24.3	29.5
TELEVISION, RADIO, SOUND EQUIPMENT	**100.0**	**19.3**	**25.1**	**32.3**	**23.3**
Television	**100.0**	**20.1**	**23.4**	**34.1**	**22.3**
Cable service and community antenna	100.0	21.7	23.1	35.0	20.2
Black-and-white TV	100.0	10.5	11.9	59.0	18.8
Color TV, console	100.0	13.5	22.3	37.7	26.6
Color TV, portable, table model	100.0	18.5	21.8	30.8	28.8
VCRs and video disc players	100.0	14.9	26.3	29.1	29.7
Video cassettes, tapes, and discs	100.0	16.1	25.4	28.4	30.0
Video game hardware and software	100.0	19.8	28.8	29.6	21.8
Repair of TV, radio, and sound equipment	100.0	15.3	23.9	39.3	21.6
Rental of television sets	100.0	0.4	14.9	56.4	28.7
Radio and sound equipment	**100.0**	**17.3**	**29.7**	**27.3**	**25.7**
Radios	100.0	8.3	35.0	30.2	27.3
Tape recorders and players	100.0	11.6	20.0	38.8	30.2
Sound components and component systems	100.0	23.0	24.4	27.6	25.1
Miscellaneous sound equipment	100.0	–	15.1	48.3	37.2
Sound equipment accessories	100.0	13.0	20.7	28.5	38.5
Satellite dishes	100.0	9.7	16.7	46.1	27.6
Compact disc, tape, record, video mail order clubs	100.0	21.2	23.8	27.1	27.9
Records, CDs, audio tapes, needles	100.0	17.9	26.1	28.2	27.7
Rental of VCR, radio, sound equipment	100.0	11.0	13.1	66.1	8.7
Musical instruments and accessories	100.0	16.3	49.1	16.1	18.5
Rental and repair of musical instruments	100.0	19.8	26.7	20.1	33.5
Rental of video cassettes, tapes, discs, films	100.0	17.4	24.5	31.2	26.9

	total consumer units	Northeast	Midwest	South	West
PETS, TOYS, PLAYGROUND EQUIPMENT	100.0%	18.2%	25.4%	32.8%	23.7%
Pets	100.0	18.4	23.5	33.1	25.1
Pet food	100.0	17.9	24.6	34.5	23.2
Pet purchase, supplies, and medicines	100.0	15.7	24.6	31.3	28.8
Pet services	100.0	17.9	19.3	31.2	31.6
Veterinarian services	100.0	20.6	22.5	33.1	23.8
Toys, games, hobbies, and tricycles	100.0	18.2	27.9	32.4	21.5
Playground equipment	100.0	6.9	54.8	22.8	15.5
OTHER ENTERTAINMENT SUPPLIES, EQUIPMENT, SERVICES	100.0	19.3	26.9	29.8	24.0
Unmotored recreational vehicles	100.0	23.2	32.2	18.3	26.3
Boat without motor and boat trailers	100.0	9.5	59.7	13.0	17.7
Trailer and other attachable campers	100.0	30.0	18.6	20.9	30.5
Motorized recreational vehicles	100.0	11.2	28.3	43.2	17.2
Motorized camper	100.0	–	39.6	45.9	14.5
Other vehicle	100.0	10.5	45.3	39.1	5.1
Motorboats	100.0	17.8	12.7	44.0	25.5
Rental of recreational vehicles	100.0	27.0	34.9	12.9	25.2
Boat and trailer rental on trips	100.0	15.0	46.2	6.5	32.2
Rental of campers on trips	100.0	42.5	17.7	–	40.2
Rental of other vehicles on trips	100.0	25.4	40.5	18.0	16.4
Rental of other RVs	100.0	–	–	23.3	89.3
Outboard motors	100.0	1.2	67.7	13.3	17.8
Docking and landing fees	100.0	29.1	22.1	25.7	23.1
Sports, recreation, exercise equipment	100.0	21.9	23.6	28.3	26.1
Athletic gear, game tables, exercise equipment	100.0	22.1	23.7	29.1	25.2
Bicycles	100.0	19.0	27.0	21.1	32.9
Camping equipment	100.0	49.8	10.0	14.2	24.6
Hunting and fishing equipment	100.0	12.6	29.0	38.6	20.1
Winter sports equipment	100.0	28.2	25.8	7.9	38.1
Water sports equipment	100.0	3.6	29.1	40.2	27.1
Other sports equipment	100.0	15.9	21.0	32.6	30.4
Rental and repair of miscellaneous sports equipment	100.0	18.5	33.8	17.0	30.9
Photographic equipment and supplies	100.0	20.0	26.4	27.0	26.6
Film	100.0	20.2	25.8	29.3	24.7
Other photographic supplies	100.0	9.6	3.9	27.2	60.4
Film processing	100.0	19.7	26.1	28.2	26.0
Repair and rental of photographic equipment	100.0	6.4	47.0	33.7	12.4
Photographic equipment	100.0	20.9	27.1	24.3	27.6
Photographer fees	100.0	20.1	28.3	25.1	26.4
Fireworks	100.0	–	56.2	26.7	18.7
Souvenirs	100.0	38.7	10.7	41.6	7.4
Visual goods	100.0	20.3	38.0	31.4	10.6
Pinball, electronic video games	100.0	15.1	25.9	37.4	21.6

Note: Numbers may not add to total because of rounding. (–) means sample is too small to make a reliable estimate.
Source: Calculations by New Strategist based on the 2000 Consumer Expenditure Survey

4

Spending on Financial Products and Services, 2000

Trends in spending on financial products and services were mixed during the 1990s. Spending on miscellaneous financial services (such as bank, accounting, credit card, and legal fees) fell 30 percent between 1990 and 2000, after adjusting for inflation. During the same time, spending on cash contributions (a category that includes child support as well as gifts to charities) rose 11 percent. Spending on pensions and Social Security barely changed during the decade, but spending on life and other personal insurance fell 12 percent. While households spent less on federal and state taxes, their local taxes rose 48 percent. Overall, Americans devoted 14 percent of their spending in 2000 to miscellaneous financial services, cash contributions, life insurance, and pensions—slightly less than the 15 percent of 1990.

Households headed by 45-to-54-year-olds spend more than other households on most financial categories. They spend 19 percent more than average on financial products services and 43 percent more on pensions and Social Security. Householders aged 55 to 64 spend the most on life and other personal insurance, an average of $587 in 2000. The biggest spenders on cash gifts to non-household members are householders aged 75 or older.

Households with incomes of $70,000 or more represent just 19 percent of consumer units but account for 52 percent of spending on personal insurance and pensions. This high-income group accounts for 63 percent of household contributions to educational organizations and 73 percent of contributions to political organizations.

Married couples with children at home spend more than other household types on most financial categories because their households are larger and more likely to include more than one wage earner. Married couples without children at home spend the most on gifts of cash, stocks, and bonds to non-household members. They are also the biggest spenders on gifts to charities.

Blacks and Hispanics spend less than average on most financial products and services. The few exceptions include funeral expenses, for which black households spend 30 percent more than average. Hispanic households spend 8 percent more than average on finance charges other than those for mortgages and vehicles.

Households in the West spend more than the average household on many financial products and services. They spend 25 percent more than average on legal fees and 56 percent more on accounting fees. Households in the South and West are the biggest spenders on bank service charges, while those in the Midwest spend the most on funerals.

Table 4.1 Financial: Average spending by age, 2000

(average annual spending of consumer units (CU) on financial products and services, cash contributions, and miscellaneous items, by age of consumer unit reference person, 2000)

	total consumer units	under 25	25 to 34	35 to 44	45 to 54	55 to 64	65 to 74	75+
Number of consumer units (in thousands, add 000)	109,367	8,306	18,887	23,983	21,874	14,161	11,538	10,617
Average number of persons per CU	2.5	1.9	2.9	3.3	2.7	2.1	1.9	1.5
Average before-tax income of CU	$44,649.00	$19,744.00	$45,498.00	$56,500.00	$58,889.00	$48,108.00	$29,349.00	$20,563.00
Average spending of CU, total	38,044.67	22,543.18	38,945.27	45,149.37	46,160.28	39,340.03	30,781.81	21,908.04
FINANCIAL PRODUCTS AND SERVICES	$775.78	$321.68	$803.59	$852.50	$926.72	$823.63	$760.79	$553.14
Miscellaneous fees, gambling losses	41.60	11.00	36.28	37.74	46.93	62.29	52.59	35.06
Legal fees	103.96	48.00	100.59	135.16	113.64	89.64	130.16	53.95
Funeral expenses	70.69	15.15	15.25	44.94	57.37	112.92	132.51	174.83
Safe deposit box rental	4.58	0.37	1.15	3.35	5.28	6.20	8.70	8.67
Checking accounts, other bank service charges	19.89	14.42	22.71	25.68	26.31	17.79	11.00	5.34
Cemetery lots, vaults, and maintenance fees	13.47	1.73	2.23	9.43	7.78	21.35	48.38	15.09
Accounting fees	55.18	8.71	30.87	56.82	59.93	80.51	68.82	72.71
Miscellaneous personal services	31.39	26.76	48.16	21.59	45.40	24.65	21.27	19.82
Finance charges, except mortgage and vehicles	253.37	157.80	352.03	300.24	319.70	211.28	133.61	96.38
Occupational expenses	96.24	27.84	121.90	121.83	141.70	101.61	19.45	28.91
Expenses for other properties	79.73	8.70	68.26	85.03	96.60	88.78	131.03	41.12
Interest paid, home equity line of credit (other property)	0.98	–	0.39	3.93	0.23	–	–	–
Credit card memberships	4.71	1.19	3.78	6.75	5.83	6.59	3.27	1.27
CASH CONTRIBUTIONS	1,192.44	189.36	647.95	1,002.96	1,536.69	1,301.30	2,022.24	1,617.65
Cash contributions to non-household members, including students, alimony, child support	296.07	32.83	182.30	362.00	554.07	324.24	191.07	100.44
Gifts of cash, stocks, bonds to non-household members	267.48	16.51	88.48	68.39	175.02	302.65	782.88	815.47
Contributions to charities	139.87	14.29	56.88	96.59	179.12	142.54	406.31	109.51
Contributions to religious organizations	445.63	106.60	273.24	456.58	567.03	466.29	589.77	558.43
Contributions to educational organizations	19.96	0.35	15.25	9.99	38.32	32.33	13.57	18.83
Political contributions	6.65	0.43	3.08	3.47	13.26	6.99	9.18	8.19
Other contributions	16.80	18.35	28.72	5.94	9.87	26.26	29.46	6.78
PERSONAL INSURANCE AND PENSIONS	3,364.92	1,215.67	3,614.28	4,570.39	4,794.77	3,838.44	1,379.26	460.17
Life and other personal insurance	398.61	54.07	241.57	412.40	549.07	586.93	514.30	229.51
Life, endowment, annuity, other personal insurance	387.97	49.40	236.67	400.86	536.73	574.77	494.06	221.94
Other nonhealth insurance	10.64	4.67	4.90	11.54	12.34	12.16	20.24	7.57
Pensions and Social Security	2,966.31	1,161.60	3,372.70	4,157.99	4,245.69	3,251.50	864.96	230.65
Deductions for government retirement	70.32	10.24	51.90	90.77	132.22	94.75	18.01	0.62
Deductions for railroad retirement	3.29	–	5.36	4.41	6.04	1.45	–	0.03
Deductions for private pensions	362.64	43.55	410.69	549.57	528.43	392.33	98.95	9.88
Nonpayroll deposit to retirement plans	389.65	24.84	302.26	515.57	637.27	620.04	121.70	19.85
Deductions for Social Security	2,140.41	1,082.97	2,602.50	2,997.68	2,941.74	2,142.94	626.29	200.28
PERSONAL TAXES	3,117.45	930.80	2,833.48	3,874.30	4,740.13	3,999.09	1,796.10	803.89
Federal income taxes	2,409.33	695.63	2,205.11	3,013.84	3,706.76	3,062.09	1,338.43	573.84
State and local income taxes	561.80	225.74	570.22	734.36	848.27	701.86	200.43	83.17
Other taxes	146.32	9.43	58.14	126.09	185.1	235.14	257.24	146.89

Note: (–) means sample is too small to make a reliable estimate.
Source: Bureau of Labor Statistics, unpublished tables from the 2000 Consumer Expenditure Survey

Table 4.2 Financial: Indexed spending by age, 2000

(indexed average annual spending of consumer units (CU) on financial products and services, cash contributions, and miscellaneous items, by age of consumer unit reference person, 2000; index definition: an index of 100 is the average for all consumer units; an index of 132 means that spending by consumer units in that group is 32 percent above the average for all consumer units; an index of 68 indicates spending that is 32 percent below the average for all consumer units)

	total consumer units	under 25	25 to 34	35 to 44	45 to 54	55 to 64	65 to 74	75+
Average spending of CU, total	$38,045	$22,543	$38,945	$45,149	$46,160	$39,340	$30,782	$21,908
Average spending of CU, index	100	59	102	119	121	103	81	58
FINANCIAL PRODUCTS AND SERVICES	**100**	**41**	**104**	**110**	**119**	**106**	**98**	**71**
Miscellaneous fees, gambling losses	100	26	87	91	113	150	126	84
Legal fees	100	46	97	130	109	86	125	52
Funeral expenses	100	21	22	64	81	160	187	247
Safe deposit box rental	100	8	25	73	115	135	190	189
Checking accounts, other bank service charges	100	72	114	129	132	89	55	27
Cemetery lots, vaults, and maintenance fees	100	13	17	70	58	159	359	112
Accounting fees	100	16	56	103	109	146	125	132
Miscellaneous personal services	100	85	153	69	145	79	68	63
Finance charges, except mortgage and vehicles	100	62	139	118	126	83	53	38
Occupational expenses	100	29	127	127	147	106	20	30
Expenses for other properties	100	11	86	107	121	111	164	52
Interest paid, home equity line of credit (other property)	100	–	40	401	23	–	–	–
Credit card memberships	100	25	80	143	124	140	69	27
CASH CONTRIBUTIONS	**100**	**16**	**54**	**84**	**129**	**109**	**170**	**136**
Cash contributions to non-household members, including students, alimony, child support	100	11	62	122	187	110	65	34
Gifts of cash, stocks, bonds to non-household members	100	6	33	26	65	113	293	305
Contributions to charities	100	10	41	69	128	102	290	78
Contributions to religious organizations	100	24	61	102	127	105	132	125
Contributions to educational organizations	100	2	76	50	192	162	68	94
Political contributions	100	6	46	52	199	105	138	123
Other contributions	100	109	171	35	59	156	175	40
PERSONAL INSURANCE AND PENSIONS	**100**	**36**	**107**	**136**	**142**	**114**	**41**	**14**
Life and other personal insurance	100	14	61	103	138	147	129	58
Life, endowment, annuity, other personal insurance	100	13	61	103	138	148	127	57
Other nonhealth insurance	100	44	46	108	116	114	190	71
Pensions and Social Security	100	39	114	140	143	110	29	8
Deductions for government retirement	100	15	74	129	188	135	26	1
Deductions for railroad retirement	100	–	163	134	184	44	–	1
Deductions for private pensions	100	12	113	152	146	108	27	3
Nonpayroll deposit to retirement plans	100	6	78	132	164	159	31	5
Deductions for Social Security	100	51	122	140	137	100	29	9
PERSONAL TAXES	**100**	**30**	**91**	**124**	**152**	**128**	**58**	**26**
Federal income taxes	100	29	92	125	154	127	56	24
State and local income taxes	100	40	101	131	151	125	36	15
Other taxes	100	6	40	86	127	161	176	100

Note: (–) means sample is too small to make a reliable estimate.
Source: Calculations by New Strategist based on the 2000 Consumer Expenditure Survey

Table 4.3 Financial: Indexed per capita spending by age, 2000

(indexed average annual per capita spending of consumer units (CU) on financial products and services, cash contributions, and miscellaneous items, by age of consumer unit reference person, 2000; index definition: an index of 100 is the average for all consumer units; an index of 132 means that spending by consumer units in that group is 32 percent above the average for all consumer units; an index of 68 indicates spending that is 32 percent below the average for all consumer units)

	total consumer units	under 25	25 to 34	35 to 44	45 to 54	55 to 64	65 to 74	75+
Per capita spending of CU, total	$15,218	$11,865	$13,429	$13,682	$17,096	$18,733	$16,201	$14,605
Per capita spending of CU, index	100	78	88	90	112	123	106	96
FINANCIAL PRODUCTS AND SERVICES	**100**	**55**	**89**	**83**	**111**	**126**	**129**	**119**
Miscellaneous fees, gambling losses	100	35	75	69	104	178	166	140
Legal fees	100	61	83	98	101	103	165	86
Funeral expenses	100	28	19	48	75	190	247	412
Safe deposit box rental	100	11	22	55	107	161	250	316
Checking accounts, other bank service charges	100	95	98	98	122	106	73	45
Cemetery lots, vaults, and maintenance fees	100	17	14	53	53	189	473	187
Accounting fees	100	21	48	78	101	174	164	220
Miscellaneous personal services	100	112	132	52	134	93	89	105
Finance charges, except mortgage and vehicles	100	82	120	90	117	99	69	63
Occupational expenses	100	38	109	96	136	126	27	50
Expenses for other properties	100	14	74	81	112	133	216	86
Interest paid, home equity line of credit (other property)	100	–	34	304	22	–	–	–
Credit card memberships	100	33	69	109	115	167	91	45
CASH CONTRIBUTIONS	**100**	**21**	**47**	**64**	**119**	**130**	**223**	**226**
Cash contributions to non-household members, including students, alimony, child support	100	15	53	93	173	130	85	57
Gifts of cash, stocks, bonds to non-household members	100	8	29	19	61	135	385	508
Contributions to charities	100	13	35	52	119	121	382	130
Contributions to religious organizations	100	31	53	78	118	125	174	209
Contributions to educational organizations	100	2	66	38	178	193	89	157
Political contributions	100	9	40	40	185	125	182	205
Other contributions	100	144	147	27	54	186	231	67
PERSONAL INSURANCE AND PENSIONS	**100**	**48**	**93**	**103**	**132**	**136**	**54**	**23**
Life and other personal insurance	100	18	52	78	128	175	170	96
Life, endowment, annuity, other personal insurance	100	17	53	78	128	176	168	95
Other nonhealth insurance	100	58	40	82	107	136	250	119
Pensions and Social Security	100	52	98	106	133	130	38	13
Deductions for government retirement	100	19	64	98	174	160	34	1
Deductions for railroad retirement	100	–	140	102	170	52	–	2
Deductions for private pensions	100	16	98	115	135	129	36	5
Nonpayroll deposit to retirement plans	100	8	67	100	151	189	41	8
Deductions for Social Security	100	67	105	106	127	119	39	16
PERSONAL TAXES	**100**	**39**	**78**	**94**	**141**	**153**	**76**	**43**
Federal income taxes	100	38	79	95	142	151	73	40
State and local income taxes	100	53	87	99	140	149	47	25
Other taxes	100	8	34	65	117	191	231	167

Note: Per capita indexes account for household size and show how much each person in a particular household demographic segment spends relative to a person in the average household. (–) means sample is too small to make a reliable estimate.
Source: Calculations by New Strategist based on the 2000 Consumer Expenditure Survey

Table 4.4 Financial: Total spending by age, 2000

(total annual spending on financial products and services, cash contributions, and miscellaneous items, by consumer unit (CU) age group, 2000; numbers in thousands)

	total consumer units	under 25	25 to 34	35 to 44	45 to 54	55 to 64	65 to 74	75+
Number of consumer units	109,367	8,306	18,887	23,983	21,874	14,161	11,538	10,617
Total spending of all CUs	$4,160,831,424	$187,243,653	$735,559,314	$1,082,817,341	$1,009,709,965	$557,094,165	$355,160,524	$232,597,661
FINANCIAL PRODUCTS, SERVICES	**$84,844,731**	**$2,671,874**	**$15,177,404**	**$20,445,508**	**$20,271,073**	**$11,663,424**	**$8,777,995**	**$5,872,687**
Miscellaneous fees, gambling losses	4,549,667	91,366	685,220	905,118	1,026,547	882,089	606,783	372,232
Legal fees	11,369,793	398,688	1,899,843	3,241,542	2,485,761	1,269,392	1,501,786	572,787
Funeral expenses	7,731,153	125,836	288,027	1,077,796	1,254,911	1,599,060	1,528,900	1,856,170
Safe deposit box rental	500,901	3,073	21,720	80,343	115,495	87,798	100,381	92,049
Checking accounts, other bank service charges	2,175,310	119,773	428,924	615,883	575,505	251,924	126,918	56,695
Cemetery lots, vaults, and maintenance fees	1,473,173	14,369	42,118	226,160	170,180	302,337	558,208	160,211
Accounting fees	6,034,871	72,345	583,042	1,362,714	1,310,909	1,140,102	794,045	771,962
Miscellaneous personal services	3,433,030	222,269	909,598	517,793	993,080	349,069	245,413	210,429
Finance charges, except mortgage, vehicles	27,710,317	1,310,687	6,648,791	7,200,656	6,993,118	2,991,936	1,541,592	1,023,266
Occupational expenses	10,525,480	231,239	2,302,325	2,921,849	3,099,546	1,438,899	224,414	306,937
Expenses for other properties	8,719,831	72,262	1,289,227	2,039,274	2,113,028	1,257,214	1,511,824	436,571
Interest paid, home equity line of credit (other property)	107,180	–	7,366	94,253	5,031	–	–	–
Credit card memberships	515,119	9,884	71,393	161,885	127,525	93,321	37,729	13,484
CASH CONTRIBUTIONS	**130,413,585**	**1,572,824**	**12,237,832**	**24,053,990**	**33,613,557**	**18,427,709**	**23,332,605**	**17,174,590**
Cash contributions to non-household members, including students, alimony, child support	32,380,288	272,686	3,443,100	8,681,846	12,119,727	4,591,563	2,204,566	1,066,371
Gifts of cash, stocks, bonds to non-household members	29,253,485	137,132	1,671,122	1,640,197	3,828,387	4,285,827	9,032,869	8,657,845
Contributions to charities	15,297,162	118,693	1,074,293	2,316,518	3,918,071	2,018,509	4,688,005	1,162,668
Contributions to religious organizations	48,737,216	885,420	5,160,684	10,950,158	12,403,214	6,603,133	6,804,766	5,928,851
Contributions to educational organizations	2,182,965	2,907	288,027	239,590	838,212	457,825	156,571	199,918
Political contributions	727,291	3,572	58,172	83,221	290,049	98,985	105,919	86,953
Other contributions	1,837,366	152,415	542,435	142,459	215,896	371,868	339,909	71,983
PERSONAL INSURANCE, PENSIONS	**368,011,206**	**10,097,355**	**68,262,906**	**109,611,663**	**104,880,799**	**54,356,149**	**15,913,902**	**4,885,625**
Life and other personal insurance	43,594,780	449,105	4,562,533	9,890,589	12,010,357	8,311,516	5,933,993	2,436,708
Life, endowment, annuity, other personal insurance	42,431,115	410,316	4,469,986	9,613,825	11,740,432	8,139,318	5,700,464	2,356,337
Other nonhealth insurance	1,163,665	38,789	92,546	276,764	269,925	172,198	233,529	80,371
Pensions and Social Security	324,416,426	9,648,250	63,700,185	99,721,074	92,870,223	46,044,492	9,979,908	2,448,811
Deductions for government retirement	7,690,687	85,053	980,235	2,176,937	2,892,180	1,341,755	207,799	6,583
Deductions for railroad retirement	359,817	–	101,234	105,765	132,119	20,533	–	319
Deductions for private pensions	39,660,849	361,726	7,756,702	13,180,337	11,558,878	5,555,785	1,141,685	104,896
Nonpayroll deposit to retirement plans	42,614,852	206,321	5,708,785	12,364,915	13,939,644	8,780,386	1,404,175	210,747
Deductions for Social Security	234,090,220	8,995,149	49,153,418	71,893,359	64,347,621	30,346,173	7,226,134	2,126,373
PERSONAL TAXES	**340,946,154**	**7,731,225**	**53,515,937**	**92,917,337**	**103,685,604**	**56,631,113**	**20,723,402**	**8,534,900**
Federal income taxes	263,501,194	5,777,903	41,647,913	72,280,925	81,081,668	43,362,256	15,442,805	6,092,459
State and local income taxes	61,442,381	1,874,996	10,769,745	17,612,156	18,555,058	9,939,039	2,312,561	883,016
Other taxes	16,002,579	78,326	1,098,090	3,024,016	4,048,877	3,329,818	2,968,035	1,559,531

Note: Numbers may not add to total because of rounding. (–) means sample is too small to make a reliable estimate.
Source: Calculations by New Strategist based on the 2000 Consumer Expenditure Survey

Table 4.5 Financial: Market shares by age, 2000

(percentage of total annual spending on financial products and services, cash contributions, and miscellaneous items accounted for by consumer unit age groups, 2000)

	total consumer units	under 25	25 to 34	35 to 44	45 to 54	55 to 64	65 to 74	75+
Share of total consumer units	100.0%	7.6%	17.3%	21.9%	20.0%	12.9%	10.5%	9.7%
Share of total before-tax income	100.0	3.4	17.6	27.7	26.4	14.0	6.9	4.5
Share of total spending	100.0	4.5	17.7	26.0	24.3	13.4	8.5	5.6
FINANCIAL PRODUCTS AND SERVICES	**100.0%**	**3.1%**	**17.9%**	**24.1%**	**23.9%**	**13.7%**	**10.3%**	**6.9%**
Miscellaneous fees, gambling losses	100.0	2.0	15.1	19.9	22.6	19.4	13.3	8.2
Legal fees	100.0	3.5	16.7	28.5	21.9	11.2	13.2	5.0
Funeral expenses	100.0	1.6	3.7	13.9	16.2	20.7	19.8	24.0
Safe deposit box rental	100.0	0.6	4.3	16.0	23.1	17.5	20.0	18.4
Checking accounts, other bank service charges	100.0	5.5	19.7	28.3	26.5	11.6	5.8	2.6
Cemetery lots, vaults, and maintenance fees	100.0	1.0	2.9	15.4	11.6	20.5	37.9	10.9
Accounting fees	100.0	1.2	9.7	22.6	21.7	18.9	13.2	12.8
Miscellaneous personal services	100.0	6.5	26.5	15.1	28.9	10.2	7.1	6.1
Finance charges, except mortgage and vehicles	100.0	4.7	24.0	26.0	25.2	10.8	5.6	3.7
Occupational expenses	100.0	2.2	21.9	27.8	29.4	13.7	2.1	2.9
Expenses for other properties	100.0	0.8	14.8	23.4	24.2	14.4	17.3	5.0
Interest paid, home equity line of credit (other property)	100.0	–	6.9	87.9	4.7	–	–	–
Credit card memberships	100.0	1.9	13.9	31.4	24.8	18.1	7.3	2.6
CASH CONTRIBUTIONS	**100.0**	**1.2**	**9.4**	**18.4**	**25.8**	**14.1**	**17.9**	**13.2**
Cash contributions to non-household members, including students, alimony, child support	100.0	0.8	10.6	26.8	37.4	14.2	6.8	3.3
Gifts of cash, stocks, bonds to non-household members	100.0	0.5	5.7	5.6	13.1	14.7	30.9	29.6
Contributions to charities	100.0	0.8	7.0	15.1	25.6	13.2	30.6	7.6
Contributions to religious organizations	100.0	1.8	10.6	22.5	25.4	13.5	14.0	12.2
Contributions to educational organizations	100.0	0.1	13.2	11.0	38.4	21.0	7.2	9.2
Political contributions	100.0	0.5	8.0	11.4	39.9	13.6	14.6	12.0
Other contributions	100.0	8.3	29.5	7.8	11.8	20.2	18.5	3.9
PERSONAL INSURANCE AND PENSIONS	**100.0**	**2.7**	**18.5**	**29.8**	**28.5**	**14.8**	**4.3**	**1.3**
Life and other personal insurance	100.0	1.0	10.5	22.7	27.5	19.1	13.6	5.6
Life, endowment, annuity, other personal insurance	100.0	1.0	10.5	22.7	27.7	19.2	13.4	5.6
Other nonhealth insurance	100.0	3.3	8.0	23.8	23.2	14.8	20.1	6.9
Pensions and Social Security	100.0	3.0	19.6	30.7	28.6	14.2	3.1	0.8
Deductions for government retirement	100.0	1.1	12.7	28.3	37.6	17.4	2.7	0.1
Deductions for railroad retirement	100.0	–	28.1	29.4	36.7	5.7	–	0.1
Deductions for private pensions	100.0	0.9	19.6	33.2	29.1	14.0	2.9	0.3
Nonpayroll deposit to retirement plans	100.0	0.5	13.4	29.0	32.7	20.6	3.3	0.5
Deductions for Social Security	100.0	3.8	21.0	30.7	27.5	13.0	3.1	0.9
PERSONAL TAXES	**100.0**	**2.3**	**15.7**	**27.3**	**30.4**	**16.6**	**6.1**	**2.5**
Federal income taxes	100.0	2.2	15.8	27.4	30.8	16.5	5.9	2.3
State and local income taxes	100.0	3.1	17.5	28.7	30.2	16.2	3.8	1.4
Other taxes	100.0	0.5	6.9	18.9	25.3	20.8	18.5	9.7

Note: Numbers may not add to total because of rounding. (–) means sample is too small to make a reliable estimate.
Source: Calculations by New Strategist based on the 2000 Consumer Expenditure Survey

Table 4.6 Financial: Average spending by income, 2000

(average annual spending on financial products and services, cash contributions, and miscellaneous items, by before-tax income of consumer units (CU), 2000; complete income reporters only)

	complete income reporters	under $10,000	$10,000– 19,999	$20,000– 29,999	$30,000– 39,999	$40,000– 49,999	$50,000– 69,999	$70,000 or more
Number of consumer units								
(in thousands, add 000)	81,454	10,810	14,714	12,039	9,477	7,653	11,337	15,424
Average number of persons per CU	2.5	1.7	2.1	2.4	2.5	2.6	2.9	3.2
Average before-tax income of CU	$44,649.00	$5,739.61	$14,586.29	$24,527.00	$34,422.00	$44,201.00	$58,561.00	$112,586.00
Average spending of CU, total	40,238.44	16,455.72	22,620.20	29,851.59	35,609.24	42,323.03	49,245.37	75,963.85
FINANCIAL PRODUCTS AND SERVICES	**$831.81**	**$386.61**	**$491.03**	**$692.31**	**$803.92**	**$1,005.69**	**$1,067.56**	**$1,328.33**
Miscellaneous fees, gambling losses	46.43	20.17	40.80	56.22	56.90	66.38	40.47	47.70
Legal fees	109.83	28.11	84.22	101.26	97.01	110.84	141.33	182.44
Funeral expenses	64.28	71.28	75.56	78.67	54.32	39.84	52.00	64.66
Safe deposit box rental	4.73	2.49	4.08	3.87	5.55	4.84	4.04	7.55
Checking accounts, other bank service charges	21.22	12.72	11.86	20.64	21.65	26.98	29.88	27.06
Cemetery lots, vaults, and maintenance fees	15.19	8.43	21.99	17.09	24.91	12.67	11.03	10.32
Accounting fees	59.45	19.10	27.98	47.41	79.85	67.69	58.74	111.04
Miscellaneous personal services	37.74	19.78	23.79	11.38	49.42	102.32	16.51	56.49
Finance charges, except mortgage and vehicles	275.41	97.22	143.47	233.75	279.34	383.48	391.85	417.06
Occupational expenses	113.93	84.62	17.30	80.01	70.80	108.11	198.77	220.14
Expenses for other properties	77.08	21.65	37.54	37.97	59.55	76.26	111.32	170.19
Interest paid, home equity line of credit (other property)	1.29	–	–	–	1.14	–	6.20	1.55
Credit card memberships	5.22	1.05	2.45	4.04	3.48	6.29	5.43	12.11
CASH CONTRIBUTIONS	**1,344.06**	**323.60**	**651.79**	**1,250.90**	**1,125.04**	**1,003.10**	**1,269.16**	**3,151.20**
Cash contributions to non-household members, including students, alimony, child support	285.06	63.44	112.94	91.57	263.22	215.65	370.41	740.72
Gifts of cash, stocks, bonds to non-household members	320.57	92.77	232.25	551.70	250.21	281.82	240.06	505.68
Contributions to charities	159.96	18.32	46.01	285.16	121.16	75.91	97.39	381.72
Contributions to religious organizations	530.36	129.36	249.29	306.90	464.81	418.38	530.47	1,349.70
Contributions to educational organizations	18.87	4.16	6.36	8.17	13.47	3.82	14.91	63.15
Political contributions	7.38	0.29	3.05	2.83	1.9i	3.47	3.15	28.42
Other contributions	21.89	15.26	1.89	4.57	10.26	4.04	12.76	81.82
PERSONAL INSURANCE AND PENSIONS	**4,308.33**	**332.77**	**811.23**	**1,908.21**	**2,999.53**	**4,303.01**	**6,050.71**	**11,830.30**
Life and other personal insurance	414.92	123.29	218.00	311.03	354.09	337.78	500.17	901.25
Life, endowment, annuity, other personal insurance	404.12	119.54	214.44	304.66	343.09	326.05	489.14	875.92
Other nonhealth insurance	10.79	3.76	3.55	6.37	11.00	11.72	11.03	25.33
Pensions and Social Security	3,893.41	209.47	593.24	1,597.18	2,645.43	3,965.23	5,550.54	10,929.05
Deductions for government retirement	93.68	0.23	5.42	25.51	65.84	80.76	136.13	288.89
Deductions for railroad retirement	4.42	–	0.20	0.03	1.96	4.41	10.18	12.25
Deductions for private pensions	481.97	2.37	14.58	90.27	192.82	346.28	673.51	1,673.91
Nonpayroll deposit to retirement plans	490.74	53.68	67.78	164.64	188.84	509.40	527.71	1,604.13
Deductions for Social Security	2,822.61	153.17	505.27	1,316.74	2,195.97	3,024.38	4,203.02	7,349.88
PERSONAL TAXES	**3,117.45**	**309.75**	**151.59**	**861.38**	**1,701.89**	**2,703.09**	**4,128.09**	**10,008.07**
Federal income taxes	2,409.33	227.02	32.42	577.64	1,235.56	2,023.61	3,094.50	8,044.98
State and local income taxes	561.80	47.96	39.40	179.29	335.82	511.36	847.24	1,672.94
Other taxes	146.32	34.76	79.78	104.44	130.51	168.12	186.35	290.16

Note: (–) means sample is too small to make a reliable estimate.
Source: Bureau of Labor Statistics, unpublished tables from the 2000 Consumer Expenditure Survey; calculations by New Strategist

Table 4.7 Financial: Indexed spending by income, 2000

(indexed average annual spending of consumer units (CU) on financial products and services, cash contributions, and miscellaneous items, by before-tax income of consumer unit, 2000; complete income reporters only; index definition: an index of 100 is the average for all consumer units; an index of 132 means that spending by consumer units in that group is 32 percent above the average for all consumer units; an index of 68 indicates spending that is 32 percent below the average for all consumer units)

	complete income reporters	under $10,000	$10,000–19,999	$20,000–29,999	$30,000–39,999	$40,000–49,999	$50,000–69,999	$70,000 or more
Average spending of CU, total	$40,238	$16,456	$22,620	$29,852	$35,609	$42,323	$49,245	$75,964
Average spending of CU, index	100	41	56	74	88	105	122	189
FINANCIAL PRODUCTS AND SERVICES	**100**	**46**	**59**	**83**	**97**	**121**	**128**	**160**
Miscellaneous fees, gambling losses	100	43	88	121	123	143	87	103
Legal fees	100	26	77	92	88	101	129	166
Funeral expenses	100	111	118	122	85	62	81	101
Safe deposit box rental	100	53	86	82	117	102	85	160
Checking accounts, other bank service charges	100	60	56	97	102	127	141	128
Cemetery lots, vaults, and maintenance fees	100	55	145	113	164	83	73	68
Accounting fees	100	32	47	80	134	114	99	187
Miscellaneous personal services	100	52	63	30	131	271	44	150
Finance charges, except mortgage and vehicles	100	35	52	85	101	139	142	151
Occupational expenses	100	74	15	70	62	95	174	193
Expenses for other properties	100	28	49	49	77	99	144	221
Interest paid, home equity line of credit (other property)	100	–	–	–	88	–	481	120
Credit card memberships	100	20	47	77	67	120	104	232
CASH CONTRIBUTIONS	**100**	**24**	**48**	**93**	**84**	**75**	**94**	**234**
Cash contributions to non-household members, including students, alimony, child support	100	22	40	32	92	76	130	260
Gifts of cash, stocks, bonds to non-household members	100	29	72	172	78	88	75	158
Contributions to charities	100	11	29	178	76	47	61	239
Contributions to religious organizations	100	24	47	58	88	79	100	254
Contributions to educational organizations	100	22	34	43	71	20	79	335
Political contributions	100	4	41	38	26	47	43	385
Other contributions	100	70	9	21	47	18	58	374
PERSONAL INSURANCE AND PENSIONS	**100**	**8**	**19**	**44**	**70**	**100**	**140**	**275**
Life and other personal insurance	100	30	53	75	85	81	121	217
Life, endowment, annuity, other personal insurance	100	30	53	75	85	81	121	217
Other nonhealth insurance	100	35	33	59	102	109	102	235
Pensions and Social Security	100	5	15	41	68	102	143	281
Deductions for government retirement	100	0	6	27	70	86	145	308
Deductions for railroad retirement	100	–	4	1	44	100	230	277
Deductions for private pensions	100	0	3	19	40	72	140	347
Nonpayroll deposit to retirement plans	100	11	14	34	38	104	108	327
Deductions for Social Security	100	5	18	47	78	107	149	260
PERSONAL TAXES	**100**	**10**	**5**	**28**	**55**	**87**	**132**	**321**
Federal income taxes	100	9	1	24	51	84	128	334
State and local income taxes	100	9	7	32	60	91	151	298
Other taxes	100	24	55	71	89	115	127	198

Note: (–) means sample is too small to make a reliable estimate.
Source: Calculations by New Strategist based on the 2000 Consumer Expenditure Survey

Table 4.8 Financial: Indexed per capita spending by income, 2000

(indexed average annual per capita spending of consumer units (CU) on financial products and services, cash contributions, and miscellaneous items, by before-tax income of consumer unit, 2000; complete income reporters only; index definition: an index of 100 is the average for all consumer units; an index of 132 means that spending by consumer units in that group is 32 percent above the average for all consumer units; an index of 68 indicates spending that is 32 percent below the average for all consumer units)

	complete income reporters	under $10,000	$10,000– 19,999	$20,000– 29,999	$30,000– 39,999	$40,000– 49,999	$50,000– 69,999	$70,000 or more
Per capita spending of CU, total	$16,095	$9,492	$10,819	$12,438	$14,244	$16,278	$16,981	$23,739
Per capita spending of CU, index	100	59	67	77	88	101	106	147
FINANCIAL PRODUCTS AND SERVICES	**100**	**67**	**71**	**87**	**97**	**116**	**111**	**125**
Miscellaneous fees, gambling losses	100	63	105	126	123	137	75	80
Legal fees	100	37	92	96	88	97	111	130
Funeral expenses	100	160	141	127	85	60	70	79
Safe deposit box rental	100	76	103	85	117	98	74	125
Checking accounts, other bank service charges	100	86	67	101	102	122	121	100
Cemetery lots, vaults, and maintenance fees	100	80	173	117	164	80	63	53
Accounting fees	100	46	56	83	134	109	85	146
Miscellaneous personal services	100	76	75	31	131	261	38	117
Finance charges, except mortgage and vehicles	100	51	62	88	101	134	123	118
Occupational expenses	100	107	18	73	62	91	150	151
Expenses for other properties	100	41	58	51	77	95	125	172
Interest paid, home equity line of credit (other property)	100	–	–	–	88	–	414	94
Credit card memberships	100	29	56	81	67	116	90	181
CASH CONTRIBUTIONS	**100**	**35**	**58**	**97**	**84**	**72**	**81**	**183**
Cash contributions to non-household members, including students, alimony, child support	100	32	47	33	92	73	112	203
Gifts of cash, stocks, bonds to non-household members	100	42	87	179	78	85	65	123
Contributions to charities	100	17	34	186	76	46	52	186
Contributions to religious organizations	100	35	56	60	88	76	86	199
Contributions to educational organizations	100	32	40	45	71	19	68	261
Political contributions	100	6	49	40	26	45	37	301
Other contributions	100	101	10	22	47	18	50	292
PERSONAL INSURANCE AND PENSIONS	**100**	**11**	**23**	**46**	**70**	**96**	**121**	**215**
Life and other personal insurance	100	43	63	78	85	78	104	170
Life, endowment, annuity, other personal insurance	100	43	63	79	85	78	104	169
Other nonhealth insurance	100	50	39	61	102	104	88	183
Pensions and Social Security	100	8	18	43	68	98	123	219
Deductions for government retirement	100	0	7	28	70	83	125	241
Deductions for railroad retirement	100	–	5	1	44	96	199	217
Deductions for private pensions	100	1	4	20	40	69	120	271
Nonpayroll deposit to retirement plans	100	16	17	35	38	100	93	255
Deductions for Social Security	100	8	21	49	78	103	128	203
PERSONAL TAXES	**100**	**14**	**6**	**29**	**55**	**83**	**114**	**251**
Federal income taxes	100	14	2	25	51	81	111	261
State and local income taxes	100	12	8	33	60	88	130	233
Other taxes	100	34	65	74	89	110	110	155

Note: Per capita indexes account for household size and show how much each person in a particular household demographic segment spends relative to a person in the average household. (–) means sample is too small to make a reliable estimate.
Source: Calculations by New Strategist based on the 2000 Consumer Expenditure Survey

Table 4.9 Financial: Total spending by income, 2000

(total annual spending on financial products and services, cash contributions, and miscellaneous items, by before-tax income group of consumer units (CU), 2000; complete income reporters only; numbers in thousands)

	complete income reporters	under $10,000	$10,000–19,999	$20,000–29,999	$30,000–39,999	$40,000–49,999	$50,000–69,999	$70,000 or more
Number of consumer units	81,454	10,810	14,714	12,039	9,477	7,653	11,337	15,424
Total spending of all CUs	$3,277,581,892	$177,886,368	$332,833,656	$359,383,292	$337,468,767	$323,898,149	$558,294,760	$1,171,666,422
FINANCIAL PRODUCTS, SERVICES	**$67,754,252**	**$4,179,218**	**$7,225,013**	**$8,334,720**	**$7,618,750**	**$7,696,546**	**$12,102,928**	**$20,488,162**
Miscellaneous fees, gambling losses	3,781,909	218,000	600,359	676,833	539,241	508,006	458,808	735,725
Legal fees	8,946,093	303,871	1,239,188	1,219,069	919,364	848,259	1,602,258	2,813,955
Funeral expenses	5,235,863	770,507	1,111,857	947,108	514,791	304,896	589,524	997,316
Safe deposit box rental	385,277	26,890	60,101	46,591	52,597	37,041	45,801	116,451
Checking accounts, other bank service charges	1,728,454	137,464	174,506	248,485	205,177	206,478	338,750	417,373
Cemetery lots, vaults, and maintenance fees	1,237,286	91,121	323,495	205,747	236,072	96,964	125,047	159,176
Accounting fees	4,842,440	206,445	411,695	570,769	756,738	518,032	665,935	1,712,681
Miscellaneous personal services	3,074,074	213,832	349,978	137,004	468,353	783,055	187,174	871,302
Finance charges, except mortgage, vehicles	22,433,246	1,050,896	2,110,945	2,814,116	2,647,305	2,934,772	4,442,403	6,432,733
Occupational expenses	9,280,054	914,771	254,560	963,240	670,972	827,366	2,253,455	3,395,439
Expenses for other properties	6,278,474	234,064	552,301	457,121	564,355	583,618	1,262,035	2,625,011
Interest paid, home equity line of credit (other property)	105,076	–	–	–	10,804	–	70,289	23,907
Credit card memberships	425,190	11,323	36,095	48,638	32,980	48,137	61,560	186,785
CASH CONTRIBUTIONS	**109,479,063**	**3,498,153**	**9,590,423**	**15,059,585**	**10,662,004**	**7,676,724**	**14,388,467**	**48,604,109**
Cash contributions to non-household members, including students, alimony, child support	23,219,277	685,784	1,661,790	1,102,411	2,494,536	1,650,369	4,199,338	11,424,865
Gifts of cash, stocks, bonds to non-household members	26,111,709	1,002,820	3,417,366	6,641,916	2,371,240	2,156,768	2,721,560	7,799,608
Contributions to charities	13,029,382	198,012	676,988	3,433,041	1,148,233	580,939	1,104,110	5,887,649
Contributions to religious organizations	43,199,943	1,398,361	3,667,984	3,694,769	4,405,004	3,201,862	6,013,938	20,817,773
Contributions to educational organizations	1,537,037	44,999	93,575	98,359	127,655	29,234	169,035	974,026
Political contributions	601,131	3,163	44,914	34,070	18,101	26,556	35,712	438,350
Other contributions	1,783,028	164,977	27,807	55,018	97,234	30,918	144,660	1,261,992
PERSONAL INSURANCE, PENSIONS	**350,930,712**	**3,597,193**	**11,936,455**	**22,972,940**	**28,426,546**	**32,930,936**	**68,596,899**	**182,470,547**
Life and other personal insurance	33,796,894	1,332,811	3,207,585	3,744,490	3,355,711	2,585,030	5,670,427	13,900,880
Life, endowment, annuity, other personal insurance	32,917,190	1,292,242	3,155,236	3,667,802	3,251,464	2,495,261	5,545,380	13,510,190
Other nonhealth insurance	878,889	40,641	52,269	76,688	104,247	89,693	125,047	390,690
Pensions and Social Security	317,133,818	2,264,382	8,728,870	19,228,450	25,070,740	30,345,905	62,926,472	168,569,667
Deductions for government retirement	7,630,611	2,521	79,678	307,115	623,966	618,056	1,543,306	4,455,839
Deductions for railroad retirement	360,027	–	2,893	361	18,575	33,750	115,411	188,944
Deductions for private pensions	39,258,384	25,657	214,565	1,086,761	1,827,355	2,650,081	7,635,583	25,818,388
Nonpayroll deposit to retirement plans	39,972,736	580,321	997,247	1,982,101	1,789,637	3,898,438	5,982,648	24,742,101
Deductions for Social Security	229,912,875	1,655,811	7,434,568	15,852,233	20,811,208	23,145,580	47,649,638	113,364,549
PERSONAL TAXES	**253,928,772**	**3,348,368**	**2,230,559**	**10,370,154**	**16,128,812**	**20,686,748**	**46,800,156**	**154,364,472**
Federal income taxes	196,249,566	2,454,071	476,962	6,954,208	11,709,402	15,486,687	35,082,347	124,085,772
State and local income taxes	45,760,857	518,453	579,711	2,158,472	3,182,566	3,913,438	9,605,160	25,803,427
Other taxes	11,918,349	375,807	1,173,886	1,257,353	1,236,843	1,286,622	2,112,650	4,475,428

Note: Numbers may not add to total because of rounding. (–) means sample is too small to make a reliable estimate.
Source: Calculations by New Strategist based on the 2000 Consumer Expenditure Survey

Table 4.10 Financial: Market shares by income, 2000

(percentage of total annual spending on financial products and services, cash contributions, and miscellaneous items accounted for by before-tax income group of consumer units, 2000; complete income reporters only)

	complete income reporters	under $10,000	$10,000–19,999	$20,000–29,999	$30,000–39,999	$40,000–49,999	$50,000–69,999	$70,000 or more
Share of total consumer units	100.0%	13.3%	18.1%	14.8%	11.6%	9.4%	13.9%	18.9%
Share of total before-tax income	100.0	1.7	5.9	8.1	9.0	9.3	18.3	47.7
Share of total spending	100.0	5.4	10.2	11.0	10.3	9.9	17.0	35.7
FINANCIAL PRODUCTS AND SERVICES	100.0%	6.2%	10.7%	12.3%	11.2%	11.4%	17.9%	30.2%
Miscellaneous fees, gambling losses	100.0	5.8	15.9	17.9	14.3	13.4	12.1	19.5
Legal fees	100.0	3.4	13.9	13.6	10.3	9.5	17.9	31.5
Funeral expenses	100.0	14.7	21.2	18.1	9.8	5.8	11.3	19.0
Safe deposit box rental	100.0	7.0	15.6	12.1	13.7	9.6	11.9	30.2
Checking accounts, other bank service charges	100.0	8.0	10.1	14.4	11.9	11.9	19.6	24.1
Cemetery lots, vaults, and maintenance fees	100.0	7.4	26.1	16.6	19.1	7.8	10.1	12.9
Accounting fees	100.0	4.3	8.5	11.8	15.6	10.7	13.8	35.4
Miscellaneous personal services	100.0	7.0	11.4	4.5	15.2	25.5	6.1	28.3
Finance charges, except mortgage and vehicles	100.0	4.7	9.4	12.5	11.8	13.1	19.8	28.7
Occupational expenses	100.0	9.9	2.7	10.4	7.2	8.9	24.3	36.6
Expenses for other properties	100.0	3.7	8.8	7.3	9.0	9.3	20.1	41.8
Interest paid, home equity line of credit (other property)	100.0	–	–	–	10.3	–	66.9	22.8
Credit card memberships	100.0	2.7	8.5	11.4	7.8	11.3	14.5	43.9
CASH CONTRIBUTIONS	100.0	3.2	8.8	13.8	9.7	7.0	13.1	44.4
Cash contributions to non-household members, including students, alimony, child support	100.0	3.0	7.2	4.7	10.7	7.1	18.1	49.2
Gifts of cash, stocks, bonds to non-household members	100.0	3.8	13.1	25.4	9.1	8.3	10.4	29.9
Contributions to charities	100.0	1.5	5.2	26.3	8.8	4.5	8.5	45.2
Contributions to religious organizations	100.0	3.2	8.5	8.6	10.2	7.4	13.9	48.2
Contributions to educational organizations	100.0	2.9	6.1	6.4	8.3	1.9	11.0	63.4
Political contributions	100.0	0.5	7.5	5.7	3.0	4.4	5.9	72.9
Other contributions	100.0	9.3	1.6	3.1	5.5	1.7	8.1	70.8
PERSONAL INSURANCE AND PENSIONS	100.0	1.0	3.4	6.5	8.1	9.4	19.5	52.0
Life and other personal insurance	100.0	3.9	9.5	11.1	9.9	7.6	16.8	41.1
Life, endowment, annuity, other personal insurance	100.0	3.9	9.6	11.1	9.9	7.6	16.8	41.0
Other nonhealth insurance	100.0	4.6	5.9	8.7	11.9	10.2	14.2	44.5
Pensions and Social Security	100.0	0.7	2.8	6.1	7.9	9.6	19.8	53.2
Deductions for government retirement	100.0	0.0	1.0	4.0	8.2	8.1	20.2	58.4
Deductions for railroad retirement	100.0	–	0.8	0.1	5.2	9.4	32.1	52.5
Deductions for private pensions	100.0	0.1	0.5	2.8	4.7	6.8	19.4	65.8
Nonpayroll deposit to retirement plans	100.0	1.5	2.5	5.0	4.5	9.8	15.0	61.9
Deductions for Social Security	100.0	0.7	3.2	6.9	9.1	10.1	20.7	49.3
PERSONAL TAXES	100.0	1.3	0.9	4.1	6.4	8.1	18.4	60.8
Federal income taxes	100.0	1.3	0.2	3.5	6.0	7.9	17.9	63.2
State and local income taxes	100.0	1.1	1.3	4.7	7.0	8.6	21.0	56.4
Other taxes	100.0	3.2	9.8	10.5	10.4	10.8	17.7	37.6

Note: Numbers may not add to total because of rounding. (–) means sample is too small to make a reliable estimate.
Source: Calculations by New Strategist based on the 2000 Consumer Expenditure Survey

Table 4.11 Financial: Average spending by household type, 2000

(average annual spending of consumer units (CU) on financial products and services, cash contributions, and miscellaneous items, by type of consumer unit, 2000)

| | total married couples | married couples, no children | married couples with children | | | | single parent, at least one child <18 | single person |
			total	oldest child under 6	oldest child 6 to 17	oldest child 18 or older		
Number of consumer units (in thousands, add 000)	56,287	22,805	28,777	5,291	15,396	8,090	6,132	32,323
Average number of persons per CU	3.2	2.0	3.9	3.5	4.1	3.8	2.9	1.0
Average before-tax income of CU	$60,588.00	$53,232.00	$66,913.00	$62,928.00	$69,472.00	$64,725.00	$25,095.00	$24,977.00
Average spending of CU, total	48,619.37	42,195.54	53,585.53	50,755.90	54,170.40	54,550.20	28,923.25	23,059.00
FINANCIAL PRODUCTS AND SERVICES	**$908.38**	**$878.15**	**$893.10**	**$686.56**	**$960.35**	**$908.61**	**$784.34**	**$560.84**
Miscellaneous fees, gambling losses	44.28	50.72	43.50	10.75	38.34	81.74	16.91	34.22
Legal fees	98.42	106.56	80.62	59.90	88.50	79.18	217.72	76.51
Funeral expenses	91.54	114.60	51.53	2.78	47.82	90.49	27.61	45.94
Safe deposit box rental	5.61	7.25	4.65	2.25	4.67	6.17	0.94	4.29
Checking accounts, other bank service charges	23.13	16.42	26.83	21.92	29.00	25.93	18.71	14.08
Cemetery lots, vaults, and maintenance fees	17.69	26.32	10.48	1.25	2.99	30.76	0.99	10.79
Accounting fees	63.68	72.10	58.73	43.53	61.17	64.03	30.73	56.50
Miscellaneous personal services	33.53	33.61	37.10	25.34	40.42	39.91	56.63	29.43
Finance charges, except mortgage and vehicles	293.69	232.27	323.50	337.55	357.13	250.31	270.48	166.55
Occupational expenses	123.56	109.65	137.07	125.44	152.55	115.21	93.10	64.42
Expenses for other properties	105.35	102.95	109.64	50.50	124.70	119.66	48.14	55.18
Interest paid, home equity line of credit (other property)	1.67	–	2.44	–	4.57	–	–	0.38
Credit card memberships	6.22	5.69	7.00	5.35	8.51	5.21	2.39	2.52
CASH CONTRIBUTIONS	**1,511.59**	**1,914.69**	**1,220.43**	**848.04**	**1,269.97**	**1,369.69**	**407.37**	**1,046.71**
Cash contributions to non-household members, including students, alimony, child support	304.79	324.14	310.88	178.37	314.92	389.87	233.64	310.23
Gifts of cash, stocks, bonds to non-household members	318.30	599.91	121.74	74.81	135.05	127.10	17.75	305.68
Contributions to charities	209.23	319.48	117.26	109.47	117.26	122.36	25.54	78.30
Contributions to religious organizations	628.07	607.52	628.17	469.10	656.55	678.21	124.99	310.52
Contributions to educational organizations	24.28	22.53	23.12	10.04	24.17	29.67	3.76	14.70
Political contributions	9.36	9.12	10.61	1.57	11.22	15.38	0.43	4.27
Other contributions	17.56	31.99	8.64	4.67	10.81	7.11	1.27	23.01
PERSONAL INSURANCE AND PENSIONS	**4,647.70**	**3,948.61**	**5,257.30**	**5,387.75**	**5,333.59**	**5,026.77**	**1,833.50**	**1,777.57**
Life and other personal insurance	608.44	613.23	601.36	481.82	589.59	701.95	150.46	154.89
Life, endowment, annuity, other personal insurance	592.42	593.00	590.26	469.41	578.95	690.83	148.80	148.85
Other nonhealth insurance	16.02	20.23	11.10	12.41	10.64	11.12	1.66	6.05
Pensions and Social Security	4,039.26	3,335.39	4,655.94	4,905.93	4,744.00	4,324.82	1,683.04	1,622.68
Deductions for government retirement	84.93	87.08	88.29	97.67	82.47	93.22	52.00	52.99
Deductions for railroad retirement	3.23	1.69	4.60	7.26	3.53	4.87	0.47	4.79
Deductions for private pensions	524.80	487.09	585.31	673.19	576.90	543.82	110.49	196.83
Nonpayroll deposit to retirement plans	521.71	534.79	538.11	605.21	551.59	468.56	234.39	278.44
Deductions for Social Security	2,904.57	2,224.75	3,439.64	3,522.60	3,529.51	3,214.34	1,285.69	1,089.62
PERSONAL TAXES	**4,307.85**	**4,357.67**	**4,457.20**	**4,163.73**	**4,734.35**	**4,120.31**	**597.37**	**2,090.23**
Federal income taxes	3,360.55	3,395.56	3,467.04	3,260.47	3,646.33	3,261.22	352.93	1,621.44
State and local income taxes	752.37	726.29	815.53	756.23	906.44	678.26	203.47	359.55
Other taxes	194.93	235.82	174.63	147.03	181.58	180.83	40.96	109.24

Note: Average spending figures for total consumer units can be found on Average Spending by Age and Average Spending by Region tables. (–) means sample is too small to make a reliable estimate.
Source: Bureau of Labor Statistics, unpublished tables from the 2000 Consumer Expenditure Survey

Table 4.12 Financial: Indexed spending by household type, 2000

(indexed average annual spending of consumer units (CU) on financial products and services, cash contributions, and miscellaneous items, by type of consumer unit, 2000; index definition: an index of 100 is the average for all consumer units; an index of 132 means that spending by consumer units in that group is 32 percent above the average for all consumer units; an index of 68 indicates spending that is 32 percent below the average for all consumer units)

| | total married couples | married couples, no children | married couples with children | | | | single parent, at least one child <18 | single person |
			total	oldest child under 6	oldest child 6 to 17	oldest child 18 or older		
Average spending of CU, total	$48,619	$42,196	$53,586	$50,756	$54,170	$54,550	$28,923	$23,059
Average spending of CU, index	128	111	141	133	142	143	76	61
FINANCIAL PRODUCTS AND SERVICES	**117**	**113**	**115**	**88**	**124**	**117**	**101**	**72**
Miscellaneous fees, gambling losses	106	122	105	26	92	196	41	82
Legal fees	95	103	78	58	85	76	209	74
Funeral expenses	129	162	73	4	68	128	39	65
Safe deposit box rental	122	158	102	49	102	135	21	94
Checking accounts, other bank service charges	116	83	135	110	146	130	94	71
Cemetery lots, vaults, and maintenance fees	131	195	78	9	22	228	7	80
Accounting fees	115	131	106	79	111	116	56	102
Miscellaneous personal services	107	107	118	81	129	127	180	94
Finance charges, except mortgage and vehicles	116	92	128	133	141	99	107	66
Occupational expenses	128	114	142	130	159	120	97	67
Expenses for other properties	132	129	138	63	156	150	60	69
Interest paid, home equity line of credit (other property)	170	–	249	–	466	–	–	39
Credit card memberships	132	121	149	114	181	111	51	54
CASH CONTRIBUTIONS	**127**	**161**	**102**	**71**	**107**	**115**	**34**	**88**
Cash contributions to non-household members, including students, alimony, child support	103	109	105	60	106	132	79	105
Gifts of cash, stocks, bonds to non-household members	119	224	46	28	50	48	7	114
Contributions to charities	150	228	84	78	84	87	18	56
Contributions to religious organizations	141	136	141	105	147	152	28	70
Contributions to educational organizations	122	113	116	50	121	149	19	74
Political contributions	141	137	160	24	169	231	6	64
Other contributions	105	190	51	28	64	42	8	137
PERSONAL INSURANCE AND PENSIONS	**138**	**117**	**156**	**160**	**159**	**149**	**54**	**53**
Life and other personal insurance	153	154	151	121	148	176	38	39
Life, endowment, annuity, other personal insurance	153	153	152	121	149	178	38	38
Other nonhealth insurance	151	190	104	117	100	105	16	57
Pensions and Social Security	136	112	157	165	160	146	57	55
Deductions for government retirement	121	124	126	139	117	133	74	75
Deductions for railroad retirement	98	51	140	221	107	148	14	146
Deductions for private pensions	145	134	161	186	159	150	30	54
Nonpayroll deposit to retirement plans	134	137	138	155	142	120	60	71
Deductions for Social Security	136	104	161	165	165	150	60	51
PERSONAL TAXES	**138**	**140**	**143**	**134**	**152**	**132**	**19**	**67**
Federal income taxes	139	141	144	135	151	135	15	67
State and local income taxes	134	129	145	135	161	121	36	64
Other taxes	133	161	119	100	124	124	28	75

Note: Spending index for total consumer units is 100. (–) means sample is too small to make a reliable estimate.
Source: Calculations by New Strategist based on the 2000 Consumer Expenditure Survey

Table 4.13 Financial: Indexed per capita spending by household type, 2000

(indexed average annual per capita spending of consumer units (CU) on financial products and services, cash contributions, and miscellaneous items, by type of consumer unit, 2000; index definition: an index of 100 is the average for all consumer units; an index of 132 means that spending by consumer units in that group is 32 percent above the average for all consumer units; an index of 68 indicates spending that is 32 percent below the average for all consumer units)

	total married couples	married couples, no children	married couples with children				single parent, at least one child <18	single person
			total	oldest child under 6	oldest child 6 to 17	oldest child 18 or older		
Per capita spending of CU, total	$15,194	$21,098	$13,740	$14,502	$13,212	$14,355	$9,974	$23,059
Per capita spending of CU, index	100	139	90	95	87	94	66	152
FINANCIAL PRODUCTS AND SERVICES	**91**	**141**	**74**	**63**	**75**	**77**	**87**	**181**
Miscellaneous fees, gambling losses	83	152	67	18	56	129	35	206
Legal fees	74	128	50	41	52	50	181	184
Funeral expenses	101	203	47	3	41	84	34	162
Safe deposit box rental	96	198	65	35	62	89	18	234
Checking accounts, other bank service charges	91	103	86	79	89	86	81	177
Cemetery lots, vaults, and maintenance fees	103	244	50	7	14	150	6	200
Accounting fees	90	163	68	56	68	76	48	256
Miscellaneous personal services	83	134	76	58	79	84	156	234
Finance charges, except mortgage and vehicles	91	115	82	95	86	65	92	164
Occupational expenses	100	142	91	93	97	79	83	167
Expenses for other properties	103	161	88	45	95	99	52	173
Interest paid, home equity line of credit (other property)	133	–	160	–	284	–	–	97
Credit card memberships	103	151	95	81	110	73	44	134
CASH CONTRIBUTIONS	**99**	**201**	**66**	**51**	**65**	**76**	**29**	**219**
Cash contributions to non-household members, including students, alimony, child support	80	137	67	43	65	87	68	262
Gifts of cash, stocks, bonds to non-household members	93	280	29	20	31	31	6	286
Contributions to charities	117	286	54	56	51	58	16	140
Contributions to religious organizations	110	170	90	75	90	100	24	174
Contributions to educational organizations	95	141	74	36	74	98	16	184
Political contributions	110	171	102	17	103	152	6	161
Other contributions	82	238	33	20	39	28	7	342
PERSONAL INSURANCE AND PENSIONS	**108**	**147**	**100**	**114**	**97**	**98**	**47**	**132**
Life and other personal insurance	119	192	97	86	90	116	33	97
Life, endowment, annuity, other personal insurance	119	191	98	86	91	117	33	96
Other nonhealth insurance	118	238	67	83	61	69	13	142
Pensions and Social Security	106	141	101	118	98	96	49	137
Deductions for government retirement	94	155	80	99	72	87	64	188
Deductions for railroad retirement	77	64	90	158	65	97	12	364
Deductions for private pensions	113	168	103	133	97	99	26	136
Nonpayroll deposit to retirement plans	105	172	89	111	86	79	52	179
Deductions for Social Security	106	130	103	118	101	99	52	127
PERSONAL TAXES	**108**	**175**	**92**	**95**	**93**	**87**	**17**	**168**
Federal income taxes	109	176	92	97	92	89	13	168
State and local income taxes	105	162	93	96	98	79	31	160
Other taxes	104	201	77	72	76	81	24	187

Note: Per capita indexes account for household size and show how much each person in a particular household demographic segment spends relative to a person in the average household. Spending index for total consumer units is 100. (–) means sample is too small to make a reliable estimate.
Source: Calculations by New Strategist based on the 2000 Consumer Expenditure Survey

Table 4.14 Financial: Total spending by household type, 2000

(total annual spending on financial products and services, cash contributions, and miscellaneous items, by consumer unit (CU) type, 2000; numbers in thousands)

	total married couples	married couples, no children	married couples with children total	oldest child under 6	oldest child 6 to 17	oldest child 18 or older	single parent, at least one child <18	single person
Number of consumer units	56,287	22,805	28,777	5,291	15,396	8,090	6,132	32,323
Total spending of all CUs	$2,736,638,479	$962,269,290	$1,542,030,797	$268,549,467	$834,007,478	$441,311,118	$177,357,369	$745,336,057
FINANCIAL PRODUCTS, SERVICES	**$51,129,985**	**$20,026,211**	**$25,700,739**	**$3,632,589**	**$14,785,549**	**$7,350,655**	**$4,809,573**	**$18,128,031**
Miscellaneous fees, gambling losses	2,492,388	1,156,670	1,251,800	56,878	590,283	661,277	103,692	1,106,093
Legal fees	5,539,767	2,430,101	2,320,002	316,931	1,362,546	640,566	1,335,059	2,473,033
Funeral expenses	5,152,512	2,613,453	1,482,879	14,709	736,237	732,064	169,305	1,484,919
Safe deposit box rental	315,770	165,336	133,813	11,905	71,899	49,915	5,764	138,666
Checking accounts, other bank service charges	1,301,918	374,458	772,087	115,979	446,484	209,774	114,730	455,108
Cemetery lots, vaults, and maintenance fees	995,717	600,228	301,583	6,614	46,034	248,848	6,071	348,765
Accounting fees	3,584,356	1,644,241	1,690,073	230,317	941,773	518,003	188,436	1,826,250
Miscellaneous personal services	1,887,303	766,476	1,067,627	134,074	622,306	322,872	347,255	951,266
Finance charges, except mortgage, vehicles	16,530,929	5,296,917	9,309,360	1,785,977	5,498,373	2,025,008	1,658,583	5,383,396
Occupational expenses	6,954,822	2,500,568	3,944,463	663,703	2,348,660	932,049	570,889	2,082,248
Expenses for other properties	5,929,835	2,347,775	3,155,110	267,196	1,919,881	968,049	295,194	1,783,583
Interest paid, home equity line of credit (other property)	93,999	–	70,216	–	70,360	–	–	12,283
Credit card memberships	350,105	129,760	201,439	28,307	131,020	42,149	14,655	81,454
CASH CONTRIBUTIONS	**85,082,866**	**43,664,505**	**35,120,314**	**4,486,980**	**19,552,458**	**11,080,792**	**2,497,993**	**33,832,807**
Cash contributions to non-household members, including students, alimony, child support	17,155,715	7,392,013	8,946,194	943,756	4,848,508	3,154,048	1,432,680	10,027,564
Gifts of cash, stocks, bonds to non-household members	17,916,152	13,680,948	3,503,312	395,820	2,079,230	1,028,239	108,843	9,880,495
Contributions to charities	11,776,929	7,285,741	3,374,391	579,206	1,805,335	989,892	156,611	2,530,891
Contributions to religious organizations	35,352,176	13,854,494	18,076,848	2,482,008	10,108,244	5,486,719	766,439	10,036,938
Contributions to educational organizations	1,366,648	513,797	665,324	53,122	372,121	240,030	23,056	475,148
Political contributions	526,846	207,982	305,324	8,307	172,743	124,424	2,637	138,019
Other contributions	988,400	729,532	248,633	24,709	166,431	57,520	7,788	743,752
PERSONAL INSURANCE, PENSIONS	**261,605,090**	**90,048,051**	**151,289,322**	**28,506,585**	**82,115,952**	**40,666,569**	**11,243,022**	**57,456,395**
Life and other personal insurance	34,247,262	13,984,710	17,305,337	2,549,310	9,077,328	5,678,776	922,621	5,006,509
Life, endowment, annuity, other personal insurance	33,345,545	13,523,365	16,985,912	2,483,648	8,913,514	5,588,815	912,442	4,811,279
Other nonhealth insurance	901,718	461,345	319,425	65,661	163,813	89,961	10,179	195,554
Pensions and Social Security	227,357,828	76,063,569	133,983,985	25,957,276	73,038,624	34,987,794	10,320,401	52,449,886
Deductions for government retirement	4,780,455	1,985,859	2,540,721	516,772	1,269,708	754,150	318,864	1,712,796
Deductions for railroad retirement	181,807	38,540	132,374	38,413	54,348	39,398	2,882	154,827
Deductions for private pensions	29,539,418	11,108,087	16,843,466	3,561,848	8,881,952	4,399,504	677,525	6,362,136
Nonpayroll deposit to retirement plans	29,365,491	12,195,886	15,485,191	3,202,166	8,492,280	3,790,650	1,437,279	9,000,016
Deductions for Social Security	163,489,532	50,735,424	98,982,520	18,638,077	54,340,336	26,004,011	7,883,851	35,219,787
PERSONAL TAXES	**242,475,953**	**99,376,664**	**128,264,844**	**22,030,295**	**72,890,053**	**33,333,308**	**3,663,073**	**67,562,504**
Federal income taxes	189,155,278	77,435,746	99,771,010	17,251,147	56,138,897	26,383,270	2,164,167	52,409,805
State and local income taxes	42,348,650	16,563,043	23,468,507	4,001,213	13,955,550	5,487,123	1,247,678	11,621,735
Other taxes	10,972,025	5,377,875	5,025,328	777,936	2,795,606	1,462,915	251,167	3,530,965

Note: Total spending figures for total consumer units can be found on Total Spending by Age and Total Spending by Region tables. Spending by type of consumer unit will not add to total because not all types of consumer units are shown. (–) means sample is too small to make a reliable estimate.
Source: Calculations by New Strategist based on the 2000 Consumer Expenditure Survey

Table 4.15 Financial: Market shares by household type, 2000

(percentage of total annual spending on financial products and services, cash contributions, and miscellaneous items accounted for by types of consumer units, 2000)

	total married couples	married couples, no children	married couples with children				single parent, at least one child <18	single person
			total	oldest child under 6	oldest child 6 to 17	oldest child 18 or older		
Share of total consumer units	51.5%	20.9%	26.3%	4.8%	14.1%	7.4%	5.6%	29.6%
Share of total before-tax income	69.8	24.9	39.4	6.8	21.9	10.7	3.2	16.5
Share of total spending	65.8	23.1	37.1	6.5	20.0	10.6	4.3	17.9
FINANCIAL PRODUCTS AND SERVICES	**60.3%**	**23.6%**	**30.3%**	**4.3%**	**17.4%**	**8.7%**	**5.7%**	**21.4%**
Miscellaneous fees, gambling losses	54.8	25.4	27.5	1.3	13.0	14.5	2.3	24.3
Legal fees	48.7	21.4	20.4	2.8	12.0	5.6	11.7	21.8
Funeral expenses	66.6	33.8	19.2	0.2	9.5	9.5	2.2	19.2
Safe deposit box rental	63.0	33.0	26.7	2.4	14.4	10.0	1.2	27.7
Checking accounts, other bank service charges	59.8	17.2	35.5	5.3	20.5	9.6	5.3	20.9
Cemetery lots, vaults, and maintenance fees	67.6	40.7	20.5	0.4	3.1	16.9	0.4	23.7
Accounting fees	59.4	27.2	28.0	3.8	15.6	8.6	3.1	30.3
Miscellaneous personal services	55.0	22.3	31.1	3.9	18.1	9.4	10.1	27.7
Finance charges, except mortgage and vehicles	59.7	19.1	33.6	6.4	19.8	7.3	6.0	19.4
Occupational expenses	66.1	23.8	37.5	6.3	22.3	8.9	5.4	19.8
Expenses for other properties	68.0	26.9	36.2	3.1	22.0	11.1	3.4	20.5
Interest paid, home equity line of credit (other property)	87.7	–	65.5	–	65.6	–	–	11.5
Credit card memberships	68.0	25.2	39.1	5.5	25.4	8.2	2.8	15.8
CASH CONTRIBUTIONS	**65.2**	**33.5**	**26.9**	**3.4**	**15.0**	**8.5**	**1.9**	**25.9**
Cash contributions to non-household members, including students, alimony, child support	53.0	22.8	27.6	2.9	15.0	9.7	4.4	31.0
Gifts of cash, stocks, bonds to non-household members	61.2	46.8	12.0	1.4	7.1	3.5	0.4	33.8
Contributions to charities	77.0	47.6	22.1	3.8	11.8	6.5	1.0	16.5
Contributions to religious organizations	72.5	28.4	37.1	5.1	20.7	11.3	1.6	20.6
Contributions to educational organizations	62.6	23.5	30.5	2.4	17.0	11.0	1.1	21.8
Political contributions	72.4	28.6	42.0	1.1	23.8	17.1	0.4	19.0
Other contributions	53.8	39.7	13.5	1.3	9.1	3.1	0.4	40.5
PERSONAL INSURANCE AND PENSIONS	**71.1**	**24.5**	**41.1**	**7.7**	**22.3**	**11.1**	**3.1**	**15.6**
Life and other personal insurance	78.6	32.1	39.7	5.8	20.8	13.0	2.1	11.5
Life, endowment, annuity, other personal insurance	78.6	31.9	40.0	5.9	21.0	13.2	2.2	11.3
Other nonhealth insurance	77.5	39.6	27.4	5.6	14.1	7.7	0.9	16.8
Pensions and Social Security	70.1	23.4	41.3	8.0	22.5	10.8	3.2	16.2
Deductions for government retirement	62.2	25.8	33.0	6.7	16.5	9.8	4.1	22.3
Deductions for railroad retirement	50.5	10.7	36.8	10.7	15.1	10.9	0.8	43.0
Deductions for private pensions	74.5	28.0	42.5	9.0	22.4	11.1	1.7	16.0
Nonpayroll deposit to retirement plans	68.9	28.6	36.3	7.5	19.9	8.9	3.4	21.1
Deductions for Social Security	69.8	21.7	42.3	8.0	23.2	11.1	3.4	15.0
PERSONAL TAXES	**71.1**	**29.1**	**37.6**	**6.5**	**21.4**	**9.8**	**1.1**	**19.8**
Federal income taxes	71.8	29.4	37.9	6.5	21.3	10.0	0.8	19.9
State and local income taxes	68.9	27.0	38.2	6.5	22.7	8.9	2.0	18.9
Other taxes	68.6	33.6	31.4	4.9	17.5	9.1	1.6	22.1

Note: Market share for total consumer units is 100.0%. Market shares by type of consumer unit will not add to total because not all types of consumer units are shown. (–) means sample is too small to make a reliable estimate.
Source: Calculations by New Strategist based on the 2000 Consumer Expenditure Survey

Table 4.16 Financial: Average spending by race and Hispanic origin, 2000

(average annual spending of consumer units (CU) on financial products and services, cash contributions, and miscellaneous items, by race and Hispanic origin of consumer unit reference person, 2000)

	total consumer units	race		Hispanic origin	
		black	white and others	Hispanic	non-Hispanic
Number of consumer units (in thousands, add 000)	109,367	13,230	96,137	9,473	99,894
Average number of persons per CU	2.5	2.7	2.5	3.4	2.4
Average before-tax income of CU	$44,649.00	$32,657.00	$46,260.00	$34,891.00	$45,669.00
Average spending of CU, total	38,044.67	28,152.24	39,406.20	32,734.95	38,548.91
FINANCIAL PRODUCTS AND SERVICES	**$775.78**	**$571.65**	**$803.88**	**$601.82**	**$792.24**
Miscellaneous fees, gambling losses	41.60	18.42	44.79	26.70	42.98
Legal fees	103.96	34.08	113.58	40.45	109.98
Funeral expenses	70.69	91.67	67.80	44.14	73.21
Safe deposit box rental	4.58	1.58	4.99	1.00	4.92
Checking accounts, other bank service charges	19.89	17.15	20.27	17.63	20.11
Cemetery lots, vaults, and maintenance fees	13.47	10.43	13.89	12.57	13.56
Accounting fees	55.18	20.26	59.99	38.31	56.78
Miscellaneous personal services	31.39	34.34	30.98	24.08	32.06
Finance charges, except mortgage and vehicles	253.37	241.46	255.01	274.64	251.35
Occupational expenses	96.24	52.94	102.20	86.00	97.21
Expenses for other properties	79.73	46.22	84.34	31.75	84.28
Interest paid, home equity line of credit (other property)	0.98	–	1.11	–	1.07
Credit card memberships	4.71	3.09	4.93	4.54	4.73
CASH CONTRIBUTIONS	**1,192.44**	**699.69**	**1,260.26**	**645.36**	**1,244.32**
Cash contributions to non-household members, including students, alimony, child support	296.07	184.15	311.47	199.87	305.19
Gifts of cash, stocks, bonds to non-household members	267.48	43.40	298.32	102.03	283.17
Contributions to charities	139.87	32.82	154.60	42.97	149.05
Contributions to religious organizations	445.63	427.82	448.08	285.61	460.80
Contributions to educational organizations	19.96	7.66	21.65	6.19	21.27
Political contributions	6.65	0.80	7.45	1.16	7.17
Other contributions	16.80	3.05	18.69	7.53	17.68
PERSONAL INSURANCE AND PENSIONS	**3,364.92**	**2,313.36**	**3,509.64**	**2,608.34**	**3,436.67**
Life and other personal insurance	398.61	358.18	404.18	188.81	418.51
Life, endowment, annuity, other personal insurance	387.97	351.21	393.03	184.70	407.25
Other nonhealth insurance	10.64	6.97	11.15	4.11	11.26
Pensions and Social Security	2,966.31	1,955.17	3,105.46	2,419.53	3,018.16
Deductions for government retirement	70.32	72.64	70.00	38.85	73.30
Deductions for railroad retirement	3.29	6.69	2.82	–	3.60
Deductions for private pensions	362.64	168.77	389.31	243.38	373.94
Nonpayroll deposit to retirement plans	389.65	119.78	426.79	162.12	411.23
Deductions for Social Security	2,140.41	1,587.30	2,216.53	1,975.18	2,156.08
PERSONAL TAXES	**3,117.45**	**1,626.16**	**3,317.68**	**1,580.63**	**3,277.99**
Federal income taxes	2,409.33	1,240.16	2,566.31	1,257.52	2,529.64
State and local income taxes	561.80	337.80	591.88	271.05	592.18
Other taxes	146.32	48.20	159.50	52.06	156.17

Note: Other races include Asians, Native Americans, and Pacific Islanders. (–) means sample is too small to make a reliable estimate.
Source: Bureau of Labor Statistics, unpublished tables from the 2000 Consumer Expenditure Survey

Table 4.17 Financial: Indexed spending by race and Hispanic origin, 2000

(indexed average annual spending of consumer units (CU) on financial products and services, cash contributions, and miscellaneous items, by race and Hispanic origin of consumer unit reference person, 2000; index definition: an index of 100 is the average for all consumer units; an index of 132 means that spending by consumer units in that group is 32 percent above the average for all consumer units; an index of 68 indicates spending that is 32 percent below the average for all consumer units)

	total consumer units	race		Hispanic origin	
		black	white and others	Hispanic	non-Hispanic
Average spending of CU, total	$38,045	$28,152	$39,406	$32,735	$38,549
Average spending of CU, index	100	74	104	86	101
FINANCIAL PRODUCTS AND SERVICES	**100**	**74**	**104**	**78**	**102**
Miscellaneous fees, gambling losses	100	44	108	64	103
Legal fees	100	33	109	39	106
Funeral expenses	100	130	96	62	104
Safe deposit box rental	100	34	109	22	107
Checking accounts, other bank service charges	100	86	102	89	101
Cemetery lots, vaults, and maintenance fees	100	77	103	93	101
Accounting fees	100	37	109	69	103
Miscellaneous personal services	100	109	99	77	102
Finance charges, except mortgage and vehicles	100	95	101	108	99
Occupational expenses	100	55	106	89	101
Expenses for other properties	100	58	106	40	106
Interest paid, home equity line of credit (other property)	100	–	113	–	109
Credit card memberships	100	66	105	96	100
CASH CONTRIBUTIONS	**100**	**59**	**106**	**54**	**104**
Cash contributions to non-household members, including students, alimony, child support	100	62	105	68	103
Gifts of cash, stocks, bonds to non-household members	100	16	112	38	106
Contributions to charities	100	23	111	31	107
Contributions to religious organizations	100	96	101	64	103
Contributions to educational organizations	100	38	108	31	107
Political contributions	100	12	112	17	108
Other contributions	100	18	111	45	105
PERSONAL INSURANCE AND PENSIONS	**100**	**69**	**104**	**78**	**102**
Life and other personal insurance	100	90	101	47	105
Life, endowment, annuity, other personal insurance	100	91	101	48	105
Other nonhealth insurance	100	66	105	39	106
Pensions and Social Security	100	66	105	82	102
Deductions for government retirement	100	103	100	55	104
Deductions for railroad retirement	100	203	86	–	109
Deductions for private pensions	100	47	107	67	103
Nonpayroll deposit to retirement plans	100	31	110	42	106
Deductions for Social Security	100	74	104	92	101
PERSONAL TAXES	**100**	**52**	**106**	**51**	**105**
Federal income taxes	100	51	107	52	105
State and local income taxes	100	60	105	48	105
Other taxes	100	33	109	36	107

Note: Other races include Asians, Native Americans, and Pacific Islanders. (–) means sample is too small to make a reliable estimate.
Source: Calculations by New Strategist based on the 2000 Consumer Expenditure Survey

Table 4.18 Financial: Indexed per capita spending by race and Hispanic origin, 2000

(indexed average annual per capita spending of consumer units (CU) on financial products and services, cash contributions, and miscellaneous items, by race and Hispanic origin of consumer unit reference person, 2000; index definition: an index of 100 is the average for all consumer units; an index of 132 means that spending by consumer units in that group is 32 percent above the average for all consumer units; an index of 68 indicates spending that is 32 percent below the average for all consumer units)

	total consumer units	race black	race white and others	Hispanic origin Hispanic	Hispanic origin non-Hispanic
Per capita spending of CU, total	$15,218	$10,427	$15,762	$9,628	$16,062
Per capita spending of CU, index	100	69	104	63	106
FINANCIAL PRODUCTS AND SERVICES	**100**	**68**	**104**	**57**	**106**
Miscellaneous fees, gambling losses	100	41	108	47	108
Legal fees	100	30	109	29	110
Funeral expenses	100	120	96	46	108
Safe deposit box rental	100	32	109	16	112
Checking accounts, other bank service charges	100	80	102	65	105
Cemetery lots, vaults, and maintenance fees	100	72	103	69	105
Accounting fees	100	34	109	51	107
Miscellaneous personal services	100	101	99	56	106
Finance charges, except mortgage and vehicles	100	88	101	80	103
Occupational expenses	100	51	106	66	105
Expenses for other properties	100	54	106	29	110
Interest paid, home equity line of credit (other property)	100	–	113	–	114
Credit card memberships	100	61	105	71	105
CASH CONTRIBUTIONS	**100**	**54**	**106**	**40**	**109**
Cash contributions to non-household members, including students, alimony, child support	100	58	105	50	107
Gifts of cash, stocks, bonds to non-household members	100	15	112	28	110
Contributions to charities	100	22	111	23	111
Contributions to religious organizations	100	89	101	47	108
Contributions to educational organizations	100	36	108	23	111
Political contributions	100	11	112	13	112
Other contributions	100	17	111	33	110
PERSONAL INSURANCE AND PENSIONS	**100**	**64**	**104**	**57**	**106**
Life and other personal insurance	100	83	101	35	109
Life, endowment, annuity, other personal insurance	100	84	101	35	109
Other nonhealth insurance	100	61	105	28	110
Pensions and Social Security	100	61	105	60	106
Deductions for government retirement	100	96	100	41	109
Deductions for railroad retirement	100	188	86	–	114
Deductions for private pensions	100	43	107	49	107
Nonpayroll deposit to retirement plans	100	28	110	31	110
Deductions for Social Security	100	69	104	68	105
PERSONAL TAXES	**100**	**48**	**106**	**37**	**110**
Federal income taxes	100	48	107	38	109
State and local income taxes	100	56	105	35	110
Other taxes	100	31	109	26	111

Note: Per capita indexes account for household size and show how much each person in a particular household demographic segment spends relative to a person in the average household. Other races include Asians, Native Americans, and Pacific Islanders. (–) means sample is too small to make a reliable estimate.
Source: Calculations by New Strategist based on the 2000 Consumer Expenditure Survey

Table 4.19 Financial: Total spending by race and Hispanic origin, 2000

(total annual spending on financial products and services, cash contributions, and miscellaneous items, by consumer unit race and Hispanic origin groups, 2000; numbers in thousands)

	total consumer units	race		Hispanic origin	
		black	white and others	Hispanic	non-Hispanic
Number of consumer units	109,367	13,230	96,137	9,473	99,894
Total spending of all consumer units	$4,160,831,424	$372,454,135	$3,788,393,849	$310,098,181	$3,850,804,816
FINANCIAL PRODUCTS AND SERVICES	**$84,844,731**	**$7,562,930**	**$77,282,612**	**$5,701,041**	**$79,140,023**
Miscellaneous fees, gambling losses	4,549,667	243,697	4,305,976	252,929	4,293,444
Legal fees	11,369,793	450,878	10,919,240	383,183	10,986,342
Funeral expenses	7,731,153	1,212,794	6,518,089	418,138	7,313,240
Safe deposit box rental	500,901	20,903	479,724	9,473	491,478
Checking accounts, other bank service charges	2,175,310	226,895	1,948,697	167,009	2,008,868
Cemetery lots, vaults, and maintenance fees	1,473,173	137,989	1,335,343	119,076	1,354,563
Accounting fees	6,034,871	268,040	5,767,259	362,911	5,671,981
Miscellaneous personal services	3,433,030	454,318	2,978,324	228,110	3,202,602
Finance charges, except mortgage and vehicles	27,710,317	3,194,516	24,515,896	2,601,665	25,108,357
Occupational expenses	10,525,480	700,396	9,825,201	814,678	9,710,696
Expenses for other properties	8,719,831	611,491	8,108,195	300,768	8,419,066
Interest paid, home equity line of credit (other property)	107,180	–	106,712	–	106,887
Credit card memberships	515,119	40,881	473,955	43,007	472,499
CASH CONTRIBUTIONS	**130,413,585**	**9,256,899**	**121,157,616**	**6,113,495**	**124,300,102**
Cash contributions to non-household members, including students, alimony, child support	32,380,288	2,436,305	29,943,791	1,893,369	30,486,650
Gifts of cash, stocks, bonds to non-household members	29,253,485	574,182	28,679,590	966,530	28,286,984
Contributions to charities	15,297,162	434,209	14,862,780	407,055	14,889,201
Contributions to religious organizations	48,737,216	5,660,059	43,077,067	2,705,584	46,031,155
Contributions to educational organizations	2,182,965	101,342	2,081,366	58,638	2,124,745
Political contributions	727,291	10,584	716,221	10,989	716,240
Other contributions	1,837,366	40,352	1,796,801	71,332	1,766,126
PERSONAL INSURANCE AND PENSIONS	**368,011,206**	**30,605,753**	**337,406,261**	**24,708,805**	**343,302,713**
Life and other personal insurance	43,594,780	4,738,721	38,856,653	1,788,597	41,806,638
Life, endowment, annuity, other personal insurance	42,431,115	4,646,508	37,784,725	1,749,663	40,681,832
Other nonhealth insurance	1,163,665	92,213	1,071,928	38,934	1,124,806
Pensions and Social Security	324,416,426	25,866,899	298,549,608	22,920,208	301,496,075
Deductions for government retirement	7,690,687	961,027	6,729,590	368,026	7,322,230
Deductions for railroad retirement	359,817	88,509	271,106	–	359,618
Deductions for private pensions	39,660,849	2,232,827	37,427,095	2,305,539	37,354,362
Nonpayroll deposit to retirement plans	42,614,852	1,584,689	41,030,310	1,535,763	41,079,410
Deductions for Social Security	234,090,220	20,999,979	213,090,545	18,710,880	215,379,456
PERSONAL TAXES	**340,946,154**	**21,514,097**	**318,951,802**	**14,973,308**	**327,451,533**
Federal income taxes	263,501,194	16,407,317	246,717,344	11,912,487	252,695,858
State and local income taxes	61,442,381	4,469,094	56,901,568	2,567,657	59,155,229
Other taxes	16,002,579	637,686	15,333,852	493,164	15,600,446

Note: Other races include Asians, Native Americans, and Pacific Islanders. Numbers may not add to total because of rounding. (–) means sample is too small to make a reliable estimate.
Source: Calculations by New Strategist based on the 2000 Consumer Expenditure Survey

Table 4.20 Financial: Market shares by race and Hispanic origin, 2000

(percentage of total annual spending on financial products and services, cash contributions, and miscellaneous items accounted for by consumer unit race and Hispanic origin groups, 2000)

	total consumer units	race black	race white and others	Hispanic origin Hispanic	Hispanic origin non-Hispanic
Share of total consumer units	100.0%	12.1%	87.9%	8.7%	91.3%
Share of total before-tax income	100.0	8.8	91.1	6.8	93.4
Share of total spending	100.0	9.0	91.0	7.5	92.5
FINANCIAL PRODUCTS AND SERVICES	100.0%	8.9%	91.1%	6.7%	93.3%
Miscellaneous fees, gambling losses	100.0	5.4	94.6	5.6	94.4
Legal fees	100.0	4.0	96.0	3.4	96.6
Funeral expenses	100.0	15.7	84.3	5.4	94.6
Safe deposit box rental	100.0	4.2	95.8	1.9	98.1
Checking accounts, other bank service charges	100.0	10.4	89.6	7.7	92.3
Cemetery lots, vaults, and maintenance fees	100.0	9.4	90.6	8.1	91.9
Accounting fees	100.0	4.4	95.6	6.0	94.0
Miscellaneous personal services	100.0	13.2	86.8	6.6	93.3
Finance charges, except mortgage and vehicles	100.0	11.5	88.5	9.4	90.6
Occupational expenses	100.0	6.7	93.3	7.7	92.3
Expenses for other properties	100.0	7.0	93.0	3.4	96.6
Interest paid, home equity line of credit (other property)	100.0	–	99.6	–	99.7
Credit card memberships	100.0	7.9	92.0	8.3	91.7
CASH CONTRIBUTIONS	100.0	7.1	92.9	4.7	95.3
Cash contributions to non-household members, including students, alimony, child support	100.0	7.5	92.5	5.8	94.2
Gifts of cash, stocks, bonds to non-household members	100.0	2.0	98.0	3.3	96.7
Contributions to charities	100.0	2.8	97.2	2.7	97.3
Contributions to religious organizations	100.0	11.6	88.4	5.6	94.4
Contributions to educational organizations	100.0	4.6	95.3	2.7	97.3
Political contributions	100.0	1.5	98.5	1.5	98.5
Other contributions	100.0	2.2	97.8	3.9	96.1
PERSONAL INSURANCE AND PENSIONS	100.0	8.3	91.7	6.7	93.3
Life and other personal insurance	100.0	10.9	89.1	4.1	95.9
Life, endowment, annuity, other personal insurance	100.0	11.0	89.0	4.1	95.9
Other nonhealth insurance	100.0	7.9	92.1	3.3	96.7
Pensions and Social Security	100.0	8.0	92.0	7.1	92.9
Deductions for government retirement	100.0	12.5	87.5	4.8	95.2
Deductions for railroad retirement	100.0	24.6	75.3	–	99.9
Deductions for private pensions	100.0	5.6	94.4	5.8	94.2
Nonpayroll deposit to retirement plans	100.0	3.7	96.3	3.6	96.4
Deductions for Social Security	100.0	9.0	91.0	8.0	92.0
PERSONAL TAXES	100.0	6.3	93.5	4.4	96.0
Federal income taxes	100.0	6.2	93.6	4.5	95.9
State and local income taxes	100.0	7.3	92.6	4.2	96.3
Other taxes	100.0	4.0	95.8	3.1	97.5

Note: Other races include Asians, Native Americans, and Pacific Islanders. Numbers may not add to total because of rounding. (–) means sample is too small to make a reliable estimate.
Source: Calculations by New Strategist based on the 2000 Consumer Expenditure Survey

Table 4.21 Financial: Average spending by region, 2000

(average annual spending of consumer units (CU) on financial products and services, cash contributions, and miscellaneous items, by region in which consumer unit lives, 2000)

	total consumer units	Northeast	Midwest	South	West
Number of consumer units (in thousands, add 000)	109,367	20,994	25,717	38,245	24,410
Average number of persons per CU	2.5	2.5	2.5	2.5	2.6
Average before-tax income of CU	$44,649.00	$47,439.00	$44,377.00	$41,984.00	$46,670.00
Average spending of CU, total	38,044.67	38,901.91	39,212.70	34,707.07	41,328.19
FINANCIAL PRODUCTS AND SERVICES	**$775.78**	**$738.05**	**$798.31**	**$729.49**	**$858.97**
Miscellaneous fees, gambling losses	41.60	47.86	62.04	21.47	46.75
Legal fees	103.96	87.59	114.70	89.28	129.71
Funeral expenses	70.69	79.67	94.32	64.12	48.36
Safe deposit box rental	4.58	4.74	6.46	3.74	3.78
Checking accounts, other bank service charges	19.89	16.45	16.63	22.40	22.37
Cemetery lots, vaults, and maintenance fees	13.47	11.45	15.35	14.27	11.98
Accounting fees	55.18	49.63	49.48	42.34	86.09
Miscellaneous personal services	31.39	16.37	30.23	24.20	58.18
Finance charges, except mortgage and vehicles	253.37	211.86	204.74	298.04	270.31
Occupational expenses	96.24	125.16	93.87	77.19	103.70
Expenses for other properties	79.73	83.25	102.74	69.56	68.39
Interest paid, home equity line of credit (other property)	0.98	0.24	0.93	0.19	2.88
Credit card memberships	4.71	3.78	6.81	2.69	6.47
CASH CONTRIBUTIONS	**1,192.44**	**1,064.27**	**1,614.83**	**952.74**	**1,233.25**
Cash contributions to non-household members, including students, alimony, child support	296.07	367.98	276.18	262.08	308.44
Gifts of cash, stocks, bonds to non-household members	267.48	250.33	532.23	116.87	239.29
Contributions to charities	139.87	108.17	254.16	93.00	120.14
Contributions to religious organizations	445.63	302.21	508.13	456.81	485.60
Contributions to educational organizations	19.96	12.83	22.27	9.01	40.83
Political contributions	6.65	6.81	7.69	4.72	8.42
Other contributions	16.80	15.95	14.17	10.26	30.54
PERSONAL INSURANCE AND PENSIONS	**3,364.92**	**3,371.21**	**3,490.42**	**3,076.85**	**3,678.65**
Life and other personal insurance	398.61	423.25	428.99	406.65	332.83
Life, endowment, annuity, other personal insurance	387.97	412.13	415.45	397.76	322.90
Other nonhealth insurance	10.64	11.12	13.54	8.89	9.93
Pensions and Social Security	2,966.31	2,947.96	3,061.43	2,670.19	3,345.82
Deductions for government retirement	70.32	24.65	77.25	85.94	77.82
Deductions for railroad retirement	3.29	1.98	5.62	3.10	2.26
Deductions for private pensions	362.64	287.64	461.95	335.27	365.39
Nonpayroll deposit to retirement plans	389.65	455.74	395.36	283.33	493.39
Deductions for Social Security	2,140.41	2,177.97	2,121.25	1,962.55	2,406.96
PERSONAL TAXES	**3,117.45**	**2,983.21**	**3,666.66**	**2,516.36**	**3,582.20**
Federal income taxes	2,409.33	2,195.97	2,698.71	2,053.44	2,827.40
State and local income taxes	561.80	633.25	814.95	321.22	614.31
Other taxes	146.32	153.99	152.99	141.7	140.49

Source: Bureau of Labor Statistics, unpublished tables from the 2000 Consumer Expenditure Survey

Table 4.22 Financial: Indexed spending by region, 2000

(indexed average annual spending of consumer units (CU) on financial products and services, cash contributions, and miscellaneous items, by region in which consumer unit lives, 2000; index definition: an index of 100 is the average for all consumer units; an index of 132 means that spending by consumer units in that group is 32 percent above the average for all consumer units; an index of 68 indicates spending that is 32 percent below the average for all consumer units)

	total consumer units	Northeast	Midwest	South	West
Average spending of CU, total	$38,045	$38,902	$39,213	$34,707	$41,328
Average spending of CU, index	100	102	103	91	109
FINANCIAL PRODUCTS AND SERVICES	**100**	**95**	**103**	**94**	**111**
Miscellaneous fees, gambling losses	100	115	149	52	112
Legal fees	100	84	110	86	125
Funeral expenses	100	113	133	91	68
Safe deposit box rental	100	103	141	82	83
Checking accounts, other bank service charges	100	83	84	113	112
Cemetery lots, vaults, and maintenance fees	100	85	114	106	89
Accounting fees	100	90	90	77	156
Miscellaneous personal services	100	52	96	77	185
Finance charges, except mortgage and vehicles	100	84	81	118	107
Occupational expenses	100	130	98	80	108
Expenses for other properties	100	104	129	87	86
Interest paid, home equity line of credit (other property)	100	24	95	19	294
Credit card memberships	100	80	145	57	137
CASH CONTRIBUTIONS	**100**	**89**	**135**	**80**	**103**
Cash contributions to non-household members, including students, alimony, child support	100	124	93	89	104
Gifts of cash, stocks, bonds to non-household members	100	94	199	44	89
Contributions to charities	100	77	182	66	86
Contributions to religious organizations	100	68	114	103	109
Contributions to educational organizations	100	64	112	45	205
Political contributions	100	102	116	71	127
Other contributions	100	95	84	61	182
PERSONAL INSURANCE AND PENSIONS	**100**	**100**	**104**	**91**	**109**
Life and other personal insurance	100	106	108	102	83
Life, endowment, annuity, other personal insurance	100	106	107	103	83
Other nonhealth insurance	100	105	127	84	93
Pensions and Social Security	100	99	103	90	113
Deductions for government retirement	100	35	110	122	111
Deductions for railroad retirement	100	60	171	94	69
Deductions for private pensions	100	79	127	92	101
Nonpayroll deposit to retirement plans	100	117	101	73	127
Deductions for Social Security	100	102	99	92	112
PERSONAL TAXES	**100**	**96**	**118**	**81**	**115**
Federal income taxes	100	91	112	85	117
State and local income taxes	100	113	145	57	109
Other taxes	100	105	105	97	96

Source: Calculations by New Strategist based on the 2000 Consumer Expenditure Survey

Table 4.23 Financial: Indexed per capita spending by region, 2000

(indexed average annual per capita spending of consumer units (CU) on financial products and services, cash contributions, and miscellaneous items, by region in which consumer unit lives, 2000; index definition: an index of 100 is the average for all consumer units; an index of 132 means that spending by consumer units in that group is 32 percent above the average for all consumer units; an index of 68 indicates spending that is 32 percent below the average for all consumer units)

	total consumer units	Northeast	Midwest	South	West
Per capita spending of CU, total	$15,218	$15,561	$15,685	$13,883	$15,895
Per capita spending of CU, index	100	102	103	91	104
FINANCIAL PRODUCTS AND SERVICES	**100**	**95**	**103**	**94**	**106**
Miscellaneous fees, gambling losses	100	115	149	52	108
Legal fees	100	84	110	86	120
Funeral expenses	100	113	133	91	66
Safe deposit box rental	100	103	141	82	79
Checking accounts, other bank service charges	100	83	84	113	108
Cemetery lots, vaults, and maintenance fees	100	85	114	106	86
Accounting fees	100	90	90	77	150
Miscellaneous personal services	100	52	96	77	178
Finance charges, except mortgage and vehicles	100	84	81	118	103
Occupational expenses	100	130	98	80	104
Expenses for other properties	100	104	129	87	82
Interest paid, home equity line of credit (other property)	100	24	95	19	283
Credit card memberships	100	80	145	57	132
CASH CONTRIBUTIONS	**100**	**89**	**135**	**80**	**99**
Cash contributions to non-household members, including students, alimony, child support	100	124	93	89	100
Gifts of cash, stocks, bonds to non-household members	100	94	199	44	86
Contributions to charities	100	77	182	66	83
Contributions to religious organizations	100	68	114	103	105
Contributions to educational organizations	100	64	112	45	197
Political contributions	100	102	116	71	122
Other contributions	100	95	84	61	175
PERSONAL INSURANCE AND PENSIONS	**100**	**100**	**104**	**91**	**105**
Life and other personal insurance	100	106	108	102	80
Life, endowment, annuity, other personal insurance	100	106	107	103	80
Other nonhealth insurance	100	105	127	84	90
Pensions and Social Security	100	99	103	90	108
Deductions for government retirement	100	35	110	122	106
Deductions for railroad retirement	100	60	171	94	66
Deductions for private pensions	100	79	127	92	97
Nonpayroll deposit to retirement plans	100	117	101	73	122
Deductions for Social Security	100	102	99	92	108
PERSONAL TAXES	**100**	**96**	**118**	**81**	**110**
Federal income taxes	100	91	112	85	113
State and local income taxes	100	113	145	57	105
Other taxes	100	105	105	97	92

Note: Per capita indexes account for household size and show how much each person in a particular household demographic segment spends relative to a person in the average household.
Source: Calculations by New Strategist based on the 2000 Consumer Expenditure Survey

Table 4.24 Financial: Total spending by region, 2000

(total annual spending on financial products and services, cash contributions, and miscellaneous items, by region in which consumer units live, 2000; numbers in thousands)

	total consumer units	Northeast	Midwest	South	West
Number of consumer units	109,367.00	20,994.00	25,717.00	38,245.00	24,410.00
Total spending of all consumer units	$4,160,831,423.89	$816,706,698.54	$1,008,433,005.90	$1,327,371,892.15	$1,008,821,117.90
FINANCIAL PRODUCTS AND SERVICES	**$84,844,731.26**	**$15,494,621.70**	**$20,530,138.27**	**$27,899,345.05**	**$20,967,457.70**
Miscellaneous fees, gambling losses	4,549,667.20	1,004,772.84	1,595,482.68	821,120.15	1,141,167.50
Legal fees	11,369,793.32	1,838,864.46	2,949,739.90	3,414,513.60	3,166,221.10
Funeral expenses	7,731,153.23	1,672,591.98	2,425,627.44	2,452,269.40	1,180,467.60
Safe deposit box rental	500,900.86	99,511.56	166,131.82	143,036.30	92,269.80
Checking accounts, other bank service charges	2,175,309.63	345,351.30	427,673.71	856,688.00	546,051.70
Cemetery lots, vaults, and maintenance fees	1,473,173.49	240,381.30	394,755.95	545,756.15	292,431.80
Accounting fees	6,034,871.06	1,041,932.22	1,272,477.16	1,619,293.30	2,101,456.90
Miscellaneous personal services	3,433,030.13	343,671.78	777,424.91	925,529.00	1,420,173.80
Finance charges, except mortgage and vehicles	27,710,316.79	4,447,788.84	5,265,298.58	11,398,539.80	6,598,267.10
Occupational expenses	10,525,480.08	2,627,609.04	2,414,054.79	2,952,131.55	2,531,317.00
Expenses for other properties	8,719,830.91	1,747,750.50	2,642,164.58	2,660,322.20	1,669,399.90
Interest paid, home equity line of credit (other property)	107,179.66	5,038.56	23,916.81	7,266.55	70,300.80
Credit card memberships	515,118.57	79,357.32	175,132.77	102,879.05	157,932.70
CASH CONTRIBUTIONS	**130,413,585.48**	**22,343,284.38**	**41,528,583.11**	**36,437,541.30**	**30,103,632.50**
Cash contributions to non-household members, including students, alimony, child support	32,380,287.69	7,725,372.12	7,102,521.06	10,023,249.60	7,529,020.40
Gifts of cash, stocks, bonds to non-household members	29,253,485.16	5,255,428.02	13,687,358.91	4,469,693.15	5,841,068.90
Contributions to charities	15,297,162.29	2,270,920.98	6,536,232.72	3,556,785.00	2,932,617.40
Contributions to religious organizations	48,737,216.21	6,344,596.74	13,067,579.21	17,470,698.45	11,853,496.00
Contributions to educational organizations	2,182,965.32	269,353.02	572,717.59	344,587.45	996,660.30
Political contributions	727,290.55	142,969.14	197,763.73	180,516.40	205,532.20
Other contributions	1,837,365.60	334,854.30	364,409.89	392,393.70	745,481.40
PERSONAL INSURANCE AND PENSIONS	**368,011,205.64**	**70,775,182.74**	**89,763,131.14**	**117,674,128.25**	**89,795,846.50**
Life and other personal insurance	43,594,779.87	8,885,710.50	11,032,335.83	15,552,329.25	8,124,380.30
Life, endowment, annuity, other personal insurance	42,431,114.99	8,652,257.22	10,684,127.65	15,212,331.20	7,881,989.00
Other nonhealth insurance	1,163,664.88	233,453.28	348,208.18	339,998.05	242,391.30
Pensions and Social Security	324,416,425.77	61,889,472.24	78,730,795.31	102,121,416.55	81,671,466.20
Deductions for government retirement	7,690,687.44	517,502.10	1,986,638.25	3,286,775.30	1,899,586.20
Deductions for railroad retirement	359,817.43	41,568.12	144,529.54	118,559.50	55,166.60
Deductions for private pensions	39,660,848.88	6,038,714.16	11,879,968.15	12,822,401.15	8,919,169.90
Nonpayroll deposit to retirement plans	42,614,851.55	9,567,805.56	10,167,473.12	10,835,955.85	12,043,649.90
Deductions for Social Security	234,090,220.47	45,724,302.18	54,552,186.25	75,057,724.75	58,753,893.60
PERSONAL TAXES	**340,946,154.15**	**62,629,510.74**	**94,295,495.22**	**96,238,188.20**	**87,441,502.00**
Federal income taxes	263,501,194.11	46,102,194.18	69,402,725.07	78,533,812.80	69,016,834.00
State and local income taxes	61,442,380.60	13,294,450.50	20,958,069.15	12,285,058.90	14,995,307.10
Other taxes	16,002,579.44	3,232,866.06	3,934,443.83	5,419,316.50	3,429,360.90

Note: Numbers may not add to total because of rounding.
Source: Calculations by New Strategist based on the 2000 Consumer Expenditure Survey

Table 4.25 Financial: Market shares by region, 2000

(percentage of total annual spending on financial products and services, cash contributions, and miscellaneous items accounted for by consumer units (CU) by region, 2000)

	total consumer units	Northeast	Midwest	South	West
Share of total consumer units	100.0%	19.2%	23.5%	35.0%	22.3%
Share of total before-tax income	100.0	20.4	23.4	32.9	23.3
Share of total spending	100.0	19.6	24.2	31.9	24.2
FINANCIAL PRODUCTS AND SERVICES	**100.0%**	**18.3%**	**24.2%**	**32.9%**	**24.7%**
Miscellaneous fees, gambling losses	100.0	22.1	35.1	18.0	25.1
Legal fees	100.0	16.2	25.9	30.0	27.8
Funeral expenses	100.0	21.6	31.4	31.7	15.3
Safe deposit box rental	100.0	19.9	33.2	28.6	18.4
Checking accounts, other bank service charges	100.0	15.9	19.7	39.4	25.1
Cemetery lots, vaults, and maintenance fees	100.0	16.3	26.8	37.0	19.9
Accounting fees	100.0	17.3	21.1	26.8	34.8
Miscellaneous personal services	100.0	10.0	22.6	27.0	41.4
Finance charges, except mortgage and vehicles	100.0	16.1	19.0	41.1	23.8
Occupational expenses	100.0	25.0	22.9	28.0	24.0
Expenses for other properties	100.0	20.0	30.3	30.5	19.1
Interest paid, home equity line of credit (other property)	100.0	4.7	22.3	6.8	65.6
Credit card memberships	100.0	15.4	34.0	20.0	30.7
CASH CONTRIBUTIONS	**100.0**	**17.1**	**31.8**	**27.9**	**23.1**
Cash contributions to non-household members, including students, alimony, child support	100.0	23.9	21.9	31.0	23.3
Gifts of cash, stocks, bonds to non-household members	100.0	18.0	46.8	15.3	20.0
Contributions to charities	100.0	14.8	42.7	23.3	19.2
Contributions to religious organizations	100.0	13.0	26.8	35.8	24.3
Contributions to educational organizations	100.0	12.3	26.2	15.8	45.7
Political contributions	100.0	19.7	27.2	24.8	28.3
Other contributions	100.0	18.2	19.8	21.4	40.6
PERSONAL INSURANCE AND PENSIONS	**100.0**	**19.2**	**24.4**	**32.0**	**24.4**
Life and other personal insurance	100.0	20.4	25.3	35.7	18.6
Life, endowment, annuity, other personal insurance	100.0	20.4	25.2	35.9	18.6
Other nonhealth insurance	100.0	20.1	29.9	29.2	20.8
Pensions and Social Security	100.0	19.1	24.3	31.5	25.2
Deductions for government retirement	100.0	6.7	25.8	42.7	24.7
Deductions for railroad retirement	100.0	11.6	40.2	32.9	15.3
Deductions for private pensions	100.0	15.2	30.0	32.3	22.5
Nonpayroll deposit to retirement plans	100.0	22.5	23.9	25.4	28.3
Deductions for Social Security	100.0	19.5	23.3	32.1	25.1
PERSONAL TAXES	**100.0**	**18.4**	**27.7**	**28.2**	**25.6**
Federal income taxes	100.0	17.5	26.3	29.8	26.2
State and local income taxes	100.0	21.6	34.1	20.0	24.4
Other taxes	100.0	20.2	24.6	33.9	21.4

Note: Numbers may not add to total because of rounding.
Source: Calculations by New Strategist based on the 2000 Consumer Expenditure Survey

5

Spending on Food and Alcoholic Beverages, 2000

The average household spent 10 percent less on food away from home (primarily sit-down meals and take-outs from restaurants) in 2000 than in 1990, after adjusting for inflation. Spending on food at home (groceries) fell 8 percent during those years. Overall, Americans devoted 13.6 percent of their expenditures to food in 2000, down from 15.1 percent in 1990. Spending on alcoholic beverages fell 4 percent between 1990 and 2000, after adjusting for inflation.

Householders aged 45 to 54 spend the most on food at home because they have the highest incomes. In 2000, they spent an average of $3,657 on food at home, 21 percent more than the average household. Spending on alcoholic beverages peaks in a younger age group, among householders aged 25 to 34. When eating out, householders spanning the ages of 35 to 54 spend the most overall, but spending differs greatly by type of restaurant. Younger householders, particularly those aged 25 to 34, are the biggest spenders at fast-food restaurants while those aged 45 to 54 spend the most at full-service establishments.

Households with incomes of $70,000 or more spend 42 percent more than the average household on food at home. They spend 83 percent more than average on food away from home and 86 percent more on alcoholic beverages. The most affluent households account for 40 percent of spending on dinners in full-service restaurants. They account for 50 percent of spending on wine consumed at home.

Married couples with adult children at home spend more on food than other household types—$7,858 in 2000. These households are not only larger than average, but they also have the highest incomes, which accounts for their above-average food spending. Empty-nesters are the best customers of full-service restaurants, while married couples with school-aged or older children spend more than other household types at fast-food restaurants. Alcohol spending is highest among married couples with adult children at home (28 percent above average) and among those without children at home (24 percent).

Hispanic households spend more on food at home than blacks, whites, or non-Hispanics—16 percent more than the average household. Behind the higher spending is their larger household size of 3.4 people versus 2.5 in the average household. Hispanics spend more than twice the average on flour and 84 percent more on rice. They spend more than three times the average on dried beans. Blacks spend 19 percent more than average on pork and 26 percent more on fish and seafood.

Households in the West spend 8 percent more than the average household on food and 21 percent more on alcoholic beverages. Spending on dinner at fast-food restaurants is highest in the Midwest and West, while dinner expenses at full-service restaurants are highest in the Northeast. Spending on wine consumed at home is 46 percent above average in the West. In the South, spending on alcohol is 18 percent below average.

Table 5.1 Food and Alcohol: Average spending by age, 2000

(average annual spending of consumer units (CU) on food and alcoholic beverages, by age of consumer unit reference person, 2000)

	total consumer units	under 25	25 to 34	35 to 44	45 to 54	55 to 64	65 to 74	75+
Number of consumer units (in thousands, add 000)	109,367	8,306	18,887	23,983	21,874	14,161	11,538	10,617
Average number of persons per CU	2.5	1.9	2.9	3.3	2.7	2.1	1.9	1.5
Average before-tax income of CU	$44,649.00	$19,744.00	$45,498.00	$56,500.00	$58,889.00	$48,108.00	$29,349.00	$20,563.00
Average spending of CU, total	38,044.67	22,543.18	38,945.27	45,149.37	46,160.28	39,340.03	30,781.81	21,908.04
Food, average spending	5,157.88	3,212.92	5,260.19	6,091.91	6,294.62	5,167.74	4,177.87	3,077.32
Alcoholic beverages, average spending	371.81	392.48	431.25	420.36	416.83	371.31	260.92	155.48
FOOD AT HOME	**$3,021.00**	**$1,643.47**	**$2,951.00**	**$3,484.42**	**$3,656.83**	**$3,070.61**	**$2,759.87**	**$2,106.16**
Cereals and bakery products	**453.33**	**237.61**	**429.34**	**530.92**	**559.89**	**440.67**	**414.33**	**334.17**
Cereals and cereal products	156.40	89.64	166.60	190.39	179.57	139.83	133.30	112.26
Flour	7.98	6.09	8.01	9.25	8.54	7.34	7.12	7.10
Prepared flour mixes	13.35	7.29	10.63	17.84	15.71	13.48	11.84	9.29
Ready-to-eat and cooked cereals	86.88	50.45	92.39	104.66	95.36	78.56	77.07	69.25
Rice	19.55	10.45	22.82	22.07	26.82	16.26	14.47	10.28
Pasta, cornmeal, and other cereal products	28.64	15.36	32.75	36.57	33.13	24.18	22.79	16.34
Bakery products	296.93	147.97	262.74	340.53	380.32	300.84	281.03	221.91
Bread	84.04	45.30	76.88	95.07	97.91	90.14	83.28	67.32
White bread	36.62	21.35	35.27	43.35	40.48	37.43	35.71	27.66
Bread, other than white	47.42	23.95	41.61	51.72	57.43	52.72	47.57	39.66
Crackers and cookies	71.03	32.54	63.64	80.02	93.54	73.26	64.29	53.76
Cookies	47.71	22.21	43.43	53.61	64.23	48.04	41.06	35.93
Crackers	23.32	10.34	20.21	26.42	29.30	25.23	23.23	17.82
Frozen and refrigerated bakery products	24.53	13.08	21.72	29.78	29.66	25.56	23.06	16.30
Other bakery products	117.33	57.04	100.50	135.65	159.21	111.87	110.41	84.54
Biscuits and rolls	38.53	20.08	31.02	45.71	48.97	41.07	35.88	28.58
Cakes and cupcakes	38.42	17.42	34.83	40.89	62.05	30.27	34.53	24.15
Bread and cracker products	4.41	1.96	3.86	6.12	5.07	3.93	4.34	2.79
Sweetrolls, coffee cakes, doughnuts	22.68	12.82	19.71	25.53	27.70	22.81	24.55	17.16
Pies, tarts, turnovers	13.28	4.76	11.09	17.41	15.42	13.79	11.11	11.86
Meats, poultry, fish, and eggs	**795.43**	**437.21**	**770.08**	**917.73**	**969.80**	**831.94**	**727.39**	**515.30**
Beef	238.19	134.51	239.25	270.49	296.12	242.86	216.55	144.16
Ground beef	87.76	64.61	90.07	102.30	102.15	86.97	71.05	57.64
Roast	39.84	15.78	31.13	43.17	57.96	38.64	42.38	30.06
Chuck roast	13.33	5.47	10.71	16.53	17.98	12.16	13.49	8.98
Round roast	11.46	6.15	8.44	11.52	14.80	12.68	14.56	9.49
Other roast	15.05	4.16	11.98	15.12	25.18	13.81	14.33	11.60
Steak	94.52	46.91	101.95	106.75	118.32	96.83	87.82	46.70
Round steak	15.31	9.11	14.28	17.08	20.54	14.44	16.42	7.47
Sirloin steak	29.86	14.36	35.22	33.68	35.65	28.63	27.90	15.78
Other steak	49.35	23.44	52.45	55.99	62.13	53.76	43.51	23.44
Other beef	16.08	7.21	16.10	18.26	17.69	20.42	15.30	9.76
Pork	166.94	89.48	155.30	186.03	198.45	185.89	168.21	115.52
Bacon	26.05	11.45	22.10	29.55	31.52	27.37	28.65	21.40
Pork chops	40.57	25.59	40.51	46.42	48.68	42.10	36.20	25.15
Ham	36.26	16.80	35.43	39.13	38.63	43.67	37.91	30.36
Ham, not canned	34.52	15.57	34.26	37.02	36.60	42.17	35.34	29.18
Canned ham	1.74	1.23	1.17	2.11	2.03	1.49	2.57	1.18
Sausage	25.24	14.17	22.09	30.25	27.63	29.08	25.55	17.70
Other pork	38.82	21.48	35.18	40.68	51.99	43.68	39.89	20.91
Other meats	100.54	54.71	98.08	120.42	121.47	99.34	85.94	70.37
Frankfurters	20.68	12.98	23.78	23.75	23.68	18.85	16.69	14.71

	total consumer units	under 25	25 to 34	35 to 44	45 to 54	55 to 64	65 to 74	75+
Lunch meats (cold cuts)	$67.99	$36.29	$63.19	$83.38	$83.89	$67.40	$58.58	$44.88
Bologna, liverwurst, salami	23.73	13.63	22.83	28.10	28.86	23.37	21.11	16.19
Other lunch meats	44.26	22.65	40.37	55.28	55.04	44.03	37.47	28.69
Lamb, organ meats, and others	11.87	5.43	11.11	13.29	13.89	13.09	10.67	10.78
Lamb and organ meats	9.71	4.98	9.73	8.10	11.63	12.08	10.22	9.85
Mutton, goat, and game	2.16	0.46	1.38	5.19	2.26	1.01	0.45	0.92
Poultry	145.16	85.79	145.25	177.73	168.52	145.91	129.94	83.84
Fresh and frozen chicken	114.43	72.35	120.17	138.41	131.90	112.79	97.04	66.66
Fresh and frozen whole chicken	31.25	24.36	31.29	36.09	38.45	29.06	28.01	17.10
Fresh and frozen chicken parts	83.18	47.99	88.89	102.32	93.45	83.73	69.03	49.57
Other poultry	30.73	13.44	25.08	39.32	36.62	33.12	32.90	17.17
Fish and seafood	110.14	52.13	101.81	126.14	145.64	115.00	94.98	73.00
Canned fish and seafood	15.67	7.86	12.65	15.13	21.46	18.78	15.17	13.56
Fresh fish and shellfish	66.82	33.44	62.66	78.49	87.56	70.01	54.98	40.46
Frozen fish and shellfish	27.65	10.83	26.50	32.51	36.62	26.22	24.82	18.98
Eggs	34.46	20.58	30.39	36.92	39.60	42.94	31.78	28.41
Dairy products	**324.63**	**174.78**	**317.33**	**382.83**	**377.36**	**321.31**	**310.24**	**236.08**
Fresh milk and cream	131.22	73.46	134.41	156.58	145.70	126.03	118.15	104.45
Fresh milk, all types	119.61	67.69	124.04	142.64	131.55	112.45	108.42	97.11
Cream	11.61	5.77	10.37	13.94	14.16	13.58	9.73	7.34
Other dairy products	193.41	101.32	182.92	226.25	231.66	195.28	192.09	131.63
Butter	17.00	6.96	15.49	20.22	21.61	17.46	17.00	10.43
Cheese	95.96	52.05	94.44	114.08	111.58	97.60	91.15	62.88
Ice cream and related products	56.56	31.70	50.89	63.97	68.91	55.09	62.12	40.86
Miscellaneous dairy products	23.89	10.61	22.09	27.98	29.57	25.13	21.81	17.46
Fruits and vegetables	**520.83**	**253.20**	**488.44**	**551.50**	**625.72**	**558.42**	**529.11**	**457.36**
Fresh fruits	163.17	76.60	145.62	169.38	186.57	184.65	164.09	175.28
Apples	29.49	16.78	27.37	31.61	34.61	32.10	27.73	26.85
Bananas	31.70	16.44	26.40	32.09	34.94	37.24	33.20	37.56
Oranges	18.93	10.88	18.73	20.27	21.55	20.20	18.11	16.61
Citrus fruits, excl. oranges	14.31	5.26	13.40	13.92	16.48	18.29	12.81	16.28
Other fresh fruits	68.74	27.24	59.72	71.48	78.99	76.83	72.24	77.98
Fresh vegetables	158.72	73.62	147.67	164.37	200.96	172.52	162.02	128.46
Potatoes	28.07	12.54	24.55	29.23	34.80	30.89	29.47	25.68
Lettuce	20.75	9.77	17.65	22.35	27.19	22.41	20.55	16.64
Tomatoes	29.53	14.56	31.61	29.73	37.12	30.48	28.82	21.81
Other fresh vegetables	80.38	36.75	73.86	83.06	101.85	88.74	83.19	64.34
Processed fruits	115.01	61.61	113.31	125.32	133.30	114.53	119.46	96.71
Frozen fruits and fruit juices	14.37	6.15	14.09	16.77	16.68	17.35	12.99	8.61
Frozen orange juice	6.90	2.77	6.23	8.11	7.66	9.16	6.20	4.81
Frozen fruits	3.62	1.27	4.03	3.53	4.82	3.68	4.18	1.94
Frozen fruit juices	3.84	2.11	3.84	5.14	4.21	4.51	2.62	1.85
Canned fruits	15.48	6.81	13.48	16.61	16.48	15.91	20.07	16.14
Dried fruits	5.50	2.01	4.41	5.63	5.83	5.53	7.48	7.32
Fresh fruit juice	23.44	11.37	22.68	24.90	28.21	22.82	24.88	21.07
Canned and bottled fruit juice	56.21	35.27	58.65	61.41	66.09	52.92	54.05	43.58
Processed vegetables	83.94	41.37	81.84	92.43	104.89	86.73	83.54	56.91
Frozen vegetables	26.42	13.58	24.62	32.09	33.44	26.61	22.44	16.57
Canned and dried vegetables and juices	57.52	27.79	57.22	60.34	71.45	60.11	61.10	40.34
Canned beans	12.67	5.99	11.95	13.54	15.20	11.82	15.23	10.79
Canned corn	6.80	2.87	7.72	7.57	8.97	5.80	5.94	4.45
Canned miscellaneous vegetables	17.95	8.30	15.43	18.25	22.72	21.40	19.76	13.59
Dried peas	0.34	0.08	0.44	0.33	0.24	0.43	0.40	0.43
Dried beans	2.53	0.82	2.69	2.78	3.49	2.46	1.94	1.91

	total consumer units	under 25	25 to 34	35 to 44	45 to 54	55 to 64	65 to 74	75+
Dried miscellaneous vegetables	$7.22	$3.88	$7.83	$6.76	$8.90	$7.99	$7.99	$4.63
Dried processed vegetables	0.41	0.22	0.65	0.57	0.30	0.41	0.12	0.30
Frozen vegetable juices	0.29	0.12	0.47	0.34	0.26	0.21	0.34	0.08
Fresh and canned vegetable juices	9.30	5.52	10.06	10.21	11.39	9.59	9.37	4.16
Other food at home	**926.77**	**540.68**	**945.81**	**1,101.44**	**1,124.06**	**918.26**	**778.80**	**563.25**
Sugar and other sweets	117.14	60.22	104.68	146.79	142.60	115.47	104.94	79.95
Candy and chewing gum	76.30	36.50	67.33	101.54	97.30	69.43	63.35	45.96
Sugar	16.80	11.01	17.14	20.38	17.16	18.61	14.19	12.01
Artificial sweeteners	4.19	0.22	1.90	3.34	6.36	6.79	5.20	4.69
Jams, preserves, other sweets	19.86	12.50	18.31	21.54	21.78	20.64	22.21	17.29
Fats and oils	83.09	42.44	76.99	89.84	101.68	90.45	86.93	59.93
Margarine	11.61	4.82	9.04	11.25	14.52	14.24	14.78	9.89
Fats and oils	23.35	13.82	23.27	23.43	27.52	26.43	25.11	16.60
Salad dressings	27.18	13.15	25.90	31.47	34.74	27.46	23.85	18.73
Nondairy cream and imitation milk	9.15	3.19	7.28	10.18	10.44	10.56	11.90	7.56
Peanut butter	11.81	7.45	11.50	13.51	14.46	11.76	11.29	7.16
Miscellaneous foods	437.02	271.50	485.49	518.10	528.08	398.23	347.63	255.51
Frozen prepared foods	90.20	60.11	93.72	102.83	113.25	82.39	73.44	60.45
Frozen meals	28.50	17.94	27.64	26.70	37.03	24.31	31.87	28.16
Other frozen prepared foods	61.70	42.17	66.07	76.14	76.22	58.08	41.57	32.29
Canned and packaged soups	35.54	19.04	33.85	36.34	41.31	38.45	35.79	34.59
Potato chips, nuts, and other snacks	92.50	54.72	88.21	112.96	122.22	87.15	75.07	48.43
Potato chips and other snacks	71.67	47.39	74.55	95.44	89.50	60.30	48.66	33.55
Nuts	20.83	7.33	13.66	17.51	32.72	26.85	26.41	14.88
Condiments and seasonings	84.61	47.64	85.15	98.50	104.52	83.24	75.46	52.26
Salt, spices, and other seasonings	20.65	10.60	21.36	23.55	23.30	23.42	19.80	12.41
Olives, pickles, relishes	9.77	4.09	9.60	10.61	13.50	7.84	10.87	6.67
Sauces and gravies	37.23	23.27	40.19	45.44	45.89	34.78	28.32	19.06
Baking needs and miscellaneous products	16.96	9.68	14.00	18.90	21.83	17.20	16.46	14.11
Other canned/packaged prepared foods	134.17	89.98	184.55	167.46	146.79	107.00	87.88	59.79
Prepared salads	18.55	7.49	17.73	21.22	24.34	20.28	15.70	11.79
Prepared desserts	9.31	6.25	9.34	10.17	10.44	7.54	10.92	8.18
Baby food	32.26	31.04	68.97	43.69	24.52	12.75	8.85	6.01
Miscellaneous prepared foods	73.91	45.20	88.37	92.23	87.20	66.36	52.27	33.80
Vitamin supplements	0.14	–	0.15	0.15	0.29	0.07	0.14	0.01
Nonalcoholic beverages	249.58	147.41	247.21	300.22	299.97	262.58	199.40	151.06
Cola	86.99	59.47	90.10	105.36	104.87	87.50	65.91	45.59
Other carbonated drinks	47.39	33.23	48.41	61.05	56.07	44.93	34.20	24.34
Coffee	41.85	10.46	30.64	45.19	51.17	58.94	44.73	35.11
Roasted coffee	27.50	6.49	19.94	30.51	33.95	38.60	29.53	21.14
Instant and freeze-dried coffee	14.35	3.97	10.70	14.68	17.23	20.35	15.20	13.97
Noncarbonated fruit-flavored drinks, incl. nonfrozen lemonade	19.42	14.53	22.60	27.86	23.70	13.78	10.02	6.47
Tea	15.68	8.12	13.89	16.27	19.53	19.90	14.34	11.66
Nonalcoholic beer	0.27	–	0.65	0.28	0.22	0.35	0.10	–
Other nonalcoholic beverages and ice	37.99	21.60	40.92	44.22	44.41	37.18	30.09	27.90
Food prepared by CU on trips	39.94	19.11	31.45	46.50	51.74	51.54	39.90	16.80
FOOD AWAY FROM HOME	**2,136.88**	**1,569.46**	**2,309.18**	**2,607.49**	**2,637.79**	**2,097.14**	**1,418.00**	**971.16**
Meals at restaurants, carry-outs, other	**1,750.33**	**1,305.72**	**2,002.41**	**2,122.65**	**2,102.72**	**1,681.99**	**1,122.02**	**814.42**
Lunch	662.90	507.99	770.98	838.18	784.91	573.43	440.78	284.70
At fast food, take-out, delivery, concession stands, buffet, and cafeteria (other than employer and school cafeteria)	368.00	356.36	469.91	451.50	423.08	300.29	225.35	122.98
At full-service restaurants	208.12	112.25	207.50	217.05	253.74	228.21	200.10	156.27
At vending machines, mobile vendors	6.52	7.30	9.05	11.19	4.97	3.92	1.29	2.34
At employer and school cafeterias	80.26	32.08	84.51	158.44	103.12	41.01	14.04	3.12

	total consumer units	under 25	25 to 34	35 to 44	45 to 54	55 to 64	65 to 74	75+
Dinner	$697.99	$474.32	$771.34	$794.35	$857.91	$751.89	$454.73	$380.87
At fast food, take-out, delivery, concession stands, buffet, and cafeteria (other than employer and school cafeteria)	206.92	166.90	278.29	262.97	238.33	179.32	101.89	60.93
At full-service restaurants	487.70	299.40	489.20	527.47	616.99	567.51	352.84	319.68
At vending machines, mobile vendors	1.02	1.98	1.50	1.66	1.10	0.11	–	–
At employer and school cafeterias	2.35	6.03	2.34	2.25	1.48	4.95	–	0.27
Snacks and nonalcoholic beverages	227.71	195.44	281.63	309.89	265.09	193.32	110.14	54.91
At fast food, take-out, delivery, concession stands, buffet, and cafeteria (other than employer and school cafeteria)	158.55	136.70	192.30	206.39	188.28	144.14	83.94	38.76
At full-service restaurants	20.15	17.34	22.10	20.41	25.87	19.30	17.04	11.20
At vending machines, mobile vendors	38.52	33.92	52.11	65.71	40.03	23.05	6.86	4.05
At employer and school cafeterias	10.49	7.47	15.13	17.38	10.91	6.82	2.31	0.90
Breakfast and brunch	161.73	127.97	178.46	180.22	194.81	163.34	116.37	93.94
At fast food, take-out, delivery, concession stands, buffet, and cafeteria (other than employer and school cafeteria)	77.12	73.00	96.94	94.56	90.52	64.18	40.10	32.42
At full-service restaurants	79.64	51.37	75.41	78.53	97.37	94.49	75.70	61.52
At vending machines, mobile vendors	1.35	0.58	1.94	1.21	2.20	1.67	0.48	–
At employer and school cafeterias	3.62	3.02	4.16	5.92	4.73	3.01	0.09	–
Board (including at school)	**39.03**	**85.83**	**8.94**	**17.24**	**112.45**	**27.5**	**5.97**	**5.21**
Catered affairs	**54.02**	**21.16**	**37.63**	**74.93**	**53.59**	**97.16**	**26.81**	**34.58**
Food on trips	**216.06**	**111.37**	**186.27**	**230.89**	**276.16**	**255.32**	**244.75**	**110.12**
School lunches	**58.46**	**15.27**	**50.99**	**137.4**	**77.78**	**12.26**	**9.86**	**1.87**
Meals as pay	**18.97**	**30.11**	**22.95**	**24.38**	**15.1**	**22.91**	**8.58**	**4.96**
ALCOHOLIC BEVERAGES	**371.81**	**392.48**	**431.25**	**420.36**	**416.83**	**371.31**	**260.92**	**155.48**
At home	**226.64**	**259.34**	**247.46**	**245.05**	**264.15**	**219.67**	**178.04**	**101.4**
Beer and ale	112.01	189.67	157.54	130.71	113.94	76.52	47.54	32.04
Whiskey	13.49	9.33	12.45	11.59	17.99	9.12	22.04	11.03
Wine	80.04	39.61	58.45	78.63	111.64	105.87	92.4	43.69
Other alcoholic beverages	21.10	20.72	19.01	24.12	20.57	28.17	16.07	14.64
Away from home	**145.17**	**133.14**	**183.79**	**175.31**	**152.69**	**151.64**	**82.87**	**54.07**
Beer and ale	62.46	62.6	79.43	79.31	64.02	63.9	28.9	21.35
At fast food, take-out, delivery, concession stands, buffet, and cafeteria	13.37	23.41	20.41	15.53	12.45	9.72	4.65	2.98
At full-service restaurants	45.05	36.35	57.95	51.86	51.37	47.47	24.25	18.38
At vending machines, mobile vendors	0.4	2.77	0.5	0.16	0.07	0.35	–	–
At catered affairs	3.64	0.08	0.57	11.76	0.13	6.36	–	–
Wine	17.79	15.31	23.01	22.19	19.58	18.83	6.17	7.04
At fast food, take-out, delivery, concession stands, buffet and cafeteria	1.23	2.22	1.3	2.47	1.08	0.45	–	–
At full-service restaurants	16.16	13.07	21.65	18.47	18.48	17.7	6.17	7.04
At catered affairs	0.39	0.01	0.06	1.25	0.01	0.67	–	–
Other alcoholic beverages	64.92	55.23	81.35	73.82	69.08	68.91	47.8	25.68
At fast food, take-out, delivery, concession stands, buffet, and cafeteria	3.04	5.96	4.67	4.58	2.63	1.15	0.55	–
At full-service restaurants	25.74	19.66	36.63	31.07	28.54	26.1	9.91	8.82
At machines and mobile vendors	0.29	0.57	0.55	0.26	0.26	0.21	0.07	0.09
At catered affairs	1.60	0.03	0.25	5.18	0.06	2.8	–	–
Alcoholic beverages purchased on trips	34.24	29.01	39.24	32.72	37.6	38.64	37.28	16.77

Note: (–) means sample is too small to make a reliable estimate.
Source: Bureau of Labor Statistics, unpublished tables from the 2000 Consumer Expenditure Survey

Table 5.2 Food and Alcohol: Indexed spending by age, 2000

(indexed average annual spending of consumer units (CU) on food and alcoholic beverages, by age of consumer unit reference person, 2000; index definition: an index of 100 is the average for all consumer units; an index of 132 means that spending by consumer units in that group is 32 percent above the average for all consumer units; an index of 68 indicates spending that is 32 percent below the average for all consumer units)

	total consumer units	under 25	25 to 34	35 to 44	45 to 54	55 to 64	65 to 74	75+
Average spending of CU, total	$38,044.67	$22,543.18	$38,945.27	$45,149.37	$46,160.28	$39,340.03	$30,781.81	$21,908.04
Average spending of CU, index	100	59	102	119	121	103	81	58
Food, spending index	100	62	102	118	122	100	81	60
Alcoholic beverages, spending index	100	106	116	113	112	100	70	42
FOOD AT HOME	**100**	**54**	**98**	**115**	**121**	**102**	**91**	**70**
Cereals and bakery products	**100**	**52**	**95**	**117**	**124**	**97**	**91**	**74**
Cereals and cereal products	100	57	107	122	115	89	85	72
Flour	100	76	100	116	107	92	89	89
Prepared flour mixes	100	55	80	134	118	101	89	70
Ready-to-eat and cooked cereals	100	58	106	120	110	90	89	80
Rice	100	53	117	113	137	83	74	53
Pasta, cornmeal, and other cereal products	100	54	114	128	116	84	80	57
Bakery products	100	50	88	115	128	101	95	75
Bread	100	54	91	113	117	107	99	80
White bread	100	58	96	118	111	102	98	76
Bread, other than white	100	51	88	109	121	111	100	84
Crackers and cookies	100	46	90	113	132	103	91	76
Cookies	100	47	91	112	135	101	86	75
Crackers	100	44	87	113	126	108	100	76
Frozen and refrigerated bakery products	100	53	89	121	121	104	94	66
Other bakery products	100	49	86	116	136	95	94	72
Biscuits and rolls	100	52	81	119	127	107	93	74
Cakes and cupcakes	100	45	91	106	162	79	90	63
Bread and cracker products	100	44	88	139	115	89	98	63
Sweetrolls, coffee cakes, doughnuts	100	57	87	113	122	101	108	76
Pies, tarts, turnovers	100	36	84	131	116	104	84	89
Meats, poultry, fish, and eggs	**100**	**55**	**97**	**115**	**122**	**105**	**91**	**65**
Beef	100	56	100	114	124	102	91	61
Ground beef	100	74	103	117	116	99	81	66
Roast	100	40	78	108	145	97	106	75
Chuck roast	100	41	80	124	135	91	101	67
Round roast	100	54	74	101	129	111	127	83
Other roast	100	28	80	100	167	92	95	77
Steak	100	50	108	113	125	102	93	49
Round steak	100	60	93	112	134	94	107	49
Sirloin steak	100	48	118	113	119	96	93	53
Other steak	100	47	106	113	126	109	88	47
Other beef	100	45	100	114	110	127	95	61
Pork	100	54	93	111	119	111	101	69
Bacon	100	44	85	113	121	105	110	82
Pork chops	100	63	100	114	120	104	89	62
Ham	100	46	98	108	107	120	105	84
Ham, not canned	100	45	99	107	106	122	102	85
Canned ham	100	71	67	121	117	86	148	68
Sausage	100	56	88	120	109	115	101	70
Other pork	100	55	91	105	134	113	103	54
Other meats	100	54	98	120	121	99	85	70
Frankfurters	100	63	115	115	115	91	81	71

	total consumer units	under 25	25 to 34	35 to 44	45 to 54	55 to 64	65 to 74	75+
Lunch meats (cold cuts)	100	53	93	123	123	99	86	66
Bologna, liverwurst, salami	100	57	96	118	122	98	89	68
Other lunch meats	100	51	91	125	124	99	85	65
Lamb, organ meats, and others	100	46	94	112	117	110	90	91
Lamb and organ meats	100	51	100	83	120	124	105	101
Mutton, goat, and game	100	21	64	240	105	47	21	43
Poultry	100	59	100	122	116	101	90	58
Fresh and frozen chicken	100	63	105	121	115	99	85	58
Fresh and frozen whole chicken	100	78	100	115	123	93	90	55
Fresh and frozen chicken parts	100	58	107	123	112	101	83	60
Other poultry	100	44	82	128	119	108	107	56
Fish and seafood	100	47	92	115	132	104	86	66
Canned fish and seafood	100	50	81	97	137	120	97	87
Fresh fish and shellfish	100	50	94	117	131	105	82	61
Frozen fish and shellfish	100	39	96	118	132	95	90	69
Eggs	100	60	88	107	115	125	92	82
Dairy products	**100**	**54**	**98**	**118**	**116**	**99**	**96**	**73**
Fresh milk and cream	100	56	102	119	111	96	90	80
Fresh milk, all types	100	57	104	119	110	94	91	81
Cream	100	50	89	120	122	117	84	63
Other dairy products	100	52	95	117	120	101	99	68
Butter	100	41	91	119	127	103	100	61
Cheese	100	54	98	119	116	102	95	66
Ice cream and related products	100	56	90	113	122	97	110	72
Miscellaneous dairy products	100	44	92	117	124	105	91	73
Fruits and vegetables	**100**	**49**	**94**	**106**	**120**	**107**	**102**	**88**
Fresh fruits	100	47	89	104	114	113	101	107
Apples	100	57	93	107	117	109	94	91
Bananas	100	52	83	101	110	117	105	118
Oranges	100	57	99	107	114	107	96	88
Citrus fruits, excl. oranges	100	37	94	97	115	128	90	114
Other fresh fruits	100	40	87	104	115	112	105	113
Fresh vegetables	100	46	93	104	127	109	102	81
Potatoes	100	45	87	104	124	110	105	91
Lettuce	100	47	85	108	131	108	99	80
Tomatoes	100	49	107	101	126	103	98	74
Other fresh vegetables	100	46	92	103	127	110	103	80
Processed fruits	100	54	99	109	116	100	104	84
Frozen fruits and fruit juices	100	43	98	117	116	121	90	60
Frozen orange juice	100	40	90	118	111	133	90	70
Frozen fruits	100	35	111	98	133	102	115	54
Frozen fruit juices	100	55	100	134	110	117	68	48
Canned fruits	100	44	87	107	106	103	130	104
Dried fruits	100	37	80	102	106	101	136	133
Fresh fruit juice	100	49	97	106	120	97	106	90
Canned and bottled fruit juice	100	63	104	109	118	94	96	78
Processed vegetables	100	49	97	110	125	103	100	68
Frozen vegetables	100	51	93	121	127	101	85	63
Canned and dried vegetables and juices	100	48	99	105	124	105	106	70
Canned beans	100	47	94	107	120	93	120	85
Canned corn	100	42	114	111	132	85	87	65
Canned miscellaneous vegetables	100	46	86	102	127	119	110	76
Dried peas	100	24	129	97	71	126	118	126
Dried beans	100	32	106	110	138	97	77	75

	total consumer units	under 25	25 to 34	35 to 44	45 to 54	55 to 64	65 to 74	75+
Dried miscellaneous vegetables	100	54	108	94	123	111	111	64
Dried processed vegetables	100	54	159	139	73	100	29	73
Frozen vegetable juices	100	41	162	117	90	72	117	28
Fresh and canned vegetable juices	100	59	108	110	122	103	101	45
Other food at home	**100**	**58**	**102**	**119**	**121**	**99**	**84**	**61**
Sugar and other sweets	100	51	89	125	122	99	90	68
Candy and chewing gum	100	48	88	133	128	91	83	60
Sugar	100	66	102	121	102	111	84	71
Artificial sweeteners	100	5	45	80	152	162	124	112
Jams, preserves, other sweets	100	63	92	108	110	104	112	87
Fats and oils	100	51	93	108	122	109	105	72
Margarine	100	42	78	97	125	123	127	85
Fats and oils	100	59	100	100	118	113	108	71
Salad dressings	100	48	95	116	128	101	88	69
Nondairy cream and imitation milk	100	35	80	111	114	115	130	83
Peanut butter	100	63	97	114	122	100	96	61
Miscellaneous foods	100	62	111	119	121	91	80	58
Frozen prepared foods	100	67	104	114	126	91	81	67
Frozen meals	100	63	97	94	130	85	112	99
Other frozen prepared foods	100	68	107	123	124	94	67	52
Canned and packaged soups	100	54	95	102	116	108	101	97
Potato chips, nuts, and other snacks	100	59	95	122	132	94	81	52
Potato chips and other snacks	100	66	104	133	125	84	68	47
Nuts	100	35	66	84	157	129	127	71
Condiments and seasonings	100	56	101	116	124	98	89	62
Salt, spices, and other seasonings	100	51	103	114	113	113	96	60
Olives, pickles, relishes	100	42	98	109	138	80	111	68
Sauces and gravies	100	63	108	122	123	93	76	51
Baking needs and miscellaneous products	100	57	83	111	129	101	97	83
Other canned/packaged prepared foods	100	67	138	125	109	80	65	45
Prepared salads	100	40	96	114	131	109	85	64
Prepared desserts	100	67	100	109	112	81	117	88
Baby food	100	96	214	135	76	40	27	19
Miscellaneous prepared foods	100	61	120	125	118	90	71	46
Vitamin supplements	100	–	107	107	207	50	100	7
Nonalcoholic beverages	100	59	99	120	120	105	80	61
Cola	100	68	104	121	121	101	76	52
Other carbonated drinks	100	70	102	129	118	95	72	51
Coffee	100	25	73	108	122	141	107	84
Roasted coffee	100	24	73	111	123	140	107	77
Instant and freeze-dried coffee	100	28	75	102	120	142	106	97
Noncarbonated fruit-flavored drinks, incl. nonfrozen lemonade	100	75	116	143	122	71	52	33
Tea	100	52	89	104	125	127	91	74
Nonalcoholic beer	100	–	241	104	81	130	37	–
Other nonalcoholic beverages and ice	100	57	108	116	117	98	79	73
Food prepared by CU on trips	100	48	79	116	130	129	100	42
FOOD AWAY FROM HOME	**100**	**73**	**108**	**122**	**123**	**98**	**66**	**45**
Meals at restaurants, carry-outs, other	**100**	**75**	**114**	**121**	**120**	**96**	**64**	**47**
Lunch	100	77	116	126	118	87	66	43
At fast food, take-out, delivery, concession stands, buffet, and cafeteria (other than employer and school cafeteria)	100	97	128	123	115	82	61	33
At full-service restaurants	100	54	100	104	122	110	96	75
At vending machines, mobile vendors	100	112	139	172	76	60	20	36
At employer and school cafeterias	100	40	105	197	128	51	17	4

	total consumer units	under 25	25 to 34	35 to 44	45 to 54	55 to 64	65 to 74	75+
Dinner	100	68	111	114	123	108	65	55
At fast food, take-out, delivery, concession stands, buffet, and cafeteria (other than employer and school cafeteria)	100	81	134	127	115	87	49	29
At full-service restaurants	100	61	100	108	127	116	72	66
At vending machines, mobile vendors	100	194	147	163	108	11	–	–
At employer and school cafeterias	100	257	100	96	63	211	–	11
Snacks and nonalcoholic beverages	100	86	124	136	116	85	48	24
At fast food, take-out, delivery, concession stands, buffet, and cafeteria (other than employer and school cafeteria)	100	86	121	130	119	91	53	24
At full-service restaurants	100	86	110	101	128	96	85	56
At vending machines, mobile vendors	100	88	135	171	104	60	18	11
At employer and school cafeterias	100	71	144	166	104	65	22	9
Breakfast and brunch	100	79	110	111	120	101	72	58
At fast food, take-out, delivery, concession stands, buffet, and cafeteria (other than employer and school cafeteria)	100	95	126	123	117	83	52	42
At full-service restaurants	100	65	95	99	122	119	95	77
At vending machines, mobile vendors	100	43	144	90	163	124	36	–
At employer and school cafeterias	100	83	115	164	131	83	2	–
Board (including at school)	**100**	**220**	**23**	**44**	**288**	**70**	**15**	**13**
Catered affairs	**100**	**39**	**70**	**139**	**99**	**180**	**50**	**64**
Food on trips	**100**	**52**	**86**	**107**	**128**	**118**	**113**	**51**
School lunches	**100**	**26**	**87**	**235**	**133**	**21**	**17**	**3**
Meals as pay	**100**	**159**	**121**	**129**	**80**	**121**	**45**	**26**
ALCOHOLIC BEVERAGES	**100**	**106**	**116**	**113**	**112**	**100**	**70**	**42**
At home	**100**	**114**	**109**	**108**	**117**	**97**	**79**	**45**
Beer and ale	100	169	141	117	102	68	42	29
Whiskey	100	69	92	86	133	68	163	82
Wine	100	49	73	98	139	132	115	55
Other alcoholic beverages	100	98	90	114	97	134	76	69
Away from home	**100**	**92**	**127**	**121**	**105**	**104**	**57**	**37**
Beer and ale	100	100	127	127	102	102	46	34
At fast food, take-out, delivery, concession stands, buffet, and cafeteria	100	175	153	116	93	73	35	22
At full-service restaurants	100	81	129	115	114	105	54	41
At vending machines, mobile vendors	100	693	125	40	18	88	–	–
At catered affairs	100	2	16	323	4	175	–	–
Wine	100	86	129	125	110	106	35	40
At fast food, take-out, delivery, concession stands, buffet and cafeteria	100	180	106	201	88	37	–	–
At full-service restaurants	100	81	134	114	114	110	38	44
At catered affairs	100	3	15	321	3	172	–	–
Other alcoholic beverages	100	85	125	114	106	106	74	40
At fast food, take-out, delivery, concession stands, buffet, and cafeteria	100	196	154	151	87	38	18	–
At full-service restaurants	100	76	142	121	111	101	39	34
At machines and mobile vendors	100	197	190	90	90	72	24	31
At catered affairs	100	2	16	324	4	175	–	–
Alcoholic beverages purchased on trips	100	85	115	96	110	113	109	49

Note: (–) means sample is too small to make a reliable estimate.
Source: Calculations by New Strategist based on the 2000 Consumer Expenditure Survey

Table 5.3 Food and Alcohol: Indexed per capita spending by age, 2000

(indexed average annual per capita spending of consumer units (CU) on food and alcoholic beverages, by age of consumer unit reference person, 2000; index definition: an index of 100 is the average for all consumer units; an index of 132 means that spending by consumer units in that group is 32 percent above the average for all consumer units; an index of 68 indicates spending that is 32 percent below the average for all consumer units)

	total consumer units	under 25	25 to 34	35 to 44	45 to 54	55 to 64	65 to 74	75+
Per capita spending of CU, total	$15,218	$11,865	$13,429	$13,682	$17,096	$18,733	$16,201	$14,605
Per capita spending of CU, index	100	78	88	90	112	123	106	96
Food, per capita spending index	100	82	88	89	113	119	107	99
Alcoholic beverages, per capita spending index	100	139	100	86	104	119	92	70
FOOD AT HOME	**100**	**72**	**84**	**87**	**112**	**121**	**120**	**116**
Cereals and bakery products	**100**	**69**	**82**	**89**	**114**	**116**	**120**	**123**
Cereals and cereal products	100	75	92	92	106	106	112	120
Flour	100	100	87	88	99	109	117	148
Prepared flour mixes	100	72	69	101	109	120	117	116
Ready-to-eat and cooked cereals	100	76	92	91	102	108	117	133
Rice	100	70	101	86	127	99	97	88
Pasta, cornmeal, and other cereal products	100	71	99	97	107	101	105	95
Bakery products	100	66	76	87	119	121	125	125
Bread	100	71	79	86	108	128	130	134
White bread	100	77	83	90	102	122	128	126
Bread, other than white	100	66	76	83	112	132	132	139
Crackers and cookies	100	60	77	85	122	123	119	126
Cookies	100	61	78	85	125	120	113	126
Crackers	100	58	75	86	116	129	131	127
Frozen and refrigerated bakery products	100	70	76	92	112	124	124	111
Other bakery products	100	64	74	88	126	114	124	120
Biscuits and rolls	100	69	69	90	118	127	123	124
Cakes and cupcakes	100	60	78	81	150	94	118	105
Bread and cracker products	100	58	75	105	106	106	129	105
Sweetrolls, coffee cakes, doughnuts	100	74	75	85	113	120	142	126
Pies, tarts, turnovers	100	47	72	99	108	124	110	149
Meats, poultry, fish, and eggs	**100**	**72**	**83**	**87**	**113**	**125**	**120**	**108**
Beef	100	74	87	86	115	121	120	101
Ground beef	100	97	88	88	108	118	107	109
Roast	100	52	67	82	135	115	140	126
Chuck roast	100	54	69	94	125	109	133	112
Round roast	100	71	63	76	120	132	167	138
Other roast	100	36	69	76	155	109	125	128
Steak	100	65	93	86	116	122	122	82
Round steak	100	78	80	85	124	112	141	81
Sirloin steak	100	63	102	85	111	114	123	88
Other steak	100	62	92	86	117	130	116	79
Other beef	100	59	86	86	102	151	125	101
Pork	100	71	80	84	110	133	133	115
Bacon	100	58	73	86	112	125	145	137
Pork chops	100	83	86	87	111	124	117	103
Ham	100	61	84	82	99	143	138	140
Ham, not canned	100	59	86	81	98	145	135	141
Canned ham	100	93	58	92	108	102	194	113
Sausage	100	74	75	91	101	137	133	117
Other pork	100	73	78	79	124	134	135	90
Other meats	100	72	84	91	112	118	112	117
Frankfurters	100	83	99	87	106	109	106	119

	total consumer units	under 25	25 to 34	35 to 44	45 to 54	55 to 64	65 to 74	75+
Lunch meats (cold cuts)	100	70	80	93	114	118	113	110
Bologna, liverwurst, salami	100	76	83	90	113	117	117	114
Other lunch meats	100	67	79	95	115	118	111	108
Lamb, organ meats, and others	100	60	81	85	108	131	118	151
Lamb and organ meats	100	67	86	63	111	148	138	169
Mutton, goat, and game	100	28	55	182	97	56	27	71
Poultry	100	78	86	93	107	120	118	96
Fresh and frozen chicken	100	83	91	92	107	117	112	97
Fresh and frozen whole chicken	100	103	86	87	114	111	118	91
Fresh and frozen chicken parts	100	76	92	93	104	120	109	99
Other poultry	100	58	70	97	110	128	141	93
Fish and seafood	100	62	80	87	122	124	113	110
Canned fish and seafood	100	66	70	73	127	143	127	144
Fresh fish and shellfish	100	66	81	89	121	125	108	101
Frozen fish and shellfish	100	52	83	89	123	113	118	114
Eggs	100	79	76	81	106	148	121	137
Dairy products	**100**	**71**	**84**	**89**	**108**	**118**	**126**	**121**
Fresh milk and cream	100	74	88	90	103	114	118	133
Fresh milk, all types	100	74	89	90	102	112	119	135
Cream	100	65	77	91	113	139	110	105
Other dairy products	100	69	82	89	111	120	131	113
Butter	100	54	79	90	118	122	132	102
Cheese	100	71	85	90	108	121	125	109
Ice cream and related products	100	74	78	86	113	116	145	120
Miscellaneous dairy products	100	58	80	89	115	125	120	122
Fruits and vegetables	**100**	**64**	**81**	**80**	**111**	**128**	**134**	**146**
Fresh fruits	100	62	77	79	106	135	132	179
Apples	100	75	80	81	109	130	124	152
Bananas	100	68	72	77	102	140	138	197
Oranges	100	76	85	81	105	127	126	146
Citrus fruits, excl. oranges	100	48	81	74	107	152	118	190
Other fresh fruits	100	52	75	79	106	133	138	189
Fresh vegetables	100	61	80	78	117	129	134	135
Potatoes	100	59	75	79	115	131	138	152
Lettuce	100	62	73	82	121	129	130	134
Tomatoes	100	65	92	76	116	123	128	123
Other fresh vegetables	100	60	79	78	117	131	136	133
Processed fruits	100	70	85	83	107	119	137	140
Frozen fruits and fruit juices	100	56	85	88	107	144	119	100
Frozen orange juice	100	53	78	89	103	158	118	116
Frozen fruits	100	46	96	74	123	121	152	89
Frozen fruit juices	100	72	86	101	102	140	90	80
Canned fruits	100	58	75	81	99	122	171	174
Dried fruits	100	48	69	78	98	120	179	222
Fresh fruit juice	100	64	83	80	111	116	140	150
Canned and bottled fruit juice	100	83	90	83	109	112	127	129
Processed vegetables	100	65	84	83	116	123	131	113
Frozen vegetables	100	68	80	92	117	120	112	105
Canned and dried vegetables and juices	100	64	86	79	115	124	140	117
Canned beans	100	62	81	81	111	111	158	142
Canned corn	100	56	98	84	122	102	115	109
Canned miscellaneous vegetables	100	61	74	77	117	142	145	126
Dried peas	100	31	112	74	65	151	155	211
Dried beans	100	43	92	83	128	116	101	126

	total consumer units	under 25	25 to 34	35 to 44	45 to 54	55 to 64	65 to 74	75+
Dried miscellaneous vegetables	100	71	93	71	114	132	146	107
Dried processed vegetables	100	71	137	105	68	119	39	122
Frozen vegetable juices	100	54	140	89	83	86	154	46
Fresh and canned vegetable juices	100	78	93	83	113	123	133	75
Other food at home	**100**	**77**	**88**	**90**	**112**	**118**	**111**	**101**
Sugar and other sweets	100	68	77	95	113	117	118	114
Candy and chewing gum	100	63	76	101	118	108	109	100
Sugar	100	86	88	92	95	132	111	119
Artificial sweeteners	100	7	39	60	141	193	163	187
Jams, preserves, other sweets	100	83	79	82	102	124	147	145
Fats and oils	100	67	80	82	113	130	138	120
Margarine	100	55	67	73	116	146	168	142
Fats and oils	100	78	86	76	109	135	141	118
Salad dressings	100	64	82	88	118	120	115	115
Nondairy cream and imitation milk	100	46	69	84	106	137	171	138
Peanut butter	100	83	84	87	113	119	126	101
Miscellaneous foods	100	82	96	90	112	108	105	97
Frozen prepared foods	100	88	90	86	116	109	107	112
Frozen meals	100	83	84	71	120	102	147	165
Other frozen prepared foods	100	90	92	93	114	112	89	87
Canned and packaged soups	100	70	82	77	108	129	133	162
Potato chips, nuts, and other snacks	100	78	82	93	122	112	107	87
Potato chips and other snacks	100	87	90	101	116	100	89	78
Nuts	100	46	57	64	145	153	167	119
Condiments and seasonings	100	74	87	88	114	117	117	103
Salt, spices, and other seasonings	100	68	89	86	104	135	126	100
Olives, pickles, relishes	100	55	85	82	128	96	146	114
Sauces and gravies	100	82	93	92	114	111	100	85
Baking needs and miscellaneous products	100	75	71	84	119	121	128	139
Other canned/packaged prepared foods	100	88	119	95	101	95	86	74
Prepared salads	100	53	82	87	121	130	111	106
Prepared desserts	100	88	86	83	104	96	154	146
Baby food	100	127	184	103	70	47	36	31
Miscellaneous prepared foods	100	80	103	95	109	107	93	76
Vitamin supplements	100	–	92	81	192	60	132	12
Nonalcoholic beverages	100	78	85	91	111	125	105	101
Cola	100	90	89	92	112	120	100	87
Other carbonated drinks	100	92	88	98	110	113	95	86
Coffee	100	33	63	82	113	168	141	140
Roasted coffee	100	31	63	84	114	167	141	128
Instant and freeze-dried coffee	100	36	64	77	111	169	139	162
Noncarbonated fruit-flavored drinks, incl. nonfrozen lemonade	100	98	100	109	113	84	68	56
Tea	100	68	76	79	115	151	120	124
Nonalcoholic beer	100	–	208	79	75	154	49	–
Other nonalcoholic beverages and ice	100	75	93	88	108	117	104	122
Food prepared by CU on trips	100	63	68	88	120	154	131	70
FOOD AWAY FROM HOME	**100**	**97**	**93**	**92**	**114**	**117**	**87**	**76**
Meals at restaurants, carry-outs, other	**100**	**98**	**99**	**92**	**111**	**114**	**84**	**78**
Lunch	100	101	100	96	110	103	87	72
At fast food, take-out, delivery, concession stands, buffet, and cafeteria (other than employer and school cafeteria)	100	127	110	93	106	97	81	56
At full-service restaurants	100	71	86	79	113	131	127	125
At vending machines, mobile vendors	100	147	120	130	71	72	26	60
At employer and school cafeterias	100	53	91	150	119	61	23	6

	total consumer units	under 25	25 to 34	35 to 44	45 to 54	55 to 64	65 to 74	75+
Dinner	100	89	95	86	114	128	86	91
At fast food, take-out, delivery, concession stands, buffet, and cafeteria (other than employer and school cafeteria)	100	106	116	96	107	103	65	49
At full-service restaurants	100	81	86	82	117	139	95	109
At vending machines, mobile vendors	100	255	127	123	100	13	–	–
At employer and school cafeterias	100	338	86	73	58	251	–	19
Snacks and nonalcoholic beverages	100	113	107	103	108	101	64	40
At fast food, take-out, delivery, concession stands, buffet, and cafeteria (other than employer and school cafeteria)	100	113	105	99	110	108	70	41
At full-service restaurants	100	113	95	77	119	114	111	93
At vending machines, mobile vendors	100	116	117	129	96	71	23	18
At employer and school cafeterias	100	94	124	126	96	77	29	14
Breakfast and brunch	100	104	95	84	112	120	95	97
At fast food, take-out, delivery, concession stands, buffet, and cafeteria (other than employer and school cafeteria)	100	125	108	93	109	99	68	70
At full-service restaurants	100	85	82	75	113	141	125	129
At vending machines, mobile vendors	100	57	124	68	151	147	47	–
At employer and school cafeterias	100	110	99	124	121	99	3	–
Board (including at school)	**100**	**289**	**20**	**33**	**267**	**84**	**20**	**22**
Catered affairs	**100**	**52**	**60**	**105**	**92**	**214**	**65**	**107**
Food on trips	**100**	**68**	**74**	**81**	**118**	**141**	**149**	**85**
School lunches	**100**	**34**	**75**	**178**	**123**	**25**	**22**	**5**
Meals as pay	**100**	**209**	**104**	**97**	**74**	**144**	**60**	**44**
ALCOHOLIC BEVERAGES	**100**	**139**	**100**	**86**	**104**	**119**	**92**	**70**
At home	**100**	**151**	**94**	**82**	**108**	**115**	**103**	**75**
Beer and ale	100	223	121	88	94	81	56	48
Whiskey	100	91	80	65	123	80	215	136
Wine	100	65	63	74	129	157	152	91
Other alcoholic beverages	100	129	78	87	90	159	100	116
Away from home	**100**	**121**	**109**	**91**	**97**	**124**	**75**	**62**
Beer and ale	100	132	110	96	95	122	61	57
At fast food, take-out, delivery, concession stands, buffet, and cafeteria	100	230	132	88	86	87	46	37
At full-service restaurants	100	106	111	87	106	125	71	68
At vending machines, mobile vendors	100	911	108	30	16	104	–	–
At catered affairs	100	3	13	245	3	208	–	–
Wine	100	113	112	94	102	126	46	66
At fast food, take-out, delivery, concession stands, buffet and cafeteria	100	237	91	152	81	44	–	–
At full-service restaurants	100	106	115	87	106	130	50	73
At catered affairs	100	3	13	243	2	205	–	–
Other alcoholic beverages	100	112	108	86	99	126	97	66
At fast food, take-out, delivery, concession stands, buffet, and cafeteria	100	258	132	114	80	45	24	–
At full-service restaurants	100	100	123	91	103	121	51	57
At machines and mobile vendors	100	259	163	68	83	86	32	52
At catered affairs	100	2	13	245	3	208	–	–
Alcoholic beverages purchased on trips	100	111	99	72	102	134	143	82

Note: Per capita indexes account for household size and show how much each person in a particular household demographic segment spends relative to a person in the average household. (–) means sample is too small to make a reliable estimate.
Source: Calculations by New Strategist based on the 2000 Consumer Expenditure Survey

Table 5.4 Food and Alcohol: Total spending by age, 2000

(total annual spending on food and alcoholic beverages, by consumer unit (CU) age group, 2000; numbers in thousands)

	total consumer units	under 25	25 to 34	35 to 44	45 to 54	55 to 64	65 to 74	75+
Number of consumer units	109,367	8,306	18,887	23,983	21,874	14,161	11,538	10,617
Total spending of all CUs	$4,160,831,424	$187,243,653	$735,559,314	$1,082,817,341	$1,009,709,965	$557,094,165	$355,160,524	$232,597,661
Food, total spending	564,101,862	26,686,514	99,349,209	146,102,278	137,688,518	73,180,366	48,204,264	32,671,906
Alcoholic beverages, total spending	40,663,744	3,259,939	8,145,019	10,081,494	9,117,739	5,258,121	3,010,495	1,650,731
FOOD AT HOME	**$330,397,707**	**$13,650,662**	**$55,735,537**	**$83,566,845**	**$79,989,499**	**$43,482,908**	**$31,843,380**	**$22,361,101**
Cereals and bakery products	**49,579,342**	**1,973,589**	**8,108,945**	**12,733,054**	**12,247,034**	**6,240,328**	**4,780,540**	**3,547,883**
Cereals and cereal products	17,104,999	744,550	3,146,574	4,566,123	3,927,914	1,980,133	1,538,015	1,191,864
Flour	872,749	50,584	151,285	221,843	186,804	103,942	82,151	75,381
Prepared flour mixes	1,460,049	60,551	200,769	427,857	343,641	190,890	136,610	98,632
Ready-to-eat and cooked cereals	9,501,805	419,038	1,744,970	2,510,061	2,085,905	1,112,488	889,234	735,227
Rice	2,138,125	86,798	431,001	529,305	586,661	230,258	166,955	109,143
Pasta, cornmeal, and other cereal products	3,132,271	127,580	618,549	877,058	724,686	342,413	262,951	173,482
Bakery products	32,474,343	1,229,039	4,962,370	8,166,931	8,319,120	4,260,195	3,242,524	2,356,018
Bread	9,191,203	376,262	1,452,033	2,280,064	2,141,683	1,276,473	960,885	714,736
White bread	4,005,020	177,333	666,144	1,039,663	885,460	530,046	412,022	293,666
Bread, other than white	5,186,183	198,929	785,888	1,240,401	1,256,224	746,568	548,863	421,070
Crackers and cookies	7,768,338	270,277	1,201,969	1,919,120	2,046,094	1,037,435	741,778	570,770
Cookies	5,217,900	184,476	820,262	1,285,729	1,404,967	680,294	473,750	381,469
Crackers	2,550,438	85,884	381,706	633,631	640,908	357,282	268,028	189,195
Frozen and refrigerated bakery products	2,682,773	108,642	410,226	714,214	648,783	361,955	266,066	173,057
Other bakery products	12,832,030	473,774	1,898,144	3,253,294	3,482,560	1,584,191	1,273,911	897,561
Biscuits and rolls	4,213,911	166,784	585,875	1,096,263	1,071,170	581,592	413,983	303,434
Cakes and cupcakes	4,201,880	144,691	657,834	980,665	1,357,282	428,653	398,407	256,401
Bread and cracker products	482,308	16,280	72,904	146,776	110,901	55,653	50,075	29,621
Sweetrolls, coffee cakes, doughnuts	2,480,444	106,483	372,263	612,286	605,910	323,012	283,258	182,188
Pies, tarts, turnovers	1,452,394	39,537	209,457	417,544	337,297	195,280	128,187	125,918
Meats, poultry, fish, and eggs	**86,993,793**	**3,631,466**	**14,544,501**	**22,009,919**	**21,213,405**	**11,781,102**	**8,392,626**	**5,470,940**
Beef	26,050,126	1,117,240	4,518,715	6,487,162	6,477,329	3,439,140	2,498,554	1,530,547
Ground beef	9,598,048	536,651	1,701,152	2,453,461	2,234,429	1,231,582	819,775	611,964
Roast	4,357,181	131,069	587,952	1,035,346	1,267,817	547,181	488,980	319,147
Chuck roast	1,457,862	45,434	202,280	396,439	393,295	172,198	155,648	95,341
Round roast	1,253,346	51,082	159,406	276,284	323,735	179,561	167,993	100,755
Other roast	1,645,973	34,553	226,266	362,623	550,787	195,563	165,340	123,157
Steak	10,337,369	389,634	1,925,530	2,560,185	2,588,132	1,371,210	1,013,267	495,814
Round steak	1,674,409	75,668	269,706	409,630	449,292	204,485	189,454	79,309
Sirloin steak	3,265,699	119,274	665,200	807,747	779,808	405,429	321,910	167,536
Other steak	5,397,261	194,693	990,623	1,342,808	1,359,032	761,295	502,018	248,862
Other beef	1,758,621	59,886	304,081	437,930	386,951	289,168	176,531	103,622
Pork	18,257,727	743,221	2,933,151	4,461,557	4,340,895	2,632,388	1,940,807	1,226,476
Bacon	2,849,010	95,104	417,403	708,698	689,468	387,587	330,564	227,204
Pork chops	4,437,019	212,551	765,112	1,113,291	1,064,826	596,178	417,676	267,018
Ham	3,965,647	139,541	669,166	938,455	844,993	618,411	437,406	322,332
Ham, not canned	3,775,349	129,324	647,069	887,851	800,588	597,169	407,753	309,804
Canned ham	190,299	10,216	22,098	50,604	44,404	21,100	29,653	12,528
Sausage	2,760,423	117,696	417,214	725,486	604,379	411,802	294,796	187,921
Other pork	4,245,627	178,413	664,445	975,628	1,137,229	618,552	460,251	222,001
Other meats	10,995,758	454,421	1,852,437	2,888,033	2,657,035	1,406,754	991,576	747,118
Frankfurters	2,261,710	107,812	449,133	569,596	517,976	266,935	192,569	156,176

	total consumer units	under 25	25 to 34	35 to 44	45 to 54	55 to 64	65 to 74	75+
Lunch meats (cold cuts)	$7,435,862	$301,425	$1,193,470	$1,999,703	$1,835,010	$954,451	$675,896	$476,491
Bologna, liverwurst, salami	2,595,279	113,211	431,190	673,922	631,284	330,943	243,567	171,889
Other lunch meats	4,840,583	188,131	762,468	1,325,780	1,203,945	623,509	432,329	304,602
Lamb, organ meats, and others	1,298,186	45,102	209,835	318,734	303,830	185,367	123,110	114,451
Lamb and organ meats	1,061,954	41,364	183,771	194,262	254,395	171,065	117,918	104,577
Mutton, goat, and game	236,233	3,821	26,064	124,472	49,435	14,303	5,192	9,768
Poultry	15,875,714	712,572	2,743,337	4,262,499	3,686,206	2,066,232	1,499,248	890,129
Fresh and frozen chicken	12,514,866	600,939	2,269,651	3,319,487	2,885,181	1,597,219	1,119,648	707,729
Fresh and frozen whole chicken	3,417,719	202,334	590,974	865,546	841,055	411,519	323,179	181,551
Fresh and frozen chicken parts	9,097,147	398,605	1,678,865	2,453,941	2,044,125	1,185,701	796,468	526,285
Other poultry	3,360,848	111,633	473,686	943,012	801,026	469,012	379,600	182,294
Fish and seafood	12,045,681	432,992	1,922,885	3,025,216	3,185,729	1,628,515	1,095,879	775,041
Canned fish and seafood	1,713,781	65,285	238,921	362,863	469,416	265,944	175,031	143,967
Fresh fish and shellfish	7,307,903	277,753	1,183,459	1,882,426	1,915,287	991,412	634,359	429,564
Frozen fish and shellfish	3,023,998	89,954	500,506	779,687	801,026	371,301	286,373	201,511
Eggs	3,768,787	170,937	573,976	885,452	866,210	608,073	366,678	301,629
Dairy products	**35,503,809**	**1,451,723**	**5,993,412**	**9,181,412**	**8,254,373**	**4,550,071**	**3,579,549**	**2,506,461**
Fresh milk and cream	14,351,138	610,159	2,538,602	3,755,258	3,187,042	1,784,711	1,363,215	1,108,946
Fresh milk, all types	13,081,387	562,233	2,342,743	3,420,935	2,877,525	1,592,404	1,250,950	1,031,017
Cream	1,269,751	47,926	195,858	334,323	309,736	192,306	112,265	77,929
Other dairy products	21,152,671	841,564	3,454,810	5,426,154	5,067,331	2,765,360	2,216,334	1,397,516
Butter	1,859,239	57,810	292,560	484,936	472,697	247,251	196,146	110,735
Cheese	10,494,857	432,327	1,783,688	2,735,981	2,440,701	1,382,114	1,051,689	667,597
Ice cream and related products	6,185,798	263,300	961,159	1,534,193	1,507,337	780,129	716,741	433,811
Miscellaneous dairy products	2,612,778	88,127	417,214	671,044	646,814	355,866	251,644	185,373
Fruits and vegetables	**56,961,615**	**2,103,079**	**9,225,166**	**13,226,625**	**13,686,999**	**7,907,786**	**6,104,871**	**4,855,791**
Fresh fruits	17,845,413	636,240	2,750,325	4,062,241	4,081,032	2,614,829	1,893,270	1,860,948
Apples	3,225,233	139,375	516,937	758,103	757,059	454,568	319,949	285,066
Bananas	3,466,934	136,551	498,617	769,614	764,278	527,356	383,062	398,775
Oranges	2,070,317	90,369	353,754	486,135	471,385	286,052	208,953	176,348
Citrus fruits, excl. oranges	1,565,042	43,690	253,086	333,843	360,484	259,005	147,802	172,845
Other fresh fruits	7,517,888	226,255	1,127,932	1,714,305	1,727,827	1,087,990	833,505	827,914
Fresh vegetables	17,358,730	611,488	2,789,043	3,942,086	4,395,799	2,443,056	1,869,387	1,363,860
Potatoes	3,069,932	104,157	463,676	701,023	761,215	437,433	340,025	272,645
Lettuce	2,269,365	81,150	333,356	536,020	594,754	317,348	237,106	176,667
Tomatoes	3,229,608	120,935	597,018	713,015	811,963	431,627	332,525	231,557
Other fresh vegetables	8,790,919	305,246	1,394,994	1,992,028	2,227,867	1,256,647	959,846	683,098
Processed fruits	12,578,299	511,733	2,140,086	3,005,550	2,915,804	1,621,859	1,378,329	1,026,770
Frozen fruits and fruit juices	1,571,604	51,082	266,118	402,195	364,858	245,693	149,879	91,412
Frozen orange juice	754,632	23,008	117,666	194,502	167,555	129,715	71,536	51,068
Frozen fruits	395,909	10,549	76,115	84,660	105,433	52,112	48,229	20,597
Frozen fruit juices	419,969	17,526	72,526	123,273	92,090	63,866	30,230	19,641
Canned fruits	1,693,001	56,564	254,597	398,358	360,484	225,302	231,568	171,358
Dried fruits	601,519	16,695	83,292	135,024	127,525	78,310	86,304	77,716
Fresh fruit juice	2,563,562	94,439	428,357	597,177	617,066	323,154	287,065	223,700
Canned and bottled fruit juice	6,147,519	292,953	1,107,723	1,472,796	1,445,653	749,400	623,629	462,689
Processed vegetables	9,180,266	343,619	1,545,712	2,216,749	2,294,364	1,228,184	963,885	604,213
Frozen vegetables	2,889,476	112,795	464,998	769,614	731,467	376,824	258,913	175,924
Canned and dried vegetables and juices	6,290,790	230,824	1,080,714	1,447,134	1,562,897	851,218	704,972	428,290
Canned beans	1,385,680	49,753	225,700	324,730	332,485	167,383	175,724	114,557
Canned corn	743,696	23,838	145,808	181,551	196,210	82,134	68,536	47,246
Canned miscellaneous vegetables	1,963,138	68,940	291,426	437,690	496,977	303,045	227,991	144,285
Dried peas	37,185	664	8,310	7,914	5,250	6,089	4,615	4,565
Dried beans	276,699	6,811	50,806	66,673	76,340	34,836	22,384	20,278

	total consumer units	under 25	25 to 34	35 to 44	45 to 54	55 to 64	65 to 74	75+
Dried miscellaneous vegetables	$789,630	$32,227	$147,885	$162,125	$194,679	$113,146	$92,189	$49,157
Dried processed vegetables	44,840	1,827	12,277	13,670	6,562	5,806	1,385	3,185
Frozen vegetable juices	31,716	997	8,877	8,154	5,687	2,974	3,923	849
Fresh and canned vegetable juices	1,017,113	45,849	190,003	244,866	249,145	135,804	108,111	44,167
Other food at home	**101,358,055**	**4,490,888**	**17,863,513**	**26,415,836**	**24,587,688**	**13,003,480**	**8,985,794**	**5,980,025**
Sugar and other sweets	12,811,250	500,187	1,977,091	3,520,465	3,119,232	1,635,171	1,210,798	848,829
Candy and chewing gum	8,344,702	303,169	1,271,662	2,435,234	2,128,340	983,198	730,932	487,957
Sugar	1,837,366	91,449	323,723	488,774	375,358	263,536	163,724	127,510
Artificial sweeteners	458,248	1,827	35,885	80,103	139,119	96,153	59,998	49,794
Jams, preserves, other sweets	2,172,029	103,825	345,821	516,594	476,416	292,283	256,259	183,568
Fats and oils	9,087,304	352,507	1,454,110	2,154,633	2,224,148	1,280,862	1,002,998	636,277
Margarine	1,269,751	40,035	170,738	269,809	317,610	201,653	170,532	105,002
Fats and oils	2,553,719	114,789	439,500	561,922	601,972	374,275	289,719	176,242
Salad dressings	2,972,595	109,224	489,173	754,745	759,903	388,861	275,181	198,856
Nondairy cream and imitation milk	1,000,708	26,496	137,497	244,147	228,365	149,540	137,302	80,265
Peanut butter	1,291,624	61,880	217,201	324,010	316,298	166,533	130,264	76,018
Miscellaneous foods	47,795,566	2,255,079	9,169,450	12,425,592	11,551,222	5,639,335	4,010,955	2,712,750
Frozen prepared foods	9,864,903	499,274	1,770,090	2,466,172	2,477,231	1,166,725	847,351	641,798
Frozen meals	3,116,960	149,010	522,037	640,346	809,994	344,254	367,716	298,975
Other frozen prepared foods	6,747,944	350,264	1,247,864	1,826,066	1,667,236	822,471	479,635	342,823
Canned and packaged soups	3,886,903	158,146	639,325	871,542	903,615	544,490	412,945	367,242
Potato chips, nuts, and other snacks	10,116,448	454,504	1,666,022	2,709,120	2,673,440	1,234,131	866,158	514,181
Potato chips and other snacks	7,838,333	393,621	1,408,026	2,288,938	1,957,723	853,908	561,439	356,200
Nuts	2,278,115	60,883	257,996	419,942	715,717	380,223	304,719	157,981
Condiments and seasonings	9,253,542	395,698	1,608,228	2,362,326	2,286,270	1,178,762	870,657	554,844
Salt, spices, and other seasonings	2,258,429	88,044	403,426	564,800	509,664	331,651	228,452	131,757
Olives, pickles, relishes	1,068,516	33,972	181,315	254,460	295,299	111,022	125,418	70,815
Sauces and gravies	4,071,733	193,281	759,069	1,089,788	1,003,798	492,520	326,756	202,360
Baking needs and miscellaneous products	1,854,864	80,402	264,418	453,279	477,509	243,569	189,915	149,806
Other canned/packaged prepared foods	14,673,770	747,374	3,485,596	4,016,193	3,210,884	1,515,227	1,013,959	634,790
Prepared salads	2,028,758	62,212	334,867	508,919	532,413	287,185	181,147	125,174
Prepared desserts	1,018,207	51,913	176,405	243,907	228,365	106,774	125,995	86,847
Baby food	3,528,179	257,818	1,302,636	1,047,817	536,350	180,553	102,111	63,808
Miscellaneous prepared foods	8,083,315	375,431	1,669,044	2,211,952	1,907,413	939,724	603,091	358,855
Vitamin supplements	15,311	–	2,833	3,597	6,343	991	1,615	106
Nonalcoholic beverages	27,295,816	1,224,387	4,669,055	7,200,176	6,561,544	3,718,395	2,300,677	1,603,804
Cola	9,513,835	493,958	1,701,719	2,526,849	2,293,926	1,239,088	760,470	484,029
Other carbonated drinks	5,182,902	276,008	914,320	1,464,162	1,226,475	636,254	394,600	258,418
Coffee	4,577,009	86,881	578,698	1,083,792	1,119,293	834,649	516,095	372,763
Roasted coffee	3,007,593	53,906	376,607	731,721	742,622	546,615	340,717	224,443
Instant and freeze-dried coffee	1,569,416	32,975	202,091	352,070	376,889	288,176	175,378	148,319
Noncarbonated fruit-flavored drinks, incl. nonfrozen lemonade	2,123,907	120,686	426,846	668,166	518,414	195,139	115,611	68,692
Tea	1,714,875	67,445	262,340	390,203	427,199	281,804	165,455	123,794
Nonalcoholic beer	29,529	–	12,277	6,715	4,812	4,956	1,154	–
Other nonalcoholic beverages and ice	4,154,852	179,410	772,856	1,060,528	971,424	526,506	347,178	296,214
Food prepared by CU on trips	4,368,118	158,728	593,996	1,115,210	1,131,761	729,858	460,366	178,366
FOOD AWAY FROM HOME	**233,704,155**	**13,035,935**	**43,613,483**	**62,535,433**	**57,699,018**	**29,697,600**	**16,360,884**	**10,310,806**
Meals at restaurants, carry-outs, other	**191,428,341**	**10,845,310**	**37,819,518**	**50,907,515**	**45,994,897**	**23,818,660**	**12,945,867**	**8,646,697**
Lunch	72,499,384	4,219,365	14,561,499	20,102,071	17,169,121	8,120,342	5,085,720	3,022,660
At fast food, take-out, delivery, concession stands, buffet, and cafeteria (other than employer and school cafeteria)	40,247,056	2,959,926	8,875,190	10,828,325	9,254,452	4,252,407	2,600,088	1,305,679
At full-service restaurants	22,761,460	932,349	3,919,053	5,205,510	5,550,309	3,231,682	2,308,754	1,659,119
At vending machines, mobile vendors	713,073	60,634	170,927	268,370	108,714	55,511	14,884	24,844
At employer and school cafeterias	8,777,795	266,456	1,596,140	3,799,867	2,255,647	580,743	161,994	33,125

	total consumer units	under 25	25 to 34	35 to 44	45 to 54	55 to 64	65 to 74	75+
Dinner	$76,337,072	$3,939,702	$14,568,299	$19,050,896	$18,765,923	$10,647,514	$5,246,675	$4,043,697
At fast food, take-out, delivery, concession stands, buffet, and cafeteria (other than employer and school cafeteria)	22,630,220	1,386,271	5,256,063	6,306,810	5,213,230	2,539,351	1,175,607	646,894
At full-service restaurants	53,338,286	2,486,816	9,239,520	12,650,313	13,496,039	8,036,509	4,071,068	3,394,043
At vending machines, mobile vendors	111,554	16,446	28,331	39,812	24,061	1,558	–	–
At employer and school cafeterias	257,012	50,085	44,196	53,962	32,374	70,097	–	2,867
Snacks and nonalcoholic beverages	24,903,960	1,623,325	5,319,146	7,432,092	5,798,579	2,737,605	1,270,795	582,979
At fast food, take–out, delivery, concession stands, buffet, and cafeteria (other than employer and school cafeteria)	17,340,138	1,135,430	3,631,970	4,949,851	4,118,437	2,041,167	968,500	411,515
At full-service restaurants	2,203,745	144,026	417,403	489,493	565,880	273,307	196,608	118,910
At vending machines, mobile vendors	4,212,817	281,740	984,202	1,575,923	875,616	326,411	79,151	42,999
At employer and school cafeterias	1,147,260	62,046	285,760	416,825	238,645	96,578	26,653	9,555
Breakfast and brunch	17,687,925	1,062,919	3,370,574	4,322,216	4,261,274	2,313,058	1,342,677	997,361
At fast food, take–out, delivery, concession stands, buffet, and cafeteria (other than employer and school cafeteria)	8,434,383	606,338	1,830,906	2,267,832	1,980,034	908,853	462,674	344,203
At full-service restaurants	8,709,988	426,679	1,424,269	1,883,385	2,129,871	1,338,073	873,427	653,158
At vending machines, mobile vendors	147,645	4,817	36,641	29,019	48,123	23,649	5,538	–
At employer and school cafeterias	395,909	25,084	78,570	141,979	103,464	42,625	1,038	–
Board (including at school)	**4,268,594**	**712,904**	**168,850**	**413,467**	**2,459,731**	**389,428**	**68,882**	**55,315**
Catered affairs	**5,908,005**	**175,755**	**710,718**	**1,797,046**	**1,172,228**	**1,375,883**	**309,334**	**367,136**
Food on trips	**23,629,834**	**925,039**	**3,518,081**	**5,537,435**	**6,040,724**	**3,615,587**	**2,823,926**	**1,169,144**
School lunches	**6,393,595**	**126,833**	**963,048**	**3,295,264**	**1,701,360**	**173,614**	**113,765**	**19,854**
Meals as pay	**2,074,692**	**250,094**	**433,457**	**584,706**	**330,297**	**324,429**	**98,996**	**52,660**
ALCOHOLIC BEVERAGES	**40,663,744**	**3,259,939**	**8,145,019**	**10,081,494**	**9,117,739**	**5,258,121**	**3,010,495**	**1,650,731**
At home	**24,786,937**	**2,154,078**	**4,673,777**	**5,877,034**	**5,778,017**	**3,110,747**	**2,054,226**	**1,076,564**
Beer and ale	12,250,198	1,575,399	2,975,458	3,134,818	2,492,324	1,083,600	548,517	340,169
Whiskey	1,475,361	77,495	235,143	277,963	393,513	129,148	254,298	117,106
Wine	8,753,735	329,001	1,103,945	1,885,783	2,442,013	1,499,225	1,066,111	463,857
Other alcoholic beverages	2,307,644	172,100	359,042	578,470	449,948	398,915	185,416	155,433
Away from home	**15,876,807**	**1,105,861**	**3,471,242**	**4,204,460**	**3,339,941**	**2,147,374**	**956,154**	**574,061**
Beer and ale	6,831,063	519,956	1,500,194	1,902,092	1,400,373	904,888	333,448	226,673
At fast food, take–out, delivery, concession stands, buffet, and cafeteria	1,462,237	194,443	385,484	372,456	272,331	137,645	53,652	31,639
At full-service restaurants	4,926,983	301,923	1,094,502	1,243,758	1,123,667	672,223	279,797	195,140
At vending machines, mobile vendors	43,747	23,008	9,444	3,837	1,531	4,956	–	–
At catered affairs	398,096	664	10,766	282,040	2,844	90,064	–	–
Wine	1,945,639	127,165	434,590	532,183	428,293	266,652	71,189	74,744
At fast food, take–out, delivery, concession stands, buffet and cafeteria	134,521	18,439	24,553	59,238	23,624	6,372	–	–
At full-service restaurants	1,767,371	108,559	408,904	442,966	404,232	250,650	71,189	74,744
At catered affairs	42,653	83	1,133	29,979	219	9,488	–	–
Other alcoholic beverages	7,100,106	458,740	1,536,457	1,770,425	1,511,056	975,835	551,516	272,645
At fast food, take–out, delivery, concession stands, buffet, and cafeteria	332,476	49,504	88,202	109,842	57,529	16,285	6,346	–
At full-service restaurants	2,815,107	163,296	691,831	745,152	624,284	369,602	114,342	93,642
At machines and mobile vendors	31,716	4,734	10,388	6,236	5,687	2,974	808	956
At catered affairs	174,987	249	4,722	124,232	1,312	39,651	–	–
Alcoholic beverages purchased on trips	3,744,726	240,957	741,126	784,724	822,462	547,181	430,137	178,047

Note: Numbers may not add to total because of rounding. (–) means sample is too small to make a reliable estimate.
Source: Calculations by New Strategist based on the 2000 Consumer Expenditure Survey

Table 5.5 Food and Alcohol: Market shares by age, 2000

(percentage of total annual spending on food and alcoholic beverages accounted for by consumer unit age groups, 2000)

	total consumer units	under 25	25 to 34	35 to 44	45 to 54	55 to 64	65 to 74	75+
Share of total consumer units	100.0%	7.6%	17.3%	21.9%	20.0%	12.9%	10.5%	9.7%
Share of total before-tax income	100.0	3.4	17.6	27.7	26.4	14.0	6.9	4.5
Share of total spending	100.0	4.5	17.7	26.0	24.3	13.4	8.5	5.6
Share of food spending	100.0	4.7	17.6	25.9	24.4	13.0	8.5	5.8
Share of alcoholic beverages spending	100.0	8.0	20.0	24.8	22.4	12.9	7.4	4.1
FOOD AT HOME	**100.0%**	**4.1%**	**16.9%**	**25.3%**	**24.2%**	**13.2%**	**9.6%**	**6.8%**
Cereals and bakery products	**100.0**	**4.0**	**16.4**	**25.7**	**24.7**	**12.6**	**9.6**	**7.2**
Cereals and cereal products	100.0	4.4	18.4	26.7	23.0	11.6	9.0	7.0
Flour	100.0	5.8	17.3	25.4	21.4	11.9	9.4	8.6
Prepared flour mixes	100.0	4.1	13.8	29.3	23.5	13.1	9.4	6.8
Ready-to-eat and cooked cereals	100.0	4.4	18.4	26.4	22.0	11.7	9.4	7.7
Rice	100.0	4.1	20.2	24.8	27.4	10.8	7.8	5.1
Pasta, cornmeal, and other cereal products	100.0	4.1	19.7	28.0	23.1	10.9	8.4	5.5
Bakery products	100.0	3.8	15.3	25.1	25.6	13.1	10.0	7.3
Bread	100.0	4.1	15.8	24.8	23.3	13.9	10.5	7.8
White bread	100.0	4.4	16.6	26.0	22.1	13.2	10.3	7.3
Bread, other than white	100.0	3.8	15.2	23.9	24.2	14.4	10.6	8.1
Crackers and cookies	100.0	3.5	15.5	24.7	26.3	13.4	9.5	7.3
Cookies	100.0	3.5	15.7	24.6	26.9	13.0	9.1	7.3
Crackers	100.0	3.4	15.0	24.8	25.1	14.0	10.5	7.4
Frozen and refrigerated bakery products	100.0	4.0	15.3	26.6	24.2	13.5	9.9	6.5
Other bakery products	100.0	3.7	14.8	25.4	27.1	12.3	9.9	7.0
Biscuits and rolls	100.0	4.0	13.9	26.0	25.4	13.8	9.8	7.2
Cakes and cupcakes	100.0	3.4	15.7	23.3	32.3	10.2	9.5	6.1
Bread and cracker products	100.0	3.4	15.1	30.4	23.0	11.5	10.4	6.1
Sweetrolls, coffee cakes, doughnuts	100.0	4.3	15.0	24.7	24.4	13.0	11.4	7.3
Pies, tarts, turnovers	100.0	2.7	14.4	28.7	23.2	13.4	8.8	8.7
Meats, poultry, fish, and eggs	**100.0**	**4.2**	**16.7**	**25.3**	**24.4**	**13.5**	**9.6**	**6.3**
Beef	100.0	4.3	17.3	24.9	24.9	13.2	9.6	5.9
Ground beef	100.0	5.6	17.7	25.6	23.3	12.8	8.5	6.4
Roast	100.0	3.0	13.5	23.8	29.1	12.6	11.2	7.3
Chuck roast	100.0	3.1	13.9	27.2	27.0	11.8	10.7	6.5
Round roast	100.0	4.1	12.7	22.0	25.8	14.3	13.4	8.0
Other roast	100.0	2.1	13.7	22.0	33.5	11.9	10.0	7.5
Steak	100.0	3.8	18.6	24.8	25.0	13.3	9.8	4.8
Round steak	100.0	4.5	16.1	24.5	26.8	12.2	11.3	4.7
Sirloin steak	100.0	3.7	20.4	24.7	23.9	12.4	9.9	5.1
Other steak	100.0	3.6	18.4	24.9	25.2	14.1	9.3	4.6
Other beef	100.0	3.4	17.3	24.9	22.0	16.4	10.0	5.9
Pork	100.0	4.1	16.1	24.4	23.8	14.4	10.6	6.7
Bacon	100.0	3.3	14.7	24.9	24.2	13.6	11.6	8.0
Pork chops	100.0	4.8	17.2	25.1	24.0	13.4	9.4	6.0
Ham	100.0	3.5	16.9	23.7	21.3	15.6	11.0	8.1
Ham, not canned	100.0	3.4	17.1	23.5	21.2	15.8	10.8	8.2
Canned ham	100.0	5.4	11.6	26.6	23.3	11.1	15.6	6.6
Sausage	100.0	4.3	15.1	26.3	21.9	14.9	10.7	6.8
Other pork	100.0	4.2	15.7	23.0	26.8	14.6	10.8	5.2
Other meats	100.0	4.1	16.8	26.3	24.2	12.8	9.0	6.8
Frankfurters	100.0	4.8	19.9	25.2	22.9	11.8	8.5	6.9

	total consumer units	under 25	25 to 34	35 to 44	45 to 54	55 to 64	65 to 74	75+
Lunch meats (cold cuts)	100.0%	4.1%	16.1%	26.9%	24.7%	12.8%	9.1%	6.4%
Bologna, liverwurst, salami	100.0	4.4	16.6	26.0	24.3	12.8	9.4	6.6
Other lunch meats	100.0	3.9	15.8	27.4	24.9	12.9	8.9	6.3
Lamb, organ meats, and others	100.0	3.5	16.2	24.6	23.4	14.3	9.5	8.8
Lamb and organ meats	100.0	3.9	17.3	18.3	24.0	16.1	11.1	9.8
Mutton, goat, and game	100.0	1.6	11.0	52.7	20.9	6.1	2.2	4.1
Poultry	100.0	4.5	17.3	26.8	23.2	13.0	9.4	5.6
Fresh and frozen chicken	100.0	4.8	18.1	26.5	23.1	12.8	8.9	5.7
Fresh and frozen whole chicken	100.0	5.9	17.3	25.3	24.6	12.0	9.5	5.3
Fresh and frozen chicken parts	100.0	4.4	18.5	27.0	22.5	13.0	8.8	5.8
Other poultry	100.0	3.3	14.1	28.1	23.8	14.0	11.3	5.4
Fish and seafood	100.0	3.6	16.0	25.1	26.4	13.5	9.1	6.4
Canned fish and seafood	100.0	3.8	13.9	21.2	27.4	15.5	10.2	8.4
Fresh fish and shellfish	100.0	3.8	16.2	25.8	26.2	13.6	8.7	5.9
Frozen fish and shellfish	100.0	3.0	16.6	25.8	26.5	12.3	9.5	6.7
Eggs	100.0	4.5	15.2	23.5	23.0	16.1	9.7	8.0
Dairy products	**100.0**	**4.1**	**16.9**	**25.9**	**23.2**	**12.8**	**10.1**	**7.1**
Fresh milk and cream	100.0	4.3	17.7	26.2	22.2	12.4	9.5	7.7
Fresh milk, all types	100.0	4.3	17.9	26.2	22.0	12.2	9.6	7.9
Cream	100.0	3.8	15.4	26.3	24.4	15.1	8.8	6.1
Other dairy products	100.0	4.0	16.3	25.7	24.0	13.1	10.5	6.6
Butter	100.0	3.1	15.7	26.1	25.4	13.3	10.5	6.0
Cheese	100.0	4.1	17.0	26.1	23.3	13.2	10.0	6.4
Ice cream and related products	100.0	4.3	15.5	24.8	24.4	12.6	11.6	7.0
Miscellaneous dairy products	100.0	3.4	16.0	25.7	24.8	13.6	9.6	7.1
Fruits and vegetables	**100.0**	**3.7**	**16.2**	**23.2**	**24.0**	**13.9**	**10.7**	**8.5**
Fresh fruits	100.0	3.6	15.4	22.8	22.9	14.7	10.6	10.4
Apples	100.0	4.3	16.0	23.5	23.5	14.1	9.9	8.8
Bananas	100.0	3.9	14.4	22.2	22.0	15.2	11.0	11.5
Oranges	100.0	4.4	17.1	23.5	22.8	13.8	10.1	8.5
Citrus fruits, excl. oranges	100.0	2.8	16.2	21.3	23.0	16.5	9.4	11.0
Other fresh fruits	100.0	3.0	15.0	22.8	23.0	14.5	11.1	11.0
Fresh vegetables	100.0	3.5	16.1	22.7	25.3	14.1	10.8	7.9
Potatoes	100.0	3.4	15.1	22.8	24.8	14.2	11.1	8.9
Lettuce	100.0	3.6	14.7	23.6	26.2	14.0	10.4	7.8
Tomatoes	100.0	3.7	18.5	22.1	25.1	13.4	10.3	7.2
Other fresh vegetables	100.0	3.5	15.9	22.7	25.3	14.3	10.9	7.8
Processed fruits	100.0	4.1	17.0	23.9	23.2	12.9	11.0	8.2
Frozen fruits and fruit juices	100.0	3.3	16.9	25.6	23.2	15.6	9.5	5.8
Frozen orange juice	100.0	3.0	15.6	25.8	22.2	17.2	9.5	6.8
Frozen fruits	100.0	2.7	19.2	21.4	26.6	13.2	12.2	5.2
Frozen fruit juices	100.0	4.2	17.3	29.4	21.9	15.2	7.2	4.7
Canned fruits	100.0	3.3	15.0	23.5	21.3	13.3	13.7	10.1
Dried fruits	100.0	2.8	13.8	22.4	21.2	13.0	14.3	12.9
Fresh fruit juice	100.0	3.7	16.7	23.3	24.1	12.6	11.2	8.7
Canned and bottled fruit juice	100.0	4.8	18.0	24.0	23.5	12.2	10.1	7.5
Processed vegetables	100.0	3.7	16.8	24.1	25.0	13.4	10.5	6.6
Frozen vegetables	100.0	3.9	16.1	26.6	25.3	13.0	9.0	6.1
Canned and dried vegetables and juices	100.0	3.7	17.2	23.0	24.8	13.5	11.2	6.8
Canned beans	100.0	3.6	16.3	23.4	24.0	12.1	12.7	8.3
Canned corn	100.0	3.2	19.6	24.4	26.4	11.0	9.2	6.4
Canned miscellaneous vegetables	100.0	3.5	14.8	22.3	25.3	15.4	11.6	7.3
Dried peas	100.0	1.8	22.3	21.3	14.1	16.4	12.4	12.3
Dried beans	100.0	2.5	18.4	24.1	27.6	12.6	8.1	7.3

	total consumer units	under 25	25 to 34	35 to 44	45 to 54	55 to 64	65 to 74	75+
Dried miscellaneous vegetables	100.0%	4.1%	18.7%	20.5%	24.7%	14.3%	11.7%	6.2%
Dried processed vegetables	100.0	4.1	27.4	30.5	14.6	12.9	3.1	7.1
Frozen vegetable juices	100.0	3.1	28.0	25.7	17.9	9.4	12.4	2.7
Fresh and canned vegetable juices	100.0	4.5	18.7	24.1	24.5	13.4	10.6	4.3
Other food at home	**100.0**	**4.4**	**17.6**	**26.1**	**24.3**	**12.8**	**8.9**	**5.9**
Sugar and other sweets	100.0	3.9	15.4	27.5	24.3	12.8	9.5	6.6
Candy and chewing gum	100.0	3.6	15.2	29.2	25.5	11.8	8.8	5.8
Sugar	100.0	5.0	17.6	26.6	20.4	14.3	8.9	6.9
Artificial sweeteners	100.0	0.4	7.8	17.5	30.4	21.0	13.1	10.9
Jams, preserves, other sweets	100.0	4.8	15.9	23.8	21.9	13.5	11.8	8.5
Fats and oils	100.0	3.9	16.0	23.7	24.5	14.1	11.0	7.0
Margarine	100.0	3.2	13.4	21.2	25.0	15.9	13.4	8.3
Fats and oils	100.0	4.5	17.2	22.0	23.6	14.7	11.3	6.9
Salad dressings	100.0	3.7	16.5	25.4	25.6	13.1	9.3	6.7
Nondairy cream and imitation milk	100.0	2.6	13.7	24.4	22.8	14.9	13.7	8.0
Peanut butter	100.0	4.8	16.8	25.1	24.5	12.9	10.1	5.9
Miscellaneous foods	100.0	4.7	19.2	26.0	24.2	11.8	8.4	5.7
Frozen prepared foods	100.0	5.1	17.9	25.0	25.1	11.8	8.6	6.5
Frozen meals	100.0	4.8	16.7	20.5	26.0	11.0	11.8	9.6
Other frozen prepared foods	100.0	5.2	18.5	27.1	24.7	12.2	7.1	5.1
Canned and packaged soups	100.0	4.1	16.4	22.4	23.2	14.0	10.6	9.4
Potato chips, nuts, and other snacks	100.0	4.5	16.5	26.8	26.4	12.2	8.6	5.1
Potato chips and other snacks	100.0	5.0	18.0	29.2	25.0	10.9	7.2	4.5
Nuts	100.0	2.7	11.3	18.4	31.4	16.7	13.4	6.9
Condiments and seasonings	100.0	4.3	17.4	25.5	24.7	12.7	9.4	6.0
Salt, spices, and other seasonings	100.0	3.9	17.9	25.0	22.6	14.7	10.1	5.8
Olives, pickles, relishes	100.0	3.2	17.0	23.8	27.6	10.4	11.7	6.6
Sauces and gravies	100.0	4.7	18.6	26.8	24.7	12.1	8.0	5.0
Baking needs and miscellaneous products	100.0	4.3	14.3	24.4	25.7	13.1	10.2	8.1
Other canned/packaged prepared foods	100.0	5.1	23.8	27.4	21.9	10.3	6.9	4.3
Prepared salads	100.0	3.1	16.5	25.1	26.2	14.2	8.9	6.2
Prepared desserts	100.0	5.1	17.3	24.0	22.4	10.5	12.4	8.5
Baby food	100.0	7.3	36.9	29.7	15.2	5.1	2.9	1.8
Miscellaneous prepared foods	100.0	4.6	20.6	27.4	23.6	11.6	7.5	4.4
Vitamin supplements	100.0	–	18.5	23.5	41.4	6.5	10.5	0.7
Nonalcoholic beverages	100.0	4.5	17.1	26.4	24.0	13.6	8.4	5.9
Cola	100.0	5.2	17.9	26.6	24.1	13.0	8.0	5.1
Other carbonated drinks	100.0	5.3	17.6	28.2	23.7	12.3	7.6	5.0
Coffee	100.0	1.9	12.6	23.7	24.5	18.2	11.3	8.1
Roasted coffee	100.0	1.8	12.5	24.3	24.7	18.2	11.3	7.5
Instant and freeze-dried coffee	100.0	2.1	12.9	22.4	24.0	18.4	11.2	9.5
Noncarbonated fruit-flavored drinks, incl. nonfrozen lemonade	100.0	5.7	20.1	31.5	24.4	9.2	5.4	3.2
Tea	100.0	3.9	15.3	22.8	24.9	16.4	9.6	7.2
Nonalcoholic beer	100.0	–	41.6	22.7	16.3	16.8	3.9	–
Other nonalcoholic beverages and ice	100.0	4.3	18.6	25.5	23.4	12.7	8.4	7.1
Food prepared by CU on trips	100.0	3.6	13.6	25.5	25.9	16.7	10.5	4.1
FOOD AWAY FROM HOME	**100.0**	**5.6**	**18.7**	**26.8**	**24.7**	**12.7**	**7.0**	**4.4**
Meals at restaurants, carry-outs, other	**100.0**	**5.7**	**19.8**	**26.6**	**24.0**	**12.4**	**6.8**	**4.5**
Lunch	100.0	5.8	20.1	27.7	23.7	11.2	7.0	4.2
At fast food, take-out, delivery, concession stands, buffet, and cafeteria (other than employer and school cafeteria)	100.0	7.4	22.1	26.9	23.0	10.6	6.5	3.2
At full-service restaurants	100.0	4.1	17.2	22.9	24.4	14.2	10.1	7.3
At vending machines, mobile vendors	100.0	8.5	24.0	37.6	15.2	7.8	2.1	3.5
At employer and school cafeterias	100.0	3.0	18.2	43.3	25.7	6.6	1.8	0.4

	total consumer units	under 25	25 to 34	35 to 44	45 to 54	55 to 64	65 to 74	75+
Dinner	100.0%	5.2%	19.1%	25.0%	24.6%	13.9%	6.9%	5.3%
At fast food, take-out, delivery, concession stands, buffet, and cafeteria (other than employer and school cafeteria)	100.0	6.1	23.2	27.9	23.0	11.2	5.2	2.9
At full-service restaurants	100.0	4.7	17.3	23.7	25.3	15.1	7.6	6.4
At vending machines, mobile vendors	100.0	14.7	25.4	35.7	21.6	1.4	–	–
At employer and school cafeterias	100.0	19.5	17.2	21.0	12.6	27.3	–	1.1
Snacks and nonalcoholic beverages	100.0	6.5	21.4	29.8	23.3	11.0	5.1	2.3
At fast food, take-out, delivery, concession stands, buffet, and cafeteria (other than employer and school cafeteria)	100.0	6.5	20.9	28.5	23.8	11.8	5.6	2.4
At full-service restaurants	100.0	6.5	18.9	22.2	25.7	12.4	8.9	5.4
At vending machines, mobile vendors	100.0	6.7	23.4	37.4	20.8	7.7	1.9	1.0
At employer and school cafeterias	100.0	5.4	24.9	36.3	20.8	8.4	2.3	0.8
Breakfast and brunch	100.0	6.0	19.1	24.4	24.1	13.1	7.6	5.6
At fast food, take-out, delivery, concession stands, buffet, and cafeteria (other than employer and school cafeteria)	100.0	7.2	21.7	26.9	23.5	10.8	5.5	4.1
At full-service restaurants	100.0	4.9	16.4	21.6	24.5	15.4	10.0	7.5
At vending machines, mobile vendors	100.0	3.3	24.8	19.7	32.6	16.0	3.8	–
At employer and school cafeterias	100.0	6.3	19.8	35.9	26.1	10.8	0.3	–
Board (including at school)	**100.0**	**16.7**	**4.0**	**9.7**	**57.6**	**9.1**	**1.6**	**1.3**
Catered affairs	**100.0**	**3.0**	**12.0**	**30.4**	**19.8**	**23.3**	**5.2**	**6.2**
Food on trips	**100.0**	**3.9**	**14.9**	**23.4**	**25.6**	**15.3**	**12.0**	**4.9**
School lunches	**100.0**	**2.0**	**15.1**	**51.5**	**26.6**	**2.7**	**1.8**	**0.3**
Meals as pay	**100.0**	**12.1**	**20.9**	**28.2**	**15.9**	**15.6**	**4.8**	**2.5**
ALCOHOLIC BEVERAGES	**100.0**	**8.0**	**20.0**	**24.8**	**22.4**	**12.9**	**7.4**	**4.1**
At home	**100.0**	**8.7**	**18.9**	**23.7**	**23.3**	**12.5**	**8.3**	**4.3**
Beer and ale	100.0	12.9	24.3	25.6	20.3	8.8	4.5	2.8
Whiskey	100.0	5.3	15.9	18.8	26.7	8.8	17.2	7.9
Wine	100.0	3.8	12.6	21.5	27.9	17.1	12.2	5.3
Other alcoholic beverages	100.0	7.5	15.6	25.1	19.5	17.3	8.0	6.7
Away from home	**100.0**	**7.0**	**21.9**	**26.5**	**21.0**	**13.5**	**6.0**	**3.6**
Beer and ale	100.0	7.6	22.0	27.8	20.5	13.2	4.9	3.3
At fast food, take-out, delivery, concession stands, buffet, and cafeteria	100.0	13.3	26.4	25.5	18.6	9.4	3.7	2.2
At full-service restaurants	100.0	6.1	22.2	25.2	22.8	13.6	5.7	4.0
At vending machines, mobile vendors	100.0	52.6	21.6	8.8	3.5	11.3	–	–
At catered affairs	100.0	0.2	2.7	70.8	0.7	22.6	–	–
Wine	100.0	6.5	22.3	27.4	22.0	13.7	3.7	3.8
At fast food, take-out, delivery, concession stands, buffet and cafeteria	100.0	13.7	18.3	44.0	17.6	4.7	–	–
At full-service restaurants	100.0	6.1	23.1	25.1	22.9	14.2	4.0	4.2
At catered affairs	100.0	0.2	2.7	70.3	0.5	22.2	–	–
Other alcoholic beverages	100.0	6.5	21.6	24.9	21.3	13.7	7.8	3.8
At fast food, take-out, delivery, concession stands, buffet, and cafeteria	100.0	14.9	26.5	33.0	17.3	4.9	1.9	–
At full-service restaurants	100.0	5.8	24.6	26.5	22.2	13.1	4.1	3.3
At machines and mobile vendors	100.0	14.9	32.8	19.7	17.9	9.4	2.5	3.0
At catered affairs	100.0	0.1	2.7	71.0	0.8	22.7	–	–
Alcoholic beverages purchased on trips	100.0	6.4	19.8	21.0	22.0	14.6	11.5	4.8

Note: Numbers may not add to total because of rounding. (–) means sample is too small to make a reliable estimate.
Source: Calculations by New Strategist based on the 2000 Consumer Expenditure Survey

Table 5.6 Food and Alcohol: Average spending by income, 2000

(average annual spending on food and alcoholic beverages, by before-tax income of consumer units (CU), 2000; complete income reporters only)

	complete income reporters	under $10,000	$10,000– $19,999	$20,000– $29,999	$30,000– $39,999	$40,000– $49,999	$50,000– $69,999	$70,000 or more
Number of consumer units								
(in thousands, add 000)	81,454	10,810	14,714	12,039	9,477	7,653	11,337	15,424
Average number of persons per CU	2.5	1.7	2.1	2.4	2.5	2.6	2.9	3.2
Average before-tax income of CU	$44,649.00	$5,739.61	$14,586.29	$24,527.00	$34,422.00	$44,201.00	$58,561.00	$112,586.00
Average spending of CU, total	40,238.44	16,455.72	22,620.20	29,851.59	35,609.24	42,323.03	49,245.37	75,963.85
Food, average spending	5,434.76	2,517.16	3,328.38	4,506.68	5,117.56	6,228.28	6,557.24	8,664.51
Alcoholic beverages, average spending	422.87	189.59	208.94	301.23	372.53	393.03	549.13	788.26
FOOD AT HOME	$3,154.43	$1,682.93	$2,311.44	$2,920.72	$2,995.31	$3,552.22	$3,604.83	$4,482.61
Cereals and bakery products	474.35	244.44	344.22	449.31	459.82	510.45	542.10	679.14
Cereals and cereal products	162.77	92.02	117.61	176.47	159.09	177.08	183.34	213.21
Flour	8.10	8.19	7.59	8.68	7.98	6.99	8.79	8.04
Prepared flour mixes	14.05	7.54	8.61	11.63	15.65	20.66	16.58	18.21
Ready-to-eat and cooked cereals	90.44	49.15	62.58	92.00	87.46	96.42	109.38	122.58
Rice	20.03	12.02	16.80	26.67	21.17	22.91	18.69	21.53
Pasta, cornmeal, and other cereal products	30.15	15.11	22.03	37.49	26.83	30.10	29.90	42.84
Bakery products	311.58	152.42	226.62	272.85	300.74	333.36	358.76	465.94
Bread	88.11	51.50	72.33	85.05	84.03	97.00	94.01	118.77
White bread	38.13	25.01	33.38	37.71	38.97	40.29	41.84	45.77
Bread, other than white	49.98	26.50	38.95	47.34	45.06	56.72	52.17	73.00
Crackers and cookies	75.31	37.28	53.09	65.09	72.87	84.91	91.04	109.36
Cookies	50.60	27.79	34.60	41.85	54.74	57.09	60.16	71.32
Crackers	24.71	9.49	18.50	23.24	18.13	27.82	30.88	38.03
Frozen and refrigerated bakery products	25.58	13.34	15.69	22.25	21.25	32.23	32.01	38.32
Other bakery products	122.57	50.31	85.50	100.46	122.59	119.23	141.70	199.49
Biscuits and rolls	40.31	16.11	28.32	29.68	37.43	41.03	49.82	66.73
Cakes and cupcakes	41.10	16.35	24.98	34.43	42.66	36.35	42.81	74.03
Bread and cracker products	4.27	1.93	2.77	2.78	3.57	4.46	6.44	6.78
Sweetrolls, coffee cakes, doughnuts	22.98	10.17	17.91	22.50	25.53	22.33	26.05	31.57
Pies, tarts, turnovers	13.90	5.75	11.51	11.06	13.40	15.06	16.57	20.38
Meats, poultry, fish, and eggs	817.18	446.16	632.84	799.55	803.10	938.33	897.94	1,095.40
Beef	243.49	124.84	194.32	230.06	243.86	278.22	268.00	329.34
Ground beef	91.26	55.68	84.18	97.60	92.48	107.15	96.17	101.46
Roast	40.42	18.76	31.69	38.17	36.12	38.30	43.44	63.51
Chuck roast	13.61	7.67	10.17	15.09	11.74	16.10	15.11	17.84
Round roast	11.74	6.36	10.73	9.88	12.63	11.29	11.20	17.09
Other roast	15.07	4.73	10.77	13.21	11.75	10.92	17.13	28.58
Steak	95.86	43.08	66.65	82.30	98.56	111.82	111.45	140.60
Round steak	16.05	10.35	12.73	15.22	14.40	21.67	17.77	19.95
Sirloin steak	30.67	13.09	19.84	24.43	34.67	36.41	32.38	48.11
Other steak	49.13	19.65	34.08	42.65	49.49	53.73	61.29	72.54
Other beef	15.95	7.32	11.81	11.99	16.71	20.95	16.95	23.77
Pork	170.62	108.90	141.01	180.53	168.65	193.06	188.13	202.45
Bacon	26.33	18.10	22.96	27.45	28.51	25.93	28.65	30.17
Pork chops	41.18	26.86	37.22	42.93	39.67	42.16	46.98	47.77
Ham	36.92	18.90	27.91	44.43	39.02	41.13	43.37	41.88
Ham, not canned	35.13	17.87	26.57	43.25	37.35	39.32	40.11	39.85
Canned ham	1.79	1.04	1.34	1.19	1.67	1.81	3.27	2.03
Sausage	26.01	19.66	23.42	23.18	23.35	28.50	25.58	34.59
Other pork	40.19	25.38	29.49	42.54	38.10	55.33	43.54	48.04
Other meats	104.34	54.88	80.04	105.48	105.14	122.07	120.52	132.68
Frankfurters	20.71	12.89	16.75	24.53	20.22	22.58	21.52	24.72

	complete income reporters	under $10,000	$10,000–$19,999	$20,000–$29,999	$30,000–$39,999	$40,000–$49,999	$50,000–$69,999	$70,000 or more
Lunch meats (cold cuts)	$71.30	$34.46	$54.39	$68.39	$70.45	$70.67	$89.49	$97.06
Bologna, liverwurst, salami	24.60	13.96	20.59	27.66	26.21	22.54	28.20	29.39
Other lunch meats	46.71	20.50	33.80	40.73	44.24	48.13	61.28	67.67
Lamb, organ meats, and others	12.32	7.54	8.90	12.56	14.47	28.83	9.50	10.90
Lamb and organ meats	9.84	6.45	8.22	11.28	12.59	13.20	8.63	9.86
Mutton, goat, and game	2.49	1.09	0.69	1.28	1.88	15.63	0.88	1.04
Poultry	149.59	82.34	109.58	145.11	151.30	173.99	159.60	206.20
Fresh and frozen chicken	118.51	67.34	89.97	114.94	123.78	136.89	123.80	159.49
Fresh and frozen whole chicken	32.77	23.26	25.10	36.13	33.69	42.98	30.64	38.63
Fresh and frozen chicken parts	85.74	44.08	64.88	78.81	90.09	93.91	93.16	120.86
Other poultry	31.08	15.00	19.60	30.17	27.52	37.10	35.81	46.70
Fish and seafood	113.53	50.98	75.76	103.32	89.55	133.54	128.02	184.22
Canned fish and seafood	15.99	8.21	11.66	15.63	13.69	20.38	16.66	23.34
Fresh fish and shellfish	68.86	31.79	45.53	64.32	50.59	75.98	75.43	116.63
Frozen fish and shellfish	28.68	10.98	18.56	23.37	25.27	37.18	35.92	44.26
Eggs	35.61	24.22	32.14	35.05	44.61	37.45	33.68	40.50
Dairy products	**339.44**	**176.80**	**251.88**	**305.32**	**338.29**	**375.55**	**400.58**	**471.93**
Fresh milk and cream	138.04	82.78	111.44	129.45	146.79	142.36	153.08	180.22
Fresh milk, all types	126.24	77.60	103.24	119.63	136.73	128.75	138.97	161.56
Cream	11.80	5.18	8.20	9.81	10.06	13.61	14.11	18.66
Other dairy products	201.40	94.02	140.43	175.87	191.51	233.19	247.50	291.71
Butter	16.52	8.21	10.74	14.58	13.93	21.86	20.52	23.83
Cheese	102.04	45.06	71.46	92.02	101.14	114.26	128.26	144.20
Ice cream and related products	57.86	28.73	41.91	50.78	54.44	68.50	69.22	82.31
Miscellaneous dairy products	24.99	12.02	16.33	18.48	21.99	28.57	29.50	41.37
Fruits and vegetables	**543.63**	**305.43**	**409.43**	**518.51**	**508.17**	**594.58**	**579.63**	**785.17**
Fresh fruits	169.59	91.52	130.66	167.73	158.73	182.33	172.24	247.79
Apples	29.73	14.46	22.69	30.51	29.36	29.11	31.98	42.81
Bananas	33.38	21.78	28.48	36.79	33.30	35.43	32.63	41.34
Oranges	18.76	9.70	14.32	19.87	21.00	22.49	16.36	25.55
Citrus fruits, excl. oranges	14.75	7.74	9.88	13.72	14.20	19.00	13.75	22.75
Other fresh fruits	72.98	37.85	55.28	66.85	60.88	76.30	77.53	115.34
Fresh vegetables	166.25	90.32	122.74	160.03	151.69	177.39	176.74	247.77
Potatoes	28.61	17.81	21.03	29.83	26.80	32.54	30.78	38.12
Lettuce	21.21	10.44	16.79	19.38	19.91	22.87	24.69	30.02
Tomatoes	31.18	15.68	24.40	32.65	31.84	33.54	34.51	40.95
Other fresh vegetables	85.24	46.38	60.52	78.18	73.14	88.44	86.75	138.68
Processed fruits	120.50	75.17	86.43	109.53	113.16	127.62	133.80	175.17
Frozen fruits and fruit juices	14.78	10.91	10.98	10.86	15.82	12.21	13.87	24.41
Frozen orange juice	6.60	3.49	5.60	6.40	5.65	5.55	7.24	9.99
Frozen fruits	4.02	6.23	1.94	2.24	5.21	2.96	2.42	6.92
Frozen fruit juices	4.16	1.19	3.45	2.22	4.96	3.70	4.22	7.51
Canned fruits	16.32	9.41	13.87	13.57	16.12	19.10	17.73	22.06
Dried fruits	5.71	3.25	4.94	4.69	5.87	4.52	5.97	8.73
Fresh fruit juice	24.32	17.79	18.16	23.66	20.48	25.17	27.47	33.43
Canned and bottled fruit juice	59.38	33.82	38.47	56.74	54.88	66.63	68.76	86.54
Processed vegetables	87.29	48.42	69.60	81.21	84.59	107.24	96.85	114.44
Frozen vegetables	27.34	13.61	19.89	21.90	22.85	35.89	32.96	40.11
Canned and dried vegetables and juices	59.96	34.81	49.72	59.31	61.74	71.35	63.89	74.33
Canned beans	13.09	6.60	12.14	15.37	13.52	15.09	13.36	14.60
Canned corn	7.26	4.45	5.79	6.52	7.60	8.51	7.92	9.40
Canned miscellaneous vegetables	18.64	10.66	14.93	17.91	18.73	21.26	19.88	24.78
Dried peas	0.35	0.27	0.35	0.44	0.38	0.08	0.39	0.43
Dried beans	2.73	1.99	2.25	3.02	3.02	4.15	2.22	2.85

	complete income reporters	under $10,000	$10,000– $19,999	$20,000– $29,999	$30,000– $39,999	$40,000– $49,999	$50,000– $69,999	$70,000 or more
Dried miscellaneous vegetables	$7.49	$5.71	$6.38	$7.70	$9.17	$8.01	$6.95	$8.42
Dried processed vegetables	0.41	–	0.40	0.26	0.38	0.15	1.11	0.40
Frozen vegetable juices	0.31	0.37	0.16	0.09	0.27	0.71	0.24	0.45
Fresh and canned vegetable juices	9.67	4.77	7.32	8.01	8.68	13.39	11.83	12.99
Other food at home	**979.82**	**510.09**	**673.07**	**848.04**	**885.92**	**1,133.31**	**1,184.58**	**1,450.97**
Sugar and other sweets	124.75	58.38	85.66	107.43	108.70	145.61	146.62	193.12
Candy and chewing gum	83.81	33.02	49.54	61.20	68.45	102.82	103.36	145.02
Sugar	17.19	13.14	16.14	21.00	18.79	16.96	17.56	16.57
Artificial sweeteners	3.70	1.93	4.55	3.99	2.03	2.85	4.13	4.86
Jams, preserves, other sweets	20.05	10.29	15.42	21.23	19.43	22.98	21.57	26.67
Fats and oils	85.51	48.45	67.47	89.59	79.71	95.71	97.24	109.75
Margarine	11.79	7.76	11.86	10.91	11.03	11.50	13.24	14.16
Fats and oils	24.18	16.83	21.49	28.63	21.82	23.33	28.39	26.31
Salad dressings	28.06	12.15	17.91	31.06	27.26	34.72	31.62	38.72
Nondairy cream and imitation milk	9.40	5.60	6.99	7.16	9.06	11.53	11.59	12.85
Peanut butter	12.09	6.11	9.22	11.84	10.54	14.63	12.40	17.71
Miscellaneous foods	460.15	222.95	311.81	376.10	405.11	522.72	569.90	710.06
Frozen prepared foods	92.95	45.76	65.12	82.72	75.10	107.27	111.48	142.11
Frozen meals	28.36	16.19	24.38	28.18	21.57	38.24	29.52	37.55
Other frozen prepared foods	64.59	29.57	40.74	54.54	53.53	69.03	81.95	104.56
Canned and packaged soups	37.47	21.24	30.90	33.09	34.18	36.95	42.62	54.08
Potato chips, nuts, and other snacks	97.35	38.00	64.21	77.41	87.80	106.52	122.72	157.74
Potato chips and other snacks	76.42	29.31	47.03	57.03	70.53	82.45	100.67	126.11
Nuts	20.94	8.68	17.18	20.37	17.27	24.07	22.05	31.62
Condiments and seasonings	89.37	41.00	62.25	76.54	78.74	103.36	108.04	136.18
Salt, spices, and other seasonings	22.15	11.21	16.17	22.19	19.87	24.59	25.25	31.61
Olives, pickles, relishes	10.22	4.11	7.62	8.20	9.11	9.71	12.42	16.75
Sauces and gravies	39.15	17.43	27.48	31.20	33.07	51.28	50.10	57.46
Baking needs and miscellaneous products	17.85	8.25	10.97	14.95	16.69	17.79	20.27	30.36
Other canned/packaged prepared foods	143.01	76.95	89.33	106.35	129.29	168.61	185.05	219.96
Prepared salads	19.54	7.82	14.02	14.92	16.46	24.15	20.49	33.40
Prepared desserts	9.94	4.88	8.06	8.44	9.41	11.33	11.22	14.28
Baby food	33.25	17.94	17.39	20.13	30.32	48.53	50.94	47.10
Miscellaneous prepared foods	80.17	46.30	49.77	62.63	73.09	84.60	101.93	125.15
Vitamin supplements	0.12	–	0.08	0.23	–	–	0.47	0.02
Nonalcoholic beverages	265.37	153.92	185.92	244.24	257.27	323.81	316.72	353.07
Cola	93.36	49.15	72.10	89.16	99.29	109.62	113.32	114.09
Other carbonated drinks	50.86	33.35	35.56	43.94	51.65	66.47	60.36	64.23
Coffee	44.54	28.21	32.80	44.12	39.81	52.72	49.17	59.88
Roasted coffee	29.01	17.56	20.74	27.07	26.02	36.56	32.04	40.06
Instant and freeze-dried coffee	15.53	10.65	12.06	17.04	13.79	16.16	17.12	19.82
Noncarbonated fruit-flavored drinks, incl. nonfrozen lemonade	20.43	11.23	11.96	16.64	17.80	27.96	25.56	30.10
Tea	16.17	10.50	10.57	16.52	15.09	23.28	16.69	21.07
Nonalcoholic beer	0.38	0.21	0.12	0.23	–	0.96	0.60	0.59
Other nonalcoholic beverages and ice	39.64	21.26	22.82	33.63	33.63	42.80	51.02	63.12
Food prepared by CU on trips	44.03	26.40	22.21	30.69	35.13	45.46	54.11	84.97
FOOD AWAY FROM HOME	**2,280.33**	**834.23**	**1,016.95**	**1,585.96**	**2,122.25**	**2,676.05**	**2,952.41**	**4,181.90**
Meals at restaurants, carry-outs, other	**1,891.38**	**661.07**	**859.57**	**1,352.51**	**1,827.33**	**2,326.54**	**2,458.66**	**3,299.11**
Lunch	722.20	258.12	347.27	539.42	679.92	915.64	935.62	1,223.63
At fast food, take-out, delivery, concession stands, buffet, and cafeteria (other than employer and school cafeteria)	393.32	158.79	200.65	341.33	385.46	497.97	503.88	607.71
At full-service restaurants	229.94	77.94	116.76	136.39	181.00	305.66	290.01	432.34
At vending machines, mobile vendors	7.65	6.70	3.40	11.17	8.43	9.46	8.78	7.09
At employer and school cafeterias	91.30	14.70	26.45	50.53	105.03	102.56	132.95	176.49

	complete income reporters	under $10,000	$10,000– $19,999	$20,000– $29,999	$30,000– $39,999	$40,000– $49,999	$50,000– $69,999	$70,000 or more
Dinner	$737.37	$218.30	$282.51	$458.66	$671.32	$899.80	$982.30	$1,414.89
At fast food, take-out, delivery, concession stands, buffet, and cafeteria (other than employer and school cafeteria)	220.81	77.69	101.96	180.56	240.01	289.21	305.66	328.95
At full-service restaurants	512.54	137.44	179.21	272.75	427.06	600.22	673.57	1,082.52
At vending machines, mobile vendors	1.01	0.25	–	1.54	2.11	1.60	0.88	1.07
At employer and school cafeterias	3.02	2.92	1.34	3.82	2.15	8.76	2.18	2.35
Snacks and nonalcoholic beverages	257.14	114.15	135.51	207.18	302.77	273.98	331.48	390.79
At fast food, take-out, delivery, concession stands, buffet, and cafeteria (other than employer and school cafeteria)	177.53	83.15	92.73	134.40	182.16	202.24	227.14	285.62
At full-service restaurants	22.40	11.62	18.73	23.21	21.19	22.33	25.95	29.50
At vending machines, mobile vendors	44.56	17.15	17.68	41.70	79.66	39.26	59.47	55.93
At employer and school cafeterias	12.65	2.24	6.37	7.87	19.75	10.15	18.91	19.73
Breakfast and brunch	174.66	70.49	94.28	147.25	173.32	237.12	209.27	269.80
At fast food, take-out, delivery, concession stands, buffet, and cafeteria (other than employer and school cafeteria)	84.29	36.77	46.40	91.03	88.81	113.91	94.88	115.12
At full-service restaurants	84.41	32.13	44.46	50.07	78.46	117.51	105.29	146.29
At vending machines, mobile vendors	1.55	–	1.65	2.69	0.97	1.12	2.45	1.47
At employer and school cafeterias	4.41	1.59	1.77	3.46	5.08	4.58	6.65	6.92
Board (including at school)	**35.79**	**46.24**	**15.98**	**10.41**	**7.39**	**25.12**	**26.70**	**96.59**
Catered affairs	**46.51**	**1.24**	**6.15**	**10.18**	**22.27**	**17.72**	**89.29**	**142.82**
Food on trips	**225.38**	**100.27**	**99.98**	**153.81**	**198.85**	**199.98**	**266.43**	**487.29**
School lunches	**60.66**	**12.82**	**16.45**	**38.03**	**41.98**	**83.24**	**94.10**	**129.69**
Meals as pay	**20.62**	**12.58**	**18.82**	**21.02**	**24.42**	**23.44**	**17.24**	**26.39**
ALCOHOLIC BEVERAGES	**422.87**	**189.59**	**208.94**	**301.23**	**372.53**	**393.03**	**549.13**	**788.26**
At home	**257.39**	**132.27**	**154.01**	**204.94**	**230.89**	**218.89**	**305.34**	**456.85**
Beer and ale	130.18	96.13	87.93	142.89	148.65	126.24	147.50	155.84
Whiskey	14.43	1.91	6.44	10.66	21.11	12.59	22.52	22.25
Wine	90.07	19.30	47.70	35.60	45.02	53.43	106.87	239.28
Other alcoholic beverages	22.70	14.93	11.94	15.78	16.12	26.63	28.45	39.49
Away from home	**165.48**	**57.32**	**54.93**	**96.29**	**141.64**	**174.14**	**243.79**	**331.41**
Beer and ale	74.34	26.05	25.23	42.38	68.91	84.48	122.01	131.60
At fast food, take-out, delivery, concession stands, buffet, and cafeteria	16.14	8.60	9.37	10.28	20.88	15.54	16.74	27.37
At full-service restaurants	52.45	17.43	15.32	30.92	45.94	63.50	77.42	100.96
At vending machines, mobile vendors	0.56	–	0.54	0.27	2.09	–	0.59	0.44
At catered affairs	5.18	–	–	0.91	–	5.44	27.25	2.84
Wine	20.16	4.66	5.44	9.12	18.86	22.76	29.21	42.76
At fast food, take-out, delivery, concession stands, buffet and cafeteria	1.54	0.56	0.99	–	2.61	1.20	1.73	3.02
At full-service restaurants	18.07	4.09	4.44	9.02	16.25	20.98	24.59	39.43
At catered affairs	0.55	–	–	0.10	–	0.58	2.89	0.30
Other alcoholic beverages	70.97	26.61	24.26	44.79	53.86	66.90	92.57	157.05
At fast food, take-out, delivery, concession stands, buffet, and cafeteria	3.74	2.34	2.03	1.19	5.60	3.85	4.06	6.36
At full-service restaurants	29.41	5.95	7.12	17.74	23.04	28.19	38.39	68.52
At machines and mobile vendors	0.32	0.18	0.09	0.28	0.80	0.07	0.49	0.35
At catered affairs	2.28	–	–	0.40	–	2.40	12.01	1.25
Alcoholic beverages purchased on trips	35.22	18.14	15.02	25.18	24.41	32.39	37.63	80.57

Note: (–) means sample is too small to make a reliable estimate.
Source: Bureau of Labor Statistics, unpublished tables from the 2000 Consumer Expenditure Survey; calculations by New Strategist

Table 5.7 Food and Alcohol: Indexed spending by income, 2000

(indexed average annual spending of consumer units (CU) on food and beverages, by before-tax income of consumer unit, 2000; complete income reporters only; index definition: an index of 100 is the average for all consumer units; an index of 132 means that spending by consumer units in that group is 32 percent above the average for all consumer units; an index of 68 indicates spending that is 32 percent below the average for all consumer units)

	complete income reporters	under $10,000	$10,000– $19,999	$20,000– $29,999	$30,000– $39,999	$40,000– $49,999	$50,000– $69,999	$70,000 or more
Average spending of CU, total	$40,238	$16,456	$22,620	$29,852	$35,609	$42,323	$49,245	$75,964
Average spending of CU, index	100	41	56	74	88	105	122	189
Food, spending index	100	46	61	83	94	115	121	159
Alcoholic beverages, spending index	100	45	49	71	88	93	130	186
FOOD AT HOME	**100**	**53**	**73**	**93**	**95**	**113**	**114**	**142**
Cereals and bakery products	**100**	**52**	**73**	**95**	**97**	**108**	**114**	**143**
Cereals and cereal products	100	57	72	108	98	109	113	131
Flour	100	101	94	107	99	86	109	99
Prepared flour mixes	100	54	61	83	111	147	118	130
Ready-to-eat and cooked cereals	100	54	69	102	97	107	121	136
Rice	100	60	84	133	106	114	93	107
Pasta, cornmeal, and other cereal products	100	50	73	124	89	100	99	142
Bakery products	100	49	73	88	97	107	115	150
Bread	100	58	82	97	95	110	107	135
White bread	100	66	88	99	102	106	110	120
Bread, other than white	100	53	78	95	90	113	104	146
Crackers and cookies	100	50	71	86	97	113	121	145
Cookies	100	55	68	83	108	113	119	141
Crackers	100	38	75	94	73	113	125	154
Frozen and refrigerated bakery products	100	52	61	87	83	126	125	150
Other bakery products	100	41	70	82	100	97	116	163
Biscuits and rolls	100	40	70	74	93	102	124	166
Cakes and cupcakes	100	40	61	84	104	88	104	180
Bread and cracker products	100	45	65	65	84	104	151	159
Sweetrolls, coffee cakes, doughnuts	100	44	78	98	111	97	113	137
Pies, tarts, turnovers	100	41	83	80	96	108	119	147
Meats, poultry, fish, and eggs	**100**	**55**	**77**	**98**	**98**	**115**	**110**	**134**
Beef	100	51	80	94	100	114	110	135
Ground beef	100	61	92	107	101	117	105	111
Roast	100	46	78	94	89	95	107	157
Chuck roast	100	56	75	111	86	118	111	131
Round roast	100	54	91	84	108	96	95	146
Other roast	100	31	71	88	78	72	114	190
Steak	100	45	70	86	103	117	116	147
Round steak	100	65	79	95	90	135	111	124
Sirloin steak	100	43	65	80	113	119	106	157
Other steak	100	40	69	87	101	109	125	148
Other beef	100	46	74	75	105	131	106	149
Pork	100	64	83	106	99	113	110	119
Bacon	100	69	87	104	108	98	109	115
Pork chops	100	65	90	104	96	102	114	116
Ham	100	51	76	120	106	111	117	113
Ham, not canned	100	51	76	123	106	112	114	113
Canned ham	100	58	75	66	93	101	183	113
Sausage	100	76	90	89	90	110	98	133
Other pork	100	63	73	106	95	138	108	120
Other meats	100	53	77	101	101	117	116	127
Frankfurters	100	62	81	118	98	109	104	119

	complete income reporters	under $10,000	$10,000– $19,999	$20,000– $29,999	$30,000– $39,999	$40,000– $49,999	$50,000– $69,999	$70,000 or more
Lunch meats (cold cuts)	100	48	76	96	99	99	126	136
Bologna, liverwurst, salami	100	57	84	112	107	92	115	119
Other lunch meats	100	44	72	87	95	103	131	145
Lamb, organ meats, and others	100	61	72	102	117	234	77	88
Lamb and organ meats	100	66	84	115	128	134	88	100
Mutton, goat, and game	100	44	28	51	76	628	35	42
Poultry	100	55	73	97	101	116	107	138
Fresh and frozen chicken	100	57	76	97	104	116	104	135
Fresh and frozen whole chicken	100	71	77	110	103	131	94	118
Fresh and frozen chicken parts	100	51	76	92	105	110	109	141
Other poultry	100	48	63	97	89	119	115	150
Fish and seafood	100	45	67	91	79	118	113	162
Canned fish and seafood	100	51	73	98	86	127	104	146
Fresh fish and shellfish	100	46	66	93	73	110	110	169
Frozen fish and shellfish	100	38	65	81	88	130	125	154
Eggs	100	68	90	98	125	105	95	114
Dairy products	**100**	**52**	**74**	**90**	**100**	**111**	**118**	**139**
Fresh milk and cream	100	60	81	94	106	103	111	131
Fresh milk, all types	100	61	82	95	108	102	110	128
Cream	100	44	69	83	85	115	120	158
Other dairy products	100	47	70	87	95	116	123	145
Butter	100	50	65	88	84	132	124	144
Cheese	100	44	70	90	99	112	126	141
Ice cream and related products	100	50	72	88	94	118	120	142
Miscellaneous dairy products	100	48	65	74	88	114	118	166
Fruits and vegetables	**100**	**56**	**75**	**95**	**93**	**109**	**107**	**144**
Fresh fruits	100	54	77	99	94	108	102	146
Apples	100	49	76	103	99	98	108	144
Bananas	100	65	85	110	100	106	98	124
Oranges	100	52	76	106	112	120	87	136
Citrus fruits, excl. oranges	100	52	67	93	96	129	93	154
Other fresh fruits	100	52	76	92	83	105	106	158
Fresh vegetables	100	54	74	96	91	107	106	149
Potatoes	100	62	73	104	94	114	108	133
Lettuce	100	49	79	91	94	108	116	142
Tomatoes	100	50	78	105	102	108	111	131
Other fresh vegetables	100	54	71	92	86	104	102	163
Processed fruits	100	62	72	91	94	106	111	145
Frozen fruits and fruit juices	100	74	74	73	107	83	94	165
Frozen orange juice	100	53	85	97	86	84	110	151
Frozen fruits	100	155	48	56	130	74	60	172
Frozen fruit juices	100	29	83	53	119	89	101	181
Canned fruits	100	58	85	83	99	117	109	135
Dried fruits	100	57	86	82	103	79	105	153
Fresh fruit juice	100	73	75	97	84	103	113	137
Canned and bottled fruit juice	100	57	65	96	92	112	116	146
Processed vegetables	100	55	80	93	97	123	111	131
Frozen vegetables	100	50	73	80	84	131	121	147
Canned and dried vegetables and juices	100	58	83	99	103	119	107	124
Canned beans	100	50	93	117	103	115	102	112
Canned corn	100	61	80	90	105	117	109	129
Canned miscellaneous vegetables	100	57	80	96	100	114	107	133
Dried peas	100	76	99	126	109	23	111	123
Dried beans	100	73	82	111	111	152	81	104

	complete income reporters	under $10,000	$10,000– $19,999	$20,000– $29,999	$30,000– $39,999	$40,000– $49,999	$50,000– $69,999	$70,000 or more
Dried miscellaneous vegetables	100	76	85	103	122	107	93	112
Dried processed vegetables	100	–	98	63	93	37	271	98
Frozen vegetable juices	100	120	53	29	87	229	77	145
Fresh and canned vegetable juices	100	49	76	83	90	138	122	134
Other food at home	**100**	**52**	**69**	**87**	**90**	**116**	**121**	**148**
Sugar and other sweets	100	47	69	86	87	117	118	155
Candy and chewing gum	100	39	59	73	82	123	123	173
Sugar	100	76	94	122	109	99	102	96
Artificial sweeteners	100	52	123	108	55	77	112	131
Jams, preserves, other sweets	100	51	77	106	97	115	108	133
Fats and oils	100	57	79	105	93	112	114	128
Margarine	100	66	101	93	94	98	112	120
Fats and oils	100	70	89	118	90	96	117	109
Salad dressings	100	43	64	111	97	124	113	138
Nondairy cream and imitation milk	100	60	74	76	96	123	123	137
Peanut butter	100	50	76	98	87	121	103	146
Miscellaneous foods	100	48	68	82	88	114	124	154
Frozen prepared foods	100	49	70	89	81	115	120	153
Frozen meals	100	57	86	99	76	135	104	132
Other frozen prepared foods	100	46	63	84	83	107	127	162
Canned and packaged soups	100	57	82	88	91	99	114	144
Potato chips, nuts, and other snacks	100	39	66	80	90	109	126	162
Potato chips and other snacks	100	38	62	75	92	108	132	165
Nuts	100	41	82	97	82	115	105	151
Condiments and seasonings	100	46	70	86	88	116	121	152
Salt, spices, and other seasonings	100	51	73	100	90	111	114	143
Olives, pickles, relishes	100	40	75	80	89	95	122	164
Sauces and gravies	100	45	70	80	84	131	128	147
Baking needs and miscellaneous products	100	46	61	84	94	100	114	170
Other canned/packaged prepared foods	100	54	62	74	90	118	129	154
Prepared salads	100	40	72	76	84	124	105	171
Prepared desserts	100	49	81	85	95	114	113	144
Baby food	100	54	52	61	91	146	153	142
Miscellaneous prepared foods	100	58	62	78	91	106	127	156
Vitamin supplements	100	–	69	192	–	–	392	17
Nonalcoholic beverages	100	58	70	92	97	122	119	133
Cola	100	53	77	96	106	117	121	122
Other carbonated drinks	100	66	70	86	102	131	119	126
Coffee	100	63	74	99	89	118	110	134
Roasted coffee	100	61	71	93	90	126	110	138
Instant and freeze-dried coffee	100	69	78	110	89	104	110	128
Noncarbonated fruit-flavored drinks, incl. nonfrozen lemonade	100	55	59	81	87	137	125	147
Tea	100	65	65	102	93	144	103	130
Nonalcoholic beer	100	56	32	61	–	253	158	155
Other nonalcoholic beverages and ice	100	54	58	85	85	108	129	159
Food prepared by CU on trips	100	60	50	70	80	103	123	193
FOOD AWAY FROM HOME	**100**	**37**	**45**	**70**	**93**	**117**	**129**	**183**
Meals at restaurants, carry-outs, other	**100**	**35**	**45**	**72**	**97**	**123**	**130**	**174**
Lunch	100	36	48	75	94	127	130	169
At fast food, take-out, delivery, concession stands, buffet, and cafeteria (other than employer and school cafeteria)	100	40	51	87	98	127	128	155
At full-service restaurants	100	34	51	59	79	133	126	188
At vending machines, mobile vendors	100	88	44	146	110	124	115	93
At employer and school cafeterias	100	16	29	55	115	112	146	193

	complete income reporters	under $10,000	$10,000–$19,999	$20,000–$29,999	$30,000–$39,999	$40,000–$49,999	$50,000–$69,999	$70,000 or more
Dinner	100	30	38	62	91	122	133	192
At fast food, take-out, delivery, concession stands, buffet, and cafeteria (other than employer and school cafeteria)	100	35	46	82	109	131	138	149
At full-service restaurants	100	27	35	53	83	117	131	211
At vending machines, mobile vendors	100	24	–	152	209	158	87	106
At employer and school cafeterias	100	97	44	126	71	290	72	78
Snacks and nonalcoholic beverages	100	44	53	81	118	107	129	152
At fast food, take-out, delivery, concession stands, buffet, and cafeteria (other than employer and school cafeteria)	100	47	52	76	103	114	128	161
At full-service restaurants	100	52	84	104	95	100	116	132
At vending machines, mobile vendors	100	38	40	94	179	88	133	126
At employer and school cafeterias	100	18	50	62	156	80	149	156
Breakfast and brunch	100	40	54	84	99	136	120	154
At fast food, take-out, delivery, concession stands, buffet, and cafeteria (other than employer and school cafeteria)	100	44	55	108	105	135	113	137
At full-service restaurants	100	38	53	59	93	139	125	173
At vending machines, mobile vendors	100	–	107	174	63	72	158	95
At employer and school cafeterias	100	36	40	78	115	104	151	157
Board (including at school)	**100**	**129**	**45**	**29**	**21**	**70**	**75**	**270**
Catered affairs	**100**	**3**	**13**	**22**	**48**	**38**	**192**	**307**
Food on trips	**100**	**44**	**44**	**68**	**88**	**89**	**118**	**216**
School lunches	**100**	**21**	**27**	**63**	**69**	**137**	**155**	**214**
Meals as pay	**100**	**61**	**91**	**102**	**118**	**114**	**84**	**128**
ALCOHOLIC BEVERAGES	**100**	**45**	**49**	**71**	**88**	**93**	**130**	**186**
At home	**100**	**51**	**60**	**80**	**90**	**85**	**119**	**177**
Beer and ale	100	74	68	110	114	97	113	120
Whiskey	100	13	45	74	146	87	156	154
Wine	100	21	53	40	50	59	119	266
Other alcoholic beverages	100	66	53	70	71	117	125	174
Away from home	**100**	**35**	**33**	**58**	**86**	**105**	**147**	**200**
Beer and ale	100	35	34	57	93	114	164	177
At fast food, take-out, delivery, concession stands, buffet, and cafeteria	100	53	58	64	129	96	104	170
At full-service restaurants	100	33	29	59	88	121	148	192
At vending machines, mobile vendors	100	–	97	48	373	–	105	79
At catered affairs	100	–	–	18	–	105	526	55
Wine	100	23	27	45	94	113	145	212
At fast food, take-out, delivery, concession stands, buffet and cafeteria	100	37	65	–	169	78	112	196
At full-service restaurants	100	23	25	50	90	116	136	218
At catered affairs	100	–	–	18	–	105	525	55
Other alcoholic beverages	100	38	34	63	76	94	130	221
At fast food, take-out, delivery, concession stands, buffet, and cafeteria	100	63	54	32	150	103	109	170
At full-service restaurants	100	20	24	60	78	96	131	233
At machines and mobile vendors	100	57	27	88	250	22	153	109
At catered affairs	100	–	–	18	–	105	527	55
Alcoholic beverages purchased on trips	100	51	43	71	69	92	107	229

Note: (–) means sample is too small to make a reliable estimate.
Source: Calculations by New Strategist based on the 2000 Consumer Expenditure Survey

Table 5.8   Food and Alcohol: Indexed per capita spending by income, 2000

(indexed average annual per capita spending of consumer units (CU) on food and alcoholic beverages, by before-tax income of consumer unit, 2000; complete income reporters only; index definition: an index of 100 is the average for all consumer units; an index of 132 means that spending by consumer units in that group is 32 percent above the average for all consumer units; an index of 68 indicates spending that is 32 percent below the average for all consumer units)

	complete income reporters	under $10,000	$10,000– $19,999	$20,000– $29,999	$30,000– $39,999	$40,000– $49,999	$50,000– $69,999	$70,000 or more
Per capita spending of CU, total	$16,095	$9,492	$10,819	$12,438	$14,244	$16,278	$16,981	$23,739
Per capita spending of CU, index	100	59	67	77	88	101	106	147
Food, per capita spending index	100	67	73	86	94	110	104	125
Alcoholic beverages, per capita spending index	100	65	59	74	88	89	112	146
FOOD AT HOME	**100**	**77**	**88**	**96**	**95**	**108**	**99**	**111**
Cereals and bakery products	**100**	**74**	**87**	**99**	**97**	**103**	**99**	**112**
Cereals and cereal products	100	82	86	113	98	105	97	102
Flour	100	146	112	112	99	83	94	78
Prepared flour mixes	100	77	73	86	111	141	102	101
Ready-to-eat and cooked cereals	100	78	83	106	97	103	104	106
Rice	100	87	100	139	106	110	80	84
Pasta, cornmeal, and other cereal products	100	72	87	130	89	96	85	111
Bakery products	100	71	87	91	97	103	99	117
Bread	100	84	98	101	95	106	92	105
White bread	100	95	105	103	102	102	95	94
Bread, other than white	100	76	93	99	90	109	90	114
Crackers and cookies	100	71	84	90	97	108	104	113
Cookies	100	79	82	86	108	108	102	110
Crackers	100	55	90	98	73	108	108	120
Frozen and refrigerated bakery products	100	75	73	91	83	121	108	117
Other bakery products	100	59	83	85	100	94	100	127
Biscuits and rolls	100	58	84	77	93	98	107	129
Cakes and cupcakes	100	57	73	87	104	85	90	141
Bread and cracker products	100	65	77	68	84	100	130	124
Sweetrolls, coffee cakes, doughnuts	100	64	93	102	111	93	98	107
Pies, tarts, turnovers	100	60	99	83	96	104	103	115
Meats, poultry, fish, and eggs	**100**	**79**	**93**	**102**	**98**	**110**	**95**	**105**
Beef	100	74	95	98	100	110	95	106
Ground beef	100	88	110	111	101	113	91	87
Roast	100	67	94	98	89	91	93	123
Chuck roast	100	81	89	115	86	114	96	102
Round roast	100	78	109	88	108	92	82	114
Other roast	100	45	85	91	78	70	98	148
Steak	100	65	83	89	103	112	100	115
Round steak	100	93	95	99	90	130	95	97
Sirloin steak	100	62	77	83	113	114	91	123
Other steak	100	58	83	90	101	105	108	115
Other beef	100	66	89	78	105	126	92	116
Pork	100	92	99	110	99	109	95	93
Bacon	100	99	104	109	108	95	94	90
Pork chops	100	94	108	109	96	98	98	91
Ham	100	74	90	125	106	107	101	89
Ham, not canned	100	73	90	128	106	108	98	89
Canned ham	100	83	89	69	93	97	157	89
Sausage	100	109	108	93	90	105	85	104
Other pork	100	91	88	110	95	132	93	93
Other meats	100	76	92	105	101	112	100	99
Frankfurters	100	90	97	123	98	105	90	93

	complete income reporters	under $10,000	$10,000– $19,999	$20,000– $29,999	$30,000– $39,999	$40,000– $49,999	$50,000– $69,999	$70,000 or more
Lunch meats (cold cuts)	100	70	91	100	99	95	108	106
Bologna, liverwurst, salami	100	82	100	117	107	88	99	93
Other lunch meats	100	63	87	91	95	99	113	113
Lamb, organ meats, and others	100	88	86	106	117	225	66	69
Lamb and organ meats	100	94	100	119	128	129	76	78
Mutton, goat, and game	100	63	33	54	76	604	30	33
Poultry	100	79	88	101	101	112	92	108
Fresh and frozen chicken	100	82	91	101	104	111	90	105
Fresh and frozen whole chicken	100	102	92	115	103	126	81	92
Fresh and frozen chicken parts	100	74	90	96	105	105	94	110
Other poultry	100	70	75	101	89	115	99	117
Fish and seafood	100	65	80	95	79	113	97	127
Canned fish and seafood	100	74	87	102	86	123	90	114
Fresh fish and shellfish	100	67	79	97	73	106	94	132
Frozen fish and shellfish	100	55	77	85	88	125	108	121
Eggs	100	98	108	103	125	101	82	89
Dairy products	**100**	**75**	**89**	**94**	**100**	**106**	**102**	**109**
Fresh milk and cream	100	86	97	98	106	99	96	102
Fresh milk, all types	100	89	98	99	108	98	95	100
Cream	100	63	83	87	85	111	103	124
Other dairy products	100	67	83	91	95	111	106	113
Butter	100	72	78	92	84	127	107	113
Cheese	100	64	84	94	99	108	108	110
Ice cream and related products	100	72	87	91	94	114	103	111
Miscellaneous dairy products	100	69	78	77	88	110	102	129
Fruits and vegetables	**100**	**81**	**90**	**99**	**93**	**105**	**92**	**113**
Fresh fruits	100	78	92	103	94	103	88	114
Apples	100	70	91	107	99	94	93	112
Bananas	100	94	102	115	100	102	84	97
Oranges	100	75	91	110	112	115	75	106
Citrus fruits, excl. oranges	100	76	80	97	96	124	80	120
Other fresh fruits	100	75	91	95	83	101	92	123
Fresh vegetables	100	78	88	100	91	103	92	116
Potatoes	100	90	88	109	94	109	93	104
Lettuce	100	71	95	95	94	104	100	111
Tomatoes	100	73	94	109	102	103	95	103
Other fresh vegetables	100	78	85	96	86	100	88	127
Processed fruits	100	90	86	95	94	102	96	114
Frozen fruits and fruit juices	100	106	89	77	107	79	81	129
Frozen orange juice	100	76	101	101	86	81	95	118
Frozen fruits	100	223	58	58	130	71	52	134
Frozen fruit juices	100	41	99	56	119	86	87	141
Canned fruits	100	83	102	87	99	113	94	106
Dried fruits	100	82	103	86	103	76	90	119
Fresh fruit juice	100	105	89	101	84	100	97	107
Canned and bottled fruit juice	100	82	77	100	92	108	100	114
Processed vegetables	100	80	95	97	97	118	96	102
Frozen vegetables	100	72	87	83	84	126	104	115
Canned and dried vegetables and juices	100	84	99	103	103	114	92	97
Canned beans	100	73	111	122	103	111	88	87
Canned corn	100	88	95	94	105	113	94	101
Canned miscellaneous vegetables	100	82	96	100	100	110	92	104
Dried peas	100	110	118	131	109	22	96	96
Dried beans	100	105	98	115	111	146	70	82

	complete income reporters	under $10,000	$10,000–$19,999	$20,000–$29,999	$30,000–$39,999	$40,000–$49,999	$50,000–$69,999	$70,000 or more
Dried miscellaneous vegetables	100	110	102	107	122	103	80	88
Dried processed vegetables	100	–	118	66	93	35	233	76
Frozen vegetable juices	100	174	63	30	87	220	67	113
Fresh and canned vegetable juices	100	71	90	86	90	133	105	105
Other food at home	**100**	**75**	**82**	**90**	**90**	**111**	**104**	**116**
Sugar and other sweets	100	67	82	90	87	112	101	121
Candy and chewing gum	100	57	71	76	82	118	106	135
Sugar	100	110	112	127	109	95	88	75
Artificial sweeteners	100	75	147	112	55	74	96	103
Jams, preserves, other sweets	100	74	92	110	97	110	93	104
Fats and oils	100	82	94	109	93	108	98	100
Margarine	100	95	120	96	94	94	97	94
Fats and oils	100	100	106	123	90	93	101	85
Salad dressings	100	62	76	115	97	119	97	108
Nondairy cream and imitation milk	100	86	89	79	96	118	106	107
Peanut butter	100	73	91	102	87	116	88	114
Miscellaneous foods	100	70	81	85	88	109	107	121
Frozen prepared foods	100	71	84	93	81	111	103	119
Frozen meals	100	82	103	104	76	130	90	103
Other frozen prepared foods	100	66	75	88	83	103	109	126
Canned and packaged soups	100	82	99	92	91	95	98	113
Potato chips, nuts, and other snacks	100	56	79	83	90	105	109	127
Potato chips and other snacks	100	55	74	78	92	104	114	129
Nuts	100	60	98	101	82	111	91	118
Condiments and seasonings	100	66	83	89	88	111	104	119
Salt, spices, and other seasonings	100	73	87	104	90	107	98	111
Olives, pickles, relishes	100	58	89	84	89	91	105	128
Sauces and gravies	100	64	84	83	84	126	110	115
Baking needs and miscellaneous products	100	67	73	87	94	96	98	133
Other canned/packaged prepared foods	100	78	75	77	90	113	112	120
Prepared salads	100	58	86	80	84	119	90	134
Prepared desserts	100	71	97	88	95	110	97	112
Baby food	100	78	63	63	91	140	132	111
Miscellaneous prepared foods	100	83	74	81	91	101	110	122
Vitamin supplements	100	–	82	200	–	–	338	13
Nonalcoholic beverages	100	84	84	96	97	117	103	104
Cola	100	76	92	99	106	113	105	95
Other carbonated drinks	100	95	84	90	102	126	102	99
Coffee	100	91	88	103	89	114	95	105
Roasted coffee	100	87	85	97	90	121	95	108
Instant and freeze-dried coffee	100	99	93	114	89	100	95	100
Noncarbonated fruit-flavored drinks, incl. nonfrozen lemonade	100	79	70	85	87	132	108	115
Tea	100	94	78	106	93	138	89	102
Nonalcoholic beer	100	81	38	63	–	243	136	121
Other nonalcoholic beverages and ice	100	77	69	88	85	104	111	124
Food prepared by CU on trips	100	86	60	73	80	99	106	151
FOOD AWAY FROM HOME	**100**	**53**	**53**	**72**	**93**	**113**	**112**	**143**
Meals at restaurants, carry-outs, other	**100**	**50**	**54**	**74**	**97**	**118**	**112**	**136**
Lunch	100	52	57	78	94	122	112	132
At fast food, take-out, delivery, concession stands, buffet, and cafeteria (other than employer and school cafeteria)	100	58	61	90	98	122	110	121
At full-service restaurants	100	49	61	62	79	128	109	147
At vending machines, mobile vendors	100	126	53	152	110	119	99	72
At employer and school cafeterias	100	23	35	58	115	108	126	151

	complete income reporters	under $10,000	$10,000– $19,999	$20,000– $29,999	$30,000– $39,999	$40,000– $49,999	$50,000– $69,999	$70,000 or more
Dinner	100	43	46	65	91	117	115	150
At fast food, take-out, delivery, concession stands, buffet, and cafeteria (other than employer and school cafeteria)	100	51	55	85	109	126	119	116
At full-service restaurants	100	39	42	55	83	113	113	165
At vending machines, mobile vendors	100	35	–	159	209	152	75	83
At employer and school cafeterias	100	140	53	132	71	279	62	61
Snacks and nonalcoholic beverages	100	64	63	84	118	102	111	119
At fast food, take-out, delivery, concession stands, buffet, and cafeteria (other than employer and school cafeteria)	100	68	62	79	103	110	110	126
At full-service restaurants	100	75	100	108	95	96	100	103
At vending machines, mobile vendors	100	55	47	97	179	85	115	98
At employer and school cafeterias	100	25	60	65	156	77	129	122
Breakfast and brunch	100	58	65	88	99	131	103	121
At fast food, take-out, delivery, concession stands, buffet, and cafeteria (other than employer and school cafeteria)	100	63	66	112	105	130	97	107
At full-service restaurants	100	55	63	62	93	134	108	135
At vending machines, mobile vendors	100	–	127	181	63	69	136	74
At employer and school cafeterias	100	52	48	82	115	100	130	123
Board (including at school)	**100**	**186**	**53**	**30**	**21**	**67**	**64**	**211**
Catered affairs	**100**	**4**	**16**	**23**	**48**	**37**	**166**	**240**
Food on trips	**100**	**64**	**53**	**71**	**88**	**85**	**102**	**169**
School lunches	**100**	**30**	**32**	**65**	**69**	**132**	**134**	**167**
Meals as pay	**100**	**88**	**109**	**106**	**118**	**109**	**72**	**100**
ALCOHOLIC BEVERAGES	**100**	**65**	**59**	**74**	**88**	**89**	**112**	**146**
At home	**100**	**74**	**72**	**83**	**90**	**82**	**102**	**139**
Beer and ale	100	106	81	114	114	93	98	94
Whiskey	100	19	53	77	146	84	135	120
Wine	100	31	63	41	50	57	102	208
Other alcoholic beverages	100	95	63	72	71	113	108	136
Away from home	**100**	**50**	**40**	**61**	**86**	**101**	**127**	**156**
Beer and ale	100	51	41	59	93	109	141	138
At fast food, take-out, delivery, concession stands, buffet, and cafeteria	100	77	69	66	129	93	89	132
At full-service restaurants	100	48	35	61	88	116	127	150
At vending machines, mobile vendors	100	–	115	50	373	–	91	61
At catered affairs	100	–	–	18	–	101	454	43
Wine	100	33	32	47	94	109	125	166
At fast food, take-out, delivery, concession stands, buffet and cafeteria	100	53	77	–	169	75	97	153
At full-service restaurants	100	33	29	52	90	112	117	170
At catered affairs	100	–	–	19	–	101	453	43
Other alcoholic beverages	100	54	41	66	76	91	112	173
At fast food, take-out, delivery, concession stands, buffet, and cafeteria	100	90	65	33	150	99	94	133
At full-service restaurants	100	29	29	63	78	92	113	182
At machines and mobile vendors	100	83	32	91	250	21	132	85
At catered affairs	100	–	–	18	–	101	454	43
Alcoholic beverages purchased on trips	100	74	51	74	69	88	92	179

Note: Per capita indexes account for household size and show how much each person in a particular household demographic segment spends relative to a person in the average household. (–) means sample is too small to make a reliable estimate.
Source: Calculations by New Strategist based on the 2000 Consumer Expenditure Survey

Table 5.9 Food and Alcohol: Total spending by income, 2000

(total annual spending on food and alcoholic beverages, by before-tax income group of consumer units (CU), 2000; complete income reporters only; numbers in thousands)

	complete income reporters	under $10,000	$10,000–$19,999	$20,000–$29,999	$30,000–$39,999	$40,000–$49,999	$50,000–$69,999	$70,000 or more
Number of consumer units	81,454	10,810	14,714	12,039	9,477	7,653	11,337	15,424
Total spending of all CUs	$3,277,581,892	$177,886,368	$332,833,656	$359,383,292	$337,468,767	$323,898,149	$558,294,760	$1,171,666,422
Food, total spending	442,682,941	27,210,487	48,973,837	54,255,921	48,499,116	47,665,027	74,339,430	133,641,402
Alcoholic beverages, total spending	34,444,453	2,049,479	3,074,337	3,626,508	3,530,467	3,007,859	6,225,487	12,158,122
FOOD AT HOME	**$256,940,941**	**$18,192,468**	**$34,010,461**	**$35,162,548**	**$28,386,553**	**$27,185,140**	**$40,867,958**	**$69,139,777**
Cereals and bakery products	**38,637,705**	**2,642,430**	**5,064,872**	**5,409,243**	**4,357,714**	**3,906,474**	**6,145,788**	**10,475,055**
Cereals and cereal products	13,258,268	994,739	1,730,457	2,124,522	1,507,696	1,355,193	2,078,526	3,288,551
Flour	659,777	88,560	111,629	104,499	75,626	53,494	99,652	124,009
Prepared flour mixes	1,144,429	81,532	126,687	140,014	148,315	158,111	187,967	280,871
Ready-to-eat and cooked cereals	7,366,700	531,324	920,737	1,107,588	828,858	737,902	1,240,041	1,890,674
Rice	1,631,524	129,938	247,131	321,080	200,628	175,330	211,889	332,079
Pasta, cornmeal, and other cereal products	2,455,838	163,384	324,207	451,342	254,268	230,355	338,976	660,764
Bakery products	25,379,437	1,647,691	3,334,482	3,284,841	2,850,113	2,551,204	4,067,262	7,186,659
Bread	7,176,912	556,742	1,064,289	1,023,917	796,352	742,341	1,065,791	1,831,908
White bread	3,105,841	270,313	491,218	453,991	369,319	308,339	474,340	705,956
Bread, other than white	4,071,071	286,429	573,071	569,926	427,034	434,078	591,451	1,125,952
Crackers and cookies	6,134,301	402,989	781,234	783,619	690,589	649,816	1,032,120	1,686,769
Cookies	4,121,572	300,463	509,038	503,832	518,771	436,910	682,034	1,100,040
Crackers	2,012,728	102,563	272,195	279,786	171,818	212,906	350,087	586,575
Frozen and refrigerated bakery products	2,083,593	144,224	230,842	267,868	201,386	246,656	362,897	591,048
Other bakery products	9,983,817	543,807	1,258,037	1,209,438	1,161,785	912,467	1,606,453	3,076,934
Biscuits and rolls	3,283,411	174,154	416,754	357,318	354,724	314,003	564,809	1,029,244
Cakes and cupcakes	3,347,759	176,749	367,596	414,503	404,289	278,187	485,337	1,141,839
Bread and cracker products	347,809	20,895	40,703	33,468	33,833	34,132	73,010	104,575
Sweetrolls, coffee cakes, doughnuts	1,871,813	109,897	263,581	270,878	241,948	170,891	295,329	486,936
Pies, tarts, turnovers	1,132,211	62,114	169,403	133,151	126,992	115,254	187,854	314,341
Meats, poultry, fish, and eggs	**66,562,580**	**4,822,990**	**9,311,653**	**9,625,782**	**7,610,979**	**7,181,039**	**10,179,946**	**16,895,450**
Beef	19,833,234	1,349,503	2,859,239	2,769,692	2,311,061	2,129,218	3,038,316	5,079,740
Ground beef	7,433,492	601,883	1,238,627	1,175,006	876,433	820,019	1,090,279	1,564,919
Roast	3,292,371	202,756	466,225	459,529	342,309	293,110	492,479	979,578
Chuck roast	1,108,589	82,893	149,621	181,669	111,260	123,213	171,302	275,164
Round roast	956,270	68,726	157,927	118,945	119,695	86,402	126,974	263,596
Other roast	1,227,512	51,101	158,530	159,035	111,355	83,571	194,203	440,818
Steak	7,808,180	465,719	980,634	990,810	934,053	855,758	1,263,509	2,168,614
Round steak	1,307,337	111,928	187,344	183,234	136,469	165,841	201,458	307,709
Sirloin steak	2,498,194	141,450	291,883	294,113	328,568	278,646	367,092	742,049
Other steak	4,001,835	212,378	501,408	513,463	469,017	411,196	694,845	1,118,857
Other beef	1,299,191	79,144	173,753	144,348	158,361	160,330	192,162	366,628
Pork	13,897,681	1,177,180	2,074,771	2,173,401	1,598,296	1,477,488	2,132,830	3,122,589
Bacon	2,144,684	195,713	337,877	330,471	270,189	198,442	324,805	465,342
Pork chops	3,354,276	290,355	547,614	516,834	375,953	322,650	532,612	736,804
Ham	3,007,282	204,340	410,631	534,893	369,793	314,768	491,686	645,957
Ham, not canned	2,861,479	193,141	390,938	520,687	353,966	300,916	454,727	614,646
Canned ham	145,803	11,200	19,693	14,326	15,827	13,852	37,072	31,311
Sausage	2,118,619	212,503	344,639	279,064	221,288	218,111	290,000	533,516
Other pork	3,273,636	274,306	433,929	512,139	361,074	423,440	493,613	740,969
Other meats	8,498,910	593,292	1,177,703	1,269,874	996,412	934,202	1,366,335	2,046,456
Frankfurters	1,686,912	139,365	246,478	295,317	191,625	172,805	243,972	381,281

	complete income reporters	under $10,000	$10,000– $19,999	$20,000– $29,999	$30,000– $39,999	$40,000– $49,999	$50,000– $69,999	$70,000 or more
Lunch meats (cold cuts)	$5,807,670	$372,511	$800,250	$823,347	$667,655	$540,838	$1,014,548	$1,497,053
Bologna, liverwurst, salami	2,003,768	150,944	302,987	332,999	248,392	172,499	319,703	453,311
Other lunch meats	3,804,716	221,567	497,263	490,348	419,262	368,339	694,731	1,043,742
Lamb, organ meats, and others	1,003,513	81,488	130,974	151,210	137,132	220,636	107,702	168,122
Lamb and organ meats	801,507	69,692	120,960	135,800	119,315	101,020	97,838	152,081
Mutton, goat, and game	202,820	11,796	10,161	15,410	17,817	119,616	9,977	16,041
Poultry	12,184,704	890,053	1,612,419	1,746,979	1,433,870	1,331,545	1,809,385	3,180,429
Fresh and frozen chicken	9,653,114	727,943	1,323,884	1,383,763	1,173,063	1,047,619	1,403,521	2,459,974
Fresh and frozen whole chicken	2,669,248	251,483	369,340	434,969	319,280	328,926	347,366	595,829
Fresh and frozen chicken parts	6,983,866	476,460	954,611	948,794	853,783	718,693	1,056,155	1,864,145
Other poultry	2,531,590	162,110	288,468	363,217	260,807	283,926	405,978	720,301
Fish and seafood	9,247,473	551,117	1,114,663	1,243,869	848,665	1,021,982	1,451,363	2,841,409
Canned fish and seafood	1,302,449	88,747	171,527	188,170	129,740	155,968	188,874	359,996
Fresh fish and shellfish	5,608,922	343,668	669,928	774,348	479,441	581,475	855,150	1,798,901
Frozen fish and shellfish	2,336,101	118,739	273,128	281,351	239,484	284,539	407,225	682,666
Eggs	2,900,577	261,844	472,938	421,967	422,769	286,605	381,830	624,672
Dairy products	**27,648,746**	**1,911,215**	**3,706,120**	**3,675,747**	**3,205,974**	**2,874,084**	**4,541,375**	**7,279,048**
Fresh milk and cream	11,243,910	894,847	1,639,674	1,558,449	1,391,129	1,089,481	1,735,468	2,779,713
Fresh milk, all types	10,282,753	838,906	1,519,080	1,440,226	1,295,790	985,324	1,575,503	2,491,901
Cream	961,157	55,977	120,594	118,103	95,339	104,157	159,965	287,812
Other dairy products	16,404,836	1,016,403	2,066,298	2,117,299	1,814,940	1,784,603	2,805,908	4,499,335
Butter	1,345,620	88,726	158,093	175,529	132,015	167,295	232,635	367,554
Cheese	8,311,566	487,062	1,051,403	1,107,829	958,504	874,432	1,454,084	2,224,141
Ice cream and related products	4,712,928	310,590	616,652	611,340	515,928	524,231	784,747	1,269,549
Miscellaneous dairy products	2,035,535	129,954	240,218	222,481	208,399	218,646	334,442	638,091
Fruits and vegetables	**44,280,838**	**3,301,751**	**6,024,376**	**6,242,342**	**4,815,927**	**4,550,321**	**6,571,265**	**12,110,462**
Fresh fruits	13,813,784	989,344	1,922,516	2,019,301	1,504,284	1,395,371	1,952,685	3,821,913
Apples	2,421,627	156,320	333,844	367,310	278,245	222,779	362,557	660,301
Bananas	2,718,935	235,447	419,078	442,915	315,584	271,146	369,926	637,628
Oranges	1,528,077	104,854	210,726	239,215	199,017	172,116	185,473	394,083
Citrus fruits, excl. oranges	1,201,447	83,686	145,395	165,175	134,573	145,407	155,884	350,896
Other fresh fruits	5,944,513	409,110	813,407	804,807	576,960	583,924	878,958	1,779,004
Fresh vegetables	13,541,728	976,339	1,805,939	1,926,601	1,437,566	1,357,566	2,003,701	3,821,604
Potatoes	2,330,399	192,557	309,411	359,123	253,984	249,029	348,953	587,963
Lettuce	1,727,639	112,878	247,004	233,316	188,687	175,024	279,911	463,028
Tomatoes	2,539,736	169,544	359,048	393,073	301,748	256,682	391,240	631,613
Other fresh vegetables	6,943,139	501,397	890,557	941,209	693,148	676,831	983,485	2,139,000
Processed fruits	9,815,207	812,580	1,271,720	1,318,632	1,072,417	976,676	1,516,891	2,701,822
Frozen fruits and fruit juices	1,203,890	117,948	161,603	130,744	149,926	93,443	157,244	376,500
Frozen orange juice	537,596	37,750	82,406	77,050	53,545	42,474	82,080	154,086
Frozen fruits	327,445	67,302	28,498	26,967	49,375	22,653	27,436	106,734
Frozen fruit juices	338,849	12,859	50,699	26,727	47,006	28,316	47,842	115,834
Canned fruits	1,329,329	101,756	204,118	163,369	152,769	146,172	201,005	340,253
Dried fruits	465,102	35,145	72,620	56,463	55,630	34,592	67,682	134,652
Fresh fruit juice	1,980,961	192,263	267,263	284,843	194,089	192,626	311,427	515,624
Canned and bottled fruit juice	4,836,739	365,540	566,115	683,093	520,098	509,919	779,532	1,334,793
Processed vegetables	7,110,120	523,415	1,024,121	977,687	801,659	820,708	1,097,988	1,765,123
Frozen vegetables	2,226,952	147,085	292,616	263,654	216,549	274,666	373,668	618,657
Canned and dried vegetables and juices	4,883,982	376,330	731,585	714,033	585,110	546,042	724,321	1,146,466
Canned beans	1,066,233	71,352	178,611	185,039	128,129	115,484	151,462	225,190
Canned corn	591,356	48,115	85,150	78,494	72,025	65,127	89,789	144,986
Canned miscellaneous vegetables	1,518,303	115,198	219,677	215,618	177,504	162,703	225,380	382,207
Dried peas	28,509	2,873	5,098	5,297	3,601	612	4,421	6,632
Dried beans	222,369	21,560	33,087	36,358	28,621	31,760	25,168	43,958

	complete income reporters	under $10,000	$10,000– $19,999	$20,000– $29,999	$30,000– $39,999	$40,000– $49,999	$50,000– $69,999	$70,000 or more
Dried miscellaneous vegetables	$610,090	$61,711	$93,868	$92,700	$86,904	$61,301	$78,792	$129,870
Dried processed vegetables	33,396	–	5,929	3,130	3,601	1,148	12,584	6,170
Frozen vegetable juices	25,251	4,035	2,411	1,084	2,559	5,434	2,721	6,941
Fresh and canned vegetable juices	787,660	51,523	107,675	96,432	82,260	102,474	134,117	200,358
Other food at home	**79,810,258**	**5,514,047**	**9,903,520**	**10,209,554**	**8,395,864**	**8,673,221**	**13,429,583**	**22,379,761**
Sugar and other sweets	10,161,387	631,036	1,260,357	1,293,350	1,030,150	1,114,353	1,662,231	2,978,683
Candy and chewing gum	6,826,660	356,949	729,005	736,787	648,701	786,881	1,171,792	2,236,788
Sugar	1,400,194	142,021	237,416	252,819	178,073	129,795	199,078	255,576
Artificial sweeteners	301,380	20,846	66,998	48,036	19,238	21,811	46,822	74,961
Jams, preserves, other sweets	1,633,153	111,219	226,871	255,588	184,138	175,866	244,539	411,358
Fats and oils	6,965,132	523,705	992,775	1,078,574	755,412	732,469	1,102,410	1,692,784
Margarine	960,343	83,845	174,503	131,345	104,531	88,010	150,102	218,404
Fats and oils	1,969,558	181,975	316,146	344,677	206,788	178,544	321,857	405,805
Salad dressings	2,285,599	131,363	263,550	373,931	258,343	265,712	358,476	597,217
Nondairy cream and imitation milk	765,668	60,523	102,888	86,199	85,862	88,239	131,396	198,198
Peanut butter	984,779	65,999	135,607	142,542	99,888	111,963	140,579	273,159
Miscellaneous foods	37,481,058	2,410,072	4,587,954	4,527,868	3,839,227	4,000,376	6,460,956	10,951,965
Frozen prepared foods	7,571,149	494,615	958,183	995,866	711,723	820,937	1,263,849	2,191,905
Frozen meals	2,310,035	175,064	358,770	339,259	204,419	292,651	334,668	579,171
Other frozen prepared foods	5,261,114	319,659	599,413	656,607	507,304	528,287	929,067	1,612,733
Canned and packaged soups	3,052,081	229,646	454,710	398,371	323,924	282,778	483,183	834,130
Potato chips, nuts, and other snacks	7,929,547	410,770	944,821	931,939	832,081	815,198	1,391,277	2,432,982
Potato chips and other snacks	6,224,715	316,849	691,973	686,584	668,413	630,990	1,141,296	1,945,121
Nuts	1,705,647	93,849	252,849	245,234	163,668	184,208	249,981	487,707
Condiments and seasonings	7,279,544	443,255	915,887	921,465	746,219	791,014	1,224,849	2,100,440
Salt, spices, and other seasonings	1,804,206	121,199	237,947	267,145	188,308	188,187	286,259	487,553
Olives, pickles, relishes	832,460	44,384	112,056	98,720	86,335	74,311	140,806	258,352
Sauces and gravies	3,188,924	188,439	404,325	375,617	313,404	392,446	567,984	886,263
Baking needs and miscellaneous products	1,453,954	89,163	161,411	179,983	158,171	136,147	229,801	468,273
Other canned/packaged prepared foods	11,648,737	831,785	1,314,434	1,280,348	1,225,281	1,290,372	2,097,912	3,392,663
Prepared salads	1,591,611	84,483	206,360	179,622	155,991	184,820	232,295	515,162
Prepared desserts	809,653	52,756	118,622	101,609	89,179	86,708	127,201	220,255
Baby food	2,708,346	193,967	255,881	242,345	287,343	371,400	577,507	726,470
Miscellaneous prepared foods	6,530,167	500,544	732,288	754,003	692,674	647,444	1,155,580	1,930,314
Vitamin supplements	9,774	–	1,217	2,769	–	–	5,328	308
Nonalcoholic beverages	21,615,448	1,663,877	2,735,644	2,940,405	2,438,148	2,478,118	3,590,655	5,445,752
Cola	7,604,545	531,361	1,060,887	1,073,397	940,971	838,922	1,284,709	1,759,724
Other carbonated drinks	4,142,750	360,482	523,183	528,994	489,487	508,695	684,301	990,684
Coffee	3,627,961	304,956	482,600	531,161	377,279	403,466	557,440	923,589
Roasted coffee	2,362,981	189,865	305,154	325,896	246,592	279,794	363,237	617,885
Instant and freeze-dried coffee	1,264,981	115,090	177,446	205,145	130,688	123,672	194,089	305,704
Noncarbonated fruit-flavored drinks, incl. nonfrozen lemonade	1,664,105	121,380	175,969	200,329	168,691	213,978	289,774	464,262
Tea	1,317,111	113,511	155,496	198,884	143,008	178,162	189,215	324,984
Nonalcoholic beer	30,953	2,299	1,768	2,769	–	7,347	6,802	9,100
Other nonalcoholic beverages and ice	3,228,837	229,780	335,742	404,872	318,712	327,548	578,414	973,563
Food prepared by CU on trips	3,586,420	285,429	326,788	369,477	332,927	347,905	613,445	1,310,577
FOOD AWAY FROM HOME	**185,742,000**	**9,017,983**	**14,963,443**	**19,093,372**	**20,112,563**	**20,479,811**	**33,471,472**	**64,501,626**
Meals at restaurants, carry-outs, other	**154,060,467**	**7,146,129**	**12,647,643**	**16,282,868**	**17,317,606**	**17,805,011**	**27,873,828**	**50,885,473**
Lunch	58,826,079	2,790,330	5,109,703	6,494,077	6,443,602	7,007,393	10,607,124	18,873,269
At fast food, take-out, delivery, concession stands, buffet, and cafeteria (other than employer and school cafeteria)	32,037,487	1,716,530	2,952,330	4,109,272	3,653,004	3,810,964	5,712,488	9,373,319
At full-service restaurants	18,729,533	842,492	1,717,955	1,641,999	1,715,337	2,339,216	3,287,843	6,668,412
At vending machines, mobile vendors	623,123	72,405	50,044	134,476	79,891	72,397	99,539	109,356
At employer and school cafeterias	7,436,750	158,903	389,227	608,331	995,369	784,892	1,507,254	2,722,182

	complete income reporters	under $10,000	$10,000– $19,999	$20,000– $29,999	$30,000– $39,999	$40,000– $49,999	$50,000– $69,999	$70,000 or more
Dinner	$60,061,736	$2,359,838	$4,156,877	$5,521,808	$6,362,100	$6,886,169	$11,136,335	$21,823,263
At fast food, take-out, delivery, concession stands, buffet, and cafeteria (other than employer and school cafeteria)	17,985,858	839,854	1,500,191	2,173,762	2,274,575	2,213,324	3,465,267	5,073,725
At full-service restaurants	41,748,433	1,485,696	2,636,962	3,283,637	4,047,248	4,593,484	7,636,263	16,696,788
At vending machines, mobile vendors	82,269	2,658	–	18,540	19,996	12,245	9,977	16,504
At employer and school cafeterias	245,991	31,594	19,724	45,989	20,376	67,040	24,715	36,246
Snacks and nonalcoholic beverages	20,945,082	1,234,009	1,993,891	2,494,240	2,869,351	2,096,769	3,757,989	6,027,545
At fast food, take-out, delivery, concession stands, buffet, and cafeteria (other than employer and school cafeteria)	14,460,529	898,798	1,364,408	1,618,042	1,726,330	1,547,743	2,575,086	4,405,403
At full-service restaurants	1,824,570	125,665	275,556	279,425	200,818	170,891	294,195	455,008
At vending machines, mobile vendors	3,629,590	185,367	260,181	502,026	754,938	300,457	674,211	862,664
At employer and school cafeterias	1,030,393	24,180	93,746	94,747	187,171	77,678	214,383	304,316
Breakfast and brunch	14,226,756	761,953	1,387,238	1,772,743	1,642,554	1,814,679	2,372,494	4,161,395
At fast food, take-out, delivery, concession stands, buffet, and cafeteria (other than employer and school cafeteria)	6,865,758	397,484	682,783	1,095,910	841,652	871,753	1,075,655	1,775,611
At full-service restaurants	6,875,532	347,329	654,223	602,793	743,565	899,304	1,193,673	2,256,377
At vending machines, mobile vendors	126,254	–	24,292	32,385	9,193	8,571	27,776	22,673
At employer and school cafeterias	359,212	17,140	26,022	41,655	48,143	35,051	75,391	106,734
Board (including at school)	**2,915,239**	**499,872**	**235,126**	**125,326**	**70,035**	**192,243**	**302,698**	**1,489,804**
Catered affairs	**3,788,426**	**13,351**	**90,495**	**122,557**	**211,053**	**135,611**	**1,012,281**	**2,202,856**
Food on trips	**18,358,103**	**1,083,871**	**1,471,116**	**1,851,719**	**1,884,501**	**1,530,447**	**3,020,517**	**7,515,961**
School lunches	**4,941,000**	**138,615**	**242,090**	**457,843**	**397,844**	**637,036**	**1,066,812**	**2,000,339**
Meals as pay	**1,679,581**	**136,002**	**276,905**	**253,060**	**231,428**	**179,386**	**195,450**	**407,039**
ALCOHOLIC BEVERAGES	**34,444,453**	**2,049,479**	**3,074,337**	**3,626,508**	**3,530,467**	**3,007,859**	**6,225,487**	**12,158,122**
At home	**20,965,445**	**1,429,811**	**2,266,109**	**2,467,273**	**2,188,145**	**1,675,165**	**3,461,640**	**7,046,454**
Beer and ale	10,603,682	1,039,175	1,293,825	1,720,253	1,408,756	966,115	1,672,208	2,403,676
Whiskey	1,175,381	20,689	94,753	128,336	200,059	96,351	255,309	343,184
Wine	7,336,562	208,614	701,888	428,588	426,655	408,900	1,211,585	3,690,655
Other alcoholic beverages	1,849,006	161,369	175,643	189,975	152,769	203,799	322,538	609,094
Away from home	**13,479,008**	**619,633**	**808,228**	**1,159,235**	**1,342,322**	**1,332,693**	**2,763,847**	**5,111,668**
Beer and ale	6,055,290	281,547	371,261	510,213	653,060	646,525	1,383,227	2,029,798
At fast food, take-out, delivery, concession stands, buffet, and cafeteria	1,314,668	93,014	137,835	123,761	197,880	118,928	189,781	422,155
At full-service restaurants	4,272,262	188,461	225,469	372,246	435,373	485,966	877,711	1,557,207
At vending machines, mobile vendors	45,614	–	7,957	3,251	19,807	–	6,689	6,787
At catered affairs	421,932	–	–	10,955	–	41,632	308,933	43,804
Wine	1,642,113	50,342	80,058	109,796	178,736	174,182	331,154	659,530
At fast food, take-out, delivery, concession stands, buffet and cafeteria	125,439	6,106	14,637	–	24,735	9,184	19,613	46,580
At full-service restaurants	1,471,874	44,237	65,273	108,592	154,001	160,560	278,777	608,168
At catered affairs	44,800	–	–	1,204	–	4,439	32,764	4,627
Other alcoholic beverages	5,780,790	287,707	356,909	539,227	510,431	511,986	1,049,466	2,422,339
At fast food, take-out, delivery, concession stands, buffet, and cafeteria	304,638	25,327	29,910	14,326	53,071	29,464	46,028	98,097
At full-service restaurants	2,395,562	64,348	104,830	213,572	218,350	215,738	435,227	1,056,852
At machines and mobile vendors	26,065	1,983	1,271	3,371	7,582	536	5,555	5,398
At catered affairs	185,715	–	–	4,816	–	18,367	136,157	19,280
Alcoholic beverages purchased on trips	2,868,810	196,050	220,965	303,142	231,334	247,881	426,611	1,242,712

Note: Numbers may not add to total because of rounding. (–) means sample is too small to make a reliable estimate.
Source: Calculations by New Strategist based on the 2000 Consumer Expenditure Survey

Table 5.10 Food and Alcohol: Market shares by income, 2000

(percentage of total annual spending on food and alcoholic beverages accounted for by before-tax income group of consumer units, 2000; complete income reporters only)

	complete income reporters	under $10,000	$10,000– $19,999	$20,000– $29,999	$30,000– $39,999	$40,000– $49,999	$50,000– $69,999	$70,000 or more
Share of total consumer units	100.0%	13.3%	18.1%	14.8%	11.6%	9.4%	13.9%	18.9%
Share of total before-tax income	100.0	1.7	5.9	8.1	9.0	9.3	18.3	47.7
Share of total spending	100.0	5.4	10.2	11.0	10.3	9.9	17.0	35.7
Share of food spending	100.0	6.1	11.1	12.3	11.0	10.8	16.8	30.2
Share of alcoholic beverages spending	100.0	6.0	8.9	10.5	10.2	8.7	18.1	35.3
FOOD AT HOME	100.0%	7.1%	13.2%	13.7%	11.0%	10.6%	15.9%	26.9%
Cereals and bakery products	100.0	6.8	13.1	14.0	11.3	10.1	15.9	27.1
Cereals and cereal products	100.0	7.5	13.1	16.0	11.4	10.2	15.7	24.8
Flour	100.0	13.4	16.9	15.8	11.5	8.1	15.1	18.8
Prepared flour mixes	100.0	7.1	11.1	12.2	13.0	13.8	16.4	24.5
Ready-to-eat and cooked cereals	100.0	7.2	12.5	15.0	11.3	10.0	16.8	25.7
Rice	100.0	8.0	15.1	19.7	12.3	10.7	13.0	20.4
Pasta, cornmeal, and other cereal products	100.0	6.7	13.2	18.4	10.4	9.4	13.8	26.9
Bakery products	100.0	6.5	13.1	12.9	11.2	10.1	16.0	28.3
Bread	100.0	7.8	14.8	14.3	11.1	10.3	14.9	25.5
White bread	100.0	8.7	15.8	14.6	11.9	9.9	15.3	22.7
Bread, other than white	100.0	7.0	14.1	14.0	10.5	10.7	14.5	27.7
Crackers and cookies	100.0	6.6	12.7	12.8	11.3	10.6	16.8	27.5
Cookies	100.0	7.3	12.4	12.2	12.6	10.6	16.5	26.7
Crackers	100.0	5.1	13.5	13.9	8.5	10.6	17.4	29.1
Frozen and refrigerated bakery products	100.0	6.9	11.1	12.9	9.7	11.8	17.4	28.4
Other bakery products	100.0	5.4	12.6	12.1	11.6	9.1	16.1	30.8
Biscuits and rolls	100.0	5.3	12.7	10.9	10.8	9.6	17.2	31.3
Cakes and cupcakes	100.0	5.3	11.0	12.4	12.1	8.3	14.5	34.1
Bread and cracker products	100.0	6.0	11.7	9.6	9.7	9.8	21.0	30.1
Sweetrolls, coffee cakes, doughnuts	100.0	5.9	14.1	14.5	12.9	9.1	15.8	26.0
Pies, tarts, turnovers	100.0	5.5	15.0	11.8	11.2	10.2	16.6	27.8
Meats, poultry, fish, and eggs	100.0	7.2	14.0	14.5	11.4	10.8	15.3	25.4
Beef	100.0	6.8	14.4	14.0	11.7	10.7	15.3	25.6
Ground beef	100.0	8.1	16.7	15.8	11.8	11.0	14.7	21.1
Roast	100.0	6.2	14.2	14.0	10.4	8.9	15.0	29.8
Chuck roast	100.0	7.5	13.5	16.4	10.0	11.1	15.5	24.8
Round roast	100.0	7.2	16.5	12.4	12.5	9.0	13.3	27.6
Other roast	100.0	4.2	12.9	13.0	9.1	6.8	15.8	35.9
Steak	100.0	6.0	12.6	12.7	12.0	11.0	16.2	27.8
Round steak	100.0	8.6	14.3	14.0	10.4	12.7	15.4	23.5
Sirloin steak	100.0	5.7	11.7	11.8	13.2	11.2	14.7	29.7
Other steak	100.0	5.3	12.5	12.8	11.7	10.3	17.4	28.0
Other beef	100.0	6.1	13.4	11.1	12.2	12.3	14.8	28.2
Pork	100.0	8.5	14.9	15.6	11.5	10.6	15.3	22.5
Bacon	100.0	9.1	15.8	15.4	12.6	9.3	15.1	21.7
Pork chops	100.0	8.7	16.3	15.4	11.2	9.6	15.9	22.0
Ham	100.0	6.8	13.7	17.8	12.3	10.5	16.3	21.5
Ham, not canned	100.0	6.7	13.7	18.2	12.4	10.5	15.9	21.5
Canned ham	100.0	7.7	13.5	9.8	10.9	9.5	25.4	21.5
Sausage	100.0	10.0	16.3	13.2	10.4	10.3	13.7	25.2
Other pork	100.0	8.4	13.3	15.6	11.0	12.9	15.1	22.6
Other meats	100.0	7.0	13.9	14.9	11.7	11.0	16.1	24.1
Frankfurters	100.0	8.3	14.6	17.5	11.4	10.2	14.5	22.6

	complete income reporters	under $10,000	$10,000– $19,999	$20,000– $29,999	$30,000– $39,999	$40,000– $49,999	$50,000– $69,999	$70,000 or more
Lunch meats (cold cuts)	100.0%	6.4%	13.8%	14.2%	11.5%	9.3%	17.5%	25.8%
Bologna, liverwurst, salami	100.0	7.5	15.1	16.6	12.4	8.6	16.0	22.6
Other lunch meats	100.0	5.8	13.1	12.9	11.0	9.7	18.3	27.4
Lamb, organ meats, and others	100.0	8.1	13.1	15.1	13.7	22.0	10.7	16.8
Lamb and organ meats	100.0	8.7	15.1	16.9	14.9	12.6	12.2	19.0
Mutton, goat, and game	100.0	5.8	5.0	7.6	8.8	59.0	4.9	7.9
Poultry	100.0	7.3	13.2	14.3	11.8	10.9	14.8	26.1
Fresh and frozen chicken	100.0	7.5	13.7	14.3	12.2	10.9	14.5	25.5
Fresh and frozen whole chicken	100.0	9.4	13.8	16.3	12.0	12.3	13.0	22.3
Fresh and frozen chicken parts	100.0	6.8	13.7	13.6	12.2	10.3	15.1	26.7
Other poultry	100.0	6.4	11.4	14.3	10.3	11.2	16.0	28.5
Fish and seafood	100.0	6.0	12.1	13.5	9.2	11.1	15.7	30.7
Canned fish and seafood	100.0	6.8	13.2	14.4	10.0	12.0	14.5	27.6
Fresh fish and shellfish	100.0	6.1	11.9	13.8	8.5	10.4	15.2	32.1
Frozen fish and shellfish	100.0	5.1	11.7	12.0	10.3	12.2	17.4	29.2
Eggs	100.0	9.0	16.3	14.5	14.6	9.9	13.2	21.5
Dairy products	**100.0**	**6.9**	**13.4**	**13.3**	**11.6**	**10.4**	**16.4**	**26.3**
Fresh milk and cream	100.0	8.0	14.6	13.9	12.4	9.7	15.4	24.7
Fresh milk, all types	100.0	8.2	14.8	14.0	12.6	9.6	15.3	24.2
Cream	100.0	5.8	12.5	12.3	9.9	10.8	16.6	29.9
Other dairy products	100.0	6.2	12.6	12.9	11.1	10.9	17.1	27.4
Butter	100.0	6.6	11.7	13.0	9.8	12.4	17.3	27.3
Cheese	100.0	5.9	12.6	13.3	11.5	10.5	17.5	26.8
Ice cream and related products	100.0	6.6	13.1	13.0	10.9	11.1	16.7	26.9
Miscellaneous dairy products	100.0	6.4	11.8	10.9	10.2	10.7	16.4	31.3
Fruits and vegetables	**100.0**	**7.5**	**13.6**	**14.1**	**10.9**	**10.3**	**14.8**	**27.3**
Fresh fruits	100.0	7.2	13.9	14.6	10.9	10.1	14.1	27.7
Apples	100.0	6.5	13.8	15.2	11.5	9.2	15.0	27.3
Bananas	100.0	8.7	15.4	16.3	11.6	10.0	13.6	23.5
Oranges	100.0	6.9	13.8	15.7	13.0	11.3	12.1	25.8
Citrus fruits, excl. oranges	100.0	7.0	12.1	13.7	11.2	12.1	13.0	29.2
Other fresh fruits	100.0	6.9	13.7	13.5	9.7	9.8	14.8	29.9
Fresh vegetables	100.0	7.2	13.3	14.2	10.6	10.0	14.8	28.2
Potatoes	100.0	8.3	13.3	15.4	10.9	10.7	15.0	25.2
Lettuce	100.0	6.5	14.3	13.5	10.9	10.1	16.2	26.8
Tomatoes	100.0	6.7	14.1	15.5	11.9	10.1	15.4	24.9
Other fresh vegetables	100.0	7.2	12.8	13.6	10.0	9.7	14.2	30.8
Processed fruits	100.0	8.3	13.0	13.4	10.9	10.0	15.5	27.5
Frozen fruits and fruit juices	100.0	9.8	13.4	10.9	12.5	7.8	13.1	31.3
Frozen orange juice	100.0	7.0	15.3	14.3	10.0	7.9	15.3	28.7
Frozen fruits	100.0	20.6	8.7	8.2	15.1	6.9	8.4	32.6
Frozen fruit juices	100.0	3.8	15.0	7.9	13.9	8.4	14.1	34.2
Canned fruits	100.0	7.7	15.4	12.3	11.5	11.0	15.1	25.6
Dried fruits	100.0	7.6	15.6	12.1	12.0	7.4	14.6	29.0
Fresh fruit juice	100.0	9.7	13.5	14.4	9.8	9.7	15.7	26.0
Canned and bottled fruit juice	100.0	7.6	11.7	14.1	10.8	10.5	16.1	27.6
Processed vegetables	100.0	7.4	14.4	13.8	11.3	11.5	15.4	24.8
Frozen vegetables	100.0	6.6	13.1	11.8	9.7	12.3	16.8	27.8
Canned and dried vegetables and juices	100.0	7.7	15.0	14.6	12.0	11.2	14.8	23.5
Canned beans	100.0	6.7	16.8	17.4	12.0	10.8	14.2	21.1
Canned corn	100.0	8.1	14.4	13.3	12.2	11.0	15.2	24.5
Canned miscellaneous vegetables	100.0	7.6	14.5	14.2	11.7	10.7	14.8	25.2
Dried peas	100.0	10.1	17.9	18.6	12.6	2.1	15.5	23.3
Dried beans	100.0	9.7	14.9	16.4	12.9	14.3	11.3	19.8

	complete income reporters	under $10,000	$10,000– $19,999	$20,000– $29,999	$30,000– $39,999	$40,000– $49,999	$50,000– $69,999	$70,000 or more
Dried miscellaneous vegetables	100.0%	10.1%	15.4%	15.2%	14.2%	10.0%	12.9%	21.3%
Dried processed vegetables	100.0	–	17.8	9.4	10.8	3.4	37.7	18.5
Frozen vegetable juices	100.0	16.0	9.5	4.3	10.1	21.5	10.8	27.5
Fresh and canned vegetable juices	100.0	6.5	13.7	12.2	10.4	13.0	17.0	25.4
Other food at home	**100.0**	**6.9**	**12.4**	**12.8**	**10.5**	**10.9**	**16.8**	**28.0**
Sugar and other sweets	100.0	6.2	12.4	12.7	10.1	11.0	16.4	29.3
Candy and chewing gum	100.0	5.2	10.7	10.8	9.5	11.5	17.2	32.8
Sugar	100.0	10.1	17.0	18.1	12.7	9.3	14.2	18.3
Artificial sweeteners	100.0	6.9	22.2	15.9	6.4	7.2	15.5	24.9
Jams, preserves, other sweets	100.0	6.8	13.9	15.6	11.3	10.8	15.0	25.2
Fats and oils	100.0	7.5	14.3	15.5	10.8	10.5	15.8	24.3
Margarine	100.0	8.7	18.2	13.7	10.9	9.2	15.6	22.7
Fats and oils	100.0	9.2	16.1	17.5	10.5	9.1	16.3	20.6
Salad dressings	100.0	5.7	11.5	16.4	11.3	11.6	15.7	26.1
Nondairy cream and imitation milk	100.0	7.9	13.4	11.3	11.2	11.5	17.2	25.9
Peanut butter	100.0	6.7	13.8	14.5	10.1	11.4	14.3	27.7
Miscellaneous foods	100.0	6.4	12.2	12.1	10.2	10.7	17.2	29.2
Frozen prepared foods	100.0	6.5	12.7	13.2	9.4	10.8	16.7	29.0
Frozen meals	100.0	7.6	15.5	14.7	8.8	12.7	14.5	25.1
Other frozen prepared foods	100.0	6.1	11.4	12.5	9.6	10.0	17.7	30.7
Canned and packaged soups	100.0	7.5	14.9	13.1	10.6	9.3	15.8	27.3
Potato chips, nuts, and other snacks	100.0	5.2	11.9	11.8	10.5	10.3	17.5	30.7
Potato chips and other snacks	100.0	5.1	11.1	11.0	10.7	10.1	18.3	31.2
Nuts	100.0	5.5	14.8	14.4	9.6	10.8	14.7	28.6
Condiments and seasonings	100.0	6.1	12.6	12.7	10.3	10.9	16.8	28.9
Salt, spices, and other seasonings	100.0	6.7	13.2	14.8	10.4	10.4	15.9	27.0
Olives, pickles, relishes	100.0	5.3	13.5	11.9	10.4	8.9	16.9	31.0
Sauces and gravies	100.0	5.9	12.7	11.8	9.8	12.3	17.8	27.8
Baking needs and miscellaneous products	100.0	6.1	11.1	12.4	10.9	9.4	15.8	32.2
Other canned/packaged prepared foods	100.0	7.1	11.3	11.0	10.5	11.1	18.0	29.1
Prepared salads	100.0	5.3	13.0	11.3	9.8	11.6	14.6	32.4
Prepared desserts	100.0	6.5	14.7	12.5	11.0	10.7	15.7	27.2
Baby food	100.0	7.2	9.4	8.9	10.6	13.7	21.3	26.8
Miscellaneous prepared foods	100.0	7.7	11.2	11.5	10.6	9.9	17.7	29.6
Vitamin supplements	100.0	–	12.4	28.3	–	–	54.5	3.2
Nonalcoholic beverages	100.0	7.7	12.7	13.6	11.3	11.5	16.6	25.2
Cola	100.0	7.0	14.0	14.1	12.4	11.0	16.9	23.1
Other carbonated drinks	100.0	8.7	12.6	12.8	11.8	12.3	16.5	23.9
Coffee	100.0	8.4	13.3	14.6	10.4	11.1	15.4	25.5
Roasted coffee	100.0	8.0	12.9	13.8	10.4	11.8	15.4	26.1
Instant and freeze-dried coffee	100.0	9.1	14.0	16.2	10.3	9.8	15.3	24.2
Noncarbonated fruit-flavored drinks, incl. nonfrozen lemonade	100.0	7.3	10.6	12.0	10.1	12.9	17.4	27.9
Tea	100.0	8.6	11.8	15.1	10.9	13.5	14.4	24.7
Nonalcoholic beer	100.0	7.4	5.7	8.9	–	23.7	22.0	29.4
Other nonalcoholic beverages and ice	100.0	7.1	10.4	12.5	9.9	10.1	17.9	30.2
Food prepared by CU on trips	100.0	8.0	9.1	10.3	9.3	9.7	17.1	36.5
FOOD AWAY FROM HOME	**100.0**	**4.9**	**8.1**	**10.3**	**10.8**	**11.0**	**18.0**	**34.7**
Meals at restaurants, carry-outs, other	**100.0**	**4.6**	**8.2**	**10.6**	**11.2**	**11.6**	**18.1**	**33.0**
Lunch	100.0	4.7	8.7	11.0	11.0	11.9	18.0	32.1
At fast food, take-out, delivery, concession stands, buffet, and cafeteria (other than employer and school cafeteria)	100.0	5.4	9.2	12.8	11.4	11.9	17.8	29.3
At full-service restaurants	100.0	4.5	9.2	8.8	9.2	12.5	17.6	35.6
At vending machines, mobile vendors	100.0	11.6	8.0	21.6	12.8	11.6	16.0	17.5
At employer and school cafeterias	100.0	2.1	5.2	8.2	13.4	10.6	20.3	36.6

	complete income reporters	under $10,000	$10,000–$19,999	$20,000–$29,999	$30,000–$39,999	$40,000–$49,999	$50,000–$69,999	$70,000 or more
Dinner	100.0%	3.9%	6.9%	9.2%	10.6%	11.5%	18.5%	36.3%
At fast food, take-out, delivery, concession stands, buffet, and cafeteria (other than employer and school cafeteria)	100.0	4.7	8.3	12.1	12.6	12.3	19.3	28.2
At full-service restaurants	100.0	3.6	6.3	7.9	9.7	11.0	18.3	40.0
At vending machines, mobile vendors	100.0	3.2	–	22.5	24.3	14.9	12.1	20.1
At employer and school cafeterias	100.0	12.8	8.0	18.7	8.3	27.3	10.0	14.7
Snacks and nonalcoholic beverages	100.0	5.9	9.5	11.9	13.7	10.0	17.9	28.8
At fast food, take-out, delivery, concession stands, buffet, and cafeteria (other than employer and school cafeteria)	100.0	6.2	9.4	11.2	11.9	10.7	17.8	30.5
At full-service restaurants	100.0	6.9	15.1	15.3	11.0	9.4	16.1	24.9
At vending machines, mobile vendors	100.0	5.1	7.2	13.8	20.8	8.3	18.6	23.8
At employer and school cafeterias	100.0	2.3	9.1	9.2	18.2	7.5	20.8	29.5
Breakfast and brunch	100.0	5.4	9.8	12.5	11.5	12.8	16.7	29.3
At fast food, take-out, delivery, concession stands, buffet, and cafeteria (other than employer and school cafeteria)	100.0	5.8	9.9	16.0	12.3	12.7	15.7	25.9
At full-service restaurants	100.0	5.1	9.5	8.8	10.8	13.1	17.4	32.8
At vending machines, mobile vendors	100.0	–	19.2	25.7	7.3	6.8	22.0	18.0
At employer and school cafeterias	100.0	4.8	7.2	11.6	13.4	9.8	21.0	29.7
Board (including at school)	**100.0**	**17.1**	**8.1**	**4.3**	**2.4**	**6.6**	**10.4**	**51.1**
Catered affairs	**100.0**	**0.4**	**2.4**	**3.2**	**5.6**	**3.6**	**26.7**	**58.1**
Food on trips	**100.0**	**5.9**	**8.0**	**10.1**	**10.3**	**8.3**	**16.5**	**40.9**
School lunches	**100.0**	**2.8**	**4.9**	**9.3**	**8.1**	**12.9**	**21.6**	**40.5**
Meals as pay	**100.0**	**8.1**	**16.5**	**15.1**	**13.8**	**10.7**	**11.6**	**24.2**
ALCOHOLIC BEVERAGES	**100.0**	**6.0**	**8.9**	**10.5**	**10.2**	**8.7**	**18.1**	**35.3**
At home	**100.0**	**6.8**	**10.8**	**11.8**	**10.4**	**8.0**	**16.5**	**33.6**
Beer and ale	100.0	9.8	12.2	16.2	13.3	9.1	15.8	22.7
Whiskey	100.0	1.8	8.1	10.9	17.0	8.2	21.7	29.2
Wine	100.0	2.8	9.6	5.8	5.8	5.6	16.5	50.3
Other alcoholic beverages	100.0	8.7	9.5	10.3	8.3	11.0	17.4	32.9
Away from home	**100.0**	**4.6**	**6.0**	**8.6**	**10.0**	**9.9**	**20.5**	**37.9**
Beer and ale	100.0	4.6	6.1	8.4	10.8	10.7	22.8	33.5
At fast food, take-out, delivery, concession stands, buffet, and cafeteria	100.0	7.1	10.5	9.4	15.1	9.0	14.4	32.1
At full-service restaurants	100.0	4.4	5.3	8.7	10.2	11.4	20.5	36.4
At vending machines, mobile vendors	100.0	–	17.4	7.1	43.4	–	14.7	14.9
At catered affairs	100.0	–	–	2.6	–	9.9	73.2	10.4
Wine	100.0	3.1	4.9	6.7	10.9	10.6	20.2	40.2
At fast food, take-out, delivery, concession stands, buffet and cafeteria	100.0	4.9	11.7	–	19.7	7.3	15.6	37.1
At full-service restaurants	100.0	3.0	4.4	7.4	10.5	10.9	18.9	41.3
At catered affairs	100.0	–	–	2.7	–	9.9	73.1	10.3
Other alcoholic beverages	100.0	5.0	6.2	9.3	8.8	8.9	18.2	41.9
At fast food, take-out, delivery, concession stands, buffet, and cafeteria	100.0	8.3	9.8	4.7	17.4	9.7	15.1	32.2
At full-service restaurants	100.0	2.7	4.4	8.9	9.1	9.0	18.2	44.1
At machines and mobile vendors	100.0	7.6	4.9	12.9	29.1	2.1	21.3	20.7
At catered affairs	100.0	–	–	2.6	–	9.9	73.3	10.4
Alcoholic beverages purchased on trips	100.0	6.8	7.7	10.6	8.1	8.6	14.9	43.3

Note: Numbers may not add to total because of rounding. (–) means sample is too small to make a reliable estimate.
Source: Calculations by New Strategist based on the 2000 Consumer Expenditure Survey

Table 5.11 Food and Alcohol: Average spending by household type, 2000

(average annual spending of consumer units (CU) on food and alcoholic beverages, by type of consumer unit, 2000)

	total married couples	married couples, no children	married couples with children				single parent, at least one child <18	single person
			total	oldest child under 6	oldest child 6 to 17	oldest child 18 or older		
Number of consumer units								
(in thousands, add 000)	56,287	22,805	28,777	5,291	15,396	8,090	6,132	32,323
Average number of persons per CU	3.2	2.0	3.9	3.5	4.1	3.8	2.9	1.0
Average before-tax income of CU	$60,588.00	$53,232.00	$66,913.00	$62,928.00	$69,472.00	$64,725.00	$25,095.00	$24,977.00
Average spending of CU, total	48,619.37	42,195.54	53,585.53	50,755.90	54,170.40	54,550.20	28,923.25	23,059.00
Food, average spending	6,575.06	5,575.09	7,251.22	5,816.77	7,508.24	7,857.60	4,255.09	2,824.80
Alcoholic beverages, average spending	420.32	461.29	395.97	375.00	365.49	477.46	187.09	325.37
FOOD AT HOME	**$3,892.15**	**$3,155.05**	**$4,356.76**	**$3,658.97**	**$4,458.13**	**$4,723.81**	**$2,646.87**	**$1,477.00**
Cereals and bakery products	**590.17**	**455.73**	**679.82**	**541.57**	**701.71**	**748.84**	**387.93**	**220.57**
Cereals and cereal products	203.26	148.55	240.10	185.69	256.22	251.37	153.47	69.48
Flour	10.36	7.73	10.82	9.02	10.56	12.86	8.14	3.20
Prepared flour mixes	18.24	16.43	19.99	15.22	21.26	21.28	12.19	5.52
Ready-to-eat and cooked cereals	112.55	81.12	134.00	106.79	143.97	135.62	85.99	40.20
Rice	25.42	17.19	30.43	23.91	28.58	39.80	18.81	7.78
Pasta, cornmeal, and other cereal products	36.69	26.07	44.85	30.76	51.85	41.80	28.33	12.78
Bakery products	386.90	307.18	439.72	355.88	445.49	497.47	234.46	151.09
Bread	105.97	87.95	117.09	97.80	117.71	131.89	72.11	46.04
White bread	45.42	34.39	51.71	41.38	53.02	57.57	35.27	19.24
Bread, other than white	60.55	53.56	65.38	56.42	64.69	74.32	36.84	26.80
Crackers and cookies	92.98	78.12	104.62	88.88	109.96	106.44	56.00	38.62
Cookies	61.50	52.98	68.39	58.03	74.04	65.08	41.86	26.26
Crackers	31.48	25.14	36.23	30.85	35.92	41.37	14.14	12.36
Frozen and refrigerated bakery products	31.54	22.83	38.53	26.85	40.31	44.51	20.66	12.83
Other bakery products	156.42	118.28	179.48	142.35	177.51	214.63	85.69	53.60
Biscuits and rolls	51.55	41.30	59.09	46.24	61.17	65.43	25.18	18.81
Cakes and cupcakes	51.14	33.49	60.20	46.09	53.74	85.63	30.97	17.06
Bread and cracker products	5.93	5.06	6.75	7.53	7.08	5.39	3.26	1.81
Sweetrolls, coffee cakes, doughnuts	30.72	25.65	33.26	26.73	33.83	37.49	16.21	9.44
Pies, tarts, turnovers	17.08	12.78	20.18	15.76	21.68	20.70	10.06	6.48
Meats, poultry, fish, and eggs	**1,018.38**	**846.14**	**1,113.10**	**818.65**	**1,154.52**	**1,271.09**	**753.82**	**352.41**
Beef	307.23	250.66	335.32	245.44	344.53	390.81	223.22	99.64
Ground beef	110.82	83.34	127.74	106.81	133.99	131.98	86.82	38.89
Roast	54.18	46.98	57.69	34.60	51.96	89.08	31.52	13.89
Chuck roast	18.29	14.90	20.23	11.01	18.23	32.18	12.34	4.15
Round roast	14.62	13.18	14.90	10.47	13.53	21.50	8.87	4.74
Other roast	21.27	18.89	22.55	13.12	20.20	35.40	10.31	5.00
Steak	121.63	103.19	126.74	88.69	132.68	145.92	90.45	41.06
Round steak	19.92	15.64	21.45	16.91	19.77	28.80	17.35	6.30
Sirloin steak	39.08	34.02	40.22	29.25	43.35	42.76	25.18	12.74
Other steak	62.63	53.53	65.07	42.53	69.56	74.36	47.92	22.02
Other beef	20.60	17.16	23.15	15.33	25.91	23.84	14.44	5.81
Pork	212.51	189.47	225.90	151.24	235.60	267.65	159.44	70.92
Bacon	32.02	30.01	33.05	23.45	34.09	38.86	28.53	12.13
Pork chops	50.68	43.90	55.03	41.48	55.86	64.60	44.46	16.27
Ham	46.65	45.03	45.84	27.14	49.20	54.32	31.76	16.81
Ham, not canned	44.45	42.90	43.76	26.93	47.51	49.86	30.11	16.31
Canned ham	2.20	2.14	2.08	0.21	1.69	4.46	1.64	0.51
Sausage	32.10	27.79	35.54	26.75	36.79	40.22	24.72	10.49
Other pork	51.06	42.74	56.44	32.42	59.67	69.65	29.97	15.23
Other meats	129.20	99.74	147.73	108.47	152.60	170.16	91.44	46.54
Frankfurters	25.74	20.14	29.45	25.55	29.96	31.62	23.04	8.98

	total married couples	married couples, no children	married couples with children			single parent, at least one child <18	single person
			total	oldest child under 6	oldest child 6 to 17	oldest child 18 or older		
Lunch meats (cold cuts)	$87.94	$69.35	$100.13	$75.11	$102.49	$116.01	$60.34	$32.26
Bologna, liverwurst, salami	28.56	24.23	30.72	20.75	34.09	31.92	28.40	12.13
Other lunch meats	59.38	45.12	69.41	54.36	68.40	84.09	31.94	20.14
Lamb, organ meats, and others	15.52	10.25	18.14	7.81	20.15	22.52	8.06	5.30
Lamb and organ meats	12.56	9.18	13.76	7.63	12.89	20.73	6.84	4.52
Mutton, goat, and game	2.97	1.07	4.38	0.17	7.26	1.79	1.22	0.78
Poultry	182.90	143.08	206.89	171.48	209.69	230.49	153.14	67.66
Fresh and frozen chicken	143.66	112.53	162.24	136.98	163.92	179.75	122.79	52.53
Fresh and frozen whole chicken	37.85	29.79	41.95	37.20	41.61	46.63	37.69	13.59
Fresh and frozen chicken parts	105.81	82.74	120.29	99.78	122.31	133.12	85.10	38.94
Other poultry	39.24	30.55	44.65	34.50	45.77	50.74	30.35	15.12
Fish and seafood	144.01	126.00	152.78	109.46	168.14	156.42	93.24	49.80
Canned fish and seafood	19.68	18.61	19.83	14.46	17.95	28.29	12.04	8.57
Fresh fish and shellfish	89.12	75.96	95.82	64.35	110.23	91.59	53.28	28.07
Frozen fish and shellfish	35.21	31.43	37.13	30.65	39.96	36.54	27.92	13.16
Eggs	42.52	37.18	44.49	32.56	43.96	55.56	33.33	17.85
Dairy products	**420.26**	**335.07**	**481.32**	**414.78**	**496.59**	**504.52**	**278.71**	**162.30**
Fresh milk and cream	168.70	120.83	201.01	176.14	208.63	205.61	116.95	64.78
Fresh milk, all types	153.12	106.84	184.22	161.00	192.62	185.83	109.08	58.70
Cream	15.58	13.98	16.78	15.15	16.01	19.79	7.87	6.08
Other dairy products	251.56	214.25	280.31	238.63	287.96	298.90	161.76	97.52
Butter	21.68	18.47	23.99	19.83	24.60	26.15	14.98	8.38
Cheese	125.86	108.07	138.74	124.28	139.89	148.37	78.03	47.94
Ice cream and related products	72.70	61.30	81.40	59.46	86.26	89.39	47.98	29.64
Miscellaneous dairy products	31.32	26.41	36.20	35.06	37.21	34.99	20.77	11.57
Fruits and vegetables	**664.76**	**578.34**	**710.01**	**618.71**	**716.98**	**771.43**	**408.03**	**279.36**
Fresh fruits	205.58	180.43	215.92	188.45	214.86	241.08	114.35	93.05
Apples	38.04	32.60	41.31	34.37	42.59	44.38	20.70	15.48
Bananas	38.20	32.53	40.71	35.58	37.93	50.86	23.68	19.87
Oranges	23.16	19.28	25.09	19.73	28.15	23.09	14.32	10.87
Citrus fruits, excl. oranges	17.95	18.16	16.28	13.21	17.92	15.38	8.78	8.34
Other fresh fruits	88.23	77.86	92.52	85.56	88.26	107.36	46.86	38.48
Fresh vegetables	204.04	183.47	211.19	183.79	213.43	229.30	116.55	86.49
Potatoes	35.91	33.29	36.07	28.28	36.95	40.69	24.14	14.39
Lettuce	26.61	24.50	27.93	24.08	27.03	33.05	14.12	11.82
Tomatoes	36.87	31.31	38.99	32.04	39.79	43.09	20.29	16.52
Other fresh vegetables	104.65	94.37	108.20	99.39	109.65	112.47	58.00	43.76
Processed fruits	147.03	123.06	163.90	152.47	168.64	163.42	104.73	59.85
Frozen fruits and fruit juices	18.98	15.73	21.71	19.15	23.67	19.70	17.75	6.36
Frozen orange juice	9.21	7.41	10.54	9.83	10.61	10.99	6.54	3.24
Frozen fruits	4.63	4.94	4.47	2.27	5.51	4.10	6.22	1.69
Frozen fruit juices	5.13	3.38	6.70	7.05	7.56	4.61	4.99	1.43
Canned fruits	20.65	18.82	21.45	17.10	23.68	20.34	9.99	8.08
Dried fruits	6.90	6.41	6.96	7.15	6.93	6.86	4.10	3.58
Fresh fruit juice	28.70	26.97	30.34	31.88	27.74	34.57	22.52	14.20
Canned and bottled fruit juice	71.81	55.12	83.44	77.18	86.62	81.95	50.38	27.63
Processed vegetables	108.10	91.39	119.00	94.00	120.05	137.63	72.40	39.97
Frozen vegetables	34.74	28.82	39.66	33.29	38.59	47.26	22.02	12.13
Canned and dried vegetables and juices	73.37	62.56	79.34	60.71	81.47	90.37	50.38	27.83
Canned beans	15.66	13.51	17.16	13.42	17.23	20.15	11.59	5.56
Canned corn	8.53	6.45	9.72	7.26	10.19	10.80	7.58	3.12
Canned miscellaneous vegetables	23.45	21.37	25.14	20.25	24.58	30.39	13.44	9.20
Dried peas	0.39	0.32	0.38	0.32	0.43	0.35	0.43	0.22
Dried beans	3.36	2.37	3.42	1.62	3.42	4.92	1.87	1.19

	total married couples	married couples, no children	married couples with children				single parent, at least one child <18	single person
			total	oldest child under 6	oldest child 6 to 17	oldest child 18 or older		
Dried miscellaneous vegetables	$9.33	$8.18	$9.48	$6.53	$10.54	$9.69	$6.63	$3.20
Dried processed vegetables	0.57	0.54	0.42	0.18	0.54	0.37	0.51	0.18
Frozen vegetable juices	0.40	0.12	0.67	0.95	0.54	0.70	0.59	0.06
Fresh and canned vegetable juices	11.68	9.72	12.95	10.18	14.01	13.01	7.75	5.11
Other food at home	**1,198.58**	**939.77**	**1,372.51**	**1,265.27**	**1,388.33**	**1,427.94**	**818.38**	**462.37**
Sugar and other sweets	155.67	122.94	172.02	127.08	175.64	201.85	107.49	55.55
Candy and chewing gum	103.61	77.74	116.60	87.52	119.84	133.98	67.50	35.76
Sugar	20.94	16.46	22.70	14.27	24.35	26.25	17.28	7.03
Artificial sweeteners	5.91	7.40	4.90	0.88	3.74	10.70	3.11	1.56
Jams, preserves, other sweets	25.22	21.35	27.83	24.42	27.71	30.92	19.60	11.21
Fats and oils	106.12	93.85	113.12	74.07	118.35	134.61	78.43	39.01
Margarine	14.90	14.92	14.60	9.44	14.53	19.06	13.32	5.14
Fats and oils	29.15	25.72	30.29	19.38	32.08	35.61	21.86	11.13
Salad dressings	35.16	30.08	38.38	23.55	43.33	40.30	25.26	12.27
Nondairy cream and imitation milk	11.96	11.41	12.51	10.09	10.85	18.04	6.14	4.50
Peanut butter	14.95	11.72	17.33	11.61	17.57	21.61	11.85	5.98
Miscellaneous foods	565.97	413.25	677.20	733.14	678.25	628.30	359.44	220.93
Frozen prepared foods	110.39	82.97	131.07	122.51	131.92	136.43	80.24	54.02
Frozen meals	29.02	26.72	30.96	34.18	29.44	31.47	26.39	24.58
Other frozen prepared foods	81.37	56.24	100.12	88.33	102.48	104.96	53.85	29.44
Canned and packaged soups	43.02	42.17	43.45	37.43	44.62	46.00	29.45	21.68
Potato chips, nuts, and other snacks	123.83	91.77	148.36	106.04	163.57	151.46	75.60	44.81
Potato chips and other snacks	97.01	65.65	120.97	88.30	135.66	117.15	61.98	32.62
Nuts	26.82	26.13	27.38	17.74	27.91	34.32	13.63	12.19
Condiments and seasonings	111.23	93.86	123.85	100.57	126.48	137.70	69.89	39.15
Salt, spices, and other seasonings	25.88	23.65	26.53	19.48	28.22	28.86	18.10	10.70
Olives, pickles, relishes	13.07	11.05	14.92	8.75	15.64	18.52	7.27	4.54
Sauces and gravies	49.28	38.34	57.16	51.68	60.36	54.95	32.74	16.39
Baking needs and miscellaneous products	23.01	20.81	25.25	20.67	22.26	35.37	11.79	7.53
Other canned/packaged prepared foods	177.50	102.49	230.47	366.59	211.65	156.72	104.25	61.27
Prepared salads	23.14	20.99	24.94	22.07	25.06	27.10	18.42	10.95
Prepared desserts	11.97	10.21	13.05	11.97	14.21	11.51	7.71	4.44
Baby food	49.80	9.67	79.79	229.16	52.41	13.11	22.91	6.13
Miscellaneous prepared foods	92.35	61.60	112.21	102.88	119.73	104.10	55.15	39.72
Vitamin supplements	0.24	0.01	0.47	0.52	0.25	0.89	0.07	0.02
Nonalcoholic beverages	315.82	251.63	356.12	285.89	357.02	412.82	241.32	124.81
Cola	109.22	83.12	126.19	96.32	125.51	152.55	88.46	43.02
Other carbonated drinks	60.36	44.32	71.16	60.07	70.63	81.52	51.22	22.47
Coffee	53.15	55.45	50.40	37.72	50.76	60.22	27.76	25.04
Roasted coffee	35.10	36.88	33.53	25.90	33.79	39.36	17.57	16.17
Instant and freeze-dried coffee	18.05	18.57	16.86	11.81	16.97	20.86	10.19	8.88
Noncarbonated fruit-flavored drinks, incl. nonfrozen lemonade	26.01	12.31	35.53	28.31	38.88	34.44	24.07	5.98
Tea	19.08	17.02	20.42	15.21	19.93	25.81	13.75	8.88
Nonalcoholic beer	0.35	0.27	0.24	0.73	0.17	–	–	0.16
Other nonalcoholic beverages and ice	47.65	39.14	52.19	47.53	51.15	58.27	36.06	19.26
Food prepared by CU on trips	55.00	58.10	54.05	45.09	59.07	50.36	31.69	22.06
FOOD AWAY FROM HOME	**2,682.91**	**2,420.04**	**2,894.47**	**2,157.80**	**3,050.10**	**3,133.79**	**1,608.22**	**1,347.79**
Meals at restaurants, carry-outs, other	**2,155.45**	**1,963.91**	**2,295.95**	**1,854.55**	**2,417.15**	**2,407.70**	**1,313.89**	**1,145.29**
Lunch	813.69	675.24	912.13	728.08	968.14	947.14	570.06	420.97
At fast food, take-out, delivery, concession stands, buffet, and cafeteria (other than employer and school cafeteria)	441.09	350.77	503.87	474.14	502.76	531.01	316.76	227.12
At full-service restaurants	258.00	291.27	231.89	208.60	215.69	285.62	115.05	160.30
At vending machines, mobile vendors	6.80	3.45	8.70	8.52	11.12	3.73	9.49	4.31
At employer and school cafeterias	107.80	29.75	167.67	36.82	238.58	126.78	128.75	29.24

	total married couples	married couples, no children	married couples with children				single parent, at least one child <18	single person
			total	oldest child under 6	oldest child 6 to 17	oldest child 18 or older		
Dinner	$877.06	$899.92	$865.99	$723.03	$894.77	$924.34	$416.90	$461.12
At fast food, take-out, delivery, concession stands, buffet, and cafeteria (other than employer and school cafeteria)	260.21	195.02	309.40	291.24	317.31	307.79	190.85	108.55
At full-service restaurants	613.40	701.81	553.50	431.40	572.39	615.37	222.00	349.10
At vending machines, mobile vendors	1.31	0.36	1.76	–	2.95	0.70	2.27	0.10
At employer and school cafeterias	2.14	2.73	1.34	0.39	2.12	0.47	1.77	3.37
Snacks and nonalcoholic beverages	274.53	208.14	322.40	272.34	342.63	321.38	213.64	145.95
At fast food, take-out, delivery, concession stands, buffet, and cafeteria (other than employer and school cafeteria)	191.77	135.83	232.66	208.41	242.65	231.76	147.84	101.41
At full-service restaurants	22.75	19.82	24.93	17.50	25.77	29.36	16.90	16.12
At vending machines, mobile vendors	47.62	43.40	49.99	40.59	54.68	47.89	35.52	23.14
At employer and school cafeterias	12.40	9.08	14.82	5.84	19.53	12.37	13.38	5.29
Breakfast and brunch	190.17	180.61	195.42	131.09	211.61	214.84	113.30	117.26
At fast food, take-out, delivery, concession stands, buffet, and cafeteria (other than employer and school cafeteria)	89.25	65.95	102.13	75.28	109.50	108.92	68.93	51.33
At full-service restaurants	95.13	110.61	86.72	53.77	93.15	100.60	38.57	61.74
At vending machines, mobile vendors	1.53	1.43	1.27	0.74	1.46	1.31	1.35	1.35
At employer and school cafeterias	4.26	2.62	5.31	1.30	7.50	4.01	4.45	2.83
Board (including at school)	**54.40**	**42.00**	**65.93**	**1.31**	**44.13**	**149.70**	**13.84**	**29.84**
Catered affairs	**75.24**	**80.33**	**71.45**	**36.35**	**51.38**	**132.59**	**15.78**	**16.31**
Food on trips	**290.37**	**318.64**	**282.62**	**226.51**	**282.33**	**319.87**	**116.35**	**137.86**
School lunches	**89.87**	**–**	**159.90**	**9.64**	**240.43**	**104.89**	**129.56**	**0.06**
Meals as pay	**17.58**	**15.16**	**18.62**	**29.44**	**14.68**	**19.04**	**18.80**	**18.44**
ALCOHOLIC BEVERAGES	**420.32**	**461.29**	**395.97**	**375.00**	**365.49**	**477.46**	**187.09**	**325.37**
At home	**267.72**	**269.29**	**266.53**	**243.44**	**247.84**	**325.35**	**123.21**	**174.59**
Beer and ale	120.06	102.88	129.01	108.85	140.58	121.35	73.53	96.61
Whiskey	14.95	19.85	12.82	17.24	9.63	15.91	8.21	13.91
Wine	108.95	118.20	105.57	99.29	81.62	161.52	30.43	47.41
Other alcoholic beverages	23.76	28.36	19.13	18.07	16.03	26.57	11.05	16.65
Away from home	**152.61**	**192.01**	**129.44**	**131.56**	**117.65**	**152.11**	**63.88**	**150.78**
Beer and ale	65.19	79.08	56.55	56.60	49.48	71.46	26.36	64.64
At fast food, take-out, delivery, concession stands, buffet, and cafeteria	12.58	10.13	14.42	13.73	13.45	17.04	4.78	16.14
At full-service restaurants	45.57	54.51	40.28	42.87	35.00	49.30	21.13	47.41
At vending machines, mobile vendors	0.23	0.47	0.06	–	0.12	–	0.44	0.72
At catered affairs	6.82	13.97	1.78	–	0.90	5.12	–	0.37
Wine	16.56	20.89	14.18	16.11	13.40	14.21	9.08	22.60
At fast food, take-out, delivery, concession stands, buffet and cafeteria	0.93	0.91	0.83	0.25	1.38	0.16	0.14	1.44
At full-service restaurants	14.90	18.50	13.15	15.86	11.92	13.51	8.94	21.11
At catered affairs	0.72	1.48	0.19	–	0.10	0.54	–	0.04
Other alcoholic beverages	70.86	92.04	58.71	58.86	54.76	66.45	28.43	63.55
At fast food, take-out, delivery, concession stands, buffet, and cafeteria	2.22	1.77	2.58	3.32	2.47	2.19	2.27	3.32
At full-service restaurants	25.20	31.50	22.03	23.61	19.67	25.69	12.97	29.19
At machines and mobile vendors	0.29	0.35	0.17	0.32	0.13	0.14	0.39	0.26
At catered affairs	3.01	6.16	0.78	–	0.40	2.26	–	0.16
Alcoholic beverages purchased on trips	40.13	52.26	33.15	31.60	32.09	36.18	12.80	30.61

Note: Average spending figures for total consumer units can be found on Average Spending by Age and Average Spending by Region tables. (–) means sample is too small to make a reliable estimate.
Source: Bureau of Labor Statistics, unpublished tables from the 2000 Consumer Expenditure Survey

Table 5.12 Food and Alcohol: Indexed spending by household type, 2000

(indexed average annual spending of consumer units (CU) on food and alcoholic beverages, by type of consumer unit, 2000; index definition: an index of 100 is the average for all consumer units; an index of 132 means that spending by consumer units in that group is 32 percent above the average for all consumer units; an index of 68 indicates spending that is 32 percent below the average for all consumer units)

	total married couples	married couples, no children	married couples with children total	oldest child under 6	oldest child 6 to 17	oldest child 18 or older	single parent, at least one child <18	single person
Average spending of CU, total	$48,619	$42,196	$53,586	$50,756	$54,170	$54,550	$28,923	$23,059
Average spending of CU, index	128	111	141	133	142	143	76	61
Food, spending index	127	108	141	113	146	152	82	55
Alcoholic beverages, spending index	113	124	106	101	98	128	50	88
FOOD AT HOME	**129**	**104**	**144**	**121**	**148**	**156**	**88**	**49**
Cereals and bakery products	**130**	**101**	**150**	**119**	**155**	**165**	**86**	**49**
Cereals and cereal products	130	95	154	119	164	161	98	44
Flour	130	97	136	113	132	161	102	40
Prepared flour mixes	137	123	150	114	159	159	91	41
Ready-to-eat and cooked cereals	130	93	154	123	166	156	99	46
Rice	130	88	156	122	146	204	96	40
Pasta, cornmeal, and other cereal products	128	91	157	107	181	146	99	45
Bakery products	130	103	148	120	150	168	79	51
Bread	126	105	139	116	140	157	86	55
White bread	124	94	141	113	145	157	96	53
Bread, other than white	128	113	138	119	136	157	78	57
Crackers and cookies	131	110	147	125	155	150	79	54
Cookies	129	111	143	122	155	136	88	55
Crackers	135	108	155	132	154	177	61	53
Frozen and refrigerated bakery products	129	93	157	109	164	181	84	52
Other bakery products	133	101	153	121	151	183	73	46
Biscuits and rolls	134	107	153	120	159	170	65	49
Cakes and cupcakes	133	87	157	120	140	223	81	44
Bread and cracker products	134	115	153	171	161	122	74	41
Sweetrolls, coffee cakes, doughnuts	135	113	147	118	149	165	71	42
Pies, tarts, turnovers	129	96	152	119	163	156	76	49
Meats, poultry, fish, and eggs	**128**	**106**	**140**	**103**	**145**	**160**	**95**	**44**
Beef	129	105	141	103	145	164	94	42
Ground beef	126	95	146	122	153	150	99	44
Roast	136	118	145	87	130	224	79	35
Chuck roast	137	112	152	83	137	241	93	31
Round roast	128	115	130	91	118	188	77	41
Other roast	141	126	150	87	134	235	69	33
Steak	129	109	134	94	140	154	96	43
Round steak	130	102	140	110	129	188	113	41
Sirloin steak	131	114	135	98	145	143	84	43
Other steak	127	108	132	86	141	151	97	45
Other beef	128	107	144	95	161	148	90	36
Pork	127	113	135	91	141	160	96	42
Bacon	123	115	127	90	131	149	110	47
Pork chops	125	108	136	102	138	159	110	40
Ham	129	124	126	75	136	150	88	46
Ham, not canned	129	124	127	78	138	144	87	47
Canned ham	126	123	120	12	97	256	94	29
Sausage	127	110	141	106	146	159	98	42
Other pork	132	110	145	84	154	179	77	39
Other meats	129	99	147	108	152	169	91	46
Frankfurters	124	97	142	124	145	153	111	43

	total married couples	married couples, no children	married couples with children				single parent, at least one child <18	single person
			total	oldest child under 6	oldest child 6 to 17	oldest child 18 or older		
Lunch meats (cold cuts)	129	102	147	110	151	171	89	47
Bologna, liverwurst, salami	120	102	129	87	144	135	120	51
Other lunch meats	134	102	157	123	155	190	72	46
Lamb, organ meats, and others	131	86	153	66	170	190	68	45
Lamb and organ meats	129	95	142	79	133	213	70	47
Mutton, goat, and game	138	50	203	8	336	83	56	36
Poultry	126	99	143	118	144	159	105	47
Fresh and frozen chicken	126	98	142	120	143	157	107	46
Fresh and frozen whole chicken	121	95	134	119	133	149	121	43
Fresh and frozen chicken parts	127	99	145	120	147	160	102	47
Other poultry	128	99	145	112	149	165	99	49
Fish and seafood	131	114	139	99	153	142	85	45
Canned fish and seafood	126	119	127	92	115	181	77	55
Fresh fish and shellfish	133	114	143	96	165	137	80	42
Frozen fish and shellfish	127	114	134	111	145	132	101	48
Eggs	123	108	129	94	128	161	97	52
Dairy products	**129**	**103**	**148**	**128**	**153**	**155**	**86**	**50**
Fresh milk and cream	129	92	153	134	159	157	89	49
Fresh milk, all types	128	89	154	135	161	155	91	49
Cream	134	120	145	130	138	170	68	52
Other dairy products	130	111	145	123	149	155	84	50
Butter	128	109	141	117	145	154	88	49
Cheese	131	113	145	130	146	155	81	50
Ice cream and related products	129	108	144	105	153	158	85	52
Miscellaneous dairy products	131	111	152	147	156	146	87	48
Fruits and vegetables	**128**	**111**	**136**	**119**	**138**	**148**	**78**	**54**
Fresh fruits	126	111	132	115	132	148	70	57
Apples	129	111	140	117	144	150	70	52
Bananas	121	103	128	112	120	160	75	63
Oranges	122	102	133	104	149	122	76	57
Citrus fruits, excl. oranges	125	127	114	92	125	107	61	58
Other fresh fruits	128	113	135	124	128	156	68	56
Fresh vegetables	129	116	133	116	134	144	73	54
Potatoes	128	119	129	101	132	145	86	51
Lettuce	128	118	135	116	130	159	68	57
Tomatoes	125	106	132	108	135	146	69	56
Other fresh vegetables	130	117	135	124	136	140	72	54
Processed fruits	128	107	143	133	147	142	91	52
Frozen fruits and fruit juices	132	109	151	133	165	137	124	44
Frozen orange juice	133	107	153	142	154	159	95	47
Frozen fruits	128	136	123	63	152	113	172	47
Frozen fruit juices	134	88	174	184	197	120	130	37
Canned fruits	133	122	139	110	153	131	65	52
Dried fruits	125	117	127	130	126	125	75	65
Fresh fruit juice	122	115	129	136	118	147	96	61
Canned and bottled fruit juice	128	98	148	137	154	146	90	49
Processed vegetables	129	109	142	112	143	164	86	48
Frozen vegetables	131	109	150	126	146	179	83	46
Canned and dried vegetables and juices	128	109	138	106	142	157	88	48
Canned beans	124	107	135	106	136	159	91	44
Canned corn	125	95	143	107	150	159	111	46
Canned miscellaneous vegetables	131	119	140	113	137	169	75	51
Dried peas	115	94	112	94	126	103	126	65
Dried beans	133	94	135	64	135	194	74	47

	total married couples	married couples, no children	married couples with children				single parent, at least one child <18	single person
			total	oldest child under 6	oldest child 6 to 17	oldest child 18 or older		
Dried miscellaneous vegetables	129	113	131	90	146	134	92	44
Dried processed vegetables	139	132	102	44	132	90	124	44
Frozen vegetable juices	138	41	231	328	186	241	203	21
Fresh and canned vegetable juices	126	105	139	109	151	140	83	55
Other food at home	**129**	**101**	**148**	**137**	**150**	**154**	**88**	**50**
Sugar and other sweets	133	105	147	108	150	172	92	47
Candy and chewing gum	136	102	153	115	157	176	88	47
Sugar	125	98	135	85	145	156	103	42
Artificial sweeteners	141	177	117	21	89	255	74	37
Jams, preserves, other sweets	127	108	140	123	140	156	99	56
Fats and oils	128	113	136	89	142	162	94	47
Margarine	128	129	126	81	125	164	115	44
Fats and oils	125	110	130	83	137	153	94	48
Salad dressings	129	111	141	87	159	148	93	45
Nondairy cream and imitation milk	131	125	137	110	119	197	67	49
Peanut butter	127	99	147	98	149	183	100	51
Miscellaneous foods	130	95	155	168	155	144	82	51
Frozen prepared foods	122	92	145	136	146	151	89	60
Frozen meals	102	94	109	120	103	110	93	86
Other frozen prepared foods	132	91	162	143	166	170	87	48
Canned and packaged soups	121	119	122	105	126	129	83	61
Potato chips, nuts, and other snacks	134	99	160	115	177	164	82	48
Potato chips and other snacks	135	92	169	123	189	163	86	46
Nuts	129	125	131	85	134	165	65	59
Condiments and seasonings	131	111	146	119	149	163	83	46
Salt, spices, and other seasonings	125	115	128	94	137	140	88	52
Olives, pickles, relishes	134	113	153	90	160	190	74	46
Sauces and gravies	132	103	154	139	162	148	88	44
Baking needs and miscellaneous products	136	123	149	122	131	209	70	44
Other canned/packaged prepared foods	132	76	172	273	158	117	78	46
Prepared salads	125	113	134	119	135	146	99	59
Prepared desserts	129	110	140	129	153	124	83	48
Baby food	154	30	247	710	162	41	71	19
Miscellaneous prepared foods	125	83	152	139	162	141	75	54
Vitamin supplements	171	7	336	371	179	636	50	14
Nonalcoholic beverages	127	101	143	115	143	165	97	50
Cola	126	96	145	111	144	175	102	49
Other carbonated drinks	127	94	150	127	149	172	108	47
Coffee	127	132	120	90	121	144	66	60
Roasted coffee	128	134	122	94	123	143	64	59
Instant and freeze-dried coffee	126	129	117	82	118	145	71	62
Noncarbonated fruit-flavored drinks, incl. nonfrozen lemonade	134	63	183	146	200	177	124	31
Tea	122	109	130	97	127	165	88	57
Nonalcoholic beer	130	100	89	270	63	–	–	59
Other nonalcoholic beverages and ice	125	103	137	125	135	153	95	51
Food prepared by CU on trips	138	145	135	113	148	126	79	55
FOOD AWAY FROM HOME	**126**	**113**	**135**	**101**	**143**	**147**	**75**	**63**
Meals at restaurants, carry-outs, other	**123**	**112**	**131**	**106**	**138**	**138**	**75**	**65**
Lunch	123	102	138	110	146	143	86	64
At fast food, take-out, delivery, concession stands, buffet, and cafeteria (other than employer and school cafeteria)	120	95	137	129	137	144	86	62
At full-service restaurants	124	140	111	100	104	137	55	77
At vending machines, mobile vendors	104	53	133	131	171	57	146	66
At employer and school cafeterias	134	37	209	46	297	158	160	36

	total married couples	married couples, no children	married couples with children				single parent, at least one child <18	single person
			total	oldest child under 6	oldest child 6 to 17	oldest child 18 or older		
Dinner	126	129	124	104	128	132	60	66
At fast food, take-out, delivery, concession stands, buffet, and cafeteria (other than employer and school cafeteria)	126	94	150	141	153	149	92	52
At full-service restaurants	126	144	113	88	117	126	46	72
At vending machines, mobile vendors	128	35	173	–	289	69	223	10
At employer and school cafeterias	91	116	57	17	90	20	75	143
Snacks and nonalcoholic beverages	121	91	142	120	150	141	94	64
At fast food, take-out, delivery, concession stands, buffet, and cafeteria (other than employer and school cafeteria)	121	86	147	131	153	146	93	64
At full-service restaurants	113	98	124	87	128	146	84	80
At vending machines, mobile vendors	124	113	130	105	142	124	92	60
At employer and school cafeterias	118	87	141	56	186	118	128	50
Breakfast and brunch	118	112	121	81	131	133	70	73
At fast food, take-out, delivery, concession stands, buffet, and cafeteria (other than employer and school cafeteria)	116	86	132	98	142	141	89	67
At full-service restaurants	119	139	109	68	117	126	48	78
At vending machines, mobile vendors	113	106	94	55	108	97	100	100
At employer and school cafeterias	118	72	147	36	207	111	123	78
Board (including at school)	**139**	**108**	**169**	**3**	**113**	**384**	**35**	**76**
Catered affairs	**139**	**149**	**132**	**67**	**95**	**245**	**29**	**30**
Food on trips	**134**	**147**	**131**	**105**	**131**	**148**	**54**	**64**
School lunches	**154**	**–**	**274**	**16**	**411**	**179**	**222**	**0**
Meals as pay	**93**	**80**	**98**	**155**	**77**	**100**	**99**	**97**
ALCOHOLIC BEVERAGES	**113**	**124**	**106**	**101**	**98**	**128**	**50**	**88**
At home	**118**	**119**	**118**	**107**	**109**	**144**	**54**	**77**
Beer and ale	107	92	115	97	126	108	66	86
Whiskey	111	147	95	128	71	118	61	103
Wine	136	148	132	124	102	202	38	59
Other alcoholic beverages	113	134	91	86	76	126	52	79
Away from home	**105**	**132**	**89**	**91**	**81**	**105**	**44**	**104**
Beer and ale	104	127	91	91	79	114	42	103
At fast food, take-out, delivery, concession stands, buffet, and cafeteria	94	76	108	103	101	127	36	121
At full-service restaurants	101	121	89	95	78	109	47	105
At vending machines, mobile vendors	58	118	15	–	30	–	110	180
At catered affairs	187	384	49	–	25	141	–	10
Wine	93	117	80	91	75	80	51	127
At fast food, take-out, delivery, concession stands, buffet and cafeteria	76	74	67	20	112	13	11	117
At full-service restaurants	92	114	81	98	74	84	55	131
At catered affairs	185	379	49	–	26	138	–	10
Other alcoholic beverages	109	142	90	91	84	102	44	98
At fast food, take-out, delivery, concession stands, buffet, and cafeteria	73	58	85	109	81	72	75	109
At full-service restaurants	98	122	86	92	76	100	50	113
At machines and mobile vendors	100	121	59	110	45	48	134	90
At catered affairs	188	385	49	–	25	141	–	10
Alcoholic beverages purchased on trips	117	153	97	92	94	106	37	89

Note: Spending index for total consumer units is 100. (–) means sample is too small to make a reliable estimate.
Source: Calculations by New Strategist based on the 2000 Consumer Expenditure Survey

Table 5.13 Food and Alcohol: Indexed per capita spending by household type, 2000

(indexed average annual per capita spending of consumer units (CU) on food and alcoholic beverages, by type of consumer unit, 2000; index definition: an index of 100 is the average for all consumer units; an index of 132 means that spending by consumer units in that group is 32 percent above the average for all consumer units; an index of 68 indicates spending that is 32 percent below the average for all consumer units)

	total married couples	married couples, no children	married couples with children — total	oldest child under 6	oldest child 6 to 17	oldest child 18 or older	single parent, at least one child <18	single person
Per capita spending of CU, total	$15,194	$21,098	$13,740	$14,502	$13,212	$14,355	$9,974	$23,059
Per capita spending of CU, index	100	139	90	95	87	94	66	152
Food, per capita spending index	100	135	90	81	89	100	71	137
Alcoholic beverages, per capita spending index	88	155	68	72	60	84	43	219
FOOD AT HOME	**101**	**131**	**92**	**87**	**90**	**103**	**76**	**122**
Cereals and bakery products	**102**	**126**	**96**	**85**	**94**	**109**	**74**	**122**
Cereals and cereal products	102	119	98	85	100	106	85	111
Flour	101	121	87	81	81	106	88	100
Prepared flour mixes	107	154	96	81	97	105	79	103
Ready-to-eat and cooked cereals	101	117	99	88	101	103	85	116
Rice	102	110	100	87	89	134	83	99
Pasta, cornmeal, and other cereal products	100	114	100	77	110	96	85	112
Bakery products	102	129	95	86	91	110	68	127
Bread	99	131	89	83	85	103	74	137
White bread	97	117	91	81	88	103	83	131
Bread, other than white	100	141	88	85	83	103	67	141
Crackers and cookies	102	137	94	89	94	99	68	136
Cookies	101	139	92	87	95	90	76	138
Crackers	105	135	100	94	94	117	52	133
Frozen and refrigerated bakery products	100	116	101	78	100	119	73	131
Other bakery products	104	126	98	87	92	120	63	114
Biscuits and rolls	105	134	98	86	97	112	56	122
Cakes and cupcakes	104	109	100	86	85	147	69	111
Bread and cracker products	105	143	98	122	98	80	64	103
Sweetrolls, coffee cakes, doughnuts	106	141	94	84	91	109	62	104
Pies, tarts, turnovers	100	120	97	85	100	103	65	122
Meats, poultry, fish, and eggs	**100**	**133**	**90**	**74**	**89**	**105**	**82**	**111**
Beef	101	132	90	74	88	108	81	105
Ground beef	99	119	93	87	93	99	85	111
Roast	106	147	93	62	80	147	68	87
Chuck roast	107	140	97	59	83	159	80	78
Round roast	100	144	83	65	72	123	67	103
Other roast	110	157	96	62	82	155	59	83
Steak	101	136	86	67	86	102	82	109
Round steak	102	128	90	79	79	124	98	103
Sirloin steak	102	142	86	70	89	94	73	107
Other steak	99	136	85	62	86	99	84	112
Other beef	100	133	92	68	98	98	77	90
Pork	99	142	87	65	86	105	82	106
Bacon	96	144	81	64	80	98	94	116
Pork chops	98	135	87	73	84	105	94	100
Ham	101	155	81	53	83	99	76	116
Ham, not canned	101	155	81	56	84	95	75	118
Canned ham	99	154	77	9	59	169	81	73
Sausage	99	138	90	76	89	105	84	104
Other pork	103	138	93	60	94	118	67	98
Other meats	100	124	94	77	93	111	78	116
Frankfurters	97	122	91	88	88	101	96	109

	total married couples	married couples, no children	married couples with children				single parent, at least one child <18	single person
			total	oldest child under 6	oldest child 6 to 17	oldest child 18 or older		
Lunch meats (cold cuts)	101	128	94	79	92	112	77	119
Bologna, liverwurst, salami	94	128	83	62	88	88	103	128
Other lunch meats	105	127	101	88	94	125	62	114
Lamb, organ meats, and others	102	108	98	47	104	125	59	112
Lamb and organ meats	101	118	91	56	81	140	61	116
Mutton, goat, and game	107	62	130	6	205	55	49	90
Poultry	98	123	91	84	88	104	91	117
Fresh and frozen chicken	98	123	91	86	87	103	93	115
Fresh and frozen whole chicken	95	119	86	85	81	98	104	109
Fresh and frozen chicken parts	99	124	93	86	90	105	88	117
Other poultry	100	124	93	80	91	109	85	123
Fish and seafood	102	143	89	71	93	93	73	113
Canned fish and seafood	98	148	81	66	70	119	66	137
Fresh fish and shellfish	104	142	92	69	101	90	69	105
Frozen fish and shellfish	99	142	86	79	88	87	87	119
Eggs	96	135	83	67	78	106	83	129
Dairy products	**101**	**129**	**95**	**91**	**93**	**102**	**74**	**125**
Fresh milk and cream	100	115	98	96	97	103	77	123
Fresh milk, all types	100	112	99	96	98	102	79	123
Cream	105	151	93	93	84	112	58	131
Other dairy products	102	138	93	88	91	102	72	126
Butter	100	136	90	83	88	101	76	123
Cheese	102	141	93	93	89	102	70	125
Ice cream and related products	100	135	92	75	93	104	73	131
Miscellaneous dairy products	102	138	97	105	95	96	75	121
Fruits and vegetables	**100**	**139**	**87**	**85**	**84**	**97**	**68**	**134**
Fresh fruits	98	138	85	82	80	97	60	143
Apples	101	138	90	83	88	99	61	131
Bananas	94	128	82	80	73	106	64	157
Oranges	96	127	85	74	91	80	65	144
Citrus fruits, excl. oranges	98	159	73	66	76	71	53	146
Other fresh fruits	100	142	86	89	78	103	59	140
Fresh vegetables	100	144	85	83	82	95	63	136
Potatoes	100	148	82	72	80	95	74	128
Lettuce	100	148	86	83	79	105	59	142
Tomatoes	98	133	85	77	82	96	59	140
Other fresh vegetables	102	147	86	88	83	92	62	136
Processed fruits	100	134	91	95	89	93	79	130
Frozen fruits and fruit juices	103	137	97	95	100	90	106	111
Frozen orange juice	104	134	98	102	94	105	82	117
Frozen fruits	100	171	79	45	93	75	148	117
Frozen fruit juices	104	110	112	131	120	79	112	93
Canned fruits	104	152	89	79	93	86	56	130
Dried fruits	98	146	81	93	77	82	64	163
Fresh fruit juice	96	144	83	97	72	97	83	151
Canned and bottled fruit juice	100	123	95	98	94	96	77	123
Processed vegetables	101	136	91	80	87	108	74	119
Frozen vegetables	103	136	96	90	89	118	72	115
Canned and dried vegetables and juices	100	136	88	75	86	103	76	121
Canned beans	97	133	87	76	83	105	79	110
Canned corn	98	119	92	76	91	104	96	115
Canned miscellaneous vegetables	102	149	90	81	83	111	65	128
Dried peas	90	118	72	67	77	68	109	162
Dried beans	104	117	87	46	82	128	64	118

	total married couples	married couples, no children	married couples with children				single parent, at least one child <18	single person
			total	oldest child under 6	oldest child 6 to 17	oldest child 18 or older		
Dried miscellaneous vegetables	101	142	84	65	89	88	79	111
Dried processed vegetables	109	165	66	31	80	59	107	110
Frozen vegetable juices	108	52	148	234	114	159	175	52
Fresh and canned vegetable juices	98	131	89	78	92	92	72	137
Other food at home	**101**	**127**	**95**	**98**	**91**	**101**	**76**	**125**
Sugar and other sweets	104	131	94	77	91	113	79	119
Candy and chewing gum	106	127	98	82	96	116	76	117
Sugar	97	122	87	61	88	103	89	105
Artificial sweeteners	110	221	75	15	54	168	64	93
Jams, preserves, other sweets	99	134	90	88	85	102	85	141
Fats and oils	100	141	87	64	87	107	81	117
Margarine	100	161	81	58	76	108	99	111
Fats and oils	98	138	83	59	84	100	81	119
Salad dressings	101	138	91	62	97	98	80	113
Nondairy cream and imitation milk	102	156	88	79	72	130	58	123
Peanut butter	99	124	94	70	91	120	86	127
Miscellaneous foods	101	118	99	120	95	95	71	126
Frozen prepared foods	96	115	93	97	89	100	77	150
Frozen meals	80	117	70	86	63	73	80	216
Other frozen prepared foods	103	114	104	102	101	112	75	119
Canned and packaged soups	95	148	78	75	77	85	71	153
Potato chips, nuts, and other snacks	105	124	103	82	108	108	70	121
Potato chips and other snacks	106	115	108	88	115	108	75	114
Nuts	101	157	84	61	82	108	56	146
Condiments and seasonings	103	139	94	85	91	107	71	116
Salt, spices, and other seasonings	98	143	82	67	83	92	76	130
Olives, pickles, relishes	105	141	98	64	98	125	64	116
Sauces and gravies	103	129	98	99	99	97	76	110
Baking needs and miscellaneous products	106	153	95	87	80	137	60	111
Other canned/packaged prepared foods	103	95	110	195	96	77	67	114
Prepared salads	97	141	86	85	82	96	86	148
Prepared desserts	100	137	90	92	93	81	71	119
Baby food	121	37	159	507	99	27	61	48
Miscellaneous prepared foods	98	104	97	99	99	93	64	134
Vitamin supplements	134	9	215	265	109	418	43	36
Nonalcoholic beverages	99	126	91	82	87	109	83	125
Cola	98	119	93	79	88	115	88	124
Other carbonated drinks	100	117	96	91	91	113	93	119
Coffee	99	166	77	64	74	95	57	150
Roasted coffee	100	168	78	67	75	94	55	147
Instant and freeze-dried coffee	98	162	75	59	72	96	61	155
Noncarbonated fruit-flavored drinks, incl. nonfrozen lemonade	105	79	117	104	122	117	107	77
Tea	95	136	83	69	78	108	76	142
Nonalcoholic beer	101	125	57	193	38	–	–	148
Other nonalcoholic beverages and ice	98	129	88	89	82	101	82	127
Food prepared by CU on trips	108	182	87	81	90	83	68	138
FOOD AWAY FROM HOME	**98**	**142**	**87**	**72**	**87**	**96**	**65**	**158**
Meals at restaurants, carry-outs, other	**96**	**140**	**84**	**76**	**84**	**90**	**65**	**164**
Lunch	96	127	88	78	89	94	74	159
At fast food, take-out, delivery, concession stands, buffet, and cafeteria (other than employer and school cafeteria)	94	119	88	92	83	95	74	154
At full-service restaurants	97	175	71	72	63	90	48	193
At vending machines, mobile vendors	81	66	86	93	104	38	125	165
At employer and school cafeterias	105	46	134	33	181	104	138	91

	total married couples	married couples, no children	married couples with children				single parent, at least one child <18	single person
			total	oldest child under 6	oldest child 6 to 17	oldest child 18 or older		
Dinner	98	161	80	74	78	87	51	165
At fast food, take-out, delivery, concession stands, buffet, and cafeteria (other than employer and school cafeteria)	98	118	96	101	94	98	80	131
At full-service restaurants	98	180	73	63	72	83	39	179
At vending machines, mobile vendors	100	44	111	–	176	45	192	25
At employer and school cafeterias	71	145	37	12	55	13	65	359
Snacks and nonalcoholic beverages	94	114	91	85	92	93	81	160
At fast food, take-out, delivery, concession stands, buffet, and cafeteria (other than employer and school cafeteria)	94	107	94	94	93	96	80	160
At full-service restaurants	88	123	79	62	78	96	72	200
At vending machines, mobile vendors	97	141	83	75	87	82	79	150
At employer and school cafeterias	92	108	91	40	114	78	110	126
Breakfast and brunch	92	140	77	58	80	87	60	181
At fast food, take-out, delivery, concession stands, buffet, and cafeteria (other than employer and school cafeteria)	90	107	85	70	87	93	77	166
At full-service restaurants	93	174	70	48	71	83	42	194
At vending machines, mobile vendors	89	132	60	39	66	64	86	250
At employer and school cafeterias	92	90	94	26	126	73	106	195
Board (including at school)	109	135	108	2	69	252	31	191
Catered affairs	109	186	85	48	58	161	25	75
Food on trips	105	184	84	75	80	97	46	160
School lunches	120	–	175	12	251	118	191	0
Meals as pay	72	100	63	111	47	66	85	243
ALCOHOLIC BEVERAGES	88	155	68	72	60	84	43	219
At home	92	149	75	77	67	94	47	193
Beer and ale	84	115	74	69	77	71	57	216
Whiskey	87	184	61	91	44	78	52	258
Wine	106	185	85	89	62	133	33	148
Other alcoholic beverages	88	168	58	61	46	83	45	197
Away from home	82	165	57	65	49	69	38	260
Beer and ale	82	158	58	65	48	75	36	259
At fast food, take-out, delivery, concession stands, buffet, and cafeteria	74	95	69	73	61	84	31	302
At full-service restaurants	79	151	57	68	47	72	40	263
At vending machines, mobile vendors	45	147	10	–	18	–	95	450
At catered affairs	146	480	31	–	15	93	–	25
Wine	73	147	51	65	46	53	44	318
At fast food, take-out, delivery, concession stands, buffet and cafeteria	59	92	43	15	68	9	10	293
At full-service restaurants	72	143	52	70	45	55	48	327
At catered affairs	144	474	31	–	16	91	–	26
Other alcoholic beverages	85	177	58	65	51	67	38	245
At fast food, take-out, delivery, concession stands, buffet, and cafeteria	57	73	54	78	50	47	64	273
At full-service restaurants	76	153	55	66	47	66	43	284
At machines and mobile vendors	78	151	38	79	27	32	116	224
At catered affairs	147	481	31	–	15	93	–	25
Alcoholic beverages purchased on trips	92	191	62	66	57	70	32	223

Note: Per capita indexes account for household size and show how much each person in a particular household demographic segment spends relative to a person in the average household. Spending index for total consumer units is 100. (–) means sample is too small to make a reliable estimate.
Source: Calculations by New Strategist based on the 2000 Consumer Expenditure Survey

Table 5.14 Food and Alcohol: Total spending by household type, 2000

(total annual spending on food and alcoholic beverages, by consumer unit (CU) type, 2000; numbers in thousands)

	total married couples	married couples, no children	married couples with children total	oldest child under 6	oldest child 6 to 17	oldest child 18 or older	single parent, at least one child <18	single person
Number of consumer units	56,287	22,805	28,777	5,291	15,396	8,090	6,132	32,323
Total spending of all CUs	$2,736,638,479	$962,269,290	$1,542,030,797	$268,549,467	$834,007,478	$441,311,118	$177,357,369	$745,336,057
Food, total spending	370,090,402	127,139,927	208,668,358	30,776,530	115,596,863	63,567,984	26,092,212	91,306,010
Alcoholic beverages, total spending	23,658,552	10,519,718	11,394,829	1,984,125	5,627,084	3,862,651	1,147,236	10,516,935
FOOD AT HOME	**$219,077,447**	**$71,950,915**	**$125,374,483**	**$19,359,610**	**$68,637,369**	**$38,215,623**	**$16,230,607**	**$47,741,071**
Cereals and bakery products	**33,218,899**	**10,392,923**	**19,563,180**	**2,865,447**	**10,803,527**	**6,058,116**	**2,378,787**	**7,129,484**
Cereals and cereal products	11,440,896	3,387,683	6,909,358	982,486	3,944,763	2,033,583	941,078	2,245,802
Flour	583,133	176,283	311,367	47,725	162,582	104,037	49,914	103,434
Prepared flour mixes	1,026,675	374,686	575,252	80,529	327,319	172,155	74,749	178,423
Ready-to-eat and cooked cereals	6,335,102	1,849,942	3,856,118	565,026	2,216,562	1,097,166	527,291	1,299,385
Rice	1,430,816	392,018	875,684	126,508	440,018	321,982	115,343	251,473
Pasta, cornmeal, and other cereal products	2,065,170	594,526	1,290,648	162,751	798,283	338,162	173,720	413,088
Bakery products	21,777,440	7,005,240	12,653,822	1,882,961	6,858,764	4,024,532	1,437,709	4,883,682
Bread	5,964,733	2,005,700	3,369,499	517,460	1,812,263	1,066,990	442,179	1,488,151
White bread	2,556,556	784,264	1,488,059	218,942	816,296	465,741	216,276	621,895
Bread, other than white	3,408,178	1,221,436	1,881,440	298,518	995,967	601,249	225,903	866,256
Crackers and cookies	5,233,565	1,781,527	3,010,650	470,264	1,692,944	861,100	343,392	1,248,314
Cookies	3,461,651	1,208,209	1,968,059	307,037	1,139,920	526,497	256,686	848,802
Crackers	1,771,915	573,318	1,042,591	163,227	553,024	334,683	86,706	399,512
Frozen and refrigerated bakery products	1,775,292	520,638	1,108,778	142,063	620,613	360,086	126,687	414,704
Other bakery products	8,804,413	2,697,375	5,164,896	753,174	2,732,944	1,736,357	525,451	1,732,513
Biscuits and rolls	2,901,595	941,847	1,700,433	244,656	941,773	529,329	154,404	607,996
Cakes and cupcakes	2,878,517	763,739	1,732,375	243,862	827,381	692,747	189,908	551,430
Bread and cracker products	333,782	115,393	194,245	39,841	109,004	43,605	19,990	58,505
Sweetrolls, coffee cakes, doughnuts	1,729,137	584,948	957,123	141,428	520,847	303,294	99,400	305,129
Pies, tarts, turnovers	961,382	291,448	580,720	83,386	333,785	167,463	61,688	209,453
Meats, poultry, fish, and eggs	**57,321,555**	**19,296,223**	**32,031,679**	**4,331,477**	**17,774,990**	**10,283,118**	**4,622,424**	**11,390,948**
Beef	17,293,055	5,716,301	9,649,504	1,298,623	5,304,384	3,161,653	1,368,785	3,220,664
Ground beef	6,237,725	1,900,569	3,675,974	565,132	2,062,910	1,067,718	532,380	1,257,041
Roast	3,049,630	1,071,379	1,660,145	183,069	799,976	720,657	193,281	448,966
Chuck roast	1,029,489	339,795	582,159	58,254	280,669	260,336	75,669	134,140
Round roast	822,916	300,570	428,777	55,397	208,308	173,935	54,391	153,211
Other roast	1,197,224	430,786	648,921	69,418	310,999	286,386	63,221	161,615
Steak	6,846,188	2,353,248	3,647,197	469,259	2,042,741	1,180,493	554,639	1,327,182
Round steak	1,121,237	356,670	617,267	89,471	304,379	232,992	106,390	203,635
Sirloin steak	2,199,696	775,826	1,157,411	154,762	667,417	345,928	154,404	411,795
Other steak	3,525,255	1,220,752	1,872,519	225,026	1,070,946	601,572	293,845	711,752
Other beef	1,159,512	391,334	666,188	81,111	398,910	192,866	88,546	187,797
Pork	11,961,550	4,320,863	6,500,724	800,211	3,627,298	2,165,289	977,686	2,292,347
Bacon	1,802,310	684,378	951,080	124,074	524,850	314,377	174,946	392,078
Pork chops	2,852,625	1,001,140	1,583,598	219,471	860,021	522,614	272,629	525,895
Ham	2,625,789	1,026,909	1,319,138	143,598	757,483	439,449	194,752	543,350
Ham, not canned	2,501,957	978,335	1,259,282	142,487	731,464	403,367	184,635	527,188
Canned ham	123,831	48,803	59,856	1,111	26,019	36,081	10,056	16,485
Sausage	1,806,813	633,751	1,022,735	141,534	566,419	325,380	151,583	339,068
Other pork	2,874,014	974,686	1,624,174	171,534	918,679	563,469	183,776	492,279
Other meats	7,272,280	2,274,571	4,251,226	573,915	2,349,430	1,376,594	560,710	1,504,312
Frankfurters	1,448,827	459,293	847,483	135,185	461,264	255,806	141,281	290,261

	total married couples	married couples, no children	married couples with children total	oldest child under 6	oldest child 6 to 17	oldest child 18 or older	single parent, at least one child <18	single person
Lunch meats (cold cuts)	$4,949,879	$1,581,527	$2,881,441	$397,407	$1,577,936	$938,521	$370,005	$1,042,740
Bologna, liverwurst, salami	1,607,557	552,565	884,029	109,788	524,850	258,233	174,149	392,078
Other lunch meats	3,342,322	1,028,962	1,997,412	287,619	1,053,086	680,288	195,856	650,985
Lamb, organ meats, and others	873,574	233,751	522,015	41,323	310,229	182,187	49,424	171,312
Lamb and organ meats	706,965	209,350	395,972	40,370	198,454	167,706	41,943	146,100
Mutton, goat, and game	167,172	24,401	126,043	899	111,775	14,481	7,481	25,212
Poultry	10,294,892	3,262,939	5,953,674	907,301	3,228,387	1,864,664	939,054	2,186,974
Fresh and frozen chicken	8,086,190	2,566,247	4,668,780	724,761	2,523,712	1,454,178	752,948	1,697,927
Fresh and frozen whole chicken	2,130,463	679,361	1,207,195	196,825	640,628	377,237	231,115	439,270
Fresh and frozen chicken parts	5,955,727	1,886,886	3,461,585	527,936	1,883,085	1,076,941	521,833	1,258,658
Other poultry	2,208,702	696,693	1,284,893	182,540	704,675	410,487	186,106	488,724
Fish and seafood	8,105,891	2,873,430	4,396,550	579,153	2,588,683	1,265,438	571,748	1,609,685
Canned fish and seafood	1,107,728	424,401	570,648	76,508	276,358	228,866	73,829	277,008
Fresh fish and shellfish	5,016,297	1,732,268	2,757,412	340,476	1,697,101	740,963	326,713	907,307
Frozen fish and shellfish	1,981,865	716,761	1,068,490	162,169	615,224	295,609	171,205	425,371
Eggs	2,393,323	847,890	1,280,289	172,275	676,808	449,480	204,380	576,966
Dairy products	**23,655,175**	**7,641,271**	**13,850,946**	**2,194,601**	**7,645,500**	**4,081,567**	**1,709,050**	**5,246,023**
Fresh milk and cream	9,495,617	2,755,528	5,784,465	931,957	3,212,067	1,663,385	717,137	2,093,884
Fresh milk, all types	8,618,665	2,436,486	5,301,299	851,851	2,965,578	1,503,365	668,879	1,897,360
Cream	876,951	318,814	482,878	80,159	246,490	160,101	48,259	196,524
Other dairy products	14,159,558	4,885,971	8,066,481	1,262,591	4,433,432	2,418,101	991,912	3,152,139
Butter	1,220,302	421,208	690,360	104,921	378,742	211,554	91,857	270,867
Cheese	7,084,282	2,464,536	3,992,521	657,565	2,153,746	1,200,313	478,480	1,549,565
Ice cream and related products	4,092,065	1,397,947	2,342,448	314,603	1,328,059	723,165	294,213	958,054
Miscellaneous dairy products	1,762,909	602,280	1,041,727	185,502	572,885	283,069	127,362	373,977
Fruits and vegetables	**37,417,346**	**13,189,044**	**20,431,958**	**3,273,595**	**11,038,624**	**6,240,869**	**2,502,040**	**9,029,753**
Fresh fruits	11,571,481	4,114,706	6,213,530	997,089	3,307,985	1,950,337	701,194	3,007,655
Apples	2,141,157	743,443	1,188,778	181,852	655,716	359,034	126,932	500,360
Bananas	2,150,163	741,847	1,171,512	188,254	583,970	411,457	145,206	642,258
Oranges	1,303,607	439,680	722,015	104,391	433,397	186,798	87,810	351,351
Citrus fruits, excl. oranges	1,010,352	414,139	468,490	69,894	275,896	124,424	53,839	269,574
Other fresh fruits	4,966,202	1,775,597	2,662,448	452,698	1,358,851	868,542	287,346	1,243,789
Fresh vegetables	11,484,799	4,184,033	6,077,415	972,433	3,285,968	1,855,037	714,685	2,795,616
Potatoes	2,021,266	759,178	1,037,986	149,629	568,882	329,182	148,026	465,128
Lettuce	1,497,797	558,723	803,742	127,407	416,154	267,375	86,584	382,058
Tomatoes	2,075,302	714,025	1,122,015	169,524	612,607	348,598	124,418	533,976
Other fresh vegetables	5,890,435	2,152,108	3,113,671	525,872	1,688,171	909,882	355,656	1,414,454
Processed fruits	8,275,878	2,806,383	4,716,550	806,719	2,596,381	1,322,068	642,204	1,934,532
Frozen fruits and fruit juices	1,068,327	358,723	624,749	101,323	364,423	159,373	108,843	205,574
Frozen orange juice	518,403	168,985	303,310	52,011	163,352	88,909	40,103	104,727
Frozen fruits	260,609	112,657	128,633	12,011	84,832	33,169	38,141	54,626
Frozen fruit juices	288,752	77,081	192,806	37,302	116,394	37,295	30,599	46,222
Canned fruits	1,162,327	429,190	617,267	90,476	364,577	164,551	61,259	261,170
Dried fruits	388,380	146,180	200,288	37,831	106,694	55,497	25,141	115,716
Fresh fruit juice	1,615,437	615,051	873,094	168,677	427,085	279,671	138,093	458,987
Canned and bottled fruit juice	4,041,969	1,257,012	2,401,153	408,359	1,333,602	662,976	308,930	893,084
Processed vegetables	6,084,625	2,084,149	3,424,463	497,354	1,848,290	1,113,427	443,957	1,291,950
Frozen vegetables	1,955,410	657,240	1,141,296	176,137	594,132	382,333	135,027	392,078
Canned and dried vegetables and juices	4,129,777	1,426,681	2,283,167	321,217	1,254,312	731,093	308,930	899,549
Canned beans	881,454	308,096	493,813	71,005	265,273	163,014	71,070	179,716
Canned corn	480,128	147,092	279,712	38,413	156,885	87,372	46,481	100,848
Canned miscellaneous vegetables	1,319,930	487,343	723,454	107,143	378,434	245,855	82,414	297,372
Dried peas	21,952	7,298	10,935	1,693	6,620	2,832	2,637	7,111
Dried beans	189,124	54,048	98,417	8,571	52,654	39,803	11,467	38,464

	total married couples	married couples, no children	married couples with children				single parent, at least one child <18	single person
			total	oldest child under 6	oldest child 6 to 17	oldest child 18 or older		
Dried miscellaneous vegetables	$525,158	$186,545	$272,806	$34,550	$162,274	$78,392	$40,655	$103,434
Dried processed vegetables	32,084	12,315	12,086	952	8,314	2,993	3,127	5,818
Frozen vegetable juices	22,515	2,737	19,281	5,026	8,314	5,663	3,618	1,939
Fresh and canned vegetable juices	657,432	221,665	372,662	53,862	215,698	105,251	47,523	165,171
Other food at home	**67,464,472**	**21,431,455**	**39,496,720**	**6,694,544**	**21,374,729**	**11,552,035**	**5,018,306**	**14,945,186**
Sugar and other sweets	8,762,197	2,803,647	4,950,220	672,380	2,704,153	1,632,967	659,129	1,795,543
Candy and chewing gum	5,831,896	1,772,861	3,355,398	463,068	1,845,057	1,083,898	413,910	1,155,870
Sugar	1,178,650	375,370	653,238	75,503	374,893	212,363	105,961	227,231
Artificial sweeteners	332,656	168,757	141,007	4,656	57,581	86,563	19,071	50,424
Jams, preserves, other sweets	1,419,558	486,887	800,864	129,206	426,623	250,143	120,187	362,341
Fats and oils	5,973,176	2,140,249	3,255,254	391,904	1,822,117	1,088,995	480,933	1,260,920
Margarine	838,676	340,251	420,144	49,947	223,704	154,195	81,678	166,140
Fats and oils	1,640,766	586,545	871,655	102,540	493,904	288,085	134,046	359,755
Salad dressings	1,979,051	685,974	1,104,461	124,603	667,109	326,027	154,894	396,603
Nondairy cream and imitation milk	673,193	260,205	360,000	53,386	167,047	145,944	37,650	145,454
Peanut butter	841,491	267,275	498,705	61,429	270,508	174,825	72,664	193,292
Miscellaneous foods	31,856,753	9,424,166	19,487,784	3,879,044	10,442,337	5,082,947	2,204,086	7,141,120
Frozen prepared foods	6,213,522	1,892,131	3,771,801	648,200	2,031,040	1,103,719	492,032	1,746,088
Frozen meals	1,633,449	609,350	890,936	180,846	453,258	254,592	161,823	794,499
Other frozen prepared foods	4,580,073	1,282,553	2,881,153	467,354	1,577,782	849,126	330,208	951,589
Canned and packaged soups	2,421,467	961,687	1,250,361	198,042	686,970	372,140	180,587	700,763
Potato chips, nuts, and other snacks	6,970,019	2,092,815	4,269,356	561,058	2,518,324	1,225,311	463,579	1,448,394
Potato chips and other snacks	5,460,402	1,497,148	3,481,154	467,195	2,088,621	947,744	380,061	1,054,376
Nuts	1,509,617	595,895	787,914	93,862	429,702	277,649	83,579	394,017
Condiments and seasonings	6,260,803	2,140,477	3,564,031	532,116	1,947,286	1,113,993	428,565	1,265,445
Salt, spices, and other seasonings	1,456,708	539,338	763,454	103,069	434,475	233,477	110,989	345,856
Olives, pickles, relishes	735,671	251,995	429,353	46,296	240,793	149,827	44,580	146,746
Sauces and gravies	2,773,823	874,344	1,644,893	273,439	929,303	444,546	200,762	529,774
Baking needs and miscellaneous products	1,295,164	474,572	726,619	109,365	342,715	286,143	72,296	243,392
Other canned/packaged prepared foods	9,990,943	2,337,284	6,632,235	1,939,628	3,258,563	1,267,865	639,261	1,980,430
Prepared salads	1,302,481	478,677	717,698	116,772	385,824	219,239	112,951	353,937
Prepared desserts	673,755	232,839	375,540	63,333	218,777	93,116	47,278	143,514
Baby food	2,803,093	220,524	2,296,117	1,212,486	806,904	106,060	140,484	198,140
Miscellaneous prepared foods	5,198,104	1,404,788	3,229,067	544,338	1,843,363	842,169	338,180	1,283,870
Vitamin supplements	13,509	228	13,525	2,751	3,849	7,200	429	646
Nonalcoholic beverages	17,776,560	5,738,422	10,248,065	1,512,644	5,496,680	3,339,714	1,479,774	4,034,234
Cola	6,147,666	1,895,552	3,631,370	509,629	1,932,352	1,234,130	542,437	1,390,535
Other carbonated drinks	3,397,483	1,010,718	2,047,771	317,830	1,087,419	659,497	314,081	726,298
Coffee	2,991,654	1,264,537	1,450,361	199,577	781,501	487,180	170,224	809,368
Roasted coffee	1,975,674	841,048	964,893	137,037	520,231	318,422	107,739	522,663
Instant and freeze-dried coffee	1,015,980	423,489	485,180	62,487	261,270	168,757	62,485	287,028
Noncarbonated fruit-flavored drinks, incl. nonfrozen lemonade	1,464,025	280,730	1,022,447	149,788	598,596	278,620	147,597	193,292
Tea	1,073,956	388,141	587,626	80,476	306,842	208,803	84,315	287,028
Nonalcoholic beer	19,700	6,157	6,906	3,862	2,617	–	–	5,172
Other nonalcoholic beverages and ice	2,682,076	892,588	1,501,872	251,481	787,505	471,404	221,120	622,541
Food prepared by CU on trips	3,095,785	1,324,971	1,555,397	238,571	909,442	407,412	194,323	713,045
FOOD AWAY FROM HOME	**151,012,955**	**55,189,012**	**83,294,163**	**11,416,920**	**46,959,340**	**25,352,361**	**9,861,605**	**43,564,616**
Meals at restaurants, carry-outs, other	**121,323,814**	**44,786,968**	**66,070,553**	**9,812,424**	**37,214,441**	**19,478,293**	**8,056,773**	**37,019,209**
Lunch	45,800,169	15,398,848	26,248,365	3,852,271	14,905,483	7,662,363	3,495,608	13,607,013
At fast food, take-out, delivery, concession stands, buffet, and cafeteria (other than employer and school cafeteria)	24,827,633	7,999,310	14,499,867	2,508,675	7,740,493	4,295,871	1,942,372	7,341,200
At full-service restaurants	14,522,046	6,642,412	6,673,099	1,103,703	3,320,763	2,310,666	705,487	5,181,377
At vending machines, mobile vendors	382,752	78,677	250,360	45,079	171,204	30,176	58,193	139,312
At employer and school cafeterias	6,067,739	678,449	4,825,040	194,815	3,673,178	1,025,650	789,495	945,125

	total married couples	married couples, no children	married couples with children total	oldest child under 6	oldest child 6 to 17	oldest child 18 or older	single parent, at least one child <18	single person
Dinner	$49,367,076	$20,522,676	$24,920,594	$3,825,552	$13,775,879	$7,477,911	$2,556,431	$14,904,782
At fast food, take-out, delivery, concession stands, buffet, and cafeteria (other than employer and school cafeteria)	14,646,440	4,447,431	8,903,604	1,540,951	4,885,305	2,490,021	1,170,292	3,508,662
At full-service restaurants	34,526,446	16,004,777	15,928,070	2,282,537	8,812,516	4,978,343	1,361,304	11,283,959
At vending machines, mobile vendors	73,736	8,210	50,648	–	45,418	5,663	13,920	3,232
At employer and school cafeterias	120,454	62,258	38,561	2,063	32,640	3,802	10,854	108,929
Snacks and nonalcoholic beverages	15,452,470	4,746,633	9,277,705	1,440,951	5,275,131	2,599,964	1,310,040	4,717,542
At fast food, take-out, delivery, concession stands, buffet, and cafeteria (other than employer and school cafeteria)	10,794,158	3,097,603	6,695,257	1,102,697	3,735,839	1,874,938	906,555	3,277,875
At full-service restaurants	1,280,529	451,995	717,411	92,593	396,755	237,522	103,631	521,047
At vending machines, mobile vendors	2,680,387	989,737	1,438,562	214,762	841,853	387,430	217,809	747,954
At employer and school cafeterias	697,959	207,069	426,475	30,899	300,684	100,073	82,046	170,989
Breakfast and brunch	10,704,099	4,118,811	5,623,601	693,597	3,257,948	1,738,056	694,756	3,790,195
At fast food, take-out, delivery, concession stands, buffet, and cafeteria (other than employer and school cafeteria)	5,023,615	1,503,990	2,938,995	398,306	1,685,862	881,163	422,679	1,659,140
At full-service restaurants	5,354,582	2,522,461	2,495,541	284,497	1,434,137	813,854	236,511	1,995,622
At vending machines, mobile vendors	86,119	32,611	36,547	3,915	22,478	10,598	8,278	43,636
At employer and school cafeterias	239,783	59,749	152,806	6,878	115,470	32,441	27,287	91,474
Board (including at school)	**3,062,013**	**957,810**	**1,897,268**	**6,931**	**679,425**	**1,211,073**	**84,867**	**964,518**
Catered affairs	**4,235,034**	**1,831,926**	**2,056,117**	**192,328**	**791,046**	**1,072,653**	**96,763**	**527,188**
Food on trips	**16,344,056**	**7,266,585**	**8,132,956**	**1,198,464**	**4,346,753**	**2,587,748**	**713,458**	**4,456,049**
School lunches	**5,058,513**	**–**	**4,601,442**	**51,005**	**3,701,660**	**848,560**	**794,462**	**1,939**
Meals as pay	**989,525**	**345,724**	**535,828**	**155,767**	**226,013**	**154,034**	**115,282**	**596,036**
ALCOHOLIC BEVERAGES	**23,658,552**	**10,519,718**	**11,394,829**	**1,984,125**	**5,627,084**	**3,862,651**	**1,147,236**	**10,516,935**
At home	**15,069,156**	**6,141,158**	**7,669,934**	**1,288,041**	**3,815,745**	**2,632,082**	**755,524**	**5,643,273**
Beer and ale	6,757,817	2,346,178	3,712,521	575,925	2,164,370	981,722	450,886	3,122,725
Whiskey	841,491	452,679	368,921	91,217	148,263	128,712	50,344	449,613
Wine	6,132,469	2,695,551	3,037,988	525,343	1,256,622	1,306,697	186,597	1,532,433
Other alcoholic beverages	1,337,379	646,750	550,504	95,608	246,798	214,951	67,759	538,178
Away from home	**8,589,959**	**4,378,788**	**3,724,895**	**696,084**	**1,811,339**	**1,230,570**	**391,712**	**4,873,662**
Beer and ale	3,669,350	1,803,419	1,627,339	299,471	761,794	578,111	161,640	2,089,359
At fast food, take-out, delivery, concession stands, buffet, and cafeteria	708,090	231,015	414,964	72,645	207,076	137,854	29,311	521,693
At full-service restaurants	2,564,999	1,243,101	1,159,138	226,825	538,860	398,837	129,569	1,532,433
At vending machines, mobile vendors	12,946	10,718	1,727	–	1,848	–	2,698	23,273
At catered affairs	383,877	318,586	51,223	–	13,856	41,421	–	11,960
Wine	932,113	476,396	408,058	85,238	206,306	114,959	55,679	730,500
At fast food, take-out, delivery, concession stands, buffet and cafeteria	52,347	20,753	23,885	1,323	21,246	1,294	858	46,545
At full-service restaurants	838,676	421,893	378,418	83,915	183,520	109,296	54,820	682,339
At catered affairs	40,527	33,751	5,468	–	1,540	4,369	–	1,293
Other alcoholic beverages	3,988,497	2,098,972	1,689,498	311,428	843,085	537,581	174,333	2,054,127
At fast food, take-out, delivery, concession stands, buffet, and cafeteria	124,957	40,365	74,245	17,566	38,028	17,717	13,920	107,312
At full-service restaurants	1,418,432	718,358	633,957	124,921	302,839	207,832	79,532	943,508
At machines and mobile vendors	16,323	7,982	4,892	1,693	2,001	1,133	2,391	8,404
At catered affairs	169,424	140,479	22,446	–	6,158	18,283	–	5,172
Alcoholic beverages purchased on trips	2,258,797	1,191,789	953,958	167,196	494,058	292,696	78,490	989,407

Note: Total spending figures for total consumer units can be found on Total Spending by Age and Total Spending by Region tables. Spending by type of consumer unit will not add to total because not all types of consumer units are shown. (–) means sample is too small to make a reliable estimate.
Source: Calculations by New Strategist based on the 2000 Consumer Expenditure Survey

Table 5.15 Food and Alcohol: Market shares by household type, 2000

(percentage of total annual spending on food and alcoholic beverages accounted for by types of consumer units, 2000)

	total married couples	married couples, no children	married couples with children				single parent, at least one child <18	single person
			total	oldest child under 6	oldest child 6 to 17	oldest child 18 or older		
Share of total consumer units	51.5%	20.9%	26.3%	4.8%	14.1%	7.4%	5.6%	29.6%
Share of total before-tax income	69.8	24.9	39.4	6.8	21.9	10.7	3.2	16.5
Share of total spending	65.8	23.1	37.1	6.5	20.0	10.6	4.3	17.9
Share of food spending	65.6	22.5	37.0	5.5	20.5	11.3	4.6	16.2
Share of alcoholic beverages spending	58.2	25.9	28.0	4.9	13.8	9.5	2.8	25.9
FOOD AT HOME	**66.3%**	**21.8%**	**37.9%**	**5.9%**	**20.8%**	**11.6%**	**4.9%**	**14.4%**
Cereals and bakery products	**67.0**	**21.0**	**39.5**	**5.8**	**21.8**	**12.2**	**4.8**	**14.4**
Cereals and cereal products	66.9	19.8	40.4	5.7	23.1	11.9	5.5	13.1
Flour	66.8	20.2	35.7	5.5	18.6	11.9	5.7	11.9
Prepared flour mixes	70.3	25.7	39.4	5.5	22.4	11.8	5.1	12.2
Ready-to-eat and cooked cereals	66.7	19.5	40.6	5.9	23.3	11.5	5.5	13.7
Rice	66.9	18.3	41.0	5.9	20.6	15.1	5.4	11.8
Pasta, cornmeal, and other cereal products	65.9	19.0	41.2	5.2	25.5	10.8	5.5	13.2
Bakery products	67.1	21.6	39.0	5.8	21.1	12.4	4.4	15.0
Bread	64.9	21.8	36.7	5.6	19.7	11.6	4.8	16.2
White bread	63.8	19.6	37.2	5.5	20.4	11.6	5.4	15.5
Bread, other than white	65.7	23.6	36.3	5.8	19.2	11.6	4.4	16.7
Crackers and cookies	67.4	22.9	38.8	6.1	21.8	11.1	4.4	16.1
Cookies	66.3	23.2	37.7	5.9	21.8	10.1	4.9	16.3
Crackers	69.5	22.5	40.9	6.4	21.7	13.1	3.4	15.7
Frozen and refrigerated bakery products	66.2	19.4	41.3	5.3	23.1	13.4	4.7	15.5
Other bakery products	68.6	21.0	40.3	5.9	21.3	13.5	4.1	13.5
Biscuits and rolls	68.9	22.4	40.4	5.8	22.3	12.6	3.7	14.4
Cakes and cupcakes	68.5	18.2	41.2	5.8	19.7	16.5	4.5	13.1
Bread and cracker products	69.2	23.9	40.3	8.3	22.6	9.0	4.1	12.1
Sweetrolls, coffee cakes, doughnuts	69.7	23.6	38.6	5.7	21.0	12.2	4.0	12.3
Pies, tarts, turnovers	66.2	20.1	40.0	5.7	23.0	11.5	4.2	14.4
Meats, poultry, fish, and eggs	**65.9**	**22.2**	**36.8**	**5.0**	**20.4**	**11.8**	**5.3**	**13.1**
Beef	66.4	21.9	37.0	5.0	20.4	12.1	5.3	12.4
Ground beef	65.0	19.8	38.3	5.9	21.5	11.1	5.5	13.1
Roast	70.0	24.6	38.1	4.2	18.4	16.5	4.4	10.3
Chuck roast	70.6	23.3	39.9	4.0	19.3	17.9	5.2	9.2
Round roast	65.7	24.0	34.2	4.4	16.6	13.9	4.3	12.2
Other roast	72.7	26.2	39.4	4.2	18.9	17.4	3.8	9.8
Steak	66.2	22.8	35.3	4.5	19.8	11.4	5.4	12.8
Round steak	67.0	21.3	36.9	5.3	18.2	13.9	6.4	12.2
Sirloin steak	67.4	23.8	35.4	4.7	20.4	10.6	4.7	12.6
Other steak	65.3	22.6	34.7	4.2	19.8	11.1	5.4	13.2
Other beef	65.9	22.3	37.9	4.6	22.7	11.0	5.0	10.7
Pork	65.5	23.7	35.6	4.4	19.9	11.9	5.4	12.6
Bacon	63.3	24.0	33.4	4.4	18.4	11.0	6.1	13.8
Pork chops	64.3	22.6	35.7	4.9	19.4	11.8	6.1	11.9
Ham	66.2	25.9	33.3	3.6	19.1	11.1	4.9	13.7
Ham, not canned	66.3	25.9	33.4	3.8	19.4	10.7	4.9	14.0
Canned ham	65.1	25.6	31.5	0.6	13.7	19.0	5.3	8.7
Sausage	65.5	23.0	37.0	5.1	20.5	11.8	5.5	12.3
Other pork	67.7	23.0	38.3	4.0	21.6	13.3	4.3	11.6
Other meats	66.1	20.7	38.7	5.2	21.4	12.5	5.1	13.7
Frankfurters	64.1	20.3	37.5	6.0	20.4	11.3	6.2	12.8

	total married couples	married couples, no children	married couples with children				single parent, at least one child <18	single person
			total	oldest child under 6	oldest child 6 to 17	oldest child 18 or older		
Lunch meats (cold cuts)	66.6%	21.3%	38.8%	5.3%	21.2%	12.6%	5.0%	14.0%
Bologna, liverwurst, salami	61.9	21.3	34.1	4.2	20.2	10.0	6.7	15.1
Other lunch meats	69.0	21.3	41.3	5.9	21.8	14.1	4.0	13.4
Lamb, organ meats, and others	67.3	18.0	40.2	3.2	23.9	14.0	3.8	13.2
Lamb and organ meats	66.6	19.7	37.3	3.8	18.7	15.8	3.9	13.8
Mutton, goat, and game	70.8	10.3	53.4	0.4	47.3	6.1	3.2	10.7
Poultry	64.8	20.6	37.5	5.7	20.3	11.7	5.9	13.8
Fresh and frozen chicken	64.6	20.5	37.3	5.8	20.2	11.6	6.0	13.6
Fresh and frozen whole chicken	62.3	19.9	35.3	5.8	18.7	11.0	6.8	12.9
Fresh and frozen chicken parts	65.5	20.7	38.1	5.8	20.7	11.8	5.7	13.8
Other poultry	65.7	20.7	38.2	5.4	21.0	12.2	5.5	14.5
Fish and seafood	67.3	23.9	36.5	4.8	21.5	10.5	4.7	13.4
Canned fish and seafood	64.6	24.8	33.3	4.5	16.1	13.4	4.3	16.2
Fresh fish and shellfish	68.6	23.7	37.7	4.7	23.2	10.1	4.5	12.4
Frozen fish and shellfish	65.5	23.7	35.3	5.4	20.3	9.8	5.7	14.1
Eggs	63.5	22.5	34.0	4.6	18.0	11.9	5.4	15.3
Dairy products	**66.6**	**21.5**	**39.0**	**6.2**	**21.5**	**11.5**	**4.8**	**14.8**
Fresh milk and cream	66.2	19.2	40.3	6.5	22.4	11.6	5.0	14.6
Fresh milk, all types	65.9	18.6	40.5	6.5	22.7	11.5	5.1	14.5
Cream	69.1	25.1	38.0	6.3	19.4	12.6	3.8	15.5
Other dairy products	66.9	23.1	38.1	6.0	21.0	11.4	4.7	14.9
Butter	65.6	22.7	37.1	5.6	20.4	11.4	4.9	14.6
Cheese	67.5	23.5	38.0	6.3	20.5	11.4	4.6	14.8
Ice cream and related products	66.2	22.6	37.9	5.1	21.5	11.7	4.8	15.5
Miscellaneous dairy products	67.5	23.1	39.9	7.1	21.9	10.8	4.9	14.3
Fruits and vegetables	**65.7**	**23.2**	**35.9**	**5.7**	**19.4**	**11.0**	**4.4**	**15.9**
Fresh fruits	64.8	23.1	34.8	5.6	18.5	10.9	3.9	16.9
Apples	66.4	23.1	36.9	5.6	20.3	11.1	3.9	15.5
Bananas	62.0	21.4	33.8	5.4	16.8	11.9	4.2	18.5
Oranges	63.0	21.2	34.9	5.0	20.9	9.0	4.2	17.0
Citrus fruits, excl. oranges	64.6	26.5	29.9	4.5	17.6	8.0	3.4	17.2
Other fresh fruits	66.1	23.6	35.4	6.0	18.1	11.6	3.8	16.5
Fresh vegetables	66.2	24.1	35.0	5.6	18.9	10.7	4.1	16.1
Potatoes	65.8	24.7	33.8	4.9	18.5	10.7	4.8	15.2
Lettuce	66.0	24.6	35.4	5.6	18.3	11.8	3.8	16.8
Tomatoes	64.3	22.1	34.7	5.2	19.0	10.8	3.9	16.5
Other fresh vegetables	67.0	24.5	35.4	6.0	19.2	10.4	4.0	16.1
Processed fruits	65.8	22.3	37.5	6.4	20.6	10.5	5.1	15.4
Frozen fruits and fruit juices	68.0	22.8	39.8	6.4	23.2	10.1	6.9	13.1
Frozen orange juice	68.7	22.4	40.2	6.9	21.6	11.8	5.3	13.9
Frozen fruits	65.8	28.5	32.5	3.0	21.4	8.4	9.6	13.8
Frozen fruit juices	68.8	18.4	45.9	8.9	27.7	8.9	7.3	11.0
Canned fruits	68.7	25.4	36.5	5.3	21.5	9.7	3.6	15.4
Dried fruits	64.6	24.3	33.3	6.3	17.7	9.2	4.2	19.2
Fresh fruit juice	63.0	24.0	34.1	6.6	16.7	10.9	5.4	17.9
Canned and bottled fruit juice	65.7	20.4	39.1	6.6	21.7	10.8	5.0	14.5
Processed vegetables	66.3	22.7	37.3	5.4	20.1	12.1	4.8	14.1
Frozen vegetables	67.7	22.7	39.5	6.1	20.6	13.2	4.7	13.6
Canned and dried vegetables and juices	65.6	22.7	36.3	5.1	19.9	11.6	4.9	14.3
Canned beans	63.6	22.2	35.6	5.1	19.1	11.8	5.1	13.0
Canned corn	64.6	19.8	37.6	5.2	21.1	11.7	6.2	13.6
Canned miscellaneous vegetables	67.2	24.8	36.9	5.5	19.3	12.5	4.2	15.1
Dried peas	59.0	19.6	29.4	4.6	17.8	7.6	7.1	19.1
Dried beans	68.4	19.5	35.6	3.1	19.0	14.4	4.1	13.9

	total married couples	married couples, no children	married couples with children				single parent, at least one child <18	single person
			total	oldest child under 6	oldest child 6 to 17	oldest child 18 or older		
Dried miscellaneous vegetables	66.5%	23.6%	34.5%	4.4%	20.6%	9.9%	5.1%	13.1%
Dried processed vegetables	71.6	27.5	27.0	2.1	18.5	6.7	7.0	13.0
Frozen vegetable juices	71.0	8.6	60.8	15.8	26.2	17.9	11.4	6.1
Fresh and canned vegetable juices	64.6	21.8	36.6	5.3	21.2	10.3	4.7	16.2
Other food at home	**66.6**	**21.1**	**39.0**	**6.6**	**21.1**	**11.4**	**5.0**	**14.7**
Sugar and other sweets	68.4	21.9	38.6	5.2	21.1	12.7	5.1	14.0
Candy and chewing gum	69.9	21.2	40.2	5.5	22.1	13.0	5.0	13.9
Sugar	64.1	20.4	35.6	4.1	20.4	11.6	5.8	12.4
Artificial sweeteners	72.6	36.8	30.8	1.0	12.6	18.9	4.2	11.0
Jams, preserves, other sweets	65.4	22.4	36.9	5.9	19.6	11.5	5.5	16.7
Fats and oils	65.7	23.6	35.8	4.3	20.1	12.0	5.3	13.9
Margarine	66.1	26.8	33.1	3.9	17.6	12.1	6.4	13.1
Fats and oils	64.3	23.0	34.1	4.0	19.3	11.3	5.2	14.1
Salad dressings	66.6	23.1	37.2	4.2	22.4	11.0	5.2	13.3
Nondairy cream and imitation milk	67.3	26.0	36.0	5.3	16.7	14.6	3.8	14.5
Peanut butter	65.1	20.7	38.6	4.8	20.9	13.5	5.6	15.0
Miscellaneous foods	66.7	19.7	40.8	8.1	21.8	10.6	4.6	14.9
Frozen prepared foods	63.0	19.2	38.2	6.6	20.6	11.2	5.0	17.7
Frozen meals	52.4	19.5	28.6	5.8	14.5	8.2	5.2	25.5
Other frozen prepared foods	67.9	19.0	42.7	6.9	23.4	12.6	4.9	14.1
Canned and packaged soups	62.3	24.7	32.2	5.1	17.7	9.6	4.6	18.0
Potato chips, nuts, and other snacks	68.9	20.7	42.2	5.5	24.9	12.1	4.6	14.3
Potato chips and other snacks	69.7	19.1	44.4	6.0	26.6	12.1	4.8	13.5
Nuts	66.3	26.2	34.6	4.1	18.9	12.2	3.7	17.3
Condiments and seasonings	67.7	23.1	38.5	5.8	21.0	12.0	4.6	13.7
Salt, spices, and other seasonings	64.5	23.9	33.8	4.6	19.2	10.3	4.9	15.3
Olives, pickles, relishes	68.8	23.6	40.2	4.3	22.5	14.0	4.2	13.7
Sauces and gravies	68.1	21.5	40.4	6.7	22.8	10.9	4.9	13.0
Baking needs and miscellaneous products	69.8	25.6	39.2	5.9	18.5	15.4	3.9	13.1
Other canned/packaged prepared foods	68.1	15.9	45.2	13.2	22.2	8.6	4.4	13.5
Prepared salads	64.2	23.6	35.4	5.8	19.0	10.8	5.6	17.4
Prepared desserts	66.2	22.9	36.9	6.2	21.5	9.1	4.6	14.1
Baby food	79.4	6.3	65.1	34.4	22.9	3.0	4.0	5.6
Miscellaneous prepared foods	64.3	17.4	39.9	6.7	22.8	10.4	4.2	15.9
Vitamin supplements	88.2	1.5	88.3	18.0	25.1	47.0	2.8	4.2
Nonalcoholic beverages	65.1	21.0	37.5	5.5	20.1	12.2	5.4	14.8
Cola	64.6	19.9	38.2	5.4	20.3	13.0	5.7	14.6
Other carbonated drinks	65.6	19.5	39.5	6.1	21.0	12.7	6.1	14.0
Coffee	65.4	27.6	31.7	4.4	17.1	10.6	3.7	17.7
Roasted coffee	65.7	28.0	32.1	4.6	17.3	10.6	3.6	17.4
Instant and freeze-dried coffee	64.7	27.0	30.9	4.0	16.6	10.8	4.0	18.3
Noncarbonated fruit-flavored drinks, incl. nonfrozen lemonade	68.9	13.2	48.1	7.1	28.2	13.1	6.9	9.1
Tea	62.6	22.6	34.3	4.7	17.9	12.2	4.9	16.7
Nonalcoholic beer	66.7	20.9	23.4	13.1	8.9	–	–	17.5
Other nonalcoholic beverages and ice	64.6	21.5	36.1	6.1	19.0	11.3	5.3	15.0
Food prepared by CU on trips	70.9	30.3	35.6	5.5	20.8	9.3	4.4	16.3
FOOD AWAY FROM HOME	**64.6**	**23.6**	**35.6**	**4.9**	**20.1**	**10.8**	**4.2**	**18.6**
Meals at restaurants, carry-outs, other	**63.4**	**23.4**	**34.5**	**5.1**	**19.4**	**10.2**	**4.2**	**19.3**
Lunch	63.2	21.2	36.2	5.3	20.6	10.6	4.8	18.8
At fast food, take-out, delivery, concession stands, buffet, and cafeteria (other than employer and school cafeteria)	61.7	19.9	36.0	6.2	19.2	10.7	4.8	18.2
At full-service restaurants	63.8	29.2	29.3	4.8	14.6	10.2	3.1	22.8
At vending machines, mobile vendors	53.7	11.0	35.1	6.3	24.0	4.2	8.2	19.5
At employer and school cafeterias	69.1	7.7	55.0	2.2	41.8	11.7	9.0	10.8

	total married couples	married couples, no children	married couples with children			single parent, at least one child <18	single person
			total	oldest child under 6	oldest child 6 to 17	oldest child 18 or older		
Dinner	64.7%	26.9%	32.6%	5.0%	18.0%	9.8%	3.3%	19.5%
At fast food, take-out, delivery, concession stands, buffet, and cafeteria (other than employer and school cafeteria)	64.7	19.7	39.3	6.8	21.6	11.0	5.2	15.5
At full-service restaurants	64.7	30.0	29.9	4.3	16.5	9.3	2.6	21.2
At vending machines, mobile vendors	66.1	7.4	45.4	–	40.7	5.1	12.5	2.9
At employer and school cafeterias	46.9	24.2	15.0	0.8	12.7	1.5	4.2	42.4
Snacks and nonalcoholic beverages	62.0	19.1	37.3	5.8	21.2	10.4	5.3	18.9
At fast food, take-out, delivery, concession stands, buffet, and cafeteria (other than employer and school cafeteria)	62.2	17.9	38.6	6.4	21.5	10.8	5.2	18.9
At full-service restaurants	58.1	20.5	32.6	4.2	18.0	10.8	4.7	23.6
At vending machines, mobile vendors	63.6	23.5	34.1	5.1	20.0	9.2	5.2	17.8
At employer and school cafeterias	60.8	18.0	37.2	2.7	26.2	8.7	7.2	14.9
Breakfast and brunch	60.5	23.3	31.8	3.9	18.4	9.8	3.9	21.4
At fast food, take-out, delivery, concession stands, buffet, and cafeteria (other than employer and school cafeteria)	59.6	17.8	34.8	4.7	20.0	10.4	5.0	19.7
At full-service restaurants	61.5	29.0	28.7	3.3	16.5	9.3	2.7	22.9
At vending machines, mobile vendors	58.3	22.1	24.8	2.7	15.2	7.2	5.6	29.6
At employer and school cafeterias	60.6	15.1	38.6	1.7	29.2	8.2	6.9	23.1
Board (including at school)	**71.7**	**22.4**	**44.4**	**0.2**	**15.9**	**28.4**	**2.0**	**22.6**
Catered affairs	**71.7**	**31.0**	**34.8**	**3.3**	**13.4**	**18.2**	**1.6**	**8.9**
Food on trips	**69.2**	**30.8**	**34.4**	**5.1**	**18.4**	**11.0**	**3.0**	**18.9**
School lunches	**79.1**	**–**	**72.0**	**0.8**	**57.9**	**13.3**	**12.4**	**0.0**
Meals as pay	**47.7**	**16.7**	**25.8**	**7.5**	**10.9**	**7.4**	**5.6**	**28.7**
ALCOHOLIC BEVERAGES	**58.2**	**25.9**	**28.0**	**4.9**	**13.8**	**9.5**	**2.8**	**25.9**
At home	**60.8**	**24.8**	**30.9**	**5.2**	**15.4**	**10.6**	**3.0**	**22.8**
Beer and ale	55.2	19.2	30.3	4.7	17.7	8.0	3.7	25.5
Whiskey	57.0	30.7	25.0	6.2	10.0	8.7	3.4	30.5
Wine	70.1	30.8	34.7	6.0	14.4	14.9	2.1	17.5
Other alcoholic beverages	58.0	28.0	23.9	4.1	10.7	9.3	2.9	23.3
Away from home	**54.1**	**27.6**	**23.5**	**4.4**	**11.4**	**7.8**	**2.5**	**30.7**
Beer and ale	53.7	26.4	23.8	4.4	11.2	8.5	2.4	30.6
At fast food, take-out, delivery, concession stands, buffet, and cafeteria	48.4	15.8	28.4	5.0	14.2	9.4	2.0	35.7
At full-service restaurants	52.1	25.2	23.5	4.6	10.9	8.1	2.6	31.1
At vending machines, mobile vendors	29.6	24.5	3.9	–	4.2	–	6.2	53.2
At catered affairs	96.4	80.0	12.9	–	3.5	10.4	–	3.0
Wine	47.9	24.5	21.0	4.4	10.6	5.9	2.9	37.5
At fast food, take-out, delivery, concession stands, buffet and cafeteria	38.9	15.4	17.8	1.0	15.8	1.0	0.6	34.6
At full-service restaurants	47.5	23.9	21.4	4.7	10.4	6.2	3.1	38.6
At catered affairs	95.0	79.1	12.8	–	3.6	10.2	–	3.0
Other alcoholic beverages	56.2	29.6	23.8	4.4	11.9	7.6	2.5	28.9
At fast food, take-out, delivery, concession stands, buffet, and cafeteria	37.6	12.1	22.3	5.3	11.4	5.3	4.2	32.3
At full-service restaurants	50.4	25.5	22.5	4.4	10.8	7.4	2.8	33.5
At machines and mobile vendors	51.5	25.2	15.4	5.3	6.3	3.6	7.5	26.5
At catered affairs	96.8	80.3	12.8	–	3.5	10.4	–	3.0
Alcoholic beverages purchased on trips	60.3	31.8	25.5	4.5	13.2	7.8	2.1	26.4

Note: Market share for total consumer units is 100.0%. Market shares by type of consumer unit will not add to total because not all types of consumer units are shown. (–) means sample is too small to make a reliable estimate.
Source: Calculations by New Strategist based on the 2000 Consumer Expenditure Survey

Table 5.16   Food and Alcohol: Average spending by race and Hispanic origin, 2000

(average annual spending of consumer units (CU) on food and alcoholic beverages, by race and Hispanic origin of consumer unit reference person, 2000)

	total consumer units	race black	race white and other	Hispanic origin Hispanic	Hispanic origin non-Hispanic
Number of consumer units					
(in thousands, add 000)	109,367	13,230	96,137	9,473	99,894
Average number of persons per CU	2.5	2.7	2.5	3.4	2.4
Average before-tax income of CU	$44,649.00	$32,657.00	$46,260.00	$34,891.00	$45,669.00
Average spending of CU, total	38,044.67	28,152.24	39,406.20	32,734.95	38,548.91
Food, average spending	5,157.88	4,094.85	5,304.24	5,361.60	5,139.23
Alcoholic beverages, average spending	371.81	211.14	393.93	284.79	379.92
FOOD AT HOME	$3,021.00	$2,690.58	$3,066.50	$3,496.40	$2,976.85
Cereals and bakery products	453.33	392.97	461.64	490.56	449.87
Cereals and cereal products	156.40	158.71	156.08	200.94	152.26
Flour	7.98	9.75	7.73	18.04	7.04
Prepared flour mixes	13.35	11.76	13.57	12.15	13.47
Ready-to-eat and cooked cereals	86.88	85.11	87.13	93.30	86.29
Rice	19.55	27.36	18.47	36.02	18.02
Pasta, cornmeal, and other cereal products	28.64	24.72	29.18	41.43	27.45
Bakery products	296.93	234.26	305.56	289.62	297.61
Bread	84.04	71.88	85.72	96.85	82.85
White bread	36.62	34.63	36.89	45.71	35.77
Bread, other than white	47.42	37.25	48.82	51.14	47.08
Crackers and cookies	71.03	53.86	73.40	56.60	72.37
Cookies	47.71	37.47	49.12	40.12	48.41
Crackers	23.32	16.39	24.28	16.49	23.96
Frozen and refrigerated bakery products	24.53	20.87	25.03	16.47	25.28
Other bakery products	117.33	87.66	121.42	119.69	117.11
Biscuits and rolls	38.53	24.28	40.49	24.79	39.80
Cakes and cupcakes	38.42	34.23	39.00	47.66	37.56
Bread and cracker products	4.41	2.30	4.70	4.03	4.45
Sweetrolls, coffee cakes, doughnuts	22.68	14.68	23.79	29.76	22.03
Pies, tarts, turnovers	13.28	12.16	13.44	13.46	13.27
Meats, poultry, fish, and eggs	795.43	908.64	779.84	1,035.90	773.09
Beef	238.19	235.66	238.54	325.97	230.04
Ground beef	87.76	91.65	87.23	114.93	85.24
Roast	39.84	31.01	41.05	52.72	38.64
Chuck roast	13.33	11.53	13.58	21.14	12.60
Round roast	11.46	7.56	11.99	13.36	11.28
Other roast	15.05	11.92	15.48	18.22	14.75
Steak	94.52	93.84	94.61	138.29	90.45
Round steak	15.31	14.54	15.42	31.49	13.81
Sirloin steak	29.86	26.84	30.28	47.32	28.24
Other steak	49.35	52.46	48.92	59.48	48.40
Other beef	16.08	19.16	15.66	20.02	15.71
Pork	166.94	199.18	162.51	212.95	162.67
Bacon	26.05	32.80	25.12	27.88	25.88
Pork chops	40.57	53.95	38.72	61.15	38.65
Ham	36.26	35.24	36.40	47.56	35.21
Ham, not canned	34.52	34.04	34.59	45.65	33.49
Canned ham	1.74	1.20	1.82	1.92	1.72
Sausage	25.24	33.54	24.10	25.16	25.25
Other pork	38.82	43.65	38.16	51.19	37.68
Other meats	100.54	106.34	99.74	115.91	99.11
Frankfurters	20.68	21.47	20.57	25.57	20.22

	total consumer units	race		Hispanic origin	
		black	white and other	Hispanic	non-Hispanic
Lunch meats (cold cuts)	$67.99	$61.20	$68.92	$66.73	$68.11
Bologna, liverwurst, salami	23.73	27.42	23.22	28.13	23.32
Other lunch meats	44.26	33.78	45.71	38.60	44.79
Lamb, organ meats, and others	11.87	23.67	10.25	23.62	10.78
Lamb and organ meats	9.71	13.14	9.24	22.51	8.52
Mutton, goat, and game	2.16	10.53	1.01	1.11	2.26
Poultry	145.16	185.19	139.65	190.04	140.99
Fresh and frozen chicken	114.43	142.12	110.62	165.12	109.73
Fresh and frozen whole chicken	31.25	42.23	29.74	62.80	28.32
Fresh and frozen chicken parts	83.18	99.89	80.88	102.32	81.40
Other poultry	30.73	43.07	29.03	24.92	31.27
Fish and seafood	110.14	138.86	106.18	136.46	107.69
Canned fish and seafood	15.67	14.20	15.87	16.33	15.61
Fresh fish and shellfish	66.82	97.86	62.54	90.26	64.64
Frozen fish and shellfish	27.65	26.81	27.77	29.86	27.45
Eggs	34.46	43.41	33.23	54.57	32.59
Dairy products	**324.63**	**244.58**	**335.66**	**359.18**	**321.43**
Fresh milk and cream	131.22	101.69	135.29	170.38	127.58
Fresh milk, all types	119.61	95.98	122.86	156.86	116.15
Cream	11.61	5.71	12.43	13.52	11.44
Other dairy products	193.41	142.89	200.37	188.80	193.84
Butter	17.00	15.99	17.14	12.81	17.39
Cheese	95.96	63.69	100.40	101.78	95.42
Ice cream and related products	56.56	45.63	58.07	51.79	57.01
Miscellaneous dairy products	23.89	17.57	24.76	22.42	24.03
Fruits and vegetables	**520.83**	**453.78**	**530.07**	**670.47**	**506.93**
Fresh fruits	163.17	131.48	167.53	228.24	157.12
Apples	29.49	25.83	29.99	37.11	28.78
Bananas	31.70	30.15	31.91	50.32	29.97
Oranges	18.93	18.60	18.97	27.92	18.09
Citrus fruits, excl. oranges	14.31	10.80	14.79	25.52	13.27
Other fresh fruits	68.74	46.10	71.86	87.38	67.01
Fresh vegetables	158.72	128.67	162.86	227.89	152.30
Potatoes	28.07	25.06	28.48	35.18	27.40
Lettuce	20.75	18.24	21.09	26.05	20.26
Tomatoes	29.53	25.67	30.06	55.33	27.13
Other fresh vegetables	80.38	59.70	83.23	111.33	77.50
Processed fruits	115.01	117.59	114.65	125.45	114.04
Frozen fruits and fruit juices	14.37	11.26	14.80	11.55	14.63
Frozen orange juice	6.90	5.57	7.09	6.25	6.96
Frozen fruits	3.62	2.31	3.80	1.67	3.80
Frozen fruit juices	3.84	3.38	3.91	3.63	3.86
Canned fruits	15.48	12.33	15.91	14.21	15.60
Dried fruits	5.50	3.63	5.76	4.28	5.62
Fresh fruit juice	23.44	24.62	23.28	25.11	23.28
Canned and bottled fruit juice	56.21	65.73	54.90	70.31	54.91
Processed vegetables	83.94	76.04	85.02	88.89	83.48
Frozen vegetables	26.42	24.70	26.66	17.65	27.24
Canned and dried vegetables and juices	57.52	51.35	58.37	71.24	56.24
Canned beans	12.67	12.11	12.75	13.59	12.59
Canned corn	6.80	7.95	6.64	8.68	6.62
Canned miscellaneous vegetables	17.95	12.70	18.68	15.99	18.14
Dried peas	0.34	0.50	0.32	0.26	0.35
Dried beans	2.53	2.42	2.55	8.98	1.93

	total consumer units	race black	race white and other	Hispanic origin Hispanic	Hispanic origin non-Hispanic
Dried miscellaneous vegetables	$7.22	$8.04	$7.10	$9.52	$7.00
Dried processed vegetables	0.41	0.25	0.43	1.57	0.30
Frozen vegetable juices	0.29	0.46	0.26	0.39	0.28
Fresh and canned vegetable juices	9.30	6.93	9.63	12.28	9.03
Other food at home	**926.77**	**690.61**	**959.29**	**940.30**	**925.53**
Sugar and other sweets	117.14	88.95	121.03	109.73	117.83
Candy and chewing gum	76.30	44.00	80.75	58.70	77.93
Sugar	16.80	21.47	16.16	29.19	15.65
Artificial sweeteners	4.19	5.80	3.96	3.27	4.27
Jams, preserves, other sweets	19.86	17.67	20.16	18.58	19.98
Fats and oils	83.09	83.29	83.06	99.50	81.56
Margarine	11.61	11.92	11.56	10.83	11.68
Fats and oils	23.35	29.90	22.44	41.90	21.62
Salad dressings	27.18	24.17	27.59	29.53	26.96
Nondairy cream and imitation milk	9.15	6.09	9.57	7.38	9.31
Peanut butter	11.81	11.20	11.89	9.86	11.99
Miscellaneous foods	437.02	315.79	453.71	405.28	439.97
Frozen prepared foods	90.20	65.97	93.53	69.69	92.10
Frozen meals	28.50	27.81	28.60	16.95	29.57
Other frozen prepared foods	61.70	38.16	64.94	52.74	62.53
Canned and packaged soups	35.54	29.08	36.43	34.01	35.68
Potato chips, nuts, and other snacks	92.50	56.85	97.41	68.26	94.75
Potato chips and other snacks	71.67	42.68	75.66	54.85	73.23
Nuts	20.83	14.17	21.75	13.41	21.52
Condiments and seasonings	84.61	66.09	87.16	76.51	85.36
Salt, spices, and other seasonings	20.65	22.70	20.37	25.64	20.19
Olives, pickles, relishes	9.77	6.44	10.23	7.58	9.97
Sauces and gravies	37.23	26.08	38.77	32.74	37.65
Baking needs and miscellaneous products	16.96	10.87	17.79	10.55	17.55
Other canned/packaged prepared foods	134.17	97.81	139.18	156.81	132.07
Prepared salads	18.55	13.34	19.26	13.49	19.02
Prepared desserts	9.31	7.17	9.61	9.64	9.28
Baby food	32.26	27.62	32.90	34.85	32.02
Miscellaneous prepared foods	73.91	49.65	77.25	98.70	71.60
Vitamin supplements	0.14	0.03	0.16	0.13	0.14
Nonalcoholic beverages	249.58	185.72	258.38	291.74	245.67
Cola	86.99	61.79	90.46	111.86	84.68
Other carbonated drinks	47.39	32.32	49.47	50.99	47.06
Coffee	41.85	24.31	44.26	44.73	41.58
Roasted coffee	27.50	16.66	28.99	27.86	27.46
Instant and freeze-dried coffee	14.35	7.64	15.27	16.86	14.12
Noncarbonated fruit-flavored drinks, incl. nonfrozen lemonade	19.42	20.85	19.22	28.16	18.61
Tea	15.68	13.56	15.97	14.63	15.77
Nonalcoholic beer	0.27	0.29	0.27	–	0.30
Other nonalcoholic beverages and ice	37.99	32.61	38.73	41.38	37.67
Food prepared by CU on trips	39.94	16.86	43.12	34.04	40.50
FOOD AWAY FROM HOME	**2,136.88**	**1,404.28**	**2,237.74**	**1,865.20**	**2,162.39**
Meals at restaurants, carry-outs, other	**1,750.33**	**1,212.70**	**1,824.37**	**1,619.58**	**1,762.48**
Lunch	662.90	535.03	680.50	670.47	662.19
At fast food, take-out, delivery, concession stands, buffet, and cafeteria (other than employer and school cafeteria)	368.00	330.93	373.10	423.56	362.84
At full-service restaurants	208.12	101.26	222.83	146.56	213.84
At vending machines, mobile vendors	6.52	7.38	6.41	18.43	5.42
At employer and school cafeterias	80.26	95.47	78.16	81.93	80.10

	total consumer units	race		Hispanic origin	
		black	white and other	Hispanic	non-Hispanic
Dinner	$697.99	$383.84	$741.25	$545.51	$712.16
At fast food, take-out, delivery, concession stands, buffet, and cafeteria (other than employer and school cafeteria)	206.92	158.87	213.53	260.83	201.91
At full-service restaurants	487.70	219.94	524.57	279.63	507.03
At vending machines, mobile vendors	1.02	2.45	0.83	2.51	0.89
At employer and school cafeterias	2.35	2.59	2.32	2.54	2.34
Snacks and nonalcoholic beverages	227.71	175.76	234.87	224.18	228.04
At fast food, take-out, delivery, concession stands, buffet, and cafeteria (other than employer and school cafeteria)	158.55	111.96	164.96	153.59	159.01
At full-service restaurants	20.15	14.49	20.94	19.93	20.18
At vending machines, mobile vendors	38.52	37.58	38.65	40.94	38.29
At employer and school cafeterias	10.49	11.74	10.32	9.73	10.56
Breakfast and brunch	161.73	118.06	167.74	179.42	160.08
At fast food, take-out, delivery, concession stands, buffet, and cafeteria (other than employer and school cafeteria)	77.12	70.35	78.05	108.16	74.23
At full-service restaurants	79.64	41.84	84.85	60.79	81.39
At vending machines, mobile vendors	1.35	1.19	1.37	3.79	1.12
At employer and school cafeterias	3.62	4.68	3.48	6.68	3.34
Board (including at school)	**39.03**	**25.80**	**40.85**	**29.31**	**39.95**
Catered affairs	**54.02**	**19.89**	**58.72**	**29.09**	**56.39**
Food on trips	**216.06**	**81.12**	**234.63**	**122.31**	**224.95**
School lunches	**58.46**	**48.33**	**59.86**	**45.88**	**59.65**
Meals as pay	**18.97**	**16.44**	**19.32**	**19.02**	**18.96**
ALCOHOLIC BEVERAGES	**371.81**	**211.14**	**393.93**	**284.79**	**379.92**
At home	**226.64**	**122.43**	**240.98**	**202.90**	**228.84**
Beer and ale	112.01	74.07	117.23	147.78	108.69
Whiskey	13.49	11.24	13.79	8.80	13.92
Wine	80.04	22.71	87.94	34.03	84.32
Other alcoholic beverages	21.10	14.42	22.02	12.29	21.91
Away from home	**145.17**	**88.71**	**152.94**	**81.89**	**151.08**
Beer and ale	62.46	48.49	64.39	36.41	64.88
At fast food, take-out, delivery, concession stands, buffet, and cafeteria	13.37	6.24	14.35	11.95	13.50
At full-service restaurants	45.05	16.69	48.95	24.39	46.97
At vending machines, mobile vendors	0.40	0.54	0.38	–	0.44
At catered affairs	3.64	25.02	0.70	0.07	3.97
Wine	17.79	8.51	19.06	10.88	18.43
At fast food, take-out, delivery, concession stands, buffet and cafeteria	1.23	0.33	1.36	1.86	1.18
At full-service restaurants	16.16	5.53	17.63	9.01	16.83
At catered affairs	0.39	2.65	0.07	0.01	0.42
Other alcoholic beverages	64.92	31.70	69.50	34.59	67.78
At fast food, take-out, delivery, concession stands, buffet, and cafeteria	3.04	1.02	3.32	3.00	3.05
At full-service restaurants	25.74	8.02	28.18	14.40	26.80
At machines and mobile vendors	0.29	0.56	0.26	0.38	0.29
At catered affairs	1.60	11.02	0.31	0.03	1.75
Alcoholic beverages purchased on trips	34.24	11.08	37.43	16.77	35.90

Note: Other races include Asians, Native Americans, and Pacific Islanders. (–) means sample is too small to make a reliable estimate.
Source: Bureau of Labor Statistics, unpublished tables from the 2000 Consumer Expenditure Survey

Table 5.17 Food and Alcohol: Indexed spending by race and Hispanic origin, 2000

(indexed average annual spending of consumer units (CU) on food and alcoholic beverages, by race and Hispanic origin of consumer unit reference person, 2000; index definition: an index of 100 is the average for all consumer units; an index of 132 means that spending by consumer units in that group is 32 percent above the average for all consumer units; an index of 68 indicates spending that is 32 percent below the average for all consumer units)

	total consumer units	race		Hispanic origin	
		black	white and other	Hispanic	non-Hispanic
Average spending of CU, total	$38,045	$28,152	$39,406	$32,735	$38,549
Average spending of CU, index	100	74	104	86	101
Food, spending index	100	79	103	104	100
Alcoholic beverages, spending index	100	57	106	77	102
FOOD AT HOME	100	89	102	116	99
Cereals and bakery products	100	87	102	108	99
Cereals and cereal products	100	101	100	128	97
Flour	100	122	97	226	88
Prepared flour mixes	100	88	102	91	101
Ready-to-eat and cooked cereals	100	98	100	107	99
Rice	100	140	94	184	92
Pasta, cornmeal, and other cereal products	100	86	102	145	96
Bakery products	100	79	103	98	100
Bread	100	86	102	115	99
White bread	100	95	101	125	98
Bread, other than white	100	79	103	108	99
Crackers and cookies	100	76	103	80	102
Cookies	100	79	103	84	101
Crackers	100	70	104	71	103
Frozen and refrigerated bakery products	100	85	102	67	103
Other bakery products	100	75	103	102	100
Biscuits and rolls	100	63	105	64	103
Cakes and cupcakes	100	89	102	124	98
Bread and cracker products	100	52	107	91	101
Sweetrolls, coffee cakes, doughnuts	100	65	105	131	97
Pies, tarts, turnovers	100	92	101	101	100
Meats, poultry, fish, and eggs	100	114	98	130	97
Beef	100	99	100	137	97
Ground beef	100	104	99	131	97
Roast	100	78	103	132	97
Chuck roast	100	86	102	159	95
Round roast	100	66	105	117	98
Other roast	100	79	103	121	98
Steak	100	99	100	146	96
Round steak	100	95	101	206	90
Sirloin steak	100	90	101	158	95
Other steak	100	106	99	121	98
Other beef	100	119	97	125	98
Pork	100	119	97	128	97
Bacon	100	126	96	107	99
Pork chops	100	133	95	151	95
Ham	100	97	100	131	97
Ham, not canned	100	99	100	132	97
Canned ham	100	69	105	110	99
Sausage	100	133	95	100	100
Other pork	100	112	98	132	97
Other meats	100	106	99	115	99
Frankfurters	100	104	99	124	98

		race		Hispanic origin	
	total consumer units	black	white and other	Hispanic	non-Hispanic
Lunch meats (cold cuts)	100	90	101	98	100
Bologna, liverwurst, salami	100	116	98	119	98
Other lunch meats	100	76	103	87	101
Lamb, organ meats, and others	100	199	86	199	91
Lamb and organ meats	100	135	95	232	88
Mutton, goat, and game	100	488	47	51	105
Poultry	100	128	96	131	97
Fresh and frozen chicken	100	124	97	144	96
Fresh and frozen whole chicken	100	135	95	201	91
Fresh and frozen chicken parts	100	120	97	123	98
Other poultry	100	140	94	81	102
Fish and seafood	100	126	96	124	98
Canned fish and seafood	100	91	101	104	100
Fresh fish and shellfish	100	146	94	135	97
Frozen fish and shellfish	100	97	100	108	99
Eggs	100	126	96	158	95
Dairy products	**100**	**75**	**103**	**111**	**99**
Fresh milk and cream	100	77	103	130	97
Fresh milk, all types	100	80	103	131	97
Cream	100	49	107	116	99
Other dairy products	100	74	104	98	100
Butter	100	94	101	75	102
Cheese	100	66	105	106	99
Ice cream and related products	100	81	103	92	101
Miscellaneous dairy products	100	74	104	94	101
Fruits and vegetables	**100**	**87**	**102**	**129**	**97**
Fresh fruits	100	81	103	140	96
Apples	100	88	102	126	98
Bananas	100	95	101	159	95
Oranges	100	98	100	147	96
Citrus fruits, excl. oranges	100	75	103	178	93
Other fresh fruits	100	67	105	127	97
Fresh vegetables	100	81	103	144	96
Potatoes	100	89	101	125	98
Lettuce	100	88	102	126	98
Tomatoes	100	87	102	187	92
Other fresh vegetables	100	74	104	139	96
Processed fruits	100	102	100	109	99
Frozen fruits and fruit juices	100	78	103	80	102
Frozen orange juice	100	81	103	91	101
Frozen fruits	100	64	105	46	105
Frozen fruit juices	100	88	102	95	101
Canned fruits	100	80	103	92	101
Dried fruits	100	66	105	78	102
Fresh fruit juice	100	105	99	107	99
Canned and bottled fruit juice	100	117	98	125	98
Processed vegetables	100	91	101	106	99
Frozen vegetables	100	93	101	67	103
Canned and dried vegetables and juices	100	89	101	124	98
Canned beans	100	96	101	107	99
Canned corn	100	117	98	128	97
Canned miscellaneous vegetables	100	71	104	89	101
Dried peas	100	147	94	76	103
Dried beans	100	96	101	355	76

	total consumer units	race black	white and other	Hispanic origin Hispanic	non-Hispanic
Dried miscellaneous vegetables	100	111	98	132	97
Dried processed vegetables	100	61	105	383	73
Frozen vegetable juices	100	159	90	134	97
Fresh and canned vegetable juices	100	75	104	132	97
Other food at home	**100**	**75**	**104**	**101**	**100**
Sugar and other sweets	100	76	103	94	101
Candy and chewing gum	100	58	106	77	102
Sugar	100	128	96	174	93
Artificial sweeteners	100	138	95	78	102
Jams, preserves, other sweets	100	89	102	94	101
Fats and oils	100	100	100	120	98
Margarine	100	103	100	93	101
Fats and oils	100	128	96	179	93
Salad dressings	100	89	102	109	99
Nondairy cream and imitation milk	100	67	105	81	102
Peanut butter	100	95	101	83	102
Miscellaneous foods	100	72	104	93	101
Frozen prepared foods	100	73	104	77	102
Frozen meals	100	98	100	59	104
Other frozen prepared foods	100	62	105	85	101
Canned and packaged soups	100	82	103	96	100
Potato chips, nuts, and other snacks	100	61	105	74	102
Potato chips and other snacks	100	60	106	77	102
Nuts	100	68	104	64	103
Condiments and seasonings	100	78	103	90	101
Salt, spices, and other seasonings	100	110	99	124	98
Olives, pickles, relishes	100	66	105	78	102
Sauces and gravies	100	70	104	88	101
Baking needs and miscellaneous products	100	64	105	62	103
Other canned/packaged prepared foods	100	73	104	117	98
Prepared salads	100	72	104	73	103
Prepared desserts	100	77	103	104	100
Baby food	100	86	102	108	99
Miscellaneous prepared foods	100	67	105	134	97
Vitamin supplements	100	21	114	93	100
Nonalcoholic beverages	100	74	104	117	98
Cola	100	71	104	129	97
Other carbonated drinks	100	68	104	108	99
Coffee	100	58	106	107	99
Roasted coffee	100	61	105	101	100
Instant and freeze-dried coffee	100	53	106	117	98
Noncarbonated fruit-flavored drinks, incl. nonfrozen lemonade	100	107	99	145	96
Tea	100	86	102	93	101
Nonalcoholic beer	100	107	100	–	111
Other nonalcoholic beverages and ice	100	86	102	109	99
Food prepared by CU on trips	100	42	108	85	101
FOOD AWAY FROM HOME	**100**	**66**	**105**	**87**	**101**
Meals at restaurants, carry-outs, other	**100**	**69**	**104**	**93**	**101**
Lunch	100	81	103	101	100
At fast food, take-out, delivery, concession stands, buffet, and cafeteria (other than employer and school cafeteria)	100	90	101	115	99
At full-service restaurants	100	49	107	70	103
At vending machines, mobile vendors	100	113	98	283	83
At employer and school cafeterias	100	119	97	102	100

	total consumer units	race		Hispanic origin	
		black	white and other	Hispanic	non-Hispanic
Dinner	100	55	106	78	102
At fast food, take-out, delivery, concession stands, buffet, and cafeteria (other than employer and school cafeteria)	100	77	103	126	98
At full-service restaurants	100	45	108	57	104
At vending machines, mobile vendors	100	240	81	246	87
At employer and school cafeterias	100	110	99	108	100
Snacks and nonalcoholic beverages	100	77	103	98	100
At fast food, take-out, delivery, concession stands, buffet, and cafeteria (other than employer and school cafeteria)	100	71	104	97	100
At full-service restaurants	100	72	104	99	100
At vending machines, mobile vendors	100	98	100	106	99
At employer and school cafeterias	100	112	98	93	101
Breakfast and brunch	100	73	104	111	99
At fast food, take-out, delivery, concession stands, buffet, and cafeteria (other than employer and school cafeteria)	100	91	101	140	96
At full-service restaurants	100	53	107	76	102
At vending machines, mobile vendors	100	88	101	281	83
At employer and school cafeterias	100	129	96	185	92
Board (including at school)	**100**	**66**	**105**	**75**	**102**
Catered affairs	**100**	**37**	**109**	**54**	**104**
Food on trips	**100**	**38**	**109**	**57**	**104**
School lunches	**100**	**83**	**102**	**78**	**102**
Meals as pay	**100**	**87**	**102**	**100**	**100**
ALCOHOLIC BEVERAGES	**100**	**57**	**106**	**77**	**102**
At home	**100**	**54**	**106**	**90**	**101**
Beer and ale	100	66	105	132	97
Whiskey	100	83	102	65	103
Wine	100	28	110	43	105
Other alcoholic beverages	100	68	104	58	104
Away from home	**100**	**61**	**105**	**56**	**104**
Beer and ale	100	78	103	58	104
At fast food, take-out, delivery, concession stands, buffet, and cafeteria	100	47	107	89	101
At full-service restaurants	100	37	109	54	104
At vending machines, mobile vendors	100	135	95	–	110
At catered affairs	100	687	19	2	109
Wine	100	48	107	61	104
At fast food, take-out, delivery, concession stands, buffet and cafeteria	100	27	111	151	96
At full-service restaurants	100	34	109	56	104
At catered affairs	100	679	18	3	108
Other alcoholic beverages	100	49	107	53	104
At fast food, take-out, delivery, concession stands, buffet, and cafeteria	100	34	109	99	100
At full-service restaurants	100	31	109	56	104
At machines and mobile vendors	100	193	90	131	100
At catered affairs	100	689	19	2	109
Alcoholic beverages purchased on trips	100	32	109	49	105

Note: Other races include Asians, Native Americans, and Pacific Islanders. (–) means sample is too small to make a reliable estimate.
Source: Calculations by New Strategist based on the 2000 Consumer Expenditure Survey

Table 5.18 Food and Alcohol: Indexed per capita spending by race and Hispanic origin, 2000

(indexed average annual per capita spending of consumer units (CU) on food and alcoholic beverages, by race and Hispanic origin of consumer unit reference person, 2000; index definition: an index of 100 is the average for all consumer units; an index of 132 means that spending by consumer units in that group is 32 percent above the average for all consumer units; an index of 68 indicates spending that is 32 percent below the average for all consumer units)

	total consumer units	race black	race white and other	Hispanic origin Hispanic	Hispanic origin non-Hispanic
Per capita spending of CU, total	$15,218	$10,427	$15,762	$9,628	$16,062
Per capita spending of CU, index	100	69	104	63	106
Food, per capita spending index	100	74	103	76	104
Alcoholic beverages, per capita spending index	100	53	106	56	106
FOOD AT HOME	**100**	**82**	**102**	**85**	**103**
Cereals and bakery products	**100**	**80**	**102**	**80**	**103**
Cereals and cereal products	100	94	100	94	101
Flour	100	113	97	166	92
Prepared flour mixes	100	82	102	67	105
Ready-to-eat and cooked cereals	100	91	100	79	103
Rice	100	130	94	135	96
Pasta, cornmeal, and other cereal products	100	80	102	106	100
Bakery products	100	73	103	72	104
Bread	100	79	102	85	103
White bread	100	88	101	92	102
Bread, other than white	100	73	103	79	103
Crackers and cookies	100	70	103	59	106
Cookies	100	73	103	62	106
Crackers	100	65	104	52	107
Frozen and refrigerated bakery products	100	79	102	49	107
Other bakery products	100	69	103	75	104
Biscuits and rolls	100	58	105	47	108
Cakes and cupcakes	100	82	102	91	102
Bread and cracker products	100	48	107	67	105
Sweetrolls, coffee cakes, doughnuts	100	60	105	96	101
Pies, tarts, turnovers	100	85	101	75	104
Meats, poultry, fish, and eggs	**100**	**106**	**98**	**96**	**101**
Beef	100	92	100	101	101
Ground beef	100	97	99	96	101
Roast	100	72	103	97	101
Chuck roast	100	80	102	117	98
Round roast	100	61	105	86	103
Other roast	100	73	103	89	102
Steak	100	92	100	108	100
Round steak	100	88	101	151	94
Sirloin steak	100	83	101	117	99
Other steak	100	98	99	89	102
Other beef	100	110	97	92	102
Pork	100	110	97	94	102
Bacon	100	117	96	79	103
Pork chops	100	123	95	111	99
Ham	100	90	100	96	101
Ham, not canned	100	91	100	97	101
Canned ham	100	64	105	81	103
Sausage	100	123	95	73	104
Other pork	100	104	98	97	101
Other meats	100	98	99	85	103
Frankfurters	100	96	99	91	102

	total consumer units	race		Hispanic origin	
		black	white and other	Hispanic	non-Hispanic
Lunch meats (cold cuts)	100	83	101	72	104
Bologna, liverwurst, salami	100	107	98	87	102
Other lunch meats	100	71	103	64	105
Lamb, organ meats, and others	100	185	86	146	95
Lamb and organ meats	100	125	95	170	91
Mutton, goat, and game	100	451	47	38	109
Poultry	100	118	96	96	101
Fresh and frozen chicken	100	115	97	106	100
Fresh and frozen whole chicken	100	125	95	148	94
Fresh and frozen chicken parts	100	111	97	90	102
Other poultry	100	130	94	60	106
Fish and seafood	100	117	96	91	102
Canned fish and seafood	100	84	101	77	104
Fresh fish and shellfish	100	136	94	99	101
Frozen fish and shellfish	100	90	100	79	103
Eggs	100	117	96	116	99
Dairy products	**100**	**70**	**103**	**81**	**103**
Fresh milk and cream	100	72	103	95	101
Fresh milk, all types	100	74	103	96	101
Cream	100	46	107	86	103
Other dairy products	100	68	104	72	104
Butter	100	87	101	55	107
Cheese	100	61	105	78	104
Ice cream and related products	100	75	103	67	105
Miscellaneous dairy products	100	68	104	69	105
Fruits and vegetables	**100**	**81**	**102**	**95**	**101**
Fresh fruits	100	75	103	103	100
Apples	100	81	102	93	102
Bananas	100	88	101	117	98
Oranges	100	91	100	108	100
Citrus fruits, excl. oranges	100	70	103	131	97
Other fresh fruits	100	62	105	93	102
Fresh vegetables	100	75	103	106	100
Potatoes	100	83	101	92	102
Lettuce	100	81	102	92	102
Tomatoes	100	80	102	138	96
Other fresh vegetables	100	69	104	102	100
Processed fruits	100	95	100	80	103
Frozen fruits and fruit juices	100	73	103	59	106
Frozen orange juice	100	75	103	67	105
Frozen fruits	100	59	105	34	109
Frozen fruit juices	100	82	102	70	105
Canned fruits	100	74	103	67	105
Dried fruits	100	61	105	57	106
Fresh fruit juice	100	97	99	79	103
Canned and bottled fruit juice	100	108	98	92	102
Processed vegetables	100	84	101	78	104
Frozen vegetables	100	87	101	49	107
Canned and dried vegetables and juices	100	83	101	91	102
Canned beans	100	89	101	79	104
Canned corn	100	108	98	94	101
Canned miscellaneous vegetables	100	66	104	66	105
Dried peas	100	136	94	56	107
Dried beans	100	89	101	261	79

	total consumer units	race		Hispanic origin	
		black	white and other	Hispanic	non-Hispanic
Dried miscellaneous vegetables	100	103	98	97	101
Dried processed vegetables	100	56	105	282	76
Frozen vegetable juices	100	147	90	99	101
Fresh and canned vegetable juices	100	69	104	97	101
Other food at home	**100**	**69**	**104**	**75**	**104**
Sugar and other sweets	100	70	103	69	105
Candy and chewing gum	100	53	106	57	106
Sugar	100	118	96	128	97
Artificial sweeteners	100	128	95	57	106
Jams, preserves, other sweets	100	82	102	69	105
Fats and oils	100	93	100	88	102
Margarine	100	95	100	69	105
Fats and oils	100	119	96	132	96
Salad dressings	100	82	102	80	103
Nondairy cream and imitation milk	100	62	105	59	106
Peanut butter	100	88	101	61	106
Miscellaneous foods	100	67	104	68	105
Frozen prepared foods	100	68	104	57	106
Frozen meals	100	90	100	44	108
Other frozen prepared foods	100	57	105	63	106
Canned and packaged soups	100	76	103	70	105
Potato chips, nuts, and other snacks	100	57	105	54	107
Potato chips and other snacks	100	55	106	56	106
Nuts	100	63	104	47	108
Condiments and seasonings	100	72	103	66	105
Salt, spices, and other seasonings	100	102	99	91	102
Olives, pickles, relishes	100	61	105	57	106
Sauces and gravies	100	65	104	65	105
Baking needs and miscellaneous products	100	59	105	46	108
Other canned/packaged prepared foods	100	68	104	86	103
Prepared salads	100	67	104	53	107
Prepared desserts	100	71	103	76	104
Baby food	100	79	102	79	103
Miscellaneous prepared foods	100	62	105	98	101
Vitamin supplements	100	20	114	68	104
Nonalcoholic beverages	100	69	104	86	103
Cola	100	66	104	95	101
Other carbonated drinks	100	63	104	79	103
Coffee	100	54	106	79	103
Roasted coffee	100	56	105	74	104
Instant and freeze-dried coffee	100	49	106	86	102
Noncarbonated fruit-flavored drinks, incl. nonfrozen lemonade	100	99	99	107	100
Tea	100	80	102	69	105
Nonalcoholic beer	100	99	100	–	116
Other nonalcoholic beverages and ice	100	79	102	80	103
Food prepared by CU on trips	100	39	108	63	106
FOOD AWAY FROM HOME	**100**	**61**	**105**	**64**	**105**
Meals at restaurants, carry-outs, other	**100**	**64**	**104**	**68**	**105**
Lunch	100	75	103	74	104
At fast food, take-out, delivery, concession stands, buffet, and cafeteria (other than employer and school cafeteria)	100	83	101	85	103
At full-service restaurants	100	45	107	52	107
At vending machines, mobile vendors	100	105	98	208	87
At employer and school cafeterias	100	110	97	75	104

	total consumer units	race		Hispanic origin	
		black	white and other	Hispanic	non-Hispanic
Dinner	100	51	106	57	106
At fast food, take-out, delivery, concession stands, buffet, and cafeteria (other than employer and school cafeteria)	100	71	103	93	102
At full-service restaurants	100	42	108	42	108
At vending machines, mobile vendors	100	222	81	181	91
At employer and school cafeterias	100	102	99	79	104
Snacks and nonalcoholic beverages	100	71	103	72	104
At fast food, take-out, delivery, concession stands, buffet, and cafeteria (other than employer and school cafeteria)	100	65	104	71	104
At full-service restaurants	100	67	104	73	104
At vending machines, mobile vendors	100	90	100	78	104
At employer and school cafeterias	100	104	98	68	105
Breakfast and brunch	100	68	104	82	103
At fast food, take-out, delivery, concession stands, buffet, and cafeteria (other than employer and school cafeteria)	100	84	101	103	100
At full-service restaurants	100	49	107	56	106
At vending machines, mobile vendors	100	82	101	206	86
At employer and school cafeterias	100	120	96	136	96
Board (including at school)	**100**	**61**	**105**	**55**	**107**
Catered affairs	**100**	**34**	**109**	**40**	**109**
Food on trips	**100**	**35**	**109**	**42**	**108**
School lunches	**100**	**77**	**102**	**58**	**106**
Meals as pay	**100**	**80**	**102**	**74**	**104**
ALCOHOLIC BEVERAGES	**100**	**53**	**106**	**56**	**106**
At home	**100**	**50**	**106**	**66**	**105**
Beer and ale	100	61	105	97	101
Whiskey	100	77	102	48	107
Wine	100	26	110	31	110
Other alcoholic beverages	100	63	104	43	108
Away from home	**100**	**57**	**105**	**41**	**108**
Beer and ale	100	72	103	43	108
At fast food, take-out, delivery, concession stands, buffet, and cafeteria	100	43	107	66	105
At full-service restaurants	100	34	109	40	109
At vending machines, mobile vendors	100	125	95	–	115
At catered affairs	100	636	19	1	114
Wine	100	44	107	45	108
At fast food, take-out, delivery, concession stands, buffet and cafeteria	100	25	111	111	100
At full-service restaurants	100	32	109	41	108
At catered affairs	100	629	18	2	112
Other alcoholic beverages	100	45	107	39	109
At fast food, take-out, delivery, concession stands, buffet, and cafeteria	100	31	109	73	105
At full-service restaurants	100	29	109	41	108
At machines and mobile vendors	100	179	90	96	104
At catered affairs	100	638	19	1	114
Alcoholic beverages purchased on trips	100	30	109	36	109

Note: Per capita indexes account for household size and show how much each person in a particular household demographic segment spends relative to a person in the average household. Other races include Asians, Native Americans, and Pacific Islanders. (–) means sample is too small to make a reliable estimate.
Source: Calculations by New Strategist based on the 2000 Consumer Expenditure Survey

Table 5.19 Food and Alcohol: Total spending by race and Hispanic origin, 2000

(total annual spending on food and alcoholic beverages, by consumer unit race and Hispanic origin groups, 2000; numbers in thousands)

	total consumer units	race		Hispanic origin	
		black	white and other	Hispanic	non-Hispanic
Total spending of all consumer units	$4,160,831,424	$372,454,135	$3,788,393,849	$310,098,181	$3,850,804,816
Food, total spending	564,101,862	54,174,866	509,933,721	50,790,437	513,378,242
Alcoholic beverages, total spending	40,663,744	2,793,382	37,871,248	2,697,816	37,951,728
FOOD AT HOME	**$330,397,707**	**$35,596,373**	**$294,804,111**	**$33,121,397**	**$297,369,454**
Cereals and bakery products	**49,579,342**	**5,198,993**	**44,380,685**	**4,647,075**	**44,939,314**
Cereals and cereal products	17,104,999	2,099,733	15,005,063	1,903,505	15,209,860
Flour	872,749	128,993	743,139	170,893	703,254
Prepared flour mixes	1,460,049	155,585	1,304,579	115,097	1,345,572
Ready-to-eat and cooked cereals	9,501,805	1,126,005	8,376,417	883,831	8,619,853
Rice	2,138,125	361,973	1,775,650	341,217	1,800,090
Pasta, cornmeal, and other cereal products	3,132,271	327,046	2,805,278	392,466	2,742,090
Bakery products	32,474,343	3,099,260	29,375,622	2,743,570	29,729,453
Bread	9,191,203	950,972	8,240,864	917,460	8,276,218
White bread	4,005,020	458,155	3,546,494	433,011	3,573,208
Bread, other than white	5,186,183	492,818	4,693,408	484,449	4,703,010
Crackers and cookies	7,768,338	712,568	7,056,456	536,172	7,229,329
Cookies	5,217,900	495,728	4,722,249	380,057	4,835,869
Crackers	2,550,438	216,840	2,334,206	156,210	2,393,460
Frozen and refrigerated bakery products	2,682,773	276,110	2,406,309	156,020	2,525,320
Other bakery products	12,832,030	1,159,742	11,672,955	1,133,823	11,698,586
Biscuits and rolls	4,213,911	321,224	3,892,587	234,836	3,975,781
Cakes and cupcakes	4,201,880	452,863	3,749,343	451,483	3,752,019
Bread and cracker products	482,308	30,429	451,844	38,176	444,528
Sweetrolls, coffee cakes, doughnuts	2,480,444	194,216	2,287,099	281,916	2,200,665
Pies, tarts, turnovers	1,452,394	160,877	1,292,081	127,507	1,325,593
Meats, poultry, fish, and eggs	**86,993,793**	**12,021,307**	**74,971,478**	**9,813,081**	**77,227,052**
Beef	26,050,126	3,117,782	22,932,520	3,087,914	22,979,616
Ground beef	9,598,048	1,212,530	8,386,031	1,088,732	8,514,965
Roast	4,357,181	410,262	3,946,424	499,417	3,859,904
Chuck roast	1,457,862	152,542	1,305,540	200,259	1,258,664
Round roast	1,253,346	100,019	1,152,683	126,559	1,126,804
Other roast	1,645,973	157,702	1,488,201	172,598	1,473,437
Steak	10,337,369	1,241,503	9,095,522	1,310,021	9,035,412
Round steak	1,674,409	192,364	1,482,433	298,305	1,379,536
Sirloin steak	3,265,699	355,093	2,911,028	448,262	2,821,007
Other steak	5,397,261	694,046	4,703,022	563,454	4,834,870
Other beef	1,758,621	253,487	1,505,505	189,649	1,569,335
Pork	18,257,727	2,635,151	15,623,224	2,017,275	16,249,757
Bacon	2,849,010	433,944	2,414,961	264,107	2,585,257
Pork chops	4,437,019	713,759	3,722,425	579,274	3,860,903
Ham	3,965,647	466,225	3,499,387	450,536	3,517,268
Ham, not canned	3,775,349	450,349	3,325,379	432,442	3,345,450
Canned ham	190,299	15,876	174,969	18,188	171,818
Sausage	2,760,423	443,734	2,316,902	238,341	2,522,324
Other pork	4,245,627	577,490	3,668,588	484,923	3,764,006
Other meats	10,995,758	1,406,878	9,588,704	1,098,015	9,900,494
Frankfurters	2,261,710	284,048	1,977,538	242,225	2,019,857

	total consumer units	race		Hispanic origin	
		black	white and other	Hispanic	non-Hispanic
Lunch meats (cold cuts)	$7,435,862	$809,676	$6,625,762	$632,133	$6,803,780
Bologna, liverwurst, salami	2,595,279	362,767	2,232,301	266,475	2,329,528
Other lunch meats	4,840,583	446,909	4,394,422	365,658	4,474,252
Lamb, organ meats, and others	1,298,186	313,154	985,404	223,752	1,076,857
Lamb and organ meats	1,061,954	173,842	888,306	213,237	851,097
Mutton, goat, and game	236,233	139,312	97,098	10,515	225,760
Poultry	15,875,714	2,450,064	13,425,532	1,800,249	14,084,055
Fresh and frozen chicken	12,514,866	1,880,248	10,634,675	1,564,182	10,961,369
Fresh and frozen whole chicken	3,417,719	558,703	2,859,114	594,904	2,828,998
Fresh and frozen chicken parts	9,097,147	1,321,545	7,775,561	969,277	8,131,372
Other poultry	3,360,848	569,816	2,790,857	236,067	3,123,685
Fish and seafood	12,045,681	1,837,118	10,207,827	1,292,686	10,757,585
Canned fish and seafood	1,713,781	187,866	1,525,694	154,694	1,559,345
Fresh fish and shellfish	7,307,903	1,294,688	6,012,408	855,033	6,457,148
Frozen fish and shellfish	3,023,998	354,696	2,669,724	282,864	2,742,090
Eggs	3,768,787	574,314	3,194,633	516,942	3,255,545
Dairy products	**35,503,809**	**3,235,793**	**32,269,345**	**3,402,512**	**32,108,928**
Fresh milk and cream	14,351,138	1,345,359	13,006,375	1,614,010	12,744,477
Fresh milk, all types	13,081,387	1,269,815	11,811,392	1,485,935	11,602,688
Cream	1,269,751	75,543	1,194,983	128,075	1,142,787
Other dairy products	21,152,671	1,890,435	19,262,971	1,788,502	19,363,453
Butter	1,859,239	211,548	1,647,788	121,349	1,737,157
Cheese	10,494,857	842,619	9,652,155	964,162	9,531,885
Ice cream and related products	6,185,798	603,685	5,582,676	490,607	5,694,957
Miscellaneous dairy products	2,612,778	232,451	2,380,352	212,385	2,400,453
Fruits and vegetables	**56,961,615**	**6,003,509**	**50,959,340**	**6,351,362**	**50,639,265**
Fresh fruits	17,845,413	1,739,480	16,105,832	2,162,118	15,695,345
Apples	3,225,233	341,731	2,883,149	351,543	2,874,949
Bananas	3,466,934	398,885	3,067,732	476,681	2,993,823
Oranges	2,070,317	246,078	1,823,719	264,486	1,807,082
Citrus fruits, excl. oranges	1,565,042	142,884	1,421,866	241,751	1,325,593
Other fresh fruits	7,517,888	609,903	6,908,405	827,751	6,693,897
Fresh vegetables	17,358,730	1,702,304	15,656,872	2,158,802	15,213,856
Potatoes	3,069,932	331,544	2,737,982	333,260	2,737,096
Lettuce	2,269,365	241,315	2,027,529	246,772	2,023,852
Tomatoes	3,229,608	339,614	2,889,878	524,141	2,710,124
Other fresh vegetables	8,790,919	789,831	8,001,483	1,054,629	7,741,785
Processed fruits	12,578,299	1,555,716	11,022,107	1,188,388	11,391,912
Frozen fruits and fruit juices	1,571,604	148,970	1,422,828	109,413	1,461,449
Frozen orange juice	754,632	73,691	681,611	59,206	695,262
Frozen fruits	395,909	30,561	365,321	15,820	379,597
Frozen fruit juices	419,969	44,717	375,896	34,387	385,591
Canned fruits	1,693,001	163,126	1,529,540	134,611	1,558,346
Dried fruits	601,519	48,025	553,749	40,544	561,404
Fresh fruit juice	2,563,562	325,723	2,238,069	237,867	2,325,532
Canned and bottled fruit juice	6,147,519	869,608	5,277,921	666,047	5,485,180
Processed vegetables	9,180,266	1,006,009	8,173,568	842,055	8,339,151
Frozen vegetables	2,889,476	326,781	2,563,012	167,198	2,721,113
Canned and dried vegetables and juices	6,290,790	679,361	5,611,517	674,857	5,618,039
Canned beans	1,385,680	160,215	1,225,747	128,738	1,257,665
Canned corn	743,696	105,179	638,350	82,226	661,298
Canned miscellaneous vegetables	1,963,138	168,021	1,795,839	151,473	1,812,077
Dried peas	37,185	6,615	30,764	2,463	34,963
Dried beans	276,699	32,017	245,149	85,068	192,795

	total consumer units	race		Hispanic origin	
		black	white and other	Hispanic	non-Hispanic
Dried miscellaneous vegetables	$789,630	$106,369	$682,573	$90,183	$699,258
Dried processed vegetables	44,840	3,308	41,339	14,873	29,968
Frozen vegetable juices	31,716	6,086	24,996	3,694	27,970
Fresh and canned vegetable juices	1,017,113	91,684	925,799	116,328	902,043
Other food at home	**101,358,055**	**9,136,770**	**92,223,263**	**8,907,462**	**92,454,894**
Sugar and other sweets	12,811,250	1,176,809	11,635,461	1,039,472	11,770,510
Candy and chewing gum	8,344,702	582,120	7,763,063	556,065	7,784,739
Sugar	1,837,366	284,048	1,553,574	276,517	1,563,341
Artificial sweeteners	458,248	76,734	380,703	30,977	426,547
Jams, preserves, other sweets	2,172,029	233,774	1,938,122	176,008	1,995,882
Fats and oils	9,087,304	1,101,927	7,985,139	942,564	8,147,355
Margarine	1,269,751	157,702	1,111,344	102,593	1,166,762
Fats and oils	2,553,719	395,577	2,157,314	396,919	2,159,708
Salad dressings	2,972,595	319,769	2,652,420	279,738	2,693,142
Nondairy cream and imitation milk	1,000,708	80,571	920,031	69,911	930,013
Peanut butter	1,291,624	148,176	1,143,069	93,404	1,197,729
Miscellaneous foods	47,795,566	4,177,902	43,618,318	3,839,217	43,950,363
Frozen prepared foods	9,864,903	872,783	8,991,694	660,173	9,200,237
Frozen meals	3,116,960	367,926	2,749,518	160,567	2,953,866
Other frozen prepared foods	6,747,944	504,857	6,243,137	499,606	6,246,372
Canned and packaged soups	3,886,903	384,728	3,502,271	322,177	3,564,218
Potato chips, nuts, and other snacks	10,116,448	752,126	9,364,705	646,627	9,464,957
Potato chips and other snacks	7,838,333	564,656	7,273,725	519,594	7,315,238
Nuts	2,278,115	187,469	2,090,980	127,033	2,149,719
Condiments and seasonings	9,253,542	874,371	8,379,301	724,779	8,526,952
Salt, spices, and other seasonings	2,258,429	300,321	1,958,311	242,888	2,016,860
Olives, pickles, relishes	1,068,516	85,201	983,482	71,805	995,943
Sauces and gravies	4,071,733	345,038	3,727,231	310,146	3,761,009
Baking needs and miscellaneous products	1,854,864	143,810	1,710,277	99,940	1,753,140
Other canned/packaged prepared foods	14,673,770	1,294,026	13,380,348	1,485,461	13,193,001
Prepared salads	2,028,758	176,488	1,851,599	127,791	1,899,984
Prepared desserts	1,018,207	94,859	923,877	91,320	927,016
Baby food	3,528,179	365,413	3,162,907	330,134	3,198,606
Miscellaneous prepared foods	8,083,315	656,870	7,426,583	934,985	7,152,410
Vitamin supplements	15,311	397	15,382	1,231	13,985
Nonalcoholic beverages	27,295,816	2,457,076	24,839,878	2,763,653	24,540,959
Cola	9,513,835	817,482	8,696,553	1,059,650	8,459,024
Other carbonated drinks	5,182,902	427,594	4,755,897	483,028	4,701,012
Coffee	4,577,009	321,621	4,255,024	423,727	4,153,593
Roasted coffee	3,007,593	220,412	2,787,012	263,918	2,743,089
Instant and freeze-dried coffee	1,569,416	101,077	1,468,012	159,715	1,410,503
Noncarbonated fruit-flavored drinks, incl. nonfrozen lemonade	2,123,907	275,846	1,847,753	266,760	1,859,027
Tea	1,714,875	179,399	1,535,308	138,590	1,575,328
Nonalcoholic beer	29,529	3,837	25,957	–	29,968
Other nonalcoholic beverages and ice	4,154,852	431,430	3,723,386	391,993	3,763,007
Food prepared by CU on trips	4,368,118	223,058	4,145,427	322,461	4,045,707
FOOD AWAY FROM HOME	**233,704,155**	**18,578,624**	**215,129,610**	**17,669,040**	**216,009,787**
Meals at restaurants, carry-outs, other	**191,428,341**	**16,044,021**	**175,389,459**	**15,342,281**	**176,061,177**
Lunch	72,499,384	7,078,447	65,421,229	6,351,362	66,148,808
At fast food, take-out, delivery, concession stands, buffet, and cafeteria (other than employer and school cafeteria)	40,247,056	4,378,204	35,868,715	4,012,384	36,245,539
At full-service restaurants	22,761,460	1,339,670	21,422,208	1,388,363	21,361,333
At vending machines, mobile vendors	713,073	97,637	616,238	174,587	541,425
At employer and school cafeterias	8,777,795	1,263,068	7,514,068	776,123	8,001,509

	total consumer units	race		Hispanic origin	
		black	white and other	Hispanic	non-Hispanic
Dinner	$76,337,072	$5,078,203	$71,261,551	$5,167,616	$71,140,511
At fast food, take-out, delivery, concession stands, buffet, and cafeteria (other than employer and school cafeteria)	22,630,220	2,101,850	20,528,134	2,470,843	20,169,598
At full-service restaurants	53,338,286	2,909,806	50,430,586	2,648,935	50,649,255
At vending machines, mobile vendors	111,554	32,414	79,794	23,777	88,906
At employer and school cafeterias	257,012	34,266	223,038	24,061	233,752
Snacks and nonalcoholic beverages	24,903,960	2,325,305	22,579,697	2,123,657	22,779,828
At fast food, take-out, delivery, concession stands, buffet, and cafeteria (other than employer and school cafeteria)	17,340,138	1,481,231	15,858,760	1,454,958	15,884,145
At full-service restaurants	2,203,745	191,703	2,013,109	188,797	2,015,861
At vending machines, mobile vendors	4,212,817	497,183	3,715,695	387,825	3,824,941
At employer and school cafeterias	1,147,260	155,320	992,134	92,172	1,054,881
Breakfast and brunch	17,687,925	1,561,934	16,126,020	1,699,646	15,991,032
At fast food, take-out, delivery, concession stands, buffet, and cafeteria (other than employer and school cafeteria)	8,434,383	930,731	7,503,493	1,024,600	7,415,132
At full-service restaurants	8,709,988	553,543	8,157,224	575,864	8,130,373
At vending machines, mobile vendors	147,645	15,744	131,708	35,903	111,881
At employer and school cafeterias	395,909	61,916	334,557	63,280	333,646
Board (including at school)	**4,268,594**	**341,334**	**3,927,196**	**277,654**	**3,990,765**
Catered affairs	**5,908,005**	**263,145**	**5,645,165**	**275,570**	**5,633,023**
Food on trips	**23,629,834**	**1,073,218**	**22,556,624**	**1,158,643**	**22,471,155**
School lunches	**6,393,595**	**639,406**	**5,754,761**	**434,621**	**5,958,677**
Meals as pay	**2,074,692**	**217,501**	**1,857,367**	**180,176**	**1,893,990**
ALCOHOLIC BEVERAGES	**40,663,744**	**2,793,382**	**37,871,248**	**2,697,816**	**37,951,728**
At home	**24,786,937**	**1,619,749**	**23,167,094**	**1,922,072**	**22,859,743**
Beer and ale	12,250,198	979,946	11,270,141	1,399,920	10,857,479
Whiskey	1,475,361	148,705	1,325,729	83,362	1,390,524
Wine	8,753,735	300,453	8,454,288	322,366	8,423,062
Other alcoholic beverages	2,307,644	190,777	2,116,937	116,423	2,188,678
Away from home	**15,876,807**	**1,173,633**	**14,703,193**	**775,744**	**15,091,986**
Beer and ale	6,831,063	641,523	6,190,261	344,912	6,481,123
At fast food, take-out, delivery, concession stands, buffet, and cafeteria	1,462,237	82,555	1,379,566	113,202	1,348,569
At full-service restaurants	4,926,983	220,809	4,705,906	231,046	4,692,021
At vending machines, mobile vendors	43,747	7,144	36,532	–	43,953
At catered affairs	398,096	331,015	67,296	663	396,579
Wine	1,945,639	112,587	1,832,371	103,066	1,841,046
At fast food, take-out, delivery, concession stands, buffet and cafeteria	134,521	4,366	130,746	17,620	117,875
At full-service restaurants	1,767,371	73,162	1,694,895	85,352	1,681,216
At catered affairs	42,653	35,060	6,730	95	41,955
Other alcoholic beverages	7,100,106	419,391	6,681,522	327,671	6,770,815
At fast food, take-out, delivery, concession stands, buffet, and cafeteria	332,476	13,495	319,175	28,419	304,677
At full-service restaurants	2,815,107	106,105	2,709,141	136,411	2,677,159
At machines and mobile vendors	31,716	7,409	24,996	3,600	28,969
At catered affairs	174,987	145,795	29,802	284	174,815
Alcoholic beverages purchased on trips	3,744,726	146,588	3,598,408	158,862	3,586,195

Note: Other races include Asians, Native Americans, and Pacific Islanders. Numbers may not add to total because of rounding. (–) means sample is too small to make a reliable estimate.
Source: Calculations by New Strategist based on the 2000 Consumer Expenditure Survey

Table 5.20 Food and Alcohol: Market shares by race and Hispanic origin, 2000

(percentage of total annual spending on food and alcoholic beverages accounted for by consumer unit race and Hispanic origin groups, 2000)

	total consumer units	race - black	race - white and other	Hispanic origin - Hispanic	Hispanic origin - non-Hispanic
Share of total consumer units	100.0%	12.1%	87.9%	8.7%	91.3%
Share of total before-tax income	100.0	8.8	91.1	6.8	93.4
Share of total spending	100.0	9.0	91.0	7.5	92.5
Share of food spending	100.0	9.6	90.4	9.0	91.0
Share of alcoholic beverages spending	100.0	6.9	93.1	6.6	93.3
FOOD AT HOME	100.0%	10.8%	89.2%	10.0%	90.0%
Cereals and bakery products	100.0	10.5	89.5	9.4	90.6
Cereals and cereal products	100.0	12.3	87.7	11.1	88.9
Flour	100.0	14.8	85.1	19.6	80.6
Prepared flour mixes	100.0	10.7	89.4	7.9	92.2
Ready-to-eat and cooked cereals	100.0	11.9	88.2	9.3	90.7
Rice	100.0	16.9	83.0	16.0	84.2
Pasta, cornmeal, and other cereal products	100.0	10.4	89.6	12.5	87.5
Bakery products	100.0	9.5	90.5	8.4	91.5
Bread	100.0	10.3	89.7	10.0	90.0
White bread	100.0	11.4	88.6	10.8	89.2
Bread, other than white	100.0	9.5	90.5	9.3	90.7
Crackers and cookies	100.0	9.2	90.8	6.9	93.1
Cookies	100.0	9.5	90.5	7.3	92.7
Crackers	100.0	8.5	91.5	6.1	93.8
Frozen and refrigerated bakery products	100.0	10.3	89.7	5.8	94.1
Other bakery products	100.0	9.0	91.0	8.8	91.2
Biscuits and rolls	100.0	7.6	92.4	5.6	94.3
Cakes and cupcakes	100.0	10.8	89.2	10.7	89.3
Bread and cracker products	100.0	6.3	93.7	7.9	92.2
Sweetrolls, coffee cakes, doughnuts	100.0	7.8	92.2	11.4	88.7
Pies, tarts, turnovers	100.0	11.1	89.0	8.8	91.3
Meats, poultry, fish, and eggs	100.0	13.8	86.2	11.3	88.8
Beef	100.0	12.0	88.0	11.9	88.2
Ground beef	100.0	12.6	87.4	11.3	88.7
Roast	100.0	9.4	90.6	11.5	88.6
Chuck roast	100.0	10.5	89.6	13.7	86.3
Round roast	100.0	8.0	92.0	10.1	89.9
Other roast	100.0	9.6	90.4	10.5	89.5
Steak	100.0	12.0	88.0	12.7	87.4
Round steak	100.0	11.5	88.5	17.8	82.4
Sirloin steak	100.0	10.9	89.1	13.7	86.4
Other steak	100.0	12.9	87.1	10.4	89.6
Other beef	100.0	14.4	85.6	10.8	89.2
Pork	100.0	14.4	85.6	11.0	89.0
Bacon	100.0	15.2	84.8	9.3	90.7
Pork chops	100.0	16.1	83.9	13.1	87.0
Ham	100.0	11.8	88.2	11.4	88.7
Ham, not canned	100.0	11.9	88.1	11.5	88.6
Canned ham	100.0	8.3	91.9	9.6	90.3
Sausage	100.0	16.1	83.9	8.6	91.4
Other pork	100.0	13.6	86.4	11.4	88.7
Other meats	100.0	12.8	87.2	10.0	90.0
Frankfurters	100.0	12.6	87.4	10.7	89.3

	total consumer units	race		Hispanic origin	
		black	white and other	Hispanic	non-Hispanic
Lunch meats (cold cuts)	100.0%	10.9%	89.1%	8.5%	91.5%
Bologna, liverwurst, salami	100.0	14.0	86.0	10.3	89.8
Other lunch meats	100.0	9.2	90.8	7.6	92.4
Lamb, organ meats, and others	100.0	24.1	75.9	17.2	83.0
Lamb and organ meats	100.0	16.4	83.6	20.1	80.1
Mutton, goat, and game	100.0	59.0	41.1	4.5	95.6
Poultry	100.0	15.4	84.6	11.3	88.7
Fresh and frozen chicken	100.0	15.0	85.0	12.5	87.6
Fresh and frozen whole chicken	100.0	16.3	83.7	17.4	82.8
Fresh and frozen chicken parts	100.0	14.5	85.5	10.7	89.4
Other poultry	100.0	17.0	83.0	7.0	92.9
Fish and seafood	100.0	15.3	84.7	10.7	89.3
Canned fish and seafood	100.0	11.0	89.0	9.0	91.0
Fresh fish and shellfish	100.0	17.7	82.3	11.7	88.4
Frozen fish and shellfish	100.0	11.7	88.3	9.4	90.7
Eggs	100.0	15.2	84.8	13.7	86.4
Dairy products	**100.0**	**9.1**	**90.9**	**9.6**	**90.4**
Fresh milk and cream	100.0	9.4	90.6	11.2	88.8
Fresh milk, all types	100.0	9.7	90.3	11.4	88.7
Cream	100.0	5.9	94.1	10.1	90.0
Other dairy products	100.0	8.9	91.1	8.5	91.5
Butter	100.0	11.4	88.6	6.5	93.4
Cheese	100.0	8.0	92.0	9.2	90.8
Ice cream and related products	100.0	9.8	90.2	7.9	92.1
Miscellaneous dairy products	100.0	8.9	91.1	8.1	91.9
Fruits and vegetables	**100.0**	**10.5**	**89.5**	**11.2**	**88.9**
Fresh fruits	100.0	9.7	90.3	12.1	88.0
Apples	100.0	10.6	89.4	10.9	89.1
Bananas	100.0	11.5	88.5	13.7	86.4
Oranges	100.0	11.9	88.1	12.8	87.3
Citrus fruits, excl. oranges	100.0	9.1	90.9	15.4	84.7
Other fresh fruits	100.0	8.1	91.9	11.0	89.0
Fresh vegetables	100.0	9.8	90.2	12.4	87.6
Potatoes	100.0	10.8	89.2	10.9	89.2
Lettuce	100.0	10.6	89.3	10.9	89.2
Tomatoes	100.0	10.5	89.5	16.2	83.9
Other fresh vegetables	100.0	9.0	91.0	12.0	88.1
Processed fruits	100.0	12.4	87.6	9.4	90.6
Frozen fruits and fruit juices	100.0	9.5	90.5	7.0	93.0
Frozen orange juice	100.0	9.8	90.3	7.8	92.1
Frozen fruits	100.0	7.7	92.3	4.0	95.9
Frozen fruit juices	100.0	10.6	89.5	8.2	91.8
Canned fruits	100.0	9.6	90.3	8.0	92.0
Dried fruits	100.0	8.0	92.1	6.7	93.3
Fresh fruit juice	100.0	12.7	87.3	9.3	90.7
Canned and bottled fruit juice	100.0	14.1	85.9	10.8	89.2
Processed vegetables	100.0	11.0	89.0	9.2	90.8
Frozen vegetables	100.0	11.3	88.7	5.8	94.2
Canned and dried vegetables and juices	100.0	10.8	89.2	10.7	89.3
Canned beans	100.0	11.6	88.5	9.3	90.8
Canned corn	100.0	14.1	85.8	11.1	88.9
Canned miscellaneous vegetables	100.0	8.6	91.5	7.7	92.3
Dried peas	100.0	17.8	82.7	6.6	94.0
Dried beans	100.0	11.6	88.6	30.7	69.7

	total consumer units	race		Hispanic origin	
		black	white and other	Hispanic	non-Hispanic
Dried miscellaneous vegetables	100.0%	13.5%	86.4%	11.4%	88.6%
Dried processed vegetables	100.0	7.4	92.2	33.2	66.8
Frozen vegetable juices	100.0	19.2	78.8	11.6	88.2
Fresh and canned vegetable juices	100.0	9.0	91.0	11.4	88.7
Other food at home	**100.0**	**9.0**	**91.0**	**8.8**	**91.2**
Sugar and other sweets	100.0	9.2	90.8	8.1	91.9
Candy and chewing gum	100.0	7.0	93.0	6.7	93.3
Sugar	100.0	15.5	84.6	15.0	85.1
Artificial sweeteners	100.0	16.7	83.1	6.8	93.1
Jams, preserves, other sweets	100.0	10.8	89.2	8.1	91.9
Fats and oils	100.0	12.1	87.9	10.4	89.7
Margarine	100.0	12.4	87.5	8.1	91.9
Fats and oils	100.0	15.5	84.5	15.5	84.6
Salad dressings	100.0	10.8	89.2	9.4	90.6
Nondairy cream and imitation milk	100.0	8.1	91.9	7.0	92.9
Peanut butter	100.0	11.5	88.5	7.2	92.7
Miscellaneous foods	100.0	8.7	91.3	8.0	92.0
Frozen prepared foods	100.0	8.8	91.1	6.7	93.3
Frozen meals	100.0	11.8	88.2	5.2	94.8
Other frozen prepared foods	100.0	7.5	92.5	7.4	92.6
Canned and packaged soups	100.0	9.9	90.1	8.3	91.7
Potato chips, nuts, and other snacks	100.0	7.4	92.6	6.4	93.6
Potato chips and other snacks	100.0	7.2	92.8	6.6	93.3
Nuts	100.0	8.2	91.8	5.6	94.4
Condiments and seasonings	100.0	9.4	90.6	7.8	92.1
Salt, spices, and other seasonings	100.0	13.3	86.7	10.8	89.3
Olives, pickles, relishes	100.0	8.0	92.0	6.7	93.2
Sauces and gravies	100.0	8.5	91.5	7.6	92.4
Baking needs and miscellaneous products	100.0	7.8	92.2	5.4	94.5
Other canned/packaged prepared foods	100.0	8.8	91.2	10.1	89.9
Prepared salads	100.0	8.7	91.3	6.3	93.7
Prepared desserts	100.0	9.3	90.7	9.0	91.0
Baby food	100.0	10.4	89.6	9.4	90.7
Miscellaneous prepared foods	100.0	8.1	91.9	11.6	88.5
Vitamin supplements	100.0	–	100.0	8.0	91.3
Nonalcoholic beverages	100.0	9.0	91.0	10.1	89.9
Cola	100.0	8.6	91.4	11.1	88.9
Other carbonated drinks	100.0	8.3	91.8	9.3	90.7
Coffee	100.0	7.0	93.0	9.3	90.7
Roasted coffee	100.0	7.3	92.7	8.8	91.2
Instant and freeze-dried coffee	100.0	6.4	93.5	10.2	89.9
Noncarbonated fruit-flavored drinks, incl. nonfrozen lemonade	100.0	13.0	87.0	12.6	87.5
Tea	100.0	10.5	89.5	8.1	91.9
Nonalcoholic beer	100.0	13.0	87.9	–	100.0
Other nonalcoholic beverages and ice	100.0	10.4	89.6	9.4	90.6
Food prepared by CU on trips	100.0	5.1	94.9	7.4	92.6
FOOD AWAY FROM HOME	**100.0**	**7.9**	**92.1**	**7.6**	**92.4**
Meals at restaurants, carry-outs, other	**100.0**	**8.4**	**91.6**	**8.0**	**92.0**
Lunch	100.0	9.8	90.2	8.8	91.2
At fast food, take-out, delivery, concession stands, buffet, and cafeteria (other than employer and school cafeteria)	100.0	10.9	89.1	10.0	90.1
At full-service restaurants	100.0	5.9	94.1	6.1	93.8
At vending machines, mobile vendors	100.0	13.7	86.4	24.5	75.9
At employer and school cafeterias	100.0	14.4	85.6	8.8	91.2

	total consumer units	race		Hispanic origin	
		black	white and other	Hispanic	non-Hispanic
Dinner	100.0%	6.7%	93.4%	6.8%	93.2%
At fast food, take-out, delivery, concession stands, buffet, and cafeteria (other than employer and school cafeteria)	100.0	9.3	90.7	10.9	89.1
At full-service restaurants	100.0	5.5	94.5	5.0	95.0
At vending machines, mobile vendors	100.0	29.1	71.5	21.3	79.7
At employer and school cafeterias	100.0	13.3	86.8	9.4	90.9
Snacks and nonalcoholic beverages	100.0	9.3	90.7	8.5	91.5
At fast food, take-out, delivery, concession stands, buffet, and cafeteria (other than employer and school cafeteria)	100.0	8.5	91.5	8.4	91.6
At full-service restaurants	100.0	8.7	91.3	8.6	91.5
At vending machines, mobile vendors	100.0	11.8	88.2	9.2	90.8
At employer and school cafeterias	100.0	13.5	86.5	8.0	91.9
Breakfast and brunch	100.0	8.8	91.2	9.6	90.4
At fast food, take-out, delivery, concession stands, buffet, and cafeteria (other than employer and school cafeteria)	100.0	11.0	89.0	12.1	87.9
At full-service restaurants	100.0	6.4	93.7	6.6	93.3
At vending machines, mobile vendors	100.0	10.7	89.2	24.3	75.8
At employer and school cafeterias	100.0	15.6	84.5	16.0	84.3
Board (including at school)	**100.0**	**8.0**	**92.0**	**6.5**	**93.5**
Catered affairs	**100.0**	**4.5**	**95.6**	**4.7**	**95.3**
Food on trips	**100.0**	**4.5**	**95.5**	**4.9**	**95.1**
School lunches	**100.0**	**10.0**	**90.0**	**6.8**	**93.2**
Meals as pay	**100.0**	**10.5**	**89.5**	**8.7**	**91.3**
ALCOHOLIC BEVERAGES	**100.0**	**6.9**	**93.1**	**6.6**	**93.3**
At home	**100.0**	**6.5**	**93.5**	**7.8**	**92.2**
Beer and ale	100.0	8.0	92.0	11.4	88.6
Whiskey	100.0	10.1	89.9	5.7	94.2
Wine	100.0	3.4	96.6	3.7	96.2
Other alcoholic beverages	100.0	8.3	91.7	5.0	94.8
Away from home	**100.0**	**7.4**	**92.6**	**4.9**	**95.1**
Beer and ale	100.0	9.4	90.6	5.0	94.9
At fast food, take-out, delivery, concession stands, buffet, and cafeteria	100.0	5.6	94.3	7.7	92.2
At full-service restaurants	100.0	4.5	95.5	4.7	95.2
At vending machines, mobile vendors	100.0	16.3	83.5	–	100.0
At catered affairs	100.0	83.1	16.9	0.2	99.6
Wine	100.0	5.8	94.2	5.3	94.6
At fast food, take-out, delivery, concession stands, buffet and cafeteria	100.0	3.2	97.2	13.1	87.6
At full-service restaurants	100.0	4.1	95.9	4.8	95.1
At catered affairs	100.0	82.2	15.8	0.2	98.4
Other alcoholic beverages	100.0	5.9	94.1	4.6	95.4
At fast food, take-out, delivery, concession stands, buffet, and cafeteria	100.0	4.1	96.0	8.5	91.6
At full-service restaurants	100.0	3.8	96.2	4.8	95.1
At machines and mobile vendors	100.0	23.4	78.8	11.3	91.3
At catered affairs	100.0	83.3	17.0	0.2	99.9
Alcoholic beverages purchased on trips	100.0	3.9	96.1	4.2	95.8

Note: Other races include Asians, Native Americans, and Pacific Islanders. Numbers may not add to total because of rounding. (–) means sample is too small to make a reliable estimate.
Source: Calculations by New Strategist based on the 2000 Consumer Expenditure Survey

Table 5.21 Food and Alcohol: Average spending by region, 2000

(average annual spending of consumer units (CU) on food and alcoholic beverages, by region in which consumer unit lives, 2000)

	total consumer units	Northeast	Midwest	South	West
Number of consumer units					
(in thousands, add 000)	109,367	20,994	25,717	38,245	24,410
Average number of persons per CU	2.5	2.5	2.5	2.5	2.6
Average before-tax income of CU	$44,649.00	$47,439.00	$44,377.00	$41,984.00	$46,670.00
Average spending of CU, total	38,044.67	38,901.91	39,212.70	34,707.07	41,328.19
Food, average spending	5,157.88	5,377.34	5,255.42	4,724.17	5,554.25
Alcoholic beverages, average spending	371.81	390.50	387.58	303.61	448.69
FOOD AT HOME	**$3,021.00**	**$3,201.88**	**$2,933.40**	**$2,822.82**	**$3,269.35**
Cereals and bakery products	**453.33**	**490.66**	**444.36**	**421.88**	**479.61**
Cereals and cereal products	156.40	164.35	152.45	148.22	166.57
Flour	7.98	6.29	6.41	9.32	9.03
Prepared flour mixes	13.35	12.33	13.73	13.30	13.99
Ready-to-eat and cooked cereals	86.88	93.26	90.68	79.75	88.54
Rice	19.55	20.71	15.14	19.35	23.50
Pasta, cornmeal, and other cereal products	28.64	31.75	26.49	26.51	31.52
Bakery products	296.93	326.31	291.91	273.65	313.04
Bread	84.04	95.63	82.61	76.13	87.75
White bread	36.62	41.28	36.37	35.97	33.63
Bread, other than white	47.42	54.34	46.24	40.16	54.12
Crackers and cookies	71.03	77.57	71.81	65.84	72.61
Cookies	47.71	54.64	47.02	43.17	49.42
Crackers	23.32	22.93	24.79	22.67	23.20
Frozen and refrigerated bakery products	24.53	21.66	25.90	26.08	23.19
Other bakery products	117.33	131.46	111.59	105.60	129.49
Biscuits and rolls	38.53	49.68	35.87	33.38	39.44
Cakes and cupcakes	38.42	41.23	32.81	35.49	46.59
Bread and cracker products	4.41	5.57	3.92	4.20	4.22
Sweetrolls, coffee cakes, doughnuts	22.68	21.11	25.73	20.09	25.11
Pies, tarts, turnovers	13.28	13.86	13.27	12.44	14.13
Meats, poultry, fish, and eggs	**795.43**	**883.13**	**720.54**	**778.84**	**821.40**
Beef	238.19	247.68	226.45	230.44	254.59
Ground beef	87.76	83.16	88.01	93.59	82.27
Roast	39.84	39.57	36.08	36.88	48.90
Chuck roast	13.33	11.00	13.04	12.94	16.43
Round roast	11.46	14.30	10.42	9.22	13.59
Other roast	15.05	14.27	12.62	14.73	18.88
Steak	94.52	106.76	87.79	84.41	106.84
Round steak	15.31	16.56	13.61	14.32	17.58
Sirloin steak	29.86	37.53	26.68	24.46	34.95
Other steak	49.35	52.66	47.50	45.62	54.31
Other beef	16.08	18.19	14.58	15.56	16.58
Pork	166.94	161.56	159.89	176.35	164.14
Bacon	26.05	22.41	24.72	30.47	23.65
Pork chops	40.57	42.16	35.67	44.89	37.28
Ham	36.26	37.68	38.98	36.67	31.37
Ham, not canned	34.52	35.52	37.93	35.48	28.41
Canned ham	1.74	2.16	1.06	1.20	2.96
Sausage	25.24	25.12	23.57	27.83	22.92
Other pork	38.82	34.18	36.95	36.48	48.92
Other meats	100.54	115.99	102.94	93.91	94.49
Frankfurters	20.68	21.35	20.80	21.09	19.26

	total consumer units	Northeast	Midwest	South	West
Lunch meats (cold cuts)	$67.99	$80.91	$74.11	$60.31	$62.03
Bologna, liverwurst, salami	23.73	28.69	25.26	21.81	20.64
Other lunch meats	44.26	52.22	48.85	38.50	41.39
Lamb, organ meats, and others	11.87	13.73	8.03	12.52	13.20
Lamb and organ meats	9.71	11.54	6.93	9.23	11.77
Mutton, goat, and game	2.16	2.19	1.10	3.29	1.43
Poultry	145.16	173.65	124.89	141.57	146.33
Fresh and frozen chicken	114.43	137.54	94.57	112.21	117.94
Fresh and frozen whole chicken	31.25	36.53	24.13	30.40	35.36
Fresh and frozen chicken parts	83.18	101.01	70.43	81.80	82.58
Other poultry	30.73	36.11	30.33	29.36	28.40
Fish and seafood	110.14	149.19	78.24	100.23	124.24
Canned fish and seafood	15.67	19.66	12.29	14.86	16.91
Fresh fish and shellfish	66.82	97.03	38.59	63.66	74.17
Frozen fish and shellfish	27.65	32.50	27.35	21.72	33.15
Eggs	34.46	35.06	28.13	36.34	37.62
Dairy products	**324.63**	**353.96**	**329.53**	**285.69**	**355.69**
Fresh milk and cream	131.22	131.93	132.18	121.65	145.12
Fresh milk, all types	119.61	120.14	121.96	111.71	129.45
Cream	11.61	11.79	10.22	9.94	15.68
Other dairy products	193.41	222.03	197.35	164.05	210.57
Butter	17.00	23.38	19.18	13.17	15.02
Cheese	95.96	107.78	101.25	80.68	104.25
Ice cream and related products	56.56	63.50	53.97	50.09	63.46
Miscellaneous dairy products	23.89	27.37	22.95	20.11	27.83
Fruits and vegetables	**520.83**	**579.43**	**481.83**	**469.60**	**591.71**
Fresh fruits	163.17	181.13	150.56	141.17	195.82
Apples	29.49	33.80	27.60	26.46	32.45
Bananas	31.70	35.99	27.32	29.13	36.60
Oranges	18.93	21.69	17.15	16.05	22.95
Citrus fruits, excl. oranges	14.31	13.83	12.09	13.06	19.15
Other fresh fruits	68.74	75.82	66.40	56.47	84.67
Fresh vegetables	158.72	184.50	136.96	139.45	189.51
Potatoes	28.07	30.27	24.69	27.60	30.40
Lettuce	20.75	24.61	18.76	18.82	22.44
Tomatoes	29.53	35.36	23.21	26.96	35.08
Other fresh vegetables	80.38	94.26	70.31	66.07	101.59
Processed fruits	115.01	130.55	113.07	102.63	122.86
Frozen fruits and fruit juices	14.37	11.31	17.20	11.14	19.43
Frozen orange juice	6.90	5.69	8.23	5.45	8.97
Frozen fruits	3.62	3.29	3.94	2.61	5.22
Frozen fruit juices	3.84	2.32	5.02	3.08	5.23
Canned fruits	15.48	16.73	16.51	14.01	15.60
Dried fruits	5.50	5.40	5.40	4.91	6.67
Fresh fruit juice	23.44	31.52	21.95	20.75	21.94
Canned and bottled fruit juice	56.21	65.59	52.01	51.80	59.22
Processed vegetables	83.94	83.26	81.23	86.36	83.51
Frozen vegetables	26.42	32.31	24.90	25.91	23.44
Canned and dried vegetables and juices	57.52	50.95	56.32	60.45	60.07
Canned beans	12.67	10.26	11.61	15.58	11.30
Canned corn	6.80	6.01	6.24	7.76	6.56
Canned miscellaneous vegetables	17.95	17.61	19.53	18.07	16.40
Dried peas	0.34	0.46	0.33	0.25	0.37
Dried beans	2.53	2.15	1.28	2.41	4.43

	total consumer units	Northeast	Midwest	South	West
Dried miscellaneous vegetables	$7.22	$5.52	$7.04	$7.61	$8.32
Dried processed vegetables	0.41	0.16	0.40	0.41	0.65
Frozen vegetable juices	0.29	0.24	0.40	0.13	0.48
Fresh and canned vegetable juices	9.30	8.54	9.48	8.23	11.57
Other food at home	**926.77**	**894.70**	**957.13**	**866.81**	**1,020.93**
Sugar and other sweets	117.14	126.49	124.04	107.34	117.09
Candy and chewing gum	76.30	86.34	87.17	64.66	74.36
Sugar	16.80	15.53	13.62	19.24	17.42
Artificial sweeteners	4.19	4.30	2.99	5.68	2.93
Jams, preserves, other sweets	19.86	20.32	20.26	17.77	22.38
Fats and oils	83.09	89.01	75.35	82.46	86.90
Margarine	11.61	11.40	11.53	11.84	11.50
Fats and oils	23.35	26.48	17.25	25.35	23.70
Salad dressings	27.18	28.56	26.36	25.52	29.46
Nondairy cream and imitation milk	9.15	8.63	8.58	9.37	9.88
Peanut butter	11.81	13.94	11.63	10.38	12.35
Miscellaneous foods	437.02	398.22	467.60	409.96	484.22
Frozen prepared foods	90.20	75.71	104.87	86.44	94.02
Frozen meals	28.50	26.52	32.63	27.78	27.09
Other frozen prepared foods	61.70	49.19	72.24	58.66	66.93
Canned and packaged soups	35.54	35.22	37.62	31.41	40.34
Potato chips, nuts, and other snacks	92.50	89.72	102.16	85.16	96.71
Potato chips and other snacks	71.67	70.54	82.31	65.51	71.38
Nuts	20.83	19.19	19.85	19.64	25.33
Condiments and seasonings	84.61	79.00	89.58	77.66	95.77
Salt, spices, and other seasonings	20.65	17.67	20.44	20.07	24.57
Olives, pickles, relishes	9.77	8.14	10.78	9.17	11.16
Sauces and gravies	37.23	38.28	37.67	33.84	41.32
Baking needs and miscellaneous products	16.96	14.92	20.69	14.58	18.71
Other canned/packaged prepared foods	134.17	118.57	133.36	129.29	157.39
Prepared salads	18.55	20.19	17.22	16.69	21.45
Prepared desserts	9.31	10.20	10.09	7.57	10.50
Baby food	32.26	26.23	31.26	36.31	32.34
Miscellaneous prepared foods	73.91	61.70	74.66	68.65	92.92
Vitamin supplements	0.14	0.24	0.13	0.07	0.17
Nonalcoholic beverages	249.58	240.46	249.35	237.85	277.35
Cola	86.99	66.48	98.51	90.28	88.29
Other carbonated drinks	47.39	44.95	53.86	44.47	47.50
Coffee	41.85	47.65	35.11	38.24	49.56
Roasted coffee	27.50	30.85	23.19	24.73	33.51
Instant and freeze-dried coffee	14.35	16.80	11.92	13.51	16.05
Noncarbonated fruit-flavored drinks, incl. nonfrozen lemonade	19.42	18.06	17.63	18.48	24.11
Tea	15.68	21.82	12.09	14.59	15.59
Nonalcoholic beer	0.27	0.30	0.38	0.10	0.42
Other nonalcoholic beverages and ice	37.99	41.19	31.77	31.70	51.90
Food prepared by CU on trips	39.94	40.52	40.80	29.19	55.37
FOOD AWAY FROM HOME	**2,136.88**	**2,175.46**	**2,322.03**	**1,901.35**	**2,284.90**
Meals at restaurants, carry-outs, other	**1,750.33**	**1,752.21**	**1,878.23**	**1,598.40**	**1,859.26**
Lunch	662.90	654.20	683.81	634.05	695.54
At fast food, take-out, delivery, concession stands, buffet, and cafeteria (other than employer and school cafeteria)	368.00	349.05	382.85	358.87	384.50
At full-service restaurants	208.12	205.93	200.02	197.55	235.97
At vending machines, mobile vendors	6.52	6.84	5.63	5.71	8.50
At employer and school cafeterias	80.26	92.38	95.30	71.92	66.57

	total consumer units	Northeast	Midwest	South	West
Dinner	$697.99	$725.78	$756.99	$613.03	$747.61
At fast food, take-out, delivery, concession stands, buffet, and cafeteria (other than employer and school cafeteria)	206.92	187.34	246.71	177.52	230.34
At full-service restaurants	487.70	537.20	505.43	430.93	515.43
At vending machines, mobile vendors	1.02	0.02	1.25	1.68	0.65
At employer and school cafeterias	2.35	1.23	3.60	2.90	1.19
Snacks and nonalcoholic beverages	227.71	229.76	254.64	203.57	236.37
At fast food, take-out, delivery, concession stands, buffet, and cafeteria (other than employer and school cafeteria)	158.55	173.26	171.69	131.52	174.90
At full-service restaurants	20.15	18.54	21.34	18.28	23.43
At vending machines, mobile vendors	38.52	27.92	50.29	42.98	28.48
At employer and school cafeterias	10.49	10.05	11.32	10.78	9.55
Breakfast and brunch	161.73	142.47	182.79	147.76	179.75
At fast food, take-out, delivery, concession stands, buffet, and cafeteria (other than employer and school cafeteria)	77.12	65.94	87.69	76.01	77.94
At full-service restaurants	79.64	71.67	90.96	66.49	96.31
At vending machines, mobile vendors	1.35	0.99	1.06	1.28	2.09
At employer and school cafeterias	3.62	3.88	3.08	3.97	3.41
Board (including at school)	**39.03**	**45.44**	**50.11**	**31.48**	**33.68**
Catered affairs	**54.02**	**60.25**	**72.52**	**23.40**	**77.16**
Food on trips	**216.06**	**248.69**	**227.16**	**176.44**	**238.38**
School lunches	**58.46**	**52.20**	**74.09**	**59.46**	**45.82**
Meals as pay	**18.97**	**16.66**	**19.92**	**12.17**	**30.61**
ALCOHOLIC BEVERAGES	**371.81**	**390.50**	**387.58**	**303.61**	**448.69**
At home	**226.64**	**239.82**	**228.06**	**186.01**	**279.05**
Beer and ale	112.01	119.56	118.70	94.15	126.94
Whiskey	13.49	11.41	16.65	15.27	9.13
Wine	80.04	82.87	68.49	63.64	116.46
Other alcoholic beverages	21.10	25.99	24.21	12.95	26.52
Away from home	**145.17**	**150.67**	**159.53**	**117.60**	**169.64**
Beer and ale	62.46	61.17	69.98	53.14	70.80
At fast food, take-out, delivery, concession stands, buffet, and cafeteria	13.37	11.35	18.90	11.03	13.11
At full-service restaurants	45.05	49.50	49.96	32.00	56.93
At vending machines, mobile vendors	0.40	–	0.86	0.41	0.27
At catered affairs	3.64	0.32	0.25	9.69	0.48
Wine	17.79	15.31	16.85	15.92	24.09
At fast food, take-out, delivery, concession stands, buffet and cafeteria	1.23	0.98	0.96	1.54	1.26
At full-service restaurants	16.16	14.29	15.87	13.36	22.78
At catered affairs	0.39	0.03	0.03	1.03	0.05
Other alcoholic beverages	64.92	74.19	72.70	48.54	74.75
At fast food, take-out, delivery, concession stands, buffet, and cafeteria	3.04	2.55	3.50	2.82	3.38
At full-service restaurants	25.74	25.02	28.82	20.57	31.55
At machines and mobile vendors	0.29	0.05	0.39	0.39	0.25
At catered affairs	1.60	0.14	0.11	4.27	0.21
Alcoholic beverages purchased on trips	34.24	46.43	39.88	20.49	39.35

Note: (–) means sample is too small to make a reliable estimate.
Source: Bureau of Labor Statistics, unpublished tables from the 2000 Consumer Expenditure Survey

Table 5.22 Food and Alcohol: Indexed spending by region, 2000

(indexed average annual spending of consumer units (CU) on food and alcoholic beverages, by region in which consumer unit lives, 2000; index definition: an index of 100 is the average for all consumer units; an index of 132 means that spending by consumer units in that group is 32 percent above the average for all consumer units; an index of 68 indicates spending that is 32 percent below the average for all consumer units)

	total consumer units	Northeast	Midwest	South	West
Average spending of CU, total	$38,045	$38,902	$39,213	$34,707	$41,328
Average spending of CU, index	100	102	103	91	109
Food, spending index	100	104	102	92	108
Alcoholic beverages, spending index	100	105	104	82	121
FOOD AT HOME	**100**	**106**	**97**	**93**	**108**
Cereals and bakery products	**100**	**108**	**98**	**93**	**106**
Cereals and cereal products	100	105	97	95	107
Flour	100	79	80	117	113
Prepared flour mixes	100	92	103	100	105
Ready-to-eat and cooked cereals	100	107	104	92	102
Rice	100	106	77	99	120
Pasta, cornmeal, and other cereal products	100	111	92	93	110
Bakery products	100	110	98	92	105
Bread	100	114	98	91	104
White bread	100	113	99	98	92
Bread, other than white	100	115	98	85	114
Crackers and cookies	100	109	101	93	102
Cookies	100	115	99	90	104
Crackers	100	98	106	97	99
Frozen and refrigerated bakery products	100	88	106	106	95
Other bakery products	100	112	95	90	110
Biscuits and rolls	100	129	93	87	102
Cakes and cupcakes	100	107	85	92	121
Bread and cracker products	100	126	89	95	96
Sweetrolls, coffee cakes, doughnuts	100	93	113	89	111
Pies, tarts, turnovers	100	104	100	94	106
Meats, poultry, fish, and eggs	**100**	**111**	**91**	**98**	**103**
Beef	100	104	95	97	107
Ground beef	100	95	100	107	94
Roast	100	99	91	93	123
Chuck roast	100	83	98	97	123
Round roast	100	125	91	80	119
Other roast	100	95	84	98	125
Steak	100	113	93	89	113
Round steak	100	108	89	94	115
Sirloin steak	100	126	89	82	117
Other steak	100	107	96	92	110
Other beef	100	113	91	97	103
Pork	100	97	96	106	98
Bacon	100	86	95	117	91
Pork chops	100	104	88	111	92
Ham	100	104	108	101	87
Ham, not canned	100	103	110	103	82
Canned ham	100	124	61	69	170
Sausage	100	100	93	110	91
Other pork	100	88	95	94	126
Other meats	100	115	102	93	94
Frankfurters	100	103	101	102	93

	total consumer units	Northeast	Midwest	South	West
Lunch meats (cold cuts)	100	119	109	89	91
Bologna, liverwurst, salami	100	121	106	92	87
Other lunch meats	100	118	110	87	94
Lamb, organ meats, and others	100	116	68	105	111
Lamb and organ meats	100	119	71	95	121
Mutton, goat, and game	100	101	51	152	66
Poultry	100	120	86	98	101
Fresh and frozen chicken	100	120	83	98	103
Fresh and frozen whole chicken	100	117	77	97	113
Fresh and frozen chicken parts	100	121	85	98	99
Other poultry	100	118	99	96	92
Fish and seafood	100	135	71	91	113
Canned fish and seafood	100	125	78	95	108
Fresh fish and shellfish	100	145	58	95	111
Frozen fish and shellfish	100	118	99	79	120
Eggs	100	102	82	105	109
Dairy products	**100**	**109**	**102**	**88**	**110**
Fresh milk and cream	100	101	101	93	111
Fresh milk, all types	100	100	102	93	108
Cream	100	102	88	86	135
Other dairy products	100	115	102	85	109
Butter	100	138	113	77	88
Cheese	100	112	106	84	109
Ice cream and related products	100	112	95	89	112
Miscellaneous dairy products	100	115	96	84	116
Fruits and vegetables	**100**	**111**	**93**	**90**	**114**
Fresh fruits	100	111	92	87	120
Apples	100	115	94	90	110
Bananas	100	114	86	92	115
Oranges	100	115	91	85	121
Citrus fruits, excl. oranges	100	97	84	91	134
Other fresh fruits	100	110	97	82	123
Fresh vegetables	100	116	86	88	119
Potatoes	100	108	88	98	108
Lettuce	100	119	90	91	108
Tomatoes	100	120	79	91	119
Other fresh vegetables	100	117	87	82	126
Processed fruits	100	114	98	89	107
Frozen fruits and fruit juices	100	79	120	78	135
Frozen orange juice	100	82	119	79	130
Frozen fruits	100	91	109	72	144
Frozen fruit juices	100	60	131	80	136
Canned fruits	100	108	107	91	101
Dried fruits	100	98	98	89	121
Fresh fruit juice	100	134	94	89	94
Canned and bottled fruit juice	100	117	93	92	105
Processed vegetables	100	99	97	103	99
Frozen vegetables	100	122	94	98	89
Canned and dried vegetables and juices	100	89	98	105	104
Canned beans	100	81	92	123	89
Canned corn	100	88	92	114	96
Canned miscellaneous vegetables	100	98	109	101	91
Dried peas	100	135	97	74	109
Dried beans	100	85	51	95	175

	total consumer units	Northeast	Midwest	South	West
Dried miscellaneous vegetables	100	76	98	105	115
Dried processed vegetables	100	39	98	100	159
Frozen vegetable juices	100	83	138	45	166
Fresh and canned vegetable juices	100	92	102	88	124
Other food at home	**100**	**97**	**103**	**94**	**110**
Sugar and other sweets	100	108	106	92	100
Candy and chewing gum	100	113	114	85	97
Sugar	100	92	81	115	104
Artificial sweeteners	100	103	71	136	70
Jams, preserves, other sweets	100	102	102	89	113
Fats and oils	100	107	91	99	105
Margarine	100	98	99	102	99
Fats and oils	100	113	74	109	101
Salad dressings	100	105	97	94	108
Nondairy cream and imitation milk	100	94	94	102	108
Peanut butter	100	118	98	88	105
Miscellaneous foods	100	91	107	94	111
Frozen prepared foods	100	84	116	96	104
Frozen meals	100	93	114	97	95
Other frozen prepared foods	100	80	117	95	108
Canned and packaged soups	100	99	106	88	114
Potato chips, nuts, and other snacks	100	97	110	92	105
Potato chips and other snacks	100	98	115	91	100
Nuts	100	92	95	94	122
Condiments and seasonings	100	93	106	92	113
Salt, spices, and other seasonings	100	86	99	97	119
Olives, pickles, relishes	100	83	110	94	114
Sauces and gravies	100	103	101	91	111
Baking needs and miscellaneous products	100	88	122	86	110
Other canned/packaged prepared foods	100	88	99	96	117
Prepared salads	100	109	93	90	116
Prepared desserts	100	110	108	81	113
Baby food	100	81	97	113	100
Miscellaneous prepared foods	100	83	101	93	126
Vitamin supplements	100	171	93	50	121
Nonalcoholic beverages	100	96	100	95	111
Cola	100	76	113	104	101
Other carbonated drinks	100	95	114	94	100
Coffee	100	114	84	91	118
Roasted coffee	100	112	84	90	122
Instant and freeze-dried coffee	100	117	83	94	112
Noncarbonated fruit-flavored drinks, incl. nonfrozen lemonade	100	93	91	95	124
Tea	100	139	77	93	99
Nonalcoholic beer	100	111	141	37	156
Other nonalcoholic beverages and ice	100	108	84	83	137
Food prepared by CU on trips	100	101	102	73	139
FOOD AWAY FROM HOME	**100**	**102**	**109**	**89**	**107**
Meals at restaurants, carry-outs, other	**100**	**100**	**107**	**91**	**106**
Lunch	100	99	103	96	105
At fast food, take-out, delivery, concession stands, buffet, and cafeteria (other than employer and school cafeteria)	100	95	104	98	104
At full-service restaurants	100	99	96	95	113
At vending machines, mobile vendors	100	105	86	88	130
At employer and school cafeterias	100	115	119	90	83

	total consumer units	Northeast	Midwest	South	West
Dinner	100	104	108	88	107
At fast food, take-out, delivery, concession stands, buffet, and cafeteria (other than employer and school cafeteria)	100	91	119	86	111
At full-service restaurants	100	110	104	88	106
At vending machines, mobile vendors	100	2	123	165	64
At employer and school cafeterias	100	52	153	123	51
Snacks and nonalcoholic beverages	100	101	112	89	104
At fast food, take-out, delivery, concession stands, buffet, and cafeteria (other than employer and school cafeteria)	100	109	108	83	110
At full-service restaurants	100	92	106	91	116
At vending machines, mobile vendors	100	72	131	112	74
At employer and school cafeterias	100	96	108	103	91
Breakfast and brunch	100	88	113	91	111
At fast food, take-out, delivery, concession stands, buffet, and cafeteria (other than employer and school cafeteria)	100	86	114	99	101
At full-service restaurants	100	90	114	83	121
At vending machines, mobile vendors	100	73	79	95	155
At employer and school cafeterias	100	107	85	110	94
Board (including at school)	**100**	**116**	**128**	**81**	**86**
Catered affairs	**100**	**112**	**134**	**43**	**143**
Food on trips	**100**	**115**	**105**	**82**	**110**
School lunches	**100**	**89**	**127**	**102**	**78**
Meals as pay	**100**	**88**	**105**	**64**	**161**
ALCOHOLIC BEVERAGES	**100**	**105**	**104**	**82**	**121**
At home	**100**	**106**	**101**	**82**	**123**
Beer and ale	100	107	106	84	113
Whiskey	100	85	123	113	68
Wine	100	104	86	80	146
Other alcoholic beverages	100	123	115	61	126
Away from home	**100**	**104**	**110**	**81**	**117**
Beer and ale	100	98	112	85	113
At fast food, take-out, delivery, concession stands, buffet, and cafeteria	100	85	141	82	98
At full-service restaurants	100	110	111	71	126
At vending machines, mobile vendors	100	–	215	103	68
At catered affairs	100	9	7	266	13
Wine	100	86	95	89	135
At fast food, take-out, delivery, concession stands, buffet and cafeteria	100	80	78	125	102
At full-service restaurants	100	88	98	83	141
At catered affairs	100	8	8	264	13
Other alcoholic beverages	100	114	112	75	115
At fast food, take-out, delivery, concession stands, buffet, and cafeteria	100	84	115	93	111
At full-service restaurants	100	97	112	80	123
At machines and mobile vendors	100	17	134	134	86
At catered affairs	100	9	7	267	13
Alcoholic beverages purchased on trips	100	136	116	60	115

Note: (–) means sample is too small to make a reliable estimate.
Source: Calculations by New Strategist based on the 2000 Consumer Expenditure Survey

Table 5.23 Food and Alcohol: Indexed per capita spending by region, 2000

(indexed average annual per capita spending of consumer units (CU) on food and alcoholic beverages, by region in which consumer unit lives, 2000; index definition: an index of 100 is the average for all consumer units; an index of 132 means that spending by consumer units in that group is 32 percent above the average for all consumer units; an index of 68 indicates spending that is 32 percent below the average for all consumer units)

	total consumer units	Northeast	Midwest	South	West
Per capita spending of CU, total	**$15,218**	**$15,561**	**$15,685**	**$13,883**	**$15,895**
Per capita spending of CU, index	**100**	**102**	**103**	**91**	**104**
Food, per capita spending index	**100**	**104**	**102**	**92**	**104**
Alcoholic beverages, per capita spending index	**100**	**105**	**104**	**82**	**116**
FOOD AT HOME	**100**	**106**	**97**	**93**	**104**
Cereals and bakery products	**100**	**108**	**98**	**93**	**102**
Cereals and cereal products	100	105	97	95	102
Flour	100	79	80	117	109
Prepared flour mixes	100	92	103	100	101
Ready-to-eat and cooked cereals	100	107	104	92	98
Rice	100	106	77	99	116
Pasta, cornmeal, and other cereal products	100	111	92	93	106
Bakery products	100	110	98	92	101
Bread	100	114	98	91	100
White bread	100	113	99	98	88
Bread, other than white	100	115	98	85	110
Crackers and cookies	100	109	101	93	98
Cookies	100	115	99	90	100
Crackers	100	98	106	97	96
Frozen and refrigerated bakery products	100	88	106	106	91
Other bakery products	100	112	95	90	106
Biscuits and rolls	100	129	93	87	98
Cakes and cupcakes	100	107	85	92	117
Bread and cracker products	100	126	89	95	92
Sweetrolls, coffee cakes, doughnuts	100	93	113	89	106
Pies, tarts, turnovers	100	104	100	94	102
Meats, poultry, fish, and eggs	**100**	**111**	**91**	**98**	**99**
Beef	100	104	95	97	103
Ground beef	100	95	100	107	90
Roast	100	99	91	93	118
Chuck roast	100	83	98	97	119
Round roast	100	125	91	80	114
Other roast	100	95	84	98	121
Steak	100	113	93	89	109
Round steak	100	108	89	94	110
Sirloin steak	100	126	89	82	113
Other steak	100	107	96	92	106
Other beef	100	113	91	97	99
Pork	100	97	96	106	95
Bacon	100	86	95	117	87
Pork chops	100	104	88	111	88
Ham	100	104	108	101	83
Ham, not canned	100	103	110	103	79
Canned ham	100	124	61	69	164
Sausage	100	100	93	110	87
Other pork	100	88	95	94	121
Other meats	100	115	102	93	90
Frankfurters	100	103	101	102	90

	total consumer units	Northeast	Midwest	South	West
Lunch meats (cold cuts)	100	119	109	89	88
Bologna, liverwurst, salami	100	121	106	92	84
Other lunch meats	100	118	110	87	90
Lamb, organ meats, and others	100	116	68	105	107
Lamb and organ meats	100	119	71	95	117
Mutton, goat, and game	100	101	51	152	64
Poultry	100	120	86	98	97
Fresh and frozen chicken	100	120	83	98	99
Fresh and frozen whole chicken	100	117	77	97	109
Fresh and frozen chicken parts	100	121	85	98	95
Other poultry	100	118	99	96	89
Fish and seafood	100	135	71	91	108
Canned fish and seafood	100	125	78	95	104
Fresh fish and shellfish	100	145	58	95	107
Frozen fish and shellfish	100	118	99	79	115
Eggs	100	102	82	105	105
Dairy products	**100**	**109**	**102**	**88**	**105**
Fresh milk and cream	100	101	101	93	106
Fresh milk, all types	100	100	102	93	104
Cream	100	102	88	86	130
Other dairy products	100	115	102	85	105
Butter	100	138	113	77	85
Cheese	100	112	106	84	104
Ice cream and related products	100	112	95	89	108
Miscellaneous dairy products	100	115	96	84	112
Fruits and vegetables	**100**	**111**	**93**	**90**	**109**
Fresh fruits	100	111	92	87	115
Apples	100	115	94	90	106
Bananas	100	114	86	92	111
Oranges	100	115	91	85	117
Citrus fruits, excl. oranges	100	97	84	91	129
Other fresh fruits	100	110	97	82	118
Fresh vegetables	100	116	86	88	115
Potatoes	100	108	88	98	104
Lettuce	100	119	90	91	104
Tomatoes	100	120	79	91	114
Other fresh vegetables	100	117	87	82	122
Processed fruits	100	114	98	89	103
Frozen fruits and fruit juices	100	79	120	78	130
Frozen orange juice	100	82	119	79	125
Frozen fruits	100	91	109	72	139
Frozen fruit juices	100	60	131	80	131
Canned fruits	100	108	107	91	97
Dried fruits	100	98	98	89	117
Fresh fruit juice	100	134	94	89	90
Canned and bottled fruit juice	100	117	93	92	101
Processed vegetables	100	99	97	103	96
Frozen vegetables	100	122	94	98	85
Canned and dried vegetables and juices	100	89	98	105	100
Canned beans	100	81	92	123	86
Canned corn	100	88	92	114	93
Canned miscellaneous vegetables	100	98	109	101	88
Dried peas	100	135	97	74	105
Dried beans	100	85	51	95	168

	total consumer units	Northeast	Midwest	South	West
Dried miscellaneous vegetables	100	76	98	105	111
Dried processed vegetables	100	39	98	100	152
Frozen vegetable juices	100	83	138	45	159
Fresh and canned vegetable juices	100	92	102	88	120
Other food at home	**100**	**97**	**103**	**94**	**106**
Sugar and other sweets	100	108	106	92	96
Candy and chewing gum	100	113	114	85	94
Sugar	100	92	81	115	100
Artificial sweeteners	100	103	71	136	67
Jams, preserves, other sweets	100	102	102	89	108
Fats and oils	100	107	91	99	101
Margarine	100	98	99	102	95
Fats and oils	100	113	74	109	98
Salad dressings	100	105	97	94	104
Nondairy cream and imitation milk	100	94	94	102	104
Peanut butter	100	118	98	88	101
Miscellaneous foods	100	91	107	94	107
Frozen prepared foods	100	84	116	96	100
Frozen meals	100	93	114	97	91
Other frozen prepared foods	100	80	117	95	104
Canned and packaged soups	100	99	106	88	109
Potato chips, nuts, and other snacks	100	97	110	92	101
Potato chips and other snacks	100	98	115	91	96
Nuts	100	92	95	94	117
Condiments and seasonings	100	93	106	92	109
Salt, spices, and other seasonings	100	86	99	97	114
Olives, pickles, relishes	100	83	110	94	110
Sauces and gravies	100	103	101	91	107
Baking needs and miscellaneous products	100	88	122	86	106
Other canned/packaged prepared foods	100	88	99	96	113
Prepared salads	100	109	93	90	111
Prepared desserts	100	110	108	81	108
Baby food	100	81	97	113	96
Miscellaneous prepared foods	100	83	101	93	121
Vitamin supplements	100	171	93	50	117
Nonalcoholic beverages	100	96	100	95	107
Cola	100	76	113	104	98
Other carbonated drinks	100	95	114	94	96
Coffee	100	114	84	91	114
Roasted coffee	100	112	84	90	117
Instant and freeze-dried coffee	100	117	83	94	108
Noncarbonated fruit-flavored drinks, incl. nonfrozen lemonade	100	93	91	95	119
Tea	100	139	77	93	96
Nonalcoholic beer	100	111	141	37	150
Other nonalcoholic beverages and ice	100	108	84	83	131
Food prepared by CU on trips	100	101	102	73	133
FOOD AWAY FROM HOME	**100**	**102**	**109**	**89**	**103**
Meals at restaurants, carry-outs, other	**100**	**100**	**107**	**91**	**102**
Lunch	100	99	103	96	101
At fast food, take-out, delivery, concession stands, buffet, and cafeteria (other than employer and school cafeteria)	100	95	104	98	100
At full-service restaurants	100	99	96	95	109
At vending machines, mobile vendors	100	105	86	88	125
At employer and school cafeterias	100	115	119	90	80

	total consumer units	Northeast	Midwest	South	West
Dinner	100	104	108	88	103
At fast food, take-out, delivery, concession stands, buffet, and cafeteria (other than employer and school cafeteria)	100	91	119	86	107
At full-service restaurants	100	110	104	88	102
At vending machines, mobile vendors	100	2	123	165	61
At employer and school cafeterias	100	52	153	123	49
Snacks and nonalcoholic beverages	100	101	112	89	100
At fast food, take-out, delivery, concession stands, buffet, and cafeteria (other than employer and school cafeteria)	100	109	108	83	106
At full-service restaurants	100	92	106	91	112
At vending machines, mobile vendors	100	72	131	112	71
At employer and school cafeterias	100	96	108	103	88
Breakfast and brunch	100	88	113	91	107
At fast food, take-out, delivery, concession stands, buffet, and cafeteria (other than employer and school cafeteria)	100	86	114	99	97
At full-service restaurants	100	90	114	83	116
At vending machines, mobile vendors	100	73	79	95	149
At employer and school cafeterias	100	107	85	110	91
Board (including at school)	**100**	**116**	**128**	**81**	**83**
Catered affairs	**100**	**112**	**134**	**43**	**137**
Food on trips	**100**	**115**	**105**	**82**	**106**
School lunches	**100**	**89**	**127**	**102**	**75**
Meals as pay	**100**	**88**	**105**	**64**	**155**
ALCOHOLIC BEVERAGES	**100**	**105**	**104**	**82**	**116**
At home	**100**	**106**	**101**	**82**	**118**
Beer and ale	100	107	106	84	109
Whiskey	100	85	123	113	65
Wine	100	104	86	80	140
Other alcoholic beverages	100	123	115	61	121
Away from home	**100**	**104**	**110**	**81**	**112**
Beer and ale	100	98	112	85	109
At fast food, take-out, delivery, concession stands, buffet, and cafeteria	100	85	141	82	94
At full-service restaurants	100	110	111	71	122
At vending machines, mobile vendors	100	–	215	103	65
At catered affairs	100	9	7	266	13
Wine	100	86	95	89	130
At fast food, take-out, delivery, concession stands, buffet and cafeteria	100	80	78	125	98
At full-service restaurants	100	88	98	83	136
At catered affairs	100	8	8	264	12
Other alcoholic beverages	100	114	112	75	111
At fast food, take-out, delivery, concession stands, buffet, and cafeteria	100	84	115	93	107
At full-service restaurants	100	97	112	80	118
At machines and mobile vendors	100	17	134	134	83
At catered affairs	100	9	7	267	13
Alcoholic beverages purchased on trips	100	136	116	60	111

Note: Per capita indexes account for household size and show how much each person in a particular household demographic segment spends relative to a person in the average household. (–) means sample is too small to make a reliable estimate.
Source: Calculations by New Strategist based on the 2000 Consumer Expenditure Survey

Table 5.24 Food and Alcohol: Total spending by region, 2000

(total annual spending on food and alcoholic beverages, by region in which consumer units live, 2000; numbers in thousands)

	total consumer units	Northeast	Midwest	South	West
Number of consumer units	109,367	20,994	25,717	38,245	24,410
Total spending of all consumer units	$4,160,831,424	$816,706,699	$1,008,433,006	$1,327,371,892	$1,008,821,118
Food, total spending	564,101,862	112,891,876	135,153,636	180,675,882	135,579,243
Alcoholic beverages, total spending	40,663,744	8,198,157	9,967,395	11,611,564	10,952,523
FOOD AT HOME	**$330,397,707**	**$67,220,269**	**$75,438,248**	**$107,958,751**	**$79,804,834**
Cereals and bakery products	**49,579,342**	**10,300,916**	**11,427,606**	**16,134,801**	**11,707,280**
Cereals and cereal products	17,104,999	3,450,364	3,920,557	5,668,674	4,065,974
Flour	872,749	132,052	164,846	356,443	220,422
Prepared flour mixes	1,460,049	258,856	353,094	508,659	341,496
Ready-to-eat and cooked cereals	9,501,805	1,957,900	2,332,018	3,050,039	2,161,261
Rice	2,138,125	434,786	389,355	740,041	573,635
Pasta, cornmeal, and other cereal products	3,132,271	666,560	681,243	1,013,875	769,403
Bakery products	32,474,343	6,850,552	7,507,049	10,465,744	7,641,306
Bread	9,191,203	2,007,656	2,124,481	2,911,592	2,141,978
White bread	4,005,020	866,632	935,327	1,375,673	820,908
Bread, other than white	5,186,183	1,140,814	1,189,154	1,535,919	1,321,069
Crackers and cookies	7,768,338	1,628,505	1,846,738	2,518,051	1,772,410
Cookies	5,217,900	1,147,112	1,209,213	1,651,037	1,206,342
Crackers	2,550,438	481,392	637,524	867,014	566,312
Frozen and refrigerated bakery products	2,682,773	454,730	666,070	997,430	566,068
Other bakery products	12,832,030	2,759,871	2,869,760	4,038,672	3,160,851
Biscuits and rolls	4,213,911	1,042,982	922,469	1,276,618	962,730
Cakes and cupcakes	4,201,880	865,583	843,775	1,357,315	1,137,262
Bread and cracker products	482,308	116,937	100,811	160,629	103,010
Sweetrolls, coffee cakes, doughnuts	2,480,444	443,183	661,698	768,342	612,935
Pies, tarts, turnovers	1,452,394	290,977	341,265	475,768	344,913
Meats, poultry, fish, and eggs	**86,993,793**	**18,540,431**	**18,530,127**	**29,786,736**	**20,050,374**
Beef	26,050,126	5,199,794	5,823,615	8,813,178	6,214,542
Ground beef	9,598,048	1,745,861	2,263,353	3,579,350	2,008,211
Roast	4,357,181	830,733	927,869	1,410,476	1,193,649
Chuck roast	1,457,862	230,934	335,350	494,890	401,056
Round roast	1,253,346	300,214	267,971	352,619	331,732
Other roast	1,645,973	299,584	324,549	563,349	460,861
Steak	10,337,369	2,241,319	2,257,695	3,228,260	2,607,964
Round steak	1,674,409	347,661	350,008	547,668	429,128
Sirloin steak	3,265,699	787,905	686,130	935,473	853,130
Other steak	5,397,261	1,105,544	1,221,558	1,744,737	1,325,707
Other beef	1,758,621	381,881	374,954	595,092	404,718
Pork	18,257,727	3,391,791	4,111,891	6,744,506	4,006,657
Bacon	2,849,010	470,476	635,724	1,165,325	577,297
Pork chops	4,437,019	885,107	917,325	1,716,818	910,005
Ham	3,965,647	791,054	1,002,449	1,402,444	765,742
Ham, not canned	3,775,349	745,707	975,446	1,356,933	693,488
Canned ham	190,299	45,347	27,260	45,894	72,254
Sausage	2,760,423	527,369	606,150	1,064,358	559,477
Other pork	4,245,627	717,575	950,243	1,395,178	1,194,137
Other meats	10,995,758	2,435,094	2,647,308	3,591,588	2,306,501
Frankfurters	2,261,710	448,222	534,914	806,587	470,137

	total consumer units	Northeast	Midwest	South	West
Lunch meats (cold cuts)	$7,435,862	$1,698,625	$1,905,887	$2,306,556	$1,514,152
Bologna, liverwurst, salami	2,595,279	602,318	649,611	834,123	503,822
Other lunch meats	4,840,583	1,096,307	1,256,275	1,472,433	1,010,330
Lamb, organ meats, and others	1,298,186	288,248	206,508	478,827	322,212
Lamb and organ meats	1,061,954	242,271	178,219	353,001	287,306
Mutton, goat, and game	236,233	45,977	28,289	125,826	34,906
Poultry	15,875,714	3,645,608	3,211,796	5,414,345	3,571,915
Fresh and frozen chicken	12,514,866	2,887,515	2,432,057	4,291,471	2,878,915
Fresh and frozen whole chicken	3,417,719	766,911	620,551	1,162,648	863,138
Fresh and frozen chicken parts	9,097,147	2,120,604	1,811,248	3,128,441	2,015,778
Other poultry	3,360,848	758,093	779,997	1,122,873	693,244
Fish and seafood	12,045,681	3,132,095	2,012,098	3,833,296	3,032,698
Canned fish and seafood	1,713,781	412,742	316,062	568,321	412,773
Fresh fish and shellfish	7,307,903	2,037,048	992,419	2,434,677	1,810,490
Frozen fish and shellfish	3,023,998	682,305	703,360	830,681	809,192
Eggs	3,768,787	736,050	723,419	1,389,823	918,304
Dairy products	**35,503,809**	**7,431,036**	**8,474,523**	**10,926,214**	**8,682,393**
Fresh milk and cream	14,351,138	2,769,738	3,399,273	4,652,504	3,542,379
Fresh milk, all types	13,081,387	2,522,219	3,136,445	4,272,349	3,159,875
Cream	1,269,751	247,519	262,828	380,155	382,749
Other dairy products	21,152,671	4,661,298	5,075,250	6,274,092	5,140,014
Butter	1,859,239	490,840	493,252	503,687	366,638
Cheese	10,494,857	2,262,733	2,603,846	3,085,607	2,544,743
Ice cream and related products	6,185,798	1,333,119	1,387,946	1,915,692	1,549,059
Miscellaneous dairy products	2,612,778	574,606	590,205	769,107	679,330
Fruits and vegetables	**56,961,615**	**12,164,553**	**12,391,222**	**17,959,852**	**14,443,641**
Fresh fruits	17,845,413	3,802,643	3,871,952	5,399,047	4,779,966
Apples	3,225,233	709,597	709,789	1,011,963	792,105
Bananas	3,466,934	755,574	702,588	1,114,077	893,406
Oranges	2,070,317	455,360	441,047	613,832	560,210
Citrus fruits, excl. oranges	1,565,042	290,347	310,919	499,480	467,452
Other fresh fruits	7,517,888	1,591,765	1,707,609	2,159,695	2,066,795
Fresh vegetables	17,358,730	3,873,393	3,522,200	5,333,265	4,625,939
Potatoes	3,069,932	635,488	634,953	1,055,562	742,064
Lettuce	2,269,365	516,662	482,451	719,771	547,760
Tomatoes	3,229,608	742,348	596,892	1,031,085	856,303
Other fresh vegetables	8,790,919	1,978,894	1,808,162	2,526,847	2,479,812
Processed fruits	12,578,299	2,740,767	2,907,821	3,925,084	2,999,013
Frozen fruits and fruit juices	1,571,604	237,442	442,332	426,049	474,286
Frozen orange juice	754,632	119,456	211,651	208,435	218,958
Frozen fruits	395,909	69,070	101,325	99,819	127,420
Frozen fruit juices	419,969	48,706	129,099	117,795	127,664
Canned fruits	1,693,001	351,230	424,588	535,812	380,796
Dried fruits	601,519	113,368	138,872	187,783	162,815
Fresh fruit juice	2,563,562	661,731	564,488	793,584	535,555
Canned and bottled fruit juice	6,147,519	1,376,996	1,337,541	1,981,091	1,445,560
Processed vegetables	9,180,266	1,747,960	2,088,992	3,302,838	2,038,479
Frozen vegetables	2,889,476	678,316	640,353	990,928	572,170
Canned and dried vegetables and juices	6,290,790	1,069,644	1,448,381	2,311,910	1,466,309
Canned beans	1,385,680	215,398	298,574	595,857	275,833
Canned corn	743,696	126,174	160,474	296,781	160,130
Canned miscellaneous vegetables	1,963,138	369,704	502,253	691,087	400,324
Dried peas	37,185	9,657	8,487	9,561	9,032
Dried beans	276,699	45,137	32,918	92,170	108,136

	total consumer units	Northeast	Midwest	South	West
Dried miscellaneous vegetables	$789,630	$115,887	$181,048	$291,044	$203,091
Dried processed vegetables	44,840	3,359	10,287	15,680	15,867
Frozen vegetable juices	31,716	5,039	10,287	4,972	11,717
Fresh and canned vegetable juices	1,017,113	179,289	243,797	314,756	282,424
Other food at home	**101,358,055**	**18,783,332**	**24,614,512**	**33,151,148**	**24,920,901**
Sugar and other sweets	12,811,250	2,655,531	3,189,937	4,105,218	2,858,167
Candy and chewing gum	8,344,702	1,812,622	2,241,751	2,472,922	1,815,128
Sugar	1,837,366	326,037	350,266	735,834	425,222
Artificial sweeteners	458,248	90,274	76,894	217,232	71,521
Jams, preserves, other sweets	2,172,029	426,598	521,026	679,614	546,296
Fats and oils	9,087,304	1,868,676	1,937,776	3,153,683	2,121,229
Margarine	1,269,751	239,332	296,517	452,821	280,715
Fats and oils	2,553,719	555,921	443,618	969,511	578,517
Salad dressings	2,972,595	599,589	677,900	976,012	719,119
Nondairy cream and imitation milk	1,000,708	181,178	220,652	358,356	241,171
Peanut butter	1,291,624	292,656	299,089	396,983	301,464
Miscellaneous foods	47,795,566	8,360,231	12,025,269	15,678,920	11,819,810
Frozen prepared foods	9,864,903	1,589,456	2,696,942	3,305,898	2,295,028
Frozen meals	3,116,960	556,761	839,146	1,062,446	661,267
Other frozen prepared foods	6,747,944	1,032,695	1,857,796	2,243,452	1,633,761
Canned and packaged soups	3,886,903	739,409	967,474	1,201,275	984,699
Potato chips, nuts, and other snacks	10,116,448	1,883,582	2,627,249	3,256,944	2,360,691
Potato chips and other snacks	7,838,333	1,480,917	2,116,766	2,505,430	1,742,386
Nuts	2,278,115	402,875	510,482	751,132	618,305
Condiments and seasonings	9,253,542	1,658,526	2,303,729	2,970,107	2,337,746
Salt, spices, and other seasonings	2,258,429	370,964	525,655	767,577	599,754
Olives, pickles, relishes	1,068,516	170,891	277,229	350,707	272,416
Sauces and gravies	4,071,733	803,650	968,759	1,294,211	1,008,621
Baking needs and miscellaneous products	1,854,864	313,230	532,085	557,612	456,711
Other canned/packaged prepared foods	14,673,770	2,489,259	3,429,619	4,944,696	3,841,890
Prepared salads	2,028,758	423,869	442,847	638,309	523,595
Prepared desserts	1,018,207	214,139	259,485	289,515	256,305
Baby food	3,528,179	550,673	803,913	1,388,676	789,419
Miscellaneous prepared foods	8,083,315	1,295,330	1,920,031	2,625,519	2,268,177
Vitamin supplements	15,311	5,039	3,343	2,677	4,150
Nonalcoholic beverages	27,295,816	5,048,217	6,412,534	9,096,573	6,770,114
Cola	9,513,835	1,395,681	2,533,382	3,452,759	2,155,159
Other carbonated drinks	5,182,902	943,680	1,385,118	1,700,755	1,159,475
Coffee	4,577,009	1,000,364	902,924	1,462,489	1,209,760
Roasted coffee	3,007,593	647,665	596,377	945,799	817,979
Instant and freeze-dried coffee	1,569,416	352,699	306,547	516,690	391,781
Noncarbonated fruit-flavored drinks, incl. nonfrozen lemonade	2,123,907	379,152	453,391	706,768	588,525
Tea	1,714,875	458,089	310,919	557,995	380,552
Nonalcoholic beer	29,529	6,298	9,772	3,825	10,252
Other nonalcoholic beverages and ice	4,154,852	864,743	817,029	1,212,367	1,266,879
Food prepared by CU on trips	4,368,118	850,677	1,049,254	1,116,372	1,351,582
FOOD AWAY FROM HOME	**233,704,155**	**45,671,607**	**59,715,646**	**72,717,131**	**55,774,409**
Meals at restaurants, carry-outs, other	**191,428,341**	**36,785,897**	**48,302,441**	**61,130,808**	**45,384,537**
Lunch	72,499,384	13,734,275	17,585,542	24,249,242	16,978,131
At fast food, take-out, delivery, concession stands, buffet, and cafeteria (other than employer and school cafeteria)	40,247,056	7,327,956	9,845,753	13,724,983	9,385,645
At full-service restaurants	22,761,460	4,323,294	5,143,914	7,555,300	5,760,028
At vending machines, mobile vendors	713,073	143,599	144,787	218,379	207,485
At employer and school cafeterias	8,777,795	1,939,426	2,450,830	2,750,580	1,624,974

	total consumer units	Northeast	Midwest	South	West
Dinner	$76,337,072	$15,237,025	$19,467,512	$23,445,332	$18,249,160
At fast food, take-out, delivery, concession stands, buffet, and cafeteria (other than employer and school cafeteria)	22,630,220	3,933,016	6,344,641	6,789,252	5,622,599
At full-service restaurants	53,338,286	11,277,977	12,998,143	16,480,918	12,581,646
At vending machines, mobile vendors	111,554	420	32,146	64,252	15,867
At employer and school cafeterias	257,012	25,823	92,581	110,911	29,048
Snacks and nonalcoholic beverages	24,903,960	4,823,581	6,548,577	7,785,535	5,769,792
At fast food, take-out, delivery, concession stands, buffet, and cafeteria (other than employer and school cafeteria)	17,340,138	3,637,420	4,415,352	5,029,982	4,269,309
At full-service restaurants	2,203,745	389,229	548,801	699,119	571,926
At vending machines, mobile vendors	4,212,817	586,152	1,293,308	1,643,770	695,197
At employer and school cafeterias	1,147,260	210,990	291,116	412,281	233,116
Breakfast and brunch	17,687,925	2,991,015	4,700,810	5,651,081	4,387,698
At fast food, take-out, delivery, concession stands, buffet, and cafeteria (other than employer and school cafeteria)	8,434,383	1,384,344	2,255,124	2,907,002	1,902,515
At full-service restaurants	8,709,988	1,504,640	2,339,218	2,542,910	2,350,927
At vending machines, mobile vendors	147,645	20,784	27,260	48,954	51,017
At employer and school cafeterias	395,909	81,457	79,208	151,833	83,238
Board (including at school)	**4,268,594**	**953,967**	**1,288,679**	**1,203,953**	**822,129**
Catered affairs	**5,908,005**	**1,264,889**	**1,864,997**	**894,933**	**1,883,476**
Food on trips	**23,629,834**	**5,220,998**	**5,841,874**	**6,747,948**	**5,818,856**
School lunches	**6,393,595**	**1,095,887**	**1,905,373**	**2,274,048**	**1,118,466**
Meals as pay	**2,074,692**	**349,760**	**512,283**	**465,442**	**747,190**
ALCOHOLIC BEVERAGES	**40,663,744**	**8,198,157**	**9,967,395**	**11,611,564**	**10,952,523**
At home	**24,786,937**	**5,034,781**	**5,865,019**	**7,113,952**	**6,811,611**
Beer and ale	12,250,198	2,510,043	3,052,608	3,600,767	3,098,605
Whiskey	1,475,361	239,542	428,188	584,001	222,863
Wine	8,753,735	1,739,773	1,761,357	2,433,912	2,842,789
Other alcoholic beverages	2,307,644	545,634	622,609	495,273	647,353
Away from home	**15,876,807**	**3,163,166**	**4,102,633**	**4,497,612**	**4,140,912**
Beer and ale	6,831,063	1,284,203	1,799,676	2,032,339	1,728,228
At fast food, take-out, delivery, concession stands, buffet, and cafeteria	1,462,237	238,282	486,051	421,842	320,015
At full-service restaurants	4,926,983	1,039,203	1,284,821	1,223,840	1,389,661
At vending machines, mobile vendors	43,747	–	22,117	15,680	6,591
At catered affairs	398,096	6,718	6,429	370,594	11,717
Wine	1,945,639	321,418	433,331	608,860	588,037
At fast food, take-out, delivery, concession stands, buffet and cafeteria	134,521	20,574	24,688	58,897	30,757
At full-service restaurants	1,767,371	300,004	408,129	510,953	556,060
At catered affairs	42,653	630	772	39,392	1,221
Other alcoholic beverages	7,100,106	1,557,545	1,869,626	1,856,412	1,824,648
At fast food, take-out, delivery, concession stands, buffet, and cafeteria	332,476	53,535	90,010	107,851	82,506
At full-service restaurants	2,815,107	525,270	741,164	786,700	770,136
At machines and mobile vendors	31,716	1,050	10,030	14,916	6,103
At catered affairs	174,987	2,939	2,829	163,306	5,126
Alcoholic beverages purchased on trips	3,744,726	974,751	1,025,594	783,640	960,534

Note: Numbers may not add to total because of rounding. (–) means sample is too small to make a reliable estimate.
Source: Calculations by New Strategist based on the 2000 Consumer Expenditure Survey

Table 5.25 Food and Alcohol: Market shares by region, 2000

(percentage of total annual spending on food and alcoholic beverages accounted for by consumer units by region, 2000)

	total consumer units	Northeast	Midwest	South	West
Share of total consumer units	100.0%	19.2%	23.5%	35.0%	22.3%
Share of total before-tax income	100.0	20.4	23.4	32.9	23.3
Share of total spending	100.0	19.6	24.2	31.9	24.2
Share of food spending	100.0	20.0	24.0	32.0	24.0
Share of alcoholic beverages spending	100.0	20.2	24.5	28.6	26.9
FOOD AT HOME	100.0%	20.3%	22.8%	32.7%	24.2%
Cereals and bakery products	100.0	20.8	23.0	32.5	23.6
Cereals and cereal products	100.0	20.2	22.9	33.1	23.8
Flour	100.0	15.1	18.9	40.8	25.3
Prepared flour mixes	100.0	17.7	24.2	34.8	23.4
Ready-to-eat and cooked cereals	100.0	20.6	24.5	32.1	22.7
Rice	100.0	20.3	18.2	34.6	26.8
Pasta, cornmeal, and other cereal products	100.0	21.3	21.7	32.4	24.6
Bakery products	100.0	21.1	23.1	32.2	23.5
Bread	100.0	21.8	23.1	31.7	23.3
White bread	100.0	21.6	23.4	34.3	20.5
Bread, other than white	100.0	22.0	22.9	29.6	25.5
Crackers and cookies	100.0	21.0	23.8	32.4	22.8
Cookies	100.0	22.0	23.2	31.6	23.1
Crackers	100.0	18.9	25.0	34.0	22.2
Frozen and refrigerated bakery products	100.0	17.0	24.8	37.2	21.1
Other bakery products	100.0	21.5	22.4	31.5	24.6
Biscuits and rolls	100.0	24.8	21.9	30.3	22.8
Cakes and cupcakes	100.0	20.6	20.1	32.3	27.1
Bread and cracker products	100.0	24.2	20.9	33.3	21.4
Sweetrolls, coffee cakes, doughnuts	100.0	17.9	26.7	31.0	24.7
Pies, tarts, turnovers	100.0	20.0	23.5	32.8	23.7
Meats, poultry, fish, and eggs	100.0	21.3	21.3	34.2	23.0
Beef	100.0	20.0	22.4	33.8	23.9
Ground beef	100.0	18.2	23.6	37.3	20.9
Roast	100.0	19.1	21.3	32.4	27.4
Chuck roast	100.0	15.8	23.0	33.9	27.5
Round roast	100.0	24.0	21.4	28.1	26.5
Other roast	100.0	18.2	19.7	34.2	28.0
Steak	100.0	21.7	21.8	31.2	25.2
Round steak	100.0	20.8	20.9	32.7	25.6
Sirloin steak	100.0	24.1	21.0	28.6	26.1
Other steak	100.0	20.5	22.6	32.3	24.6
Other beef	100.0	21.7	21.3	33.8	23.0
Pork	100.0	18.6	22.5	36.9	21.9
Bacon	100.0	16.5	22.3	40.9	20.3
Pork chops	100.0	19.9	20.7	38.7	20.5
Ham	100.0	19.9	25.3	35.4	19.3
Ham, not canned	100.0	19.8	25.8	35.9	18.4
Canned ham	100.0	23.8	14.3	24.1	38.0
Sausage	100.0	19.1	22.0	38.6	20.3
Other pork	100.0	16.9	22.4	32.9	28.1
Other meats	100.0	22.1	24.1	32.7	21.0
Frankfurters	100.0	19.8	23.7	35.7	20.8

	total consumer units	Northeast	Midwest	South	West
Lunch meats (cold cuts)	100.0%	22.8%	25.6%	31.0%	20.4%
Bologna, liverwurst, salami	100.0	23.2	25.0	32.1	19.4
Other lunch meats	100.0	22.6	26.0	30.4	20.9
Lamb, organ meats, and others	100.0	22.2	15.9	36.9	24.8
Lamb and organ meats	100.0	22.8	16.8	33.2	27.1
Mutton, goat, and game	100.0	19.5	12.0	53.3	14.8
Poultry	100.0	23.0	20.2	34.1	22.5
Fresh and frozen chicken	100.0	23.1	19.4	34.3	23.0
Fresh and frozen whole chicken	100.0	22.4	18.2	34.0	25.3
Fresh and frozen chicken parts	100.0	23.3	19.9	34.4	22.2
Other poultry	100.0	22.6	23.2	33.4	20.6
Fish and seafood	100.0	26.0	16.7	31.8	25.2
Canned fish and seafood	100.0	24.1	18.4	33.2	24.1
Fresh fish and shellfish	100.0	27.9	13.6	33.3	24.8
Frozen fish and shellfish	100.0	22.6	23.3	27.5	26.8
Eggs	100.0	19.5	19.2	36.9	24.4
Dairy products	**100.0**	**20.9**	**23.9**	**30.8**	**24.5**
Fresh milk and cream	100.0	19.3	23.7	32.4	24.7
Fresh milk, all types	100.0	19.3	24.0	32.7	24.2
Cream	100.0	19.5	20.7	29.9	30.1
Other dairy products	100.0	22.0	24.0	29.7	24.3
Butter	100.0	26.4	26.5	27.1	19.7
Cheese	100.0	21.6	24.8	29.4	24.2
Ice cream and related products	100.0	21.6	22.4	31.0	25.0
Miscellaneous dairy products	100.0	22.0	22.6	29.4	26.0
Fruits and vegetables	**100.0**	**21.4**	**21.8**	**31.5**	**25.4**
Fresh fruits	100.0	21.3	21.7	30.3	26.8
Apples	100.0	22.0	22.0	31.4	24.6
Bananas	100.0	21.8	20.3	32.1	25.8
Oranges	100.0	22.0	21.3	29.6	27.1
Citrus fruits, excl. oranges	100.0	18.6	19.9	31.9	29.9
Other fresh fruits	100.0	21.2	22.7	28.7	27.5
Fresh vegetables	100.0	22.3	20.3	30.7	26.6
Potatoes	100.0	20.7	20.7	34.4	24.2
Lettuce	100.0	22.8	21.3	31.7	24.1
Tomatoes	100.0	23.0	18.5	31.9	26.5
Other fresh vegetables	100.0	22.5	20.6	28.7	28.2
Processed fruits	100.0	21.8	23.1	31.2	23.8
Frozen fruits and fruit juices	100.0	15.1	28.1	27.1	30.2
Frozen orange juice	100.0	15.8	28.0	27.6	29.0
Frozen fruits	100.0	17.4	25.6	25.2	32.2
Frozen fruit juices	100.0	11.6	30.7	28.0	30.4
Canned fruits	100.0	20.7	25.1	31.6	22.5
Dried fruits	100.0	18.8	23.1	31.2	27.1
Fresh fruit juice	100.0	25.8	22.0	31.0	20.9
Canned and bottled fruit juice	100.0	22.4	21.8	32.2	23.5
Processed vegetables	100.0	19.0	22.8	36.0	22.2
Frozen vegetables	100.0	23.5	22.2	34.3	19.8
Canned and dried vegetables and juices	100.0	17.0	23.0	36.8	23.3
Canned beans	100.0	15.5	21.5	43.0	19.9
Canned corn	100.0	17.0	21.6	39.9	21.5
Canned miscellaneous vegetables	100.0	18.8	25.6	35.2	20.4
Dried peas	100.0	26.0	22.8	25.7	24.3
Dried beans	100.0	16.3	11.9	33.3	39.1

	total consumer units	Northeast	Midwest	South	West
Dried miscellaneous vegetables	100.0%	14.7%	22.9%	36.9%	25.7%
Dried processed vegetables	100.0	7.5	22.9	35.0	35.4
Frozen vegetable juices	100.0	15.9	32.4	15.7	36.9
Fresh and canned vegetable juices	100.0	17.6	24.0	30.9	27.8
Other food at home	**100.0**	**18.5**	**24.3**	**32.7**	**24.6**
Sugar and other sweets	100.0	20.7	24.9	32.0	22.3
Candy and chewing gum	100.0	21.7	26.9	29.6	21.8
Sugar	100.0	17.7	19.1	40.0	23.1
Artificial sweeteners	100.0	19.7	16.8	47.4	15.6
Jams, preserves, other sweets	100.0	19.6	24.0	31.3	25.2
Fats and oils	100.0	20.6	21.3	34.7	23.3
Margarine	100.0	18.8	23.4	35.7	22.1
Fats and oils	100.0	21.8	17.4	38.0	22.7
Salad dressings	100.0	20.2	22.8	32.8	24.2
Nondairy cream and imitation milk	100.0	18.1	22.0	35.8	24.1
Peanut butter	100.0	22.7	23.2	30.7	23.3
Miscellaneous foods	100.0	17.5	25.2	32.8	24.7
Frozen prepared foods	100.0	16.1	27.3	33.5	23.3
Frozen meals	100.0	17.9	26.9	34.1	21.2
Other frozen prepared foods	100.0	15.3	27.5	33.2	24.2
Canned and packaged soups	100.0	19.0	24.9	30.9	25.3
Potato chips, nuts, and other snacks	100.0	18.6	26.0	32.2	23.3
Potato chips and other snacks	100.0	18.9	27.0	32.0	22.2
Nuts	100.0	17.7	22.4	33.0	27.1
Condiments and seasonings	100.0	17.9	24.9	32.1	25.3
Salt, spices, and other seasonings	100.0	16.4	23.3	34.0	26.6
Olives, pickles, relishes	100.0	16.0	25.9	32.8	25.5
Sauces and gravies	100.0	19.7	23.8	31.8	24.8
Baking needs and miscellaneous products	100.0	16.9	28.7	30.1	24.6
Other canned/packaged prepared foods	100.0	17.0	23.4	33.7	26.2
Prepared salads	100.0	20.9	21.8	31.5	25.8
Prepared desserts	100.0	21.0	25.5	28.4	25.2
Baby food	100.0	15.6	22.8	39.4	22.4
Miscellaneous prepared foods	100.0	16.0	23.8	32.5	28.1
Vitamin supplements	100.0	32.9	21.8	17.5	27.1
Nonalcoholic beverages	100.0	18.5	23.5	33.3	24.8
Cola	100.0	14.7	26.6	36.3	22.7
Other carbonated drinks	100.0	18.2	26.7	32.8	22.4
Coffee	100.0	21.9	19.7	32.0	26.4
Roasted coffee	100.0	21.5	19.8	31.4	27.2
Instant and freeze-dried coffee	100.0	22.5	19.5	32.9	25.0
Noncarbonated fruit-flavored drinks, incl. nonfrozen lemonade	100.0	17.9	21.3	33.3	27.7
Tea	100.0	26.7	18.1	32.5	22.2
Nonalcoholic beer	100.0	21.3	33.1	13.0	34.7
Other nonalcoholic beverages and ice	100.0	20.8	19.7	29.2	30.5
Food prepared by CU on trips	100.0	19.5	24.0	25.6	30.9
FOOD AWAY FROM HOME	**100.0**	**19.5**	**25.6**	**31.1**	**23.9**
Meals at restaurants, carry-outs, other	**100.0**	**19.2**	**25.2**	**31.9**	**23.7**
Lunch	100.0	18.9	24.3	33.4	23.4
At fast food, take-out, delivery, concession stands, buffet, and cafeteria (other than employer and school cafeteria)	100.0	18.2	24.5	34.1	23.3
At full-service restaurants	100.0	19.0	22.6	33.2	25.3
At vending machines, mobile vendors	100.0	20.1	20.3	30.6	29.1
At employer and school cafeterias	100.0	22.1	27.9	31.3	18.5

	total consumer units	Northeast	Midwest	South	West
Dinner	100.0%	20.0%	25.5%	30.7%	23.9%
At fast food, take-out, delivery, concession stands, buffet, and cafeteria (other than employer and school cafeteria)	100.0	17.4	28.0	30.0	24.8
At full-service restaurants	100.0	21.1	24.4	30.9	23.6
At vending machines, mobile vendors	100.0	0.4	28.8	57.6	14.2
At employer and school cafeterias	100.0	10.0	36.0	43.2	11.3
Snacks and nonalcoholic beverages	100.0	19.4	26.3	31.3	23.2
At fast food, take-out, delivery, concession stands, buffet, and cafeteria (other than employer and school cafeteria)	100.0	21.0	25.5	29.0	24.6
At full-service restaurants	100.0	17.7	24.9	31.7	26.0
At vending machines, mobile vendors	100.0	13.9	30.7	39.0	16.5
At employer and school cafeterias	100.0	18.4	25.4	35.9	20.3
Breakfast and brunch	100.0	16.9	26.6	31.9	24.8
At fast food, take-out, delivery, concession stands, buffet, and cafeteria (other than employer and school cafeteria)	100.0	16.4	26.7	34.5	22.6
At full-service restaurants	100.0	17.3	26.9	29.2	27.0
At vending machines, mobile vendors	100.0	14.1	18.5	33.2	34.6
At employer and school cafeterias	100.0	20.6	20.0	38.4	21.0
Board (including at school)	**100.0**	**22.3**	**30.2**	**28.2**	**19.3**
Catered affairs	**100.0**	**21.4**	**31.6**	**15.1**	**31.9**
Food on trips	**100.0**	**22.1**	**24.7**	**28.6**	**24.6**
School lunches	**100.0**	**17.1**	**29.8**	**35.6**	**17.5**
Meals as pay	**100.0**	**16.9**	**24.7**	**22.4**	**36.0**
ALCOHOLIC BEVERAGES	**100.0**	**20.2**	**24.5**	**28.6**	**26.9**
At home	**100.0**	**20.3**	**23.7**	**28.7**	**27.5**
Beer and ale	100.0	20.5	24.9	29.4	25.3
Whiskey	100.0	16.2	29.0	39.6	15.1
Wine	100.0	19.9	20.1	27.8	32.5
Other alcoholic beverages	100.0	23.6	27.0	21.5	28.1
Away from home	**100.0**	**19.9**	**25.8**	**28.3**	**26.1**
Beer and ale	100.0	18.8	26.3	29.8	25.3
At fast food, take-out, delivery, concession stands, buffet, and cafeteria	100.0	16.3	33.2	28.8	21.9
At full-service restaurants	100.0	21.1	26.1	24.8	28.2
At vending machines, mobile vendors	100.0	–	50.6	35.8	15.1
At catered affairs	100.0	1.7	1.6	93.1	2.9
Wine	100.0	16.5	22.3	31.3	30.2
At fast food, take-out, delivery, concession stands, buffet and cafeteria	100.0	15.3	18.4	43.8	22.9
At full-service restaurants	100.0	17.0	23.1	28.9	31.5
At catered affairs	100.0	1.5	1.8	92.4	2.9
Other alcoholic beverages	100.0	21.9	26.3	26.1	25.7
At fast food, take-out, delivery, concession stands, buffet, and cafeteria	100.0	16.1	27.1	32.4	24.8
At full-service restaurants	100.0	18.7	26.3	27.9	27.4
At machines and mobile vendors	100.0	3.3	31.6	47.0	19.2
At catered affairs	100.0	1.7	1.6	93.3	2.9
Alcoholic beverages purchased on trips	100.0	26.0	27.4	20.9	25.7

Note: Numbers may not add to total because of rounding. (–) means sample is too small to make a reliable estimate.
Source: Calculations by New Strategist based on the 2000 Consumer Expenditure Survey

Spending on Gifts, 2000

Gift spending fell 10 percent between 1990 and 2000, to $1,083 after adjusting for inflation. This figure represents the amount households spend on gifts for non-household members. Gift spending fell sharply, as much as 32 percent for traditional gifts such as women's apparel. Gift spending rose 8 percent for entertainment items and climbed 6 percent for miscellaneous household equipment. Gifts of educational expenses also rose.

Households headed by 45-to-54-year-olds spend the most on gifts, a total of $1,724 in 2000—59 percent more than the average household. This age group is the most affluent and accounts for 32 percent of all spending on gifts although it represents just 20 percent of households. Householders aged 55 to 64 spend 24 percent more than the average household on gifts, or $1,345 in 2000. All other age groups spend less than average on gifts.

Households with incomes of $70,000 or more spent $2,577 on gifts in 2000, more than twice the average. While overall spending on gifts is less in lower-income households, gift spending by category varies by household income. Lower-income households spend more than the average household on practical gifts such as helping a relative pay for housing repairs, electric or phone bills.

Among household types, married couples with adult children at home (many of whom also have children living away from home) spend the most on gifts for non-household members—60 percent more than the average household. Married couples without children at home, many of them empty-nesters, spend 36 percent more than average on gifts. Spending on gifts for non-household members is well below average for married couples with preschoolers and for single parents. Typically, these households have little discretionary income.

Black and Hispanic households spend less than average on gifts for non-household members, but they spend more than average on a variety of individual gift categories. Black and Hispanic households spend more than average on gifts of telephone service. Black households spend more than twice the average and Hispanics more than three times the average on gifts of men's coats and jackets. Hispanics spend 50 percent more than average on gifts of infant clothing.

Households in the Midwest spend the most on gifts for non-household members, 19 percent more than the average household. In the South, spending on gifts is 16 percent below average.

Table 6.1 Gifts: Average spending by age, 2000

(average annual spending of consumer units (CU) on gifts of products and services for non–household members, by age of consumer unit reference person, 2000)

	total consumer units	under 25	25 to 34	35 to 44	45 to 54	55 to 64	65 to 74	75+
Number of consumer units (in thousands, add 000)	109,367	8,306	18,887	23,983	21,874	14,161	11,538	10,617
Average number of persons per CU	2.5	1.9	2.9	3.3	2.7	2.1	1.9	1.5
Average before-tax income of CU	$44,649.00	$19,744.00	$45,498.00	$56,500.00	$58,889.00	$48,108.00	$29,349.00	$20,563.00
Average spending of CU, total	38,044.67	22,543.18	38,945.27	45,149.37	46,160.28	39,340.03	30,781.81	21,908.04
Gifts, average spending	1,083.14	597.01	715.83	1,001.08	1,724.18	1,345.18	968.45	755.25
FOOD	**$70.09**	**$11.43**	**$32.01**	**$67.42**	**$136.72**	**$121.17**	**$28.59**	**$29.43**
Fresh fruits	4.58	0.15	3.19	3.35	2.75	8.64	2.87	13.89
Candy and chewing gum	12.50	1.42	9.32	23.59	16.57	6.73	7.64	5.83
Board (including at school)	20.21	4.70	1.06	9.69	74.66	20.04	0.17	–
Catered affairs	15.59	0.18	5.76	12.39	18.61	53.11	7.98	4.39
ALCOHOLIC BEVERAGES	**14.49**	**5.89**	**26.67**	**17.50**	**16.80**	**9.67**	**3.39**	**5.97**
Beer and ale	3.64	3.26	5.38	3.28	5.22	3.90	0.60	1.39
Wine	6.76	2.23	12.61	8.60	7.14	3.83	2.54	3.16
Whiskey and other alcoholic beverages	3.73	0.37	8.61	5.11	3.76	1.40	–	1.36
HOUSING	**291.10**	**143.41**	**214.84**	**274.29**	**428.33**	**334.61**	**268.05**	**268.69**
Housekeeping supplies	**39.10**	**27.45**	**35.53**	**45.74**	**43.50**	**45.43**	**36.74**	**24.15**
Miscellaneous household products	7.32	10.04	5.96	10.15	8.35	6.85	4.48	2.25
Lawn and garden supplies	3.08	0.61	1.73	5.49	2.22	3.85	2.92	2.65
Postage and stationery	24.95	15.39	23.94	25.72	28.24	29.18	27.38	17.77
Stationery, stationery supplies, giftwraps	20.28	13.85	18.40	22.80	22.93	24.09	18.90	13.83
Postage	4.57	1.54	5.54	2.79	5.31	5.09	8.48	3.12
Household textiles	**13.20**	**3.23**	**8.20**	**12.01**	**20.95**	**22.67**	**12.44**	**5.39**
Bathroom linens	2.79	–	3.45	1.70	7.08	1.30	1.95	0.83
Bedroom linens	6.85	1.90	2.60	6.92	8.99	17.90	4.85	1.13
Appliances and miscellaneous housewares	**28.14**	**10.03**	**19.12**	**26.48**	**41.53**	**38.16**	**31.41**	**18.17**
Major appliances	7.61	0.56	3.92	4.00	15.83	8.79	10.99	6.08
Electric floor cleaning equipment	3.01	–	3.01	1.92	6.33	3.90	–	3.53
Small appliances and miscellaneous housewares	20.53	9.47	15.20	22.48	25.70	29.37	20.42	12.10
Glassware	3.60	0.27	6.14	4.00	2.95	1.61	5.16	3.13
Nonelectric cookware	3.66	0.94	2.72	1.89	5.36	10.33	1.83	1.27
Tableware, nonelectric kitchenware	4.34	5.71	1.34	6.77	3.88	4.58	3.29	4.57
Small electric kitchen appliances	2.68	0.88	2.37	2.70	3.56	3.88	3.10	0.72
Miscellaneous household equipment	**70.31**	**30.03**	**46.22**	**73.24**	**97.92**	**81.25**	**93.15**	**42.48**
Infants' equipment	2.72	0.29	2.30	5.58	3.36	2.07	1.07	–
Outdoor equipment	2.86	1.80	1.83	1.75	1.78	3.79	1.27	11.07
Household decorative items	27.33	11.28	19.14	34.74	32.39	23.36	47.13	11.55
Indoor plants, fresh flowers	16.04	9.54	9.89	12.47	23.98	25.00	19.19	8.41
Computers and computer hardware, nonbusiness use	8.97	1.08	5.23	7.23	20.74	5.06	14.82	0.31
Miscellaneous household equipment and parts	2.53	2.04	2.41	2.37	3.81	1.59	3.56	1.11
Other housing	**140.36**	**72.67**	**105.77**	**116.82**	**224.44**	**147.10**	**94.30**	**178.49**
Repair or maintenance services	3.74	0.19	1.68	3.73	2.50	1.40	1.34	18.49
Housing while attending school	42.32	9.01	0.99	16.23	146.27	62.76	3.78	1.22
Natural gas (renter)	3.11	2.81	2.35	2.87	2.02	5.68	2.75	4.44
Electricity (renter)	13.28	12.06	17.81	11.94	7.44	12.34	16.16	19.34
Telephone services in home city, excl. mobile phones	13.64	30.60	16.78	13.82	9.63	10.17	10.87	10.24

	total consumer units	under 25	25 to 34	35 to 44	45 to 54	55 to 64	65 to 74	75+
Water, sewerage maintenance (renter)	$2.67	$2.05	$3.65	$1.89	$1.49	$2.79	$4.17	$3.79
Care for elderly, invalids, handicapped	2.10	–	–	0.69	4.94	1.04	0.65	7.80
Day-care centers, nurseries, and preschools	21.46	4.48	42.78	39.08	11.82	15.53	6.26	1.29
Housekeeping services	3.44	0.04	1.34	1.68	7.67	2.16	5.77	4.24
Gardening, lawn care service	3.14	0.18	0.87	0.91	3.07	2.84	5.95	12.04
Repair of miscellaneous household equipment and furnishings	7.78	–	–	1.87	–	–	–	78.56
Bedroom furniture except mattress and springs	2.06	–	0.92	0.10	5.77	2.88	3.35	–
APPAREL AND SERVICES	**244.25**	**143.30**	**219.69**	**278.53**	**314.10**	**296.04**	**208.96**	**113.29**
Men and boys, aged 2 or older	**67.55**	**32.85**	**56.88**	**65.28**	**90.10**	**106.83**	**52.60**	**36.89**
Men's coats and jackets	3.30	0.47	4.32	1.69	7.18	4.09	2.12	–
Men's underwear	2.10	4.55	1.63	1.30	3.49	1.67	0.49	2.38
Men's accessories	3.40	2.19	2.77	3.68	2.84	2.56	3.50	7.07
Men's sweaters and vests	2.72	1.69	1.29	3.17	4.03	3.72	2.02	1.82
Men's active sportswear	4.35	–	6.27	3.24	9.98	3.90	0.94	–
Men's shirts	20.77	15.68	16.79	21.45	18.02	44.73	10.71	14.13
Men's pants	7.11	0.58	5.49	6.99	14.48	9.34	3.45	1.76
Boys' shirts	5.56	1.62	6.33	6.23	5.75	7.10	6.46	2.38
Boys' pants	2.84	0.49	2.52	2.78	3.08	4.80	4.02	0.94
Women and girls, aged 2 or older	**85.28**	**45.81**	**65.55**	**101.03**	**131.03**	**83.58**	**69.48**	**42.34**
Women's coats and jackets	3.57	2.18	2.88	6.26	3.32	3.96	2.45	0.65
Women's dresses	10.62	7.15	2.36	7.85	35.23	3.24	5.08	1.63
Women's vests and sweaters	8.86	5.70	4.31	14.11	10.87	5.85	5.97	10.41
Women's shirts, tops, blouses	10.59	8.54	10.34	15.12	9.90	8.45	10.01	6.79
Women's pants	5.94	0.58	2.92	8.28	10.18	4.10	4.34	6.04
Women's active sportswear	3.47	4.90	1.46	3.28	9.32	1.37	1.05	–
Women's sleepwear	6.15	0.50	5.53	6.86	6.66	14.54	2.92	1.16
Women's undergarments	2.69	0.43	1.29	4.26	2.43	3.68	4.80	0.22
Women's accessories	4.17	4.33	3.08	5.75	6.49	2.18	2.39	2.18
Girls' dresses and suits	4.03	–	8.93	3.01	5.03	4.15	1.40	1.52
Girls' shirts, blouses, sweaters	6.18	2.58	5.54	6.42	6.13	9.37	7.69	3.85
Girls' skirts and pants	2.78	0.71	2.50	1.78	3.08	4.50	5.59	1.21
Girls' active sportswear	2.10	2.03	4.06	1.57	2.29	2.37	–	1.38
Girls' accessories	2.18	0.43	1.17	5.02	2.65	1.00	1.01	0.53
Children under age 2	**40.71**	**22.84**	**49.66**	**53.41**	**43.29**	**48.26**	**27.48**	**6.82**
Infant dresses, outerwear	14.51	7.15	13.60	13.75	18.62	25.14	11.50	4.18
Infant underwear	18.27	8.36	28.72	27.81	16.88	14.46	10.40	0.85
Infant nightwear, loungewear	2.46	1.10	2.17	2.66	3.34	3.47	1.97	0.93
Infant accessories	4.02	5.20	4.05	7.87	2.54	2.75	2.35	0.23
Other apparel products and services	**50.71**	**41.80**	**47.59**	**58.81**	**49.68**	**57.36**	**59.41**	**27.24**
Watches	3.43	2.31	2.69	2.63	3.89	7.33	1.20	3.70
Jewelry	16.85	9.18	15.41	15.84	13.13	21.30	33.99	10.78
Men's footwear	8.66	15.07	9.25	14.90	7.35	3.68	1.22	4.75
Boys' footwear	4.70	3.42	6.09	3.72	4.03	8.40	4.59	1.91
Women's footwear	10.06	8.02	7.82	13.86	13.34	11.48	5.26	3.19
Girls' footwear	5.21	3.80	4.93	5.85	6.07	3.18	8.54	2.79
TRANSPORTATION	**70.27**	**166.24**	**32.46**	**43.97**	**92.57**	**121.98**	**57.14**	**21.43**
New cars	6.08	43.85	–	–	13.77	–	–	–
New trucks	14.04	78.68	–	–	–	47.63	17.95	–
Used cars	12.52	26.62	–	11.48	29.67	12.86	1.06	2.78
Used trucks	2.82	–	11.37	–	–	6.61	–	–
Gasoline on trips	12.55	7.49	7.61	12.18	15.93	17.80	16.95	7.35

	total consumer units	under 25	25 to 34	35 to 44	45 to 54	55 to 64	65 to 74	75+
Airline fares	$8.51	$4.55	$4.39	$7.82	$12.46	$15.45	$8.47	$3.15
Local transportation on trips	2.13	0.94	1.46	1.56	2.44	3.33	2.23	3.24
Intercity train fares	2.23	0.58	0.91	2.29	3.74	3.82	1.82	0.92
Ship fares	2.98	1.37	1.21	2.93	4.42	5.40	3.33	0.91
HEALTH CARE	**38.08**	**1.33**	**9.06**	**12.96**	**39.87**	**44.89**	**107.65**	**86.94**
Physician's services	2.66	0.02	0.48	2.14	5.33	1.29	1.88	7.00
Dental services	3.49	–	1.88	3.13	3.65	4.64	10.66	0.23
Hospital room	2.73	–	–	–	9.40	–	0.59	8.16
Care in convalescent or nursing home	18.42	–	–	3.33	–	19.63	84.92	63.75
Nonprescription drugs	2.15	0.17	3.10	1.01	0.95	5.79	1.51	2.91
ENTERTAINMENT	**93.76**	**32.27**	**80.85**	**102.32**	**106.43**	**124.02**	**112.82**	**56.68**
Toys, games, hobbies, and tricycles	29.58	11.31	27.01	25.60	30.57	50.93	39.74	15.89
Movie, other admissions, on trips	9.17	3.97	8.20	9.60	7.99	16.72	8.46	7.14
Admission to sports events on trips	3.06	1.32	2.73	3.20	2.66	5.57	2.82	2.38
Fees for recreational lessons	6.30	1.99	3.74	8.11	12.87	7.07	0.96	1.38
Cable service and community antenna	4.65	6.28	5.50	5.35	3.43	2.69	6.16	3.80
Color TV, portable, table model	2.10	0.15	1.11	2.51	2.87	3.53	2.32	0.68
Musical instruments and accessories	2.32	–	0.62	1.60	4.50	0.27	1.54	7.90
Athletic gear, game tables, and exercise equipment	9.47	1.63	11.38	17.21	7.76	6.11	7.36	4.24
PERSONAL CARE PRODUCTS AND SERVICES	**19.20**	**11.71**	**15.53**	**32.13**	**21.29**	**24.79**	**7.05**	**2.15**
Hair care products	2.14	1.33	1.77	3.93	1.67	3.16	0.50	0.51
Cosmetics, perfume, bath preparation	13.00	8.00	10.00	24.00	14.00	13.00	3.00	0.00
Deodorants, feminine hygiene, misc. personal care	2.00	1.00	1.00	1.00	3.00	4.00	2.00	1.00
READING	**2.00**	**0.00**	**1.00**	**1.00**	**2.00**	**3.00**	**4.00**	**3.00**
EDUCATION	**151.00**	**55.00**	**41.00**	**100.00**	**463.00**	**125.00**	**44.00**	**44.00**
College tuition	114.00	32.00	26.00	49.00	398.00	96.00	16.00	31.00
Elementary and high school tuition	11.00	1.00	5.00	26.00	11.00	5.00	13.00	–
Other school tuition	3.00	0.00	1.00	2.00	5.00	2.00	3.00	11.00
Other school expenses including rentals	5.00	1.00	1.00	6.00	13.00	3.00	2.00	0.00
College books and supplies	10.00	16.00	2.00	7.00	29.00	10.00	2.00	–
Miscellaneous school supplies	5.00	4.00	4.00	6.00	5.00	8.00	7.00	2.00
ALL OTHER GIFTS	**89.00**	**26.00**	**43.00**	**70.00**	**103.00**	**141.00**	**127.00**	**124.00**
Gifts of trip expenses	49.00	21.00	30.00	31.00	59.00	69.00	63.00	83.00
Miscellaneous fees, gambling losses	2.00	0.00	0.00	4.00	2.00	1.00	1.00	1.00
Legal fees	4.00	3.00	4.00	5.00	3.00	5.00	5.00	5.00
Funeral expenses	28.00	2.00	6.00	23.00	33.00	60.00	45.00	30.00
Cemetery lots, vaults, maintenance fees	3.00	–	2.00	1.00	3.00	4.00	10.00	2.00
Accounting fees	2.00	–	1.00	4.00	1.00	1.00	2.00	1.00

Note: (–) means sample is too small to make a reliable estimate. Expenditures for items in a given category may not add to category total because categories with annual spending of less than $2.00 for the average household are omitted. Spending on gifts is also included in the product and service categories in other chapters.
Source: Bureau of Labor Statistics, unpublished tables from the 2000 Consumer Expenditure Survey

Table 6.2 Gifts: Indexed spending by age, 2000

(indexed average annual spending of consumer units (CU) on gifts of products and services for non–household members, by age of consumer unit reference person, 2000; index definition: an index of 100 is the average for all consumer units; an index of 132 means that spending by consumer units in that group is 32 percent above the average for all consumer units; an index of 68 indicates spending that is 32 percent below the average for all consumer units)

	total consumer units	under 25	25 to 34	35 to 44	45 to 54	55 to 64	65 to 74	75+
Average spending of CU, total	$38,045	$22,543	$38,945	$45,149	$46,160	$39,340	$30,782	$21,908
Average spending of CU, index	100	59	102	119	121	103	81	58
Gifts, spending index	100	55	66	92	159	124	89	70
FOOD	**100**	**16**	**46**	**96**	**195**	**173**	**41**	**42**
Fresh fruits	100	3	70	73	60	189	63	303
Candy and chewing gum	100	11	75	189	133	54	61	47
Board (including at school)	100	23	5	48	369	99	1	–
Catered affairs	100	1	37	79	119	341	51	28
ALCOHOLIC BEVERAGES	**100**	**41**	**184**	**121**	**116**	**67**	**23**	**41**
Beer and ale	100	90	148	90	143	107	16	38
Wine	100	33	187	127	106	57	38	47
Whiskey and other alcoholic beverages	100	10	231	137	101	38	–	36
HOUSING	**100**	**49**	**74**	**94**	**147**	**115**	**92**	**92**
Housekeeping supplies	**100**	**70**	**91**	**117**	**111**	**116**	**94**	**62**
Miscellaneous household products	100	137	81	139	114	94	61	31
Lawn and garden supplies	100	20	56	178	72	125	95	86
Postage and stationery	100	62	96	103	113	117	110	71
Stationery, stationery supplies, giftwraps	100	68	91	112	113	119	93	68
Postage	100	34	121	61	116	111	186	68
Household textiles	**100**	**24**	**62**	**91**	**159**	**172**	**94**	**41**
Bathroom linens	100	–	124	61	254	47	70	30
Bedroom linens	100	28	38	101	131	261	71	16
Appliances and miscellaneous housewares	**100**	**36**	**68**	**94**	**148**	**136**	**112**	**65**
Major appliances	100	7	52	53	208	116	144	80
Electric floor cleaning equipment	100	–	100	64	210	130	–	117
Small appliances and miscellaneous housewares	100	46	74	109	125	143	99	59
Glassware	100	8	171	111	82	45	143	87
Nonelectric cookware	100	26	74	52	146	282	50	35
Tableware, nonelectric kitchenware	100	132	31	156	89	106	76	105
Small electric kitchen appliances	100	33	88	101	133	145	116	27
Miscellaneous household equipment	**100**	**43**	**66**	**104**	**139**	**116**	**132**	**60**
Infants' equipment	100	11	85	205	124	76	39	–
Outdoor equipment	100	63	64	61	62	133	44	387
Household decorative items	100	41	70	127	119	85	172	42
Indoor plants, fresh flowers	100	59	62	78	150	156	120	52
Computers and computer hardware, nonbusiness use	100	12	58	81	231	56	165	3
Miscellaneous household equipment and parts	100	81	95	94	151	63	141	44
Other housing	**100**	**52**	**75**	**83**	**160**	**105**	**67**	**127**
Repair or maintenance services	100	5	45	100	67	37	36	494
Housing while attending school	100	21	2	38	346	148	9	3
Natural gas (renter)	100	90	76	92	65	183	88	143
Electricity (renter)	100	91	134	90	56	93	122	146
Telephone services in home city, excl. mobile phones	100	224	123	101	71	75	80	75

	total consumer units	under 25	25 to 34	35 to 44	45 to 54	55 to 64	65 to 74	75+
Water, sewerage maintenance (renter)	100	77	137	71	56	104	156	142
Care for elderly, invalids, handicapped	100	–	–	33	235	50	31	371
Day-care centers, nurseries, and preschools	100	21	199	182	55	72	29	6
Housekeeping services	100	1	39	49	223	63	168	123
Gardening, lawn care service	100	6	28	29	98	90	189	383
Repair of miscellaneous household equipment and furnishings	100	–	–	24	–	–	–	1,010
Bedroom furniture except mattress and springs	100	–	45	5	280	140	163	–
APPAREL AND SERVICES	**100**	**59**	**90**	**114**	**129**	**121**	**86**	**46**
Men and boys, aged 2 or older	**100**	**49**	**84**	**97**	**133**	**158**	**78**	**55**
Men's coats and jackets	100	14	131	51	218	124	64	–
Men's underwear	100	217	78	62	166	80	23	113
Men's accessories	100	64	81	108	84	75	103	208
Men's sweaters and vests	100	62	47	117	148	137	74	67
Men's active sportswear	100	–	144	74	229	90	22	–
Men's shirts	100	75	81	103	87	215	52	68
Men's pants	100	8	77	98	204	131	49	25
Boys' shirts	100	29	114	112	103	128	116	43
Boys' pants	100	17	89	98	108	169	142	33
Women and girls, aged 2 or older	**100**	**54**	**77**	**118**	**154**	**98**	**81**	**50**
Women's coats and jackets	100	61	81	175	93	111	69	18
Women's dresses	100	67	22	74	332	31	48	15
Women's vests and sweaters	100	64	49	159	123	66	67	117
Women's shirts, tops, blouses	100	81	98	143	93	80	95	64
Women's pants	100	10	49	139	171	69	73	102
Women's active sportswear	100	141	42	95	269	39	30	–
Women's sleepwear	100	8	90	112	108	236	47	19
Women's undergarments	100	16	48	158	90	137	178	8
Women's accessories	100	104	74	138	156	52	57	52
Girls' dresses and suits	100	–	222	75	125	103	35	38
Girls' shirts, blouses, sweaters	100	42	90	104	99	152	124	62
Girls' skirts and pants	100	26	90	64	111	162	201	44
Girls' active sportswear	100	97	193	75	109	113	–	66
Girls' accessories	100	20	54	230	122	46	46	24
Children under age 2	**100**	**56**	**122**	**131**	**106**	**119**	**68**	**17**
Infant dresses, outerwear	100	49	94	95	128	173	79	29
Infant underwear	100	46	157	152	92	79	57	5
Infant nightwear, loungewear	100	45	88	108	136	141	80	38
Infant accessories	100	129	101	196	63	68	58	6
Other apparel products and services	**100**	**82**	**94**	**116**	**98**	**113**	**117**	**54**
Watches	100	67	78	77	113	214	35	108
Jewelry	100	54	91	94	78	126	202	64
Men's footwear	100	174	107	172	85	42	14	55
Boys' footwear	100	73	130	79	86	179	98	41
Women's footwear	100	80	78	138	133	114	52	32
Girls' footwear	100	73	95	112	117	61	164	54
TRANSPORTATION	**100**	**237**	**46**	**63**	**132**	**174**	**81**	**30**
New cars	100	721	–	–	226	–	–	–
New trucks	100	560	–	–	–	339	128	–
Used cars	100	213	–	92	237	103	8	22
Used trucks	100	–	403	–	–	234	–	–
Gasoline on trips	100	60	61	97	127	142	135	59

	total consumer units	under 25	25 to 34	35 to 44	45 to 54	55 to 64	65 to 74	75+
Airline fares	100	53	52	92	146	182	100	37
Local transportation on trips	100	44	69	73	115	156	105	152
Intercity train fares	100	26	41	103	168	171	82	41
Ship fares	100	46	41	98	148	181	112	31
HEALTH CARE	**100**	**3**	**24**	**34**	**105**	**118**	**283**	**228**
Physician's services	100	1	18	80	200	48	71	263
Dental services	100	–	54	90	105	133	305	7
Hospital room	100	–	–	–	344	–	22	299
Care in convalescent or nursing home	100	–	–	18	–	107	461	346
Nonprescription drugs	100	8	144	47	44	269	70	135
ENTERTAINMENT	**100**	**34**	**86**	**109**	**114**	**132**	**120**	**60**
Toys, games, hobbies, and tricycles	100	38	91	87	103	172	134	54
Movie, other admissions, on trips	100	43	89	105	87	182	92	78
Admission to sports events on trips	100	43	89	105	87	182	92	78
Fees for recreational lessons	100	32	59	129	204	112	15	22
Cable service and community antenna	100	135	118	115	74	58	132	82
Color TV, portable, table model	100	7	53	120	137	168	110	32
Musical instruments and accessories	100	–	27	69	194	12	66	341
Athletic gear, game tables, and exercise equipment	100	17	120	182	82	65	78	45
PERSONAL CARE PRODUCTS AND SERVICES	**100**	**61**	**81**	**167**	**111**	**129**	**37**	**11**
Hair care products	100	62	83	184	78	148	23	24
Cosmetics, perfume, bath preparation	100	62	77	185	108	100	23	0
Deodorants, feminine hygiene, misc. personal care	100	50	50	50	150	200	100	50
READING	**100**	**0**	**50**	**50**	**100**	**150**	**200**	**150**
EDUCATION	**100**	**36**	**27**	**66**	**307**	**83**	**29**	**29**
College tuition	100	28	23	43	349	84	14	27
Elementary and high school tuition	100	9	45	236	100	45	118	–
Other school tuition	100	0	33	67	167	67	100	367
Other school expenses including rentals	100	20	20	120	260	60	40	0
College books and supplies	100	160	20	70	290	100	20	–
Miscellaneous school supplies	100	80	80	120	100	160	140	40
ALL OTHER GIFTS	**100**	**29**	**48**	**79**	**116**	**158**	**143**	**139**
Gifts of trip expenses	100	43	61	63	120	141	129	169
Miscellaneous fees, gambling losses	100	0	0	200	100	50	50	50
Legal fees	100	75	100	125	75	125	125	125
Funeral expenses	100	7	21	82	118	214	161	107
Cemetery lots, vaults, maintenance fees	100	–	67	33	100	133	333	67
Accounting fees	100	–	50	200	50	50	100	50

Note: (–) means sample is too small to make a reliable estimate. Categories with annual spending of less than $2.00 for the average household are omitted. Spending on gifts is also included in the product and service categories in other chapters.
Source: Calculations by New Strategist based on the 2000 Consumer Expenditure Survey

Table 6.3 Gifts: Indexed per capita spending by age, 2000

(indexed average annual per capita spending of consumer units (CU) on gifts of products and services for non–household members, by age of consumer unit reference person, 2000; index definition: an index of 100 is the average for all consumer units; an index of 132 means that spending by consumer units in that group is 32 percent above the average for all consumer units; an index of 68 indicates spending that is 32 percent below the average for all consumer units)

	total consumer units	under 25	25 to 34	35 to 44	45 to 54	55 to 64	65 to 74	75+
Per capita spending of CU, total	$15,218	$11,865	$13,429	$13,682	$17,096	$18,733	$16,201	$14,605
Per capita spending of CU, index	100	78	88	90	112	123	106	96
Gifts, per capita spending index	100	73	57	70	147	148	118	116
FOOD	**100**	**21**	**39**	**73**	**181**	**206**	**54**	**70**
Fresh fruits	100	4	60	55	56	225	82	505
Candy and chewing gum	100	15	64	143	123	64	80	78
Board (including at school)	100	31	5	36	342	118	1	–
Catered affairs	100	2	32	60	111	406	67	47
ALCOHOLIC BEVERAGES	**100**	**53**	**159**	**91**	**107**	**79**	**31**	**69**
Beer and ale	100	118	127	68	133	128	22	64
Wine	100	43	161	96	98	67	49	78
Whiskey and other alcoholic beverages	100	13	199	104	93	45	–	61
HOUSING	**100**	**65**	**64**	**71**	**136**	**137**	**121**	**154**
Housekeeping supplies	**100**	**92**	**78**	**89**	**103**	**138**	**124**	**103**
Miscellaneous household products	100	180	70	105	106	111	81	51
Lawn and garden supplies	100	26	48	135	67	149	125	143
Postage and stationery	100	81	83	78	105	139	144	119
Stationery, stationery supplies, giftwraps	100	90	78	85	105	141	123	114
Postage	100	44	105	46	108	133	244	114
Household textiles	**100**	**32**	**54**	**69**	**147**	**204**	**124**	**68**
Bathroom linens	100	–	107	46	235	55	92	50
Bedroom linens	100	36	33	77	122	311	93	27
Appliances and miscellaneous housewares	**100**	**47**	**59**	**71**	**137**	**161**	**147**	**108**
Major appliances	100	10	44	40	193	138	190	133
Electric floor cleaning equipment	100	–	86	48	195	154	–	195
Small appliances and miscellaneous housewares	100	61	64	83	116	170	131	98
Glassware	100	10	147	84	76	53	189	145
Nonelectric cookware	100	34	64	39	136	336	66	58
Tableware, nonelectric kitchenware	100	173	27	118	83	126	100	175
Small electric kitchen appliances	100	43	76	76	123	172	152	45
Miscellaneous household equipment	**100**	**56**	**57**	**79**	**129**	**138**	**174**	**101**
Infants' equipment	100	14	73	155	114	91	52	–
Outdoor equipment	100	83	55	46	58	158	58	645
Household decorative items	100	54	60	96	110	102	227	70
Indoor plants, fresh flowers	100	78	53	59	138	186	157	87
Computers and computer hardware, nonbusiness use	100	16	50	61	214	67	217	6
Miscellaneous household equipment and parts	100	106	82	71	139	75	185	73
Other housing	**100**	**68**	**65**	**63**	**148**	**125**	**88**	**212**
Repair or maintenance services	100	7	39	76	62	45	47	824
Housing while attending school	100	28	2	29	320	177	12	5
Natural gas (renter)	100	119	65	70	60	217	116	238
Electricity (renter)	100	119	116	68	52	111	160	243
Telephone services in home city, excl. mobile phones	100	295	106	77	65	89	105	125

	total consumer units	under 25	25 to 34	35 to 44	45 to 54	55 to 64	65 to 74	75+
Water, sewerage maintenance (renter)	100	101	118	54	52	124	205	237
Care for elderly, invalids, handicapped	100	–	–	25	218	59	41	619
Day-care centers, nurseries, and preschools	100	27	172	138	51	86	38	10
Housekeeping services	100	2	34	37	206	75	221	205
Gardening, lawn care service	100	8	24	22	91	108	249	639
Repair of miscellaneous household equipment and furnishings	100	–	–	18	–	–	–	1,683
Bedroom furniture except mattress and springs	100	–	39	4	259	166	214	–
APPAREL AND SERVICES	**100**	**77**	**78**	**86**	**119**	**144**	**113**	**77**
Men and boys, aged 2 or older	**100**	**64**	**73**	**73**	**124**	**188**	**102**	**91**
Men's coats and jackets	100	19	113	39	201	148	85	–
Men's underwear	100	285	67	47	154	95	31	189
Men's accessories	100	85	70	82	77	90	135	347
Men's sweaters and vests	100	82	41	88	137	163	98	112
Men's active sportswear	100	–	124	56	212	107	28	–
Men's shirts	100	99	70	78	80	256	68	113
Men's pants	100	11	67	74	189	156	64	41
Boys' shirts	100	38	98	85	96	152	153	71
Boys' pants	100	23	76	74	100	201	186	55
Women and girls, aged 2 or older	**100**	**71**	**66**	**90**	**142**	**117**	**107**	**83**
Women's coats and jackets	100	80	70	133	86	132	90	30
Women's dresses	100	89	19	56	307	36	63	26
Women's vests and sweaters	100	85	42	121	114	79	89	196
Women's shirts, tops, blouses	100	106	84	108	87	95	124	107
Women's pants	100	13	42	106	159	82	96	169
Women's active sportswear	100	186	36	72	249	47	40	–
Women's sleepwear	100	11	78	85	100	281	62	31
Women's undergarments	100	21	41	120	84	163	235	14
Women's accessories	100	137	64	104	144	62	75	87
Girls' dresses and suits	100	–	191	57	116	123	46	63
Girls' shirts, blouses, sweaters	100	55	77	79	92	180	164	104
Girls' skirts and pants	100	34	78	49	103	193	265	73
Girls' active sportswear	100	127	167	57	101	134	–	110
Girls' accessories	100	26	46	174	113	55	61	41
Children under age 2	**100**	**74**	**105**	**99**	**98**	**141**	**89**	**28**
Infant dresses, outerwear	100	65	81	72	119	206	104	48
Infant underwear	100	60	136	115	86	94	75	8
Infant nightwear, loungewear	100	59	76	82	126	168	105	63
Infant accessories	100	170	87	148	59	81	77	10
Other apparel products and services	**100**	**108**	**81**	**88**	**91**	**135**	**154**	**90**
Watches	100	89	68	58	105	254	46	180
Jewelry	100	72	79	71	72	150	265	107
Men's footwear	100	229	92	130	79	51	19	91
Boys' footwear	100	96	112	60	79	213	128	68
Women's footwear	100	105	67	104	123	136	69	53
Girls' footwear	100	96	82	85	108	73	216	89
TRANSPORTATION	**100**	**311**	**40**	**47**	**122**	**207**	**107**	**51**
New cars	100	949	–	–	210	–	–	–
New trucks	100	737	–	–	–	404	168	–
Used cars	100	280	–	69	219	122	11	37
Used trucks	100	–	348	–	–	279	–	–
Gasoline on trips	100	79	52	74	118	169	178	98

	total consumer units	under 25	25 to 34	35 to 44	45 to 54	55 to 64	65 to 74	75+
Airline fares	100	70	44	70	136	216	131	62
Local transportation on trips	100	58	59	55	106	186	138	254
Intercity train fares	100	34	35	78	155	204	107	69
Ship fares	100	60	35	74	137	216	147	51
HEALTH CARE	**100**	**5**	**21**	**26**	**97**	**140**	**372**	**381**
Physician's services	100	1	16	61	186	58	93	439
Dental services	100	–	46	68	97	158	402	11
Hospital room	100	–	–	–	319	–	28	498
Care in convalescent or nursing home	100	–	–	14	–	127	607	577
Nonprescription drugs	100	10	124	36	41	321	92	226
ENTERTAINMENT	**100**	**45**	**74**	**83**	**105**	**157**	**158**	**101**
Toys, games, hobbies, and tricycles	100	50	79	66	96	205	177	90
Movie, other admissions, on trips	100	57	77	79	81	217	121	130
Admission to sports events on trips	100	57	77	79	80	217	121	130
Fees for recreational lessons	100	42	51	98	189	134	20	37
Cable service and community antenna	100	178	102	87	68	69	174	136
Color TV, portable, table model	100	9	46	91	127	200	145	54
Musical instruments and accessories	100	–	23	52	180	14	87	568
Athletic gear, game tables, exercise equipment	100	23	104	138	76	77	102	75
PERSONAL CARE PRODUCTS AND SERVICES	**100**	**80**	**70**	**127**	**103**	**154**	**48**	**19**
Hair care products	100	82	71	139	72	176	31	40
Cosmetics, perfume, bath preparation	100	81	66	140	100	119	30	0
Deodorants, feminine hygiene, misc. personal care	100	66	43	38	139	238	132	83
READING	**100**	**0**	**43**	**38**	**93**	**179**	**263**	**250**
EDUCATION	**100**	**48**	**23**	**50**	**284**	**99**	**38**	**49**
College tuition	100	37	20	33	323	100	18	45
Elementary and high school tuition	100	12	39	179	93	54	156	–
Other school tuition	100	0	29	51	154	79	132	611
Other school expenses including rentals	100	26	17	91	241	71	53	0
College books and supplies	100	211	17	53	269	119	26	–
Miscellaneous school supplies	100	105	69	91	93	190	184	67
ALL OTHER GIFTS	**100**	**38**	**42**	**60**	**107**	**189**	**188**	**232**
Gifts of trip expenses	100	56	53	48	111	168	169	282
Miscellaneous fees, gambling losses	100	0	0	152	93	60	66	83
Legal fees	100	99	86	95	69	149	164	208
Funeral expenses	100	9	18	62	109	255	211	179
Cemetery lots, vaults, maintenance fees	100	–	57	25	93	159	439	111
Accounting fees	100	–	43	152	46	60	132	83

Note: Per capita indexes account for household size and show how much each person in a particular household demographic segment spends relative to a person in the average household. (–) means sample is too small to make a reliable estimate. Categories with annual spending of less than $2.00 for the average household are omitted. Spending on gifts is also included in the product and service categories in other chapters.
Source: Calculations by New Strategist based on the 2000 Consumer Expenditure Survey

Table 6.4 Gifts: Total spending by age, 2000

(total annual spending on selected gifts, by consumer unit (CU) age group, 2000; numbers in thousands)

	total consumer units	under 25	25 to 34	35 to 44	45 to 54	55 to 64	65 to 74	75+
Number of consumer units	109,367	8,306	18,887	23,983	21,874	14,161	11,538	10,617
Total spending of all CUs	$4,160,831,424	$187,243,653	$735,559,314	$1,082,817,341	$1,009,709,965	$557,094,165	$355,160,524	$232,597,661
Gifts, total spending	118,459,772	4,958,765	13,519,881	24,008,902	37,714,713	19,049,094	11,173,976	8,018,489
FOOD	**$7,665,533**	**$94,938**	**$604,573**	**$1,616,934**	**$2,990,613**	**$1,715,888**	**$329,871**	**$312,458**
Fresh fruits	500,901	1,246	60,250	80,343	60,154	122,351	33,114	147,470
Candy and chewing gum	1,367,088	11,795	176,027	565,759	362,452	95,304	88,150	61,897
Board (including at school)	2,210,307	39,038	20,020	232,395	1,633,113	283,786	1,961	–
Catered affairs	1,705,032	1,495	108,789	297,149	407,075	752,091	92,073	46,609
ALCOHOLIC BEVERAGES	**1,584,728**	**48,922**	**503,716**	**419,703**	**367,483**	**136,937**	**39,114**	**63,383**
Beer and ale	398,096	27,078	101,612	78,664	114,182	55,228	6,923	14,758
Wine	739,321	18,522	238,165	206,254	156,180	54,237	29,307	33,550
Whiskey and other alcoholic beverages	407,939	3,073	162,617	122,553	82,246	19,825	–	14,439
HOUSING	**31,836,734**	**1,191,163**	**4,057,683**	**6,578,297**	**9,369,290**	**4,738,412**	**3,092,761**	**2,852,682**
Housekeeping supplies	**4,276,250**	**228,000**	**671,055**	**1,096,982**	**951,519**	**643,334**	**423,906**	**256,401**
Miscellaneous household products	800,566	83,392	112,567	243,427	182,648	97,003	51,690	23,888
Lawn and garden supplies	336,850	5,067	32,675	131,667	48,560	54,520	33,691	28,135
Postage and stationery	2,728,707	127,829	452,155	616,843	617,722	413,218	315,910	188,664
Stationery, stationery supplies, giftwraps	2,217,963	115,038	347,521	546,812	501,571	341,138	218,068	146,833
Postage	499,807	12,791	104,634	66,913	116,151	72,079	97,842	33,125
Household textiles	**1,443,644**	**26,828**	**154,873**	**288,036**	**458,260**	**321,030**	**143,533**	**57,226**
Bathroom linens	305,134	–	65,160	40,771	154,868	18,409	22,499	8,812
Bedroom linens	749,164	15,781	49,106	165,962	196,647	253,482	55,959	11,997
Appliances and miscellaneous housewares	**3,077,587**	**83,309**	**361,119**	**635,070**	**908,427**	**540,384**	**362,409**	**192,911**
Major appliances	832,283	4,651	74,037	95,932	346,265	124,475	126,803	64,551
Electric floor cleaning equipment	329,195	–	56,850	46,047	138,462	55,228	–	37,478
Small appliances and misc. housewares	2,245,305	78,658	287,082	539,138	562,162	415,909	235,606	128,466
Glassware	393,721	2,243	115,966	95,932	64,528	22,799	59,536	33,231
Nonelectric cookware	400,283	7,808	51,373	45,328	117,245	146,283	21,115	13,484
Tableware, nonelectric kitchenware	474,653	47,427	25,309	162,365	84,871	64,857	37,960	48,520
Small electric kitchen appliances	293,104	7,309	44,762	64,754	77,871	54,945	35,768	7,644
Miscellaneous household equipment	**7,689,594**	**249,429**	**872,957**	**1,756,515**	**2,141,902**	**1,150,581**	**1,074,765**	**451,010**
Infants' equipment	297,478	2,409	43,440	133,825	73,497	29,313	12,346	–
Outdoor equipment	312,790	14,951	34,563	41,970	38,936	53,670	14,653	117,530
Household decorative items	2,989,000	93,692	361,497	833,169	708,499	330,801	543,786	122,626
Indoor plants, fresh flowers	1,754,247	79,239	186,792	299,068	524,539	354,025	221,414	89,289
Computers and computer hardware, nonbusiness use	981,022	8,970	98,779	173,397	453,667	71,655	170,993	3,291
Miscellaneous household equipment and parts	276,699	16,944	45,518	56,840	83,340	22,516	41,075	11,785
Other housing	**15,350,752**	**603,597**	**1,997,678**	**2,801,694**	**4,909,401**	**2,083,083**	**1,088,033**	**1,895,028**
Repair or maintenance services	409,033	1,578	31,730	89,457	54,685	19,825	15,461	196,308
Housing while attending school	4,628,411	74,837	18,698	389,244	3,199,510	888,744	43,614	12,953
Natural gas (renter)	340,131	23,340	44,384	68,831	44,185	80,434	31,730	47,139
Electricity (renter)	1,452,394	100,170	336,377	286,357	162,743	174,747	186,454	205,333
Telephone services in home city, excl. mobile phones	1,491,766	254,164	316,924	331,445	210,647	144,017	125,418	108,718

	total consumer units	under 25	25 to 34	35 to 44	45 to 54	55 to 64	65 to 74	75+
Water, sewerage maintenance (renter)	$292,010	$17,027	$68,938	$45,328	$32,592	$39,509	$48,113	$40,238
Care for elderly, invalids, handicapped	229,671	–	–	16,548	108,058	14,727	7,500	82,813
Day-care centers, nurseries, and preschools	2,347,016	37,211	807,986	937,256	258,551	219,920	72,228	13,696
Housekeeping services	376,222	332	25,309	40,291	167,774	30,588	66,574	45,016
Gardening, lawn care service	343,412	1,495	16,432	21,825	67,153	40,217	68,651	127,829
Repair of miscellaneous household equipment and furnishings	850,875	–	–	44,848	–	–	–	834,072
Bedroom furniture except mattress and springs	225,296	–	17,376	2,398	126,213	40,784	38,652	–
APPAREL AND SERVICES	**26,712,890**	**1,190,250**	**4,149,285**	**6,679,985**	**6,870,623**	**4,192,222**	**2,410,980**	**1,202,800**
Men and boys, aged 2 or older	**7,387,741**	**272,852**	**1,074,293**	**1,565,610**	**1,970,847**	**1,512,820**	**606,899**	**391,661**
Men's coats and jackets	360,911	3,904	81,592	40,531	157,055	57,918	24,461	–
Men's underwear	229,671	37,792	30,786	31,178	76,340	23,649	5,654	25,268
Men's accessories	371,848	18,190	52,317	88,257	62,122	36,252	40,383	75,062
Men's sweaters and vests	297,478	14,037	24,364	76,026	88,152	52,679	23,307	19,323
Men's active sportswear	475,746	–	118,421	77,705	218,303	55,228	10,846	–
Men's shirts	2,271,553	130,238	317,113	514,435	394,169	633,422	123,572	150,018
Men's pants	777,599	4,817	103,690	167,641	316,736	132,264	39,806	18,686
Boys' shirts	608,081	13,456	119,555	149,414	125,776	100,543	74,535	25,268
Boys' pants	310,602	4,070	47,595	66,673	67,372	67,973	46,383	9,980
Women and girls, aged 2 or older	**9,326,818**	**380,498**	**1,238,043**	**2,423,002**	**2,866,150**	**1,183,576**	**801,660**	**449,524**
Women's coats and jackets	390,440	18,107	54,395	150,134	72,622	56,078	28,268	6,901
Women's dresses	1,161,478	59,388	44,573	188,267	770,621	45,882	58,613	17,306
Women's vests and sweaters	968,992	47,344	81,403	338,400	237,770	82,842	68,882	110,523
Women's shirts, tops, blouses	1,158,197	70,933	195,292	362,623	216,553	119,660	115,495	72,089
Women's pants	649,640	4,817	55,150	198,579	222,677	58,060	50,075	64,127
Women's active sportswear	379,503	40,699	27,575	78,664	203,866	19,401	12,115	–
Women's sleepwear	672,607	4,153	104,445	164,523	145,681	205,901	33,691	12,316
Women's undergarments	294,197	3,572	24,364	102,168	53,154	52,112	55,382	2,336
Women's accessories	456,060	35,965	58,172	137,902	141,962	30,871	27,576	23,145
Girls' dresses and suits	440,749	–	168,661	72,189	110,026	58,768	16,153	16,138
Girls' shirts, blouses, sweaters	675,888	21,429	104,634	153,971	134,088	132,689	88,727	40,875
Girls' skirts and pants	304,040	5,897	47,218	42,690	67,372	63,725	64,497	12,847
Girls' active sportswear	229,671	16,861	76,681	37,653	50,091	33,562	–	14,651
Girls' accessories	238,420	3,572	22,098	120,395	57,966	14,161	11,653	5,627
Children under age 2	**4,452,331**	**189,709**	**937,928**	**1,280,932**	**946,925**	**683,410**	**317,064**	**72,408**
Infant dresses, outerwear	1,586,915	59,388	256,863	329,766	407,294	356,008	132,687	44,379
Infant underwear	1,998,135	69,438	542,435	666,967	369,233	204,768	119,995	9,024
Infant nightwear, loungewear	269,043	9,137	40,985	63,795	73,059	49,139	22,730	9,874
Infant accessories	439,655	43,191	76,492	188,746	55,560	38,943	27,114	2,442
Other apparel products and services	**5,546,001**	**347,191**	**898,832**	**1,410,440**	**1,086,700**	**812,275**	**685,473**	**289,207**
Watches	375,129	19,187	50,806	63,075	85,090	103,800	13,846	39,283
Jewelry	1,842,834	76,249	291,049	379,891	287,206	301,629	392,177	114,451
Men's footwear	947,118	125,171	174,705	357,347	160,774	52,112	14,076	50,431
Boys' footwear	514,025	28,407	115,022	89,217	88,152	118,952	52,959	20,278
Women's footwear	1,100,232	66,614	147,696	332,404	291,799	162,568	60,690	33,868
Girls' footwear	569,802	31,563	93,113	140,301	132,775	45,032	98,535	29,621
TRANSPORTATION	**7,685,219**	**1,380,789**	**613,072**	**1,054,533**	**2,024,876**	**1,727,359**	**659,281**	**227,522**
New cars	664,951	364,218	–	–	301,205	–	–	–
New trucks	1,535,513	653,516	–	–	–	674,488	207,107	–
Used cars	1,369,275	221,106	–	275,325	649,002	182,110	12,230	29,515
Used trucks	308,415	–	214,745	–	–	93,604	–	–
Gasoline on trips	1,372,556	62,212	143,730	292,113	348,453	252,066	195,569	78,035

	total consumer units	under 25	25 to 34	35 to 44	45 to 54	55 to 64	65 to 74	75+
Airline fares	$930,713	$37,792	$82,914	$187,547	$272,550	$218,787	$97,727	$33,444
Local transportation on trips	232,952	7,808	27,575	37,413	53,373	47,156	25,730	34,399
Intercity train fares	243,888	4,817	17,187	54,921	81,809	54,095	20,999	9,768
Ship fares	325,914	11,379	22,853	70,270	96,683	76,469	38,422	9,661
HEALTH CARE	**4,164,695**	**11,047**	**171,116**	**310,820**	**872,116**	**635,687**	**1,242,066**	**923,042**
Physician's services	290,916	166	9,066	51,324	116,588	18,268	21,691	74,319
Dental services	381,691	–	35,508	75,067	79,840	65,707	122,995	2,442
Hospital room	298,572	–	–	–	205,616	–	6,807	86,635
Care in convalescent or nursing home	2,014,540	–	–	79,863	–	277,980	979,807	676,834
Nonprescription drugs	235,139	1,412	58,550	24,223	20,780	81,992	17,422	30,895
ENTERTAINMENT	**10,254,250**	**268,035**	**1,527,014**	**2,453,941**	**2,328,050**	**1,756,247**	**1,301,717**	**601,772**
Toys, games, hobbies, and tricycles	3,235,076	93,941	510,138	613,965	668,688	721,220	458,520	168,704
Movie, other admissions, on trips	1,002,895	32,975	154,873	230,237	174,773	236,772	97,611	75,805
Admission to sports events on trips	334,663	10,964	51,562	76,746	58,185	78,877	32,537	25,268
Fees for recreational lessons	689,012	16,529	70,637	194,502	281,518	100,118	11,076	14,651
Cable service and community antenna	508,557	52,162	103,879	128,309	75,028	38,093	71,074	40,345
Color TV, portable, table model	229,671	1,246	20,965	60,197	62,778	49,988	26,768	7,220
Musical instruments and accessories	253,731	–	11,710	38,373	98,433	3,823	17,769	83,874
Athletic gear, game tables, exercise equipment	1,035,705	13,539	214,934	412,747	169,742	86,524	84,920	45,016
PERSONAL CARE PRODUCTS AND SERVICES	**2,099,846**	**97,263**	**293,315**	**770,574**	**465,697**	**351,051**	**81,343**	**22,827**
Hair care products	234,045	11,047	33,430	94,253	36,530	44,749	5,769	5,415
Cosmetics, perfume, bath preparation	1,421,771	66,448	188,870	575,592	306,236	184,093	34,614	0
Deodorants, feminine hygiene, misc. personal care	218,734	8,306	18,887	23,983	65,622	56,644	23,076	10,617
READING	**218,734**	**0**	**18,887**	**23,983**	**43,748**	**42,483**	**46,152**	**31,851**
EDUCATION	**16,514,417**	**456,830**	**774,367**	**2,398,300**	**10,127,662**	**1,770,125**	**507,672**	**467,148**
College tuition	12,467,838	265,792	491,062	1,175,167	8,705,852	1,359,456	184,608	329,127
Elementary and high school tuition	1,203,037	8,306	94,435	623,558	240,614	70,805	149,994	–
Other school tuition	328,101	0	18,887	47,966	109,370	28,322	34,614	116,787
Other school expenses including rentals	546,835	8,306	18,887	143,898	284,362	42,483	23,076	0
College books and supplies	1,093,670	132,896	37,774	167,881	634,346	141,610	23,076	–
Miscellaneous school supplies	546,835	33,224	75,548	143,898	109,370	113,288	80,766	21,234
ALL OTHER GIFTS	**9,733,663**	**215,956**	**812,141**	**1,678,810**	**2,253,022**	**1,996,701**	**1,465,326**	**1,316,508**
Gifts of trip expenses	5,358,983	174,426	566,610	743,473	1,290,566	977,109	726,894	881,211
Miscellaneous fees, gambling losses	218,734	0	0	95,932	43,748	14,161	11,538	10,617
Legal fees	437,468	24,918	75,548	119,915	65,622	70,805	57,690	53,085
Funeral expenses	3,062,276	16,612	113,322	551,609	721,842	849,660	519,210	318,510
Cemetery lots, vaults, maintenance fees	328,101	–	37,774	23,983	65,622	56,644	115,380	21,234
Accounting fees	218,734	–	18,887	95,932	21,874	14,161	23,076	10,617

Note: Numbers may not add to total because of rounding. (–) means sample is too small to make a reliable estimate. Expenditures for items in a given category may not add to category total because categories with annual spending of less than $2.00 for the average household are omitted. Spending on gifts is also included in the product and service categories in other chapters.
Source: Calculations by New Strategist based on the 2000 Consumer Expenditure Survey

Table 6.5 Gifts: Market shares by age, 2000

(percentage of total annual spending on gifts of products and services for non-household members accounted for by consumer unit age groups, 2000)

	total consumer units	under 25	25 to 34	35 to 44	45 to 54	55 to 64	65 to 74	75+
Share of total consumer units	100.0%	7.6%	17.3%	21.9%	20.0%	12.9%	10.5%	9.7%
Share of total before-tax income	100.0	3.4	17.6	27.7	26.4	14.0	6.9	4.5
Share of total spending	100.0	4.5	17.7	26.0	24.3	13.4	8.5	5.6
Share of gifts spending	100.0	4.2	11.4	20.3	31.8	16.1	9.4	6.8
FOOD	100.0%	1.2%	7.9%	21.1%	39.0%	22.4%	4.3%	4.1%
Fresh fruits	100.0	0.2	12.0	16.0	12.0	24.4	6.6	29.4
Candy and chewing gum	100.0	0.9	12.9	41.4	26.5	7.0	6.4	4.5
Board (including at school)	100.0	1.8	0.9	10.5	73.9	12.8	0.1	–
Catered affairs	100.0	0.1	6.4	17.4	23.9	44.1	5.4	2.7
ALCOHOLIC BEVERAGES	100.0	3.1	31.8	26.5	23.2	8.6	2.5	4.0
Beer and ale	100.0	6.8	25.5	19.8	28.7	13.9	1.7	3.7
Wine	100.0	2.5	32.2	27.9	21.1	7.3	4.0	4.5
Whiskey and other alcoholic beverages	100.0	0.8	39.9	30.0	20.2	4.9	–	3.5
HOUSING	100.0	3.7	12.7	20.7	29.4	14.9	9.7	9.0
Housekeeping supplies	100.0	5.3	15.7	25.7	22.3	15.0	9.9	6.0
Miscellaneous household products	100.0	10.4	14.1	30.4	22.8	12.1	6.5	3.0
Lawn and garden supplies	100.0	1.5	9.7	39.1	14.4	16.2	10.0	8.4
Postage and stationery	100.0	4.7	16.6	22.6	22.6	15.1	11.6	6.9
Stationery, stationery supplies, giftwraps	100.0	5.2	15.7	24.7	22.6	15.4	9.8	6.6
Postage	100.0	2.6	20.9	13.4	23.2	14.4	19.6	6.6
Household textiles	100.0	1.9	10.7	20.0	31.7	22.2	9.9	4.0
Bathroom linens	100.0	–	21.4	13.4	50.8	6.0	7.4	2.9
Bedroom linens	100.0	2.1	6.6	22.2	26.2	33.8	7.5	1.6
Appliances and miscellaneous housewares	100.0	2.7	11.7	20.6	29.5	17.6	11.8	6.3
Major appliances	100.0	0.6	8.9	11.5	41.6	15.0	15.2	7.8
Electric floor cleaning equipment	100.0	–	17.3	14.0	42.1	16.8	–	11.4
Small appliances and miscellaneous housewares	100.0	3.5	12.8	24.0	25.0	18.5	10.5	5.7
Glassware	100.0	0.6	29.5	24.4	16.4	5.8	15.1	8.4
Nonelectric cookware	100.0	2.0	12.8	11.3	29.3	36.5	5.3	3.4
Tableware, nonelectric kitchenware	100.0	10.0	5.3	34.2	17.9	13.7	8.0	10.2
Small electric kitchen appliances	100.0	2.5	15.3	22.1	26.6	18.7	12.2	2.6
Miscellaneous household equipment	100.0	3.2	11.4	22.8	27.9	15.0	14.0	5.9
Infants' equipment	100.0	0.8	14.6	45.0	24.7	9.9	4.2	–
Outdoor equipment	100.0	4.8	11.0	13.4	12.4	17.2	4.7	37.6
Household decorative items	100.0	3.1	12.1	27.9	23.7	11.1	18.2	4.1
Indoor plants, fresh flowers	100.0	4.5	10.6	17.0	29.9	20.2	12.6	5.1
Computers and computer hardware, nonbusiness use	100.0	0.9	10.1	17.7	46.2	7.3	17.4	0.3
Miscellaneous household equipment and parts	100.0	6.1	16.5	20.5	30.1	8.1	14.8	4.3
Other housing	100.0	3.9	13.0	18.3	32.0	13.6	7.1	12.3
Repair or maintenance services	100.0	0.4	7.8	21.9	13.4	4.8	3.8	48.0
Housing while attending school	100.0	1.6	0.4	8.4	69.1	19.2	0.9	0.3
Natural gas (renter)	100.0	6.9	13.0	20.2	13.0	23.6	9.3	13.9
Electricity (renter)	100.0	6.9	23.2	19.7	11.2	12.0	12.8	14.1
Telephone services in home city, excl. mobile phones	100.0	17.0	21.2	22.2	14.1	9.7	8.4	7.3

	total consumer units	under 25	25 to 34	35 to 44	45 to 54	55 to 64	65 to 74	75+
Water, sewerage maintenance (renter)	100.0%	5.8%	23.6%	15.5%	11.2%	13.5%	16.5%	13.8%
Care for elderly, invalids, handicapped	100.0	–	–	7.2	47.0	6.4	3.3	36.1
Day-care centers, nurseries, and preschools	100.0	1.6	34.4	39.9	11.0	9.4	3.1	0.6
Housekeeping services	100.0	0.1	6.7	10.7	44.6	8.1	17.7	12.0
Gardening, lawn care service	100.0	0.4	4.8	6.4	19.6	11.7	20.0	37.2
Repair of miscellaneous household equipment and furnishings	100.0	–	–	5.3	–	–	–	98.0
Bedroom furniture except mattress and springs	100.0	–	7.7	1.1	56.0	18.1	17.2	–
APPAREL AND SERVICES	**100.0**	**4.5**	**15.5**	**25.0**	**25.7**	**15.7**	**9.0**	**4.5**
Men and boys, aged 2 or older	**100.0**	**3.7**	**14.5**	**21.2**	**26.7**	**20.5**	**8.2**	**5.3**
Men's coats and jackets	100.0	1.1	22.6	11.2	43.5	16.0	6.8	–
Men's underwear	100.0	16.5	13.4	13.6	33.2	10.3	2.5	11.0
Men's accessories	100.0	4.9	14.1	23.7	16.7	9.7	10.9	20.2
Men's sweaters and vests	100.0	4.7	8.2	25.6	29.6	17.7	7.8	6.5
Men's active sportswear	100.0	–	24.9	16.3	45.9	11.6	2.3	–
Men's shirts	100.0	5.7	14.0	22.6	17.4	27.9	5.4	6.6
Men's pants	100.0	0.6	13.3	21.6	40.7	17.0	5.1	2.4
Boys' shirts	100.0	2.2	19.7	24.6	20.7	16.5	12.3	4.2
Boys' pants	100.0	1.3	15.3	21.5	21.7	21.9	14.9	3.2
Women and girls, aged 2 or older	**100.0**	**4.1**	**13.3**	**26.0**	**30.7**	**12.7**	**8.6**	**4.8**
Women's coats and jackets	100.0	4.6	13.9	38.5	18.6	14.4	7.2	1.8
Women's dresses	100.0	5.1	3.8	16.2	66.3	4.0	5.0	1.5
Women's vests and sweaters	100.0	4.9	8.4	34.9	24.5	8.5	7.1	11.4
Women's shirts, tops, blouses	100.0	6.1	16.9	31.3	18.7	10.3	10.0	6.2
Women's pants	100.0	0.7	8.5	30.6	34.3	8.9	7.7	9.9
Women's active sportswear	100.0	10.7	7.3	20.7	53.7	5.1	3.2	–
Women's sleepwear	100.0	0.6	15.5	24.5	21.7	30.6	5.0	1.8
Women's undergarments	100.0	1.2	8.3	34.7	18.1	17.7	18.8	0.8
Women's accessories	100.0	7.9	12.8	30.2	31.1	6.8	6.0	5.1
Girls' dresses and suits	100.0	–	38.3	16.4	25.0	13.3	3.7	3.7
Girls' shirts, blouses, sweaters	100.0	3.2	15.5	22.8	19.8	19.6	13.1	6.0
Girls' skirts and pants	100.0	1.9	15.5	14.0	22.2	21.0	21.2	4.2
Girls' active sportswear	100.0	7.3	33.4	16.4	21.8	14.6	–	6.4
Girls' accessories	100.0	1.5	9.3	50.5	24.3	5.9	4.9	2.4
Children under age 2	**100.0**	**4.3**	**21.1**	**28.8**	**21.3**	**15.3**	**7.1**	**1.6**
Infant dresses, outerwear	100.0	3.7	16.2	20.8	25.7	22.4	8.4	2.8
Infant underwear	100.0	3.5	27.1	33.4	18.5	10.2	6.0	0.5
Infant nightwear, loungewear	100.0	3.4	15.2	23.7	27.2	18.3	8.4	3.7
Infant accessories	100.0	9.8	17.4	42.9	12.6	8.9	6.2	0.6
Other apparel products and services	**100.0**	**6.3**	**16.2**	**25.4**	**19.6**	**14.6**	**12.4**	**5.2**
Watches	100.0	5.1	13.5	16.8	22.7	27.7	3.7	10.5
Jewelry	100.0	4.1	15.8	20.6	15.6	16.4	21.3	6.2
Men's footwear	100.0	13.2	18.4	37.7	17.0	5.5	1.5	5.3
Boys' footwear	100.0	5.5	22.4	17.4	17.1	23.1	10.3	3.9
Women's footwear	100.0	6.1	13.4	30.2	26.5	14.8	5.5	3.1
Girls' footwear	100.0	5.5	16.3	24.6	23.3	7.9	17.3	5.2
TRANSPORTATION	**100.0**	**18.0**	**8.0**	**13.7**	**26.3**	**22.5**	**8.6**	**3.0**
New cars	100.0	54.8	–	–	45.3	–	–	–
New trucks	100.0	42.6	–	–	–	43.9	13.5	–
Used cars	100.0	16.1	–	20.1	47.4	13.3	0.9	2.2
Used trucks	100.0	–	69.6	–	–	30.4	–	–
Gasoline on trips	100.0	4.5	10.5	21.3	25.4	18.4	14.2	5.7

	total consumer units	under 25	25 to 34	35 to 44	45 to 54	55 to 64	65 to 74	75+
Airline fares	100.0%	4.1%	8.9%	20.2%	29.3%	23.5%	10.5%	3.6%
Local transportation on trips	100.0	3.4	11.8	16.1	22.9	20.2	11.0	14.8
Intercity train fares	100.0	2.0	7.0	22.5	33.5	22.2	8.6	4.0
Ship fares	100.0	3.5	7.0	21.6	29.7	23.5	11.8	3.0
HEALTH CARE	**100.0**	**0.3**	**4.1**	**7.5**	**20.9**	**15.3**	**29.8**	**22.2**
Physician's services	100.0	0.1	3.1	17.6	40.1	6.3	7.5	25.5
Dental services	100.0	–	9.3	19.7	20.9	17.2	32.2	0.6
Hospital room	100.0	–	–	–	68.9	–	2.3	29.0
Care in convalescent or nursing home	100.0	–	–	4.0	–	13.8	48.6	33.6
Nonprescription drugs	100.0	0.6	24.9	10.3	8.8	34.9	7.4	13.1
ENTERTAINMENT	**100.0**	**2.6**	**14.9**	**23.9**	**22.7**	**17.1**	**12.7**	**5.9**
Toys, games, hobbies, and tricycles	100.0	2.9	15.8	19.0	20.7	22.3	14.2	5.2
Movie, other admissions, on trips	100.0	3.3	15.4	23.0	17.4	23.6	9.7	7.6
Admission to sports events on trips	100.0	3.3	15.4	22.9	17.4	23.6	9.7	7.6
Fees for recreational lessons	100.0	2.4	10.3	28.2	40.9	14.5	1.6	2.1
Cable service and community antenna	100.0	10.3	20.4	25.2	14.8	7.5	14.0	7.9
Color TV, portable, table model	100.0	0.5	9.1	26.2	27.3	21.8	11.7	3.1
Musical instruments and accessories	100.0	–	4.6	15.1	38.8	1.5	7.0	33.1
Athletic gear, game tables, and exercise equipment	100.0	1.3	20.8	39.9	16.4	8.4	8.2	4.3
PERSONAL CARE PRODUCTS								
AND SERVICES	**100.0**	**4.6**	**14.0**	**36.7**	**22.2**	**16.7**	**3.9**	**1.1**
Hair care products	100.0	4.7	14.3	40.3	15.6	19.1	2.5	2.3
Cosmetics, perfume, bath preparation	100.0	4.7	13.3	40.5	21.5	12.9	2.4	0.0
Deodorants, feminine hygiene, misc. personal care	100.0	3.8	8.6	11.0	30.0	25.9	10.5	4.9
READING	**100.0**	**0.0**	**8.6**	**11.0**	**20.0**	**19.4**	**21.1**	**14.6**
EDUCATION	**100.0**	**2.8**	**4.7**	**14.5**	**61.3**	**10.7**	**3.1**	**2.8**
College tuition	100.0	2.1	3.9	9.4	69.8	10.9	1.5	2.6
Elementary and high school tuition	100.0	0.7	7.8	51.8	20.0	5.9	12.5	–
Other school tuition	100.0	0.0	5.8	14.6	33.3	8.6	10.5	35.6
Other school expenses including rentals	100.0	1.5	3.5	26.3	52.0	7.8	4.2	0.0
College books and supplies	100.0	12.2	3.5	15.4	58.0	12.9	2.1	–
Miscellaneous school supplies	100.0	6.1	13.8	26.3	20.0	20.7	14.8	3.9
ALL OTHER GIFTS	**100.0**	**2.2**	**8.3**	**17.2**	**23.1**	**20.5**	**15.1**	**13.5**
Gifts of trip expenses	100.0	3.3	10.6	13.9	24.1	18.2	13.6	16.4
Miscellaneous fees, gambling losses	100.0	0.0	0.0	43.9	20.0	6.5	5.3	4.9
Legal fees	100.0	5.7	17.3	27.4	15.0	16.2	13.2	12.1
Funeral expenses	100.0	0.5	3.7	18.0	23.6	27.7	17.0	10.4
Cemetery lots, vaults, maintenance fees	100.0	–	11.5	7.3	20.0	17.3	35.2	6.5
Accounting fees	100.0	–	8.6	43.9	10.0	6.5	10.5	4.9

Note: Numbers may not add to total because of rounding. (–) means sample is too small to make a reliable estimate. Expenditures for items in a given category may not add to category total because categories with annual spending of less than $2.00 for the average household are omitted. Spending on gifts is also included in the product and service categories in other chapters.
Source: Calculations by New Strategist based on the 2000 Consumer Expenditure Survey

Table 6.6 Gifts: Average spending by income, 2000

(average annual spending on gifts of products and services for non–household members, by before-tax income of consumer units (CU), 2000; complete income reporters only)

	complete income reporters	under $10,000	$10,000–$19,999	$20,000–$29,999	$30,000–$39,999	$40,000–$49,999	$50,000–$69,999	$70,000 or more
Number of consumer units (in thousands, add 000)	81,454	10,810	14,714	12,039	9,477	7,653	11,337	15,424
Average number of persons per CU	2.5	1.7	2.1	2.4	2.5	2.6	2.9	3.2
Average before-tax income of CU	$44,649.00	$5,739.61	$14,586.29	$24,527.00	$34,422.00	$44,201.00	$58,561.00	$112,586.00
Average spending of CU, total	40,238.44	16,455.72	22,620.20	29,851.59	35,609.24	42,323.03	49,245.37	75,963.85
Gifts, average spending	1,163.45	527.17	625.04	769.81	890.96	1,025.82	1,200.21	2,577.44
FOOD	**$66.26**	**$18.78**	**$19.35**	**$29.73**	**$32.53**	**$56.45**	**$80.68**	**$182.53**
Fresh fruits	4.51	2.05	0.25	4.13	3.41	15.41	2.87	6.60
Candy and chewing gum	15.31	1.98	6.28	6.52	6.50	15.02	15.91	42.12
Board (including at school)	18.19	5.38	3.12	4.21	2.28	5.43	15.03	70.90
Catered affairs	11.78	0.62	2.55	1.67	10.49	5.50	30.91	26.15
ALCOHOLIC BEVERAGES	**16.54**	**4.62**	**6.24**	**9.79**	**11.81**	**7.45**	**20.25**	**41.64**
Beer and ale	3.99	1.28	3.51	4.25	2.60	2.60	3.92	7.34
Wine	8.00	2.41	2.45	3.12	4.45	4.12	4.54	25.91
Whiskey and other alcoholic beverages	4.22	0.78	0.27	2.08	4.67	0.62	11.38	7.39
HOUSING	**316.35**	**123.91**	**168.97**	**222.40**	**223.41**	**306.30**	**330.66**	**694.88**
Housekeeping supplies	**43.80**	**13.61**	**19.90**	**36.79**	**34.25**	**45.63**	**59.19**	**80.83**
Miscellaneous household products	8.17	0.43	3.88	4.17	6.70	7.14	8.38	20.33
Lawn and garden supplies	2.40	0.23	1.05	1.70	0.86	1.28	7.96	2.77
Postage and stationery	29.12	12.24	13.13	24.65	22.54	32.99	39.90	50.42
Stationery, stationery supplies, giftwraps	23.75	9.34	10.79	17.53	19.38	26.80	30.70	43.97
Postage	5.31	2.90	2.35	7.12	3.16	6.19	8.80	6.45
Household textiles	**15.83**	**3.47**	**5.02**	**21.23**	**6.91**	**22.78**	**22.51**	**26.29**
Bathroom linens	2.78	0.39	1.33	2.85	2.77	3.57	5.08	3.34
Bedroom linens	8.52	2.54	1.07	16.89	2.36	12.88	10.86	12.52
Appliances and miscellaneous housewares	**33.66**	**11.85**	**14.81**	**13.59**	**25.04**	**50.94**	**49.73**	**63.22**
Major appliances	9.52	6.08	5.46	2.81	8.37	14.42	11.80	16.82
Electric floor cleaning equipment	4.32	3.92	–	–	4.87	7.65	5.17	8.75
Small appliances and miscellaneous housewares	24.14	5.77	9.35	10.78	16.67	36.52	37.93	46.40
Glassware	4.71	0.09	3.21	1.09	3.53	5.15	12.15	6.35
Nonelectric cookware	3.06	2.24	1.20	1.08	0.71	2.29	7.92	4.81
Tableware, nonelectric kitchenware	5.38	1.46	2.44	4.46	4.58	8.65	5.85	9.44
Small electric kitchen appliances	3.06	0.93	1.41	2.09	2.56	3.82	5.39	5.10
Miscellaneous household equipment	**77.78**	**21.79**	**51.20**	**59.03**	**76.99**	**63.09**	**83.44**	**153.99**
Infants' equipment	2.52	–	0.86	2.45	1.96	4.00	5.17	3.21
Outdoor equipment	3.06	1.88	8.75	0.60	0.82	3.00	2.06	2.51
Household decorative items	32.99	7.19	21.18	18.27	40.70	30.17	29.23	67.97
Indoor plants, fresh flowers	16.57	8.16	10.05	12.06	13.92	12.18	18.35	34.68
Computers and computer hardware, nonbusiness use	7.79	2.25	3.75	3.26	8.37	0.51	9.03	21.39
Miscellaneous household equipment and parts	2.87	0.75	0.97	4.28	5.52	1.84	1.67	4.45
Other housing	**145.28**	**73.20**	**78.02**	**91.75**	**80.21**	**123.87**	**115.80**	**370.54**
Repair or maintenance services	4.76	–	13.09	3.79	1.88	3.31	4.43	3.66
Housing while attending school	41.71	9.14	7.37	6.88	8.51	18.86	31.44	163.77
Natural gas (renter)	2.43	2.87	2.98	1.29	4.57	1.83	2.13	1.71
Electricity (renter)	12.48	21.03	17.39	14.37	13.33	8.95	8.86	4.19
Telephone services in home city, excl. mobile phones	12.89	20.24	14.02	14.58	16.40	11.06	9.79	6.38

	complete income reporters	under $10,000	$10,000–$19,999	$20,000–$29,999	$30,000–$39,999	$40,000–$49,999	$50,000–$69,999	$70,000 or more
Water, sewerage maintenance (renter)	$2.42	$4.57	$2.15	$3.52	$2.73	$2.44	$1.03	$1.11
Care for elderly, invalids, handicapped	1.71	0.26	–	6.88	0.83	0.78	3.50	0.03
Day-care centers, nurseries, and preschools	23.15	1.61	4.09	9.70	5.33	22.38	30.95	72.53
Housekeeping services	4.35	0.64	2.73	2.47	1.03	5.62	6.13	10.05
Gardening, lawn care service	3.30	1.63	0.79	2.33	0.67	1.21	1.43	11.64
Repair of miscellaneous household equipment and furnishings	10.55	–	–	–	–	–	–	52.21
Bedroom furniture except mattress and springs	2.53	–	–	3.27	1.83	10.75	0.85	3.70
APPAREL AND SERVICES	**276.30**	**154.44**	**169.27**	**179.76**	**225.53**	**280.97**	**299.33**	**526.74**
Men and boys, aged 2 or older	**74.66**	**30.86**	**58.45**	**50.88**	**50.90**	**49.35**	**77.44**	**156.50**
Men's coats and jackets	4.36	–	–	3.78	–	3.72	8.67	10.95
Men's underwear	1.91	3.67	0.18	2.04	0.98	2.67	2.38	2.24
Men's accessories	3.95	4.43	4.72	3.38	2.72	2.15	3.91	4.91
Men's sweaters and vests	2.63	1.44	1.33	1.25	3.01	2.72	3.84	4.61
Men's active sportswear	5.79	–	2.06	1.85	8.44	2.06	1.46	18.39
Men's shirts	23.97	12.49	22.57	16.93	13.42	11.20	23.45	49.52
Men's pants	8.69	2.74	11.19	5.11	1.83	7.56	5.18	19.60
Boys' shirts	5.27	0.83	3.69	2.73	4.49	3.56	8.12	10.18
Boys' pants	2.84	0.72	2.47	2.39	3.22	3.31	3.63	3.96
Women and girls, aged 2 or older	**97.35**	**55.03**	**50.75**	**54.56**	**83.02**	**102.91**	**98.33**	**198.59**
Women's coats and jackets	4.18	–	1.87	3.11	–	8.93	7.06	7.58
Women's dresses	13.80	7.71	3.01	5.10	4.56	10.29	7.95	44.16
Women's vests and sweaters	9.82	3.43	0.66	4.32	7.83	12.10	10.98	24.54
Women's shirts, tops, blouses	12.04	6.64	14.51	7.67	13.66	12.17	8.57	17.33
Women's pants	5.92	3.83	1.48	2.94	4.23	6.67	10.32	10.65
Women's active sportswear	4.21	3.51	0.66	0.79	2.11	8.86	1.07	11.50
Women's sleepwear	7.24	4.37	3.44	1.82	0.69	8.67	15.60	13.36
Women's undergarments	3.23	3.20	1.03	0.35	2.99	3.53	2.23	7.96
Women's accessories	4.17	1.97	2.05	1.57	3.44	0.21	3.54	11.91
Girls' dresses and suits	4.78	2.78	1.44	4.25	10.81	8.00	2.92	5.40
Girls' shirts, blouses, sweaters	6.32	5.27	6.02	4.09	7.61	6.17	6.87	7.81
Girls' skirts and pants	3.09	1.13	2.73	4.34	3.19	4.35	2.54	3.55
Girls' active sportswear	2.40	1.36	2.08	1.55	5.29	1.36	2.28	2.61
Girls' accessories	2.64	0.31	1.14	2.60	4.81	0.21	2.93	4.89
Children under age 2	**47.11**	**20.56**	**28.47**	**31.61**	**43.70**	**56.54**	**56.07**	**83.23**
Infant dresses, outerwear	15.70	4.37	7.86	14.64	13.08	15.67	22.97	28.24
Infant underwear	22.26	9.24	16.10	10.86	21.03	31.94	20.29	40.81
Infant nightwear, loungewear	2.57	1.32	1.20	2.03	1.97	3.86	3.39	4.33
Infant accessories	5.03	5.35	2.21	3.23	5.69	3.62	6.70	7.50
Other apparel products and services	**57.18**	**48.00**	**31.62**	**42.71**	**47.91**	**72.17**	**67.49**	**88.41**
Watches	3.88	4.46	3.21	0.72	3.72	3.58	5.40	5.74
Jewelry	19.73	12.34	9.64	15.96	12.90	22.46	22.68	38.13
Men's footwear	9.66	3.48	9.50	7.22	2.99	16.16	8.10	17.27
Boys' footwear	3.45	1.59	–	2.02	1.15	0.59	14.03	3.69
Women's footwear	12.20	8.05	6.30	9.16	13.22	28.90	10.24	14.54
Girls' footwear	6.34	17.93	2.45	4.15	12.63	–	4.80	4.95
TRANSPORTATION	**72.13**	**41.35**	**19.76**	**54.69**	**44.71**	**33.47**	**47.94**	**210.58**
New cars	1.21	–	–	–	–	–	–	6.40
New trucks	16.30	–	–	–	–	–	–	86.10
Used cars	13.63	20.46	0.57	33.86	1.68	–	5.18	25.83
Used trucks	1.15	–	3.22	–	–	–	–	3.00
Gasoline on trips	14.37	6.23	8.23	11.08	17.37	15.76	16.83	24.14

	complete income reporters	under $10,000	$10,000– $19,999	$20,000– $29,999	$30,000– $39,999	$40,000– $49,999	$50,000– $69,999	$70,000 or more
Airline fares	$9.98	$7.49	$3.37	$3.89	$7.93	$5.29	$9.83	$26.47
Local transportation on trips	2.31	1.68	1.36	1.96	1.97	1.12	2.35	4.72
Intercity train fares	2.28	0.98	0.88	0.44	1.71	1.42	2.46	6.60
Ship fares	3.82	0.68	0.08	0.20	5.05	4.92	4.35	10.72
HEALTH CARE	**42.61**	**10.30**	**77.61**	**49.43**	**36.85**	**9.85**	**31.46**	**54.54**
Physician's services	2.88	0.87	5.37	1.75	1.10	2.33	1.11	5.47
Dental services	3.52	0.16	5.00	3.11	2.56	2.88	3.53	5.67
Hospital room	3.36	–	5.88	–	–	–	–	12.14
Care in convalescent or nursing home	20.89	7.18	50.00	33.38	27.84	–	19.48	0.08
Nonprescription drugs	2.10	0.70	5.28	1.51	1.73	0.47	0.34	2.85
ENTERTAINMENT	**101.70**	**42.75**	**49.23**	**100.18**	**112.81**	**104.67**	**105.96**	**180.55**
Toys, games, hobbies, and tricycles	31.66	11.62	21.27	33.88	32.77	36.02	34.66	48.80
Movie, other admissions, on trips	9.56	3.73	5.93	7.50	6.16	7.55	10.03	21.44
Admission to sports events on trips	3.19	1.24	1.97	2.50	2.05	2.52	3.34	7.15
Fees for recreational lessons	6.36	0.17	0.71	2.31	3.58	6.05	3.09	23.50
Cable service and community antenna	4.70	6.73	5.59	5.02	6.55	4.03	4.15	1.76
Color TV, portable, table model	2.59	0.08	1.80	3.20	1.96	4.68	1.88	4.52
Musical instruments and accessories	2.84	–	1.17	0.49	10.29	10.08	0.77	1.62
Athletic gear, game tables, and exercise equipment	9.73	3.04	2.27	6.07	14.85	4.38	10.91	21.32
PERSONAL CARE PRODUCTS AND SERVICES	**22.57**	**9.01**	**16.69**	**13.41**	**17.21**	**35.01**	**25.95**	**36.80**
Hair care products	2.81	1.61	0.64	2.28	2.60	8.40	1.85	3.94
Cosmetics, perfume, bath preparation	14.00	2.66	14.08	6.00	11.00	20.00	18.00	22.00
Deodorants, feminine hygiene, misc. personal care	2.00	3.32	0.55	2.00	1.00	3.00	1.00	4.00
READING	**2.00**	**1.66**	**1.55**	**2.00**	**2.00**	**3.00**	**3.00**	**3.00**
EDUCATION	**149.00**	**47.49**	**42.64**	**19.00**	**92.00**	**87.00**	**151.00**	**486.00**
College tuition	115.00	30.12	31.92	12.00	61.00	60.00	107.00	401.00
Elementary and high school tuition	7.00	3.33	2.45	0.00	6.00	5.00	10.00	18.00
Other school tuition	3.00	0.00	–	1.00	3.00	5.00	5.00	6.00
Other school expenses including rentals	5.00	0.66	0.45	1.00	3.00	2.00	14.00	10.00
College books and supplies	11.00	9.37	2.55	1.00	7.00	6.00	8.00	36.00
Miscellaneous school supplies	7.00	3.34	4.82	3.00	11.00	5.00	5.00	12.00
ALL OTHER GIFTS	**98.00**	**73.30**	**54.08**	**90.00**	**92.00**	**101.00**	**104.00**	**160.00**
Gifts of trip expenses	57.00	34.74	27.08	41.00	57.00	71.00	59.00	107.00
Miscellaneous fees, gambling losses	2.00	–	–	0.00	2.00	7.00	3.00	2.00
Legal fees	4.00	0.34	5.08	8.00	12.00	4.00	1.00	2.00
Funeral expenses	28.00	33.58	18.09	36.00	7.00	12.00	37.00	41.00
Cemetery lots, vaults, maintenance fees	3.00	3.99	2.36	4.00	4.00	4.00	2.00	3.00
Accounting fees	2.00	0.66	0.55	1.00	9.00	1.00	1.00	3.00

Note: (–) means sample is too small to make a reliable estimate. Expenditures for items in a given category may not add to category total because categories with annual spending of less than $2.00 for the average household are omitted. Spending on gifts is also included in the product and service categories in other chapters.
Source: Bureau of Labor Statistics, unpublished tables from the 2000 Consumer Expenditure Survey; calculations by New Strategist

Table 6.7 Gifts: Indexed spending by income, 2000

(indexed average annual spending of consumer units (CU) on gifts of products and services for non–household members, by before-tax income of consumer unit, 2000; complete income reporters only; index definition: an index of 100 is the average for all consumer units; an index of 132 means that spending by consumer units in that group is 32 percent above the average for all consumer units; an index of 68 indicates spending that is 32 percent below the average for all consumer units)

	complete income reporters	under $10,000	$10,000–$19,999	$20,000–$29,999	$30,000–$39,999	$40,000–$49,999	$50,000–$69,999	$70,000 or more
Average spending of CU, total	$40,238	$16,456	$22,620	$29,852	$35,609	$42,323	$49,245	$75,964
Average spending of CU, index	100	41	56	74	88	105	122	189
Gifts, spending index	100	45	54	66	77	88	103	222
FOOD	100	28	29	45	49	85	122	275
Fresh fruits	100	45	5	92	76	342	64	146
Candy and chewing gum	100	13	41	43	42	98	104	275
Board (including at school)	100	30	17	23	13	30	83	390
Catered affairs	100	5	22	14	89	47	262	222
ALCOHOLIC BEVERAGES	100	28	38	59	71	45	122	252
Beer and ale	100	32	88	107	65	65	98	184
Wine	100	30	31	39	56	52	57	324
Whiskey and other alcoholic beverages	100	18	6	49	111	15	270	175
HOUSING	100	39	53	70	71	97	105	220
Housekeeping supplies	100	31	45	84	78	104	135	185
Miscellaneous household products	100	5	48	51	82	87	103	249
Lawn and garden supplies	100	9	44	71	36	53	332	115
Postage and stationery	100	42	45	85	77	113	137	173
Stationery, stationery supplies, giftwraps	100	39	45	74	82	113	129	185
Postage	100	55	44	134	60	117	166	121
Household textiles	100	22	32	134	44	144	142	166
Bathroom linens	100	14	48	103	100	128	183	120
Bedroom linens	100	30	13	198	28	151	127	147
Appliances and miscellaneous housewares	100	35	44	40	74	151	148	188
Major appliances	100	64	57	30	88	151	124	177
Electric floor cleaning equipment	100	91	–	–	113	177	120	203
Small appliances and miscellaneous housewares	100	24	39	45	69	151	157	192
Glassware	100	2	68	23	75	109	258	135
Nonelectric cookware	100	73	39	35	23	75	259	157
Tableware, nonelectric kitchenware	100	27	45	83	85	161	109	175
Small electric kitchen appliances	100	30	46	68	84	125	176	167
Miscellaneous household equipment	100	28	66	76	99	81	107	198
Infants' equipment	100	–	34	97	78	159	205	127
Outdoor equipment	100	61	286	20	27	98	67	82
Household decorative items	100	22	64	55	123	91	89	206
Indoor plants, fresh flowers	100	49	61	73	84	74	111	209
Computers and computer hardware, nonbusiness use	100	29	48	42	107	7	116	275
Miscellaneous household equipment and parts	100	26	34	149	192	64	58	155
Other housing	100	50	54	63	55	85	80	255
Repair or maintenance services	100	–	275	80	39	70	93	77
Housing while attending school	100	22	18	16	20	45	75	393
Natural gas (renter)	100	118	123	53	188	75	88	70
Electricity (renter)	100	169	139	115	107	72	71	34
Telephone services in home city, excl. mobile phones	100	157	109	113	127	86	76	49

	complete income reporters	under $10,000	$10,000– $19,999	$20,000– $29,999	$30,000– $39,999	$40,000– $49,999	$50,000– $69,999	$70,000 or more
Water, sewerage maintenance (renter)	100	189	89	145	113	101	43	46
Care for elderly, invalids, handicapped	100	15	–	402	49	46	205	2
Day-care centers, nurseries, and preschools	100	7	18	42	23	97	134	313
Housekeeping services	100	15	63	57	24	129	141	231
Gardening, lawn care service	100	50	24	71	20	37	43	353
Repair of miscellaneous household equipment and furnishings	100	–	–	–	–	–	–	495
Bedroom furniture except mattress and springs	100	–	–	129	72	425	34	146
APPAREL AND SERVICES	**100**	**56**	**61**	**65**	**82**	**102**	**108**	**191**
Men and boys, aged 2 or older	**100**	**41**	**78**	**68**	**68**	**66**	**104**	**210**
Men's coats and jackets	100	–	–	87	–	85	199	251
Men's underwear	100	192	9	107	51	140	125	117
Men's accessories	100	112	120	86	69	54	99	124
Men's sweaters and vests	100	55	51	48	114	103	146	175
Men's active sportswear	100	–	36	32	146	36	25	318
Men's shirts	100	52	94	71	56	47	98	207
Men's pants	100	32	129	59	21	87	60	226
Boys' shirts	100	16	70	52	85	68	154	193
Boys' pants	100	25	87	84	113	117	128	139
Women and girls, aged 2 or older	**100**	**57**	**52**	**56**	**85**	**106**	**101**	**204**
Women's coats and jackets	100	–	45	74	–	214	169	181
Women's dresses	100	56	22	37	33	75	58	320
Women's vests and sweaters	100	35	7	44	80	123	112	250
Women's shirts, tops, blouses	100	55	121	64	113	101	71	144
Women's pants	100	65	25	50	71	113	174	180
Women's active sportswear	100	83	16	19	50	210	25	273
Women's sleepwear	100	60	48	25	10	120	215	185
Women's undergarments	100	99	32	11	93	109	69	246
Women's accessories	100	47	49	38	82	5	85	286
Girls' dresses and suits	100	58	30	89	226	167	61	113
Girls' shirts, blouses, sweaters	100	83	95	65	120	98	109	124
Girls' skirts and pants	100	37	88	140	103	141	82	115
Girls' active sportswear	100	56	87	65	220	57	95	109
Girls' accessories	100	12	43	98	182	8	111	185
Children under age 2	**100**	**44**	**60**	**67**	**93**	**120**	**119**	**177**
Infant dresses, outerwear	100	28	50	93	83	100	146	180
Infant underwear	100	42	72	49	94	143	91	183
Infant nightwear, loungewear	100	51	47	79	77	150	132	168
Infant accessories	100	106	44	64	113	72	133	149
Other apparel products and services	**100**	**84**	**55**	**75**	**84**	**126**	**118**	**155**
Watches	100	115	83	19	96	92	139	148
Jewelry	100	63	49	81	65	114	115	193
Men's footwear	100	36	98	75	31	167	84	179
Boys' footwear	100	46	–	59	33	17	407	107
Women's footwear	100	66	52	75	108	237	84	119
Girls' footwear	100	283	39	65	199	–	76	78
TRANSPORTATION	**100**	**57**	**27**	**76**	**62**	**46**	**66**	**292**
New cars	100	–	–	–	–	–	–	529
New trucks	100	–	–	–	–	–	–	528
Used cars	100	150	4	248	12	–	38	190
Used trucks	100	–	280	–	–	–	–	261
Gasoline on trips	100	43	57	77	121	110	117	168

	complete income reporters	under $10,000	$10,000– $19,999	$20,000– $29,999	$30,000– $39,999	$40,000– $49,999	$50,000– $69,999	$70,000 or more
Airline fares	100	75	34	39	79	53	98	265
Local transportation on trips	100	73	59	85	85	48	102	204
Intercity train fares	100	43	39	19	75	62	108	289
Ship fares	100	18	2	5	132	129	114	281
HEALTH CARE	**100**	**24**	**182**	**116**	**86**	**23**	**74**	**128**
Physician's services	100	30	186	61	38	81	39	190
Dental services	100	5	142	88	73	82	100	161
Hospital room	100	–	175	–	–	–	–	361
Care in convalescent or nursing home	100	34	239	160	133	–	93	0
Nonprescription drugs	100	33	252	72	82	22	16	136
ENTERTAINMENT	**100**	**42**	**48**	**99**	**111**	**103**	**104**	**178**
Toys, games, hobbies, and tricycles	100	37	67	107	104	114	109	154
Movie, other admissions, on trips	100	39	62	78	64	79	105	224
Admission to sports events on trips	100	39	62	78	64	79	105	224
Fees for recreational lessons	100	3	11	36	56	95	49	369
Cable service and community antenna	100	143	119	107	139	86	88	37
Color TV, portable, table model	100	3	70	124	76	181	73	175
Musical instruments and accessories	100	–	41	17	362	355	27	57
Athletic gear, game tables, and exercise equipment	100	31	23	62	153	45	112	219
PERSONAL CARE PRODUCTS AND SERVICES	**100**	**40**	**74**	**59**	**76**	**155**	**115**	**163**
Hair care products	100	57	23	81	93	299	66	140
Cosmetics, perfume, bath preparation	100	19	101	43	79	143	129	157
Deodorants, feminine hygiene, misc. personal care	100	166	27	100	50	150	50	200
READING	**100**	**83**	**77**	**100**	**100**	**150**	**150**	**150**
EDUCATION	**100**	**32**	**29**	**13**	**62**	**58**	**101**	**326**
College tuition	100	26	28	10	53	52	93	349
Elementary and high school tuition	100	48	35	0	86	71	143	257
Other school tuition	100	0	–	33	100	167	167	200
Other school expenses including rentals	100	13	9	20	60	40	280	200
College books and supplies	100	85	23	9	64	55	73	327
Miscellaneous school supplies	100	48	69	43	157	71	71	171
ALL OTHER GIFTS	**100**	**75**	**55**	**92**	**94**	**103**	**106**	**163**
Gifts of trip expenses	100	61	48	72	100	125	104	188
Miscellaneous fees, gambling losses	100	–	–	0	100	350	150	100
Legal fees	100	8	127	200	300	100	25	50
Funeral expenses	100	120	65	129	25	43	132	146
Cemetery lots, vaults, maintenance fees	100	133	79	133	133	133	67	100
Accounting fees	100	33	27	50	450	50	50	150

Note: (–) means sample is too small to make a reliable estimate. Categories with annual spending of less than $2.00 for the average household are omitted. Spending on gifts is also included in the product and service categories in other chapters.
Source: Calculations by New Strategist based on the 2000 Consumer Expenditure Survey

Table 6.8 Gifts: Indexed per capita spending by income, 2000

(indexed average annual per capita spending of consumer units (CU) on gifts of products and services for non–household members, by before-tax income of consumer unit, 2000; complete income reporters only; index definition: an index of 100 is the average for all consumer units; an index of 132 means that spending by consumer units in that group is 32 percent above the average for all consumer units; an index of 68 indicates spending that is 32 percent below the average for all consumer units)

	complete income reporters	under $10,000	$10,000– $19,999	$20,000– $29,999	$30,000– $39,999	$40,000– $49,999	$50,000– $69,999	$70,000 or more
Per capita spending of CU, total	$16,095	$9,492	$10,819	$12,438	$14,244	$16,278	$16,981	$23,739
Per capita spending of CU, index	100	59	67	77	88	101	106	147
Gifts, per capita spending index	100	65	64	69	77	85	89	173
FOOD	**100**	**41**	**35**	**47**	**49**	**82**	**105**	**215**
Fresh fruits	100	66	6	95	76	329	55	114
Candy and chewing gum	100	19	49	44	42	94	90	215
Board (including at school)	100	43	20	24	13	29	71	305
Catered affairs	100	8	26	15	89	45	226	173
ALCOHOLIC BEVERAGES	**100**	**40**	**45**	**62**	**71**	**43**	**106**	**197**
Beer and ale	100	46	105	111	65	63	85	144
Wine	100	43	37	41	56	50	49	253
Whiskey and other alcoholic beverages	100	27	8	51	111	14	232	137
HOUSING	**100**	**56**	**64**	**73**	**71**	**93**	**90**	**172**
Housekeeping supplies	**100**	**45**	**54**	**87**	**78**	**100**	**116**	**144**
Miscellaneous household products	100	8	57	53	82	84	88	194
Lawn and garden supplies	100	14	52	74	36	51	286	90
Postage and stationery	100	61	54	88	77	109	118	135
Stationery, stationery supplies, giftwraps	100	57	54	77	82	109	111	145
Postage	100	79	53	140	60	112	143	95
Household textiles	**100**	**32**	**38**	**140**	**44**	**138**	**123**	**130**
Bathroom linens	100	20	57	107	100	123	158	94
Bedroom linens	100	43	15	206	28	145	110	115
Appliances and miscellaneous housewares	**100**	**51**	**53**	**42**	**74**	**146**	**127**	**147**
Major appliances	100	92	69	31	88	146	107	138
Electric floor cleaning equipment	100	131	–	–	113	170	103	158
Small appliances and miscellaneous housewares	100	34	46	47	69	145	135	150
Glassware	100	3	81	24	75	105	222	105
Nonelectric cookware	100	106	47	37	23	72	223	123
Tableware, nonelectric kitchenware	100	39	54	86	85	155	94	137
Small electric kitchen appliances	100	44	55	71	84	120	152	130
Miscellaneous household equipment	**100**	**40**	**79**	**79**	**99**	**78**	**92**	**155**
Infants' equipment	100	–	41	101	78	153	177	100
Outdoor equipment	100	89	342	20	27	94	58	64
Household decorative items	100	31	77	58	123	88	76	161
Indoor plants, fresh flowers	100	71	73	76	84	71	95	164
Computers and computer hardware, nonbusiness use	100	42	58	44	107	6	100	215
Miscellaneous household equipment and parts	100	38	40	155	192	62	50	121
Other housing	**100**	**73**	**64**	**66**	**55**	**82**	**69**	**199**
Repair or maintenance services	100	–	329	83	39	67	80	60
Housing while attending school	100	32	21	17	20	43	65	307
Natural gas (renter)	100	170	147	55	188	72	76	55
Electricity (renter)	100	243	167	120	107	69	61	26
Telephone services in home city, excl. mobile phones	100	226	130	118	127	83	65	39

	complete income reporters	under $10,000	$10,000–$19,999	$20,000–$29,999	$30,000–$39,999	$40,000–$49,999	$50,000–$69,999	$70,000 or more
Water, sewerage maintenance (renter)	100	272	106	152	113	97	37	36
Care for elderly, invalids, handicapped	100	22	–	419	49	44	176	1
Day-care centers, nurseries, and preschools	100	10	21	44	23	93	115	245
Housekeeping services	100	21	75	59	24	124	121	180
Gardening, lawn care service	100	71	29	74	20	35	37	276
Repair of misc. household equipment and furnishings	100	–	–	–	–	–	–	387
Bedroom furniture except mattress and springs	100	–	–	135	72	409	29	114
APPAREL AND SERVICES	**100**	**81**	**73**	**68**	**82**	**98**	**93**	**149**
Men and boys, aged 2 or older	**100**	**60**	**94**	**71**	**68**	**64**	**89**	**164**
Men's coats and jackets	100	–	–	90	–	82	171	196
Men's underwear	100	277	11	111	51	134	107	92
Men's accessories	100	162	143	89	69	52	85	97
Men's sweaters and vests	100	79	61	50	114	99	126	137
Men's active sportswear	100	–	42	33	146	34	22	248
Men's shirts	100	75	113	74	56	45	84	161
Men's pants	100	45	154	61	21	84	51	176
Boys' shirts	100	23	84	54	85	65	133	151
Boys' pants	100	37	104	88	113	112	110	109
Women and girls, aged 2 or older	**100**	**82**	**62**	**58**	**85**	**102**	**87**	**159**
Women's coats and jackets	100	–	53	78	–	205	146	142
Women's dresses	100	81	26	38	33	72	50	250
Women's vests and sweaters	100	50	8	46	80	118	96	195
Women's shirts, tops, blouses	100	80	144	66	113	97	61	112
Women's pants	100	93	30	52	71	108	150	141
Women's active sportswear	100	120	19	20	50	202	22	213
Women's sleepwear	100	87	57	26	10	115	186	144
Women's undergarments	100	143	38	11	93	105	60	193
Women's accessories	100	68	59	39	82	5	73	223
Girls' dresses and suits	100	84	36	93	226	161	53	88
Girls' shirts, blouses, sweaters	100	120	114	67	120	94	94	97
Girls' skirts and pants	100	53	106	146	103	135	71	90
Girls' active sportswear	100	81	104	67	220	54	82	85
Girls' accessories	100	17	52	103	182	8	96	145
Children under age 2	**100**	**63**	**72**	**70**	**93**	**115**	**103**	**138**
Infant dresses, outerwear	100	40	60	97	83	96	126	141
Infant underwear	100	60	87	51	94	138	79	143
Infant nightwear, loungewear	100	74	56	82	77	144	114	132
Infant accessories	100	153	53	67	113	69	115	116
Other apparel products and services	**100**	**121**	**66**	**78**	**84**	**121**	**102**	**121**
Watches	100	166	99	19	96	89	120	116
Jewelry	100	90	58	84	65	109	99	151
Men's footwear	100	52	118	78	31	161	72	140
Boys' footwear	100	66	–	61	33	16	351	84
Women's footwear	100	95	62	78	108	228	72	93
Girls' footwear	100	408	46	68	199	–	65	61
TRANSPORTATION	**100**	**83**	**33**	**79**	**62**	**45**	**57**	**228**
New cars	100	–	–	–	–	–	–	413
New trucks	100	–	–	–	–	–	–	413
Used cars	100	216	5	259	12	–	33	148
Used trucks	100	–	335	–	–	–	–	204
Gasoline on trips	100	63	68	80	121	105	101	131

	complete income reporters	under $10,000	$10,000– $19,999	$20,000– $29,999	$30,000– $39,999	$40,000– $49,999	$50,000– $69,999	$70,000 or more
Airline fares	100	108	40	41	79	51	85	207
Local transportation on trips	100	105	70	88	85	47	88	160
Intercity train fares	100	62	46	20	75	60	93	226
Ship fares	100	26	2	5	132	124	98	219
HEALTH CARE	**100**	**35**	**218**	**121**	**86**	**22**	**64**	**100**
Physician's services	100	44	223	63	38	78	33	148
Dental services	100	7	170	92	73	79	86	126
Hospital room	100	–	209	–	–	–	–	282
Care in convalescent or nursing home	100	50	286	166	133	–	80	0
Nonprescription drugs	100	48	301	75	82	22	14	106
ENTERTAINMENT	**100**	**61**	**58**	**103**	**111**	**99**	**90**	**139**
Toys, games, hobbies, and tricycles	100	53	80	111	104	109	94	120
Movie, other admissions, on trips	100	56	74	82	64	76	90	175
Admission to sports events on trips	100	56	74	82	64	76	90	175
Fees for recreational lessons	100	4	13	38	56	91	42	289
Cable service and community antenna	100	206	142	111	139	82	76	29
Color TV, portable, table model	100	5	83	129	76	174	63	136
Musical instruments and accessories	100	–	49	18	362	341	23	45
Athletic gear, game tables, and exercise equipment	100	45	28	65	153	43	97	171
PERSONAL CARE PRODUCTS AND SERVICES	**100**	**58**	**88**	**62**	**76**	**149**	**99**	**127**
Hair care products	100	83	27	85	93	287	57	110
Cosmetics, perfume, bath preparation	100	27	120	45	79	137	111	123
Deodorants, feminine hygiene, misc. personal care	100	240	33	104	50	144	43	156
READING	**100**	**120**	**92**	**104**	**100**	**144**	**129**	**117**
EDUCATION	**100**	**46**	**34**	**13**	**62**	**56**	**87**	**255**
College tuition	100	38	33	11	53	50	80	272
Elementary and high school tuition	100	69	42	0	86	69	123	201
Other school tuition	100	0	–	35	100	160	144	156
Other school expenses including rentals	100	19	11	21	60	38	241	156
College books and supplies	100	123	28	9	64	52	63	256
Miscellaneous school supplies	100	69	82	45	157	69	62	134
ALL OTHER GIFTS	**100**	**108**	**66**	**96**	**94**	**99**	**91**	**128**
Gifts of trip expenses	100	88	57	75	100	120	89	147
Miscellaneous fees, gambling losses	100	–	–	0	100	337	129	78
Legal fees	100	12	152	208	300	96	22	39
Funeral expenses	100	173	77	134	25	41	114	114
Cemetery lots, vaults, maintenance fees	100	192	94	139	133	128	57	78
Accounting fees	100	48	33	52	450	48	43	117

Note: Per capita indexes account for household size and show how much each person in a particular household demographic segment spends relative to a person in the average household. (–) means sample is too small to make a reliable estimate. Categories with annual spending of less than $2.00 for the average household are omitted. Spending on gifts is also included in the product and service categories in other chapters.
Source: Calculations by New Strategist based on the 2000 Consumer Expenditure Survey

Table 6.9 Gifts: Total spending by income, 2000

(total annual spending on selected gifts, by before-tax income group of consumer units (CU), 2000; complete income reporters only; numbers in thousands)

	complete income reporters	under $10,000	$10,000– $19,999	$20,000– $29,999	$30,000– $39,999	$40,000– $49,999	$50,000– $69,999	$70,000 or more
Number of consumer units	81,454	10,810	14,714	12,039	9,477	7,653	11,337	15,424
Total spending of all CUs	$3,277,581,892	$177,886,368	$332,833,656	$359,383,292	$337,468,767	$323,898,149	$558,294,760	$1,171,666,422
Gifts, total spending	94,767,656	5,698,696	9,196,849	9,267,743	8,443,628	7,850,600	13,606,781	39,754,435
FOOD	**$5,397,142**	**$203,024**	**$284,664**	**$357,919**	**$308,287**	**$432,012**	**$914,669**	**$2,815,343**
Fresh fruits	367,358	22,178	3,606	49,721	32,317	117,933	32,537	101,798
Candy and chewing gum	1,247,061	21,422	92,369	78,494	61,601	114,948	180,372	649,659
Board (including at school)	1,481,648	58,116	45,847	50,684	21,608	41,556	170,395	1,093,562
Catered affairs	959,528	6,680	37,528	20,105	99,414	42,092	350,427	403,338
ALCOHOLIC BEVERAGES	**1,347,249**	**49,921**	**91,742**	**117,862**	**111,923**	**57,015**	**229,574**	**642,255**
Beer and ale	325,001	13,886	51,576	51,166	24,640	19,898	44,441	113,212
Wine	651,632	26,074	36,080	37,562	42,173	31,530	51,470	399,636
Whiskey and other alcoholic beverages	343,736	8,404	3,939	25,041	44,258	4,745	129,015	113,983
HOUSING	**25,767,973**	**1,339,483**	**2,486,172**	**2,677,474**	**2,117,257**	**2,344,114**	**3,748,692**	**10,717,829**
Housekeeping supplies	**3,567,685**	**147,112**	**292,852**	**442,915**	**324,587**	**349,206**	**671,037**	**1,246,722**
Miscellaneous household products	665,479	4,665	57,114	50,203	63,496	54,642	95,004	313,570
Lawn and garden supplies	195,490	2,442	15,463	20,466	8,150	9,796	90,243	42,724
Postage and stationery	2,371,940	132,287	193,261	296,761	213,612	252,472	452,346	777,678
Stationery, stationery supplies, giftwraps	1,934,533	100,977	158,736	211,044	183,664	205,100	348,046	678,193
Postage	432,521	31,310	34,526	85,718	29,947	47,372	99,766	99,485
Household textiles	**1,289,417**	**37,461**	**73,904**	**255,588**	**65,486**	**174,335**	**255,196**	**405,497**
Bathroom linens	226,442	4,166	19,613	34,311	26,251	27,321	57,592	51,516
Bedroom linens	693,988	27,439	15,711	203,339	22,366	98,571	123,120	193,108
Appliances and miscellaneous housewares	**2,741,742**	**128,094**	**217,980**	**163,610**	**237,304**	**389,844**	**563,789**	**975,105**
Major appliances	775,442	65,738	80,337	33,830	79,322	110,356	133,777	259,432
Electric floor cleaning equipment	351,881	42,380	–	–	46,153	58,545	58,612	134,960
Small appliances and misc. housewares	1,966,300	62,357	137,643	129,780	157,982	279,488	430,012	715,674
Glassware	383,648	934	47,179	13,123	33,454	39,413	137,745	97,942
Nonelectric cookware	249,249	24,207	17,647	13,002	6,729	17,525	89,789	74,189
Tableware, nonelectric kitchenware	438,223	15,731	35,863	53,694	43,405	66,198	66,321	145,603
Small electric kitchen appliances	249,249	10,070	20,731	25,162	24,261	29,234	61,106	78,662
Miscellaneous household equipment	**6,335,492**	**235,530**	**753,332**	**710,662**	**729,634**	**482,828**	**945,959**	**2,375,142**
Infants' equipment	205,264	–	12,605	29,496	18,575	30,612	58,612	49,511
Outdoor equipment	249,249	20,328	128,711	7,223	7,771	22,959	23,354	38,714
Household decorative items	2,687,167	77,682	311,582	219,953	385,714	230,891	331,381	1,048,369
Indoor plants, fresh flowers	1,349,693	88,233	147,835	145,190	131,920	93,214	208,034	534,904
Computers and computer hardware, nonbusiness use	634,527	24,288	55,152	39,247	79,322	3,903	102,373	329,919
Miscellaneous household equipment and parts	233,773	8,157	14,289	51,527	52,313	14,082	18,933	68,637
Other housing	**11,833,637**	**791,321**	**1,148,037**	**1,104,578**	**760,150**	**947,977**	**1,312,825**	**5,715,209**
Repair or maintenance services	387,721	–	192,647	45,628	17,817	25,331	50,223	56,452
Housing while attending school	3,397,446	98,772	108,434	82,828	80,649	144,336	356,435	2,525,988
Natural gas (renter)	197,933	31,000	43,877	15,530	43,310	14,005	24,148	26,375
Electricity (renter)	1,016,546	227,365	255,921	173,000	126,328	68,494	100,446	64,627
Telephone services in home city, excl. mobile phones	1,049,942	218,842	206,319	175,529	155,423	84,642	110,989	98,405

	complete income reporters	under $10,000	$10,000– $19,999	$20,000– $29,999	$30,000– $39,999	$40,000– $49,999	$50,000– $69,999	$70,000 or more
Water, sewerage maintenance (renter)	$197,119	$49,378	$31,655	$42,377	$25,872	$18,673	$11,677	$17,121
Care for elderly, invalids, handicapped	139,286	2,829	–	82,828	7,866	5,969	39,680	463
Day-care centers, nurseries, and preschools	1,885,660	17,442	60,206	116,778	50,512	171,274	350,880	1,118,703
Housekeeping services	354,325	6,946	40,127	29,736	9,761	43,010	69,496	155,011
Gardening, lawn care service	268,798	17,670	11,641	28,051	6,350	9,260	16,212	179,535
Repair of miscellaneous household equipment and furnishings	859,340	–	–	–	–	–	–	805,287
Bedroom furniture except mattress and springs	206,079	–	–	39,368	17,343	82,270	9,636	57,069
APPAREL AND SERVICES	**22,505,740**	**1,669,462**	**2,490,700**	**2,164,131**	**2,137,348**	**2,150,263**	**3,393,504**	**8,124,438**
Men and boys, aged 2 or older	**6,081,356**	**333,575**	**859,963**	**612,544**	**482,379**	**377,676**	**877,937**	**2,413,856**
Men's coats and jackets	355,139	–	–	45,507	–	28,469	98,292	168,893
Men's underwear	155,577	39,683	2,609	24,560	9,287	20,434	26,982	34,550
Men's accessories	321,743	47,897	69,495	40,692	25,777	16,454	44,328	75,732
Men's sweaters and vests	214,224	15,612	19,626	15,049	28,526	20,816	43,534	71,105
Men's active sportswear	471,619	–	30,262	22,272	79,986	15,765	16,552	283,647
Men's shirts	1,952,452	135,004	332,139	203,820	127,181	85,714	265,853	763,796
Men's pants	707,835	29,632	164,722	61,519	17,343	57,857	58,726	302,310
Boys' shirts	429,263	8,950	54,294	32,866	42,552	27,245	92,056	157,016
Boys' pants	231,329	7,795	36,404	28,773	30,516	25,331	41,153	61,079
Women and girls, aged 2 or older	**7,929,547**	**594,890**	**746,681**	**656,848**	**786,781**	**787,570**	**1,114,767**	**3,063,052**
Women's coats and jackets	340,478	–	27,442	37,441	–	68,341	80,039	116,914
Women's dresses	1,124,065	83,313	44,301	61,399	43,215	78,749	90,129	681,124
Women's vests and sweaters	799,878	37,064	9,748	52,008	74,205	92,601	124,480	378,505
Women's shirts, tops, blouses	980,706	71,790	213,503	92,339	129,456	93,137	97,158	267,298
Women's pants	482,208	41,363	21,795	35,395	40,088	51,046	116,998	164,266
Women's active sportswear	342,921	37,913	9,748	9,511	19,996	67,806	12,131	177,376
Women's sleepwear	589,727	47,243	50,688	21,911	6,539	66,352	176,857	206,065
Women's undergarments	263,096	34,573	15,097	4,214	28,336	27,015	25,282	122,775
Women's accessories	339,663	21,247	30,218	18,901	32,601	1,607	40,133	183,700
Girls' dresses and suits	389,350	30,101	21,236	51,166	102,446	61,224	33,104	83,290
Girls' shirts, blouses, sweaters	514,789	56,995	88,566	49,240	72,120	47,219	77,885	120,461
Girls' skirts and pants	251,693	12,198	40,138	52,249	30,232	33,291	28,796	54,755
Girls' active sportswear	195,490	14,653	30,578	18,660	50,133	10,408	25,848	40,257
Girls' accessories	215,039	3,304	16,819	31,301	45,584	1,607	33,217	75,423
Children under age 2	**3,837,298**	**222,207**	**418,874**	**380,553**	**414,145**	**432,701**	**635,666**	**1,283,740**
Infant dresses, outerwear	1,278,828	47,223	115,672	176,251	123,959	119,923	260,411	435,574
Infant underwear	1,813,166	99,867	236,963	130,744	199,301	244,437	230,028	629,453
Infant nightwear, loungewear	209,337	14,247	17,616	24,439	18,670	29,541	38,432	66,786
Infant accessories	409,714	57,834	32,564	38,886	53,924	27,704	75,958	115,680
Other apparel products and services	**4,657,540**	**518,863**	**465,263**	**514,186**	**454,043**	**552,317**	**765,134**	**1,363,636**
Watches	316,042	48,206	47,177	8,668	35,254	27,398	61,220	88,534
Jewelry	1,607,087	133,408	141,880	192,142	122,253	171,886	257,123	588,117
Men's footwear	786,846	37,639	139,844	86,922	28,336	123,672	91,830	266,372
Boys' footwear	281,016	17,173	–	24,319	10,899	4,515	159,058	56,915
Women's footwear	993,739	87,015	92,676	110,277	125,286	221,172	116,091	224,265
Girls' footwear	516,418	193,792	35,991	49,962	119,695	–	54,418	76,349
TRANSPORTATION	**5,875,277**	**446,950**	**290,745**	**658,413**	**423,717**	**256,146**	**543,496**	**3,247,986**
New cars	98,559	–	–	–	–	–	–	98,714
New trucks	1,327,700	–	–	–	–	–	–	1,328,006
Used cars	1,110,218	221,138	8,346	407,641	15,921	–	58,726	398,402
Used trucks	93,672	–	47,338	–	–	–	–	46,272
Gasoline on trips	1,170,494	67,388	121,126	133,392	164,615	120,611	190,802	372,335

	complete income reporters	under $10,000	$10,000–$19,999	$20,000–$29,999	$30,000–$39,999	$40,000–$49,999	$50,000–$69,999	$70,000 or more
Airline fares	$812,911	$80,987	$49,633	$46,832	$75,153	$40,484	$111,443	$408,273
Local transportation on trips	188,159	18,210	19,970	23,596	18,670	8,571	26,642	72,801
Intercity train fares	185,715	10,562	12,946	5,297	16,206	10,867	27,889	101,798
Ship fares	311,154	7,398	1,135	2,408	47,859	37,653	49,316	165,345
HEALTH CARE	**3,470,755**	**111,371**	**1,141,943**	**595,088**	**349,227**	**75,382**	**356,662**	**841,225**
Physician's services	234,588	9,433	79,010	21,068	10,425	17,831	12,584	84,369
Dental services	286,718	1,741	73,542	37,441	24,261	22,041	40,020	87,454
Hospital room	273,685	–	86,558	–	–	–	–	187,247
Care in convalescent or nursing home	1,701,574	77,618	735,760	401,862	263,840	–	220,845	1,234
Nonprescription drugs	171,053	7,542	77,726	18,179	16,395	3,597	3,855	43,958
ENTERTAINMENT	**8,283,872**	**462,151**	**724,378**	**1,206,067**	**1,069,100**	**801,040**	**1,201,269**	**2,784,803**
Toys, games, hobbies, and tricycles	2,578,834	125,646	312,951	407,881	310,561	275,661	392,940	752,691
Movie, other admissions, on trips	778,700	40,319	87,223	90,293	58,378	57,780	113,710	330,691
Admission to sports events on trips	259,838	13,416	29,052	30,098	19,428	19,286	37,866	110,282
Fees for recreational lessons	518,047	1,837	10,487	27,810	33,928	46,301	35,031	362,464
Cable service and community antenna	382,834	72,716	82,311	60,436	62,074	30,842	47,049	27,146
Color TV, portable, table model	210,966	907	26,490	38,525	18,575	35,816	21,314	69,716
Musical instruments and accessories	231,329	–	17,149	5,899	97,518	77,142	8,729	24,987
Athletic gear, game tables, exercise equipment	792,547	32,901	33,377	73,077	140,733	33,520	123,687	328,840
PERSONAL CARE PRODUCTS AND SERVICES	**1,838,417**	**97,400**	**245,566**	**161,443**	**163,099**	**267,932**	**294,195**	**567,603**
Hair care products	228,886	17,456	9,381	27,449	24,640	64,285	20,973	60,771
Cosmetics, perfume, bath preparation	1,140,356	28,803	207,233	72,234	104,247	153,060	204,066	339,328
Deodorants, feminine hygiene, misc. personal care	162,908	35,915	8,037	24,078	9,477	22,959	11,337	61,696
READING	**162,908**	**17,993**	**22,751**	**24,078**	**18,954**	**22,959**	**34,011**	**46,272**
EDUCATION	**12,136,646**	**513,330**	**627,385**	**228,741**	**871,884**	**665,811**	**1,711,887**	**7,496,064**
College tuition	9,367,210	325,649	469,611	144,468	578,097	459,180	1,213,059	6,185,024
Elementary and high school tuition	570,178	35,986	36,105	0	56,862	38,265	113,370	277,632
Other school tuition	244,362	0	–	12,039	28,431	38,265	56,685	92,544
Other school expenses including rentals	407,270	7,183	6,677	12,039	28,431	15,306	158,718	154,240
College books and supplies	895,994	101,272	37,465	12,039	66,339	45,918	90,696	555,264
Miscellaneous school supplies	570,178	36,057	70,850	36,117	104,247	38,265	56,685	185,088
ALL OTHER GIFTS	**7,982,492**	**792,402**	**795,670**	**1,083,510**	**871,884**	**772,953**	**1,179,048**	**2,467,840**
Gifts of trip expenses	4,642,878	375,504	398,515	493,599	540,189	543,363	668,883	1,650,368
Miscellaneous fees, gambling losses	162,908	–	–	0	18,954	53,571	34,011	30,848
Legal fees	325,816	3,627	74,807	96,312	113,724	30,612	11,337	30,848
Funeral expenses	2,280,712	362,990	266,212	433,404	66,339	91,836	419,469	632,384
Cemetery lots, vaults, maintenance fees	244,362	43,098	34,745	48,156	37,908	30,612	22,674	46,272
Accounting fees	162,908	7,183	8,037	12,039	85,293	7,653	11,337	46,272

Note: Numbers may not add to total because of rounding. (–) means sample is too small to make a reliable estimate. Expenditures for items in a given category may not add to category total because categories with annual spending of less than $2.00 for the average household are omitted. Spending on gifts is also included in the product and service categories in other chapters.
Source: Calculations by New Strategist based on the 2000 Consumer Expenditure Survey

Table 6.10 Gifts: Market shares by income, 2000

(percentage of total annual spending on gifts of products and services for non-household members accounted for by before-tax income group of consumer units, 2000; complete income reporters only)

	complete income reporters	under $10,000	$10,000–$19,999	$20,000–$29,999	$30,000–$39,999	$40,000–$49,999	$50,000–$69,999	$70,000 or more
Share of total consumer units	100.0%	13.3%	18.1%	14.8%	11.6%	9.4%	13.9%	18.9%
Share of total before-tax income	100.0	1.7	5.9	8.1	9.0	9.3	18.3	47.7
Share of total spending	100.0	5.4	10.2	11.0	10.3	9.9	17.0	35.7
Share of gifts spending	100.0	6.0	9.7	9.8	8.9	8.3	14.4	41.9
FOOD	**100.0%**	**3.8%**	**5.3%**	**6.6%**	**5.7%**	**8.0%**	**16.9%**	**52.2%**
Fresh fruits	100.0	6.0	1.0	13.5	8.8	32.1	8.9	27.7
Candy and chewing gum	100.0	1.7	7.4	6.3	4.9	9.2	14.5	52.1
Board (including at school)	100.0	3.9	3.1	3.4	1.5	2.8	11.5	73.8
Catered affairs	100.0	0.7	3.9	2.1	10.4	4.4	36.5	42.0
ALCOHOLIC BEVERAGES	**100.0**	**3.7**	**6.8**	**8.7**	**8.3**	**4.2**	**17.0**	**47.7**
Beer and ale	100.0	4.3	15.9	15.7	7.6	6.1	13.7	34.8
Wine	100.0	4.0	5.5	5.8	6.5	4.8	7.9	61.3
Whiskey and other alcoholic beverages	100.0	2.4	1.1	7.3	12.9	1.4	37.5	33.2
HOUSING	**100.0**	**5.2**	**9.6**	**10.4**	**8.2**	**9.1**	**14.5**	**41.6**
Housekeeping supplies	**100.0**	**4.1**	**8.2**	**12.4**	**9.1**	**9.8**	**18.8**	**34.9**
Miscellaneous household products	100.0	0.7	8.6	7.5	9.5	8.2	14.3	47.1
Lawn and garden supplies	100.0	1.2	7.9	10.5	4.2	5.0	46.2	21.9
Postage and stationery	100.0	5.6	8.1	12.5	9.0	10.6	19.1	32.8
Stationery, stationery supplies, giftwraps	100.0	5.2	8.2	10.9	9.5	10.6	18.0	35.1
Postage	100.0	7.2	8.0	19.8	6.9	11.0	23.1	23.0
Household textiles	**100.0**	**2.9**	**5.7**	**19.8**	**5.1**	**13.5**	**19.8**	**31.4**
Bathroom linens	100.0	1.8	8.7	15.2	11.6	12.1	25.4	22.8
Bedroom linens	100.0	4.0	2.3	29.3	3.2	14.2	17.7	27.8
Appliances and miscellaneous housewares	**100.0**	**4.7**	**8.0**	**6.0**	**8.7**	**14.2**	**20.6**	**35.6**
Major appliances	100.0	8.5	10.4	4.4	10.2	14.2	17.3	33.5
Electric floor cleaning equipment	100.0	12.0	–	–	13.1	16.6	16.7	38.4
Small appliances and miscellaneous housewares	100.0	3.2	7.0	6.6	8.0	14.2	21.9	36.4
Glassware	100.0	0.2	12.3	3.4	8.7	10.3	35.9	25.5
Nonelectric cookware	100.0	9.7	7.1	5.2	2.7	7.0	36.0	29.8
Tableware, nonelectric kitchenware	100.0	3.6	8.2	12.3	9.9	15.1	15.1	33.2
Small electric kitchen appliances	100.0	4.0	8.3	10.1	9.7	11.7	24.5	31.6
Miscellaneous household equipment	**100.0**	**3.7**	**11.9**	**11.2**	**11.5**	**7.6**	**14.9**	**37.5**
Infants' equipment	100.0	–	6.1	14.4	9.0	14.9	28.6	24.1
Outdoor equipment	100.0	8.2	51.6	2.9	3.1	9.2	9.4	15.5
Household decorative items	100.0	2.9	11.6	8.2	14.4	8.6	12.3	39.0
Indoor plants, fresh flowers	100.0	6.5	11.0	10.8	9.8	6.9	15.4	39.6
Computers and computer hardware, nonbusiness use	100.0	3.8	8.7	6.2	12.5	0.6	16.1	52.0
Miscellaneous household equipment and parts	100.0	3.5	6.1	22.0	22.4	6.0	8.1	29.4
Other housing	**100.0**	**6.7**	**9.7**	**9.3**	**6.4**	**8.0**	**11.1**	**48.3**
Repair or maintenance services	100.0	–	49.7	11.8	4.6	6.5	13.0	14.6
Housing while attending school	100.0	2.9	3.2	2.4	2.4	4.2	10.5	74.3
Natural gas (renter)	100.0	15.7	22.2	7.8	21.9	7.1	12.2	13.3
Electricity (renter)	100.0	22.4	25.2	17.0	12.4	6.7	9.9	6.4
Telephone services in home city, excl. mobile phones	100.0	20.8	19.7	16.7	14.8	8.1	10.6	9.4

	complete income reporters	under $10,000	$10,000– $19,999	$20,000– $29,999	$30,000– $39,999	$40,000– $49,999	$50,000– $69,999	$70,000 or more
Water, sewerage maintenance (renter)	100.0%	25.1%	16.1%	21.5%	13.1%	9.5%	5.9%	8.7%
Care for elderly, invalids, handicapped	100.0	2.0	–	59.5	5.6	4.3	28.5	0.3
Day-care centers, nurseries, and preschools	100.0	0.9	3.2	6.2	2.7	9.1	18.6	59.3
Housekeeping services	100.0	2.0	11.3	8.4	2.8	12.1	19.6	43.7
Gardening, lawn care service	100.0	6.6	4.3	10.4	2.4	3.4	6.0	66.8
Repair of miscellaneous household equipment and furnishings	100.0	–	–	–	–	–	–	93.7
Bedroom furniture except mattress and springs	100.0	–	–	19.1	8.4	39.9	4.7	27.7
APPAREL AND SERVICES	**100.0**	**7.4**	**11.1**	**9.6**	**9.5**	**9.6**	**15.1**	**36.1**
Men and boys, aged 2 or older	**100.0**	**5.5**	**14.1**	**10.1**	**7.9**	**6.2**	**14.4**	**39.7**
Men's coats and jackets	100.0	–	–	12.8	–	8.0	27.7	47.6
Men's underwear	100.0	25.5	1.7	15.8	6.0	13.1	17.3	22.2
Men's accessories	100.0	14.9	21.6	12.6	8.0	5.1	13.8	23.5
Men's sweaters and vests	100.0	7.3	9.2	7.0	13.3	9.7	20.3	33.2
Men's active sportswear	100.0	–	6.4	4.7	17.0	3.3	3.5	60.1
Men's shirts	100.0	6.9	17.0	10.4	6.5	4.4	13.6	39.1
Men's pants	100.0	4.2	23.3	8.7	2.5	8.2	8.3	42.7
Boys' shirts	100.0	2.1	12.6	7.7	9.9	6.3	21.4	36.6
Boys' pants	100.0	3.4	15.7	12.4	13.2	11.0	17.8	26.4
Women and girls, aged 2 or older	**100.0**	**7.5**	**9.4**	**8.3**	**9.9**	**9.9**	**14.1**	**38.6**
Women's coats and jackets	100.0	–	8.1	11.0	–	20.1	23.5	34.3
Women's dresses	100.0	7.4	3.9	5.5	3.8	7.0	8.0	60.6
Women's vests and sweaters	100.0	4.6	1.2	6.5	9.3	11.6	15.6	47.3
Women's shirts, tops, blouses	100.0	7.3	21.8	9.4	13.2	9.5	9.9	27.3
Women's pants	100.0	8.6	4.5	7.3	8.3	10.6	24.3	34.1
Women's active sportswear	100.0	11.1	2.8	2.8	5.8	19.8	3.5	51.7
Women's sleepwear	100.0	8.0	8.6	3.7	1.1	11.3	30.0	34.9
Women's undergarments	100.0	13.1	5.7	1.6	10.8	10.3	9.6	46.7
Women's accessories	100.0	6.3	8.9	5.6	9.6	0.5	11.8	54.1
Girls' dresses and suits	100.0	7.7	5.5	13.1	26.3	15.7	8.5	21.4
Girls' shirts, blouses, sweaters	100.0	11.1	17.2	9.6	14.0	9.2	15.1	23.4
Girls' skirts and pants	100.0	4.8	15.9	20.8	12.0	13.2	11.4	21.8
Girls' active sportswear	100.0	7.5	15.6	9.5	25.6	5.3	13.2	20.6
Girls' accessories	100.0	1.5	7.8	14.6	21.2	0.7	15.4	35.1
Children under age 2	**100.0**	**5.8**	**10.9**	**9.9**	**10.8**	**11.3**	**16.6**	**33.5**
Infant dresses, outerwear	100.0	3.7	9.0	13.8	9.7	9.4	20.4	34.1
Infant underwear	100.0	5.5	13.1	7.2	11.0	13.5	12.7	34.7
Infant nightwear, loungewear	100.0	6.8	8.4	11.7	8.9	14.1	18.4	31.9
Infant accessories	100.0	14.1	7.9	9.5	13.2	6.8	18.5	28.2
Other apparel products and services	**100.0**	**11.1**	**10.0**	**11.0**	**9.7**	**11.9**	**16.4**	**29.3**
Watches	100.0	15.3	14.9	2.7	11.2	8.7	19.4	28.0
Jewelry	100.0	8.3	8.8	12.0	7.6	10.7	16.0	36.6
Men's footwear	100.0	4.8	17.8	11.0	3.6	15.7	11.7	33.9
Boys' footwear	100.0	6.1	–	8.7	3.9	1.6	56.6	20.3
Women's footwear	100.0	8.8	9.3	11.1	12.6	22.3	11.7	22.6
Girls' footwear	100.0	37.5	7.0	9.7	23.2	–	10.5	14.8
TRANSPORTATION	**100.0**	**7.6**	**4.9**	**11.2**	**7.2**	**4.4**	**9.3**	**55.3**
New cars	100.0	–	–	–	–	–	–	100.2
New trucks	100.0	–	–	–	–	–	–	100.0
Used cars	100.0	19.9	0.8	36.7	1.4	–	5.3	35.9
Used trucks	100.0	–	50.5	–	–	–	–	49.4
Gasoline on trips	100.0	5.8	10.3	11.4	14.1	10.3	16.3	31.8

	complete income reporters	under $10,000	$10,000– $19,999	$20,000– $29,999	$30,000– $39,999	$40,000– $49,999	$50,000– $69,999	$70,000 or more
Airline fares	100.0%	10.0%	6.1%	5.8%	9.2%	5.0%	13.7%	50.2%
Local transportation on trips	100.0	9.7	10.6	12.5	9.9	4.6	14.2	38.7
Intercity train fares	100.0	5.7	7.0	2.9	8.7	5.9	15.0	54.8
Ship fares	100.0	2.4	0.4	0.8	15.4	12.1	15.8	53.1
HEALTH CARE	**100.0**	**3.2**	**32.9**	**17.1**	**10.1**	**2.2**	**10.3**	**24.2**
Physician's services	100.0	4.0	33.7	9.0	4.4	7.6	5.4	36.0
Dental services	100.0	0.6	25.6	13.1	8.5	7.7	14.0	30.5
Hospital room	100.0	–	31.6	–	–	–	–	68.4
Care in convalescent or nursing home	100.0	4.6	43.2	23.6	15.5	–	13.0	0.1
Nonprescription drugs	100.0	4.4	45.4	10.6	9.6	2.1	2.3	25.7
ENTERTAINMENT	**100.0**	**5.6**	**8.7**	**14.6**	**12.9**	**9.7**	**14.5**	**33.6**
Toys, games, hobbies, and tricycles	100.0	4.9	12.1	15.8	12.0	10.7	15.2	29.2
Movie, other admissions, on trips	100.0	5.2	11.2	11.6	7.5	7.4	14.6	42.5
Admission to sports events on trips	100.0	5.2	11.2	11.6	7.5	7.4	14.6	42.4
Fees for recreational lessons	100.0	0.4	2.0	5.4	6.5	8.9	6.8	70.0
Cable service and community antenna	100.0	19.0	21.5	15.8	16.2	8.1	12.3	7.1
Color TV, portable, table model	100.0	0.4	12.6	18.3	8.8	17.0	10.1	33.0
Musical instruments and accessories	100.0	–	7.4	2.6	42.2	33.3	3.8	10.8
Athletic gear, game tables, and exercise equipment	100.0	4.2	4.2	9.2	17.8	4.2	15.6	41.5
PERSONAL CARE PRODUCTS **AND SERVICES**	**100.0**	**5.3**	**13.4**	**8.8**	**8.9**	**14.6**	**16.0**	**30.9**
Hair care products	100.0	7.6	4.1	12.0	10.8	28.1	9.2	26.6
Cosmetics, perfume, bath preparation	100.0	2.5	18.2	6.3	9.1	13.4	17.9	29.8
Deodorants, feminine hygiene, misc. personal care	100.0	22.0	4.9	14.8	5.8	14.1	7.0	37.9
READING	**100.0**	**11.0**	**14.0**	**14.8**	**11.6**	**14.1**	**20.9**	**28.4**
EDUCATION	**100.0**	**4.2**	**5.2**	**1.9**	**7.2**	**5.5**	**14.1**	**61.8**
College tuition	100.0	3.5	5.0	1.5	6.2	4.9	13.0	66.0
Elementary and high school tuition	100.0	6.3	6.3	0.0	10.0	6.7	19.9	48.7
Other school tuition	100.0	0.0	–	4.9	11.6	15.7	23.2	37.9
Other school expenses including rentals	100.0	1.8	1.6	3.0	7.0	3.8	39.0	37.9
College books and supplies	100.0	11.3	4.2	1.3	7.4	5.1	10.1	62.0
Miscellaneous school supplies	100.0	6.3	12.4	6.3	18.3	6.7	9.9	32.5
ALL OTHER GIFTS	**100.0**	**9.9**	**10.0**	**13.6**	**10.9**	**9.7**	**14.8**	**30.9**
Gifts of trip expenses	100.0	8.1	8.6	10.6	11.6	11.7	14.4	35.5
Miscellaneous fees, gambling losses	100.0	–	–	0.0	11.6	32.9	20.9	18.9
Legal fees	100.0	1.1	23.0	29.6	34.9	9.4	3.5	9.5
Funeral expenses	100.0	15.9	11.7	19.0	2.9	4.0	18.4	27.7
Cemetery lots, vaults, maintenance fees	100.0	17.6	14.2	19.7	15.5	12.5	9.3	18.9
Accounting fees	100.0	4.4	4.9	7.4	52.4	4.7	7.0	28.4

Note: Numbers may not add to total because of rounding. (–) means sample is too small to make a reliable estimate. Expenditures for items in a given category may not add to category total because categories with annual spending of less than $2.00 for the average household are omitted. Spending on gifts is also included in the product and service categories in other chapters.
Source: Calculations by New Strategist based on the 2000 Consumer Expenditure Survey

Table 6.11 Gifts: Average spending by household type, 2000

(average annual spending of consumer units (CU) on gifts of products and services for non–household members, by type of consumer unit, 2000)

	total married couples	married couples, no children	married couples with children				single parent, at least one child <18	single person
			total	oldest child under 6	oldest child 6 to 17	oldest child 18 or older		
Number of consumer units (in thousands, add 000)	56,287	22,805	28,777	5,291	15,396	8,090	6,132	32,323
Average number of persons per CU	3.2	2.0	3.9	3.5	4.1	3.8	2.9	1.0
Average before-tax income of CU	$60,588.00	$53,232.00	$66,913.00	$62,928.00	$69,472.00	$64,725.00	$25,095.00	$24,977.00
Average spending of CU, total	48,619.37	42,195.54	53,585.53	50,755.90	54,170.40	54,550.20	28,923.25	23,059.00
Gifts, average spending	1,354.78	1,476.76	1,265.88	917.98	1,146.92	1,728.15	683.26	807.21
FOOD	**$108.72**	**$100.75**	**$116.44**	**$58.46**	**$86.86**	**$212.83**	**$30.33**	**$31.01**
Fresh fruits	6.49	9.11	3.80	2.33	3.75	5.05	2.36	1.82
Candy and chewing gum	19.31	12.92	20.29	20.27	16.38	28.60	6.99	4.98
Board (including at school)	34.70	37.41	33.96	0.14	33.77	56.44	6.16	5.32
Catered affairs	27.50	26.03	32.31	9.52	9.85	89.96	2.55	2.55
ALCOHOLIC BEVERAGES	**18.90**	**14.42**	**23.83**	**44.84**	**14.15**	**26.94**	**7.93**	**9.64**
Beer and ale	4.25	2.79	5.56	6.15	3.14	10.18	1.80	3.12
Wine	8.64	7.27	10.61	22.34	5.39	11.86	5.78	4.86
Whiskey and other alcoholic beverages	5.52	3.98	7.03	14.33	5.43	4.34	0.26	1.34
HOUSING	**378.86**	**416.71**	**357.60**	**345.07**	**323.67**	**435.69**	**213.56**	**192.31**
Housekeeping supplies	**50.26**	**49.84**	**51.61**	**48.76**	**44.65**	**68.72**	**22.69**	**24.69**
Miscellaneous household products	8.99	8.15	9.99	5.70	7.70	18.40	5.27	5.25
Lawn and garden supplies	4.84	7.36	2.12	–	1.66	4.87	1.02	0.84
Postage and stationery	31.05	30.58	32.83	32.31	29.49	40.33	14.34	16.56
Stationery, stationery supplies, giftwraps	26.15	25.74	27.71	28.36	23.54	35.99	12.14	13.99
Postage	4.75	4.48	5.12	3.95	5.95	4.34	1.73	2.56
Household textiles	**19.04**	**14.37**	**23.85**	**10.42**	**15.36**	**52.77**	**4.56**	**7.74**
Bathroom linens	3.25	3.15	3.77	4.37	3.24	4.37	–	2.92
Bedroom linens	11.35	6.51	16.69	2.82	10.14	42.13	4.19	1.98
Appliances and miscellaneous housewares	**35.30**	**44.02**	**27.19**	**35.43**	**23.20**	**28.33**	**8.26**	**19.02**
Major appliances	9.91	10.96	5.80	1.70	7.39	5.45	2.96	5.46
Electric floor cleaning equipment	4.15	2.38	1.58	–	2.95	–	–	1.23
Small appliances and miscellaneous housewares	25.38	33.06	21.39	33.73	15.81	22.88	5.30	13.56
Glassware	4.40	5.82	3.75	6.04	3.50	2.36	1.68	2.79
Nonelectric cookware	4.78	7.45	2.92	2.61	0.47	8.36	–	1.57
Tableware, nonelectric kitchenware	6.05	7.07	5.91	9.02	5.57	4.04	0.19	2.58
Small electric kitchen appliances	3.20	4.45	2.38	2.21	1.97	3.27	0.41	2.29
Miscellaneous household equipment	**84.66**	**87.19**	**82.60**	**69.93**	**66.47**	**122.00**	**50.48**	**63.55**
Infants' equipment	4.40	1.42	7.36	8.73	5.51	10.12	1.29	1.16
Outdoor equipment	2.23	3.19	1.71	4.58	1.22	0.37	2.65	4.50
Household decorative items	34.33	31.61	33.66	33.21	31.31	39.00	21.44	22.20
Indoor plants, fresh flowers	18.16	18.25	18.89	11.48	13.50	34.00	9.10	15.77
Computers and computer hardware, nonbusiness use	11.68	13.22	11.04	5.37	3.54	29.03	3.42	7.84
Miscellaneous household equipment and parts	2.90	1.92	3.67	1.15	5.45	2.00	7.21	1.37
Other housing	**189.60**	**221.29**	**172.35**	**180.53**	**173.98**	**163.87**	**127.57**	**77.31**
Repair or maintenance services	5.03	9.05	2.56	0.18	4.55	0.35	5.98	1.09
Housing while attending school	70.04	89.00	62.76	2.38	58.95	109.50	15.69	14.26
Natural gas (renter)	3.03	4.02	2.43	0.88	3.67	1.06	1.46	2.64
Electricity (renter)	12.25	11.11	12.81	10.75	16.71	6.75	25.65	11.93
Telephone services in home city, excl. mobile phones	12.60	11.17	13.86	17.55	16.58	6.28	22.71	13.66

	total married couples	married couples, no children	married couples with children			single parent, at least one child <18	single person
			total	oldest child under 6	oldest child 6 to 17	oldest child 18 or older		

	total married couples	married couples, no children	total	oldest child under 6	oldest child 6 to 17	oldest child 18 or older	single parent, at least one child <18	single person
Water, sewerage maintenance (renter)	$2.49	$2.53	$2.28	$1.82	$3.50	$0.27	$4.01	$2.35
Care for elderly, invalids, handicapped	0.70	0.99	0.54	–	1.01	–	–	3.75
Day-care centers, nurseries, and preschools	30.47	16.54	43.04	109.15	38.58	8.30	23.63	6.38
Housekeeping services	4.50	2.91	2.54	0.61	3.59	1.79	3.98	2.65
Gardening, lawn care service	3.57	6.64	1.16	1.23	1.14	1.14	2.70	2.88
Repair of miscellaneous household equipment and furnishings	15.05	34.36	1.61	–	3.00	–	–	–
Bedroom furniture except mattress and springs	3.08	4.99	0.69	–	0.42	1.65	0.01	0.94
APPAREL AND SERVICES	**279.62**	**300.95**	**260.80**	**269.78**	**220.93**	**333.89**	**202.60**	**186.96**
Men and boys, aged 2 or older	**74.45**	**86.88**	**68.45**	**58.61**	**45.10**	**124.04**	**46.71**	**50.95**
Men's coats and jackets	5.23	5.78	5.16	5.27	2.14	11.47	–	1.96
Men's underwear	2.09	1.81	2.39	1.99	1.75	4.10	1.46	2.14
Men's accessories	3.33	3.58	3.12	3.30	2.39	4.52	5.75	3.16
Men's sweaters and vests	3.20	4.40	2.55	0.84	1.52	5.61	0.88	2.74
Men's active sportswear	6.72	10.75	4.37	3.29	2.52	9.18	–	2.54
Men's shirts	16.97	19.52	15.24	19.39	7.44	28.29	20.55	17.33
Men's pants	7.53	9.28	6.76	4.33	4.49	13.61	7.73	4.82
Boys' shirts	6.48	6.52	6.33	5.75	4.36	10.98	4.36	3.58
Boys' pants	3.49	3.73	3.30	2.04	3.51	3.71	1.61	2.31
Women and girls, aged 2 or older	**99.92**	**121.56**	**81.51**	**65.17**	**78.90**	**100.22**	**74.03**	**59.94**
Women's coats and jackets	4.10	4.18	4.60	2.29	6.30	2.95	2.91	3.24
Women's dresses	13.01	19.88	8.85	–	6.93	20.29	0.74	7.06
Women's vests and sweaters	11.70	14.16	10.28	16.25	8.04	10.05	8.33	3.71
Women's shirts, tops, blouses	9.25	11.58	6.88	7.55	3.40	13.68	10.79	11.01
Women's pants	7.54	8.85	5.00	0.96	5.24	7.88	3.86	3.23
Women's active sportswear	4.64	9.08	1.72	0.13	2.34	1.72	3.66	2.59
Women's sleepwear	6.78	5.79	4.13	2.15	4.44	5.12	6.51	2.90
Women's undergarments	2.68	2.90	2.34	–	3.22	2.44	3.15	2.87
Women's accessories	5.05	3.45	6.49	12.90	3.30	7.91	2.68	2.21
Girls' dresses and suits	4.97	3.93	5.45	5.29	5.42	5.63	10.60	2.64
Girls' shirts, blouses, sweaters	8.48	9.71	8.03	6.50	9.96	5.21	4.39	3.46
Girls' skirts and pants	2.95	4.28	1.96	1.95	1.74	2.38	3.17	2.60
Girls' active sportswear	2.68	3.62	2.29	–	3.62	1.36	–	2.54
Girls' accessories	2.74	3.15	2.74	1.19	3.90	1.60	2.22	1.13
Children under age 2	**56.80**	**38.23**	**64.84**	**105.32**	**50.98**	**59.71**	**38.94**	**17.27**
Infant dresses, outerwear	20.20	23.08	17.80	18.45	14.08	24.46	9.62	6.57
Infant underwear	25.54	6.93	35.25	73.50	27.62	19.47	23.68	6.45
Infant nightwear, loungewear	3.17	3.19	3.13	3.62	2.51	3.98	2.06	1.33
Infant accessories	5.97	2.89	6.90	6.81	5.90	9.11	2.84	2.04
Other apparel products and services	**48.44**	**54.28**	**46.00**	**40.68**	**45.95**	**49.92**	**42.91**	**58.80**
Watches	3.33	3.34	3.48	4.40	1.19	7.24	1.81	4.18
Jewelry	10.35	13.16	9.18	11.39	7.15	11.59	5.17	31.42
Men's footwear	10.92	10.55	12.75	13.87	13.64	9.93	4.78	8.50
Boys' footwear	6.91	10.78	3.38	3.91	2.12	5.59	1.59	1.46
Women's footwear	10.15	11.03	9.03	4.90	11.51	7.24	22.17	7.71
Girls' footwear	4.96	3.40	6.59	1.96	9.39	4.52	6.38	5.21
TRANSPORTATION	**72.43**	**100.93**	**56.51**	**15.11**	**61.27**	**74.54**	**19.41**	**58.19**
New cars	1.75	4.33	–	–	–	–	–	6.26
New trucks	15.66	38.66	–	–	–	–	–	–
Used cars	11.22	3.25	19.37	–	23.89	23.44	–	14.19
Used trucks	0.82	2.03	–	–	–	–	–	8.11
Gasoline on trips	15.91	19.59	13.68	6.93	14.35	16.81	6.99	9.86

	total married couples	married couples, no children	married couples with children				single parent, at least one child <18	single person
			total	oldest child under 6	oldest child 6 to 17	oldest child 18 or older		
Airline fares	$10.41	$13.18	$8.80	$3.87	$6.39	$16.61	$5.58	$7.54
Local transportation on trips	1.78	2.52	1.33	0.77	1.46	1.43	0.51	3.32
Intercity train fares	2.89	3.27	2.67	0.88	1.88	5.34	0.85	1.79
Ship fares	3.59	4.47	2.80	1.31	2.13	5.03	3.50	1.64
HEALTH CARE	**28.45**	**28.82**	**13.94**	**2.75**	**14.18**	**21.05**	**7.79**	**62.37**
Physician's services	2.75	2.58	2.63	0.09	1.69	6.06	1.70	3.53
Dental services	3.10	4.21	2.47	0.46	1.69	5.28	1.47	5.66
Hospital room	3.65	0.80	–	–	–	–	–	2.89
Care in convalescent or nursing home	4.72	4.63	–	–	–	–	–	41.75
Nonprescription drugs	2.00	2.64	1.17	–	1.62	1.20	0.26	3.33
ENTERTAINMENT	**112.03**	**122.65**	**96.41**	**100.18**	**92.11**	**101.91**	**50.85**	**73.38**
Toys, games, hobbies, and tricycles	36.01	47.06	27.17	33.51	24.01	29.04	12.96	24.33
Movie, other admissions, on trips	10.71	10.69	10.71	14.88	10.29	8.78	5.12	7.56
Admission to sports events on trips	3.57	3.56	3.57	4.96	3.43	2.93	1.71	2.52
Fees for recreational lessons	9.57	6.77	12.77	4.30	17.40	9.50	3.99	2.09
Cable service and community antenna	3.51	2.85	4.13	4.03	5.23	2.10	5.01	5.24
Color TV, portable, table model	2.60	2.60	2.38	1.71	1.45	4.60	1.01	1.88
Musical instruments and accessories	1.17	0.93	1.24	0.47	0.26	3.61	1.72	5.33
Athletic gear, game tables, and exercise equipment	11.50	15.17	9.21	12.39	7.65	9.85	3.44	3.94
PERSONAL CARE PRODUCTS AND SERVICES	**22.98**	**14.90**	**29.37**	**26.01**	**31.31**	**28.08**	**28.94**	**14.48**
Hair care products	2.94	1.25	4.47	1.88	5.93	3.53	2.26	1.16
Cosmetics, perfume, bath preparation	15.00	10.00	19.00	20.00	20.00	17.00	21.00	9.00
Deodorants, feminine hygiene, misc. personal care	2.00	1.00	3.00	2.00	3.00	3.00	2.00	1.00
READING	**2.00**	**3.00**	**2.00**	**2.00**	**1.00**	**2.00**	**0.00**	**2.00**
EDUCATION	**237.00**	**271.00**	**229.00**	**19.00**	**234.00**	**355.00**	**67.00**	**72.00**
College tuition	184.00	211.00	178.00	4.00	177.00	292.00	34.00	53.00
Elementary and high school tuition	16.00	17.00	17.00	9.00	26.00	5.00	4.00	7.00
Other school tuition	5.00	8.00	4.00	1.00	1.00	11.00	2.00	1.00
Other school expenses including rentals	6.00	7.00	7.00	1.00	7.00	10.00	14.00	2.00
College books and supplies	15.00	18.00	15.00	0.00	13.00	29.00	7.00	6.00
Miscellaneous school supplies	7.00	7.00	5.00	4.00	6.00	5.00	2.00	4.00
ALL OTHER GIFTS	**94.00**	**102.00**	**81.00**	**35.00**	**67.00**	**136.00**	**54.00**	**105.00**
Gifts of trip expenses	45.00	62.00	34.00	17.00	29.00	54.00	20.00	71.00
Miscellaneous fees, gambling losses	3.00	3.00	2.00	3.00	2.00	2.00	–	1.00
Legal fees	5.00	8.00	3.00	2.00	2.00	6.00	9.00	1.00
Funeral expenses	35.00	22.00	35.00	1.00	30.00	66.00	21.00	25.00
Cemetery lots, vaults, maintenance fees	3.00	3.00	2.00	1.00	1.00	4.00	1.00	4.00
Accounting fees	2.00	2.00	2.00	1.00	1.00	2.00	1.00	2.00

Note: Average spending figures for total consumer units can be found on Average Spending by Age and Average Spending by Region tables. (–) means sample is too small to make a reliable estimate. Expenditures for items in a given category may not add to category total because categories with annual spending of less than $2.00 for the average household are omitted. Spending on gifts is also included in the product and service categories in other chapters.
Source: Bureau of Labor Statistics, unpublished tables from the 2000 Consumer Expenditure Survey

Table 6.12 Gifts: Indexed spending by household type, 2000

(indexed average annual spending of consumer units (CU) on gifts of products and services for non–household members, by type of consumer unit, 2000; index definition: an index of 100 is the average for all consumer units; an index of 132 means that spending by consumer units in that group is 32 percent above the average for all consumer units; an index of 68 indicates spending that is 32 percent below the average for all consumer units)

	total married couples	married couples, no children	married couples with children				single parent, at least one child <18	single person
			total	oldest child under 6	oldest child 6 to 17	oldest child 18 or older		
Average spending of CU, total	$48,619	$42,196	$53,586	$50,756	$54,170	$54,550	$28,923	$23,059
Average spending of CU, index	128	111	141	133	142	143	76	61
Gifts, spending index	125	136	117	85	106	160	63	75
FOOD	**155**	**144**	**166**	**83**	**124**	**304**	**43**	**44**
Fresh fruits	142	199	83	51	82	110	52	40
Candy and chewing gum	154	103	162	162	131	229	56	40
Board (including at school)	172	185	168	1	167	279	30	26
Catered affairs	176	167	207	61	63	577	16	16
ALCOHOLIC BEVERAGES	**130**	**100**	**164**	**309**	**98**	**186**	**55**	**67**
Beer and ale	117	77	153	169	86	280	49	86
Wine	128	108	157	330	80	175	86	72
Whiskey and other alcoholic beverages	148	107	188	384	146	116	7	36
HOUSING	**130**	**143**	**123**	**119**	**111**	**150**	**73**	**66**
Housekeeping supplies	**129**	**127**	**132**	**125**	**114**	**176**	**58**	**63**
Miscellaneous household products	123	111	136	78	105	251	72	72
Lawn and garden supplies	157	239	69	–	54	158	33	27
Postage and stationery	124	123	132	129	118	162	57	66
Stationery, stationery supplies, giftwraps	129	127	137	140	116	177	60	69
Postage	104	98	112	86	130	95	38	56
Household textiles	**144**	**109**	**181**	**79**	**116**	**400**	**35**	**59**
Bathroom linens	116	113	135	157	116	157	–	105
Bedroom linens	166	95	244	41	148	615	61	29
Appliances and miscellaneous housewares	**125**	**156**	**97**	**126**	**82**	**101**	**29**	**68**
Major appliances	130	144	76	22	97	72	39	72
Electric floor cleaning equipment	138	79	52	–	98	–	–	41
Small appliances and miscellaneous housewares	124	161	104	164	77	111	26	66
Glassware	122	162	104	168	97	66	47	78
Nonelectric cookware	131	204	80	71	13	228	–	43
Tableware, nonelectric kitchenware	139	163	136	208	128	93	4	59
Small electric kitchen appliances	119	166	89	82	74	122	15	85
Miscellaneous household equipment	**120**	**124**	**117**	**99**	**95**	**174**	**72**	**90**
Infants' equipment	162	52	271	321	203	372	47	43
Outdoor equipment	78	112	60	160	43	13	93	157
Household decorative items	126	116	123	122	115	143	78	81
Indoor plants, fresh flowers	113	114	118	72	84	212	57	98
Computers and computer hardware, nonbusiness use	130	147	123	60	39	324	38	87
Miscellaneous household equipment and parts	115	76	145	45	215	79	285	54
Other housing	**135**	**158**	**123**	**129**	**124**	**117**	**91**	**55**
Repair or maintenance services	134	242	68	5	122	9	160	29
Housing while attending school	166	210	148	6	139	259	37	34
Natural gas (renter)	97	129	78	28	118	34	47	85
Electricity (renter)	92	84	96	81	126	51	193	90
Telephone services in home city, excl. mobile phones	92	82	102	129	122	46	166	100

	total married couples	married couples, no children	married couples with children				single parent, at least one child <18	single person
			total	oldest child under 6	oldest child 6 to 17	oldest child 18 or older		
Water, sewerage maintenance (renter)	93	95	85	68	131	10	150	88
Care for elderly, invalids, handicapped	33	47	26	–	48	–	–	179
Day-care centers, nurseries, and preschools	142	77	201	509	180	39	110	30
Housekeeping services	131	85	74	18	104	52	116	77
Gardening, lawn care service	114	211	37	39	36	36	86	92
Repair of miscellaneous household equipment and furnishings	193	442	21	–	39	–	–	–
Bedroom furniture except mattress and springs	150	242	33	–	20	80	0	46
APPAREL AND SERVICES	**114**	**123**	**107**	**110**	**90**	**137**	**83**	**77**
Men and boys, aged 2 or older	**110**	**129**	**101**	**87**	**67**	**184**	**69**	**75**
Men's coats and jackets	158	175	156	160	65	348	–	59
Men's underwear	100	86	114	95	83	195	70	102
Men's accessories	98	105	92	97	70	133	169	93
Men's sweaters and vests	118	162	94	31	56	206	32	101
Men's active sportswear	154	247	100	76	58	211	–	58
Men's shirts	82	94	73	93	36	136	99	83
Men's pants	106	131	95	61	63	191	109	68
Boys' shirts	117	117	114	103	78	197	78	64
Boys' pants	123	131	116	72	124	131	57	81
Women and girls, aged 2 or older	**117**	**143**	**96**	**76**	**93**	**118**	**87**	**70**
Women's coats and jackets	115	117	129	64	176	83	82	91
Women's dresses	123	187	83	–	65	191	7	66
Women's vests and sweaters	132	160	116	183	91	113	94	42
Women's shirts, tops, blouses	87	109	65	71	32	129	102	104
Women's pants	127	149	84	16	88	133	65	54
Women's active sportswear	134	262	50	4	67	50	105	75
Women's sleepwear	110	94	67	35	72	83	106	47
Women's undergarments	100	108	87	–	120	91	117	107
Women's accessories	121	83	156	309	79	190	64	53
Girls' dresses and suits	123	98	135	131	134	140	263	66
Girls' shirts, blouses, sweaters	137	157	130	105	161	84	71	56
Girls' skirts and pants	106	154	71	70	63	86	114	94
Girls' active sportswear	128	172	109	–	172	65	–	121
Girls' accessories	126	144	126	55	179	73	102	52
Children under age 2	**140**	**94**	**159**	**259**	**125**	**147**	**96**	**42**
Infant dresses, outerwear	139	159	123	127	97	169	66	45
Infant underwear	140	38	193	402	151	107	130	35
Infant nightwear, loungewear	129	130	127	147	102	162	84	54
Infant accessories	149	72	172	169	147	227	71	51
Other apparel products and services	**96**	**107**	**91**	**80**	**91**	**98**	**85**	**116**
Watches	97	97	101	128	35	211	53	122
Jewelry	61	78	54	68	42	69	31	186
Men's footwear	126	122	147	160	158	115	55	98
Boys' footwear	147	229	72	83	45	119	34	31
Women's footwear	101	110	90	49	114	72	220	77
Girls' footwear	95	65	126	38	180	87	122	100
TRANSPORTATION	**103**	**144**	**80**	**22**	**87**	**106**	**28**	**83**
New cars	29	71	–	–	–	–	–	103
New trucks	112	275	–	–	–	–	–	–
Used cars	90	26	155	–	191	187	–	113
Used trucks	29	72	–	–	–	–	–	288
Gasoline on trips	127	156	109	55	114	134	56	79

	total married couples	married couples, no children	married couples with children				single parent, at least one child <18	single person
			total	oldest child under 6	oldest child 6 to 17	oldest child 18 or older		
Airline fares	122	155	103	45	75	195	66	89
Local transportation on trips	84	118	62	36	69	67	24	156
Intercity train fares	130	147	120	39	84	239	38	80
Ship fares	120	150	94	44	71	169	117	55
HEALTH CARE	**75**	**76**	**37**	**7**	**37**	**55**	**20**	**164**
Physician's services	103	97	99	3	64	228	64	133
Dental services	89	121	71	13	48	151	42	162
Hospital room	134	29	–	–	–	–	–	106
Care in convalescent or nursing home	26	25	–	–	–	–	–	227
Nonprescription drugs	93	123	54	–	75	56	12	155
ENTERTAINMENT	**119**	**131**	**103**	**107**	**98**	**109**	**54**	**78**
Toys, games, hobbies, and tricycles	122	159	92	113	81	98	44	82
Movie, other admissions, on trips	117	117	117	162	112	96	56	82
Admission to sports events on trips	117	116	117	162	112	96	56	82
Fees for recreational lessons	152	107	203	68	276	151	63	33
Cable service and community antenna	75	61	89	87	112	45	108	113
Color TV, portable, table model	124	124	113	81	69	219	48	90
Musical instruments and accessories	50	40	53	20	11	156	74	230
Athletic gear, game tables, and exercise equipment	121	160	97	131	81	104	36	42
PERSONAL CARE PRODUCTS AND SERVICES	**120**	**78**	**153**	**135**	**163**	**146**	**151**	**75**
Hair care products	137	58	209	88	277	165	106	54
Cosmetics, perfume, bath preparation	115	77	146	154	154	131	162	69
Deodorants, feminine hygiene, misc. personal care	100	50	150	100	150	150	100	50
READING	**100**	**150**	**100**	**100**	**50**	**100**	**0**	**100**
EDUCATION	**157**	**179**	**152**	**13**	**155**	**235**	**44**	**48**
College tuition	161	185	156	4	155	256	30	46
Elementary and high school tuition	145	155	155	82	236	45	36	64
Other school tuition	167	267	133	33	33	367	67	33
Other school expenses including rentals	120	140	140	20	140	200	280	40
College books and supplies	150	180	150	0	130	290	70	60
Miscellaneous school supplies	140	140	100	80	120	100	40	80
ALL OTHER GIFTS	**106**	**115**	**91**	**39**	**75**	**153**	**61**	**118**
Gifts of trip expenses	92	127	69	35	59	110	41	145
Miscellaneous fees, gambling losses	150	150	100	150	100	100	–	50
Legal fees	125	200	75	50	50	150	225	25
Funeral expenses	125	79	125	4	107	236	75	89
Cemetery lots, vaults, maintenance fees	100	100	67	33	33	133	33	133
Accounting fees	100	100	100	50	50	100	50	100

Note: Spending index for total consumer units is 100. (–) means sample is too small to make a reliable estimate. Categories with annual spending of less than $2.00 for the average household are omitted. Spending on gifts is also included in the product and service categories in other chapters.
Source: Calculations by New Strategist based on the 2000 Consumer Expenditure Survey

Table 6.13 Gifts: Indexed per capita spending by household type, 2000

(indexed average annual per capita spending of consumer units (CU) on gifts of products and services for non–household members, by type of consumer unit, 2000; index definition: an index of 100 is the average for all consumer units; an index of 132 means that spending by consumer units in that group is 32 percent above the average for all consumer units; an index of 68 indicates spending that is 32 percent below the average for all consumer units)

	total married couples	married couples, no children	married couples with children				single parent, at least one child <18	single person
			total	oldest child under 6	oldest child 6 to 17	oldest child 18 or older		
Per capita spending of CU, total	$15,194	$21,098	$13,740	$14,502	$13,212	$14,355	$9,974	$23,059
Per capita spending of CU, index	100	139	90	95	87	94	66	152
Gifts, per capita spending index	98	170	75	61	65	105	54	186
FOOD	**121**	**180**	**106**	**60**	**76**	**200**	**37**	**111**
Fresh fruits	111	249	53	36	50	73	44	99
Candy and chewing gum	121	129	104	116	80	151	48	100
Board (including at school)	134	231	108	0	102	184	26	66
Catered affairs	138	209	133	44	39	380	14	41
ALCOHOLIC BEVERAGES	**102**	**124**	**105**	**221**	**60**	**122**	**47**	**166**
Beer and ale	91	96	98	121	53	184	43	214
Wine	100	134	101	236	49	115	74	180
Whiskey and other alcoholic beverages	116	133	121	274	89	77	6	90
HOUSING	**102**	**179**	**79**	**85**	**68**	**98**	**63**	**165**
Housekeeping supplies	**100**	**159**	**85**	**89**	**70**	**116**	**50**	**158**
Miscellaneous household products	96	139	87	56	64	165	62	179
Lawn and garden supplies	123	299	44	–	33	104	29	68
Postage and stationery	97	153	84	92	72	106	50	166
Stationery, stationery supplies, giftwraps	101	159	88	100	71	117	52	172
Postage	81	123	72	62	79	62	33	140
Household textiles	**113**	**136**	**116**	**56**	**71**	**263**	**30**	**147**
Bathroom linens	91	141	87	112	71	103	–	262
Bedroom linens	129	119	156	29	90	405	53	72
Appliances and miscellaneous housewares	**98**	**196**	**62**	**90**	**50**	**66**	**25**	**169**
Major appliances	102	180	49	16	59	47	34	179
Electric floor cleaning equipment	108	99	34	–	60	–	–	102
Small appliances and miscellaneous housewares	97	201	67	117	47	73	22	165
Glassware	95	202	67	120	59	43	40	194
Nonelectric cookware	102	254	51	51	8	150	–	107
Tableware, nonelectric kitchenware	109	204	87	148	78	61	4	149
Small electric kitchen appliances	93	208	57	59	45	80	13	214
Miscellaneous household equipment	**94**	**155**	**75**	**71**	**58**	**114**	**62**	**226**
Infants' equipment	126	65	173	229	124	245	41	107
Outdoor equipment	61	139	38	114	26	9	80	393
Household decorative items	98	145	79	87	70	94	68	203
Indoor plants, fresh flowers	88	142	75	51	51	139	49	246
Computers and computer hardware, nonbusiness use	102	184	79	43	24	213	33	219
Miscellaneous household equipment and parts	90	95	93	32	131	52	246	135
Other housing	**106**	**197**	**79**	**92**	**76**	**77**	**78**	**138**
Repair or maintenance services	105	302	44	3	74	6	138	73
Housing while attending school	129	263	95	4	85	170	32	84
Natural gas (renter)	76	162	50	20	72	22	40	212
Electricity (renter)	72	105	62	58	77	33	167	225
Telephone services in home city, excl. mobile phones	72	102	65	92	74	30	144	250

	total married couples	married couples, no children	married couples with children				single parent, at least one child <18	single person
			total	oldest child under 6	oldest child 6 to 17	oldest child 18 or older		
Water, sewerage maintenance (renter)	73	118	55	49	80	7	129	220
Care for elderly, invalids, handicapped	26	59	16	–	29	–	–	446
Day-care centers, nurseries, and preschools	111	96	129	363	110	25	95	74
Housekeeping services	102	106	47	13	64	34	100	193
Gardening, lawn care service	89	264	24	28	22	24	74	229
Repair of miscellaneous household equipment and furnishings	151	552	13	–	24	–	–	–
Bedroom furniture except mattress and springs	117	303	21	–	12	53	0	114
APPAREL AND SERVICES	**89**	**154**	**68**	**79**	**55**	**90**	**72**	**191**
Men and boys, aged 2 or older	**86**	**161**	**65**	**62**	**41**	**121**	**60**	**189**
Men's coats and jackets	124	219	100	114	40	229	–	148
Men's underwear	78	108	73	68	51	128	60	255
Men's accessories	77	132	59	69	43	87	146	232
Men's sweaters and vests	92	202	60	22	34	136	28	252
Men's active sportswear	121	309	64	54	35	139	–	146
Men's shirts	64	117	47	67	22	90	85	209
Men's pants	83	163	61	44	39	126	94	169
Boys' shirts	91	147	73	74	48	130	68	161
Boys' pants	96	164	74	51	75	86	49	203
Women and girls, aged 2 or older	**92**	**178**	**61**	**55**	**56**	**77**	**75**	**176**
Women's coats and jackets	90	146	83	46	108	54	70	227
Women's dresses	96	234	53	–	40	126	6	166
Women's vests and sweaters	103	200	74	131	55	75	81	105
Women's shirts, tops, blouses	68	137	42	51	20	85	88	260
Women's pants	99	186	54	12	54	87	56	136
Women's active sportswear	104	327	32	3	41	33	91	187
Women's sleepwear	86	118	43	25	44	55	91	118
Women's undergarments	78	135	56	–	73	60	101	267
Women's accessories	95	103	100	221	48	125	55	132
Girls' dresses and suits	96	122	87	94	82	92	227	164
Girls' shirts, blouses, sweaters	107	196	83	75	98	55	61	140
Girls' skirts and pants	83	192	45	50	38	56	98	234
Girls' active sportswear	100	215	70	–	105	43	–	302
Girls' accessories	98	181	81	39	109	48	88	130
Children under age 2	**109**	**117**	**102**	**185**	**76**	**96**	**82**	**106**
Infant dresses, outerwear	109	199	79	91	59	111	57	113
Infant underwear	109	47	124	287	92	70	112	88
Infant nightwear, loungewear	101	162	82	105	62	106	72	135
Infant accessories	116	90	110	121	89	149	61	127
Other apparel products and services	**75**	**134**	**58**	**57**	**55**	**65**	**73**	**290**
Watches	76	122	65	92	21	139	45	305
Jewelry	48	98	35	48	26	45	26	466
Men's footwear	99	152	94	114	96	75	48	245
Boys' footwear	115	287	46	59	28	78	29	78
Women's footwear	79	137	58	35	70	47	190	192
Girls' footwear	74	82	81	27	110	57	106	250
TRANSPORTATION	**81**	**180**	**52**	**15**	**53**	**70**	**24**	**207**
New cars	22	89	–	–	–	–	–	257
New trucks	87	344	–	–	–	–	–	–
Used cars	70	32	99	–	116	123	–	283
Used trucks	23	90	–	–	–	–	–	719
Gasoline on trips	99	195	70	39	70	88	48	196

	total married couples	married couples, no children	married couples with children				single parent, at least one child <18	single person
			total	oldest child under 6	oldest child 6 to 17	oldest child 18 or older		
Airline fares	96	194	66	32	46	128	57	222
Local transportation on trips	65	148	40	26	42	44	21	390
Intercity train fares	101	183	77	28	51	158	33	201
Ship fares	94	188	60	31	44	111	101	138
HEALTH CARE	**58**	**95**	**23**	**5**	**23**	**36**	**18**	**409**
Physician's services	81	121	63	2	39	150	55	332
Dental services	69	151	45	9	30	100	36	405
Hospital room	104	37	–	–	–	–	–	265
Care in convalescent or nursing home	20	31	–	–	–	–	–	567
Nonprescription drugs	73	153	35	–	46	37	10	387
ENTERTAINMENT	**93**	**164**	**66**	**76**	**60**	**72**	**47**	**196**
Toys, games, hobbies, and tricycles	95	199	59	81	49	65	38	206
Movie, other admissions, on trips	91	146	75	116	68	63	48	206
Admission to sports events on trips	91	145	75	116	68	63	48	206
Fees for recreational lessons	119	134	130	49	168	99	55	83
Cable service and community antenna	59	77	57	62	69	30	93	282
Color TV, portable, table model	97	155	73	58	42	144	41	224
Musical instruments and accessories	39	50	34	14	7	102	64	574
Athletic gear, game tables, and exercise equipment	95	200	62	93	49	68	31	104
PERSONAL CARE PRODUCTS AND SERVICES	**94**	**97**	**98**	**97**	**99**	**96**	**130**	**189**
Hair care products	107	73	134	63	169	109	91	136
Cosmetics, perfume, bath preparation	90	96	94	110	94	86	139	173
Deodorants, feminine hygiene, misc. personal care	78	63	96	71	91	99	86	125
READING	**78**	**188**	**64**	**71**	**30**	**66**	**0**	**250**
EDUCATION	**123**	**224**	**97**	**9**	**94**	**155**	**38**	**119**
College tuition	126	231	100	3	95	169	26	116
Elementary and high school tuition	114	193	99	58	144	30	31	159
Other school tuition	130	333	85	24	20	241	57	83
Other school expenses including rentals	94	175	90	14	85	132	241	100
College books and supplies	117	225	96	0	79	191	60	150
Miscellaneous school supplies	109	175	64	57	73	66	34	200
ALL OTHER GIFTS	**83**	**143**	**58**	**28**	**46**	**101**	**52**	**295**
Gifts of trip expenses	72	158	44	25	36	73	35	362
Miscellaneous fees, gambling losses	117	188	64	107	61	66	–	125
Legal fees	98	250	48	36	30	99	194	63
Funeral expenses	98	98	80	3	65	155	65	223
Cemetery lots, vaults, maintenance fees	78	125	43	24	20	88	29	333
Accounting fees	78	125	64	36	30	66	43	250

Note: Per capita indexes account for household size and show how much each person in a particular household demographic segment spends relative to a person in the average household. Spending index for total consumer units is 100. (–) means sample is too small to make a reliable estimate. Categories with annual spending of less than $2.00 for the average household are omitted. Spending on gifts is also included in the product and service categories in other chapters.
Source: Calculations by New Strategist based on the 2000 Consumer Expenditure Survey

Table 6.14 Gifts: Total spending by household type, 2000

(total annual spending on selected gifts, by consumer unit (CU) type, 2000; numbers in thousands)

	total married couples	married couples, no children	married couples with children				single parent, at least one child <18	single person
			total	oldest child under 6	oldest child 6 to 17	oldest child 18 or older		
Number of consumer units	56,287	22,805	28,777	5,291	15,396	8,090	6,132	32,323
Total spending of all CUs	$2,736,638,479	$962,269,290	$1,542,030,797	$268,549,467	$834,007,478	$441,311,118	$177,357,369	$745,336,057
Gifts, total spending	76,256,502	33,677,512	36,428,229	4,857,032	17,657,980	13,980,734	4,189,750	26,091,449
FOOD	**$6,119,523**	**$2,297,604**	**$3,350,794**	**$309,312**	**$1,337,297**	**$1,721,795**	**$185,984**	**$1,002,336**
Fresh fruits	365,303	207,754	109,353	12,328	57,735	40,855	14,472	58,828
Candy and chewing gum	1,086,902	294,641	583,885	107,249	252,186	231,374	42,863	160,969
Board (including at school)	1,953,159	853,135	977,267	741	519,923	456,600	37,773	171,958
Catered affairs	1,547,893	593,614	929,785	50,370	151,651	727,776	15,637	82,424
ALCOHOLIC BEVERAGES	**1,063,824**	**328,848**	**685,756**	**237,248**	**217,853**	**217,945**	**48,627**	**311,594**
Beer and ale	239,220	63,626	160,000	32,540	48,343	82,356	11,038	100,848
Wine	486,320	165,792	305,324	118,201	82,984	95,947	35,443	157,090
Whiskey and other alcoholic beverages	310,704	90,764	202,302	75,820	83,600	35,111	1,594	43,313
HOUSING	**21,324,893**	**9,503,072**	**10,290,655**	**1,825,765**	**4,983,223**	**3,524,732**	**1,309,550**	**6,216,036**
Housekeeping supplies	**2,828,985**	**1,136,601**	**1,485,181**	**257,989**	**687,431**	**555,945**	**139,135**	**798,055**
Miscellaneous household products	506,020	185,861	287,482	30,159	118,549	148,856	32,316	169,696
Lawn and garden supplies	272,429	167,845	61,007	–	25,557	39,398	6,255	27,151
Postage and stationery	1,747,711	697,377	944,749	170,952	454,028	326,270	87,933	535,269
Stationery, stationery supplies, giftwraps	1,471,905	587,001	797,411	150,053	362,422	291,159	74,442	452,199
Postage	267,363	102,166	147,338	20,899	91,606	35,111	10,608	82,747
Household textiles	**1,071,704**	**327,708**	**686,331**	**55,132**	**236,483**	**426,909**	**27,962**	**250,180**
Bathroom linens	182,933	71,836	108,489	23,122	49,883	35,353	–	94,383
Bedroom linens	638,857	148,461	480,288	14,921	156,115	340,832	25,693	64,000
Appliances and miscellaneous housewares	**1,986,931**	**1,003,876**	**782,447**	**187,460**	**357,187**	**229,190**	**50,650**	**614,783**
Major appliances	557,804	249,943	166,907	8,995	113,776	44,091	18,151	176,484
Electric floor cleaning equipment	233,591	54,276	45,468	–	45,418	–	–	39,757
Small appliances and misc. housewares	1,428,564	753,933	615,540	178,465	243,411	185,099	32,500	438,300
Glassware	247,663	132,725	107,914	31,958	53,886	19,092	10,302	90,181
Nonelectric cookware	269,052	169,897	84,029	13,810	7,236	67,632	–	50,747
Tableware, nonelectric kitchenware	340,536	161,231	170,072	47,725	85,756	32,684	1,165	83,393
Small electric kitchen appliances	180,118	101,482	68,489	11,693	30,330	26,454	2,514	74,020
Miscellaneous household equipment	**4,765,257**	**1,988,368**	**2,376,980**	**370,000**	**1,023,372**	**986,980**	**309,543**	**2,054,127**
Infants' equipment	247,663	32,383	211,799	46,190	84,832	81,871	7,910	37,495
Outdoor equipment	125,520	72,748	49,209	24,233	18,783	2,993	16,250	145,454
Household decorative items	1,932,333	720,866	968,634	175,714	482,049	315,510	131,470	717,571
Indoor plants, fresh flowers	1,022,172	416,191	543,598	60,741	207,846	275,060	55,801	509,734
Computers and computer hardware, nonbusiness use	657,432	301,482	317,698	28,413	54,502	234,853	20,971	253,412
Miscellaneous household equipment, parts	163,232	43,786	105,612	6,085	83,908	16,180	44,212	44,283
Other housing	**10,672,015**	**5,046,518**	**4,959,716**	**955,184**	**2,678,596**	**1,325,708**	**782,259**	**2,498,891**
Repair or maintenance services	283,124	206,385	73,669	952	70,052	2,832	36,669	35,232
Housing while attending school	3,942,341	2,029,645	1,806,045	12,593	907,594	885,855	96,211	460,926
Natural gas (renter)	170,550	91,676	69,928	4,656	56,503	8,575	8,953	85,333
Electricity (renter)	689,516	253,364	368,633	56,878	257,267	54,608	157,286	385,613
Telephone services in home city, excl. mobile phones	709,216	254,732	398,849	92,857	255,266	50,805	139,258	441,532

	total married couples	married couples, no children	married couples with children				single parent, at least one child <18	single person
			total	oldest child under 6	oldest child 6 to 17	oldest child 18 or older		
Water, sewerage maintenance (renter)	$140,155	$57,697	$65,612	$9,630	$53,886	$2,184	$24,589	$75,959
Care for elderly, invalids, handicapped	39,401	22,577	15,540	–	15,550	–	–	121,211
Day-care centers, nurseries, and preschools	1,715,065	377,195	1,238,562	577,513	593,978	67,147	144,899	206,221
Housekeeping services	253,292	66,363	73,094	3,228	55,272	14,481	24,405	85,656
Gardening, lawn care service	200,945	151,425	33,381	6,508	17,551	9,223	16,556	93,090
Repair of miscellaneous household equipment and furnishings	847,119	783,580	46,331	–	46,188	–	–	–
Bedroom furniture except mattress and springs	173,364	113,797	19,856	–	6,466	13,349	61	30,384
APPAREL AND SERVICES	**15,738,971**	**6,863,165**	**7,505,042**	**1,427,406**	**3,401,438**	**2,701,170**	**1,242,343**	**6,043,108**
Men and boys, aged 2 or older	**4,190,567**	**1,981,298**	**1,969,786**	**310,106**	**694,360**	**1,003,484**	**286,426**	**1,646,857**
Men's coats and jackets	294,381	131,813	148,489	27,884	32,947	92,792	–	63,353
Men's underwear	117,640	41,277	68,777	10,529	26,943	33,169	8,953	69,171
Men's accessories	187,436	81,642	89,784	17,460	36,796	36,567	35,259	102,141
Men's sweaters and vests	180,118	100,342	73,381	4,444	23,402	45,385	5,396	88,565
Men's active sportswear	378,249	245,154	125,755	17,407	38,798	74,266	–	82,100
Men's shirts	955,190	445,154	438,561	102,592	114,546	228,866	126,013	560,158
Men's pants	423,841	211,630	194,533	22,910	69,128	110,105	47,400	155,797
Boys' shirts	364,740	148,689	182,158	30,423	67,127	88,828	26,736	115,716
Boys' pants	196,442	85,063	94,964	10,794	54,040	30,014	9,873	74,666
Women and girls, aged 2 or older	**5,624,197**	**2,772,176**	**2,345,613**	**344,814**	**1,214,744**	**810,780**	**453,952**	**1,937,441**
Women's coats and jackets	230,777	95,325	132,374	12,116	96,995	23,866	17,844	104,727
Women's dresses	732,294	453,363	254,676	–	106,694	164,146	4,538	228,200
Women's vests and sweaters	658,558	322,919	295,828	85,979	123,784	81,305	51,080	119,918
Women's shirts, tops, blouses	520,655	264,082	197,986	39,947	52,346	110,671	66,164	355,876
Women's pants	424,404	201,824	143,885	5,079	80,675	63,749	23,670	104,403
Women's active sportswear	261,172	207,069	49,496	688	36,027	13,915	22,443	83,717
Women's sleepwear	381,626	132,041	118,849	11,376	68,358	41,421	39,919	93,737
Women's undergarments	150,849	66,135	67,338	–	49,575	19,740	19,316	92,767
Women's accessories	284,249	78,677	186,763	68,254	50,807	63,992	16,434	71,434
Girls' dresses and suits	279,746	89,624	156,835	27,989	83,446	45,547	64,999	85,333
Girls' shirts, blouses, sweaters	477,314	221,437	231,079	34,392	153,344	42,149	26,919	111,838
Girls' skirts and pants	166,047	97,605	56,403	10,317	26,789	19,254	19,438	84,040
Girls' active sportswear	150,849	82,554	65,899	–	55,734	11,002	–	82,100
Girls' accessories	154,226	71,836	78,849	6,296	60,044	12,944	13,613	36,525
Children under age 2	**3,197,102**	**871,835**	**1,865,901**	**557,248**	**784,888**	**483,054**	**238,780**	**558,218**
Infant dresses, outerwear	1,136,997	526,339	512,231	97,619	216,776	197,881	58,990	212,362
Infant underwear	1,437,570	158,039	1,014,389	388,889	425,238	157,512	145,206	208,483
Infant nightwear, loungewear	178,430	72,748	90,072	19,153	38,644	32,198	12,632	42,990
Infant accessories	336,033	65,906	198,561	36,032	90,836	73,700	17,415	65,939
Other apparel products and services	**2,726,542**	**1,237,855**	**1,323,742**	**215,238**	**707,446**	**403,853**	**263,124**	**1,900,592**
Watches	187,436	76,169	100,144	23,280	18,321	58,572	11,099	135,110
Jewelry	582,570	300,114	264,173	60,264	110,081	93,763	31,702	1,015,589
Men's footwear	614,654	240,593	366,907	73,386	210,001	80,334	29,311	274,746
Boys' footwear	388,943	245,838	97,266	20,688	32,640	45,223	9,750	47,192
Women's footwear	571,313	251,539	259,856	25,926	177,208	58,572	135,946	249,210
Girls' footwear	279,184	77,537	189,640	10,370	144,568	36,567	39,122	168,403
TRANSPORTATION	**4,076,867**	**2,301,709**	**1,626,188**	**79,947**	**943,313**	**603,029**	**119,022**	**1,880,875**
New cars	98,502	98,746	–	–	–	–	–	202,342
New trucks	881,454	881,641	–	–	–	–	–	–
Used cars	631,540	74,116	557,410	–	367,810	189,630	–	458,663
Used trucks	46,155	46,294	–	–	–	–	–	262,140
Gasoline on trips	895,526	446,750	393,669	36,667	220,933	135,993	42,863	318,705

	total married couples	married couples, no children	married couples with children				single parent, at least one child <18	single person
			total	oldest child under 6	oldest child 6 to 17	oldest child 18 or older		
Airline fares	$585,948	$300,570	$253,238	$20,476	$98,380	$134,375	$34,217	$243,715
Local transportation on trips	100,191	57,469	38,273	4,074	22,478	11,569	3,127	107,312
Intercity train fares	162,669	74,572	76,835	4,656	28,944	43,201	5,212	57,858
Ship fares	202,070	101,938	80,576	6,931	32,793	40,693	21,462	53,010
HEALTH CARE	**1,601,365**	**657,240**	**401,151**	**14,550**	**218,315**	**170,295**	**47,768**	**2,015,986**
Physician's services	154,789	58,837	75,684	476	26,019	49,025	10,424	114,100
Dental services	174,490	96,009	71,079	2,434	26,019	42,715	9,014	182,948
Hospital room	205,448	18,244	–	–	–	–	–	93,413
Care in convalescent or nursing home	265,675	105,587	–	–	–	–	–	1,349,485
Nonprescription drugs	112,574	60,205	33,669	–	24,942	9,708	1,594	107,636
ENTERTAINMENT	**6,305,833**	**2,797,033**	**2,774,391**	**530,052**	**1,418,126**	**824,452**	**311,812**	**2,371,862**
Toys, games, hobbies, and tricycles	2,026,895	1,073,203	781,871	177,301	369,658	234,934	79,471	786,419
Movie, other admissions, on trips	602,834	243,785	308,202	78,730	158,425	71,030	31,396	244,362
Admission to sports events on trips	200,945	81,186	102,734	26,243	52,808	23,704	10,486	81,454
Fees for recreational lessons	538,667	154,390	367,482	22,751	267,890	76,855	24,467	67,555
Cable service and community antenna	197,567	64,994	118,849	21,323	80,521	16,989	30,721	169,373
Color TV, portable, table model	146,346	59,293	68,489	9,048	22,324	37,214	6,193	60,767
Musical instruments and accessories	65,856	21,209	35,683	2,487	4,003	29,205	10,547	172,282
Athletic gear, game tables, and exercise equipment	647,301	345,952	265,036	65,555	117,779	79,687	21,094	127,353
PERSONAL CARE PRODUCTS AND SERVICES	**1,293,475**	**339,795**	**845,180**	**137,619**	**482,049**	**227,167**	**177,460**	**468,037**
Hair care products	165,484	28,506	128,633	9,947	91,298	28,558	13,858	37,495
Cosmetics, perfume, bath preparation	844,305	228,050	546,763	105,820	307,920	137,530	128,772	290,907
Deodorants, feminine hygiene, misc. personal care	112,574	22,805	86,331	10,582	46,188	24,270	12,264	32,323
READING	**112,574**	**68,415**	**57,554**	**10,582**	**15,396**	**16,180**	**0**	**64,646**
EDUCATION	**13,340,019**	**6,180,155**	**6,589,933**	**100,529**	**3,602,664**	**2,871,950**	**410,844**	**2,327,256**
College tuition	10,356,808	4,811,855	5,122,306	21,164	2,725,092	2,362,280	208,488	1,713,119
Elementary and high school tuition	900,592	387,685	489,209	47,619	400,296	40,450	24,528	226,261
Other school tuition	281,435	182,440	115,108	5,291	15,396	88,990	12,264	32,323
Other school expenses including rentals	337,722	159,635	201,439	5,291	107,772	80,900	85,848	64,646
College books and supplies	844,305	410,490	431,655	0	200,148	234,610	42,924	193,938
Miscellaneous school supplies	394,009	159,635	143,885	21,164	92,376	40,450	12,264	129,292
ALL OTHER GIFTS	**5,290,978**	**2,326,110**	**2,330,937**	**185,185**	**1,031,532**	**1,100,240**	**331,128**	**3,393,915**
Gifts of trip expenses	2,532,915	1,413,910	978,418	89,947	446,484	436,860	122,640	2,294,933
Miscellaneous fees, gambling losses	168,861	68,415	57,554	15,873	30,792	16,180	–	32,323
Legal fees	281,435	182,440	86,331	10,582	30,792	48,540	55,188	32,323
Funeral expenses	1,970,045	501,710	1,007,195	5,291	461,880	533,940	128,772	808,075
Cemetery lots, vaults, maintenance fees	168,861	68,415	57,554	5,291	15,396	32,360	6,132	129,292
Accounting fees	112,574	45,610	57,554	5,291	15,396	16,180	6,132	64,646

Note: Total spending figures for total consumer units can be found on Total Spending by Age and Total Spending by Region tables. Spending by type of consumer unit will not add to total because not all types of consumer units are shown. (–) means sample is too small to make a reliable estimate. Expenditures for items in a given category may not add to category total because categories with annual spending of less than $2.00 for the average household are omitted. Spending on gifts is also included in the product and service categories in other chapters.
Source: Calculations by New Strategist based on the 2000 Consumer Expenditure Survey

Table 6.15 Gifts: Market shares by household type, 2000

(percentage of total annual spending on gifts of products and services for non-household members accounted for by types of consumer units, 2000)

	total married couples	married couples, no children	married couples with children				single parent, at least one child <18	single person
			total	oldest child under 6	oldest child 6 to 17	oldest child 18 or older		
Share of total consumer units	51.5%	20.9%	26.3%	4.8%	14.1%	7.4%	5.6%	29.6%
Share of total before-tax income	69.8	24.9	39.4	6.8	21.9	10.7	3.2	16.5
Share of total spending	65.8	23.1	37.1	6.5	20.0	10.6	4.3	17.9
Share of gifts spending	64.4	28.4	30.8	4.1	14.9	11.8	3.5	22.0
FOOD	**79.8%**	**30.0%**	**43.7%**	**4.0%**	**17.4%**	**22.5%**	**2.4%**	**13.1%**
Fresh fruits	72.9	41.5	21.8	2.5	11.5	8.2	2.9	11.7
Candy and chewing gum	79.5	21.6	42.7	7.8	18.4	16.9	3.1	11.8
Board (including at school)	88.4	38.6	44.2	0.0	23.5	20.7	1.7	7.8
Catered affairs	90.8	34.8	54.5	3.0	8.9	42.7	0.9	4.8
ALCOHOLIC BEVERAGES	**67.1**	**20.8**	**43.3**	**15.0**	**13.7**	**13.8**	**3.1**	**19.7**
Beer and ale	60.1	16.0	40.2	8.2	12.1	20.7	2.8	25.3
Wine	65.8	22.4	41.3	16.0	11.2	13.0	4.8	21.2
Whiskey and other alcoholic beverages	76.2	22.2	49.6	18.6	20.5	8.6	0.4	10.6
HOUSING	**67.0**	**29.8**	**32.3**	**5.7**	**15.7**	**11.1**	**4.1**	**19.5**
Housekeeping supplies	**66.2**	**26.6**	**34.7**	**6.0**	**16.1**	**13.0**	**3.3**	**18.7**
Miscellaneous household products	63.2	23.2	35.9	3.8	14.8	18.6	4.0	21.2
Lawn and garden supplies	80.9	49.8	18.1	–	7.6	11.7	1.9	8.1
Postage and stationery	64.0	25.6	34.6	6.3	16.6	12.0	3.2	19.6
Stationery, stationery supplies, giftwraps	66.4	26.5	36.0	6.8	16.3	13.1	3.4	20.4
Postage	53.5	20.4	29.5	4.2	18.3	7.0	2.1	16.6
Household textiles	**74.2**	**22.7**	**47.5**	**3.8**	**16.4**	**29.6**	**1.9**	**17.3**
Bathroom linens	60.0	23.5	35.6	7.6	16.3	11.6	–	30.9
Bedroom linens	85.3	19.8	64.1	2.0	20.8	45.5	3.4	8.5
Appliances and miscellaneous housewares	**64.6**	**32.6**	**25.4**	**6.1**	**11.6**	**7.4**	**1.6**	**20.0**
Major appliances	67.0	30.0	20.1	1.1	13.7	5.3	2.2	21.2
Electric floor cleaning equipment	71.0	16.5	13.8	–	13.8	–	–	12.1
Small appliances and miscellaneous housewares	63.6	33.6	27.4	7.9	10.8	8.2	1.4	19.5
Glassware	62.9	33.7	27.4	8.1	13.7	4.8	2.6	22.9
Nonelectric cookware	67.2	42.4	21.0	3.4	1.8	16.9	–	12.7
Tableware, nonelectric kitchenware	71.7	34.0	35.8	10.1	18.1	6.9	0.2	17.6
Small electric kitchen appliances	61.5	34.6	23.4	4.0	10.3	9.0	0.9	25.3
Miscellaneous household equipment	**62.0**	**25.9**	**30.9**	**4.8**	**13.3**	**12.8**	**4.0**	**26.7**
Infants' equipment	83.3	10.9	71.2	15.5	28.5	27.5	2.7	12.6
Outdoor equipment	40.1	23.3	15.7	7.7	6.0	1.0	5.2	46.5
Household decorative items	64.6	24.1	32.4	5.9	16.1	10.6	4.4	24.0
Indoor plants, fresh flowers	58.3	23.7	31.0	3.5	11.8	15.7	3.2	29.1
Computers and computer hardware, nonbusiness use	67.0	30.7	32.4	2.9	5.6	23.9	2.1	25.8
Miscellaneous household equipment and parts	59.0	15.8	38.2	2.2	30.3	5.8	16.0	16.0
Other housing	**69.5**	**32.9**	**32.3**	**6.2**	**17.4**	**8.6**	**5.1**	**16.3**
Repair or maintenance services	69.2	50.5	18.0	0.2	17.1	0.7	9.0	8.6
Housing while attending school	85.2	43.9	39.0	0.3	19.6	19.1	2.1	10.0
Natural gas (renter)	50.1	27.0	20.6	1.4	16.6	2.5	2.6	25.1
Electricity (renter)	47.5	17.4	25.4	3.9	17.7	3.8	10.8	26.6
Telephone services in home city, excl. mobile phones	47.5	17.1	26.7	6.2	17.1	3.4	9.3	29.6

	total married couples	married couples, no children	married couples with children			single parent, at least one child <18	single person
			total	oldest child under 6	oldest child 6 to 17	oldest child 18 or older	
Water, sewerage maintenance (renter)	48.0%	19.8%	22.5%	3.3%	18.5%	0.7%	8.4%	26.0%
Care for elderly, invalids, handicapped	17.2	9.8	6.8	–	6.8	–	–	52.8
Day-care centers, nurseries, and preschools	73.1	16.1	52.8	24.6	25.3	2.9	6.2	8.8
Housekeeping services	67.3	17.6	19.4	0.9	14.7	3.8	6.5	22.8
Gardening, lawn care service	58.5	44.1	9.7	1.9	5.1	2.7	4.8	27.1
Repair of miscellaneous household equipment and furnishings	99.6	92.1	5.4	–	5.4	–	–	–
Bedroom furniture except mattress and springs	76.9	50.5	8.8	–	2.9	5.9	0.0	13.5
APPAREL AND SERVICES	**58.9**	**25.7**	**28.1**	**5.3**	**12.7**	**10.1**	**4.7**	**22.6**
Men and boys, aged 2 or older	**56.7**	**26.8**	**26.7**	**4.2**	**9.4**	**13.6**	**3.9**	**22.3**
Men's coats and jackets	81.6	36.5	41.1	7.7	9.1	25.7	–	17.6
Men's underwear	51.2	18.0	29.9	4.6	11.7	14.4	3.9	30.1
Men's accessories	50.4	22.0	24.1	4.7	9.9	9.8	9.5	27.5
Men's sweaters and vests	60.5	33.7	24.7	1.5	7.9	15.3	1.8	29.8
Men's active sportswear	79.5	51.5	26.4	3.7	8.2	15.6	–	17.3
Men's shirts	42.1	19.6	19.3	4.5	5.0	10.1	5.5	24.7
Men's pants	54.5	27.2	25.0	2.9	8.9	14.2	6.1	20.0
Boys' shirts	60.0	24.5	30.0	5.0	11.0	14.6	4.4	19.0
Boys' pants	63.2	27.4	30.6	3.5	17.4	9.7	3.2	24.0
Women and girls, aged 2 or older	**60.3**	**29.7**	**25.1**	**3.7**	**13.0**	**8.7**	**4.9**	**20.8**
Women's coats and jackets	59.1	24.4	33.9	3.1	24.8	6.1	4.6	26.8
Women's dresses	63.0	39.0	21.9	–	9.2	14.1	0.4	19.6
Women's vests and sweaters	68.0	33.3	30.5	8.9	12.8	8.4	5.3	12.4
Women's shirts, tops, blouses	45.0	22.8	17.1	3.4	4.5	9.6	5.7	30.7
Women's pants	65.3	31.1	22.1	0.8	12.4	9.8	3.6	16.1
Women's active sportswear	68.8	54.6	13.0	0.2	9.5	3.7	5.9	22.1
Women's sleepwear	56.7	19.6	17.7	1.7	10.2	6.2	5.9	13.9
Women's undergarments	51.3	22.5	22.9	–	16.9	6.7	6.6	31.5
Women's accessories	62.3	17.3	41.0	15.0	11.1	14.0	3.6	15.7
Girls' dresses and suits	63.5	20.3	35.6	6.4	18.9	10.3	14.7	19.4
Girls' shirts, blouses, sweaters	70.6	32.8	34.2	5.1	22.7	6.2	4.0	16.5
Girls' skirts and pants	54.6	32.1	18.6	3.4	8.8	6.3	6.4	27.6
Girls' active sportswear	65.7	35.9	28.7	–	24.3	4.8	–	35.7
Girls' accessories	64.7	30.1	33.1	2.6	25.2	5.4	5.7	15.3
Children under age 2	**71.8**	**19.6**	**41.9**	**12.5**	**17.6**	**10.8**	**5.4**	**12.5**
Infant dresses, outerwear	71.6	33.2	32.3	6.2	13.7	12.5	3.7	13.4
Infant underwear	71.9	7.9	50.8	19.5	21.3	7.9	7.3	10.4
Infant nightwear, loungewear	66.3	27.0	33.5	7.1	14.4	12.0	4.7	16.0
Infant accessories	76.4	15.0	45.2	8.2	20.7	16.8	4.0	15.0
Other apparel products and services	**49.2**	**22.3**	**23.9**	**3.9**	**12.8**	**7.3**	**4.7**	**34.3**
Watches	50.0	20.3	26.7	6.2	4.9	15.6	3.0	36.0
Jewelry	31.6	16.3	14.3	3.3	6.0	5.1	1.7	55.1
Men's footwear	64.9	25.4	38.7	7.7	22.2	8.5	3.1	29.0
Boys' footwear	75.7	47.8	18.9	4.0	6.3	8.8	1.9	9.2
Women's footwear	51.9	22.9	23.6	2.4	16.1	5.3	12.4	22.7
Girls' footwear	49.0	13.6	33.3	1.8	25.4	6.4	6.9	29.6
TRANSPORTATION	**53.0**	**29.9**	**21.2**	**1.0**	**12.3**	**7.8**	**1.5**	**24.5**
New cars	14.8	14.9	–	–	–	–	–	30.4
New trucks	57.4	57.4	–	–	–	–	–	–
Used cars	46.1	5.4	40.7	–	26.9	13.8	–	33.5
Used trucks	15.0	15.0	–	–	–	–	–	85.0
Gasoline on trips	65.2	32.5	28.7	2.7	16.1	9.9	3.1	23.2

	total married couples	married couples, no children	married couples with children			single parent, at least one child <18	single person
			total	oldest child under 6	oldest child 6 to 17	oldest child 18 or older		
Airline fares	63.0%	32.3%	27.2%	2.2%	10.6%	14.4%	3.7%	26.2%
Local transportation on trips	43.0	24.7	16.4	1.7	9.6	5.0	1.3	46.1
Intercity train fares	66.7	30.6	31.5	1.9	11.9	17.7	2.1	23.7
Ship fares	62.0	31.3	24.7	2.1	10.1	12.5	6.6	16.3
HEALTH CARE	**38.5**	**15.8**	**9.6**	**0.3**	**5.2**	**4.1**	**1.1**	**48.4**
Physician's services	53.2	20.2	26.0	0.2	8.9	16.9	3.6	39.2
Dental services	45.7	25.2	18.6	0.6	6.8	11.2	2.4	47.9
Hospital room	68.8	6.1	–	–	–	–	–	31.3
Care in convalescent or nursing home	13.2	5.2	–	–	–	–	–	67.0
Nonprescription drugs	47.9	25.6	14.3	–	10.6	4.1	0.7	45.8
ENTERTAINMENT	**61.5**	**27.3**	**27.1**	**5.2**	**13.8**	**8.0**	**3.0**	**23.1**
Toys, games, hobbies, and tricycles	62.7	33.2	24.2	5.5	11.4	7.3	2.5	24.3
Movie, other admissions, on trips	60.1	24.3	30.7	7.9	15.8	7.1	3.1	24.4
Admission to sports events on trips	60.0	24.3	30.7	7.8	15.8	7.1	3.1	24.3
Fees for recreational lessons	78.2	22.4	53.3	3.3	38.9	11.2	3.6	9.8
Cable service and community antenna	38.8	12.8	23.4	4.2	15.8	3.3	6.0	33.3
Color TV, portable, table model	63.7	25.8	29.8	3.9	9.7	16.2	2.7	26.5
Musical instruments and accessories	26.0	8.4	14.1	1.0	1.6	11.5	4.2	67.9
Athletic gear, game tables, and exercise equipment	62.5	33.4	25.6	6.3	11.4	7.7	2.0	12.3
PERSONAL CARE PRODUCTS AND SERVICES	**61.6**	**16.2**	**40.2**	**6.6**	**23.0**	**10.8**	**8.5**	**22.3**
Hair care products	70.7	12.2	55.0	4.3	39.0	12.2	5.9	16.0
Cosmetics, perfume, bath preparation	59.4	16.0	38.5	7.4	21.7	9.7	9.1	20.5
Deodorants, feminine hygiene, misc. personal care	51.5	10.4	39.5	4.8	21.1	11.1	5.6	14.8
READING	**51.5**	**31.3**	**26.3**	**4.8**	**7.0**	**7.4**	**0.0**	**29.6**
EDUCATION	**80.8**	**37.4**	**39.9**	**0.6**	**21.8**	**17.4**	**2.5**	**14.1**
College tuition	83.1	38.6	41.1	0.2	21.9	18.9	1.7	13.7
Elementary and high school tuition	74.9	32.2	40.7	4.0	33.3	3.4	2.0	18.8
Other school tuition	85.8	55.6	35.1	1.6	4.7	27.1	3.7	9.9
Other school expenses including rentals	61.8	29.2	36.8	1.0	19.7	14.8	15.7	11.8
College books and supplies	77.2	37.5	39.5	0.0	18.3	21.5	3.9	17.7
Miscellaneous school supplies	72.1	29.2	26.3	3.9	16.9	7.4	2.2	23.6
ALL OTHER GIFTS	**54.4**	**23.9**	**23.9**	**1.9**	**10.6**	**11.3**	**3.4**	**34.9**
Gifts of trip expenses	47.3	26.4	18.3	1.7	8.3	8.2	2.3	42.8
Miscellaneous fees, gambling losses	77.2	31.3	26.3	7.3	14.1	7.4	–	14.8
Legal fees	64.3	41.7	19.7	2.4	7.0	11.1	12.6	7.4
Funeral expenses	64.3	16.4	32.9	0.2	15.1	17.4	4.2	26.4
Cemetery lots, vaults, maintenance fees	51.5	20.9	17.5	1.6	4.7	9.9	1.9	39.4
Accounting fees	51.5	20.9	26.3	2.4	7.0	7.4	2.8	29.6

Note: Market share for total consumer units is 100.0%. Market shares by type of consumer unit will not add to total because not all types of consumer units are shown. (–) means sample is too small to make a reliable estimate.
Source: Calculations by New Strategist based on the 2000 Consumer Expenditure Survey

Table 6.16 Gifts: Average spending by race and Hispanic origin, 2000

(average annual spending of consumer units (CU) on gifts of products and services for non–household members, by race and Hispanic origin of consumer unit reference person, 2000)

	total consumer units	race		Hispanic origin	
		black	white and other	Hispanic	non-Hispanic
Number of consumer units (in thousands, add 000)	109,367	13,230	96,137	9,473	99,894
Average number of persons per CU	2.5	2.7	2.5	3.4	2.4
Average before-tax income of CU	$44,649.00	$32,657.00	$46,260.00	$34,891.00	$45,669.00
Average spending of CU, total	38,044.67	28,152.24	39,406.20	32,734.95	38,548.91
Gifts, average spending	1,083.14	571.18	1,153.61	825.28	1,107.63
FOOD	**$70.09**	**$26.12**	**$76.14**	**$43.56**	**$72.58**
Fresh fruits	4.58	1.19	5.05	4.65	4.58
Candy and chewing gum	12.50	2.26	13.91	4.81	13.22
Board (including at school)	20.21	14.96	20.93	21.03	20.13
Catered affairs	15.59	1.71	17.50	2.17	16.87
ALCOHOLIC BEVERAGES	**14.49**	**9.76**	**15.14**	**11.37**	**14.78**
Beer and ale	3.64	3.82	3.62	2.75	3.73
Wine	6.76	3.88	7.15	5.75	6.85
Whiskey and other alcoholic beverages	3.73	1.75	4.00	2.66	3.82
HOUSING	**291.10**	**132.93**	**312.88**	**207.50**	**298.96**
Housekeeping supplies	**39.10**	**13.63**	**42.60**	**35.74**	**39.41**
Miscellaneous household products	7.32	1.04	8.18	7.52	7.30
Lawn and garden supplies	3.08	1.62	3.28	3.46	3.04
Postage and stationery	24.95	9.09	27.13	16.97	25.69
Stationery, stationery supplies, giftwraps	20.28	6.60	22.16	8.62	21.36
Postage	4.57	2.49	4.85	8.35	4.21
Household textiles	**13.20**	**2.55**	**14.67**	**12.61**	**13.26**
Bathroom linens	2.79	1.29	3.00	2.12	2.86
Bedroom linens	6.85	–	7.79	9.41	6.61
Appliances and miscellaneous housewares	**28.14**	**5.52**	**31.25**	**12.41**	**29.61**
Major appliances	7.61	2.45	8.32	8.13	7.57
Electric floor cleaning equipment	3.01	–	3.43	6.15	2.72
Small appliances and miscellaneous housewares	20.53	3.07	22.93	4.28	22.04
Glassware	3.60	0.61	4.01	0.41	3.90
Nonelectric cookware	3.66	0.09	4.15	0.68	3.94
Tableware, nonelectric kitchenware	4.34	0.58	4.86	0.45	4.70
Small electric kitchen appliances	2.68	1.36	2.86	1.57	2.79
Miscellaneous household equipment	**70.31**	**19.43**	**77.31**	**35.45**	**73.59**
Infants' equipment	2.72	1.13	2.94	3.22	2.68
Outdoor equipment	2.86	–	3.26	–	3.13
Household decorative items	27.33	10.47	29.65	12.92	28.67
Indoor plants, fresh flowers	16.04	5.32	17.52	6.32	16.96
Computers and computer hardware, nonbusiness use	8.97	0.89	10.08	1.18	9.71
Miscellaneous household equipment and parts	2.53	0.25	2.84	0.77	2.69
Other housing	**140.36**	**91.80**	**147.04**	**111.28**	**143.10**
Repair or maintenance services	3.74	1.09	4.11	1.40	3.96
Housing while attending school	42.32	16.22	45.91	33.52	43.15
Natural gas (renter)	3.11	4.00	2.99	3.26	3.09
Electricity (renter)	13.28	12.67	13.36	14.28	13.18
Telephone services in home city, excl. mobile phones	13.64	16.71	13.21	15.83	13.43

	total consumer units	race		Hispanic origin	
		black	white and other	Hispanic	non-Hispanic
Water, sewerage maintenance (renter)	$2.67	$2.69	$2.66	$3.13	$2.62
Care for elderly, invalids, handicapped	2.10	2.14	2.09	0.59	2.24
Day-care centers, nurseries, and preschools	21.46	19.06	21.79	15.98	21.98
Housekeeping services	3.44	0.62	3.82	1.31	3.64
Gardening, lawn care service	3.14	1.71	3.34	0.47	3.39
Repair of miscellaneous household equipment and furnishings	7.78	–	8.85	–	8.50
Bedroom furniture except mattress and springs	2.06	0.94	2.22	0.59	2.20
APPAREL AND SERVICES	**244.25**	**193.59**	**251.22**	**291.41**	**239.89**
Men and boys, aged 2 or older	**67.55**	**38.23**	**71.59**	**64.58**	**67.82**
Men's coats and jackets	3.30	7.09	2.78	11.26	2.56
Men's underwear	2.10	1.94	2.12	1.53	2.15
Men's accessories	3.40	0.56	3.79	0.89	3.63
Men's sweaters and vests	2.72	2.30	2.78	1.04	2.88
Men's active sportswear	4.35	1.00	4.81	1.09	4.65
Men's shirts	20.77	6.97	22.67	14.83	21.33
Men's pants	7.11	0.70	7.99	8.58	6.97
Boys' shirts	5.56	4.63	5.69	5.69	5.55
Boys' pants	2.84	2.41	2.89	4.88	2.64
Women and girls, aged 2 or older	**85.28**	**87.04**	**85.03**	**96.18**	**84.27**
Women's coats and jackets	3.57	4.39	3.45	4.48	3.48
Women's dresses	10.62	14.25	10.12	11.63	10.53
Women's vests and sweaters	8.86	6.43	9.19	3.16	9.39
Women's shirts, tops, blouses	10.59	10.12	10.66	13.35	10.33
Women's pants	5.94	6.38	5.88	10.18	5.55
Women's active sportswear	3.47	3.00	3.53	0.76	3.72
Women's sleepwear	6.15	11.40	5.42	9.72	5.82
Women's undergarments	2.69	6.37	2.18	0.71	2.87
Women's accessories	4.17	1.51	4.54	3.51	4.23
Girls' dresses and suits	4.03	3.42	4.11	11.28	3.36
Girls' shirts, blouses, sweaters	6.18	4.00	6.48	6.11	6.19
Girls' skirts and pants	2.78	2.47	2.83	3.25	2.74
Girls' active sportswear	2.10	2.04	2.11	3.86	1.94
Girls' accessories	2.18	0.42	2.42	1.55	2.23
Children under age 2	**40.71**	**33.59**	**41.69**	**61.14**	**38.82**
Infant dresses, outerwear	14.51	13.27	14.68	12.87	14.66
Infant underwear	18.27	13.39	18.95	36.28	16.60
Infant nightwear, loungewear	2.46	2.10	2.50	2.40	2.46
Infant accessories	4.02	3.59	4.08	8.15	3.64
Other apparel products and services	**50.71**	**34.73**	**52.91**	**69.52**	**48.98**
Watches	3.43	1.42	3.71	3.45	3.43
Jewelry	16.85	6.78	18.24	7.49	17.74
Men's footwear	8.66	2.51	9.51	21.89	7.44
Boys' footwear	4.70	3.43	4.87	6.66	4.52
Women's footwear	10.06	13.13	9.63	18.26	9.29
Girls' footwear	5.21	4.81	5.27	11.69	4.61
TRANSPORTATION	**70.27**	**23.41**	**76.72**	**25.70**	**74.51**
New cars	6.08	–	6.92	–	6.66
New trucks	14.04	–	15.97	–	15.37
Used cars	12.52	–	14.25	0.42	13.67
Used trucks	2.82	3.58	2.72	–	3.09
Gasoline on trips	12.55	4.46	13.66	6.42	13.13

	total consumer units	race black	race white and other	Hispanic origin Hispanic	Hispanic origin non-Hispanic
Airline fares	$8.51	$6.86	$8.74	$4.70	$8.87
Local transportation on trips	2.13	0.67	2.34	1.46	2.20
Intercity train fares	2.23	1.82	2.28	1.24	2.32
Ship fares	2.98	1.95	3.12	2.94	2.98
HEALTH CARE	**38.08**	**5.60**	**42.55**	**12.09**	**40.55**
Physician's services	2.66	0.89	2.91	1.65	2.76
Dental services	3.49	0.85	3.85	1.41	3.68
Hospital room	2.73	–	3.11	–	2.99
Care in convalescent or nursing home	18.42	–	20.96	0.05	20.16
Nonprescription drugs	2.15	0.96	2.31	2.86	2.08
ENTERTAINMENT	**93.76**	**42.99**	**100.75**	**69.09**	**96.09**
Toys, games, hobbies, and tricycles	29.58	16.59	31.37	22.62	30.24
Movie, other admissions, on trips	9.17	3.20	9.99	7.12	9.37
Admission to sports events on trips	3.06	1.07	3.33	2.37	3.12
Fees for recreational lessons	6.30	1.39	6.98	5.63	6.37
Cable service and community antenna	4.65	6.35	4.42	5.11	4.61
Color TV, portable, table model	2.10	0.51	2.31	0.89	2.21
Musical instruments and accessories	2.32	0.19	2.62	1.79	2.37
Athletic gear, game tables, and exercise equipment	9.47	6.94	9.82	8.25	9.59
PERSONAL CARE PRODUCTS AND SERVICES	**19.20**	**10.47**	**20.41**	**30.85**	**18.12**
Hair care products	2.14	1.13	2.28	9.52	1.45
Cosmetics, perfume, bath preparation	13.00	6.00	13.00	17.00	12.00
Deodorants, feminine hygiene, misc. personal care	2.00	2.00	2.00	2.00	2.00
READING	**2.00**	**–**	**2.00**	**1.00**	**2.00**
EDUCATION	**151.00**	**39.00**	**166.00**	**71.00**	**159.00**
College tuition	114.00	30.00	126.00	47.00	121.00
Elementary and high school tuition	11.00	1.00	12.00	5.00	11.00
Other school tuition	3.00	–	3.00	2.00	3.00
Other school expenses including rentals	5.00	1.00	5.00	3.00	5.00
College books and supplies	10.00	3.00	11.00	–	11.00
Miscellaneous school supplies	5.00	–	6.00	6.00	5.00
ALL OTHER GIFTS	**89.00**	**87.00**	**89.00**	**62.00**	**91.00**
Gifts of trip expenses	49.00	14.00	54.00	27.00	51.00
Miscellaneous fees, gambling losses	2.00	–	2.00	–	2.00
Legal fees	4.00	5.00	4.00	1.00	4.00
Funeral expenses	28.00	63.00	23.00	30.00	28.00
Cemetery lots, vaults, maintenance fees	3.00	3.00	3.00	3.00	3.00
Accounting fees	2.00	–	2.00	1.00	2.00

Note: Other races include Asians, Native Americans, and Pacific Islanders. (–) means sample is too small to make a reliable estimate. Expenditures for items in a given category may not add to category total because categories with annual spending of less than $2.00 for the average household are omitted. Spending on gifts is also included in the product and service categories in other chapters.
Source: Bureau of Labor Statistics, unpublished tables from the 2000 Consumer Expenditure Survey

Table 6.17 Gifts: Indexed spending by race and Hispanic origin, 2000

(indexed average annual spending of consumer units (CU) on gifts of products and services for non–household members, by race and Hispanic origin of consumer unit reference person, 2000; index definition: an index of 100 is the average for all consumer units; an index of 132 means that spending by consumer units in that group is 32 percent above the average for all consumer units; an index of 68 indicates spending that is 32 percent below the average for all consumer units)

	total consumer units	race black	race white and other	Hispanic origin Hispanic	Hispanic origin non-Hispanic
Average spending of CU, total	$38,045	$28,152	$39,406	$32,735	$38,549
Average spending of CU, index	100	74	104	86	101
Gifts, spending index	100	53	107	76	102
FOOD	100	37	109	62	104
Fresh fruits	100	26	110	102	100
Candy and chewing gum	100	18	111	38	106
Board (including at school)	100	74	104	104	100
Catered affairs	100	11	112	14	108
ALCOHOLIC BEVERAGES	100	67	104	78	102
Beer and ale	100	105	99	76	102
Wine	100	57	106	85	101
Whiskey and other alcoholic beverages	100	47	107	71	102
HOUSING	100	46	107	71	103
Housekeeping supplies	100	35	109	91	101
Miscellaneous household products	100	14	112	103	100
Lawn and garden supplies	100	53	106	112	99
Postage and stationery	100	36	109	68	103
Stationery, stationery supplies, giftwraps	100	33	109	43	105
Postage	100	54	106	183	92
Household textiles	100	19	111	96	100
Bathroom linens	100	46	108	76	103
Bedroom linens	100	–	114	137	96
Appliances and miscellaneous housewares	100	20	111	44	105
Major appliances	100	32	109	107	99
Electric floor cleaning equipment	100	–	114	204	90
Small appliances and miscellaneous housewares	100	15	112	21	107
Glassware	100	17	111	11	108
Nonelectric cookware	100	2	113	19	108
Tableware, nonelectric kitchenware	100	13	112	10	108
Small electric kitchen appliances	100	51	107	59	104
Miscellaneous household equipment	100	28	110	50	105
Infants' equipment	100	42	108	118	99
Outdoor equipment	100	–	114	–	109
Household decorative items	100	38	108	47	105
Indoor plants, fresh flowers	100	33	109	39	106
Computers and computer hardware, nonbusiness use	100	10	112	13	108
Miscellaneous household equipment and parts	100	10	112	30	106
Other housing	100	65	105	79	102
Repair or maintenance services	100	29	110	37	106
Housing while attending school	100	38	108	79	102
Natural gas (renter)	100	129	96	105	99
Electricity (renter)	100	95	101	108	99
Telephone services in home city, excl. mobile phones	100	123	97	116	98

	total consumer units	race		Hispanic origin	
		black	white and other	Hispanic	non-Hispanic
Water, sewerage maintenance (renter)	100	101	100	117	98
Care for elderly, invalids, handicapped	100	102	100	28	107
Day-care centers, nurseries, and preschools	100	89	102	74	102
Housekeeping services	100	18	111	38	106
Gardening, lawn care service	100	54	106	15	108
Repair of miscellaneous household equipment and furnishings	100	–	114	–	109
Bedroom furniture except mattress and springs	100	46	108	29	107
APPAREL AND SERVICES	**100**	**79**	**103**	**119**	**98**
Men and boys, aged 2 or older	**100**	**57**	**106**	**96**	**100**
Men's coats and jackets	100	215	84	341	78
Men's underwear	100	92	101	73	102
Men's accessories	100	16	111	26	107
Men's sweaters and vests	100	85	102	38	106
Men's active sportswear	100	23	111	25	107
Men's shirts	100	34	109	71	103
Men's pants	100	10	112	121	98
Boys' shirts	100	83	102	102	100
Boys' pants	100	85	102	172	93
Women and girls, aged 2 or older	**100**	**102**	**100**	**113**	**99**
Women's coats and jackets	100	123	97	125	97
Women's dresses	100	134	95	110	99
Women's vests and sweaters	100	73	104	36	106
Women's shirts, tops, blouses	100	96	101	126	98
Women's pants	100	107	99	171	93
Women's active sportswear	100	86	102	22	107
Women's sleepwear	100	185	88	158	95
Women's undergarments	100	237	81	26	107
Women's accessories	100	36	109	84	101
Girls' dresses and suits	100	85	102	280	83
Girls' shirts, blouses, sweaters	100	65	105	99	100
Girls' skirts and pants	100	89	102	117	99
Girls' active sportswear	100	97	100	184	92
Girls' accessories	100	19	111	71	102
Children under age 2	**100**	**83**	**102**	**150**	**95**
Infant dresses, outerwear	100	91	101	89	101
Infant underwear	100	73	104	199	91
Infant nightwear, loungewear	100	85	102	98	100
Infant accessories	100	89	101	203	91
Other apparel products and services	**100**	**68**	**104**	**137**	**97**
Watches	100	41	108	101	100
Jewelry	100	40	108	44	105
Men's footwear	100	29	110	253	86
Boys' footwear	100	73	104	142	96
Women's footwear	100	131	96	182	92
Girls' footwear	100	92	101	224	88
TRANSPORTATION	**100**	**33**	**109**	**37**	**106**
New cars	100	–	114	–	110
New trucks	100	–	114	–	109
Used cars	100	–	114	3	109
Used trucks	100	127	96	–	110
Gasoline on trips	100	36	109	51	105

	total consumer units	race		Hispanic origin	
		black	white and other	Hispanic	non-Hispanic
Airline fares	100	81	103	55	104
Local transportation on trips	100	31	110	69	103
Intercity train fares	100	82	102	56	104
Ship fares	100	65	105	99	100
HEALTH CARE	**100**	**15**	**112**	**32**	**106**
Physician's services	100	33	109	62	104
Dental services	100	24	110	40	105
Hospital room	100	–	114	–	110
Care in convalescent or nursing home	100	–	114	0	109
Nonprescription drugs	100	45	107	133	97
ENTERTAINMENT	**100**	**46**	**107**	**74**	**102**
Toys, games, hobbies, and tricycles	100	56	106	76	102
Movie, other admissions, on trips	100	35	109	78	102
Admission to sports events on trips	100	35	109	77	102
Fees for recreational lessons	100	22	111	89	101
Cable service and community antenna	100	137	95	110	99
Color TV, portable, table model	100	24	110	42	105
Musical instruments and accessories	100	8	113	77	102
Athletic gear, game tables, and exercise equipment	100	73	104	87	101
PERSONAL CARE PRODUCTS AND SERVICES	**100**	**55**	**106**	**161**	**94**
Hair care products	100	53	107	445	68
Cosmetics, perfume, bath preparation	100	46	100	131	92
Deodorants, feminine hygiene, misc. personal care	100	100	100	100	100
READING	**100**	**–**	**100**	**50**	**100**
EDUCATION	**100**	**26**	**110**	**47**	**105**
College tuition	100	26	111	41	106
Elementary and high school tuition	100	9	109	45	100
Other school tuition	100	–	100	67	100
Other school expenses including rentals	100	20	100	60	100
College books and supplies	100	30	110	–	110
Miscellaneous school supplies	100	–	120	120	100
ALL OTHER GIFTS	**100**	**98**	**100**	**70**	**102**
Gifts of trip expenses	100	29	110	55	104
Miscellaneous fees, gambling losses	100	–	100	–	100
Legal fees	100	125	100	25	100
Funeral expenses	100	225	82	107	100
Cemetery lots, vaults, maintenance fees	100	100	100	100	100
Accounting fees	100	–	100	50	100

Note: Other races include Asians, Native Americans, and Pacific Islanders. (–) means sample is too small to make a reliable estimate. Categories with annual spending of less than $2.00 for the average household are omitted. Spending on gifts is also included in the product and service categories in other chapters.
Source: Calculations by New Strategist based on the 2000 Consumer Expenditure Survey

Table 6.18 Gifts: Indexed per capita spending by race and Hispanic origin, 2000

(indexed average annual per capita spending of consumer units (CU) on gifts of products and services for non–household members, by race and Hispanic origin of consumer unit reference person, 2000; index definition: an index of 100 is the average for all consumer units; an index of 132 means that spending by consumer units in that group is 32 percent above the average for all consumer units; an index of 68 indicates spending that is 32 percent below the average for all consumer units)

	total consumer units	race		Hispanic origin	
		black	white and other	Hispanic	non-Hispanic
Per capita spending of CU, total	$15,218	$10,427	$15,762	$9,628	$16,062
Per capita spending of CU, index	100	69	104	63	106
Gifts, per capita spending index	100	49	107	56	107
FOOD	100	35	109	46	108
Fresh fruits	100	24	110	75	104
Candy and chewing gum	100	17	111	28	110
Board (including at school)	100	69	104	77	104
Catered affairs	100	10	112	10	113
ALCOHOLIC BEVERAGES	100	62	104	58	106
Beer and ale	100	97	99	56	107
Wine	100	53	106	63	106
Whiskey and other alcoholic beverages	100	43	107	52	107
HOUSING	100	42	107	52	107
Housekeeping supplies	100	32	109	67	105
Miscellaneous household products	100	13	112	76	104
Lawn and garden supplies	100	49	106	83	103
Postage and stationery	100	34	109	50	107
Stationery, stationery supplies, giftwraps	100	30	109	31	110
Postage	100	50	106	134	96
Household textiles	100	18	111	70	105
Bathroom linens	100	43	108	56	107
Bedroom linens	100	–	114	101	101
Appliances and miscellaneous housewares	100	18	111	32	110
Major appliances	100	30	109	79	104
Electric floor cleaning equipment	100	–	114	150	94
Small appliances and miscellaneous housewares	100	14	112	15	112
Glassware	100	16	111	8	113
Nonelectric cookware	100	2	113	14	112
Tableware, nonelectric kitchenware	100	12	112	8	113
Small electric kitchen appliances	100	47	107	43	108
Miscellaneous household equipment	100	26	110	37	109
Infants' equipment	100	38	108	87	103
Outdoor equipment	100	–	114	–	114
Household decorative items	100	35	108	35	109
Indoor plants, fresh flowers	100	31	109	29	110
Computers and computer hardware, nonbusiness use	100	9	112	10	113
Miscellaneous household equipment and parts	100	9	112	22	111
Other housing	100	61	105	58	106
Repair or maintenance services	100	27	110	28	110
Housing while attending school	100	35	108	58	106
Natural gas (renter)	100	119	96	77	103
Electricity (renter)	100	88	101	79	103
Telephone services in home city, excl. mobile phones	100	113	97	85	103

	total consumer units	race		Hispanic origin	
		black	white and other	Hispanic	non-Hispanic
Water, sewerage maintenance (renter)	100	93	100	86	102
Care for elderly, invalids, handicapped	100	94	100	21	111
Day-care centers, nurseries, and preschools	100	82	102	55	107
Housekeeping services	100	17	111	28	110
Gardening, lawn care service	100	50	106	11	112
Repair of miscellaneous household equipment and furnishings	100	–	114	–	114
Bedroom furniture except mattress and springs	100	42	108	21	111
APPAREL AND SERVICES	**100**	**73**	**103**	**88**	**102**
Men and boys, aged 2 or older	**100**	**52**	**106**	**70**	**105**
Men's coats and jackets	100	199	84	251	81
Men's underwear	100	86	101	54	107
Men's accessories	100	15	111	19	111
Men's sweaters and vests	100	78	102	28	110
Men's active sportswear	100	21	111	18	111
Men's shirts	100	31	109	53	107
Men's pants	100	9	112	89	102
Boys' shirts	100	77	102	75	104
Boys' pants	100	79	102	126	97
Women and girls, aged 2 or older	**100**	**95**	**100**	**83**	**103**
Women's coats and jackets	100	114	97	92	102
Women's dresses	100	124	95	81	103
Women's vests and sweaters	100	67	104	26	110
Women's shirts, tops, blouses	100	88	101	93	102
Women's pants	100	99	99	126	97
Women's active sportswear	100	80	102	16	112
Women's sleepwear	100	172	88	116	99
Women's undergarments	100	219	81	19	111
Women's accessories	100	34	109	62	106
Girls' dresses and suits	100	79	102	206	87
Girls' shirts, blouses, sweaters	100	60	105	73	104
Girls' skirts and pants	100	82	102	86	103
Girls' active sportswear	100	90	100	135	96
Girls' accessories	100	18	111	52	107
Children under age 2	**100**	**76**	**102**	**110**	**99**
Infant dresses, outerwear	100	85	101	65	105
Infant underwear	100	68	104	146	95
Infant nightwear, loungewear	100	79	102	72	104
Infant accessories	100	83	101	149	94
Other apparel products and services	**100**	**63**	**104**	**101**	**101**
Watches	100	38	108	74	104
Jewelry	100	37	108	33	110
Men's footwear	100	27	110	186	89
Boys' footwear	100	68	104	104	100
Women's footwear	100	121	96	133	96
Girls' footwear	100	85	101	165	92
TRANSPORTATION	**100**	**31**	**109**	**27**	**110**
New cars	100	–	114	–	114
New trucks	100	–	114	–	114
Used cars	100	–	114	2	114
Used trucks	100	118	96	–	114
Gasoline on trips	100	33	109	38	109

	total consumer units	race		Hispanic origin	
		black	white and other	Hispanic	non-Hispanic
Airline fares	100	75	103	41	109
Local transportation on trips	100	29	110	50	108
Intercity train fares	100	76	102	41	108
Ship fares	100	61	105	73	104
HEALTH CARE	**100**	**14**	**112**	**23**	**111**
Physician's services	100	31	109	46	108
Dental services	100	23	110	30	110
Hospital room	100	–	114	–	114
Care in convalescent or nursing home	100	–	114	0	114
Nonprescription drugs	100	41	107	98	101
ENTERTAINMENT	**100**	**42**	**107**	**54**	**107**
Toys, games, hobbies, and tricycles	100	52	106	56	106
Movie, other admissions, on trips	100	32	109	57	106
Admission to sports events on trips	100	32	109	57	106
Fees for recreational lessons	100	20	111	66	105
Cable service and community antenna	100	126	95	81	103
Color TV, portable, table model	100	22	110	31	110
Musical instruments and accessories	100	8	113	57	106
Athletic gear, game tables, and exercise equipment	100	68	104	64	105
PERSONAL CARE PRODUCTS AND SERVICES	**100**	**50**	**106**	**118**	**98**
Hair care products	100	49	107	327	71
Cosmetics, perfume, bath preparation	100	43	100	96	96
Deodorants, feminine hygiene, misc. personal care	100	93	100	74	104
READING	**100**	**–**	**100**	**37**	**104**
EDUCATION	**100**	**24**	**110**	**35**	**110**
College tuition	100	24	111	30	111
Elementary and high school tuition	100	8	109	33	104
Other school tuition	100	–	100	49	104
Other school expenses including rentals	100	19	100	44	104
College books and supplies	100	28	110	–	115
Miscellaneous school supplies	100	–	120	88	104
ALL OTHER GIFTS	**100**	**91**	**100**	**51**	**107**
Gifts of trip expenses	100	26	110	41	108
Miscellaneous fees, gambling losses	100	–	100	–	104
Legal fees	100	116	100	18	104
Funeral expenses	100	208	82	79	104
Cemetery lots, vaults, maintenance fees	100	93	100	74	104
Accounting fees	100	–	100	37	104

Note: Per capita indexes account for household size and show how much each person in a particular household demographic segment spends relative to a person in the average household. Other races include Asians, Native Americans, and Pacific Islanders. (–) means sample is too small to make a reliable estimate. Categories with annual spending of less than $2.00 for the average household are omitted. Spending on gifts is also included in the product and service categories in other chapters.
Source: Calculations by New Strategist based on the 2000 Consumer Expenditure Survey

Table 6.19 Gifts: Total spending by race and Hispanic origin, 2000

(total annual spending on gifts of products and services for non-household members, by consumer unit race and Hispanic origin groups, 2000; numbers in thousands)

	total consumer units	race black	race white and other	Hispanic origin Hispanic	Hispanic origin non-Hispanic
Number of consumer units	109,367	13,230	96,137	9,473	99,894
Total spending of all consumer units	$4,160,831,424	$372,454,135	$3,788,393,849	$310,098,181	$3,850,804,816
Gifts, total spending	118,459,772	7,556,711	110,904,605	7,817,877	110,645,591
FOOD	**$7,665,533**	**$345,568**	**$7,319,871**	**$412,644**	**$7,250,307**
Fresh fruits	500,901	15,744	485,492	44,049	457,515
Candy and chewing gum	1,367,088	29,900	1,337,266	45,565	1,320,599
Board (including at school)	2,210,307	197,921	2,012,147	199,217	2,010,866
Catered affairs	1,705,032	22,623	1,682,398	20,556	1,685,212
ALCOHOLIC BEVERAGES	**1,584,728**	**129,125**	**1,455,514**	**107,708**	**1,476,433**
Beer and ale	398,096	50,539	348,016	26,051	372,605
Wine	739,321	51,332	687,380	54,470	684,274
Whiskey and other alcoholic beverages	407,939	23,153	384,548	25,198	381,595
HOUSING	**31,836,734**	**1,758,664**	**30,079,345**	**1,965,648**	**29,864,310**
Housekeeping supplies	**4,276,250**	**180,325**	**4,095,436**	**338,565**	**3,936,823**
Miscellaneous household products	800,566	13,759	786,401	71,237	729,226
Lawn and garden supplies	336,850	21,433	315,329	32,777	303,678
Postage and stationery	2,728,707	120,261	2,608,197	160,757	2,566,277
Stationery, stationery supplies, giftwraps	2,217,963	87,318	2,130,396	81,657	2,133,736
Postage	499,807	32,943	466,264	79,100	420,554
Household textiles	**1,443,644**	**33,737**	**1,410,330**	**119,455**	**1,324,594**
Bathroom linens	305,134	17,067	288,411	20,083	285,697
Bedroom linens	749,164	–	748,907	89,141	660,299
Appliances and miscellaneous housewares	**3,077,587**	**73,030**	**3,004,281**	**117,560**	**2,957,861**
Major appliances	832,283	32,414	799,860	77,015	756,198
Electric floor cleaning equipment	329,195	–	329,750	58,259	271,712
Small appliances and miscellaneous housewares	2,245,305	40,616	2,204,421	40,544	2,201,664
Glassware	393,721	8,070	385,509	3,884	389,587
Nonelectric cookware	400,283	1,191	398,969	6,442	393,582
Tableware, nonelectric kitchenware	474,653	7,673	467,226	4,263	469,502
Small electric kitchen appliances	293,104	17,993	274,952	14,873	278,704
Miscellaneous household equipment	**7,689,594**	**257,059**	**7,432,351**	**335,818**	**7,351,199**
Infants' equipment	297,478	14,950	282,643	30,503	267,716
Outdoor equipment	312,790	–	313,407	–	312,668
Household decorative items	2,989,000	138,518	2,850,462	122,391	2,863,961
Indoor plants, fresh flowers	1,754,247	70,384	1,684,320	59,869	1,694,202
Computers and computer hardware, nonbusiness use	981,022	11,775	969,061	11,178	969,971
Miscellaneous household equipment and parts	276,699	3,308	273,029	7,294	268,715
Other housing	**15,350,752**	**1,214,514**	**14,135,984**	**1,054,155**	**14,294,831**
Repair or maintenance services	409,033	14,421	395,123	13,262	395,580
Housing while attending school	4,628,411	214,591	4,413,650	317,535	4,310,426
Natural gas (renter)	340,131	52,920	287,450	30,882	308,672
Electricity (renter)	1,452,394	167,624	1,284,390	135,274	1,316,603
Telephone services in home city, excl. mobile phones	1,491,766	221,073	1,269,970	149,958	1,341,576

	total consumer units	race		Hispanic origin	
		black	white and other	Hispanic	non-Hispanic
Water, sewerage maintenance (renter)	$292,010	$35,589	$255,724	$29,650	$261,722
Care for elderly, invalids, handicapped	229,671	28,312	200,926	5,589	223,763
Day-care centers, nurseries, and preschools	2,347,016	252,164	2,094,825	151,379	2,195,670
Housekeeping services	376,222	8,203	367,243	12,410	363,614
Gardening, lawn care service	343,412	22,623	321,098	4,452	338,641
Repair of miscellaneous household equipment and furnishings	850,875	–	850,812	–	849,099
Bedroom furniture except mattress and springs	225,296	12,436	213,424	5,589	219,767
APPAREL AND SERVICES	**26,712,890**	**2,561,196**	**24,151,537**	**2,760,527**	**23,963,572**
Men and boys, aged 2 or older	**7,387,741**	**505,783**	**6,882,448**	**611,766**	**6,774,811**
Men's coats and jackets	360,911	93,801	267,261	106,666	255,729
Men's underwear	229,671	25,666	203,810	14,494	214,772
Men's accessories	371,848	7,409	364,359	8,431	362,615
Men's sweaters and vests	297,478	30,429	267,261	9,852	287,695
Men's active sportswear	475,746	13,230	462,419	10,326	464,507
Men's shirts	2,271,553	92,213	2,179,426	140,485	2,130,739
Men's pants	777,599	9,261	768,135	81,278	696,261
Boys' shirts	608,081	61,255	547,020	53,901	554,412
Boys' pants	310,602	31,884	277,836	46,228	263,720
Women and girls, aged 2 or older	**9,326,818**	**1,151,539**	**8,174,529**	**911,113**	**8,418,067**
Women's coats and jackets	390,440	58,080	331,673	42,439	347,631
Women's dresses	1,161,478	188,528	972,906	110,171	1,051,884
Women's vests and sweaters	968,992	85,069	883,499	29,935	938,005
Women's shirts, tops, blouses	1,158,197	133,888	1,024,820	126,465	1,031,905
Women's pants	649,640	84,407	565,286	96,435	554,412
Women's active sportswear	379,503	39,690	339,364	7,199	371,606
Women's sleepwear	672,607	150,822	521,063	92,078	581,383
Women's undergarments	294,197	84,275	209,579	6,726	286,696
Women's accessories	456,060	19,977	436,462	33,250	422,552
Girls' dresses and suits	440,749	45,247	395,123	106,855	335,644
Girls' shirts, blouses, sweaters	675,888	52,920	622,968	57,880	618,344
Girls' skirts and pants	304,040	32,678	272,068	30,787	273,710
Girls' active sportswear	229,671	26,989	202,849	36,566	193,794
Girls' accessories	238,420	5,557	232,652	14,683	222,764
Children under age 2	**4,452,331**	**444,396**	**4,007,952**	**579,179**	**3,877,885**
Infant dresses, outerwear	1,586,915	175,562	1,411,291	121,918	1,464,446
Infant underwear	1,998,135	177,150	1,821,796	343,680	1,658,240
Infant nightwear, loungewear	269,043	27,783	240,343	22,735	245,739
Infant accessories	439,655	47,496	392,239	77,205	363,614
Other apparel products and services	**5,546,001**	**459,478**	**5,086,609**	**658,563**	**4,892,808**
Watches	375,129	18,787	356,668	32,682	342,636
Jewelry	1,842,834	89,699	1,753,539	70,953	1,772,120
Men's footwear	947,118	33,207	914,263	207,364	743,211
Boys' footwear	514,025	45,379	468,187	63,090	451,521
Women's footwear	1,100,232	173,710	925,799	172,977	928,015
Girls' footwear	569,802	63,636	506,642	110,739	460,511
TRANSPORTATION	**7,685,219**	**309,714**	**7,375,631**	**243,456**	**7,443,102**
New cars	664,951	–	665,268	–	665,294
New trucks	1,535,513	–	1,535,308	–	1,535,371
Used cars	1,369,275	–	1,369,952	3,979	1,365,551
Used trucks	308,415	47,363	261,493	–	308,672
Gasoline on trips	1,372,556	59,006	1,313,231	60,817	1,311,608

	total consumer units	race		Hispanic origin	
		black	white and other	Hispanic	non-Hispanic
Airline fares	$930,713	$90,758	$840,237	$44,523	$886,060
Local transportation on trips	232,952	8,864	224,961	13,831	219,767
Intercity train fares	243,888	24,079	219,192	11,747	231,754
Ship fares	325,914	25,799	299,947	27,851	297,684
HEALTH CARE	**4,164,695**	**74,088**	**4,090,629**	**114,529**	**4,050,702**
Physician's services	290,916	11,775	279,759	15,630	275,707
Dental services	381,691	11,246	370,127	13,357	367,610
Hospital room	298,572	–	298,986	–	298,683
Care in convalescent or nursing home	2,014,540	–	2,015,032	474	2,013,863
Nonprescription drugs	235,139	12,701	222,076	27,093	207,780
ENTERTAINMENT	**10,254,250**	**568,758**	**9,685,803**	**654,490**	**9,598,814**
Toys, games, hobbies, and tricycles	3,235,076	219,486	3,015,818	214,279	3,020,795
Movie, other admissions, on trips	1,002,895	42,336	960,409	67,448	936,007
Admission to sports events on trips	334,663	14,156	320,136	22,451	311,669
Fees for recreational lessons	689,012	18,390	671,036	53,333	636,325
Cable service and community antenna	508,557	84,011	424,926	48,407	460,511
Color TV, portable, table model	229,671	6,747	222,076	8,431	220,766
Musical instruments and accessories	253,731	2,514	251,879	16,957	236,749
Athletic gear, game tables, and exercise equipment	1,035,705	91,816	944,065	78,152	957,983
PERSONAL CARE PRODUCTS AND SERVICES	**2,099,846**	**138,518**	**1,962,156**	**292,242**	**1,810,079**
Hair care products	234,045	14,950	219,192	90,183	144,846
Cosmetics, perfume, bath preparation	1,421,771	79,380	1,249,781	161,041	1,198,728
Deodorants, feminine hygiene, misc. personal care	218,734	26,460	192,274	18,946	199,788
READING	**218,734**	**–**	**192,274**	**9,473**	**199,788**
EDUCATION	**16,514,417**	**515,970**	**15,958,742**	**672,583**	**15,883,146**
College tuition	12,467,838	396,900	12,113,262	445,231	12,087,174
Elementary and high school tuition	1,203,037	13,230	1,153,644	47,365	1,098,834
Other school tuition	328,101	–	288,411	18,946	299,682
Other school expenses including rentals	546,835	13,230	480,685	28,419	499,470
College books and supplies	1,093,670	39,690	1,057,507	–	1,098,834
Miscellaneous school supplies	546,835	–	576,822	56,838	499,470
ALL OTHER GIFTS	**9,733,663**	**1,151,010**	**8,556,193**	**587,326**	**9,090,354**
Gifts of trip expenses	5,358,983	185,220	5,191,398	255,771	5,094,594
Miscellaneous fees, gambling losses	218,734	–	192,274	–	199,788
Legal fees	437,468	66,150	384,548	9,473	399,576
Funeral expenses	3,062,276	833,490	2,211,151	284,190	2,797,032
Cemetery lots, vaults, maintenance fees	328,101	39,690	288,411	28,419	299,682
Accounting fees	218,734	–	192,274	9,473	199,788

Note: Other races include Asians, Native Americans, and Pacific Islanders. Numbers may not add to total because of rounding. (–) means sample is too small to make a reliable estimate. Expenditures for items in a given category may not add to category total because categories with annual spending of less than $2.00 for the average household are omitted. Spending on gifts is also included in the product and service categories in other chapters.
Source: Calculations by New Strategist based on the 2000 Consumer Expenditure Survey

Table 6.20 Gifts: Market shares by race and Hispanic origin, 2000

(percentage of total annual spending on gifts of products and services for non-household members accounted for by consumer unit race and Hispanic origin groups, 2000)

	total consumer units	race black	race white and other	Hispanic origin Hispanic	Hispanic origin non-Hispanic
Share of total consumer units	100.0%	12.1%	87.9%	8.7%	91.3%
Share of total before-tax income	100.0	8.8	91.1	6.8	93.4
Share of total spending	100.0	9.0	91.0	7.5	92.5
Share of gifts spending	100.0	6.4	93.6	6.6	93.4
FOOD	100.0%	4.5%	95.5%	5.4%	94.6%
Fresh fruits	100.0	3.1	96.9	8.8	91.3
Candy and chewing gum	100.0	2.2	97.8	3.3	96.6
Board (including at school)	100.0	9.0	91.0	9.0	91.0
Catered affairs	100.0	1.3	98.7	1.2	98.8
ALCOHOLIC BEVERAGES	100.0	8.1	91.8	6.8	93.2
Beer and ale	100.0	12.7	87.4	6.5	93.6
Wine	100.0	6.9	93.0	7.4	92.6
Whiskey and other alcoholic beverages	100.0	5.7	94.3	6.2	93.5
HOUSING	100.0	5.5	94.5	6.2	93.8
Housekeeping supplies	100.0	4.2	95.8	7.9	92.1
Miscellaneous household products	100.0	1.7	98.2	8.9	91.1
Lawn and garden supplies	100.0	6.4	93.6	9.7	90.2
Postage and stationery	100.0	4.4	95.6	5.9	94.0
Stationery, stationery supplies, giftwraps	100.0	3.9	96.1	3.7	96.2
Postage	100.0	6.6	93.3	15.8	84.1
Household textiles	100.0	2.3	97.7	8.3	91.8
Bathroom linens	100.0	5.6	94.5	6.6	93.6
Bedroom linens	100.0	–	100.0	11.9	88.1
Appliances and miscellaneous housewares	100.0	2.4	97.6	3.8	96.1
Major appliances	100.0	3.9	96.1	9.3	90.9
Electric floor cleaning equipment	100.0	–	100.0	17.7	82.5
Small appliances and miscellaneous housewares	100.0	1.8	98.2	1.8	98.1
Glassware	100.0	2.0	97.9	1.0	98.9
Nonelectric cookware	100.0	0.3	99.7	1.6	98.3
Tableware, nonelectric kitchenware	100.0	1.6	98.4	0.9	98.9
Small electric kitchen appliances	100.0	6.1	93.8	5.1	95.1
Miscellaneous household equipment	100.0	3.3	96.7	4.4	95.6
Infants' equipment	100.0	5.0	95.0	10.3	90.0
Outdoor equipment	100.0	–	100.0	–	100.0
Household decorative items	100.0	4.6	95.4	4.1	95.8
Indoor plants, fresh flowers	100.0	4.0	96.0	3.4	96.6
Computers and computer hardware, nonbusiness use	100.0	1.2	98.8	1.1	98.9
Miscellaneous household equipment and parts	100.0	1.2	98.7	2.6	97.1
Other housing	100.0	7.9	92.1	6.9	93.1
Repair or maintenance services	100.0	3.5	96.6	3.2	96.7
Housing while attending school	100.0	4.6	95.4	6.9	93.1
Natural gas (renter)	100.0	15.6	84.5	9.1	90.8
Electricity (renter)	100.0	11.5	88.4	9.3	90.7
Telephone services in home city, excl. mobile phones	100.0	14.8	85.1	10.1	89.9

	total consumer units	race		Hispanic origin	
		black	white and other	Hispanic	non-Hispanic
Water, sewerage maintenance (renter)	100.0%	12.2%	87.6%	10.2%	89.6%
Care for elderly, invalids, handicapped	100.0	12.3	87.5	2.4	97.4
Day-care centers, nurseries, and preschools	100.0	10.7	89.3	6.4	93.6
Housekeeping services	100.0	2.2	97.6	3.3	96.6
Gardening, lawn care service	100.0	6.6	93.5	1.3	98.6
Repair of miscellaneous household equipment and furnishings	100.0	–	100.0	–	99.8
Bedroom furniture except mattress and springs	100.0	5.5	94.7	2.5	97.5
APPAREL AND SERVICES	**100.0**	**9.6**	**90.4**	**10.3**	**89.7**
Men and boys, aged 2 or older	**100.0**	**6.8**	**93.2**	**8.3**	**91.7**
Men's coats and jackets	100.0	26.0	74.1	29.6	70.9
Men's underwear	100.0	11.2	88.7	6.3	93.5
Men's accessories	100.0	2.0	98.0	2.3	97.5
Men's sweaters and vests	100.0	10.2	89.8	3.3	96.7
Men's active sportswear	100.0	2.8	97.2	2.2	97.6
Men's shirts	100.0	4.1	95.9	6.2	93.8
Men's pants	100.0	1.2	98.8	10.5	89.5
Boys' shirts	100.0	10.1	90.0	8.9	91.2
Boys' pants	100.0	10.3	89.5	14.9	84.9
Women and girls, aged 2 or older	**100.0**	**12.3**	**87.6**	**9.8**	**90.3**
Women's coats and jackets	100.0	14.9	84.9	10.9	89.0
Women's dresses	100.0	16.2	83.8	9.5	90.6
Women's vests and sweaters	100.0	8.8	91.2	3.1	96.8
Women's shirts, tops, blouses	100.0	11.6	88.5	10.9	89.1
Women's pants	100.0	13.0	87.0	14.8	85.3
Women's active sportswear	100.0	10.5	89.4	1.9	97.9
Women's sleepwear	100.0	22.4	77.5	13.7	86.4
Women's undergarments	100.0	28.6	71.2	2.3	97.5
Women's accessories	100.0	4.4	95.7	7.3	92.7
Girls' dresses and suits	100.0	10.3	89.6	24.2	76.2
Girls' shirts, blouses, sweaters	100.0	7.8	92.2	8.6	91.5
Girls' skirts and pants	100.0	10.7	89.5	10.1	90.0
Girls' active sportswear	100.0	11.8	88.3	15.9	84.4
Girls' accessories	100.0	2.3	97.6	6.2	93.4
Children under age 2	**100.0**	**10.0**	**90.0**	**13.0**	**87.1**
Infant dresses, outerwear	100.0	11.1	88.9	7.7	92.3
Infant underwear	100.0	8.9	91.2	17.2	83.0
Infant nightwear, loungewear	100.0	10.3	89.3	8.5	91.3
Infant accessories	100.0	10.8	89.2	17.6	82.7
Other apparel products and services	**100.0**	**8.3**	**91.7**	**11.9**	**88.2**
Watches	100.0	5.0	95.1	8.7	91.3
Jewelry	100.0	4.9	95.2	3.9	96.2
Men's footwear	100.0	3.5	96.5	21.9	78.5
Boys' footwear	100.0	8.8	91.1	12.3	87.8
Women's footwear	100.0	15.8	84.1	15.7	84.3
Girls' footwear	100.0	11.2	88.9	19.4	80.8
TRANSPORTATION	**100.0**	**4.0**	**96.0**	**3.2**	**96.8**
New cars	100.0	–	100.0	–	100.0
New trucks	100.0	–	100.0	–	100.0
Used cars	100.0	–	100.0	0.3	99.7
Used trucks	100.0	15.4	84.8	–	100.0
Gasoline on trips	100.0	4.3	95.7	4.4	95.6

	total consumer units	race		Hispanic origin	
		black	white and other	Hispanic	non-Hispanic
Airline fares	100.0%	9.8%	90.3%	4.8%	95.2%
Local transportation on trips	100.0	3.8	96.6	5.9	94.3
Intercity train fares	100.0	9.9	89.9	4.8	95.0
Ship fares	100.0	7.9	92.0	8.5	91.3
HEALTH CARE	**100.0**	**1.8**	**98.2**	**2.7**	**97.3**
Physician's services	100.0	4.0	96.2	5.4	94.8
Dental services	100.0	2.9	97.0	3.5	96.3
Hospital room	100.0	–	100.0	–	100.0
Care in convalescent or nursing home	100.0	–	100.0	–	100.0
Nonprescription drugs	100.0	5.4	94.4	11.5	88.4
ENTERTAINMENT	**100.0**	**5.5**	**94.5**	**6.4**	**93.6**
Toys, games, hobbies, and tricycles	100.0	6.8	93.2	6.6	93.4
Movie, other admissions, on trips	100.0	4.2	95.8	6.7	93.3
Admission to sports events on trips	100.0	4.2	95.7	6.7	93.1
Fees for recreational lessons	100.0	2.7	97.4	7.7	92.4
Cable service and community antenna	100.0	16.5	83.6	9.5	90.6
Color TV, portable, table model	100.0	2.9	96.7	3.7	96.1
Musical instruments and accessories	100.0	1.0	99.3	6.7	93.3
Athletic gear, game tables, and exercise equipment	100.0	8.9	91.2	7.5	92.5
PERSONAL CARE PRODUCTS AND SERVICES	**100.0**	**6.6**	**93.4**	**13.9**	**86.2**
Hair care products	100.0	6.4	93.7	38.5	61.9
Cosmetics, perfume, bath preparation	100.0	5.6	87.9	11.3	84.3
Deodorants, feminine hygiene, misc. personal care	100.0	12.1	87.9	8.7	91.3
READING	**100.0**	**–**	**87.9**	**4.3**	**91.3**
EDUCATION	**100.0**	**3.1**	**96.6**	**4.1**	**96.2**
College tuition	100.0	3.2	97.2	3.6	96.9
Elementary and high school tuition	100.0	1.1	95.9	3.9	91.3
Other school tuition	100.0	–	87.9	5.8	91.3
Other school expenses including rentals	100.0	2.4	87.9	5.2	91.3
College books and supplies	100.0	3.6	96.7	–	100.0
Miscellaneous school supplies	100.0	–	100.0	10.4	91.3
ALL OTHER GIFTS	**100.0**	**11.8**	**87.9**	**6.0**	**93.4**
Gifts of trip expenses	100.0	3.5	96.9	4.8	95.1
Miscellaneous fees, gambling losses	100.0	–	87.9	–	91.3
Legal fees	100.0	15.1	87.9	2.2	91.3
Funeral expenses	100.0	27.2	72.2	9.3	91.3
Cemetery lots, vaults, maintenance fees	100.0	12.1	87.9	8.7	91.3
Accounting fees	100.0	–	87.9	4.3	91.3

Note: Other races include Asians, Native Americans, and Pacific Islanders. Numbers may not add to total because of rounding. (–) means sample is too small to make a reliable estimate. Expenditures for items in a given category may not add to category total because categories with annual spending of less than $2.00 for the average household are omitted. Spending on gifts is also included in the product and service categories in other chapters.
Source: Calculations by New Strategist based on the 2000 Consumer Expenditure Survey

Table 6.21 Gifts: Average spending by region, 2000

(average annual spending of consumer units (CU) on gifts of products and services for non–household members, by region in which consumer unit lives, 2000)

	total consumer units	Northeast	Midwest	South	West
Number of consumer units (in thousands, add 000)	109,367	20,994	25,717	38,245	24,410
Average number of persons per CU	2.5	2.5	2.5	2.5	2.6
Average before-tax income of CU	$44,649.00	$47,439.00	$44,377.00	$41,984.00	$46,670.00
Average spending of CU, total	38,044.67	38,901.91	39,212.70	34,707.07	41,328.19
Gifts, average spending	1,083.14	1,095.67	1,290.51	908.03	1,130.74
FOOD	$70.09	$65.54	$103.19	$49.47	$71.69
Fresh fruits	4.58	6.62	5.46	3.10	4.17
Candy and chewing gum	12.50	19.14	17.56	8.56	7.39
Board (including at school)	20.21	20.32	29.15	18.51	13.37
Catered affairs	15.59	7.97	31.92	6.09	19.85
ALCOHOLIC BEVERAGES	14.49	13.28	19.22	12.69	13.47
Beer and ale	3.64	2.57	6.28	2.21	4.16
Wine	6.76	6.89	7.12	6.32	6.96
Whiskey and other alcoholic beverages	3.73	3.40	5.40	3.99	1.81
HOUSING	291.10	277.46	348.62	269.57	276.07
Housekeeping supplies	39.10	49.30	44.49	28.18	41.67
Miscellaneous household products	7.32	12.94	7.38	3.43	8.37
Lawn and garden supplies	3.08	7.37	1.79	2.07	2.12
Postage and stationery	24.95	25.03	32.47	19.44	25.81
Stationery, stationery supplies, giftwraps	20.28	20.60	27.61	15.18	20.44
Postage	4.57	4.25	4.69	4.17	5.37
Household textiles	13.20	19.50	14.12	9.16	12.97
Bathroom linens	2.79	1.56	2.48	2.72	4.38
Bedroom linens	6.85	14.85	5.64	3.73	5.82
Appliances and miscellaneous housewares	28.14	24.70	40.95	26.15	20.83
Major appliances	7.61	5.01	9.86	9.50	4.51
Electric floor cleaning equipment	3.01	–	3.63	6.12	0.08
Small appliances and miscellaneous housewares	20.53	19.68	31.09	16.64	16.33
Glassware	3.60	1.29	7.63	3.18	2.11
Nonelectric cookware	3.66	5.12	5.87	1.99	2.68
Tableware, nonelectric kitchenware	4.34	2.21	7.01	4.17	3.74
Small electric kitchen appliances	2.68	2.85	3.39	1.98	2.87
Miscellaneous household equipment	70.31	63.38	94.69	56.09	73.39
Infants' equipment	2.72	2.10	5.74	1.76	1.63
Outdoor equipment	2.86	4.30	2.72	3.42	0.78
Household decorative items	27.33	19.05	43.33	22.41	25.90
Indoor plants, fresh flowers	16.04	14.55	20.81	13.12	16.89
Computers and computer hardware, nonbusiness use	8.97	8.37	9.43	6.48	12.88
Miscellaneous household equipment and parts	2.53	4.85	2.55	0.80	3.17
Other housing	140.36	120.59	154.36	149.99	127.20
Repair or maintenance services	3.74	1.82	8.11	1.10	4.92
Housing while attending school	42.32	40.77	61.47	36.65	32.33
Natural gas (renter)	3.11	2.77	5.30	2.69	1.75
Electricity (renter)	13.28	8.33	11.73	21.03	7.01
Telephone services in home city, excl. mobile phones	13.64	12.52	13.34	16.16	10.95

	total consumer units	Northeast	Midwest	South	West
Water, sewerage maintenance (renter)	$2.67	$1.02	$2.94	$3.85	$1.94
Care for elderly, invalids, handicapped	2.10	4.13	3.27	1.20	0.53
Day-care centers, nurseries, and preschools	21.46	15.98	25.52	19.02	25.71
Housekeeping services	3.44	1.84	1.46	1.90	9.31
Gardening, lawn care service	3.14	1.66	1.05	1.45	9.28
Repair of miscellaneous household equipment and furnishings	7.78	2.14	–	20.87	–
Bedroom furniture except mattress and springs	2.06	1.75	3.82	1.89	0.75
APPAREL AND SERVICES	**244.25**	**269.21**	**257.73**	**206.11**	**269.50**
Men and boys, aged 2 or older	**67.55**	**69.22**	**77.26**	**49.01**	**86.10**
Men's coats and jackets	3.30	2.53	4.93	2.89	2.95
Men's underwear	2.10	1.73	2.93	1.43	2.65
Men's accessories	3.40	2.70	5.44	2.61	3.14
Men's sweaters and vests	2.72	4.07	3.67	1.83	1.96
Men's active sportswear	4.35	5.07	2.21	5.61	3.92
Men's shirts	20.77	16.74	25.50	10.33	36.43
Men's pants	7.11	7.27	8.38	4.42	9.97
Boys' shirts	5.56	5.46	7.76	3.39	6.86
Boys' pants	2.84	3.34	1.99	2.98	3.07
Women and girls, aged 2 or older	**85.28**	**103.15**	**85.79**	**72.07**	**89.86**
Women's coats and jackets	3.57	8.07	3.83	0.22	4.57
Women's dresses	10.62	6.99	4.51	14.00	14.99
Women's vests and sweaters	8.86	12.41	12.00	3.18	11.46
Women's shirts, tops, blouses	10.59	11.05	15.72	7.66	9.45
Women's pants	5.94	10.90	3.50	4.85	5.73
Women's active sportswear	3.47	3.51	3.61	4.45	1.66
Women's sleepwear	6.15	9.45	4.86	4.67	6.87
Women's undergarments	2.69	2.59	2.95	3.26	1.58
Women's accessories	4.17	3.81	6.10	1.97	6.02
Girls' dresses and suits	4.03	5.63	3.60	3.99	3.08
Girls' shirts, blouses, sweaters	6.18	5.74	7.30	7.43	3.36
Girls' skirts and pants	2.78	3.71	2.09	2.71	2.83
Girls' active sportswear	2.10	1.48	2.91	2.50	1.18
Girls' accessories	2.18	3.83	2.20	1.70	1.40
Children under age 2	**40.71**	**49.45**	**42.23**	**37.32**	**36.73**
Infant dresses, outerwear	14.51	16.77	16.14	14.07	11.53
Infant underwear	18.27	22.63	17.38	16.73	17.71
Infant nightwear, loungewear	2.46	3.03	2.99	1.69	2.60
Infant accessories	4.02	4.33	4.62	3.76	3.52
Other apparel products and services	**50.71**	**47.39**	**52.45**	**47.71**	**56.82**
Watches	3.43	3.01	4.20	2.44	4.53
Jewelry	16.85	21.87	14.33	14.59	18.72
Men's footwear	8.66	5.27	7.34	8.17	14.03
Boys' footwear	4.70	2.37	9.43	3.32	4.02
Women's footwear	10.06	10.94	9.53	11.54	7.38
Girls' footwear	5.21	3.53	4.69	6.28	5.58
TRANSPORTATION	**70.27**	**59.82**	**73.60**	**49.02**	**109.05**
New cars	6.08	–	18.00	5.29	–
New trucks	14.04	31.13	–	–	36.12
Used cars	12.52	2.80	9.73	18.06	15.15
Used trucks	2.82	–	–	2.45	8.80
Gasoline on trips	12.55	7.47	15.89	7.64	21.08

	total consumer units	Northeast	Midwest	South	West
Airline fares	$8.51	$5.89	$13.03	$5.37	$10.92
Local transportation on trips	2.13	2.59	2.63	0.87	3.21
Intercity train fares	2.23	1.99	3.43	1.21	2.75
Ship fares	2.98	2.09	4.71	1.87	3.66
HEALTH CARE	**38.08**	**16.73**	**69.33**	**40.49**	**19.63**
Physician's services	2.66	0.53	2.92	2.46	4.55
Dental services	3.49	0.67	5.51	3.82	3.26
Hospital room	2.73	–	3.37	5.38	0.28
Care in convalescent or nursing home	18.42	2.31	47.97	16.55	4.07
Nonprescription drugs	2.15	3.51	1.02	2.62	1.33
ENTERTAINMENT	**93.76**	**88.17**	**109.34**	**84.64**	**96.70**
Toys, games, hobbies, and tricycles	29.58	31.85	38.91	23.40	27.48
Movie, other admissions, on trips	9.17	9.87	10.78	4.53	14.16
Admission to sports events on trips	3.06	3.29	3.59	1.51	4.72
Fees for recreational lessons	6.30	5.02	5.16	7.75	6.33
Cable service and community antenna	4.65	4.31	3.05	6.78	3.31
Color TV, portable, table model	2.10	2.96	2.66	1.75	1.30
Musical instruments and accessories	2.32	0.20	3.50	2.93	1.95
Athletic gear, game tables, and exercise equipment	9.47	11.09	6.44	7.27	14.80
PERSONAL CARE PRODUCTS AND SERVICES	**19.20**	**14.12**	**24.29**	**15.37**	**24.70**
Hair care products	2.14	0.89	2.05	2.55	2.73
Cosmetics, perfume, bath preparation	13.00	11.00	16.00	8.00	17.00
Deodorants, feminine hygiene, misc. personal care	2.00	1.00	3.00	2.00	1.00
READING	**2.00**	**2.00**	**2.00**	**1.00**	**2.00**
EDUCATION	**151.00**	**193.00**	**183.00**	**117.00**	**135.00**
College tuition	114.00	164.00	148.00	76.00	96.00
Elementary and high school tuition	11.00	8.00	6.00	16.00	11.00
Other school tuition	3.00	2.00	2.00	2.00	6.00
Other school expenses including rentals	5.00	2.00	5.00	5.00	7.00
College books and supplies	10.00	13.00	13.00	9.00	7.00
Miscellaneous school supplies	5.00	3.00	6.00	5.00	7.00
ALL OTHER GIFTS	**89.00**	**96.00**	**100.00**	**63.00**	**112.00**
Gifts of trip expenses	49.00	47.00	58.00	31.00	68.00
Miscellaneous fees, gambling losses	2.00	2.00	3.00	0.00	2.00
Legal fees	4.00	2.00	4.00	6.00	4.00
Funeral expenses	28.00	39.00	27.00	23.00	28.00
Cemetery lots, vaults, maintenance fees	3.00	4.00	3.00	2.00	3.00
Accounting fees	2.00	1.00	1.00	1.00	5.00

Note: (–) means sample is too small to make a reliable estimate. Expenditures for items in a given category may not add to category total because categories with annual spending of less than $2.00 for the average household are omitted. Spending on gifts is also included in the product and service categories in other chapters.
Source: Bureau of Labor Statistics, unpublished tables from the 2000 Consumer Expenditure Survey

Table 6.22 Gifts: Indexed spending by region, 2000

(indexed average annual spending of consumer units (CU) on gifts of products and services for non–household members, by region in which consumer unit lives, 2000; index definition: an index of 100 is the average for all consumer units; an index of 132 means that spending by consumer units in that group is 32 percent above the average for all consumer units; an index of 68 indicates spending that is 32 percent below the average for all consumer units)

	total consumer units	Northeast	Midwest	South	West
Average spending of CU, total	$38,045	$38,902	$39,213	$34,707	$41,328
Average spending of CU, index	100	102	103	91	109
Gifts, spending index	100	101	119	84	104
FOOD	100	94	147	71	102
Fresh fruits	100	145	119	68	91
Candy and chewing gum	100	153	140	68	59
Board (including at school)	100	101	144	92	66
Catered affairs	100	51	205	39	127
ALCOHOLIC BEVERAGES	100	92	133	88	93
Beer and ale	100	71	173	61	114
Wine	100	102	105	93	103
Whiskey and other alcoholic beverages	100	91	145	107	49
HOUSING	100	95	120	93	95
Housekeeping supplies	100	126	114	72	107
Miscellaneous household products	100	177	101	47	114
Lawn and garden supplies	100	239	58	67	69
Postage and stationery	100	100	130	78	103
Stationery, stationery supplies, giftwraps	100	102	136	75	101
Postage	100	93	103	91	118
Household textiles	100	148	107	69	98
Bathroom linens	100	56	89	97	157
Bedroom linens	100	217	82	54	85
Appliances and miscellaneous housewares	100	88	146	93	74
Major appliances	100	66	130	125	59
Electric floor cleaning equipment	100	–	121	203	3
Small appliances and miscellaneous housewares	100	96	151	81	80
Glassware	100	36	212	88	59
Nonelectric cookware	100	140	160	54	73
Tableware, nonelectric kitchenware	100	51	162	96	86
Small electric kitchen appliances	100	106	126	74	107
Miscellaneous household equipment	100	90	135	80	104
Infants' equipment	100	77	211	65	60
Outdoor equipment	100	150	95	120	27
Household decorative items	100	70	159	82	95
Indoor plants, fresh flowers	100	91	130	82	105
Computers and computer hardware, nonbusiness use	100	93	105	72	144
Miscellaneous household equipment and parts	100	192	101	32	125
Other housing	100	86	110	107	91
Repair or maintenance services	100	49	217	29	132
Housing while attending school	100	96	145	87	76
Natural gas (renter)	100	89	170	86	56
Electricity (renter)	100	63	88	158	53
Telephone services in home city, excl. mobile phones	100	92	98	118	80

	total consumer units	Northeast	Midwest	South	West
Water, sewerage maintenance (renter)	100	38	110	144	73
Care for elderly, invalids, handicapped	100	197	156	57	25
Day-care centers, nurseries, and preschools	100	74	119	89	120
Housekeeping services	100	53	42	55	271
Gardening, lawn care service	100	53	33	46	296
Repair of miscellaneous household equipment and furnishings	100	28	–	268	–
Bedroom furniture except mattress and springs	100	85	185	92	36
APPAREL AND SERVICES	**100**	**110**	**106**	**84**	**110**
Men and boys, aged 2 or older	**100**	**102**	**114**	**73**	**127**
Men's coats and jackets	100	77	149	88	89
Men's underwear	100	82	140	68	126
Men's accessories	100	79	160	77	92
Men's sweaters and vests	100	150	135	67	72
Men's active sportswear	100	117	51	129	90
Men's shirts	100	81	123	50	175
Men's pants	100	102	118	62	140
Boys' shirts	100	98	140	61	123
Boys' pants	100	118	70	105	108
Women and girls, aged 2 or older	**100**	**121**	**101**	**85**	**105**
Women's coats and jackets	100	226	107	6	128
Women's dresses	100	66	42	132	141
Women's vests and sweaters	100	140	135	36	129
Women's shirts, tops, blouses	100	104	148	72	89
Women's pants	100	184	59	82	96
Women's active sportswear	100	101	104	128	48
Women's sleepwear	100	154	79	76	112
Women's undergarments	100	96	110	121	59
Women's accessories	100	91	146	47	144
Girls' dresses and suits	100	140	89	99	76
Girls' shirts, blouses, sweaters	100	93	118	120	54
Girls' skirts and pants	100	133	75	97	102
Girls' active sportswear	100	70	139	119	56
Girls' accessories	100	176	101	78	64
Children under age 2	**100**	**121**	**104**	**92**	**90**
Infant dresses, outerwear	100	116	111	97	79
Infant underwear	100	124	95	92	97
Infant nightwear, loungewear	100	123	122	69	106
Infant accessories	100	108	115	94	88
Other apparel products and services	**100**	**93**	**103**	**94**	**112**
Watches	100	88	122	71	132
Jewelry	100	130	85	87	111
Men's footwear	100	61	85	94	162
Boys' footwear	100	50	201	71	86
Women's footwear	100	109	95	115	73
Girls' footwear	100	68	90	121	107
TRANSPORTATION	**100**	**85**	**105**	**70**	**155**
New cars	100	–	296	87	–
New trucks	100	222	–	–	257
Used cars	100	22	78	144	121
Used trucks	100	–	–	87	312
Gasoline on trips	100	60	127	61	168

	total consumer units	Northeast	Midwest	South	West
Airline fares	100	69	153	63	128
Local transportation on trips	100	122	123	41	151
Intercity train fares	100	89	154	54	123
Ship fares	100	70	158	63	123
HEALTH CARE	**100**	**44**	**182**	**106**	**52**
Physician's services	100	20	110	92	171
Dental services	100	19	158	109	93
Hospital room	100	–	123	197	10
Care in convalescent or nursing home	100	13	260	90	22
Nonprescription drugs	100	163	47	122	62
ENTERTAINMENT	**100**	**94**	**117**	**90**	**103**
Toys, games, hobbies, and tricycles	100	108	132	79	93
Movie, other admissions, on trips	100	108	118	49	154
Admission to sports events on trips	100	108	117	49	154
Fees for recreational lessons	100	80	82	123	100
Cable service and community antenna	100	93	66	146	71
Color TV, portable, table model	100	141	127	83	62
Musical instruments and accessories	100	9	151	126	84
Athletic gear, game tables, and exercise equipment	100	117	68	77	156
PERSONAL CARE PRODUCTS AND SERVICES	**100**	**74**	**127**	**80**	**129**
Hair care products	100	42	96	119	128
Cosmetics, perfume, bath preparation	100	85	123	62	131
Deodorants, feminine hygiene, misc. personal care	100	50	150	100	50
READING	**100**	**100**	**100**	**50**	**100**
EDUCATION	**100**	**128**	**121**	**77**	**89**
College tuition	100	144	130	67	84
Elementary and high school tuition	100	73	55	145	100
Other school tuition	100	67	67	67	200
Other school expenses including rentals	100	40	100	100	140
College books and supplies	100	130	130	90	70
Miscellaneous school supplies	100	60	120	100	140
ALL OTHER GIFTS	**100**	**108**	**112**	**71**	**126**
Gifts of trip expenses	100	96	118	63	139
Miscellaneous fees, gambling losses	100	100	150	0	100
Legal fees	100	50	100	150	100
Funeral expenses	100	139	96	82	100
Cemetery lots, vaults, maintenance fees	100	133	100	67	100
Accounting fees	100	50	50	50	250

Note: (–) means sample is too small to make a reliable estimate. Categories with annual spending of less than $2.00 for the average household are omitted. Spending on gifts is also included in the product and service categories in other chapters.
Source: Calculations by New Strategist based on the 2000 Consumer Expenditure Survey

Table 6.23 Gifts: Indexed per capita spending by region, 2000

(indexed average annual per capita spending of consumer units (CU) on gifts of products and services for non–household members, by region in which consumer unit lives, 2000; index definition: an index of 100 is the average for all consumer units; an index of 132 means that spending by consumer units in that group is 32 percent above the average for all consumer units; an index of 68 indicates spending that is 32 percent below the average for all consumer units)

	total consumer units	Northeast	Midwest	South	West
Per capita spending of CU, total	$15,218	$15,561	$15,685	$13,883	$15,895
Per capita spending of CU, index	100	102	103	91	104
Gifts, per capita spending index	100	101	119	84	100
FOOD	**100**	**94**	**147**	**71**	**98**
Fresh fruits	100	145	119	68	88
Candy and chewing gum	100	153	140	68	57
Board (including at school)	100	101	144	92	64
Catered affairs	100	51	205	39	122
ALCOHOLIC BEVERAGES	**100**	**92**	**133**	**88**	**89**
Beer and ale	100	71	173	61	110
Wine	100	102	105	93	99
Whiskey and other alcoholic beverages	100	91	145	107	47
HOUSING	**100**	**95**	**120**	**93**	**91**
Housekeeping supplies	**100**	**126**	**114**	**72**	**102**
Miscellaneous household products	100	177	101	47	110
Lawn and garden supplies	100	239	58	67	66
Postage and stationery	100	100	130	78	99
Stationery, stationery supplies, giftwraps	100	102	136	75	97
Postage	100	93	103	91	113
Household textiles	**100**	**148**	**107**	**69**	**94**
Bathroom linens	100	56	89	97	151
Bedroom linens	100	217	82	54	82
Appliances and miscellaneous housewares	**100**	**88**	**146**	**93**	**71**
Major appliances	100	66	130	125	57
Electric floor cleaning equipment	100	–	121	203	3
Small appliances and miscellaneous housewares	100	96	151	81	76
Glassware	100	36	212	88	56
Nonelectric cookware	100	140	160	54	70
Tableware, nonelectric kitchenware	100	51	162	96	83
Small electric kitchen appliances	100	106	126	74	103
Miscellaneous household equipment	**100**	**90**	**135**	**80**	**100**
Infants' equipment	100	77	211	65	58
Outdoor equipment	100	150	95	120	26
Household decorative items	100	70	159	82	91
Indoor plants, fresh flowers	100	91	130	82	101
Computers and computer hardware, nonbusiness use	100	93	105	72	138
Miscellaneous household equipment and parts	100	192	101	32	120
Other housing	**100**	**86**	**110**	**107**	**87**
Repair or maintenance services	100	49	217	29	126
Housing while attending school	100	96	145	87	73
Natural gas (renter)	100	89	170	86	54
Electricity (renter)	100	63	88	158	51
Telephone services in home city, excl. mobile phones	100	92	98	118	77

	total consumer units	Northeast	Midwest	South	West
Water, sewerage maintenance (renter)	100	38	110	144	70
Care for elderly, invalids, handicapped	100	197	156	57	24
Day-care centers, nurseries, and preschools	100	74	119	89	115
Housekeeping services	100	53	42	55	260
Gardening, lawn care service	100	53	33	46	284
Repair of miscellaneo%us household equipment and furnishings	100	28	–	268	–
Bedroom furniture except mattress and springs	100	85	185	92	35
APPAREL AND SERVICES	**100**	**110**	**106**	**84**	**106**
Men and boys, aged 2 or older	**100**	**102**	**114**	**73**	**123**
Men's coats and jackets	100	77	149	88	86
Men's underwear	100	82	140	68	121
Men's accessories	100	79	160	77	89
Men's sweaters and vests	100	150	135	67	69
Men's active sportswear	100	117	51	129	87
Men's shirts	100	81	123	50	169
Men's pants	100	102	118	62	135
Boys' shirts	100	98	140	61	119
Boys' pants	100	118	70	105	104
Women and girls, aged 2 or older	**100**	**121**	**101**	**85**	**101**
Women's coats and jackets	100	226	107	6	123
Women's dresses	100	66	42	132	136
Women's vests and sweaters	100	140	135	36	124
Women's shirts, tops, blouses	100	104	148	72	86
Women's pants	100	184	59	82	93
Women's active sportswear	100	101	104	128	46
Women's sleepwear	100	154	79	76	107
Women's undergarments	100	96	110	121	56
Women's accessories	100	91	146	47	139
Girls' dresses and suits	100	140	89	99	73
Girls' shirts, blouses, sweaters	100	93	118	120	52
Girls' skirts and pants	100	133	75	97	98
Girls' active sportswear	100	70	139	119	54
Girls' accessories	100	176	101	78	62
Children under age 2	**100**	**121**	**104**	**92**	**87**
Infant dresses, outerwear	100	116	111	97	76
Infant underwear	100	124	95	92	93
Infant nightwear, loungewear	100	123	122	69	102
Infant accessories	100	108	115	94	84
Other apparel products and services	**100**	**93**	**103**	**94**	**108**
Watches	100	88	122	71	127
Jewelry	100	130	85	87	107
Men's footwear	100	61	85	94	156
Boys' footwear	100	50	201	71	82
Women's footwear	100	109	95	115	71
Girls' footwear	100	68	90	121	103
TRANSPORTATION	**100**	**85**	**105**	**70**	**149**
New cars	100	–	296	87	–
New trucks	100	222	–	–	247
Used cars	100	22	78	144	116
Used trucks	100	–	–	87	300
Gasoline on trips	100	60	127	61	162

	total consumer units	Northeast	Midwest	South	West
Airline fares	100	69	153	63	123
Local transportation on trips	100	122	123	41	145
Intercity train fares	100	89	154	54	119
Ship fares	100	70	158	63	118
HEALTH CARE	**100**	**44**	**182**	**106**	**50**
Physician's services	100	20	110	92	164
Dental services	100	19	158	109	90
Hospital room	100	–	123	197	10
Care in convalescent or nursing home	100	13	260	90	21
Nonprescription drugs	100	163	47	122	59
ENTERTAINMENT	**100**	**94**	**117**	**90**	**99**
Toys, games, hobbies, and tricycles	100	108	132	79	89
Movie, other admissions, on trips	100	108	118	49	148
Admission to sports events on trips	100	108	117	49	148
Fees for recreational lessons	100	80	82	123	97
Cable service and community antenna	100	93	66	146	68
Color TV, portable, table model	100	141	127	83	60
Musical instruments and accessories	100	9	151	126	81
Athletic gear, game tables, and exercise equipment	100	117	68	77	150
PERSONAL CARE PRODUCTS AND SERVICES	**100**	**74**	**127**	**80**	**124**
Hair care products	100	42	96	119	123
Cosmetics, perfume, bath preparation	100	85	123	62	126
Deodorants, feminine hygiene, misc. personal care	100	50	150	100	48
READING	**100**	**100**	**100**	**50**	**96**
EDUCATION	**100**	**128**	**121**	**77**	**86**
College tuition	100	144	130	67	81
Elementary and high school tuition	100	73	55	145	96
Other school tuition	100	67	67	67	192
Other school expenses including rentals	100	40	100	100	135
College books and supplies	100	130	130	90	67
Miscellaneous school supplies	100	60	120	100	135
ALL OTHER GIFTS	**100**	**108**	**112**	**71**	**121**
Gifts of trip expenses	100	96	118	63	133
Miscellaneous fees, gambling losses	100	100	150	0	96
Legal fees	100	50	100	150	96
Funeral expenses	100	139	96	82	96
Cemetery lots, vaults, maintenance fees	100	133	100	67	96
Accounting fees	100	50	50	50	240

Note: Per capita indexes account for household size and show how much each person in a particular household demographic segment spends relative to a person in the average household. (–) means sample is too small to make a reliable estimate. Categories with annual spending of less than $2.00 for the average household are omitted. Spending on gifts is also included in the product and service categories in other chapters.
Source: Calculations by New Strategist based on the 2000 Consumer Expenditure Survey

Table 6.24 Gifts: Total spending by region, 2000

(total annual spending on selected gifts, by region in which consumer units live, 2000; numbers in thousands)

	total consumer units	Northeast	Midwest	South	West
Number of consumer units	109,367	20,994	25,717	38,245	24,410
Total spending of all consumer units	$4,160,831,424	$816,706,699	$1,008,433,006	$1,327,371,892	$1,008,821,118
Gifts, total spending	118,459,772	23,002,496	33,188,046	34,727,607	27,601,363
FOOD	**$7,665,533**	**$1,375,947**	**$2,653,737**	**$1,891,980**	**$1,749,953**
Fresh fruits	500,901	138,980	140,415	118,560	101,790
Candy and chewing gum	1,367,088	401,825	451,591	327,377	180,390
Board (including at school)	2,210,307	426,598	749,651	707,915	326,362
Catered affairs	1,705,032	167,322	820,887	232,912	484,539
ALCOHOLIC BEVERAGES	**1,584,728**	**278,800**	**494,281**	**485,329**	**328,803**
Beer and ale	398,096	53,955	161,503	84,521	101,546
Wine	739,321	144,649	183,105	241,708	169,894
Whiskey and other alcoholic beverages	407,939	71,380	138,872	152,598	44,182
HOUSING	**31,836,734**	**5,824,995**	**8,965,461**	**10,309,705**	**6,738,869**
Housekeeping supplies	**4,276,250**	**1,035,004**	**1,144,149**	**1,077,744**	**1,017,165**
Miscellaneous household products	800,566	271,662	189,791	131,180	204,312
Lawn and garden supplies	336,850	154,726	46,033	79,167	51,749
Postage and stationery	2,728,707	525,480	835,031	743,483	630,022
Stationery, stationery supplies, giftwraps	2,217,963	432,476	710,046	580,559	498,940
Postage	499,807	89,225	120,613	159,482	131,082
Household textiles	**1,443,644**	**409,383**	**363,124**	**350,324**	**316,598**
Bathroom linens	305,134	32,751	63,778	104,026	106,916
Bedroom linens	749,164	311,761	145,044	142,654	142,066
Appliances and miscellaneous housewares	**3,077,587**	**518,552**	**1,053,111**	**1,000,107**	**508,460**
Major appliances	832,283	105,180	253,570	363,328	110,089
Electric floor cleaning equipment	329,195	–	93,353	234,059	1,953
Small appliances and miscellaneous housewares	2,245,305	413,162	799,542	636,397	398,615
Glassware	393,721	27,082	196,221	121,619	51,505
Nonelectric cookware	400,283	107,489	150,959	76,108	65,419
Tableware, nonelectric kitchenware	474,653	46,397	180,276	159,482	91,293
Small electric kitchen appliances	293,104	59,833	87,181	75,725	70,057
Miscellaneous household equipment	**7,689,594**	**1,330,600**	**2,435,143**	**2,145,162**	**1,791,450**
Infants' equipment	297,478	44,087	147,616	67,311	39,788
Outdoor equipment	312,790	90,274	69,950	130,798	19,040
Household decorative items	2,989,000	399,936	1,114,318	857,070	632,219
Indoor plants, fresh flowers	1,754,247	305,463	535,171	501,774	412,285
Computers and computer hardware, nonbusiness use	981,022	175,720	242,511	247,828	314,401
Miscellaneous household equipment and parts	276,699	101,821	65,578	30,596	77,380
Other housing	**15,350,752**	**2,531,666**	**3,969,676**	**5,736,368**	**3,104,952**
Repair or maintenance services	409,033	38,209	208,565	42,070	120,097
Housing while attending school	4,628,411	855,925	1,580,824	1,401,679	789,175
Natural gas (renter)	340,131	58,153	136,300	102,879	42,718
Electricity (renter)	1,452,394	174,880	301,660	804,292	171,114
Telephone services in home city, excl. mobile phones	1,491,766	262,845	343,065	618,039	267,290

	total consumer units	Northeast	Midwest	South	West
Water, sewerage maintenance (renter)	$292,010	$21,414	$75,608	$147,243	$47,355
Care for elderly, invalids, handicapped	229,671	86,705	84,095	45,894	12,937
Day-care centers, nurseries, and preschools	2,347,016	335,484	656,298	727,420	627,581
Housekeeping services	376,222	38,629	37,547	72,666	227,257
Gardening, lawn care service	343,412	34,850	27,003	55,455	226,525
Repair of miscellaneous household equipment and furnishings	850,875	44,927	–	798,173	–
Bedroom furniture except mattress and springs	225,296	36,740	98,239	72,283	18,308
APPAREL AND SERVICES	**26,712,890**	**5,651,795**	**6,628,042**	**7,882,677**	**6,578,495**
Men and boys, aged 2 or older	**7,387,741**	**1,453,205**	**1,986,895**	**1,874,387**	**2,101,701**
Men's coats and jackets	360,911	53,115	126,785	110,528	72,010
Men's underwear	229,671	36,320	75,351	54,690	64,687
Men's accessories	371,848	56,684	139,900	99,819	76,647
Men's sweaters and vests	297,478	85,446	94,381	69,988	47,844
Men's active sportswear	475,746	106,440	56,835	214,554	95,687
Men's shirts	2,271,553	351,440	655,784	395,071	889,256
Men's pants	777,599	152,626	215,508	169,043	243,368
Boys' shirts	608,081	114,627	199,564	129,651	167,453
Boys' pants	310,602	70,120	51,177	113,970	74,939
Women and girls, aged 2 or older	**9,326,818**	**2,165,531**	**2,206,261**	**2,756,317**	**2,193,483**
Women's coats and jackets	390,440	169,422	98,496	8,414	111,554
Women's dresses	1,161,478	146,748	115,984	535,430	365,906
Women's vests and sweaters	968,992	260,536	308,604	121,619	279,739
Women's shirts, tops, blouses	1,158,197	231,984	404,271	292,957	230,675
Women's pants	649,640	228,835	90,010	185,488	139,869
Women's active sportswear	379,503	73,689	92,838	170,190	40,521
Women's sleepwear	672,607	198,393	124,985	178,604	167,697
Women's undergarments	294,197	54,374	75,865	124,679	38,568
Women's accessories	456,060	79,987	156,874	75,343	146,948
Girls' dresses and suits	440,749	118,196	92,581	152,598	75,183
Girls' shirts, blouses, sweaters	675,888	120,506	187,734	284,160	82,018
Girls' skirts and pants	304,040	77,888	53,749	103,644	69,080
Girls' active sportswear	229,671	31,071	74,836	95,613	28,804
Girls' accessories	238,420	80,407	56,577	65,017	34,174
Children under age 2	**4,452,331**	**1,038,153**	**1,086,029**	**1,427,303**	**896,579**
Infant dresses, outerwear	1,586,915	352,069	415,072	538,107	281,447
Infant underwear	1,998,135	475,094	446,961	639,839	432,301
Infant nightwear, loungewear	269,043	63,612	76,894	64,634	63,466
Infant accessories	439,655	90,904	118,813	143,801	85,923
Other apparel products and services	**5,546,001**	**994,906**	**1,348,857**	**1,824,669**	**1,386,976**
Watches	375,129	63,192	108,011	93,318	110,577
Jewelry	1,842,834	459,139	368,525	557,995	456,955
Men's footwear	947,118	110,638	188,763	312,462	342,472
Boys' footwear	514,025	49,756	242,511	126,973	98,128
Women's footwear	1,100,232	229,674	245,083	441,347	180,146
Girls' footwear	569,802	74,109	120,613	240,179	136,208
TRANSPORTATION	**7,685,219**	**1,255,861**	**1,892,771**	**1,874,770**	**2,661,911**
New cars	664,951	–	462,906	202,316	–
New trucks	1,535,513	653,543	–	–	881,689
Used cars	1,369,275	58,783	250,226	690,705	369,812
Used trucks	308,415	–	–	93,700	214,808
Gasoline on trips	1,372,556	156,825	408,643	292,192	514,563

	total consumer units	Northeast	Midwest	South	West
Airline fares	$930,713	$123,655	$335,093	$205,376	$266,557
Local transportation on trips	232,952	54,374	67,636	33,273	78,356
Intercity train fares	243,888	41,778	88,209	46,276	67,128
Ship fares	325,914	43,877	121,127	71,518	89,341
HEALTH CARE	**4,164,695**	**351,230**	**1,782,960**	**1,548,540**	**479,168**
Physician's services	290,916	11,127	75,094	94,083	111,066
Dental services	381,691	14,066	141,701	146,096	79,577
Hospital room	298,572	–	86,666	205,758	6,835
Care in convalescent or nursing home	2,014,540	48,496	1,233,644	632,955	99,349
Nonprescription drugs	235,139	73,689	26,231	100,202	32,465
ENTERTAINMENT	**10,254,250**	**1,851,041**	**2,811,897**	**3,237,057**	**2,360,447**
Toys, games, hobbies, and tricycles	3,235,076	668,659	1,000,648	894,933	670,787
Movie, other admissions, on trips	1,002,895	207,211	277,229	173,250	345,646
Admission to sports events on trips	334,663	69,070	92,324	57,750	115,215
Fees for recreational lessons	689,012	105,390	132,700	296,399	154,515
Cable service and community antenna	508,557	90,484	78,437	259,301	80,797
Color TV, portable, table model	229,671	62,142	68,407	66,929	31,733
Musical instruments and accessories	253,731	4,199	90,010	112,058	47,600
Athletic gear, game tables, and exercise equipment	1,035,705	232,823	165,617	278,041	361,268
PERSONAL CARE PRODUCTS AND SERVICES	**2,099,846**	**296,435**	**624,666**	**587,826**	**602,927**
Hair care products	234,045	18,685	52,720	97,525	66,639
Cosmetics, perfume, bath preparation	1,421,771	230,934	411,472	305,960	414,970
Deodorants, feminine hygiene, misc. personal care	218,734	20,994	77,151	76,490	24,410
READING	**218,734**	**41,988**	**51,434**	**38,245**	**48,820**
EDUCATION	**16,514,417**	**4,051,842**	**4,706,211**	**4,474,665**	**3,295,350**
College tuition	12,467,838	3,443,016	3,806,116	2,906,620	2,343,360
Elementary and high school tuition	1,203,037	167,952	154,302	611,920	268,510
Other school tuition	328,101	41,988	51,434	76,490	146,460
Other school expenses including rentals	546,835	41,988	128,585	191,225	170,870
College books and supplies	1,093,670	272,922	334,321	344,205	170,870
Miscellaneous school supplies	546,835	62,982	154,302	191,225	170,870
ALL OTHER GIFTS	**9,733,663**	**2,015,424**	**2,571,700**	**2,409,435**	**2,733,920**
Gifts of trip expenses	5,358,983	986,718	1,491,586	1,185,595	1,659,880
Miscellaneous fees, gambling losses	218,734	41,988	77,151	0	48,820
Legal fees	437,468	41,988	102,868	229,470	97,640
Funeral expenses	3,062,276	818,766	694,359	879,635	683,480
Cemetery lots, vaults, maintenance fees	328,101	83,976	77,151	76,490	73,230
Accounting fees	218,734	20,994	25,717	38,245	122,050

Note: Numbers may not add to total because of rounding. (–) means sample is too small to make a reliable estimate. Expenditures for items in a given category may not add to category total because categories with annual spending of less than $2.00 for the average household are omitted. Spending on gifts is also included in the product and service categories in other chapters.
Source: Calculations by New Strategist based on the 2000 Consumer Expenditure Survey

Table 6.25 Gifts: Market shares by region, 2000

(percentage of total annual spending on gifts of products and services for non-household members accounted for by consumer units by region, 2000)

	total consumer units	Northeast	Midwest	South	West
Share of total consumer units	100.0%	19.2%	23.5%	35.0%	22.3%
Share of total before-tax income	100.0	20.4	23.4	32.9	23.3
Share of total spending	100.0	19.6	24.2	31.9	24.2
Share of gifts spending	100.0	19.4	28.0	29.3	23.3
FOOD	**100.0%**	**17.9%**	**34.6%**	**24.7%**	**22.8%**
Fresh fruits	100.0	27.7	28.0	23.7	20.3
Candy and chewing gum	100.0	29.4	33.0	23.9	13.2
Board (including at school)	100.0	19.3	33.9	32.0	14.8
Catered affairs	100.0	9.8	48.1	13.7	28.4
ALCOHOLIC BEVERAGES	**100.0**	**17.6**	**31.2**	**30.6**	**20.7**
Beer and ale	100.0	13.6	40.6	21.2	25.5
Wine	100.0	19.6	24.8	32.7	23.0
Whiskey and other alcoholic beverages	100.0	17.5	34.0	37.4	10.8
HOUSING	**100.0**	**18.3**	**28.2**	**32.4**	**21.2**
Housekeeping supplies	**100.0**	**24.2**	**26.8**	**25.2**	**23.8**
Miscellaneous household products	100.0	33.9	23.7	16.4	25.5
Lawn and garden supplies	100.0	45.9	13.7	23.5	15.4
Postage and stationery	100.0	19.3	30.6	27.2	23.1
Stationery, stationery supplies, giftwraps	100.0	19.5	32.0	26.2	22.5
Postage	100.0	17.9	24.1	31.9	26.2
Household textiles	**100.0**	**28.4**	**25.2**	**24.3**	**21.9**
Bathroom linens	100.0	10.7	20.9	34.1	35.0
Bedroom linens	100.0	41.6	19.4	19.0	19.0
Appliances and miscellaneous housewares	**100.0**	**16.8**	**34.2**	**32.5**	**16.5**
Major appliances	100.0	12.6	30.5	43.7	13.2
Electric floor cleaning equipment	100.0	–	28.4	71.1	0.6
Small appliances and miscellaneous housewares	100.0	18.4	35.6	28.3	17.8
Glassware	100.0	6.9	49.8	30.9	13.1
Nonelectric cookware	100.0	26.9	37.7	19.0	16.3
Tableware, nonelectric kitchenware	100.0	9.8	38.0	33.6	19.2
Small electric kitchen appliances	100.0	20.4	29.7	25.8	23.9
Miscellaneous household equipment	**100.0**	**17.3**	**31.7**	**27.9**	**23.3**
Infants' equipment	100.0	14.8	49.6	22.6	13.4
Outdoor equipment	100.0	28.9	22.4	41.8	6.1
Household decorative items	100.0	13.4	37.3	28.7	21.2
Indoor plants, fresh flowers	100.0	17.4	30.5	28.6	23.5
Computers and computer hardware, nonbusiness use	100.0	17.9	24.7	25.3	32.0
Miscellaneous household equipment and parts	100.0	36.8	23.7	11.1	28.0
Other housing	**100.0**	**16.5**	**25.9**	**37.4**	**20.2**
Repair or maintenance services	100.0	9.3	51.0	10.3	29.4
Housing while attending school	100.0	18.5	34.2	30.3	17.1
Natural gas (renter)	100.0	17.1	40.1	30.2	12.6
Electricity (renter)	100.0	12.0	20.8	55.4	11.8
Telephone services in home city, excl. mobile phones	100.0	17.6	23.0	41.4	17.9

	total consumer units	Northeast	Midwest	South	West
Water, sewerage maintenance (renter)	100.0%	7.3%	25.9%	50.4%	16.2%
Care for elderly, invalids, handicapped	100.0	37.8	36.6	20.0	5.6
Day-care centers, nurseries, and preschools	100.0	14.3	28.0	31.0	26.7
Housekeeping services	100.0	10.3	10.0	19.3	60.4
Gardening, lawn care service	100.0	10.1	7.9	16.1	66.0
Repair of miscellaneous household equipment and furnishings	100.0	5.3	–	93.8	–
Bedroom furniture except mattress and springs	100.0	16.3	43.6	32.1	8.1
APPAREL AND SERVICES	**100.0**	**21.2**	**24.8**	**29.5**	**24.6**
Men and boys, aged 2 or older	**100.0**	**19.7**	**26.9**	**25.4**	**28.4**
Men's coats and jackets	100.0	14.7	35.1	30.6	20.0
Men's underwear	100.0	15.8	32.8	23.8	28.2
Men's accessories	100.0	15.2	37.6	26.8	20.6
Men's sweaters and vests	100.0	28.7	31.7	23.5	16.1
Men's active sportswear	100.0	22.4	11.9	45.1	20.1
Men's shirts	100.0	15.5	28.9	17.4	39.1
Men's pants	100.0	19.6	27.7	21.7	31.3
Boys' shirts	100.0	18.9	32.8	21.3	27.5
Boys' pants	100.0	22.6	16.5	36.7	24.1
Women and girls, aged 2 or older	**100.0**	**23.2**	**23.7**	**29.6**	**23.5**
Women's coats and jackets	100.0	43.4	25.2	2.2	28.6
Women's dresses	100.0	12.6	10.0	46.1	31.5
Women's vests and sweaters	100.0	26.9	31.8	12.6	28.9
Women's shirts, tops, blouses	100.0	20.0	34.9	25.3	19.9
Women's pants	100.0	35.2	13.9	28.6	21.5
Women's active sportswear	100.0	19.4	24.5	44.8	10.7
Women's sleepwear	100.0	29.5	18.6	26.6	24.9
Women's undergarments	100.0	18.5	25.8	42.4	13.1
Women's accessories	100.0	17.5	34.4	16.5	32.2
Girls' dresses and suits	100.0	26.8	21.0	34.6	17.1
Girls' shirts, blouses, sweaters	100.0	17.8	27.8	42.0	12.1
Girls' skirts and pants	100.0	25.6	17.7	34.1	22.7
Girls' active sportswear	100.0	13.5	32.6	41.6	12.5
Girls' accessories	100.0	33.7	23.7	27.3	14.3
Children under age 2	**100.0**	**23.3**	**24.4**	**32.1**	**20.1**
Infant dresses, outerwear	100.0	22.2	26.2	33.9	17.7
Infant underwear	100.0	23.8	22.4	32.0	21.6
Infant nightwear, loungewear	100.0	23.6	28.6	24.0	23.6
Infant accessories	100.0	20.7	27.0	32.7	19.5
Other apparel products and services	**100.0**	**17.9**	**24.3**	**32.9**	**25.0**
Watches	100.0	16.8	28.8	24.9	29.5
Jewelry	100.0	24.9	20.0	30.3	24.8
Men's footwear	100.0	11.7	19.9	33.0	36.2
Boys' footwear	100.0	9.7	47.2	24.7	19.1
Women's footwear	100.0	20.9	22.3	40.1	16.4
Girls' footwear	100.0	13.0	21.2	42.2	23.9
TRANSPORTATION	**100.0**	**16.3**	**24.6**	**24.4**	**34.6**
New cars	100.0	–	69.6	30.4	–
New trucks	100.0	42.6	–	–	57.4
Used cars	100.0	4.3	18.3	50.4	27.0
Used trucks	100.0	–	–	30.4	69.6
Gasoline on trips	100.0	11.4	29.8	21.3	37.5

	total consumer units	Northeast	Midwest	South	West
Airline fares	100.0%	13.3%	36.0%	22.1%	28.6%
Local transportation on trips	100.0	23.3	29.0	14.3	33.6
Intercity train fares	100.0	17.1	36.2	19.0	27.5
Ship fares	100.0	13.5	37.2	21.9	27.4
HEALTH CARE	**100.0**	**8.4**	**42.8**	**37.2**	**11.5**
Physician's services	100.0	3.8	25.8	32.3	38.2
Dental services	100.0	3.7	37.1	38.3	20.8
Hospital room	100.0	–	29.0	68.9	2.3
Care in convalescent or nursing home	100.0	2.4	61.2	31.4	4.9
Nonprescription drugs	100.0	31.3	11.2	42.6	13.8
ENTERTAINMENT	**100.0**	**18.1**	**27.4**	**31.6**	**23.0**
Toys, games, hobbies, and tricycles	100.0	20.7	30.9	27.7	20.7
Movie, other admissions, on trips	100.0	20.7	27.6	17.3	34.5
Admission to sports events on trips	100.0	20.6	27.6	17.3	34.4
Fees for recreational lessons	100.0	15.3	19.3	43.0	22.4
Cable service and community antenna	100.0	17.8	15.4	51.0	15.9
Color TV, portable, table model	100.0	27.1	29.8	29.1	13.8
Musical instruments and accessories	100.0	1.7	35.5	44.2	18.8
Athletic gear, game tables, and exercise equipment	100.0	22.5	16.0	26.8	34.9
PERSONAL CARE PRODUCTS AND SERVICES	**100.0**	**14.1**	**29.7**	**28.0**	**28.7**
Hair care products	100.0	8.0	22.5	41.7	28.5
Cosmetics, perfume, bath preparation	100.0	16.2	28.9	21.5	29.2
Deodorants, feminine hygiene, misc. personal care	100.0	9.6	35.3	35.0	11.2
READING	**100.0**	**19.2**	**23.5**	**17.5**	**22.3**
EDUCATION	**100.0**	**24.5**	**28.5**	**27.1**	**20.0**
College tuition	100.0	27.6	30.5	23.3	18.8
Elementary and high school tuition	100.0	14.0	12.8	50.9	22.3
Other school tuition	100.0	12.8	15.7	23.3	44.6
Other school expenses including rentals	100.0	7.7	23.5	35.0	31.2
College books and supplies	100.0	25.0	30.6	31.5	15.6
Miscellaneous school supplies	100.0	11.5	28.2	35.0	31.2
ALL OTHER GIFTS	**100.0**	**20.7**	**26.4**	**24.8**	**28.1**
Gifts of trip expenses	100.0	18.4	27.8	22.1	31.0
Miscellaneous fees, gambling losses	100.0	19.2	35.3	0.0	22.3
Legal fees	100.0	9.6	23.5	52.5	22.3
Funeral expenses	100.0	26.7	22.7	28.7	22.3
Cemetery lots, vaults, maintenance fees	100.0	25.6	23.5	23.3	22.3
Accounting fees	100.0	9.6	11.8	17.5	55.8

Note: Numbers may not add to total because of rounding. (–) means sample is too small to make a reliable estimate. Expenditures for items in a given category may not add to category total because categories with annual spending of less than $2.00 for the average household are omitted. Spending on gifts is also included in the product and service categories in other chapters.
Source: Calculations by New Strategist based on the 2000 Consumer Expenditure Survey

7

Spending on Health Care, 2000

American households spent 6 percent more out-of-pocket on health care costs in 2000 than in 1990, after adjusting for inflation. Out-of-pocket spending on health insurance rose 28 percent during the decade, while drug spending was up 25 percent. Spending on medical services fell 23 percent, however, as managed care limited services and reduced costs. Out-of-pocket health care costs absorbed 5.4 percent of the household budget in 2000, up slightly from 5.2 percent of 1990.

Not surprisingly, out-of-pocket health care spending rises with age and is highest among householders aged 75 or older, at $3,338 in 2000. The oldest householders spend more than any other age group out-of-pocket on health insurance ($1,631 in 2000, despite Medicare coverage), drugs ($908), and medical supplies ($141). Householders aged 55 to 64 spend the most on medical services ($721).

Households with incomes below $20,000 account for 31 percent of all out-of-pocket spending on prescription drugs. Many low-income householders are elderly retirees, which accounts for their above-average spending on drugs. The most affluent households account for 34 percent of spending on dental services and 42 percent of spending on eyeglasses and contact lenses.

Married couples without children at home, most of them older empty-nesters, spend the most out-of-pocket on health care, $3,044 in 2000—47 percent more than the average household. Married couples with children at home spend just 12 percent more than the average household on health care, but they spend 32 percent more than average on physician services.

Blacks and Hispanics spend far less than average out-of-pocket on almost every health care category. Black households spent $1,107 on health care in 2000 versus the $2,066 spent by the average household. Hispanics spent only slightly more than blacks, $1,243.

Households in the Midwest spend 5 percent more out-of-pocket on health care than the average household. Households in the Northeast spend 10 percent less than average. Western households spend the most on medical services, including 44 percent more on medical services by a professional other than a physician. Those in the South spend the most on prescription drugs.

Table 7.1 Health Care: Average spending by age, 2000

(average annual spending of consumer units (CU) on health care, by age of consumer unit reference person, 2000)

	total consumer units	under 25	25 to 34	35 to 44	45 to 54	55 to 64	65 to 74	75+
Number of consumer units (in thousands, add 000)	109,367	8,306	18,887	23,983	21,874	14,161	11,538	10,617
Average number of persons per CU	2.5	1.9	2.9	3.3	2.7	2.1	1.9	1.5
Average before-tax income of CU	$44,649.00	$19,744.00	$45,498.00	$56,500.00	$58,889.00	$48,108.00	$29,349.00	$20,563.00
Average spending of CU, total	38,044.67	22,543.18	38,945.27	45,149.37	46,160.28	39,340.03	30,781.81	21,908.04
Health care, average spending	2,065.67	504.12	1,255.79	1,773.60	2,199.85	2,507.77	3,162.74	3,337.73
HEALTH INSURANCE	**$982.65**	**$211.14**	**$640.07**	**$849.92**	**$975.69**	**$1,132.22**	**$1,607.65**	**$1,631.09**
Commercial health insurance	194.39	40.69	143.23	229.95	256.72	280.44	167.17	111.70
Traditional fee-for-service health plan (not BCBS)	77.07	15.39	36.93	76.85	103.05	101.85	101.58	84.04
Preferred-provider health plan (not BCBS)	117.32	25.31	106.30	153.10	153.67	178.59	65.59	27.66
Blue Cross, Blue Shield	**232.50**	**46.48**	**160.22**	**214.15**	**253.69**	**302.81**	**305.60**	**331.19**
Traditional fee-for-service health plan	49.89	12.91	27.35	30.23	56.33	86.60	61.72	88.27
Preferred-provider health plan	60.94	12.07	46.19	66.56	101.26	82.02	42.26	21.80
Health maintenance organization	73.18	18.49	64.10	100.57	78.44	103.87	53.73	39.60
Commercial Medicare supplement	43.77	1.73	16.59	11.58	12.04	26.58	143.31	177.88
Other BCBS health insurance	4.71	1.28	5.98	5.20	5.61	3.74	4.58	3.65
Health maintenance plans (HMOs)	**254.81**	**84.85**	**251.42**	**312.23**	**330.26**	**329.21**	**157.83**	**114.77**
Medicare payments	**164.04**	**12.40**	**17.33**	**28.13**	**44.65**	**103.15**	**650.08**	**649.70**
Commercial Medicare supplements/ other health insurance	**136.91**	**26.71**	**67.87**	**65.47**	**90.37**	**116.60**	**326.97**	**423.73**
Commercial Medicare supplement (not BCBS)	88.22	20.81	43.23	29.28	43.93	57.05	241.01	320.93
Other health insurance (not BCBS)	48.69	5.91	24.64	36.19	46.44	59.55	85.95	102.80
MEDICAL SERVICES	**567.85**	**177.87**	**366.62**	**554.85**	**699.23**	**720.61**	**685.92**	**657.69**
Physician's services	134.41	74.22	118.14	153.09	160.05	169.31	109.11	96.33
Dental services	220.79	49.06	116.69	240.25	267.39	265.79	305.68	248.12
Eye care services	35.05	7.46	20.30	35.84	53.20	47.46	29.23	33.49
Service by professionals other than physician	36.87	6.56	22.42	35.78	51.71	48.28	37.21	42.56
Lab tests, X-rays	20.12	8.21	10.81	18.65	24.70	39.67	17.13	17.03
Hospital room	35.95	15.03	31.20	19.46	66.29	41.48	42.31	21.25
Hospital services other than room	41.13	15.13	37.90	40.79	53.09	63.18	30.94	24.97
Care in convalescent or nursing home	32.35	0.64	0.55	3.99	13.24	25.17	95.79	157.82
Repair of medical equipment	0.61	–	–	–	–	–	5.53	0.41
Other medical services	10.56	1.55	8.61	6.97	9.51	20.27	13.01	15.71
DRUGS	**416.45**	**80.91**	**180.53**	**283.67**	**406.68**	**538.21**	**743.60**	**907.54**
Nonprescription drugs	65.09	25.96	51.31	63.12	70.26	69.71	79.22	96.22
Nonprescription vitamins	46.19	4.00	24.20	46.37	55.84	71.03	57.61	55.57
Prescription drugs	305.17	50.95	105.02	174.18	280.57	397.48	606.77	755.75
MEDICAL SUPPLIES	**98.73**	**34.21**	**68.58**	**85.17**	**118.25**	**116.72**	**125.56**	**141.41**
Eyeglasses and contact lenses	58.43	22.39	38.37	61.48	82.86	77.75	57.05	40.80
Hearing aids	11.78	0.03	4.80	3.93	3.57	5.91	26.92	59.39
Topicals and dressings	20.99	10.71	22.14	16.80	24.47	21.61	28.36	21.76
Medical equipment for general use	2.04	0.50	1.26	0.98	2.28	2.67	4.16	3.36
Supportive, convalescent medical equipment	3.18	0.25	1.42	1.08	2.57	5.49	6.35	8.11
Rental of medical equipment	0.85	–	0.16	0.39	1.39	1.17	1.02	2.04
Rental of supportive, convalescent medical equip.	1.46	0.33	0.43	0.49	1.13	2.11	1.69	5.95

Note: (–) means sample is too small to make a reliable estimate.
Source: Bureau of Labor Statistics, unpublished tables from the 2000 Consumer Expenditure Survey

Table 7.2 Health Care: Indexed spending by age, 2000

(indexed average annual spending of consumer units (CU) on health care, by age of consumer unit reference person, 2000; index definition: an index of 100 is the average for all consumer units; an index of 132 means that spending by consumer units in that group is 32 percent above the average for all consumer units; an index of 68 indicates spending that is 32 percent below the average for all consumer units)

	total consumer units	under 25	25 to 34	35 to 44	45 to 54	55 to 64	65 to 74	75+
Average spending of CU, total	$38,045	$22,543	$38,945	$45,149	$46,160	$39,340	$30,782	$21,908
Average spending of CU, index	100	59	102	119	121	103	81	58
Health care, spending index	100	24	61	86	106	121	153	162
HEALTH INSURANCE	**100**	**21**	**65**	**86**	**99**	**115**	**164**	**166**
Commercial health insurance	**100**	**21**	**74**	**118**	**132**	**144**	**86**	**57**
Traditional fee-for-service health plan (not BCBS)	100	20	48	100	134	132	132	109
Preferred-provider health plan (not BCBS)	100	22	91	130	131	152	56	24
Blue Cross, Blue Shield	**100**	**20**	**69**	**92**	**109**	**130**	**131**	**142**
Traditional fee-for-service health plan	100	26	55	61	113	174	124	177
Preferred-provider health plan	100	20	76	109	166	135	69	36
Health maintenance organization	100	25	88	137	107	142	73	54
Commercial Medicare supplement	100	4	38	26	28	61	327	406
Other BCBS health insurance	100	27	127	110	119	79	97	77
Health maintenance plans (HMOs)	**100**	**33**	**99**	**123**	**130**	**129**	**62**	**45**
Medicare payments	**100**	**8**	**11**	**17**	**27**	**63**	**396**	**396**
Commercial Medicare supplements/ other health insurance	**100**	**20**	**50**	**48**	**66**	**85**	**239**	**309**
Commercial Medicare supplement (not BCBS)	100	24	49	33	50	65	273	364
Other health insurance (not BCBS)	100	12	51	74	95	122	177	211
MEDICAL SERVICES	**100**	**31**	**65**	**98**	**123**	**127**	**121**	**116**
Physician's services	100	55	88	114	119	126	81	72
Dental services	100	22	53	109	121	120	138	112
Eye care services	100	21	58	102	152	135	83	96
Service by professionals other than physician	100	18	61	97	140	131	101	115
Lab tests, X-rays	100	41	54	93	123	197	85	85
Hospital room	100	42	87	54	184	115	118	59
Hospital services other than room	100	37	92	99	129	154	75	61
Care in convalescent or nursing home	100	2	2	12	41	78	296	488
Repair of medical equipment	100	–	–	–	–	–	907	67
Other medical services	100	15	82	66	90	192	123	149
DRUGS	**100**	**19**	**43**	**68**	**98**	**129**	**179**	**218**
Nonprescription drugs	100	40	79	97	108	107	122	148
Nonprescription vitamins	100	9	52	100	121	154	125	120
Prescription drugs	100	17	34	57	92	130	199	248
MEDICAL SUPPLIES	**100**	**35**	**69**	**86**	**120**	**118**	**127**	**143**
Eyeglasses and contact lenses	100	38	66	105	142	133	98	70
Hearing aids	100	0	41	33	30	50	229	504
Topicals and dressings	100	51	105	80	117	103	135	104
Medical equipment for general use	100	25	62	48	112	131	204	165
Supportive, convalescent medical equipment	100	8	45	34	81	173	200	255
Rental of medical equipment	100	–	19	46	164	138	120	240
Rental of supportive, convalescent medical equip.	100	23	29	34	77	145	116	408

Note: (–) means sample is too small to make a reliable estimate.
Source: Calculations by New Strategist based on the 2000 Consumer Expenditure Survey

Table 7.3 Health Care: Indexed per capita spending by age, 2000

(indexed average annual per capita spending of consumer units (CU) on health care, by age of consumer unit reference person, 2000; index definition: an index of 100 is the average for all consumer units; an index of 132 means that spending by consumer units in that group is 32 percent above the average for all consumer units; an index of 68 indicates spending that is 32 percent below the average for all consumer units)

	total consumer units	under 25	25 to 34	35 to 44	45 to 54	55 to 64	65 to 74	75+
Per capita spending of CU, total	$15,218	$11,865	$13,429	$13,682	$17,096	$18,733	$16,201	$14,605
Per capita spending of CU, index	100	78	88	90	112	123	106	96
Health care, per capita spending index	100	32	52	65	99	145	201	269
HEALTH INSURANCE	**100**	**28**	**56**	**66**	**92**	**137**	**215**	**277**
Commercial health insurance	**100**	**28**	**64**	**90**	**122**	**172**	**113**	**96**
Traditional fee-for-service health plan (not BCBS)	100	26	41	76	124	157	173	182
Preferred-provider health plan (not BCBS)	100	28	78	99	121	181	74	39
Blue Cross, Blue Shield	**100**	**26**	**59**	**70**	**101**	**155**	**173**	**237**
Traditional fee-for-service health plan	100	34	47	46	105	207	163	295
Preferred-provider health plan	100	26	65	83	154	160	91	60
Health maintenance organization	100	33	76	104	99	169	97	90
Commercial Medicare supplement	100	5	33	20	25	72	431	677
Other BCBS health insurance	100	36	109	84	110	95	128	129
Health maintenance plans (HMOs)	**100**	**44**	**85**	**93**	**120**	**154**	**82**	**75**
Medicare payments	**100**	**10**	**9**	**13**	**25**	**75**	**521**	**660**
Commercial Medicare supplements/ other health insurance	**100**	**26**	**43**	**36**	**61**	**101**	**314**	**516**
Commercial Medicare supplement (not BCBS)	100	31	42	25	46	77	359	606
Other health insurance (not BCBS)	100	16	44	56	88	146	232	352
MEDICAL SERVICES	**100**	**41**	**56**	**74**	**114**	**151**	**159**	**193**
Physician's services	100	73	76	86	110	150	107	119
Dental services	100	29	46	82	112	143	182	187
Eye care services	100	28	50	77	141	161	110	159
Service by professionals other than physician	100	23	52	74	130	156	133	192
Lab tests, X-rays	100	54	46	70	114	235	112	141
Hospital room	100	55	75	41	171	137	155	99
Hospital services other than room	100	48	79	75	120	183	99	101
Care in convalescent or nursing home	100	3	1	9	38	93	390	813
Repair of medical equipment	100	–	–	–	–	–	1,193	112
Other medical services	100	19	70	50	83	229	162	248
DRUGS	**100**	**26**	**37**	**52**	**90**	**154**	**235**	**363**
Nonprescription drugs	100	52	68	73	100	127	160	246
Nonprescription vitamins	100	11	45	76	112	183	164	201
Prescription drugs	100	22	30	43	85	155	262	413
MEDICAL SUPPLIES	**100**	**46**	**60**	**65**	**111**	**141**	**167**	**239**
Eyeglasses and contact lenses	100	50	57	80	131	158	128	116
Hearing aids	100	0	35	25	28	60	301	840
Topicals and dressings	100	67	91	61	108	123	178	173
Medical equipment for general use	100	32	53	36	103	156	268	275
Supportive, convalescent medical equipment	100	10	38	26	75	206	263	425
Rental of medical equipment	100	–	16	35	151	164	158	400
Rental of supportive, convalescent medical equip.	100	30	25	25	72	172	152	679

Note: Per capita indexes account for household size and show how much each person in a particular household demographic segment spends relative to a person in the average household. (–) means sample is too small to make a reliable estimate.
Source: Calculations by New Strategist based on the 2000 Consumer Expenditure Survey

Table 7.4 Health Care: Total spending by age, 2000

(total annual spending on health care, by consumer unit (CU) age group, 2000; numbers in thousands)

	total consumer units	under 25	25 to 34	35 to 44	45 to 54	55 to 64	65 to 74	75+
Number of consumer units	109,367	8,306	18,887	23,983	21,874	14,161	11,538	10,617
Total spending of all CUs	$4,160,831,424	$187,243,653	$735,559,314	$1,082,817,341	$1,009,709,965	$557,094,165	$355,160,524	$232,597,661
Health care, total spending	225,916,131	4,187,221	23,718,106	42,536,249	48,119,519	35,512,531	36,491,694	35,436,679
HEALTH INSURANCE	**$107,469,483**	**$1,753,729**	**$12,089,002**	**$20,383,631**	**$21,342,243**	**$16,033,367**	**$18,549,066**	**$17,317,283**
Commercial health insurance	**21,259,851**	**337,971**	**2,705,185**	**5,514,891**	**5,615,493**	**3,971,311**	**1,928,807**	**1,185,919**
Traditional fee-for-service health plan (not BCBS)	8,428,915	127,829	697,497	1,843,094	2,254,116	1,442,298	1,172,030	892,253
Preferred-provider health plan (not BCBS)	12,830,936	210,225	2,007,688	3,671,797	3,361,378	2,529,013	756,777	293,666
Blue Cross, Blue Shield	**25,427,828**	**386,063**	**3,026,075**	**5,135,959**	**5,549,215**	**4,288,092**	**3,526,013**	**3,516,244**
Traditional fee-for-service health plan	5,456,320	107,230	516,559	725,006	1,232,162	1,226,343	712,125	937,163
Preferred-provider health plan	6,664,825	100,253	872,391	1,596,308	2,214,961	1,161,485	487,596	231,451
Health maintenance organization	8,003,477	153,578	1,210,657	2,411,970	1,715,797	1,470,903	619,937	420,433
Commercial Medicare supplement	4,786,994	14,369	313,335	277,723	263,363	376,399	1,653,511	1,888,552
Other BCBS health insurance	515,119	10,632	112,944	124,712	122,713	52,962	52,844	38,752
Health maintenance plans (HMOs)	**27,867,805**	**704,764**	**4,748,570**	**7,488,212**	**7,224,107**	**4,661,943**	**1,821,043**	**1,218,513**
Medicare payments	**17,940,563**	**102,994**	**327,312**	**674,642**	**976,674**	**1,460,707**	**7,500,623**	**6,897,865**
Commercial Medicare supplements/ other health insurance	**14,973,436**	**221,853**	**1,281,861**	**1,570,167**	**1,976,753**	**1,651,173**	**3,772,580**	**4,498,741**
Commercial Medicare supplement (not BCBS)	9,648,357	172,848	816,485	702,222	960,925	807,885	2,780,773	3,407,314
Other health insurance (not BCBS)	5,325,079	49,088	465,376	867,945	1,015,829	843,288	991,691	1,091,428
MEDICAL SERVICES	**62,104,051**	**1,477,388**	**6,924,352**	**13,306,968**	**15,294,957**	**10,204,558**	**7,914,145**	**6,982,695**
Physician's services	14,700,018	616,471	2,231,310	3,671,557	3,500,934	2,397,599	1,258,911	1,022,736
Dental services	24,147,140	407,492	2,203,924	5,761,916	5,848,889	3,763,852	3,526,936	2,634,290
Eye care services	3,833,313	61,963	383,406	859,551	1,163,697	672,081	337,256	355,563
Service by professionals other than physician	4,032,361	54,487	423,447	858,112	1,131,105	683,693	429,329	451,860
Lab tests, X-rays	2,200,464	68,192	204,168	447,283	540,288	561,767	197,646	180,808
Hospital room	3,931,744	124,839	589,274	466,709	1,450,027	587,398	488,173	225,611
Hospital services other than room	4,498,265	125,670	715,817	978,267	1,161,291	894,692	356,986	265,106
Care in convalescent or nursing home	3,538,022	5,316	10,388	95,692	289,612	356,432	1,105,225	1,675,575
Repair of medical equipment	66,714	–	–	–	–	–	63,805	4,353
Other medical services	1,154,916	12,874	162,617	167,162	208,022	287,043	150,109	166,793
DRUGS	**45,545,887**	**672,038**	**3,409,670**	**6,803,258**	**8,895,718**	**7,621,592**	**8,579,657**	**9,635,352**
Nonprescription drugs	7,118,698	215,624	969,092	1,513,807	1,536,867	987,163	914,040	1,021,568
Nonprescription vitamins	5,051,662	33,224	457,065	1,112,092	1,221,444	1,005,856	664,704	589,987
Prescription drugs	33,375,527	423,191	1,983,513	4,177,359	6,137,188	5,628,714	7,000,912	8,023,798
MEDICAL SUPPLIES	**10,797,804**	**284,148**	**1,295,270**	**2,042,632**	**2,586,601**	**1,652,872**	**1,448,711**	**1,501,350**
Eyeglasses and contact lenses	6,390,314	185,971	724,694	1,474,475	1,812,480	1,101,018	658,243	433,174
Hearing aids	1,288,343	249	90,658	94,253	78,090	83,692	310,603	630,544
Topicals and dressings	2,295,613	88,957	418,158	402,914	535,257	306,019	327,218	231,026
Medical equipment for general use	223,109	4,153	23,798	23,503	49,873	37,810	47,998	35,673
Supportive, convalescent medical equipment	347,787	2,077	26,820	25,902	56,216	77,744	73,266	86,104
Rental of medical equipment	92,962	–	3,022	9,353	30,405	16,568	11,769	21,659
Rental of supportive, convalescent medical equipment	159,676	2,741	8,121	11,752	24,718	29,880	19,499	63,171

Note: Numbers may not add to total because of rounding. (–) means sample is too small to make a reliable estimate.
Source: Calculations by New Strategist based on the 2000 Consumer Expenditure Survey

Table 7.5 Health Care: Market shares by age, 2000

(percentage of total annual spending on health care accounted for by consumer unit age groups, 2000)

	total consumer units	under 25	25 to 34	35 to 44	45 to 54	55 to 64	65 to 74	75+
Share of total consumer units	100.0%	7.6%	17.3%	21.9%	20.0%	12.9%	10.5%	9.7%
Share of total before-tax income	100.0	3.4	17.6	27.7	26.4	14.0	6.9	4.5
Share of total spending	100.0	4.5	17.7	26.0	24.3	13.4	8.5	5.6
Share of health care spending	100.0	1.9	10.5	18.8	21.3	15.7	16.2	15.7
HEALTH INSURANCE	100.0%	1.6%	11.2%	19.0%	19.9%	14.9%	17.3%	16.1%
Commercial health insurance	100.0	1.6	12.7	25.9	26.4	18.7	9.1	5.6
Traditional fee-for-service health plan (not BCBS)	100.0	1.5	8.3	21.9	26.7	17.1	13.9	10.6
Preferred-provider health plan (not BCBS)	100.0	1.6	15.6	28.6	26.2	19.7	5.9	2.3
Blue Cross, Blue Shield	100.0	1.5	11.9	20.2	21.8	16.9	13.9	13.8
Traditional fee-for-service health plan	100.0	2.0	9.5	13.3	22.6	22.5	13.1	17.2
Preferred-provider health plan	100.0	1.5	13.1	24.0	33.2	17.4	7.3	3.5
Health maintenance organization	100.0	1.9	15.1	30.1	21.4	18.4	7.7	5.3
Commercial Medicare supplement	100.0	0.3	6.5	5.8	5.5	7.9	34.5	39.5
Other BCBS health insurance	100.0	2.1	21.9	24.2	23.8	10.3	10.3	7.5
Health maintenance plans (HMOs)	100.0	2.5	17.0	26.9	25.9	16.7	6.5	4.4
Medicare payments	100.0	0.6	1.8	3.8	5.4	8.1	41.8	38.4
Commercial Medicare supplements/ other health insurance	100.0	1.5	8.6	10.5	13.2	11.0	25.2	30.0
Commercial Medicare supplement (not BCBS)	100.0	1.8	8.5	7.3	10.0	8.4	28.8	35.3
Other health insurance (not BCBS)	100.0	0.9	8.7	16.3	19.1	15.8	18.6	20.5
MEDICAL SERVICES	100.0	2.4	11.1	21.4	24.6	16.4	12.7	11.2
Physician's services	100.0	4.2	15.2	25.0	23.8	16.3	8.6	7.0
Dental services	100.0	1.7	9.1	23.9	24.2	15.6	14.6	10.9
Eye care services	100.0	1.6	10.0	22.4	30.4	17.5	8.8	9.3
Service by professionals other than physician	100.0	1.4	10.5	21.3	28.1	17.0	10.6	11.2
Lab tests, X-rays	100.0	3.1	9.3	20.3	24.6	25.5	9.0	8.2
Hospital room	100.0	3.2	15.0	11.9	36.9	14.9	12.4	5.7
Hospital services other than room	100.0	2.8	15.9	21.7	25.8	19.9	7.9	5.9
Care in convalescent or nursing home	100.0	0.2	0.3	2.7	8.2	10.1	31.2	47.4
Repair of medical equipment	100.0	–	–	–	–	–	95.6	6.5
Other medical services	100.0	1.1	14.1	14.5	18.0	24.9	13.0	14.4
DRUGS	100.0	1.5	7.5	14.9	19.5	16.7	18.8	21.2
Nonprescription drugs	100.0	3.0	13.6	21.3	21.6	13.9	12.8	14.4
Nonprescription vitamins	100.0	0.7	9.0	22.0	24.2	19.9	13.2	11.7
Prescription drugs	100.0	1.3	5.9	12.5	18.4	16.9	21.0	24.0
MEDICAL SUPPLIES	100.0	2.6	12.0	18.9	24.0	15.3	13.4	13.9
Eyeglasses and contact lenses	100.0	2.9	11.3	23.1	28.4	17.2	10.3	6.8
Hearing aids	100.0	0.0	7.0	7.3	6.1	6.5	24.1	48.9
Topicals and dressings	100.0	3.9	18.2	17.6	23.3	13.3	14.3	10.1
Medical equipment for general use	100.0	1.9	10.7	10.5	22.4	16.9	21.5	16.0
Supportive, convalescent medical equipment	100.0	0.6	7.7	7.4	16.2	22.4	21.1	24.8
Rental of medical equipment	100.0	–	3.3	10.1	32.7	17.8	12.7	23.3
Rental of supportive, convalescent medical equip.	100.0	1.7	5.1	7.4	15.5	18.7	12.2	39.6

Note: Numbers may not add to total because of rounding. (–) means sample is too small to make a reliable estimate.
Source: Calculations by New Strategist based on the 2000 Consumer Expenditure Survey

Table 7.6 Health Care: Average spending by income, 2000

(average annual spending on health care, by before-tax income of consumer units (CU), 2000; complete income reporters only)

	complete income reporters	under $10,000	$10,000–$19,999	$20,000–$29,999	$30,000–$39,999	$40,000–$49,999	$50,000–$69,999	$70,000 or more
Number of consumer units (in thousands, add 000)	81,454	10,810	14,714	12,039	9,477	7,653	11,337	15,424
Average number of persons per CU	2.5	1.7	2.1	2.4	2.5	2.6	2.9	3.2
Average before-tax income of CU	$44,649.00	$5,739.61	$14,586.29	$24,527.00	$34,422.00	$44,201.00	$58,561.00	$112,586.00
Average spending of CU, total	40,238.44	16,455.72	22,620.20	29,851.59	35,609.24	42,323.03	49,245.37	75,963.85
Health care, average spending	2,120.04	1,247.70	1,943.02	2,018.43	1,976.91	2,173.18	2,319.62	2,882.09
HEALTH INSURANCE	**$984.66**	**$606.14**	**$901.35**	**$976.85**	**$953.49**	**$1,031.00**	**$1,083.41**	**$1,259.11**
Commercial health insurance	188.03	70.28	90.09	162.03	174.71	245.78	267.48	305.45
Traditional fee-for-service health plan (not BCBS)	74.18	43.84	54.23	78.38	75.85	78.26	87.57	98.30
Preferred-provider health plan (not BCBS)	113.85	26.44	35.86	83.65	98.86	167.52	179.90	207.15
Blue Cross, Blue Shield	**230.60**	**151.00**	**200.26**	**201.03**	**228.69**	**258.14**	**240.53**	**318.63**
Traditional fee-for-service health plan	45.92	32.34	45.63	37.87	47.66	47.67	38.95	65.20
Preferred-provider health plan	58.76	22.64	31.07	37.09	45.19	72.27	90.75	105.53
Health maintenance organization	76.74	36.03	35.35	54.72	91.10	107.12	88.46	129.45
Commercial Medicare supplement	44.44	56.77	84.69	63.92	41.93	24.14	14.84	15.54
Other BCBS health insurance	4.74	3.22	3.51	7.44	2.80	6.95	7.53	2.90
Health maintenance plans (HMOs)	**258.76**	**60.88**	**128.03**	**210.20**	**262.75**	**307.04**	**383.32**	**442.13**
Medicare payments	**169.31**	**226.03**	**324.93**	**225.36**	**148.96**	**102.36**	**74.18**	**52.99**
Commercial Medicare supplements/ other health insurance	**137.95**	**97.94**	**158.05**	**178.24**	**138.38**	**117.67**	**117.90**	**139.91**
Commercial Medicare supplement (not BCBS)	85.72	65.89	121.31	129.69	97.25	59.04	53.24	61.37
Other health insurance (not BCBS)	52.23	32.07	36.75	48.54	41.13	58.63	64.67	78.54
MEDICAL SERVICES	**582.98**	**282.55**	**422.70**	**473.58**	**529.46**	**604.58**	**679.18**	**983.73**
Physician's services	136.18	66.05	89.13	124.00	116.66	164.30	157.71	221.92
Dental services	232.75	102.53	124.26	186.38	226.61	261.29	280.06	418.54
Eye care services	39.00	11.77	26.42	18.46	34.17	48.38	35.41	87.08
Service by professionals other than physician	42.56	14.93	40.02	26.00	26.65	38.64	54.53	80.19
Lab tests, X-rays	21.82	22.72	20.72	16.82	16.71	20.69	17.98	32.65
Hospital room	31.53	11.89	31.15	25.16	39.42	20.69	31.23	51.38
Hospital services other than room	37.19	20.02	23.65	26.07	31.86	38.85	40.00	71.18
Care in convalescent or nursing home	32.37	17.95	63.81	39.30	31.41	1.32	50.32	9.90
Repair of medical equipment	0.87	7.18	–	–	–	–	–	–
Other medical services	8.70	7.52	3.54	11.40	5.96	10.41	11.94	10.82
DRUGS	**446.97**	**307.07**	**539.30**	**480.37**	**410.51**	**433.46**	**423.21**	**467.05**
Nonprescription drugs	74.08	49.73	63.08	68.06	79.53	69.80	77.11	98.05
Nonprescription vitamins	55.40	20.30	45.94	44.59	35.38	63.20	78.17	83.62
Prescription drugs	317.49	237.03	430.29	367.73	295.60	300.46	267.93	285.38
MEDICAL SUPPLIES	**105.42**	**51.95**	**79.67**	**87.62**	**83.46**	**104.14**	**133.83**	**172.20**
Eyeglasses and contact lenses	63.29	24.69	31.86	48.52	50.74	66.33	82.18	124.16
Hearing aids	11.95	12.86	21.50	10.78	7.02	5.18	14.28	7.80
Topicals and dressings	22.60	8.81	16.88	20.20	18.10	23.24	30.02	34.13
Medical equipment for general use	2.07	1.45	1.93	3.73	2.44	1.68	1.77	1.50
Supportive, convalescent medical equipment	2.84	1.04	4.18	2.07	3.56	4.61	1.53	3.05
Rental of medical equipment	1.00	1.08	1.15	0.49	0.44	0.74	2.30	0.70
Rental of supportive, convalescent medical equip.	1.69	2.02	2.15	1.83	1.15	2.34	1.74	0.86

Note: (–) means sample is too small to make a reliable estimate.
Source: Bureau of Labor Statistics, unpublished tables from the 2000 Consumer Expenditure Survey; calculations by New Strategist

Table 7.7 Health Care: Indexed spending by income, 2000

(indexed average annual spending of consumer units (CU) on health care, by before-tax income of consumer unit, 2000; complete income reporters only; index definition: an index of 100 is the average for all consumer units; an index of 132 means that spending by consumer units in that group is 32 percent above the average for all consumer units; an index of 68 indicates spending that is 32 percent below the average for all consumer units)

	complete income reporters	under $10,000	$10,000– $19,999	$20,000– $29,999	$30,000– $39,999	$40,000– $49,999	$50,000– $69,999	$70,000 or more
Average spending of CU, total	$40,238	$16,456	$22,620	$29,852	$35,609	$42,323	$49,245	$75,964
Average spending of CU, index	100	41	56	74	88	105	122	189
Health care, spending index	100	59	92	95	93	103	109	136
HEALTH INSURANCE	**100**	**62**	**92**	**99**	**97**	**105**	**110**	**128**
Commercial health insurance	**100**	**37**	**48**	**86**	**93**	**131**	**142**	**162**
Traditional fee-for-service health plan (not BCBS)	100	59	73	106	102	106	118	133
Preferred-provider health plan (not BCBS)	100	23	31	73	87	147	158	182
Blue Cross, Blue Shield	**100**	**65**	**87**	**87**	**99**	**112**	**104**	**138**
Traditional fee-for-service health plan	100	70	99	82	104	104	85	142
Preferred-provider health plan	100	39	53	63	77	123	154	180
Health maintenance organization	100	47	46	71	119	140	115	169
Commercial Medicare supplement	100	128	191	144	94	54	33	35
Other BCBS health insurance	100	68	74	157	59	147	159	61
Health maintenance plans (HMOs)	**100**	**24**	**49**	**81**	**102**	**119**	**148**	**171**
Medicare payments	**100**	**134**	**192**	**133**	**88**	**60**	**44**	**31**
Commercial Medicare supplements/ other health insurance	**100**	**71**	**115**	**129**	**100**	**85**	**85**	**101**
Commercial Medicare supplement (not BCBS)	100	77	142	151	113	69	62	72
Other health insurance (not BCBS)	100	61	70	93	79	112	124	150
MEDICAL SERVICES	**100**	**48**	**73**	**81**	**91**	**104**	**117**	**169**
Physician's services	100	49	65	91	86	121	116	163
Dental services	100	44	53	80	97	112	120	180
Eye care services	100	30	68	47	88	124	91	223
Service by professionals other than physician	100	35	94	61	63	91	128	188
Lab tests, X-rays	100	104	95	77	77	95	82	150
Hospital room	100	38	99	80	125	66	99	163
Hospital services other than room	100	54	64	70	86	104	108	191
Care in convalescent or nursing home	100	55	197	121	97	4	155	31
Repair of medical equipment	100	825	–	–	–	–	–	–
Other medical services	100	86	41	131	69	120	137	124
DRUGS	**100**	**69**	**121**	**107**	**92**	**97**	**95**	**104**
Nonprescription drugs	100	67	85	92	107	94	104	132
Nonprescription vitamins	100	37	83	80	64	114	141	151
Prescription drugs	100	75	136	116	93	95	84	90
MEDICAL SUPPLIES	**100**	**49**	**76**	**83**	**79**	**99**	**127**	**163**
Eyeglasses and contact lenses	100	39	50	77	80	105	130	196
Hearing aids	100	108	180	90	59	43	119	65
Topicals and dressings	100	39	75	89	80	103	133	151
Medical equipment for general use	100	70	93	180	118	81	86	72
Supportive, convalescent medical equipment	100	37	147	73	125	162	54	107
Rental of medical equipment	100	108	115	49	44	74	230	70
Rental of supportive, convalescent medical equip.	100	119	127	108	68	138	103	51

Note: (–) means sample is too small to make a reliable estimate.
Source: Calculations by New Strategist based on the 2000 Consumer Expenditure Survey

Table 7.8 Health Care: Indexed per capita spending by income, 2000

(indexed average annual per capita spending of consumer units (CU) on health care, by before-tax income of consumer unit, 2000; complete income reporters only; index definition: an index of 100 is the average for all consumer units; an index of 132 means that spending by consumer units in that group is 32 percent above the average for all consumer units; an index of 68 indicates spending that is 32 percent below the average for all consumer units)

	complete income reporters	under $10,000	$10,000– $19,999	$20,000– $29,999	$30,000– $39,999	$40,000– $49,999	$50,000– $69,999	$70,000 or more
Per capita spending of CU, total	$16,095	$9,492	$10,819	$12,438	$14,244	$16,278	$16,981	$23,739
Per capita spending of CU, index	100	59	67	77	88	101	106	147
Health care, per capita spending index	100	85	110	99	93	99	94	106
HEALTH INSURANCE	100	89	109	103	97	101	95	100
Commercial health insurance	100	54	57	90	93	126	123	127
Traditional fee-for-service health plan (not BCBS)	100	85	87	110	102	101	102	104
Preferred-provider health plan (not BCBS)	100	33	38	77	87	141	136	142
Blue Cross, Blue Shield	100	94	104	91	99	108	90	108
Traditional fee-for-service health plan	100	102	119	86	104	100	73	111
Preferred-provider health plan	100	56	63	66	77	118	133	140
Health maintenance organization	100	68	55	74	119	134	99	132
Commercial Medicare supplement	100	184	228	150	94	52	29	27
Other BCBS health insurance	100	98	88	164	59	141	137	48
Health maintenance plans (HMOs)	100	34	59	85	102	114	128	133
Medicare payments	100	193	229	139	88	58	38	24
Commercial Medicare supplements/ other health insurance	100	102	137	135	100	82	74	79
Commercial Medicare supplement (not BCBS)	100	111	169	158	113	66	54	56
Other health insurance (not BCBS)	100	89	84	97	79	108	107	117
MEDICAL SERVICES	100	70	87	85	91	100	100	132
Physician's services	100	70	78	95	86	116	100	127
Dental services	100	64	64	83	97	108	104	140
Eye care services	100	44	81	49	88	119	78	174
Service by professionals other than physician	100	51	112	64	63	87	110	147
Lab tests, X-rays	100	150	114	80	77	91	71	117
Hospital room	100	54	118	83	125	63	85	127
Hospital services other than room	100	78	76	73	86	100	93	150
Care in convalescent or nursing home	100	80	236	126	97	4	134	24
Repair of medical equipment	100	1,190	–	–	–	–	–	–
Other medical services	100	125	49	136	69	115	118	97
DRUGS	100	99	144	112	92	93	82	82
Nonprescription drugs	100	97	102	96	107	91	90	103
Nonprescription vitamins	100	53	99	84	64	110	122	118
Prescription drugs	100	108	162	121	93	91	73	70
MEDICAL SUPPLIES	100	71	90	87	79	95	109	128
Eyeglasses and contact lenses	100	56	60	80	80	101	112	153
Hearing aids	100	155	215	94	59	42	103	51
Topicals and dressings	100	56	89	93	80	99	115	118
Medical equipment for general use	100	101	112	188	118	78	74	57
Supportive, convalescent medical equipment	100	53	176	76	125	156	46	84
Rental of medical equipment	100	156	138	51	44	71	198	55
Rental of supportive, convalescent medical equip.	100	172	152	113	68	133	89	40

Note: Per capita indexes account for household size and show how much each person in a particular household demographic segment spends relative to a person in the average household. (–) means sample is too small to make a reliable estimate.
Source: Calculations by New Strategist based on the 2000 Consumer Expenditure Survey

Table 7.9 Health Care: Total spending by income, 2000

(total annual spending on health care, by before-tax income group of consumer units (CU), 2000; complete income reporters only; numbers in thousands)

	complete income reporters	under $10,000	$10,000– $19,999	$20,000– $29,999	$30,000– $39,999	$40,000– $49,999	$50,000– $69,999	$70,000 or more
Number of consumer units	81,454	10,810	14,714	12,039	9,477	7,653	11,337	15,424
Total spending of all CUs	$3,277,581,892	$177,886,368	$332,833,656	$359,383,292	$337,468,767	$323,898,149	$558,294,760	$1,171,666,422
Health care, total spending	172,685,738	13,487,688	28,589,670	24,299,879	18,735,176	16,631,347	26,297,532	44,453,356
HEALTH INSURANCE	**$80,204,496**	**$6,552,379**	**$13,262,466**	**$11,760,297**	**$9,036,225**	**$7,890,243**	**$12,282,619**	**$19,420,513**
Commercial health insurance	15,315,796	759,684	1,325,514	1,950,679	1,655,727	1,880,954	3,032,421	4,711,261
Traditional fee-for-service health plan (not BCBS)	6,042,258	473,910	797,888	943,617	718,830	598,924	992,781	1,516,179
Preferred-provider health plan (not BCBS)	9,273,538	285,774	527,626	1,007,062	936,896	1,282,031	2,039,526	3,195,082
Blue Cross, Blue Shield	**18,783,292**	**1,632,278**	**2,946,633**	**2,420,200**	**2,167,295**	**1,975,545**	**2,726,889**	**4,914,549**
Traditional fee-for-service health plan	3,740,368	349,577	671,469	455,917	451,674	364,819	441,576	1,005,645
Preferred-provider health plan	4,786,237	244,704	457,195	446,527	428,266	553,082	1,028,833	1,627,695
Health maintenance organization	6,250,780	389,510	520,098	658,774	863,355	819,789	1,002,871	1,996,637
Commercial Medicare supplement	3,619,816	613,707	1,246,194	769,533	397,371	184,743	168,241	239,689
Other BCBS health insurance	386,092	34,782	51,597	89,570	26,536	53,188	85,368	44,730
Health maintenance plans (HMOs)	**21,077,037**	**658,134**	**1,883,761**	**2,530,598**	**2,490,082**	**2,349,777**	**4,345,699**	**6,819,413**
Medicare payments	**13,790,977**	**2,443,436**	**4,781,054**	**2,713,109**	**1,411,694**	**783,361**	**840,979**	**817,318**
Commercial Medicare supplements/ other health insurance	**11,236,579**	**1,058,774**	**2,325,584**	**2,145,831**	**1,311,427**	**900,529**	**1,336,632**	**2,157,972**
Commercial Medicare supplement (not BCBS)	6,982,237	712,219	1,784,952	1,561,338	921,638	451,833	603,582	946,571
Other health insurance (not BCBS)	4,254,342	346,627	540,699	584,373	389,789	448,695	733,164	1,211,401
MEDICAL SERVICES	**47,486,053**	**3,054,399**	**6,219,656**	**5,701,430**	**5,017,692**	**4,626,851**	**7,699,864**	**15,173,052**
Physician's services	11,092,406	714,015	1,311,485	1,492,836	1,105,587	1,257,388	1,787,958	3,422,894
Dental services	18,958,419	1,108,375	1,828,377	2,243,829	2,147,583	1,999,652	3,175,040	6,455,561
Eye care services	3,176,706	127,239	388,763	222,240	323,829	370,252	401,443	1,343,122
Service by professionals other than physician	3,466,682	161,346	588,856	313,014	252,562	295,712	618,207	1,236,851
Lab tests, X-rays	1,777,326	245,648	304,852	202,496	158,361	158,341	203,839	503,594
Hospital room	2,568,245	128,490	458,268	302,901	373,583	158,341	354,055	792,485
Hospital services other than room	3,029,274	216,402	348,043	313,857	301,937	297,319	453,480	1,097,880
Care in convalescent or nursing home	2,636,666	194,054	938,832	473,133	297,673	10,102	570,478	152,698
Repair of medical equipment	70,865	77,576	–	–	–	–	–	–
Other medical services	708,650	81,325	52,114	137,245	56,483	79,668	135,364	166,888
DRUGS	**36,407,494**	**3,319,428**	**7,935,238**	**5,783,174**	**3,890,403**	**3,317,269**	**4,797,932**	**7,203,779**
Nonprescription drugs	6,034,112	537,603	928,132	819,374	753,706	534,179	874,196	1,512,323
Nonprescription vitamins	4,512,552	219,452	675,905	536,819	335,296	483,670	886,213	1,289,755
Prescription drugs	25,860,830	2,562,338	6,331,268	4,427,101	2,801,401	2,299,420	3,037,522	4,401,701
MEDICAL SUPPLIES	**8,586,881**	**561,589**	**1,172,230**	**1,054,857**	**790,950**	**796,983**	**1,517,231**	**2,656,013**
Eyeglasses and contact lenses	5,155,224	266,864	468,763	584,132	480,863	507,623	931,675	1,915,044
Hearing aids	973,375	139,012	316,418	129,780	66,529	39,643	161,892	120,307
Topicals and dressings	1,840,860	95,207	248,395	243,188	171,534	177,856	340,337	526,421
Medical equipment for general use	168,610	15,711	28,459	44,905	23,124	12,857	20,066	23,136
Supportive, convalescent medical equipment	231,329	11,262	61,508	24,921	33,738	35,280	17,346	47,043
Rental of medical equipment	81,454	11,709	16,957	5,899	4,170	5,663	26,075	10,797
Rental of supportive, convalescent medical equipment	137,657	21,823	31,650	22,031	10,899	17,908	19,726	13,265

Note: Numbers may not add to total because of rounding. (–) means sample is too small to make a reliable estimate.
Source: Calculations by New Strategist based on the 2000 Consumer Expenditure Survey

Table 7.10 Health Care: Market shares by income, 2000

(percentage of total annual spending on health care accounted for by before-tax income group of consumer units, 2000; complete income reporters only)

	complete income reporters	under $10,000	$10,000– $19,999	$20,000– $29,999	$30,000– $39,999	$40,000– $49,999	$50,000– $69,999	$70,000 or more
Share of total consumer units	100.0%	13.3%	18.1%	14.8%	11.6%	9.4%	13.9%	18.9%
Share of total before-tax income	100.0	1.7	5.9	8.1	9.0	9.3	18.3	47.7
Share of total spending	100.0	5.4	10.2	11.0	10.3	9.9	17.0	35.7
Share of health care spending	100.0	7.8	16.6	14.1	10.8	9.6	15.2	25.7
HEALTH INSURANCE	**100.0%**	**8.2%**	**16.5%**	**14.7%**	**11.3%**	**9.8%**	**15.3%**	**24.2%**
Commercial health insurance	**100.0**	**5.0**	**8.7**	**12.7**	**10.8**	**12.3**	**19.8**	**30.8**
Traditional fee-for-service health plan (not BCBS)	100.0	7.8	13.2	15.6	11.9	9.9	16.4	25.1
Preferred-provider health plan (not BCBS)	100.0	3.1	5.7	10.9	10.1	13.8	22.0	34.5
Blue Cross, Blue Shield	**100.0**	**8.7**	**15.7**	**12.9**	**11.5**	**10.5**	**14.5**	**26.2**
Traditional fee-for-service health plan	100.0	9.3	18.0	12.2	12.1	9.8	11.8	26.9
Preferred-provider health plan	100.0	5.1	9.6	9.3	8.9	11.6	21.5	34.0
Health maintenance organization	100.0	6.2	8.3	10.5	13.8	13.1	16.0	31.9
Commercial Medicare supplement	100.0	17.0	34.4	21.3	11.0	5.1	4.6	6.6
Other BCBS health insurance	100.0	9.0	13.4	23.2	6.9	13.8	22.1	11.6
Health maintenance plans (HMOs)	**100.0**	**3.1**	**8.9**	**12.0**	**11.8**	**11.1**	**20.6**	**32.4**
Medicare payments	**100.0**	**17.7**	**34.7**	**19.7**	**10.2**	**5.7**	**6.1**	**5.9**
Commercial Medicare supplements/ other health insurance	**100.0**	**9.4**	**20.7**	**19.1**	**11.7**	**8.0**	**11.9**	**19.2**
Commercial Medicare supplement (not BCBS)	100.0	10.2	25.6	22.4	13.2	6.5	8.6	13.6
Other health insurance (not BCBS)	100.0	8.1	12.7	13.7	9.2	10.5	17.2	28.5
MEDICAL SERVICES	**100.0**	**6.4**	**13.1**	**12.0**	**10.6**	**9.7**	**16.2**	**32.0**
Physician's services	100.0	6.4	11.8	13.5	10.0	11.3	16.1	30.9
Dental services	100.0	5.8	9.6	11.8	11.3	10.5	16.7	34.1
Eye care services	100.0	4.0	12.2	7.0	10.2	11.7	12.6	42.3
Service by professionals other than physician	100.0	4.7	17.0	9.0	7.3	8.5	17.8	35.7
Lab tests, X-rays	100.0	13.8	17.2	11.4	8.9	8.9	11.5	28.3
Hospital room	100.0	5.0	17.8	11.8	14.5	6.2	13.8	30.9
Hospital services other than room	100.0	7.1	11.5	10.4	10.0	9.8	15.0	36.2
Care in convalescent or nursing home	100.0	7.4	35.6	17.9	11.3	0.4	21.6	5.8
Repair of medical equipment	100.0	100.0	–	–	–	–	–	–
Other medical services	100.0	11.5	7.4	19.4	8.0	11.2	19.1	23.6
DRUGS	**100.0**	**9.1**	**21.8**	**15.9**	**10.7**	**9.1**	**13.2**	**19.8**
Nonprescription drugs	100.0	8.9	15.4	13.6	12.5	8.9	14.5	25.1
Nonprescription vitamins	100.0	4.9	15.0	11.9	7.4	10.7	19.6	28.6
Prescription drugs	100.0	9.9	24.5	17.1	10.8	8.9	11.7	17.0
MEDICAL SUPPLIES	**100.0**	**6.5**	**13.7**	**12.3**	**9.2**	**9.3**	**17.7**	**30.9**
Eyeglasses and contact lenses	100.0	5.2	9.1	11.3	9.3	9.8	18.1	37.1
Hearing aids	100.0	14.3	32.5	13.3	6.8	4.1	16.6	12.4
Topicals and dressings	100.0	5.2	13.5	13.2	9.3	9.7	18.5	28.6
Medical equipment for general use	100.0	9.3	16.9	26.6	13.7	7.6	11.9	13.7
Supportive, convalescent medical equipment	100.0	4.9	26.6	10.8	14.6	15.3	7.5	20.3
Rental of medical equipment	100.0	14.4	20.8	7.2	5.1	7.0	32.0	13.3
Rental of supportive, convalescent medical equip.	100.0	15.9	23.0	16.0	7.9	13.0	14.3	9.6

Note: Numbers may not add to total because of rounding. (–) means sample is too small to make a reliable estimate.
Source: Calculations by New Strategist based on the 2000 Consumer Expenditure Survey

Table 7.11 Health Care: Average spending by household type, 2000

(average annual spending of consumer units (CU) on health care, by type of consumer unit, 2000)

	total married couples	married couples, no children	married couples with children				single parent, at least one child <18	single person
			total	oldest child under 6	oldest child 6 to 17	oldest child 18 or older		
Number of consumer units								
(in thousands, add 000)	56,287	22,805	28,777	5,291	15,396	8,090	6,132	32,323
Average number of persons per CU	3.2	2.0	3.9	3.5	4.1	3.8	2.9	1.0
Average before-tax income of CU	$60,588.00	$53,232.00	$66,913.00	$62,928.00	$69,472.00	$64,725.00	$25,095.00	$24,977.00
Average spending of CU, total	48,619.37	42,195.54	53,585.53	50,755.90	54,170.40	54,550.20	28,923.25	23,059.00
Health care, average spending	2,640.10	3,043.86	2,305.93	1,896.70	2,251.26	2,681.17	1,014.50	1,487.78
HEALTH INSURANCE	**$1,287.70**	**$1,478.63**	**$1,131.44**	**$1,024.69**	**$1,077.95**	**$1,303.07**	**$452.70**	**$657.35**
Commercial health insurance	**286.13**	**267.08**	**316.67**	**315.38**	**318.40**	**314.24**	**85.56**	**92.02**
Traditional fee-for-service health plan (not BCBS)	106.23	119.84	101.46	68.16	102.12	121.98	25.11	46.11
Preferred-provider health plan (not BCBS)	179.89	147.24	215.22	247.22	216.28	192.26	60.45	45.91
Blue Cross, Blue Shield	**304.09**	**322.07**	**283.01**	**231.05**	**266.62**	**348.19**	**111.25**	**155.93**
Traditional fee-for-service health plan	59.06	70.09	48.32	34.79	43.72	65.93	13.17	38.43
Preferred-provider health plan	89.23	81.89	97.40	73.61	88.03	130.79	37.75	26.51
Health maintenance organization	102.24	78.95	114.46	104.65	116.10	117.78	56.82	35.82
Commercial Medicare supplement	47.11	83.50	17.05	16.53	11.79	27.41	3.08	51.95
Other BCBS health insurance	6.44	7.65	5.77	1.47	6.98	6.28	0.42	3.22
Health maintenance plans (HMOs)	**358.34**	**290.84**	**408.23**	**403.77**	**404.84**	**417.60**	**193.60**	**108.86**
Medicare payments	**172.63**	**333.47**	**33.94**	**5.82**	**11.85**	**94.37**	**19.41**	**183.84**
Commercial Medicare supplements/ other health insurance	**166.51**	**265.17**	**89.59**	**68.66**	**76.24**	**128.67**	**42.88**	**116.70**
Commercial Medicare supplement (not BCBS)	103.39	172.60	43.77	41.42	30.66	70.27	15.60	82.31
Other health insurance (not BCBS)	63.12	92.57	45.82	27.24	45.59	58.40	27.28	34.39
MEDICAL SERVICES	**716.78**	**737.55**	**697.67**	**547.69**	**731.27**	**731.82**	**362.59**	**417.76**
Physician's services	177.17	173.79	177.41	181.71	171.09	186.60	88.63	80.30
Dental services	292.65	301.71	298.04	136.85	351.80	301.14	153.92	147.79
Eye care services	49.13	51.60	49.35	32.97	44.68	68.97	12.73	22.70
Service by professionals other than physician	39.36	35.32	45.02	22.63	48.29	53.45	22.01	38.85
Lab tests, X-rays	24.89	27.96	18.75	10.75	21.58	18.60	15.19	13.62
Hospital room	43.62	46.69	37.74	73.47	31.73	25.80	20.32	23.40
Hospital services other than room	57.72	56.85	56.76	83.41	53.03	46.43	32.92	20.96
Care in convalescent or nursing home	19.57	31.99	3.99	1.94	0.57	11.86	0.47	59.98
Repair of medical equipment	1.10	2.65	–	–	–	–	–	0.13
Other medical services	11.57	8.94	10.61	3.97	8.49	18.96	16.40	10.01
DRUGS	**504.06**	**670.92**	**360.94**	**240.80**	**326.58**	**508.67**	**145.32**	**351.12**
Nonprescription drugs	78.88	79.83	72.58	77.50	70.68	72.49	40.54	48.69
Nonprescription vitamins	54.91	67.22	47.96	28.40	44.58	71.42	17.62	40.53
Prescription drugs	370.27	523.87	240.40	134.91	211.32	364.76	87.16	261.90
MEDICAL SUPPLIES	**131.56**	**156.77**	**115.88**	**83.52**	**115.46**	**137.60**	**53.89**	**61.54**
Eyeglasses and contact lenses	79.94	81.87	79.92	52.41	80.27	97.25	35.01	31.03
Hearing aids	15.63	32.22	4.97	0.43	5.43	7.06	0.29	10.80
Topicals and dressings	26.90	29.19	26.11	26.62	26.76	24.30	16.78	13.86
Medical equipment for general use	2.44	4.00	1.41	1.20	1.27	1.80	0.73	1.49
Supportive, convalescent medical equipment	3.82	6.09	1.94	2.15	0.73	4.10	0.86	2.16
Rental of medical equipment	1.03	1.07	0.36	0.27	0.31	0.52	0.07	0.56
Rental of supportive, convalescent medical equip.	1.80	2.33	1.18	0.44	0.69	2.59	0.15	1.64

Note: Average spending figures for total consumer units can be found on Average Spending by Age and Average Spending by Region tables. (–) means sample is too small to make a reliable estimate.
Source: Bureau of Labor Statistics, unpublished tables from the 2000 Consumer Expenditure Survey

Table 7.12 Health Care: Indexed spending by household type, 2000

(indexed average annual spending of consumer units (CU) on health care, by type of consumer unit, 2000; index definition: an index of 100 is the average for all consumer units; an index of 132 means that spending by consumer units in that group is 32 percent above the average for all consumer units; an index of 68 indicates spending that is 32 percent below the average for all consumer units)

| | total married couples | married couples, no children | married couples with children | | | | single parent, at least one child <18 | single person |
			total	oldest child under 6	oldest child 6 to 17	oldest child 18 or older		
Average spending of CU, total	$48,619	$42,196	$53,586	$50,756	$54,170	$54,550	$28,923	$23,059
Average spending of CU, index	128	111	141	133	142	143	76	61
Health care, spending index	128	147	112	92	109	130	49	72
HEALTH INSURANCE	**131**	**150**	**115**	**104**	**110**	**133**	**46**	**67**
Commercial health insurance	**147**	**137**	**163**	**162**	**164**	**162**	**44**	**47**
Traditional fee-for-service health plan (not BCBS)	138	155	132	88	133	158	33	60
Preferred-provider health plan (not BCBS)	153	126	183	211	184	164	52	39
Blue Cross, Blue Shield	**131**	**139**	**122**	**99**	**115**	**150**	**48**	**67**
Traditional fee-for-service health plan	118	140	97	70	88	132	26	77
Preferred-provider health plan	146	134	160	121	144	215	62	44
Health maintenance organization	140	108	156	143	159	161	78	49
Commercial Medicare supplement	108	191	39	38	27	63	7	119
Other BCBS health insurance	137	162	123	31	148	133	9	68
Health maintenance plans (HMOs)	**141**	**114**	**160**	**158**	**159**	**164**	**76**	**43**
Medicare payments	**105**	**203**	**21**	**4**	**7**	**58**	**12**	**112**
Commercial Medicare supplements/ other health insurance	**122**	**194**	**65**	**50**	**56**	**94**	**31**	**85**
Commercial Medicare supplement (not BCBS)	117	196	50	47	35	80	18	93
Other health insurance (not BCBS)	130	190	94	56	94	120	56	71
MEDICAL SERVICES	**126**	**130**	**123**	**96**	**129**	**129**	**64**	**74**
Physician's services	132	129	132	135	127	139	66	60
Dental services	133	137	135	62	159	136	70	67
Eye care services	140	147	141	94	127	197	36	65
Service by professionals other than physician	107	96	122	61	131	145	60	105
Lab tests, X-rays	124	139	93	53	107	92	75	68
Hospital room	121	130	105	204	88	72	57	65
Hospital services other than room	140	138	138	203	129	113	80	51
Care in convalescent or nursing home	60	99	12	6	2	37	1	185
Repair of medical equipment	180	434	–	–	–	–	–	21
Other medical services	110	85	100	38	80	180	155	95
DRUGS	**121**	**161**	**87**	**58**	**78**	**122**	**35**	**84**
Nonprescription drugs	121	123	112	119	109	111	62	75
Nonprescription vitamins	119	146	104	61	97	155	38	88
Prescription drugs	121	172	79	44	69	120	29	86
MEDICAL SUPPLIES	**133**	**159**	**117**	**85**	**117**	**139**	**55**	**62**
Eyeglasses and contact lenses	137	140	137	90	137	166	60	53
Hearing aids	133	274	42	4	46	60	2	92
Topicals and dressings	128	139	124	127	127	116	80	66
Medical equipment for general use	120	196	69	59	62	88	36	73
Supportive, convalescent medical equipment	120	192	61	68	23	129	27	68
Rental of medical equipment	121	126	42	32	36	61	8	66
Rental of supportive, convalescent medical equip.	123	160	81	30	47	177	10	112

Note: Spending index for total consumer units is 100. (–) means sample is too small to make a reliable estimate.
Source: Calculations by New Strategist based on the 2000 Consumer Expenditure Survey

Table 7.13 Health Care: Indexed per capita spending by household type, 2000

(indexed average annual per capita spending of consumer units (CU) on health care, by type of consumer unit, 2000; index definition: an index of 100 is the average for all consumer units; an index of 132 means that spending by consumer units in that group is 32 percent above the average for all consumer units; an index of 68 indicates spending that is 32 percent below the average for all consumer units)

	total married couples	married couples, no children	married couples with children				single parent, at least one child <18	single person
			total	oldest child under 6	oldest child 6 to 17	oldest child 18 or older		
Per capita spending of CU, total	$15,194	$21,098	$13,740	$14,502	$13,212	$14,355	$9,974	$23,059
Per capita spending of CU, index	100	139	90	95	87	94	66	152
Health care, per capita spending index	100	184	72	66	66	85	42	180
HEALTH INSURANCE	102	188	74	74	67	87	40	167
Commercial health insurance	115	172	104	116	100	106	38	118
Traditional fee-for-service health plan (not BCBS)	108	194	84	63	81	104	28	150
Preferred-provider health plan (not BCBS)	120	157	118	151	112	108	44	98
Blue Cross, Blue Shield	102	173	78	71	70	99	41	168
Traditional fee-for-service health plan	92	176	62	50	53	87	23	193
Preferred-provider health plan	114	168	102	86	88	141	53	109
Health maintenance organization	109	135	100	102	97	106	67	122
Commercial Medicare supplement	84	238	25	27	16	41	6	297
Other BCBS health insurance	107	203	79	22	90	88	8	171
Health maintenance plans (HMOs)	110	143	103	113	97	108	65	107
Medicare payments	82	254	13	3	4	38	10	280
Commercial Medicare supplements/ other health insurance	95	242	42	36	34	62	27	213
Commercial Medicare supplement (not BCBS)	92	245	32	34	21	52	15	233
Other health insurance (not BCBS)	101	238	60	40	57	79	48	177
MEDICAL SERVICES	99	162	79	69	79	85	55	184
Physician's services	103	162	85	97	78	91	57	149
Dental services	104	171	87	44	97	90	60	167
Eye care services	110	184	90	67	78	129	31	162
Service by professionals other than physician	83	120	78	44	80	95	51	263
Lab tests, X-rays	97	174	60	38	65	61	65	169
Hospital room	95	162	67	146	54	47	49	163
Hospital services other than room	110	173	88	145	79	74	69	127
Care in convalescent or nursing home	47	124	8	4	1	24	1	464
Repair of medical equipment	141	543	–	–	–	–	–	53
Other medical services	86	106	64	27	49	118	134	237
DRUGS	95	201	56	41	48	80	30	211
Nonprescription drugs	95	153	71	85	66	73	54	187
Nonprescription vitamins	93	182	67	44	59	102	33	219
Prescription drugs	95	215	50	32	42	79	25	215
MEDICAL SUPPLIES	104	198	75	60	71	92	47	156
Eyeglasses and contact lenses	107	175	88	64	84	109	52	133
Hearing aids	104	342	27	3	28	39	2	229
Topicals and dressings	100	174	80	91	78	76	69	165
Medical equipment for general use	93	245	44	42	38	58	31	183
Supportive, convalescent medical equipment	94	239	39	48	14	85	23	170
Rental of medical equipment	95	157	27	23	22	40	7	165
Rental of supportive, convalescent medical equip.	96	199	52	22	29	117	9	281

Note: Per capita indexes account for household size and show how much each person in a particular household demographic segment spends relative to a person in the average household. Spending index for total consumer units is 100. (–) means sample is too small to make a reliable estimate.
Source: Calculations by New Strategist based on the 2000 Consumer Expenditure Survey

Table 7.14 Health Care: Total spending by household type, 2000

(total annual spending on health care, by consumer unit (CU) type, 2000; numbers in thousands)

	total married couples	married couples, no children	married couples with children				single parent, at least one child <18	single person
			total	oldest child under 6	oldest child 6 to 17	oldest child 18 or older		
Number of consumer units	56,287	22,805	28,777	5,291	15,396	8,090	6,132	32,323
Total spending of all CUs	$2,736,638,479	$962,269,290	$1,542,030,797	$268,549,467	$834,007,478	$441,311,118	$177,357,369	$745,336,057
Health care, total spending	148,603,309	69,415,227	66,357,748	10,035,440	34,660,399	21,690,665	6,220,914	48,089,513
HEALTH INSURANCE	**$72,480,770**	**$33,720,157**	**$32,559,449**	**$5,421,635**	**$16,596,118**	**$10,541,836**	**$2,775,956**	**$21,247,524**
Commercial health insurance	**16,105,399**	**6,090,759**	**9,112,813**	**1,668,676**	**4,902,086**	**2,542,202**	**524,654**	**2,974,362**
Traditional fee-for-service health plan (not BCBS)	5,979,368	2,732,951	2,919,714	360,635	1,572,240	986,818	153,975	1,490,414
Preferred-provider health plan (not BCBS)	10,125,468	3,357,808	6,193,386	1,308,041	3,329,847	1,555,383	370,679	1,483,949
Blue Cross, Blue Shield	**17,116,314**	**7,344,806**	**8,144,179**	**1,222,486**	**4,104,882**	**2,816,857**	**682,185**	**5,040,125**
Traditional fee-for-service health plan	3,324,310	1,598,402	1,390,505	184,074	673,113	533,374	80,758	1,242,173
Preferred-provider health plan	5,022,489	1,867,501	2,802,880	389,471	1,355,310	1,058,091	231,483	856,883
Health maintenance organization	5,754,783	1,800,455	3,293,815	553,703	1,787,476	952,840	348,420	1,157,810
Commercial Medicare supplement	2,651,681	1,904,218	490,648	87,460	181,519	221,747	18,887	1,679,180
Other BCBS health insurance	362,488	174,458	166,043	7,778	107,464	50,805	2,575	104,080
Health maintenance plans (HMOs)	**20,169,884**	**6,632,606**	**11,747,635**	**2,136,347**	**6,232,917**	**3,378,384**	**1,187,155**	**3,518,682**
Medicare payments	**9,716,825**	**7,604,783**	**976,691**	**30,794**	**182,443**	**763,453**	**119,022**	**5,942,260**
Commercial Medicare supplements/ other health insurance	**9,372,348**	**6,047,202**	**2,578,131**	**363,280**	**1,173,791**	**1,040,940**	**262,940**	**3,772,094**
Commercial Medicare supplement (not BCBS)	5,819,513	3,936,143	1,259,569	219,153	472,041	568,484	95,659	2,660,506
Other health insurance (not BCBS)	3,552,835	2,111,059	1,318,562	144,127	701,904	472,456	167,281	1,111,588
MEDICAL SERVICES	**40,345,396**	**16,819,828**	**20,076,850**	**2,897,828**	**11,258,633**	**5,920,424**	**2,223,402**	**13,503,256**
Physician's services	9,972,368	3,963,281	5,105,328	961,428	2,634,102	1,509,594	543,479	2,595,537
Dental services	16,472,391	6,880,497	8,576,697	724,073	5,416,313	2,436,223	943,837	4,777,016
Eye care services	2,765,380	1,176,738	1,420,145	174,444	687,893	557,967	78,060	733,732
Service by professionals other than physician	2,215,456	805,473	1,295,541	119,735	743,473	432,411	134,965	1,255,749
Lab tests, X-rays	1,400,983	637,628	539,569	56,878	332,246	150,474	93,145	440,239
Hospital room	2,455,239	1,064,765	1,086,044	388,730	488,515	208,722	124,602	756,358
Hospital services other than room	3,248,886	1,296,464	1,633,383	441,322	816,450	375,619	201,865	677,490
Care in convalescent or nursing home	1,101,537	729,532	114,820	10,265	8,776	95,947	2,882	1,938,734
Repair of medical equipment	61,916	60,433	–	–	–	–	–	4,202
Other medical services	651,241	203,877	305,324	21,005	130,712	153,386	100,565	323,553
DRUGS	**28,372,025**	**15,300,331**	**10,386,770**	**1,274,073**	**5,028,026**	**4,115,140**	**891,102**	**11,349,252**
Nonprescription drugs	4,439,919	1,820,523	2,088,635	410,053	1,088,189	586,444	248,591	1,573,807
Nonprescription vitamins	3,090,719	1,532,952	1,380,145	150,264	686,354	577,788	108,046	1,310,051
Prescription drugs	20,841,387	11,946,855	6,917,991	713,809	3,253,483	2,950,908	534,465	8,465,394
MEDICAL SUPPLIES	**7,405,118**	**3,575,140**	**3,334,679**	**441,904**	**1,777,622**	**1,113,184**	**330,453**	**1,989,157**
Eyeglasses and contact lenses	4,499,583	1,867,045	2,299,858	277,301	1,235,837	786,753	214,681	1,002,983
Hearing aids	879,766	734,777	143,022	2,275	83,600	57,115	1,778	349,088
Topicals and dressings	1,514,120	665,678	751,367	140,846	411,997	196,587	102,895	447,997
Medical equipment for general use	137,340	91,220	40,576	6,349	19,553	14,562	4,476	48,161
Supportive, convalescent medical equipment	215,016	138,882	55,827	11,376	11,239	33,169	5,274	69,818
Rental of medical equipment	57,976	24,401	10,360	1,429	4,773	4,207	429	18,101
Rental of supportive, convalescent medical equipment	101,317	53,136	33,957	2,328	10,623	20,953	920	53,010

Note: Total spending figures for total consumer units can be found on Total Spending by Age and Total Spending by Region tables. Spending by type of consumer unit will not add to total because not all types of consumer units are shown. (–) means sample is too small to make a reliable estimate.
Source: Calculations by New Strategist based on the 2000 Consumer Expenditure Survey

Table 7.15   Health Care: Market shares by household type, 2000

(percentage of total annual spending on health care accounted for by types of consumer units, 2000)

	total married couples	married couples, no children	married couples with children				single parent, at least one child <18	single person
			total	oldest child under 6	oldest child 6 to 17	oldest child 18 or older		
Share of total consumer units	51.5%	20.9%	26.3%	4.8%	14.1%	7.4%	5.6%	29.6%
Share of total before-tax income	69.8	24.9	39.4	6.8	21.9	10.7	3.2	16.5
Share of total spending	65.8	23.1	37.1	6.5	20.0	10.6	4.3	17.9
Share of health care spending	65.8	30.7	29.4	4.4	15.3	9.6	2.8	21.3
HEALTH INSURANCE	67.4%	31.4%	30.3%	5.0%	15.4%	9.8%	2.6%	19.8%
Commercial health insurance	75.8	28.6	42.9	7.8	23.1	12.0	2.5	14.0
Traditional fee-for-service health plan (not BCBS)	70.9	32.4	34.6	4.3	18.7	11.7	1.8	17.7
Preferred-provider health plan (not BCBS)	78.9	26.2	48.3	10.2	26.0	12.1	2.9	11.6
Blue Cross, Blue Shield	67.3	28.9	32.0	4.8	16.1	11.1	2.7	19.8
Traditional fee-for-service health plan	60.9	29.3	25.5	3.4	12.3	9.8	1.5	22.8
Preferred-provider health plan	75.4	28.0	42.1	5.8	20.3	15.9	3.5	12.9
Health maintenance organization	71.9	22.5	41.2	6.9	22.3	11.9	4.4	14.5
Commercial Medicare supplement	55.4	39.8	10.2	1.8	3.8	4.6	0.4	35.1
Other BCBS health insurance	70.4	33.9	32.2	1.5	20.9	9.9	0.5	20.2
Health maintenance plans (HMOs)	72.4	23.8	42.2	7.7	22.4	12.1	4.3	12.6
Medicare payments	54.2	42.4	5.4	0.2	1.0	4.3	0.7	33.1
Commercial Medicare supplements/ other health insurance	62.6	40.4	17.2	2.4	7.8	7.0	1.8	25.2
Commercial Medicare supplement (not BCBS)	60.3	40.8	13.1	2.3	4.9	5.9	1.0	27.6
Other health insurance (not BCBS)	66.7	39.6	24.8	2.7	13.2	8.9	3.1	20.9
MEDICAL SERVICES	65.0	27.1	32.3	4.7	18.1	9.5	3.6	21.7
Physician's services	67.8	27.0	34.7	6.5	17.9	10.3	3.7	17.7
Dental services	68.2	28.5	35.5	3.0	22.4	10.1	3.9	19.8
Eye care services	72.1	30.7	37.0	4.6	17.9	14.6	2.0	19.1
Service by professionals other than physician	54.9	20.0	32.1	3.0	18.4	10.7	3.3	31.1
Lab tests, X-rays	63.7	29.0	24.5	2.6	15.1	6.8	4.2	20.0
Hospital room	62.4	27.1	27.6	9.9	12.4	5.3	3.2	19.2
Hospital services other than room	72.2	28.8	36.3	9.8	18.2	8.4	4.5	15.1
Care in convalescent or nursing home	31.1	20.6	3.2	0.3	0.2	2.7	0.1	54.8
Repair of medical equipment	92.8	90.6	–	–	–	–	–	6.3
Other medical services	56.4	17.7	26.4	1.8	11.3	13.3	8.7	28.0
DRUGS	62.3	33.6	22.8	2.8	11.0	9.0	2.0	24.9
Nonprescription drugs	62.4	25.6	29.3	5.8	15.3	8.2	3.5	22.1
Nonprescription vitamins	61.2	30.3	27.3	3.0	13.6	11.4	2.1	25.9
Prescription drugs	62.4	35.8	20.7	2.1	9.7	8.8	1.6	25.4
MEDICAL SUPPLIES	68.6	33.1	30.9	4.1	16.5	10.3	3.1	18.4
Eyeglasses and contact lenses	70.4	29.2	36.0	4.3	19.3	12.3	3.4	15.7
Hearing aids	68.3	57.0	11.1	0.2	6.5	4.4	0.1	27.1
Topicals and dressings	66.0	29.0	32.7	6.1	17.9	8.6	4.5	19.5
Medical equipment for general use	61.6	40.9	18.2	2.8	8.8	6.5	2.0	21.6
Supportive, convalescent medical equipment	61.8	39.9	16.1	3.3	3.2	9.5	1.5	20.1
Rental of medical equipment	62.4	26.2	11.1	1.5	5.1	4.5	0.5	19.5
Rental of supportive, convalescent medical equip.	63.5	33.3	21.3	1.5	6.7	13.1	0.6	33.2

Note: Market share for total consumer units is 100.0%. Market shares by type of consumer unit will not add to total because not all types of consumer units are shown. (–) means sample is too small to make a reliable estimate.
Source: Calculations by New Strategist based on the 2000 Consumer Expenditure Survey

Table 7.16 Health Care: Average spending by race and Hispanic origin, 2000

(average annual spending of consumer units (CU) on health care, by race and Hispanic origin of consumer unit reference person, 2000)

	total consumer units	race		Hispanic origin	
		black	white and other	Hispanic	non-Hispanic
Number of consumer units					
(in thousands, add 000)	109,367	13,230	96,137	9,473	99,894
Average number of persons per CU	2.5	2.7	2.5	3.4	2.4
Average before-tax income of CU	$44,649.00	$32,657.00	$46,260.00	$34,891.00	$45,669.00
Average spending of CU, total	38,044.67	28,152.24	39,406.20	32,734.95	38,548.91
Health care, average spending	2,065.67	1,106.60	2,197.66	1,243.46	2,143.61
HEALTH INSURANCE	$982.65	$639.29	$1,029.90	$599.96	$1,018.94
Commercial health insurance	194.39	81.59	209.91	92.68	204.03
Traditional fee-for-service health plan (not BCBS)	77.07	33.69	83.04	36.17	80.95
Preferred-provider health plan (not BCBS)	117.32	47.90	126.87	56.50	123.08
Blue Cross, Blue Shield	232.50	127.91	246.89	113.20	243.81
Traditional fee-for-service health plan	49.89	34.02	52.08	7.54	53.91
Preferred-provider health plan	60.94	31.51	64.99	32.85	63.60
Health maintenance organization	73.18	48.25	76.61	61.85	74.25
Commercial Medicare supplement	43.77	10.56	48.35	8.78	47.09
Other BCBS health insurance	4.71	3.58	4.87	2.18	4.95
Health maintenance plans (HMOs)	254.81	234.96	257.54	226.54	257.49
Medicare payments	164.04	125.94	169.29	110.72	169.10
Commercial Medicare supplements/					
other health insurance	136.91	68.89	146.27	56.82	144.50
Commercial Medicare supplement (not BCBS)	88.22	51.21	93.31	29.37	93.80
Other health insurance (not BCBS)	48.69	17.68	52.96	27.46	50.70
MEDICAL SERVICES	567.85	190.67	619.75	363.74	587.21
Physician's services	134.41	51.60	145.80	100.85	137.59
Dental services	220.79	67.47	241.89	119.81	230.37
Eye care services	35.05	12.32	38.18	31.19	35.42
Service by professionals other than physician	36.87	9.87	40.58	10.80	39.34
Lab tests, X-rays	20.12	7.55	21.85	13.51	20.74
Hospital room	35.95	10.60	39.44	32.39	36.29
Hospital services other than room	41.13	20.85	43.92	43.13	40.94
Care in convalescent or nursing home	32.35	4.28	36.22	0.20	35.40
Repair of medical equipment	0.61	–	0.69	–	–
Other medical services	10.56	6.12	11.17	5.19	11.07
DRUGS	416.45	235.30	441.38	211.11	435.88
Nonprescription drugs	65.09	33.45	69.45	63.39	65.25
Nonprescription vitamins	46.19	15.08	50.48	25.08	48.15
Prescription drugs	305.17	186.77	321.46	122.64	322.47
MEDICAL SUPPLIES	98.73	41.34	106.63	68.65	101.59
Eyeglasses and contact lenses	58.43	27.39	62.70	42.69	59.92
Hearing aids	11.78	0.48	13.33	1.01	12.80
Topicals and dressings	20.99	11.38	22.32	21.59	20.94
Medical equipment for general use	2.04	0.77	2.21	1.29	2.11
Supportive, convalescent medical equipment	3.18	0.67	3.53	1.76	3.32
Rental of medical equipment	0.85	0.32	0.92	0.06	0.92
Rental of supportive, convalescent medical equipment	1.46	0.34	1.62	0.26	1.58

Note: Other races include Asians, Native Americans, and Pacific Islanders. (–) means sample is too small to make a reliable estimate.
Source: Bureau of Labor Statistics, unpublished tables from the 2000 Consumer Expenditure Survey

Table 7.17 Health Care: Indexed spending by race and Hispanic origin, 2000

(indexed average annual spending of consumer units (CU) on health care, by race and Hispanic origin of consumer unit reference person, 2000; index definition: an index of 100 is the average for all consumer units; an index of 132 means that spending by consumer units in that group is 32 percent above the average for all consumer units; an index of 68 indicates spending that is 32 percent below the average for all consumer units)

	total consumer units	race		Hispanic origin	
		black	*white and other*	*Hispanic*	*non-Hispanic*
Average spending of CU, total	$38,045	$28,152	$39,406	$32,735	$38,549
Average spending of CU, index	100	74	104	86	101
Health care, spending index	100	54	106	60	104
HEALTH INSURANCE	**100**	**65**	**105**	**61**	**104**
Commercial health insurance	**100**	**42**	**108**	**48**	**105**
Traditional fee-for-service health plan (not BCBS)	100	44	108	47	105
Preferred-provider health plan (not BCBS)	100	41	108	48	105
Blue Cross, Blue Shield	**100**	**55**	**106**	**49**	**105**
Traditional fee-for-service health plan	100	68	104	15	108
Preferred-provider health plan	100	52	107	54	104
Health maintenance organization	100	66	105	85	101
Commercial Medicare supplement	100	24	110	20	108
Other BCBS health insurance	100	76	103	46	105
Health maintenance plans (HMOs)	**100**	**92**	**101**	**89**	**101**
Medicare payments	**100**	**77**	**103**	**67**	**103**
Commercial Medicare supplements/ other health insurance	**100**	**50**	**107**	**42**	**106**
Commercial Medicare supplement (not BCBS)	100	58	106	33	106
Other health insurance (not BCBS)	100	36	109	56	104
MEDICAL SERVICES	**100**	**34**	**109**	**64**	**103**
Physician's services	100	38	108	75	102
Dental services	100	31	110	54	104
Eye care services	100	35	109	89	101
Service by professionals other than physician	100	27	110	29	107
Lab tests, X-rays	100	38	109	67	103
Hospital room	100	29	110	90	101
Hospital services other than room	100	51	107	105	100
Care in convalescent or nursing home	100	13	112	1	109
Repair of medical equipment	100	–	113	–	–
Other medical services	100	58	106	49	105
DRUGS	**100**	**57**	**106**	**51**	**105**
Nonprescription drugs	100	51	107	97	100
Nonprescription vitamins	100	33	109	54	104
Prescription drugs	100	61	105	40	106
MEDICAL SUPPLIES	**100**	**42**	**108**	**70**	**103**
Eyeglasses and contact lenses	100	47	107	73	103
Hearing aids	100	4	113	9	109
Topicals and dressings	100	54	106	103	100
Medical equipment for general use	100	38	108	63	103
Supportive, convalescent medical equipment	100	21	111	55	104
Rental of medical equipment	100	38	108	7	108
Rental of supportive, convalescent medical equipment	100	23	111	18	108

Note: Other races include Asians, Native Americans, and Pacific Islanders. (–) means sample is too small to make a reliable estimate.
Source: Calculations by New Strategist based on the 2000 Consumer Expenditure Survey

Table 7.18 Health Care: Indexed per capita spending by race and Hispanic origin, 2000

(indexed average annual per capita spending of consumer units (CU) on health care, by race and Hispanic origin of consumer unit reference person, 2000; index definition: an index of 100 is the average for all consumer units; an index of 132 means that spending by consumer units in that group is 32 percent above the average for all consumer units; an index of 68 indicates spending that is 32 percent below the average for all consumer units)

	total consumer units	race		Hispanic origin	
		black	white and other	Hispanic	non-Hispanic
Per capita spending of CU, total	$15,218	$10,427	$15,762	$9,628	$16,062
Per capita spending of CU, index	100	69	104	63	106
Health care, per capita spending index	100	50	106	44	108
HEALTH INSURANCE	**100**	**60**	**105**	**45**	**108**
Commercial health insurance	**100**	**39**	**108**	**35**	**109**
Traditional fee-for-service health plan (not BCBS)	100	40	108	35	109
Preferred-provider health plan (not BCBS)	100	38	108	35	109
Blue Cross, Blue Shield	**100**	**51**	**106**	**36**	**109**
Traditional fee-for-service health plan	100	63	104	11	113
Preferred-provider health plan	100	48	107	40	109
Health maintenance organization	100	61	105	62	106
Commercial Medicare supplement	100	22	110	15	112
Other BCBS health insurance	100	70	103	34	109
Health maintenance plans (HMOs)	**100**	**85**	**101**	**65**	**105**
Medicare payments	**100**	**71**	**103**	**50**	**107**
Commercial Medicare supplements/ other health insurance	**100**	**47**	**107**	**31**	**110**
Commercial Medicare supplement (not BCBS)	100	54	106	24	111
Other health insurance (not BCBS)	100	34	109	41	108
MEDICAL SERVICES	**100**	**31**	**109**	**47**	**108**
Physician's services	100	36	108	55	107
Dental services	100	28	110	40	109
Eye care services	100	33	109	65	105
Service by professionals other than physician	100	25	110	22	111
Lab tests, X-rays	100	35	109	49	107
Hospital room	100	27	110	66	105
Hospital services other than room	100	47	107	77	104
Care in convalescent or nursing home	100	12	112	0	114
Repair of medical equipment	100	–	113	–	–
Other medical services	100	54	106	36	109
DRUGS	**100**	**52**	**106**	**37**	**109**
Nonprescription drugs	100	48	107	72	104
Nonprescription vitamins	100	30	109	40	109
Prescription drugs	100	57	105	30	110
MEDICAL SUPPLIES	**100**	**39**	**108**	**51**	**107**
Eyeglasses and contact lenses	100	43	107	54	107
Hearing aids	100	4	113	6	113
Topicals and dressings	100	50	106	76	104
Medical equipment for general use	100	35	108	46	108
Supportive, convalescent medical equipment	100	20	111	41	109
Rental of medical equipment	100	35	108	5	113
Rental of supportive, convalescent medical equipment	100	22	111	13	113

Note: Per capita indexes account for household size and show how much each person in a particular household demographic segment spends relative to a person in the average household. Other races include Asians, Native Americans, and Pacific Islanders. (–) means sample is too small to make a reliable estimate.
Source: Calculations by New Strategist based on the 2000 Consumer Expenditure Survey

Table 7.19 Health Care: Total spending by race and Hispanic origin, 2000

(total annual spending on health care, by consumer unit race and Hispanic origin groups, 2000; numbers in thousands)

	total consumer units	race		Hispanic origin	
		black	white and other	Hispanic	non-Hispanic
Number of consumer units	109,367	13,230	96,137	9,473	99,894
Total spending of all consumer units	$4,160,831,424	$372,454,135	$3,788,393,849	$310,098,181	$3,850,804,816
Health care, total spending	225,916,131	14,640,318	211,276,439	11,779,297	214,133,777
HEALTH INSURANCE	**$107,469,483**	**$8,457,807**	**$99,011,496**	**$5,683,421**	**$101,785,992**
Commercial health insurance	**21,259,851**	**1,079,436**	**20,180,118**	**877,958**	**20,381,373**
Traditional fee-for-service health plan (not BCBS)	8,428,915	445,719	7,983,216	342,638	8,086,419
Preferred-provider health plan (not BCBS)	12,830,936	633,717	12,196,901	535,225	12,294,954
Blue Cross, Blue Shield	**25,427,828**	**1,692,249**	**23,735,264**	**1,072,344**	**24,355,156**
Traditional fee-for-service health plan	5,456,320	450,085	5,006,815	71,426	5,385,286
Preferred-provider health plan	6,664,825	416,877	6,247,944	311,188	6,353,258
Health maintenance organization	8,003,477	638,348	7,365,056	585,905	7,417,130
Commercial Medicare supplement	4,786,994	139,709	4,648,224	83,173	4,704,008
Other BCBS health insurance	515,119	47,363	468,187	20,651	494,475
Health maintenance plans (HMOs)	**27,867,805**	**3,108,521**	**24,759,123**	**2,146,013**	**25,721,706**
Medicare payments	**17,940,563**	**1,666,186**	**16,275,033**	**1,048,851**	**16,892,075**
Commercial Medicare supplements/ other health insurance	**14,973,436**	**911,415**	**14,061,959**	**538,256**	**14,434,683**
Commercial Medicare supplement (not BCBS)	9,648,357	677,508	8,970,543	278,222	9,370,057
Other health insurance (not BCBS)	5,325,079	233,906	5,091,416	260,129	5,064,626
MEDICAL SERVICES	**62,104,051**	**2,522,564**	**59,580,906**	**3,445,709**	**58,658,756**
Physician's services	14,700,018	682,668	14,016,775	955,352	13,744,415
Dental services	24,147,140	892,628	23,254,579	1,134,960	23,012,581
Eye care services	3,833,313	162,994	3,670,511	295,463	3,538,245
Service by professionals other than physician	4,032,361	130,580	3,901,239	102,308	3,929,830
Lab tests, X-rays	2,200,464	99,887	2,100,593	127,980	2,071,802
Hospital room	3,931,744	140,238	3,791,643	306,830	3,625,153
Hospital services other than room	4,498,265	275,846	4,222,337	408,570	4,089,660
Care in convalescent or nursing home	3,538,022	56,624	3,482,082	1,895	3,536,248
Repair of medical equipment	66,714	–	66,335	–	–
Other medical services	1,154,916	80,968	1,073,850	49,165	1,105,827
DRUGS	**45,545,887**	**3,113,019**	**42,432,949**	**1,999,845**	**43,541,797**
Nonprescription drugs	7,118,698	442,544	6,676,715	600,493	6,518,084
Nonprescription vitamins	5,051,662	199,508	4,852,996	237,583	4,809,896
Prescription drugs	33,375,527	2,470,967	30,904,200	1,161,769	32,212,818
MEDICAL SUPPLIES	**10,797,804**	**546,928**	**10,251,088**	**650,321**	**10,148,231**
Eyeglasses and contact lenses	6,390,314	362,370	6,027,790	404,402	5,985,648
Hearing aids	1,288,343	6,350	1,281,506	9,568	1,278,643
Topicals and dressings	2,295,613	150,557	2,145,778	204,522	2,091,780
Medical equipment for general use	223,109	10,187	212,463	12,220	210,776
Supportive, convalescent medical equipment	347,787	8,864	339,364	16,672	331,648
Rental of medical equipment	92,962	4,234	88,446	568	91,902
Rental of supportive, convalescent medical equipment	159,676	4,498	155,742	2,463	157,833

Note: Other races include Asians, Native Americans, and Pacific Islanders. Numbers may not add to total because of rounding. (–) means sample is too small to make a reliable estimate.
Source: Calculations by New Strategist based on the 2000 Consumer Expenditure Survey

Table 7.20 Health Care: Market shares by race and Hispanic origin, 2000

(percentage of total annual spending on health care accounted for by consumer unit race and Hispanic origin groups, 2000)

	total consumer units	race		Hispanic origin	
		black	white and other	Hispanic	non-Hispanic
Share of total consumer units	100.0%	12.1%	87.9%	8.7%	91.3%
Share of total before-tax income	100.0	8.8	91.1	6.8	93.4
Share of total spending	100.0	9.0	91.0	7.5	92.5
Share of health care spending	100.0	6.5	93.5	5.2	94.8
HEALTH INSURANCE	100.0%	7.9%	92.1%	5.3%	94.7%
Commercial health insurance	100.0	5.1	94.9	4.1	95.9
Traditional fee-for-service health plan (not BCBS)	100.0	5.3	94.7	4.1	95.9
Preferred-provider health plan (not BCBS)	100.0	4.9	95.1	4.2	95.8
Blue Cross, Blue Shield	100.0	6.7	93.3	4.2	95.8
Traditional fee-for-service health plan	100.0	8.2	91.8	1.3	98.7
Preferred-provider health plan	100.0	6.3	93.7	4.7	95.3
Health maintenance organization	100.0	8.0	92.0	7.3	92.7
Commercial Medicare supplement	100.0	2.9	97.1	1.7	98.3
Other BCBS health insurance	100.0	9.2	90.9	4.0	96.0
Health maintenance plans (HMOs)	100.0	11.2	88.8	7.7	92.3
Medicare payments	100.0	9.3	90.7	5.8	94.2
Commercial Medicare supplements/ other health insurance	100.0	6.1	93.9	3.6	96.4
Commercial Medicare supplement (not BCBS)	100.0	7.0	93.0	2.9	97.1
Other health insurance (not BCBS)	100.0	4.4	95.6	4.9	95.1
MEDICAL SERVICES	100.0	4.1	95.9	5.5	94.5
Physician's services	100.0	4.6	95.4	6.5	93.5
Dental services	100.0	3.7	96.3	4.7	95.3
Eye care services	100.0	4.3	95.8	7.7	92.3
Service by professionals other than physician	100.0	3.2	96.7	2.5	97.5
Lab tests, X-rays	100.0	4.5	95.5	5.8	94.2
Hospital room	100.0	3.6	96.4	7.8	92.2
Hospital services other than room	100.0	6.1	93.9	9.1	90.9
Care in convalescent or nursing home	100.0	1.6	98.4	0.1	99.9
Repair of medical equipment	100.0	–	99.4	–	–
Other medical services	100.0	7.0	93.0	4.3	95.7
DRUGS	100.0	6.8	93.2	4.4	95.6
Nonprescription drugs	100.0	6.2	93.8	8.4	91.6
Nonprescription vitamins	100.0	3.9	96.1	4.7	95.2
Prescription drugs	100.0	7.4	92.6	3.5	96.5
MEDICAL SUPPLIES	100.0	5.1	94.9	6.0	94.0
Eyeglasses and contact lenses	100.0	5.7	94.3	6.3	93.7
Hearing aids	100.0	0.5	99.5	0.7	99.2
Topicals and dressings	100.0	6.6	93.5	8.9	91.1
Medical equipment for general use	100.0	4.6	95.2	5.5	94.5
Supportive, convalescent medical equipment	100.0	2.5	97.6	4.8	95.4
Rental of medical equipment	100.0	4.6	95.1	0.6	98.9
Rental of supportive, convalescent medical equipment	100.0	2.8	97.5	1.5	98.8

Note: Other races include Asians, Native Americans, and Pacific Islanders. Numbers may not add to total because of rounding. (–) means sample is too small to make a reliable estimate.
Source: Calculations by New Strategist based on the 2000 Consumer Expenditure Survey

Table 7.21 Health Care: Average spending by region, 2000

(average annual spending of consumer units (CU) on health care, by region in which consumer unit lives, 2000)

	total consumer units	Northeast	Midwest	South	West
Number of consumer units					
(in thousands, add 000)	109,367	20,994	25,717	38,245	24,410
Average number of persons per CU	2.5	2.5	2.5	2.5	2.6
Average before-tax income of CU	$44,649.00	$47,439.00	$44,377.00	$41,984.00	$46,670.00
Average spending of CU, total	38,044.67	38,901.91	39,212.70	34,707.07	41,328.19
Health care, average spending	2,065.67	1,862.39	2,172.31	2,147.36	2,001.18
HEALTH INSURANCE	$982.65	$908.47	$1,047.35	$1,062.68	$852.89
Commercial health insurance	194.39	124.26	236.51	232.06	151.30
Traditional fee-for-service health plan (not BCBS)	77.07	70.68	94.08	81.58	57.59
Preferred-provider health plan (not BCBS)	117.32	53.58	142.43	150.48	93.71
Blue Cross, Blue Shield	232.50	233.72	265.75	241.20	182.79
Traditional fee-for-service health plan	49.89	67.80	55.37	41.97	41.14
Preferred-provider health plan	60.94	31.22	65.94	80.90	49.95
Health maintenance organization	73.18	97.45	67.11	68.98	65.29
Commercial Medicare supplement	43.77	33.19	73.93	43.60	21.39
Other BCBS health insurance	4.71	4.06	3.40	5.75	5.03
Health maintenance plans (HMOs)	254.81	265.08	257.21	241.69	264.00
Medicare payments	164.04	174.98	159.18	175.55	141.73
Commercial Medicare supplements/ other health insurance	136.91	110.43	128.71	172.17	113.06
Commercial Medicare supplement (not BCBS)	88.22	70.52	79.52	119.05	64.31
Other health insurance (not BCBS)	48.69	39.92	49.19	53.12	48.75
MEDICAL SERVICES	567.85	504.50	574.69	533.13	669.49
Physician's services	134.41	128.16	135.85	128.09	148.16
Dental services	220.79	232.20	196.08	208.47	256.31
Eye care services	35.05	29.68	39.17	33.38	37.95
Service by professionals other than physician	36.87	42.04	38.03	22.97	52.97
Lab tests, X-rays	20.12	13.12	23.54	21.11	20.97
Hospital room	35.95	22.63	37.01	37.56	43.79
Hospital services other than room	41.13	21.71	38.50	48.85	48.50
Care in convalescent or nursing home	32.35	7.78	54.30	19.24	50.92
Repair of medical equipment	0.61	–	–	1.61	0.18
Other medical services	10.56	7.18	12.18	11.85	9.74
DRUGS	416.45	348.78	438.95	469.96	367.94
Nonprescription drugs	65.09	62.63	69.97	63.10	65.40
Nonprescription vitamins	46.19	42.04	36.37	42.35	66.75
Prescription drugs	305.17	244.11	332.61	364.51	235.79
MEDICAL SUPPLIES	98.73	100.64	111.32	81.60	110.86
Eyeglasses and contact lenses	58.43	55.83	66.65	50.40	64.60
Hearing aids	11.78	17.94	9.56	6.92	16.42
Topicals and dressings	20.99	20.28	24.84	17.91	22.55
Medical equipment for general use	2.04	2.38	2.59	1.55	1.93
Supportive, convalescent medical equipment	3.18	2.39	3.91	2.70	3.86
Rental of medical equipment	0.85	0.46	1.24	0.89	0.71
Rental of supportive, convalescent medical equipment	1.46	1.37	2.53	1.23	0.79

Note: (–) means sample is too small to make a reliable estimate.
Source: Bureau of Labor Statistics, unpublished tables from the 2000 Consumer Expenditure Survey

Table 7.22 Health Care: Indexed spending by region, 2000

(indexed average annual spending of consumer units (CU) on health care, by region in which consumer unit lives, 2000; index definition: an index of 100 is the average for all consumer units; an index of 132 means that spending by consumer units in that group is 32 percent above the average for all consumer units; an index of 68 indicates spending that is 32 percent below the average for all consumer units)

	total consumer units	Northeast	Midwest	South	West
Average spending of CU, total	$38,045	$38,902	$39,213	$34,707	$41,328
Average spending of CU, index	100	102	103	91	109
Health care, spending index	100	90	105	104	97
HEALTH INSURANCE	**100**	**92**	**107**	**108**	**87**
Commercial health insurance	**100**	**64**	**122**	**119**	**78**
Traditional fee-for-service health plan (not BCBS)	100	92	122	106	75
Preferred-provider health plan (not BCBS)	100	46	121	128	80
Blue Cross, Blue Shield	**100**	**101**	**114**	**104**	**79**
Traditional fee-for-service health plan	100	136	111	84	82
Preferred-provider health plan	100	51	108	133	82
Health maintenance organization	100	133	92	94	89
Commercial Medicare supplement	100	76	169	100	49
Other BCBS health insurance	100	86	72	122	107
Health maintenance plans (HMOs)	**100**	**104**	**101**	**95**	**104**
Medicare payments	**100**	**107**	**97**	**107**	**86**
Commercial Medicare supplements/ other health insurance	**100**	**81**	**94**	**126**	**83**
Commercial Medicare supplement (not BCBS)	100	80	90	135	73
Other health insurance (not BCBS)	100	82	101	109	100
MEDICAL SERVICES	**100**	**89**	**101**	**94**	**118**
Physician's services	100	95	101	95	110
Dental services	100	105	89	94	116
Eye care services	100	85	112	95	108
Service by professionals other than physician	100	114	103	62	144
Lab tests, X-rays	100	65	117	105	104
Hospital room	100	63	103	104	122
Hospital services other than room	100	53	94	119	118
Care in convalescent or nursing home	100	24	168	59	157
Repair of medical equipment	100	–	–	264	30
Other medical services	100	68	115	112	92
DRUGS	**100**	**84**	**105**	**113**	**88**
Nonprescription drugs	100	96	107	97	100
Nonprescription vitamins	100	91	79	92	145
Prescription drugs	100	80	109	119	77
MEDICAL SUPPLIES	**100**	**102**	**113**	**83**	**112**
Eyeglasses and contact lenses	100	96	114	86	111
Hearing aids	100	152	81	59	139
Topicals and dressings	100	97	118	85	107
Medical equipment for general use	100	117	127	76	95
Supportive, convalescent medical equipment	100	75	123	85	121
Rental of medical equipment	100	54	146	105	84
Rental of supportive, convalescent medical equipment	100	94	173	84	54

Note: (–) means sample is too small to make a reliable estimate.
Source: Calculations by New Strategist based on the 2000 Consumer Expenditure Survey

Table 7.23 Health Care: Indexed per capita spending by region, 2000

(indexed average annual per capita spending of consumer units (CU) on health care, by region in which consumer unit lives, 2000; index definition: an index of 100 is the average for all consumer units; an index of 132 means that spending by consumer units in that group is 32 percent above the average for all consumer units; an index of 68 indicates spending that is 32 percent below the average for all consumer units)

	total consumer units	Northeast	Midwest	South	West
Per capita spending of CU, total	$15,218	$15,561	$15,685	$13,883	$15,895
Per capita spending of CU, index	100	102	103	91	104
Health care, per capita spending index	100	90	105	104	93
HEALTH INSURANCE	100	92	107	108	83
Commercial health insurance	100	64	122	119	75
Traditional fee-for-service health plan (not BCBS)	100	92	122	106	72
Preferred-provider health plan (not BCBS)	100	46	121	128	77
Blue Cross, Blue Shield	100	101	114	104	76
Traditional fee-for-service health plan	100	136	111	84	79
Preferred-provider health plan	100	51	108	133	79
Health maintenance organization	100	133	92	94	86
Commercial Medicare supplement	100	76	169	100	47
Other BCBS health insurance	100	86	72	122	103
Health maintenance plans (HMOs)	100	104	101	95	100
Medicare payments	100	107	97	107	83
Commercial Medicare supplements/ other health insurance	100	81	94	126	79
Commercial Medicare supplement (not BCBS)	100	80	90	135	70
Other health insurance (not BCBS)	100	82	101	109	96
MEDICAL SERVICES	100	89	101	94	113
Physician's services	100	95	101	95	106
Dental services	100	105	89	94	112
Eye care services	100	85	112	95	104
Service by professionals other than physician	100	114	103	62	138
Lab tests, X-rays	100	65	117	105	100
Hospital room	100	63	103	104	117
Hospital services other than room	100	53	94	119	113
Care in convalescent or nursing home	100	24	168	59	151
Repair of medical equipment	100	–	–	264	28
Other medical services	100	68	115	112	89
DRUGS	100	84	105	113	85
Nonprescription drugs	100	96	107	97	97
Nonprescription vitamins	100	91	79	92	139
Prescription drugs	100	80	109	119	74
MEDICAL SUPPLIES	100	102	113	83	108
Eyeglasses and contact lenses	100	96	114	86	106
Hearing aids	100	152	81	59	134
Topicals and dressings	100	97	118	85	103
Medical equipment for general use	100	117	127	76	91
Supportive, convalescent medical equipment	100	75	123	85	117
Rental of medical equipment	100	54	146	105	80
Rental of supportive, convalescent medical equipment	100	94	173	84	52

Note: Per capita indexes account for household size and show how much each person in a particular household demographic segment spends relative to a person in the average household. (–) means sample is too small to make a reliable estimate.
Source: Calculations by New Strategist based on the 2000 Consumer Expenditure Survey

Table 7.24 Health Care: Total spending by region, 2000

(total annual spending on health care, by region in which consumer units live, 2000; numbers in thousands)

	total consumer units	Northeast	Midwest	South	West
Number of consumer units	109,367	20,994	25,717	38,245	24,410
Total spending of all consumer units	$4,160,831,424	$816,706,699	$1,008,433,006	$1,327,371,892	$1,008,821,118
Health care, total spending	225,916,131	39,099,016	55,865,296	82,125,783	48,848,804
HEALTH INSURANCE	**$107,469,483**	**$19,072,419**	**$26,934,700**	**$40,642,197**	**$20,819,045**
Commercial health insurance	**21,259,851**	**2,608,714**	**6,082,328**	**8,875,135**	**3,693,233**
Traditional fee-for-service health plan (not BCBS)	8,428,915	1,483,856	2,419,455	3,120,027	1,405,772
Preferred-provider health plan (not BCBS)	12,830,936	1,124,859	3,662,872	5,755,108	2,287,461
Blue Cross, Blue Shield	**25,427,828**	**4,906,718**	**6,834,293**	**9,224,694**	**4,461,904**
Traditional fee-for-service health plan	5,456,320	1,423,393	1,423,950	1,605,143	1,004,227
Preferred-provider health plan	6,664,825	655,433	1,695,779	3,094,021	1,219,280
Health maintenance organization	8,003,477	2,045,865	1,725,868	2,638,140	1,593,729
Commercial Medicare supplement	4,786,994	696,791	1,901,258	1,667,482	522,130
Other BCBS health insurance	515,119	85,236	87,438	219,909	122,782
Health maintenance plans (HMOs)	**27,867,805**	**5,565,090**	**6,614,670**	**9,243,434**	**6,444,240**
Medicare payments	**17,940,563**	**3,673,530**	**4,093,632**	**6,713,910**	**3,459,629**
Commercial Medicare supplements/ other health insurance	**14,973,436**	**2,318,367**	**3,310,035**	**6,584,642**	**2,759,795**
Commercial Medicare supplement (not BCBS)	9,648,357	1,480,497	2,045,016	4,553,067	1,569,807
Other health insurance (not BCBS)	5,325,079	838,080	1,265,019	2,031,574	1,189,988
MEDICAL SERVICES	**62,104,051**	**10,591,473**	**14,779,303**	**20,389,557**	**16,342,251**
Physician's services	14,700,018	2,690,591	3,493,654	4,898,802	3,616,586
Dental services	24,147,140	4,874,807	5,042,589	7,972,935	6,256,527
Eye care services	3,833,313	623,102	1,007,335	1,276,618	926,360
Service by professionals other than physician	4,032,361	882,588	978,018	878,488	1,292,998
Lab tests, X-rays	2,200,464	275,441	605,378	807,352	511,878
Hospital room	3,931,744	475,094	951,786	1,436,482	1,068,914
Hospital services other than room	4,498,265	455,780	990,105	1,868,268	1,183,885
Care in convalescent or nursing home	3,538,022	163,333	1,396,433	735,834	1,242,957
Repair of medical equipment	66,714	–	–	61,574	4,394
Other medical services	1,154,916	150,737	313,233	453,203	237,753
DRUGS	**45,545,887**	**7,322,287**	**11,288,477**	**17,973,620**	**8,981,415**
Nonprescription drugs	7,118,698	1,314,854	1,799,418	2,413,260	1,596,414
Nonprescription vitamins	5,051,662	882,588	935,327	1,619,676	1,629,368
Prescription drugs	33,375,527	5,124,845	8,553,731	13,940,685	5,755,634
MEDICAL SUPPLIES	**10,797,804**	**2,112,836**	**2,862,816**	**3,120,792**	**2,706,093**
Eyeglasses and contact lenses	6,390,314	1,172,095	1,714,038	1,927,548	1,576,886
Hearing aids	1,288,343	376,632	245,855	264,655	400,812
Topicals and dressings	2,295,613	425,758	638,810	684,968	550,446
Medical equipment for general use	223,109	49,966	66,607	59,280	47,111
Supportive, convalescent medical equipment	347,787	50,176	100,553	103,262	94,223
Rental of medical equipment	92,962	9,657	31,889	34,038	17,331
Rental of supportive, convalescent medical equipment	159,676	28,762	65,064	47,041	19,284

Note: Numbers may not add to total because of rounding. (–) means sample is too small to make a reliable estimate.
Source: Calculations by New Strategist based on the 2000 Consumer Expenditure Survey

Table 7.25 Health Care: Market shares by region, 2000

(percentage of total annual spending on health care accounted for by consumer units by region, 2000)

	total consumer units	Northeast	Midwest	South	West
Share of total consumer units	100.0%	19.2%	23.5%	35.0%	22.3%
Share of total before-tax income	100.0	20.4	23.4	32.9	23.3
Share of total spending	100.0	19.6	24.2	31.9	24.2
Share of health care spending	100.0	17.3	24.7	36.4	21.6
HEALTH INSURANCE	100.0%	17.7%	25.1%	37.8%	19.4%
Commercial health insurance	100.0	12.3	28.6	41.7	17.4
Traditional fee-for-service health plan (not BCBS)	100.0	17.6	28.7	37.0	16.7
Preferred-provider health plan (not BCBS)	100.0	8.8	28.5	44.9	17.8
Blue Cross, Blue Shield	100.0	19.3	26.9	36.3	17.5
Traditional fee-for-service health plan	100.0	26.1	26.1	29.4	18.4
Preferred-provider health plan	100.0	9.8	25.4	46.4	18.3
Health maintenance organization	100.0	25.6	21.6	33.0	19.9
Commercial Medicare supplement	100.0	14.6	39.7	34.8	10.9
Other BCBS health insurance	100.0	16.5	17.0	42.7	23.8
Health maintenance plans (HMOs)	100.0	20.0	23.7	33.2	23.1
Medicare payments	100.0	20.5	22.8	37.4	19.3
Commercial Medicare supplements/ other health insurance	100.0	15.5	22.1	44.0	18.4
Commercial Medicare supplement (not BCBS)	100.0	15.3	21.2	47.2	16.3
Other health insurance (not BCBS)	100.0	15.7	23.8	38.2	22.3
MEDICAL SERVICES	100.0	17.1	23.8	32.8	26.3
Physician's services	100.0	18.3	23.8	33.3	24.6
Dental services	100.0	20.2	20.9	33.0	25.9
Eye care services	100.0	16.3	26.3	33.3	24.2
Service by professionals other than physician	100.0	21.9	24.3	21.8	32.1
Lab tests, X-rays	100.0	12.5	27.5	36.7	23.3
Hospital room	100.0	12.1	24.2	36.5	27.2
Hospital services other than room	100.0	10.1	22.0	41.5	26.3
Care in convalescent or nursing home	100.0	4.6	39.5	20.8	35.1
Repair of medical equipment	100.0	–	–	92.3	6.6
Other medical services	100.0	13.1	27.1	39.2	20.6
DRUGS	100.0	16.1	24.8	39.5	19.7
Nonprescription drugs	100.0	18.5	25.3	33.9	22.4
Nonprescription vitamins	100.0	17.5	18.5	32.1	32.3
Prescription drugs	100.0	15.4	25.6	41.8	17.2
MEDICAL SUPPLIES	100.0	19.6	26.5	28.9	25.1
Eyeglasses and contact lenses	100.0	18.3	26.8	30.2	24.7
Hearing aids	100.0	29.2	19.1	20.5	31.1
Topicals and dressings	100.0	18.5	27.8	29.8	24.0
Medical equipment for general use	100.0	22.4	29.9	26.6	21.1
Supportive, convalescent medical equipment	100.0	14.4	28.9	29.7	27.1
Rental of medical equipment	100.0	10.4	34.3	36.6	18.6
Rental of supportive, convalescent medical equipment	100.0	18.0	40.7	29.5	12.1

Note: Numbers may not add to total because of rounding. (–) means sample is too small to make a reliable estimate.
Source: Calculations by New Strategist based on the 2000 Consumer Expenditure Survey

8

Spending on Household Operations, 2000

Housing is Americans' biggest expense. In 2000, spending for shelter, utilities, and household operations (which includes household services, housekeeping supplies, furniture, and equipment) absorbed 32.4 percent of the expenditures of the average household. That figure was 30.7 percent in 1990. Spending on household services rose 16 percent between 1990 and 2000, after adjusting for inflation. Spending on housekeeping supplies fell 10 percent, while spending on household furnishings and equipment rose 5 percent.

Housing costs are highest for householders aged 35 to 44, at $15,111 in 2000. The 35-to-44 age group spends the most on household services, $896 in 2000, because of the high cost of day care. Householders aged 55 to 64 spend the most on laundry and cleaning supplies, while those aged 65 to 74 spend the most on postage. Spending on computers and computer hardware for nonbusiness use is greatest among 45-to-54-year-olds, the most affluent householders.

Households with incomes of $70,000 or more spent $22,932 on housing in 2000 versus the $12,527 the average household spent. The most affluent households spend far more than average on just about every category of household operations, particularly household services, furnishings, and equipment.

Among household types, married couples with preschoolers spend the most on housing, $18,702 in 2000. Behind this figure is the high cost of housing for recent home buyers as many married couples with young children are new homeowners. In addition, these householders spend the most on day care. Married couples with preschoolers spent an average of $1,527 at day care centers in 2000.

Black and Hispanic householders spend less than average on housing, but they spend more on some household products and services. Hispanics spend 53 percent more than average on soaps and detergents and 56 percent more on bathroom linens. Blacks spend 10 percent more than average on day care and 37 percent more on home security system service fees.

Households in the West spend the most on housing, $13,972 in 2000, because of the high cost of housing in California and other Western states. Spending on housing is lowest in the South, at $10,855. Southern households spend the most on lawn and garden supplies and equipment, however. Households in the West spend the most on computer hardware and software and computer information services.

Table 8.1 (Housing) Household Operations: Average spending by age, 2000

(average annual spending of consumer units (CU) on household services, supplies, furnishings, and equipment, by age of consumer unit reference person, 2000)

	total consumer units	under 25	25 to 34	35 to 44	45 to 54	55 to 64	65 to 74	75+
Number of consumer units (in thousands, add 000)	109,367	8,306	18,887	23,983	21,874	14,161	11,538	10,617
Average number of persons per CU	2.5	1.9	2.9	3.3	2.7	2.1	1.9	1.5
Average before-tax income of CU	$44,649.00	$19,744.00	$45,498.00	$56,500.00	$58,889.00	$48,108.00	$29,349.00	$20,563.00
Average spending of CU, total	38,044.67	22,543.18	38,945.27	45,149.37	46,160.28	39,340.03	30,781.81	21,908.04
Housing, average spending	12,318.51	7,109.16	13,049.56	15,111.45	14,179.31	12,362.20	9,671.46	7,766.01
HOUSEHOLD SERVICES	$684.38	$225.97	$871.17	$895.68	$582.55	$542.16	$498.29	$838.50
Personal services	326.20	153.59	641.13	541.81	147.18	93.24	99.02	340.41
Babysitting, child care in your own home	32.21	7.63	61.76	80.21	13.66	2.02	3.55	0.11
Babysitting, child care in someone else's home	32.59	29.39	97.51	50.38	8.56	5.05	0.04	1.07
Care for elderly, invalids, handicapped, etc.	50.38	1.18	0.80	5.02	23.77	34.94	69.95	333.72
Adult day care centers	2.60	–	–	2.88	1.17	10.43	0.81	3.04
Day care centers, nurseries, and preschools	208.42	115.39	481.06	403.32	100.02	40.79	24.69	2.47
Other household services	358.18	72.38	230.04	353.87	435.36	448.92	399.26	498.10
Housekeeping services	88.15	6.04	42.72	87.68	129.22	98.64	90.08	133.54
Gardening, lawn care service	78.26	3.64	25.47	61.51	89.07	118.63	113.25	154.18
Water softening service	3.11	1.52	3.04	3.04	3.36	4.65	2.74	2.45
Nonclothing laundry, dry cleaning, sent out	1.48	0.96	0.90	1.42	1.47	2.28	1.66	1.76
Nonclothing laundry, dry cleaning, coin-operated	4.64	9.23	6.61	4.97	4.30	2.90	2.51	2.17
Termite/pest control services	9.57	0.94	4.56	12.75	7.67	11.09	15.45	13.56
Home security system service fee	18.67	1.81	16.41	20.64	21.06	25.26	21.53	14.61
Other home services	14.28	1.04	10.30	13.79	17.38	20.68	14.65	17.45
Termite/pest control products	0.49	0.00	0.18	0.57	0.37	0.68	0.76	0.98
Moving, storage, and freight express	32.43	10.04	30.79	32.09	46.41	41.56	35.92	8.88
Appliance repair, including service center	12.58	2.50	7.28	11.78	17.67	15.05	16.70	13.44
Reupholstering and furniture repair	9.26	0.38	8.64	8.17	5.91	13.09	23.71	5.92
Repairs/rentals of lawn/garden equipment, hand/power tools, etc.	4.96	0.02	2.86	5.73	5.41	6.23	7.00	6.02
Appliance rental	3.77	3.29	3.48	3.51	4.31	5.20	3.78	2.16
Rental of office equipment for nonbusiness use	0.53	0.96	0.71	0.58	0.57	0.24	0.44	0.14
Repair of misc. household equipment and furnishings	11.73	1.83	–	1.89	0.19	11.30	0.75	102.24
Repair of computer systems for nonbusiness use	2.75	1.12	2.34	2.45	2.70	2.56	5.94	2.37
Computer information services	61.36	26.98	63.69	81.23	78.30	68.13	42.12	16.22
Rental, installation of dishwashers, range hoods, and garbage disposals	0.15	0.06	0.06	0.05	–	0.75	0.26	–
HOUSEKEEPING SUPPLIES	482.32	193.61	437.45	569.66	531.67	585.30	510.56	322.42
Laundry and cleaning supplies	130.76	54.84	124.74	156.72	137.33	183.91	109.56	78.85
Soaps and detergents	69.27	33.09	71.70	85.78	76.34	75.53	57.89	44.47
Other laundry cleaning products	61.49	21.74	53.04	70.94	60.98	108.37	51.67	34.38
Other household products	225.90	88.99	200.88	279.99	246.97	262.25	241.20	146.20
Cleansing and toilet tissue, paper towels, and napkins	68.45	29.14	62.30	74.01	78.00	82.76	71.35	56.99
Miscellaneous household products	90.48	52.04	80.74	110.11	106.92	97.08	91.87	48.99
Lawn and garden supplies	66.97	7.80	57.84	95.87	62.05	82.40	77.98	40.22
Postage and stationery	125.66	49.79	111.82	132.95	147.38	139.14	159.79	97.37
Stationery, stationery supplies, giftwrap	63.65	31.35	69.73	73.50	75.76	62.85	54.99	41.60
Postage	60.60	18.25	41.47	58.74	68.32	74.77	102.80	54.87
Delivery services	1.41	0.18	0.63	0.71	3.30	1.52	2.01	0.90

	total consumer units	under 25	25 to 34	35 to 44	45 to 54	55 to 64	65 to 74	75+
HOUSEHOLD FURNISHINGS AND EQUIPMENT	$1,548.63	$867.49	$1,495.26	$1,906.13	$1,910.84	$1,891.48	$1,110.14	$634.13
Household textiles	106.49	34.60	119.96	124.18	124.92	125.20	100.73	42.52
Bathroom linens	17.55	3.48	25.34	17.28	20.99	16.74	16.67	10.79
Bedroom linens	44.52	22.40	62.54	44.06	54.14	48.82	37.59	12.93
Kitchen and dining room linens	9.31	2.44	10.15	9.93	8.33	12.65	12.33	6.10
Curtains and draperies	21.06	3.16	12.33	39.75	24.01	16.13	24.14	5.53
Slipcovers and decorative pillows	2.75	–	1.79	3.00	2.01	9.94	–	0.81
Sewing materials for household items	9.75	2.51	6.82	8.36	13.34	18.48	9.18	5.35
Other linens	1.53	0.62	1.00	1.79	2.10	2.43	0.84	1.00
Furniture	390.63	270.35	456.55	499.42	471.22	361.21	256.12	141.08
Mattresses and springs	52.89	50.16	60.16	61.90	62.58	49.02	35.88	25.39
Other bedroom furniture	69.11	58.20	110.98	71.11	88.51	44.21	47.33	15.58
Sofas	89.15	67.63	98.70	125.81	99.54	85.40	53.28	28.78
Living room chairs	43.84	23.96	36.77	45.52	44.37	65.62	45.65	36.04
Living room tables	17.19	13.39	18.39	24.12	20.11	19.23	7.29	4.42
Kitchen and dining room furniture	46.46	15.69	53.38	63.58	65.66	33.77	33.38	11.17
Infants' furniture	6.22	8.57	13.32	9.65	3.21	3.07	0.90	0.14
Outdoor furniture	15.16	1.17	9.47	20.63	26.28	16.03	9.86	5.53
Wall units, cabinets, and other furniture	50.61	31.58	55.38	77.09	60.96	44.86	22.55	14.03
Floor coverings	44.38	6.46	42.44	52.78	50.59	55.50	40.17	35.50
Wall-to-wall carpet (renter)	1.38	2.10	0.76	2.98	0.78	0.42	1.69	0.48
Wall-to-wall carpet (replacement) (owner)	27.78	0.45	24.41	30.25	35.07	31.48	27.83	29.63
Room-size rugs and other floor coverings, nonpermanent	15.22	3.91	17.27	19.54	14.74	23.60	10.66	5.39
Major appliances	188.96	76.92	181.08	211.53	222.81	221.44	195.63	122.08
Dishwashers (built-in), garbage disposals, range hoods (renter)	0.87	1.67	1.14	1.51	0.18	1.23	–	0.21
Dishwashers (built-in), garbage disposals, range hoods (owner)	14.10	0.09	9.96	12.11	20.00	22.20	18.57	9.06
Refrigerators and freezers (renter)	7.35	12.92	13.14	8.77	4.46	3.74	2.74	5.24
Refrigerators and freezers (owner)	44.34	6.79	36.17	61.76	46.99	51.91	49.10	28.15
Washing machines (renter)	4.79	8.16	8.48	5.87	4.32	1.60	2.13	1.25
Washing machines (owner)	18.53	3.57	13.59	24.69	24.58	22.31	17.09	9.22
Clothes dryers (renter)	3.36	8.17	6.15	3.76	2.13	0.96	1.68	1.30
Clothes dryers (owner)	12.02	3.35	9.60	15.68	16.23	11.05	6.26	13.69
Cooking stoves, ovens (renter)	2.80	3.01	2.64	4.82	2.49	2.86	1.83	–
Cooking stoves, ovens (owner)	23.95	6.24	18.37	25.20	25.92	43.83	22.64	15.71
Microwave ovens (renter)	2.38	5.75	4.31	2.75	0.90	1.17	1.56	1.04
Microwave ovens (owner)	7.36	0.31	6.16	7.58	9.08	11.82	7.88	4.43
Portable dishwasher (renter)	0.16	1.28	–	0.28	–	–	–	–
Portable dishwasher (owner)	0.76	–	0.78	0.47	1.02	1.90	0.71	–
Window air conditioners (renter)	1.85	2.53	2.58	2.32	1.24	1.35	0.50	2.33
Window air conditioners (owner)	4.82	4.98	3.18	2.96	3.68	5.15	9.57	8.58
Electric floor-cleaning equipment	25.98	6.63	36.27	21.62	39.72	12.88	32.15	17.34
Sewing machines	4.78	–	0.87	2.29	7.08	11.14	11.35	0.72
Miscellaneous household appliances	8.77	1.48	7.71	7.09	12.77	14.35	9.88	3.82
Small appliances and misc. housewares	87.37	50.07	78.26	92.72	126.10	106.12	67.90	38.82
Housewares	64.87	36.69	57.62	68.66	97.73	78.31	46.66	27.16
Plastic dinnerware	1.45	1.87	2.80	1.30	1.37	1.40	0.56	0.29
China and other dinnerware	11.43	4.09	5.06	14.33	25.64	8.52	7.20	2.02
Flatware	3.61	2.61	2.78	3.56	3.86	7.20	3.59	0.66
Glassware	8.02	2.87	14.41	6.86	7.65	6.85	7.68	6.11
Silver serving pieces	2.35	0.61	1.77	3.99	3.22	1.87	1.48	0.80

	total consumer units	under 25	25 to 34	35 to 44	45 to 54	55 to 64	65 to 74	75+
Other serving pieces	$1.43	$2.28	$1.23	$1.35	$1.80	$1.77	$1.12	$0.42
Nonelectric cookware	16.67	10.14	18.29	12.97	19.67	30.74	12.95	6.57
Tableware, nonelectric kitchenware	19.90	12.22	11.27	24.31	34.51	19.95	12.10	10.29
Small appliances	22.51	13.37	20.64	24.06	28.37	27.81	21.24	11.66
Small electric kitchen appliances	17.04	10.46	15.78	17.64	20.95	21.43	18.25	7.80
Portable heating and cooling equipment	5.47	2.91	4.87	6.42	7.42	6.38	2.99	3.85
Miscellaneous household equipment	**730.81**	**429.09**	**616.96**	**925.51**	**915.20**	**1,022.01**	**449.58**	**254.12**
Window coverings	13.02	2.52	8.95	14.98	22.15	11.96	13.38	6.25
Infants' equipment	8.01	2.47	14.73	14.26	7.86	2.29	1.29	0.60
Laundry and cleaning equipment	10.08	5.91	8.68	10.03	11.94	14.20	9.91	7.00
Outdoor equipment	18.39	13.07	8.75	18.70	18.13	35.09	5.56	31.36
Clocks	13.91	0.20	5.69	10.30	17.61	51.11	3.41	1.65
Lamps and lighting fixtures	10.80	6.51	8.49	14.40	15.00	12.97	6.51	3.25
Other household decorative items	177.30	45.08	123.37	244.58	184.45	347.62	115.19	41.74
Telephones and accessories	29.19	13.91	22.48	43.09	47.46	19.93	22.06	4.02
Lawn and garden equipment	46.82	8.34	25.78	62.22	73.15	47.16	41.82	30.33
Power tools	21.32	8.33	33.46	28.36	15.01	29.88	7.64	8.62
Office furniture for home use	13.67	5.67	15.31	21.31	14.90	15.97	5.70	2.81
Hand tools	7.26	4.27	7.46	9.25	8.89	9.59	4.92	0.80
Indoor plants and fresh flowers	57.01	21.02	42.82	64.15	74.62	75.08	59.36	31.38
Closet and storage items	8.03	5.39	7.82	7.92	12.19	10.27	5.23	2.34
Rental of furniture	3.12	3.84	5.66	5.12	2.00	2.01	0.57	–
Luggage	8.32	3.95	7.96	10.79	10.57	7.96	6.40	4.77
Computers and computer hardware, nonbusiness use	187.83	176.88	188.57	238.81	250.90	193.36	93.09	45.56
Computer software and accessories, nonbusiness use	17.49	12.09	20.22	21.81	22.46	19.37	9.64	2.88
Telephone answering devices	1.97	1.61	2.32	2.44	2.02	1.28	2.50	0.79
Calculators	1.64	1.69	1.39	2.48	2.34	1.42	0.44	0.29
Business equipment for home use	1.83	0.89	1.77	2.24	1.77	1.76	1.59	2.18
Other hardware	24.09	3.08	3.28	31.04	47.19	50.51	1.38	4.43
Smoke alarms (owner)	0.56	0.20	0.66	0.53	0.51	0.53	0.64	0.82
Smoke alarms (renter)	0.16	0.15	0.43	0.12	0.11	0.13	–	0.08
Other household appliances (owner)	7.59	0.26	7.06	7.31	10.52	11.12	7.16	4.64
Other household appliances (renter)	1.22	1.55	2.61	1.61	0.95	0.33	0.31	0.31
Miscellaneous household equipment and parts	40.18	80.20	41.21	37.65	40.49	49.10	23.88	15.21

Note: (–) means sample is too small to make a reliable estimate.
Source: Bureau of Labor Statistics, unpublished tables from the 2000 Consumer Expenditure Survey

Table 8.2 (Housing) Household Operations: Indexed spending by age, 2000

(indexed average annual spending of consumer units (CU) on household services, supplies, furnishings, and equipment, by age of consumer unit reference person, 2000; index definition: an index of 100 is the average for all consumer units; an index of 132 means that spending by consumer units in that group is 32 percent above the average for all consumer units; an index of 68 indicates spending that is 32 percent below the average for all consumer units)

	total consumer units	under 25	25 to 34	35 to 44	45 to 54	55 to 64	65 to 74	75+
Average spending of CU, total	$38,045	$22,543	$38,945	$45,149	$46,160	$39,340	$30,782	$21,908
Average spending of CU, index	100	59	102	119	121	103	81	58
Housing, spending index	100	58	106	123	115	100	79	63
HOUSEHOLD SERVICES	100	33	127	131	85	79	73	123
Personal services	100	47	197	166	45	29	30	104
Babysitting and child care in your own home	100	24	192	249	42	6	11	0
Babysitting and child care in someone else's home	100	90	299	155	26	15	0	3
Care for elderly, invalids, handicapped, etc.	100	2	2	10	47	69	139	662
Adult day care centers	100	–	–	111	45	401	31	117
Day care centers, nurseries, and preschools	100	55	231	194	48	20	12	1
Other household services	100	20	64	99	122	125	111	139
Housekeeping services	100	7	48	99	147	112	102	151
Gardening, lawn care service	100	5	33	79	114	152	145	197
Water softening service	100	49	98	98	108	150	88	79
Nonclothing laundry and dry cleaning, sent out	100	65	61	96	99	154	112	119
Nonclothing laundry and dry cleaning, coin-operated	100	199	142	107	93	63	54	47
Termite/pest control services	100	10	48	133	80	116	161	142
Home security system service fee	100	10	88	111	113	135	115	78
Other home services	100	7	72	97	122	145	103	122
Termite/pest control products	100	0	37	116	76	139	155	200
Moving, storage, and freight express	100	31	95	99	143	128	111	27
Appliance repair, including service center	100	20	58	94	140	120	133	107
Reupholstering and furniture repair	100	4	93	88	64	141	256	64
Repairs/rentals of lawn/garden equipment, hand/power tools, etc.	100	0	58	116	109	126	141	121
Appliance rental	100	87	92	93	114	138	100	57
Rental of office equipment for nonbusiness use	100	181	134	109	108	45	83	26
Repair of misc. household equipment and furnishings	100	16	–	16	2	96	6	872
Repair of computer systems for nonbusiness use	100	41	85	89	98	93	216	86
Computer information services	100	44	104	132	128	111	69	26
Rental, installation of dishwashers, range hoods, and garbage disposals	100	40	40	33	–	500	173	–
HOUSEKEEPING SUPPLIES	100	40	91	118	110	121	106	67
Laundry and cleaning supplies	100	42	95	120	105	141	84	60
Soaps and detergents	100	48	104	124	110	109	84	64
Other laundry cleaning products	100	35	86	115	99	176	84	56
Other household products	100	39	89	124	109	116	107	65
Cleansing and toilet tissue, paper towels, napkins	100	43	91	108	114	121	104	83
Miscellaneous household products	100	58	89	122	118	107	102	54
Lawn and garden supplies	100	12	86	143	93	123	116	60
Postage and stationery	100	40	89	106	117	111	127	77
Stationery, stationery supplies, giftwrap	100	49	110	115	119	99	86	65
Postage	100	30	68	97	113	123	170	91
Delivery services	100	13	45	50	234	108	143	64

	total consumer units	under 25	25 to 34	35 to 44	45 to 54	55 to 64	65 to 74	75+
HOUSEHOLD FURNISHINGS AND EQUIPMENT	**100**	**56**	**97**	**123**	**123**	**122**	**72**	**41**
Household textiles	**100**	**32**	**113**	**117**	**117**	**118**	**95**	**40**
Bathroom linens	100	20	144	98	120	95	95	61
Bedroom linens	100	50	140	99	122	110	84	29
Kitchen and dining room linens	100	26	109	107	89	136	132	66
Curtains and draperies	100	15	59	189	114	77	115	26
Slipcovers and decorative pillows	100	–	65	109	73	361	–	29
Sewing materials for household items	100	26	70	86	137	190	94	55
Other linens	100	41	65	117	137	159	55	65
Furniture	**100**	**69**	**117**	**128**	**121**	**92**	**66**	**36**
Mattresses and springs	100	95	114	117	118	93	68	48
Other bedroom furniture	100	84	161	103	128	64	68	23
Sofas	100	76	111	141	112	96	60	32
Living room chairs	100	55	84	104	101	150	104	82
Living room tables	100	78	107	140	117	112	42	26
Kitchen and dining room furniture	100	34	115	137	141	73	72	24
Infants' furniture	100	138	214	155	52	49	14	2
Outdoor furniture	100	8	62	136	173	106	65	36
Wall units, cabinets, and other furniture	100	62	109	152	120	89	45	28
Floor coverings	**100**	**15**	**96**	**119**	**114**	**125**	**91**	**80**
Wall-to-wall carpet (renter)	100	152	55	216	57	30	122	35
Wall-to-wall carpet (replacement) (owner)	100	2	88	109	126	113	100	107
Room-size rugs and other floor coverings, nonpermanent	100	26	113	128	97	155	70	35
Major appliances	**100**	**41**	**96**	**112**	**118**	**117**	**104**	**65**
Dishwashers (built-in), garbage disposals, range hoods (renter)	100	192	131	174	21	141	–	24
Dishwashers (built-in), garbage disposals, range hoods (owner)	100	1	71	86	142	157	132	64
Refrigerators and freezers (renter)	100	176	179	119	61	51	37	71
Refrigerators and freezers (owner)	100	15	82	139	106	117	111	63
Washing machines (renter)	100	170	177	123	90	33	44	26
Washing machines (owner)	100	19	73	133	133	120	92	50
Clothes dryers (renter)	100	243	183	112	63	29	50	39
Clothes dryers (owner)	100	28	80	130	135	92	52	114
Cooking stoves, ovens (renter)	100	108	94	172	89	102	65	–
Cooking stoves, ovens (owner)	100	26	77	105	108	183	95	66
Microwave ovens (renter)	100	242	181	116	38	49	66	44
Microwave ovens (owner)	100	4	84	103	123	161	107	60
Portable dishwasher (renter)	100	800	–	175	–	–	–	–
Portable dishwasher (owner)	100	–	103	62	134	250	93	–
Window air conditioners (renter)	100	137	139	125	67	73	27	126
Window air conditioners (owner)	100	103	66	61	76	107	199	178
Electric floor-cleaning equipment	100	26	140	83	153	50	124	67
Sewing machines	100	–	18	48	148	233	237	15
Miscellaneous household appliances	100	17	88	81	146	164	113	44
Small appliances and misc. housewares	**100**	**57**	**90**	**106**	**144**	**121**	**78**	**44**
Housewares	100	57	89	106	151	121	72	42
Plastic dinnerware	100	129	193	90	94	97	39	20
China and other dinnerware	100	36	44	125	224	75	63	18
Flatware	100	72	77	99	107	199	99	18
Glassware	100	36	180	86	95	85	96	76
Silver serving pieces	100	26	75	170	137	80	63	34

	total consumer units	under 25	25 to 34	35 to 44	45 to 54	55 to 64	65 to 74	75+
Other serving pieces	100	159	86	94	126	124	78	29
Nonelectric cookware	100	61	110	78	118	184	78	39
Tableware, nonelectric kitchenware	100	61	57	122	173	100	61	52
Small appliances	100	59	92	107	126	124	94	52
Small electric kitchen appliances	100	61	93	104	123	126	107	46
Portable heating and cooling equipment	100	53	89	117	136	117	55	70
Miscellaneous household equipment	**100**	**59**	**84**	**127**	**125**	**140**	**62**	**35**
Window coverings	100	19	69	115	170	92	103	48
Infants' equipment	100	31	184	178	98	29	16	7
Laundry and cleaning equipment	100	59	86	100	118	141	98	69
Outdoor equipment	100	71	48	102	99	191	30	171
Clocks	100	1	41	74	127	367	25	12
Lamps and lighting fixtures	100	60	79	133	139	120	60	30
Other household decorative items	100	25	70	138	104	196	65	24
Telephones and accessories	100	48	77	148	163	68	76	14
Lawn and garden equipment	100	18	55	133	156	101	89	65
Power tools	100	39	157	133	70	140	36	40
Office furniture for home use	100	41	112	156	109	117	42	21
Hand tools	100	59	103	127	122	132	68	11
Indoor plants and fresh flowers	100	37	75	113	131	132	104	55
Closet and storage items	100	67	97	99	152	128	65	29
Rental of furniture	100	123	181	164	64	64	18	–
Luggage	100	47	96	130	127	96	77	57
Computers and computer hardware, nonbusiness use	100	94	100	127	134	103	50	24
Computer software and accessories, nonbusiness use	100	69	116	125	128	111	55	16
Telephone answering devices	100	82	118	124	103	65	127	40
Calculators	100	103	85	151	143	87	27	18
Business equipment for home use	100	49	97	122	97	96	87	119
Other hardware	100	13	14	129	196	210	6	18
Smoke alarms (owner)	100	36	118	95	91	95	114	146
Smoke alarms (renter)	100	94	269	75	69	81	–	50
Other household appliances (owner)	100	3	93	96	139	147	94	61
Other household appliances (renter)	100	127	214	132	78	27	25	25
Miscellaneous household equipment and parts	100	200	103	94	101	122	59	38

Note: (–) means sample is too small to make a reliable estimate.
Source: Calculations by New Strategist based on the 2000 Consumer Expenditure Survey

Table 8.3 (Housing) Household Operations: Indexed per capita spending by age, 2000

(indexed average annual per capita spending of consumer units (CU) on household services, supplies, furnishings, and equipment, by age of consumer unit reference person, 2000; index definition: an index of 100 is the average for all consumer units; an index of 132 means that spending by consumer units in that group is 32 percent above the average for all consumer units; an index of 68 indicates spending that is 32 percent below the average for all consumer units)

	total consumer units	under 25	25 to 34	35 to 44	45 to 54	55 to 64	65 to 74	75+
Per capita spending of CU, total	$15,218	$11,865	$13,429	$13,682	$17,096	$18,733	$16,201	$14,605
Per capita spending of CU, index	100	78	88	90	112	123	106	96
Housing, per capita spending index	100	76	91	93	107	119	103	105
HOUSEHOLD SERVICES	**100**	**43**	**110**	**99**	**79**	**94**	**96**	**204**
Personal services	**100**	**62**	**169**	**126**	**42**	**34**	**40**	**174**
Babysitting and child care in your own home	100	31	165	189	39	7	15	1
Babysitting and child care in someone else's home	100	119	258	117	24	18	0	5
Care for elderly, invalids, handicapped, etc.	100	3	1	8	44	83	183	1,104
Adult day care centers	100	–	–	84	42	478	41	195
Day care centers, nurseries, and preschools	100	73	199	147	44	23	16	2
Other household services	**100**	**27**	**55**	**75**	**113**	**149**	**147**	**232**
Housekeeping services	100	9	42	75	136	133	134	252
Gardening, lawn care service	100	6	28	60	105	180	190	328
Water softening service	100	64	84	74	100	178	116	131
Nonclothing laundry and dry cleaning, sent out	100	85	52	73	92	183	148	198
Nonclothing laundry and dry cleaning, coin-operated	100	262	123	81	86	74	71	78
Termite/pest control services	100	13	41	101	74	138	212	236
Home security system service fee	100	13	76	84	104	161	152	130
Other home services	100	10	62	73	113	172	135	204
Termite/pest control products	100	0	32	88	70	165	204	333
Moving, storage, and freight express	100	41	82	75	133	153	146	46
Appliance repair, including service center	100	26	50	71	130	142	175	178
Reupholstering and furniture repair	100	5	80	67	59	168	337	107
Repairs/rentals of lawn/garden equipment, hand/power tools, etc.	100	1	50	88	101	150	186	202
Appliance rental	100	115	80	71	106	164	132	95
Rental of office equipment for nonbusiness use	100	238	115	83	100	54	109	44
Repair of misc. household equipment and furnishings	100	21	–	12	1	115	8	1,453
Repair of computer systems for nonbusiness use	100	54	73	67	91	111	284	144
Computer information services	100	58	89	100	118	132	90	44
Rental, installation of dishwashers, range hoods, and garbage disposals	100	53	34	25	–	595	228	–
HOUSEKEEPING SUPPLIES	**100**	**53**	**78**	**89**	**102**	**144**	**139**	**111**
Laundry and cleaning supplies	**100**	**55**	**82**	**91**	**97**	**167**	**110**	**101**
Soaps and detergents	100	63	89	94	102	130	110	107
Other laundry cleaning products	100	47	74	87	92	210	111	93
Other household products	**100**	**52**	**77**	**94**	**101**	**138**	**140**	**108**
Cleansing and toilet tissue, paper towels, napkins	100	56	78	82	106	144	137	139
Miscellaneous household products	100	76	77	92	109	128	134	90
Lawn and garden supplies	100	15	74	108	86	146	153	100
Postage and stationery	**100**	**52**	**77**	**80**	**109**	**132**	**167**	**129**
Stationery, stationery supplies, giftwrap	100	65	94	87	110	118	114	109
Postage	100	40	59	73	104	147	223	151
Delivery services	100	17	39	38	217	128	188	106

	total consumer units	under 25	25 to 34	35 to 44	45 to 54	55 to 64	65 to 74	75+
HOUSEHOLD FURNISHINGS AND EQUIPMENT	**100**	**74**	**83**	**93**	**114**	**145**	**94**	**68**
Household textiles	**100**	**43**	**97**	**88**	**109**	**140**	**124**	**67**
Bathroom linens	100	26	124	75	111	114	125	102
Bedroom linens	100	66	121	75	113	131	111	48
Kitchen and dining room linens	100	34	94	81	83	162	174	109
Curtains and draperies	100	20	50	143	106	91	151	44
Slipcovers and decorative pillows	100	–	56	83	68	430	–	49
Sewing materials for household items	100	34	60	65	127	226	124	91
Other linens	100	53	56	89	127	189	72	109
Furniture	**100**	**91**	**101**	**97**	**112**	**110**	**86**	**60**
Mattresses and springs	100	125	98	89	110	110	89	80
Other bedroom furniture	100	111	138	78	119	76	90	38
Sofas	100	100	95	107	103	114	79	54
Living room chairs	100	72	72	79	94	178	137	137
Living room tables	100	102	92	106	108	133	56	43
Kitchen and dining room furniture	100	44	99	104	131	87	95	40
Infants' furniture	100	181	185	118	48	59	19	4
Outdoor furniture	100	10	54	103	161	126	86	61
Wall units, cabinets, and other furniture	100	82	94	115	112	106	59	46
Floor coverings	**100**	**19**	**82**	**90**	**106**	**149**	**119**	**133**
Wall-to-wall carpet (renter)	100	200	47	164	52	36	161	58
Wall-to-wall carpet (replacement) (owner)	100	2	76	82	117	135	132	178
Room-size rugs and other floor coverings, nonpermanent	100	34	98	97	90	185	92	59
Major appliances	**100**	**54**	**83**	**85**	**109**	**140**	**136**	**108**
Dishwashers (built-in), garbage disposals, range hoods (renter)	100	253	113	131	19	168	–	40
Dishwashers (built-in), garbage disposals, range hoods (owner)	100	1	61	65	131	187	173	107
Refrigerators and freezers (renter)	100	231	154	90	56	61	49	119
Refrigerators and freezers (owner)	100	20	70	106	98	139	146	106
Washing machines (renter)	100	224	153	93	84	40	59	43
Washing machines (owner)	100	25	63	101	123	143	121	83
Clothes dryers (renter)	100	320	158	85	59	34	66	64
Clothes dryers (owner)	100	37	69	99	125	109	69	190
Cooking stoves, ovens (renter)	100	141	81	130	82	122	86	–
Cooking stoves, ovens (owner)	100	34	66	80	100	218	124	109
Microwave ovens (renter)	100	318	156	88	35	59	86	73
Microwave ovens (owner)	100	6	72	78	114	191	141	100
Portable dishwasher (renter)	100	1,053	–	133	–	–	–	–
Portable dishwasher (owner)	100	–	88	47	124	298	123	–
Window air conditioners (renter)	100	180	120	95	62	87	36	210
Window air conditioners (owner)	100	136	57	47	71	127	261	297
Electric floor-cleaning equipment	100	34	120	63	142	59	163	111
Sewing machines	100	–	16	36	137	277	312	25
Miscellaneous household appliances	100	22	76	61	135	195	148	73
Small appliances and misc. housewares	**100**	**75**	**77**	**80**	**134**	**145**	**102**	**74**
Housewares	100	74	77	80	139	144	95	70
Plastic dinnerware	100	170	166	68	87	115	51	33
China and other dinnerware	100	47	38	95	208	89	83	29
Flatware	100	95	66	75	99	237	131	30
Glassware	100	47	155	65	88	102	126	127
Silver serving pieces	100	34	65	129	127	95	83	57

	total consumer units	under 25	25 to 34	35 to 44	45 to 54	55 to 64	65 to 74	75+
Other serving pieces	100	210	74	72	117	147	103	49
Nonelectric cookware	100	80	95	59	109	220	102	66
Tableware, nonelectric kitchenware	100	81	49	93	161	119	80	86
Small appliances	100	78	79	81	117	147	124	86
Small electric kitchen appliances	100	81	80	78	114	150	141	76
Portable heating and cooling equipment	100	70	77	89	126	139	72	117
Miscellaneous household equipment	**100**	**77**	**73**	**96**	**116**	**166**	**81**	**58**
Window coverings	100	25	59	87	158	109	135	80
Infants' equipment	100	41	159	135	91	34	21	12
Laundry and cleaning equipment	100	77	74	75	110	168	129	116
Outdoor equipment	100	94	41	77	91	227	40	284
Clocks	100	2	35	56	117	437	32	20
Lamps and lighting fixtures	100	79	68	101	129	143	79	50
Other household decorative items	100	33	60	105	96	233	85	39
Telephones and accessories	100	63	66	112	151	81	99	23
Lawn and garden equipment	100	23	47	101	145	120	118	108
Power tools	100	51	135	101	65	167	47	67
Office furniture for home use	100	55	97	118	101	139	55	34
Hand tools	100	77	89	97	113	157	89	18
Indoor plants and fresh flowers	100	49	65	85	121	157	137	92
Closet and storage items	100	88	84	75	141	152	86	49
Rental of furniture	100	162	156	124	59	77	24	–
Luggage	100	62	82	98	118	114	101	96
Computers and computer hardware, nonbusiness use	100	124	87	96	124	123	65	40
Computer software and accessories, nonbusiness use	100	91	100	94	119	132	73	27
Telephone answering devices	100	108	102	94	95	77	167	67
Calculators	100	136	73	115	132	103	35	29
Business equipment for home use	100	64	83	93	90	114	114	199
Other hardware	100	17	12	98	181	250	8	31
Smoke alarms (owner)	100	47	102	72	84	113	150	244
Smoke alarms (renter)	100	123	232	57	64	97	–	83
Other household appliances (owner)	100	5	80	73	128	174	124	102
Other household appliances (renter)	100	167	184	100	72	32	33	42
Miscellaneous household equipment and parts	100	263	88	71	93	145	78	63

Note: Per capita indexes account for household size and show how much each person in a particular household demographic segment spends relative to a person in the average household. (–) means sample is too small to make a reliable estimate.
Source: Calculations by New Strategist based on the 2000 Consumer Expenditure Survey

Table 8.4 (Housing) Household Operations: Total spending by age, 2000

(total annual spending on household services, supplies, furnishings, and equipment, by consumer unit (CU) age group, 2000; numbers in thousands)

	total consumer units	under 25	25 to 34	35 to 44	45 to 54	55 to 64	65 to 74	75+
Number of consumer units	109,367	8,306	18,887	23,983	21,874	14,161	11,538	10,617
Total spending of all CUs	$4,160,831,424	$187,243,653	$735,559,314	$1,082,817,341	$1,009,709,965	$557,094,165	$355,160,524	$232,597,661
Housing, total spending	1,347,238,483	59,048,683	246,467,040	362,417,905	310,158,227	175,061,114	111,589,305	82,451,728
HOUSEHOLD SERVICES	**$74,848,587**	**$1,876,907**	**$16,453,788**	**$21,481,093**	**$12,742,699**	**$7,677,528**	**$5,749,270**	**$8,902,355**
Personal services	**35,675,515**	**1,275,719**	**12,109,022**	**12,994,229**	**3,219,415**	**1,320,372**	**1,142,493**	**3,614,133**
Babysitting and child care in your own home	3,522,711	63,375	1,166,461	1,923,676	298,799	28,605	40,960	1,168
Babysitting and child care in someone else's home	3,564,271	244,113	1,841,671	1,208,264	187,241	71,513	462	11,360
Care for elderly, invalids, handicapped, etc.	5,509,909	9,801	15,110	120,395	519,945	494,785	807,083	3,543,105
Adult day care centers	284,354	–	–	69,071	25,593	147,699	9,346	32,276
Day care centers, nurseries, and preschools	22,794,270	958,429	9,085,780	9,672,824	2,187,837	577,627	284,873	26,224
Other household services	**39,173,072**	**601,188**	**4,344,765**	**8,486,864**	**9,523,065**	**6,357,156**	**4,606,662**	**5,288,328**
Housekeeping services	9,640,701	50,168	806,853	2,102,829	2,826,558	1,396,841	1,039,343	1,417,794
Gardening, lawn care service	8,559,061	30,234	481,052	1,475,194	1,948,317	1,679,919	1,306,679	1,636,929
Water softening service	340,131	12,625	57,416	72,908	73,497	65,849	31,614	26,012
Nonclothing laundry and dry cleaning, sent out	161,863	7,974	16,998	34,056	32,155	32,287	19,153	18,686
Nonclothing laundry and dry cleaning, coin-operated	507,463	76,664	124,843	119,196	94,058	41,067	28,960	23,039
Termite/pest control services	1,046,642	7,808	86,125	305,783	167,774	157,045	178,262	143,967
Home security system service fee	2,041,882	15,034	309,936	495,009	460,666	357,707	248,413	155,114
Other home services	1,561,761	8,638	194,536	330,726	380,170	292,849	169,032	185,267
Termite/pest control products	53,590	–	3,400	13,670	8,093	9,629	8,769	10,405
Moving, storage, and freight express	3,546,772	83,392	581,531	769,614	1,015,172	588,531	414,445	94,279
Appliance repair, including service center	1,375,837	20,765	137,497	282,520	386,514	213,123	192,685	142,692
Reupholstering and furniture repair	1,012,738	3,156	163,184	195,941	129,275	185,367	273,566	62,853
Repairs/rentals of lawn/garden equipment, hand/power tools, etc.	542,460	166	54,017	137,423	118,338	88,223	80,766	63,914
Appliance rental	412,314	27,327	65,727	84,180	94,277	73,637	43,614	22,933
Rental of office equipment for nonbusiness use	57,965	7,974	13,410	13,910	12,468	3,399	5,077	1,486
Repair of misc. household equipment and furnishings	1,282,875	15,200	–	45,328	4,156	160,019	8,654	1,085,482
Repair of computer systems for nonbusiness use	300,759	9,303	44,196	58,758	59,060	36,252	68,536	25,162
Computer information services	6,710,759	224,096	1,202,913	1,948,139	1,712,734	964,789	485,981	172,208
Rental, installation of dishwashers, range hoods, and garbage disposals	16,405	498	1,133	1,199	–	10,621	3,000	–
HOUSEKEEPING SUPPLIES	**52,749,891**	**1,608,125**	**8,262,118**	**13,662,156**	**11,629,750**	**8,288,433**	**5,890,841**	**3,423,133**
Laundry and cleaning supplies	**14,300,829**	**455,501**	**2,355,964**	**3,758,616**	**3,003,956**	**2,604,350**	**1,264,103**	**837,150**
Soaps and detergents	7,575,852	274,846	1,354,198	2,057,262	1,669,861	1,069,580	667,935	472,138
Other laundry cleaning products	6,724,977	180,572	1,001,766	1,701,354	1,333,877	1,534,628	596,168	365,012
Other household products	**24,706,005**	**739,151**	**3,794,021**	**6,715,000**	**5,402,222**	**3,713,722**	**2,782,966**	**1,552,205**
Cleansing and toilet tissue, paper towels, and napkins	7,486,171	242,037	1,176,660	1,774,982	1,706,172	1,171,964	823,236	605,063
Miscellaneous household products	9,895,526	432,244	1,524,936	2,640,768	2,338,768	1,374,750	1,059,996	520,127
Lawn and garden supplies	7,324,308	64,787	1,092,424	2,299,250	1,357,282	1,166,866	899,733	427,016
Postage and stationery	**13,743,057**	**413,556**	**2,111,944**	**3,188,540**	**3,223,790**	**1,970,362**	**1,843,657**	**1,033,777**
Stationery, stationery supplies, giftwrap	6,961,210	260,393	1,316,991	1,762,751	1,657,174	890,019	634,475	441,667
Postage	6,627,640	151,585	783,244	1,408,761	1,494,432	1,058,818	1,186,106	582,555
Delivery services	154,207	1,495	11,899	17,028	72,184	21,525	23,191	9,555

	total consumer units	under 25	25 to 34	35 to 44	45 to 54	55 to 64	65 to 74	75+
HOUSEHOLD FURNISHINGS AND EQUIPMENT	**$169,369,017**	**$7,205,372**	**$28,240,976**	**$45,714,716**	**$41,797,714**	**$26,785,248**	**$12,808,795**	**$6,732,558**
Household textiles	**11,646,492**	**287,388**	**2,265,685**	**2,978,209**	**2,732,500**	**1,772,957**	**1,162,223**	**451,435**
Bathroom linens	1,919,391	28,905	478,597	414,426	459,135	237,055	192,338	114,557
Bedroom linens	4,869,019	186,054	1,181,193	1,056,691	1,184,258	691,340	433,713	137,278
Kitchen and dining room linens	1,018,207	20,267	191,703	238,151	182,210	179,137	142,264	64,764
Curtains and draperies	2,303,269	26,247	232,877	953,324	525,195	228,417	278,527	58,712
Slipcovers and decorative pillows	300,759	–	33,808	71,949	43,967	140,760	–	8,600
Sewing materials for household items	1,066,328	20,848	128,809	200,498	291,799	261,695	105,919	56,801
Other linens	167,332	5,150	18,887	42,930	45,935	34,411	9,692	10,617
Furniture	**42,722,031**	**2,245,527**	**8,622,860**	**11,977,590**	**10,307,466**	**5,115,095**	**2,955,113**	**1,497,846**
Mattresses and springs	5,784,421	416,629	1,136,242	1,484,548	1,368,875	694,172	413,983	269,566
Other bedroom furniture	7,558,353	483,409	2,096,079	1,705,431	1,936,068	626,058	546,094	165,413
Sofas	9,750,068	561,735	1,864,147	3,017,301	2,177,338	1,209,349	614,745	305,557
Living room chairs	4,794,649	199,012	694,475	1,091,706	970,549	929,245	526,710	382,637
Living room tables	1,880,019	111,217	347,332	578,470	439,886	272,316	84,112	46,927
Kitchen and dining room furniture	5,081,191	130,321	1,008,188	1,524,839	1,436,247	478,217	385,138	118,592
Infants' furniture	680,263	71,182	251,575	231,436	70,216	43,474	10,384	1,486
Outdoor furniture	1,658,004	9,718	178,860	494,769	574,849	227,001	113,765	58,712
Wall units, cabinets, and other furniture	5,535,064	262,303	1,045,962	1,848,849	1,333,439	635,262	260,182	148,957
Floor coverings	**4,853,707**	**53,657**	**801,564**	**1,265,823**	**1,106,606**	**785,936**	**463,481**	**376,904**
Wall-to-wall carpet (renter)	150,926	17,443	14,354	71,469	17,062	5,948	19,499	5,096
Wall-to-wall carpet (replacement) (owner)	3,038,215	3,738	461,032	725,486	767,121	445,788	321,103	314,582
Room-size rugs and other floor coverings, nonpermanent	1,664,566	32,476	326,178	468,628	322,423	334,200	122,995	57,226
Major appliances	**20,665,988**	**638,898**	**3,420,058**	**5,073,124**	**4,873,746**	**3,135,812**	**2,257,179**	**1,296,123**
Dishwashers (built-in), garbage disposals, range hoods (renter)	95,149	13,871	21,531	36,214	3,937	17,418	–	2,230
Dishwashers (built-in), garbage disposals, range hoods (owner)	1,542,075	748	188,115	290,434	437,480	314,374	214,261	96,190
Refrigerators and freezers (renter)	803,847	107,314	248,175	210,331	97,558	52,962	31,614	55,633
Refrigerators and freezers (owner)	4,849,333	56,398	683,143	1,481,190	1,027,859	735,098	566,516	298,869
Washing machines (renter)	523,868	67,777	160,162	140,780	94,496	22,658	24,576	13,271
Washing machines (owner)	2,026,571	29,652	256,674	592,140	537,663	315,932	197,184	97,889
Clothes dryers (renter)	367,473	67,860	116,155	90,176	46,592	13,595	19,384	13,802
Clothes dryers (owner)	1,314,591	27,825	181,315	376,053	355,015	156,479	72,228	145,347
Cooking stoves, ovens (renter)	306,228	25,001	49,862	115,598	54,466	40,500	21,115	–
Cooking stoves, ovens (owner)	2,619,340	51,829	346,954	604,372	566,974	620,677	261,220	166,793
Microwave ovens (renter)	260,293	47,760	81,403	65,953	19,687	16,568	17,999	11,042
Microwave ovens (owner)	804,941	2,575	116,344	181,791	198,616	167,383	90,919	47,033
Portable dishwasher (renter)	17,499	10,632	–	6,715	–	–	–	–
Portable dishwasher (owner)	83,119	–	14,732	11,272	22,311	26,906	8,192	–
Window air conditioners (renter)	202,329	21,014	48,728	55,641	27,124	19,117	5,769	24,738
Window air conditioners (owner)	527,149	41,364	60,061	70,990	80,496	72,929	110,419	91,094
Electric floor-cleaning equipment	2,841,355	55,069	685,031	518,512	868,835	182,394	370,947	184,099
Sewing machines	522,774	–	16,432	54,921	154,868	157,754	130,956	7,644
Miscellaneous household appliances	959,149	12,293	145,619	170,039	279,331	203,210	113,995	40,557
Small appliances and misc. housewares	**9,555,395**	**415,881**	**1,478,097**	**2,223,704**	**2,758,311**	**1,502,765**	**783,430**	**412,152**
Housewares	7,094,637	304,747	1,088,269	1,646,673	2,137,746	1,108,948	538,363	288,358
Plastic dinnerware	158,582	15,532	52,884	31,178	29,967	19,825	6,461	3,079
China and other dinnerware	1,250,065	33,972	95,568	343,676	560,849	120,652	83,074	21,446
Flatware	394,815	21,679	52,506	85,379	84,434	101,959	41,421	7,007
Glassware	877,123	23,838	272,162	164,523	167,336	97,003	88,612	64,870
Silver serving pieces	257,012	5,067	33,430	95,692	70,434	26,481	17,076	8,494

	total consumer units	under 25	25 to 34	35 to 44	45 to 54	55 to 64	65 to 74	75+
Other serving pieces	$156,395	$18,938	$23,231	$32,377	$39,373	$25,065	$12,923	$4,459
Nonelectric cookware	1,823,148	84,223	345,443	311,060	430,262	435,309	149,417	69,754
Tableware, nonelectric kitchenware	2,176,403	101,499	212,856	583,027	754,872	282,512	139,610	109,249
Small appliances	2,461,851	111,051	389,828	577,031	620,565	393,817	245,067	123,794
Small electric kitchen appliances	1,863,614	86,881	298,037	423,060	458,260	303,470	210,569	82,813
Portable heating and cooling equipment	598,237	24,170	91,980	153,971	162,305	90,347	34,499	40,875
Miscellaneous household equipment	**79,926,497**	**3,564,022**	**11,652,524**	**22,196,506**	**20,019,085**	**14,472,684**	**5,187,254**	**2,697,992**
Window coverings	1,423,958	20,931	169,039	359,265	484,509	169,366	154,378	66,356
Infants' equipment	876,030	20,516	278,206	341,998	171,930	32,429	14,884	6,370
Laundry and cleaning equipment	1,102,419	49,088	163,939	240,549	261,176	201,086	114,342	74,319
Outdoor equipment	2,011,259	108,559	165,261	448,482	396,576	496,909	64,151	332,949
Clocks	1,521,295	1,661	107,467	247,025	385,201	723,769	39,345	17,518
Lamps and lighting fixtures	1,181,164	54,072	160,351	345,355	328,110	183,668	75,112	34,505
Other household decorative items	19,390,769	374,434	2,330,089	5,865,762	4,034,659	4,922,647	1,329,062	443,154
Telephones and accessories	3,192,423	115,536	424,580	1,033,427	1,038,140	282,229	254,528	42,680
Lawn and garden equipment	5,120,563	69,272	486,907	1,492,222	1,600,083	667,833	482,519	322,014
Power tools	2,331,704	69,189	631,959	680,158	328,329	423,131	88,150	91,519
Office furniture for home use	1,495,047	47,095	289,160	511,078	325,923	226,151	65,767	29,834
Hand tools	794,004	35,467	140,897	221,843	194,460	135,804	56,767	8,494
Indoor plants and fresh flowers	6,235,013	174,592	808,741	1,538,509	1,632,238	1,063,208	684,896	333,161
Closet and storage items	878,217	44,769	147,696	189,945	266,644	145,433	60,344	24,844
Rental of furniture	341,225	31,895	106,900	122,793	43,748	28,464	6,577	–
Luggage	909,933	32,809	150,341	258,777	231,208	112,722	73,843	50,643
Computers and computer hardware, nonbusiness use	20,542,404	1,469,165	3,561,522	5,727,380	5,488,187	2,738,171	1,074,072	483,711
Computer software and accessories, nonbusiness use	1,912,829	100,420	381,895	523,069	491,290	274,299	111,226	30,577
Telephone answering devices	215,453	13,373	43,818	58,519	44,185	18,126	28,845	8,387
Calculators	179,362	14,037	26,253	59,478	51,185	20,109	5,077	3,079
Business equipment for home use	200,142	7,392	33,430	53,722	38,717	24,923	18,345	23,145
Other hardware	2,634,651	25,582	61,949	744,432	1,032,234	715,272	15,922	47,033
Smoke alarms (owner)	61,246	1,661	12,465	12,711	11,156	7,505	7,384	8,706
Smoke alarms (renter)	17,499	1,246	8,121	2,878	2,406	1,841	–	849
Other household appliances (owner)	830,096	2,160	133,342	175,316	230,114	157,470	82,612	49,263
Other household appliances (renter)	133,428	12,874	49,295	38,613	20,780	4,673	3,577	3,291
Miscellaneous household equipment and parts	4,394,366	666,141	778,333	902,960	885,678	695,305	275,527	161,485

Note: Numbers may not add to total because of rounding. (–) means sample is too small to make a reliable estimate.
Source: Calculations by New Strategist based on the 2000 Consumer Expenditure Survey

Table 8.5 (Housing) Household Operations: Market shares by age, 2000

(percentage of total annual spending on household services, supplies, furnishings, and equipment accounted for by consumer unit age groups, 2000)

	total consumer units	under 25	25 to 34	35 to 44	45 to 54	55 to 64	65 to 74	75+
Share of total consumer units	100.0%	7.6%	17.3%	21.9%	20.0%	12.9%	10.5%	9.7%
Share of total before-tax income	100.0	3.4	17.6	27.7	26.4	14.0	6.9	4.5
Share of total spending	100.0	4.5	17.7	26.0	24.3	13.4	8.5	5.6
Share of housing spending	100.0	4.4	18.3	26.9	23.0	13.0	8.3	6.1
HOUSEHOLD SERVICES	100.0%	2.5%	22.0%	28.7%	17.0%	10.3%	7.7%	11.9%
Personal services	100.0	3.6	33.9	36.4	9.0	3.7	3.2	10.1
Babysitting and child care in your own home	100.0	1.8	33.1	54.6	8.5	0.8	1.2	0.0
Babysitting and child care in someone else's home	100.0	6.8	51.7	33.9	5.3	2.0	0.0	0.3
Care for elderly, invalids, handicapped, etc.	100.0	0.2	0.3	2.2	9.4	9.0	14.6	64.3
Adult day care centers	100.0	–	–	24.3	9.0	51.9	3.3	11.4
Day care centers, nurseries, and preschools	100.0	4.2	39.9	42.4	9.6	2.5	1.2	0.1
Other household services	100.0	1.5	11.1	21.7	24.3	16.2	11.8	13.5
Housekeeping services	100.0	0.5	8.4	21.8	29.3	14.5	10.8	14.7
Gardening, lawn care service	100.0	0.4	5.6	17.2	22.8	19.6	15.3	19.1
Water softening service	100.0	3.7	16.9	21.4	21.6	19.4	9.3	7.6
Nonclothing laundry and dry cleaning, sent out	100.0	4.9	10.5	21.0	19.9	19.9	11.8	11.5
Nonclothing laundry and dry cleaning, coin-operated	100.0	15.1	24.6	23.5	18.5	8.1	5.7	4.5
Termite/pest control services	100.0	0.7	8.2	29.2	16.0	15.0	17.0	13.8
Home security system service fee	100.0	0.7	15.2	24.2	22.6	17.5	12.2	7.6
Other home services	100.0	0.6	12.5	21.2	24.3	18.8	10.8	11.9
Termite/pest control products	100.0	0.0	6.3	25.5	15.1	18.0	16.4	19.4
Moving, storage, and freight express	100.0	2.4	16.4	21.7	28.6	16.6	11.7	2.7
Appliance repair, including service center	100.0	1.5	10.0	20.5	28.1	15.5	14.0	10.4
Reupholstering and furniture repair	100.0	0.3	16.1	19.3	12.8	18.3	27.0	6.2
Repairs/rentals of lawn/garden equipment, hand/power tools, etc.	100.0	0.0	10.0	25.3	21.8	16.3	14.9	11.8
Appliance rental	100.0	6.6	15.9	20.4	22.9	17.9	10.6	5.6
Rental of office equipment for nonbusiness use	100.0	13.8	23.1	24.0	21.5	5.9	8.8	2.6
Repair of misc. household equipment and furnishings	100.0	1.2	–	3.5	0.3	12.5	0.7	84.6
Repair of computer systems for nonbusiness use	100.0	3.1	14.7	19.5	19.6	12.1	22.8	8.4
Computer information services	100.0	3.3	17.9	29.0	25.5	14.4	7.2	2.6
Rental, installation of dishwashers, range hoods, and garbage disposals	100.0	3.0	6.9	7.3	–	64.7	18.3	–
HOUSEKEEPING SUPPLIES	100.0	3.0	15.7	25.9	22.0	15.7	11.2	6.5
Laundry and cleaning supplies	100.0	3.2	16.5	26.3	21.0	18.2	8.8	5.9
Soaps and detergents	100.0	3.6	17.9	27.2	22.0	14.1	8.8	6.2
Other laundry cleaning products	100.0	2.7	14.9	25.3	19.8	22.8	8.9	5.4
Other household products	100.0	3.0	15.4	27.2	21.9	15.0	11.3	6.3
Cleansing and toilet tissue, paper towels, and napkins	100.0	3.2	15.7	23.7	22.8	15.7	11.0	8.1
Miscellaneous household products	100.0	4.4	15.4	26.7	23.6	13.9	10.7	5.3
Lawn and garden supplies	100.0	0.9	14.9	31.4	18.5	15.9	12.3	5.8
Postage and stationery	100.0	3.0	15.4	23.2	23.5	14.3	13.4	7.5
Stationery, stationery supplies, giftwrap	100.0	3.7	18.9	25.3	23.8	12.8	9.1	6.3
Postage	100.0	2.3	11.8	21.3	22.5	16.0	17.9	8.8
Delivery services	100.0	1.0	7.7	11.0	46.8	14.0	15.0	6.2

	total consumer units	under 25	25 to 34	35 to 44	45 to 54	55 to 64	65 to 74	75+
HOUSEHOLD FURNISHINGS AND EQUIPMENT	100.0%	4.3%	16.7%	27.0%	24.7%	15.8%	7.6%	4.0%
Household textiles	100.0	2.5	19.5	25.6	23.5	15.2	10.0	3.9
Bathroom linens	100.0	1.5	24.9	21.6	23.9	12.4	10.0	6.0
Bedroom linens	100.0	3.8	24.3	21.7	24.3	14.2	8.9	2.8
Kitchen and dining room linens	100.0	2.0	18.8	23.4	17.9	17.6	14.0	6.4
Curtains and draperies	100.0	1.1	10.1	41.4	22.8	9.9	12.1	2.5
Slipcovers and decorative pillows	100.0	–	11.2	23.9	14.6	46.8	–	2.9
Sewing materials for household items	100.0	2.0	12.1	18.8	27.4	24.5	9.9	5.3
Other linens	100.0	3.1	11.3	25.7	27.5	20.6	5.8	6.3
Furniture	100.0	5.3	20.2	28.0	24.1	12.0	6.9	3.5
Mattresses and springs	100.0	7.2	19.6	25.7	23.7	12.0	7.2	4.7
Other bedroom furniture	100.0	6.4	27.7	22.6	25.6	8.3	7.2	2.2
Sofas	100.0	5.8	19.1	30.9	22.3	12.4	6.3	3.1
Living room chairs	100.0	4.2	14.5	22.8	20.2	19.4	11.0	8.0
Living room tables	100.0	5.9	18.5	30.8	23.4	14.5	4.5	2.5
Kitchen and dining room furniture	100.0	2.6	19.8	30.0	28.3	9.4	7.6	2.3
Infants' furniture	100.0	10.5	37.0	34.0	10.3	6.4	1.5	0.2
Outdoor furniture	100.0	0.6	10.8	29.8	34.7	13.7	6.9	3.5
Wall units, cabinets, and other furniture	100.0	4.7	18.9	33.4	24.1	11.5	4.7	2.7
Floor coverings	100.0	1.1	16.5	26.1	22.8	16.2	9.5	7.8
Wall-to-wall carpet (renter)	100.0	11.6	9.5	47.4	11.3	3.9	12.9	3.4
Wall-to-wall carpet (replacement) (owner)	100.0	0.1	15.2	23.9	25.2	14.7	10.6	10.4
Room-size rugs and other floor coverings, nonpermanent	100.0	2.0	19.6	28.2	19.4	20.1	7.4	3.4
Major appliances	100.0	3.1	16.5	24.5	23.6	15.2	10.9	6.3
Dishwashers (built-in), garbage disposals, range hoods (renter)	100.0	14.6	22.6	38.1	4.1	18.3	–	2.3
Dishwashers (built-in), garbage disposals, range hoods (owner)	100.0	0.0	12.2	18.8	28.4	20.4	13.9	6.2
Refrigerators and freezers (renter)	100.0	13.3	30.9	26.2	12.1	6.6	3.9	6.9
Refrigerators and freezers (owner)	100.0	1.2	14.1	30.5	21.2	15.2	11.7	6.2
Washing machines (renter)	100.0	12.9	30.6	26.9	18.0	4.3	4.7	2.5
Washing machines (owner)	100.0	1.5	12.7	29.2	26.5	15.6	9.7	4.8
Clothes dryers (renter)	100.0	18.5	31.6	24.5	12.7	3.7	5.3	3.8
Clothes dryers (owner)	100.0	2.1	13.8	28.6	27.0	11.9	5.5	11.1
Cooking stoves, ovens (renter)	100.0	8.2	16.3	37.7	17.8	13.2	6.9	–
Cooking stoves, ovens (owner)	100.0	2.0	13.2	23.1	21.6	23.7	10.0	6.4
Microwave ovens (renter)	100.0	18.3	31.3	25.3	7.6	6.4	6.9	4.2
Microwave ovens (owner)	100.0	0.3	14.5	22.6	24.7	20.8	11.3	5.8
Portable dishwasher (renter)	100.0	60.8	–	38.4	–	–	–	–
Portable dishwasher (owner)	100.0	–	17.7	13.6	26.8	32.4	9.9	–
Window air conditioners (renter)	100.0	10.4	24.1	27.5	13.4	9.4	2.9	12.2
Window air conditioners (owner)	100.0	7.8	11.4	13.5	15.3	13.8	20.9	17.3
Electric floor-cleaning equipment	100.0	1.9	24.1	18.2	30.6	6.4	13.1	6.5
Sewing machines	100.0	–	3.1	10.5	29.6	30.2	25.1	1.5
Miscellaneous household appliances	100.0	1.3	15.2	17.7	29.1	21.2	11.9	4.2
Small appliances and misc. housewares	100.0	4.4	15.5	23.3	28.9	15.7	8.2	4.3
Housewares	100.0	4.3	15.3	23.2	30.1	15.6	7.6	4.1
Plastic dinnerware	100.0	9.8	33.3	19.7	18.9	12.5	4.1	1.9
China and other dinnerware	100.0	2.7	7.6	27.5	44.9	9.7	6.6	1.7
Flatware	100.0	5.5	13.3	21.6	21.4	25.8	10.5	1.8
Glassware	100.0	2.7	31.0	18.8	19.1	11.1	10.1	7.4
Silver serving pieces	100.0	2.0	13.0	37.2	27.4	10.3	6.6	3.3

	total consumer units	under 25	25 to 34	35 to 44	45 to 54	55 to 64	65 to 74	75+
Other serving pieces	100.0%	12.1%	14.9%	20.7%	25.2%	16.0%	8.3%	2.9%
Nonelectric cookware	100.0	4.6	18.9	17.1	23.6	23.9	8.2	3.8
Tableware, nonelectric kitchenware	100.0	4.7	9.8	26.8	34.7	13.0	6.4	5.0
Small appliances	100.0	4.5	15.8	23.4	25.2	16.0	10.0	5.0
Small electric kitchen appliances	100.0	4.7	16.0	22.7	24.6	16.3	11.3	4.4
Portable heating and cooling equipment	100.0	4.0	15.4	25.7	27.1	15.1	5.8	6.8
Miscellaneous household equipment	**100.0**	**4.5**	**14.6**	**27.8**	**25.0**	**18.1**	**6.5**	**3.4**
Window coverings	100.0	1.5	11.9	25.2	34.0	11.9	10.8	4.7
Infants' equipment	100.0	2.3	31.8	39.0	19.6	3.7	1.7	0.7
Laundry and cleaning equipment	100.0	4.5	14.9	21.8	23.7	18.2	10.4	6.7
Outdoor equipment	100.0	5.4	8.2	22.3	19.7	24.7	3.2	16.6
Clocks	100.0	0.1	7.1	16.2	25.3	47.6	2.6	1.2
Lamps and lighting fixtures	100.0	4.6	13.6	29.2	27.8	15.5	6.4	2.9
Other household decorative items	100.0	1.9	12.0	30.3	20.8	25.4	6.9	2.3
Telephones and accessories	100.0	3.6	13.3	32.4	32.5	8.8	8.0	1.3
Lawn and garden equipment	100.0	1.4	9.5	29.1	31.2	13.0	9.4	6.3
Power tools	100.0	3.0	27.1	29.2	14.1	18.1	3.8	3.9
Office furniture for home use	100.0	3.2	19.3	34.2	21.8	15.1	4.4	2.0
Hand tools	100.0	4.5	17.7	27.9	24.5	17.1	7.1	1.1
Indoor plants and fresh flowers	100.0	2.8	13.0	24.7	26.2	17.1	11.0	5.3
Closet and storage items	100.0	5.1	16.8	21.6	30.4	16.6	6.9	2.8
Rental of furniture	100.0	9.3	31.3	36.0	12.8	8.3	1.9	–
Luggage	100.0	3.6	16.5	28.4	25.4	12.4	8.1	5.6
Computers and computer hardware, nonbusiness use	100.0	7.2	17.3	27.9	26.7	13.3	5.2	2.4
Computer software and accessories, nonbusiness use	100.0	5.2	20.0	27.3	25.7	14.3	5.8	1.6
Telephone answering devices	100.0	6.2	20.3	27.2	20.5	8.4	13.4	3.9
Calculators	100.0	7.8	14.6	33.2	28.5	11.2	2.8	1.7
Business equipment for home use	100.0	3.7	16.7	26.8	19.3	12.5	9.2	11.6
Other hardware	100.0	1.0	2.4	28.3	39.2	27.1	0.6	1.8
Smoke alarms (owner)	100.0	2.7	20.4	20.8	18.2	12.3	12.1	14.2
Smoke alarms (renter)	100.0	7.1	46.4	16.4	13.8	10.5	–	4.9
Other household appliances (owner)	100.0	0.3	16.1	21.1	27.7	19.0	10.0	5.9
Other household appliances (renter)	100.0	9.6	36.9	28.9	15.6	3.5	2.7	2.5
Miscellaneous household equipment and parts	100.0	15.2	17.7	20.5	20.2	15.8	6.3	3.7

Note: Numbers may not add to total because of rounding. (–) means sample is too small to make a reliable estimate.
Source: Calculations by New Strategist based on the 2000 Consumer Expenditure Survey

Table 8.6 (Housing) Household Operations: Average spending by income, 2000

(average annual spending on household services, supplies, furnishings, and equipment, by before-tax income of consumer units (CU), 2000; complete income reporters only)

	complete income reporters	under $10,000	$10,000–$19,999	$20,000–$29,999	$30,000–$39,999	$40,000–$49,999	$50,000–$69,999	$70,000 or more
Number of consumer units (in thousands, add 000)	81,454	10,810	14,714	12,039	9,477	7,653	11,337	15,424
Average number of persons per CU	2.5	1.7	2.1	2.4	2.5	2.6	2.9	3.2
Average before-tax income of CU	$44,649.00	$5,739.61	$14,586.29	$24,527.00	$34,422.00	$44,201.00	$58,561.00	$112,586.00
Average spending of CU, total	40,238.44	16,455.72	22,620.20	29,851.59	35,609.24	42,323.03	49,245.37	75,963.85
Housing, average spending	12,527.38	5,931.71	7,766.01	9,372.13	11,114.58	12,872.14	14,913.70	22,932.20
HOUSEHOLD SERVICES	$708.32	$232.44	$367.51	$433.16	$411.54	$569.19	$844.28	$1,729.11
Personal services	337.92	87.54	164.86	180.91	171.60	247.32	478.92	844.52
Babysitting and child care in your own home	34.46	3.89	12.39	7.98	27.99	19.18	25.86	115.47
Babysitting and child care in someone else's home	36.35	4.06	21.70	26.48	33.08	52.31	62.47	55.54
Care for elderly, invalids, handicapped, etc.	42.34	50.44	66.06	52.87	2.37	15.63	50.69	37.50
Adult day care centers	2.88	1.23	9.66	0.10	4.18	1.75	1.40	0.57
Day care centers, nurseries, and preschools	221.89	27.92	55.06	93.48	103.98	158.44	338.50	635.44
Other household services	370.41	144.89	202.64	252.25	239.94	321.87	365.35	884.59
Housekeeping services	85.90	20.72	46.01	44.17	31.85	49.98	67.44	266.79
Gardening, lawn care service	76.59	37.07	60.24	50.80	46.13	50.12	66.90	178.98
Water softening service	3.28	1.30	3.51	1.32	3.09	3.53	3.37	5.90
Nonclothing laundry and dry cleaning, sent out	1.54	0.92	0.46	1.45	1.13	1.16	2.19	3.06
Nonclothing laundry and dry cleaning, coin-operated	4.85	5.97	6.38	6.43	4.72	5.47	3.06	2.48
Termite/pest control services	10.35	2.84	7.14	7.98	5.05	11.58	13.93	20.53
Home security system service fee	19.89	6.97	9.79	14.90	19.99	19.37	23.19	40.24
Other home services	14.27	3.29	9.32	9.37	14.02	14.97	13.27	31.03
Termite/pest control products	0.57	0.20	0.62	0.27	0.11	0.70	0.32	1.40
Moving, storage, and freight express	36.19	28.26	12.31	33.23	25.87	45.80	35.79	68.73
Appliance repair, including service center	13.51	5.73	8.44	12.32	12.84	13.98	15.97	23.11
Reupholstering and furniture repair	9.25	3.13	2.24	3.86	3.58	17.30	10.75	22.84
Repairs/rentals of lawn/garden equipment, hand/power tools, etc.	5.59	2.38	3.81	3.37	3.90	6.62	4.86	12.34
Appliance rental	3.97	3.31	4.41	1.89	4.51	5.97	2.98	5.05
Rental of office equipment for nonbusiness use	0.63	0.08	0.87	0.59	0.53	0.65	0.93	0.63
Repair of misc. household equipment and furnishings	15.96	–	1.44	13.92	1.93	–	–	66.73
Repair of computer systems for nonbusiness use	2.75	0.69	1.90	3.24	1.75	2.36	3.56	4.83
Computer information services	65.11	22.00	23.74	43.10	58.93	72.32	96.46	129.15
Rental, installation of dishwashers, range hoods, and garbage disposals	0.20	–	–	0.04	–	–	0.39	0.75
HOUSEKEEPING SUPPLIES	545.74	207.81	333.15	416.26	468.87	563.86	685.46	953.45
Laundry and cleaning supplies	146.21	70.64	95.45	126.41	135.32	140.03	164.82	243.55
Soaps and detergents	77.30	44.15	59.10	75.30	70.91	73.73	94.83	106.36
Other laundry cleaning products	68.91	26.48	36.34	51.11	64.41	66.30	69.99	137.18
Other household products	257.63	90.45	149.88	176.10	234.96	256.06	356.45	447.84
Cleansing and toilet tissue, paper towels, and napkins	76.01	40.65	55.65	82.30	69.11	82.55	90.44	100.05
Miscellaneous household products	105.06	38.29	53.02	65.19	87.60	120.19	153.80	185.34
Lawn and garden supplies	76.56	11.51	41.20	28.60	78.25	53.32	112.21	162.45
Postage and stationery	141.89	46.73	87.83	113.76	98.59	167.78	164.18	262.06
Stationery, stationery supplies, giftwrap	73.84	23.65	28.93	54.06	48.66	88.46	89.02	153.25
Postage	66.62	22.99	58.70	58.51	49.70	78.34	72.62	105.27
Delivery services	1.42	0.09	0.19	1.19	0.23	0.97	2.54	3.55

	complete income reporters	under $10,000	$10,000– $19,999	$20,000– $29,999	$30,000– $39,999	$40,000– $49,999	$50,000– $69,999	$70,000 or more
HOUSEHOLD FURNISHINGS AND EQUIPMENT	**$1,652.03**	**$515.61**	**$749.21**	**$1,089.37**	**$1,228.41**	**$1,772.01**	**$2,131.54**	**$3,504.02**
Household textiles	**114.94**	**19.88**	**61.55**	**94.90**	**96.76**	**115.81**	**130.23**	**235.86**
Bathroom linens	19.47	4.13	21.82	13.58	14.58	18.00	22.51	32.18
Bedroom linens	50.03	6.77	17.24	55.14	50.88	56.03	65.32	85.21
Kitchen and dining room linens	10.76	2.48	7.96	5.08	4.69	14.66	12.84	22.35
Curtains and draperies	20.42	2.99	7.44	8.68	15.65	10.17	12.51	68.04
Slipcovers and decorative pillows	3.28	–	0.59	3.10	1.47	3.95	5.37	6.92
Sewing materials for household items	9.67	2.74	5.45	8.40	8.89	11.76	10.06	18.69
Other linens	1.31	0.76	1.05	0.92	0.60	1.24	1.61	2.48
Furniture	**413.26**	**135.39**	**186.87**	**248.11**	**301.10**	**378.11**	**437.43**	**1,021.50**
Mattresses and springs	55.97	31.65	27.00	39.59	56.62	60.87	53.72	112.26
Other bedroom furniture	76.93	10.18	38.74	45.21	64.43	75.42	89.32	184.23
Sofas	87.11	31.80	36.44	75.09	52.00	84.99	87.98	205.59
Living room chairs	45.32	19.16	33.28	24.80	28.93	38.18	62.64	92.04
Living room tables	17.88	4.30	8.23	12.53	10.91	16.17	15.15	47.89
Kitchen and dining room furniture	53.23	10.93	16.54	21.95	36.84	41.46	40.65	167.48
Infants' furniture	7.14	2.36	2.25	3.82	10.99	6.93	8.65	14.37
Outdoor furniture	15.54	8.28	6.09	5.25	5.56	9.11	15.23	47.22
Wall units, cabinets, and other furniture	54.15	16.75	18.30	19.87	34.84	44.98	64.09	150.42
Floor coverings	**49.09**	**9.92**	**22.64**	**19.54**	**36.30**	**46.18**	**68.77**	**119.65**
Wall-to-wall carpet (renter)	1.20	–	0.69	2.06	2.24	0.70	–	2.36
Wall-to-wall carpet (replacement) (owner)	31.76	5.66	14.04	10.05	24.71	35.67	54.72	69.42
Room-size rugs and other floor coverings, nonpermanent	16.12	4.26	7.91	7.43	9.36	9.80	14.05	47.86
Major appliances	**195.47**	**91.84**	**124.56**	**142.87**	**151.43**	**215.66**	**230.26**	**361.96**
Dishwashers (built-in), garbage disposals, range hoods (renter)	1.05	1.48	0.54	0.35	0.94	1.03	1.63	1.43
Dishwashers (built-in), garbage disposals, range hoods (owner)	13.34	5.76	5.31	7.77	14.18	15.51	16.35	26.88
Refrigerators and freezers (renter)	7.70	7.57	9.35	5.96	8.60	19.57	1.73	5.51
Refrigerators and freezers (owner)	43.31	16.70	31.46	30.47	24.87	34.93	68.93	79.95
Washing machines (renter)	5.07	4.79	7.07	6.67	4.50	8.16	2.81	2.60
Washing machines (owner)	19.24	10.81	8.33	15.98	13.40	17.65	24.17	38.88
Clothes dryers (renter)	3.41	1.90	4.63	3.62	2.09	6.99	2.78	2.66
Clothes dryers (owner)	12.69	4.96	6.32	10.20	8.18	12.04	15.85	26.92
Cooking stoves, ovens (renter)	3.11	4.81	1.86	2.48	2.71	4.50	4.67	2.02
Cooking stoves, ovens (owner)	23.85	11.56	10.72	16.41	13.95	19.35	41.86	45.87
Microwave ovens (renter)	2.56	2.27	4.49	3.70	2.60	2.04	1.42	1.11
Microwave ovens (owner)	7.79	1.23	2.92	6.07	5.38	4.30	10.15	19.84
Portable dishwasher (renter)	0.21	0.04	–	–	1.12	–	–	0.40
Portable dishwasher (owner)	0.64	–	0.52	0.65	–	0.97	1.09	1.12
Window air conditioners (renter)	1.92	3.35	2.07	2.74	1.75	4.04	0.65	0.13
Window air conditioners (owner)	4.99	2.76	6.37	5.68	8.34	1.99	3.08	5.56
Electric floor-cleaning equipment	29.07	8.47	12.62	14.07	30.62	42.02	14.04	69.68
Sewing machines	5.18	0.86	1.39	3.14	0.75	9.42	9.74	10.68
Miscellaneous household appliances	10.31	2.50	8.60	6.91	7.47	11.18	9.32	20.70
Small appliances and misc. housewares	**95.31**	**37.53**	**42.55**	**61.46**	**77.42**	**118.33**	**129.46**	**176.99**
Housewares	70.79	25.29	26.82	42.80	57.00	85.56	100.32	135.83
Plastic dinnerware	1.63	0.69	0.51	1.51	2.00	3.00	1.95	2.29
China and other dinnerware	13.75	4.77	2.60	4.23	5.91	17.69	13.72	38.41
Flatware	4.06	1.19	1.29	3.24	3.90	2.26	3.08	11.07
Glassware	9.15	2.40	4.65	4.58	8.96	10.59	21.98	10.30
Silver serving pieces	2.72	1.04	1.18	1.55	2.42	3.10	2.42	6.03

	complete income reporters	under $10,000	$10,000–$19,999	$20,000–$29,999	$30,000–$39,999	$40,000–$49,999	$50,000–$69,999	$70,000 or more
Other serving pieces	$1.50	$0.64	$0.61	$2.78	$1.07	$0.87	$1.78	$2.33
Nonelectric cookware	17.73	7.92	8.42	13.77	20.77	14.30	30.99	24.30
Tableware, nonelectric kitchenware	20.25	6.65	7.55	11.15	11.96	33.76	24.40	41.10
Small appliances	24.52	12.23	15.72	18.66	20.41	32.77	29.14	41.15
Small electric kitchen appliances	18.44	8.21	11.79	14.52	16.15	24.79	21.63	30.92
Portable heating and cooling equipment	6.08	4.03	3.93	4.14	4.26	7.97	7.50	10.23
Miscellaneous household equipment	**783.96**	**221.06**	**311.04**	**522.51**	**565.39**	**897.92**	**1,135.39**	**1,588.07**
Window coverings	14.09	4.00	4.23	5.56	7.27	7.45	17.36	42.32
Infants' equipment	7.46	2.27	3.55	2.95	5.70	6.28	13.17	14.57
Laundry and cleaning equipment	11.42	5.55	7.47	11.97	10.10	9.92	15.53	16.38
Outdoor equipment	20.49	3.51	13.72	13.17	8.15	15.31	25.69	47.41
Clocks	18.39	0.55	2.80	1.70	3.17	95.07	22.72	23.90
Lamps and lighting fixtures	12.08	3.05	4.24	11.47	8.02	11.35	18.55	24.45
Other household decorative items	208.05	33.83	59.34	114.09	105.37	196.29	421.66	418.90
Telephones and accessories	31.46	8.17	18.63	30.18	30.60	32.46	28.97	58.84
Lawn and garden equipment	46.52	16.52	19.84	24.97	60.53	46.78	59.24	91.75
Power tools	23.36	2.19	9.28	14.24	29.63	37.59	29.57	39.16
Office furniture for home use	14.80	2.98	3.09	7.34	5.77	19.78	21.61	38.14
Hand tools	8.01	2.97	3.58	4.67	6.20	9.92	11.10	16.27
Indoor plants and fresh flowers	57.44	19.10	26.55	38.89	43.10	44.23	66.41	137.05
Closet and storage items	9.17	2.30	2.22	8.13	8.41	12.79	11.54	16.91
Rental of furniture	3.26	1.51	3.85	6.66	5.83	1.06	1.82	1.82
Luggage	9.17	2.27	3.43	3.49	8.80	9.27	13.45	20.96
Computers and computer hardware, nonbusiness use	190.71	70.38	81.31	146.71	151.80	237.52	238.82	379.07
Computer software and accessories, nonbusiness use	18.43	6.05	7.49	8.86	14.66	20.52	26.23	40.53
Telephone answering devices	2.33	1.83	1.41	2.42	2.20	2.26	2.14	3.71
Calculators	1.78	1.29	0.44	0.90	1.97	3.03	2.27	2.99
Business equipment for home use	2.05	1.24	1.07	1.64	1.64	2.66	3.16	3.03
Other hardware	20.86	0.50	0.91	22.25	13.44	13.44	39.76	43.35
Smoke alarms (owner)	0.63	0.73	0.25	0.50	0.42	0.62	0.83	1.02
Smoke alarms (renter)	0.19	0.03	0.58	0.13	0.30	–	0.11	0.05
Other household appliances (owner)	7.75	3.57	3.47	4.81	8.71	8.54	12.96	12.26
Other household appliances (renter)	1.44	0.93	1.91	0.57	0.96	0.71	1.19	2.87
Miscellaneous household equipment and parts	42.62	23.77	26.36	34.25	22.67	53.08	29.51	90.37

Note: (–) means sample is too small to make a reliable estimate.
Source: Bureau of Labor Statistics, unpublished tables from the 2000 Consumer Expenditure Survey; calculations by New Strategist

Table 8.7 (Housing) Household Operations: Indexed spending by income, 2000

(indexed average annual spending of consumer units (CU) on household services, supplies, furnishings, and equipment, by before-tax income of consumer unit, 2000; complete income reporters only; index definition: an index of 100 is the average for all consumer units; an index of 132 means that spending by consumer units in that group is 32 percent above the average for all consumer units; an index of 68 indicates spending that is 32 percent below the average for all consumer units)

	complete income reporters	under $10,000	$10,000–$19,999	$20,000–$29,999	$30,000–$39,999	$40,000–$49,999	$50,000–$69,999	$70,000 or more
Average spending of CU, total	$40,238	$16,456	$22,620	$29,852	$35,609	$42,323	$49,245	$75,964
Average spending of CU, index	100	41	56	74	88	105	122	189
Housing, spending index	100	47	62	75	89	103	119	183
HOUSEHOLD SERVICES	100	33	52	61	58	80	119	244
Personal services	100	26	49	54	51	73	142	250
Babysitting and child care in your own home	100	11	36	23	81	56	75	335
Babysitting and child care in someone else's home	100	11	60	73	91	144	172	153
Care for elderly, invalids, handicapped, etc.	100	119	156	125	6	37	120	89
Adult day care centers	100	43	335	3	145	61	49	20
Day care centers, nurseries, and preschools	100	13	25	42	47	71	153	286
Other household services	100	39	55	68	65	87	99	239
Housekeeping services	100	24	54	51	37	58	79	311
Gardening, lawn care service	100	48	79	66	60	65	87	234
Water softening service	100	40	107	40	94	108	103	180
Nonclothing laundry and dry cleaning, sent out	100	60	30	94	73	75	142	199
Nonclothing laundry and dry cleaning, coin-operated	100	123	131	133	97	113	63	51
Termite/pest control services	100	27	69	77	49	112	135	198
Home security system service fee	100	35	49	75	101	97	117	202
Other home services	100	23	65	66	98	105	93	217
Termite/pest control products	100	36	109	47	19	123	56	246
Moving, storage, and freight express	100	78	34	92	71	127	99	190
Appliance repair, including service center	100	42	62	91	95	103	118	171
Reupholstering and furniture repair	100	34	24	42	39	187	116	247
Repairs/rentals of lawn/garden equipment, hand/power tools, etc.	100	43	68	60	70	118	87	221
Appliance rental	100	83	111	48	114	150	75	127
Rental of office equipment for nonbusiness use	100	13	138	94	84	103	148	100
Repair of misc. household equipment and furnishings	100	–	9	87	12	–	–	418
Repair of computer systems for nonbusiness use	100	25	69	118	64	86	129	176
Computer information services	100	34	36	66	91	111	148	198
Rental, installation of dishwashers, range hoods, and garbage disposals	100	–	–	20	–	–	195	375
HOUSEKEEPING SUPPLIES	100	38	61	76	86	103	126	175
Laundry and cleaning supplies	100	48	65	86	93	96	113	167
Soaps and detergents	100	57	76	97	92	95	123	138
Other laundry cleaning products	100	38	53	74	93	96	102	199
Other household products	100	35	58	68	91	99	138	174
Cleansing and toilet tissue, paper towels, and napkins	100	53	73	108	91	109	119	132
Miscellaneous household products	100	36	50	62	83	114	146	176
Lawn and garden supplies	100	15	54	37	102	70	147	212
Postage and stationery	100	33	62	80	69	118	116	185
Stationery, stationery supplies, giftwrap	100	32	39	73	66	120	121	208
Postage	100	35	88	88	75	118	109	158
Delivery services	100	6	13	84	16	68	179	250

	complete income reporters	under $10,000	$10,000–$19,999	$20,000–$29,999	$30,000–$39,999	$40,000–$49,999	$50,000–$69,999	$70,000 or more
HOUSEHOLD FURNISHINGS AND EQUIPMENT	**100**	**31**	**45**	**66**	**74**	**107**	**129**	**212**
Household textiles	**100**	**17**	**54**	**83**	**84**	**101**	**113**	**205**
Bathroom linens	100	21	112	70	75	92	116	165
Bedroom linens	100	14	34	110	102	112	131	170
Kitchen and dining room linens	100	23	74	47	44	136	119	208
Curtains and draperies	100	15	36	43	77	50	61	333
Slipcovers and decorative pillows	100	–	18	95	45	120	164	211
Sewing materials for household items	100	28	56	87	92	122	104	193
Other linens	100	58	80	70	46	95	123	189
Furniture	**100**	**33**	**45**	**60**	**73**	**91**	**106**	**247**
Mattresses and springs	100	57	48	71	101	109	96	201
Other bedroom furniture	100	13	50	59	84	98	116	239
Sofas	100	37	42	86	60	98	101	236
Living room chairs	100	42	73	55	64	84	138	203
Living room tables	100	24	46	70	61	90	85	268
Kitchen and dining room furniture	100	21	31	41	69	78	76	315
Infants' furniture	100	33	32	54	154	97	121	201
Outdoor furniture	100	53	39	34	36	59	98	304
Wall units, cabinets, and other furniture	100	31	34	37	64	83	118	278
Floor coverings	**100**	**20**	**46**	**40**	**74**	**94**	**140**	**244**
Wall-to-wall carpet (renter)	100	–	57	172	187	58	–	197
Wall-to-wall carpet (replacement) (owner)	100	18	44	32	78	112	172	219
Room-size rugs and other floor coverings, nonpermanent	100	26	49	46	58	61	87	297
Major appliances	**100**	**47**	**64**	**73**	**77**	**110**	**118**	**185**
Dishwashers (built-in), garbage disposals, range hoods (renter)	100	141	52	33	90	98	155	136
Dishwashers (built-in), garbage disposals, range hoods (owner)	100	43	40	58	106	116	123	201
Refrigerators and freezers (renter)	100	98	121	77	112	254	22	72
Refrigerators and freezers (owner)	100	39	73	70	57	81	159	185
Washing machines (renter)	100	94	139	132	89	161	55	51
Washing machines (owner)	100	56	43	83	70	92	126	202
Clothes dryers (renter)	100	56	136	106	61	205	82	78
Clothes dryers (owner)	100	39	50	80	64	95	125	212
Cooking stoves, ovens (renter)	100	155	60	80	87	145	150	65
Cooking stoves, ovens (owner)	100	48	45	69	58	81	176	192
Microwave ovens (renter)	100	89	176	145	102	80	55	43
Microwave ovens (owner)	100	16	37	78	69	55	130	255
Portable dishwasher (renter)	100	19	–	–	533	–	–	190
Portable dishwasher (owner)	100	–	82	102	–	152	170	175
Window air conditioners (renter)	100	174	108	143	91	210	34	7
Window air conditioners (owner)	100	55	128	114	167	40	62	111
Electric floor-cleaning equipment	100	29	43	48	105	145	48	240
Sewing machines	100	17	27	61	14	182	188	206
Miscellaneous household appliances	100	24	83	67	72	108	90	201
Small appliances and misc. housewares	**100**	**39**	**45**	**64**	**81**	**124**	**136**	**186**
Housewares	100	36	38	60	81	121	142	192
Plastic dinnerware	100	42	31	93	123	184	120	140
China and other dinnerware	100	35	19	31	43	129	100	279
Flatware	100	29	32	80	96	56	76	273
Glassware	100	26	51	50	98	116	240	113
Silver serving pieces	100	38	43	57	89	114	89	222

	complete income reporters	under $10,000	$10,000– $19,999	$20,000– $29,999	$30,000– $39,999	$40,000– $49,999	$50,000– $69,999	$70,000 or more
Other serving pieces	100	42	41	185	71	58	119	155
Nonelectric cookware	100	45	48	78	117	81	175	137
Tableware, nonelectric kitchenware	100	33	37	55	59	167	120	203
Small appliances	100	50	64	76	83	134	119	168
Small electric kitchen appliances	100	45	64	79	88	134	117	168
Portable heating and cooling equipment	100	66	65	68	70	131	123	168
Miscellaneous household equipment	**100**	**28**	**40**	**67**	**72**	**115**	**145**	**203**
Window coverings	100	28	30	39	52	53	123	300
Infants' equipment	100	30	48	40	76	84	177	195
Laundry and cleaning equipment	100	49	65	105	88	87	136	143
Outdoor equipment	100	17	67	64	40	75	125	231
Clocks	100	3	15	9	17	517	124	130
Lamps and lighting fixtures	100	25	35	95	66	94	154	202
Other household decorative items	100	16	29	55	51	94	203	201
Telephones and accessories	100	26	59	96	97	103	92	187
Lawn and garden equipment	100	36	43	54	130	101	127	197
Power tools	100	9	40	61	127	161	127	168
Office furniture for home use	100	20	21	50	39	134	146	258
Hand tools	100	37	45	58	77	124	139	203
Indoor plants and fresh flowers	100	33	46	68	75	77	116	239
Closet and storage items	100	25	24	89	92	139	126	184
Rental of furniture	100	46	118	204	179	33	56	56
Luggage	100	25	37	38	96	101	147	229
Computers and computer hardware, nonbusiness use	100	37	43	77	80	125	125	199
Computer software and accessories, nonbusiness use	100	33	41	48	80	111	142	220
Telephone answering devices	100	79	61	104	94	97	92	159
Calculators	100	73	24	51	111	170	128	168
Business equipment for home use	100	60	52	80	80	130	154	148
Other hardware	100	2	4	107	64	64	191	208
Smoke alarms (owner)	100	115	40	79	67	98	132	162
Smoke alarms (renter)	100	14	307	68	158	–	58	26
Other household appliances (owner)	100	46	45	62	112	110	167	158
Other household appliances (renter)	100	64	133	40	67	49	83	199
Miscellaneous household equipment and parts	100	56	62	80	53	125	69	212

Note: (–) means sample is too small to make a reliable estimate.
Source: Calculations by New Strategist based on the 2000 Consumer Expenditure Survey

Table 8.8 (Housing) Household Operations: Indexed per capita spending by income, 2000

(indexed average annual per capita spending of consumer units (CU) on household services, supplies, furnishings, and equipment, by before-tax income of consumer unit, 2000; complete income reporters only; index definition: an index of 100 is the average for all consumer units; an index of 132 means that spending by consumer units in that group is 32 percent above the average for all consumer units; an index of 68 indicates spending that is 32 percent below the average for all consumer units)

	complete income reporters	under $10,000	$10,000–$19,999	$20,000–$29,999	$30,000–$39,999	$40,000–$49,999	$50,000–$69,999	$70,000 or more
Per capita spending of CU, total	$16,095	$9,492	$10,819	$12,438	$14,244	$16,278	$16,981	$23,739
Per capita spending of CU, index	100	59	67	77	88	101	106	147
Housing, per capita spending index	100	68	74	78	89	99	103	143
HOUSEHOLD SERVICES	100	47	62	64	58	77	103	191
Personal services	100	37	58	56	51	70	122	195
Babysitting and child care in your own home	100	16	43	24	81	54	65	262
Babysitting and child care in someone else's home	100	16	71	76	91	138	148	119
Care for elderly, invalids, handicapped, etc.	100	172	187	130	6	35	103	69
Adult day care centers	100	62	401	4	145	58	42	15
Day care centers, nurseries, and preschools	100	18	30	44	47	69	132	224
Other household services	100	56	65	71	65	84	85	187
Housekeeping services	100	35	64	54	37	56	68	243
Gardening, lawn care service	100	70	94	69	60	63	75	183
Water softening service	100	57	128	42	94	103	89	141
Nonclothing laundry and dry cleaning, sent out	100	87	36	98	73	72	123	155
Nonclothing laundry and dry cleaning, coin-operated	100	178	157	138	97	108	54	40
Termite/pest control services	100	40	83	80	49	108	116	155
Home security system service fee	100	51	59	78	101	94	101	158
Other home services	100	33	78	68	98	101	80	170
Termite/pest control products	100	52	130	49	19	118	48	192
Moving, storage, and freight express	100	113	41	96	71	122	85	148
Appliance repair, including service center	100	61	75	95	95	99	102	134
Reupholstering and furniture repair	100	49	29	43	39	180	100	193
Repairs/rentals of lawn/garden equipment, hand/power tools, etc.	100	62	82	63	70	114	75	172
Appliance rental	100	120	133	50	114	145	65	99
Rental of office equipment for nonbusiness use	100	18	165	98	84	99	127	78
Repair of misc. household equipment and furnishings	100	–	11	91	12	–	–	327
Repair of computer systems for nonbusiness use	100	36	82	123	64	83	112	137
Computer information services	100	49	44	69	91	107	128	155
Rental, installation of dishwashers, range hoods, and garbage disposals	100	–	–	21	–	–	168	293
HOUSEKEEPING SUPPLIES	100	55	73	79	86	99	108	136
Laundry and cleaning supplies	100	70	78	90	93	92	97	130
Soaps and detergents	100	82	91	101	92	92	106	107
Other laundry cleaning products	100	55	63	77	93	93	88	156
Other household products	100	51	70	71	91	96	119	136
Cleansing and toilet tissue, paper towels, and napkins	100	77	88	113	91	104	103	103
Miscellaneous household products	100	53	60	65	83	110	126	138
Lawn and garden supplies	100	22	64	39	102	67	126	166
Postage and stationery	100	47	74	84	69	114	100	144
Stationery, stationery supplies, giftwrap	100	46	47	76	66	115	104	162
Postage	100	50	105	91	75	113	94	123
Delivery services	100	9	16	87	16	66	154	195

HOUSEHOLD FURNISHINGS AND EQUIPMENT	complete income reporters	under $10,000	$10,000–$19,999	$20,000–$29,999	$30,000–$39,999	$40,000–$49,999	$50,000–$69,999	$70,000 or more
HOUSEHOLD FURNISHINGS AND EQUIPMENT	**100**	**45**	**54**	**69**	**74**	**103**	**111**	**166**
Household textiles	**100**	**25**	**64**	**86**	**84**	**97**	**98**	**160**
Bathroom linens	100	31	134	73	75	89	100	129
Bedroom linens	100	20	41	115	102	108	113	133
Kitchen and dining room linens	100	33	88	49	44	131	103	162
Curtains and draperies	100	21	44	44	77	48	53	260
Slipcovers and decorative pillows	100	–	22	98	45	116	141	165
Sewing materials for household items	100	41	67	90	92	117	90	151
Other linens	100	83	96	73	46	91	106	148
Furniture	**100**	**47**	**54**	**63**	**73**	**88**	**91**	**193**
Mattresses and springs	100	82	58	74	101	105	83	157
Other bedroom furniture	100	19	60	61	84	94	100	187
Sofas	100	53	50	90	60	94	87	184
Living room chairs	100	61	88	57	64	81	119	159
Living room tables	100	35	55	73	61	87	73	209
Kitchen and dining room furniture	100	30	37	43	69	75	66	246
Infants' furniture	100	48	38	56	154	93	104	157
Outdoor furniture	100	77	47	35	36	56	84	237
Wall units, cabinets, and other furniture	100	45	40	38	64	80	102	217
Floor coverings	**100**	**29**	**55**	**41**	**74**	**90**	**121**	**190**
Wall-to-wall carpet (renter)	100	–	69	179	187	56	–	154
Wall-to-wall carpet (replacement) (owner)	100	26	53	33	78	108	149	171
Room-size rugs and other floor coverings, nonpermanent	100	38	59	48	58	58	75	232
Major appliances	**100**	**68**	**76**	**76**	**77**	**106**	**102**	**145**
Dishwashers (built-in), garbage disposals, range hoods (renter)	100	203	62	35	90	94	134	106
Dishwashers (built-in), garbage disposals, range hoods (owner)	100	62	48	61	106	112	106	157
Refrigerators and freezers (renter)	100	142	145	81	112	244	19	56
Refrigerators and freezers (owner)	100	56	87	73	57	78	137	144
Washing machines (renter)	100	136	167	137	89	155	48	40
Washing machines (owner)	100	81	52	87	70	88	108	158
Clothes dryers (renter)	100	80	163	111	61	197	70	61
Clothes dryers (owner)	100	56	60	84	64	91	108	166
Cooking stoves, ovens (renter)	100	223	72	83	87	139	129	51
Cooking stoves, ovens (owner)	100	70	54	72	58	78	151	150
Microwave ovens (renter)	100	128	210	151	102	77	48	34
Microwave ovens (owner)	100	23	45	81	69	53	112	199
Portable dishwasher (renter)	100	27	–	–	533	–	–	149
Portable dishwasher (owner)	100	–	98	106	–	146	147	137
Window air conditioners (renter)	100	251	129	149	91	202	29	5
Window air conditioners (owner)	100	80	153	119	167	38	53	87
Electric floor-cleaning equipment	100	42	52	50	105	139	42	187
Sewing machines	100	24	32	63	14	175	162	161
Miscellaneous household appliances	100	35	100	70	72	104	78	157
Small appliances and misc. housewares	**100**	**57**	**53**	**67**	**81**	**119**	**117**	**145**
Housewares	100	52	45	63	81	116	122	150
Plastic dinnerware	100	61	37	96	123	177	103	110
China and other dinnerware	100	50	23	32	43	124	86	218
Flatware	100	42	38	83	96	54	65	213
Glassware	100	38	61	52	98	111	207	88
Silver serving pieces	100	55	52	59	89	110	77	173

	complete income reporters	under $10,000	$10,000–$19,999	$20,000–$29,999	$30,000–$39,999	$40,000–$49,999	$50,000–$69,999	$70,000 or more
Other serving pieces	100	61	49	193	71	56	102	121
Nonelectric cookware	100	64	57	81	117	78	151	107
Tableware, nonelectric kitchenware	100	47	45	57	59	160	104	159
Small appliances	100	72	77	79	83	129	102	131
Small electric kitchen appliances	100	64	76	82	88	129	101	131
Portable heating and cooling equipment	100	96	77	71	70	126	106	131
Miscellaneous household equipment	**100**	**41**	**47**	**69**	**72**	**110**	**125**	**158**
Window coverings	100	41	36	41	52	51	106	235
Infants' equipment	100	44	57	41	76	81	152	153
Laundry and cleaning equipment	100	70	78	109	88	84	117	112
Outdoor equipment	100	25	80	67	40	72	108	181
Clocks	100	4	18	10	17	497	107	102
Lamps and lighting fixtures	100	36	42	99	66	90	132	158
Other household decorative items	100	23	34	57	51	91	175	157
Telephones and accessories	100	37	71	100	97	99	79	146
Lawn and garden equipment	100	51	51	56	130	97	110	154
Power tools	100	14	48	63	127	155	109	131
Office furniture for home use	100	29	25	52	39	129	126	201
Hand tools	100	53	53	61	77	119	119	159
Indoor plants and fresh flowers	100	48	55	71	75	74	100	186
Closet and storage items	100	36	29	92	92	134	108	144
Rental of furniture	100	67	141	213	179	31	48	44
Luggage	100	36	45	40	96	97	126	179
Computers and computer hardware, nonbusiness use	100	53	51	80	80	120	108	155
Computer software and accessories, nonbusiness use	100	47	49	50	80	107	123	172
Telephone answering devices	100	114	73	108	94	93	79	124
Calculators	100	105	29	53	111	164	110	131
Business equipment for home use	100	87	62	83	80	125	133	115
Other hardware	100	3	5	111	64	62	164	162
Smoke alarms (owner)	100	167	47	83	67	95	114	126
Smoke alarms (renter)	100	20	367	71	158	–	50	21
Other household appliances (owner)	100	66	54	65	112	106	144	124
Other household appliances (renter)	100	93	159	41	67	47	71	156
Miscellaneous household equipment and parts	100	80	74	84	53	120	60	166

Note: Per capita indexes account for household size and show how much each person in a particular household demographic segment spends relative to a person in the average household. (–) means sample is too small to make a reliable estimate.
Source: Calculations by New Strategist based on the 2000 Consumer Expenditure Survey

Table 8.9 (Housing) Household Operations: Total spending by income, 2000

(total annual spending on household services, supplies, furnishings, and equipment, by before-tax income group of consumer units (CU), 2000; complete income reporters only; numbers in thousands)

	complete income reporters	under $10,000	$10,000–$19,999	$20,000–$29,999	$30,000–$39,999	$40,000–$49,999	$50,000–$69,999	$70,000 or more
Number of consumer units	81,454	10,810	14,714	12,039	9,477	7,653	11,337	15,424
Total spending of all CUs	$3,277,581,892	$177,886,368	$332,833,656	$359,383,292	$337,468,767	$323,898,149	$558,294,760	$1,171,666,422
Housing, total spending	1,020,405,211	64,121,738	114,269,029	112,831,073	105,332,875	98,510,487	169,076,617	353,706,253
HOUSEHOLD SERVICES	**$57,695,497**	**$2,512,668**	**$5,407,505**	**$5,214,813**	**$3,900,165**	**$4,356,011**	**$9,571,602**	**$26,669,793**
Personal services	**27,524,936**	**946,357**	**2,425,778**	**2,177,975**	**1,626,253**	**1,892,740**	**5,429,516**	**13,025,876**
Babysitting and child care in your own home	2,806,905	42,092	182,297	96,071	265,261	146,785	293,175	1,781,009
Babysitting and child care in someone else's home	2,960,853	43,882	319,340	318,793	313,499	400,328	708,222	856,649
Care for elderly, invalids, handicapped, etc.	3,448,762	545,267	971,943	636,502	22,460	119,616	574,673	578,400
Adult day care centers	234,588	13,289	142,151	1,204	39,614	13,393	15,872	8,792
Day care centers, nurseries, and preschools	18,073,828	301,791	810,114	1,125,406	985,418	1,212,541	3,837,575	9,801,027
Other household services	**30,171,376**	**1,566,311**	**2,981,646**	**3,036,838**	**2,273,911**	**2,463,271**	**4,141,973**	**13,643,916**
Housekeeping services	6,996,899	223,948	677,052	531,763	301,842	382,497	764,567	4,114,969
Gardening, lawn care service	6,238,562	400,730	886,384	611,581	437,174	383,568	758,445	2,760,588
Water softening service	267,169	14,062	51,620	15,891	29,284	27,015	38,206	91,002
Nonclothing laundry and dry cleaning, sent out	125,439	9,989	6,740	17,457	10,709	8,877	24,828	47,197
Nonclothing laundry and dry cleaning, coin-operated	395,052	64,585	93,809	77,411	44,731	41,862	34,691	38,252
Termite/pest control services	843,049	30,740	105,130	96,071	47,859	88,622	157,924	316,655
Home security system service fee	1,620,120	75,375	144,115	179,381	189,445	148,239	262,905	620,662
Other home services	1,162,349	35,541	137,179	112,805	132,868	114,565	150,442	478,607
Termite/pest control products	46,429	2,205	9,131	3,251	1,042	5,357	3,628	21,594
Moving, storage, and freight express	2,947,820	305,538	181,074	400,056	245,170	350,507	405,751	1,060,092
Appliance repair, including service center	1,100,444	61,951	124,214	148,320	121,685	106,989	181,052	356,449
Reupholstering and furniture repair	753,450	33,822	33,030	46,471	33,928	132,397	121,873	352,284
Repairs/rentals of lawn/garden equipment, hand/power tools, etc.	455,328	25,777	56,124	40,571	36,960	50,663	55,098	190,332
Appliance rental	323,372	35,757	64,898	22,754	42,741	45,688	33,784	77,891
Rental of office equipment for nonbusiness use	51,316	866	12,768	7,103	5,023	4,974	10,543	9,717
Repair of misc. household equipment and furnishings	1,300,006	–	21,115	167,583	18,291	–	–	1,029,244
Repair of computer systems for nonbusiness use	223,999	7,410	27,906	39,006	16,585	18,061	40,360	74,498
Computer information services	5,303,470	237,838	349,344	518,881	558,480	553,465	1,093,567	1,992,010
Rental, installation of dishwashers, range hoods, and garbage disposals	16,291	–	–	482	–	–	4,421	11,568
HOUSEKEEPING SUPPLIES	**44,452,706**	**2,246,469**	**4,902,007**	**5,011,354**	**4,443,481**	**4,315,221**	**7,771,060**	**14,706,013**
Laundry and cleaning supplies	**11,909,389**	**763,571**	**1,404,403**	**1,521,850**	**1,282,428**	**1,071,650**	**1,868,564**	**3,756,515**
Soaps and detergents	6,296,394	477,313	869,607	906,537	672,014	564,256	1,075,088	1,640,497
Other laundry cleaning products	5,612,995	286,295	534,716	615,313	610,414	507,394	793,477	2,115,864
Other household products	**20,984,994**	**977,733**	**2,205,268**	**2,120,068**	**2,226,716**	**1,959,627**	**4,041,074**	**6,907,484**
Cleansing and toilet tissue, paper towels, and napkins	6,191,319	439,382	818,880	990,810	654,955	631,755	1,025,318	1,543,171
Miscellaneous household products	8,557,557	413,966	780,134	784,822	830,185	919,814	1,743,631	2,858,684
Lawn and garden supplies	6,236,118	124,421	606,187	344,315	741,575	408,058	1,272,125	2,505,629
Postage and stationery	**11,557,508**	**505,129**	**1,292,335**	**1,369,557**	**934,337**	**1,284,020**	**1,861,309**	**4,042,013**
Stationery, stationery supplies, giftwrap	6,014,563	255,634	425,697	650,828	461,151	676,984	1,009,220	2,363,728
Postage	5,426,465	248,526	863,750	704,402	471,007	599,536	823,293	1,623,684
Delivery services	115,665	934	2,741	14,326	2,180	7,423	28,796	54,755

	complete income reporters	under $10,000	$10,000–$19,999	$20,000–$29,999	$30,000–$39,999	$40,000–$49,999	$50,000–$69,999	$70,000 or more
HOUSEHOLD FURNISHINGS AND EQUIPMENT	$134,564,452	$5,573,760	$11,023,907	$13,114,925	$11,641,642	$13,561,193	$24,165,269	$54,046,004
Household textiles	9,362,323	214,883	905,681	1,142,501	916,995	886,294	1,476,418	3,637,905
Bathroom linens	1,585,909	44,654	321,002	163,490	138,175	137,754	255,196	496,344
Bedroom linens	4,075,144	73,182	253,694	663,830	482,190	428,798	740,533	1,314,279
Kitchen and dining room linens	876,445	26,834	117,078	61,158	44,447	112,193	145,567	344,726
Curtains and draperies	1,663,291	32,285	109,426	104,499	148,315	77,831	141,826	1,049,449
Slipcovers and decorative pillows	267,169	–	8,747	37,321	13,931	30,229	60,880	106,734
Sewing materials for household items	787,660	29,663	80,162	101,128	84,251	89,999	114,050	288,275
Other linens	106,705	8,194	15,492	11,076	5,686	9,490	18,253	38,252
Furniture	33,661,680	1,463,565	2,749,602	2,986,996	2,853,525	2,893,676	4,959,144	15,755,616
Mattresses and springs	4,558,980	342,171	397,253	476,624	536,588	465,838	609,024	1,731,498
Other bedroom furniture	6,266,256	110,018	570,000	544,283	610,603	577,189	1,012,621	2,841,564
Sofas	7,095,458	343,755	536,155	904,009	492,804	650,428	997,429	3,171,020
Living room chairs	3,691,495	207,134	489,635	298,567	274,170	292,192	710,150	1,419,625
Living room tables	1,456,398	46,483	121,135	150,849	103,394	123,749	171,756	738,655
Kitchen and dining room furniture	4,335,796	118,114	243,347	264,256	349,133	317,293	460,849	2,583,212
Infants' furniture	581,582	25,481	33,176	45,989	104,152	53,035	98,065	221,643
Outdoor furniture	1,265,795	89,538	89,535	63,205	52,692	69,719	172,663	728,321
Wall units, cabinets, and other furniture	4,410,734	181,014	269,272	239,215	330,179	344,232	726,588	2,320,078
Floor coverings	3,998,577	107,200	333,183	235,242	344,015	353,416	779,645	1,845,482
Wall-to-wall carpet (renter)	97,745	–	10,149	24,800	21,228	5,357	–	36,401
Wall-to-wall carpet (replacement) (owner)	2,586,979	61,175	206,517	120,992	234,177	272,983	620,361	1,070,734
Room-size rugs and other floor coverings, nonpermanent	1,313,038	46,097	116,437	89,450	88,705	74,999	159,285	738,193
Major appliances	15,921,813	992,761	1,832,843	1,720,012	1,435,102	1,650,446	2,610,458	5,582,871
Dishwashers (built-in), garbage disposals, range hoods (renter)	85,527	16,012	7,995	4,214	8,908	7,883	18,479	22,056
Dishwashers (built-in), garbage disposals, range hoods (owner)	1,086,596	62,262	78,193	93,543	134,384	118,698	185,360	414,597
Refrigerators and freezers (renter)	627,196	81,849	137,505	71,752	81,502	149,769	19,613	84,986
Refrigerators and freezers (owner)	3,527,773	180,558	462,931	366,828	235,693	267,319	781,459	1,233,149
Washing machines (renter)	412,972	51,769	104,051	80,300	42,647	62,448	31,857	40,102
Washing machines (owner)	1,567,175	116,814	122,504	192,383	126,992	135,075	274,015	599,685
Clothes dryers (renter)	277,758	20,565	68,188	43,581	19,807	53,494	31,517	41,028
Clothes dryers (owner)	1,033,651	53,593	92,973	122,798	77,522	92,142	179,691	415,214
Cooking stoves, ovens (renter)	253,322	52,000	27,416	29,857	25,683	34,439	52,944	31,156
Cooking stoves, ovens (owner)	1,942,678	124,982	157,768	197,560	132,204	148,086	474,567	707,499
Microwave ovens (renter)	208,522	24,593	66,109	44,544	24,640	15,612	16,099	17,121
Microwave ovens (owner)	634,527	13,315	42,969	73,077	50,986	32,908	115,071	306,012
Portable dishwasher (renter)	17,105	431	–	–	10,614	–	–	6,170
Portable dishwasher (owner)	52,131	–	7,716	7,825	–	7,423	12,357	17,275
Window air conditioners (renter)	156,392	36,173	30,413	32,987	16,585	30,918	7,369	2,005
Window air conditioners (owner)	406,455	29,835	93,694	68,382	79,038	15,229	34,918	85,757
Electric floor-cleaning equipment	2,367,868	91,589	185,622	169,389	290,186	321,579	159,171	1,074,744
Sewing machines	421,932	9,307	20,422	37,802	7,108	72,091	110,422	164,728
Miscellaneous household appliances	839,791	27,008	126,523	83,189	70,793	85,561	105,661	319,277
Small appliances and misc. housewares	7,763,381	405,680	626,011	739,917	733,709	905,579	1,467,688	2,729,894
Housewares	5,766,129	273,436	394,654	515,269	540,189	654,791	1,137,328	2,095,042
Plastic dinnerware	132,770	7,437	7,515	18,179	18,954	22,959	22,107	35,321
China and other dinnerware	1,119,993	51,597	38,254	50,925	56,009	135,382	155,544	592,436
Flatware	330,703	12,838	18,970	39,006	36,960	17,296	34,918	170,744
Glassware	745,304	25,980	68,424	55,139	84,914	81,045	249,187	158,867
Silver serving pieces	221,555	11,289	17,312	18,660	22,934	23,724	27,436	93,007

	complete income reporters	under $10,000	$10,000– $19,999	$20,000– $29,999	$30,000– $39,999	$40,000– $49,999	$50,000– $69,999	$70,000 or more
Other serving pieces	$122,181	$6,890	$8,995	$33,468	$10,140	$6,658	$20,180	$35,938
Nonelectric cookware	1,444,179	85,578	123,949	165,777	196,837	109,438	351,334	374,803
Tableware, nonelectric kitchenware	1,649,444	71,864	111,087	134,235	113,345	258,365	276,623	633,926
Small appliances	1,997,252	132,244	231,357	224,648	193,426	250,789	330,360	634,698
Small electric kitchen appliances	1,502,012	88,705	173,478	174,806	153,054	189,718	245,219	476,910
Portable heating and cooling equipment	495,240	43,539	57,879	49,841	40,372	60,994	85,028	157,788
Miscellaneous household equipment	**63,856,678**	**2,389,707**	**4,576,600**	**6,290,498**	**5,358,201**	**6,871,782**	**12,871,916**	**24,494,392**
Window coverings	1,147,687	43,260	62,280	66,937	68,898	57,015	196,810	652,744
Infants' equipment	607,647	24,546	52,225	35,515	54,019	48,061	149,308	224,728
Laundry and cleaning equipment	930,205	59,958	109,983	144,107	95,718	75,918	176,064	252,645
Outdoor equipment	1,668,992	37,926	201,911	158,554	77,238	117,167	291,248	731,252
Clocks	1,497,939	5,962	41,158	20,466	30,042	727,571	257,577	368,634
Lamps and lighting fixtures	983,964	32,932	62,369	138,087	76,006	86,862	210,301	377,117
Other household decorative items	16,946,505	365,699	873,155	1,373,530	998,591	1,502,207	4,780,359	6,461,114
Telephones and accessories	2,562,543	88,272	274,178	363,337	289,996	248,416	328,433	907,548
Lawn and garden equipment	3,789,240	178,548	291,948	300,614	573,643	358,007	671,604	1,415,152
Power tools	1,902,765	23,716	136,585	171,435	280,804	287,676	335,235	604,004
Office furniture for home use	1,205,519	32,197	45,433	88,366	54,682	151,376	244,993	588,271
Hand tools	652,447	32,066	52,706	56,222	58,757	75,918	125,841	250,948
Indoor plants and fresh flowers	4,678,718	206,506	390,730	468,197	408,459	338,492	752,890	2,113,859
Closet and storage items	746,933	24,818	32,643	97,877	79,702	97,882	130,829	260,820
Rental of furniture	265,540	16,280	56,708	80,180	55,251	8,112	20,633	28,072
Luggage	746,933	24,574	50,427	42,016	83,398	70,943	152,483	323,287
Computers and computer hardware, nonbusiness use	15,534,092	760,782	1,196,370	1,766,242	1,438,609	1,817,741	2,707,502	5,846,776
Computer software and accessories, nonbusiness use	1,501,197	65,414	110,217	106,666	138,933	157,040	297,370	625,135
Telephone answering devices	189,788	19,836	20,816	29,134	20,849	17,296	24,261	57,223
Calculators	144,988	13,991	6,412	10,835	18,670	23,189	25,735	46,118
Business equipment for home use	166,981	13,377	15,735	19,744	15,542	20,357	35,825	46,735
Other hardware	1,699,130	5,387	13,349	267,868	127,371	102,856	450,759	668,630
Smoke alarms (owner)	51,316	7,866	3,665	6,020	3,980	4,745	9,410	15,732
Smoke alarms (renter)	15,476	290	8,572	1,565	2,843	–	1,247	771
Other household appliances (owner)	631,269	38,538	51,122	57,908	82,545	65,357	146,928	189,098
Other household appliances (renter)	117,294	10,024	28,123	6,862	9,098	5,434	13,491	44,267
Miscellaneous household equipment and parts	3,471,569	256,976	387,927	412,336	214,844	406,221	334,555	1,393,867

Note: Numbers may not add to total because of rounding. (–) means sample is too small to make a reliable estimate.
Source: Calculations by New Strategist based on the 2000 Consumer Expenditure Survey

Table 8.10 (Housing) Household Operations: Market shares by income, 2000

(percentage of total annual spending on household services, supplies, furnishings, and equipment accounted for by before-tax income group of consumer units, 2000; complete income reporters only)

	complete income reporters	under $10,000	$10,000– $19,999	$20,000– $29,999	$30,000– $39,999	$40,000– $49,999	$50,000– $69,999	$70,000 or more
Share of total consumer units	100.0%	13.3%	18.1%	14.8%	11.6%	9.4%	13.9%	18.9%
Share of total before-tax income	100.0	1.7	5.9	8.1	9.0	9.3	18.3	47.7
Share of total spending	100.0	5.4	10.2	11.0	10.3	9.9	17.0	35.7
Share of housing spending	100.0	6.3	11.2	11.1	10.3	9.7	16.6	34.7
HOUSEHOLD SERVICES	**100.0%**	**4.4%**	**9.4%**	**9.0%**	**6.8%**	**7.6%**	**16.6%**	**46.2%**
Personal services	**100.0**	**3.4**	**8.8**	**7.9**	**5.9**	**6.9**	**19.7**	**47.3**
Babysitting and child care in your own home	100.0	1.5	6.5	3.4	9.5	5.2	10.4	63.5
Babysitting and child care in someone else's home	100.0	1.5	10.8	10.8	10.6	13.5	23.9	28.9
Care for elderly, invalids, handicapped, etc.	100.0	15.8	28.2	18.5	0.7	3.5	16.7	16.8
Adult day care centers	100.0	5.7	60.6	0.5	16.9	5.7	6.8	3.7
Day care centers, nurseries, and preschools	100.0	1.7	4.5	6.2	5.5	6.7	21.2	54.2
Other household services	**100.0**	**5.2**	**9.9**	**10.1**	**7.5**	**8.2**	**13.7**	**45.2**
Housekeeping services	100.0	3.2	9.7	7.6	4.3	5.5	10.9	58.8
Gardening, lawn care service	100.0	6.4	14.2	9.8	7.0	6.1	12.2	44.3
Water softening service	100.0	5.3	19.3	5.9	11.0	10.1	14.3	34.1
Nonclothing laundry and dry cleaning, sent out	100.0	8.0	5.4	13.9	8.5	7.1	19.8	37.6
Nonclothing laundry and dry cleaning, coin-operated	100.0	16.3	23.7	19.6	11.3	10.6	8.8	9.7
Termite/pest control services	100.0	3.6	12.5	11.4	5.7	10.5	18.7	37.6
Home security system service fee	100.0	4.7	8.9	11.1	11.7	9.1	16.2	38.3
Other home services	100.0	3.1	11.8	9.7	11.4	9.9	12.9	41.2
Termite/pest control products	100.0	4.7	19.7	7.0	2.2	11.5	7.8	46.5
Moving, storage, and freight express	100.0	10.4	6.1	13.6	8.3	11.9	13.8	36.0
Appliance repair, including service center	100.0	5.6	11.3	13.5	11.1	9.7	16.5	32.4
Reupholstering and furniture repair	100.0	4.5	4.4	6.2	4.5	17.6	16.2	46.8
Repairs/rentals of lawn/garden equipment, hand/power tools, etc.	100.0	5.7	12.3	8.9	8.1	11.1	12.1	41.8
Appliance rental	100.0	11.1	20.1	7.0	13.2	14.1	10.4	24.1
Rental of office equipment for nonbusiness use	100.0	1.7	24.9	13.8	9.8	9.7	20.5	18.9
Repair of misc. household equipment and furnishings	100.0	–	1.6	12.9	1.4	–	–	79.2
Repair of computer systems for nonbusiness use	100.0	3.3	12.5	17.4	7.4	8.1	18.0	33.3
Computer information services	100.0	4.5	6.6	9.8	10.5	10.4	20.6	37.6
Rental, installation of dishwashers, range hoods, and garbage disposals	100.0	–	–	3.0	–	–	27.1	71.0
HOUSEKEEPING SUPPLIES	**100.0**	**5.1**	**11.0**	**11.3**	**10.0**	**9.7**	**17.5**	**33.1**
Laundry and cleaning supplies	**100.0**	**6.4**	**11.8**	**12.8**	**10.8**	**9.0**	**15.7**	**31.5**
Soaps and detergents	100.0	7.6	13.8	14.4	10.7	9.0	17.1	26.1
Other laundry cleaning products	100.0	5.1	9.5	11.0	10.9	9.0	14.1	37.7
Other household products	**100.0**	**4.7**	**10.5**	**10.1**	**10.6**	**9.3**	**19.3**	**32.9**
Cleansing and toilet tissue, paper towels, and napkins	100.0	7.1	13.2	16.0	10.6	10.2	16.6	24.9
Miscellaneous household products	100.0	4.8	9.1	9.2	9.7	10.7	20.4	33.4
Lawn and garden supplies	100.0	2.0	9.7	5.5	11.9	6.5	20.4	40.2
Postage and stationery	**100.0**	**4.4**	**11.2**	**11.8**	**8.1**	**11.1**	**16.1**	**35.0**
Stationery, stationery supplies, giftwrap	100.0	4.3	7.1	10.8	7.7	11.3	16.8	39.3
Postage	100.0	4.6	15.9	13.0	8.7	11.0	15.2	29.9
Delivery services	100.0	0.8	2.4	12.4	1.9	6.4	24.9	47.3

	complete income reporters	under $10,000	$10,000– $19,999	$20,000– $29,999	$30,000– $39,999	$40,000– $49,999	$50,000– $69,999	$70,000 or more
HOUSEHOLD FURNISHINGS AND EQUIPMENT	**100.0%**	**4.1%**	**8.2%**	**9.7%**	**8.7%**	**10.1%**	**18.0%**	**40.2%**
Household textiles	**100.0**	**2.3**	**9.7**	**12.2**	**9.8**	**9.5**	**15.8**	**38.9**
Bathroom linens	100.0	2.8	20.2	10.3	8.7	8.7	16.1	31.3
Bedroom linens	100.0	1.8	6.2	16.3	11.8	10.5	18.2	32.3
Kitchen and dining room linens	100.0	3.1	13.4	7.0	5.1	12.8	16.6	39.3
Curtains and draperies	100.0	1.9	6.6	6.3	8.9	4.7	8.5	63.1
Slipcovers and decorative pillows	100.0	–	3.3	14.0	5.2	11.3	22.8	40.0
Sewing materials for household items	100.0	3.8	10.2	12.8	10.7	11.4	14.5	36.6
Other linens	100.0	7.7	14.5	10.4	5.3	8.9	17.1	35.8
Furniture	**100.0**	**4.3**	**8.2**	**8.9**	**8.5**	**8.6**	**14.7**	**46.8**
Mattresses and springs	100.0	7.5	8.7	10.5	11.8	10.2	13.4	38.0
Other bedroom furniture	100.0	1.8	9.1	8.7	9.7	9.2	16.2	45.3
Sofas	100.0	4.8	7.6	12.7	6.9	9.2	14.1	44.7
Living room chairs	100.0	5.6	13.3	8.1	7.4	7.9	19.2	38.5
Living room tables	100.0	3.2	8.3	10.4	7.1	8.5	11.8	50.7
Kitchen and dining room furniture	100.0	2.7	5.6	6.1	8.1	7.3	10.6	59.6
Infants' furniture	100.0	4.4	5.7	7.9	17.9	9.1	16.9	38.1
Outdoor furniture	100.0	7.1	7.1	5.0	4.2	5.5	13.6	57.5
Wall units, cabinets, and other furniture	100.0	4.1	6.1	5.4	7.5	7.8	16.5	52.6
Floor coverings	**100.0**	**2.7**	**8.3**	**5.9**	**8.6**	**8.8**	**19.5**	**46.2**
Wall-to-wall carpet (renter)	100.0	–	10.4	25.4	21.7	5.5	–	37.2
Wall-to-wall carpet (replacement) (owner)	100.0	2.4	8.0	4.7	9.1	10.6	24.0	41.4
Room-size rugs and other floor coverings, nonpermanent	100.0	3.5	8.9	6.8	6.8	5.7	12.1	56.2
Major appliances	**100.0**	**6.2**	**11.5**	**10.8**	**9.0**	**10.4**	**16.4**	**35.1**
Dishwashers (built-in), garbage disposals, range hoods (renter)	100.0	18.7	9.3	4.9	10.4	9.2	21.6	25.8
Dishwashers (built-in), garbage disposals, range hoods (owner)	100.0	5.7	7.2	8.6	12.4	10.9	17.1	38.2
Refrigerators and freezers (renter)	100.0	13.0	21.9	11.4	13.0	23.9	3.1	13.6
Refrigerators and freezers (owner)	100.0	5.1	13.1	10.4	6.7	7.6	22.2	35.0
Washing machines (renter)	100.0	12.5	25.2	19.4	10.3	15.1	7.7	9.7
Washing machines (owner)	100.0	7.5	7.8	12.3	8.1	8.6	17.5	38.3
Clothes dryers (renter)	100.0	7.4	24.5	15.7	7.1	19.3	11.3	14.8
Clothes dryers (owner)	100.0	5.2	9.0	11.9	7.5	8.9	17.4	40.2
Cooking stoves, ovens (renter)	100.0	20.5	10.8	11.8	10.1	13.6	20.9	12.3
Cooking stoves, ovens (owner)	100.0	6.4	8.1	10.2	6.8	7.6	24.4	36.4
Microwave ovens (renter)	100.0	11.8	31.7	21.4	11.8	7.5	7.7	8.2
Microwave ovens (owner)	100.0	2.1	6.8	11.5	8.0	5.2	18.1	48.2
Portable dishwasher (renter)	100.0	2.5	–	–	62.1	–	–	36.1
Portable dishwasher (owner)	100.0	–	14.8	15.0	–	14.2	23.7	33.1
Window air conditioners (renter)	100.0	23.1	19.4	21.1	10.6	19.8	4.7	1.3
Window air conditioners (owner)	100.0	7.3	23.1	16.8	19.4	3.7	8.6	21.1
Electric floor-cleaning equipment	100.0	3.9	7.8	7.2	12.3	13.6	6.7	45.4
Sewing machines	100.0	2.2	4.8	9.0	1.7	17.1	26.2	39.0
Miscellaneous household appliances	100.0	3.2	15.1	9.9	8.4	10.2	12.6	38.0
Small appliances and misc. housewares	**100.0**	**5.2**	**8.1**	**9.5**	**9.5**	**11.7**	**18.9**	**35.2**
Housewares	100.0	4.7	6.8	8.9	9.4	11.4	19.7	36.3
Plastic dinnerware	100.0	5.6	5.7	13.7	14.3	17.3	16.7	26.6
China and other dinnerware	100.0	4.6	3.4	4.5	5.0	12.1	13.9	52.9
Flatware	100.0	3.9	5.7	11.8	11.2	5.2	10.6	51.6
Glassware	100.0	3.5	9.2	7.4	11.4	10.9	33.4	21.3
Silver serving pieces	100.0	5.1	7.8	8.4	10.4	10.7	12.4	42.0

	complete income reporters	under $10,000	$10,000– $19,999	$20,000– $29,999	$30,000– $39,999	$40,000– $49,999	$50,000– $69,999	$70,000 or more
Other serving pieces	100.0%	5.6%	7.4%	27.4%	8.3%	5.4%	16.5%	29.4%
Nonelectric cookware	100.0	5.9	8.6	11.5	13.6	7.6	24.3	26.0
Tableware, nonelectric kitchenware	100.0	4.4	6.7	8.1	6.9	15.7	16.8	38.4
Small appliances	100.0	6.6	11.6	11.2	9.7	12.6	16.5	31.8
Small electric kitchen appliances	100.0	5.9	11.5	11.6	10.2	12.6	16.3	31.8
Portable heating and cooling equipment	100.0	8.8	11.7	10.1	8.2	12.3	17.2	31.9
Miscellaneous household equipment	**100.0**	**3.7**	**7.2**	**9.9**	**8.4**	**10.8**	**20.2**	**38.4**
Window coverings	100.0	3.8	5.4	5.8	6.0	5.0	17.1	56.9
Infants' equipment	100.0	4.0	8.6	5.8	8.9	7.9	24.6	37.0
Laundry and cleaning equipment	100.0	6.4	11.8	15.5	10.3	8.2	18.9	27.2
Outdoor equipment	100.0	2.3	12.1	9.5	4.6	7.0	17.5	43.8
Clocks	100.0	0.4	2.7	1.4	2.0	48.6	17.2	24.6
Lamps and lighting fixtures	100.0	3.3	6.3	14.0	7.7	8.8	21.4	38.3
Other household decorative items	100.0	2.2	5.2	8.1	5.9	8.9	28.2	38.1
Telephones and accessories	100.0	3.4	10.7	14.2	11.3	9.7	12.8	35.4
Lawn and garden equipment	100.0	4.7	7.7	7.9	15.1	9.4	17.7	37.3
Power tools	100.0	1.2	7.2	9.0	14.8	15.1	17.6	31.7
Office furniture for home use	100.0	2.7	3.8	7.3	4.5	12.6	20.3	48.8
Hand tools	100.0	4.9	8.1	8.6	9.0	11.6	19.3	38.5
Indoor plants and fresh flowers	100.0	4.4	8.4	10.0	8.7	7.2	16.1	45.2
Closet and storage items	100.0	3.3	4.4	13.1	10.7	13.1	17.5	34.9
Rental of furniture	100.0	6.1	21.4	30.2	20.8	3.1	7.8	10.6
Luggage	100.0	3.3	6.8	5.6	11.2	9.5	20.4	43.3
Computers and computer hardware, nonbusiness use	100.0	4.9	7.7	11.4	9.3	11.7	17.4	37.6
Computer software and accessories, nonbusiness use	100.0	4.4	7.3	7.1	9.3	10.5	19.8	41.6
Telephone answering devices	100.0	10.5	11.0	15.4	11.0	9.1	12.8	30.2
Calculators	100.0	9.6	4.4	7.5	12.9	16.0	17.7	31.8
Business equipment for home use	100.0	8.0	9.4	11.8	9.3	12.2	21.5	28.0
Other hardware	100.0	0.3	0.8	15.8	7.5	6.1	26.5	39.4
Smoke alarms (owner)	100.0	15.3	7.1	11.7	7.8	9.2	18.3	30.7
Smoke alarms (renter)	100.0	1.9	55.4	10.1	18.4	–	8.1	5.0
Other household appliances (owner)	100.0	6.1	8.1	9.2	13.1	10.4	23.3	30.0
Other household appliances (renter)	100.0	8.5	24.0	5.9	7.8	4.6	11.5	37.7
Miscellaneous household equipment and parts	100.0	7.4	11.2	11.9	6.2	11.7	9.6	40.2

Note: Numbers may not add to total because of rounding. (–) means sample is too small to make a reliable estimate.
Source: Calculations by New Strategist based on the 2000 Consumer Expenditure Survey

Table 8.11 (Housing) Household Operations: Average spending by household type, 2000

(average annual spending of consumer units (CU) on household services, supplies, furnishings, and equipment, by type of consumer unit, 2000)

	total married couples	married couples, no children	married couples with children				single parent, at least one child <18	single person
			total	oldest child under 6	oldest child 6 to 17	oldest child 18 or older		
Number of consumer units (in thousands, add 000)	56,287	22,805	28,777	5,291	15,396	8,090	6,132	32,323
Average number of persons per CU	3.2	2.0	3.9	3.5	4.1	3.8	2.9	1.0
Average before-tax income of CU	$60,588.00	$53,232.00	$66,913.00	$62,928.00	$69,472.00	$64,725.00	$25,095.00	$24,977.00
Average spending of CU, total	48,619.37	42,195.54	53,585.53	50,755.90	54,170.40	54,550.20	28,923.25	23,059.00
Housing, average spending	15,203.59	12,831.51	17,132.38	18,702.09	17,432.55	15,536.72	10,732.20	8,188.63
HOUSEHOLD SERVICES	$911.27	$532.58	$1,220.62	$2,379.97	$1,183.23	$533.54	$786.14	$387.40
Personal services	443.80	54.33	749.51	1,990.42	660.71	106.90	586.20	123.86
Babysitting and child care in your own home	48.48	0.11	89.04	226.49	85.79	5.34	68.84	0.07
Babysitting and child care in someone else's home	45.16	1.08	80.75	233.75	66.35	8.07	104.75	2.39
Care for elderly, invalids, handicapped, etc.	22.57	35.01	4.00	2.11	1.79	9.43	1.79	114.17
Adult day care centers	3.85	1.32	0.62	1.29	0.21	0.95	1.89	0.56
Day care centers, nurseries, and preschools	323.75	16.81	575.10	1,526.79	506.57	83.11	408.92	6.67
Other household services	467.46	478.25	471.11	389.55	522.52	426.64	199.94	263.54
Housekeeping services	124.57	102.44	144.16	104.08	177.96	106.06	30.32	61.44
Gardening, lawn care service	88.53	105.99	78.31	59.65	87.19	73.61	35.61	80.39
Water softening service	4.34	3.79	5.04	7.42	4.66	4.20	1.29	1.82
Nonclothing laundry and dry cleaning, sent out	1.81	1.77	1.84	1.58	1.99	1.74	1.21	1.05
Nonclothing laundry and dry cleaning, coin-operated	3.36	2.43	3.76	4.92	3.41	3.69	10.61	4.35
Termite/pest control services	12.17	11.40	12.65	10.24	12.22	15.04	6.54	7.82
Home security system service fee	24.31	23.30	25.02	30.32	27.89	16.10	9.26	14.10
Other home services	18.99	20.40	17.44	9.70	20.06	17.53	7.30	9.75
Termite/pest control products	0.67	0.82	0.60	0.09	0.44	1.24	0.03	0.38
Moving, storage, and freight express	42.92	45.84	41.78	42.25	35.43	53.55	31.11	19.07
Appliance repair, including service center	16.51	15.73	17.12	15.39	16.78	18.92	9.48	7.65
Reupholstering and furniture repair	13.48	16.76	12.10	7.42	18.09	3.78	4.15	6.13
Repairs/rentals of lawn/garden equipment, hand/power tools, etc.	7.09	7.63	7.00	2.45	8.86	6.44	1.80	3.03
Appliance rental	4.66	4.97	5.05	5.93	4.41	5.72	2.77	1.63
Rental of office equipment for nonbusiness use	0.49	0.35	0.66	1.06	0.44	0.80	0.30	0.48
Repair of misc. household equipment and furnishings	19.52	45.01	1.73	–	3.00	0.50	–	4.66
Repair of computer systems for nonbusiness use	3.10	3.59	2.55	1.29	1.87	4.67	2.92	2.55
Computer information services	80.66	65.73	93.96	85.54	97.84	92.09	45.24	37.23
Rental, installation of dishwashers, range hoods, and garbage disposals	0.28	0.30	0.31	0.21	–	0.98	–	0.01
HOUSEKEEPING SUPPLIES	647.02	573.39	703.24	617.54	724.17	730.45	367.81	224.46
Laundry and cleaning supplies	173.48	133.81	203.33	149.51	225.92	200.43	150.92	53.33
Soaps and detergents	89.18	69.13	102.97	90.27	107.10	104.85	76.44	30.20
Other laundry cleaning products	84.29	64.68	100.36	59.24	118.82	95.58	74.48	23.13
Other household products	317.26	285.69	338.25	302.26	345.49	352.95	139.83	101.75
Cleansing and toilet tissue, paper towels, and napkins	89.08	80.36	94.78	84.40	91.91	109.53	56.79	33.73
Miscellaneous household products	125.56	103.34	141.03	130.45	134.16	164.39	64.94	40.68
Lawn and garden supplies	102.62	101.98	102.44	87.42	119.43	79.03	18.10	27.34
Postage and stationery	156.29	153.89	161.66	165.77	152.76	177.06	77.07	69.38
Stationery, stationery supplies, giftwrap	80.63	73.74	87.91	83.96	89.27	88.35	49.25	31.75
Postage	73.71	79.01	71.79	80.38	61.82	85.71	26.47	36.66
Delivery services	1.94	1.14	1.96	1.42	1.67	3.01	1.35	0.97

	total married couples	married couples, no children	married couples with children			single parent, at least one child <18	single person
			total	oldest child under 6	oldest child 6 to 17	oldest child 18 or older	
HOUSEHOLD FURNISHINGS AND EQUIPMENT	**$2,103.44**	**$1,883.62**	**$2,335.57**	**$2,502.46**	**$2,297.00**	**$2,291.06**	**$911.76**	**$895.21**
Household textiles	**144.20**	**128.56**	**162.14**	**179.46**	**156.65**	**162.71**	**59.73**	**63.37**
Bathroom linens	23.38	17.58	27.97	30.04	27.89	26.42	4.72	11.48
Bedroom linens	57.41	43.81	71.83	52.29	73.43	84.74	32.70	28.27
Kitchen and dining room linens	13.06	13.53	12.86	21.70	11.23	8.95	1.47	5.45
Curtains and draperies	29.62	26.86	31.77	63.54	23.40	26.92	15.60	11.63
Slipcovers and decorative pillows	4.63	7.19	3.21	3.34	3.77	1.93	1.25	0.57
Sewing materials for household items	14.35	17.47	13.01	7.60	15.64	11.54	3.44	4.62
Other linens	1.74	2.11	1.49	0.97	1.29	2.20	0.54	1.35
Furniture	**521.19**	**436.63**	**608.43**	**722.38**	**634.78**	**483.75**	**272.39**	**225.65**
Mattresses and springs	68.54	53.92	80.79	99.73	72.02	85.09	45.47	28.27
Other bedroom furniture	90.56	64.79	114.29	178.71	110.33	79.70	61.62	32.64
Sofas	117.42	101.57	131.61	137.63	139.61	112.46	67.34	56.42
Living room chairs	54.93	61.36	50.55	53.44	49.66	50.35	25.04	35.26
Living room tables	22.37	16.38	27.48	27.84	31.60	19.42	10.95	11.05
Kitchen and dining room furniture	65.07	55.29	78.96	102.24	93.18	36.65	22.44	24.47
Infants' furniture	9.98	8.64	10.84	36.25	7.37	0.81	5.43	0.99
Outdoor furniture	23.32	17.06	30.74	20.07	32.88	33.66	4.32	4.06
Wall units, cabinets, and other furniture	68.99	57.63	83.17	66.48	98.12	65.62	29.78	32.50
Floor coverings	**64.93**	**61.27**	**70.72**	**46.10**	**59.63**	**107.93**	**22.44**	**19.73**
Wall-to-wall carpet (renter)	1.28	0.70	0.50	–	0.49	0.86	2.84	0.68
Wall-to-wall carpet (replacement) (owner)	43.84	42.07	48.28	23.19	39.31	81.77	14.71	9.24
Room-size rugs and other floor coverings, nonpermanent	19.81	18.50	21.94	22.91	19.84	25.30	4.90	9.81
Major appliances	**257.58**	**217.59**	**289.99**	**264.79**	**273.71**	**341.92**	**104.47**	**104.33**
Dishwashers (built-in), garbage disposals, range hoods (renter)	0.78	0.22	1.12	1.94	1.42	–	0.99	0.72
Dishwashers (built-in), garbage disposals, range hoods (owner)	19.93	20.58	19.91	17.55	20.30	20.73	4.58	8.28
Refrigerators and freezers (renter)	6.64	2.35	10.10	7.78	14.50	3.25	10.81	4.32
Refrigerators and freezers (owner)	64.31	56.36	73.04	45.95	79.39	78.67	11.95	19.18
Washing machines (renter)	4.75	3.22	5.44	8.18	5.88	2.81	9.61	2.78
Washing machines (owner)	27.22	24.30	29.55	28.31	27.99	33.34	9.85	7.54
Clothes dryers (renter)	3.60	2.62	4.26	5.72	4.76	2.36	6.53	1.89
Clothes dryers (owner)	17.33	14.87	18.40	18.86	20.06	14.95	6.64	5.86
Cooking stoves, ovens (renter)	3.49	2.25	4.79	3.33	6.16	3.14	5.41	1.32
Cooking stoves, ovens (owner)	33.24	28.04	38.63	31.92	38.06	44.11	10.71	14.54
Microwave ovens (renter)	1.70	1.30	1.77	2.74	2.36	0.03	6.32	2.58
Microwave ovens (owner)	10.54	9.72	11.80	13.05	12.12	10.39	3.31	3.60
Portable dishwasher (renter)	0.30	–	0.59	2.01	0.40	–	0.07	–
Portable dishwasher (owner)	1.04	0.94	0.61	2.86	0.17	–	0.50	0.58
Window air conditioners (renter)	1.54	0.85	1.99	3.37	1.33	2.34	1.81	1.50
Window air conditioners (owner)	5.99	7.15	5.21	1.83	5.44	6.96	2.66	3.66
Electric floor-cleaning equipment	36.26	20.84	47.62	54.46	18.70	103.13	7.38	18.00
Sewing machines	8.37	9.21	7.31	3.34	7.78	9.00	0.68	0.88
Miscellaneous household appliances	10.56	12.75	7.83	11.58	6.90	6.69	4.66	7.10
Small appliances and misc. housewares	**116.59**	**110.20**	**122.11**	**125.05**	**120.20**	**123.56**	**35.86**	**49.19**
Housewares	87.42	82.45	91.86	96.50	90.62	90.91	25.35	34.95
Plastic dinnerware	1.59	1.30	1.93	4.17	1.59	1.12	0.83	1.22
China and other dinnerware	14.27	9.29	18.66	16.55	16.81	24.36	8.70	6.65
Flatware	4.92	6.40	4.06	4.00	4.39	3.48	2.08	1.80
Glassware	10.52	14.83	7.59	7.83	8.16	6.19	2.41	5.25
Silver serving pieces	3.25	2.60	3.94	7.43	3.00	3.01	1.41	0.71

	total married couples	married couples, no children	married couples with children				single parent, at least one child <18	single person
			total	oldest child under 6	oldest child 6 to 17	oldest child 18 or older		
Other serving pieces	$1.55	$1.62	$1.63	$1.26	$1.48	$2.15	$0.81	$1.20
Nonelectric cookware	22.23	21.75	19.94	23.48	14.42	28.68	4.26	7.21
Tableware, nonelectric kitchenware	29.09	24.66	34.10	31.78	40.77	21.93	4.86	10.91
Small appliances	29.17	27.74	30.25	28.55	29.58	32.65	10.51	14.24
Small electric kitchen appliances	21.78	21.35	22.53	20.34	21.17	26.55	8.28	11.55
Portable heating and cooling equipment	7.39	6.39	7.72	8.21	8.41	6.10	2.23	2.69
Miscellaneous household equipment	**998.95**	**929.38**	**1,082.17**	**1,164.68**	**1,052.03**	**1,071.20**	**416.88**	**432.94**
Window coverings	20.65	15.29	24.55	33.70	19.03	29.08	2.71	3.83
Infants' equipment	12.08	1.72	20.66	43.41	16.48	10.54	3.74	3.44
Laundry and cleaning equipment	12.82	10.87	13.95	13.78	13.30	15.46	8.38	6.44
Outdoor equipment	24.33	31.24	21.45	19.51	24.97	15.60	10.20	14.20
Clocks	20.61	35.41	11.48	6.97	7.66	23.33	3.03	8.76
Lamps and lighting fixtures	13.67	11.83	16.47	13.97	20.45	10.53	5.66	7.92
Other household decorative items	260.46	260.95	273.57	404.69	236.37	242.91	126.29	78.42
Telephones and accessories	37.14	30.92	40.86	39.64	38.73	46.36	7.78	26.16
Lawn and garden equipment	73.18	81.74	68.91	51.61	78.03	62.87	6.61	17.31
Power tools	33.29	26.48	40.95	51.16	42.20	29.78	6.64	9.67
Office furniture for home use	19.07	16.26	21.65	41.46	20.58	10.75	4.98	8.03
Hand tools	9.95	9.96	10.20	10.23	10.46	9.68	2.04	4.25
Indoor plants and fresh flowers	75.35	77.76	76.21	55.35	71.73	98.37	31.21	33.69
Closet and storage items	11.29	8.87	13.24	12.82	10.80	18.76	3.84	4.68
Rental of furniture	2.43	1.01	3.74	6.82	3.36	2.45	18.97	0.42
Luggage	11.05	10.75	11.69	14.91	10.54	11.79	2.84	5.92
Computers and computer hardware, nonbusiness use	235.60	189.38	273.39	241.98	274.39	292.03	123.64	134.40
Computer software and accessories, nonbusiness use	23.78	19.72	27.67	21.25	29.92	27.59	10.74	10.64
Telephone answering devices	1.94	1.55	2.27	2.15	2.54	1.83	2.42	2.16
Calculators	2.00	0.83	3.02	1.46	3.67	2.80	2.89	0.70
Business equipment for home use	2.43	2.50	2.35	4.03	1.91	2.09	1.44	1.02
Other hardware	27.80	9.84	38.34	25.09	52.75	18.91	0.51	27.65
Smoke alarms (owner)	0.80	0.74	0.92	1.45	0.69	1.00	0.07	0.18
Smoke alarms (renter)	0.21	0.05	0.36	1.22	0.18	0.15	0.07	0.14
Other household appliances (owner)	10.78	11.33	9.82	17.77	6.35	11.21	0.96	3.43
Other household appliances (renter)	1.25	0.30	2.15	0.97	3.37	0.62	0.83	0.82
Miscellaneous household equipment and parts	54.98	62.09	52.30	27.25	51.58	74.70	28.38	18.69

Note: Average spending figures for total consumer units can be found on Average Spending by Age and Average Spending by Region tables. (–) means sample is too small to make a reliable estimate.
Source: Bureau of Labor Statistics, unpublished tables from the 2000 Consumer Expenditure Survey

Table 8.12 (Housing) Household Operations: Indexed spending by household type, 2000

(indexed average annual spending of consumer units (CU) on household services, supplies, furnishings, and equipment, by type of consumer unit, 2000; index definition: an index of 100 is the average for all consumer units; an index of 132 means that spending by consumer units in that group is 32 percent above the average for all consumer units; an index of 68 indicates spending that is 32 percent below the average for all consumer units)

	total married couples	married couples, no children	married couples with children				single parent, at least one child <18	single person
			total	oldest child under 6	oldest child 6 to 17	oldest child 18 or older		
Average spending of CU, total	$48,619	$42,196	$53,586	$50,756	$54,170	$54,550	$28,923	$23,059
Average spending of CU, index	128	111	141	133	142	143	76	61
Housing, spending index	123	104	139	152	142	126	87	66
HOUSEHOLD SERVICES	**133**	**78**	**178**	**348**	**173**	**78**	**115**	**57**
Personal services	**136**	**17**	**230**	**610**	**203**	**33**	**180**	**38**
Babysitting and child care in your own home	151	0	276	703	266	17	214	0
Babysitting and child care in someone else's home	139	3	248	717	204	25	321	7
Care for elderly, invalids, handicapped, etc.	45	69	8	4	4	19	4	227
Adult day care centers	148	51	24	50	8	37	73	22
Day care centers, nurseries, and preschools	155	8	276	733	243	40	196	3
Other household services	**131**	**134**	**132**	**109**	**146**	**119**	**56**	**74**
Housekeeping services	141	116	164	118	202	120	34	70
Gardening, lawn care service	113	135	100	76	111	94	46	103
Water softening service	140	122	162	239	150	135	41	59
Nonclothing laundry and dry cleaning, sent out	122	120	124	107	134	118	82	71
Nonclothing laundry and dry cleaning, coin-operated	72	52	81	106	73	80	229	94
Termite/pest control services	127	119	132	107	128	157	68	82
Home security system service fee	130	125	134	162	149	86	50	76
Other home services	133	143	122	68	140	123	51	68
Termite/pest control products	137	167	122	18	90	253	6	78
Moving, storage, and freight express	132	141	129	130	109	165	96	59
Appliance repair, including service center	131	125	136	122	133	150	75	61
Reupholstering and furniture repair	146	181	131	80	195	41	45	66
Repairs/rentals of lawn/garden equipment, hand/power tools, etc.	143	154	141	49	179	130	36	61
Appliance rental	124	132	134	157	117	152	73	43
Rental of office equipment for nonbusiness use	92	66	125	200	83	151	57	91
Repair of misc. household equipment and furnishings	166	384	15	–	26	4	–	40
Repair of computer systems for nonbusiness use	113	131	93	47	68	170	106	93
Computer information services	131	107	153	139	159	150	74	61
Rental, installation of dishwashers, range hoods, and garbage disposals	187	200	207	140	–	653	–	7
HOUSEKEEPING SUPPLIES	**134**	**119**	**146**	**128**	**150**	**151**	**76**	**47**
Laundry and cleaning supplies	**133**	**102**	**155**	**114**	**173**	**153**	**115**	**41**
Soaps and detergents	129	100	149	130	155	151	110	44
Other laundry cleaning products	137	105	163	96	193	155	121	38
Other household products	**140**	**126**	**150**	**134**	**153**	**156**	**62**	**45**
Cleansing and toilet tissue, paper towels, and napkins	130	117	138	123	134	160	83	49
Miscellaneous household products	139	114	156	144	148	182	72	45
Lawn and garden supplies	153	152	153	131	178	118	27	41
Postage and stationery	**124**	**122**	**129**	**132**	**122**	**141**	**61**	**55**
Stationery, stationery supplies, giftwrap	127	116	138	132	140	139	77	50
Postage	122	130	118	133	102	141	44	60
Delivery services	138	81	139	101	118	213	96	69

	total married couples	married couples, no children	married couples with children				single parent, at least one child <18	single person
			total	oldest child under 6	oldest child 6 to 17	oldest child 18 or older		
HOUSEHOLD FURNISHINGS AND EQUIPMENT	**136**	**122**	**151**	**162**	**148**	**148**	**59**	**58**
Household textiles	**135**	**121**	**152**	**169**	**147**	**153**	**56**	**60**
Bathroom linens	133	100	159	171	159	151	27	65
Bedroom linens	129	98	161	117	165	190	73	63
Kitchen and dining room linens	140	145	138	233	121	96	16	59
Curtains and draperies	141	128	151	302	111	128	74	55
Slipcovers and decorative pillows	168	261	117	121	137	70	45	21
Sewing materials for household items	147	179	133	78	160	118	35	47
Other linens	114	138	97	63	84	144	35	88
Furniture	**133**	**112**	**156**	**185**	**163**	**124**	**70**	**58**
Mattresses and springs	130	102	153	189	136	161	86	53
Other bedroom furniture	131	94	165	259	160	115	89	47
Sofas	132	114	148	154	157	126	76	63
Living room chairs	125	140	115	122	113	115	57	80
Living room tables	130	95	160	162	184	113	64	64
Kitchen and dining room furniture	140	119	170	220	201	79	48	53
Infants' furniture	160	139	174	583	118	13	87	16
Outdoor furniture	154	113	203	132	217	222	28	27
Wall units, cabinets, and other furniture	136	114	164	131	194	130	59	64
Floor coverings	**146**	**138**	**159**	**104**	**134**	**243**	**51**	**44**
Wall-to-wall carpet (renter)	93	51	36	–	36	62	206	49
Wall-to-wall carpet (replacement) (owner)	158	151	174	83	142	294	53	33
Room-size rugs and other floor coverings, nonpermanent	130	122	144	151	130	166	32	64
Major appliances	**136**	**115**	**153**	**140**	**145**	**181**	**55**	**55**
Dishwashers (built-in), garbage disposals, range hoods (renter)	90	25	129	223	163	–	114	83
Dishwashers (built-in), garbage disposals, range hoods (owner)	141	146	141	124	144	147	32	59
Refrigerators and freezers (renter)	90	32	137	106	197	44	147	59
Refrigerators and freezers (owner)	145	127	165	104	179	177	27	43
Washing machines (renter)	99	67	114	171	123	59	201	58
Washing machines (owner)	147	131	159	153	151	180	53	41
Clothes dryers (renter)	107	78	127	170	142	70	194	56
Clothes dryers (owner)	144	124	153	157	167	124	55	49
Cooking stoves, ovens (renter)	125	80	171	119	220	112	193	47
Cooking stoves, ovens (owner)	139	117	161	133	159	184	45	61
Microwave ovens (renter)	71	55	74	115	99	1	266	108
Microwave ovens (owner)	143	132	160	177	165	141	45	49
Portable dishwasher (renter)	188	–	369	1,256	250	–	44	–
Portable dishwasher (owner)	137	124	80	376	22	–	66	76
Window air conditioners (renter)	83	46	108	182	72	126	98	81
Window air conditioners (owner)	124	148	108	38	113	144	55	76
Electric floor-cleaning equipment	140	80	183	210	72	397	28	69
Sewing machines	175	193	153	70	163	188	14	18
Miscellaneous household appliances	120	145	89	132	79	76	53	81
Small appliances and misc. housewares	**133**	**126**	**140**	**143**	**138**	**141**	**41**	**56**
Housewares	135	127	142	149	140	140	39	54
Plastic dinnerware	110	90	133	288	110	77	57	84
China and other dinnerware	125	81	163	145	147	213	76	58
Flatware	136	177	112	111	122	96	58	50
Glassware	131	185	95	98	102	77	30	65
Silver serving pieces	138	111	168	316	128	128	60	30

	total married couples	married couples, no children	married couples with children				single parent, at least one child <18	single person
			total	oldest child under 6	oldest child 6 to 17	oldest child 18 or older		
Other serving pieces	108	113	114	88	103	150	57	84
Nonelectric cookware	133	130	120	141	87	172	26	43
Tableware, nonelectric kitchenware	146	124	171	160	205	110	24	55
Small appliances	130	123	134	127	131	145	47	63
Small electric kitchen appliances	128	125	132	119	124	156	49	68
Portable heating and cooling equipment	135	117	141	150	154	112	41	49
Miscellaneous household equipment	**137**	**127**	**148**	**159**	**144**	**147**	**57**	**59**
Window coverings	159	117	189	259	146	223	21	29
Infants' equipment	151	21	258	542	206	132	47	43
Laundry and cleaning equipment	127	108	138	137	132	153	83	64
Outdoor equipment	132	170	117	106	136	85	55	77
Clocks	148	255	83	50	55	168	22	63
Lamps and lighting fixtures	127	110	153	129	189	98	52	73
Other household decorative items	147	147	154	228	133	137	71	44
Telephones and accessories	127	106	140	136	133	159	27	90
Lawn and garden equipment	156	175	147	110	167	134	14	37
Power tools	156	124	192	240	198	140	31	45
Office furniture for home use	140	119	158	303	151	79	36	59
Hand tools	137	137	140	141	144	133	28	59
Indoor plants and fresh flowers	132	136	134	97	126	173	55	59
Closet and storage items	141	110	165	160	134	234	48	58
Rental of furniture	78	32	120	219	108	79	608	13
Luggage	133	129	141	179	127	142	34	71
Computers and computer hardware, nonbusiness use	125	101	146	129	146	155	66	72
Computer software and accessories, nonbusiness use	136	113	158	121	171	158	61	61
Telephone answering devices	98	79	115	109	129	93	123	110
Calculators	122	51	184	89	224	171	176	43
Business equipment for home use	133	137	128	220	104	114	79	56
Other hardware	115	41	159	104	219	78	2	115
Smoke alarms (owner)	143	132	164	259	123	179	13	32
Smoke alarms (renter)	131	31	225	763	113	94	44	88
Other household appliances (owner)	142	149	129	234	84	148	13	45
Other household appliances (renter)	102	25	176	80	276	51	68	67
Miscellaneous household equipment and parts	137	155	130	68	128	186	71	47

Note: Spending index for total consumer units is 100. (–) means sample is too small to make a reliable estimate.
Source: Calculations by New Strategist based on the 2000 Consumer Expenditure Survey

Table 8.13 (Housing) Household Operations: Indexed per capita spending by household type, 2000

(indexed average annual per capita spending of consumer units (CU) on household services, supplies, furnishings, and equipment, by type of consumer unit, 2000; index definition: an index of 100 is the average for all consumer units; an index of 132 means that spending by consumer units in that group is 32 percent above the average for all consumer units; an index of 68 indicates spending that is 32 percent below the average for all consumer units)

	total married couples	married couples, no children	married couples with children				single parent, at least one child <18	single person
			total	oldest child under 6	oldest child 6 to 17	oldest child 18 or older		
Per capita spending of CU, total	$15,194	$21,098	$13,740	$14,502	$13,212	$14,355	$9,974	$23,059
Per capita spending of CU, index	100	139	90	95	87	94	66	152
Housing, per capita spending index	96	130	89	108	86	83	75	166
HOUSEHOLD SERVICES	**104**	**97**	**114**	**248**	**105**	**51**	**99**	**142**
Personal services	**106**	**21**	**147**	**436**	**124**	**22**	**155**	**95**
Babysitting and child care in your own home	118	0	177	502	162	11	184	1
Babysitting and child care in someone else's home	108	4	159	512	124	16	277	18
Care for elderly, invalids, handicapped, etc.	35	87	5	3	2	12	3	567
Adult day care centers	116	63	15	35	5	24	63	54
Day care centers, nurseries, and preschools	121	10	177	523	148	26	169	8
Other household services	**102**	**167**	**84**	**78**	**89**	**78**	**48**	**184**
Housekeeping services	110	145	105	84	123	79	30	174
Gardening, lawn care service	88	169	64	54	68	62	39	257
Water softening service	109	152	104	170	91	89	36	146
Nonclothing laundry and dry cleaning, sent out	96	149	80	76	82	77	70	177
Nonclothing laundry and dry cleaning, coin-operated	57	65	52	76	45	52	197	234
Termite/pest control services	99	149	85	76	78	103	59	204
Home security system service fee	102	156	86	116	91	57	43	189
Other home services	104	179	78	49	86	81	44	171
Termite/pest control products	107	209	78	13	55	166	5	194
Moving, storage, and freight express	103	177	83	93	67	109	83	147
Appliance repair, including service center	103	156	87	87	81	99	65	152
Reupholstering and furniture repair	114	226	84	57	119	27	39	165
Repairs/rentals of lawn/garden equipment, hand/power tools, etc.	112	192	90	35	109	85	31	153
Appliance rental	97	165	86	112	71	100	63	108
Rental of office equipment for nonbusiness use	72	83	80	143	51	99	49	226
Repair of misc. household equipment and furnishings	130	480	9	–	16	3	–	99
Repair of computer systems for nonbusiness use	88	163	59	34	41	112	92	232
Computer information services	103	134	98	100	97	99	64	152
Rental, installation of dishwashers, range hoods, and garbage disposals	146	250	132	100	–	430	–	17
HOUSEKEEPING SUPPLIES	**105**	**149**	**93**	**91**	**92**	**100**	**66**	**116**
Laundry and cleaning supplies	**104**	**128**	**100**	**82**	**105**	**101**	**99**	**102**
Soaps and detergents	101	125	95	93	94	100	95	109
Other laundry cleaning products	107	131	105	69	118	102	104	94
Other household products	**110**	**158**	**96**	**96**	**93**	**103**	**53**	**113**
Cleansing and toilet tissue, paper towels, and napkins	102	147	89	88	82	105	72	123
Miscellaneous household products	108	143	100	103	90	120	62	112
Lawn and garden supplies	120	190	98	93	109	78	23	102
Postage and stationery	**97**	**153**	**82**	**94**	**74**	**93**	**53**	**138**
Stationery, stationery supplies, giftwrap	99	145	89	94	86	91	67	125
Postage	95	163	76	95	62	93	38	151
Delivery services	107	101	89	72	72	140	83	172

	total married couples	married couples, no children	married couples with children			single parent, at least one child <18	single person
			total	oldest child under 6	oldest child 6 to 17	oldest child 18 or older		
HOUSEHOLD FURNISHINGS AND EQUIPMENT	**106**	**152**	**97**	**115**	**90**	**97**	**51**	**145**
Household textiles	**106**	**151**	**98**	**120**	**90**	**101**	**48**	**149**
Bathroom linens	104	125	102	122	97	99	23	164
Bedroom linens	101	123	103	84	101	125	63	159
Kitchen and dining room linens	110	182	89	166	74	63	14	146
Curtains and draperies	110	159	97	216	68	84	64	138
Slipcovers and decorative pillows	132	327	75	87	84	46	39	52
Sewing materials for household items	115	224	86	56	98	78	30	118
Other linens	89	172	62	45	51	95	30	221
Furniture	**104**	**140**	**100**	**132**	**99**	**81**	**60**	**144**
Mattresses and springs	101	127	98	135	83	106	74	134
Other bedroom furniture	102	117	106	185	97	76	77	118
Sofas	103	142	95	110	95	83	65	158
Living room chairs	98	175	74	87	69	76	49	201
Living room tables	102	119	102	116	112	74	55	161
Kitchen and dining room furniture	109	149	109	157	122	52	42	132
Infants' furniture	125	174	112	416	72	9	75	40
Outdoor furniture	120	141	130	95	132	146	25	67
Wall units, cabinets, and other furniture	106	142	105	94	118	85	51	161
Floor coverings	**114**	**173**	**102**	**74**	**82**	**160**	**44**	**111**
Wall-to-wall carpet (renter)	72	63	23	–	22	41	177	123
Wall-to-wall carpet (replacement) (owner)	123	189	111	60	86	194	46	83
Room-size rugs and other floor coverings, nonpermanent	102	152	92	108	79	109	28	161
Major appliances	**106**	**144**	**98**	**100**	**88**	**119**	**48**	**138**
Dishwashers (built-in), garbage disposals, range hoods (renter)	70	32	83	159	100	–	98	207
Dishwashers (built-in), garbage disposals, range hoods (owner)	110	182	91	89	88	97	28	147
Refrigerators and freezers (renter)	71	40	88	76	120	29	127	147
Refrigerators and freezers (owner)	113	159	106	74	109	117	23	108
Washing machines (renter)	77	84	73	122	75	39	173	145
Washing machines (owner)	115	164	102	109	92	118	46	102
Clothes dryers (renter)	84	97	81	122	86	46	168	141
Clothes dryers (owner)	113	155	98	112	102	82	48	122
Cooking stoves, ovens (renter)	97	100	110	85	134	74	167	118
Cooking stoves, ovens (owner)	108	146	103	95	97	121	39	152
Microwave ovens (renter)	56	68	48	82	60	1	229	271
Microwave ovens (owner)	112	165	103	127	100	93	39	122
Portable dishwasher (renter)	146	–	236	897	152	–	38	–
Portable dishwasher (owner)	107	155	51	269	14	–	57	191
Window air conditioners (renter)	65	57	69	130	44	83	84	203
Window air conditioners (owner)	97	185	69	27	69	95	48	190
Electric floor-cleaning equipment	109	100	117	150	44	261	24	173
Sewing machines	137	241	98	50	99	124	12	46
Miscellaneous household appliances	94	182	57	94	48	50	46	202
Small appliances and misc. housewares	**104**	**158**	**90**	**102**	**84**	**93**	**35**	**141**
Housewares	105	159	91	106	85	92	34	135
Plastic dinnerware	86	112	85	205	67	51	49	210
China and other dinnerware	98	102	105	103	90	140	66	145
Flatware	106	222	72	79	74	63	50	125
Glassware	102	231	61	70	62	51	26	164
Silver serving pieces	108	138	107	226	78	84	52	76

	total married couples	married couples, no children	married couples with children				single parent, at least one child <18	single person
			total	oldest child under 6	oldest child 6 to 17	oldest child 18 or older		
Other serving pieces	85	142	73	63	63	99	49	210
Nonelectric cookware	104	163	77	101	53	113	22	108
Tableware, nonelectric kitchenware	114	155	110	114	125	73	21	137
Small appliances	101	154	86	91	80	95	40	158
Small electric kitchen appliances	100	157	85	85	76	103	42	169
Portable heating and cooling equipment	106	146	90	107	94	73	35	123
Miscellaneous household equipment	**107**	**159**	**95**	**114**	**88**	**96**	**49**	**148**
Window coverings	124	147	121	185	89	147	18	74
Infants' equipment	118	27	165	387	125	87	40	107
Laundry and cleaning equipment	99	135	89	98	80	101	72	160
Outdoor equipment	103	212	75	76	83	56	48	193
Clocks	116	318	53	36	34	110	19	157
Lamps and lighting fixtures	99	137	98	92	115	64	45	183
Other household decorative items	115	184	99	163	81	90	61	111
Telephones and accessories	99	132	90	97	81	104	23	224
Lawn and garden equipment	122	218	94	79	102	88	12	92
Power tools	122	155	123	171	121	92	27	113
Office furniture for home use	109	149	102	217	92	52	31	147
Hand tools	107	171	90	101	88	88	24	146
Indoor plants and fresh flowers	103	170	86	69	77	114	47	148
Closet and storage items	110	138	106	114	82	154	41	146
Rental of furniture	61	40	77	156	66	52	524	34
Luggage	104	162	90	128	77	93	29	178
Computers and computer hardware, nonbusiness use	98	126	93	92	89	102	57	179
Computer software and accessories, nonbusiness use	106	141	101	87	104	104	53	152
Telephone answering devices	77	98	74	78	79	61	106	274
Calculators	95	63	118	64	136	112	152	107
Business equipment for home use	104	171	82	157	64	75	68	139
Other hardware	90	51	102	74	134	52	2	287
Smoke alarms (owner)	112	165	105	185	75	117	11	80
Smoke alarms (renter)	103	39	144	545	69	62	38	219
Other household appliances (owner)	111	187	83	167	51	97	11	113
Other household appliances (renter)	80	31	113	57	168	33	59	168
Miscellaneous household equipment and parts	107	193	83	48	78	122	61	116

Note: Per capita indexes account for household size and show how much each person in a particular household demographic segment spends relative to a person in the average household. Spending index for total consumer units is 100. (−) means sample is too small to make a reliable estimate.
Source: Calculations by New Strategist based on the 2000 Consumer Expenditure Survey

Table 8.14 (Housing) Household Operations: Total spending by household type, 2000

(total annual spending on household services, supplies, furnishings, and equipment, by consumer unit (CU) type, 2000; numbers in thousands)

	total married couples	married couples, no children	married couples with children				single parent, at least one child <18	single person
			total	oldest child under 6	oldest child 6 to 17	oldest child 18 or older		
Number of consumer units	56,287	22,805	28,777	5,291	15,396	8,090	6,132	32,323
Total spending of all CUs	$2,736,638,479	$962,269,290	$1,542,030,797	$268,549,467	$834,007,478	$441,311,118	$177,357,369	$745,336,057
Housing, total spending	855,764,470	292,622,586	493,018,499	98,952,758	268,391,540	125,692,065	65,809,850	264,681,087
HOUSEHOLD SERVICES	**$51,292,654**	**$12,145,487**	**$35,125,782**	**$12,592,421**	**$18,217,009**	**$4,316,339**	**$4,820,610**	**$12,521,930**
Personal services	**24,980,171**	**1,238,996**	**21,568,649**	**10,531,312**	**10,172,291**	**864,821**	**3,594,578**	**4,003,527**
Babysitting and child care in your own home	2,728,794	2,509	2,562,304	1,198,359	1,320,823	43,201	422,127	2,263
Babysitting and child care in someone else's home	2,541,921	24,629	2,323,743	1,236,771	1,021,525	65,286	642,327	77,252
Care for elderly, invalids, handicapped, etc.	1,270,398	798,403	115,108	11,164	27,559	76,289	10,976	3,690,317
Adult day care centers	216,705	30,103	17,842	6,825	3,233	7,686	11,589	18,101
Day care centers, nurseries, and preschools	18,222,916	383,352	16,549,653	8,078,246	7,799,152	672,360	2,507,497	215,594
Other household services	**26,311,921**	**10,906,491**	**13,557,132**	**2,061,109**	**8,044,718**	**3,451,518**	**1,226,032**	**8,518,403**
Housekeeping services	7,011,672	2,336,144	4,148,492	550,687	2,739,872	858,025	185,922	1,985,925
Gardening, lawn care service	4,983,088	2,417,102	2,253,527	315,608	1,342,377	595,505	218,361	2,598,446
Water softening service	244,286	86,431	145,036	39,259	71,745	33,978	7,910	58,828
Nonclothing laundry and dry cleaning, sent out	101,879	40,365	52,950	8,360	30,638	14,077	7,420	33,939
Nonclothing laundry and dry cleaning, coin-operated	189,124	55,416	108,202	26,032	52,500	29,852	65,061	140,605
Termite/pest control services	685,013	259,977	364,029	54,180	188,139	121,674	40,103	252,766
Home security system service fee	1,368,337	531,357	720,001	160,423	429,394	130,249	56,782	455,754
Other home services	1,068,890	465,222	501,871	51,323	308,844	141,818	44,764	315,149
Termite/pest control products	37,712	18,700	17,266	476	6,774	10,032	184	12,283
Moving, storage, and freight express	2,415,838	1,045,381	1,202,303	223,545	545,480	433,220	190,767	616,400
Appliance repair, including service center	929,298	358,723	492,662	81,428	258,345	153,063	58,131	247,271
Reupholstering and furniture repair	758,749	382,212	348,202	39,259	278,514	30,580	25,448	198,140
Repairs/rentals of lawn/garden equipment, hand/power tools, etc.	399,075	174,002	201,439	12,963	136,409	52,100	11,038	97,939
Appliance rental	262,297	113,341	145,324	31,376	67,896	46,275	16,986	52,686
Rental of office equipment for nonbusiness use	27,581	7,982	18,993	5,608	6,774	6,472	1,840	15,515
Repair of misc. household equipment and furnishings	1,098,722	1,026,453	49,784	–	46,188	4,045	–	150,625
Repair of computer systems for nonbusiness use	174,490	81,870	73,381	6,825	28,791	37,780	17,905	82,424
Computer information services	4,540,109	1,498,973	2,703,887	452,592	1,506,345	745,008	277,412	1,203,385
Rental, installation of dishwashers, range hoods, and garbage disposals	15,760	6,842	8,921	1,111	–	7,928	–	323
HOUSEKEEPING SUPPLIES	**36,418,815**	**13,076,159**	**20,237,137**	**3,267,404**	**11,149,321**	**5,909,341**	**2,255,411**	**7,255,221**
Laundry and cleaning supplies	**9,764,669**	**3,051,537**	**5,851,227**	**791,057**	**3,478,264**	**1,621,479**	**925,441**	**1,723,786**
Soaps and detergents	5,019,675	1,576,510	2,963,168	477,619	1,648,912	848,237	468,730	976,155
Other laundry cleaning products	4,744,431	1,475,027	2,888,060	313,439	1,829,353	773,242	456,711	747,631
Other household products	**17,857,614**	**6,515,160**	**9,733,820**	**1,599,258**	**5,319,164**	**2,855,366**	**857,438**	**3,288,865**
Cleansing and toilet tissue, paper towels, and napkins	5,014,046	1,832,610	2,727,484	446,560	1,415,046	886,098	348,236	1,090,255
Miscellaneous household products	7,067,396	2,356,669	4,058,420	690,211	2,065,527	1,329,915	398,212	1,314,900
Lawn and garden supplies	5,776,172	2,325,654	2,947,916	462,539	1,838,744	639,353	110,989	883,711
Postage and stationery	**8,797,095**	**3,509,461**	**4,652,090**	**877,089**	**2,351,893**	**1,432,415**	**472,593**	**2,242,570**
Stationery, stationery supplies, giftwrap	4,538,421	1,681,641	2,529,786	444,232	1,374,401	714,752	302,001	1,026,255
Postage	4,148,915	1,801,823	2,065,901	425,291	951,781	693,394	162,314	1,184,961
Delivery services	109,197	25,998	56,403	7,513	25,711	24,351	8,278	31,353

	total married couples	married couples, no children	married couples with children				single parent, at least one child <18	single person
			total	oldest child under 6	oldest child 6 to 17	oldest child 18 or older		
HOUSEHOLD FURNISHINGS AND EQUIPMENT	$118,396,327	$42,955,954	$67,210,698	$13,240,516	$35,364,612	$18,534,675	$5,590,912	$28,935,873
Household textiles	8,116,585	2,931,811	4,665,903	949,523	2,411,783	1,316,324	366,264	2,048,309
Bathroom linens	1,315,990	400,912	804,893	158,942	429,394	213,738	28,943	371,068
Bedroom linens	3,231,437	999,087	2,067,052	276,666	1,130,528	685,547	200,516	913,771
Kitchen and dining room linens	735,108	308,552	370,072	114,815	172,897	72,406	9,014	176,160
Curtains and draperies	1,667,221	612,542	914,245	336,190	360,266	217,783	95,659	375,916
Slipcovers and decorative pillows	260,609	163,968	92,374	17,672	58,043	15,614	7,665	18,424
Sewing materials for household items	807,718	398,403	374,389	40,212	240,793	93,359	21,094	149,332
Other linens	97,939	48,119	42,878	5,132	19,861	17,798	3,311	43,636
Furniture	29,336,222	9,957,347	17,508,790	3,822,113	9,773,073	3,913,538	1,670,295	7,293,685
Mattresses and springs	3,857,911	1,229,646	2,324,894	527,671	1,108,820	688,378	278,822	913,771
Other bedroom furniture	5,097,351	1,477,536	3,288,923	945,555	1,698,641	644,773	377,854	1,055,023
Sofas	6,609,220	2,316,304	3,787,341	728,200	2,149,436	909,801	412,929	1,823,664
Living room chairs	3,091,845	1,399,315	1,454,677	282,751	764,565	407,332	153,545	1,139,709
Living room tables	1,259,140	373,546	790,792	147,301	486,514	157,108	67,145	357,169
Kitchen and dining room furniture	3,662,595	1,260,888	2,272,232	540,952	1,434,599	296,499	137,602	790,944
Infants' furniture	561,744	197,035	311,943	191,799	113,469	6,553	33,297	32,000
Outdoor furniture	1,312,613	389,053	884,605	106,190	506,220	272,309	26,490	131,231
Wall units, cabinets, and other furniture	3,883,240	1,314,252	2,393,383	351,746	1,510,656	530,866	182,611	1,050,498
Floor coverings	3,654,715	1,397,262	2,035,109	243,915	918,063	873,154	137,602	637,733
Wall-to-wall carpet (renter)	72,047	15,964	14,389	–	7,544	6,957	17,415	21,980
Wall-to-wall carpet (replacement) (owner)	2,467,622	959,406	1,389,354	122,698	605,217	661,519	90,202	298,665
Room-size rugs and other floor coverings, nonpermanent	1,115,045	421,893	631,367	121,217	305,457	204,677	30,047	317,089
Major appliances	14,498,405	4,962,140	8,345,042	1,401,004	4,214,039	2,766,133	640,610	3,372,259
Dishwashers (built-in), garbage disposals, range hoods (renter)	43,904	5,017	32,230	10,265	21,862	–	6,071	23,273
Dishwashers (built-in), garbage disposals, range hoods (owner)	1,121,800	469,327	572,950	92,857	312,539	167,706	28,085	267,634
Refrigerators and freezers (renter)	373,746	53,592	290,648	41,164	223,242	26,293	66,287	139,635
Refrigerators and freezers (owner)	3,619,817	1,285,290	2,101,872	243,121	1,222,288	636,440	73,277	619,955
Washing machines (renter)	267,363	73,432	156,547	43,280	90,528	22,733	58,929	89,858
Washing machines (owner)	1,532,132	554,162	850,360	149,788	430,934	269,721	60,400	243,715
Clothes dryers (renter)	202,633	59,749	122,590	30,265	73,285	19,092	40,042	61,090
Clothes dryers (owner)	975,454	339,110	529,497	99,788	308,844	120,946	40,716	189,413
Cooking stoves, ovens (renter)	196,442	51,311	137,842	17,619	94,839	25,403	33,174	42,666
Cooking stoves, ovens (owner)	1,870,980	639,452	1,111,656	168,889	585,972	356,850	65,674	469,976
Microwave ovens (renter)	95,688	29,647	50,935	14,497	36,335	243	38,754	83,393
Microwave ovens (owner)	593,265	221,665	339,569	69,048	186,600	84,055	20,297	116,363
Portable dishwasher (renter)	16,886	–	16,978	10,635	6,158	–	429	–
Portable dishwasher (owner)	58,538	21,437	17,554	15,132	2,617	–	3,066	18,747
Window air conditioners (renter)	86,682	19,384	57,266	17,831	20,477	18,931	11,099	48,485
Window air conditioners (owner)	337,159	163,056	149,928	9,683	83,754	56,306	16,311	118,302
Electric floor-cleaning equipment	2,040,967	475,256	1,370,361	288,148	287,905	834,322	45,254	581,814
Sewing machines	471,122	210,034	210,360	17,672	119,781	72,810	4,170	28,444
Miscellaneous household appliances	594,391	290,764	225,324	61,270	106,232	54,122	28,575	229,493
Small appliances and misc. housewares	6,562,501	2,513,111	3,513,959	661,640	1,850,599	999,600	219,894	1,589,968
Housewares	4,920,610	1,880,272	2,643,455	510,582	1,395,186	735,462	155,446	1,129,689
Plastic dinnerware	89,496	29,647	55,540	22,063	24,480	9,061	5,090	39,434
China and other dinnerware	803,215	211,858	536,979	87,566	258,807	197,072	53,348	214,948
Flatware	276,932	145,952	116,835	21,164	67,588	28,153	12,755	58,181
Glassware	592,139	338,198	218,417	41,429	125,631	50,077	14,778	169,696
Silver serving pieces	182,933	59,293	113,381	39,312	46,188	24,351	8,646	22,949

	total married couples	married couples, no children	married couples with children				single parent, at least one child <18	single person
			total	oldest child under 6	oldest child 6 to 17	oldest child 18 or older		
Other serving pieces	$87,245	$36,944	$46,907	$6,667	$22,786	$17,394	$4,967	$38,788
Nonelectric cookware	1,251,260	496,009	573,813	124,233	222,010	232,021	26,122	233,049
Tableware, nonelectric kitchenware	1,637,389	562,371	981,296	168,148	627,695	177,414	29,802	352,644
Small appliances	1,641,892	632,611	870,504	151,058	455,414	264,139	64,447	460,280
Small electric kitchen appliances	1,225,931	486,887	648,346	107,619	325,933	214,790	50,773	373,331
Portable heating and cooling equipment	415,961	145,724	222,158	43,439	129,480	49,349	13,674	86,949
Miscellaneous household equipment	**56,227,899**	**21,194,511**	**31,141,606**	**6,162,322**	**16,197,054**	**8,666,008**	**2,556,308**	**13,993,920**
Window coverings	1,162,327	348,688	706,475	178,307	292,986	235,257	16,618	123,797
Infants' equipment	679,947	39,225	594,533	229,682	253,726	85,269	22,934	111,191
Laundry and cleaning equipment	721,599	247,890	401,439	72,910	204,767	125,071	51,386	208,160
Outdoor equipment	1,369,463	712,428	617,267	103,227	384,438	126,204	62,546	458,987
Clocks	1,160,075	807,525	330,360	36,878	117,933	188,740	18,580	283,149
Lamps and lighting fixtures	769,443	269,783	473,957	73,915	314,848	85,188	34,707	255,998
Other household decorative items	14,660,512	5,950,965	7,872,524	2,141,215	3,639,153	1,965,142	774,410	2,534,770
Telephones and accessories	2,090,499	705,131	1,175,828	209,735	596,287	375,052	47,707	845,570
Lawn and garden equipment	4,119,083	1,864,081	1,983,023	273,069	1,201,350	508,618	40,533	559,511
Power tools	1,873,794	603,876	1,178,418	270,688	649,711	240,920	40,716	312,563
Office furniture for home use	1,073,393	370,809	623,022	219,365	316,850	86,968	30,537	259,554
Hand tools	560,056	227,138	293,525	54,127	161,042	78,311	12,509	137,373
Indoor plants and fresh flowers	4,241,225	1,773,317	2,193,095	292,857	1,104,355	795,813	191,380	1,088,962
Closet and storage items	635,480	202,280	381,007	67,831	166,277	151,768	23,547	151,272
Rental of furniture	136,777	23,033	107,626	36,085	51,731	19,821	116,324	13,576
Luggage	621,971	245,154	336,403	78,889	162,274	95,381	17,415	191,352
Computers and computer hardware, nonbusiness use	13,261,217	4,318,811	7,867,344	1,280,316	4,224,508	2,362,523	758,160	4,344,211
Computer software and accessories, nonbusiness use	1,338,505	449,715	796,260	112,434	460,648	223,203	65,858	343,917
Telephone answering devices	109,197	35,348	65,324	11,376	39,106	14,805	14,839	69,818
Calculators	112,574	18,928	86,907	7,725	56,503	22,652	17,721	22,626
Business equipment for home use	136,777	57,013	67,626	21,323	29,406	16,908	8,830	32,969
Other hardware	1,564,779	224,401	1,103,310	132,751	812,139	152,982	3,127	893,731
Smoke alarms (owner)	45,030	16,876	26,475	7,672	10,623	8,090	429	5,818
Smoke alarms (renter)	11,820	1,140	10,360	6,455	2,771	1,214	429	4,525
Other household appliances (owner)	606,774	258,381	282,590	94,021	97,765	90,689	5,887	110,868
Other household appliances (renter)	70,359	6,842	61,871	5,132	51,885	5,016	5,090	26,505
Miscellaneous household equipment and parts	3,094,659	1,415,962	1,505,037	144,180	794,126	604,323	174,026	604,117

Note: Total spending figures for total consumer units can be found on Total Spending by Age and Total Spending by Region tables. Spending by type of consumer unit will not add to total because not all types of consumer units are shown. (–) means sample is too small to make a reliable estimate.
Source: Calculations by New Strategist based on the 2000 Consumer Expenditure Survey

Table 8.15 (Housing) Household Operations: Market shares by household type, 2000

(percentage of total annual spending on household services, supplies, furnishings, and equipment accounted for by types of consumer units, 2000)

	total married couples	married couples, no children	married couples with children				single parent, at least one child <18	single person
			total	oldest child under 6	oldest child 6 to 17	oldest child 18 or older		
Share of total consumer units	51.5%	20.9%	26.3%	4.8%	14.1%	7.4%	5.6%	29.6%
Share of total before-tax income	69.8	24.9	39.4	6.8	21.9	10.7	3.2	16.5
Share of total spending	65.8	23.1	37.1	6.5	20.0	10.6	4.3	17.9
Share of housing spending	63.5	21.7	36.6	7.3	19.9	9.3	4.9	19.6
HOUSEHOLD SERVICES	**68.5%**	**16.2%**	**46.9%**	**16.8%**	**24.3%**	**5.8%**	**6.4%**	**16.7%**
Personal services	**70.0**	**3.5**	**60.5**	**29.5**	**28.5**	**2.4**	**10.1**	**11.2**
Babysitting and child care in your own home	77.5	0.1	72.7	34.0	37.5	1.2	12.0	0.1
Babysitting and child care in someone else's home	71.3	0.7	65.2	34.7	28.7	1.8	18.0	2.2
Care for elderly, invalids, handicapped, etc.	23.1	14.5	2.1	0.2	0.5	1.4	0.2	67.0
Adult day care centers	76.2	10.6	6.3	2.4	1.1	2.7	4.1	6.4
Day care centers, nurseries, and preschools	79.9	1.7	72.6	35.4	34.2	2.9	11.0	0.9
Other household services	**67.2**	**27.8**	**34.6**	**5.3**	**20.5**	**8.8**	**3.1**	**21.7**
Housekeeping services	72.7	24.2	43.0	5.7	28.4	8.9	1.9	20.6
Gardening, lawn care service	58.2	28.2	26.3	3.7	15.7	7.0	2.6	30.4
Water softening service	71.8	25.4	42.6	11.5	21.1	10.0	2.3	17.3
Nonclothing laundry and dry cleaning, sent out	62.9	24.9	32.7	5.2	18.9	8.7	4.6	21.0
Nonclothing laundry and dry cleaning, coin-operated	37.3	10.9	21.3	5.1	10.3	5.9	12.8	27.7
Termite/pest control services	65.4	24.8	34.8	5.2	18.0	11.6	3.8	24.2
Home security system service fee	67.0	26.0	35.3	7.9	21.0	6.4	2.8	22.3
Other home services	68.4	29.8	32.1	3.3	19.8	9.1	2.9	20.2
Termite/pest control products	70.4	34.9	32.2	0.9	12.6	18.7	0.3	22.9
Moving, storage, and freight express	68.1	29.5	33.9	6.3	15.4	12.2	5.4	17.4
Appliance repair, including service center	67.5	26.1	35.8	5.9	18.8	11.1	4.2	18.0
Reupholstering and furniture repair	74.9	37.7	34.4	3.9	27.5	3.0	2.5	19.6
Repairs/rentals of lawn/garden equipment, hand/power tools, etc.	73.6	32.1	37.1	2.4	25.1	9.6	2.0	18.1
Appliance rental	63.6	27.5	35.2	7.6	16.5	11.2	4.1	12.8
Rental of office equipment for nonbusiness use	47.6	13.8	32.8	9.7	11.7	11.2	3.2	26.8
Repair of misc. household equipment and furnishings	85.6	80.0	3.9	–	3.6	0.3	–	11.7
Repair of computer systems for nonbusiness use	58.0	27.2	24.4	2.3	9.6	12.6	6.0	27.4
Computer information services	67.7	22.3	40.3	6.7	22.4	11.1	4.1	17.9
Rental, installation of dishwashers, range hoods, and garbage disposals	96.1	41.7	54.4	6.8	–	48.3	–	2.0
HOUSEKEEPING SUPPLIES	**69.0**	**24.8**	**38.4**	**6.2**	**21.1**	**11.2**	**4.3**	**13.8**
Laundry and cleaning supplies	**68.3**	**21.3**	**40.9**	**5.5**	**24.3**	**11.3**	**6.5**	**12.1**
Soaps and detergents	66.3	20.8	39.1	6.3	21.8	11.2	6.2	12.9
Other laundry cleaning products	70.5	21.9	42.9	4.7	27.2	11.5	6.8	11.1
Other household products	**72.3**	**26.4**	**39.4**	**6.5**	**21.5**	**11.6**	**3.5**	**13.3**
Cleansing and toilet tissue, paper towels, and napkins	67.0	24.5	36.4	6.0	18.9	11.8	4.7	14.6
Miscellaneous household products	71.4	23.8	41.0	7.0	20.9	13.4	4.0	13.3
Lawn and garden supplies	78.9	31.8	40.2	6.3	25.1	8.7	1.5	12.1
Postage and stationery	**64.0**	**25.5**	**33.9**	**6.4**	**17.1**	**10.4**	**3.4**	**16.3**
Stationery, stationery supplies, giftwrap	65.2	24.2	36.3	6.4	19.7	10.3	4.3	14.7
Postage	62.6	27.2	31.2	6.4	14.4	10.5	2.4	17.9
Delivery services	70.8	16.9	36.6	4.9	16.7	15.8	5.4	20.3

	total married couples	married couples, no children	married couples with children				single parent, at least one child <18	single person
			total	oldest child under 6	oldest child 6 to 17	oldest child 18 or older		
HOUSEHOLD FURNISHINGS AND EQUIPMENT	**69.9%**	**25.4%**	**39.7%**	**7.8%**	**20.9%**	**10.9%**	**3.3%**	**17.1%**
Household textiles	**69.7**	**25.2**	**40.1**	**8.2**	**20.7**	**11.3**	**3.1**	**17.6**
Bathroom linens	68.6	20.9	41.9	8.3	22.4	11.1	1.5	19.3
Bedroom linens	66.4	20.5	42.5	5.7	23.2	14.1	4.1	18.8
Kitchen and dining room linens	72.2	30.3	36.3	11.3	17.0	7.1	0.9	17.3
Curtains and draperies	72.4	26.6	39.7	14.6	15.6	9.5	4.2	16.3
Slipcovers and decorative pillows	86.7	54.5	30.7	5.9	19.3	5.2	2.5	6.1
Sewing materials for household items	75.7	37.4	35.1	3.8	22.6	8.8	2.0	14.0
Other linens	58.5	28.8	25.6	3.1	11.9	10.6	2.0	26.1
Furniture	**68.7**	**23.3**	**41.0**	**8.9**	**22.9**	**9.2**	**3.9**	**17.1**
Mattresses and springs	66.7	21.3	40.2	9.1	19.2	11.9	4.8	15.8
Other bedroom furniture	67.4	19.5	43.5	12.5	22.5	8.5	5.0	14.0
Sofas	67.8	23.8	38.8	7.5	22.0	9.3	4.2	18.7
Living room chairs	64.5	29.2	30.3	5.9	15.9	8.5	3.2	23.8
Living room tables	67.0	19.9	42.1	7.8	25.9	8.4	3.6	19.0
Kitchen and dining room furniture	72.1	24.8	44.7	10.6	28.2	5.8	2.7	15.6
Infants' furniture	82.6	29.0	45.9	28.2	16.7	1.0	4.9	4.7
Outdoor furniture	79.2	23.5	53.4	6.4	30.5	16.4	1.6	7.9
Wall units, cabinets, and other furniture	70.2	23.7	43.2	6.4	27.3	9.6	3.3	19.0
Floor coverings	**75.3**	**28.8**	**41.9**	**5.0**	**18.9**	**18.0**	**2.8**	**13.1**
Wall-to-wall carpet (renter)	47.7	10.6	9.5	–	5.0	4.6	11.5	14.6
Wall-to-wall carpet (replacement) (owner)	81.2	31.6	45.7	4.0	19.9	21.8	3.0	9.8
Room-size rugs and other floor coverings, nonpermanent	67.0	25.3	37.9	7.3	18.4	12.3	1.8	19.0
Major appliances	**70.2**	**24.0**	**40.4**	**6.8**	**20.4**	**13.4**	**3.1**	**16.3**
Dishwashers (built-in), garbage disposals, range hoods (renter)	46.1	5.3	33.9	10.8	23.0	–	6.4	24.5
Dishwashers (built-in), garbage disposals, range hoods (owner)	72.7	30.4	37.2	6.0	20.3	10.9	1.8	17.4
Refrigerators and freezers (renter)	46.5	6.7	36.2	5.1	27.8	3.3	8.2	17.4
Refrigerators and freezers (owner)	74.6	26.5	43.3	5.0	25.2	13.1	1.5	12.8
Washing machines (renter)	51.0	14.0	29.9	8.3	17.3	4.3	11.2	17.2
Washing machines (owner)	75.6	27.3	42.0	7.4	21.3	13.3	3.0	12.0
Clothes dryers (renter)	55.1	16.3	33.4	8.2	19.9	5.2	10.9	16.6
Clothes dryers (owner)	74.2	25.8	40.3	7.6	23.5	9.2	3.1	14.4
Cooking stoves, ovens (renter)	64.1	16.8	45.0	5.8	31.0	8.3	10.8	13.9
Cooking stoves, ovens (owner)	71.4	24.4	42.4	6.4	22.4	13.6	2.5	17.9
Microwave ovens (renter)	36.8	11.4	19.6	5.6	14.0	0.1	14.9	32.0
Microwave ovens (owner)	73.7	27.5	42.2	8.6	23.2	10.4	2.5	14.5
Portable dishwasher (renter)	96.5	–	97.0	60.8	35.2	–	2.5	–
Portable dishwasher (owner)	70.4	25.8	21.1	18.2	3.1	–	3.7	22.6
Window air conditioners (renter)	42.8	9.6	28.3	8.8	10.1	9.4	5.5	24.0
Window air conditioners (owner)	64.0	30.9	28.4	1.8	15.9	10.7	3.1	22.4
Electric floor-cleaning equipment	71.8	16.7	48.2	10.1	10.1	29.4	1.6	20.5
Sewing machines	90.1	40.2	40.2	3.4	22.9	13.9	0.8	5.4
Miscellaneous household appliances	62.0	30.3	23.5	6.4	11.1	5.6	3.0	23.9
Small appliances and misc. housewares	**68.7**	**26.3**	**36.8**	**6.9**	**19.4**	**10.5**	**2.3**	**16.6**
Housewares	69.4	26.5	37.3	7.2	19.7	10.4	2.2	15.9
Plastic dinnerware	56.4	18.7	35.0	13.9	15.4	5.7	3.2	24.9
China and other dinnerware	64.3	16.9	43.0	7.0	20.7	15.8	4.3	17.2
Flatware	70.1	37.0	29.6	5.4	17.1	7.1	3.2	14.7
Glassware	67.5	38.6	24.9	4.7	14.3	5.7	1.7	19.3
Silver serving pieces	71.2	23.1	44.1	15.3	18.0	9.5	3.4	8.9

	total married couples	married couples, no children	married couples with children			single parent, at least one child <18	single person
			total	oldest child under 6	oldest child 6 to 17	oldest child 18 or older		
Other serving pieces	55.8%	23.6%	30.0%	4.3%	14.6%	11.1%	3.2%	24.8%
Nonelectric cookware	68.6	27.2	31.5	6.8	12.2	12.7	1.4	12.8
Tableware, nonelectric kitchenware	75.2	25.8	45.1	7.7	28.8	8.2	1.4	16.2
Small appliances	66.7	25.7	35.4	6.1	18.5	10.7	2.6	18.7
Small electric kitchen appliances	65.8	26.1	34.8	5.8	17.5	11.5	2.7	20.0
Portable heating and cooling equipment	69.5	24.4	37.1	7.3	21.6	8.2	2.3	14.5
Miscellaneous household equipment	**70.3**	**26.5**	**39.0**	**7.7**	**20.3**	**10.8**	**3.2**	**17.5**
Window coverings	81.6	24.5	49.6	12.5	20.6	16.5	1.2	8.7
Infants' equipment	77.6	4.5	67.9	26.2	29.0	9.7	2.6	12.7
Laundry and cleaning equipment	65.5	22.5	36.4	6.6	18.6	11.3	4.7	18.9
Outdoor equipment	68.1	35.4	30.7	5.1	19.1	6.3	3.1	22.8
Clocks	76.3	53.1	21.7	2.4	7.8	12.4	1.2	18.6
Lamps and lighting fixtures	65.1	22.8	40.1	6.3	26.7	7.2	2.9	21.7
Other household decorative items	75.6	30.7	40.6	11.0	18.8	10.1	4.0	13.1
Telephones and accessories	65.5	22.1	36.8	6.6	18.7	11.7	1.5	26.5
Lawn and garden equipment	80.4	36.4	38.7	5.3	23.5	9.9	0.8	10.9
Power tools	80.4	25.9	50.5	11.6	27.9	10.3	1.7	13.4
Office furniture for home use	71.8	24.8	41.7	14.7	21.2	5.8	2.0	17.4
Hand tools	70.5	28.6	37.0	6.8	20.3	9.9	1.6	17.3
Indoor plants and fresh flowers	68.0	28.4	35.2	4.7	17.7	12.8	3.1	17.5
Closet and storage items	72.4	23.0	43.4	7.7	18.9	17.3	2.7	17.2
Rental of furniture	40.1	6.8	31.5	10.6	15.2	5.8	34.1	4.0
Luggage	68.4	26.9	37.0	8.7	17.8	10.5	1.9	21.0
Computers and computer hardware, nonbusiness use	64.6	21.0	38.3	6.2	20.6	11.5	3.7	21.1
Computer software and accessories, nonbusiness use	70.0	23.5	41.6	5.9	24.1	11.7	3.4	18.0
Telephone answering devices	50.7	16.4	30.3	5.3	18.2	6.9	6.9	32.4
Calculators	62.8	10.6	48.5	4.3	31.5	12.6	9.9	12.6
Business equipment for home use	68.3	28.5	33.8	10.7	14.7	8.4	4.4	16.5
Other hardware	59.4	8.5	41.9	5.0	30.8	5.8	0.1	33.9
Smoke alarms (owner)	73.5	27.6	43.2	12.5	17.3	13.2	0.7	9.5
Smoke alarms (renter)	67.5	6.5	59.2	36.9	15.8	6.9	2.5	25.9
Other household appliances (owner)	73.1	31.1	34.0	11.3	11.8	10.9	0.7	13.4
Other household appliances (renter)	52.7	5.1	46.4	3.8	38.9	3.8	3.8	19.9
Miscellaneous household equipment and parts	70.4	32.2	34.2	3.3	18.1	13.8	4.0	13.7

Note: Market share for total consumer units is 100.0%. Market shares by type of consumer unit will not add to total because not all types of consumer units are shown. (–) means sample is too small to make a reliable estimate.
Source: Calculations by New Strategist based on the 2000 Consumer Expenditure Survey

Table 8.16 (Housing) Household Operations: Average spending by race and Hispanic origin, 2000

(average annual spending of consumer units (CU) on household services, supplies, furnishings, and equipment, by race and Hispanic origin of consumer unit reference person, 2000)

	total consumer units	race		Hispanic origin	
		black	white and other	Hispanic	non-Hispanic
Number of consumer units					
(in thousands, add 000)	109,367	13,230	96,137	9,473	99,894
Average number of persons per CU	2.5	2.7	2.5	3.4	2.4
Average before-tax income of CU	$44,649.00	$32,657.00	$46,260.00	$34,891.00	$45,669.00
Average spending of CU, total	38,044.67	28,152.24	39,406.20	32,734.95	38,548.91
Housing, average spending	12,318.51	9,905.54	12,650.61	10,849.81	12,457.64
HOUSEHOLD SERVICES	**$684.38**	**$468.22**	**$714.13**	**$465.48**	**$705.17**
Personal services	**326.20**	**292.10**	**330.90**	**254.71**	**332.98**
Babysitting and child care in your own home	32.21	11.17	35.11	58.49	29.72
Babysitting and child care in someone else's home	32.59	36.35	32.08	65.83	29.44
Care for elderly, invalids, handicapped, etc.	50.38	14.13	55.37	2.16	54.95
Adult day care centers	2.60	0.88	2.84	0.14	2.83
Day care centers, nurseries, and preschools	208.42	229.57	205.51	128.09	216.03
Other household services	**358.18**	**176.12**	**383.24**	**210.77**	**372.18**
Housekeeping services	88.15	20.02	97.52	46.36	92.11
Gardening, lawn care service	78.26	40.82	83.41	29.22	82.91
Water softening service	3.11	0.82	3.42	1.28	3.28
Nonclothing laundry and dry cleaning, sent out	1.48	2.04	1.40	0.66	1.55
Nonclothing laundry and dry cleaning, coin-operated	4.64	7.57	4.24	12.32	3.92
Termite/pest control services	9.57	4.94	10.21	5.37	9.97
Home security system service fee	18.67	25.59	17.72	11.34	19.37
Other home services	14.28	5.74	15.45	8.94	14.78
Termite/pest control products	0.49	0.45	0.50	0.14	0.53
Moving, storage, and freight express	32.43	13.26	35.07	22.93	33.33
Appliance repair, including service center	12.58	8.99	13.07	5.26	13.27
Reupholstering and furniture repair	9.26	2.35	10.22	3.21	9.84
Repairs/rentals of lawn/garden equipment, hand/power tools, etc.	4.96	2.56	5.29	1.47	5.29
Appliance rental	3.77	4.15	3.71	4.97	3.65
Rental of office equipment for nonbusiness use	0.53	0.36	0.55	0.32	0.55
Repair of misc. household equipment and furnishings	11.73	–	13.35	24.06	10.59
Repair of computer systems for nonbusiness use	2.75	3.49	2.65	1.51	2.87
Computer information services	61.36	32.97	65.27	31.27	64.21
Rental, installation of dishwashers, range hoods, and garbage disposals	0.15	–	0.17	0.12	0.15
HOUSEKEEPING SUPPLIES	**482.32**	**302.65**	**507.06**	**473.77**	**483.11**
Laundry and cleaning supplies	**130.76**	**125.75**	**131.45**	**171.68**	**126.96**
Soaps and detergents	69.27	69.58	69.23	105.92	65.86
Other laundry cleaning products	61.49	56.17	62.23	65.76	61.10
Other household products	**225.90**	**125.66**	**239.70**	**226.57**	**225.84**
Cleansing and toilet tissue, paper towels, and napkins	68.45	60.95	69.48	92.02	66.26
Miscellaneous household products	90.48	40.57	97.35	85.66	90.93
Lawn and garden supplies	66.97	24.15	72.87	48.89	68.65
Postage and stationery	**125.66**	**51.23**	**135.91**	**75.51**	**130.32**
Stationery, stationery supplies, giftwrap	63.65	22.27	69.35	33.54	66.45
Postage	60.60	27.40	65.17	41.80	62.35
Delivery services	1.41	1.56	1.39	0.17	1.52

	total consumer units	race		Hispanic origin	
		black	white and other	Hispanic	non-Hispanic
HOUSEHOLD FURNISHINGS AND EQUIPMENT	**$1,548.63**	**$886.62**	**$1,639.76**	**$1,303.33**	**$1,571.75**
Household textiles	**106.49**	**57.00**	**113.30**	**88.70**	**108.17**
Bathroom linens	17.55	9.30	18.69	27.42	16.64
Bedroom linens	44.52	28.21	46.77	33.64	45.53
Kitchen and dining room linens	9.31	4.14	10.02	9.00	9.34
Curtains and draperies	21.06	11.99	22.31	10.84	22.03
Slipcovers and decorative pillows	2.75	0.12	3.12	1.71	2.85
Sewing materials for household items	9.75	2.44	10.76	4.32	10.27
Other linens	1.53	0.80	1.63	1.78	1.51
Furniture	**390.63**	**283.26**	**405.41**	**447.40**	**385.25**
Mattresses and springs	52.89	48.20	53.53	76.05	50.69
Other bedroom furniture	69.11	72.64	68.63	109.57	65.28
Sofas	89.15	63.36	92.70	92.64	88.82
Living room chairs	43.84	14.78	47.84	35.40	44.64
Living room tables	17.19	10.76	18.08	16.98	17.21
Kitchen and dining room furniture	46.46	33.32	48.27	58.97	45.28
Infants' furniture	6.22	7.29	6.07	7.24	6.12
Outdoor furniture	15.16	5.69	16.46	4.04	16.21
Wall units, cabinets, and other furniture	50.61	27.23	53.83	46.53	51.00
Floor coverings	**44.38**	**24.88**	**47.07**	**27.40**	**45.99**
Wall-to-wall carpet (renter)	1.38	1.98	1.30	0.82	1.43
Wall-to-wall carpet (replacement) (owner)	27.78	14.84	29.57	21.97	28.34
Room-size rugs and other floor coverings, nonpermanent	15.22	8.05	16.20	4.60	16.22
Major appliances	**188.96**	**108.41**	**200.05**	**166.17**	**191.14**
Dishwashers (built-in), garbage disposals, range hoods (renter)	0.87	0.74	0.89	0.35	0.92
Dishwashers (built-in), garbage disposals, range hoods (owner)	14.10	2.42	15.70	4.22	15.03
Refrigerators and freezers (renter)	7.35	11.30	6.80	7.74	7.31
Refrigerators and freezers (owner)	44.34	17.96	47.97	28.73	45.82
Washing machines (renter)	4.79	11.39	3.88	3.15	4.94
Washing machines (owner)	18.53	10.69	19.61	18.32	18.55
Clothes dryers (renter)	3.36	5.51	3.06	1.69	3.52
Clothes dryers (owner)	12.02	7.40	12.65	9.13	12.29
Cooking stoves, ovens (renter)	2.80	5.04	2.50	3.04	2.78
Cooking stoves, ovens (owner)	23.95	9.99	25.87	21.15	24.21
Microwave ovens (renter)	2.38	3.99	2.16	3.45	2.28
Microwave ovens (owner)	7.36	3.10	7.94	4.71	7.61
Portable dishwasher (renter)	0.16	–	0.18	–	0.17
Portable dishwasher (owner)	0.76	0.28	0.83	–	0.83
Window air conditioners (renter)	1.85	3.51	1.62	3.09	1.73
Window air conditioners (owner)	4.82	5.09	4.78	3.78	4.92
Electric floor-cleaning equipment	25.98	3.89	29.02	37.17	24.94
Sewing machines	4.78	1.74	5.20	8.81	4.40
Miscellaneous household appliances	8.77	4.36	9.38	7.63	8.87
Small appliances and misc. housewares	**87.37**	**35.91**	**94.46**	**66.09**	**89.36**
Housewares	64.87	22.26	70.74	48.06	66.43
Plastic dinnerware	1.45	0.67	1.56	1.72	1.43
China and other dinnerware	11.43	1.54	12.79	6.27	11.91
Flatware	3.61	1.59	3.88	2.19	3.74
Glassware	8.02	3.08	8.70	5.51	8.25
Silver serving pieces	2.35	1.24	2.51	1.04	2.48

	total consumer units	race		Hispanic origin	
		black	white and other	Hispanic	non-Hispanic
Other serving pieces	$1.43	$1.20	$1.46	$0.67	$1.50
Nonelectric cookware	16.67	6.82	18.03	23.54	16.04
Tableware, nonelectric kitchenware	19.90	6.11	21.80	7.11	21.09
Small appliances	22.51	13.65	23.72	18.04	22.93
Small electric kitchen appliances	17.04	10.35	17.96	13.28	17.39
Portable heating and cooling equipment	5.47	3.30	5.77	4.75	5.54
Miscellaneous household equipment	**730.81**	**377.16**	**779.49**	**507.57**	**751.84**
Window coverings	13.02	8.94	13.58	2.50	14.02
Infants' equipment	8.01	3.49	8.63	10.27	7.80
Laundry and cleaning equipment	10.08	6.54	10.57	10.57	10.04
Outdoor equipment	18.39	5.49	20.17	7.91	19.37
Clocks	13.91	3.36	15.36	10.22	14.25
Lamps and lighting fixtures	10.80	7.32	11.28	5.98	11.26
Other household decorative items	177.30	102.29	187.63	95.77	184.88
Telephones and accessories	29.19	13.02	31.41	35.36	28.61
Lawn and garden equipment	46.82	13.57	51.40	13.51	49.98
Power tools	21.32	3.74	23.74	37.97	19.77
Office furniture for home use	13.67	8.20	14.42	8.01	14.21
Hand tools	7.26	2.05	7.97	4.88	7.48
Indoor plants and fresh flowers	57.01	27.15	61.12	28.99	59.67
Closet and storage items	8.03	2.56	8.78	6.78	8.14
Rental of furniture	3.12	4.40	2.94	6.07	2.84
Luggage	8.32	4.28	8.88	4.74	8.66
Computers and computer hardware, nonbusiness use	187.83	124.32	196.57	122.67	194.01
Computer software and accessories, nonbusiness use	17.49	8.06	18.79	13.66	17.85
Telephone answering devices	1.97	1.56	2.02	0.93	2.07
Calculators	1.64	1.58	1.64	1.20	1.68
Business equipment for home use	1.83	1.69	1.85	1.68	1.84
Other hardware	24.09	1.30	27.23	16.61	24.79
Smoke alarms (owner)	0.56	0.80	0.53	0.05	0.61
Smoke alarms (renter)	0.16	0.16	0.16	0.15	0.16
Other household appliances (owner)	7.59	3.66	8.13	7.61	7.59
Other household appliances (renter)	1.22	1.60	1.17	4.74	0.88
Miscellaneous household equipment and parts	40.18	16.04	43.50	48.76	39.38

Note: Other races include Asians, Native Americans, and Pacific Islanders. (–) means sample is too small to make a reliable estimate.
Source: Bureau of Labor Statistics, unpublished tables from the 2000 Consumer Expenditure Survey

Table 8.17 (Housing) Household Operations: Indexed spending by race and Hispanic origin, 2000

(indexed average annual spending of consumer units (CU) on household services, supplies, furnishings, and equipment, by race and Hispanic origin of consumer unit reference person, 2000; index definition: an index of 100 is the average for all consumer units; an index of 132 means that spending by consumer units in that group is 32 percent above the average for all consumer units; an index of 68 indicates spending that is 32 percent below the average for all consumer units)

	total consumer units	race black	race white and other	Hispanic origin Hispanic	Hispanic origin non-Hispanic
Average spending of CU, total	$38,045	$28,152	$39,406	$32,735	$38,549
Average spending of CU, index	100	74	104	86	101
Housing, spending index	100	80	103	88	101
HOUSEHOLD SERVICES	**100**	**68**	**104**	**68**	**103**
Personal services	**100**	**90**	**101**	**78**	**102**
Babysitting and child care in your own home	100	35	109	182	92
Babysitting and child care in someone else's home	100	112	98	202	90
Care for elderly, invalids, handicapped, etc.	100	28	110	4	109
Adult day care centers	100	34	109	5	109
Day care centers, nurseries, and preschools	100	110	99	61	104
Other household services	**100**	**49**	**107**	**59**	**104**
Housekeeping services	100	23	111	53	104
Gardening, lawn care service	100	52	107	37	106
Water softening service	100	26	110	41	105
Nonclothing laundry and dry cleaning, sent out	100	138	95	45	105
Nonclothing laundry and dry cleaning, coin-operated	100	163	91	266	84
Termite/pest control services	100	52	107	56	104
Home security system service fee	100	137	95	61	104
Other home services	100	40	108	63	104
Termite/pest control products	100	92	102	29	108
Moving, storage, and freight express	100	41	108	71	103
Appliance repair, including service center	100	71	104	42	105
Reupholstering and furniture repair	100	25	110	35	106
Repairs/rentals of lawn/garden equipment, hand/power tools, etc.	100	52	107	30	107
Appliance rental	100	110	98	132	97
Rental of office equipment for nonbusiness use	100	68	104	60	104
Repair of misc. household equipment and furnishings	100	–	114	205	90
Repair of computer systems for nonbusiness use	100	127	96	55	104
Computer information services	100	54	106	51	105
Rental, installation of dishwashers, range hoods, and garbage disposals	100	–	113	80	100
HOUSEKEEPING SUPPLIES	**100**	**63**	**105**	**98**	**100**
Laundry and cleaning supplies	**100**	**96**	**101**	**131**	**97**
Soaps and detergents	100	100	100	153	95
Other laundry cleaning products	100	91	101	107	99
Other household products	**100**	**56**	**106**	**100**	**100**
Cleansing and toilet tissue, paper towels, and napkins	100	89	102	134	97
Miscellaneous household products	100	45	108	95	100
Lawn and garden supplies	100	36	109	73	103
Postage and stationery	**100**	**41**	**108**	**60**	**104**
Stationery, stationery supplies, giftwrap	100	35	109	53	104
Postage	100	45	108	69	103
Delivery services	100	111	99	12	108

	total consumer units	race		Hispanic origin	
		black	white and other	Hispanic	non-Hispanic
HOUSEHOLD FURNISHINGS AND EQUIPMENT	**100**	**57**	**106**	**84**	**101**
Household textiles	**100**	**54**	**106**	**83**	**102**
Bathroom linens	100	53	106	156	95
Bedroom linens	100	63	105	76	102
Kitchen and dining room linens	100	44	108	97	100
Curtains and draperies	100	57	106	51	105
Slipcovers and decorative pillows	100	4	113	62	104
Sewing materials for household items	100	25	110	44	105
Other linens	100	52	107	116	99
Furniture	**100**	**73**	**104**	**115**	**99**
Mattresses and springs	100	91	101	144	96
Other bedroom furniture	100	105	99	159	94
Sofas	100	71	104	104	100
Living room chairs	100	34	109	81	102
Living room tables	100	63	105	99	100
Kitchen and dining room furniture	100	72	104	127	97
Infants' furniture	100	117	98	116	98
Outdoor furniture	100	38	109	27	107
Wall units, cabinets, and other furniture	100	54	106	92	101
Floor coverings	**100**	**56**	**106**	**62**	**104**
Wall-to-wall carpet (renter)	100	143	94	59	104
Wall-to-wall carpet (replacement) (owner)	100	53	106	79	102
Room-size rugs and other floor coverings, nonpermanent	100	53	106	30	107
Major appliances	**100**	**57**	**106**	**88**	**101**
Dishwashers (built-in), garbage disposals, range hoods (renter)	100	85	102	40	106
Dishwashers (built-in), garbage disposals, range hoods (owner)	100	17	111	30	107
Refrigerators and freezers (renter)	100	154	93	105	99
Refrigerators and freezers (owner)	100	41	108	65	103
Washing machines (renter)	100	238	81	66	103
Washing machines (owner)	100	58	106	99	100
Clothes dryers (renter)	100	164	91	50	105
Clothes dryers (owner)	100	62	105	76	102
Cooking stoves, ovens (renter)	100	180	89	109	99
Cooking stoves, ovens (owner)	100	42	108	88	101
Microwave ovens (renter)	100	168	91	145	96
Microwave ovens (owner)	100	42	108	64	103
Portable dishwasher (renter)	100	–	113	–	106
Portable dishwasher (owner)	100	37	109	–	109
Window air conditioners (renter)	100	190	88	167	94
Window air conditioners (owner)	100	106	99	78	102
Electric floor-cleaning equipment	100	15	112	143	96
Sewing machines	100	36	109	184	92
Miscellaneous household appliances	100	50	107	87	101
Small appliances and misc. housewares	**100**	**41**	**108**	**76**	**102**
Housewares	100	34	109	74	102
Plastic dinnerware	100	46	108	119	99
China and other dinnerware	100	13	112	55	104
Flatware	100	44	107	61	104
Glassware	100	38	108	69	103
Silver serving pieces	100	53	107	44	106

	total consumer units	race		Hispanic origin	
		black	white and other	Hispanic	non-Hispanic
Other serving pieces	100	84	102	47	105
Nonelectric cookware	100	41	108	141	96
Tableware, nonelectric kitchenware	100	31	110	36	106
Small appliances	100	61	105	80	102
Small electric kitchen appliances	100	61	105	78	102
Portable heating and cooling equipment	100	60	105	87	101
Miscellaneous household equipment	**100**	**52**	**107**	**69**	**103**
Window coverings	100	69	104	19	108
Infants' equipment	100	44	108	128	97
Laundry and cleaning equipment	100	65	105	105	100
Outdoor equipment	100	30	110	43	105
Clocks	100	24	110	73	102
Lamps and lighting fixtures	100	68	104	55	104
Other household decorative items	100	58	106	54	104
Telephones and accessories	100	45	108	121	98
Lawn and garden equipment	100	29	110	29	107
Power tools	100	18	111	178	93
Office furniture for home use	100	60	105	59	104
Hand tools	100	28	110	67	103
Indoor plants and fresh flowers	100	48	107	51	105
Closet and storage items	100	32	109	84	101
Rental of furniture	100	141	94	195	91
Luggage	100	51	107	57	104
Computers and computer hardware, nonbusiness use	100	66	105	65	103
Computer software and accessories, nonbusiness use	100	46	107	78	102
Telephone answering devices	100	79	103	47	105
Calculators	100	96	100	73	102
Business equipment for home use	100	92	101	92	101
Other hardware	100	5	113	69	103
Smoke alarms (owner)	100	143	95	9	109
Smoke alarms (renter)	100	100	100	94	100
Other household appliances (owner)	100	48	107	100	100
Other household appliances (renter)	100	131	96	389	72
Miscellaneous household equipment and parts	100	40	108	121	98

Note: Other races include Asians, Native Americans, and Pacific Islanders. (–) means sample is too small to make a reliable estimate.
Source: Calculations by New Strategist based on the 2000 Consumer Expenditure Survey

Table 8.18 (Housing) Household Operations: Indexed per capita spending by race and Hispanic origin, 2000

(indexed average annual per capita spending of consumer units (CU) on household services, supplies, furnishings, and equipment, by race and Hispanic origin of consumer unit reference person, 2000; index definition: an index of 100 is the average for all consumer units; an index of 132 means that spending by consumer units in that group is 32 percent above the average for all consumer units; an index of 68 indicates spending that is 32 percent below the average for all consumer units)

	total consumer units	race black	race white and other	Hispanic origin Hispanic	Hispanic origin non-Hispanic
Per capita spending of CU, total	$15,218	$10,427	$15,762	$9,628	$16,062
Per capita spending of CU, index	100	69	104	63	106
Housing, per capita spending index	100	74	103	65	105
HOUSEHOLD SERVICES	100	63	104	50	107
Personal services	100	83	101	57	106
Babysitting and child care in your own home	100	32	109	134	96
Babysitting and child care in someone else's home	100	103	98	149	94
Care for elderly, invalids, handicapped, etc.	100	26	110	3	114
Adult day care centers	100	31	109	4	113
Day care centers, nurseries, and preschools	100	102	99	45	108
Other household services	100	46	107	43	108
Housekeeping services	100	21	111	39	109
Gardening, lawn care service	100	48	107	27	110
Water softening service	100	24	110	30	110
Nonclothing laundry and dry cleaning, sent out	100	128	95	33	109
Nonclothing laundry and dry cleaning, coin-operated	100	151	91	195	88
Termite/pest control services	100	48	107	41	109
Home security system service fee	100	127	95	45	108
Other home services	100	37	108	46	108
Termite/pest control products	100	85	102	21	113
Moving, storage, and freight express	100	38	108	52	107
Appliance repair, including service center	100	66	104	31	110
Reupholstering and furniture repair	100	23	110	25	111
Repairs/rentals of lawn/garden equipment, hand/power tools, etc.	100	48	107	22	111
Appliance rental	100	102	98	97	101
Rental of office equipment for nonbusiness use	100	63	104	44	108
Repair of misc. household equipment and furnishings	100	–	114	151	94
Repair of computer systems for nonbusiness use	100	118	96	40	109
Computer information services	100	50	106	37	109
Rental, installation of dishwashers, range hoods, and garbage disposals	100	–	113	59	104
HOUSEKEEPING SUPPLIES	100	58	105	72	104
Laundry and cleaning supplies	100	89	101	97	101
Soaps and detergents	100	93	100	112	99
Other laundry cleaning products	100	85	101	79	104
Other household products	100	52	106	74	104
Cleansing and toilet tissue, paper towels, and napkins	100	82	102	99	101
Miscellaneous household products	100	42	108	70	105
Lawn and garden supplies	100	33	109	54	107
Postage and stationery	100	38	108	44	108
Stationery, stationery supplies, giftwrap	100	32	109	39	109
Postage	100	42	108	51	107
Delivery services	100	102	99	9	112

	total consumer units	race		Hispanic origin	
		black	white and other	Hispanic	non-Hispanic
HOUSEHOLD FURNISHINGS AND EQUIPMENT	**100**	**53**	**106**	**62**	**106**
Household textiles	**100**	**50**	**106**	**61**	**106**
Bathroom linens	100	49	106	115	99
Bedroom linens	100	59	105	56	107
Kitchen and dining room linens	100	41	108	71	105
Curtains and draperies	100	53	106	38	109
Slipcovers and decorative pillows	100	4	113	46	108
Sewing materials for household items	100	23	110	33	110
Other linens	100	48	107	86	103
Furniture	**100**	**67**	**104**	**84**	**103**
Mattresses and springs	100	84	101	106	100
Other bedroom furniture	100	97	99	117	98
Sofas	100	66	104	76	104
Living room chairs	100	31	109	59	106
Living room tables	100	58	105	73	104
Kitchen and dining room furniture	100	66	104	93	102
Infants' furniture	100	109	98	86	102
Outdoor furniture	100	35	109	20	111
Wall units, cabinets, and other furniture	100	50	106	68	105
Floor coverings	**100**	**52**	**106**	**45**	**108**
Wall-to-wall carpet (renter)	100	133	94	44	108
Wall-to-wall carpet (replacement) (owner)	100	49	106	58	106
Room-size rugs and other floor coverings, nonpermanent	100	49	106	22	111
Major appliances	**100**	**53**	**106**	**65**	**105**
Dishwashers (built-in), garbage disposals, range hoods (renter)	100	79	102	30	110
Dishwashers (built-in), garbage disposals, range hoods (owner)	100	16	111	22	111
Refrigerators and freezers (renter)	100	142	93	77	104
Refrigerators and freezers (owner)	100	38	108	48	108
Washing machines (renter)	100	220	81	48	107
Washing machines (owner)	100	53	106	73	104
Clothes dryers (renter)	100	152	91	37	109
Clothes dryers (owner)	100	57	105	56	107
Cooking stoves, ovens (renter)	100	167	89	80	103
Cooking stoves, ovens (owner)	100	39	108	65	105
Microwave ovens (renter)	100	155	91	107	100
Microwave ovens (owner)	100	39	108	47	108
Portable dishwasher (renter)	100	–	113	–	111
Portable dishwasher (owner)	100	34	109	–	114
Window air conditioners (renter)	100	176	88	123	97
Window air conditioners (owner)	100	98	99	58	106
Electric floor-cleaning equipment	100	14	112	105	100
Sewing machines	100	34	109	136	96
Miscellaneous household appliances	100	46	107	64	105
Small appliances and misc. housewares	**100**	**38**	**108**	**56**	**107**
Housewares	100	32	109	54	107
Plastic dinnerware	100	43	108	87	103
China and other dinnerware	100	12	112	40	109
Flatware	100	41	107	45	108
Glassware	100	36	108	51	107
Silver serving pieces	100	49	107	33	110

	total consumer units	race		Hispanic origin	
		black	white and other	Hispanic	non-Hispanic
Other serving pieces	100	78	102	34	109
Nonelectric cookware	100	38	108	104	100
Tableware, nonelectric kitchenware	100	28	110	26	110
Small appliances	100	56	105	59	106
Small electric kitchen appliances	100	56	105	57	106
Portable heating and cooling equipment	100	56	105	64	105
Miscellaneous household equipment	**100**	**48**	**107**	**51**	**107**
Window coverings	100	64	104	14	112
Infants' equipment	100	40	108	94	101
Laundry and cleaning equipment	100	60	105	77	104
Outdoor equipment	100	28	110	32	110
Clocks	100	22	110	54	107
Lamps and lighting fixtures	100	63	104	41	109
Other household decorative items	100	53	106	40	109
Telephones and accessories	100	41	108	89	102
Lawn and garden equipment	100	27	110	21	111
Power tools	100	16	111	131	97
Office furniture for home use	100	56	105	43	108
Hand tools	100	26	110	49	107
Indoor plants and fresh flowers	100	44	107	37	109
Closet and storage items	100	30	109	62	106
Rental of furniture	100	131	94	143	95
Luggage	100	48	107	42	108
Computers and computer hardware, nonbusiness use	100	61	105	48	108
Computer software and accessories, nonbusiness use	100	43	107	57	106
Telephone answering devices	100	73	103	35	109
Calculators	100	89	100	54	107
Business equipment for home use	100	86	101	68	105
Other hardware	100	5	113	51	107
Smoke alarms (owner)	100	132	95	7	113
Smoke alarms (renter)	100	93	100	69	104
Other household appliances (owner)	100	45	107	74	104
Other household appliances (renter)	100	121	96	286	75
Miscellaneous household equipment and parts	100	37	108	89	102

Note: Per capita indexes account for household size and show how much each person in a particular household demographic segment spends relative to a person in the average household. Other races include Asians, Native Americans, and Pacific Islanders. (–) means sample is too small to make a reliable estimate.
Source: Calculations by New Strategist based on the 2000 Consumer Expenditure Survey

Table 8.19 (Housing) Household Operations: Total spending by race and Hispanic origin, 2000

(total annual spending on household services, supplies, furnishings, and equipment, by consumer unit race and Hispanic origin groups, 2000; numbers in thousands)

	total consumer units	race		Hispanic origin	
		black	white and other	Hispanic	non-Hispanic
Number of consumer units	109,367	13,230	96,137	9,473	99,894
Total spending of all consumer units	$4,160,831,424	$372,454,135	$3,788,393,849	$310,098,181	$3,850,804,816
Housing, total spending	1,347,238,483	131,050,294	1,216,191,694	102,780,250	1,244,443,490
HOUSEHOLD SERVICES	**$74,848,587**	**$6,194,551**	**$68,654,316**	**$4,409,492**	**$70,442,252**
Personal services	**35,675,515**	**3,864,483**	**31,811,733**	**2,412,868**	**33,262,704**
Babysitting and child care in your own home	3,522,711	147,779	3,375,370	554,076	2,968,850
Babysitting and child care in someone else's home	3,564,271	480,911	3,084,075	623,608	2,940,879
Care for elderly, invalids, handicapped, etc.	5,509,909	186,940	5,323,106	20,462	5,489,175
Adult day care centers	284,354	11,642	273,029	1,326	282,700
Day care centers, nurseries, and preschools	22,794,270	3,037,211	19,757,115	1,213,397	21,580,101
Other household services	**39,173,072**	**2,330,068**	**36,843,544**	**1,996,624**	**37,178,549**
Housekeeping services	9,640,701	264,865	9,375,280	439,168	9,201,236
Gardening, lawn care service	8,559,061	540,049	8,018,787	276,801	8,282,212
Water softening service	340,131	10,849	328,789	12,125	327,652
Nonclothing laundry and dry cleaning, sent out	161,863	26,989	134,592	6,252	154,836
Nonclothing laundry and dry cleaning, coin-operated	507,463	100,151	407,621	116,707	391,584
Termite/pest control services	1,046,642	65,356	981,559	50,870	995,943
Home security system service fee	2,041,882	338,556	1,703,548	107,424	1,934,947
Other home services	1,561,761	75,940	1,485,317	84,689	1,476,433
Termite/pest control products	53,590	5,954	48,069	1,326	52,944
Moving, storage, and freight express	3,546,772	175,430	3,371,525	217,216	3,329,467
Appliance repair, including service center	1,375,837	118,938	1,256,511	49,828	1,325,593
Reupholstering and furniture repair	1,012,738	31,091	982,520	30,408	982,957
Repairs/rentals of lawn/garden equipment, hand/power tools, etc.	542,460	33,869	508,565	13,925	528,439
Appliance rental	412,314	54,905	356,668	47,081	364,613
Rental of office equipment for nonbusiness use	57,965	4,763	52,875	3,031	54,942
Repair of misc. household equipment and furnishings	1,282,875	–	1,283,429	227,920	1,057,877
Repair of computer systems for nonbusiness use	300,759	46,173	254,763	14,304	286,696
Computer information services	6,710,759	436,193	6,274,862	296,221	6,414,194
Rental, installation of dishwashers, range hoods, and garbage disposals	16,405	–	16,343	1,137	14,984
HOUSEKEEPING SUPPLIES	**52,749,891**	**4,004,060**	**48,747,227**	**4,488,023**	**48,259,790**
Laundry and cleaning supplies	**14,300,829**	**1,663,673**	**12,637,209**	**1,626,325**	**12,682,542**
Soaps and detergents	7,575,852	920,543	6,655,565	1,003,380	6,579,019
Other laundry cleaning products	6,724,977	743,129	5,982,606	622,944	6,103,523
Other household products	**24,706,005**	**1,662,482**	**23,044,039**	**2,146,298**	**22,560,061**
Cleansing and toilet tissue, paper towels, and napkins	7,486,171	806,369	6,679,599	871,705	6,618,976
Miscellaneous household products	9,895,526	536,741	9,358,937	811,457	9,083,361
Lawn and garden supplies	7,324,308	319,505	7,005,503	463,135	6,857,723
Postage and stationery	**13,743,057**	**677,773**	**13,065,980**	**715,306**	**13,018,186**
Stationery, stationery supplies, giftwrap	6,961,210	294,632	6,667,101	317,724	6,637,956
Postage	6,627,640	362,502	6,265,248	395,971	6,228,391
Delivery services	154,207	20,639	133,630	1,610	151,839

		race		Hispanic origin	
	total consumer units	black	white and other	Hispanic	non-Hispanic
HOUSEHOLD FURNISHINGS AND EQUIPMENT	**$169,369,017**	**$11,729,983**	**$157,641,607**	**$12,346,445**	**$157,008,395**
Household textiles	**11,646,492**	**754,110**	**10,892,322**	**840,255**	**10,805,534**
Bathroom linens	1,919,391	123,039	1,796,801	259,750	1,662,236
Bedroom linens	4,869,019	373,218	4,496,327	318,672	4,548,174
Kitchen and dining room linens	1,018,207	54,772	963,293	85,257	933,010
Curtains and draperies	2,303,269	158,628	2,144,816	102,687	2,200,665
Slipcovers and decorative pillows	300,759	1,588	299,947	16,199	284,698
Sewing materials for household items	1,066,328	32,281	1,034,434	40,923	1,025,911
Other linens	167,332	10,584	156,703	16,862	150,840
Furniture	**42,722,031**	**3,747,530**	**38,974,901**	**4,238,220**	**38,484,164**
Mattresses and springs	5,784,421	637,686	5,146,214	720,422	5,063,627
Other bedroom furniture	7,558,353	961,027	6,597,882	1,037,957	6,521,080
Sofas	9,750,068	838,253	8,911,900	877,579	8,872,585
Living room chairs	4,794,649	195,539	4,599,194	335,344	4,459,268
Living room tables	1,880,019	142,355	1,738,157	160,852	1,719,176
Kitchen and dining room furniture	5,081,191	440,824	4,640,533	558,623	4,523,200
Infants' furniture	680,263	96,447	583,552	68,585	611,351
Outdoor furniture	1,658,004	75,279	1,582,415	38,271	1,619,282
Wall units, cabinets, and other furniture	5,535,064	360,253	5,175,055	440,779	5,094,594
Floor coverings	**4,853,707**	**329,162**	**4,525,169**	**259,560**	**4,594,125**
Wall-to-wall carpet (renter)	150,926	26,195	124,978	7,768	142,848
Wall-to-wall carpet (replacement) (owner)	3,038,215	196,333	2,842,771	208,122	2,830,996
Room-size rugs and other floor coverings, nonpermanent	1,664,566	106,502	1,557,419	43,576	1,620,281
Major appliances	**20,665,988**	**1,434,264**	**19,232,207**	**1,574,128**	**19,093,739**
Dishwashers (built-in), garbage disposals, range hoods (renter)	95,149	9,790	85,562	3,316	91,902
Dishwashers (built-in), garbage disposals, range hoods (owner)	1,542,075	32,017	1,509,351	39,976	1,501,407
Refrigerators and freezers (renter)	803,847	149,499	653,732	73,321	730,225
Refrigerators and freezers (owner)	4,849,333	237,611	4,611,692	272,159	4,577,143
Washing machines (renter)	523,868	150,690	373,012	29,840	493,476
Washing machines (owner)	2,026,571	141,429	1,885,247	173,545	1,853,034
Clothes dryers (renter)	367,473	72,897	294,179	16,009	351,627
Clothes dryers (owner)	1,314,591	97,902	1,216,133	86,488	1,227,697
Cooking stoves, ovens (renter)	306,228	66,679	240,343	28,798	277,705
Cooking stoves, ovens (owner)	2,619,340	132,168	2,487,064	200,354	2,418,434
Microwave ovens (renter)	260,293	52,788	207,656	32,682	227,758
Microwave ovens (owner)	804,941	41,013	763,328	44,618	760,193
Portable dishwasher (renter)	17,499	–	17,305	–	16,982
Portable dishwasher (owner)	83,119	3,704	79,794	–	82,912
Window air conditioners (renter)	202,329	46,437	155,742	29,272	172,817
Window air conditioners (owner)	527,149	67,341	459,535	35,808	491,478
Electric floor-cleaning equipment	2,841,355	51,465	2,789,896	352,111	2,491,356
Sewing machines	522,774	23,020	499,912	83,457	439,534
Miscellaneous household appliances	959,149	57,683	901,765	72,279	886,060
Small appliances and misc. housewares	**9,555,395**	**475,089**	**9,081,101**	**626,071**	**8,926,528**
Housewares	7,094,637	294,500	6,800,731	455,272	6,635,958
Plastic dinnerware	158,582	8,864	149,974	16,294	142,848
China and other dinnerware	1,250,065	20,374	1,229,592	59,396	1,189,738
Flatware	394,815	21,036	373,012	20,746	373,604
Glassware	877,123	40,748	836,392	52,196	824,126
Silver serving pieces	257,012	16,405	241,304	9,852	247,737

	total consumer units	race		Hispanic origin	
		black	white and other	Hispanic	non-Hispanic
Other serving pieces	$156,395	$15,876	$140,360	$6,347	$149,841
Nonelectric cookware	1,823,148	90,229	1,733,350	222,994	1,602,300
Tableware, nonelectric kitchenware	2,176,403	80,835	2,095,787	67,353	2,106,764
Small appliances	2,461,851	180,590	2,280,370	170,893	2,290,569
Small electric kitchen appliances	1,863,614	136,931	1,726,621	125,801	1,737,157
Portable heating and cooling equipment	598,237	43,659	554,710	44,997	553,413
Miscellaneous household equipment	**79,926,497**	**4,989,827**	**74,937,830**	**4,808,211**	**75,104,305**
Window coverings	1,423,958	118,276	1,305,540	23,683	1,400,514
Infants' equipment	876,030	46,173	829,662	97,288	779,173
Laundry and cleaning equipment	1,102,419	86,524	1,016,168	100,130	1,002,936
Outdoor equipment	2,011,259	72,633	1,939,083	74,931	1,934,947
Clocks	1,521,295	44,453	1,476,664	96,814	1,423,490
Lamps and lighting fixtures	1,181,164	96,844	1,084,425	56,649	1,124,806
Other household decorative items	19,390,769	1,353,297	18,038,185	907,229	18,468,403
Telephones and accessories	3,192,423	172,255	3,019,663	334,965	2,857,967
Lawn and garden equipment	5,120,563	179,531	4,941,442	127,980	4,992,702
Power tools	2,331,704	49,480	2,282,292	359,690	1,974,904
Office furniture for home use	1,495,047	108,486	1,386,296	75,879	1,419,494
Hand tools	794,004	27,122	766,212	46,228	747,207
Indoor plants and fresh flowers	6,235,013	359,195	5,875,893	274,622	5,960,675
Closet and storage items	878,217	33,869	844,083	64,227	813,137
Rental of furniture	341,225	58,212	282,643	57,501	283,699
Luggage	909,933	56,624	853,697	44,902	865,082
Computers and computer hardware, nonbusiness use	20,542,404	1,644,754	18,897,650	1,162,053	19,380,435
Computer software and accessories, nonbusiness use	1,912,829	106,634	1,806,414	129,401	1,783,108
Telephone answering devices	215,453	20,639	194,197	8,810	206,781
Calculators	179,362	20,903	157,665	11,368	167,822
Business equipment for home use	200,142	22,359	177,853	15,915	183,805
Other hardware	2,634,651	17,199	2,617,811	157,347	2,476,372
Smoke alarms (owner)	61,246	10,584	50,953	474	60,935
Smoke alarms (renter)	17,499	2,117	15,382	1,421	15,983
Other household appliances (owner)	830,096	48,422	781,594	72,090	758,195
Other household appliances (renter)	133,428	21,168	112,480	44,902	87,907
Miscellaneous household equipment and parts	4,394,366	212,209	4,181,960	461,903	3,933,826

Note: Other races include Asians, Native Americans, and Pacific Islanders. Numbers may not add to total because of rounding. (–) means sample is too small to make a reliable estimate.
Source: Calculations by New Strategist based on the 2000 Consumer Expenditure Survey

Table 8.20 (Housing) Household Operations: Market shares by race and Hispanic origin, 2000

(percentage of total annual spending on household services, supplies, furnishings, and equipment accounted for by consumer unit race and Hispanic origin groups, 2000)

	total consumer units	race		Hispanic origin	
		black	white and other	Hispanic	non-Hispanic
Share of total consumer units	100.0%	12.1%	87.9%	8.7%	91.3%
Share of total before-tax income	100.0	8.8	91.1	6.8	93.4
Share of total spending	100.0	9.0	91.0	7.5	92.5
Share of housing spending	100.0	9.7	90.3	7.6	92.4
HOUSEHOLD SERVICES	**100.0%**	**8.3%**	**91.7%**	**5.9%**	**94.1%**
Personal services	**100.0**	**10.8**	**89.2**	**6.8**	**93.2**
Babysitting and child care in your own home	100.0	4.2	95.8	15.7	84.3
Babysitting and child care in someone else's home	100.0	13.5	86.5	17.5	82.5
Care for elderly, invalids, handicapped, etc.	100.0	3.4	96.6	0.4	99.6
Adult day care centers	100.0	4.1	96.0	0.5	99.4
Day care centers, nurseries, and preschools	100.0	13.3	86.7	5.3	94.7
Other household services	**100.0**	**5.9**	**94.1**	**5.1**	**94.9**
Housekeeping services	100.0	2.7	97.2	4.6	95.4
Gardening, lawn care service	100.0	6.3	93.7	3.2	96.8
Water softening service	100.0	3.2	96.7	3.6	96.3
Nonclothing laundry and dry cleaning, sent out	100.0	16.7	83.2	3.9	95.7
Nonclothing laundry and dry cleaning, coin-operated	100.0	19.7	80.3	23.0	77.2
Termite/pest control services	100.0	6.2	93.8	4.9	95.2
Home security system service fee	100.0	16.6	83.4	5.3	94.8
Other home services	100.0	4.9	95.1	5.4	94.5
Termite/pest control products	100.0	11.1	89.7	2.5	98.8
Moving, storage, and freight express	100.0	4.9	95.1	6.1	93.9
Appliance repair, including service center	100.0	8.6	91.3	3.6	96.3
Reupholstering and furniture repair	100.0	3.1	97.0	3.0	97.1
Repairs/rentals of lawn/garden equipment, hand/power tools, etc.	100.0	6.2	93.8	2.6	97.4
Appliance rental	100.0	13.3	86.5	11.4	88.4
Rental of office equipment for nonbusiness use	100.0	8.2	91.2	5.2	94.8
Repair of misc. household equipment and furnishings	100.0	–	100.0	17.8	82.5
Repair of computer systems for nonbusiness use	100.0	15.4	84.7	4.8	95.3
Computer information services	100.0	6.5	93.5	4.4	95.6
Rental, installation of dishwashers, range hoods, and garbage disposals	100.0	–	99.6	6.9	91.3
HOUSEKEEPING SUPPLIES	**100.0**	**7.6**	**92.4**	**8.5**	**91.5**
Laundry and cleaning supplies	**100.0**	**11.6**	**88.4**	**11.4**	**88.7**
Soaps and detergents	100.0	12.2	87.9	13.2	86.8
Other laundry cleaning products	100.0	11.1	89.0	9.3	90.8
Other household products	**100.0**	**6.7**	**93.3**	**8.7**	**91.3**
Cleansing and toilet tissue, paper towels, and napkins	100.0	10.8	89.2	11.6	88.4
Miscellaneous household products	100.0	5.4	94.6	8.2	91.8
Lawn and garden supplies	100.0	4.4	95.6	6.3	93.6
Postage and stationery	**100.0**	**4.9**	**95.1**	**5.2**	**94.7**
Stationery, stationery supplies, giftwrap	100.0	4.2	95.8	4.6	95.4
Postage	100.0	5.5	94.5	6.0	94.0
Delivery services	100.0	13.4	86.7	1.0	98.5

	total consumer units	race		Hispanic origin	
		black	white and other	Hispanic	non-Hispanic
HOUSEHOLD FURNISHINGS AND EQUIPMENT	100.0%	6.9%	93.1%	7.3%	92.7%
Household textiles	100.0	6.5	93.5	7.2	92.8
Bathroom linens	100.0	6.4	93.6	13.5	86.6
Bedroom linens	100.0	7.7	92.3	6.5	93.4
Kitchen and dining room linens	100.0	5.4	94.6	8.4	91.6
Curtains and draperies	100.0	6.9	93.1	4.5	95.5
Slipcovers and decorative pillows	100.0	0.5	99.7	5.4	94.7
Sewing materials for household items	100.0	3.0	97.0	3.8	96.2
Other linens	100.0	6.3	93.6	10.1	90.1
Furniture	100.0	8.8	91.2	9.9	90.1
Mattresses and springs	100.0	11.0	89.0	12.5	87.5
Other bedroom furniture	100.0	12.7	87.3	13.7	86.3
Sofas	100.0	8.6	91.4	9.0	91.0
Living room chairs	100.0	4.1	95.9	7.0	93.0
Living room tables	100.0	7.6	92.5	8.6	91.4
Kitchen and dining room furniture	100.0	8.7	91.3	11.0	89.0
Infants' furniture	100.0	14.2	85.8	10.1	89.9
Outdoor furniture	100.0	4.5	95.4	2.3	97.7
Wall units, cabinets, and other furniture	100.0	6.5	93.5	8.0	92.0
Floor coverings	100.0	6.8	93.2	5.3	94.7
Wall-to-wall carpet (renter)	100.0	17.4	82.8	5.1	94.6
Wall-to-wall carpet (replacement) (owner)	100.0	6.5	93.6	6.9	93.2
Room-size rugs and other floor coverings, nonpermanent	100.0	6.4	93.6	2.6	97.3
Major appliances	100.0	6.9	93.1	7.6	92.4
Dishwashers (built-in), garbage disposals, range hoods (renter)	100.0	10.3	89.9	3.5	96.6
Dishwashers (built-in), garbage disposals, range hoods (owner)	100.0	2.1	97.9	2.6	97.4
Refrigerators and freezers (renter)	100.0	18.6	81.3	9.1	90.8
Refrigerators and freezers (owner)	100.0	4.9	95.1	5.6	94.4
Washing machines (renter)	100.0	28.8	71.2	5.7	94.2
Washing machines (owner)	100.0	7.0	93.0	8.6	91.4
Clothes dryers (renter)	100.0	19.8	80.1	4.4	95.7
Clothes dryers (owner)	100.0	7.4	92.5	6.6	93.4
Cooking stoves, ovens (renter)	100.0	21.8	78.5	9.4	90.7
Cooking stoves, ovens (owner)	100.0	5.0	95.0	7.6	92.3
Microwave ovens (renter)	100.0	20.3	79.8	12.6	87.5
Microwave ovens (owner)	100.0	5.1	94.8	5.5	94.4
Portable dishwasher (renter)	100.0	–	98.9	–	97.0
Portable dishwasher (owner)	100.0	4.5	96.0	–	99.8
Window air conditioners (renter)	100.0	23.0	77.0	14.5	85.4
Window air conditioners (owner)	100.0	12.8	87.2	6.8	93.2
Electric floor-cleaning equipment	100.0	1.8	98.2	12.4	87.7
Sewing machines	100.0	4.4	95.6	16.0	84.1
Miscellaneous household appliances	100.0	6.0	94.0	7.5	92.4
Small appliances and misc. housewares	100.0	5.0	95.0	6.6	93.4
Housewares	100.0	4.2	95.9	6.4	93.5
Plastic dinnerware	100.0	5.6	94.6	10.3	90.1
China and other dinnerware	100.0	1.6	98.4	4.8	95.2
Flatware	100.0	5.3	94.5	5.3	94.6
Glassware	100.0	4.6	95.4	6.0	94.0
Silver serving pieces	100.0	6.4	93.9	3.8	96.4

	total consumer units	race		Hispanic origin	
		black	white and other	Hispanic	non-Hispanic
Other serving pieces	100.0%	10.2%	89.7%	4.1%	95.8%
Nonelectric cookware	100.0	4.9	95.1	12.2	87.9
Tableware, nonelectric kitchenware	100.0	3.7	96.3	3.1	96.8
Small appliances	100.0	7.3	92.6	6.9	93.0
Small electric kitchen appliances	100.0	7.3	92.6	6.8	93.2
Portable heating and cooling equipment	100.0	7.3	92.7	7.5	92.5
Miscellaneous household equipment	**100.0**	**6.2**	**93.8**	**6.0**	**94.0**
Window coverings	100.0	8.3	91.7	1.7	98.4
Infants' equipment	100.0	5.3	94.7	11.1	88.9
Laundry and cleaning equipment	100.0	7.8	92.2	9.1	91.0
Outdoor equipment	100.0	3.6	96.4	3.7	96.2
Clocks	100.0	2.9	97.1	6.4	93.6
Lamps and lighting fixtures	100.0	8.2	91.8	4.8	95.2
Other household decorative items	100.0	7.0	93.0	4.7	95.2
Telephones and accessories	100.0	5.4	94.6	10.5	89.5
Lawn and garden equipment	100.0	3.5	96.5	2.5	97.5
Power tools	100.0	2.1	97.9	15.4	84.7
Office furniture for home use	100.0	7.3	92.7	5.1	94.9
Hand tools	100.0	3.4	96.5	5.8	94.1
Indoor plants and fresh flowers	100.0	5.8	94.2	4.4	95.6
Closet and storage items	100.0	3.9	96.1	7.3	92.6
Rental of furniture	100.0	17.1	82.8	16.9	83.1
Luggage	100.0	6.2	93.8	4.9	95.1
Computers and computer hardware, nonbusiness use	100.0	8.0	92.0	5.7	94.3
Computer software and accessories, nonbusiness use	100.0	5.6	94.4	6.8	93.2
Telephone answering devices	100.0	9.6	90.1	4.1	96.0
Calculators	100.0	11.7	87.9	6.3	93.6
Business equipment for home use	100.0	11.2	88.9	8.0	91.8
Other hardware	100.0	0.7	99.4	6.0	94.0
Smoke alarms (owner)	100.0	17.3	83.2	0.8	99.5
Smoke alarms (renter)	100.0	12.1	87.9	8.1	91.3
Other household appliances (owner)	100.0	5.8	94.2	8.7	91.3
Other household appliances (renter)	100.0	15.9	84.3	33.7	65.9
Miscellaneous household equipment and parts	100.0	4.8	95.2	10.5	89.5

Note: Other races include Asians, Native Americans, and Pacific Islanders. Numbers may not add to total because of rounding. (–) means sample is too small to make a reliable estimate.
Source: Calculations by New Strategist based on the 2000 Consumer Expenditure Survey

Table 8.21 (Housing) Household Operations: Average spending by region, 2000

(average annual spending of consumer units (CU) on household services, supplies, furnishings, and equipment, by region in which consumer unit lives, 2000)

	total consumer units	Northeast	Midwest	South	West
Number of consumer units (in thousands, add 000)	109,367	20,994	25,717	38,245	24,410
Average number of persons per CU	2.5	2.5	2.5	2.5	2.6
Average before-tax income of CU	$44,649.00	$47,439.00	$44,377.00	$41,984.00	$46,670.00
Average spending of CU, total	38,044.67	38,901.91	39,212.70	34,707.07	41,328.19
Housing, average spending	12,318.51	13,504.65	11,961.22	10,854.51	13,972.45
HOUSEHOLD SERVICES	**$684.38**	**$643.00**	**$670.28**	**$645.05**	**$796.05**
Personal services	**326.20**	**312.13**	**368.96**	**283.62**	**359.99**
Babysitting and child care in your own home	32.21	52.77	32.21	17.70	37.28
Babysitting and child care in someone else's home	32.59	25.84	50.96	28.25	25.87
Care for elderly, invalids, handicapped, etc.	50.38	32.09	57.35	37.81	78.47
Adult day care centers	2.60	0.71	2.33	4.24	1.92
Day care centers, nurseries, and preschools	208.42	200.72	226.11	195.62	216.45
Other household services	**358.18**	**330.86**	**301.32**	**361.44**	**436.06**
Housekeeping services	88.15	94.45	66.29	82.30	114.92
Gardening, lawn care service	78.26	79.75	58.83	79.47	95.54
Water softening service	3.11	1.48	4.49	2.77	3.57
Nonclothing laundry and dry cleaning, sent out	1.48	1.51	1.28	0.93	2.52
Nonclothing laundry and dry cleaning, coin-operated	4.64	5.95	4.43	3.87	4.96
Termite/pest control services	9.57	5.42	3.54	13.07	14.01
Home security system service fee	18.67	15.52	14.11	23.38	18.82
Other home services	14.28	13.90	11.24	10.84	23.19
Termite/pest control products	0.49	0.46	0.23	0.55	0.71
Moving, storage, and freight express	32.43	13.00	36.59	28.61	50.75
Appliance repair, including service center	12.58	14.11	12.85	11.58	12.53
Reupholstering and furniture repair	9.26	10.88	9.40	6.04	12.80
Repairs/rentals of lawn/garden equipment, hand/power tools, etc.	4.96	5.11	6.07	4.33	4.66
Appliance rental	3.77	2.71	4.83	3.59	3.83
Rental of office equipment for nonbusiness use	0.53	0.46	0.91	0.50	0.23
Repair of misc. household equipment and furnishings	11.73	2.14	1.31	31.09	0.23
Repair of computer systems for nonbusiness use	2.75	1.97	2.73	2.43	3.96
Computer information services	61.36	62.05	62.18	55.77	68.66
Rental, installation of dishwashers, range hoods, and garbage disposals	0.15	–	–	0.32	0.17
HOUSEKEEPING SUPPLIES	**482.32**	**529.75**	**514.44**	**440.46**	**472.36**
Laundry and cleaning supplies	**130.76**	**146.37**	**133.04**	**125.89**	**121.83**
Soaps and detergents	69.27	69.59	70.61	67.97	69.66
Other laundry cleaning products	61.49	76.78	62.43	57.92	52.18
Other household products	**225.90**	**244.50**	**238.48**	**213.27**	**215.84**
Cleansing and toilet tissue, paper towels, and napkins	68.45	77.81	70.91	61.77	68.05
Miscellaneous household products	90.48	99.55	98.01	78.88	92.94
Lawn and garden supplies	66.97	67.14	69.56	72.61	54.86
Postage and stationery	**125.66**	**138.87**	**142.91**	**101.30**	**134.68**
Stationery, stationery supplies, giftwrap	63.65	60.80	86.85	46.88	68.80
Postage	60.60	76.64	55.29	52.82	64.13
Delivery services	1.41	1.44	0.77	1.60	1.75

	total consumer units	Northeast	Midwest	South	West
HOUSEHOLD FURNISHINGS AND EQUIPMENT	**$1,548.63**	**$1,540.43**	**$1,630.88**	**$1,333.65**	**$1,811.16**
Household textiles	**106.49**	**133.77**	**116.53**	**84.64**	**106.09**
Bathroom linens	17.55	17.76	17.37	14.34	22.79
Bedroom linens	44.52	62.61	43.47	35.76	43.20
Kitchen and dining room linens	9.31	11.65	9.58	6.93	10.72
Curtains and draperies	21.06	26.74	32.50	15.77	12.41
Slipcovers and decorative pillows	2.75	5.39	1.49	2.70	1.77
Sewing materials for household items	9.75	8.01	10.98	7.93	12.81
Other linens	1.53	1.59	1.14	1.21	2.40
Furniture	**390.63**	**387.53**	**378.00**	**338.05**	**488.97**
Mattresses and springs	52.89	36.90	55.12	49.88	69.01
Other bedroom furniture	69.11	64.95	62.29	61.10	92.43
Sofas	89.15	84.70	95.43	73.82	110.40
Living room chairs	43.84	37.33	45.59	43.33	48.39
Living room tables	17.19	22.51	16.73	14.59	17.20
Kitchen and dining room furniture	46.46	53.95	47.50	34.68	57.39
Infants' furniture	6.22	6.39	5.43	6.19	6.94
Outdoor furniture	15.16	21.35	13.09	10.81	18.83
Wall units, cabinets, and other furniture	50.61	59.46	36.84	43.66	68.38
Floor coverings	**44.38**	**47.06**	**53.66**	**41.17**	**37.34**
Wall-to-wall carpet (renter)	1.38	1.96	2.80	0.92	0.11
Wall-to-wall carpet (replacement) (owner)	27.78	23.68	38.59	28.38	18.99
Room-size rugs and other floor coverings, nonpermanent	15.22	21.41	12.27	11.86	18.25
Major appliances	**188.96**	**179.02**	**198.00**	**168.38**	**221.08**
Dishwashers (built-in), garbage disposals, range hoods (renter)	0.87	0.27	0.46	1.63	0.65
Dishwashers (built-in), garbage disposals, range hoods (owner)	14.10	17.24	14.68	10.21	16.86
Refrigerators and freezers (renter)	7.35	4.94	7.66	6.24	10.84
Refrigerators and freezers (owner)	44.34	49.88	43.09	41.26	45.72
Washing machines (renter)	4.79	2.55	4.67	5.36	5.95
Washing machines (owner)	18.53	14.06	18.37	17.27	24.53
Clothes dryers (renter)	3.36	1.98	2.32	3.76	5.01
Clothes dryers (owner)	12.02	10.43	12.13	9.92	16.56
Cooking stoves, ovens (renter)	2.80	2.01	2.72	4.21	1.37
Cooking stoves, ovens (owner)	23.95	25.11	25.87	21.30	25.07
Microwave ovens (renter)	2.38	1.90	2.50	2.00	3.26
Microwave ovens (owner)	7.36	7.13	8.62	6.36	7.77
Portable dishwasher (renter)	0.16	0.02	0.24	0.28	0.00
Portable dishwasher (owner)	0.76	0.65	1.27	0.46	0.79
Window air conditioners (renter)	1.85	4.82	1.79	1.05	0.60
Window air conditioners (owner)	4.82	6.35	4.45	6.03	2.00
Electric floor-cleaning equipment	25.98	18.52	38.90	20.13	28.60
Sewing machines	4.78	5.24	1.54	2.05	12.06
Miscellaneous household appliances	8.77	5.93	6.72	8.86	13.43
Small appliances and misc. housewares	**87.37**	**91.17**	**102.58**	**71.53**	**93.17**
Housewares	64.87	70.23	78.71	52.70	64.99
Plastic dinnerware	1.45	1.22	1.43	1.20	2.08
China and other dinnerware	11.43	14.87	15.96	7.44	9.91
Flatware	3.61	6.22	3.70	2.29	3.33
Glassware	8.02	5.33	13.67	5.67	8.29
Silver serving pieces	2.35	1.47	2.78	2.49	2.50

	total consumer units	Northeast	Midwest	South	West
Other serving pieces	$1.43	$1.82	$1.58	$0.92	$1.73
Nonelectric cookware	16.67	21.30	18.91	12.97	16.04
Tableware, nonelectric kitchenware	19.90	18.01	20.69	19.73	21.10
Small appliances	22.51	20.94	23.88	18.82	28.18
Small electric kitchen appliances	17.04	16.47	17.37	13.75	22.31
Portable heating and cooling equipment	5.47	4.47	6.50	5.07	5.87
Miscellaneous household equipment	**730.81**	**701.88**	**782.10**	**629.89**	**864.51**
Window coverings	13.02	10.25	11.12	10.91	20.71
Infants' equipment	8.01	8.49	9.54	4.58	11.49
Laundry and cleaning equipment	10.08	10.03	10.51	8.29	12.60
Outdoor equipment	18.39	26.75	23.43	15.80	9.52
Clocks	13.91	32.08	5.71	9.20	13.52
Lamps and lighting fixtures	10.80	12.24	13.81	8.59	9.85
Other household decorative items	177.30	115.68	170.92	163.47	263.51
Telephones and accessories	29.19	26.68	28.80	20.79	45.57
Lawn and garden equipment	46.82	38.54	54.39	60.73	24.18
Power tools	21.32	10.71	36.99	19.37	17.55
Office furniture for home use	13.67	9.52	15.67	14.07	14.50
Hand tools	7.26	5.81	8.65	5.38	9.98
Indoor plants and fresh flowers	57.01	62.99	68.22	41.81	63.89
Closet and storage items	8.03	8.56	10.20	6.76	7.28
Rental of furniture	3.12	1.97	2.45	5.40	1.22
Luggage	8.32	6.99	10.21	6.60	10.19
Computers and computer hardware, nonbusiness use	187.83	194.01	187.75	163.47	220.77
Computer software and accessories, nonbusiness use	17.49	16.78	18.79	12.71	24.23
Telephone answering devices	1.97	2.42	2.08	1.51	2.17
Calculators	1.64	1.79	2.03	1.17	1.83
Business equipment for home use	1.83	1.53	1.86	1.61	2.38
Other hardware	24.09	42.64	21.01	10.69	32.07
Smoke alarms (owner)	0.56	0.84	0.90	0.36	0.30
Smoke alarms (renter)	0.16	0.11	0.34	0.07	0.16
Other household appliances (owner)	7.59	6.33	12.19	4.18	9.18
Other household appliances (renter)	1.22	1.58	0.90	0.96	1.65
Miscellaneous household equipment and parts	40.18	46.55	53.65	31.39	34.22

Note: (–) means sample is too small to make a reliable estimate.
Source: Bureau of Labor Statistics, unpublished tables from the 2000 Consumer Expenditure Survey

Table 8.22 (Housing) Household Operations: Indexed spending by region, 2000

(indexed average annual spending of consumer units (CU) on household services, supplies, furnishings, and equipment, by region in which consumer unit lives, 2000; index definition: an index of 100 is the average for all consumer units; an index of 132 means that spending by consumer units in that group is 32 percent above the average for all consumer units; an index of 68 indicates spending that is 32 percent below the average for all consumer units)

	total consumer units	Northeast	Midwest	South	West
Average spending of CU, total	$38,045	$38,902	$39,213	$34,707	$41,328
Average spending of CU, index	100	102	103	91	109
Housing, spending index	100	110	97	88	113
HOUSEHOLD SERVICES	**100**	**94**	**98**	**94**	**116**
Personal services	**100**	**96**	**113**	**87**	**110**
Babysitting and child care in your own home	100	164	100	55	116
Babysitting and child care in someone else's home	100	79	156	87	79
Care for elderly, invalids, handicapped, etc.	100	64	114	75	156
Adult day care centers	100	27	90	163	74
Day care centers, nurseries, and preschools	100	96	108	94	104
Other household services	**100**	**92**	**84**	**101**	**122**
Housekeeping services	100	107	75	93	130
Gardening, lawn care service	100	102	75	102	122
Water softening service	100	48	144	89	115
Nonclothing laundry and dry cleaning, sent out	100	102	86	63	170
Nonclothing laundry and dry cleaning, coin-operated	100	128	95	83	107
Termite/pest control services	100	57	37	137	146
Home security system service fee	100	83	76	125	101
Other home services	100	97	79	76	162
Termite/pest control products	100	94	47	112	145
Moving, storage, and freight express	100	40	113	88	156
Appliance repair, including service center	100	112	102	92	100
Reupholstering and furniture repair	100	117	102	65	138
Repairs/rentals of lawn/garden equipment, hand/power tools, etc.	100	103	122	87	94
Appliance rental	100	72	128	95	102
Rental of office equipment for nonbusiness use	100	87	172	94	43
Repair of misc. household equipment and furnishings	100	18	11	265	2
Repair of computer systems for nonbusiness use	100	72	99	88	144
Computer information services	100	101	101	91	112
Rental, installation of dishwashers, range hoods, and garbage disposals	100	–	–	213	113
HOUSEKEEPING SUPPLIES	**100**	**110**	**107**	**91**	**98**
Laundry and cleaning supplies	**100**	**112**	**102**	**96**	**93**
Soaps and detergents	100	100	102	98	101
Other laundry cleaning products	100	125	102	94	85
Other household products	**100**	**108**	**106**	**94**	**96**
Cleansing and toilet tissue, paper towels, and napkins	100	114	104	90	99
Miscellaneous household products	100	110	108	87	103
Lawn and garden supplies	100	100	104	108	82
Postage and stationery	**100**	**111**	**114**	**81**	**107**
Stationery, stationery supplies, giftwrap	100	96	136	74	108
Postage	100	126	91	87	106
Delivery services	100	102	55	113	124

	total consumer units	Northeast	Midwest	South	West
HOUSEHOLD FURNISHINGS AND EQUIPMENT	**100**	**99**	**105**	**86**	**117**
Household textiles	**100**	**126**	**109**	**79**	**100**
Bathroom linens	100	101	99	82	130
Bedroom linens	100	141	98	80	97
Kitchen and dining room linens	100	125	103	74	115
Curtains and draperies	100	127	154	75	59
Slipcovers and decorative pillows	100	196	54	98	64
Sewing materials for household items	100	82	113	81	131
Other linens	100	104	75	79	157
Furniture	**100**	**99**	**97**	**87**	**125**
Mattresses and springs	100	70	104	94	130
Other bedroom furniture	100	94	90	88	134
Sofas	100	95	107	83	124
Living room chairs	100	85	104	99	110
Living room tables	100	131	97	85	100
Kitchen and dining room furniture	100	116	102	75	124
Infants' furniture	100	103	87	100	112
Outdoor furniture	100	141	86	71	124
Wall units, cabinets, and other furniture	100	117	73	86	135
Floor coverings	**100**	**106**	**121**	**93**	**84**
Wall-to-wall carpet (renter)	100	142	203	67	8
Wall-to-wall carpet (replacement) (owner)	100	85	139	102	68
Room-size rugs and other floor coverings, nonpermanent	100	141	81	78	120
Major appliances	**100**	**95**	**105**	**89**	**117**
Dishwashers (built-in), garbage disposals, range hoods (renter)	100	31	53	187	75
Dishwashers (built-in), garbage disposals, range hoods (owner)	100	122	104	72	120
Refrigerators and freezers (renter)	100	67	104	85	147
Refrigerators and freezers (owner)	100	112	97	93	103
Washing machines (renter)	100	53	97	112	124
Washing machines (owner)	100	76	99	93	132
Clothes dryers (renter)	100	59	69	112	149
Clothes dryers (owner)	100	87	101	83	138
Cooking stoves, ovens (renter)	100	72	97	150	49
Cooking stoves, ovens (owner)	100	105	108	89	105
Microwave ovens (renter)	100	80	105	84	137
Microwave ovens (owner)	100	97	117	86	106
Portable dishwasher (renter)	100	13	150	175	0
Portable dishwasher (owner)	100	86	167	61	104
Window air conditioners (renter)	100	261	97	57	32
Window air conditioners (owner)	100	132	92	125	41
Electric floor-cleaning equipment	100	71	150	77	110
Sewing machines	100	110	32	43	252
Miscellaneous household appliances	100	68	77	101	153
Small appliances and misc. housewares	**100**	**104**	**117**	**82**	**107**
Housewares	100	108	121	81	100
Plastic dinnerware	100	84	99	83	143
China and other dinnerware	100	130	140	65	87
Flatware	100	172	102	63	92
Glassware	100	66	170	71	103
Silver serving pieces	100	63	118	106	106

	total consumer units	Northeast	Midwest	South	West
Other serving pieces	100	127	110	64	121
Nonelectric cookware	100	128	113	78	96
Tableware, nonelectric kitchenware	100	91	104	99	106
Small appliances	100	93	106	84	125
Small electric kitchen appliances	100	97	102	81	131
Portable heating and cooling equipment	100	82	119	93	107
Miscellaneous household equipment	**100**	**96**	**107**	**86**	**118**
Window coverings	100	79	85	84	159
Infants' equipment	100	106	119	57	143
Laundry and cleaning equipment	100	100	104	82	125
Outdoor equipment	100	145	127	86	52
Clocks	100	231	41	66	97
Lamps and lighting fixtures	100	113	128	80	91
Other household decorative items	100	65	96	92	149
Telephones and accessories	100	91	99	71	156
Lawn and garden equipment	100	82	116	130	52
Power tools	100	50	173	91	82
Office furniture for home use	100	70	115	103	106
Hand tools	100	80	119	74	137
Indoor plants and fresh flowers	100	110	120	73	112
Closet and storage items	100	107	127	84	91
Rental of furniture	100	63	79	173	39
Luggage	100	84	123	79	122
Computers and computer hardware, nonbusiness use	100	103	100	87	118
Computer software and accessories, nonbusiness use	100	96	107	73	139
Telephone answering devices	100	123	106	77	110
Calculators	100	109	124	71	112
Business equipment for home use	100	84	102	88	130
Other hardware	100	177	87	44	133
Smoke alarms (owner)	100	150	161	64	54
Smoke alarms (renter)	100	69	213	44	100
Other household appliances (owner)	100	83	161	55	121
Other household appliances (renter)	100	130	74	79	135
Miscellaneous household equipment and parts	100	116	134	78	85

Note: (–) means sample is too small to make a reliable estimate.
Source: Calculations by New Strategist based on the 2000 Consumer Expenditure Survey

Table 8.23 (Housing) Household Operations: Indexed per capita spending by region, 2000

(indexed average annual per capita spending of consumer units (CU) on household services, supplies, furnishings, and equipment, by region in which consumer unit lives, 2000; index definition: an index of 100 is the average for all consumer units; an index of 132 means that spending by consumer units in that group is 32 percent above the average for all consumer units; an index of 68 indicates spending that is 32 percent below the average for all consumer units)

	total consumer units	Northeast	Midwest	South	West
Per capita spending of CU, total	$15,218	$15,561	$15,685	$13,883	$15,895
Per capita spending of CU, index	100	102	103	91	104
Housing, per capita spending index	100	110	97	88	109
HOUSEHOLD SERVICES	100	94	98	94	112
Personal services	100	96	113	87	106
Babysitting and child care in your own home	100	164	100	55	111
Babysitting and child care in someone else's home	100	79	156	87	76
Care for elderly, invalids, handicapped, etc.	100	64	114	75	150
Adult day care centers	100	27	90	163	71
Day care centers, nurseries, and preschools	100	96	108	94	100
Other household services	100	92	84	101	117
Housekeeping services	100	107	75	93	125
Gardening, lawn care service	100	102	75	102	117
Water softening service	100	48	144	89	110
Nonclothing laundry and dry cleaning, sent out	100	102	86	63	164
Nonclothing laundry and dry cleaning, coin-operated	100	128	95	83	103
Termite/pest control services	100	57	37	137	141
Home security system service fee	100	83	76	125	97
Other home services	100	97	79	76	156
Termite/pest control products	100	94	47	112	139
Moving, storage, and freight express	100	40	113	88	150
Appliance repair, including service center	100	112	102	92	96
Reupholstering and furniture repair	100	117	102	65	133
Repairs/rentals of lawn/garden equipment, hand/power tools, etc.	100	103	122	87	90
Appliance rental	100	72	128	95	98
Rental of office equipment for nonbusiness use	100	87	172	94	42
Repair of misc. household equipment and furnishings	100	18	11	265	2
Repair of computer systems for nonbusiness use	100	72	99	88	138
Computer information services	100	101	101	91	108
Rental, installation of dishwashers, range hoods, and garbage disposals	100	–	–	213	109
HOUSEKEEPING SUPPLIES	100	110	107	91	94
Laundry and cleaning supplies	100	112	102	96	90
Soaps and detergents	100	100	102	98	97
Other laundry cleaning products	100	125	102	94	82
Other household products	100	108	106	94	92
Cleansing and toilet tissue, paper towels, and napkins	100	114	104	90	96
Miscellaneous household products	100	116	108	87	99
Lawn and garden supplies	100	100	104	108	79
Postage and stationery	100	111	114	81	103
Stationery, stationery supplies, giftwrap	100	96	136	74	104
Postage	100	126	91	87	102
Delivery services	100	102	55	113	119

	total consumer units	Northeast	Midwest	South	West
HOUSEHOLD FURNISHINGS AND EQUIPMENT	**100**	**99**	**105**	**86**	**112**
Household textiles	**100**	**126**	**109**	**79**	**96**
Bathroom linens	100	101	99	82	125
Bedroom linens	100	141	98	80	93
Kitchen and dining room linens	100	125	103	74	111
Curtains and draperies	100	127	154	75	57
Slipcovers and decorative pillows	100	196	54	98	62
Sewing materials for household items	100	82	113	81	126
Other linens	100	104	75	79	151
Furniture	**100**	**99**	**97**	**87**	**120**
Mattresses and springs	100	70	104	94	125
Other bedroom furniture	100	94	90	88	129
Sofas	100	95	107	83	119
Living room chairs	100	85	104	99	106
Living room tables	100	131	97	85	96
Kitchen and dining room furniture	100	116	102	75	119
Infants' furniture	100	103	87	100	107
Outdoor furniture	100	141	86	71	119
Wall units, cabinets, and other furniture	100	117	73	86	130
Floor coverings	**100**	**106**	**121**	**93**	**81**
Wall-to-wall carpet (renter)	100	142	203	67	8
Wall-to-wall carpet (replacement) (owner)	100	85	139	102	66
Room-size rugs and other floor coverings, nonpermanent	100	141	81	78	115
Major appliances	**100**	**95**	**105**	**89**	**112**
Dishwashers (built-in), garbage disposals, range hoods (renter)	100	31	53	187	72
Dishwashers (built-in), garbage disposals, range hoods (owner)	100	122	104	72	115
Refrigerators and freezers (renter)	100	67	104	85	142
Refrigerators and freezers (owner)	100	112	97	93	99
Washing machines (renter)	100	53	97	112	119
Washing machines (owner)	100	76	99	93	127
Clothes dryers (renter)	100	59	69	112	143
Clothes dryers (owner)	100	87	101	83	132
Cooking stoves, ovens (renter)	100	72	97	150	47
Cooking stoves, ovens (owner)	100	105	108	89	101
Microwave ovens (renter)	100	80	105	84	132
Microwave ovens (owner)	100	97	117	86	102
Portable dishwasher (renter)	100	13	150	175	0
Portable dishwasher (owner)	100	86	167	61	100
Window air conditioners (renter)	100	261	97	57	31
Window air conditioners (owner)	100	132	92	125	40
Electric floor-cleaning equipment	100	71	150	77	106
Sewing machines	100	110	32	43	243
Miscellaneous household appliances	100	68	77	101	147
Small appliances and misc. housewares	**100**	**104**	**117**	**82**	**103**
Housewares	100	108	121	81	96
Plastic dinnerware	100	84	99	83	138
China and other dinnerware	100	130	140	65	83
Flatware	100	172	102	63	89
Glassware	100	66	170	71	99
Silver serving pieces	100	63	118	106	102

	total consumer units	Northeast	Midwest	South	West
Other serving pieces	100	127	110	64	116
Nonelectric cookware	100	128	113	78	93
Tableware, nonelectric kitchenware	100	91	104	99	102
Small appliances	100	93	106	84	120
Small electric kitchen appliances	100	97	102	81	126
Portable heating and cooling equipment	100	82	119	93	103
Miscellaneous household equipment	**100**	**96**	**107**	**86**	**114**
Window coverings	100	79	85	84	153
Infants' equipment	100	106	119	57	138
Laundry and cleaning equipment	100	100	104	82	120
Outdoor equipment	100	145	127	86	50
Clocks	100	231	41	66	93
Lamps and lighting fixtures	100	113	128	80	88
Other household decorative items	100	65	96	92	143
Telephones and accessories	100	91	99	71	150
Lawn and garden equipment	100	82	116	130	50
Power tools	100	50	173	91	79
Office furniture for home use	100	70	115	103	102
Hand tools	100	80	119	74	132
Indoor plants and fresh flowers	100	110	120	73	108
Closet and storage items	100	107	127	84	87
Rental of furniture	100	63	79	173	38
Luggage	100	84	123	79	118
Computers and computer hardware, nonbusiness use	100	103	100	87	113
Computer software and accessories, nonbusiness use	100	96	107	73	133
Telephone answering devices	100	123	106	77	106
Calculators	100	109	124	71	107
Business equipment for home use	100	84	102	88	125
Other hardware	100	177	87	44	128
Smoke alarms (owner)	100	150	161	64	52
Smoke alarms (renter)	100	69	213	44	96
Other household appliances (owner)	100	83	161	55	116
Other household appliances (renter)	100	130	74	79	130
Miscellaneous household equipment and parts	100	116	134	78	82

Note: Per capita indexes account for household size and show how much each person in a particular household demographic segment spends relative to a person in the average household. (–) means sample is too small to make a reliable estimate.
Source: Calculations by New Strategist based on the 2000 Consumer Expenditure Survey

Table 8.24 (Housing) Household Operations: Total spending by region, 2000

(total annual spending on household services, supplies, furnishings, and equipment, by region in which consumer units live, 2000; numbers in thousands)

	total consumer units	Northeast	Midwest	South	West
Number of consumer units	109,367	20,994	25,717	38,245	24,410
Total spending of all consumer units	$4,160,831,424	$816,706,699	$1,008,433,006	$1,327,371,892	$1,008,821,118
Housing, total spending	1,347,238,483	283,516,622	307,606,695	415,130,735	341,067,505
HOUSEHOLD SERVICES	**$74,848,587**	**$13,499,142**	**$17,237,591**	**$24,669,937**	**$19,431,581**
Personal services	**35,675,515**	**6,552,857**	**9,488,544**	**10,847,047**	**8,787,356**
Babysitting and child care in your own home	3,522,711	1,107,853	828,345	676,937	910,005
Babysitting and child care in someone else's home	3,564,271	542,485	1,310,538	1,080,421	631,487
Care for elderly, invalids, handicapped, etc.	5,509,909	673,697	1,474,870	1,446,043	1,915,453
Adult day care centers	284,354	14,906	59,921	162,159	46,867
Day care centers, nurseries, and preschools	22,794,270	4,213,916	5,814,871	7,481,487	5,283,545
Other household services	**39,173,072**	**6,946,075**	**7,749,046**	**13,823,273**	**10,644,225**
Housekeeping services	9,640,701	1,982,883	1,704,780	3,147,564	2,805,197
Gardening, lawn care service	8,559,061	1,674,272	1,512,931	3,039,330	2,332,131
Water softening service	340,131	31,071	115,469	105,939	87,144
Nonclothing laundry and dry cleaning, sent out	161,863	31,701	32,918	35,568	61,513
Nonclothing laundry and dry cleaning, coin-operated	507,463	124,914	113,926	148,008	121,074
Termite/pest control services	1,046,642	113,787	91,038	499,862	341,984
Home security system service fee	2,041,882	325,827	362,867	894,168	459,396
Other home services	1,561,761	291,817	289,059	414,576	566,068
Termite/pest control products	53,590	9,657	5,915	21,035	17,331
Moving, storage, and freight express	3,546,772	272,922	940,985	1,094,189	1,238,808
Appliance repair, including service center	1,375,837	296,225	330,463	442,877	305,857
Reupholstering and furniture repair	1,012,738	228,415	241,740	231,000	312,448
Repairs/rentals of lawn/garden equipment, hand/power tools, etc.	542,460	107,279	156,102	165,601	113,751
Appliance rental	412,314	56,894	124,213	137,300	93,490
Rental of office equipment for nonbusiness use	57,965	9,657	23,402	19,123	5,614
Repair of misc. household equipment and furnishings	1,282,875	44,927	33,689	1,189,037	5,614
Repair of computer systems for nonbusiness use	300,759	41,358	70,207	92,935	96,664
Computer information services	6,710,759	1,302,678	1,599,083	2,132,924	1,675,991
Rental, installation of dishwashers, range hoods, and garbage disposals	16,405	–	–	12,238	4,150
HOUSEKEEPING SUPPLIES	**52,749,891**	**11,121,572**	**13,229,853**	**16,845,393**	**11,530,308**
Laundry and cleaning supplies	**14,300,829**	**3,072,892**	**3,421,390**	**4,814,663**	**2,973,870**
Soaps and detergents	7,575,852	1,460,972	1,815,877	2,599,513	1,700,401
Other laundry cleaning products	6,724,977	1,611,919	1,605,512	2,215,150	1,273,714
Other household products	**24,706,005**	**5,133,033**	**6,132,990**	**8,156,511**	**5,268,654**
Cleansing and toilet tissue, paper towels, and napkins	7,486,171	1,633,543	1,823,592	2,362,394	1,661,101
Miscellaneous household products	9,895,526	2,089,953	2,520,523	3,016,766	2,268,665
Lawn and garden supplies	7,324,308	1,409,537	1,788,875	2,776,969	1,339,133
Postage and stationery	**13,743,057**	**2,915,437**	**3,675,216**	**3,874,219**	**3,287,539**
Stationery, stationery supplies, giftwrap	6,961,210	1,276,435	2,233,521	1,792,926	1,679,408
Postage	6,627,640	1,608,980	1,421,893	2,020,101	1,565,413
Delivery services	154,207	30,231	19,802	61,192	42,718

	total consumer units	Northeast	Midwest	South	West
HOUSEHOLD FURNISHINGS AND EQUIPMENT	$169,369,017	$32,339,787	$41,941,341	$51,005,444	$44,210,416
Household textiles	11,646,492	2,808,367	2,996,802	3,237,057	2,589,657
Bathroom linens	1,919,391	372,853	446,704	548,433	556,304
Bedroom linens	4,869,019	1,314,434	1,117,918	1,367,641	1,054,512
Kitchen and dining room linens	1,018,207	244,580	246,369	265,038	261,675
Curtains and draperies	2,303,269	561,380	835,803	603,124	302,928
Slipcovers and decorative pillows	300,759	113,158	38,318	103,262	43,206
Sewing materials for household items	1,066,328	168,162	282,373	303,283	312,692
Other linens	167,332	33,380	29,317	46,276	58,584
Furniture	42,722,031	8,135,805	9,721,026	12,928,722	11,935,758
Mattresses and springs	5,784,421	774,679	1,417,521	1,907,661	1,684,534
Other bedroom furniture	7,558,353	1,363,560	1,601,912	2,336,770	2,256,216
Sofas	9,750,068	1,778,192	2,454,173	2,823,246	2,694,864
Living room chairs	4,794,649	783,706	1,172,438	1,657,156	1,181,200
Living room tables	1,880,019	472,575	430,245	557,995	419,852
Kitchen and dining room furniture	5,081,191	1,132,626	1,221,558	1,326,337	1,400,890
Infants' furniture	680,263	134,152	139,643	236,737	169,405
Outdoor furniture	1,658,004	448,222	336,636	413,428	459,640
Wall units, cabinets, and other furniture	5,535,064	1,248,303	947,414	1,669,777	1,669,156
Floor coverings	4,853,707	987,978	1,379,974	1,574,547	911,469
Wall-to-wall carpet (renter)	150,926	41,148	72,008	35,185	2,685
Wall-to-wall carpet (replacement) (owner)	3,038,215	497,138	992,419	1,085,393	463,546
Room-size rugs and other floor coverings, nonpermanent	1,664,566	449,482	315,548	453,586	445,483
Major appliances	20,665,988	3,758,346	5,091,966	6,439,693	5,396,563
Dishwashers (built-in), garbage disposals, range hoods (renter)	95,149	5,668	11,830	62,339	15,867
Dishwashers (built-in), garbage disposals, range hoods (owner)	1,542,075	361,937	377,526	390,481	411,553
Refrigerators and freezers (renter)	803,847	103,710	196,992	238,649	264,604
Refrigerators and freezers (owner)	4,849,333	1,047,181	1,108,146	1,577,989	1,116,025
Washing machines (renter)	523,868	53,535	120,098	204,993	145,240
Washing machines (owner)	2,026,571	295,176	472,421	660,491	598,777
Clothes dryers (renter)	367,473	41,568	59,663	143,801	122,294
Clothes dryers (owner)	1,314,591	218,967	311,947	379,390	404,230
Cooking stoves, ovens (renter)	306,228	42,198	69,950	161,011	33,442
Cooking stoves, ovens (owner)	2,619,340	527,159	665,299	814,619	611,959
Microwave ovens (renter)	260,293	39,889	64,293	76,490	79,577
Microwave ovens (owner)	804,941	149,687	221,681	243,238	189,666
Portable dishwasher (renter)	17,499	420	6,172	10,709	0
Portable dishwasher (owner)	83,119	13,646	32,661	17,593	19,284
Window air conditioners (renter)	202,329	101,191	46,033	40,157	14,646
Window air conditioners (owner)	527,149	133,312	114,441	230,617	48,820
Electric floor-cleaning equipment	2,841,355	388,809	1,000,391	769,872	698,126
Sewing machines	522,774	110,009	39,604	78,402	294,385
Miscellaneous household appliances	959,149	124,494	172,818	338,851	327,826
Small appliances and misc. housewares	9,555,395	1,914,023	2,638,050	2,735,665	2,274,280
Housewares	7,094,637	1,474,409	2,024,185	2,015,512	1,586,406
Plastic dinnerware	158,582	25,613	36,775	45,894	50,773
China and other dinnerware	1,250,065	312,181	410,443	284,543	241,903
Flatware	394,815	130,583	95,153	87,581	81,285
Glassware	877,123	111,898	351,551	216,849	202,359
Silver serving pieces	257,012	30,861	71,493	95,230	61,025

	total consumer units	Northeast	Midwest	South	West
Other serving pieces	$156,395	$38,209	$40,633	$35,185	$42,229
Nonelectric cookware	1,823,148	447,172	486,308	496,038	391,536
Tableware, nonelectric kitchenware	2,176,403	378,102	532,085	754,574	515,051
Small appliances	2,461,851	439,614	614,122	719,771	687,874
Small electric kitchen appliances	1,863,614	345,771	446,704	525,869	544,587
Portable heating and cooling equipment	598,237	93,843	167,161	193,902	143,287
Miscellaneous household equipment	**79,926,497**	**14,735,269**	**20,113,266**	**24,090,143**	**21,102,689**
Window coverings	1,423,958	215,189	285,973	417,253	505,531
Infants' equipment	876,030	178,239	245,340	175,162	280,471
Laundry and cleaning equipment	1,102,419	210,570	270,286	317,051	307,566
Outdoor equipment	2,011,259	561,590	602,549	604,271	232,383
Clocks	1,521,295	673,488	146,844	351,854	330,023
Lamps and lighting fixtures	1,181,164	256,967	355,152	328,525	240,439
Other household decorative items	19,390,769	2,428,586	4,395,550	6,251,910	6,432,279
Telephones and accessories	3,192,423	560,120	740,650	795,114	1,112,364
Lawn and garden equipment	5,120,563	809,109	1,398,748	2,322,619	590,234
Power tools	2,331,704	224,846	951,272	740,806	428,396
Office furniture for home use	1,495,047	199,863	402,985	538,107	353,945
Hand tools	794,004	121,975	222,452	205,758	243,612
Indoor plants and fresh flowers	6,235,013	1,322,412	1,754,414	1,599,023	1,559,555
Closet and storage items	878,217	179,709	262,313	258,536	177,705
Rental of furniture	341,225	41,358	63,007	206,523	29,780
Luggage	909,933	146,748	262,571	252,417	248,738
Computers and computer hardware, nonbusiness use	20,542,404	4,073,046	4,828,367	6,251,910	5,388,996
Computer software and accessories, nonbusiness use	1,912,829	352,279	483,222	486,094	591,454
Telephone answering devices	215,453	50,805	53,491	57,750	52,970
Calculators	179,362	37,579	52,206	44,747	44,670
Business equipment for home use	200,142	32,121	47,834	61,574	58,096
Other hardware	2,634,651	895,184	540,314	408,839	782,829
Smoke alarms (owner)	61,246	17,635	23,145	13,768	7,323
Smoke alarms (renter)	17,499	2,309	8,744	2,677	3,906
Other household appliances (owner)	830,096	132,892	313,490	159,864	224,084
Other household appliances (renter)	133,428	33,171	23,145	36,715	40,277
Miscellaneous household equipment and parts	4,394,366	977,271	1,379,717	1,200,511	835,310

Note: Numbers may not add to total because of rounding. (–) means sample is too small to make a reliable estimate.
Source: Calculations by New Strategist based on the 2000 Consumer Expenditure Survey

Table 8.25 (Housing) Household Operations: Market shares by region, 2000

(percentage of total annual spending on household services, supplies, furnishings, and equipment accounted for by consumer units by region, 2000)

	total consumer units	Northeast	Midwest	South	West
Share of total consumer units	100.0%	19.2%	23.5%	35.0%	22.3%
Share of total before-tax income	100.0	20.4	23.4	32.9	23.3
Share of total spending	100.0	19.6	24.2	31.9	24.2
Share of housing spending	100.0	21.0	22.8	30.8	25.3
HOUSEHOLD SERVICES	**100.0%**	**18.0%**	**23.0%**	**33.0%**	**26.0%**
Personal services	**100.0**	**18.4**	**26.6**	**30.4**	**24.6**
Babysitting and child care in your own home	100.0	31.4	23.5	19.2	25.8
Babysitting and child care in someone else's home	100.0	15.2	36.8	30.3	17.7
Care for elderly, invalids, handicapped, etc.	100.0	12.2	26.8	26.2	34.8
Adult day care centers	100.0	5.2	21.1	57.0	16.5
Day care centers, nurseries, and preschools	100.0	18.5	25.5	32.8	23.2
Other household services	**100.0**	**17.7**	**19.8**	**35.3**	**27.2**
Housekeeping services	100.0	20.6	17.7	32.6	29.1
Gardening, lawn care service	100.0	19.6	17.7	35.5	27.2
Water softening service	100.0	9.1	33.9	31.1	25.6
Nonclothing laundry and dry cleaning, sent out	100.0	19.6	20.3	22.0	38.0
Nonclothing laundry and dry cleaning, coin-operated	100.0	24.6	22.5	29.2	23.9
Termite/pest control services	100.0	10.9	8.7	47.8	32.7
Home security system service fee	100.0	16.0	17.8	43.8	22.5
Other home services	100.0	18.7	18.5	26.5	36.2
Termite/pest control products	100.0	18.0	11.0	39.3	32.3
Moving, storage, and freight express	100.0	7.7	26.5	30.9	34.9
Appliance repair, including service center	100.0	21.5	24.0	32.2	22.2
Reupholstering and furniture repair	100.0	22.6	23.9	22.8	30.9
Repairs/rentals of lawn/garden equipment, hand/power tools, etc.	100.0	19.8	28.8	30.5	21.0
Appliance rental	100.0	13.8	30.1	33.3	22.7
Rental of office equipment for nonbusiness use	100.0	16.7	40.4	33.0	9.7
Repair of misc. household equipment and furnishings	100.0	3.5	2.6	92.7	0.4
Repair of computer systems for nonbusiness use	100.0	13.8	23.3	30.9	32.1
Computer information services	100.0	19.4	23.8	31.8	25.0
Rental, installation of dishwashers, range hoods, and garbage disposals	100.0	–	–	74.6	25.3
HOUSEKEEPING SUPPLIES	**100.0**	**21.1**	**25.1**	**31.9**	**21.9**
Laundry and cleaning supplies	**100.0**	**21.5**	**23.9**	**33.7**	**20.8**
Soaps and detergents	100.0	19.3	24.0	34.3	22.4
Other laundry cleaning products	100.0	24.0	23.9	32.9	18.9
Other household products	**100.0**	**20.8**	**24.8**	**33.0**	**21.3**
Cleansing and toilet tissue, paper towels, and napkins	100.0	21.8	24.4	31.6	22.2
Miscellaneous household products	100.0	21.1	25.5	30.5	22.9
Lawn and garden supplies	100.0	19.2	24.4	37.9	18.3
Postage and stationery	**100.0**	**21.2**	**26.7**	**28.2**	**23.9**
Stationery, stationery supplies, giftwrap	100.0	18.3	32.1	25.8	24.1
Postage	100.0	24.3	21.5	30.5	23.6
Delivery services	100.0	19.6	12.8	39.7	27.7

	total consumer units	Northeast	Midwest	South	West
HOUSEHOLD FURNISHINGS AND EQUIPMENT	100.0%	19.1%	24.8%	30.1%	26.1%
Household textiles	100.0	24.1	25.7	27.8	22.2
Bathroom linens	100.0	19.4	23.3	28.6	29.0
Bedroom linens	100.0	27.0	23.0	28.1	21.7
Kitchen and dining room linens	100.0	24.0	24.2	26.0	25.7
Curtains and draperies	100.0	24.4	36.3	26.2	13.2
Slipcovers and decorative pillows	100.0	37.6	12.7	34.3	14.4
Sewing materials for household items	100.0	15.8	26.5	28.4	29.3
Other linens	100.0	19.9	17.5	27.7	35.0
Furniture	100.0	19.0	22.8	30.3	27.9
Mattresses and springs	100.0	13.4	24.5	33.0	29.1
Other bedroom furniture	100.0	18.0	21.2	30.9	29.9
Sofas	100.0	18.2	25.2	29.0	27.6
Living room chairs	100.0	16.3	24.5	34.6	24.6
Living room tables	100.0	25.1	22.9	29.7	22.3
Kitchen and dining room furniture	100.0	22.3	24.0	26.1	27.6
Infants' furniture	100.0	19.7	20.5	34.8	24.9
Outdoor furniture	100.0	27.0	20.3	24.9	27.7
Wall units, cabinets, and other furniture	100.0	22.6	17.1	30.2	30.2
Floor coverings	100.0	20.4	28.4	32.4	18.8
Wall-to-wall carpet (renter)	100.0	27.3	47.7	23.3	1.8
Wall-to-wall carpet (replacement) (owner)	100.0	16.4	32.7	35.7	15.3
Room-size rugs and other floor coverings, nonpermanent	100.0	27.0	19.0	27.2	26.8
Major appliances	100.0	18.2	24.6	31.2	26.1
Dishwashers (built-in), garbage disposals, range hoods (renter)	100.0	6.0	12.4	65.5	16.7
Dishwashers (built-in), garbage disposals, range hoods (owner)	100.0	23.5	24.5	25.3	26.7
Refrigerators and freezers (renter)	100.0	12.9	24.5	29.7	32.9
Refrigerators and freezers (owner)	100.0	21.6	22.9	32.5	23.0
Washing machines (renter)	100.0	10.2	22.9	39.1	27.7
Washing machines (owner)	100.0	14.6	23.3	32.6	29.5
Clothes dryers (renter)	100.0	11.3	16.2	39.1	33.3
Clothes dryers (owner)	100.0	16.7	23.7	28.9	30.7
Cooking stoves, ovens (renter)	100.0	13.8	22.8	52.6	10.9
Cooking stoves, ovens (owner)	100.0	20.1	25.4	31.1	23.4
Microwave ovens (renter)	100.0	15.3	24.7	29.4	30.6
Microwave ovens (owner)	100.0	18.6	27.5	30.2	23.6
Portable dishwasher (renter)	100.0	2.4	35.3	61.2	0.0
Portable dishwasher (owner)	100.0	16.4	39.3	21.2	23.2
Window air conditioners (renter)	100.0	50.0	22.8	19.8	7.2
Window air conditioners (owner)	100.0	25.3	21.7	43.7	9.3
Electric floor-cleaning equipment	100.0	13.7	35.2	27.1	24.6
Sewing machines	100.0	21.0	7.6	15.0	56.3
Miscellaneous household appliances	100.0	13.0	18.0	35.3	34.2
Small appliances and misc. housewares	100.0	20.0	27.6	28.6	23.8
Housewares	100.0	20.8	28.5	28.4	22.4
Plastic dinnerware	100.0	16.2	23.2	28.9	32.0
China and other dinnerware	100.0	25.0	32.8	22.8	19.4
Flatware	100.0	33.1	24.1	22.2	20.6
Glassware	100.0	12.8	40.1	24.7	23.1
Silver serving pieces	100.0	12.0	27.8	37.1	23.7

	total consumer units	Northeast	Midwest	South	West
Other serving pieces	100.0%	24.4%	26.0%	22.5%	27.0%
Nonelectric cookware	100.0	24.5	26.7	27.2	21.5
Tableware, nonelectric kitchenware	100.0	17.4	24.4	34.7	23.7
Small appliances	100.0	17.9	24.9	29.2	27.9
Small electric kitchen appliances	100.0	18.6	24.0	28.2	29.2
Portable heating and cooling equipment	100.0	15.7	27.9	32.4	24.0
Miscellaneous household equipment	**100.0**	**18.4**	**25.2**	**30.1**	**26.4**
Window coverings	100.0	15.1	20.1	29.3	35.5
Infants' equipment	100.0	20.3	28.0	20.0	32.0
Laundry and cleaning equipment	100.0	19.1	24.5	28.8	27.9
Outdoor equipment	100.0	27.9	30.0	30.0	11.6
Clocks	100.0	44.3	9.7	23.1	21.7
Lamps and lighting fixtures	100.0	21.8	30.1	27.8	20.4
Other household decorative items	100.0	12.5	22.7	32.2	33.2
Telephones and accessories	100.0	17.5	23.2	24.9	34.8
Lawn and garden equipment	100.0	15.8	27.3	45.4	11.5
Power tools	100.0	9.6	40.8	31.8	18.4
Office furniture for home use	100.0	13.4	27.0	36.0	23.7
Hand tools	100.0	15.4	28.0	25.9	30.7
Indoor plants and fresh flowers	100.0	21.2	28.1	25.6	25.0
Closet and storage items	100.0	20.5	29.9	29.4	20.2
Rental of furniture	100.0	12.1	18.5	60.5	8.7
Luggage	100.0	16.1	28.9	27.7	27.3
Computers and computer hardware, nonbusiness use	100.0	19.8	23.5	30.4	26.2
Computer software and accessories, nonbusiness use	100.0	18.4	25.3	25.4	30.9
Telephone answering devices	100.0	23.6	24.8	26.8	24.6
Calculators	100.0	21.0	29.1	24.9	24.9
Business equipment for home use	100.0	16.0	23.9	30.8	29.0
Other hardware	100.0	34.0	20.5	15.5	29.7
Smoke alarms (owner)	100.0	28.8	37.8	22.5	12.0
Smoke alarms (renter)	100.0	13.2	50.0	15.3	22.3
Other household appliances (owner)	100.0	16.0	37.8	19.3	27.0
Other household appliances (renter)	100.0	24.9	17.3	27.5	30.2
Miscellaneous household equipment and parts	100.0	22.2	31.4	27.3	19.0

Note: Numbers may not add to total because of rounding. (–) means sample is too small to make a reliable estimate.
Source: Calculations by New Strategist based on the 2000 Consumer Expenditure Survey

9

Spending on Shelter and Utilities, 2000

Housing is Americans' biggest expense. In 2000, costs for shelter, utilities, and household operations (household services, housekeeping supplies, furniture, and equipment) absorbed 32.4 percent of the expenditures of the average household. That figure was 30.7 percent in 1990. Spending on shelter rose 12 percent between 1990 and 2000, after adjusting for inflation. Spending on owned homes rose 18 percent, while spending on rented homes rose less than 1 percent during the decade. Spending on "other lodging," such as hotels and motels, rose 4 percent. Spending on utilities and fuels was the same in 2000 as in 1990, although spending on fuel oil fell 26 percent.

Housing costs are highest for householders aged 35 to 44, at $15,111 in 2000. This age group spends the most on owned homes, $6,433 in 2000. Close behind are householders aged 45 to 54, spending $5,964, most of it mortgage interest charges. Spending on maintenance and repair services for owned homes is greatest among householders aged 65 to 74. Householders aged 55 to 64 spend the most on owned vacation homes.

Households with incomes of $70,000 or more spent $22,932 on housing in 2000, versus the $12,527 spent by the average household. The most affluent households account for a large share of the market in a number of shelter categories: 47 percent of the market for painting and wallpapering owned homes, 49 percent of the market for landscape maintenance of owned homes, 53 percent of the market for owned vacations homes, and 45 percent of the market for lodging on out-of-town trips.

Among household types, married couples with preschoolers spend the most on housing, $18,702 in 2000. Behind this figure is the high cost of housing for recent home buyers, as many married couples with young children are new homeowners. This household type spends twice as much as the average household on mortgage interest. Married couples without children at home (most of them older empty-nesters) spend the most on owned vacation homes and lodging on out-of-town trips.

Black and Hispanic householders spend less than average on housing, but they spend more on some shelter categories. Blacks spend 40 percent more than the average household on rent, while Hispanics spend 63 percent more. Blacks spend 12 percent more than average on telephone services.

Households in the West spend the most on housing, $13,972 in 2000, because of the high cost of housing in California and other Western states. Housing costs are lowest in the South, at $10,855. Western households spend 34 percent more than the average household on mortgage interest. Households in the Northeast spend 31 percent more than average on lodging on out-of-town trips, while households in the South spend 26 percent more than average on electricity.

Table 9.1 (Housing) Shelter and Utilities: Average spending by age, 2000

(average annual spending of consumer units (CU) on shelter and utilities, by age of consumer unit reference person, 2000)

	total consumer units	under 25	25 to 34	35 to 44	45 to 54	55 to 64	65 to 74	75+
Number of consumer units								
(in thousands, add 000)	109,367	8,306	18,887	23,983	21,874	14,161	11,538	10,617
Average number of persons per CU	2.5	1.9	2.9	3.3	2.7	2.1	1.9	1.5
Average before-tax income of CU	$44,649.00	$19,744.00	$45,498.00	$56,500.00	$58,889.00	$48,108.00	$29,349.00	$20,563.00
Average spending of CU, total	38,044.67	22,543.18	38,945.27	45,149.37	46,160.28	39,340.03	30,781.81	21,908.04
Housing, average spending	12,318.51	7,109.16	13,049.56	15,111.45	14,179.31	12,362.20	9,671.46	7,766.01
SHELTER	**$7,114.26**	**$4,574.35**	**$7,904.51**	**$8,930.13**	**$8,296.78**	**$6,587.11**	**$5,114.16**	**$4,034.01**
Owned dwellings*	**4,602.32**	**633.74**	**4,142.16**	**6,432.87**	**5,963.55**	**4,779.80**	**3,619.04**	**2,417.96**
Mortgage interest and charges	2,638.81	385.95	2,887.85	4,302.48	3,557.76	2,278.02	1,178.60	374.95
Mortgage interest	2,460.48	384.80	2,792.14	4,056.61	3,292.33	2,012.24	1,016.98	341.54
Interest paid, home equity loan	98.22	1.15	71.60	136.99	146.88	126.09	79.11	17.27
Interest paid, home equity line of credit	79.76	–	24.08	107.98	117.90	139.59	82.50	16.14
Prepayment penalty charges	0.34	–	0.03	0.89	0.65	0.10	–	–
Property taxes	1,138.55	175.98	755.28	1,246.03	1,470.91	1,461.79	1,272.03	1,069.72
Maintenance, repairs, insurance, other expenses	824.96	71.81	499.03	884.36	934.89	1,039.99	1,168.40	973.29
Homeowner's and related insurance	234.84	23.16	160.18	242.51	282.11	304.40	302.79	251.96
Ground rent	38.67	26.73	38.76	21.21	33.46	37.22	44.91	93.22
Maintenance and repair services	438.92	9.71	193.76	495.02	492.27	575.55	669.63	541.28
Painting and papering	49.93	0.86	21.20	61.92	52.06	81.24	76.76	37.05
Plumbing and water heating	41.62	1.12	16.76	32.74	42.30	66.18	65.22	77.73
Heat, air conditioning, electrical work	79.19	1.92	37.07	83.75	117.96	90.67	108.38	77.41
Roofing and gutters	75.27	0.43	19.40	80.68	68.29	96.58	148.01	127.87
Other repair and maintenance services	157.99	4.63	65.65	197.65	158.01	209.86	231.80	203.23
Repair, replacement of hard-surface flooring	33.61	0.40	32.93	36.60	52.67	29.45	37.62	15.96
Repair of built-in appliances	1.31	0.34	0.75	1.68	0.97	1.57	1.85	2.04
Maintenance and repair materials	78.08	10.51	84.36	99.09	94.88	81.36	87.68	22.89
Paints, wallpaper, and supplies	16.03	2.52	25.66	20.45	12.11	16.44	19.76	2.94
Tools, equipment for painting, wallpapering	1.72	0.27	2.76	2.20	1.30	1.77	2.12	0.32
Plumbing supplies and equipment	6.13	1.03	4.59	5.46	6.61	9.04	9.24	6.10
Electrical supplies, heating and cooling equip.	4.35	0.16	3.21	7.26	3.69	1.93	8.33	3.38
Hard-surface flooring, repair and replacement	6.98	1.18	5.39	9.89	12.99	3.42	7.10	0.06
Roofing and gutters	6.41	0.10	2.19	12.13	6.37	11.79	4.08	1.36
Plaster, paneling, siding, windows, doors, screens, awnings	12.14	0.25	15.67	12.37	16.50	13.46	13.94	1.93
Patio, walk, fence, driveway, masonry, brick, and stucco materials	0.60	0.07	0.41	0.90	0.67	0.67	0.77	0.22
Landscape maintenance	2.92	0.09	2.74	3.83	4.34	3.24	2.34	0.66
Miscellaneous supplies and equipment	20.80	4.85	21.76	24.61	30.29	19.60	20.00	5.93
Insulation, other maintenance, repair	13.45	3.56	15.42	18.40	19.65	9.28	10.03	3.05
Finish basement, remodel rooms, build patios, walks, etc.	7.35	1.29	6.34	6.21	10.64	10.33	9.97	2.88
Property management and security	30.99	1.30	18.61	23.82	29.43	36.75	57.69	58.89
Property management	21.49	1.15	14.35	19.01	20.41	24.88	36.36	37.25
Management and upkeep services for security	9.50	0.15	4.26	4.82	9.02	11.88	21.34	21.64
Parking	3.45	0.41	3.35	2.70	2.75	4.72	5.70	5.05

	total consumer units	under 25	25 to 34	35 to 44	45 to 54	55 to 64	65 to 74	75+
Rented dwellings	**$2,034.11**	**$3,618.31**	**$3,514.36**	**$2,067.03**	**$1,614.16**	**$1,122.52**	**$951.67**	**$1,344.46**
Rent	1,977.33	3,537.59	3,452.53	2,003.02	1,567.46	1,075.88	906.48	1,284.84
Rent as pay	29.24	55.54	32.18	36.53	23.04	20.40	20.43	21.13
Maintenance, insurance, and other expenses	27.54	25.18	29.65	27.48	23.65	26.24	24.76	38.49
Tenant's insurance	8.86	8.51	14.89	6.36	7.66	7.54	7.47	9.79
Maintenance and repair services	11.13	5.10	8.70	9.59	8.55	12.57	10.28	27.94
Repair and maintenance services	9.98	3.84	6.24	9.20	8.46	12.54	6.36	26.87
Repair and replacement of hard-surface flooring	1.08	0.88	2.44	0.31	0.08	–	3.83	1.07
Repair of built-in appliances	0.07	0.38	0.02	0.09	0.01	0.03	0.09	–
Maintenance and repair materials	7.55	11.57	6.06	11.52	7.44	6.13	7.01	0.76
Paint, wallpaper, and supplies	1.54	2.52	1.29	3.38	0.90	0.59	0.95	0.28
Painting and wallpapering tools	0.17	0.27	0.14	0.36	0.10	0.06	0.10	0.03
Plastering, paneling, roofing, gutters, etc.	0.48	0.61	0.16	0.35	1.59	0.02	0.06	0.01
Patio, walk, fence, driveway, masonry, brick, and stucco materials	0.03	–	–	–	–	–	–	–
Plumbing supplies and equipment	0.39	2.03	0.47	0.27	0.27	0.26	0.05	0.04
Electrical supplies, heating, cooling equipment	0.25	0.03	0.29	0.24	0.64	0.10	–	0.00
Miscellaneous supplies and equipment	3.60	4.23	2.86	6.05	2.29	2.83	5.82	0.25
Insulation, other maintenance and repair	0.92	1.69	1.47	0.26	0.53	2.60	0.19	0.19
Materials for additions, finishing basements, remodeling rooms	2.67	2.54	1.35	5.79	1.76	0.23	5.57	0.06
Construction materials for jobs not started	0.01	–	0.05	–	–	–	0.05	–
Hard-surface flooring	0.49	1.56	0.72	0.33	0.83	–	–	0.09
Landscape maintenance	0.60	0.31	0.13	0.54	0.68	2.26	0.02	0.06
Other lodging	**477.84**	**322.30**	**247.99**	**430.24**	**719.08**	**684.79**	**543.45**	**271.59**
Owned vacation homes	147.91	9.72	51.06	125.77	187.22	296.05	228.50	112.17
Mortgage interest and charges	63.65	3.18	27.33	74.63	77.55	118.51	100.13	9.29
Mortgage interest	61.19	3.18	25.38	72.67	74.61	110.29	100.13	8.84
Interest paid, home equity loan	1.35	–	1.95	1.10	2.34	2.35	–	–
Interest paid, home equity line of credit	1.11	–	–	0.86	0.59	5.87	–	0.45
Property taxes	51.97	6.44	13.49	37.68	63.01	117.16	72.69	56.16
Maintenance, insurance and other expenses	32.29	0.09	10.24	13.47	46.67	60.38	55.68	46.72
Homeowner's and related insurance	10.74	–	4.88	10.00	16.39	14.25	15.52	9.72
Homeowner's insurance	10.74	–	4.88	10.00	16.39	14.25	15.52	9.72
Ground rent	2.97	–	0.18	–	1.36	9.64	5.73	8.38
Maintenance and repair services	13.56	0.06	3.26	1.36	22.53	25.12	24.94	23.74
Maintenance and repair materials	0.48	–	0.14	0.30	0.15	2.30	0.58	–
Property management and security	3.89	0.03	1.69	1.41	5.56	7.88	7.39	3.83
Property management	2.56	0.03	1.37	1.09	3.43	5.18	4.71	2.37
Management and upkeep services for security	1.33	–	0.32	0.33	2.13	2.70	2.68	1.46
Parking	0.65	0.00	0.09	0.39	0.68	1.18	1.51	1.06
Housing while attending school	78.31	233.98	12.69	32.93	197.18	79.34	6.23	7.80
Lodging on trips	251.62	78.60	184.24	271.54	334.68	309.39	308.71	151.62
UTILITIES, FUELS, AND PUBLIC SERVICES	**2,488.90**	**1,247.75**	**2,341.16**	**2,809.84**	**2,857.47**	**2,756.16**	**2,438.31**	**1,936.94**
Natural gas	**307.35**	**102.31**	**273.12**	**350.07**	**344.04**	**340.50**	**318.17**	**300.53**
Natural gas (renter)	60.47	76.12	101.59	73.14	47.03	44.12	30.69	28.30
Natural gas (owner)	244.63	26.08	171.16	275.60	293.78	291.01	284.62	269.76
Natural gas (vacation)	2.25	0.11	0.37	1.33	3.24	5.37	2.86	2.47

	total consumer units	under 25	25 to 34	35 to 44	45 to 54	55 to 64	65 to 74	75+
Electricity	**$911.44**	**$444.46**	**$826.12**	**$1,008.73**	**$1,045.36**	**$1,048.45**	**$920.84**	**$739.89**
Electricity (renter)	213.85	354.14	367.11	236.15	168.88	129.07	101.57	108.82
Electricity (owner)	690.09	89.69	457.70	767.18	867.41	904.15	805.66	622.61
Electricity (vacation)	7.50	0.62	1.31	5.40	9.07	15.22	13.61	8.46
Fuel oil and other fuels	**96.94**	**21.20**	**57.73**	**96.86**	**109.06**	**112.92**	**151.08**	**121.06**
Fuel oil	55.08	8.97	34.24	48.83	59.37	66.53	92.96	77.07
Fuel oil (renter)	6.54	6.74	9.92	5.14	7.37	3.75	7.30	4.67
Fuel oil (owner)	47.74	2.23	24.32	43.69	51.17	62.50	81.84	70.30
Fuel oil (vacation)	0.81	–	–	–	0.83	0.27	3.82	2.10
Coal	0.58	0.13	0.41	0.79	0.70	0.86	0.33	0.41
Coal (renter)	0.14	0.13	–	0.53	–	0.10	–	–
Coal (owner)	0.44	–	0.41	0.26	0.70	0.76	0.33	0.41
Bottled/tank gas	35.26	8.62	18.90	40.59	42.62	38.36	48.10	39.91
Gas (renter)	4.76	2.68	6.47	5.02	3.99	2.89	5.25	6.29
Gas (owner)	28.79	5.59	10.83	33.47	36.45	33.36	41.26	32.90
Gas (vacation)	1.71	0.35	1.61	2.11	2.18	2.11	1.58	0.72
Wood and other fuels	6.02	3.48	4.18	6.64	6.37	7.17	9.68	3.68
Wood and other fuels (renter)	1.09	2.62	1.61	1.32	0.20	0.78	0.02	1.87
Wood and other fuels (owner)	4.88	0.85	2.57	5.32	5.92	6.38	9.63	1.80
Wood and other fuels (vacation)	0.05	–	–	–	0.24	–	0.03	–
Telephone services	**876.75**	**589.26**	**949.72**	**1,017.82**	**1,007.26**	**909.37**	**720.07**	**511.10**
Telephone services in home city, excl. mobile phones	757.26	504.62	812.00	860.09	860.83	777.75	661.80	488.30
Telephone services for mobile phones	119.49	84.65	137.72	157.72	146.43	131.62	58.27	22.80
Water and other public services	**296.42**	**90.51**	**234.47**	**336.37**	**351.75**	**344.92**	**328.15**	**264.36**
Water and sewerage maintenance	212.72	67.85	169.86	247.00	254.59	242.28	230.32	180.07
Water and sewerage maintenance (renter)	29.99	46.89	47.43	34.21	25.75	20.66	15.12	13.54
Water and sewerage maintenance (owner)	181.10	20.78	122.26	212.04	226.92	218.76	210.91	164.30
Water and sewerage maintenance (vacation)	1.63	0.19	0.16	0.74	1.92	2.85	4.29	2.24
Trash and garbage collection	81.74	22.30	62.71	87.60	94.74	100.82	95.18	82.08
Trash and garbage collection (renter)	8.30	11.84	13.13	9.27	6.82	6.51	5.44	3.33
Trash and garbage collection (owner)	71.34	10.25	49.05	77.62	84.94	90.56	84.85	76.31
Trash and garbage collection (vacation)	2.10	0.21	0.53	0.72	2.99	3.76	4.89	2.44
Septic tank cleaning	1.96	0.36	1.91	1.77	2.43	1.83	2.65	2.21
Septic tank cleaning (renter)	0.04	0.03	0.04	0.05	–	–	–	0.19
Septic tank cleaning (owner)	1.92	0.33	1.87	1.71	2.43	1.83	2.65	2.02

See appendix for information about mortgage principle reduction.
Note: (–) means sample is too small to make a reliable estimate.
Source: Bureau of Labor Statistics, unpublished tables from the 2000 Consumer Expenditure Survey

Table 9.2 (Housing) Shelter and Utilities: Indexed spending by age, 2000

(indexed average annual spending of consumer units (CU) on shelter and utilities, by age of consumer unit reference person, 2000; index definition: an index of 100 is the average for all consumer units; an index of 132 means that spending by consumer units in that group is 32 percent above the average for all consumer units; an index of 68 indicates spending that is 32 percent below the average for all consumer units)

	total consumer units	under 25	25 to 34	35 to 44	45 to 54	55 to 64	65 to 74	75+
Average spending of CU, total	$38,045	$22,543	$38,945	$45,149	$46,160	$39,340	$30,782	$21,908
Average spending of CU, index	100	59	102	119	121	103	81	58
Housing, spending index	100	58	106	123	115	100	79	63
SHELTER	**100**	**64**	**111**	**126**	**117**	**93**	**72**	**57**
Owned dwellings*	**100**	**14**	**90**	**140**	**130**	**104**	**79**	**53**
Mortgage interest and charges	100	15	109	163	135	86	45	14
Mortgage interest	100	16	113	165	134	82	41	14
Interest paid, home equity loan	100	1	73	139	150	128	81	18
Interest paid, home equity line of credit	100	–	30	135	148	175	103	20
Prepayment penalty charges	100	–	9	262	191	29	–	–
Property taxes	100	15	66	109	129	128	112	94
Maintenance, repairs, insurance, other expenses	100	9	60	107	113	126	142	118
Homeowner's and related insurance	100	10	68	103	120	130	129	107
Ground rent	100	69	100	55	87	96	116	241
Maintenance and repair services	100	2	44	113	112	131	153	123
Painting and papering	100	2	42	124	104	163	154	74
Plumbing and water heating	100	3	40	79	102	159	157	187
Heat, air conditioning, electrical work	100	2	47	106	149	114	137	98
Roofing and gutters	100	1	26	107	91	128	197	170
Other repair and maintenance services	100	3	42	125	100	133	147	129
Repair, replacement of hard-surface flooring	100	1	98	109	157	88	112	47
Repair of built-in appliances	100	26	57	128	74	120	141	156
Maintenance and repair materials	100	13	108	127	122	104	112	29
Paints, wallpaper, and supplies	100	16	160	128	76	103	123	18
Tools, equipment for painting, wallpapering	100	16	160	128	76	103	123	19
Plumbing supplies and equipment	100	17	75	89	108	147	151	100
Electrical supplies, heating and cooling equipment	100	4	74	167	85	44	191	78
Hard-surface flooring, repair and replacement	100	17	77	142	186	49	102	1
Roofing and gutters	100	2	34	189	99	184	64	21
Plaster, paneling, siding, windows, doors, screens, awnings	100	2	129	102	136	111	115	16
Patio, walk, fence, driveway, masonry, brick, and stucco materials	100	12	68	150	112	112	128	37
Landscape maintenance	100	3	94	131	149	111	80	23
Miscellaneous supplies and equipment	100	23	105	118	146	94	96	29
Insulation, other maintenance, repair	100	26	115	137	146	69	75	23
Finish basement, remodel rooms, build patios, walks, etc.	100	18	86	84	145	141	136	39
Property management and security	100	4	60	77	95	119	186	190
Property management	100	5	67	88	95	116	169	173
Management and upkeep services for security	100	2	45	51	95	125	225	228
Parking	100	12	97	78	80	137	165	146

	total consumer units	under 25	25 to 34	35 to 44	45 to 54	55 to 64	65 to 74	75+
Rented dwellings	**100**	**178**	**173**	**102**	**79**	**55**	**47**	**66**
Rent	100	179	175	101	79	54	46	65
Rent as pay	100	190	110	125	79	70	70	72
Maintenance, insurance, and other expenses	100	91	108	100	86	95	90	140
Tenant's insurance	100	96	168	72	86	85	84	110
Maintenance and repair services	100	46	78	86	77	113	92	251
Repair and maintenance services	100	38	63	92	85	126	64	269
Repair and replacement of hard-surface flooring	100	81	226	29	7	–	355	99
Repair of built-in appliances	100	543	29	129	14	43	129	–
Maintenance and repair materials	100	153	80	153	99	81	93	10
Paint, wallpaper, and supplies	100	164	84	219	58	38	62	18
Painting and wallpapering tools	100	159	82	212	59	35	59	18
Plastering, paneling, roofing, gutters, etc.	100	127	33	73	331	4	13	2
Patio, walk, fence, driveway, masonry, brick, and stucco materials	100	–	–	–	–	–	–	–
Plumbing supplies and equipment	100	521	121	69	69	67	13	10
Electrical supplies, heating and cooling equip.	100	12	116	96	256	40	–	0
Miscellaneous supplies and equipment	100	118	79	168	64	79	162	7
Insulation, other maintenance and repair	100	184	160	28	58	283	21	21
Materials for additions, finishing basements, remodeling rooms	100	95	51	217	66	9	209	2
Construction materials for jobs not started	100	–	500	–	–	–	500	–
Hard-surface flooring	100	318	147	67	169	–	–	18
Landscape maintenance	100	52	22	90	113	377	3	10
Other lodging	**100**	**67**	**52**	**90**	**150**	**143**	**114**	**57**
Owned vacation homes	100	7	35	85	127	200	154	76
Mortgage interest and charges	100	5	43	117	122	186	157	15
Mortgage interest	100	5	41	119	122	180	164	14
Interest paid, home equity loan	100	–	144	81	173	174	–	–
Interest paid, home equity line of credit	100	–	–	77	53	529	–	41
Property taxes	100	12	26	73	121	225	140	108
Maintenance, insurance and other expenses	100	0	32	42	145	187	172	145
Homeowner's and related insurance	100	–	45	93	153	133	145	91
Homeowner's insurance	100	–	45	93	153	133	145	91
Ground rent	100	–	6	–	46	325	193	282
Maintenance and repair services	100	0	24	10	166	185	184	175
Maintenance and repair materials	100	–	29	63	31	479	121	–
Property management and security	100	1	43	36	143	203	190	98
Property management	100	1	54	43	134	202	184	93
Management and upkeep services for security	100	–	24	25	160	203	202	110
Parking	100	0	14	60	105	182	232	163
Housing while attending school	100	299	16	42	252	101	8	10
Lodging on trips	100	31	73	108	133	123	123	60
UTILITIES, FUELS, AND PUBLIC SERVICES	**100**	**50**	**94**	**113**	**115**	**111**	**98**	**78**
Natural gas	**100**	**33**	**89**	**114**	**112**	**111**	**104**	**98**
Natural gas (renter)	100	126	168	121	78	73	51	47
Natural gas (owner)	100	11	70	113	120	119	116	110
Natural gas (vacation)	100	5	16	59	144	239	127	110

	total consumer units	under 25	25 to 34	35 to 44	45 to 54	55 to 64	65 to 74	75+
Electricity	**100**	**49**	**91**	**111**	**115**	**115**	**101**	**81**
Electricity (renter)	100	166	172	110	79	60	47	51
Electricity (owner)	100	13	66	111	126	131	117	90
Electricity (vacation)	100	8	17	72	121	203	181	113
Fuel oil and other fuels	**100**	**22**	**60**	**100**	**113**	**116**	**156**	**125**
Fuel oil	100	16	62	89	108	121	169	140
Fuel oil (renter)	100	103	152	79	113	57	112	71
Fuel oil (owner)	100	5	51	92	107	131	171	147
Fuel oil (vacation)	100	–	–	–	102	33	472	259
Coal	100	22	71	136	121	148	57	71
Coal (renter)	100	93	–	379	–	71	–	–
Coal (owner)	100	–	93	59	159	173	75	93
Bottled/tank gas	100	24	54	115	121	109	136	113
Gas (renter)	100	56	136	105	84	61	110	132
Gas (owner)	100	19	38	116	127	116	143	114
Gas (vacation)	100	20	94	123	127	123	92	42
Wood and other fuels	100	58	69	110	106	119	161	61
Wood and other fuels (renter)	100	240	148	121	18	72	2	172
Wood and other fuels (owner)	100	17	53	109	121	131	197	37
Wood and other fuels (vacation)	100	–	–	–	480	–	60	–
Telephone services	**100**	**67**	**108**	**116**	**115**	**104**	**82**	**58**
Telephone services in home city, excl. mobile phones	100	67	107	114	114	103	87	64
Telephone services for mobile phones	100	71	115	132	123	110	49	19
Water and other public services	**100**	**31**	**79**	**113**	**119**	**116**	**111**	**89**
Water and sewerage maintenance	100	32	80	116	120	114	108	85
Water and sewerage maintenance (renter)	100	156	158	114	86	69	50	45
Water and sewerage maintenance (owner)	100	11	68	117	125	121	116	91
Water and sewerage maintenance (vacation)	100	12	10	45	118	175	263	137
Trash and garbage collection	100	27	77	107	116	123	116	100
Trash and garbage collection (renter)	100	143	158	112	82	78	66	40
Trash and garbage collection (owner)	100	14	69	109	119	127	119	107
Trash and garbage collection (vacation)	100	10	25	34	142	179	233	116
Septic tank cleaning	100	18	97	90	124	93	135	113
Septic tank cleaning (renter)	100	75	100	125	–	–	–	475
Septic tank cleaning (owner)	100	17	97	89	127	95	138	105

See appendix for information about mortgage principle reduction.
Note: (–) means sample is too small to make a reliable estimate.
Source: Calculations by New Strategist based on the 2000 Consumer Expenditure Survey

Table 9.3 (Housing) Shelter and Utilities: Indexed per capita spending by age, 2000

(indexed average annual per capita spending of consumer units (CU) on shelter and utilities, by age of consumer unit reference person, 2000; index definition: an index of 100 is the average for all consumer units; an index of 132 means that spending by consumer units in that group is 32 percent above the average for all consumer units; an index of 68 indicates spending that is 32 percent below the average for all consumer units)

	total consumer units	under 25	25 to 34	35 to 44	45 to 54	55 to 64	65 to 74	75+
Per capita spending of CU, total	$15,218	$11,865	$13,429	$13,682	$17,096	$18,733	$16,201	$14,605
Per capita spending of CU, index	100	78	88	90	112	123	106	96
Housing, per capita spending index	100	76	91	93	107	119	103	105
SHELTER	100	85	96	95	108	110	95	95
Owned dwellings*	100	18	78	106	120	124	103	88
Mortgage interest and charges	100	19	94	124	125	103	59	24
Mortgage interest	100	21	98	125	124	97	54	23
Interest paid, home equity loan	100	2	63	106	138	153	106	29
Interest paid, home equity line of credit	100	–	26	103	137	208	136	34
Prepayment penalty charges	100	–	8	198	177	35	–	–
Property taxes	100	20	57	83	120	153	147	157
Maintenance, repairs, insurance, other expenses	100	11	52	81	105	150	186	197
Homeowner's and related insurance	100	13	59	78	111	154	170	179
Ground rent	100	91	86	42	80	115	153	402
Maintenance and repair services	100	3	38	85	104	156	201	206
Painting and papering	100	2	37	94	97	194	202	124
Plumbing and water heating	100	4	35	60	94	189	206	311
Heat, air conditioning, electrical work	100	3	40	80	138	136	180	163
Roofing and gutters	100	1	22	81	84	153	259	283
Other repair and maintenance services	100	4	36	95	93	158	193	214
Repair, replacement of hard-surface flooring	100	2	84	82	145	104	147	79
Repair of built-in appliances	100	34	49	97	69	143	186	260
Maintenance and repair materials	100	18	93	96	113	124	148	49
Paints, wallpaper, and supplies	100	21	138	97	70	122	162	31
Tools, equipment for painting, wallpapering	100	21	138	97	70	123	162	31
Plumbing supplies and equipment	100	22	65	67	100	176	198	166
Electrical supplies, heating and cooling equipment	100	5	64	126	79	53	252	130
Hard-surface flooring, repair and replacement	100	22	67	107	172	58	134	1
Roofing and gutters	100	2	29	143	92	219	84	35
Plaster, paneling, siding, windows, doors, screens, awnings	100	3	111	77	126	132	151	26
Patio, walk, fence, driveway, masonry, brick, and stucco materials	100	15	59	114	103	133	169	61
Landscape maintenance	100	4	81	99	138	132	105	38
Miscellaneous supplies and equipment	100	31	90	90	135	112	127	48
Insulation, other maintenance, repair	100	35	99	104	135	82	98	38
Finish basement, remodel rooms, build patios, walks, etc.	100	23	74	64	134	167	178	65
Property management and security	100	6	52	58	88	141	245	317
Property management	100	7	58	67	88	138	223	289
Management and upkeep services for security	100	2	39	38	88	149	296	380
Parking	100	16	84	59	74	163	217	244

	total consumer units	under 25	25 to 34	35 to 44	45 to 54	55 to 64	65 to 74	75+
Rented dwellings	**100**	**234**	**149**	**77**	**73**	**66**	**62**	**110**
Rent	100	235	151	77	73	65	60	108
Rent as pay	100	250	95	95	73	83	92	120
Maintenance, insurance, and other expenses	100	120	93	76	80	113	118	233
Tenant's insurance	100	126	145	54	80	101	111	184
Maintenance and repair services	100	60	67	65	71	134	122	418
Repair and maintenance services	100	51	54	70	78	150	84	449
Repair and replacement of hard-surface flooring	100	107	195	22	7	–	467	165
Repair of built-in appliances	100	714	25	97	13	51	169	–
Maintenance and repair materials	100	202	69	116	91	97	122	17
Paint, wallpaper, and supplies	100	215	72	166	54	46	81	30
Painting and wallpapering tools	100	209	71	160	54	42	77	29
Plastering, paneling, roofing, gutters, etc.	100	167	29	55	307	5	16	3
Patio, walk, fence, driveway, masonry, brick, and stucco materials	100	–	–	–	–	–	–	–
Plumbing supplies and equipment	100	685	104	52	64	79	17	17
Electrical supplies, heating and cooling equip.	100	16	100	73	237	48	–	0
Miscellaneous supplies and equipment	100	155	68	127	59	94	213	12
Insulation, other maintenance and repair	100	242	138	21	53	336	27	34
Materials for additions, finishing basements, remodeling rooms	100	125	44	164	61	10	274	4
Construction materials for jobs not started	100	–	431	–	–	–	658	–
Hard-surface flooring	100	419	127	51	157	–	–	31
Landscape maintenance	100	68	19	68	105	448	4	17
Other lodging	**100**	**89**	**45**	**68**	**139**	**171**	**150**	**95**
Owned vacation homes	100	9	30	64	117	238	203	126
Mortgage interest and charges	100	7	37	89	113	222	207	24
Mortgage interest	100	7	36	90	113	215	215	24
Interest paid, home equity loan	100	–	125	62	160	207	–	–
Interest paid, home equity line of credit	100	–	–	59	49	630	–	68
Property taxes	100	16	22	55	112	268	184	180
Maintenance, insurance and other expenses	100	0	27	32	134	223	227	241
Homeowner's and related insurance	100	–	39	71	141	158	190	151
Homeowner's insurance	100	–	39	71	141	158	190	151
Ground rent	100	–	5	–	42	386	254	470
Maintenance and repair services	100	1	21	8	154	221	242	292
Maintenance and repair materials	100	–	25	47	29	570	159	–
Property management and security	100	1	37	27	132	241	250	164
Property management	100	2	46	32	124	241	242	154
Management and upkeep services for security	100	–	21	19	148	242	265	183
Parking	100	0	12	45	97	216	306	272
Housing while attending school	100	393	14	32	233	121	10	17
Lodging on trips	100	41	63	82	123	146	161	100
UTILITIES, FUELS, AND PUBLIC SERVICES	**100**	**66**	**81**	**86**	**106**	**132**	**129**	**130**
Natural gas	**100**	**44**	**77**	**86**	**104**	**132**	**136**	**163**
Natural gas (renter)	100	166	145	92	72	87	67	78
Natural gas (owner)	100	14	60	85	111	142	153	184
Natural gas (vacation)	100	6	14	45	133	284	167	183

	total consumer units	under 25	25 to 34	35 to 44	45 to 54	55 to 64	65 to 74	75+
Electricity	100	64	78	84	106	137	133	135
Electricity (renter)	100	218	148	84	73	72	62	85
Electricity (owner)	100	17	57	84	116	156	154	150
Electricity (vacation)	100	11	15	55	112	242	239	188
Fuel oil and other fuels	100	29	51	76	104	139	205	208
Fuel oil	100	21	54	67	100	144	222	233
Fuel oil (renter)	100	136	131	60	104	68	147	119
Fuel oil (owner)	100	6	44	69	99	156	226	245
Fuel oil (vacation)	100	–	–	–	95	40	621	432
Coal	100	29	61	103	112	177	75	118
Coal (renter)	100	122	–	287	–	85	–	–
Coal (owner)	100	–	80	45	147	206	99	155
Bottled/tank gas	100	32	46	87	112	130	179	189
Gas (renter)	100	74	117	80	78	72	145	220
Gas (owner)	100	26	32	88	117	138	189	190
Gas (vacation)	100	27	81	93	118	147	122	70
Wood and other fuels	100	76	60	84	98	142	212	102
Wood and other fuels (renter)	100	316	127	92	17	85	2	286
Wood and other fuels (owner)	100	23	45	83	112	156	260	61
Wood and other fuels (vacation)	100	–	–	–	444	–	79	–
Telephone services	100	88	93	88	106	123	108	97
Telephone services in home city, excl. mobile phones	100	88	92	86	105	122	115	107
Telephone services for mobile phones	100	93	99	100	113	131	64	32
Water and other public services	100	40	68	86	110	139	146	149
Water and sewerage maintenance	100	42	69	88	111	136	142	141
Water and sewerage maintenance (renter)	100	206	136	86	80	82	66	75
Water and sewerage maintenance (owner)	100	15	58	89	116	144	153	151
Water and sewerage maintenance (vacation)	100	15	8	34	109	208	346	229
Trash and garbage collection	100	36	66	81	107	147	153	167
Trash and garbage collection (renter)	100	188	136	85	76	93	86	67
Trash and garbage collection (owner)	100	19	59	82	110	151	156	178
Trash and garbage collection (vacation)	100	13	22	26	132	213	306	194
Septic tank cleaning	100	24	84	68	115	111	178	188
Septic tank cleaning (renter)	100	99	86	95	–	–	–	792
Septic tank cleaning (owner)	100	23	84	67	117	113	182	175

See appendix for information about mortgage principle reduction.
Note: Per capita indexes account for household size and show how much each person in a particular household demographic segment spends relative to a person in the average household. (–) means sample is too small to make a reliable estimate.
Source: Calculations by New Strategist based on the 2000 Consumer Expenditure Survey

Table 9.4 (Housing) Shelter and Utilities: Total spending by age, 2000

(total annual spending on shelter and utilities, by consumer unit (CU) age group, 2000; numbers in thousands)

	total consumer units	under 25	25 to 34	35 to 44	45 to 54	55 to 64	65 to 74	75+
Number of consumer units	109,367	8,306	18,887	23,983	21,874	14,161	11,538	10,617
Total spending of all CUs	$4,160,831,424	$187,243,653	$735,559,314	$1,082,817,341	$1,009,709,965	$557,094,165	$355,160,524	$232,597,661
Housing, total spending	1,347,238,483	59,048,683	246,467,040	362,417,905	310,158,227	175,061,114	111,589,305	82,451,728
SHELTER	**$778,065,273**	**$37,994,551**	**$149,292,480**	**$214,171,308**	**$181,483,766**	**$93,280,065**	**$59,007,178**	**$42,829,084**
Owned dwellings*	**503,341,931**	**5,263,844**	**78,232,976**	**154,279,521**	**130,446,693**	**67,686,748**	**41,756,484**	**25,671,481**
Mortgage interest and charges	288,598,733	3,205,701	54,542,823	103,186,378	77,822,442	32,259,041	13,598,687	3,980,844
Mortgage interest	269,095,316	3,196,149	52,735,148	97,289,678	72,016,426	28,495,331	11,733,915	3,626,130
Interest paid, home equity loan	10,742,027	9,552	1,352,309	3,285,431	3,212,853	1,785,560	912,771	183,356
Interest paid, home equity line of credit	8,723,112	–	454,799	2,589,684	2,578,945	1,976,734	951,885	171,358
Prepayment penalty charges	37,185	–	567	21,345	14,218	1,416	–	–
Property taxes	124,519,798	1,461,690	14,264,973	29,883,537	32,174,685	20,700,408	14,676,682	11,357,217
Maintenance, repairs, insurance, other expenses	90,223,400	596,454	9,425,180	21,209,606	20,449,784	14,727,298	13,480,999	10,333,420
Homeowner's and related insurance	25,683,746	192,367	3,025,320	5,816,117	6,170,874	4,310,608	3,493,591	2,675,059
Ground rent	4,229,222	222,019	732,060	508,679	731,904	527,072	518,172	989,717
Maintenance and repair services	48,003,364	80,651	3,659,545	11,872,065	10,767,914	8,150,364	7,726,191	5,746,770
Painting and papering	5,460,694	7,143	400,404	1,485,027	1,138,760	1,150,440	885,657	393,360
Plumbing and water heating	4,551,855	9,303	316,546	785,203	925,270	937,175	752,508	825,259
Heat, air conditioning, electrical work	8,660,773	15,948	700,141	2,008,576	2,580,257	1,283,978	1,250,488	821,862
Roofing and gutters	8,232,054	3,572	366,408	1,934,948	1,493,775	1,367,669	1,707,739	1,357,596
Other repair and maintenance services	17,278,892	38,457	1,239,932	4,740,240	3,456,311	2,971,827	2,674,508	2,157,693
Repair, replacement of hard-surface flooring	3,675,825	3,322	621,949	877,778	1,152,104	417,041	434,060	169,447
Repair of built-in appliances	143,271	2,824	14,165	40,291	21,218	22,233	21,345	21,659
Maintenance and repair materials	8,539,375	87,296	1,593,307	2,376,475	2,075,405	1,152,139	1,011,652	243,023
Paints, wallpaper, and supplies	1,753,153	20,931	484,640	490,452	264,894	232,807	227,991	31,214
Tools, equipment for painting, wallpapering	188,111	2,243	52,128	52,763	28,436	25,065	24,461	3,397
Plumbing supplies and equipment	670,420	8,555	86,691	130,947	144,587	128,015	106,611	64,764
Electrical supplies, heating and cooling equip.	475,746	1,329	60,627	174,117	80,715	27,331	96,112	35,885
Hard-surface flooring, repair and replacement	763,382	9,801	101,801	237,192	284,143	48,431	81,920	637
Roofing and gutters	701,042	831	41,363	290,914	139,337	166,958	47,075	14,439
Plaster, paneling, siding, windows, doors, screens, awnings	1,327,715	2,077	295,959	296,670	360,921	190,607	160,840	20,491
Patio, walk, fence, driveway, masonry, brick, and stucco materials	65,620	581	7,744	21,585	14,656	9,488	8,884	2,336
Landscape maintenance	319,352	748	51,750	91,855	94,933	45,882	26,999	7,007
Miscellaneous supplies and equipment	2,274,834	40,284	410,981	590,222	662,563	277,556	230,760	62,959
Insulation, other maintenance, repair	1,470,986	29,569	291,238	441,287	429,824	131,414	115,726	32,382
Finish basement, remodel rooms, build patios, walks, etc.	803,847	10,715	119,744	148,934	232,739	146,283	115,034	30,577
Property management and security	3,389,283	10,798	351,487	571,275	643,752	520,417	665,627	625,235
Property management	2,350,297	9,552	271,028	455,917	446,448	352,326	419,522	395,483
Management and upkeep services for security	1,038,987	1,246	80,459	115,598	197,303	168,233	246,221	229,752
Parking	377,316	3,405	63,271	64,754	60,154	66,840	65,767	53,616

	total consumer units	under 25	25 to 34	35 to 44	45 to 54	55 to 64	65 to 74	75+
Rented dwellings	**$222,464,508**	**$30,053,683**	**$66,375,717**	**$49,573,580**	**$35,308,136**	**$15,896,006**	**$10,980,368**	**$14,274,132**
Rent	216,254,650	29,383,223	65,207,934	48,038,429	34,286,620	15,235,537	10,458,966	13,641,146
Rent as pay	3,197,891	461,315	607,784	876,099	503,977	288,884	235,721	224,337
Maintenance, insurance, and other expenses	3,011,967	209,145	560,000	659,053	517,320	371,585	285,681	408,648
Tenant's insurance	968,992	70,684	281,227	152,532	167,555	106,774	86,189	103,940
Maintenance and repair services	1,217,255	42,361	164,317	229,997	187,023	178,004	118,611	296,639
Repair and maintenance services	1,091,483	31,895	117,855	220,644	185,054	177,579	73,382	285,279
Repair and replacement of hard-surface flooring	118,116	7,309	46,084	7,435	1,750	–	44,191	11,360
Repair of built-in appliances	7,656	3,156	378	2,158	219	425	1,038	–
Maintenance and repair materials	825,721	96,100	114,455	276,284	162,743	86,807	80,881	8,069
Paint, wallpaper, and supplies	168,425	20,931	24,364	81,063	19,687	8,355	10,961	2,973
Painting and wallpapering tools	18,592	2,243	2,644	8,634	2,187	850	1,154	319
Plastering, paneling, roofing, gutters, etc.	52,496	5,067	3,022	8,394	34,780	283	692	106
Patio, walk, fence, driveway, masonry, brick, and stucco materials	3,281	–	–	–	–	–	–	–
Plumbing supplies and equipment	42,653	16,861	8,877	6,475	5,906	3,682	577	425
Electrical supplies, heating and cooling equip.	27,342	249	5,477	5,756	13,999	1,416	–	0
Miscellaneous supplies and equipment	393,721	35,134	54,017	145,097	50,091	40,076	67,151	2,654
Insulation, other maintenance and repair	100,618	14,037	27,764	6,236	11,593	36,819	2,192	2,017
Materials for additions, finishing basements, remodeling rooms	292,010	21,097	25,497	138,862	38,498	3,257	64,267	637
Construction materials for jobs not started	1,094	–	944	–	–	–	577	–
Hard-surface flooring	53,590	12,957	13,599	7,914	18,155	–	–	956
Landscape maintenance	65,620	2,575	2,455	12,951	14,874	32,004	231	637
Other lodging	**52,259,927**	**2,677,024**	**4,683,787**	**10,318,446**	**15,729,156**	**9,697,311**	**6,270,326**	**2,883,471**
Owned vacation homes	16,176,473	80,734	964,370	3,016,342	4,095,250	4,192,364	2,636,433	1,190,909
Mortgage interest and charges	6,961,210	26,413	516,182	1,789,851	1,696,329	1,678,220	1,155,300	98,632
Mortgage interest	6,692,167	26,413	479,352	1,742,845	1,632,019	1,561,817	1,155,300	93,854
Interest paid, home equity loan	147,645	–	36,830	26,381	51,185	33,278	–	–
Interest paid, home equity line of credit	121,397	–	–	20,625	12,906	83,125	–	4,778
Property taxes	5,683,803	53,491	254,786	903,679	1,378,281	1,659,103	838,697	596,251
Maintenance, insurance and other expenses	3,531,460	748	193,403	323,051	1,020,860	855,041	642,436	496,026
Homeowner's and related insurance	1,174,602	–	92,169	239,830	358,515	201,794	179,070	103,197
Homeowner's insurance	1,174,602	–	92,169	239,830	358,515	201,794	179,070	103,197
Ground rent	324,820	–	3,400	–	29,749	136,512	66,113	88,970
Maintenance and repair services	1,483,017	498	61,572	32,617	492,821	355,724	287,758	252,048
Maintenance and repair materials	52,496	–	2,644	7,195	3,281	32,570	6,692	–
Property management and security	425,438	249	31,919	33,816	121,619	111,589	85,266	40,663
Property management	279,980	249	25,875	26,141	75,028	73,354	54,344	25,162
Management and upkeep services for security	145,458	–	6,044	7,914	46,592	38,235	30,922	15,501
Parking	71,089	0	1,700	9,353	14,874	16,710	17,422	11,254
Housing while attending school	8,564,530	1,943,438	239,676	789,760	4,313,115	1,123,534	71,882	82,813
Lodging on trips	27,518,925	652,852	3,479,741	6,512,344	7,320,790	4,381,272	3,561,896	1,609,750
UTILITIES, FUELS, AND PUBLIC SERVICES	**272,203,526**	**10,363,812**	**44,217,489**	**67,388,393**	**62,504,299**	**39,029,982**	**28,133,221**	**20,564,492**
Natural gas	**33,613,947**	**849,787**	**5,158,417**	**8,395,729**	**7,525,531**	**4,821,821**	**3,671,045**	**3,190,727**
Natural gas (renter)	6,613,422	632,253	1,918,730	1,754,117	1,028,734	624,783	354,101	300,461
Natural gas (owner)	26,754,449	216,620	3,232,699	6,609,715	6,426,144	4,120,993	3,283,946	2,864,042
Natural gas (vacation)	246,076	914	6,988	31,897	70,872	76,045	32,999	26,224

	total consumer units	under 25	25 to 34	35 to 44	45 to 54	55 to 64	65 to 74	75+
Electricity	**$99,681,458**	**$3,691,685**	**$15,602,928**	**$24,192,372**	**$22,866,205**	**$14,847,100**	**$10,624,652**	**$7,855,412**
Electricity (renter)	23,388,133	2,941,487	6,933,607	5,663,585	3,694,081	1,827,760	1,171,915	1,155,342
Electricity (owner)	75,473,073	744,965	8,644,580	18,399,278	18,973,726	12,803,668	9,295,705	6,610,250
Electricity (vacation)	820,253	5,150	24,742	129,508	198,397	215,530	157,032	89,820
Fuel oil and other fuels	**10,602,037**	**176,087**	**1,090,347**	**2,322,993**	**2,385,578**	**1,599,060**	**1,743,161**	**1,285,294**
Fuel oil	6,023,934	74,505	646,691	1,171,090	1,298,659	942,131	1,072,572	818,252
Fuel oil (renter)	715,260	55,982	187,359	123,273	161,211	53,104	84,227	49,581
Fuel oil (owner)	5,221,181	18,522	459,332	1,047,817	1,119,293	885,063	944,270	746,375
Fuel oil (vacation)	88,587	–	–	–	18,155	3,823	44,075	22,296
Coal	63,433	1,080	7,744	18,947	15,312	12,178	3,808	4,353
Coal (renter)	15,311	1,080	–	12,711	–	1,416	–	–
Coal (owner)	48,121	–	7,744	6,236	15,312	10,762	3,808	4,353
Bottled/tank gas	3,856,280	71,598	356,964	973,470	932,270	543,216	554,978	423,724
Gas (renter)	520,587	22,260	122,199	120,395	87,277	40,925	60,575	66,781
Gas (owner)	3,148,676	46,431	204,546	802,711	797,307	472,411	476,058	349,299
Gas (vacation)	187,018	2,907	30,408	50,604	47,685	29,880	18,230	7,644
Wood and other fuels	658,389	28,905	78,948	159,247	139,337	101,534	111,688	39,071
Wood and other fuels (renter)	119,210	21,762	30,408	31,658	4,375	11,046	231	19,854
Wood and other fuels (owner)	533,711	7,060	48,540	127,590	129,494	90,347	111,111	19,111
Wood and other fuels (vacation)	5,468	–	–	–	5,250	–	346	–
Telephone services	**95,887,517**	**4,894,394**	**17,937,362**	**24,410,377**	**22,032,805**	**12,877,589**	**8,308,168**	**5,426,349**
Telephone services in home city, excl. mobile phones	82,819,254	4,191,374	15,336,244	20,627,538	18,829,795	11,013,718	7,635,848	5,184,281
Telephone services for mobile phones	13,068,263	703,103	2,601,118	3,782,599	3,203,010	1,863,871	672,319	242,068
Water and other public services	**32,418,566**	**751,776**	**4,428,435**	**8,067,162**	**7,694,180**	**4,884,412**	**3,786,195**	**2,806,710**
Water and sewerage maintenance	23,264,548	563,562	3,208,146	5,923,801	5,568,902	3,430,927	2,657,432	1,911,803
Water and sewerage maintenance (renter)	3,279,916	389,468	895,810	820,458	563,256	292,566	174,455	143,754
Water and sewerage maintenance (owner)	19,806,364	172,599	2,309,125	5,085,355	4,963,648	3,097,860	2,433,480	1,744,373
Water and sewerage maintenance (vacation)	178,268	1,578	3,022	17,747	41,998	40,359	49,498	23,782
Trash and garbage collection	8,939,659	185,224	1,184,404	2,100,911	2,072,343	1,427,712	1,098,187	871,443
Trash and garbage collection (renter)	907,746	98,343	247,986	222,322	149,181	92,188	62,767	35,355
Trash and garbage collection (owner)	7,802,242	85,137	926,407	1,861,560	1,857,978	1,282,420	978,999	810,183
Trash and garbage collection (vacation)	229,671	1,744	10,010	17,268	65,403	53,245	56,421	25,905
Septic tank cleaning	214,359	2,990	36,074	42,450	53,154	25,915	30,576	23,464
Septic tank cleaning (renter)	4,375	249	755	1,199	–	–	–	2,017
Septic tank cleaning (owner)	209,985	2,741	35,319	41,011	53,154	25,915	30,576	21,446

See appendix for information about mortgage principle reduction.
Note: Numbers may not add to total because of rounding. (–) means sample is too small to make a reliable estimate.
Source: Calculations by New Strategist based on the 2000 Consumer Expenditure Survey

Table 9.5 (Housing) Shelter and Utilities: Market shares by age, 2000

(percentage of total annual spending on shelter and utilities accounted for by consumer unit age groups, 2000)

	total consumer units	under 25	25 to 34	35 to 44	45 to 54	55 to 64	65 to 74	75+
Share of total consumer units	100.0%	7.6%	17.3%	21.9%	20.0%	12.9%	10.5%	9.7%
Share of total before-tax income	100.0	3.4	17.6	27.7	26.4	14.0	6.9	4.5
Share of total spending	100.0	4.5	17.7	26.0	24.3	13.4	8.5	5.6
Share of housing spending	100.0	4.4	18.3	26.9	23.0	13.0	8.3	6.1
SHELTER	100.0%	4.9%	19.2%	27.5%	23.3%	12.0%	7.6%	5.5%
Owned dwellings*	100.0	1.0	15.5	30.7	25.9	13.4	8.3	5.1
Mortgage interest and charges	100.0	1.1	18.9	35.8	27.0	11.2	4.7	1.4
Mortgage interest	100.0	1.2	19.6	36.2	26.8	10.6	4.4	1.3
Interest paid, home equity loan	100.0	0.1	12.6	30.6	29.9	16.6	8.5	1.7
Interest paid, home equity line of credit	100.0	–	5.2	29.7	29.6	22.7	10.9	2.0
Prepayment penalty charges	100.0	–	1.5	57.4	38.2	3.8	–	–
Property taxes	100.0	1.2	11.5	24.0	25.8	16.6	11.8	9.1
Maintenance, repairs, insurance, other expenses	100.0	0.7	10.4	23.5	22.7	16.3	14.9	11.5
Homeowner's and related insurance	100.0	0.7	11.8	22.6	24.0	16.8	13.6	10.4
Ground rent	100.0	5.2	17.3	12.0	17.3	12.5	12.3	23.4
Maintenance and repair services	100.0	0.2	7.6	24.7	22.4	17.0	16.1	12.0
Painting and papering	100.0	0.1	7.3	27.2	20.9	21.1	16.2	7.2
Plumbing and water heating	100.0	0.2	7.0	17.3	20.3	20.6	16.5	18.1
Heat, air conditioning, electrical work	100.0	0.2	8.1	23.2	29.8	14.8	14.4	9.5
Roofing and gutters	100.0	0.0	4.5	23.5	18.1	16.6	20.7	16.5
Other repair and maintenance services	100.0	0.2	7.2	27.4	20.0	17.2	15.5	12.5
Repair, replacement of hard-surface flooring	100.0	0.1	16.9	23.9	31.3	11.3	11.8	4.6
Repair of built-in appliances	100.0	2.0	9.9	28.1	14.8	15.5	14.9	15.1
Maintenance and repair materials	100.0	1.0	18.7	27.8	24.3	13.5	11.8	2.8
Paints, wallpaper, and supplies	100.0	1.2	27.6	28.0	15.1	13.3	13.0	1.8
Tools, equipment for painting, wallpapering	100.0	1.2	27.7	28.0	15.1	13.3	13.0	1.8
Plumbing supplies and equipment	100.0	1.3	12.9	19.5	21.6	19.1	15.9	9.7
Electrical supplies, heating and cooling equip.	100.0	0.3	12.7	36.6	17.0	5.7	20.2	7.5
Hard-surface flooring, repair and replacement	100.0	1.3	13.3	31.1	37.2	6.3	10.7	0.1
Roofing and gutters	100.0	0.1	5.9	41.5	19.9	23.8	6.7	2.1
Plaster, paneling, siding, windows, doors, screens, awnings	100.0	0.2	22.3	22.3	27.2	14.4	12.1	1.5
Patio, walk, fence, driveway, masonry, brick, and stucco materials	100.0	0.9	11.8	32.9	22.3	14.5	13.5	3.6
Landscape maintenance	100.0	0.2	16.2	28.8	29.7	14.4	8.5	2.2
Miscellaneous supplies and equipment	100.0	1.8	18.1	25.9	29.1	12.2	10.1	2.8
Insulation, other maintenance, repair	100.0	2.0	19.8	30.0	29.2	8.9	7.9	2.2
Finish basement, remodel rooms, build patios, walks, etc.	100.0	1.3	14.9	18.5	29.0	18.2	14.3	3.8
Property management and security	100.0	0.3	10.4	16.9	19.0	15.4	19.6	18.4
Property management	100.0	0.4	11.5	19.4	19.0	15.0	17.8	16.8
Management and upkeep services for security	100.0	0.1	7.7	11.1	19.0	16.2	23.7	22.1
Parking	100.0	0.9	16.8	17.2	15.9	17.7	17.4	14.2

	total consumer units	under 25	25 to 34	35 to 44	45 to 54	55 to 64	65 to 74	75+
Rented dwellings	**100.0%**	**13.5%**	**29.8%**	**22.3%**	**15.9%**	**7.1%**	**4.9%**	**6.4%**
Rent	100.0	13.6	30.2	22.2	15.9	7.0	4.8	6.3
Rent as pay	100.0	14.4	19.0	27.4	15.8	9.0	7.4	7.0
Maintenance, insurance, and other expenses	100.0	6.9	18.6	21.9	17.2	12.3	9.5	13.6
Tenant's insurance	100.0	7.3	29.0	15.7	17.3	11.0	8.9	10.7
Maintenance and repair services	100.0	3.5	13.5	18.9	15.4	14.6	9.7	24.4
Repair and maintenance services	100.0	2.9	10.8	20.2	17.0	16.3	6.7	26.1
Repair and replacement of hard-surface flooring	100.0	6.2	39.0	6.3	1.5	–	37.4	9.6
Repair of built-in appliances	100.0	41.2	4.9	28.2	2.9	5.5	13.6	–
Maintenance and repair materials	100.0	11.6	13.9	33.5	19.7	10.5	9.8	1.0
Paint, wallpaper, and supplies	100.0	12.4	14.5	48.1	11.7	5.0	6.5	1.8
Painting and wallpapering tools	100.0	12.1	14.2	46.4	11.8	4.6	6.2	1.7
Plastering, paneling, roofing, gutters, etc.	100.0	9.7	5.8	16.0	66.3	0.5	1.3	0.2
Patio, walk, fence, driveway, masonry, brick, and stucco materials	100.0	–	–	–	–	–	–	–
Plumbing supplies and equipment	100.0	39.5	20.8	15.2	13.8	8.6	1.4	1.0
Electrical supplies, heating and cooling equip.	100.0	0.9	20.0	21.1	51.2	5.2	–	0.0
Miscellaneous supplies and equipment	100.0	8.9	13.7	36.9	12.7	10.2	17.1	0.7
Insulation, other maintenance and repair	100.0	14.0	27.6	6.2	11.5	36.6	2.2	2.0
Materials for additions, finishing basements, remodeling rooms	100.0	7.2	8.7	47.6	13.2	1.1	22.0	0.2
Construction materials for jobs not started	100.0	–	86.3	–	–	–	52.7	–
Hard-surface flooring	100.0	24.2	25.4	14.8	33.9	–	–	1.8
Landscape maintenance	100.0	3.9	3.7	19.7	22.7	48.8	0.4	1.0
Other lodging	**100.0**	**5.1**	**9.0**	**19.7**	**30.1**	**18.6**	**12.0**	**5.5**
Owned vacation homes	100.0	0.5	6.0	18.6	25.3	25.9	16.3	7.4
Mortgage interest and charges	100.0	0.4	7.4	25.7	24.4	24.1	16.6	1.4
Mortgage interest	100.0	0.4	7.2	26.0	24.4	23.3	17.3	1.4
Interest paid, home equity loan	100.0	–	24.9	17.9	34.7	22.5	–	–
Interest paid, home equity line of credit	100.0	–	–	17.0	10.6	68.5	–	3.9
Property taxes	100.0	0.9	4.5	15.9	24.2	29.2	14.8	10.5
Maintenance, insurance and other expenses	100.0	0.0	5.5	9.1	28.9	24.2	18.2	14.0
Homeowner's and related insurance	100.0	–	7.8	20.4	30.5	17.2	15.2	8.8
Homeowner's insurance	100.0	–	7.8	20.4	30.5	17.2	15.2	8.8
Ground rent	100.0	–	1.0	–	9.2	42.0	20.4	27.4
Maintenance and repair services	100.0	0.0	4.2	2.2	33.2	24.0	19.4	17.0
Maintenance and repair materials	100.0	–	5.0	13.7	6.3	62.0	12.7	–
Property management and security	100.0	0.1	7.5	7.9	28.6	26.2	20.0	9.6
Property management	100.0	0.1	9.2	9.3	26.8	26.2	19.4	9.0
Management and upkeep services for security	100.0	–	4.2	5.4	32.0	26.3	21.3	10.7
Parking	100.0	0.0	2.4	13.2	20.9	23.5	24.5	15.8
Housing while attending school	100.0	22.7	2.8	9.2	50.4	13.1	0.8	1.0
Lodging on trips	100.0	2.4	12.6	23.7	26.6	15.9	12.9	5.8
UTILITIES, FUELS, AND PUBLIC SERVICES	**100.0**	**3.8**	**16.2**	**24.8**	**23.0**	**14.3**	**10.3**	**7.6**
Natural gas	**100.0**	**2.5**	**15.3**	**25.0**	**22.4**	**14.3**	**10.9**	**9.5**
Natural gas (renter)	100.0	9.6	29.0	26.5	15.6	9.4	5.4	4.5
Natural gas (owner)	100.0	0.8	12.1	24.7	24.0	15.4	12.3	10.7
Natural gas (vacation)	100.0	0.4	2.8	13.0	28.8	30.9	13.4	10.7

	total consumer units	under 25	25 to 34	35 to 44	45 to 54	55 to 64	65 to 74	75+
Electricity	**100.0%**	**3.7%**	**15.7%**	**24.3%**	**22.9%**	**14.9%**	**10.7%**	**7.9%**
Electricity (renter)	100.0	12.6	29.6	24.2	15.8	7.8	5.0	4.9
Electricity (owner)	100.0	1.0	11.5	24.4	25.1	17.0	12.3	8.8
Electricity (vacation)	100.0	0.6	3.0	15.8	24.2	26.3	19.1	11.0
Fuel oil and other fuels	**100.0**	**1.7**	**10.3**	**21.9**	**22.5**	**15.1**	**16.4**	**12.1**
Fuel oil	100.0	1.2	10.7	19.4	21.6	15.6	17.8	13.6
Fuel oil (renter)	100.0	7.8	26.2	17.2	22.5	7.4	11.8	6.9
Fuel oil (owner)	100.0	0.4	8.8	20.1	21.4	17.0	18.1	14.3
Fuel oil (vacation)	100.0	–	–	–	20.5	4.3	49.8	25.2
Coal	100.0	1.7	12.2	29.9	24.1	19.2	6.0	6.9
Coal (renter)	100.0	7.1	–	83.0	–	9.2	–	–
Coal (owner)	100.0	–	16.1	13.0	31.8	22.4	7.9	9.0
Bottled/tank gas	100.0	1.9	9.3	25.2	24.2	14.1	14.4	11.0
Gas (renter)	100.0	4.3	23.5	23.1	16.8	7.9	11.6	12.8
Gas (owner)	100.0	1.5	6.5	25.5	25.3	15.0	15.1	11.1
Gas (vacation)	100.0	1.6	16.3	27.1	25.5	16.0	9.7	4.1
Wood and other fuels	100.0	4.4	12.0	24.2	21.2	15.4	17.0	5.9
Wood and other fuels (renter)	100.0	18.3	25.5	26.6	3.7	9.3	0.2	16.7
Wood and other fuels (owner)	100.0	1.3	9.1	23.9	24.3	16.9	20.8	3.6
Wood and other fuels (vacation)	100.0	–	–	–	96.0	–	6.3	–
Telephone services	**100.0**	**5.1**	**18.7**	**25.5**	**23.0**	**13.4**	**8.7**	**5.7**
Telephone services in home city, excl. mobile phones	100.0	5.1	18.5	24.9	22.7	13.3	9.2	6.3
Telephone services for mobile phones	100.0	5.4	19.9	28.9	24.5	14.3	5.1	1.9
Water and other public services	**100.0**	**2.3**	**13.7**	**24.9**	**23.7**	**15.1**	**11.7**	**8.7**
Water and sewerage maintenance	100.0	2.4	13.8	25.5	23.9	14.7	11.4	8.2
Water and sewerage maintenance (renter)	100.0	11.9	27.3	25.0	17.2	8.9	5.3	4.4
Water and sewerage maintenance (owner)	100.0	0.9	11.7	25.7	25.1	15.6	12.3	8.8
Water and sewerage maintenance (vacation)	100.0	0.9	1.7	10.0	23.6	22.6	27.8	13.3
Trash and garbage collection	100.0	2.1	13.2	23.5	23.2	16.0	12.3	9.7
Trash and garbage collection (renter)	100.0	10.8	27.3	24.5	16.4	10.2	6.9	3.9
Trash and garbage collection (owner)	100.0	1.1	11.9	23.9	23.8	16.4	12.5	10.4
Trash and garbage collection (vacation)	100.0	0.8	4.4	7.5	28.5	23.2	24.6	11.3
Septic tank cleaning	100.0	1.4	16.8	19.8	24.8	12.1	14.3	10.9
Septic tank cleaning (renter)	100.0	5.7	17.3	27.4	–	–	–	46.1
Septic tank cleaning (owner)	100.0	1.3	16.8	19.5	25.3	12.3	14.6	10.2

*See appendix for information about mortgage principle reduction.
Note: Numbers may not add to total because of rounding. (–) means sample is too small to make a reliable estimate.
Source: Calculations by New Strategist based on the 2000 Consumer Expenditure Survey

Table 9.6 (Housing) Shelter and Utilities: Average spending by income, 2000

(average annual spending on shelter and utilities, by before-tax income of consumer units (CU), 2000; complete income reporters only)

	complete income reporters	under $10,000	$10,000– $19,999	$20,000– $29,999	$30,000– $39,999	$40,000– $49,999	$50,000– $69,999	$70,000 or more
Number of consumer units								
(in thousands, add 000)	81,454	10,810	14,714	12,039	9,477	7,653	11,337	15,424
Average number of persons per CU	2.5	1.7	2.1	2.4	2.5	2.6	2.9	3.2
Average before-tax income of CU	$44,649.00	$5,739.61	$14,586.29	$24,527.00	$34,422.00	$44,201.00	$58,561.00	$112,586.00
Average spending of CU, total	40,238.44	16,455.72	22,620.20	29,851.59	35,609.24	42,323.03	49,245.37	75,963.85
Housing, average spending	12,527.38	5,931.71	7,766.01	9,372.13	11,114.58	12,872.14	14,913.70	22,932.20
SHELTER	$7,134.13	$3,447.20	$4,342.73	$5,209.12	$6,561.85	$7,371.25	$8,379.36	$13,202.33
Owned dwellings*	4,598.75	1,228.55	1,961.11	2,466.38	3,734.99	4,466.42	6,121.32	10,618.69
Mortgage interest and charges	2,672.67	462.52	664.26	1,095.94	2,030.00	2,755.58	3,871.37	6,841.03
Mortgage interest	2,484.16	432.45	612.93	985.20	1,885.66	2,587.11	3,581.59	6,387.24
Interest paid, home equity loan	102.89	16.22	35.98	62.20	97.06	122.11	162.17	209.70
Interest paid, home equity line of credit	85.32	13.86	15.34	48.49	47.09	46.29	127.53	242.74
Prepayment penalty charges	0.30	–	–	0.05	0.18	0.08	0.08	1.35
Property taxes	1,084.22	446.24	658.59	716.74	923.95	920.04	1,301.51	2,244.42
Maintenance, repairs, insurance, other expenses	841.86	319.79	638.26	653.69	781.05	790.80	948.44	1,533.24
Homeowner's and related insurance	236.96	93.39	155.36	207.62	218.21	243.85	290.70	406.96
Ground rent	39.85	32.58	64.22	50.88	54.27	39.58	27.01	13.82
Maintenance and repair services	447.39	146.04	341.51	318.97	398.82	385.41	475.10	900.06
Painting and papering	50.98	18.67	22.63	32.83	33.12	40.88	57.50	126.04
Plumbing and water heating	42.16	23.01	36.93	30.70	35.95	36.54	40.48	77.36
Heat, air conditioning, electrical work	81.77	22.23	50.91	72.71	105.26	87.03	79.05	144.98
Roofing and gutters	82.38	41.91	88.76	57.17	69.88	63.33	83.45	140.69
Other repair and maintenance services	153.52	34.62	124.40	106.56	129.50	119.04	179.12	314.35
Repair, replacement of hard-surface flooring	35.17	5.25	17.22	18.26	24.47	35.38	34.44	93.47
Repair of built-in appliances	1.40	0.35	0.67	0.74	0.63	3.21	1.06	3.17
Maintenance and repair materials	82.80	23.62	47.58	51.40	80.74	84.17	122.29	153.94
Paints, wallpaper, and supplies	17.18	2.99	7.75	7.76	28.20	11.77	26.11	32.80
Tools, equipment for painting, wallpapering	1.85	0.32	0.83	0.83	3.03	1.26	2.81	3.52
Plumbing supplies and equipment	6.65	4.84	5.90	5.66	4.63	5.15	11.91	7.53
Electrical supplies, heating and cooling equip.	4.84	0.29	8.26	0.95	2.81	4.74	9.36	5.77
Hard-surface flooring, repair and replacement	7.62	0.04	11.68	1.97	8.89	5.25	6.57	14.65
Roofing and gutters	5.85	3.78	1.30	2.79	3.40	20.32	6.95	7.52
Plaster, paneling, siding, windows, doors, screens, awnings	13.47	1.24	4.00	7.96	10.79	12.32	17.25	34.83
Patio, walk, fence, driveway, masonry, brick, and stucco materials	0.57	0.02	0.28	0.55	1.00	0.48	0.98	0.74
Landscape maintenance	3.05	0.06	0.62	1.54	2.24	2.87	4.99	7.82
Miscellaneous supplies and equipment	21.72	10.03	6.96	21.39	15.74	20.00	35.35	38.74
Insulation, other maintenance, repair	13.70	8.29	2.71	7.64	9.83	15.77	21.78	28.10
Finish basement, remodel rooms, build patios, walks, etc.	8.02	1.73	4.26	13.75	5.92	4.23	13.58	10.64
Property management and security	31.34	22.60	27.54	21.71	24.36	34.88	29.34	52.60
Property management	21.57	16.97	16.71	15.11	17.29	24.64	20.42	36.42
Management and upkeep services for security	9.77	5.63	10.83	6.61	7.07	10.24	8.91	16.18
Parking	3.51	1.56	2.05	3.11	4.64	2.90	4.01	5.85

	complete income reporters	under $10,000	$10,000–$19,999	$20,000–$29,999	$30,000–$39,999	$40,000–$49,999	$50,000–$69,999	$70,000 or more
Rented dwellings	**$2,062.21**	**$1,945.07**	**$2,207.56**	**$2,474.70**	**$2,529.76**	**$2,567.38**	**$1,742.12**	**$1,381.02**
Rent	2,004.55	1,854.92	2,112.61	2,423.33	2,482.65	2,508.86	1,699.91	1,359.38
Rent as pay	29.01	74.49	54.63	24.84	17.29	13.68	13.45	2.17
Maintenance, insurance, and other expenses	28.65	15.66	40.32	26.53	29.81	44.85	28.76	19.47
Tenant's insurance	9.37	4.63	9.10	8.77	13.29	11.23	9.47	10.03
Maintenance and repair services	11.76	7.23	22.50	13.24	5.76	8.72	13.05	7.76
Repair and maintenance services	10.24	5.76	22.44	8.36	5.12	7.72	10.20	7.65
Repair and replacement of hard-surface flooring	1.43	1.19	–	4.88	0.64	0.96	2.75	–
Repair of built-in appliances	0.09	0.29	0.06	–	0.01	0.04	0.10	0.11
Maintenance and repair materials	7.52	3.80	8.71	4.52	10.76	24.89	6.25	1.68
Paint, wallpaper, and supplies	1.66	0.69	1.55	1.59	3.12	3.78	1.89	0.40
Painting and wallpapering tools	0.18	0.07	0.16	0.17	0.34	0.41	0.20	0.04
Plastering, paneling, roofing, gutters, etc.	0.57	2.14	0.51	0.21	0.66	0.56	0.21	0.00
Patio, walk, fence, driveway, masonry, brick, and stucco materials	0.04	–	–	–	0.36	0.01	0.00	–
Plumbing supplies and equipment	0.48	0.28	1.34	0.38	0.18	0.41	0.26	0.26
Electrical supplies, heating and cooling equip.	0.31	0.03	0.93	0.18	0.00	0.70	0.11	0.17
Miscellaneous supplies and equipment	3.10	0.25	3.54	1.10	4.59	15.30	1.61	0.37
Insulation, other maintenance and repair	0.78	0.25	1.90	0.58	1.44	0.66	0.21	0.30
Materials for additions, finishing basements, remodeling rooms	2.31	–	1.64	0.52	3.09	14.64	1.41	0.01
Construction materials for jobs not started	0.02	–	–	–	0.07	–	–	0.06
Hard-surface flooring	0.43	0.09	0.28	0.41	0.49	0.05	1.73	0.02
Landscape maintenance	0.75	0.24	0.38	0.48	1.02	3.69	0.24	0.43
Other lodging	**473.17**	**273.58**	**174.06**	**268.04**	**297.10**	**337.45**	**515.92**	**1,202.62**
Owned vacation homes	142.20	26.88	55.36	94.50	90.12	76.74	158.75	395.42
Mortgage interest and charges	59.22	7.29	15.89	31.13	46.02	23.07	69.67	177.25
Mortgage interest	56.37	7.29	15.89	29.21	37.91	23.07	61.58	174.62
Interest paid, home equity loan	1.61	–	–	–	4.47	–	4.23	2.63
Interest paid, home equity line of credit	1.24	–	–	1.92	3.64	–	3.86	–
Property taxes	48.24	16.32	22.26	35.91	30.38	34.52	52.07	120.01
Maintenance, insurance and other expenses	34.74	3.27	17.22	27.47	13.72	19.15	37.01	98.15
Homeowner's and related insurance	11.34	2.17	6.93	13.36	6.21	10.39	13.72	22.27
Homeowner's insurance	11.34	2.17	6.93	13.36	6.21	10.39	13.72	22.27
Ground rent	2.18	–	0.82	3.61	1.62	1.98	3.63	3.27
Maintenance and repair services	15.95	0.76	6.94	5.94	2.26	4.04	14.54	58.38
Maintenance and repair materials	0.44	–	0.93	–	0.06	1.01	0.42	0.58
Property management and security	4.13	0.25	1.29	3.87	2.71	1.24	3.91	12.23
Property management	2.78	0.17	1.08	2.34	1.70	0.76	2.49	8.46
Management and upkeep services for security	1.35	0.08	0.22	1.53	1.02	0.48	1.42	3.78
Parking	0.69	0.08	0.30	0.69	0.85	0.48	0.79	1.42
Housing while attending school	79.38	154.57	24.43	19.50	12.45	43.62	49.47	206.67
Lodging on trips	251.59	92.13	94.26	154.03	194.53	217.09	307.70	600.53
UTILITIES, FUELS, AND PUBLIC SERVICES	**2,487.16**	**1,528.64**	**1,973.41**	**2,224.22**	**2,443.92**	**2,595.83**	**2,873.06**	**3,543.28**
Natural gas	**304.51**	**169.52**	**241.57**	**262.70**	**291.87**	**306.76**	**359.50**	**458.03**
Natural gas (renter)	60.38	69.00	64.12	73.59	76.48	69.73	49.87	33.63
Natural gas (owner)	241.87	99.79	176.45	187.10	215.11	236.60	307.62	417.35
Natural gas (vacation)	2.26	0.73	1.00	2.01	0.28	0.43	2.01	7.04

	complete income reporters	under $10,000	$10,000–$19,999	$20,000–$29,999	$30,000–$39,999	$40,000–$49,999	$50,000–$69,999	$70,000 or more
Electricity	**$897.41**	**$576.01**	**$764.28**	**$858.85**	**$883.04**	**$930.44**	**$1,018.06**	**$1,183.55**
Electricity (renter)	217.06	258.05	274.52	280.32	244.82	216.87	173.03	99.54
Electricity (owner)	672.82	315.26	484.58	571.31	634.99	708.09	836.03	1,068.00
Electricity (vacation)	7.54	2.70	5.18	7.22	3.24	5.49	9.00	16.00
Fuel oil and other fuels	**95.49**	**80.24**	**91.89**	**87.33**	**85.22**	**95.12**	**98.08**	**120.56**
Fuel oil	53.23	36.14	50.00	46.83	43.03	49.10	54.76	80.47
Fuel oil (renter)	6.09	3.46	5.71	7.19	6.72	9.23	3.78	7.21
Fuel oil (owner)	46.33	31.86	41.81	39.64	36.31	39.88	50.97	71.93
Fuel oil (vacation)	0.81	0.82	2.47	–	–	–	0.01	1.34
Coal	0.46	0.52	1.03	0.26	0.14	0.28	0.91	–
Coal (renter)	0.06	0.20	–	–	0.14	0.14	–	–
Coal (owner)	0.41	0.33	1.03	0.26	–	0.14	0.91	–
Bottled/tank gas	35.17	34.08	35.18	31.60	37.51	42.62	35.68	33.19
Gas (renter)	5.32	6.66	11.84	7.80	2.77	3.19	1.96	1.30
Gas (owner)	28.17	27.07	22.74	22.74	33.60	37.46	30.67	28.55
Gas (vacation)	1.69	0.35	0.59	1.07	1.14	1.98	3.05	3.34
Wood and other fuels	6.63	9.49	5.69	8.64	4.53	3.11	6.73	6.89
Wood and other fuels (renter)	1.36	2.55	1.05	3.01	0.70	0.75	0.45	0.92
Wood and other fuels (owner)	5.22	6.80	4.51	5.63	3.83	2.32	6.28	5.98
Wood and other fuels (vacation)	0.04	0.14	0.13	–	–	0.04	–	–
Telephone services	**889.98**	**552.49**	**653.30**	**754.35**	**899.16**	**955.40**	**1,040.81**	**1,309.23**
Telephone services in home city, excl. mobile phones	765.41	510.54	609.71	683.08	781.66	812.34	877.96	1,040.85
Telephone services for mobile phones	124.57	41.95	43.59	71.27	117.49	143.06	162.85	268.38
Water and other public services	**299.76**	**150.38**	**222.37**	**260.99**	**284.64**	**308.12**	**356.61**	**471.92**
Water and sewerage maintenance	213.74	108.19	158.31	193.58	199.14	220.19	253.65	332.75
Water and sewerage maintenance (renter)	31.05	32.26	35.29	40.17	35.02	34.03	26.82	18.21
Water and sewerage maintenance (owner)	181.04	75.85	122.15	151.30	163.54	185.54	224.16	311.01
Water and sewerage maintenance (vacation)	1.64	0.07	0.86	2.11	0.57	0.61	2.68	3.53
Trash and garbage collection	83.72	41.33	63.08	66.55	83.18	84.28	100.36	134.35
Trash and garbage collection (renter)	8.33	7.93	9.41	10.46	10.90	10.06	6.94	4.49
Trash and garbage collection (owner)	73.09	33.14	51.94	54.55	71.08	73.08	90.75	124.00
Trash and garbage collection (vacation)	2.31	0.26	1.75	1.54	1.20	1.14	2.67	5.86
Septic tank cleaning	2.30	0.86	0.98	0.86	2.31	3.66	2.60	4.82
Septic tank cleaning (renter)	0.04	–	0.02	0.10	–	0.22	–	–
Septic tank cleaning (owner)	2.27	0.86	0.96	0.75	2.31	3.44	2.60	4.82

See appendix for information about mortgage principle reduction.
Note: (–) means sample is too small to make a reliable estimate.
Source: Bureau of Labor Statistics, unpublished tables from the 2000 Consumer Expenditure Survey; calculations by New Strategist

Table 9.7 (Housing) Shelter and Utilities: Indexed spending by income, 2000

(indexed average annual spending of consumer units (CU) on shelter and utilities, by before-tax income of consumer unit, 2000; complete income reporters only; index definition: an index of 100 is the average for all consumer units; an index of 132 means that spending by consumer units in that group is 32 percent above the average for all consumer units; an index of 68 indicates spending that is 32 percent below the average for all consumer units)

	complete income reporters	under $10,000	$10,000–$19,999	$20,000–$29,999	$30,000–$39,999	$40,000–$49,999	$50,000–$69,999	$70,000 or more
Average spending of CU, total	$40,238	$16,456	$22,620	$29,852	$35,609	$42,323	$49,245	$75,964
Average spending of CU, index	100	41	56	74	88	105	122	189
Housing, spending index	100	47	62	75	89	103	119	183
SHELTER	100	48	61	73	92	103	117	185
Owned dwellings*	100	27	43	54	81	97	133	231
Mortgage interest and charges	100	17	25	41	76	103	145	256
Mortgage interest	100	17	25	40	76	104	144	257
Interest paid, home equity loan	100	16	35	60	94	119	158	204
Interest paid, home equity line of credit	100	16	18	57	55	54	149	285
Prepayment penalty charges	100	–	–	17	60	27	27	450
Property taxes	100	41	61	66	85	85	120	207
Maintenance, repairs, insurance, other expenses	100	38	76	78	93	94	113	182
Homeowner's and related insurance	100	39	66	88	92	103	123	172
Ground rent	100	82	161	128	136	99	68	35
Maintenance and repair services	100	33	76	71	89	86	106	201
Painting and papering	100	37	44	64	65	80	113	247
Plumbing and water heating	100	55	88	73	85	87	96	183
Heat, air conditioning, electrical work	100	27	62	89	129	106	97	177
Roofing and gutters	100	51	108	69	85	77	101	171
Other repair and maintenance services	100	23	81	69	84	78	117	205
Repair, replacement of hard-surface flooring	100	15	49	52	70	101	98	266
Repair of built-in appliances	100	25	48	53	45	229	76	226
Maintenance and repair materials	100	29	57	62	98	102	148	186
Paints, wallpaper, and supplies	100	17	45	45	164	69	152	191
Tools, equipment for painting, wallpapering	100	17	45	45	164	68	152	190
Plumbing supplies and equipment	100	73	89	85	70	77	179	113
Electrical supplies, heating and cooling equip.	100	6	171	20	58	98	193	119
Hard-surface flooring, repair and replacement	100	1	153	26	117	69	86	192
Roofing and gutters	100	65	22	48	58	347	119	129
Plaster, paneling, siding, windows, doors, screens, awnings	100	9	30	59	80	91	128	259
Patio, walk, fence, driveway, masonry, brick, and stucco materials	100	4	48	96	175	84	172	130
Landscape maintenance	100	2	20	50	73	94	164	256
Miscellaneous supplies and equipment	100	46	32	98	72	92	163	178
Insulation, other maintenance, repair	100	61	20	56	72	115	159	205
Finish basement, remodel rooms, build patios, walks, etc.	100	22	53	171	74	53	169	133
Property management and security	100	72	88	69	78	111	94	168
Property management	100	79	77	70	80	114	95	169
Management and upkeep services for security	100	58	111	68	72	105	91	166
Parking	100	44	58	89	132	83	114	167

	complete income reporters	under $10,000	$10,000– $19,999	$20,000– $29,999	$30,000– $39,999	$40,000– $49,999	$50,000– $69,999	$70,000 or more
Rented dwellings	**100**	**94**	**107**	**120**	**123**	**124**	**84**	**67**
Rent	100	93	105	121	124	125	85	68
Rent as pay	100	257	188	86	60	47	46	7
Maintenance, insurance, and other expenses	100	55	141	93	104	157	100	68
Tenant's insurance	100	49	97	94	142	120	101	107
Maintenance and repair services	100	62	191	113	49	74	111	66
Repair and maintenance services	100	56	219	82	50	75	100	75
Repair and replacement of hard-surface flooring	100	83	–	341	45	67	192	–
Repair of built-in appliances	100	325	67	–	11	44	111	122
Maintenance and repair materials	100	51	116	60	143	331	83	22
Paint, wallpaper, and supplies	100	42	93	96	188	228	114	24
Painting and wallpapering tools	100	39	91	94	189	228	111	22
Plastering, paneling, roofing, gutters, etc.	100	375	90	37	116	98	37	0
Patio, walk, fence, driveway, masonry, brick, and stucco materials	100	–	–	–	900	25	0	–
Plumbing supplies and equipment	100	59	280	79	38	85	54	54
Electrical supplies, heating and cooling equip.	100	9	301	58	0	226	35	55
Miscellaneous supplies and equipment	100	8	114	35	148	494	52	12
Insulation, other maintenance and repair	100	32	244	74	185	85	27	38
Materials for additions, finishing basements, remodeling rooms	100	–	71	23	134	634	61	0
Construction materials for jobs not started	100	–	–	–	350	–	–	300
Hard-surface flooring	100	21	64	95	114	12	402	5
Landscape maintenance	100	32	51	64	136	492	32	57
Other lodging	**100**	**58**	**37**	**57**	**63**	**71**	**109**	**254**
Owned vacation homes	100	19	39	66	63	54	112	278
Mortgage interest and charges	100	12	27	53	78	39	118	299
Mortgage interest	100	13	28	52	67	41	109	310
Interest paid, home equity loan	100	–	–	–	278	–	263	163
Interest paid, home equity line of credit	100	–	–	155	294	–	311	–
Property taxes	100	34	46	74	63	72	108	249
Maintenance, insurance and other expenses	100	9	50	79	39	55	107	283
Homeowner's and related insurance	100	19	61	118	55	92	121	196
Homeowner's insurance	100	19	61	118	55	92	121	196
Ground rent	100	–	38	166	74	91	167	150
Maintenance and repair services	100	5	43	37	14	25	91	366
Maintenance and repair materials	100	–	211	–	14	230	95	132
Property management and security	100	6	31	94	66	30	95	296
Property management	100	6	39	84	61	27	90	304
Management and upkeep services for security	100	6	16	113	76	36	105	280
Parking	100	12	43	100	123	70	114	206
Housing while attending school	100	195	31	25	16	55	62	260
Lodging on trips	100	37	37	61	77	86	122	239
UTILITIES, FUELS, AND PUBLIC SERVICES	**100**	**61**	**79**	**89**	**98**	**104**	**116**	**142**
Natural gas	**100**	**56**	**79**	**86**	**96**	**101**	**118**	**150**
Natural gas (renter)	100	114	106	122	127	115	83	56
Natural gas (owner)	100	41	73	77	89	98	127	173
Natural gas (vacation)	100	32	44	89	12	19	89	312

	complete income reporters	under $10,000	$10,000– $19,999	$20,000– $29,999	$30,000– $39,999	$40,000– $49,999	$50,000– $69,999	$70,000 or more
Electricity	**100**	**64**	**85**	**96**	**98**	**104**	**113**	**132**
Electricity (renter)	100	119	126	129	113	100	80	46
Electricity (owner)	100	47	72	85	94	105	124	159
Electricity (vacation)	100	36	69	96	43	73	119	212
Fuel oil and other fuels	**100**	**84**	**96**	**91**	**89**	**100**	**103**	**126**
Fuel oil	100	68	94	88	81	92	103	151
Fuel oil (renter)	100	57	94	118	110	152	62	118
Fuel oil (owner)	100	69	90	86	78	86	110	155
Fuel oil (vacation)	100	101	305	–	–	–	1	165
Coal	100	114	224	57	30	61	198	–
Coal (renter)	100	332	–	–	233	233	–	–
Coal (owner)	100	79	251	63	–	34	222	–
Bottled/tank gas	100	97	100	90	107	121	101	94
Gas (renter)	100	125	223	147	52	60	37	24
Gas (owner)	100	96	81	81	119	133	109	101
Gas (vacation)	100	21	35	63	67	117	180	198
Wood and other fuels	100	143	86	130	68	47	102	104
Wood and other fuels (renter)	100	188	77	221	51	55	33	68
Wood and other fuels (owner)	100	130	86	108	73	44	120	115
Wood and other fuels (vacation)	100	352	314	–	–	100	–	–
Telephone services	**100**	**62**	**73**	**85**	**101**	**107**	**117**	**147**
Telephone services in home city, excl. mobile phones	100	67	80	89	102	106	115	136
Telephone services for mobile phones	100	34	35	57	94	115	131	215
Water and other public services	**100**	**50**	**74**	**87**	**95**	**103**	**119**	**157**
Water and sewerage maintenance	100	51	74	91	93	103	119	156
Water and sewerage maintenance (renter)	100	104	114	129	113	110	86	59
Water and sewerage maintenance (owner)	100	42	67	84	90	102	124	172
Water and sewerage maintenance (vacation)	100	4	53	129	35	37	163	215
Trash and garbage collection	100	49	75	79	99	101	120	160
Trash and garbage collection (renter)	100	95	113	126	131	121	83	54
Trash and garbage collection (owner)	100	45	71	75	97	100	124	170
Trash and garbage collection (vacation)	100	11	76	67	52	49	116	254
Septic tank cleaning	100	38	43	37	100	159	113	210
Septic tank cleaning (renter)	100	–	41	250	–	550	–	–
Septic tank cleaning (owner)	100	38	42	33	102	152	115	212

See appendix for information about mortgage principle reduction.
Note: (–) means sample is too small to make a reliable estimate.
Source: Calculations by New Strategist based on the 2000 Consumer Expenditure Survey

Table 9.8 (Housing) Shelter and Utilities: Indexed per capita spending by income, 2000

(indexed average annual per capita spending of consumer units (CU) on shelter and utilities, by before-tax income of consumer unit, 2000; complete income reporters only; index definition: an index of 100 is the average for all consumer units; an index of 132 means that spending by consumer units in that group is 32 percent above the average for all consumer units; an index of 68 indicates spending that is 32 percent below the average for all consumer units)

	complete income reporters	under $10,000	$10,000–$19,999	$20,000–$29,999	$30,000–$39,999	$40,000–$49,999	$50,000–$69,999	$70,000 or more
Per capita spending of CU, total	$16,095	$9,492	$10,819	$12,438	$14,244	$16,278	$16,981	$23,739
Per capita spending of CU, index	100	59	67	77	88	101	106	147
Housing, per capita spending index	100	68	74	78	89	99	103	143
SHELTER	100	70	73	76	92	99	101	145
Owned dwellings*	100	39	51	56	81	93	115	180
Mortgage interest and charges	100	25	30	43	76	99	125	200
Mortgage interest	100	25	30	41	76	100	124	201
Interest paid, home equity loan	100	23	42	63	94	114	136	159
Interest paid, home equity line of credit	100	23	22	59	55	52	129	222
Prepayment penalty charges	100	–	–	17	60	26	23	352
Property taxes	100	59	73	69	85	82	103	162
Maintenance, repairs, insurance, other expenses	100	55	91	81	93	90	97	142
Homeowner's and related insurance	100	57	78	91	92	99	106	134
Ground rent	100	118	193	133	136	96	58	27
Maintenance and repair services	100	47	91	74	89	83	92	157
Painting and papering	100	53	53	67	65	77	97	193
Plumbing and water heating	100	79	105	76	85	83	83	143
Heat, air conditioning, electrical work	100	39	74	93	129	102	83	139
Roofing and gutters	100	73	129	72	85	74	87	133
Other repair and maintenance services	100	33	97	72	84	75	101	160
Repair, replacement of hard-surface flooring	100	22	59	54	70	97	84	208
Repair of built-in appliances	100	36	58	55	45	220	65	177
Maintenance and repair materials	100	41	69	65	98	98	127	145
Paints, wallpaper, and supplies	100	25	54	47	164	66	131	149
Tools, equipment for painting, wallpapering	100	25	54	47	164	65	131	149
Plumbing supplies and equipment	100	105	106	89	70	74	154	88
Electrical supplies, heating and cooling equip.	100	9	204	20	58	94	167	93
Hard-surface flooring, repair and replacement	100	1	183	27	117	66	74	150
Roofing and gutters	100	93	27	50	58	334	102	100
Plaster, paneling, siding, windows, doors, screens, awnings	100	13	35	62	80	88	110	202
Patio, walk, fence, driveway, masonry, brick, and stucco materials	100	5	58	101	175	81	148	101
Landscape maintenance	100	3	24	53	73	90	141	200
Miscellaneous supplies and equipment	100	67	38	103	72	89	140	139
Insulation, other maintenance, repair	100	87	24	58	72	111	137	160
Finish basement, remodel rooms, build patios, walks, etc.	100	31	64	179	74	51	146	104
Property management and security	100	104	105	72	78	107	81	131
Property management	100	113	93	73	80	110	82	132
Management and upkeep services for security	100	83	133	70	72	101	79	129
Parking	100	64	70	92	132	79	98	130

	complete income reporters	under $10,000	$10,000– $19,999	$20,000– $29,999	$30,000– $39,999	$40,000– $49,999	$50,000– $69,999	$70,000 or more
Rented dwellings	**100**	**136**	**128**	**125**	**123**	**120**	**73**	**52**
Rent	100	133	126	126	124	120	73	53
Rent as pay	100	370	225	89	60	45	40	6
Maintenance, insurance, and other expenses	100	79	168	96	104	151	87	53
Tenant's insurance	100	71	116	97	142	115	87	84
Maintenance and repair services	100	89	229	117	49	71	96	52
Repair and maintenance services	100	81	262	85	50	72	86	58
Repair and replacement of hard-surface flooring	100	120	–	355	45	65	166	–
Repair of built-in appliances	100	468	80	–	11	43	96	95
Maintenance and repair materials	100	73	139	63	143	318	72	17
Paint, wallpaper, and supplies	100	60	112	100	188	219	98	19
Painting and wallpapering tools	100	56	109	98	189	219	96	17
Plastering, paneling, roofing, gutters, etc.	100	541	107	38	116	94	32	0
Patio, walk, fence, driveway, masonry, brick, and stucco materials	100	–	–	–	900	24	0	–
Plumbing supplies and equipment	100	85	334	82	38	82	47	42
Electrical supplies, heating and cooling equip.	100	12	360	60	0	217	31	43
Miscellaneous supplies and equipment	100	12	136	37	148	475	45	9
Insulation, other maintenance and repair	100	46	291	77	185	81	23	30
Materials for additions, finishing basements, remodeling rooms	100	–	85	23	134	609	53	0
Construction materials for jobs not started	100	–	–	–	350	–	–	234
Hard-surface flooring	100	30	77	99	114	11	347	4
Landscape maintenance	100	46	60	67	136	473	28	45
Other lodging	**100**	**83**	**44**	**59**	**63**	**69**	**94**	**199**
Owned vacation homes	100	27	47	69	63	52	96	217
Mortgage interest and charges	100	18	32	55	78	37	101	234
Mortgage interest	100	19	34	54	67	39	94	242
Interest paid, home equity loan	100	–	–	–	278	–	226	128
Interest paid, home equity line of credit	100	–	–	161	294	–	268	–
Property taxes	100	49	55	78	63	69	93	194
Maintenance, insurance and other expenses	100	14	59	82	39	53	92	221
Homeowner's and related insurance	100	28	73	123	55	88	104	153
Homeowner's insurance	100	28	73	123	55	88	104	153
Ground rent	100	–	45	172	74	87	144	117
Maintenance and repair services	100	7	52	39	14	24	79	286
Maintenance and repair materials	100	–	253	–	14	221	82	103
Property management and security	100	9	37	98	66	29	82	231
Property management	100	9	46	88	61	26	77	238
Management and upkeep services for security	100	9	19	118	76	34	91	219
Parking	100	18	52	104	123	67	99	161
Housing while attending school	100	281	37	26	16	53	54	203
Lodging on trips	100	53	45	64	77	83	105	186
UTILITIES, FUELS, AND PUBLIC SERVICES	**100**	**89**	**95**	**93**	**98**	**100**	**100**	**111**
Natural gas	**100**	**80**	**95**	**90**	**96**	**97**	**102**	**118**
Natural gas (renter)	100	165	127	127	127	111	71	44
Natural gas (owner)	100	59	87	81	89	94	110	135
Natural gas (vacation)	100	46	53	93	12	18	77	243

	complete income reporters	under $10,000	$10,000– $19,999	$20,000– $29,999	$30,000– $39,999	$40,000– $49,999	$50,000– $69,999	$70,000 or more
Electricity	**100**	**93**	**102**	**100**	**98**	**100**	**98**	**103**
Electricity (renter)	100	171	151	135	113	96	69	36
Electricity (owner)	100	68	86	88	94	101	107	124
Electricity (vacation)	100	52	82	100	43	70	103	166
Fuel oil and other fuels	**100**	**121**	**115**	**95**	**89**	**96**	**89**	**99**
Fuel oil	100	98	112	92	81	89	89	118
Fuel oil (renter)	100	82	112	123	110	146	54	92
Fuel oil (owner)	100	99	108	89	78	83	95	121
Fuel oil (vacation)	100	146	365	–	–	–	1	129
Coal	100	165	268	59	30	59	171	–
Coal (renter)	100	479	–	–	233	224	–	–
Coal (owner)	100	115	301	66	–	33	191	–
Bottled/tank gas	100	140	120	94	107	117	87	74
Gas (renter)	100	181	266	153	52	58	32	19
Gas (owner)	100	139	97	84	119	128	94	79
Gas (vacation)	100	30	42	66	67	113	156	154
Wood and other fuels	100	206	103	136	68	45	88	81
Wood and other fuels (renter)	100	271	92	231	51	53	29	53
Wood and other fuels (owner)	100	188	103	112	73	43	104	89
Wood and other fuels (vacation)	100	508	376	–	–	96	–	–
Telephone services	**100**	**90**	**88**	**88**	**101**	**103**	**101**	**115**
Telephone services in home city, excl. mobile phones	100	96	95	93	102	102	99	106
Telephone services for mobile phones	100	49	42	60	94	110	113	168
Water and other public services	**100**	**72**	**89**	**91**	**95**	**99**	**103**	**123**
Water and sewerage maintenance	100	73	89	94	93	99	102	122
Water and sewerage maintenance (renter)	100	150	136	135	113	105	74	46
Water and sewerage maintenance (owner)	100	60	81	87	90	99	107	134
Water and sewerage maintenance (vacation)	100	6	63	134	35	36	141	168
Trash and garbage collection	100	71	90	83	99	97	103	125
Trash and garbage collection (renter)	100	137	135	131	131	116	72	42
Trash and garbage collection (owner)	100	65	85	78	97	96	107	133
Trash and garbage collection (vacation)	100	16	90	69	52	47	100	198
Septic tank cleaning	100	54	51	39	100	153	97	164
Septic tank cleaning (renter)	100	–	49	260	–	529	–	–
Septic tank cleaning (owner)	100	55	51	34	102	146	99	166

*See appendix for information about mortgage principle reduction.
Note: Per capita indexes account for household size and show how much each person in a particular household demographic segment spends relative to a person in the average household. (–) means sample is too small to make a reliable estimate.
Source: Calculations by New Strategist based on the 2000 Consumer Expenditure Survey

Table 9.9 (Housing) Shelter and Utilities: Total spending by income, 2000

(total annual spending on shelter and utilities, by before-tax income group of consumer units (CU), 2000; complete income reporters only; numbers in thousands)

	complete income reporters	under $10,000	$10,000– $19,999	$20,000– $29,999	$30,000– $39,999	$40,000– $49,999	$50,000– $69,999	$70,000 or more
Number of consumer units	81,454	10,810	14,714	12,039	9,477	7,653	11,337	15,424
Total spending of all CUs	$3,277,581,892	$177,886,368	$332,833,656	$359,383,292	$337,468,767	$323,898,149	$558,294,760	$1,171,666,422
Housing, total spending	1,020,405,211	64,121,738	114,269,029	112,831,073	105,332,875	98,510,487	169,076,617	353,706,253
SHELTER	**$581,103,425**	**$37,264,285**	**$63,898,881**	**$62,712,596**	**$62,186,652**	**$56,412,176**	**$94,996,804**	**$203,632,738**
Owned dwellings*	**374,586,583**	**13,280,664**	**28,855,780**	**29,692,749**	**35,396,500**	**34,181,512**	**69,397,405**	**163,782,675**
Mortgage interest and charges	217,699,662	4,999,885	9,773,880	13,194,022	19,238,310	21,088,454	43,889,722	105,516,047
Mortgage interest	202,344,769	4,674,767	9,018,700	11,860,823	17,870,400	19,799,153	40,604,486	98,516,790
Interest paid, home equity loan	8,380,802	175,297	529,439	748,826	919,838	934,508	1,838,521	3,234,413
Interest paid, home equity line of credit	6,949,655	149,784	225,741	583,771	446,272	354,257	1,445,808	3,744,022
Prepayment penalty charges	24,436	–	–	602	1,706	612	907	20,822
Property taxes	88,314,056	4,823,883	9,690,530	8,628,833	8,756,274	7,041,066	14,755,219	34,617,934
Maintenance, repairs, insurance, other expenses	68,572,864	3,456,897	9,391,369	7,869,774	7,402,011	6,051,992	10,752,464	23,648,694
Homeowner's and related insurance	19,301,340	1,009,514	2,285,947	2,499,537	2,067,976	1,866,184	3,295,666	6,276,951
Ground rent	3,245,942	352,144	944,893	612,544	514,317	302,906	306,212	213,160
Maintenance and repair services	36,441,705	1,578,745	5,025,051	3,840,080	3,779,617	2,949,543	5,386,209	13,882,525
Painting and papering	4,152,525	201,870	332,967	395,240	313,878	312,855	651,878	1,944,041
Plumbing and water heating	3,434,101	248,728	543,326	369,597	340,698	279,641	458,922	1,193,201
Heat, air conditioning, electrical work	6,660,494	240,270	749,147	875,356	997,549	666,041	896,190	2,236,172
Roofing and gutters	6,710,181	453,087	1,305,994	688,270	662,253	484,664	946,073	2,170,003
Other repair and maintenance services	12,504,818	374,277	1,830,360	1,282,876	1,227,272	911,013	2,030,683	4,848,534
Repair, replacement of hard-surface flooring	2,864,737	56,751	253,426	219,832	231,902	270,763	390,446	1,441,681
Repair of built-in appliances	114,036	3,799	9,912	8,909	5,971	24,566	12,017	48,894
Maintenance and repair materials	6,744,391	255,328	700,111	618,805	765,173	644,153	1,386,402	2,374,371
Paints, wallpaper, and supplies	1,399,380	32,352	114,016	93,423	267,251	90,076	296,009	505,907
Tools, equipment for painting, wallpapering	150,690	3,466	12,215	9,992	28,715	9,643	31,857	54,292
Plumbing supplies and equipment	541,669	52,272	86,847	68,141	43,879	39,413	135,024	116,143
Electrical supplies, heating and cooling equip.	394,237	3,168	121,466	11,437	26,630	36,275	106,114	88,996
Hard-surface flooring, repair and replacement	620,679	431	171,806	23,717	84,251	40,178	74,484	225,962
Roofing and gutters	476,506	40,911	19,100	33,589	32,222	155,509	78,792	115,988
Plaster, paneling, siding, windows, doors, screens, awnings	1,097,185	13,423	58,806	95,830	102,257	94,285	195,563	537,218
Patio, walk, fence, driveway, masonry, brick, and stucco materials	46,429	216	4,062	6,621	9,477	3,673	11,110	11,414
Landscape maintenance	248,435	653	9,145	18,540	21,228	21,964	56,572	120,616
Miscellaneous supplies and equipment	1,769,181	108,400	102,420	257,514	149,168	153,060	400,763	597,526
Insulation, other maintenance, repair	1,115,920	89,652	39,817	91,978	93,159	120,688	246,920	433,414
Finish basement, remodel rooms, build patios, walks, etc.	653,261	18,748	62,683	165,536	56,104	32,372	153,956	164,111
Property management and security	2,552,768	244,311	405,271	261,367	230,860	266,937	332,628	811,302
Property management	1,756,963	183,500	245,944	181,909	163,857	188,570	231,502	561,742
Management and upkeep services for security	795,806	60,847	159,328	79,578	67,002	78,367	101,013	249,560
Parking	285,904	16,819	30,096	37,441	43,973	22,194	45,461	90,230

	complete income reporters	under $10,000	$10,000–$19,999	$20,000–$29,999	$30,000–$39,999	$40,000–$49,999	$50,000–$69,999	$70,000 or more
Rented dwellings	**$167,975,253**	**$21,026,239**	**$32,482,003**	**$29,792,913**	**$23,974,536**	**$19,648,159**	**$19,750,414**	**$21,300,852**
Rent	163,278,616	20,051,636	31,084,951	29,174,470	23,528,074	19,200,306	19,271,880	20,967,077
Rent as pay	2,362,981	805,283	803,786	299,049	163,857	104,693	152,483	33,470
Maintenance, insurance, and other expenses	2,333,657	169,320	593,199	319,395	282,509	343,237	326,052	300,305
Tenant's insurance	763,224	50,043	133,891	105,582	125,949	85,943	107,361	154,703
Maintenance and repair services	957,899	78,208	331,137	159,396	54,588	66,734	147,948	119,690
Repair and maintenance services	834,089	62,213	330,253	100,646	48,522	59,081	115,637	117,994
Repair and replacement of hard-surface flooring	116,479	12,906	–	58,750	6,065	7,347	31,177	–
Repair of built-in appliances	7,331	3,161	884	–	95	306	1,134	1,697
Maintenance and repair materials	612,534	41,070	128,172	54,416	101,973	190,483	70,856	25,912
Paint, wallpaper, and supplies	135,214	7,465	22,823	19,142	29,568	28,928	21,427	6,170
Painting and wallpapering tools	14,662	757	2,419	2,047	3,222	3,138	2,267	617
Plastering, paneling, roofing, gutters, etc.	46,429	23,129	7,535	2,528	6,255	4,286	2,381	0
Patio, walk, fence, driveway, masonry, brick, and stucco materials	3,258	–	–	–	3,412	77	0	–
Plumbing supplies and equipment	39,098	3,059	19,745	4,575	1,706	3,138	2,948	4,010
Electrical supplies, heating and cooling equip.	25,251	287	13,716	2,167	0	5,357	1,247	2,622
Miscellaneous supplies and equipment	252,507	2,699	52,064	13,243	43,499	117,091	18,253	5,707
Insulation, other maintenance and repair	63,534	2,699	27,977	6,983	13,647	5,051	2,381	4,627
Materials for additions, finishing basements, remodeling rooms	188,159	–	24,087	6,260	29,284	112,040	15,985	154
Construction materials for jobs not started	1,629	–	–	–	663	–	–	925
Hard-surface flooring	35,025	979	4,073	4,936	4,644	383	19,613	308
Landscape maintenance	61,091	2,586	5,583	5,779	9,667	28,240	2,721	6,632
Other lodging	**38,541,589**	**2,957,419**	**2,561,098**	**3,226,934**	**2,815,617**	**2,582,505**	**5,848,985**	**18,549,211**
Owned vacation homes	11,582,759	290,558	814,619	1,137,686	854,067	587,291	1,799,749	6,098,958
Mortgage interest and charges	4,823,706	78,814	233,755	374,774	436,132	176,555	789,849	2,733,904
Mortgage interest	4,591,562	78,814	233,755	351,659	359,273	176,555	698,132	2,693,339
Interest paid, home equity loan	131,141	–	–	–	42,362	–	47,956	40,565
Interest paid, home equity line of credit	101,003	–	–	23,115	34,496	–	43,761	–
Property taxes	3,929,341	176,434	327,547	432,320	287,911	264,182	590,318	1,851,034
Maintenance, insurance and other expenses	2,829,712	35,310	253,317	330,711	130,024	146,555	419,582	1,513,866
Homeowner's and related insurance	923,688	23,442	102,029	160,841	58,852	79,515	155,544	343,492
Homeowner's insurance	923,688	23,442	102,029	160,841	58,852	79,515	155,544	343,492
Ground rent	177,570	–	12,056	43,461	15,353	15,153	41,153	50,436
Maintenance and repair services	1,299,191	8,172	102,062	71,512	21,418	30,918	164,840	900,453
Maintenance and repair materials	35,840	–	13,688	–	569	7,730	4,762	8,946
Property management and security	336,405	2,717	19,037	46,591	25,683	9,490	44,328	188,636
Property management	226,442	1,813	15,832	28,171	16,111	5,816	28,229	130,487
Management and upkeep services for security	109,963	905	3,205	18,420	9,667	3,673	16,099	58,303
Parking	56,203	907	4,380	8,307	8,055	3,673	8,956	21,902
Housing while attending school	6,465,819	1,670,869	359,480	234,761	117,989	333,824	560,841	3,187,678
Lodging on trips	20,493,012	995,884	1,387,000	1,854,367	1,843,561	1,661,390	3,488,395	9,262,575
UTILITIES, FUELS, AND PUBLIC SERVICES	**202,589,131**	**16,524,555**	**29,036,743**	**26,777,385**	**23,161,030**	**19,865,887**	**32,571,881**	**54,651,551**
Natural gas	**24,803,558**	**1,832,554**	**3,554,434**	**3,162,645**	**2,766,052**	**2,347,634**	**4,075,652**	**7,064,655**
Natural gas (renter)	4,918,193	745,896	943,478	885,950	724,801	533,644	565,376	518,709
Natural gas (owner)	19,701,279	1,078,728	2,596,352	2,252,497	2,038,597	1,810,700	3,487,488	6,437,206
Natural gas (vacation)	184,086	7,859	14,684	24,198	2,654	3,291	22,787	108,585

	complete income reporters	under $10,000	$10,000–$19,999	$20,000–$29,999	$30,000–$39,999	$40,000–$49,999	$50,000–$69,999	$70,000 or more
Electricity	**$73,097,634**	**$6,226,623**	**$11,245,543**	**$10,339,695**	**$8,368,570**	**$7,120,657**	**$11,541,746**	**$18,255,075**
Electricity (renter)	17,680,405	2,789,531	4,039,262	3,374,772	2,320,159	1,659,706	1,961,641	1,535,305
Electricity (owner)	54,803,880	3,407,913	7,130,125	6,878,001	6,017,800	5,419,013	9,478,072	16,472,832
Electricity (vacation)	614,163	29,179	76,156	86,922	30,705	42,015	102,033	246,784
Fuel oil and other fuels	**7,778,042**	**867,375**	**1,352,076**	**1,051,366**	**807,630**	**727,953**	**1,111,933**	**1,859,517**
Fuel oil	4,335,796	390,703	735,650	563,786	407,795	375,762	620,814	1,241,169
Fuel oil (renter)	496,055	37,406	84,074	86,560	63,685	70,637	42,854	111,207
Fuel oil (owner)	3,773,764	344,454	615,237	477,226	344,110	305,202	577,847	1,109,448
Fuel oil (vacation)	65,978	8,844	36,352	–	–	–	113	20,668
Coal	37,469	5,675	15,172	3,130	1,327	2,143	10,317	–
Coal (renter)	4,887	2,155	–	–	1,327	1,071	–	–
Coal (owner)	33,396	3,520	15,172	3,130	–	1,071	10,317	–
Bottled/tank gas	2,864,737	368,402	517,584	380,432	355,482	326,171	404,504	511,923
Gas (renter)	433,335	71,983	174,258	93,904	26,251	24,413	22,221	20,051
Gas (owner)	2,294,559	292,657	334,589	273,767	318,427	286,681	347,706	440,355
Gas (vacation)	137,657	3,761	8,670	12,882	10,804	15,153	34,578	51,516
Wood and other fuels	540,040	102,596	83,738	104,017	42,931	23,801	76,298	106,271
Wood and other fuels (renter)	110,777	27,593	15,474	36,237	6,634	5,740	5,102	14,190
Wood and other fuels (owner)	425,190	73,516	66,415	67,780	36,297	17,755	71,196	92,236
Wood and other fuels (vacation)	3,258	1,523	1,849	–	–	306	–	–
Telephone services	**72,492,431**	**5,972,401**	**9,612,656**	**9,081,620**	**8,521,339**	**7,311,676**	**11,799,663**	**20,193,564**
Telephone services in home city, excl. mobile phones	62,345,706	5,518,959	8,971,234	8,223,600	7,407,792	6,216,838	9,953,433	16,054,070
Telephone services for mobile phones	10,146,725	453,478	641,422	858,020	1,113,453	1,094,838	1,846,230	4,139,493
Water and other public services	**24,416,651**	**1,625,602**	**3,271,966**	**3,142,059**	**2,697,533**	**2,358,042**	**4,042,888**	**7,278,894**
Water and sewerage maintenance	17,409,978	1,169,488	2,329,427	2,330,510	1,887,250	1,685,114	2,875,630	5,132,336
Water and sewerage maintenance (renter)	2,529,147	348,782	519,312	483,607	331,885	260,432	304,058	280,871
Water and sewerage maintenance (owner)	14,746,432	819,951	1,797,298	1,821,501	1,549,869	1,419,938	2,541,302	4,797,018
Water and sewerage maintenance (vacation)	133,585	792	12,669	25,402	5,402	4,668	30,383	54,447
Trash and garbage collection	6,819,329	446,735	928,219	801,195	788,297	644,995	1,137,781	2,072,214
Trash and garbage collection (renter)	678,512	85,701	138,422	125,928	103,299	76,989	78,679	69,254
Trash and garbage collection (owner)	5,953,473	358,245	764,191	656,727	673,625	559,281	1,028,833	1,912,576
Trash and garbage collection (vacation)	188,159	2,825	25,686	18,540	11,372	8,724	30,270	90,385
Septic tank cleaning	187,344	9,342	14,388	10,354	21,892	28,010	29,476	74,344
Septic tank cleaning (renter)	3,258	–	241	1,204	–	1,684	–	–
Septic tank cleaning (owner)	184,901	9,342	14,147	9,029	21,892	26,326	29,476	74,344

See appendix for information about mortgage principle reduction.
Note: Numbers may not add to total because of rounding. (–) means sample is too small to make a reliable estimate.
Source: Calculations by New Strategist based on the 2000 Consumer Expenditure Survey

Table 9.10 (Housing) Shelter and Utilities: Market shares by income, 2000

(percentage of total annual spending on shelter and utilities accounted for by before-tax income group of consumer units, 2000; complete income reporters only)

	complete income reporters	under $10,000	$10,000–$19,999	$20,000–$29,999	$30,000–$39,999	$40,000–$49,999	$50,000–$69,999	$70,000 or more
Share of total consumer units	100.0%	13.3%	18.1%	14.8%	11.6%	9.4%	13.9%	18.9%
Share of total before-tax income	100.0	1.7	5.9	8.1	9.0	9.3	18.3	47.7
Share of total spending	100.0	5.4	10.2	11.0	10.3	9.9	17.0	35.7
Share of housing spending	100.0	6.3	11.2	11.1	10.3	9.7	16.6	34.7
SHELTER	100.0%	6.4%	11.0%	10.8%	10.7%	9.7%	16.3%	35.0%
Owned dwellings*	100.0	3.5	7.7	7.9	9.4	9.1	18.5	43.7
Mortgage interest and charges	100.0	2.3	4.5	6.1	8.8	9.7	20.2	48.5
Mortgage interest	100.0	2.3	4.5	5.9	8.8	9.8	20.1	48.7
Interest paid, home equity loan	100.0	2.1	6.3	8.9	11.0	11.2	21.9	38.6
Interest paid, home equity line of credit	100.0	2.2	3.2	8.4	6.4	5.1	20.8	53.9
Prepayment penalty charges	100.0	–	–	2.5	7.0	2.5	3.7	85.2
Property taxes	100.0	5.5	11.0	9.8	9.9	8.0	16.7	39.2
Maintenance, repairs, insurance, other expenses	100.0	5.0	13.7	11.5	10.8	8.8	15.7	34.5
Homeowner's and related insurance	100.0	5.2	11.8	13.0	10.7	9.7	17.1	32.5
Ground rent	100.0	10.8	29.1	18.9	15.8	9.3	9.4	6.6
Maintenance and repair services	100.0	4.3	13.8	10.5	10.4	8.1	14.8	38.1
Painting and papering	100.0	4.9	8.0	9.5	7.6	7.5	15.7	46.8
Plumbing and water heating	100.0	7.2	15.8	10.8	9.9	8.1	13.4	34.7
Heat, air conditioning, electrical work	100.0	3.6	11.2	13.1	15.0	10.0	13.5	33.6
Roofing and gutters	100.0	6.8	19.5	10.3	9.9	7.2	14.1	32.3
Other repair and maintenance services	100.0	3.0	14.6	10.3	9.8	7.3	16.2	38.8
Repair, replacement of hard-surface flooring	100.0	2.0	8.8	7.7	8.1	9.5	13.6	50.3
Repair of built-in appliances	100.0	3.3	8.7	7.8	5.2	21.5	10.5	42.9
Maintenance and repair materials	100.0	3.8	10.4	9.2	11.3	9.6	20.6	35.2
Paints, wallpaper, and supplies	100.0	2.3	8.1	6.7	19.1	6.4	21.2	36.2
Tools, equipment for painting, wallpapering	100.0	2.3	8.1	6.6	19.1	6.4	21.1	36.0
Plumbing supplies and equipment	100.0	9.7	16.0	12.6	8.1	7.3	24.9	21.4
Electrical supplies, heating and cooling equip.	100.0	0.8	30.8	2.9	6.8	9.2	26.9	22.6
Hard-surface flooring, repair and replacement	100.0	0.1	27.7	3.8	13.6	6.5	12.0	36.4
Roofing and gutters	100.0	8.6	4.0	7.0	6.8	32.6	16.5	24.3
Plaster, paneling, siding, windows, doors, screens, awnings	100.0	1.2	5.4	8.7	9.3	8.6	17.8	49.0
Patio, walk, fence, driveway, masonry, brick, and stucco materials	100.0	0.5	8.7	14.3	20.4	7.9	23.9	24.6
Landscape maintenance	100.0	0.3	3.7	7.5	8.5	8.8	22.8	48.6
Miscellaneous supplies and equipment	100.0	6.1	5.8	14.6	8.4	8.7	22.7	33.8
Insulation, other maintenance, repair	100.0	8.0	3.6	8.2	8.3	10.8	22.1	38.8
Finish basement, remodel rooms, build patios, walks, etc.	100.0	2.9	9.6	25.3	8.6	5.0	23.6	25.1
Property management and security	100.0	9.6	15.9	10.2	9.0	10.5	13.0	31.8
Property management	100.0	10.4	14.0	10.4	9.3	10.7	13.2	32.0
Management and upkeep services for security	100.0	7.6	20.0	10.0	8.4	9.8	12.7	31.4
Parking	100.0	5.9	10.5	13.1	15.4	7.8	15.9	31.6

	complete income reporters	under $10,000	$10,000– $19,999	$20,000– $29,999	$30,000– $39,999	$40,000– $49,999	$50,000– $69,999	$70,000 or more
Rented dwellings	100.0%	12.5%	19.3%	17.7%	14.3%	11.7%	11.8%	12.7%
Rent	100.0	12.3	19.0	17.9	14.4	11.8	11.8	12.8
Rent as pay	100.0	34.1	34.0	12.7	6.9	4.4	6.5	1.4
Maintenance, insurance, and other expenses	100.0	7.3	25.4	13.7	12.1	14.7	14.0	12.9
Tenant's insurance	100.0	6.6	17.5	13.8	16.5	11.3	14.1	20.3
Maintenance and repair services	100.0	8.2	34.6	16.6	5.7	7.0	15.4	12.5
Repair and maintenance services	100.0	7.5	39.6	12.1	5.8	7.1	13.9	14.1
Repair and replacement of hard-surface flooring	100.0	11.1	–	50.4	5.2	6.3	26.8	–
Repair of built-in appliances	100.0	43.1	12.1	–	1.3	4.2	15.5	23.1
Maintenance and repair materials	100.0	6.7	20.9	8.9	16.6	31.1	11.6	4.2
Paint, wallpaper, and supplies	100.0	5.5	16.9	14.2	21.9	21.4	15.8	4.6
Painting and wallpapering tools	100.0	5.2	16.5	14.0	22.0	21.4	15.5	4.2
Plastering, paneling, roofing, gutters, etc.	100.0	49.8	16.2	5.4	13.5	9.2	5.1	0.0
Patio, walk, fence, driveway, masonry, brick, and stucco materials	100.0	–	–	–	104.7	2.3	0.0	–
Plumbing supplies and equipment	100.0	7.8	50.5	11.7	4.4	8.0	7.5	10.3
Electrical supplies, heating and cooling equip.	100.0	1.1	54.3	8.6	0.0	21.2	4.9	10.4
Miscellaneous supplies and equipment	100.0	1.1	20.6	5.2	17.2	46.4	7.2	2.3
Insulation, other maintenance and repair	100.0	4.2	44.0	11.0	21.5	8.0	3.7	7.3
Materials for additions, finishing basements, remodeling rooms	100.0	–	12.8	3.3	15.6	59.5	8.5	0.1
Construction materials for jobs not started	100.0	–	–	–	40.7	–	–	56.8
Hard-surface flooring	100.0	2.8	11.6	14.1	13.3	1.1	56.0	0.9
Landscape maintenance	100.0	4.2	9.1	9.5	15.8	46.2	4.5	10.9
Other lodging	**100.0**	**7.7**	**6.6**	**8.4**	**7.3**	**6.7**	**15.2**	**48.1**
Owned vacation homes	100.0	2.5	7.0	9.8	7.4	5.1	15.5	52.7
Mortgage interest and charges	100.0	1.6	4.8	7.8	9.0	3.7	16.4	56.7
Mortgage interest	100.0	1.7	5.1	7.7	7.8	3.8	15.2	58.7
Interest paid, home equity loan	100.0	–	–	–	32.3	–	36.6	30.9
Interest paid, home equity line of credit	100.0	–	–	22.9	34.2	–	43.3	–
Property taxes	100.0	4.5	8.3	11.0	7.3	6.7	15.0	47.1
Maintenance, insurance and other expenses	100.0	1.2	9.0	11.7	4.6	5.2	14.8	53.5
Homeowner's and related insurance	100.0	2.5	11.0	17.4	6.4	8.6	16.8	37.2
Homeowner's insurance	100.0	2.5	11.0	17.4	6.4	8.6	16.8	37.2
Ground rent	100.0	–	6.8	24.5	8.6	8.5	23.2	28.4
Maintenance and repair services	100.0	0.6	7.9	5.5	1.6	2.4	12.7	69.3
Maintenance and repair materials	100.0	–	38.2	–	1.6	21.6	13.3	25.0
Property management and security	100.0	0.8	5.7	13.8	7.6	2.8	13.2	56.1
Property management	100.0	0.8	7.0	12.4	7.1	2.6	12.5	57.6
Management and upkeep services for security	100.0	0.8	2.9	16.8	8.8	3.3	14.6	53.0
Parking	100.0	1.6	7.8	14.8	14.3	6.5	15.9	39.0
Housing while attending school	100.0	25.8	5.6	3.6	1.8	5.2	8.7	49.3
Lodging on trips	100.0	4.9	6.8	9.0	9.0	8.1	17.0	45.2
UTILITIES, FUELS, AND PUBLIC SERVICES	**100.0**	**8.2**	**14.3**	**13.2**	**11.4**	**9.8**	**16.1**	**27.0**
Natural gas	100.0	7.4	14.3	12.8	11.2	9.5	16.4	28.5
Natural gas (renter)	100.0	15.2	19.2	18.0	14.7	10.9	11.5	10.5
Natural gas (owner)	100.0	5.5	13.2	11.4	10.3	9.2	17.7	32.7
Natural gas (vacation)	100.0	4.3	8.0	13.1	1.4	1.8	12.4	59.0

	complete income reporters	under $10,000	$10,000–$19,999	$20,000–$29,999	$30,000–$39,999	$40,000–$49,999	$50,000–$69,999	$70,000 or more
Electricity	**100.0%**	**8.5%**	**15.4%**	**14.1%**	**11.4%**	**9.7%**	**15.8%**	**25.0%**
Electricity (renter)	100.0	15.8	22.8	19.1	13.1	9.4	11.1	8.7
Electricity (owner)	100.0	6.2	13.0	12.6	11.0	9.9	17.3	30.1
Electricity (vacation)	100.0	4.8	12.4	14.2	5.0	6.8	16.6	40.2
Fuel oil and other fuels	**100.0**	**11.2**	**17.4**	**13.5**	**10.4**	**9.4**	**14.3**	**23.9**
Fuel oil	100.0	9.0	17.0	13.0	9.4	8.7	14.3	28.6
Fuel oil (renter)	100.0	7.5	16.9	17.4	12.8	14.2	8.6	22.4
Fuel oil (owner)	100.0	9.1	16.3	12.6	9.1	8.1	15.3	29.4
Fuel oil (vacation)	100.0	13.4	55.1	–	–	–	0.2	31.3
Coal	100.0	15.1	40.5	8.4	3.5	5.7	27.5	–
Coal (renter)	100.0	44.1	–	–	27.1	21.9	–	–
Coal (owner)	100.0	10.5	45.4	9.4	–	3.2	30.9	–
Bottled/tank gas	100.0	12.9	18.1	13.3	12.4	11.4	14.1	17.9
Gas (renter)	100.0	16.6	40.2	21.7	6.1	5.6	5.1	4.6
Gas (owner)	100.0	12.8	14.6	11.9	13.9	12.5	15.2	19.2
Gas (vacation)	100.0	2.7	6.3	9.4	7.8	11.0	25.1	37.4
Wood and other fuels	100.0	19.0	15.5	19.3	7.9	4.4	14.1	19.7
Wood and other fuels (renter)	100.0	24.9	14.0	32.7	6.0	5.2	4.6	12.8
Wood and other fuels (owner)	100.0	17.3	15.6	15.9	8.5	4.2	16.7	21.7
Wood and other fuels (vacation)	100.0	46.8	56.7	–	–	9.4	–	–
Telephone services	**100.0**	**8.2**	**13.3**	**12.5**	**11.8**	**10.1**	**16.3**	**27.9**
Telephone services in home city, excl. mobile phones	100.0	8.9	14.4	13.2	11.9	10.0	16.0	25.8
Telephone services for mobile phones	100.0	4.5	6.3	8.5	11.0	10.8	18.2	40.8
Water and other public services	**100.0**	**6.7**	**13.4**	**12.9**	**11.0**	**9.7**	**16.6**	**29.8**
Water and sewerage maintenance	100.0	6.7	13.4	13.4	10.8	9.7	16.5	29.5
Water and sewerage maintenance (renter)	100.0	13.8	20.5	19.1	13.1	10.3	12.0	11.1
Water and sewerage maintenance (owner)	100.0	5.6	12.2	12.4	10.5	9.6	17.2	32.5
Water and sewerage maintenance (vacation)	100.0	0.6	9.5	19.0	4.0	3.5	22.7	40.8
Trash and garbage collection	100.0	6.6	13.6	11.7	11.6	9.5	16.7	30.4
Trash and garbage collection (renter)	100.0	12.6	20.4	18.6	15.2	11.3	11.6	10.2
Trash and garbage collection (owner)	100.0	6.0	12.8	11.0	11.3	9.4	17.3	32.1
Trash and garbage collection (vacation)	100.0	1.5	13.7	9.9	6.0	4.6	16.1	48.0
Septic tank cleaning	100.0	5.0	7.7	5.5	11.7	15.0	15.7	39.7
Septic tank cleaning (renter)	100.0	–	7.4	37.0	–	51.7	–	–
Septic tank cleaning (owner)	100.0	5.1	7.7	4.9	11.8	14.2	15.9	40.2

See appendix for information about mortgage principle reduction.
Note: Numbers may not add to total because of rounding. (–) means sample is too small to make a reliable estimate.
Source: Calculations by New Strategist based on the 2000 Consumer Expenditure Survey

Table 9.11 (Housing) Shelter and Utilities: Average spending by household type, 2000

(average annual spending of consumer units (CU) on shelter and utilities, by type of consumer unit, 2000)

	total married couples	married couples, no children	married couples with children				single parent, at least one child <18	single person
			total	oldest child under 6	oldest child 6 to 17	oldest child 18 or older		
Number of consumer units								
(in thousands, add 000)	56,287	22,805	28,777	5,291	15,396	8,090	6,132	32,323
Average number of persons per CU	3.2	2.0	3.9	3.5	4.1	3.8	2.9	1.0
Average before-tax income of CU	$60,588.00	$53,232.00	$66,913.00	$62,928.00	$69,472.00	$64,725.00	$25,095.00	$24,977.00
Average spending of CU, total	48,619.37	42,195.54	53,585.53	50,755.90	54,170.40	54,550.20	28,923.25	23,059.00
Housing, average spending	15,203.59	12,831.51	17,132.38	18,702.09	17,432.55	15,536.72	10,732.20	8,188.63
SHELTER	**$8,535.59**	**$7,153.31**	**$9,693.21**	**$10,398.44**	**$10,035.31**	**$8,580.87**	**$6,331.44**	**$5,053.52**
Owned dwellings*	6,505.40	5,234.01	7,587.46	7,863.60	7,936.52	6,742.52	2,797.38	2,331.93
Mortgage interest and charges	3,921.76	2,691.95	4,940.26	5,485.30	5,279.84	3,937.50	1,694.21	1,004.66
Mortgage interest	3,641.80	2,446.08	4,653.29	5,320.03	4,987.26	3,581.60	1,630.06	951.85
Interest paid, home equity loan	149.91	127.25	147.19	84.58	159.38	164.93	48.52	33.51
Interest paid, home equity line of credit	129.76	118.56	139.28	80.69	133.16	189.26	15.63	18.64
Prepayment penalty charges	0.29	0.06	0.50	–	0.04	1.71	–	0.65
Property taxes	1,533.70	1,460.43	1,618.11	1,504.03	1,604.12	1,719.36	645.89	723.11
Maintenance, repairs, insurance, other expenses	1,049.95	1,081.63	1,029.09	874.28	1,052.56	1,085.66	457.28	604.17
Homeowner's and related insurance	317.90	340.20	302.25	260.13	305.05	324.47	104.67	144.39
Ground rent	31.83	38.72	22.93	20.76	21.68	26.73	33.49	45.28
Maintenance and repair services	556.22	559.19	559.12	436.84	588.14	583.85	273.70	328.78
Painting and papering	66.79	63.13	74.08	82.72	79.39	58.32	17.26	42.09
Plumbing and water heating	48.05	59.13	40.78	26.22	43.68	44.79	22.58	31.94
Heat, air conditioning, electrical work	97.59	97.71	101.19	46.12	123.40	94.94	53.14	65.50
Roofing and gutters	92.64	115.40	81.83	76.40	64.16	119.00	44.95	50.96
Other repair and maintenance services	200.20	177.51	203.97	164.11	226.29	187.55	119.32	120.12
Repair, replacement of hard-surface flooring	49.34	44.58	55.73	39.67	50.03	77.08	16.00	17.15
Repair of built-in appliances	1.61	1.75	1.54	1.60	1.19	2.18	0.46	1.03
Maintenance and repair materials	112.50	100.49	120.00	126.96	114.62	125.70	27.78	37.45
Paints, wallpaper, and supplies	22.00	18.80	23.84	31.10	24.84	17.19	6.87	9.23
Tools, equipment for painting, wallpapering	2.36	2.02	2.56	3.34	2.67	1.85	0.74	0.99
Plumbing supplies and equipment	7.72	8.06	6.41	4.58	4.06	12.07	0.71	3.79
Electrical supplies, heating and cooling equip.	5.75	5.29	6.13	5.39	8.87	1.41	9.05	1.50
Hard-surface flooring, repair and replacement	10.30	4.94	14.18	5.17	8.88	30.18	1.29	3.00
Roofing and gutters	10.21	6.72	12.16	8.74	16.42	6.30	3.59	2.35
Plaster, paneling, siding, windows, doors, screens, awnings	20.21	19.20	22.58	35.66	21.27	16.53	2.41	2.20
Patio, walk, fence, driveway, masonry, brick, and stucco materials	0.87	0.94	0.81	0.43	0.69	1.26	0.05	0.22
Landscape maintenance	4.43	5.00	3.94	3.07	4.73	3.03	0.47	1.20
Miscellaneous supplies and equipment	28.65	29.53	27.38	29.48	22.20	35.87	2.60	12.96
Insulation, other maintenance, repair	19.31	20.21	18.01	23.69	17.69	14.90	1.54	7.29
Finish basement, remodel rooms, build patios, walks, etc.	9.33	9.32	9.38	5.79	4.52	20.97	1.06	5.68
Property management and security	28.54	38.54	22.71	25.80	21.36	23.27	14.82	43.28
Property management	19.27	25.62	15.95	19.50	15.49	14.48	12.21	29.65
Management and upkeep services for security	9.27	12.92	6.77	6.30	5.87	8.79	2.62	13.62
Parking	2.95	4.49	2.07	3.78	1.71	1.64	2.81	5.00

	total married couples	married couples, no children	married couples with children				single parent, at least one child <18	single person
			total	oldest child under 6	oldest child 6 to 17	oldest child 18 or older		
Rented dwellings	**$1,355.20**	**$1,121.30**	**$1,502.19**	**$2,162.42**	**$1,542.85**	**$992.99**	**$3,314.85**	**$2,435.08**
Rent	1,316.54	1,076.49	1,472.28	2,130.33	1,508.41	973.15	3,196.07	2,367.58
Rent as pay	12.97	12.83	10.64	13.96	10.88	8.00	81.53	40.86
Maintenance, insurance, and other expenses	25.69	31.98	19.27	18.13	23.57	11.84	37.26	26.64
Tenant's insurance	6.56	9.10	4.54	8.91	4.53	1.71	7.65	13.02
Maintenance and repair services	10.98	14.53	6.69	2.28	8.18	6.75	19.43	9.56
Repair and maintenance services	9.50	11.27	6.41	1.13	8.04	6.75	19.15	8.74
Repair and replacement of hard-surface flooring	1.45	3.26	0.21	1.15	–	–	0.21	0.77
Repair of built-in appliances	0.04	–	0.07	–	0.14	–	0.07	0.05
Maintenance and repair materials	8.15	8.34	8.04	6.94	10.86	3.38	10.18	4.07
Paint, wallpaper, and supplies	1.34	0.77	1.51	0.67	1.70	1.69	5.29	1.24
Painting and wallpapering tools	0.14	0.08	0.16	0.07	0.18	0.18	0.57	0.13
Plastering, paneling, roofing, gutters, etc.	0.56	0.12	0.97	0.42	1.61	0.13	0.39	0.29
Patio, walk, fence, driveway, masonry, brick, and stucco materials	0.00	–	0.00	0.00	0.00	–	–	0.00
Plumbing supplies and equipment	0.38	0.05	0.70	0.05	1.24	0.10	0.57	0.44
Electrical supplies, heating and cooling equip.	0.08	0.04	0.13	0.04	0.23	–	0.79	0.45
Miscellaneous supplies and equipment	4.01	4.80	3.63	5.24	4.64	0.65	2.01	1.02
Insulation, other maintenance and repair	1.10	1.93	0.55	0.94	0.65	0.10	0.70	0.53
Materials for additions, finishing basements, remodeling rooms	2.91	2.86	3.08	4.31	3.99	0.55	1.31	0.47
Construction materials for jobs not started	–	–	–	–	–	–	–	0.02
Hard-surface flooring	0.79	0.78	0.72	0.37	1.10	0.24	0.14	0.19
Landscape maintenance	0.84	1.71	0.21	0.08	0.17	0.38	0.43	0.31
Other lodging	**674.99**	**798.00**	**603.55**	**372.42**	**555.93**	**845.36**	**219.21**	**286.50**
Owned vacation homes	221.77	300.08	153.06	114.51	152.51	179.33	57.58	61.62
Mortgage interest and charges	100.40	127.17	75.33	56.16	82.05	75.07	36.04	18.55
Mortgage interest	97.40	121.71	74.07	51.85	81.80	73.88	33.93	15.85
Interest paid, home equity loan	1.85	3.71	0.40	0.53	0.25	0.61	–	1.35
Interest paid, home equity line of credit	1.15	1.75	0.86	3.79	–	0.58	2.11	1.35
Property taxes	74.95	107.48	50.02	42.61	48.03	58.65	15.72	28.39
Maintenance, insurance and other expenses	46.41	65.43	27.72	15.73	22.43	45.61	5.81	14.68
Homeowner's and related insurance	14.78	18.02	12.37	4.97	13.07	15.90	4.28	4.74
Homeowner's insurance	14.78	18.02	12.37	4.97	13.07	15.90	4.28	4.74
Ground rent	3.48	4.11	1.08	–	0.64	2.61	–	2.80
Maintenance and repair services	20.02	31.81	8.57	3.53	6.08	16.58	0.55	5.46
Maintenance and repair materials	0.84	1.73	0.28	–	0.33	0.38	–	0.08
Property management and security	6.22	8.10	4.66	5.91	1.97	8.98	0.98	1.38
Property management	4.04	5.50	2.83	5.11	1.07	4.67	0.78	0.90
Management and upkeep services for security	2.18	2.60	1.84	0.80	0.90	4.31	0.20	0.48
Parking	1.08	1.66	0.75	1.32	0.34	1.16	–	0.23
Housing while attending school	97.07	91.66	110.02	8.10	62.11	267.85	30.27	77.89
Lodging on trips	356.16	406.27	340.47	249.81	341.31	398.18	131.37	146.99
UTILITIES, FUELS, AND PUBLIC SERVICES	**3,006.27**	**2,688.61**	**3,179.75**	**2,803.67**	**3,192.84**	**3,400.80**	**2,335.04**	**1,628.05**
Natural gas	**367.93**	**318.38**	**396.30**	**360.26**	**397.25**	**418.05**	**305.91**	**208.04**
Natural gas (renter)	46.54	32.41	55.63	75.61	57.78	38.48	166.27	48.28
Natural gas (owner)	317.91	281.18	337.93	284.51	337.69	373.33	139.45	158.99
Natural gas (vacation)	3.47	4.79	2.73	0.14	1.78	6.25	0.19	0.78

	total married couples	married couples, no children	married couples with children				single parent, at least one child <18	single person
			total	oldest child under 6	oldest child 6 to 17	oldest child 18 or older		
Electricity	**$1,116.40**	**$1,022.34**	**$1,160.98**	**$955.63**	**$1,170.44**	**$1,277.26**	**$862.97**	**$569.45**
Electricity (renter)	154.77	108.19	181.13	237.51	193.74	120.24	492.54	194.13
Electricity (owner)	950.58	895.24	974.95	716.10	973.43	1,147.12	369.70	372.14
Electricity (vacation)	11.04	18.91	4.91	2.01	3.27	9.91	0.73	3.18
Fuel oil and other fuels	**120.45**	**128.95**	**120.32**	**113.97**	**117.53**	**129.79**	**42.88**	**68.26**
Fuel oil	68.24	69.68	71.50	81.71	65.44	76.35	20.20	40.16
Fuel oil (renter)	5.97	4.04	7.45	11.11	6.58	6.72	8.30	4.61
Fuel oil (owner)	61.36	63.93	63.61	70.60	58.28	69.18	11.90	35.27
Fuel oil (vacation)	0.91	1.70	0.44	–	0.58	0.45	–	0.28
Coal	0.51	0.60	0.29	–	0.51	0.06	–	1.01
Coal (renter)	0.23	0.57	–	–	–	–	–	–
Coal (owner)	0.28	0.03	0.29	–	0.51	0.06	–	1.01
Bottled/tank gas	44.32	52.39	39.52	25.72	41.84	44.12	19.95	23.00
Gas (renter)	2.94	2.31	3.74	6.16	4.08	1.52	9.60	4.22
Gas (owner)	38.80	46.99	33.54	17.23	35.49	40.48	9.80	17.95
Gas (vacation)	2.57	3.09	2.24	2.32	2.27	2.12	0.55	0.83
Wood and other fuels	7.38	6.28	9.02	6.54	9.75	9.25	2.73	4.08
Wood and other fuels (renter)	1.10	0.72	1.47	2.09	1.98	0.10	0.58	0.55
Wood and other fuels (owner)	6.21	5.40	7.55	4.45	7.77	9.15	2.15	3.48
Wood and other fuels (vacation)	0.07	0.16	–	–	–	–	–	0.06
Telephone services	**1,015.95**	**870.73**	**1,097.07**	**1,044.97**	**1,096.03**	**1,133.12**	**892.87**	**606.80**
Telephone services in home city, excl. mobile phones	855.89	746.19	913.42	860.17	910.12	954.54	807.10	541.24
Telephone services for mobile phones	160.06	124.54	183.65	184.80	185.91	178.58	85.78	65.56
Water and other public services	**385.54**	**348.20**	**405.09**	**328.84**	**411.59**	**442.58**	**230.42**	**175.50**
Water and sewerage maintenance	278.54	242.37	297.32	230.66	303.22	329.70	171.00	119.33
Water and sewerage maintenance (renter)	27.41	16.96	33.99	36.52	35.71	29.07	67.85	19.86
Water and sewerage maintenance (owner)	248.43	220.13	262.55	193.82	266.97	299.08	103.00	98.97
Water and sewerage maintenance (vacation)	2.70	5.28	0.78	0.32	0.54	1.55	0.15	0.50
Trash and garbage collection	104.12	103.42	104.35	93.72	106.01	108.14	58.77	55.26
Trash and garbage collection (renter)	7.84	5.14	9.52	12.51	9.69	7.23	15.53	5.52
Trash and garbage collection (owner)	92.73	93.35	92.43	79.60	93.90	98.04	42.94	49.13
Trash and garbage collection (vacation)	3.54	4.93	2.40	1.61	2.41	2.87	0.30	0.60
Septic tank cleaning	2.89	2.41	3.42	4.46	2.37	4.74	0.64	0.91
Septic tank cleaning (renter)	0.02	0.02	0.03	–	0.05	–	0.21	0.06
Septic tank cleaning (owner)	2.87	2.40	3.39	4.46	2.32	4.74	0.44	0.85

*See appendix for information about mortgage principle reduction.

Note: Average spending figures for total consumer units can be found on Average Spending by Age and Average Spending by Region tables. (–) means sample is too small to make a reliable estimate.

Source: Bureau of Labor Statistics, unpublished tables from the 2000 Consumer Expenditure Survey

Table 9.12 (Housing) Shelter and Utilities: Indexed spending by household type, 2000

(indexed average annual spending of consumer units (CU) on shelter and utilities, by type of consumer unit, 2000; index definition: an index of 100 is the average for all consumer units; an index of 132 means that spending by consumer units in that group is 32 percent above the average for all consumer units; an index of 68 indicates spending that is 32 percent below the average for all consumer units)

| | total married couples | married couples, no children | married couples with children | | | | single parent, at least one child <18 | single person |
			total	oldest child under 6	oldest child 6 to 17	oldest child 18 or older		
Average spending of CU, total	$48,619	$42,196	$53,586	$50,756	$54,170	$54,550	$28,923	$23,059
Average spending of CU, index	128	111	141	133	142	143	76	61
Housing, spending index	123	104	139	152	142	126	87	66
SHELTER	120	101	136	146	141	121	89	71
Owned dwellings*	141	114	165	171	172	147	61	51
Mortgage interest and charges	149	102	187	208	200	149	64	38
Mortgage interest	148	99	189	216	203	146	66	39
Interest paid, home equity loan	153	130	150	86	162	168	49	34
Interest paid, home equity line of credit	163	149	175	101	167	237	20	23
Prepayment penalty charges	85	18	147	–	12	503	–	191
Property taxes	135	128	142	132	141	151	57	64
Maintenance, repairs, insurance, other expenses	127	131	125	106	128	132	55	73
Homeowner's and related insurance	135	145	129	111	130	138	45	61
Ground rent	82	100	59	54	56	69	87	117
Maintenance and repair services	127	127	127	100	134	133	62	75
Painting and papering	134	126	148	166	159	117	35	84
Plumbing and water heating	115	142	98	63	105	108	54	77
Heat, air conditioning, electrical work	123	123	128	58	156	120	67	83
Roofing and gutters	123	153	109	102	85	158	60	68
Other repair and maintenance services	127	112	129	104	143	119	76	76
Repair, replacement of hard-surface flooring	147	133	166	118	149	229	48	51
Repair of built-in appliances	123	134	118	122	91	166	35	79
Maintenance and repair materials	144	129	154	163	147	161	36	48
Paints, wallpaper, and supplies	137	117	149	194	155	107	43	58
Tools, equipment for painting, wallpapering	137	117	149	194	155	108	43	58
Plumbing supplies and equipment	126	131	105	75	66	197	12	62
Electrical supplies, heating and cooling equip.	132	122	141	124	204	32	208	34
Hard-surface flooring, repair and replacement	148	71	203	74	127	432	18	43
Roofing and gutters	159	105	190	136	256	98	56	37
Plaster, paneling, siding, windows, doors, screens, awnings	166	158	186	294	175	136	20	18
Patio, walk, fence, driveway, masonry, brick, and stucco materials	145	157	135	72	115	210	8	37
Landscape maintenance	152	171	135	105	162	104	16	41
Miscellaneous supplies and equipment	138	142	132	142	107	172	13	62
Insulation, other maintenance, repair	144	150	134	176	132	111	11	54
Finish basement, remodel rooms, build patios, walks, etc.	127	127	128	79	61	285	14	77
Property management and security	92	124	73	83	69	75	48	140
Property management	90	119	74	91	72	67	57	138
Management and upkeep services for security	98	136	71	66	62	93	28	143
Parking	86	130	60	110	50	48	81	145

	total married couples	married couples, no children	married couples with children			single parent, at least one child <18	single person
			total	oldest child under 6	oldest child 6 to 17	oldest child 18 or older	
Rented dwellings	**67**	**55**	**74**	**106**	**76**	**49**	**163**	**120**
Rent	67	54	74	108	76	49	162	120
Rent as pay	44	44	36	48	37	27	279	140
Maintenance, insurance, and other expenses	93	116	70	66	86	43	135	97
Tenant's insurance	74	103	51	101	51	19	86	147
Maintenance and repair services	99	131	60	20	73	61	175	86
Repair and maintenance services	95	113	64	11	81	68	192	88
Repair and replacement of hard-surface flooring	134	302	19	106	–	–	19	71
Repair of built-in appliances	57	–	100	–	200	–	100	71
Maintenance and repair materials	108	110	106	92	144	45	135	54
Paint, wallpaper, and supplies	87	50	98	44	110	110	344	81
Painting and wallpapering tools	82	47	94	41	106	106	335	76
Plastering, paneling, roofing, gutters, etc.	117	25	202	88	335	27	81	60
Patio, walk, fence, driveway, masonry, brick, and stucco materials	0	–	0	0	0	–	–	0
Plumbing supplies and equipment	97	13	179	13	318	26	146	113
Electrical supplies, heating and cooling equip.	32	16	52	16	92	–	316	180
Miscellaneous supplies and equipment	111	133	101	146	129	18	56	28
Insulation, other maintenance and repair	120	210	60	102	71	11	76	58
Materials for additions, finishing basements, remodeling rooms	109	107	115	161	149	21	49	18
Construction materials for jobs not started	–	–	–	–	–	–	–	200
Hard-surface flooring	161	159	147	76	224	49	29	39
Landscape maintenance	140	285	35	13	28	63	72	52
Other lodging	**141**	**167**	**126**	**78**	**116**	**177**	**46**	**60**
Owned vacation homes	150	203	103	77	103	121	39	42
Mortgage interest and charges	158	200	118	88	129	118	57	29
Mortgage interest	159	199	121	85	134	121	55	26
Interest paid, home equity loan	137	275	30	39	19	45	–	100
Interest paid, home equity line of credit	104	158	77	341	–	52	190	122
Property taxes	144	207	96	82	92	113	30	55
Maintenance, insurance and other expenses	144	203	86	49	69	141	18	45
Homeowner's and related insurance	138	168	115	46	122	148	40	44
Homeowner's insurance	138	168	115	46	122	148	40	44
Ground rent	117	138	36	–	22	88	–	94
Maintenance and repair services	148	235	63	26	45	122	4	40
Maintenance and repair materials	175	360	58	–	69	79	–	17
Property management and security	160	208	120	152	51	231	25	35
Property management	158	215	111	200	42	182	30	35
Management and upkeep services for security	164	195	138	60	68	324	15	36
Parking	166	255	115	203	52	178	–	35
Housing while attending school	124	117	140	10	79	342	39	99
Lodging on trips	142	161	135	99	136	158	52	58
UTILITIES, FUELS, AND PUBLIC SERVICES	**121**	**108**	**128**	**113**	**128**	**137**	**94**	**65**
Natural gas	**120**	**104**	**129**	**117**	**129**	**136**	**100**	**68**
Natural gas (renter)	77	54	92	125	96	64	275	80
Natural gas (owner)	130	115	138	116	138	153	57	65
Natural gas (vacation)	154	213	121	6	79	278	8	35

	total married couples	married couples, no children	married couples with children				single parent, at least one child <18	single person
			total	oldest child under 6	oldest child 6 to 17	oldest child 18 or older		
Electricity	**122**	**112**	**127**	**105**	**128**	**140**	**95**	**62**
Electricity (renter)	72	51	85	111	91	56	230	91
Electricity (owner)	138	130	141	104	141	166	54	54
Electricity (vacation)	147	252	65	27	44	132	10	42
Fuel oil and other fuels	**124**	**133**	**124**	**118**	**121**	**134**	**44**	**70**
Fuel oil	124	127	130	148	119	139	37	73
Fuel oil (renter)	91	62	114	170	101	103	127	70
Fuel oil (owner)	129	134	133	148	122	145	25	74
Fuel oil (vacation)	112	210	54	–	72	56	–	35
Coal	88	103	50	–	88	10	–	174
Coal (renter)	164	407	–	–	–	–	–	–
Coal (owner)	64	7	66	–	116	14	–	230
Bottled/tank gas	126	149	112	73	119	125	57	65
Gas (renter)	62	49	79	129	86	32	202	89
Gas (owner)	135	163	116	60	123	141	34	62
Gas (vacation)	150	181	131	136	133	124	32	49
Wood and other fuels	123	104	150	109	162	154	45	68
Wood and other fuels (renter)	101	66	135	192	182	9	53	50
Wood and other fuels (owner)	127	111	155	91	159	188	44	71
Wood and other fuels (vacation)	140	320	–	–	–	–	–	120
Telephone services	**116**	**99**	**125**	**119**	**125**	**129**	**102**	**69**
Telephone services in home city, excl. mobile phones	113	99	121	114	120	126	107	71
Telephone services for mobile phones	134	104	154	155	156	149	72	55
Water and other public services	**130**	**117**	**137**	**111**	**139**	**149**	**78**	**59**
Water and sewerage maintenance	131	114	140	108	143	155	80	56
Water and sewerage maintenance (renter)	91	57	113	122	119	97	226	66
Water and sewerage maintenance (owner)	137	122	145	107	147	165	57	55
Water and sewerage maintenance (vacation)	166	324	48	20	33	95	9	31
Trash and garbage collection	127	127	128	115	130	132	72	68
Trash and garbage collection (renter)	94	62	115	151	117	87	187	67
Trash and garbage collection (owner)	130	131	130	112	132	137	60	69
Trash and garbage collection (vacation)	169	235	114	77	115	137	14	29
Septic tank cleaning	147	123	174	228	121	242	33	46
Septic tank cleaning (renter)	50	50	75	–	125	–	525	150
Septic tank cleaning (owner)	149	125	177	232	121	247	23	44

See appendix for information about mortgage principle reduction.
Note: Spending index for total consumer units is 100. (–) means sample is too small to make a reliable estimate.
Source: Calculations by New Strategist based on the 2000 Consumer Expenditure Survey

Table 9.13 (Housing) Shelter and Utilities: Indexed per capita spending by household type, 2000

(indexed average annual per capita spending of consumer units (CU) on shelter and utilities, by type of consumer unit, 2000; index definition: an index of 100 is the average for all consumer units; an index of 132 means that spending by consumer units in that group is 32 percent above the average for all consumer units; an index of 68 indicates spending that is 32 percent below the average for all consumer units)

	total married couples	married couples, no children	married couples with children				single parent, at least one child <18	single person
			total	oldest child under 6	oldest child 6 to 17	oldest child 18 or older		
Per capita spending of CU, total	$15,194	$21,098	$13,740	$14,502	$13,212	$14,355	$9,974	$23,059
Per capita spending of CU, index	100	139	90	95	87	94	66	152
Housing, per capita spending index	96	130	89	108	86	83	75	166
SHELTER	**94**	**126**	**87**	**104**	**86**	**79**	**77**	**178**
Owned dwellings*	**110**	**142**	**106**	**122**	**105**	**96**	**52**	**127**
Mortgage interest and charges	116	128	120	148	122	98	55	95
Mortgage interest	116	124	121	154	124	96	57	97
Interest paid, home equity loan	119	162	96	62	99	110	43	85
Interest paid, home equity line of credit	127	186	112	72	102	156	17	58
Prepayment penalty charges	67	22	94	–	7	331	–	478
Property taxes	105	160	91	94	86	99	49	159
Maintenance, repairs, insurance, other expenses	99	164	80	76	78	87	48	183
Homeowner's and related insurance	106	181	83	79	79	91	38	154
Ground rent	64	125	38	38	34	45	75	293
Maintenance and repair services	99	159	82	71	82	88	54	187
Painting and papering	105	158	95	118	97	77	30	211
Plumbing and water heating	90	178	63	45	64	71	47	192
Heat, air conditioning, electrical work	96	154	82	42	95	79	58	207
Roofing and gutters	96	192	70	73	52	104	51	169
Other repair and maintenance services	99	140	83	74	87	78	65	190
Repair, replacement of hard-surface flooring	115	166	106	84	91	151	41	128
Repair of built-in appliances	96	167	75	87	55	109	30	197
Maintenance and repair materials	113	161	99	116	90	106	31	120
Paints, wallpaper, and supplies	107	147	95	139	94	71	37	144
Tools, equipment for painting, wallpapering	107	147	95	139	95	71	37	144
Plumbing supplies and equipment	98	164	67	53	40	130	10	155
Electrical supplies, heating and cooling equip.	103	152	90	89	124	21	179	86
Hard-surface flooring, repair and replacement	115	88	130	53	78	284	16	107
Roofing and gutters	124	131	122	97	156	65	48	92
Plaster, paneling, siding, windows, doors, screens, awnings	130	198	119	210	107	90	17	45
Patio, walk, fence, driveway, masonry, brick, and stucco materials	113	196	87	51	70	138	7	92
Landscape maintenance	119	214	86	75	99	68	14	103
Miscellaneous supplies and equipment	108	177	84	101	65	113	11	156
Insulation, other maintenance, repair	112	188	86	126	80	73	10	136
Finish basement, remodel rooms, build patios, walks, etc.	99	159	82	56	37	188	12	193
Property management and security	72	155	47	59	42	49	41	349
Property management	70	149	48	65	44	44	49	345
Management and upkeep services for security	76	170	46	47	38	61	24	358
Parking	67	163	38	78	30	31	70	362

	total married couples	married couples, no children	married couples with children				single parent, at least one child <18	single person
			total	oldest child under 6	oldest child 6 to 17	oldest child 18 or older		
Rented dwellings	**52**	**69**	**47**	**76**	**46**	**32**	**140**	**299**
Rent	52	68	48	77	47	32	139	299
Rent as pay	35	55	23	34	23	18	240	349
Maintenance, insurance, and other expenses	73	145	45	47	52	28	117	242
Tenant's insurance	58	128	33	72	31	13	74	367
Maintenance and repair services	77	163	39	15	45	40	150	215
Repair and maintenance services	74	141	41	8	49	44	165	219
Repair and replacement of hard-surface flooring	105	377	12	76	–	–	17	178
Repair of built-in appliances	45	–	64	–	122	–	86	179
Maintenance and repair materials	84	138	68	66	88	29	116	135
Paint, wallpaper, and supplies	68	63	63	31	67	72	296	201
Painting and wallpapering tools	64	59	60	29	65	70	289	191
Plastering, paneling, roofing, gutters, etc.	91	31	130	63	205	18	70	151
Patio, walk, fence, driveway, masonry, brick, and stucco materials	0	–	0	0	0	–	–	0
Plumbing supplies and equipment	76	16	115	9	194	17	126	282
Electrical supplies, heating and cooling equip.	25	20	33	11	56	–	272	450
Miscellaneous supplies and equipment	87	167	65	104	79	12	48	71
Insulation, other maintenance and repair	93	262	38	73	43	7	66	144
Materials for additions, finishing basements, remodeling rooms	85	134	74	115	91	14	42	44
Construction materials for jobs not started	–	–	–	–	–	–	–	500
Hard-surface flooring	126	199	94	54	137	32	25	97
Landscape maintenance	109	356	22	10	17	42	62	129
Other lodging	**110**	**209**	**81**	**56**	**71**	**116**	**40**	**150**
Owned vacation homes	117	254	66	55	63	80	34	104
Mortgage interest and charges	123	250	76	63	79	78	49	73
Mortgage interest	124	249	78	61	82	79	48	65
Interest paid, home equity loan	107	344	19	28	11	30	–	250
Interest paid, home equity line of credit	81	197	50	244	–	34	164	304
Property taxes	113	259	62	59	56	74	26	137
Maintenance, insurance and other expenses	112	253	55	35	42	93	16	114
Homeowner's and related insurance	108	210	74	33	74	97	34	110
Homeowner's insurance	108	210	74	33	74	97	34	110
Ground rent	92	173	23	–	13	58	–	236
Maintenance and repair services	115	293	41	19	27	80	3	101
Maintenance and repair materials	137	451	37	–	42	52	–	42
Property management and security	125	260	77	109	31	152	22	89
Property management	123	269	71	143	25	120	26	88
Management and upkeep services for security	128	244	89	43	41	213	13	90
Parking	130	319	74	145	32	117	–	88
Housing while attending school	97	146	90	7	48	225	33	249
Lodging on trips	111	202	87	71	83	104	45	146
UTILITIES, FUELS, AND PUBLIC SERVICES	**94**	**135**	**82**	**80**	**78**	**90**	**81**	**164**
Natural gas	**94**	**129**	**83**	**84**	**79**	**89**	**86**	**169**
Natural gas (renter)	60	67	59	89	58	42	237	200
Natural gas (owner)	102	144	89	83	84	100	49	162
Natural gas (vacation)	120	266	78	4	48	183	7	87

	total married couples	married couples, no children	married couples with children				single parent, at least one child <18	single person
			total	oldest child under 6	oldest child 6 to 17	oldest child 18 or older		
Electricity	**96**	**140**	**82**	**75**	**78**	**92**	**82**	**156**
Electricity (renter)	57	63	54	79	55	37	199	227
Electricity (owner)	108	162	91	74	86	109	46	135
Electricity (vacation)	115	315	42	19	27	87	8	106
Fuel oil and other fuels	**97**	**166**	**80**	**84**	**74**	**88**	**38**	**176**
Fuel oil	97	158	83	106	72	91	32	182
Fuel oil (renter)	71	77	73	121	61	68	109	176
Fuel oil (owner)	100	167	85	106	74	95	21	185
Fuel oil (vacation)	88	262	35	–	44	37	–	86
Coal	69	129	32	–	54	7	–	435
Coal (renter)	128	509	–	–	–	–	–	–
Coal (owner)	50	9	42	–	71	9	–	574
Bottled/tank gas	98	186	72	52	72	82	49	163
Gas (renter)	48	61	50	92	52	21	174	222
Gas (owner)	105	204	75	43	75	93	29	156
Gas (vacation)	117	226	84	97	81	82	28	121
Wood and other fuels	96	130	96	78	99	101	39	169
Wood and other fuels (renter)	79	83	86	137	111	6	46	126
Wood and other fuels (owner)	99	138	99	65	97	123	38	178
Wood and other fuels (vacation)	109	400	–	–	–	–	–	300
Telephone services	**91**	**124**	**80**	**85**	**76**	**85**	**88**	**173**
Telephone services in home city, excl. mobile phones	88	123	77	81	73	83	92	179
Telephone services for mobile phones	105	130	99	110	95	98	62	137
Water and other public services	**102**	**147**	**88**	**79**	**85**	**98**	**67**	**148**
Water and sewerage maintenance	102	142	90	77	87	102	69	140
Water and sewerage maintenance (renter)	71	71	73	87	73	64	195	166
Water and sewerage maintenance (owner)	107	152	93	76	90	109	49	137
Water and sewerage maintenance (vacation)	129	405	31	14	20	63	8	77
Trash and garbage collection	100	158	82	82	79	87	62	169
Trash and garbage collection (renter)	74	77	74	108	71	57	161	166
Trash and garbage collection (owner)	102	164	83	80	80	90	52	172
Trash and garbage collection (vacation)	132	293	73	55	70	90	12	71
Septic tank cleaning	115	154	112	163	74	159	28	116
Septic tank cleaning (renter)	39	63	48	–	76	–	453	375
Septic tank cleaning (owner)	117	156	113	166	74	162	20	111

See appendix for information about mortgage principle reduction.
Note: Per capita indexes account for household size and show how much each person in a particular household demographic segment spends relative to a person in the average household. Spending index for total consumer units is 100. (–) means sample is too small to make a reliable estimate.
Source: Calculations by New Strategist based on the 2000 Consumer Expenditure Survey

Table 9.14 (Housing) Shelter and Utilities: Total spending by household type, 2000

(total annual spending on shelter and utilities, by consumer unit (CU) type, 2000; numbers in thousands)

	total married couples	married couples, no children	married couples with children				single parent, at least one child <18	single person
			total	oldest child under 6	oldest child 6 to 17	oldest child 18 or older		
Number of consumer units	56,287	22,805	28,777	5,291	15,396	8,090	6,132	32,323
Total spending of all CUs	$2,736,638,479	$962,269,290	$1,542,030,797	$268,549,467	$834,007,478	$441,311,118	$177,357,369	$745,336,057
Housing, total spending	855,764,470	292,622,586	493,018,499	98,952,758	268,391,540	125,692,065	65,809,850	264,681,087
SHELTER	**$480,442,754**	**$163,131,235**	**$278,941,504**	**$55,018,146**	**$154,503,633**	**$69,419,238**	**$38,824,390**	**$163,344,927**
Owned dwellings*	**366,169,450**	**119,361,598**	**218,344,336**	**41,606,308**	**122,190,662**	**54,546,987**	**17,153,534**	**75,374,973**
Mortgage interest and charges	220,744,105	61,389,920	142,165,862	29,022,722	81,288,417	31,854,375	10,388,896	32,473,625
Mortgage interest	204,985,997	55,782,854	133,907,726	28,148,279	76,783,855	28,975,144	9,995,528	30,766,648
Interest paid, home equity loan	8,437,984	2,901,936	4,235,687	447,513	2,453,814	1,334,284	297,525	1,083,144
Interest paid, home equity line of credit	7,303,801	2,703,761	4,008,061	426,931	2,050,131	1,531,113	95,843	602,501
Prepayment penalty charges	16,323	1,368	14,389	#VALUE!	616	13,834	#VALUE!	21,010
Property taxes	86,327,372	33,305,106	46,564,351	7,957,823	24,697,032	13,909,622	3,960,597	23,373,085
Maintenance, repairs, insurance, other expenses	59,098,536	24,666,572	29,614,123	4,625,815	16,205,214	8,782,989	2,804,041	19,528,587
Homeowner's and related insurance	17,893,637	7,758,261	8,697,848	1,376,348	4,696,550	2,624,962	641,836	4,667,118
Ground rent	1,791,615	883,010	659,857	109,841	333,785	216,246	205,361	1,463,585
Maintenance and repair services	31,307,955	12,752,328	16,089,796	2,311,320	9,055,003	4,723,347	1,678,328	10,627,156
Painting and papering	3,759,409	1,439,680	2,131,800	437,672	1,222,288	471,809	105,838	1,360,475
Plumbing and water heating	2,704,590	1,348,460	1,173,526	138,730	672,497	362,351	138,461	1,032,397
Heat, air conditioning, electrical work	5,493,048	2,228,277	2,911,945	244,021	1,899,866	768,065	325,854	2,117,157
Roofing and gutters	5,214,428	2,631,697	2,354,822	404,232	987,807	962,710	275,633	1,647,180
Other repair and maintenance services	11,268,657	4,048,116	5,869,645	868,306	3,483,961	1,517,280	731,670	3,882,639
Repair, replacement of hard-surface flooring	2,777,201	1,016,647	1,603,742	209,894	770,262	623,577	98,112	554,339
Repair of built-in appliances	90,622	39,909	44,317	8,466	18,321	17,636	2,821	33,293
Maintenance and repair materials	6,332,288	2,291,674	3,453,240	671,745	1,764,690	1,016,913	170,347	1,210,496
Paints, wallpaper, and supplies	1,238,314	428,734	686,044	164,550	382,437	139,067	42,127	298,341
Tools, equipment for painting, wallpapering	132,837	46,066	73,669	17,672	41,107	14,967	4,538	32,000
Plumbing supplies and equipment	434,536	183,808	184,461	24,233	62,508	97,646	4,354	122,504
Electrical supplies, heating and cooling equip.	323,650	120,638	176,403	28,518	136,563	11,407	55,495	48,485
Hard-surface flooring, repair and replacement	579,756	112,657	408,058	27,354	136,716	244,156	7,910	96,969
Roofing and gutters	574,690	153,250	349,928	46,243	252,802	50,967	22,014	75,959
Plaster, paneling, siding, windows, doors, screens, awnings	1,137,560	437,856	649,785	188,677	327,473	133,728	14,778	71,111
Patio, walk, fence, driveway, masonry, brick, and stucco materials	48,970	21,437	23,309	2,275	10,623	10,193	307	7,111
Landscape maintenance	249,351	114,025	113,381	16,243	72,823	24,513	2,882	38,788
Miscellaneous supplies and equipment	1,612,623	673,432	787,914	155,979	341,791	290,188	15,943	418,906
Insulation, other maintenance, repair	1,086,902	460,889	518,274	125,344	272,355	120,541	9,443	235,635
Finish basement, remodel rooms, build patios, walks, etc.	525,158	212,543	269,928	30,635	69,590	169,647	6,500	183,595
Property management and security	1,606,431	878,905	653,526	136,508	328,859	188,254	90,876	1,398,939
Property management	1,084,650	584,264	458,993	103,175	238,484	117,143	74,872	958,377
Management and upkeep services for security	521,780	294,641	194,820	33,333	90,375	71,111	16,066	440,239
Parking	166,047	102,394	59,568	20,000	26,327	13,268	17,231	161,615

	total married couples	married couples, no children	married couples with children				single parent, at least one child <18	single person
			total	oldest child under 6	oldest child 6 to 17	oldest child 18 or older		
Rented dwellings	**$76,280,142**	**$25,571,247**	**$43,228,522**	**$11,441,364**	**$23,753,719**	**$8,033,289**	**$20,326,660**	**$78,709,091**
Rent	74,104,087	24,549,354	42,367,802	11,271,576	23,223,480	7,872,784	19,598,301	76,527,288
Rent as pay	730,042	292,588	306,187	73,862	167,508	64,720	499,942	1,320,718
Maintenance, insurance, and other expenses	1,446,013	729,304	554,533	95,926	362,884	95,786	228,478	861,085
Tenant's insurance	369,243	207,526	130,648	47,143	69,744	13,834	46,910	420,845
Maintenance and repair services	618,031	331,357	192,518	12,063	125,939	54,608	119,145	309,008
Repair and maintenance services	534,727	257,012	184,461	5,979	123,784	54,608	117,428	282,503
Repair and replacement of hard-surface flooring	81,616	74,344	6,043	6,085	–	–	1,288	24,889
Repair of built-in appliances	2,251	–	2,014	–	2,155	–	429	1,616
Maintenance and repair materials	458,739	190,194	231,367	36,720	167,201	27,344	62,424	131,555
Paint, wallpaper, and supplies	75,425	17,560	43,453	3,545	26,173	13,672	32,438	40,081
Painting and wallpapering tools	7,880	1,824	4,604	370	2,771	1,456	3,495	4,202
Plastering, paneling, roofing, gutters, etc.	31,521	2,737	27,914	2,222	24,788	1,052	2,391	9,374
Patio, walk, fence, driveway, masonry, brick, and stucco materials	0	–	0	0	0	–	–	0
Plumbing supplies and equipment	21,389	1,140	20,144	265	19,091	809	3,495	14,222
Electrical supplies, heating and cooling equip.	4,503	912	3,741	212	3,541	–	4,844	14,545
Miscellaneous supplies and equipment	225,711	109,464	104,461	27,725	71,437	5,259	12,325	32,969
Insulation, other maintenance and repair	61,916	44,014	15,827	4,974	10,007	809	4,292	17,131
Materials for additions, finishing basements, remodeling rooms	163,795	65,222	88,633	22,804	61,430	4,450	8,033	15,192
Construction materials for jobs not started	–	–	–	–	–	–	–	646
Hard-surface flooring	44,467	17,788	20,719	1,958	16,936	1,942	858	6,141
Landscape maintenance	47,281	38,997	6,043	423	2,617	3,074	2,637	10,020
Other lodging	**37,993,162**	**18,198,390**	**17,368,358**	**1,970,474**	**8,559,098**	**6,838,962**	**1,344,196**	**9,260,540**
Owned vacation homes	12,482,768	6,843,324	4,404,608	605,872	2,348,044	1,450,780	353,081	1,991,743
Mortgage interest and charges	5,651,215	2,900,112	2,167,771	297,143	1,263,242	607,316	220,997	599,592
Mortgage interest	5,482,354	2,775,597	2,131,512	274,338	1,259,393	597,689	208,059	512,320
Interest paid, home equity loan	104,131	84,607	11,511	2,804	3,849	4,935	–	43,636
Interest paid, home equity line of credit	64,730	39,909	24,748	20,053	–	4,692	12,939	43,636
Property taxes	4,218,711	2,451,081	1,439,426	225,450	739,470	474,479	96,395	917,650
Maintenance, insurance and other expenses	2,612,280	1,492,131	797,698	83,227	345,332	368,985	35,627	474,502
Homeowner's and related insurance	831,922	410,946	355,971	26,296	201,226	128,631	26,245	153,211
Homeowner's insurance	831,922	410,946	355,971	26,296	201,226	128,631	26,245	153,211
Ground rent	195,879	93,729	31,079	–	9,853	21,115	–	90,504
Maintenance and repair services	1,126,866	725,427	246,619	18,677	93,608	134,132	3,373	176,484
Maintenance and repair materials	47,281	39,453	8,058	–	5,081	3,074	–	2,586
Property management and security	350,105	184,721	134,101	31,270	30,330	72,648	6,009	44,606
Property management	227,399	125,428	81,439	27,037	16,474	37,780	4,783	29,091
Management and upkeep services for security	122,706	59,293	52,950	4,233	13,856	34,868	1,226	15,515
Parking	60,790	37,856	21,583	6,984	5,235	9,384	–	7,434
Housing while attending school	5,463,779	2,090,306	3,166,046	42,857	956,246	2,166,907	185,616	2,517,638
Lodging on trips	20,047,178	9,264,987	9,797,705	1,321,745	5,254,809	3,221,276	805,561	4,751,158
UTILITIES, FUELS, AND PUBLIC SERVICES	**169,213,919**	**61,313,751**	**91,503,666**	**14,834,218**	**49,156,965**	**27,512,472**	**14,318,465**	**52,623,460**
Natural gas	**20,709,676**	**7,260,656**	**11,404,325**	**1,906,136**	**6,116,061**	**3,382,025**	**1,875,840**	**6,724,477**
Natural gas (renter)	2,619,597	739,110	1,600,865	400,053	889,581	311,303	1,019,568	1,560,554
Natural gas (owner)	17,894,200	6,412,310	9,724,612	1,505,342	5,199,075	3,020,240	855,107	5,139,034
Natural gas (vacation)	195,316	109,236	78,561	741	27,405	50,563	1,165	25,212

	total married couples	married couples, no children	married couples with children			single parent, at least one child <18	single person
			total	oldest child under 6	oldest child 6 to 17	oldest child 18 or older		
Electricity	**$62,838,807**	**$23,314,464**	**$33,409,521**	**$5,056,238**	**$18,020,094**	**$10,333,033**	**$5,291,732**	**$18,406,332**
Electricity (renter)	8,711,539	2,467,273	5,212,378	1,256,665	2,982,821	972,742	3,020,255	6,274,864
Electricity (owner)	53,505,296	20,415,948	28,056,136	3,788,885	14,986,928	9,280,201	2,267,000	12,028,681
Electricity (vacation)	621,408	431,243	141,295	10,635	50,345	80,172	4,476	102,787
Fuel oil and other fuels	**6,779,769**	**2,940,705**	**3,462,449**	**603,015**	**1,809,492**	**1,050,001**	**262,940**	**2,206,368**
Fuel oil	3,841,025	1,589,052	2,057,556	432,328	1,007,514	617,672	123,866	1,298,092
Fuel oil (renter)	336,033	92,132	214,389	58,783	101,306	54,365	50,896	149,009
Fuel oil (owner)	3,453,770	1,457,924	1,830,505	373,545	897,279	559,666	72,971	1,140,032
Fuel oil (vacation)	51,221	38,769	12,662	–	8,930	3,641	–	9,050
Coal	28,706	13,683	8,345	–	7,852	485	–	32,646
Coal (renter)	12,946	12,999	–	–	–	–	–	–
Coal (owner)	15,760	684	8,345	–	7,852	485	–	32,646
Bottled/tank gas	2,494,640	1,194,754	1,137,267	136,085	644,169	356,931	122,333	743,429
Gas (renter)	165,484	52,680	107,626	32,593	62,816	12,297	58,867	136,403
Gas (owner)	2,183,936	1,071,607	965,181	91,164	546,404	327,483	60,094	580,198
Gas (vacation)	144,658	70,467	64,460	12,275	34,949	17,151	3,373	26,828
Wood and other fuels	415,398	143,215	259,569	34,603	150,111	74,833	16,740	131,878
Wood and other fuels (renter)	61,916	16,420	42,302	11,058	30,484	809	3,557	17,778
Wood and other fuels (owner)	349,542	123,147	217,266	23,545	119,627	74,024	13,184	112,484
Wood and other fuels (vacation)	3,940	3,649	–	–	–	–	–	1,939
Telephone services	**57,184,778**	**19,856,998**	**31,570,383**	**5,528,936**	**16,874,478**	**9,166,941**	**5,475,079**	**19,613,596**
Telephone services in home city, excl. mobile phones	48,175,480	17,016,863	26,285,487	4,551,159	14,012,208	7,722,229	4,949,137	17,494,501
Telephone services for mobile phones	9,009,297	2,840,135	5,284,896	977,777	2,862,270	1,444,712	526,003	2,119,096
Water and other public services	**21,700,890**	**7,940,701**	**11,657,275**	**1,739,892**	**6,336,840**	**3,580,472**	**1,412,935**	**5,672,687**
Water and sewerage maintenance	15,678,181	5,527,248	8,555,978	1,220,422	4,668,375	2,667,273	1,048,572	3,857,104
Water and sewerage maintenance (renter)	1,542,827	386,773	978,130	193,227	549,791	235,176	416,056	641,935
Water and sewerage maintenance (owner)	13,983,379	5,020,065	7,555,401	1,025,502	4,110,270	2,419,557	631,596	3,199,007
Water and sewerage maintenance (vacation)	151,975	120,410	22,446	1,693	8,314	12,540	920	16,162
Trash and garbage collection	5,860,602	2,358,493	3,002,880	495,873	1,632,130	874,853	360,378	1,786,169
Trash and garbage collection (renter)	441,290	117,218	273,957	66,190	149,187	58,491	95,230	178,423
Trash and garbage collection (owner)	5,219,494	2,128,847	2,659,858	421,164	1,445,684	793,144	263,308	1,588,029
Trash and garbage collection (vacation)	199,256	112,429	69,065	8,519	37,104	23,218	1,840	19,394
Septic tank cleaning	162,669	54,960	98,417	23,598	36,489	38,347	3,924	29,414
Septic tank cleaning (renter)	1,126	456	863	–	770	–	1,288	1,939
Septic tank cleaning (owner)	161,544	54,732	97,554	23,598	35,719	38,347	2,698	27,475

See appendix for information about mortgage principle reduction.
Note: Total spending figures for total consumer units can be found on Total Spending by Age and Total Spending by Region tables. Spending by type of consumer unit will not add to total because not all types of consumer units are shown. (–) means sample is too small to make a reliable estimate.
Source: Calculations by New Strategist based on the 2000 Consumer Expenditure Survey

Table 9.15 (Housing) Shelter and Utilities: Market shares by household type, 2000

(percentage of total annual spending on shelter and utilities accounted for by types of consumer units, 2000)

	total married couples	married couples, no children	married couples with children				single parent, at least one child <18	single person
			total	oldest child under 6	oldest child 6 to 17	oldest child 18 or older		
Share of total consumer units	51.5%	20.9%	26.3%	4.8%	14.1%	7.4%	5.6%	29.6%
Share of total before-tax income	69.8	24.9	39.4	6.8	21.9	10.7	3.2	16.5
Share of total spending	65.8	23.1	37.1	6.5	20.0	10.6	4.3	17.9
Share of housing spending	63.5	21.7	36.6	7.3	19.9	9.3	4.9	19.6
SHELTER	**61.7%**	**21.0%**	**35.9%**	**7.1%**	**19.9%**	**8.9%**	**5.0%**	**21.0%**
Owned dwellings*	**72.7**	**23.7**	**43.4**	**8.3**	**24.3**	**10.8**	**3.4**	**15.0**
Mortgage interest and charges	76.5	21.3	49.3	10.1	28.2	11.0	3.6	11.3
Mortgage interest	76.2	20.7	49.8	10.5	28.5	10.8	3.7	11.4
Interest paid, home equity loan	78.6	27.0	39.4	4.2	22.8	12.4	2.8	10.1
Interest paid, home equity line of credit	83.7	31.0	45.9	4.9	23.5	17.6	1.1	6.9
Prepayment penalty charges	43.9	3.7	38.7	–	1.7	37.2	–	56.5
Property taxes	69.3	26.7	37.4	6.4	19.8	11.2	3.2	18.8
Maintenance, repairs, insurance, other expenses	65.5	27.3	32.8	5.1	18.0	9.7	3.1	21.6
Homeowner's and related insurance	69.7	30.2	33.9	5.4	18.3	10.2	2.5	18.2
Ground rent	42.4	20.9	15.6	2.6	7.9	5.1	4.9	34.6
Maintenance and repair services	65.2	26.6	33.5	4.8	18.9	9.8	3.5	22.1
Painting and papering	68.8	26.4	39.0	8.0	22.4	8.6	1.9	24.9
Plumbing and water heating	59.4	29.6	25.8	3.0	14.8	8.0	3.0	22.7
Heat, air conditioning, electrical work	63.4	25.7	33.6	2.8	21.9	8.9	3.8	24.4
Roofing and gutters	63.3	32.0	28.6	4.9	12.0	11.7	3.3	20.0
Other repair and maintenance services	65.2	23.4	34.0	5.0	20.2	8.8	4.2	22.5
Repair, replacement of hard-surface flooring	75.6	27.7	43.6	5.7	21.0	17.0	2.7	15.1
Repair of built-in appliances	63.3	27.9	30.9	5.9	12.8	12.3	2.0	23.2
Maintenance and repair materials	74.2	26.8	40.4	7.9	20.7	11.9	2.0	14.2
Paints, wallpaper, and supplies	70.6	24.5	39.1	9.4	21.8	7.9	2.4	17.0
Tools, equipment for painting, wallpapering	70.6	24.5	39.2	9.4	21.9	8.0	2.4	17.0
Plumbing supplies and equipment	64.8	27.4	27.5	3.6	9.3	14.6	0.6	18.3
Electrical supplies, heating and cooling equip.	68.0	25.4	37.1	6.0	28.7	2.4	11.7	10.2
Hard-surface flooring, repair and replacement	75.9	14.8	53.5	3.6	17.9	32.0	1.0	12.7
Roofing and gutters	82.0	21.9	49.9	6.6	36.1	7.3	3.1	10.8
Plaster, paneling, siding, windows, doors, screens, awnings	85.7	33.0	48.9	14.2	24.7	10.1	1.1	5.4
Patio, walk, fence, driveway, masonry, brick, and stucco materials	74.6	32.7	35.5	3.5	16.2	15.5	0.5	10.8
Landscape maintenance	78.1	35.7	35.5	5.1	22.8	7.7	0.9	12.1
Miscellaneous supplies and equipment	70.9	29.6	34.6	6.9	15.0	12.8	0.7	18.4
Insulation, other maintenance, repair	73.9	31.3	35.2	8.5	18.5	8.2	0.6	16.0
Finish basement, remodel rooms, build patios, walks, etc.	65.3	26.4	33.6	3.8	8.7	21.1	0.8	22.8
Property management and security	47.4	25.9	19.3	4.0	9.7	5.6	2.7	41.3
Property management	46.1	24.9	19.5	4.4	10.1	5.0	3.2	40.8
Management and upkeep services for security	50.2	28.4	18.8	3.2	8.7	6.8	1.5	42.4
Parking	44.0	27.1	15.8	5.3	7.0	3.5	4.6	42.8

	total married couples	married couples, no children	married couples with children			single parent, at least one child <18	single person
			total	oldest child under 6	oldest child 6 to 17	oldest child 18 or older		
Rented dwellings	**34.3%**	**11.5%**	**19.4%**	**5.1%**	**10.7%**	**3.6%**	**9.1%**	**35.4%**
Rent	34.3	11.4	19.6	5.2	10.7	3.6	9.1	35.4
Rent as pay	22.8	9.1	9.6	2.3	5.2	2.0	15.6	41.3
Maintenance, insurance, and other expenses	48.0	24.2	18.4	3.2	12.0	3.2	7.6	28.6
Tenant's insurance	38.1	21.4	13.5	4.9	7.2	1.4	4.8	43.4
Maintenance and repair services	50.8	27.2	15.8	1.0	10.3	4.5	9.8	25.4
Repair and maintenance services	49.0	23.5	16.9	0.5	11.3	5.0	10.8	25.9
Repair and replacement of hard-surface flooring	69.1	62.9	5.1	5.2	–	–	1.1	21.1
Repair of built-in appliances	29.4	–	26.3	–	28.2	–	5.6	21.1
Maintenance and repair materials	55.6	23.0	28.0	4.4	20.2	3.3	7.6	15.9
Paint, wallpaper, and supplies	44.8	10.4	25.8	2.1	15.5	8.1	19.3	23.8
Painting and wallpapering tools	42.4	9.8	24.8	2.0	14.9	7.8	18.8	22.6
Plastering, paneling, roofing, gutters, etc.	60.0	5.2	53.2	4.2	47.2	2.0	4.6	17.9
Patio, walk, fence, driveway, masonry, brick, and stucco materials	0.0	–	0.0	0.0	0.0	–	–	0.0
Plumbing supplies and equipment	50.1	2.7	47.2	0.6	44.8	1.9	8.2	33.3
Electrical supplies, heating and cooling equip.	16.5	3.3	13.7	0.8	13.0	–	17.7	53.2
Miscellaneous supplies and equipment	57.3	27.8	26.5	7.0	18.1	1.3	3.1	8.4
Insulation, other maintenance and repair	61.5	43.7	15.7	4.9	9.9	0.8	4.3	17.0
Materials for additions, finishing basements, remodeling rooms	56.1	22.3	30.4	7.8	21.0	1.5	2.8	5.2
Construction materials for jobs not started	–	–	–	–	–	–	–	59.1
Hard-surface flooring	83.0	33.2	38.7	3.7	31.6	3.6	1.6	11.5
Landscape maintenance	72.1	59.4	9.2	0.6	4.0	4.7	4.0	15.3
Other lodging	**72.7**	**34.8**	**33.2**	**3.8**	**16.4**	**13.1**	**2.6**	**17.7**
Owned vacation homes	77.2	42.3	27.2	3.7	14.5	9.0	2.2	12.3
Mortgage interest and charges	81.2	41.7	31.1	4.3	18.1	8.7	3.2	8.6
Mortgage interest	81.9	41.5	31.9	4.1	18.8	8.9	3.1	7.7
Interest paid, home equity loan	70.5	57.3	7.8	1.9	2.6	3.3	–	29.6
Interest paid, home equity line of credit	53.3	32.9	20.4	16.5	–	3.9	10.7	35.9
Property taxes	74.2	43.1	25.3	4.0	13.0	8.3	1.7	16.1
Maintenance, insurance and other expenses	74.0	42.3	22.6	2.4	9.8	10.4	1.0	13.4
Homeowner's and related insurance	70.8	35.0	30.3	2.2	17.1	11.0	2.2	13.0
Homeowner's insurance	70.8	35.0	30.3	2.2	17.1	11.0	2.2	13.0
Ground rent	60.3	28.9	9.6	–	3.0	6.5	–	27.9
Maintenance and repair services	76.0	48.9	16.6	1.3	6.3	9.0	0.2	11.9
Maintenance and repair materials	90.1	75.2	15.3	–	9.7	5.9	–	4.9
Property management and security	82.3	43.4	31.5	7.4	7.1	17.1	1.4	10.5
Property management	81.2	44.8	29.1	9.7	5.9	13.5	1.7	10.4
Management and upkeep services for security	84.4	40.8	36.4	2.9	9.5	24.0	0.8	10.7
Parking	85.5	53.3	30.4	9.8	7.4	13.2	–	10.5
Housing while attending school	63.8	24.4	37.0	0.5	11.2	25.3	2.2	29.4
Lodging on trips	72.8	33.7	35.6	4.8	19.1	11.7	2.9	17.3
UTILITIES, FUELS, AND PUBLIC SERVICES	**62.2**	**22.5**	**33.6**	**5.4**	**18.1**	**10.1**	**5.3**	**19.3**
Natural gas	**61.6**	**21.6**	**33.9**	**5.7**	**18.2**	**10.1**	**5.6**	**20.0**
Natural gas (renter)	39.6	11.2	24.2	6.0	13.5	4.7	15.4	23.6
Natural gas (owner)	66.9	24.0	36.3	5.6	19.4	11.3	3.2	19.2
Natural gas (vacation)	79.4	44.4	31.9	0.3	11.1	20.5	0.5	10.2

| | total married couples | married couples, no children | married couples with children | | | | single parent, at least one child <18 | single person |
			total	oldest child under 6	oldest child 6 to 17	oldest child 18 or older		
Electricity	**63.0%**	**23.4%**	**33.5%**	**5.1%**	**18.1%**	**10.4%**	**5.3%**	**18.5%**
Electricity (renter)	37.2	10.5	22.3	5.4	12.8	4.2	12.9	26.8
Electricity (owner)	70.9	27.1	37.2	5.0	19.9	12.3	3.0	15.9
Electricity (vacation)	75.8	52.6	17.2	1.3	6.1	9.8	0.5	12.5
Fuel oil and other fuels	**63.9**	**27.7**	**32.7**	**5.7**	**17.1**	**9.9**	**2.5**	**20.8**
Fuel oil	63.8	26.4	34.2	7.2	16.7	10.3	2.1	21.5
Fuel oil (renter)	47.0	12.9	30.0	8.2	14.2	7.6	7.1	20.8
Fuel oil (owner)	66.1	27.9	35.1	7.2	17.2	10.7	1.4	21.8
Fuel oil (vacation)	57.8	43.8	14.3	–	10.1	4.1	–	10.2
Coal	45.3	21.6	13.2	–	12.4	0.8	–	51.5
Coal (renter)	84.6	84.9	–	–	–	–	–	–
Coal (owner)	32.8	1.4	17.3	–	16.3	1.0	–	67.8
Bottled/tank gas	64.7	31.0	29.5	3.5	16.7	9.3	3.2	19.3
Gas (renter)	31.8	10.1	20.7	6.3	12.1	2.4	11.3	26.2
Gas (owner)	69.4	34.0	30.7	2.9	17.4	10.4	1.9	18.4
Gas (vacation)	77.3	37.7	34.5	6.6	18.7	9.2	1.8	14.3
Wood and other fuels	63.1	21.8	39.4	5.3	22.8	11.4	2.5	20.0
Wood and other fuels (renter)	51.9	13.8	35.5	9.3	25.6	0.7	3.0	14.9
Wood and other fuels (owner)	65.5	23.1	40.7	4.4	22.4	13.9	2.5	21.1
Wood and other fuels (vacation)	72.1	66.7	–	–	–	–	–	35.5
Telephone services	**59.6**	**20.7**	**32.9**	**5.8**	**17.6**	**9.6**	**5.7**	**20.5**
Telephone services in home city, excl. mobile phones	58.2	20.5	31.7	5.5	16.9	9.3	6.0	21.1
Telephone services for mobile phones	68.9	21.7	40.4	7.5	21.9	11.1	4.0	16.2
Water and other public services	**66.9**	**24.5**	**36.0**	**5.4**	**19.5**	**11.0**	**4.4**	**17.5**
Water and sewerage maintenance	67.4	23.8	36.8	5.2	20.1	11.5	4.5	16.6
Water and sewerage maintenance (renter)	47.0	11.8	29.8	5.9	16.8	7.2	12.7	19.6
Water and sewerage maintenance (owner)	70.6	25.3	38.1	5.2	20.8	12.2	3.2	16.2
Water and sewerage maintenance (vacation)	85.3	67.5	12.6	0.9	4.7	7.0	0.5	9.1
Trash and garbage collection	65.6	26.4	33.6	5.5	18.3	9.8	4.0	20.0
Trash and garbage collection (renter)	48.6	12.9	30.2	7.3	16.4	6.4	10.5	19.7
Trash and garbage collection (owner)	66.9	27.3	34.1	5.4	18.5	10.2	3.4	20.4
Trash and garbage collection (vacation)	86.8	49.0	30.1	3.7	16.2	10.1	0.8	8.4
Septic tank cleaning	75.9	25.6	45.9	11.0	17.0	17.9	1.8	13.7
Septic tank cleaning (renter)	25.7	10.4	19.7	–	17.6	–	29.4	44.3
Septic tank cleaning (owner)	76.9	26.1	46.5	11.2	17.0	18.3	1.3	13.1

See appendix for information about mortgage principle reduction.
Note: Market share for total consumer units is 100.0%. Market shares by type of consumer unit will not add to total because not all types of consumer units are shown. (–) means sample is too small to make a reliable estimate.
Source: Calculations by New Strategist based on the 2000 Consumer Expenditure Survey

Table 9.16 (Housing) Shelter and Utilities: Average spending by race and Hispanic origin, 2000

(average annual spending of consumer units (CU) on shelter and utilities, by race and Hispanic origin of consumer unit reference person, 2000)

	total consumer units	race		Hispanic origin	
		black	white and other	Hispanic	non-Hispanic
Number of consumer units					
(in thousands, add 000)	109,367	13,230	96,137	9,473	99,894
Average number of persons per CU	2.5	2.7	2.5	3.4	2.4
Average before-tax income of CU	$44,649.00	$32,657.00	$46,260.00	$34,891.00	$45,669.00
Average spending of CU, total	38,044.67	28,152.24	39,406.20	32,734.95	38,548.91
Housing, average spending	12,318.51	9,905.54	12,650.61	10,849.81	12,457.64
SHELTER	$7,114.26	$5,677.51	$7,311.99	$6,437.15	$7,178.47
Owned dwellings*	4,602.32	2,607.38	4,876.86	2,948.92	4,759.11
Mortgage interest and charges	2,638.81	1,574.25	2,785.31	1,751.04	2,722.99
Mortgage interest	2,460.48	1,476.34	2,595.91	1,661.11	2,536.28
Interest paid, home equity loan	98.22	78.84	100.89	52.84	102.52
Interest paid, home equity line of credit	79.76	19.06	88.12	35.61	83.95
Prepayment penalty charges	0.34	–	0.39	1.48	0.24
Property taxes	1,138.55	639.98	1,207.17	664.62	1,183.50
Maintenance, repairs, insurance, other expenses	824.96	393.15	884.38	533.26	852.62
Homeowner's and related insurance	234.84	152.84	246.13	130.30	244.76
Ground rent	38.67	10.46	42.56	33.62	39.15
Maintenance and repair services	438.92	180.70	474.46	270.61	454.88
Painting and papering	49.93	22.44	53.71	23.06	52.48
Plumbing and water heating	41.62	30.14	43.19	19.58	43.70
Heat, air conditioning, electrical work	79.19	29.63	86.01	33.68	83.51
Roofing and gutters	75.27	20.58	82.80	67.53	76.00
Other repair and maintenance services	157.99	66.33	170.61	106.34	162.89
Repair, replacement of hard-surface flooring	33.61	10.97	36.73	20.32	34.87
Repair of built-in appliances	1.31	0.62	1.41	0.10	1.43
Maintenance and repair materials	78.08	21.29	85.89	79.83	77.91
Paints, wallpaper, and supplies	16.03	4.86	17.56	15.97	16.03
Tools, equipment for painting, wallpapering	1.72	0.52	1.89	1.72	1.72
Plumbing supplies and equipment	6.13	4.74	6.32	3.35	6.39
Electrical supplies, heating and cooling equipment	4.35	0.54	4.88	4.39	4.35
Hard-surface flooring, repair and replacement	6.98	2.33	7.62	6.52	7.03
Roofing and gutters	6.41	1.83	7.04	8.06	6.25
Plaster, paneling, siding, windows, doors, screens, awnings	12.14	3.21	13.37	13.81	11.98
Patio, walk, fence, driveway, masonry, brick, and stucco materials	0.60	0.32	0.63	0.41	0.61
Landscape maintenance	2.92	0.13	3.30	2.27	2.98
Miscellaneous supplies and equipment	20.80	2.80	23.28	23.33	20.56
Insulation, other maintenance, repair	13.45	1.37	15.12	19.42	12.89
Finish basement, remodel rooms, build patios, walks, etc.	7.35	1.43	8.16	3.91	7.67
Property management and security	30.99	25.26	31.77	16.79	32.33
Property management	21.49	19.90	21.71	13.27	22.27
Management and upkeep services for security	9.50	5.36	10.07	3.52	10.06
Parking	3.45	2.59	3.57	2.11	3.58

	total consumer units	race		Hispanic origin	
		black	white and other	Hispanic	non-Hispanic
Rented dwellings	**$2,034.11**	**$2,843.04**	**$1,922.78**	**$3,307.05**	**$1,913.39**
Rent	1,977.33	2,750.44	1,870.93	3,225.26	1,858.99
Rent as pay	29.24	76.46	22.74	54.89	26.81
Maintenance, insurance, and other expenses	27.54	16.15	29.10	26.90	27.60
Tenant's insurance	8.86	5.12	9.38	2.52	9.46
Maintenance and repair services	11.13	8.06	11.55	3.54	11.85
Repair and maintenance services	9.98	7.91	10.27	3.54	10.59
Repair and replacement of hard-surface flooring	1.08	0.10	1.21	–	1.18
Repair of built-in appliances	0.07	0.06	0.07	–	0.07
Maintenance and repair materials	7.55	2.97	8.18	20.83	6.29
Paint, wallpaper, and supplies	1.54	1.02	1.61	3.16	1.39
Painting and wallpapering tools	0.17	0.11	0.17	0.34	0.15
Plastering, paneling, roofing, gutters, etc.	0.48	0.38	0.49	0.33	0.49
Patio, walk, fence, driveway, masonry, brick, and stucco materials	0.03	–	–	–	–
Plumbing supplies and equipment	0.39	0.28	0.40	1.43	0.29
Electrical supplies, heating and cooling equipment	0.25	–	0.28	0.03	0.27
Miscellaneous supplies and equipment	3.60	0.24	4.07	13.40	2.67
Insulation, other maintenance and repair	0.92	0.24	1.01	1.16	0.90
Materials for additions, finishing basements, remodeling rooms	2.67	–	3.04	12.24	1.76
Construction materials for jobs not started	0.01	–	–	–	–
Hard-surface flooring	0.49	0.94	0.43	1.77	0.37
Landscape maintenance	0.60	–	0.68	–	0.66
Other lodging	**477.84**	**227.09**	**512.35**	**181.19**	**505.97**
Owned vacation homes	147.91	84.99	156.57	30.45	159.05
Mortgage interest and charges	63.65	47.97	65.80	8.75	68.85
Mortgage interest	61.19	47.97	63.00	8.45	66.19
Interest paid, home equity loan	1.35	–	1.54	0.29	1.45
Interest paid, home equity line of credit	1.11	–	1.26	–	1.21
Property taxes	51.97	25.24	55.65	12.32	55.73
Maintenance, insurance and other expenses	32.29	11.78	35.11	9.38	34.46
Homeowner's and related insurance	10.74	8.66	11.03	5.00	11.29
Homeowner's insurance	10.74	8.66	11.03	5.00	11.29
Ground rent	2.97	0.26	3.35	2.23	3.04
Maintenance and repair services	13.56	0.65	15.34	0.77	14.77
Maintenance and repair materials	0.48	0.22	0.52	–	0.52
Property management and security	3.89	1.78	4.18	1.39	4.13
Property management	2.56	0.83	2.80	0.76	2.73
Management and upkeep services for security	1.33	0.95	1.38	0.63	1.40
Parking	0.65	0.21	0.71	–	0.71
Housing while attending school	78.31	37.54	83.92	52.99	80.71
Lodging on trips	251.62	104.56	271.86	97.75	266.21
UTILITIES, FUELS, AND PUBLIC SERVICES	**2,488.90**	**2,570.54**	**2,477.67**	**2,170.08**	**2,519.14**
Natural gas	307.35	342.08	302.57	242.49	313.50
Natural gas (renter)	60.47	114.80	52.99	99.05	56.81
Natural gas (owner)	244.63	226.44	247.13	143.11	254.26
Natural gas (vacation)	2.25	0.84	2.44	0.32	2.43

	total consumer units	race black	race white and other	Hispanic origin Hispanic	Hispanic origin non-Hispanic
Electricity	**$911.44**	**$938.17**	**$907.76**	**$749.43**	**$926.80**
Electricity (renter)	213.85	410.39	186.80	304.07	205.29
Electricity (owner)	690.09	524.92	712.82	442.76	713.54
Electricity (vacation)	7.50	2.85	8.14	2.59	7.96
Fuel oil and other fuels	**96.94**	**42.94**	**104.38**	**29.94**	**103.30**
Fuel oil	55.08	27.95	58.81	6.55	59.68
Fuel oil (renter)	6.54	4.95	6.75	0.57	7.10
Fuel oil (owner)	47.74	21.79	51.31	5.98	51.70
Fuel oil (vacation)	0.81	1.21	0.76	–	0.89
Coal	0.58	–	0.66	–	0.63
Coal (renter)	0.14	–	0.16	–	0.15
Coal (owner)	0.44	–	0.50	–	0.48
Bottled/tank gas	35.26	12.46	38.40	18.76	36.83
Gas (renter)	4.76	1.83	5.16	2.17	5.00
Gas (owner)	28.79	10.41	31.32	16.13	29.99
Gas (vacation)	1.71	0.22	1.92	0.46	1.83
Wood and other fuels	6.02	2.54	6.50	4.63	6.15
Wood and other fuels (renter)	1.09	0.28	1.21	0.43	1.16
Wood and other fuels (owner)	4.88	2.11	5.26	4.20	4.94
Wood and other fuels (vacation)	0.05	0.14	0.04	–	0.06
Telephone services	**876.75**	**986.30**	**861.68**	**888.85**	**875.61**
Telephone services in home city, excl. mobile phones	757.26	891.17	738.83	788.83	754.27
Telephone services for mobile phones	119.49	95.13	122.84	100.01	121.34
Water and other public services	**296.42**	**261.06**	**301.29**	**259.37**	**299.94**
Water and sewerage maintenance	212.72	201.81	214.22	192.18	214.67
Water and sewerage maintenance (renter)	29.99	55.64	26.46	41.95	28.86
Water and sewerage maintenance (owner)	181.10	145.07	186.06	149.77	184.07
Water and sewerage maintenance (vacation)	1.63	1.09	1.71	0.46	1.74
Trash and garbage collection	81.74	58.66	84.92	66.27	83.21
Trash and garbage collection (renter)	8.30	14.45	7.46	11.89	7.96
Trash and garbage collection (owner)	71.34	43.21	75.21	54.12	72.98
Trash and garbage collection (vacation)	2.10	1.00	2.25	0.26	2.28
Septic tank cleaning	1.96	0.59	2.15	0.91	2.06
Septic tank cleaning (renter)	0.04	0.10	0.03	0.13	0.03
Septic tank cleaning (owner)	1.92	0.50	2.12	0.78	2.03

*See appendix for information about mortgage principle reduction.
Note: Other races include Asians, Native Americans, and Pacific Islanders. (–) means sample is too small to make a reliable estimate.
Source: Bureau of Labor Statistics, unpublished tables from the 2000 Consumer Expenditure Survey

Table 9.17 (Housing) Shelter and Utilities: Indexed spending by race and Hispanic origin, 2000

(indexed average annual spending of consumer units (CU) on shelter and utilities, by race and Hispanic origin of consumer unit reference person, 2000; index definition: an index of 100 is the average for all consumer units; an index of 132 means that spending by consumer units in that group is 32 percent above the average for all consumer units; an index of 68 indicates spending that is 32 percent below the average for all consumer units)

	total consumer units	race		Hispanic origin	
		black	white and other	Hispanic	non-Hispanic
Average spending of CU, total	$38,045	$28,152	$39,406	$32,735	$38,549
Average spending of CU, index	100	74	104	86	101
Housing, spending index	100	80	103	88	101
SHELTER	**100**	**80**	**103**	**90**	**101**
Owned dwellings*	**100**	**57**	**106**	**64**	**103**
Mortgage interest and charges	100	60	106	66	103
Mortgage interest	100	60	106	68	103
Interest paid, home equity loan	100	80	103	54	104
Interest paid, home equity line of credit	100	24	110	45	105
Prepayment penalty charges	100	–	115	435	71
Property taxes	100	56	106	58	104
Maintenance, repairs, insurance, other expenses	100	48	107	65	103
Homeowner's and related insurance	100	65	105	55	104
Ground rent	100	27	110	87	101
Maintenance and repair services	100	41	108	62	104
Painting and papering	100	45	108	46	105
Plumbing and water heating	100	72	104	47	105
Heat, air conditioning, electrical work	100	37	109	43	105
Roofing and gutters	100	27	110	90	101
Other repair and maintenance services	100	42	108	67	103
Repair, replacement of hard-surface flooring	100	33	109	60	104
Repair of built-in appliances	100	47	108	8	109
Maintenance and repair materials	100	27	110	102	100
Paints, wallpaper, and supplies	100	30	110	100	100
Tools, equipment for painting, wallpapering	100	30	110	100	100
Plumbing supplies and equipment	100	77	103	55	104
Electrical supplies, heating and cooling equipment	100	12	112	101	100
Hard-surface flooring, repair and replacement	100	33	109	93	101
Roofing and gutters	100	29	110	126	98
Plaster, paneling, siding, windows, doors, screens, awnings	100	26	110	114	99
Patio, walk, fence, driveway, masonry, brick, and stucco materials	100	53	105	68	102
Landscape maintenance	100	4	113	78	102
Miscellaneous supplies and equipment	100	13	112	112	99
Insulation, other maintenance, repair	100	10	112	144	96
Finish basement, remodel rooms, build patios, walks, etc.	100	19	111	53	104
Property management and security	100	82	103	54	104
Property management	100	93	101	62	104
Management and upkeep services for security	100	56	106	37	106
Parking	100	75	103	61	104

	total consumer units	race		Hispanic origin	
		black	white and other	Hispanic	non-Hispanic
Rented dwellings	**100**	**140**	**95**	**163**	**94**
Rent	100	139	95	163	94
Rent as pay	100	261	78	188	92
Maintenance, insurance, and other expenses	100	59	106	98	100
Tenant's insurance	100	58	106	28	107
Maintenance and repair services	100	72	104	32	106
Repair and maintenance services	100	79	103	35	106
Repair and replacement of hard-surface flooring	100	9	112	–	109
Repair of built-in appliances	100	86	100	–	100
Maintenance and repair materials	100	39	108	276	83
Paint, wallpaper, and supplies	100	66	105	205	90
Painting and wallpapering tools	100	65	100	200	88
Plastering, paneling, roofing, gutters, etc.	100	79	102	69	102
Patio, walk, fence, driveway, masonry, brick, and stucco materials	100	–	–	–	–
Plumbing supplies and equipment	100	72	103	367	74
Electrical supplies, heating and cooling equipment	100	–	112	12	108
Miscellaneous supplies and equipment	100	7	113	372	74
Insulation, other maintenance and repair	100	26	110	126	98
Materials for additions, finishing basements, remodeling rooms	100	–	114	458	66
Construction materials for jobs not started	100	–	–	–	–
Hard-surface flooring	100	192	88	361	76
Landscape maintenance	100	–	113	–	110
Other lodging	**100**	**48**	**107**	**38**	**106**
Owned vacation homes	100	57	106	21	108
Mortgage interest and charges	100	75	103	14	108
Mortgage interest	100	78	103	14	108
Interest paid, home equity loan	100	–	114	21	107
Interest paid, home equity line of credit	100	–	114	–	109
Property taxes	100	49	107	24	107
Maintenance, insurance and other expenses	100	36	109	29	107
Homeowner's and related insurance	100	81	103	47	105
Homeowner's insurance	100	81	103	47	105
Ground rent	100	9	113	75	102
Maintenance and repair services	100	5	113	6	109
Maintenance and repair materials	100	46	108	–	108
Property management and security	100	46	107	36	106
Property management	100	32	109	30	107
Management and upkeep services for security	100	71	104	47	105
Parking	100	32	109	–	109
Housing while attending school	100	48	107	68	103
Lodging on trips	100	42	108	39	106
UTILITIES, FUELS, AND PUBLIC SERVICES	**100**	**103**	**100**	**87**	**101**
Natural gas	**100**	**111**	**98**	**79**	**102**
Natural gas (renter)	100	190	88	164	94
Natural gas (owner)	100	93	101	59	104
Natural gas (vacation)	100	37	108	14	108

	total consumer units	race black	race white and other	Hispanic origin Hispanic	Hispanic origin non-Hispanic
Electricity	**100**	**103**	**100**	**82**	**102**
Electricity (renter)	100	192	87	142	96
Electricity (owner)	100	76	103	64	103
Electricity (vacation)	100	38	109	35	106
Fuel oil and other fuels	**100**	**44**	**108**	**31**	**107**
Fuel oil	100	51	107	12	108
Fuel oil (renter)	100	76	103	9	109
Fuel oil (owner)	100	46	107	13	108
Fuel oil (vacation)	100	149	94	–	110
Coal	100	–	114	–	109
Coal (renter)	100	–	114	–	107
Coal (owner)	100	–	114	–	109
Bottled/tank gas	100	35	109	53	104
Gas (renter)	100	38	108	46	105
Gas (owner)	100	36	109	56	104
Gas (vacation)	100	13	112	27	107
Wood and other fuels	100	42	108	77	102
Wood and other fuels (renter)	100	26	111	39	106
Wood and other fuels (owner)	100	43	108	86	101
Wood and other fuels (vacation)	100	280	80	–	120
Telephone services	**100**	**112**	**98**	**101**	**100**
Telephone services in home city, excl. mobile phones	100	118	98	104	100
Telephone services for mobile phones	100	80	103	84	102
Water and other public services	**100**	**88**	**102**	**88**	**101**
Water and sewerage maintenance	100	95	101	90	101
Water and sewerage maintenance (renter)	100	186	88	140	96
Water and sewerage maintenance (owner)	100	80	103	83	102
Water and sewerage maintenance (vacation)	100	67	105	28	107
Trash and garbage collection	100	72	104	81	102
Trash and garbage collection (renter)	100	174	90	143	96
Trash and garbage collection (owner)	100	61	105	76	102
Trash and garbage collection (vacation)	100	48	107	12	109
Septic tank cleaning	100	30	110	46	105
Septic tank cleaning (renter)	100	250	75	325	75
Septic tank cleaning (owner)	100	26	110	41	106

See appendix for information about mortgage principle reduction.
Note: Other races include Asians, Native Americans, and Pacific Islanders. (–) means sample is too small to make a reliable estimate.
Source: Calculations by New Strategist based on the 2000 Consumer Expenditure Survey

Table 9.18 (Housing) Shelter and Utilities: Indexed per capita spending by race and Hispanic origin, 2000

(indexed average annual per capita spending of consumer units (CU) on shelter and utilities, by race and Hispanic origin of consumer unit reference person, 2000; index definition: an index of 100 is the average for all consumer units; an index of 132 means that spending by consumer units in that group is 32 percent above the average for all consumer units; an index of 68 indicates spending that is 32 percent below the average for all consumer units)

	total consumer units	race black	race white and other	Hispanic origin Hispanic	Hispanic origin non-Hispanic
Per capita spending of CU, total	$15,218	$10,427	$15,762	$9,628	$16,062
Per capita spending of CU, index	100	69	104	63	106
Housing, per capita spending index	100	74	103	65	105
SHELTER	100	74	103	67	105
Owned dwellings*	100	52	106	47	108
Mortgage interest and charges	100	55	106	49	107
Mortgage interest	100	56	106	50	107
Interest paid, home equity loan	100	74	103	40	109
Interest paid, home equity line of credit	100	22	110	33	110
Prepayment penalty charges	100	–	115	320	74
Property taxes	100	52	106	43	108
Maintenance, repairs, insurance, other expenses	100	44	107	48	108
Homeowner's and related insurance	100	60	105	41	109
Ground rent	100	25	110	64	105
Maintenance and repair services	100	38	108	45	108
Painting and papering	100	42	108	34	109
Plumbing and water heating	100	67	104	35	109
Heat, air conditioning, electrical work	100	35	109	31	110
Roofing and gutters	100	25	110	66	105
Other repair and maintenance services	100	39	108	49	107
Repair, replacement of hard-surface flooring	100	30	109	44	108
Repair of built-in appliances	100	44	108	6	114
Maintenance and repair materials	100	25	110	75	104
Paints, wallpaper, and supplies	100	28	110	73	104
Tools, equipment for painting, wallpapering	100	28	110	74	104
Plumbing supplies and equipment	100	72	103	40	109
Electrical supplies, heating and cooling equipment	100	11	112	74	104
Hard-surface flooring, repair and replacement	100	31	109	69	105
Roofing and gutters	100	26	110	92	102
Plaster, paneling, siding, windows, doors, screens, awnings	100	24	110	84	103
Patio, walk, fence, driveway, masonry, brick, and stucco materials	100	49	105	50	106
Landscape maintenance	100	4	113	57	106
Miscellaneous supplies and equipment	100	12	112	82	103
Insulation, other maintenance, repair	100	9	112	106	100
Finish basement, remodel rooms, build patios, walks, etc.	100	18	111	39	109
Property management and security	100	75	103	40	109
Property management	100	86	101	45	108
Management and upkeep services for security	100	52	106	27	110
Parking	100	70	103	45	108

	total consumer units	race		Hispanic origin	
		black	white and other	Hispanic	non-Hispanic
Rented dwellings	**100**	**129**	**95**	**120**	**98**
Rent	100	129	95	120	98
Rent as pay	100	242	78	138	96
Maintenance, insurance, and other expenses	100	54	106	72	104
Tenant's insurance	100	54	106	21	111
Maintenance and repair services	100	67	104	23	111
Repair and maintenance services	100	73	103	26	111
Repair and replacement of hard-surface flooring	100	9	112	–	114
Repair of built-in appliances	100	79	100	–	104
Maintenance and repair materials	100	36	108	203	87
Paint, wallpaper, and supplies	100	61	105	151	94
Painting and wallpapering tools	100	60	100	147	92
Plastering, paneling, roofing, gutters, etc.	100	73	102	51	106
Patio, walk, fence, driveway, masonry, brick, and stucco materials	100	–	–	–	–
Plumbing supplies and equipment	100	66	103	270	77
Electrical supplies, heating and cooling equipment	100	–	112	9	113
Miscellaneous supplies and equipment	100	6	113	274	77
Insulation, other maintenance and repair	100	24	110	93	102
Materials for additions, finishing basements, remodeling rooms	100	–	114	337	69
Construction materials for jobs not started	100	–	–	–	–
Hard-surface flooring	100	178	88	266	79
Landscape maintenance	100	–	113	–	115
Other lodging	**100**	**44**	**107**	**28**	**110**
Owned vacation homes	100	53	106	15	112
Mortgage interest and charges	100	70	103	10	113
Mortgage interest	100	73	103	10	113
Interest paid, home equity loan	100	–	114	16	112
Interest paid, home equity line of credit	100	–	114	–	114
Property taxes	100	45	107	17	112
Maintenance, insurance and other expenses	100	34	109	21	111
Homeowner's and related insurance	100	75	103	34	110
Homeowner's insurance	100	75	103	34	110
Ground rent	100	8	113	55	107
Maintenance and repair services	100	4	113	4	113
Maintenance and repair materials	100	42	108	–	113
Property management and security	100	42	107	26	111
Property management	100	30	109	22	111
Management and upkeep services for security	100	66	104	35	110
Parking	100	30	109	–	114
Housing while attending school	100	44	107	50	107
Lodging on trips	100	38	108	29	110
UTILITIES, FUELS, AND PUBLIC SERVICES	**100**	**96**	**100**	**64**	**105**
Natural gas	**100**	**103**	**98**	**58**	**106**
Natural gas (renter)	100	176	88	120	98
Natural gas (owner)	100	86	101	43	108
Natural gas (vacation)	100	35	108	10	113

	total consumer units	race		Hispanic origin	
		black	white and other	Hispanic	non-Hispanic
Electricity	**100**	**95**	**100**	**60**	**106**
Electricity (renter)	100	178	87	105	100
Electricity (owner)	100	70	103	47	108
Electricity (vacation)	100	35	109	25	111
Fuel oil and other fuels	**100**	**41**	**108**	**23**	**111**
Fuel oil	100	47	107	9	113
Fuel oil (renter)	100	70	103	6	113
Fuel oil (owner)	100	42	107	9	113
Fuel oil (vacation)	100	138	94	–	114
Coal	100	–	114	–	113
Coal (renter)	100	–	114	–	112
Coal (owner)	100	–	114	–	114
Bottled/tank gas	100	33	109	39	109
Gas (renter)	100	36	108	34	109
Gas (owner)	100	33	109	41	109
Gas (vacation)	100	12	112	20	111
Wood and other fuels	100	39	108	57	106
Wood and other fuels (renter)	100	24	111	29	111
Wood and other fuels (owner)	100	40	108	63	105
Wood and other fuels (vacation)	100	259	80	–	125
Telephone services	**100**	**104**	**98**	**75**	**104**
Telephone services in home city, excl. mobile phones	100	109	98	77	104
Telephone services for mobile phones	100	74	103	62	106
Water and other public services	**100**	**82**	**102**	**64**	**105**
Water and sewerage maintenance	100	88	101	66	105
Water and sewerage maintenance (renter)	100	172	88	103	100
Water and sewerage maintenance (owner)	100	74	103	61	106
Water and sewerage maintenance (vacation)	100	62	105	21	111
Trash and garbage collection	100	66	104	60	106
Trash and garbage collection (renter)	100	161	90	105	100
Trash and garbage collection (owner)	100	56	105	56	107
Trash and garbage collection (vacation)	100	44	107	9	113
Septic tank cleaning	100	28	110	34	109
Septic tank cleaning (renter)	100	231	75	239	78
Septic tank cleaning (owner)	100	24	110	30	110

See appendix for information about mortgage principle reduction.
Note: Per capita indexes account for household size and show how much each person in a particular household demographic segment spends relative to a person in the average household. Other races include Asians, Native Americans, and Pacific Islanders. (–) means sample is too small to make a reliable estimate.
Source: Calculations by New Strategist based on the 2000 Consumer Expenditure Survey

Table 9.19 (Housing) Shelter and Utilities: Total spending by race and Hispanic origin, 2000

(total annual spending on shelter and utilities, by consumer unit race and Hispanic origin groups, 2000; numbers in thousands)

	total consumer units	race		Hispanic origin	
		black	white and other	Hispanic	non-Hispanic
Number of consumer units	109,367	13,230	96,137	9,473	99,894
Total spending of all consumer units	$4,160,831,424	$372,454,135	$3,788,393,849	$310,098,181	$3,850,804,816
Housing, total spending	1,347,238,483	131,050,294	1,216,191,694	102,780,250	1,244,443,490
SHELTER	**$778,065,273**	**$75,113,457**	**$702,952,783**	**$60,979,122**	**$717,086,082**
Owned dwellings*	**503,341,931**	**34,495,637**	**468,846,690**	**27,935,119**	**475,406,534**
Mortgage interest and charges	288,598,733	20,827,328	267,771,347	16,587,602	272,010,363
Mortgage interest	269,095,316	19,531,978	249,563,000	15,735,695	253,359,154
Interest paid, home equity loan	10,742,027	1,043,053	9,699,262	500,553	10,241,133
Interest paid, home equity line of credit	8,723,112	252,164	8,471,592	337,334	8,386,101
Prepayment penalty charges	37,185	–	37,493	14,020	23,975
Property taxes	124,519,798	8,466,935	116,053,702	6,295,945	118,224,549
Maintenance, repairs, insurance, other expenses	90,223,400	5,201,375	85,021,640	5,051,572	85,171,622
Homeowner's and related insurance	25,683,746	2,022,073	23,662,200	1,234,332	24,450,055
Ground rent	4,229,222	138,386	4,091,591	318,482	3,910,850
Maintenance and repair services	48,003,364	2,390,661	45,613,161	2,563,489	45,439,783
Painting and papering	5,460,694	296,881	5,163,518	218,447	5,242,437
Plumbing and water heating	4,551,855	398,752	4,152,157	185,481	4,365,368
Heat, air conditioning, electrical work	8,660,773	392,005	8,268,743	319,051	8,342,148
Roofing and gutters	8,232,054	272,273	7,960,144	639,712	7,591,944
Other repair and maintenance services	17,278,892	877,546	16,401,934	1,007,359	16,271,734
Repair, replacement of hard-surface flooring	3,675,825	145,133	3,531,112	192,491	3,483,304
Repair of built-in appliances	143,271	8,203	135,553	947	142,848
Maintenance and repair materials	8,539,375	281,667	8,257,207	756,230	7,782,742
Paints, wallpaper, and supplies	1,753,153	64,298	1,688,166	151,284	1,601,301
Tools, equipment for painting, wallpapering	188,111	6,880	181,699	16,294	171,818
Plumbing supplies and equipment	670,420	62,710	607,586	31,735	638,323
Electrical supplies, heating and cooling equipment	475,746	7,144	469,149	41,586	434,539
Hard-surface flooring, repair and replacement	763,382	30,826	732,564	61,764	702,255
Roofing and gutters	701,042	24,211	676,804	76,352	624,338
Plaster, paneling, siding, windows, doors, screens, awnings	1,327,715	42,468	1,285,352	130,822	1,196,730
Patio, walk, fence, driveway, masonry, brick, and stucco materials	65,620	4,234	60,566	3,884	60,935
Landscape maintenance	319,352	1,720	317,252	21,504	297,684
Miscellaneous supplies and equipment	2,274,834	37,044	2,238,069	221,005	2,053,821
Insulation, other maintenance, repair	1,470,986	18,125	1,453,591	183,966	1,287,634
Finish basement, remodel rooms, build patios, walks, etc.	803,847	18,919	784,478	37,039	766,187
Property management and security	3,389,283	334,190	3,054,272	159,052	3,229,573
Property management	2,350,297	263,277	2,087,134	125,707	2,224,639
Management and upkeep services for security	1,038,987	70,913	968,100	33,345	1,004,934
Parking	377,316	34,266	343,209	19,988	357,621

	total consumer units	race		Hispanic origin	
		black	white and other	Hispanic	non-Hispanic
Rented dwellings	**$222,464,508**	**$37,613,419**	**$184,850,301**	**$31,327,685**	**$191,136,181**
Rent	216,254,650	36,388,321	179,865,597	30,552,888	185,701,947
Rent as pay	3,197,891	1,011,566	2,186,155	519,973	2,678,158
Maintenance, insurance, and other expenses	3,011,967	213,665	2,797,587	254,824	2,757,074
Tenant's insurance	968,992	67,738	901,765	23,872	944,997
Maintenance and repair services	1,217,255	106,634	1,110,382	33,534	1,183,744
Repair and maintenance services	1,091,483	104,649	987,327	33,534	1,057,877
Repair and replacement of hard-surface flooring	118,116	1,323	116,326	–	117,875
Repair of built-in appliances	7,656	794	6,730	–	6,993
Maintenance and repair materials	825,721	39,293	786,401	197,323	628,333
Paint, wallpaper, and supplies	168,425	13,495	154,781	29,935	138,853
Painting and wallpapering tools	18,592	1,455	16,343	3,221	14,984
Plastering, paneling, roofing, gutters, etc.	52,496	5,027	47,107	3,126	48,948
Patio, walk, fence, driveway, masonry, brick, and stucco materials	3,281	–	–	–	–
Plumbing supplies and equipment	42,653	3,704	38,455	13,546	28,969
Electrical supplies, heating and cooling equipment	27,342	–	26,918	284	26,971
Miscellaneous supplies and equipment	393,721	3,175	391,278	126,938	266,717
Insulation, other maintenance and repair	100,618	3,175	97,098	10,989	89,905
Materials for additions, finishing basements, remodeling rooms	292,010	–	292,256	115,950	175,813
Construction materials for jobs not started	1,094	–	–	–	–
Hard-surface flooring	53,590	12,436	41,339	16,767	36,961
Landscape maintenance	65,620	–	65,373	–	65,930
Other lodging	**52,259,927**	**3,004,401**	**49,255,792**	**1,716,413**	**50,543,367**
Owned vacation homes	16,176,473	1,124,418	15,052,170	288,453	15,888,141
Mortgage interest and charges	6,961,210	634,643	6,325,815	82,889	6,877,702
Mortgage interest	6,692,167	634,643	6,056,631	80,047	6,611,984
Interest paid, home equity loan	147,645	–	148,051	2,747	144,846
Interest paid, home equity line of credit	121,397	–	121,133	–	120,872
Property taxes	5,683,803	333,925	5,350,024	116,707	5,567,093
Maintenance, insurance and other expenses	3,531,460	155,849	3,375,370	88,857	3,442,347
Homeowner's and related insurance	1,174,602	114,572	1,060,391	47,365	1,127,803
Homeowner's insurance	1,174,602	114,572	1,060,391	47,365	1,127,803
Ground rent	324,820	3,440	322,059	21,125	303,678
Maintenance and repair services	1,483,017	8,600	1,474,742	7,294	1,475,434
Maintenance and repair materials	52,496	2,911	49,991	–	51,945
Property management and security	425,438	23,549	401,853	13,167	412,562
Property management	279,980	10,981	269,184	7,199	272,711
Management and upkeep services for security	145,458	12,569	132,669	5,968	139,852
Parking	71,089	2,778	68,257	–	70,925
Housing while attending school	8,564,530	496,654	8,067,817	501,974	8,062,445
Lodging on trips	27,518,925	1,383,329	26,135,805	925,986	26,592,782
UTILITIES, FUELS, AND PUBLIC SERVICES	**272,203,526**	**34,008,244**	**238,195,761**	**20,557,168**	**251,646,971**
Natural gas	**33,613,947**	**4,525,718**	**29,088,172**	**2,297,108**	**31,316,769**
Natural gas (renter)	6,613,422	1,518,804	5,094,300	938,301	5,674,978
Natural gas (owner)	26,754,449	2,995,801	23,758,337	1,355,681	25,399,048
Natural gas (vacation)	246,076	11,113	234,574	3,031	242,742

	total consumer units	race		Hispanic origin	
		black	white and other	Hispanic	non-Hispanic
Electricity	**$99,681,458**	**$12,411,989**	**$87,269,323**	**$7,099,350**	**$92,581,759**
Electricity (renter)	23,388,133	5,429,460	17,958,392	2,880,455	20,507,239
Electricity (owner)	75,473,073	6,944,692	68,528,376	4,194,265	71,278,365
Electricity (vacation)	820,253	37,706	782,555	24,535	795,156
Fuel oil and other fuels	**10,602,037**	**568,096**	**10,034,780**	**283,622**	**10,319,050**
Fuel oil	6,023,934	369,779	5,653,817	62,048	5,961,674
Fuel oil (renter)	715,260	65,489	648,925	5,400	709,247
Fuel oil (owner)	5,221,181	288,282	4,932,789	56,649	5,164,520
Fuel oil (vacation)	88,587	16,008	73,064	–	88,906
Coal	63,433	–	63,450	–	62,933
Coal (renter)	15,311	–	15,382	–	14,984
Coal (owner)	48,121	–	48,069	–	47,949
Bottled/tank gas	3,856,280	164,846	3,691,661	177,713	3,679,096
Gas (renter)	520,587	24,211	496,067	20,556	499,470
Gas (owner)	3,148,676	137,724	3,011,011	152,799	2,995,821
Gas (vacation)	187,018	2,911	184,583	4,358	182,806
Wood and other fuels	658,389	33,604	624,891	43,860	614,348
Wood and other fuels (renter)	119,210	3,704	116,326	4,073	115,877
Wood and other fuels (owner)	533,711	27,915	505,681	39,787	493,476
Wood and other fuels (vacation)	5,468	1,852	3,845	–	5,994
Telephone services	**95,887,517**	**13,048,749**	**82,839,330**	**8,420,076**	**87,468,185**
Telephone services in home city, excl. mobile phones	82,819,254	11,790,179	71,028,900	7,472,587	75,347,047
Telephone services for mobile phones	13,068,263	1,258,570	11,809,469	947,395	12,121,138
Water and other public services	**32,418,566**	**3,453,824**	**28,965,117**	**2,457,012**	**29,962,206**
Water and sewerage maintenance	23,264,548	2,669,946	20,594,468	1,820,521	21,444,245
Water and sewerage maintenance (renter)	3,279,916	736,117	2,543,785	397,392	2,882,941
Water and sewerage maintenance (owner)	19,806,364	1,919,276	17,887,250	1,418,771	18,387,489
Water and sewerage maintenance (vacation)	178,268	14,421	164,394	4,358	173,816
Trash and garbage collection	8,939,659	776,072	8,163,954	627,776	8,312,180
Trash and garbage collection (renter)	907,746	191,174	717,182	112,634	795,156
Trash and garbage collection (owner)	7,802,242	571,668	7,230,464	512,679	7,290,264
Trash and garbage collection (vacation)	229,671	13,230	216,308	2,463	227,758
Septic tank cleaning	214,359	7,806	206,695	8,620	205,782
Septic tank cleaning (renter)	4,375	1,323	2,884	1,231	2,997
Septic tank cleaning (owner)	209,985	6,615	203,810	7,389	202,785

See appendix for information about mortgage principle reduction.
Note: Other races include Asians, Native Americans, and Pacific Islanders. Numbers may not add to total because of rounding. (–) means sample is too small to make a reliable estimate.
Source: Calculations by New Strategist based on the 2000 Consumer Expenditure Survey

Table 9.20 (Housing) Shelter and Utilities: Market shares by race and Hispanic origin, 2000

(percentage of total annual spending on shelter and utilities accounted for by consumer unit race and Hispanic origin groups, 2000)

	total consumer units	race — black	race — white and other	Hispanic origin — Hispanic	Hispanic origin — non-Hispanic
Share of total consumer units	100.0%	12.1%	87.9%	8.7%	91.3%
Share of total before-tax income	100.0	8.8	91.1	6.8	93.4
Share of total spending	100.0	9.0	91.0	7.5	92.5
Share of housing spending	100.0	9.7	90.3	7.6	92.4
SHELTER	100.0%	9.7%	90.3%	7.8%	92.2%
Owned dwellings*	100.0	6.9	93.1	5.5	94.5
Mortgage interest and charges	100.0	7.2	92.8	5.7	94.3
Mortgage interest	100.0	7.3	92.7	5.8	94.2
Interest paid, home equity loan	100.0	9.7	90.3	4.7	95.3
Interest paid, home equity line of credit	100.0	2.9	97.1	3.9	96.1
Prepayment penalty charges	100.0	–	100.0	37.7	64.5
Property taxes	100.0	6.8	93.2	5.1	94.9
Maintenance, repairs, insurance, other expenses	100.0	5.8	94.2	5.6	94.4
Homeowner's and related insurance	100.0	7.9	92.1	4.8	95.2
Ground rent	100.0	3.3	96.7	7.5	92.5
Maintenance and repair services	100.0	5.0	95.0	5.3	94.7
Painting and papering	100.0	5.4	94.6	4.0	96.0
Plumbing and water heating	100.0	8.8	91.2	4.1	95.9
Heat, air conditioning, electrical work	100.0	4.5	95.5	3.7	96.3
Roofing and gutters	100.0	3.3	96.7	7.8	92.2
Other repair and maintenance services	100.0	5.1	94.9	5.8	94.2
Repair, replacement of hard-surface flooring	100.0	3.9	96.1	5.2	94.8
Repair of built-in appliances	100.0	5.7	94.6	0.7	99.7
Maintenance and repair materials	100.0	3.3	96.7	8.9	91.1
Paints, wallpaper, and supplies	100.0	3.7	96.3	8.6	91.3
Tools, equipment for painting, wallpapering	100.0	3.7	96.6	8.7	91.3
Plumbing supplies and equipment	100.0	9.4	90.6	4.7	95.2
Electrical supplies, heating and cooling equipment	100.0	1.5	98.6	8.7	91.3
Hard-surface flooring, repair and replacement	100.0	4.0	96.0	8.1	92.0
Roofing and gutters	100.0	3.5	96.5	10.9	89.1
Plaster, paneling, siding, windows, doors, screens, awnings	100.0	3.2	96.8	9.9	90.1
Patio, walk, fence, driveway, masonry, brick, and stucco materials	100.0	6.5	92.3	5.9	92.9
Landscape maintenance	100.0	0.5	99.3	6.7	93.2
Miscellaneous supplies and equipment	100.0	1.6	98.4	9.7	90.3
Insulation, other maintenance, repair	100.0	1.2	98.8	12.5	87.5
Finish basement, remodel rooms, build patios, walks, etc.	100.0	2.4	97.6	4.6	95.3
Property management and security	100.0	9.9	90.1	4.7	95.3
Property management	100.0	11.2	88.8	5.3	94.7
Management and upkeep services for security	100.0	6.8	93.2	3.2	96.7
Parking	100.0	9.1	91.0	5.3	94.8

	total consumer units	race		Hispanic origin	
		black	white and other	Hispanic	non-Hispanic
Rented dwellings	**100.0%**	**16.9%**	**83.1%**	**14.1%**	**85.9%**
Rent	100.0	16.8	83.2	14.1	85.9
Rent as pay	100.0	31.6	68.4	16.3	83.7
Maintenance, insurance, and other expenses	100.0	7.1	92.9	8.5	91.5
Tenant's insurance	100.0	7.0	93.1	2.5	97.5
Maintenance and repair services	100.0	8.8	91.2	2.8	97.2
Repair and maintenance services	100.0	9.6	90.5	3.1	96.9
Repair and replacement of hard-surface flooring	100.0	1.1	98.5	–	99.8
Repair of built-in appliances	100.0	10.4	87.9	–	91.3
Maintenance and repair materials	100.0	4.8	95.2	23.9	76.1
Paint, wallpaper, and supplies	100.0	8.0	91.9	17.8	82.4
Painting and wallpapering tools	100.0	7.8	87.9	17.3	80.6
Plastering, paneling, roofing, gutters, etc.	100.0	9.6	89.7	6.0	93.2
Patio, walk, fence, driveway, masonry, brick, and stucco materials	100.0	–	–	–	–
Plumbing supplies and equipment	100.0	8.7	90.2	31.8	67.9
Electrical supplies, heating and cooling equipment	100.0	–	98.5	1.0	98.6
Miscellaneous supplies and equipment	100.0	0.8	99.4	32.2	67.7
Insulation, other maintenance and repair	100.0	3.2	96.5	10.9	89.4
Materials for additions, finishing basements, remodeling rooms	100.0	–	100.0	39.7	60.2
Construction materials for jobs not started	100.0	–	–	–	–
Hard-surface flooring	100.0	23.2	77.1	31.3	69.0
Landscape maintenance	100.0	–	99.6	–	100.0
Other lodging	**100.0**	**5.7**	**94.3**	**3.3**	**96.7**
Owned vacation homes	100.0	7.0	93.0	1.8	98.2
Mortgage interest and charges	100.0	9.1	90.9	1.2	98.8
Mortgage interest	100.0	9.5	90.5	1.2	98.8
Interest paid, home equity loan	100.0	–	100.0	1.9	98.1
Interest paid, home equity line of credit	100.0	–	99.8	–	99.6
Property taxes	100.0	5.9	94.1	2.1	97.9
Maintenance, insurance and other expenses	100.0	4.4	95.6	2.5	97.5
Homeowner's and related insurance	100.0	9.8	90.3	4.0	96.0
Homeowner's insurance	100.0	9.8	90.3	4.0	96.0
Ground rent	100.0	1.1	99.1	6.5	93.5
Maintenance and repair services	100.0	0.6	99.4	0.5	99.5
Maintenance and repair materials	100.0	5.5	95.2	–	98.9
Property management and security	100.0	5.5	94.5	3.1	97.0
Property management	100.0	3.9	96.1	2.6	97.4
Management and upkeep services for security	100.0	8.6	91.2	4.1	96.1
Parking	100.0	3.9	96.0	–	99.8
Housing while attending school	100.0	5.8	94.2	5.9	94.1
Lodging on trips	100.0	5.0	95.0	3.4	96.6
UTILITIES, FUELS, AND PUBLIC SERVICES	**100.0**	**12.5**	**87.5**	**7.6**	**92.4**
Natural gas	**100.0**	**13.5**	**86.5**	**6.8**	**93.2**
Natural gas (renter)	100.0	23.0	77.0	14.2	85.8
Natural gas (owner)	100.0	11.2	88.8	5.1	94.9
Natural gas (vacation)	100.0	4.5	95.3	1.2	98.6

	total consumer units	race		Hispanic origin	
		black	white and other	Hispanic	non-Hispanic
Electricity	100.0%	12.5%	87.5%	7.1%	92.9%
Electricity (renter)	100.0	23.2	76.8	12.3	87.7
Electricity (owner)	100.0	9.2	90.8	5.6	94.4
Electricity (vacation)	100.0	4.6	95.4	3.0	96.9
Fuel oil and other fuels	**100.0**	**5.4**	**94.6**	**2.7**	**97.3**
Fuel oil	100.0	6.1	93.9	1.0	99.0
Fuel oil (renter)	100.0	9.2	90.7	0.8	99.2
Fuel oil (owner)	100.0	5.5	94.5	1.1	98.9
Fuel oil (vacation)	100.0	18.1	82.5	–	100.0
Coal	100.0	–	100.0	–	99.2
Coal (renter)	100.0	–	100.0	–	97.9
Coal (owner)	100.0	–	99.9	–	99.6
Bottled/tank gas	100.0	4.3	95.7	4.6	95.4
Gas (renter)	100.0	4.7	95.3	3.9	95.9
Gas (owner)	100.0	4.4	95.6	4.9	95.1
Gas (vacation)	100.0	1.6	98.7	2.3	97.7
Wood and other fuels	100.0	5.1	94.9	6.7	93.3
Wood and other fuels (renter)	100.0	3.1	97.6	3.4	97.2
Wood and other fuels (owner)	100.0	5.2	94.7	7.5	92.5
Wood and other fuels (vacation)	100.0	33.9	70.3	–	100.0
Telephone services	**100.0**	**13.6**	**86.4**	**8.8**	**91.2**
Telephone services in home city, excl. mobile phones	100.0	14.2	85.8	9.0	91.0
Telephone services for mobile phones	100.0	9.6	90.4	7.2	92.8
Water and other public services	**100.0**	**10.7**	**89.3**	**7.6**	**92.4**
Water and sewerage maintenance	100.0	11.5	88.5	7.8	92.2
Water and sewerage maintenance (renter)	100.0	22.4	77.6	12.1	87.9
Water and sewerage maintenance (owner)	100.0	9.7	90.3	7.2	92.8
Water and sewerage maintenance (vacation)	100.0	8.1	92.2	2.4	97.5
Trash and garbage collection	100.0	8.7	91.3	7.0	93.0
Trash and garbage collection (renter)	100.0	21.1	79.0	12.4	87.6
Trash and garbage collection (owner)	100.0	7.3	92.7	6.6	93.4
Trash and garbage collection (vacation)	100.0	5.8	94.2	1.1	99.2
Septic tank cleaning	100.0	3.6	96.4	4.0	96.0
Septic tank cleaning (renter)	100.0	30.2	65.9	28.2	68.5
Septic tank cleaning (owner)	100.0	3.2	97.1	3.5	96.6

See appendix for information about mortgage principle reduction.
Note: Other races include Asians, Native Americans, and Pacific Islanders. Numbers may not add to total because of rounding. (–) means sample is too small to make a reliable estimate.
Source: Calculations by New Strategist based on the 2000 Consumer Expenditure Survey

Table 9.21 (Housing) Shelter and Utilities: Average spending by region, 2000

(average annual spending of consumer units (CU) on shelter and utilities, by region in which consumer unit lives, 2000)

	total consumer units	Northeast	Midwest	South	West
Number of consumer units					
(in thousands, add 000)	109,367	20,994	25,717	38,245	24,410
Average number of persons per CU	2.5	2.5	2.5	2.5	2.6
Average before-tax income of CU	$44,649.00	$47,439.00	$44,377.00	$41,984.00	$46,670.00
Average spending of CU, total	38,044.67	38,901.91	39,212.70	34,707.07	41,328.19
Housing, average spending	12,318.51	13,504.65	11,961.22	10,854.51	13,972.45
SHELTER	**$7,114.26**	**$8,221.86**	**$6,633.06**	**$5,838.96**	**$8,666.72**
Owned dwellings*	4,602.32	5,228.85	4,599.01	3,802.61	5,319.90
Mortgage interest and charges	2,638.81	2,574.43	2,471.25	2,238.16	3,498.42
Mortgage interest	2,460.48	2,362.62	2,279.14	2,107.78	3,288.27
Interest paid, home equity loan	98.22	116.28	98.50	78.86	112.72
Interest paid, home equity line of credit	79.76	95.52	93.10	51.41	96.58
Prepayment penalty charges	0.34	–	0.50	0.10	0.85
Property taxes	1,138.55	1,780.44	1,224.27	825.13	987.25
Maintenance, repairs, insurance, other expenses	824.96	873.98	903.49	739.33	834.23
Homeowner's and related insurance	234.84	215.91	237.15	256.27	215.13
Ground rent	38.67	18.69	25.22	37.51	71.85
Maintenance and repair services	438.92	522.61	515.09	355.23	417.83
Painting and papering	49.93	49.95	42.33	46.48	63.34
Plumbing and water heating	41.62	53.66	40.91	38.31	37.19
Heat, air conditioning, electrical work	79.19	81.77	113.17	64.94	63.52
Roofing and gutters	75.27	84.95	115.48	44.27	73.14
Other repair and maintenance services	157.99	217.08	179.42	110.00	159.79
Repair, replacement of hard-surface flooring	33.61	33.62	22.16	50.43	19.31
Repair of built-in appliances	1.31	1.59	1.62	0.81	1.55
Maintenance and repair materials	78.08	62.44	105.37	61.84	88.22
Paints, wallpaper, and supplies	16.03	20.59	18.16	10.06	19.20
Tools, equipment for painting, wallpapering	1.72	2.21	1.95	1.08	2.06
Plumbing supplies and equipment	6.13	4.83	8.09	5.41	6.30
Electrical supplies, heating and cooling equipment	4.35	3.24	6.89	2.72	5.19
Hard-surface flooring, repair and replacement	6.98	1.57	7.33	9.83	6.82
Roofing and gutters	6.41	1.07	8.82	8.09	5.82
Plaster, paneling, siding, windows, doors, screens, awnings	12.14	6.14	21.60	8.01	13.80
Patio, walk, fence, driveway, masonry, brick, and stucco materials	0.60	0.73	0.45	0.44	0.88
Landscape maintenance	2.92	3.03	4.24	1.97	2.92
Miscellaneous supplies and equipment	20.80	19.03	27.82	14.23	25.23
Insulation, other maintenance, repair	13.45	13.60	17.01	8.76	16.94
Finish basement, remodel rooms, build patios, walks, etc.	7.35	5.43	10.81	5.47	8.29
Property management and security	30.99	51.23	17.56	25.71	35.99
Property management	21.49	36.82	12.31	17.50	24.23
Management and upkeep services for security	9.50	14.41	5.25	8.21	11.76
Parking	3.45	3.10	3.11	2.76	5.21

	total consumer units	Northeast	Midwest	South	West
Rented dwellings	**$2,034.11**	**$2,434.17**	**$1,531.42**	**$1,643.12**	**$2,832.21**
Rent	1,977.33	2,380.81	1,476.86	1,601.44	2,746.49
Rent as pay	29.24	27.58	26.01	17.46	52.55
Maintenance, insurance, and other expenses	27.54	25.78	28.55	24.22	33.17
Tenant's insurance	8.86	8.32	11.74	7.52	8.40
Maintenance and repair services	11.13	12.59	13.41	6.90	14.08
Repair and maintenance services	9.98	10.94	12.71	5.89	12.70
Repair and replacement of hard-surface flooring	1.08	1.60	0.69	0.87	1.37
Repair of built-in appliances	0.07	0.05	0.02	0.14	0.01
Maintenance and repair materials	7.55	4.87	3.39	9.80	10.69
Paint, wallpaper, and supplies	1.54	2.39	1.17	1.39	1.42
Painting and wallpapering tools	0.17	0.26	0.13	0.15	0.15
Plastering, paneling, roofing, gutters, etc.	0.48	0.39	0.23	0.91	0.14
Patio, walk, fence, driveway, masonry, brick, and stucco materials	0.03	–	–	–	–
Plumbing supplies and equipment	0.39	0.19	0.26	0.57	0.40
Electrical supplies, heating and cooling equipment	0.25	0.12	0.60	0.11	0.20
Miscellaneous supplies and equipment	3.60	1.09	0.49	4.80	7.16
Insulation, other maintenance and repair	0.92	1.06	0.19	1.09	1.30
Materials for additions, finishing basements, remodeling rooms	2.67	0.04	0.27	3.71	5.83
Construction materials for jobs not started	0.01	–	0.03	–	0.03
Hard-surface flooring	0.49	0.23	0.04	1.13	0.18
Landscape maintenance	0.60	0.19	0.46	0.73	0.90
Other lodging	**477.84**	**558.84**	**502.64**	**393.23**	**514.61**
Owned vacation homes	147.91	157.85	156.65	133.00	153.53
Mortgage interest and charges	63.65	54.69	58.28	62.46	78.86
Mortgage interest	61.19	50.12	56.23	61.22	75.87
Interest paid, home equity loan	1.35	0.61	2.03	0.78	2.17
Interest paid, home equity line of credit	1.11	3.96	0.02	0.46	0.82
Property taxes	51.97	67.50	59.87	41.18	47.21
Maintenance, insurance and other expenses	32.29	35.66	38.50	29.35	27.46
Homeowner's and related insurance	10.74	7.06	10.59	11.95	12.17
Homeowner's insurance	10.74	7.06	10.59	11.95	12.17
Ground rent	2.97	4.48	4.27	2.19	1.53
Maintenance and repair services	13.56	19.63	15.47	12.09	8.63
Maintenance and repair materials	0.48	0.13	0.93	0.50	0.27
Property management and security	3.89	3.77	5.82	2.51	4.11
Property management	2.56	2.72	3.41	1.91	2.55
Management and upkeep services for security	1.33	1.05	2.41	0.61	1.56
Parking	0.65	0.59	1.42	0.11	0.74
Housing while attending school	78.31	72.22	90.43	58.48	101.83
Lodging on trips	251.62	328.77	255.56	201.75	259.25
UTILITIES, FUELS, AND PUBLIC SERVICES	**2,488.90**	**2,569.62**	**2,512.56**	**2,596.39**	**2,226.16**
Natural gas	**307.35**	**412.87**	**430.23**	**189.59**	**271.63**
Natural gas (renter)	60.47	85.15	70.62	35.04	68.39
Natural gas (owner)	244.63	323.54	356.32	153.81	201.38
Natural gas (vacation)	2.25	4.18	3.28	0.73	1.86

	total consumer units	Northeast	Midwest	South	West
Electricity	$911.44	$816.28	$834.42	$1,147.56	$704.47
Electricity (renter)	213.85	182.40	167.62	279.51	186.72
Electricity (owner)	690.09	624.28	658.33	861.19	512.08
Electricity (vacation)	7.50	9.61	8.47	6.86	5.67
Fuel oil and other fuels	96.94	270.75	73.10	57.22	34.81
Fuel oil	55.08	227.99	15.53	16.78	8.04
Fuel oil (renter)	6.54	26.44	2.31	1.51	1.74
Fuel oil (owner)	47.74	198.92	12.70	14.88	6.10
Fuel oil (vacation)	0.81	2.63	0.51	0.40	0.21
Coal	0.58	2.91	–	0.06	–
Coal (renter)	0.14	0.60	–	0.06	–
Coal (owner)	0.44	2.30	–	–	–
Bottled/tank gas	35.26	28.28	54.49	35.35	20.87
Gas (renter)	4.76	1.46	10.08	4.89	1.77
Gas (owner)	28.79	25.83	42.49	28.94	16.67
Gas (vacation)	1.71	0.99	1.92	1.51	2.43
Wood and other fuels	6.02	11.58	3.08	5.03	5.89
Wood and other fuels (renter)	1.09	1.88	0.45	1.41	0.61
Wood and other fuels (owner)	4.88	9.69	2.64	3.53	5.21
Wood and other fuels (vacation)	0.05	0.01	–	0.09	0.08
Telephone services	876.75	855.64	884.07	891.46	864.16
Telephone services in home city, excl. mobile phones	757.26	761.05	764.40	748.95	759.51
Telephone services for mobile phones	119.49	94.60	119.67	142.50	104.66
Water and other public services	296.42	214.07	290.75	310.56	351.08
Water and sewerage maintenance	212.72	162.91	207.25	225.72	240.96
Water and sewerage maintenance (renter)	29.99	10.92	25.30	43.44	30.25
Water and sewerage maintenance (owner)	181.10	150.35	180.61	180.77	208.59
Water and sewerage maintenance (vacation)	1.63	1.64	1.35	1.50	2.12
Trash and garbage collection	81.74	49.25	81.30	82.80	108.50
Trash and garbage collection (renter)	8.30	3.29	5.33	11.02	11.49
Trash and garbage collection (owner)	71.34	44.65	72.20	70.41	94.85
Trash and garbage collection (vacation)	2.10	1.31	3.77	1.37	2.16
Septic tank cleaning	1.96	1.92	2.20	2.04	1.62
Septic tank cleaning (renter)	0.04	0.14	0.03	–	0.02
Septic tank cleaning (owner)	1.92	1.78	2.17	2.04	1.59

See appendix for information about mortgage principle reduction.
Note: (–) means sample is too small to make a reliable estimate.
Source: Bureau of Labor Statistics, unpublished tables from the 2000 Consumer Expenditure Survey

Table. 9.22 (Housing) Shelter and Utilities: Indexed spending by region, 2000

(indexed average annual spending of consumer units (CU) on shelter and utilities, by region in which consumer unit lives, 2000; index definition: an index of 100 is the average for all consumer units; an index of 132 means that spending by consumer units in that group is 32 percent above the average for all consumer units; an index of 68 indicates spending that is 32 percent below the average for all consumer units)

	total consumer units	Northeast	Midwest	South	West
Average spending of CU, total	**$38,045**	**$38,902**	**$39,213**	**$34,707**	**$41,328**
Average spending of CU, index	**100**	**102**	**103**	**91**	**109**
Housing, spending index	**100**	**110**	**97**	**88**	**113**
SHELTER	**100**	**116**	**93**	**82**	**122**
Owned dwellings*	**100**	**114**	**100**	**83**	**116**
Mortgage interest and charges	100	98	94	85	133
Mortgage interest	100	96	93	86	134
Interest paid, home equity loan	100	118	100	80	115
Interest paid, home equity line of credit	100	120	117	64	121
Prepayment penalty charges	100	–	147	29	250
Property taxes	100	156	108	72	87
Maintenance, repairs, insurance, other expenses	100	106	110	90	101
Homeowner's and related insurance	100	92	101	109	92
Ground rent	100	48	65	97	186
Maintenance and repair services	100	119	117	81	95
Painting and papering	100	100	85	93	127
Plumbing and water heating	100	129	98	92	89
Heat, air conditioning, electrical work	100	103	143	82	80
Roofing and gutters	100	113	153	59	97
Other repair and maintenance services	100	137	114	70	101
Repair, replacement of					
hard-surface flooring	100	100	66	150	57
Repair of built-in appliances	100	121	124	62	118
Maintenance and repair materials	100	80	135	79	113
Paints, wallpaper, and supplies	100	128	113	63	120
Tools, equipment for painting, wallpapering	100	128	113	63	120
Plumbing supplies and equipment	100	79	132	88	103
Electrical supplies, heating and cooling equipment	100	74	158	63	119
Hard-surface flooring, repair and replacement	100	22	105	141	98
Roofing and gutters	100	17	138	126	91
Plaster, paneling, siding, windows,					
doors, screens, awnings	100	51	178	66	114
Patio, walk, fence, driveway, masonry,					
brick, and stucco materials	100	122	75	73	147
Landscape maintenance	100	104	145	67	100
Miscellaneous supplies and equipment	100	91	134	68	121
Insulation, other maintenance, repair	100	101	126	65	126
Finish basement, remodel rooms,					
build patios, walks, etc.	100	74	147	74	113
Property management and security	100	165	57	83	116
Property management	100	171	57	81	113
Management and upkeep services for security	100	152	55	86	124
Parking	100	90	90	80	151

	total consumer units	Northeast	Midwest	South	West
Rented dwellings	**100**	**120**	**75**	**81**	**139**
Rent	100	120	75	81	139
Rent as pay	100	94	89	60	180
Maintenance, insurance, and other expenses	100	94	104	88	120
Tenant's insurance	100	94	133	85	95
Maintenance and repair services	100	113	120	62	127
Repair and maintenance services	100	110	127	59	127
Repair and replacement of hard-surface flooring	100	148	64	81	127
Repair of built-in appliances	100	71	29	200	14
Maintenance and repair materials	100	65	45	130	142
Paint, wallpaper, and supplies	100	155	76	90	92
Painting and wallpapering tools	100	153	76	88	88
Plastering, paneling, roofing, gutters, etc.	100	81	48	190	29
Patio, walk, fence, driveway, masonry, brick, and stucco materials	100	–	–	–	–
Plumbing supplies and equipment	100	49	67	146	103
Electrical supplies, heating and cooling equipment	100	48	240	44	80
Miscellaneous supplies and equipment	100	30	14	133	199
Insulation, other maintenance and repair	100	115	21	118	141
Materials for additions, finishing basements, remodeling rooms	100	1	10	139	218
Construction materials for jobs not started	100	–	–	–	–
Hard-surface flooring	100	47	8	231	37
Landscape maintenance	100	32	77	122	150
Other lodging	**100**	**117**	**105**	**82**	**108**
Owned vacation homes	100	107	106	90	104
Mortgage interest and charges	100	86	92	98	124
Mortgage interest	100	82	92	100	124
Interest paid, home equity loan	100	45	150	58	161
Interest paid, home equity line of credit	100	357	2	41	74
Property taxes	100	130	115	79	91
Maintenance, insurance and other expenses	100	110	119	91	85
Homeowner's and related insurance	100	66	99	111	113
Homeowner's insurance	100	66	99	111	113
Ground rent	100	151	144	74	52
Maintenance and repair services	100	145	114	89	64
Maintenance and repair materials	100	27	194	104	56
Property management and security	100	97	150	65	106
Property management	100	106	133	75	100
Management and upkeep services for security	100	79	181	46	117
Parking	100	91	218	17	114
Housing while attending school	100	92	115	75	130
Lodging on trips	100	131	102	80	103
UTILITIES, FUELS, AND PUBLIC SERVICES	**100**	**103**	**101**	**104**	**89**
Natural gas	**100**	**134**	**140**	**62**	**88**
Natural gas (renter)	100	141	117	58	113
Natural gas (owner)	100	132	146	63	82
Natural gas (vacation)	100	186	146	32	83

	total consumer units	Northeast	Midwest	South	West
Electricity	**100**	**90**	**92**	**126**	**77**
Electricity (renter)	100	85	78	131	87
Electricity (owner)	100	90	95	125	74
Electricity (vacation)	100	128	113	91	76
Fuel oil and other fuels	**100**	**279**	**75**	**59**	**36**
Fuel oil	100	414	28	30	15
Fuel oil (renter)	100	404	35	23	27
Fuel oil (owner)	100	417	27	31	13
Fuel oil (vacation)	100	325	63	49	26
Coal	100	502	–	10	–
Coal (renter)	100	429	–	43	–
Coal (owner)	100	523	–	–	–
Bottled/tank gas	100	80	155	100	59
Gas (renter)	100	31	212	103	37
Gas (owner)	100	90	148	101	58
Gas (vacation)	100	58	112	88	142
Wood and other fuels	100	192	51	84	98
Wood and other fuels (renter)	100	172	41	129	56
Wood and other fuels (owner)	100	199	54	72	107
Wood and other fuels (vacation)	100	20	–	180	160
Telephone services	**100**	**98**	**101**	**102**	**99**
Telephone services in home city, excl. mobile phones	100	101	101	99	100
Telephone services for mobile phones	100	79	100	119	88
Water and other public services	**100**	**72**	**98**	**105**	**118**
Water and sewerage maintenance	100	77	97	106	113
Water and sewerage maintenance (renter)	100	36	84	145	101
Water and sewerage maintenance (owner)	100	83	100	100	115
Water and sewerage maintenance (vacation)	100	101	83	92	130
Trash and garbage collection	100	60	99	101	133
Trash and garbage collection (renter)	100	40	64	133	138
Trash and garbage collection (owner)	100	63	101	99	133
Trash and garbage collection (vacation)	100	62	180	65	103
Septic tank cleaning	100	98	112	104	83
Septic tank cleaning (renter)	100	350	75	–	50
Septic tank cleaning (owner)	100	93	113	106	83

See appendix for information about mortgage principle reduction.
Note: (–) means sample is too small to make a reliable estimate.
Source: Calculations by New Strategist based on the 2000 Consumer Expenditure Survey

Table 9.23 (Housing) Shelter and Utilities: Indexed per capita spending by region, 2000

(indexed average annual per capita spending of consumer units (CU) on shelter and utilities, by region in which consumer unit lives, 2000; index definition: an index of 100 is the average for all consumer units; an index of 132 means that spending by consumer units in that group is 32 percent above the average for all consumer units; an index of 68 indicates spending that is 32 percent below the average for all consumer units)

	total consumer units	Northeast	Midwest	South	West
Per capita spending of CU, total	$15,218	$15,561	$15,685	$13,883	$15,895
Per capita spending of CU, index	100	102	103	91	104
Housing, per capita spending index	100	110	97	88	109
SHELTER	100	116	93	82	117
Owned dwellings*	100	114	100	83	111
Mortgage interest and charges	100	98	94	85	127
Mortgage interest	100	96	93	86	129
Interest paid, home equity loan	100	118	100	80	110
Interest paid, home equity line of credit	100	120	117	64	116
Prepayment penalty charges	100	–	147	29	240
Property taxes	100	156	108	72	83
Maintenance, repairs, insurance, other expenses	100	106	110	90	97
Homeowner's and related insurance	100	92	101	109	88
Ground rent	100	48	65	97	179
Maintenance and repair services	100	119	117	81	92
Painting and papering	100	100	85	93	122
Plumbing and water heating	100	129	98	92	86
Heat, air conditioning, electrical work	100	103	143	82	77
Roofing and gutters	100	113	153	59	93
Other repair and maintenance services	100	137	114	70	97
Repair, replacement of hard-surface flooring	100	100	66	150	55
Repair of built-in appliances	100	121	124	62	114
Maintenance and repair materials	100	80	135	79	109
Paints, wallpaper, and supplies	100	128	113	63	115
Tools, equipment for painting, wallpapering	100	128	113	63	115
Plumbing supplies and equipment	100	79	132	88	99
Electrical supplies, heating and cooling equipment	100	74	158	63	115
Hard-surface flooring, repair and replacement	100	22	105	141	94
Roofing and gutters	100	17	138	126	87
Plaster, paneling, siding, windows, doors, screens, awnings	100	51	178	66	109
Patio, walk, fence, driveway, masonry, brick, and stucco materials	100	122	75	73	141
Landscape maintenance	100	104	145	67	96
Miscellaneous supplies and equipment	100	91	134	68	117
Insulation, other maintenance, repair	100	101	126	65	121
Finish basement, remodel rooms, build patios, walks, etc.	100	74	147	74	108
Property management and security	100	165	57	83	112
Property management	100	171	57	81	108
Management and upkeep services for security	100	152	55	86	119
Parking	100	90	90	80	145

	total consumer units	Northeast	Midwest	South	West
Rented dwellings	**100**	**120**	**75**	**81**	**134**
Rent	100	120	75	81	134
Rent as pay	100	94	89	60	173
Maintenance, insurance, and other expenses	100	94	104	88	116
Tenant's insurance	100	94	133	85	91
Maintenance and repair services	100	113	120	62	122
Repair and maintenance services	100	110	127	59	122
Repair and replacement of hard-surface flooring	100	148	64	81	122
Repair of built-in appliances	100	71	29	200	14
Maintenance and repair materials	100	65	45	130	136
Paint, wallpaper, and supplies	100	155	76	90	89
Painting and wallpapering tools	100	153	76	88	85
Plastering, paneling, roofing, gutters, etc.	100	81	48	190	28
Patio, walk, fence, driveway, masonry, brick, and stucco materials	100	–	–	–	–
Plumbing supplies and equipment	100	49	67	146	99
Electrical supplies, heating and cooling equipment	100	48	240	44	77
Miscellaneous supplies and equipment	100	30	14	133	191
Insulation, other maintenance and repair	100	115	21	118	136
Materials for additions, finishing basements, remodeling rooms	100	1	10	139	210
Construction materials for jobs not started	100	–	–	–	–
Hard-surface flooring	100	47	8	231	35
Landscape maintenance	100	32	77	122	144
Other lodging	**100**	**117**	**105**	**82**	**104**
Owned vacation homes	100	107	106	90	100
Mortgage interest and charges	100	86	92	98	119
Mortgage interest	100	82	92	100	119
Interest paid, home equity loan	100	45	150	58	155
Interest paid, home equity line of credit	100	357	2	41	71
Property taxes	100	130	115	79	87
Maintenance, insurance and other expenses	100	110	119	91	82
Homeowner's and related insurance	100	66	99	111	109
Homeowner's insurance	100	66	99	111	109
Ground rent	100	151	144	74	50
Maintenance and repair services	100	145	114	89	61
Maintenance and repair materials	100	27	194	104	54
Property management and security	100	97	150	65	102
Property management	100	106	133	75	96
Management and upkeep services for security	100	79	181	46	113
Parking	100	91	218	17	109
Housing while attending school	100	92	115	75	125
Lodging on trips	100	131	102	80	99
UTILITIES, FUELS, AND PUBLIC SERVICES	**100**	**103**	**101**	**104**	**86**
Natural gas	**100**	**134**	**140**	**62**	**85**
Natural gas (renter)	100	141	117	58	109
Natural gas (owner)	100	132	146	63	79
Natural gas (vacation)	100	186	146	32	79

	total consumer units	Northeast	Midwest	South	West
Electricity	**100**	**90**	**92**	**126**	**74**
Electricity (renter)	100	85	78	131	84
Electricity (owner)	100	90	95	125	71
Electricity (vacation)	100	128	113	91	73
Fuel oil and other fuels	**100**	**279**	**75**	**59**	**35**
Fuel oil	100	414	28	30	14
Fuel oil (renter)	100	404	35	23	26
Fuel oil (owner)	100	417	27	31	12
Fuel oil (vacation)	100	325	63	49	25
Coal	100	502	–	10	–
Coal (renter)	100	429	–	43	–
Coal (owner)	100	523	–	–	–
Bottled/tank gas	100	80	155	100	57
Gas (renter)	100	31	212	103	36
Gas (owner)	100	90	148	101	56
Gas (vacation)	100	58	112	88	137
Wood and other fuels	100	192	51	84	94
Wood and other fuels (renter)	100	172	41	129	54
Wood and other fuels (owner)	100	199	54	72	103
Wood and other fuels (vacation)	100	20	–	180	154
Telephone services	**100**	**98**	**101**	**102**	**95**
Telephone services in home city, excl. mobile phones	100	101	101	99	96
Telephone services for mobile phones	100	79	100	119	84
Water and other public services	**100**	**72**	**98**	**105**	**114**
Water and sewerage maintenance	100	77	97	106	109
Water and sewerage maintenance (renter)	100	36	84	145	97
Water and sewerage maintenance (owner)	100	83	100	100	111
Water and sewerage maintenance (vacation)	100	101	83	92	125
Trash and garbage collection	100	60	99	101	128
Trash and garbage collection (renter)	100	40	64	133	133
Trash and garbage collection (owner)	100	63	101	99	128
Trash and garbage collection (vacation)	100	62	180	65	99
Septic tank cleaning	100	98	112	104	79
Septic tank cleaning (renter)	100	350	75	–	48
Septic tank cleaning (owner)	100	93	113	106	80

See appendix for information about mortgage principle reduction.
Note: Per capita indexes account for household size and show how much each person in a particular household demographic segment spends relative to a person in the average household. (–) means sample is too small to make a reliable estimate.
Source: Calculations by New Strategist based on the 2000 Consumer Expenditure Survey

Table 9.24 (Housing) Shelter and Utilities: Total spending by region, 2000

(total annual spending on shelter and utilities, by region in which consumer units live, 2000; numbers in thousands)

	total consumer units	Northeast	Midwest	South	West
Number of consumer units	109,367	20,994	25,717	38,245	24,410
Total spending of all consumer units	$4,160,831,424	$816,706,699	$1,008,433,006	$1,327,371,892	$1,008,821,118
Housing, total spending	1,347,238,483	283,516,622	307,606,695	415,130,735	341,067,505
SHELTER	$778,065,273	$172,609,729	$170,582,404	$223,311,025	$211,554,635
Owned dwellings*	503,341,931	109,774,477	118,272,740	145,430,819	129,858,759
Mortgage interest and charges	288,598,733	54,047,583	63,553,136	85,598,429	85,396,432
Mortgage interest	269,095,316	49,600,844	58,612,643	80,612,046	80,266,671
Interest paid, home equity loan	10,742,027	2,441,182	2,533,125	3,016,001	2,751,495
Interest paid, home equity line of credit	8,723,112	2,005,347	2,394,253	1,966,175	2,357,518
Prepayment penalty charges	37,185	–	12,859	3,825	20,749
Property taxes	124,519,798	37,378,557	31,484,552	31,557,097	24,098,773
Maintenance, repairs, insurance, other expenses	90,223,400	18,348,336	23,235,052	28,275,676	20,363,554
Homeowner's and related insurance	25,683,746	4,532,815	6,098,787	9,801,046	5,251,323
Ground rent	4,229,222	392,378	648,583	1,434,570	1,753,859
Maintenance and repair services	48,003,364	10,971,674	13,246,570	13,585,771	10,199,230
Painting and papering	5,460,694	1,048,650	1,088,601	1,777,628	1,546,129
Plumbing and water heating	4,551,855	1,126,538	1,052,082	1,465,166	907,808
Heat, air conditioning, electrical work	8,660,773	1,716,679	2,910,393	2,483,630	1,550,523
Roofing and gutters	8,232,054	1,783,440	2,969,799	1,693,106	1,785,347
Other repair and maintenance services	17,278,892	4,557,378	4,614,144	4,206,950	3,900,474
Repair, replacement of hard-surface flooring	3,675,825	705,818	569,889	1,928,695	471,357
Repair of built-in appliances	143,271	33,380	41,662	30,978	37,836
Maintenance and repair materials	8,539,375	1,310,865	2,709,800	2,365,071	2,153,450
Paints, wallpaper, and supplies	1,753,153	432,266	467,021	384,745	468,672
Tools, equipment for painting, wallpapering	188,111	46,397	50,148	41,305	50,285
Plumbing supplies and equipment	670,420	101,401	208,051	206,905	153,783
Electrical supplies, heating and cooling equipment	475,746	68,021	177,190	104,026	126,688
Hard-surface flooring, repair and replacement	763,382	32,961	188,506	375,948	166,476
Roofing and gutters	701,042	22,464	226,824	309,402	142,066
Plaster, paneling, siding, windows, doors, screens, awnings	1,327,715	128,903	555,487	306,342	336,858
Patio, walk, fence, driveway, masonry, brick, and stucco materials	65,620	15,326	11,573	16,828	21,481
Landscape maintenance	319,352	63,612	109,040	75,343	71,277
Miscellaneous supplies and equipment	2,274,834	399,516	715,447	544,226	615,864
Insulation, other maintenance, repair	1,470,986	285,518	437,446	335,026	413,505
Finish basement, remodel rooms, build patios, walks, etc.	803,847	113,997	278,001	209,200	202,359
Property management and security	3,389,283	1,075,523	451,591	983,279	878,516
Property management	2,350,297	772,999	316,576	669,288	591,454
Management and upkeep services for security	1,038,987	302,524	135,014	313,991	287,062
Parking	377,316	65,081	79,980	105,556	127,176

	total consumer units	Northeast	Midwest	South	West
Rented dwellings	**$222,464,508**	**$51,102,965**	**$39,383,528**	**$62,841,124**	**$69,134,246**
Rent	216,254,650	49,982,725	37,980,409	61,247,073	67,041,821
Rent as pay	3,197,891	579,015	668,899	667,758	1,282,746
Maintenance, insurance, and other expenses	3,011,967	541,225	734,220	926,294	809,680
Tenant's insurance	968,992	174,670	301,918	287,602	205,044
Maintenance and repair services	1,217,255	264,314	344,865	263,891	343,693
Repair and maintenance services	1,091,483	229,674	326,863	225,263	310,007
Repair and replacement of hard-surface flooring	118,116	33,590	17,745	33,273	33,442
Repair of built-in appliances	7,656	1,050	514	5,354	244
Maintenance and repair materials	825,721	102,241	87,181	374,801	260,943
Paint, wallpaper, and supplies	168,425	50,176	30,089	53,161	34,662
Painting and wallpapering tools	18,592	5,458	3,343	5,737	3,662
Plastering, paneling, roofing, gutters, etc.	52,496	8,188	5,915	34,803	3,417
Patio, walk, fence, driveway, masonry, brick, and stucco materials	3,281	–	–	–	–
Plumbing supplies and equipment	42,653	3,989	6,686	21,800	9,764
Electrical supplies, heating and cooling equipment	27,342	2,519	15,430	4,207	4,882
Miscellaneous supplies and equipment	393,721	22,883	12,601	183,576	174,776
Insulation, other maintenance and repair	100,618	22,254	4,886	41,687	31,733
Materials for additions, finishing basements, remodeling rooms	292,010	840	6,944	141,889	142,310
Construction materials for jobs not started	1,094	–	–	–	–
Hard-surface flooring	53,590	4,829	1,029	43,217	4,394
Landscape maintenance	65,620	3,989	11,830	27,919	21,969
Other lodging	**52,259,927**	**11,732,287**	**12,926,393**	**15,039,081**	**12,561,630**
Owned vacation homes	16,176,473	3,313,903	4,028,568	5,086,585	3,747,667
Mortgage interest and charges	6,961,210	1,148,162	1,498,787	2,388,783	1,924,973
Mortgage interest	6,692,167	1,052,219	1,446,067	2,341,359	1,851,987
Interest paid, home equity loan	147,645	12,806	52,206	29,831	52,970
Interest paid, home equity line of credit	121,397	83,136	514	17,593	20,016
Property taxes	5,683,803	1,417,095	1,539,677	1,574,929	1,152,396
Maintenance, insurance and other expenses	3,531,460	748,646	990,105	1,122,491	670,299
Homeowner's and related insurance	1,174,602	148,218	272,343	457,028	297,070
Homeowner's insurance	1,174,602	148,218	272,343	457,028	297,070
Ground rent	324,820	94,053	109,812	83,757	37,347
Maintenance and repair services	1,483,017	412,112	397,842	462,382	210,658
Maintenance and repair materials	52,496	2,729	23,917	19,123	6,591
Property management and security	425,438	79,147	149,673	95,995	100,325
Property management	279,980	57,104	87,695	73,048	62,246
Management and upkeep services for security	145,458	22,044	61,978	23,329	38,080
Parking	71,089	12,386	36,518	4,207	18,063
Housing while attending school	8,564,530	1,516,187	2,325,588	2,236,568	2,485,670
Lodging on trips	27,518,925	6,902,197	6,572,237	7,715,929	6,328,293
UTILITIES, FUELS, AND PUBLIC SERVICES	**272,203,526**	**53,946,602**	**64,615,506**	**99,298,936**	**54,340,566**
Natural gas	**33,613,947**	**8,667,793**	**11,064,225**	**7,250,870**	**6,630,488**
Natural gas (renter)	6,613,422	1,787,639	1,816,135	1,340,105	1,669,400
Natural gas (owner)	26,754,449	6,792,399	9,163,481	5,882,463	4,915,686
Natural gas (vacation)	246,076	87,755	84,352	27,919	45,403

	total consumer units	Northeast	Midwest	South	West
Electricity	**$99,681,458**	**$17,136,982**	**$21,458,779**	**$43,888,432**	**$17,196,113**
Electricity (renter)	23,388,133	3,829,306	4,310,684	10,689,860	4,557,835
Electricity (owner)	75,473,073	13,106,134	16,930,273	32,936,212	12,499,873
Electricity (vacation)	820,253	201,752	217,823	262,361	138,405
Fuel oil and other fuels	**10,602,037**	**5,684,126**	**1,879,913**	**2,188,379**	**849,712**
Fuel oil	6,023,934	4,786,422	399,385	641,751	196,256
Fuel oil (renter)	715,260	555,081	59,406	57,750	42,473
Fuel oil (owner)	5,221,181	4,176,126	326,606	569,086	148,901
Fuel oil (vacation)	88,587	55,214	13,116	15,298	5,126
Coal	63,433	61,093	–	2,295	–
Coal (renter)	15,311	12,596	–	2,295	–
Coal (owner)	48,121	48,286	–	–	–
Bottled/tank gas	3,856,280	593,710	1,401,319	1,351,961	509,437
Gas (renter)	520,587	30,651	259,227	187,018	43,206
Gas (owner)	3,148,676	542,275	1,092,715	1,106,810	406,915
Gas (vacation)	187,018	20,784	49,377	57,750	59,316
Wood and other fuels	658,389	243,111	79,208	192,372	143,775
Wood and other fuels (renter)	119,210	39,469	11,573	53,925	14,890
Wood and other fuels (owner)	533,711	203,432	67,893	135,005	127,176
Wood and other fuels (vacation)	5,468	210	–	3,442	1,953
Telephone services	**95,887,517**	**17,963,306**	**22,735,628**	**34,093,888**	**21,094,146**
Telephone services in home city, excl. mobile phones	82,819,254	15,977,484	19,658,075	28,643,593	18,539,639
Telephone services for mobile phones	13,068,263	1,986,032	3,077,553	5,449,913	2,554,751
Water and other public services	**32,418,566**	**4,494,186**	**7,477,218**	**11,877,367**	**8,569,863**
Water and sewerage maintenance	23,264,548	3,420,133	5,329,848	8,632,661	5,881,834
Water and sewerage maintenance (renter)	3,279,916	229,254	650,640	1,661,363	738,403
Water and sewerage maintenance (owner)	19,806,364	3,156,448	4,644,747	6,913,549	5,091,682
Water and sewerage maintenance (vacation)	178,268	34,430	34,718	57,368	51,749
Trash and garbage collection	8,939,659	1,033,955	2,090,792	3,166,686	2,648,485
Trash and garbage collection (renter)	907,746	69,070	137,072	421,460	280,471
Trash and garbage collection (owner)	7,802,242	937,382	1,856,767	2,692,830	2,315,289
Trash and garbage collection (vacation)	229,671	27,502	96,953	52,396	52,726
Septic tank cleaning	214,359	40,308	56,577	78,020	39,544
Septic tank cleaning (renter)	4,375	2,939	772	–	488
Septic tank cleaning (owner)	209,985	37,369	55,806	78,020	38,812

See appendix for information about mortgage principle reduction.
Note: Numbers may not add to total because of rounding. (–) means sample is too small to make a reliable estimate.
Source: Calculations by New Strategist based on the 2000 Consumer Expenditure Survey

Table 9.25 (Housing) Shelter and Utilities: Market shares by region, 2000

(percentage of total annual spending on shelter and utilities accounted for by consumer units by region, 2000)

	total consumer units	Northeast	Midwest	South	West
Share of total consumer units	**100.0%**	**19.2%**	**23.5%**	**35.0%**	**22.3%**
Share of total before-tax income	**100.0**	**20.4**	**23.4**	**32.9**	**23.3**
Share of total spending	**100.0**	**19.6**	**24.2**	**31.9**	**24.2**
Share of housing spending	**100.0**	**21.0**	**22.8**	**30.8**	**25.3**
SHELTER	**100.0%**	**22.2%**	**21.9%**	**28.7%**	**27.2%**
Owned dwellings*	**100.0**	**21.8**	**23.5**	**28.9**	**25.8**
Mortgage interest and charges	100.0	18.7	22.0	29.7	29.6
Mortgage interest	100.0	18.4	21.8	30.0	29.8
Interest paid, home equity loan	100.0	22.7	23.6	28.1	25.6
Interest paid, home equity line of credit	100.0	23.0	27.4	22.5	27.0
Prepayment penalty charges	100.0	–	34.6	10.3	55.8
Property taxes	100.0	30.0	25.3	25.3	19.4
Maintenance, repairs, insurance, other expenses	100.0	20.3	25.8	31.3	22.6
Homeowner's and related insurance	100.0	17.6	23.7	38.2	20.4
Ground rent	100.0	9.3	15.3	33.9	41.5
Maintenance and repair services	100.0	22.9	27.6	28.3	21.2
Painting and papering	100.0	19.2	19.9	32.6	28.3
Plumbing and water heating	100.0	24.7	23.1	32.2	19.9
Heat, air conditioning, electrical work	100.0	19.8	33.6	28.7	17.9
Roofing and gutters	100.0	21.7	36.1	20.6	21.7
Other repair and maintenance services	100.0	26.4	26.7	24.3	22.6
Repair, replacement of hard-surface flooring	100.0	19.2	15.5	52.5	12.8
Repair of built-in appliances	100.0	23.3	29.1	21.6	26.4
Maintenance and repair materials	100.0	15.4	31.7	27.7	25.2
Paints, wallpaper, and supplies	100.0	24.7	26.6	21.9	26.7
Tools, equipment for painting, wallpapering	100.0	24.7	26.7	22.0	26.7
Plumbing supplies and equipment	100.0	15.1	31.0	30.9	22.9
Electrical supplies, heating and cooling equipment	100.0	14.3	37.2	21.9	26.6
Hard-surface flooring, repair and replacement	100.0	4.3	24.7	49.2	21.8
Roofing and gutters	100.0	3.2	32.4	44.1	20.3
Plaster, paneling, siding, windows, doors, screens, awnings	100.0	9.7	41.8	23.1	25.4
Patio, walk, fence, driveway, masonry, brick, and stucco materials	100.0	23.4	17.6	25.6	32.7
Landscape maintenance	100.0	19.9	34.1	23.6	22.3
Miscellaneous supplies and equipment	100.0	17.6	31.5	23.9	27.1
Insulation, other maintenance, repair	100.0	19.4	29.7	22.8	28.1
Finish basement, remodel rooms, build patios, walks, etc.	100.0	14.2	34.6	26.0	25.2
Property management and security	100.0	31.7	13.3	29.0	25.9
Property management	100.0	32.9	13.5	28.5	25.2
Management and upkeep services for security	100.0	29.1	13.0	30.2	27.6
Parking	100.0	17.2	21.2	28.0	33.7

	total consumer units	Northeast	Midwest	South	West
Rented dwellings	**100.0%**	**23.0%**	**17.7%**	**28.2%**	**31.1%**
Rent	100.0	23.1	17.6	28.3	31.0
Rent as pay	100.0	18.1	20.9	20.9	40.1
Maintenance, insurance, and other expenses	100.0	18.0	24.4	30.8	26.9
Tenant's insurance	100.0	18.0	31.2	29.7	21.2
Maintenance and repair services	100.0	21.7	28.3	21.7	28.2
Repair and maintenance services	100.0	21.0	29.9	20.6	28.4
Repair and replacement of hard-surface flooring	100.0	28.4	15.0	28.2	28.3
Repair of built-in appliances	100.0	13.7	6.7	69.9	3.2
Maintenance and repair materials	100.0	12.4	10.6	45.4	31.6
Paint, wallpaper, and supplies	100.0	29.8	17.9	31.6	20.6
Painting and wallpapering tools	100.0	29.4	18.0	30.9	19.7
Plastering, paneling, roofing, gutters, etc.	100.0	15.6	11.3	66.3	6.5
Patio, walk, fence, driveway, masonry, brick, and stucco materials	100.0	–	–	–	–
Plumbing supplies and equipment	100.0	9.4	15.7	51.1	22.9
Electrical supplies, heating and cooling equipment	100.0	9.2	56.4	15.4	17.9
Miscellaneous supplies and equipment	100.0	5.8	3.2	46.6	44.4
Insulation, other maintenance and repair	100.0	22.1	4.9	41.4	31.5
Materials for additions, finishing basements, remodeling rooms	100.0	0.3	2.4	48.6	48.7
Construction materials for jobs not started	100.0	–	–	–	–
Hard-surface flooring	100.0	9.0	1.9	80.6	8.2
Landscape maintenance	100.0	6.1	18.0	42.5	33.5
Other lodging	**100.0**	**22.4**	**24.7**	**28.8**	**24.0**
Owned vacation homes	100.0	20.5	24.9	31.4	23.2
Mortgage interest and charges	100.0	16.5	21.5	34.3	27.7
Mortgage interest	100.0	15.7	21.6	35.0	27.7
Interest paid, home equity loan	100.0	8.7	35.4	20.2	35.9
Interest paid, home equity line of credit	100.0	68.5	0.4	14.5	16.5
Property taxes	100.0	24.9	27.1	27.7	20.3
Maintenance, insurance and other expenses	100.0	21.2	28.0	31.8	19.0
Homeowner's and related insurance	100.0	12.6	23.2	38.9	25.3
Homeowner's insurance	100.0	12.6	23.2	38.9	25.3
Ground rent	100.0	29.0	33.8	25.8	11.5
Maintenance and repair services	100.0	27.8	26.8	31.2	14.2
Maintenance and repair materials	100.0	5.2	45.6	36.4	12.6
Property management and security	100.0	18.6	35.2	22.6	23.6
Property management	100.0	20.4	31.3	26.1	22.2
Management and upkeep services for security	100.0	15.2	42.6	16.0	26.2
Parking	100.0	17.4	51.4	5.9	25.4
Housing while attending school	100.0	17.7	27.2	26.1	29.0
Lodging on trips	100.0	25.1	23.9	28.0	23.0
UTILITIES, FUELS, AND PUBLIC SERVICES	**100.0**	**19.8**	**23.7**	**36.5**	**20.0**
Natural gas	**100.0**	**25.8**	**32.9**	**21.6**	**19.7**
Natural gas (renter)	100.0	27.0	27.5	20.3	25.2
Natural gas (owner)	100.0	25.4	34.3	22.0	18.4
Natural gas (vacation)	100.0	35.7	34.3	11.3	18.5

	total consumer units	Northeast	Midwest	South	West
Electricity	100.0%	17.2%	21.5%	44.0%	17.3%
Electricity (renter)	100.0	16.4	18.4	45.7	19.5
Electricity (owner)	100.0	17.4	22.4	43.6	16.6
Electricity (vacation)	100.0	24.6	26.6	32.0	16.9
Fuel oil and other fuels	100.0	53.6	17.7	20.6	8.0
Fuel oil	100.0	79.5	6.6	10.7	3.3
Fuel oil (renter)	100.0	77.6	8.3	8.1	5.9
Fuel oil (owner)	100.0	80.0	6.3	10.9	2.9
Fuel oil (vacation)	100.0	62.3	14.8	17.3	5.8
Coal	100.0	96.3	–	3.6	–
Coal (renter)	100.0	82.3	–	15.0	–
Coal (owner)	100.0	100.3	–	–	–
Bottled/tank gas	100.0	15.4	36.3	35.1	13.2
Gas (renter)	100.0	5.9	49.8	35.9	8.3
Gas (owner)	100.0	17.2	34.7	35.2	12.9
Gas (vacation)	100.0	11.1	26.4	30.9	31.7
Wood and other fuels	100.0	36.9	12.0	29.2	21.8
Wood and other fuels (renter)	100.0	33.1	9.7	45.2	12.5
Wood and other fuels (owner)	100.0	38.1	12.7	25.3	23.8
Wood and other fuels (vacation)	100.0	3.8	–	62.9	35.7
Telephone services	100.0	18.7	23.7	35.6	22.0
Telephone services in home city, excl. mobile phones	100.0	19.3	23.7	34.6	22.4
Telephone services for mobile phones	100.0	15.2	23.5	41.7	19.5
Water and other public services	100.0	13.9	23.1	36.6	26.4
Water and sewerage maintenance	100.0	14.7	22.9	37.1	25.3
Water and sewerage maintenance (renter)	100.0	7.0	19.8	50.7	22.5
Water and sewerage maintenance (owner)	100.0	15.9	23.5	34.9	25.7
Water and sewerage maintenance (vacation)	100.0	19.3	19.5	32.2	29.0
Trash and garbage collection	100.0	11.6	23.4	35.4	29.6
Trash and garbage collection (renter)	100.0	7.6	15.1	46.4	30.9
Trash and garbage collection (owner)	100.0	12.0	23.8	34.5	29.7
Trash and garbage collection (vacation)	100.0	12.0	42.2	22.8	23.0
Septic tank cleaning	100.0	18.8	26.4	36.4	18.4
Septic tank cleaning (renter)	100.0	67.2	17.6	–	11.2
Septic tank cleaning (owner)	100.0	17.8	26.6	37.2	18.5

See appendix for information about mortgage principle reduction.
Note: Numbers may not add to total because of rounding. (–) means sample is too small to make a reliable estimate.
Source: Calculations by New Strategist based on the 2000 Consumer Expenditure Survey

Spending on Personal Care, Reading, Education, and Tobacco, 2000

The average American household spent 18 percent more on personal care products and services in 2000 than in 1990, after adjusting for inflation. Spending on tobacco fell 12 percent during those years, and spending on reading material declined 28 percent. But education spending rose 18 percent as college costs soared.

Spending on personal care products and services is highest among householders aged 45 to 54, the most affluent age group. The biggest spenders on newspaper subscriptions are householders aged 65 and older, spending 62 to 63 percent more than the average household on this item. The biggest spenders on books are 45-to-54-year-olds. Householders aged 35 to 44 spend the most on tobacco, while those under age 25 spend the most on education because many are in college.

Households with incomes of $70,000 or more spend 67 percent more than average on personal care products and services. This income group spends 89 percent more than the average household on reading material and more than twice the average on education. Households with incomes below $40,000 account for the 54 percent majority of spending on tobacco products and smoking supplies.

Not surprisingly, spending on education is highest among married couples with children aged 18 or older at home because many have children in college. This household type also spends the most on personal care products and services and on tobacco, in part because their households are relatively large. Married couples without children at home spend the most on reading material, particularly on newspaper and magazine subscriptions.

Black and Hispanic householders spend an average amount on personal care products and services, but on many individual personal care items their spending is well above average. Blacks spend more than five times the average amount on wigs and hairpieces, for example. Hispanics spend 50 percent more than average on hair care products. Black and Hispanic householders spend less than average on reading material, education, and tobacco.

Households in the Northeast spend the most on reading material, particularly nonsubscription newspapers. Households in the Northeast also spend the most on education, including 42 percent more than average on college tuition. Households in the Midwest spend the most on tobacco, while those in the South spend 21 percent more than average on wigs and hairpieces.

Table 10.1 Personal Care, Reading, Education, Tobacco: Average spending by age, 2000

(average annual spending of consumer units (CU) on personal care, reading, education, and tobacco products, by age of consumer unit reference person, 2000)

	total consumer units	under 25	25 to 34	35 to 44	45 to 54	55 to 64	65 to 74	75+
Number of consumer units (in thousands, add 000)	109,367	8,306	18,887	23,983	21,874	14,161	11,538	10,617
Average number of persons per CU	2.5	1.9	2.9	3.3	2.7	2.1	1.9	1.5
Average before-tax income of CU	$44,649.00	$19,744.00	$45,498.00	$56,500.00	$58,889.00	$48,108.00	$29,349.00	$20,563.00
Average spending of CU, total	38,044.67	22,543.18	38,945.27	45,149.37	46,160.28	39,340.03	30,781.81	21,908.04
PERSONAL CARE PRODUCTS AND SERVICES	$563.62	$345.43	$576.02	$643.78	$682.39	$569.08	$479.31	$368.12
Personal care products	256.30	159.73	290.78	300.34	322.34	259.86	176.50	114.32
Hair care products	51.46	36.59	62.26	63.36	61.00	53.17	29.50	17.14
Hair accessories	6.59	3.54	7.01	8.85	9.33	4.87	4.60	1.88
Wigs and hairpieces	1.17	2.38	1.09	1.20	0.95	1.07	1.48	0.55
Oral hygiene products	25.78	10.52	25.40	27.38	30.45	31.10	26.96	17.28
Shaving products	13.19	10.12	14.76	15.52	14.20	14.22	10.18	6.98
Cosmetics, perfume, and bath products	119.91	68.96	139.82	143.35	157.67	111.93	79.14	47.58
Deodorants, feminine hygiene, misc. products	29.21	23.74	29.12	34.28	37.61	26.95	21.45	16.15
Electric personal care appliances	8.99	3.87	11.32	6.40	11.14	16.56	3.18	6.76
Personal care services	307.31	185.70	285.24	343.44	360.05	309.22	302.81	253.80
READING	146.47	57.15	118.25	150.50	178.20	179.01	165.96	127.55
Newspaper subscriptions	47.43	5.61	19.85	40.13	53.81	65.07	76.67	77.28
Newspaper, nonsubscription	12.26	6.47	11.49	12.64	15.40	13.80	12.73	8.29
Magazine subscriptions	19.10	9.21	13.99	17.42	22.75	24.48	24.77	18.85
Magazines, nonsubscription	9.50	9.31	11.31	11.77	11.36	8.62	5.84	2.58
Books purchased through book clubs	8.03	1.99	7.59	11.32	8.39	9.57	8.44	2.88
Books not purchased through book clubs	49.52	24.53	53.88	55.73	66.11	57.38	35.85	17.46
Encyclopedia and other reference book sets	0.51	0.02	0.15	1.49	0.38	0.10	0.40	0.21
EDUCATION	631.93	1,257.43	585.13	615.39	1,145.98	379.88	148.91	63.32
College tuition	363.29	909.82	336.47	198.04	756.36	246.88	57.64	34.34
Elementary and high school tuition	101.42	3.79	89.51	211.20	157.79	30.38	31.45	5.66
Other school tuition	24.42	36.25	16.50	34.22	33.17	12.12	19.46	10.84
Other school expenses including rentals	24.00	25.29	21.16	37.99	42.06	9.20	3.70	1.04
Books, supplies for college	52.66	249.36	44.02	33.76	71.74	25.10	10.11	0.54
Books, supplies for elementary, high school	13.92	1.25	14.93	30.88	18.38	4.06	1.75	0.91
Books, supplies for day care, nursery school	3.09	1.80	3.76	4.98	3.97	2.11	1.21	0.14
Miscellaneous school expenses and supplies	49.13	29.87	58.77	64.31	62.51	50.04	23.61	9.86
TOBACCO PRODUCTS AND SMOKING SUPPLIES	318.62	237.21	310.32	426.91	375.64	348.85	222.63	98.84
Cigarettes	293.90	214.92	280.44	400.72	348.35	319.51	202.83	90.94
Other tobacco products	22.52	20.76	27.82	22.85	24.46	27.74	18.12	7.56
Smoking accessories	2.03	1.52	2.06	2.61	2.83	1.59	1.67	0.34

Source: Bureau of Labor Statistics, unpublished tables from the 2000 Consumer Expenditure Survey

Table 10.2 Personal Care, Reading, Education, Tobacco: Indexed spending by age, 2000

(indexed average annual spending of consumer units (CU) on personal care, reading, education, and tobacco products, by age of consumer unit reference person, 2000; index definition: an index of 100 is the average for all consumer units; an index of 132 means that spending by consumer units in that group is 32 percent above the average for all consumer units; an index of 68 indicates spending that is 32 percent below the average for all consumer units)

	total consumer units	under 25	25 to 34	35 to 44	45 to 54	55 to 64	65 to 74	75+
Average spending of CU, total	$38,045	$22,543	$38,945	$45,149	$46,160	$39,340	$30,782	$21,908
Average spending of CU, index	100	59	102	119	121	103	81	58
PERSONAL CARE PRODUCTS								
AND SERVICES	**100**	**61**	**102**	**114**	**121**	**101**	**85**	**65**
Personal care products	**100**	**62**	**113**	**117**	**126**	**101**	**69**	**45**
Hair care products	100	71	121	123	119	103	57	33
Hair accessories	100	54	106	134	142	74	70	29
Wigs and hairpieces	100	203	93	103	81	91	126	47
Oral hygiene products	100	41	99	106	118	121	105	67
Shaving products	100	77	112	118	108	108	77	53
Cosmetics, perfume, and bath products	100	58	117	120	131	93	66	40
Deodorants, feminine hygiene, misc. products	100	81	100	117	129	92	73	55
Electric personal care appliances	100	43	126	71	124	184	35	75
Personal care services	**100**	**60**	**93**	**112**	**117**	**101**	**99**	**83**
READING	**100**	**39**	**81**	**103**	**122**	**122**	**113**	**87**
Newspaper subscriptions	100	12	42	85	113	137	162	163
Newspaper, nonsubscription	100	53	94	103	126	113	104	68
Magazine subscriptions	100	48	73	91	119	128	130	99
Magazines, nonsubscription	100	98	119	124	120	91	61	27
Books purchased through book clubs	100	25	95	141	104	119	105	36
Books not purchased through book clubs	100	50	109	113	134	116	72	35
Encyclopedia and other reference book sets	100	4	29	292	75	20	78	41
EDUCATION	**100**	**199**	**93**	**97**	**181**	**60**	**24**	**10**
College tuition	100	250	93	55	208	68	16	9
Elementary and high school tuition	100	4	88	208	156	30	31	6
Other school tuition	100	148	68	140	136	50	80	44
Other school expenses including rentals	100	105	88	158	175	38	15	4
Books, supplies for college	100	474	84	64	136	48	19	1
Books, supplies for elementary, high school	100	9	107	222	132	29	13	7
Books, supplies for day care, nursery school	100	58	122	161	128	68	39	5
Miscellaneous school expenses and supplies	100	61	120	131	127	102	48	20
TOBACCO PRODUCTS AND								
SMOKING SUPPLIES	**100**	**74**	**97**	**134**	**118**	**109**	**70**	**31**
Cigarettes	100	73	95	136	119	109	69	31
Other tobacco products	100	92	124	101	109	123	80	34
Smoking accessories	100	75	101	129	139	78	82	17

Source: Calculations by New Strategist based on the 2000 Consumer Expenditure Survey

Table 10.3 Personal Care, Reading, Education, Tobacco: Indexed per capita spending by age, 2000

(indexed average annual per capita spending of consumer units (CU) on personal care, reading, education, and tobacco products, by age of consumer unit reference person, 2000; index definition: an index of 100 is the average for all consumer units; an index of 132 means that spending by consumer units in that group is 32 percent above the average for all consumer units; an index of 68 indicates spending that is 32 percent below the average for all consumer units)

	total consumer units	under 25	25 to 34	35 to 44	45 to 54	55 to 64	65 to 74	75+
Per capita spending of CU, total	$15,218	$11,865	$13,429	$13,682	$17,096	$18,733	$16,201	$14,605
Per capita spending of CU, index	100	78	88	90	112	123	106	96
PERSONAL CARE PRODUCTS AND SERVICES	**100**	**81**	**88**	**87**	**112**	**120**	**112**	**109**
Personal care products	**100**	**82**	**98**	**89**	**116**	**121**	**91**	**74**
Hair care products	100	94	104	93	110	123	75	56
Hair accessories	100	71	92	102	131	88	92	48
Wigs and hairpieces	100	268	80	78	75	109	166	78
Oral hygiene products	100	54	85	80	109	144	138	112
Shaving products	100	101	96	89	100	128	102	88
Cosmetics, perfume, and bath products	100	76	101	91	122	111	87	66
Deodorants, feminine hygiene, misc. products	100	107	86	89	119	110	97	92
Electric personal care appliances	100	57	109	54	115	219	47	125
Personal care services	**100**	**80**	**80**	**85**	**108**	**120**	**130**	**138**
READING	**100**	**51**	**70**	**78**	**113**	**145**	**149**	**145**
Newspaper subscriptions	100	16	36	64	105	163	213	272
Newspaper, nonsubscription	100	69	81	78	116	134	137	113
Magazine subscriptions	100	63	63	69	110	153	171	164
Magazines, nonsubscription	100	129	103	94	111	108	81	45
Books purchased through book clubs	100	33	81	107	97	142	138	60
Books not purchased through book clubs	100	65	94	85	124	138	95	59
Encyclopedia and other reference book sets	100	5	25	221	69	23	103	69
EDUCATION	**100**	**262**	**80**	**74**	**168**	**72**	**31**	**17**
College tuition	100	330	80	41	193	81	21	16
Elementary and high school tuition	100	5	76	158	144	36	41	9
Other school tuition	100	195	58	106	126	59	105	74
Other school expenses including rentals	100	139	76	120	162	46	20	7
Books, supplies for college	100	623	72	49	126	57	25	2
Books, supplies for elementary, high school	100	12	92	168	122	35	17	11
Books, supplies for day care, nursery school	100	77	105	122	119	81	52	8
Miscellaneous school expenses and supplies	100	80	103	99	118	121	63	33
TOBACCO PRODUCTS AND SMOKING SUPPLIES	**100**	**98**	**84**	**102**	**109**	**130**	**92**	**52**
Cigarettes	100	96	82	103	110	129	91	52
Other tobacco products	100	121	106	77	101	147	106	56
Smoking accessories	100	99	87	97	129	93	108	28

Note: Per capita indexes account for household size and show how much each person in a particular household demographic segment spends relative to a person in the average household.
Source: Calculations by New Strategist based on the 2000 Consumer Expenditure Survey

Table 10.4 Personal Care, Reading, Education, Tobacco: Total spending by age, 2000

(total annual spending on personal care, reading, education, and tobacco products, by consumer unit (CU) age group, 2000; numbers in thousands)

	total consumer units	under 25	25 to 34	35 to 44	45 to 54	55 to 64	65 to 74	75+
Number of consumer units	109,367	8,306	18,887	23,983	21,874	14,161	11,538	10,617
Total spending of all CUs	$4,160,831,424	$187,243,653	$735,559,314	$1,082,817,341	$1,009,709,965	$557,094,165	$355,160,524	$232,597,661
PERSONAL CARE PRODUCTS								
AND SERVICES	**$61,641,429**	**$2,869,142**	**$10,879,290**	**$15,439,776**	**$14,926,599**	**$8,058,742**	**$5,530,279**	**$3,908,330**
Personal care products	**28,030,762**	**1,326,717**	**5,491,962**	**7,203,054**	**7,050,865**	**3,679,877**	**2,036,457**	**1,213,735**
Hair care products	5,628,026	303,917	1,175,905	1,519,563	1,334,314	752,940	340,371	181,975
Hair accessories	720,729	29,403	132,398	212,250	204,084	68,964	53,075	19,960
Wigs and hairpieces	127,959	19,768	20,587	28,780	20,780	15,152	17,076	5,839
Oral hygiene products	2,819,481	87,379	479,730	656,655	666,063	440,407	311,064	183,462
Shaving products	1,442,551	84,057	278,772	372,216	310,611	201,369	117,457	74,107
Cosmetics, perfume, and bath products	13,114,197	572,782	2,640,780	3,437,963	3,448,874	1,585,041	913,117	505,157
Deodorants, feminine hygiene, misc. products	3,194,610	197,184	549,989	822,137	822,681	381,639	247,490	171,465
Electric personal care appliances	983,209	32,144	213,801	153,491	243,676	234,506	36,691	71,771
Personal care services	**33,609,573**	**1,542,424**	**5,387,328**	**8,236,722**	**7,875,734**	**4,378,864**	**3,493,822**	**2,694,595**
READING	**16,018,984**	**474,688**	**2,233,388**	**3,609,442**	**3,897,947**	**2,534,961**	**1,914,846**	**1,354,198**
Newspaper subscriptions	5,187,277	46,597	374,907	962,438	1,177,040	921,456	884,618	820,482
Newspaper, nonsubscription	1,340,839	53,740	217,012	303,145	336,860	195,422	146,879	88,015
Magazine subscriptions	2,088,910	76,498	264,229	417,784	497,634	346,661	285,796	200,130
Magazines, nonsubscription	1,038,987	77,329	213,612	282,280	248,489	122,068	67,382	27,392
Books purchased through book clubs	878,217	16,529	143,352	271,488	183,523	135,521	97,381	30,577
Books not purchased through book clubs	5,415,854	203,746	1,017,632	1,336,573	1,446,090	812,558	413,637	185,373
Encyclopedia and other reference book sets	55,777	166	2,833	35,735	8,312	1,416	4,615	2,230
EDUCATION	**69,112,288**	**10,444,214**	**11,051,350**	**14,758,898**	**25,067,167**	**5,379,481**	**1,718,124**	**672,268**
College tuition	39,731,937	7,556,965	6,354,909	4,749,593	16,544,619	3,496,068	665,050	364,588
Elementary and high school tuition	11,092,001	31,480	1,690,575	5,065,210	3,451,498	430,211	362,870	60,092
Other school tuition	2,670,742	301,093	311,636	820,698	725,561	171,631	224,529	115,088
Other school expenses including rentals	2,624,808	210,059	399,649	911,114	920,020	130,281	42,691	11,042
Books, supplies for college	5,759,266	2,071,184	831,406	809,666	1,569,241	355,441	116,649	5,733
Books, supplies for elementary, high school	1,522,389	10,383	281,983	740,595	402,044	57,494	20,192	9,661
Books, supplies for day care, nursery school	337,944	14,951	71,015	119,435	86,840	29,880	13,961	1,486
Miscellaneous school expenses and supplies	5,373,201	248,100	1,109,989	1,542,347	1,367,344	708,616	272,412	104,684
TOBACCO PRODUCTS AND								
SMOKING SUPPLIES	**34,846,514**	**1,970,266**	**5,861,014**	**10,238,583**	**8,216,749**	**4,940,065**	**2,568,705**	**1,049,384**
Cigarettes	32,142,961	1,785,126	5,296,670	9,610,468	7,619,808	4,524,581	2,340,253	965,510
Other tobacco products	2,462,945	172,433	525,436	548,012	535,038	392,826	209,069	80,265
Smoking accessories	222,015	12,625	38,907	62,596	61,903	22,516	19,268	3,610

Note: Numbers may not add to total because of rounding.
Source: Calculations by New Strategist based on the 2000 Consumer Expenditure Survey

Table 10.5 Personal Care, Reading, Education, Tobacco: Market shares by age, 2000

(percentage of total annual spending on personal care, reading, education, and tobacco products accounted for by consumer unit age groups, 2000)

	total consumer units	under 25	25 to 34	35 to 44	45 to 54	55 to 64	65 to 74	75+
Share of total consumer units	100.0%	7.6%	17.3%	21.9%	20.0%	12.9%	10.5%	9.7%
Share of total before-tax income	100.0	3.4	17.6	27.7	26.4	14.0	6.9	4.5
Share of total spending	100.0	4.5	17.7	26.0	24.3	13.4	8.5	5.6
PERSONAL CARE PRODUCTS								
AND SERVICES	100.0%	4.7%	17.6%	25.0%	24.2%	13.1%	9.0%	6.3%
Personal care products	100.0	4.7	19.6	25.7	25.2	13.1	7.3	4.3
Hair care products	100.0	5.4	20.9	27.0	23.7	13.4	6.0	3.2
Hair accessories	100.0	4.1	18.4	29.4	28.3	9.6	7.4	2.8
Wigs and hairpieces	100.0	15.4	16.1	22.5	16.2	11.8	13.3	4.6
Oral hygiene products	100.0	3.1	17.0	23.3	23.6	15.6	11.0	6.5
Shaving products	100.0	5.8	19.3	25.8	21.5	14.0	8.1	5.1
Cosmetics, perfume, and bath products	100.0	4.4	20.1	26.2	26.3	12.1	7.0	3.9
Deodorants, feminine hygiene, misc. products	100.0	6.2	17.2	25.7	25.8	11.9	7.7	5.4
Electric personal care appliances	100.0	3.3	21.7	15.6	24.8	23.9	3.7	7.3
Personal care services	100.0	4.6	16.0	24.5	23.4	13.0	10.4	8.0
READING	100.0	3.0	13.9	22.5	24.3	15.8	12.0	8.5
Newspaper subscriptions	100.0	0.9	7.2	18.6	22.7	17.8	17.1	15.8
Newspaper, nonsubscription	100.0	4.0	16.2	22.6	25.1	14.6	11.0	6.6
Magazine subscriptions	100.0	3.7	12.6	20.0	23.8	16.6	13.7	9.6
Magazines, nonsubscription	100.0	7.4	20.6	27.2	23.9	11.7	6.5	2.6
Books purchased through book clubs	100.0	1.9	16.3	30.9	20.9	15.4	11.1	3.5
Books not purchased through book clubs	100.0	3.8	18.8	24.7	26.7	15.0	7.6	3.4
Encyclopedia and other reference book sets	100.0	0.3	5.1	64.1	14.9	2.5	8.3	4.0
EDUCATION	100.0	15.1	16.0	21.4	36.3	7.8	2.5	1.0
College tuition	100.0	19.0	16.0	12.0	41.6	8.8	1.7	0.9
Elementary and high school tuition	100.0	0.3	15.2	45.7	31.1	3.9	3.3	0.5
Other school tuition	100.0	11.3	11.7	30.7	27.2	6.4	8.4	4.3
Other school expenses including rentals	100.0	8.0	15.2	34.7	35.1	5.0	1.6	0.4
Books, supplies for college	100.0	36.0	14.4	14.1	27.2	6.2	2.0	0.1
Books, supplies for elementary, high school	100.0	0.7	18.5	48.6	26.4	3.8	1.3	0.6
Books, supplies for day care, nursery school	100.0	4.4	21.0	35.3	25.7	8.8	4.1	0.4
Miscellaneous school expenses and supplies	100.0	4.6	20.7	28.7	25.4	13.2	5.1	1.9
TOBACCO PRODUCTS AND								
SMOKING SUPPLIES	100.0	5.7	16.8	29.4	23.6	14.2	7.4	3.0
Cigarettes	100.0	5.6	16.5	29.9	23.7	14.1	7.3	3.0
Other tobacco products	100.0	7.0	21.3	22.3	21.7	15.9	8.5	3.3
Smoking accessories	100.0	5.7	17.5	28.2	27.9	10.1	8.7	1.6

Note: Numbers may not add to total because of rounding.
Source: Calculations by New Strategist based on the 2000 Consumer Expenditure Survey

Table 10.6 Personal Care, Reading, Education, Tobacco: Average spending by income, 2000

(average annual spending on personal care, reading, education, and tobacco products, by before-tax income of consumer units (CU), 2000; complete income reporters only)

	complete income reporters	under $10,000	$10,000– 19,999	$20,000– 29,999	$30,000– 39,999	$40,000– 49,999	$50,000– 69,999	$70,000 or more
Number of consumer units (in thousands, add 000)	81,454	10,810	14,714	12,039	9,477	7,653	11,337	15,424
Average number of persons per CU	2.5	1.7	2.1	2.4	2.5	2.6	2.9	3.2
Average before-tax income of CU	$44,649.00	$5,739.61	$14,586.29	$24,527.00	$34,422.00	$44,201.00	$58,561.00	$112,586.00
Average spending of CU, total	40,238.44	16,455.72	22,620.20	29,851.59	35,609.24	42,323.03	49,245.37	75,963.85
PERSONAL CARE PRODUCTS								
AND SERVICES	**$595.33**	**$306.14**	**$376.05**	**$478.52**	**$521.54**	**$652.32**	**$718.22**	**$992.81**
Personal care products	**288.03**	**135.20**	**168.98**	**228.01**	**246.21**	**353.50**	**346.96**	**473.18**
Hair care products	57.63	28.22	30.02	46.10	57.65	80.01	68.14	88.19
Hair accessories	7.32	3.57	4.17	5.59	3.69	9.98	6.05	15.31
Wigs and hairpieces	1.29	1.15	0.90	1.53	1.27	0.42	1.86	1.61
Oral hygiene products	29.44	13.11	20.55	23.69	31.48	28.31	36.15	45.07
Shaving products	15.94	4.87	10.27	15.11	13.45	19.21	20.23	24.69
Cosmetics, perfume, and bath products	134.33	60.77	77.78	100.80	97.57	175.30	169.25	227.27
Deodorants, feminine hygiene, misc. products	33.47	21.04	20.14	30.43	30.77	29.56	35.07	56.42
Electric personal care appliances	8.61	2.48	5.15	4.76	10.34	10.70	10.21	14.61
Personal care services	**307.30**	**170.94**	**207.07**	**250.51**	**275.33**	**298.82**	**371.27**	**519.63**
READING	**156.11**	**69.24**	**86.32**	**127.39**	**137.56**	**151.40**	**190.57**	**294.34**
Newspaper subscriptions	48.63	25.65	37.57	39.84	42.30	42.64	54.60	84.62
Newspaper, nonsubscription	13.12	7.70	9.24	12.91	14.95	13.93	16.12	17.06
Magazine subscriptions	21.00	9.74	11.14	18.52	19.94	20.59	27.86	36.03
Magazines, nonsubscription	10.23	4.56	5.54	7.47	9.41	11.16	13.09	18.79
Books purchased through book clubs	9.38	2.55	3.57	7.57	6.76	10.38	12.73	19.78
Books not purchased through book clubs	52.91	18.91	19.06	41.02	43.74	52.69	65.91	114.49
Encyclopedia and other reference book sets	0.66	0.14	0.21	0.05	0.47	–	0.25	2.65
EDUCATION	**635.52**	**532.73**	**254.83**	**302.85**	**436.88**	**445.98**	**703.76**	**1,488.89**
College tuition	359.04	369.39	171.47	171.57	223.08	221.41	370.06	820.81
Elementary and high school tuition	99.47	13.71	11.30	17.70	62.12	50.68	118.06	341.02
Other school tuition	25.06	3.25	4.07	20.70	41.43	17.19	31.21	53.12
Other school expenses including rentals	25.11	12.82	10.75	11.24	14.60	18.31	38.53	58.20
Books, supplies for college	53.73	100.91	36.32	30.16	33.58	31.95	45.44	84.96
Books, supplies for elementary, high school	13.76	5.50	5.71	7.68	10.51	18.08	15.67	30.41
Books, supplies for day care, nursery school	3.17	1.73	0.88	1.56	2.93	4.48	3.96	6.54
Miscellaneous school expenses and supplies	56.17	25.43	14.32	42.25	48.63	83.88	80.84	93.83
TOBACCO PRODUCTS AND								
SMOKING SUPPLIES	**333.30**	**259.73**	**277.57**	**357.77**	**356.56**	**411.29**	**383.58**	**328.84**
Cigarettes	306.30	243.49	261.51	329.46	335.25	381.26	348.45	289.03
Other tobacco products	24.81	15.07	14.22	26.51	17.99	27.71	32.44	37.56
Smoking accessories	2.19	1.17	1.84	1.80	3.31	2.32	2.68	2.25

Note: (–) means sample is too small to make a reliable estimate.
Source: Bureau of Labor Statistics, unpublished tables from the 2000 Consumer Expenditure Survey; calculations by New Strategist

Table 10.7 Personal Care, Reading, Education, Tobacco: Indexed spending by income, 2000

(indexed average annual spending of consumer units (CU) on personal care, reading, education, and tobacco products, by before-tax income of consumer unit, 2000; complete income reporters only; index definition: an index of 100 is the average for all consumer units; an index of 132 means that spending by consumer units in that group is 32 percent above the average for all consumer units; an index of 68 indicates spending that is 32 percent below the average for all consumer units)

	complete income reporters	under $10,000	$10,000– 19,999	$20,000– 29,999	$30,000– 39,999	$40,000– 49,999	$50,000– 69,999	$70,000 or more
Average spending of CU, total	$40,238	$16,456	$22,620	$29,852	$35,609	$42,323	$49,245	$75,964
Average spending of CU, index	100	41	56	74	88	105	122	189
PERSONAL CARE PRODUCTS								
AND SERVICES	100	51	63	80	88	110	121	167
Personal care products	100	47	59	79	85	123	120	164
Hair care products	100	49	52	80	100	139	118	153
Hair accessories	100	49	57	76	50	136	83	209
Wigs and hairpieces	100	89	70	119	98	33	144	125
Oral hygiene products	100	45	70	80	107	96	123	153
Shaving products	100	31	64	95	84	121	127	155
Cosmetics, perfume, and bath products	100	45	58	75	73	130	126	169
Deodorants, feminine hygiene, misc. products	100	63	60	91	92	88	105	169
Electric personal care appliances	100	29	60	55	120	124	119	170
Personal care services	100	56	67	82	90	97	121	169
READING	100	44	55	82	88	97	122	189
Newspaper subscriptions	100	53	77	82	87	88	112	174
Newspaper, nonsubscription	100	59	70	98	114	106	123	130
Magazine subscriptions	100	46	53	88	95	98	133	172
Magazines, nonsubscription	100	45	54	73	92	109	128	184
Books purchased through book clubs	100	27	38	81	72	111	136	211
Books not purchased through book clubs	100	36	36	78	83	100	125	216
Encyclopedia and other reference book sets	100	21	32	8	71	–	38	402
EDUCATION	100	84	40	48	69	70	111	234
College tuition	100	103	48	48	62	62	103	229
Elementary and high school tuition	100	14	11	18	62	51	119	343
Other school tuition	100	13	16	83	165	69	125	212
Other school expenses including rentals	100	51	43	45	58	73	153	232
Books, supplies for college	100	188	68	56	62	59	85	158
Books, supplies for elementary, high school	100	40	42	56	76	131	114	221
Books, supplies for day care, nursery school	100	55	28	49	92	141	125	206
Miscellaneous school expenses and supplies	100	45	25	75	87	149	144	167
TOBACCO PRODUCTS AND								
SMOKING SUPPLIES	100	78	83	107	107	123	115	99
Cigarettes	100	79	85	108	109	124	114	94
Other tobacco products	100	61	57	107	73	112	131	151
Smoking accessories	100	53	84	82	151	106	122	103

Note: (–) means sample is too small to make a reliable estimate.
Source: Calculations by New Strategist based on the 2000 Consumer Expenditure Survey

Table 10.8 Personal Care, Reading, Education, Tobacco: Indexed per capita spending by income, 2000

(indexed average annual per capita spending of consumer units (CU) on personal care, reading, education, and tobacco products, by before-tax income of consumer unit, 2000; complete income reporters only; index definition: an index of 100 is the average for all consumer units; an index of 132 means that spending by consumer units in that group is 32 percent above the average for all consumer units; an index of 68 indicates spending that is 32 percent below the average for all consumer units)

	complete income reporters	under $10,000	$10,000– 19,999	$20,000– 29,999	$30,000– 39,999	$40,000– 49,999	$50,000– 69,999	$70,000 or more
Per capita spending of CU, total	$16,095	$9,492	$10,819	$12,438	$14,244	$16,278	$16,981	$23,739
Per capita spending of CU, index	100	59	67	77	88	101	106	147
PERSONAL CARE PRODUCTS AND SERVICES	**100**	**74**	**76**	**84**	**88**	**105**	**104**	**130**
Personal care products	**100**	**68**	**70**	**82**	**85**	**118**	**104**	**128**
Hair care products	100	71	62	83	100	133	102	120
Hair accessories	100	70	68	80	50	131	71	163
Wigs and hairpieces	100	128	84	124	98	31	124	98
Oral hygiene products	100	64	83	84	107	92	106	120
Shaving products	100	44	77	99	84	116	109	121
Cosmetics, perfume, and bath products	100	65	69	78	73	125	109	132
Deodorants, feminine hygiene, misc. products	100	91	72	95	92	85	90	132
Electric personal care appliances	100	42	71	58	120	119	102	133
Personal care services	**100**	**80**	**81**	**85**	**90**	**94**	**104**	**132**
READING	**100**	**64**	**66**	**85**	**88**	**93**	**105**	**147**
Newspaper subscriptions	100	76	92	85	87	84	97	136
Newspaper, nonsubscription	100	85	84	102	114	102	106	102
Magazine subscriptions	100	67	63	92	95	94	114	134
Magazines, nonsubscription	100	64	65	76	92	105	110	143
Books purchased through book clubs	100	39	46	84	72	106	117	165
Books not purchased through book clubs	100	52	43	81	83	96	107	169
Encyclopedia and other reference book sets	100	30	38	8	71	–	33	314
EDUCATION	**100**	**121**	**48**	**50**	**69**	**67**	**95**	**183**
College tuition	100	148	57	50	62	59	89	179
Elementary and high school tuition	100	20	14	19	62	49	102	268
Other school tuition	100	19	19	86	165	66	107	166
Other school expenses including rentals	100	74	51	47	58	70	132	181
Books, supplies for college	100	271	81	58	62	57	73	124
Books, supplies for elementary, high school	100	58	50	58	76	126	98	173
Books, supplies for day care, nursery school	100	79	33	51	92	136	108	161
Miscellaneous school expenses and supplies	100	65	30	78	87	144	124	131
TOBACCO PRODUCTS AND SMOKING SUPPLIES	**100**	**112**	**100**	**112**	**107**	**119**	**99**	**77**
Cigarettes	100	115	102	112	109	120	98	74
Other tobacco products	100	88	69	111	73	107	113	118
Smoking accessories	100	77	101	86	151	102	105	80

Note: Per capita indexes account for household size and show how much each person in a particular household demographic segment spends relative to a person in the average household. (–) means sample is too small to make a reliable estimate.
Source: Calculations by New Strategist based on the 2000 Consumer Expenditure Survey

Table 10.9 Personal Care, Reading, Education, Tobacco: Total spending by income, 2000

(total annual spending on personal care, reading, education, and tobacco products, by before-tax income group of consumer units (CU), 2000; complete income reporters only; numbers in thousands)

	complete income reporters	under $10,000	$10,000– 19,999	$20,000– 29,999	$30,000– 39,999	$40,000– 49,999	$50,000– 69,999	$70,000 or more
Number of consumer units	81,454	10,810	14,714	12,039	9,477	7,653	11,337	15,424
Total spending of all CUs	$3,277,581,892	$177,886,368	$332,833,656	$359,383,292	$337,468,767	$323,898,149	$558,294,760	$1,171,666,422
PERSONAL CARE PRODUCTS								
AND SERVICES	**$48,492,010**	**$3,309,414**	**$5,533,173**	**$5,760,902**	**$4,942,635**	**$4,992,205**	**$8,142,460**	**$15,313,101**
Personal care products	**23,461,196**	**1,461,554**	**2,486,307**	**2,745,012**	**2,333,332**	**2,705,336**	**3,933,486**	**7,298,328**
Hair care products	4,694,194	305,029	441,714	554,998	546,349	612,317	772,503	1,360,243
Hair accessories	596,243	38,620	61,424	67,298	34,970	76,377	68,589	236,141
Wigs and hairpieces	105,076	12,415	13,261	18,420	12,036	3,214	21,087	24,833
Oral hygiene products	2,398,006	141,716	302,355	285,204	298,336	216,656	409,833	695,160
Shaving products	1,298,377	52,617	151,112	181,909	127,466	147,014	229,348	380,819
Cosmetics, perfume, and bath products	10,941,716	656,964	1,144,429	1,213,531	924,671	1,341,571	1,918,787	3,505,412
Deodorants, feminine hygiene, misc. products	2,726,265	227,458	296,297	366,347	291,607	226,223	397,589	870,222
Electric personal care appliances	701,319	26,843	75,728	57,306	97,992	81,887	115,751	225,345
Personal care services	**25,030,814**	**1,847,860**	**3,046,866**	**3,015,890**	**2,609,302**	**2,286,869**	**4,209,088**	**8,014,773**
READING	**12,715,784**	**748,498**	**1,270,065**	**1,533,648**	**1,303,656**	**1,158,664**	**2,160,492**	**4,539,900**
Newspaper subscriptions	3,961,108	277,304	552,770	479,634	400,877	326,324	619,000	1,305,179
Newspaper, nonsubscription	1,068,676	83,247	135,920	155,423	141,681	106,606	182,752	263,133
Magazine subscriptions	1,710,534	105,268	163,863	222,962	188,971	157,575	315,849	555,727
Magazines, nonsubscription	833,274	49,267	81,521	89,931	89,179	85,407	148,401	289,817
Books purchased through book clubs	764,039	27,513	52,519	91,135	64,065	79,438	144,320	305,087
Books not purchased through book clubs	4,309,731	204,415	280,438	493,840	414,524	403,237	747,222	1,765,894
Encyclopedia and other reference book sets	53,760	1,484	3,100	602	4,454	–	2,834	40,874
EDUCATION	**51,765,646**	**5,758,843**	**3,749,561**	**3,646,011**	**4,140,312**	**3,413,085**	**7,978,527**	**22,964,639**
College tuition	29,245,244	3,993,101	2,523,013	2,065,531	2,114,129	1,694,451	4,195,370	12,660,173
Elementary and high school tuition	8,102,229	148,222	166,269	213,090	588,711	387,854	1,338,446	5,259,892
Other school tuition	2,041,237	35,134	59,920	249,207	392,632	131,555	353,828	819,323
Other school expenses including rentals	2,045,310	138,579	158,158	135,318	138,364	140,126	436,815	897,677
Books, supplies for college	4,376,523	1,090,822	534,346	363,096	318,238	244,513	515,153	1,310,423
Books, supplies for elementary, high school	1,120,807	59,421	84,076	92,460	99,603	138,366	177,651	469,044
Books, supplies for day care, nursery school	258,209	18,679	12,910	18,781	27,768	34,285	44,895	100,873
Miscellaneous school expenses and supplies	4,575,271	274,849	210,721	508,648	460,867	641,934	916,483	1,447,234
TOBACCO PRODUCTS AND								
SMOKING SUPPLIES	**27,148,618**	**2,807,695**	**4,084,101**	**4,307,193**	**3,379,119**	**3,147,602**	**4,348,646**	**5,072,028**
Cigarettes	24,949,360	2,632,134	3,847,811	3,966,369	3,177,164	2,917,783	3,950,378	4,457,999
Other tobacco products	2,020,874	162,959	209,176	319,154	170,491	212,065	367,772	579,325
Smoking accessories	178,384	12,603	27,115	21,670	31,369	17,755	30,383	34,704

Note: Numbers may not add to total because of rounding. (–) means sample is too small to make a reliable estimate.
Source: Calculations by New Strategist based on the 2000 Consumer Expenditure Survey

Table 10.10 Personal Care, Reading, Education, Tobacco: Market shares by income, 2000

(percentage of total annual spending on personal care, reading, education, and tobacco products accounted for by before-tax income group of consumer units, 2000; complete income reporters only)

	complete income reporters	under $10,000	$10,000– 19,999	$20,000– 29,999	$30,000– 39,999	$40,000– 49,999	$50,000– 69,999	$70,000 or more
Share of total consumer units	100.0%	13.3%	18.1%	14.8%	11.6%	9.4%	13.9%	18.9%
Share of total before-tax income	100.0	1.7	5.9	8.1	9.0	9.3	18.3	47.7
Share of total spending	100.0	5.4	10.2	11.0	10.3	9.9	17.0	35.7
PERSONAL CARE PRODUCTS								
AND SERVICES	100.0%	6.8%	11.4%	11.9%	10.2%	10.3%	16.8%	31.6%
Personal care products	100.0	6.2	10.6	11.7	9.9	11.5	16.8	31.1
Hair care products	100.0	6.5	9.4	11.8	11.6	13.0	16.5	29.0
Hair accessories	100.0	6.5	10.3	11.3	5.9	12.8	11.5	39.6
Wigs and hairpieces	100.0	11.8	12.6	17.5	11.5	3.1	20.1	23.6
Oral hygiene products	100.0	5.9	12.6	11.9	12.4	9.0	17.1	29.0
Shaving products	100.0	4.1	11.6	14.0	9.8	11.3	17.7	29.3
Cosmetics, perfume, and bath products	100.0	6.0	10.5	11.1	8.5	12.3	17.5	32.0
Deodorants, feminine hygiene, misc. products	100.0	8.3	10.9	13.4	10.7	8.3	14.6	31.9
Electric personal care appliances	100.0	3.8	10.8	8.2	14.0	11.7	16.5	32.1
Personal care services	100.0	7.4	12.2	12.0	10.4	9.1	16.8	32.0
READING	100.0	5.9	10.0	12.1	10.3	9.1	17.0	35.7
Newspaper subscriptions	100.0	7.0	14.0	12.1	10.1	8.2	15.6	32.9
Newspaper, nonsubscription	100.0	7.8	12.7	14.5	13.3	10.0	17.1	24.6
Magazine subscriptions	100.0	6.2	9.6	13.0	11.0	9.2	18.5	32.5
Magazines, nonsubscription	100.0	5.9	9.8	10.8	10.7	10.2	17.8	34.8
Books purchased through book clubs	100.0	3.6	6.9	11.9	8.4	10.4	18.9	39.9
Books not purchased through book clubs	100.0	4.7	6.5	11.5	9.6	9.4	17.3	41.0
Encyclopedia and other reference book sets	100.0	2.8	5.8	1.1	8.3	–	5.3	76.0
EDUCATION	100.0	11.1	7.2	7.0	8.0	6.6	15.4	44.4
College tuition	100.0	13.7	8.6	7.1	7.2	5.8	14.3	43.3
Elementary and high school tuition	100.0	1.8	2.1	2.6	7.3	4.8	16.5	64.9
Other school tuition	100.0	1.7	2.9	12.2	19.2	6.4	17.3	40.1
Other school expenses including rentals	100.0	6.8	7.7	6.6	6.8	6.9	21.4	43.9
Books, supplies for college	100.0	24.9	12.2	8.3	7.3	5.6	11.8	29.9
Books, supplies for elementary, high school	100.0	5.3	7.5	8.2	8.9	12.3	15.9	41.8
Books, supplies for day care, nursery school	100.0	7.2	5.0	7.3	10.8	13.3	17.4	39.1
Miscellaneous school expenses and supplies	100.0	6.0	4.6	11.1	10.1	14.0	20.0	31.6
TOBACCO PRODUCTS AND								
SMOKING SUPPLIES	100.0	10.3	15.0	15.9	12.4	11.6	16.0	18.7
Cigarettes	100.0	10.5	15.4	15.9	12.7	11.7	15.8	17.9
Other tobacco products	100.0	8.1	10.4	15.8	8.4	10.5	18.2	28.7
Smoking accessories	100.0	7.1	15.2	12.1	17.6	10.0	17.0	19.5

Note: Numbers may not add to total because of rounding. (–) means sample is too small to make a reliable estimate.
Source: Calculations by New Strategist based on the 2000 Consumer Expenditure Survey

Table 10.11 Personal Care, Reading, Education, Tobacco: Average spending by household type, 2000

(average annual spending of consumer units (CU) on personal care, reading, education, and tobacco products, by type of consumer unit, 2000)

	total married couples	married couples, no children	married couples with children				single parent, at least one child <18	single person
			total	oldest child under 6	oldest child 6 to 17	oldest child 18 or older		
Number of consumer units (in thousands, add 000)	56,287	22,805	28,777	5,291	15,396	8,090	6,132	32,323
Average number of persons per CU	3.2	2.0	3.9	3.5	4.1	3.8	2.9	1.0
Average before-tax income of CU	$60,588.00	$53,232.00	$66,913.00	$62,928.00	$69,472.00	$64,725.00	$25,095.00	$24,977.00
Average spending of CU, total	48,619.37	42,195.54	53,585.53	50,755.90	54,170.40	54,550.20	28,923.25	23,059.00
PERSONAL CARE PRODUCTS AND SERVICES	**$700.36**	**$610.82**	**$768.58**	**$648.89**	**$774.41**	**$845.49**	**$568.99**	**$338.33**
Personal care products	**321.52**	**265.24**	**365.19**	**309.65**	**366.90**	**407.98**	**274.62**	**145.55**
Hair care products	63.98	48.09	75.51	58.75	80.74	78.44	63.91	25.39
Hair accessories	8.47	5.73	9.19	5.07	10.98	8.85	8.87	3.63
Wigs and hairpieces	1.02	0.89	0.93	1.39	0.90	0.70	3.26	0.76
Oral hygiene products	33.97	29.97	37.47	37.84	33.79	44.97	16.07	15.26
Shaving products	15.53	14.96	15.84	13.96	16.09	16.90	9.24	8.55
Cosmetics, perfume, and bath products	149.43	126.59	170.02	149.62	167.26	192.88	133.49	73.91
Deodorants, feminine hygiene, misc. products	35.62	25.98	42.87	33.98	45.78	44.14	33.80	14.25
Electric personal care appliances	13.48	13.03	13.35	9.06	11.37	21.11	5.99	3.78
Personal care services	**378.84**	**345.57**	**403.39**	**339.24**	**407.51**	**437.51**	**294.37**	**192.78**
READING	**181.55**	**196.72**	**176.14**	**173.53**	**174.34**	**181.27**	**75.83**	**113.28**
Newspaper subscriptions	61.86	76.90	52.32	39.94	49.39	66.00	15.53	35.90
Newspaper, nonsubscription	13.20	12.87	13.61	11.32	13.21	15.89	10.01	10.25
Magazine subscriptions	24.02	29.22	20.65	17.91	21.64	20.55	8.51	15.72
Magazines, nonsubscription	11.09	9.07	12.80	15.09	12.25	12.34	7.33	7.18
Books purchased through book clubs	10.14	7.53	12.11	19.82	11.54	8.16	5.64	5.05
Books not purchased through book clubs	60.34	59.79	64.01	69.31	65.52	57.68	28.62	38.64
Encyclopedia and other reference book sets	0.89	1.35	0.63	0.13	0.79	0.64	0.19	0.09
EDUCATION	**810.90**	**446.72**	**1,125.72**	**419.84**	**1,032.03**	**1,768.65**	**395.46**	**406.71**
College tuition	437.85	329.36	534.10	212.37	258.61	1,268.85	103.00	289.71
Elementary and high school tuition	172.47	17.47	308.64	95.34	462.78	154.77	106.56	6.81
Other school tuition	32.21	13.77	45.53	22.74	56.04	40.42	22.12	15.18
Other school expenses including rentals	32.12	11.77	47.79	17.80	52.07	59.25	41.53	11.35
Books, supplies for college	49.99	37.89	61.20	26.54	25.44	151.95	25.55	59.71
Books, supplies for elementary, high school	21.20	2.51	36.69	2.63	57.09	20.16	31.85	0.69
Books, supplies for day care, nursery school	4.18	1.41	5.98	4.16	7.86	3.60	3.18	1.56
Miscellaneous school expenses and supplies	60.88	32.54	85.78	38.26	112.14	69.65	61.65	21.70
TOBACCO PRODUCTS AND SMOKING SUPPLIES	**343.35**	**285.55**	**358.17**	**275.14**	**335.84**	**455.13**	**298.67**	**202.66**
Cigarettes	311.74	258.80	322.27	234.51	301.89	418.44	292.21	186.60
Other tobacco products	29.65	24.94	33.97	39.56	32.01	34.07	4.09	13.43
Smoking accessories	1.96	1.82	1.93	1.07	1.95	2.63	2.37	2.05

Note: Average spending figures for total consumer units can be found on Average Spending by Age and Average Spending by Region tables.
Source: Bureau of Labor Statistics, unpublished tables from the 2000 Consumer Expenditure Survey

Table 10.12 Personal Care, Reading, Education, Tobacco: Indexed spending by household type, 2000

(indexed average annual spending of consumer units (CU) on personal care, reading, education, and tobacco products, by type of consumer unit, 2000; index definition: an index of 100 is the average for all consumer units; an index of 132 means that spending by consumer units in that group is 32 percent above the average for all consumer units; an index of 68 indicates spending that is 32 percent below the average for all consumer units)

| | total married couples | married couples, no children | married couples with children | | | | single parent, at least one child <18 | single person |
			total	oldest child under 6	oldest child 6 to 17	oldest child 18 or older		
Average spending of CU, total	$48,619	$42,196	$53,586	$50,756	$54,170	$54,550	$28,923	$23,059
Average spending of CU, index	128	111	141	133	142	143	76	61
PERSONAL CARE PRODUCTS								
AND SERVICES	**124**	**108**	**136**	**115**	**137**	**150**	**101**	**60**
Personal care products	**125**	**103**	**142**	**121**	**143**	**159**	**107**	**57**
Hair care products	124	93	147	114	157	152	124	49
Hair accessories	129	87	139	77	167	134	135	55
Wigs and hairpieces	87	76	79	119	77	60	279	65
Oral hygiene products	132	116	145	147	131	174	62	59
Shaving products	118	113	120	106	122	128	70	65
Cosmetics, perfume, and bath products	125	106	142	125	139	161	111	62
Deodorants, feminine hygiene, misc. products	122	89	147	116	157	151	116	49
Electric personal care appliances	150	145	148	101	126	235	67	42
Personal care services	**123**	**112**	**131**	**110**	**133**	**142**	**96**	**63**
READING	**124**	**134**	**120**	**118**	**119**	**124**	**52**	**77**
Newspaper subscriptions	130	162	110	84	104	139	33	76
Newspaper, nonsubscription	108	105	111	92	108	130	82	84
Magazine subscriptions	126	153	108	94	113	108	45	82
Magazines, nonsubscription	117	95	135	159	129	130	77	76
Books purchased through book clubs	126	94	151	247	144	102	70	63
Books not purchased through book clubs	122	121	129	140	132	116	58	78
Encyclopedia and other reference book sets	175	265	124	25	155	125	37	18
EDUCATION	**128**	**71**	**178**	**66**	**163**	**280**	**63**	**64**
College tuition	121	91	147	58	71	349	28	80
Elementary and high school tuition	170	17	304	94	456	153	105	7
Other school tuition	132	56	186	93	229	166	91	62
Other school expenses including rentals	134	49	199	74	217	247	173	47
Books, supplies for college	95	72	116	50	48	289	49	113
Books, supplies for elementary, high school	152	18	264	19	410	145	229	5
Books, supplies for day care, nursery school	135	46	194	135	254	117	103	50
Miscellaneous school expenses and supplies	124	66	175	78	228	142	125	44
TOBACCO PRODUCTS AND								
SMOKING SUPPLIES	**108**	**90**	**112**	**86**	**105**	**143**	**94**	**64**
Cigarettes	106	88	110	80	103	142	99	63
Other tobacco products	132	111	151	176	142	151	18	60
Smoking accessories	97	90	95	53	96	130	117	101

Note: Spending index for total consumer units is 100.
Source: Calculations by New Strategist based on the 2000 Consumer Expenditure Survey

Table 10.13 Personal Care, Reading, Education, Tobacco: Indexed per capita spending by household type, 2000

(indexed average annual per capita spending of consumer units (CU) on personal care, reading, education, and tobacco products, by type of consumer unit, 2000; index definition: an index of 100 is the average for all consumer units; an index of 132 means that spending by consumer units in that group is 32 percent above the average for all consumer units; an index of 68 indicates spending that is 32 percent below the average for all consumer units)

	total married couples	married couples, no children	married couples with children				single parent, at least one child <18	single person
			total	oldest child under 6	oldest child 6 to 17	oldest child 18 or older		
Per capita spending of CU, total	$15,194	$21,098	$13,740	$14,502	$13,212	$14,355	$9,974	$23,059
Per capita spending of CU, index	100	139	90	95	87	94	66	152
PERSONAL CARE PRODUCTS AND SERVICES	**97**	**135**	**87**	**82**	**84**	**99**	**87**	**150**
Personal care products	**98**	**129**	**91**	**86**	**87**	**105**	**92**	**142**
Hair care products	97	117	94	82	96	100	107	123
Hair accessories	100	109	89	55	102	88	116	138
Wigs and hairpieces	68	95	51	85	47	39	240	162
Oral hygiene products	103	145	93	105	80	115	54	148
Shaving products	92	142	77	76	74	84	60	162
Cosmetics, perfume, and bath products	97	132	91	89	85	106	96	154
Deodorants, feminine hygiene, misc. products	95	111	94	83	96	99	100	122
Electric personal care appliances	117	181	95	72	77	154	57	105
Personal care services	**96**	**141**	**84**	**79**	**81**	**94**	**83**	**157**
READING	**97**	**168**	**77**	**85**	**73**	**81**	**45**	**193**
Newspaper subscriptions	102	203	71	60	63	92	28	189
Newspaper, nonsubscription	84	131	71	66	66	85	70	209
Magazine subscriptions	98	191	69	67	69	71	38	206
Magazines, nonsubscription	91	119	86	113	79	85	67	189
Books purchased through book clubs	99	117	97	176	88	67	61	157
Books not purchased through book clubs	95	151	83	100	81	77	50	195
Encyclopedia and other reference book sets	136	331	79	18	94	83	32	44
EDUCATION	**100**	**88**	**114**	**47**	**100**	**184**	**54**	**161**
College tuition	94	113	94	42	43	230	24	199
Elementary and high school tuition	133	22	195	67	278	100	91	17
Other school tuition	103	70	120	67	140	109	78	155
Other school expenses including rentals	105	61	128	53	132	162	149	118
Books, supplies for college	74	90	74	36	29	190	42	283
Books, supplies for elementary, high school	119	23	169	13	250	95	197	12
Books, supplies for day care, nursery school	106	57	124	96	155	77	89	126
Miscellaneous school expenses and supplies	97	83	112	56	139	93	108	110
TOBACCO PRODUCTS AND SMOKING SUPPLIES	**84**	**112**	**72**	**62**	**64**	**94**	**81**	**159**
Cigarettes	83	110	70	57	63	94	86	159
Other tobacco products	103	138	97	125	87	100	16	149
Smoking accessories	75	112	61	38	59	85	101	252

Note: Per capita indexes account for household size and show how much each person in a particular household demographic segment spends relative to a person in the average household. Spending index for total consumer units is 100.
Source: Calculations by New Strategist based on the 2000 Consumer Expenditure Survey

Table 10.14 Personal Care, Reading, Education, Tobacco: Total spending by household type, 2000

(total annual spending on personal care, reading, education, and tobacco products, by consumer unit (CU) type, 2000; numbers in thousands)

	total married couples	married couples, no children	married couples with children total	oldest child under 6	oldest child 6 to 17	oldest child 18 or older	single parent, at least one child <18	single person
Number of consumer units	56,287	22,805	28,777	5,291	15,396	8,090	6,132	32,323
Total spending of all CUs	$2,736,638,479	$962,269,290	$1,542,030,797	$268,549,467	$834,007,478	$441,311,118	$177,357,369	$745,336,057
PERSONAL CARE PRODUCTS AND SERVICES	**$39,421,163**	**$13,929,750**	**$22,117,427**	**$3,433,277**	**$11,922,816**	**$6,840,014**	**$3,489,047**	**$10,935,841**
Personal care products	**18,097,396**	**6,048,798**	**10,509,073**	**1,638,358**	**5,648,792**	**3,300,558**	**1,683,970**	**4,704,613**
Hair care products	3,601,242	1,096,692	2,172,951	310,846	1,243,073	634,580	391,896	820,681
Hair accessories	476,751	130,673	264,461	26,825	169,048	71,597	54,391	117,332
Wigs and hairpieces	57,413	20,296	26,763	7,354	13,856	5,663	19,990	24,565
Oral hygiene products	1,912,069	683,466	1,078,274	200,211	520,231	363,807	98,541	493,249
Shaving products	874,137	341,163	455,828	73,862	247,722	136,721	56,660	276,362
Cosmetics, perfume, and bath products	8,410,966	2,886,885	4,892,666	791,639	2,575,135	1,560,399	818,561	2,388,993
Deodorants, feminine hygiene, misc. products	2,004,943	592,474	1,233,670	179,788	704,829	357,093	207,262	460,603
Electric personal care appliances	758,749	297,149	384,173	47,936	175,053	170,780	36,731	122,181
Personal care services	**21,323,767**	**7,880,724**	**11,608,354**	**1,794,919**	**6,274,024**	**3,539,456**	**1,805,077**	**6,231,228**
READING	**10,218,905**	**4,486,200**	**5,068,781**	**918,147**	**2,684,139**	**1,466,474**	**464,990**	**3,661,549**
Newspaper subscriptions	3,481,914	1,753,705	1,505,613	211,323	760,408	533,940	95,230	1,160,396
Newspaper, nonsubscription	742,988	293,500	391,655	59,894	203,381	128,550	61,381	331,311
Magazine subscriptions	1,352,014	666,362	594,245	94,762	333,169	166,250	52,183	508,118
Magazines, nonsubscription	624,223	206,841	368,346	79,841	188,601	99,831	44,948	232,079
Books purchased through book clubs	570,750	171,722	348,489	104,868	177,670	66,014	34,584	163,231
Books not purchased through book clubs	3,396,358	1,363,511	1,842,016	366,719	1,008,746	466,631	175,498	1,248,961
Encyclopedia and other reference book sets	50,095	30,787	18,130	688	12,163	5,178	1,165	2,909
EDUCATION	**45,643,128**	**10,187,450**	**32,394,844**	**2,221,373**	**15,889,134**	**14,308,379**	**2,424,961**	**13,146,087**
College tuition	24,645,263	7,511,055	15,369,796	1,123,650	3,981,560	10,264,997	631,596	9,364,296
Elementary and high school tuition	9,707,819	398,403	8,881,733	504,444	7,124,961	1,252,089	653,426	220,120
Other school tuition	1,813,004	314,025	1,310,217	120,317	862,792	326,998	135,640	490,663
Other school expenses including rentals	1,807,938	268,415	1,375,253	94,180	801,670	479,333	254,662	366,866
Books, supplies for college	2,813,787	864,081	1,761,152	140,423	391,674	1,229,276	156,673	1,930,006
Books, supplies for elementary, high school	1,193,284	57,241	1,055,828	13,915	878,958	163,094	195,304	22,303
Books, supplies for day care, nursery school	235,280	32,155	172,086	22,011	121,013	29,124	19,500	50,424
Miscellaneous school expenses and supplies	3,426,753	742,075	2,468,491	202,434	1,726,507	563,469	378,038	701,409
TOBACCO PRODUCTS AND SMOKING SUPPLIES	**19,326,141**	**6,511,968**	**10,307,058**	**1,455,766**	**5,170,593**	**3,682,002**	**1,831,444**	**6,550,579**
Cigarettes	17,546,909	5,901,934	9,273,964	1,240,792	4,647,898	3,385,180	1,791,832	6,031,472
Other tobacco products	1,668,910	568,757	977,555	209,312	492,826	275,626	25,080	434,098
Smoking accessories	110,323	41,505	55,540	5,661	30,022	21,277	14,533	66,262

Note: Total spending figures for total consumer units can be found on Total Spending by Age and Total Spending by Region tables. Spending by type of consumer unit will not add to total because not all types of consumer units are shown.
Source: Calculations by New Strategist based on the 2000 Consumer Expenditure Survey

Table 10.15 Personal Care, Reading, Education, Tobacco: Market shares by household type, 2000

(percentage of total annual spending on personal care, reading, education, and tobacco products accounted for by types of consumer units, 2000)

	total married couples	married couples, no children	married couples with children			single parent, at least one child <18	single person
			total	oldest child under 6	oldest child 6 to 17	oldest child 18 or older	
Share of total consumer units	51.5%	20.9%	26.3%	4.8%	14.1%	7.4%	5.6%	29.6%
Share of total before-tax income	69.8	24.9	39.4	6.8	21.9	10.7	3.2	16.5
Share of total spending	65.8	23.1	37.1	6.5	20.0	10.6	4.3	17.9
PERSONAL CARE PRODUCTS								
AND SERVICES	**64.0%**	**22.6%**	**35.9%**	**5.6%**	**19.3%**	**11.1%**	**5.7%**	**17.7%**
Personal care products	**64.6**	**21.6**	**37.5**	**5.8**	**20.2**	**11.8**	**6.0**	**16.8**
Hair care products	64.0	19.5	38.6	5.5	22.1	11.3	7.0	14.6
Hair accessories	66.1	18.1	36.7	3.7	23.5	9.9	7.5	16.3
Wigs and hairpieces	44.9	15.9	20.9	5.7	10.8	4.4	15.6	19.2
Oral hygiene products	67.8	24.2	38.2	7.1	18.5	12.9	3.5	17.5
Shaving products	60.6	23.6	31.6	5.1	17.2	9.5	3.9	19.2
Cosmetics, perfume, and bath products	64.1	22.0	37.3	6.0	19.6	11.9	6.2	18.2
Deodorants, feminine hygiene, misc. products	62.8	18.5	38.6	5.6	22.1	11.2	6.5	14.4
Electric personal care appliances	77.2	30.2	39.1	4.9	17.8	17.4	3.7	12.4
Personal care services	**63.4**	**23.4**	**34.5**	**5.3**	**18.7**	**10.5**	**5.4**	**18.5**
READING	**63.8**	**28.0**	**31.6**	**5.7**	**16.8**	**9.2**	**2.9**	**22.9**
Newspaper subscriptions	67.1	33.8	29.0	4.1	14.7	10.3	1.8	22.4
Newspaper, nonsubscription	55.4	21.9	29.2	4.5	15.2	9.6	4.6	24.7
Magazine subscriptions	64.7	31.9	28.4	4.5	15.9	8.0	2.5	24.3
Magazines, nonsubscription	60.1	19.9	35.5	7.7	18.2	9.6	4.3	22.3
Books purchased through book clubs	65.0	19.6	39.7	11.9	20.2	7.5	3.9	18.6
Books not purchased through book clubs	62.7	25.2	34.0	6.8	18.6	8.6	3.2	23.1
Encyclopedia and other reference book sets	89.8	55.2	32.5	1.2	21.8	9.3	2.1	5.2
EDUCATION	**66.0**	**14.7**	**46.9**	**3.2**	**23.0**	**20.7**	**3.5**	**19.0**
College tuition	62.0	18.9	38.7	2.8	10.0	25.8	1.6	23.6
Elementary and high school tuition	87.5	3.6	80.1	4.5	64.2	11.3	5.9	2.0
Other school tuition	67.9	11.8	49.1	4.5	32.3	12.2	5.1	18.4
Other school expenses including rentals	68.9	10.2	52.4	3.6	30.5	18.3	9.7	14.0
Books, supplies for college	48.9	15.0	30.6	2.4	6.8	21.3	2.7	33.5
Books, supplies for elementary, high school	78.4	3.8	69.4	0.9	57.7	10.7	12.8	1.5
Books, supplies for day care, nursery school	69.6	9.5	50.9	6.5	35.8	8.6	5.8	14.9
Miscellaneous school expenses and supplies	63.8	13.8	45.9	3.8	32.1	10.5	7.0	13.1
TOBACCO PRODUCTS AND								
SMOKING SUPPLIES	**55.5**	**18.7**	**29.6**	**4.2**	**14.8**	**10.6**	**5.3**	**18.8**
Cigarettes	54.6	18.4	28.9	3.9	14.5	10.5	5.6	18.8
Other tobacco products	67.8	23.1	39.7	8.5	20.0	11.2	1.0	17.6
Smoking accessories	49.7	18.7	25.0	2.5	13.5	9.6	6.5	29.8

Note: Market share for total consumer units is 100.0%. Market shares by type of consumer unit will not add to total because not all types of consumer units are shown.
Source: Calculations by New Strategist based on the 2000 Consumer Expenditure Survey

Table 10.16 Personal Care, Reading, Education, Tobacco: Average spending by race and Hispanic origin, 2000

(average annual spending of consumer units (CU) on personal care, reading, education, and tobacco products, by race and Hispanic origin of consumer unit reference person, 2000)

	total consumer units	race		Hispanic origin	
		black	white and other	Hispanic	non-Hispanic
Number of consumer units (in thousands, add 000)	109,367	13,230	96,137	9,473	99,894
Average number of persons per CU	2.5	2.7	2.5	3.4	2.4
Average before-tax income of CU	$44,649.00	$32,657.00	$46,260.00	$34,891.00	$45,669.00
Average spending of CU, total	38,044.67	28,152.24	39,406.20	32,734.95	38,548.91
PERSONAL CARE PRODUCTS AND SERVICES	$563.62	$627.43	$554.84	$564.29	$563.64
Personal care products	256.30	221.29	261.13	301.58	252.10
Hair care products	51.46	42.61	52.68	77.18	49.07
Hair accessories	6.59	5.01	6.50	7.30	6.52
Wigs and hairpieces	1.17	6.02	0.50	0.21	1.26
Oral hygiene products	25.78	21.05	26.43	34.88	24.93
Shaving products	13.19	7.74	13.94	13.03	13.20
Cosmetics, perfume, and bath products	119.91	107.46	121.63	132.47	118.75
Deodorants, feminine hygiene, misc. products	29.21	28.61	29.30	27.12	29.41
Electric personal care appliances	8.99	2.79	9.84	9.40	8.95
Personal care services	307.31	406.14	293.71	262.70	311.54
READING	146.47	71.98	156.72	58.60	154.80
Newspaper subscriptions	47.43	21.65	50.98	15.78	50.43
Newspaper, nonsubscription	12.26	12.86	12.18	8.63	12.61
Magazine subscriptions	19.10	8.66	20.53	6.30	20.31
Magazines, nonsubscription	9.50	5.47	10.05	4.88	9.93
Books purchased through book clubs	8.03	3.56	8.65	4.20	8.40
Books not purchased through book clubs	49.52	19.69	53.62	18.48	52.46
Encyclopedia and other reference book sets	0.51	0.08	0.56	0.34	0.52
EDUCATION	631.93	382.90	666.20	362.52	657.47
College tuition	363.29	205.88	384.96	147.65	383.74
Elementary and high school tuition	101.42	51.25	108.33	77.09	103.73
Other school tuition	24.42	12.23	26.09	25.35	24.33
Other school expenses including rentals	24.00	18.27	24.79	17.17	24.65
Books, supplies for college	52.66	37.04	54.81	30.16	54.79
Books, supplies for elementary, high school	13.92	13.09	14.03	15.27	13.79
Books, supplies for day care, nursery school	3.09	2.71	3.14	2.82	3.11
Miscellaneous school expenses and supplies	49.13	42.42	50.05	47.01	49.33
TOBACCO PRODUCTS AND SMOKING SUPPLIES	318.62	243.41	328.97	173.26	332.40
Cigarettes	293.90	234.49	302.07	163.11	306.30
Other tobacco products	22.52	7.94	24.53	8.57	23.85
Smoking accessories	2.03	0.99	2.17	1.59	2.07

Note: Other races include Asians, Native Americans, and Pacific Islanders.
Source: Bureau of Labor Statistics, unpublished tables from the 2000 Consumer Expenditure Survey

Table 10.17 Personal Care, Reading, Education, Tobacco: Indexed spending by race and Hispanic origin, 2000

(indexed average annual spending of consumer units (CU) on personal care, reading, education, and tobacco products, by race and Hispanic origin of consumer unit reference person, 2000; index definition: an index of 100 is the average for all consumer units; an index of 132 means that spending by consumer units in that group is 32 percent above the average for all consumer units; an index of 68 indicates spending that is 32 percent below the average for all consumer units)

	total consumer units	race		Hispanic origin	
		black	white and other	Hispanic	non-Hispanic
Average spending of CU, total	$38,045	$28,152	$39,406	$32,735	$38,549
Average spending of CU, index	100	74	104	86	101
PERSONAL CARE PRODUCTS					
AND SERVICES	100	111	98	100	100
Personal care products	100	86	102	118	98
Hair care products	100	83	102	150	95
Hair accessories	100	76	103	111	99
Wigs and hairpieces	100	515	43	18	108
Oral hygiene products	100	82	103	135	97
Shaving products	100	59	106	99	100
Cosmetics, perfume, and bath products	100	90	101	110	99
Deodorants, feminine hygiene, misc. products	100	98	100	93	101
Electric personal care appliances	100	31	109	105	100
Personal care services	100	132	96	85	101
READING	100	49	107	40	106
Newspaper subscriptions	100	46	107	33	106
Newspaper, nonsubscription	100	105	99	70	103
Magazine subscriptions	100	45	107	33	106
Magazines, nonsubscription	100	58	106	51	105
Books purchased through book clubs	100	44	108	52	105
Books not purchased through book clubs	100	40	108	37	106
Encyclopedia and other reference book sets	100	16	110	67	102
EDUCATION	100	61	105	57	104
College tuition	100	57	106	41	106
Elementary and high school tuition	100	51	107	76	102
Other school tuition	100	50	107	104	100
Other school expenses including rentals	100	76	103	72	103
Books, supplies for college	100	70	104	57	104
Books, supplies for elementary, high school	100	94	101	110	99
Books, supplies for day care, nursery school	100	88	102	91	101
Miscellaneous school expenses and supplies	100	86	102	96	100
TOBACCO PRODUCTS AND					
SMOKING SUPPLIES	100	76	103	54	104
Cigarettes	100	80	103	55	104
Other tobacco products	100	35	109	38	106
Smoking accessories	100	49	107	78	102

Note: Other races include Asians, Native Americans, and Pacific Islanders.
Source: Calculations by New Strategist based on the 2000 Consumer Expenditure Survey

Table 10.18 Personal Care, Reading, Education, Tobacco: Indexed per capita spending by race and Hispanic origin, 2000

(indexed average annual per capita spending of consumer units (CU) on personal care, reading, education, and tobacco products, by race and Hispanic origin of consumer unit reference person, 2000; index definition: an index of 100 is the average for all consumer units; an index of 132 means that spending by consumer units in that group is 32 percent above the average for all consumer units; an index of 68 indicates spending that is 32 percent below the average for all consumer units)

	total consumer units	race		Hispanic origin	
		black	white and other	Hispanic	non-Hispanic
Per capita spending of CU, total	$15,218	$10,427	$15,762	$9,628	$16,062
Per capita spending of CU, index	100	69	104	63	106
PERSONAL CARE PRODUCTS					
AND SERVICES	**100**	**103**	**98**	**74**	**104**
Personal care products	**100**	**80**	**102**	**87**	**102**
Hair care products	100	77	102	110	99
Hair accessories	100	70	103	81	103
Wigs and hairpieces	100	476	43	13	112
Oral hygiene products	100	76	103	99	101
Shaving products	100	54	106	73	104
Cosmetics, perfume, and bath products	100	83	101	81	103
Deodorants, feminine hygiene, misc. products	100	91	100	68	105
Electric personal care appliances	100	29	109	77	104
Personal care services	**100**	**122**	**96**	**63**	**106**
READING	**100**	**46**	**107**	**29**	**110**
Newspaper subscriptions	100	42	107	24	111
Newspaper, nonsubscription	100	97	99	52	107
Magazine subscriptions	100	42	107	24	111
Magazines, nonsubscription	100	53	106	38	109
Books purchased through book clubs	100	41	108	38	109
Books not purchased through book clubs	100	37	108	27	110
Encyclopedia and other reference book sets	100	15	110	49	106
EDUCATION	**100**	**56**	**105**	**42**	**108**
College tuition	100	52	106	30	110
Elementary and high school tuition	100	47	107	56	107
Other school tuition	100	46	107	76	104
Other school expenses including rentals	100	70	103	53	107
Books, supplies for college	100	65	104	42	108
Books, supplies for elementary, high school	100	87	101	81	103
Books, supplies for day care, nursery school	100	81	102	67	105
Miscellaneous school expenses and supplies	100	80	102	70	105
TOBACCO PRODUCTS AND					
SMOKING SUPPLIES	**100**	**71**	**103**	**40**	**109**
Cigarettes	100	74	103	41	109
Other tobacco products	100	33	109	28	110
Smoking accessories	100	45	107	58	106

Note: Per capita indexes account for household size and show how much each person in a particular household demographic segment spends relative to a person in the average household. Other races include Asians, Native Americans, and Pacific Islanders.
Source: Calculations by New Strategist based on the 2000 Consumer Expenditure Survey

Table 10.19 Personal Care, Reading, Education, Tobacco: Total spending by race and Hispanic origin, 2000

(total annual spending on personal care, reading, education, and tobacco products, by consumer unit race and Hispanic origin groups, 2000; numbers in thousands)

	total consumer units	race		Hispanic origin	
		black	white and other	Hispanic	non-Hispanic
Number of consumer units	109,367	13,230	96,137	9,473	99,894
Total spending of all consumer units	$4,160,831,424	$372,454,135	$3,788,393,849	$310,098,181	$3,850,804,816
PERSONAL CARE PRODUCTS					
AND SERVICES	**$61,641,429**	**$8,300,899**	**$53,340,653**	**$5,345,519**	**$56,304,254**
Personal care products	**28,030,762**	**2,927,667**	**25,104,255**	**2,856,867**	**25,183,277**
Hair care products	5,628,026	563,730	5,064,497	731,126	4,901,799
Hair accessories	720,729	66,282	654,693	69,153	651,309
Wigs and hairpieces	127,959	79,645	48,069	1,989	125,866
Oral hygiene products	2,819,481	278,492	2,540,901	330,418	2,490,357
Shaving products	1,442,551	102,400	1,340,150	123,433	1,318,601
Cosmetics, perfume, and bath products	13,114,197	1,421,696	11,693,143	1,254,888	11,862,413
Deodorants, feminine hygiene, misc. products	3,194,610	378,510	2,816,814	256,908	2,937,883
Electric personal care appliances	983,209	36,912	945,988	89,046	894,051
Personal care services	**33,609,573**	**5,373,232**	**28,236,398**	**2,488,557**	**31,120,977**
READING	**16,018,984**	**952,295**	**15,066,591**	**555,118**	**15,463,591**
Newspaper subscriptions	5,187,277	286,430	4,901,064	149,484	5,037,654
Newspaper, nonsubscription	1,340,839	170,138	1,170,949	81,752	1,259,663
Magazine subscriptions	2,088,910	114,572	1,973,693	59,680	2,028,847
Magazines, nonsubscription	1,038,987	72,368	966,177	46,228	991,947
Books purchased through book clubs	878,217	47,099	831,585	39,787	839,110
Books not purchased through book clubs	5,415,854	260,499	5,154,866	175,061	5,240,439
Encyclopedia and other reference book sets	55,777	1,058	53,837	3,221	51,945
EDUCATION	**69,112,288**	**5,065,767**	**64,046,469**	**3,434,152**	**65,677,308**
College tuition	39,731,937	2,723,792	37,008,900	1,398,688	38,333,324
Elementary and high school tuition	11,092,001	678,038	10,414,521	730,274	10,362,005
Other school tuition	2,670,742	161,803	2,508,214	240,141	2,430,421
Other school expenses including rentals	2,624,808	241,712	2,383,236	162,651	2,462,387
Books, supplies for college	5,759,266	490,039	5,269,269	285,706	5,473,192
Books, supplies for elementary, high school	1,522,389	173,181	1,348,802	144,653	1,377,538
Books, supplies for day care, nursery school	337,944	35,853	301,870	26,714	310,670
Miscellaneous school expenses and supplies	5,373,201	561,217	4,811,657	445,326	4,927,771
TOBACCO PRODUCTS AND					
SMOKING SUPPLIES	**34,846,514**	**3,220,314**	**31,626,189**	**1,641,292**	**33,204,766**
Cigarettes	32,142,961	3,102,303	29,040,104	1,545,141	30,597,532
Other tobacco products	2,462,945	105,046	2,358,241	81,184	2,382,472
Smoking accessories	222,015	13,098	208,617	15,062	206,781

Note: Other races include Asians, Native Americans, and Pacific Islanders. Numbers may not add to total because of rounding.
Source: Calculations by New Strategist based on the 2000 Consumer Expenditure Survey

Table 10.20 Personal Care, Reading, Education, Tobacco: Market shares by race and Hispanic origin, 2000

(percentage of total annual spending on personal care, reading, education, and tobacco products accounted for by consumer unit race and Hispanic origin groups, 2000)

	total consumer units	race		Hispanic origin	
		black	white and other	Hispanic	non-Hispanic
Share of total consumer units	100.0%	12.1%	87.9%	8.7%	91.3%
Share of total before-tax income	100.0	8.8	91.1	6.8	93.4
Share of total spending	100.0	9.0	91.0	7.5	92.5
PERSONAL CARE PRODUCTS AND SERVICES	**100.0%**	**13.5%**	**86.5%**	**8.7%**	**91.3%**
Personal care products	**100.0**	**10.4**	**89.6**	**10.2**	**89.8**
Hair care products	100.0	10.0	90.0	13.0	87.1
Hair accessories	100.0	9.2	90.8	9.6	90.4
Wigs and hairpieces	100.0	62.2	37.6	1.6	98.4
Oral hygiene products	100.0	9.9	90.1	11.7	88.3
Shaving products	100.0	7.1	92.9	8.6	91.4
Cosmetics, perfume, and bath products	100.0	10.8	89.2	9.6	90.5
Deodorants, feminine hygiene, misc. products	100.0	11.8	88.2	8.0	92.0
Electric personal care appliances	100.0	3.8	96.2	9.1	90.9
Personal care services	**100.0**	**16.0**	**84.0**	**7.4**	**92.6**
READING	**100.0**	**5.9**	**94.1**	**3.5**	**96.5**
Newspaper subscriptions	100.0	5.5	94.5	2.9	97.1
Newspaper, nonsubscription	100.0	12.7	87.3	6.1	93.9
Magazine subscriptions	100.0	5.5	94.5	2.9	97.1
Magazines, nonsubscription	100.0	7.0	93.0	4.4	95.5
Books purchased through book clubs	100.0	5.4	94.7	4.5	95.5
Books not purchased through book clubs	100.0	4.8	95.2	3.2	96.8
Encyclopedia and other reference book sets	100.0	1.9	96.5	5.8	93.1
EDUCATION	**100.0**	**7.3**	**92.7**	**5.0**	**95.0**
College tuition	100.0	6.9	93.1	3.5	96.5
Elementary and high school tuition	100.0	6.1	93.9	6.6	93.4
Other school tuition	100.0	6.1	93.9	9.0	91.0
Other school expenses including rentals	100.0	9.2	90.8	6.2	93.8
Books, supplies for college	100.0	8.5	91.5	5.0	95.0
Books, supplies for elementary, high school	100.0	11.4	88.6	9.5	90.5
Books, supplies for day care, nursery school	100.0	10.6	89.3	7.9	91.9
Miscellaneous school expenses and supplies	100.0	10.4	89.5	8.3	91.7
TOBACCO PRODUCTS AND SMOKING SUPPLIES	**100.0**	**9.2**	**90.8**	**4.7**	**95.3**
Cigarettes	100.0	9.7	90.3	4.8	95.2
Other tobacco products	100.0	4.3	95.7	3.3	96.7
Smoking accessories	100.0	5.9	94.0	6.8	93.1

Note: Other races include Asians, Native Americans, and Pacific Islanders. Numbers may not add to total because of rounding.
Source: Calculations by New Strategist based on the 2000 Consumer Expenditure Survey

Table 10.21 Personal Care, Reading, Education, Tobacco: Average spending by region, 2000

(average annual spending of consumer units (CU) on personal care, reading, education, and tobacco products, by region in which consumer unit lives, 2000)

	total consumer units	Northeast	Midwest	South	West
Number of consumer units					
(in thousands, add 000)	109,367	20,994	25,717	38,245	24,410
Average number of persons per CU	2.5	2.5	2.5	2.5	2.6
Average before-tax income of CU	$44,649.00	$47,439.00	$44,377.00	$41,984.00	$46,670.00
Average spending of CU, total	38,044.67	38,901.91	39,212.70	34,707.07	41,328.19
PERSONAL CARE PRODUCTS					
AND SERVICES	$563.62	$578.23	$544.41	$549.99	$594.31
Personal care products	256.30	235.14	257.77	250.33	283.99
Hair care products	51.46	43.18	52.39	51.23	58.48
Hair accessories	6.59	7.07	6.81	5.53	7.64
Wigs and hairpieces	1.17	0.88	1.35	1.42	0.84
Oral hygiene products	25.78	27.81	23.44	24.35	28.72
Shaving products	13.19	12.42	13.72	12.77	14.01
Cosmetics, perfume, and bath products	119.91	108.09	120.27	119.60	130.96
Deodorants, feminine hygiene, misc. products	29.21	27.83	33.31	26.15	31.11
Electric personal care appliances	8.99	7.86	6.49	9.28	12.23
Personal care services	307.31	343.09	286.64	299.66	310.33
READING	146.47	172.32	163.80	113.54	157.59
Newspaper subscriptions	47.43	60.08	57.41	36.89	42.56
Newspaper, nonsubscription	12.26	21.85	12.78	8.41	9.51
Magazine subscriptions	19.10	20.30	22.84	14.51	21.31
Magazines, nonsubscription	9.50	9.56	11.00	7.87	10.41
Books purchased through book clubs	8.03	7.38	9.04	6.88	9.35
Books not purchased through book clubs	49.52	52.95	50.21	38.86	62.53
Encyclopedia and other reference book sets	0.51	0.21	0.54	0.12	1.33
EDUCATION	631.93	823.25	666.86	476.58	674.18
College tuition	363.29	517.06	410.20	234.05	384.12
Elementary and high school tuition	101.42	140.25	85.20	99.35	88.36
Other school tuition	24.42	26.97	23.15	17.69	34.09
Other school expenses including rentals	24.00	20.28	25.76	19.82	31.89
Books, supplies for college	52.66	53.08	53.86	45.59	62.10
Books, supplies for elementary, high school	13.92	8.99	14.65	17.26	12.17
Books, supplies for day care, nursery school	3.09	2.20	2.58	3.54	3.69
Miscellaneous school expenses and supplies	49.13	54.42	51.46	39.29	57.76
TOBACCO PRODUCTS AND					
SMOKING SUPPLIES	318.62	325.69	359.54	334.08	245.12
Cigarettes	293.90	299.87	339.66	302.94	226.39
Other tobacco products	22.52	22.51	17.99	28.99	17.16
Smoking accessories	2.03	2.48	1.88	2.15	1.57

Source: Bureau of Labor Statistics, unpublished tables from the 2000 Consumer Expenditure Survey

Table 10.22 Personal Care, Reading, Education, Tobacco: Indexed spending by region, 2000

(indexed average annual spending of consumer units (CU) on personal care, reading, education, and tobacco products, by region in which consumer unit lives, 2000; index definition: an index of 100 is the average for all consumer units; an index of 132 means that spending by consumer units in that group is 32 percent above the average for all consumer units; an index of 68 indicates spending that is 32 percent below the average for all consumer units)

	total consumer units	Northeast	Midwest	South	West
Average spending of CU, total	$38,045	$38,902	$39,213	$34,707	$41,328
Average spending of CU, index	100	102	103	91	109
PERSONAL CARE PRODUCTS AND SERVICES	**100**	**103**	**97**	**98**	**105**
Personal care products	**100**	**92**	**101**	**98**	**111**
Hair care products	100	84	102	100	114
Hair accessories	100	107	103	84	116
Wigs and hairpieces	100	75	115	121	72
Oral hygiene products	100	108	91	94	111
Shaving products	100	94	104	97	106
Cosmetics, perfume, and bath products	100	90	100	100	109
Deodorants, feminine hygiene, misc. products	100	95	114	90	107
Electric personal care appliances	100	87	72	103	136
Personal care services	**100**	**112**	**93**	**98**	**101**
READING	**100**	**118**	**112**	**78**	**108**
Newspaper subscriptions	100	127	121	78	90
Newspaper, nonsubscription	100	178	104	69	78
Magazine subscriptions	100	106	120	76	112
Magazines, nonsubscription	100	101	116	83	110
Books purchased through book clubs	100	92	113	86	116
Books not purchased through book clubs	100	107	101	78	126
Encyclopedia and other reference book sets	100	41	106	24	261
EDUCATION	**100**	**130**	**106**	**75**	**107**
College tuition	100	142	113	64	106
Elementary and high school tuition	100	138	84	98	87
Other school tuition	100	110	95	72	140
Other school expenses including rentals	100	85	107	83	133
Books, supplies for college	100	101	102	87	118
Books, supplies for elementary, high school	100	65	105	124	87
Books, supplies for day care, nursery school	100	71	83	115	119
Miscellaneous school expenses and supplies	100	111	105	80	118
TOBACCO PRODUCTS AND SMOKING SUPPLIES	**100**	**102**	**113**	**105**	**77**
Cigarettes	100	102	116	103	77
Other tobacco products	100	100	80	129	76
Smoking accessories	100	122	93	106	77

Source: Calculations by New Strategist based on the 2000 Consumer Expenditure Survey

Table 10.23 Personal Care, Reading, Education, Tobacco: Indexed per capita spending by region, 2000

(indexed average annual per capita spending of consumer units (CU) on personal care, reading, education, and tobacco products, by region in which consumer unit lives, 2000; index definition: an index of 100 is the average for all consumer units; an index of 132 means that spending by consumer units in that group is 32 percent above the average for all consumer units; an index of 68 indicates spending that is 32 percent below the average for all consumer units)

	total consumer units	Northeast	Midwest	South	West
Per capita spending of CU, total	**$15,218**	**$15,561**	**$15,685**	**$13,883**	**$15,895**
Per capita spending of CU, index	**100**	**102**	**103**	**91**	**104**
PERSONAL CARE PRODUCTS AND SERVICES	**100**	**103**	**97**	**98**	**101**
Personal care products	**100**	**92**	**101**	**98**	**107**
Hair care products	100	84	102	100	109
Hair accessories	100	107	103	84	111
Wigs and hairpieces	100	75	115	121	69
Oral hygiene products	100	108	91	94	107
Shaving products	100	94	104	97	102
Cosmetics, perfume, and bath products	100	90	100	100	105
Deodorants, feminine hygiene, misc. products	100	95	114	90	102
Electric personal care appliances	100	87	72	103	131
Personal care services	**100**	**112**	**93**	**98**	**97**
READING	**100**	**118**	**112**	**78**	**103**
Newspaper subscriptions	100	127	121	78	86
Newspaper, nonsubscription	100	178	104	69	75
Magazine subscriptions	100	106	120	76	107
Magazines, nonsubscription	100	101	116	83	105
Books purchased through book clubs	100	92	113	86	112
Books not purchased through book clubs	100	107	101	78	121
Encyclopedia and other reference book sets	100	41	106	24	251
EDUCATION	**100**	**130**	**106**	**75**	**103**
College tuition	100	142	113	64	102
Elementary and high school tuition	100	138	84	98	84
Other school tuition	100	110	95	72	134
Other school expenses including rentals	100	85	107	83	128
Books, supplies for college	100	101	102	87	113
Books, supplies for elementary, high school	100	65	105	124	84
Books, supplies for day care, nursery school	100	71	83	115	115
Miscellaneous school expenses and supplies	100	111	105	80	113
TOBACCO PRODUCTS AND SMOKING SUPPLIES	**100**	**102**	**113**	**105**	**74**
Cigarettes	100	102	116	103	74
Other tobacco products	100	100	80	129	73
Smoking accessories	100	122	93	106	74

Note: Per capita indexes account for household size and show how much each person in a particular household demographic segment spends relative to a person in the average household.
Source: Calculations by New Strategist based on the 2000 Consumer Expenditure Survey

Table 10.24 Personal Care, Reading, Education, Tobacco: Total spending by region, 2000

(total annual spending on personal care, reading, education, and tobacco products, by region in which consumer units live, 2000; numbers in thousands)

	total consumer units	Northeast	Midwest	South	West
Number of consumer units	109,367	20,994	25,717	38,245	24,410
Total spending of all consumer units	$4,160,831,424	$816,706,699	$1,008,433,006	$1,327,371,892	$1,008,821,118
PERSONAL CARE PRODUCTS					
AND SERVICES	**$61,641,429**	**$12,139,361**	**$14,000,592**	**$21,034,368**	**$14,507,107**
Personal care products	**28,030,762**	**4,936,529**	**6,629,071**	**9,573,871**	**6,932,196**
Hair care products	5,628,026	906,521	1,347,314	1,959,291	1,427,497
Hair accessories	720,729	148,428	175,133	211,495	186,492
Wigs and hairpieces	127,959	18,475	34,718	54,308	20,504
Oral hygiene products	2,819,481	583,843	602,806	931,266	701,055
Shaving products	1,442,551	260,745	352,837	488,389	341,984
Cosmetics, perfume, and bath products	13,114,197	2,269,241	3,092,984	4,574,102	3,196,734
Deodorants, feminine hygiene, misc. products	3,194,610	584,263	856,633	1,000,107	759,395
Electric personal care appliances	983,209	165,013	166,903	354,914	298,534
Personal care services	**33,609,573**	**7,202,831**	**7,371,521**	**11,460,497**	**7,575,155**
READING	**16,018,984**	**3,617,686**	**4,212,445**	**4,342,337**	**3,846,772**
Newspaper subscriptions	5,187,277	1,261,320	1,476,413	1,410,858	1,038,890
Newspaper, nonsubscription	1,340,839	458,719	328,663	321,640	232,139
Magazine subscriptions	2,088,910	426,178	587,376	554,935	520,177
Magazines, nonsubscription	1,038,987	200,703	282,887	300,988	254,108
Books purchased through book clubs	878,217	154,936	232,482	263,126	228,234
Books not purchased through book clubs	5,415,854	1,111,632	1,291,251	1,486,201	1,526,357
Encyclopedia and other reference book sets	55,777	4,409	13,887	4,589	32,465
EDUCATION	**69,112,288**	**17,283,311**	**17,149,639**	**18,226,802**	**16,456,734**
College tuition	39,731,937	10,855,158	10,549,113	8,951,242	9,376,369
Elementary and high school tuition	11,092,001	2,944,409	2,191,088	3,799,641	2,156,868
Other school tuition	2,670,742	566,208	595,349	676,554	832,137
Other school expenses including rentals	2,624,808	425,758	662,470	758,016	778,435
Books, supplies for college	5,759,266	1,114,362	1,385,118	1,743,590	1,515,861
Books, supplies for elementary, high school	1,522,389	188,736	376,754	660,109	297,070
Books, supplies for day care, nursery school	337,944	46,187	66,350	135,387	90,073
Miscellaneous school expenses and supplies	5,373,201	1,142,493	1,323,397	1,502,646	1,409,922
TOBACCO PRODUCTS AND					
SMOKING SUPPLIES	**34,846,514**	**6,837,536**	**9,246,290**	**12,776,890**	**5,983,379**
Cigarettes	32,142,961	6,295,471	8,735,036	11,585,940	5,526,180
Other tobacco products	2,462,945	472,575	462,649	1,108,723	418,876
Smoking accessories	222,015	52,065	48,348	82,227	38,324

Note: Numbers may not add to total because of rounding.
Source: Calculations by New Strategist based on the 2000 Consumer Expenditure Survey

Table 10.25 Personal Care, Reading, Education, Tobacco: Market shares by region, 2000

(percentage of total annual spending on personal care, reading, education, and tobacco products accounted for by consumer units by region, 2000)

	total consumer units	Northeast	Midwest	South	West
Share of total consumer units	100.0%	19.2%	23.5%	35.0%	22.3%
Share of total before-tax income	100.0	20.4	23.4	32.9	23.3
Share of total spending	100.0	19.6	24.2	31.9	24.2
PERSONAL CARE PRODUCTS AND SERVICES	100.0%	19.7%	22.7%	34.1%	23.5%
Personal care products	100.0	17.6	23.6	34.2	24.7
Hair care products	100.0	16.1	23.9	34.8	25.4
Hair accessories	100.0	20.6	24.3	29.3	25.9
Wigs and hairpieces	100.0	14.4	27.1	42.4	16.0
Oral hygiene products	100.0	20.7	21.4	33.0	24.9
Shaving products	100.0	18.1	24.5	33.9	23.7
Cosmetics, perfume, and bath products	100.0	17.3	23.6	34.9	24.4
Deodorants, feminine hygiene, misc. products	100.0	18.3	26.8	31.3	23.8
Electric personal care appliances	100.0	16.8	17.0	36.1	30.4
Personal care services	100.0	21.4	21.9	34.1	22.5
READING	100.0	22.6	26.3	27.1	24.0
Newspaper subscriptions	100.0	24.3	28.5	27.2	20.0
Newspaper, nonsubscription	100.0	34.2	24.5	24.0	17.3
Magazine subscriptions	100.0	20.4	28.1	26.6	24.9
Magazines, nonsubscription	100.0	19.3	27.2	29.0	24.5
Books purchased through book clubs	100.0	17.6	26.5	30.0	26.0
Books not purchased through book clubs	100.0	20.5	23.8	27.4	28.2
Encyclopedia and other reference book sets	100.0	7.9	24.9	8.2	58.2
EDUCATION	100.0	25.0	24.8	26.4	23.8
College tuition	100.0	27.3	26.6	22.5	23.6
Elementary and high school tuition	100.0	26.5	19.8	34.3	19.4
Other school tuition	100.0	21.2	22.3	25.3	31.2
Other school expenses including rentals	100.0	16.2	25.2	28.9	29.7
Books, supplies for college	100.0	19.3	24.1	30.3	26.3
Books, supplies for elementary, high school	100.0	12.4	24.7	43.4	19.5
Books, supplies for day care, nursery school	100.0	13.7	19.6	40.1	26.7
Miscellaneous school expenses and supplies	100.0	21.3	24.6	28.0	26.2
TOBACCO PRODUCTS AND SMOKING SUPPLIES	100.0	19.6	26.5	36.7	17.2
Cigarettes	100.0	19.6	27.2	36.0	17.2
Other tobacco products	100.0	19.2	18.8	45.0	17.0
Smoking accessories	100.0	23.5	21.8	37.0	17.3

Note: Numbers may not add to total because of rounding.
Source: Calculations by New Strategist based on the 2000 Consumer Expenditure Survey

11

Spending on Transportation, 2000

Household spending on transportation rose 10 percent between 1990 and 2000, after adjusting for inflation. Spending on new cars and trucks rose 5 percent, while spending on used cars and trucks increased a substantial 42 percent. Spending on gasoline and motor oil fell 6 percent, while spending on vehicle rentals and leasing rose an enormous 120 percent. Transportation is the second largest household expenditure category, consuming 19.5 percent of the average household budget in 2000 as compared to 18.0 percent in 1990.

Householders aged 45 to 54 spend the most on transportation, $8,827 in 2000, or 19 percent more than the average household. These are the most affluent households, which accounts for their above-average spending. Householders aged 55 to 64 spend the most on new cars, however, while those aged 35 to 44 spend the most on used cars. Spending on public transportation peaks in the 45-to-64 age group. Householders aged 55 to 64 spend 70 percent more than average on ship fares, while those aged 65 to 74 spend 71 percent more than average on intercity train fares.

The most affluent households account for 33 percent of the transportation market. They spend 77 percent more than average on transportation and control 48 percent of the new truck market. Affluent households also account for 51 percent of spending on vehicle leases and 44 percent of spending on airline fares. Households with incomes below $40,000 dominate spending on taxi fares.

Married couples with children aged 18 or older at home spend the most on transportation because they are most likely to have two or more cars. In 2000, this household type spent $12,158 on transportation. They spend 76 percent more than average on used cars and trucks. Single-parent households spend 48 percent more than the average household on intracity mass transit fares, while married couples without children at home (most of them empty-nesters) spend the most on ship fares.

Black and Hispanic households spend less than average on transportation, but on some categories their spending is well above average. Hispanics spend 20 percent more than average on used cars, while blacks spend 12 percent more than average on vehicle finance charges. Black and Hispanic households spend about twice the average on intracity mass transit fares, and they are also above-average spenders on taxi fares.

Households in the West spend the most on transportation, $7,943 in 2000. Households in the South spend the most on new trucks, however, a full 25 percent more than average . Households in both the Northeast and West spend significantly more than the average household on public transportation.

Table 11.1 Transportation: Average spending by age, 2000

(average annual spending of consumer units (CU) on transportation, by age of consumer unit reference person, 2000)

	total consumer units	under 25	25 to 34	35 to 44	45 to 54	55 to 64	65 to 74	75+
Number of consumer units								
(in thousands, add 000)	109,367	8,306	18,887	23,983	21,874	14,161	11,538	10,617
Average number of persons per CU	2.5	1.9	2.9	3.3	2.7	2.1	1.9	1.5
Average before-tax income of CU	$44,649.00	$19,744.00	$45,498.00	$56,500.00	$58,889.00	$48,108.00	$29,349.00	$20,563.00
Average spending of CU, total	38,044.67	22,543.18	38,945.27	45,149.37	46,160.28	39,340.03	30,781.81	21,908.04
Transportation, average spending	7,417.36	5,189.09	8,357.23	8,702.16	8,827.21	7,841.84	5,797.01	2,875.31
VEHICLE PURCHASES	$3,418.27	$2,628.43	$4,139.47	$3,996.48	$3,862.71	$3,622.75	$2,630.83	$1,114.42
Cars and trucks, new	1,604.95	1,061.18	1,845.33	1,724.45	1,689.76	2,096.98	1,447.46	673.01
New cars	917.02	666.89	988.97	900.60	1,023.03	1,091.13	969.45	514.17
New trucks	687.94	394.29	856.36	823.85	666.73	1,005.85	478.01	158.84
Cars and trucks, used	1,769.85	1,546.99	2,216.69	2,198.26	2,128.17	1,507.52	1,173.38	441.41
Used cars	1,011.25	962.06	1,151.47	1,287.01	1,242.96	863.15	652.04	287.87
Used trucks	758.60	584.93	1,065.22	911.26	885.20	644.38	521.34	153.53
Other vehicles	43.46	20.26	77.44	73.77	44.79	18.25	10.00	–
New motorcycles	18.45	–	16.59	38.17	28.16	12.23	–	–
Used motorcycles	17.38	20.26	25.55	35.60	16.63	0.17	2.65	–
GASOLINE AND MOTOR OIL	1,291.25	947.12	1,340.79	1,577.30	1,592.09	1,348.88	958.38	491.22
Gasoline	1,175.50	851.72	1,237.38	1,447.57	1,451.02	1,209.39	843.30	452.33
Diesel fuel	12.98	4.43	13.80	18.89	15.07	13.40	9.74	3.49
Gasoline on trips	91.79	82.41	78.01	96.71	112.76	114.02	98.21	32.69
Motor oil	10.05	7.74	10.82	13.15	12.10	10.91	6.13	2.38
Motor oil on trips	0.93	0.83	0.79	0.98	1.14	1.15	0.99	0.33
OTHER VEHICLE EXPENSES	2,281.28	1,397.06	2,482.02	2,677.32	2,867.53	2,375.18	1,765.74	947.36
Vehicle finance charges	328.24	227.77	436.50	405.58	390.70	348.50	181.65	43.12
Automobile finance charges	169.25	137.38	220.71	192.81	206.82	187.20	96.85	26.73
Truck finance charges	138.62	81.27	197.10	191.86	160.87	132.10	57.28	10.43
Motorcycle and plane finance charges	1.58	0.45	2.10	2.46	2.09	1.37	0.16	0.29
Other vehicle finance charges	18.79	8.66	16.59	18.45	20.92	27.83	27.36	5.67
Maintenance and repairs	623.76	442.06	569.67	707.62	801.03	671.98	557.89	313.65
Coolant, additives, brake and transmission fluids	4.47	3.26	6.69	5.49	5.03	3.57	2.74	1.06
Tires	87.23	55.43	86.50	103.74	117.54	84.16	69.60	36.88
Parts, equipment, and accessories	48.46	39.84	53.34	56.93	58.55	54.14	37.53	10.95
Vehicle audio equipment	2.41	0.17	2.69	7.64	–	1.44	–	–
Vehicle products	4.10	1.74	8.38	3.15	4.31	2.25	3.13	3.69
Miscellaneous auto repair, servicing	26.74	19.11	23.46	29.88	29.28	43.41	17.84	12.93
Body work and painting	26.35	24.03	22.24	25.39	37.18	26.87	28.29	12.51
Clutch, transmission repair	42.61	37.10	42.00	42.95	64.70	38.23	40.03	10.33
Drive shaft and rear-end repair	3.66	2.17	5.36	2.84	3.67	5.09	2.35	3.10
Brake work	54.04	38.79	48.24	60.95	72.12	63.01	39.17	27.69
Repair to steering or front-end	18.02	11.40	15.73	22.35	22.95	17.35	16.88	9.45
Repair to engine cooling system	20.55	13.15	17.11	22.81	25.98	27.78	15.74	11.78
Motor tune-up	44.41	27.79	38.24	50.81	60.25	43.66	41.06	25.93
Lube, oil change, and oil filters	58.75	36.16	57.49	65.88	72.20	64.76	53.85	32.18
Front-end alignment, wheel balance, rotation	10.79	7.94	8.22	13.92	13.19	10.75	10.96	5.42
Shock absorber replacement	4.25	2.21	3.60	5.03	5.57	4.93	3.50	2.39
Gas tank repair, replacement	3.55	0.42	1.68	4.32	3.70	1.78	9.87	3.03
Tire repair and other repair work	29.75	17.66	26.35	37.72	29.94	35.91	32.35	15.82
Vehicle air conditioning repair	19.80	11.99	11.68	22.24	24.37	20.89	27.20	15.91
Exhaust system repair	13.34	9.67	12.19	13.41	16.10	15.50	12.17	10.78
Electrical system repair	30.31	23.22	23.97	34.96	37.97	29.17	32.18	20.39
Motor repair, replacement	64.46	52.51	53.30	67.59	87.45	70.47	56.57	39.82
Auto repair service policy	5.71	6.30	1.20	7.62	8.97	6.85	4.86	1.64

	total consumer units	under 25	25 to 34	35 to 44	45 to 54	55 to 64	65 to 74	75+
Vehicle insurance	$778.13	$449.10	$774.38	$884.32	$1,002.00	$795.84	$673.28	$431.48
Vehicle rental, leases, licenses, other charges	551.15	278.14	701.47	679.80	673.80	558.85	352.92	159.12
Leased and rented vehicles	392.88	186.58	537.30	498.68	477.28	395.05	212.66	77.46
Rented vehicles	44.95	15.49	46.81	57.87	48.97	51.77	43.80	19.38
Auto rental	7.21	4.34	8.75	7.90	6.34	8.35	6.19	6.54
Auto rental on trips	29.62	7.85	25.26	39.27	35.26	35.94	30.03	12.10
Truck rental	3.21	2.06	6.43	4.54	1.56	4.58	0.07	0.40
Truck rental on trips	4.71	1.07	5.70	6.09	5.70	2.67	7.51	0.34
Leased vehicles	347.93	171.09	490.49	440.80	428.31	343.28	168.86	58.08
Car lease payments	174.84	80.58	216.98	195.20	215.86	203.83	142.12	39.96
Cash down payment (car lease)	13.99	40.04	8.49	13.47	23.94	5.32	6.04	4.32
Termination fee (car lease)	1.81	1.19	4.32	3.19	0.28	–	1.26	0.91
Truck lease payments	148.45	43.42	250.74	217.00	176.92	123.22	15.88	12.90
Cash down payment (truck lease)	7.72	5.86	6.80	10.27	10.81	10.16	3.56	–
Termination fee (truck lease)	1.11	–	3.15	1.67	0.50	0.75	–	–
State and local registration	85.19	39.17	89.90	95.02	106.22	89.01	80.88	46.94
Driver's license	6.85	5.10	7.48	7.15	7.92	8.23	5.30	4.11
Vehicle inspection	9.41	3.96	9.43	10.55	11.58	9.77	9.17	6.44
Parking fees	29.38	29.86	32.67	36.95	33.55	26.25	22.33	9.31
Parking fees in home city, excluding residence	25.33	27.85	28.54	32.37	28.66	22.11	19.35	5.70
Parking fees on trips	4.05	2.01	4.13	4.58	4.88	4.14	2.98	3.62
Tolls	10.90	1.93	13.37	14.67	15.99	10.26	4.23	2.51
Tolls on trips	3.51	2.01	3.29	3.84	4.61	4.21	3.26	1.37
Towing charges	4.68	8.25	4.01	5.95	5.55	3.78	3.00	1.42
Automobile service clubs	8.35	1.27	4.03	7.00	11.11	12.30	12.10	9.57
PUBLIC TRANSPORTATION	426.56	216.49	394.95	451.06	504.88	495.03	442.06	322.31
Airline fares	274.02	113.13	248.18	293.22	334.94	318.86	280.82	209.82
Intercity bus fares	16.10	13.72	8.62	15.72	17.83	19.70	19.58	19.94
Intracity mass transit fares	47.41	40.46	64.02	57.71	61.29	34.08	24.45	14.12
Local transportation on trips	10.66	4.22	8.03	9.80	13.15	14.19	13.05	9.92
Taxi fares and limousine service on trips	6.26	2.48	4.71	5.75	7.72	8.33	7.66	5.83
Taxi fares and limousine service	12.15	15.38	20.90	8.21	14.29	10.74	2.95	10.41
Intercity train fares	21.12	15.29	11.76	23.20	20.32	26.45	36.06	15.97
Ship fares	36.58	10.51	26.70	34.57	30.80	62.12	55.57	36.30
School bus	2.26	1.28	2.03	2.87	4.54	0.55	1.92	–

Note: (–) means sample is too small to make a reliable estimate.
Source: Bureau of Labor Statistics, unpublished tables from the 2000 Consumer Expenditure Survey

Table 11.2 Transportation: Indexed spending by age, 2000

(indexed average annual spending of consumer units (CU) on transportation, by age of consumer unit reference person, 2000; index definition: an index of 100 is the average for all consumer units; an index of 132 means that spending by consumer units in that group is 32 percent above the average for all consumer units; an index of 68 indicates spending that is 32 percent below the average for all consumer units)

	total consumer units	under 25	25 to 34	35 to 44	45 to 54	55 to 64	65 to 74	75+
Average spending of CU, total	$38,045	$22,543	$38,945	$45,149	$46,160	$39,340	$30,782	$21,908
Average spending of CU, index	100	59	102	119	121	103	81	58
Transportation, spending index	100	70	113	117	119	106	78	39
VEHICLE PURCHASES	100	77	121	117	113	106	77	33
Cars and trucks, new	100	66	115	107	105	131	90	42
New cars	100	73	108	98	112	119	106	56
New trucks	100	57	124	120	97	146	69	23
Cars and trucks, used	100	87	125	124	120	85	66	25
Used cars	100	95	114	127	123	85	64	28
Used trucks	100	77	140	120	117	85	69	20
Other vehicles	100	47	178	170	103	42	23	–
New motorcycles	100	–	90	207	153	66	–	–
Used motorcycles	100	117	147	205	96	1	15	–
GASOLINE AND MOTOR OIL	100	73	104	122	123	104	74	38
Gasoline	100	72	105	123	123	103	72	38
Diesel fuel	100	34	106	146	116	103	75	27
Gasoline on trips	100	90	85	105	123	124	107	36
Motor oil	100	77	108	131	120	109	61	24
Motor oil on trips	100	89	85	105	123	124	106	35
OTHER VEHICLE EXPENSES	100	61	109	117	126	104	77	42
Vehicle finance charges	100	69	133	124	119	106	55	13
Automobile finance charges	100	81	130	114	122	111	57	16
Truck finance charges	100	59	142	138	116	95	41	8
Motorcycle and plane finance charges	100	28	133	156	132	87	10	18
Other vehicle finance charges	100	46	88	98	111	148	146	30
Maintenance and repairs	100	71	91	113	128	108	89	50
Coolant, additives, brake and transmission fluids	100	73	150	123	113	80	61	24
Tires	100	64	99	119	135	96	80	42
Parts, equipment, and accessories	100	82	110	117	121	112	77	23
Vehicle audio equipment	100	7	112	317	–	60	–	–
Vehicle products	100	42	204	77	105	55	76	90
Miscellaneous auto repair, servicing	100	71	88	112	109	162	67	48
Body work and painting	100	91	84	96	141	102	107	47
Clutch, transmission repair	100	87	99	101	152	90	94	24
Drive shaft and rear-end repair	100	59	146	78	100	139	64	85
Brake work	100	72	89	113	133	117	72	51
Repair to steering or front-end	100	63	87	124	127	96	94	52
Repair to engine cooling system	100	64	83	111	126	135	77	57
Motor tune-up	100	63	86	114	136	98	92	58
Lube, oil change, and oil filters	100	62	98	112	123	110	92	55
Front-end alignment, wheel balance, rotation	100	74	76	129	122	100	102	50
Shock absorber replacement	100	52	85	118	131	116	82	56
Gas tank repair, replacement	100	12	47	122	104	50	278	85
Tire repair and other repair work	100	59	89	127	101	121	109	53
Vehicle air conditioning repair	100	61	59	112	123	106	137	80
Exhaust system repair	100	72	91	101	121	116	91	81
Electrical system repair	100	77	79	115	125	96	106	67
Motor repair, replacement	100	81	83	105	136	109	88	62
Auto repair service policy	100	110	21	133	157	120	85	29

	total consumer units	under 25	25 to 34	35 to 44	45 to 54	55 to 64	65 to 74	75+
Vehicle insurance	**100**	**58**	**100**	**114**	**129**	**102**	**87**	**55**
Vehicle rental, leases, licenses, other charges	**100**	**50**	**127**	**123**	**122**	**101**	**64**	**29**
Leased and rented vehicles	100	47	137	127	121	101	54	20
Rented vehicles	100	34	104	129	109	115	97	43
Auto rental	100	60	121	110	88	116	86	91
Auto rental on trips	100	27	85	133	119	121	101	41
Truck rental	100	64	200	141	49	143	2	12
Truck rental on trips	100	23	121	129	121	57	159	7
Leased vehicles	100	49	141	127	123	99	49	17
Car lease payments	100	46	124	112	123	117	81	23
Cash down payment (car lease)	100	286	61	96	171	38	43	31
Termination fee (car lease)	100	66	239	176	15	–	70	50
Truck lease payments	100	29	169	146	119	83	11	9
Cash down payment (truck lease)	100	76	88	133	140	132	46	–
Termination fee (truck lease)	100	–	284	150	45	68	–	–
State and local registration	100	46	106	112	125	104	95	55
Driver's license	100	74	109	104	116	120	77	60
Vehicle inspection	100	42	100	112	123	104	97	68
Parking fees	100	102	111	126	114	89	76	32
Parking fees in home city, excluding residence	100	110	113	128	113	87	76	23
Parking fees on trips	100	50	102	113	120	102	74	89
Tolls	100	18	123	135	147	94	39	23
Tolls on trips	100	57	94	109	131	120	93	39
Towing charges	100	176	86	127	119	81	64	30
Automobile service clubs	100	15	48	84	133	147	145	115
PUBLIC TRANSPORTATION	**100**	**51**	**93**	**106**	**118**	**116**	**104**	**76**
Airline fares	100	41	91	107	122	116	102	77
Intercity bus fares	100	85	54	98	111	122	122	124
Intracity mass transit fares	100	85	135	122	129	72	52	30
Local transportation on trips	100	40	75	92	123	133	122	93
Taxi fares and limousine service on trips	100	40	75	92	123	133	122	93
Taxi fares and limousine service	100	127	172	68	118	88	24	86
Intercity train fares	100	72	56	110	96	125	171	76
Ship fares	100	29	73	95	84	170	152	99
School bus	100	57	90	127	201	24	85	–

Note: (–) means sample is too small to make a reliable estimate.
Source: Calculations by New Strategist based on the 2000 Consumer Expenditure Survey

Table 11.3 Transportation: Indexed per capita spending by age, 2000

(indexed average annual per capita spending of consumer units (CU) on transportation, by age of consumer unit reference person, 2000; index definition: an index of 100 is the average for all consumer units; an index of 132 means that spending by consumer units in that group is 32 percent above the average for all consumer units; an index of 68 indicates spending that is 32 percent below the average for all consumer units)

	total consumer units	under 25	25 to 34	35 to 44	45 to 54	55 to 64	65 to 74	75+
Per capita spending of CU, total	$15,218	$11,865	$13,429	$13,682	$17,096	$18,733	$16,201	$14,605
Per capita spending of CU, index	100	78	88	90	112	123	106	96
Transportation, per capita spending index	100	92	97	89	110	126	103	65
VEHICLE PURCHASES	100	101	104	89	105	126	101	54
Cars and trucks, new	100	87	99	81	97	156	119	70
New cars	100	96	93	74	103	142	139	93
New trucks	100	75	107	91	90	174	91	38
Cars and trucks, used	100	115	108	94	111	101	87	42
Used cars	100	125	98	96	114	102	85	47
Used trucks	100	101	121	91	108	101	90	34
Other vehicles	100	61	154	129	95	50	30	–
New motorcycles	100	–	78	157	141	79	–	–
Used motorcycles	100	153	127	155	89	1	20	–
GASOLINE AND MOTOR OIL	100	97	90	93	114	124	98	63
Gasoline	100	95	91	93	114	122	94	64
Diesel fuel	100	45	92	110	108	123	99	45
Gasoline on trips	100	118	73	80	114	148	141	59
Motor oil	100	101	93	99	111	129	80	39
Motor oil on trips	100	117	73	80	114	147	140	59
OTHER VEHICLE EXPENSES	100	81	94	89	116	124	102	69
Vehicle finance charges	100	91	115	94	110	126	73	22
Automobile finance charges	100	107	112	86	113	132	75	26
Truck finance charges	100	77	123	105	107	113	54	13
Motorcycle and plane finance charges	100	37	115	118	122	103	13	31
Other vehicle finance charges	100	61	76	74	103	176	192	50
Maintenance and repairs	100	93	79	86	119	128	118	84
Coolant, additives, brake and transmission fluids	100	96	129	93	104	95	81	40
Tires	100	84	85	90	125	115	105	70
Parts, equipment, and accessories	100	108	95	89	112	133	102	38
Vehicle audio equipment	100	9	96	240	–	71	–	–
Vehicle products	100	56	176	58	97	65	100	150
Miscellaneous auto repair, servicing	100	94	76	85	101	193	88	81
Body work and painting	100	120	73	73	131	121	141	79
Clutch, transmission repair	100	115	85	76	141	107	124	40
Drive shaft and rear-end repair	100	78	126	59	93	166	84	141
Brake work	100	94	77	85	124	139	95	85
Repair to steering or front-end	100	83	75	94	118	115	123	87
Repair to engine cooling system	100	84	72	84	117	161	101	96
Motor tune-up	100	82	74	87	126	117	122	97
Lube, oil change, and oil filters	100	81	84	85	114	131	121	91
Front-end alignment, wheel balance, rotation	100	97	66	98	113	119	134	84
Shock absorber replacement	100	68	73	90	121	138	108	94
Gas tank repair, replacement	100	16	41	92	97	60	366	142
Tire repair and other repair work	100	78	76	96	93	144	143	89
Vehicle air conditioning repair	100	80	51	85	114	126	181	134
Exhaust system repair	100	95	79	76	112	138	120	135
Electrical system repair	100	101	68	87	116	115	140	112
Motor repair, replacement	100	107	71	79	126	130	115	103
Auto repair service policy	100	145	18	101	145	143	112	48

	total consumer units	under 25	25 to 34	35 to 44	45 to 54	55 to 64	65 to 74	75+
Vehicle insurance	**100**	**76**	**86**	**86**	**119**	**122**	**114**	**92**
Vehicle rental, leases, licenses, other charges	**100**	**66**	**110**	**93**	**113**	**121**	**84**	**48**
Leased and rented vehicles	100	62	118	96	112	120	71	33
Rented vehicles	100	45	90	98	101	137	128	72
Auto rental	100	79	105	83	81	138	113	151
Auto rental on trips	100	35	74	100	110	144	133	68
Truck rental	100	84	173	107	45	170	3	21
Truck rental on trips	100	30	104	98	112	67	210	12
Leased vehicles	100	65	122	96	114	117	64	28
Car lease payments	100	61	107	85	114	139	107	38
Cash down payment (car lease)	100	377	52	73	158	45	57	51
Termination fee (car lease)	100	87	206	134	14	–	92	84
Truck lease payments	100	38	146	111	110	99	14	14
Cash down payment (truck lease)	100	100	76	101	130	157	61	–
Termination fee (truck lease)	100	–	245	114	42	80	–	–
State and local registration	100	60	91	84	115	124	125	92
Driver's license	100	98	94	79	107	143	102	100
Vehicle inspection	100	55	86	85	114	124	128	114
Parking fees	100	134	96	95	106	106	100	53
Parking fees in home city, excluding residence	100	145	97	97	105	104	101	38
Parking fees on trips	100	65	88	86	112	122	97	149
Tolls	100	23	106	102	136	112	51	38
Tolls on trips	100	75	81	83	122	143	122	65
Towing charges	100	232	74	96	110	96	84	51
Automobile service clubs	100	20	42	64	123	175	191	191
PUBLIC TRANSPORTATION	**100**	**67**	**80**	**80**	**110**	**138**	**136**	**126**
Airline fares	100	54	78	81	113	139	135	128
Intercity bus fares	100	112	46	74	103	146	160	206
Intracity mass transit fares	100	112	116	92	120	86	68	50
Local transportation on trips	100	52	65	70	114	158	161	155
Taxi fares and limousine service on trips	100	52	65	70	114	158	161	155
Taxi fares and limousine service	100	167	148	51	109	105	32	143
Intercity train fares	100	95	48	83	89	149	225	126
Ship fares	100	38	63	72	78	202	200	165
School bus	100	75	77	96	186	29	112	–

Note: Per capita indexes account for household size and show how much each person in a particular household demographic segment spends relative to a person in the average household. (–) means sample is too small to make a reliable estimate.
Source: Calculations by New Strategist based on the 2000 Consumer Expenditure Survey

Table 11.4 Transportation: Total spending by age, 2000

(total annual spending on transportation, by consumer unit (CU) age group, 2000; numbers in thousands)

	total consumer units	under 25	25 to 34	35 to 44	45 to 54	55 to 64	65 to 74	75+
Number of consumer units	109,367	8,306	18,887	23,983	21,874	14,161	11,538	10,617
Total spending of all CUs	$4,160,831,424	$187,243,653	$735,559,314	$1,082,817,341	$1,009,709,965	$557,094,165	$355,160,524	$232,597,661
Transportation, total spending	811,214,411	43,100,582	157,843,003	208,703,903	193,086,392	111,048,296	66,885,901	30,527,166
VEHICLE PURCHASES	**$373,845,935**	**$21,831,740**	**$78,182,170**	**$95,847,580**	**$84,492,919**	**$51,301,763**	**$30,354,517**	**$11,831,797**
Cars and trucks, new	**175,528,567**	**8,814,161**	**34,852,748**	**41,357,484**	**36,961,810**	**29,695,334**	**16,700,793**	**7,145,347**
New cars	100,291,726	5,539,188	18,678,676	21,599,090	22,377,758	15,451,492	11,185,514	5,458,943
New trucks	75,237,934	3,274,973	16,174,071	19,758,395	14,584,052	14,243,842	5,515,279	1,686,404
Cars and trucks, used	**193,563,185**	**12,849,299**	**41,866,624**	**52,720,870**	**46,551,591**	**21,347,991**	**13,538,458**	**4,686,450**
Used cars	110,597,379	7,990,870	21,747,814	30,866,361	27,188,507	12,223,067	7,523,238	3,056,316
Used trucks	82,965,806	4,858,429	20,118,810	21,854,749	19,362,865	9,125,065	6,015,221	1,630,028
Other vehicles	**4,753,090**	**168,280**	**1,462,609**	**1,769,226**	**979,736**	**258,438**	**115,380**	**–**
New motorcycles	2,017,821	–	313,335	915,431	615,972	173,189	–	–
Used motorcycles	1,900,798	168,280	482,563	853,795	363,765	2,407	30,576	–
GASOLINE AND MOTOR OIL	**141,220,139**	**7,866,779**	**25,323,501**	**37,828,386**	**34,825,377**	**19,101,490**	**11,057,788**	**5,215,283**
Gasoline	128,560,909	7,074,386	23,370,396	34,717,071	31,739,611	17,126,172	9,729,995	4,802,388
Diesel fuel	1,419,584	36,796	260,641	453,039	329,641	189,757	112,380	37,053
Gasoline on trips	10,038,797	684,497	1,473,375	2,319,396	2,466,512	1,614,637	1,133,147	347,070
Motor oil	1,099,138	64,288	204,357	315,376	264,675	154,497	70,728	25,268
Motor oil on trips	101,711	6,894	14,921	23,503	24,936	16,285	11,423	3,504
OTHER VEHICLE EXPENSES	**249,496,750**	**11,603,980**	**46,877,912**	**64,210,166**	**62,724,351**	**33,634,924**	**20,373,108**	**10,058,121**
Vehicle finance charges	**35,898,624**	**1,891,858**	**8,244,176**	**9,727,025**	**8,546,172**	**4,935,109**	**2,095,878**	**457,805**
Automobile finance charges	18,510,365	1,141,078	4,168,550	4,624,162	4,523,981	2,650,939	1,117,455	283,792
Truck finance charges	15,160,454	675,029	3,722,628	4,601,378	3,518,870	1,870,668	660,897	110,735
Motorcycle and plane finance charges	172,800	3,738	39,663	58,998	45,717	19,401	1,846	3,079
Other vehicle finance charges	2,055,006	71,930	313,335	442,486	457,604	394,101	315,680	60,198
Maintenance and repairs	**68,218,760**	**3,671,750**	**10,759,357**	**16,970,850**	**17,521,730**	**9,515,909**	**6,436,935**	**3,330,022**
Coolant, additives, brake, transmission fluids	488,870	27,078	126,354	131,667	110,026	50,555	31,614	11,254
Tires	9,540,083	460,402	1,633,726	2,487,996	2,571,070	1,191,790	803,045	391,555
Parts, equipment, and accessories	5,299,925	330,911	1,007,433	1,365,352	1,280,723	766,677	433,021	116,256
Vehicle audio equipment	263,574	1,412	50,806	183,230	–	20,392	–	–
Vehicle products	448,405	14,452	158,273	75,546	94,277	31,862	36,114	39,177
Miscellaneous auto repair, servicing	2,924,474	158,728	443,089	716,612	640,471	614,729	205,838	137,278
Body work and painting	2,881,820	199,593	420,047	608,928	813,275	380,506	326,410	132,819
Clutch, transmission repair	4,660,128	308,153	793,254	1,030,070	1,415,248	541,375	461,866	109,674
Drive shaft and rear-end repair	400,283	18,024	101,234	68,112	80,278	72,079	27,114	32,913
Brake work	5,910,193	322,190	911,109	1,461,764	1,577,553	892,285	451,943	293,985
Repair to steering or front-end	1,970,793	94,688	297,093	536,020	502,008	245,693	194,761	100,331
Repair to engine cooling system	2,247,492	109,224	323,157	547,052	568,287	393,393	181,608	125,068
Motor tune-up	4,856,988	230,824	722,239	1,218,576	1,317,909	618,269	473,750	275,299
Lube, oil change, and oil filters	6,425,311	300,345	1,085,814	1,580,000	1,579,303	917,066	621,321	341,655
Front-end alignment, wheel balance, rotation	1,180,070	65,950	155,251	333,843	288,518	152,231	126,456	57,544
Shock absorber replacement	464,810	18,356	67,993	120,634	121,838	69,814	40,383	25,375
Gas tank repair, replacement	388,253	3,489	31,730	103,607	80,934	25,207	113,880	32,170
Tire repair and other repair work	3,253,668	146,684	497,672	904,639	654,908	508,522	373,254	167,961
Vehicle air conditioning repair	2,165,467	99,589	220,600	533,382	533,069	295,823	313,834	168,916
Exhaust system repair	1,458,956	80,319	230,233	321,612	352,171	219,496	140,417	114,451
Electrical system repair	3,314,914	192,865	452,721	838,446	830,556	413,076	371,293	216,481
Motor repair, replacement	7,049,797	436,148	1,006,677	1,621,011	1,912,881	997,926	652,705	422,769
Auto repair service policy	624,486	52,328	22,664	182,750	196,210	97,003	56,075	17,412

	total consumer units	under 25	25 to 34	35 to 44	45 to 54	55 to 64	65 to 74	75+
Vehicle insurance	$85,101,744	$3,730,225	$14,625,715	$21,208,647	$21,917,748	$11,269,890	$7,768,305	$4,581,023
Vehicle rental, leases, licenses, other charges	**60,277,622**	**2,310,231**	**13,248,664**	**16,303,643**	**14,738,701**	**7,913,875**	**4,071,991**	**1,689,377**
Leased and rented vehicles	42,968,107	1,549,733	10,147,985	11,959,842	10,440,023	5,594,303	2,453,671	822,393
Rented vehicles	4,916,047	128,660	884,100	1,387,896	1,071,170	733,115	505,364	205,757
Auto rental	788,536	36,048	165,261	189,466	138,681	118,244	71,420	69,435
Auto rental on trips	3,239,451	65,202	477,086	941,812	771,277	508,946	346,486	128,466
Truck rental	351,068	17,110	121,443	108,883	34,123	64,857	808	4,247
Truck rental on trips	515,119	8,887	107,656	146,056	124,682	37,810	86,650	3,610
Leased vehicles	38,052,060	1,421,074	9,263,885	10,571,706	9,368,853	4,861,188	1,948,307	616,635
Car lease payments	19,121,726	669,297	4,098,101	4,681,482	4,721,722	2,886,437	1,639,781	424,255
Cash down payment (car lease)	1,530,044	332,572	160,351	323,051	523,664	75,337	69,690	45,865
Termination fee (car lease)	197,954	9,884	81,592	76,506	6,125	–	14,538	9,661
Truck lease payments	16,235,531	360,647	4,735,726	5,204,311	3,869,948	1,744,918	183,223	136,959
Cash down payment (truck lease)	844,313	48,673	128,432	246,305	236,458	143,876	41,075	–
Termination fee (truck lease)	121,397	–	59,494	40,052	10,937	10,621	–	–
State and local registration	9,316,975	325,346	1,697,941	2,278,865	2,323,456	1,260,471	933,193	498,362
Driver's license	749,164	42,361	141,275	171,478	173,242	116,545	61,151	43,636
Vehicle inspection	1,029,143	32,892	178,104	253,021	253,301	138,353	105,803	68,373
Parking fees	3,213,202	248,017	617,038	886,172	733,873	371,726	257,644	98,844
Parking fees in home city, excl. residence	2,770,266	231,322	539,035	776,330	626,909	313,100	223,260	60,517
Parking fees on trips	442,936	16,695	78,003	109,842	106,745	58,627	34,383	38,434
Tolls	1,192,100	16,031	252,519	351,831	349,765	145,292	48,806	26,649
Tolls on trips	383,878	16,695	62,138	92,095	100,839	59,618	37,614	14,545
Towing charges	511,838	68,525	75,737	142,699	121,401	53,529	34,614	15,076
Automobile service clubs	913,214	10,549	76,115	167,881	243,020	174,180	139,610	101,605
PUBLIC TRANSPORTATION	**46,651,588**	**1,798,166**	**7,459,421**	**10,817,772**	**11,043,745**	**7,010,120**	**5,100,488**	**3,421,965**
Airline fares	29,968,745	939,658	4,687,376	7,032,295	7,326,478	4,515,376	3,240,101	2,227,659
Intercity bus fares	1,760,809	113,958	162,806	377,013	390,013	278,972	225,914	211,703
Intracity mass transit fares	5,185,089	336,061	1,209,146	1,384,059	1,340,657	482,607	282,104	149,912
Local transportation on trips	1,165,852	35,051	151,663	235,033	287,643	200,945	150,571	105,321
Taxi fares and limousine service on trips	684,637	20,599	88,958	137,902	168,867	117,961	88,381	61,897
Taxi fares and limousine service	1,328,809	127,746	394,738	196,900	312,579	152,089	34,037	110,523
Intercity train fares	2,309,831	126,999	222,111	556,406	444,480	374,558	416,060	169,553
Ship fares	4,000,645	87,296	504,283	829,092	673,719	879,681	641,167	385,397
School bus	247,169	10,632	38,341	68,831	99,308	7,789	22,153	–

Note: Numbers may not add to total because of rounding. (–) means sample is too small to make a reliable estimate.
Source: Calculations by New Strategist based on the 2000 Consumer Expenditure Survey

Table 11.5 Transportation: Market shares by age, 2000

(percentage of total annual spending on transportation accounted for by consumer unit age groups, 2000)

	total consumer units	under 25	25 to 34	35 to 44	45 to 54	55 to 64	65 to 74	75+
Share of total consumer units	100.0%	7.6%	17.3%	21.9%	20.0%	12.9%	10.5%	9.7%
Share of total before-tax income	100.0	3.4	17.6	27.7	26.4	14.0	6.9	4.5
Share of total spending	100.0	4.5	17.7	26.0	24.3	13.4	8.5	5.6
Share of transportation spending	100.0	5.3	19.5	25.7	23.8	13.7	8.2	3.8
VEHICLE PURCHASES	**100.0%**	**5.8%**	**20.9%**	**25.6%**	**22.6%**	**13.7%**	**8.1%**	**3.2%**
Cars and trucks, new	**100.0**	**5.0**	**19.9**	**23.6**	**21.1**	**16.9**	**9.5**	**4.1**
New cars	100.0	5.5	18.6	21.5	22.3	15.4	11.2	5.4
New trucks	100.0	4.4	21.5	26.3	19.4	18.9	7.3	2.2
Cars and trucks, used	**100.0**	**6.6**	**21.6**	**27.2**	**24.0**	**11.0**	**7.0**	**2.4**
Used cars	100.0	7.2	19.7	27.9	24.6	11.1	6.8	2.8
Used trucks	100.0	5.9	24.2	26.3	23.3	11.0	7.3	2.0
Other vehicles	**100.0**	**3.5**	**30.8**	**37.2**	**20.6**	**5.4**	**2.4**	**–**
New motorcycles	100.0	–	15.5	45.4	30.5	8.6	–	–
Used motorcycles	100.0	8.9	25.4	44.9	19.1	0.1	1.6	–
GASOLINE AND MOTOR OIL	**100.0**	**5.6**	**17.9**	**26.8**	**24.7**	**13.5**	**7.8**	**3.7**
Gasoline	100.0	5.5	18.2	27.0	24.7	13.3	7.6	3.7
Diesel fuel	100.0	2.6	18.4	31.9	23.2	13.4	7.9	2.6
Gasoline on trips	100.0	6.8	14.7	23.1	24.6	16.1	11.3	3.5
Motor oil	100.0	5.8	18.6	28.7	24.1	14.1	6.4	2.3
Motor oil on trips	100.0	6.8	14.7	23.1	24.5	16.0	11.2	3.4
OTHER VEHICLE EXPENSES	**100.0**	**4.7**	**18.8**	**25.7**	**25.1**	**13.5**	**8.2**	**4.0**
Vehicle finance charges	**100.0**	**5.3**	**23.0**	**27.1**	**23.8**	**13.7**	**5.8**	**1.3**
Automobile finance charges	100.0	6.2	22.5	25.0	24.4	14.3	6.0	1.5
Truck finance charges	100.0	4.5	24.6	30.4	23.2	12.3	4.4	0.7
Motorcycle and plane finance charges	100.0	2.2	23.0	34.1	26.5	11.2	1.1	1.8
Other vehicle finance charges	100.0	3.5	15.2	21.5	22.3	19.2	15.4	2.9
Maintenance and repairs	**100.0**	**5.4**	**15.8**	**24.9**	**25.7**	**13.9**	**9.4**	**4.9**
Coolant, additives, brake and transmission fluids	100.0	5.5	25.8	26.9	22.5	10.3	6.5	2.3
Tires	100.0	4.8	17.1	26.1	27.0	12.5	8.4	4.1
Parts, equipment, and accessories	100.0	6.2	19.0	25.8	24.2	14.5	8.2	2.2
Vehicle audio equipment	100.0	0.5	19.3	69.5	–	7.7	–	–
Vehicle products	100.0	3.2	35.3	16.8	21.0	7.1	8.1	8.7
Miscellaneous auto repair, servicing	100.0	5.4	15.2	24.5	21.9	21.0	7.0	4.7
Body work and painting	100.0	6.9	14.6	21.1	28.2	13.2	11.3	4.6
Clutch, transmission repair	100.0	6.6	17.0	22.1	30.4	11.6	9.9	2.4
Drive shaft and rear-end repair	100.0	4.5	25.3	17.0	20.1	18.0	6.8	8.2
Brake work	100.0	5.5	15.4	24.7	26.7	15.1	7.6	5.0
Repair to steering or front-end	100.0	4.8	15.1	27.2	25.5	12.5	9.9	5.1
Repair to engine cooling system	100.0	4.9	14.4	24.3	25.3	17.5	8.1	5.6
Motor tune-up	100.0	4.8	14.9	25.1	27.1	12.7	9.8	5.7
Lube, oil change, and oil filters	100.0	4.7	16.9	24.6	24.6	14.3	9.7	5.3
Front-end alignment, wheel balance, rotation	100.0	5.6	13.2	28.3	24.4	12.9	10.7	4.9
Shock absorber replacement	100.0	3.9	14.6	26.0	26.2	15.0	8.7	5.5
Gas tank repair, replacement	100.0	0.9	8.2	26.7	20.8	6.5	29.3	8.3
Tire repair and other repair work	100.0	4.5	15.3	27.8	20.1	15.6	11.5	5.2
Vehicle air conditioning repair	100.0	4.6	10.2	24.6	24.6	13.7	14.5	7.8
Exhaust system repair	100.0	5.5	15.8	22.0	24.1	15.0	9.6	7.8
Electrical system repair	100.0	5.8	13.7	25.3	25.1	12.5	11.2	6.5
Motor repair, replacement	100.0	6.2	14.3	23.0	27.1	14.2	9.3	6.0
Auto repair service policy	100.0	8.4	3.6	29.3	31.4	15.5	9.0	2.8

	total consumer units	under 25	25 to 34	35 to 44	45 to 54	55 to 64	65 to 74	75+
Vehicle insurance	**100.0**	**4.4**	**17.2**	**24.9**	**25.8**	**13.2**	**9.1**	**5.4**
Vehicle rental, leases, licenses, other charges	**100.0**	**3.8**	**22.0**	**27.0**	**24.5**	**13.1**	**6.8**	**2.8**
Leased and rented vehicles	100.0	3.6	23.6	27.8	24.3	13.0	5.7	1.9
Rented vehicles	100.0	2.6	18.0	28.2	21.8	14.9	10.3	4.2
Auto rental	100.0	4.6	21.0	24.0	17.6	15.0	9.1	8.8
Auto rental on trips	100.0	2.0	14.7	29.1	23.8	15.7	10.7	4.0
Truck rental	100.0	4.9	34.6	31.0	9.7	18.5	0.2	1.2
Truck rental on trips	100.0	1.7	20.9	28.4	24.2	7.3	16.8	0.7
Leased vehicles	100.0	3.7	24.3	27.8	24.6	12.8	5.1	1.6
Car lease payments	100.0	3.5	21.4	24.5	24.7	15.1	8.6	2.2
Cash down payment (car lease)	100.0	21.7	10.5	21.1	34.2	4.9	4.6	3.0
Termination fee (car lease)	100.0	5.0	41.2	38.6	3.1	–	7.3	4.9
Truck lease payments	100.0	2.2	29.2	32.1	23.8	10.7	1.1	0.8
Cash down payment (truck lease)	100.0	5.8	15.2	29.2	28.0	17.0	4.9	–
Termination fee (truck lease)	100.0	–	49.0	33.0	9.0	8.7	–	–
State and local registration	100.0	3.5	18.2	24.5	24.9	13.5	10.0	5.3
Driver's license	100.0	5.7	18.9	22.9	23.1	15.6	8.2	5.8
Vehicle inspection	100.0	3.2	17.3	24.6	24.6	13.4	10.3	6.6
Parking fees	100.0	7.7	19.2	27.6	22.8	11.6	8.0	3.1
Parking fees in home city, excluding residence	100.0	8.4	19.5	28.0	22.6	11.3	8.1	2.2
Parking fees on trips	100.0	3.8	17.6	24.8	24.1	13.2	7.8	8.7
Tolls	100.0	1.3	21.2	29.5	29.3	12.2	4.1	2.2
Tolls on trips	100.0	4.3	16.2	24.0	26.3	15.5	9.8	3.8
Towing charges	100.0	13.4	14.8	27.9	23.7	10.5	6.8	2.9
Automobile service clubs	100.0	1.2	8.3	18.4	26.6	19.1	15.3	11.1
PUBLIC TRANSPORTATION	**100.0**	**3.9**	**16.0**	**23.2**	**23.7**	**15.0**	**10.9**	**7.3**
Airline fares	100.0	3.1	15.6	23.5	24.4	15.1	10.8	7.4
Intercity bus fares	100.0	6.5	9.2	21.4	22.1	15.8	12.8	12.0
Intracity mass transit fares	100.0	6.5	23.3	26.7	25.9	9.3	5.4	2.9
Local transportation on trips	100.0	3.0	13.0	20.2	24.7	17.2	12.9	9.0
Taxi fares and limousine service on trips	100.0	3.0	13.0	20.1	24.7	17.2	12.9	9.0
Taxi fares and limousine service	100.0	9.6	29.7	14.8	23.5	11.4	2.6	8.3
Intercity train fares	100.0	5.5	9.6	24.1	19.2	16.2	18.0	7.3
Ship fares	100.0	2.2	12.6	20.7	16.8	22.0	16.0	9.6
School bus	100.0	4.3	15.5	27.8	40.2	3.2	9.0	–

Note: Numbers may not add to total because of rounding. (–) means sample is too small to make a reliable estimate.
Source: Calculations by New Strategist based on the 2000 Consumer Expenditure Survey

Table 11.6 Transportation: Average spending by income, 2000

(average annual spending on transportation, by before-tax income of consumer unit (CU), 2000; complete income reporters only)

	complete income reporters	under $10,000	$10,000– 19,999	$20,000– 29,999	$30,000– 39,999	$40,000– 49,999	$50,000– 69,999	$70,000 or more
Number of consumer units (in thousands, add 000)	81,454	10,810	14,714	12,039	9,477	7,653	11,337	15,424
Average number of persons per CU	2.5	1.7	2.1	2.4	2.5	2.6	2.9	3.2
Average before-tax income of CU	$44,649.00	$5,739.61	$14,586.29	$24,527.00	$34,422.00	$44,201.00	$58,561.00	$112,586.00
Average spending of CU, total	40,238.44	16,455.72	22,620.20	29,851.59	35,609.24	42,323.03	49,245.37	75,963.85
Transportation, average spending	7,567.51	2,727.94	4,489.31	5,745.19	7,303.20	8,715.30	9,655.60	13,365.69
VEHICLE PURCHASES	**$3,465.58**	**$1,100.43**	**$2,199.14**	**$2,545.23**	**$3,379.95**	**$4,260.61**	**$4,407.69**	**$6,015.43**
Cars and trucks, new	**1,611.67**	**344.96**	**661.46**	**1,168.01**	**1,452.75**	**1,896.40**	**1,985.72**	**3,433.64**
New cars	935.98	196.82	432.06	798.76	1,016.21	1,010.39	1,261.79	1,716.16
New trucks	675.69	148.15	229.40	369.25	436.54	886.01	723.93	1,717.48
Cars and trucks, used	**1,804.04**	**753.27**	**1,528.72**	**1,353.13**	**1,925.78**	**2,302.25**	**2,316.88**	**2,456.15**
Used cars	1,052.96	532.27	982.45	1,019.64	1,040.52	1,257.43	1,435.01	1,136.55
Used trucks	751.08	221.00	546.27	333.48	885.26	1,044.82	881.86	1,319.59
Other vehicles	**49.88**	**2.21**	**8.96**	**24.09**	**1.42**	**61.97**	**105.09**	**125.64**
New motorcycles	19.99	–	–	–	–	13.74	63.44	52.13
Used motorcycles	19.64	2.21	3.20	24.09	1.42	48.22	41.65	24.92
GASOLINE AND MOTOR OIL	**1,315.89**	**597.46**	**829.21**	**1,087.91**	**1,340.37**	**1,483.62**	**1,729.33**	**2,059.47**
Gasoline	1,190.68	527.90	757.05	997.44	1,211.34	1,345.28	1,573.94	1,848.59
Diesel fuel	14.01	3.98	13.90	7.91	13.94	13.05	19.03	22.76
Gasoline on trips	99.39	59.18	51.21	70.95	100.49	111.36	120.27	173.78
Motor oil	10.80	5.80	6.53	10.90	13.59	12.80	14.86	12.59
Motor oil on trips	1.00	0.60	0.52	0.72	1.02	1.12	1.21	1.76
OTHER VEHICLE EXPENSES	**2,344.80**	**835.84**	**1,232.08**	**1,811.88**	**2,222.87**	**2,604.87**	**3,029.40**	**4,312.90**
Vehicle finance charges	**337.19**	**71.69**	**135.05**	**250.72**	**339.81**	**411.18**	**542.00**	**594.74**
Automobile finance charges	173.27	36.39	79.94	150.46	192.63	222.61	265.31	272.03
Truck finance charges	140.60	31.92	43.99	87.08	130.89	174.06	234.92	270.74
Motorcycle and plane finance charges	1.68	0.01	0.42	0.57	0.27	1.20	3.99	4.35
Other vehicle finance charges	21.64	3.36	10.71	12.61	16.03	13.31	37.78	47.62
Maintenance and repairs	**659.40**	**290.76**	**415.90**	**556.41**	**633.52**	**745.24**	**771.37**	**1,114.62**
Coolant, additives, brake and transmission fluids	4.77	2.05	3.05	4.96	4.38	5.66	5.01	7.80
Tires	92.39	42.14	52.45	75.78	88.28	114.36	110.99	156.62
Parts, equipment, and accessories	53.37	22.00	36.96	54.51	60.36	70.96	74.58	61.53
Vehicle audio equipment	3.46	0.18	–	–	5.43	–	0.05	13.68
Vehicle products	4.22	0.62	1.36	4.35	3.73	6.64	10.58	3.27
Miscellaneous auto repair, servicing	31.22	4.22	13.16	24.20	21.34	77.81	21.70	58.18
Body work and painting	26.97	20.42	18.88	16.25	19.21	34.58	23.05	51.51
Clutch, transmission repair	44.77	15.51	31.50	33.43	36.03	57.65	60.68	74.07
Drive shaft and rear-end repair	3.80	1.77	2.25	4.03	4.03	4.13	5.54	4.95
Brake work	56.64	28.01	32.18	48.78	49.48	57.33	66.32	103.14
Repair to steering or front-end	19.01	9.13	15.24	18.60	21.38	13.99	22.65	28.22
Repair to engine cooling system	21.81	13.31	15.53	15.24	17.97	23.63	23.47	39.13
Motor tune-up	45.45	21.06	31.37	31.99	42.22	37.91	52.47	87.07
Lube, oil change, and oil filters	61.50	27.18	38.54	50.09	55.79	67.22	78.61	104.48
Front-end alignment, wheel balance, rotation	11.88	7.08	8.35	11.11	9.44	6.25	15.70	20.69
Shock absorber replacement	4.20	1.01	2.64	4.43	2.19	5.97	4.44	7.95
Gas tank repair, replacement	3.86	0.72	2.50	2.42	9.88	3.00	2.97	5.24
Tire repair and other repair work	30.47	8.50	19.34	22.64	36.91	19.95	34.65	60.80
Vehicle air conditioning repair	20.60	8.16	16.89	16.47	18.08	21.29	22.38	36.01
Exhaust system repair	14.31	9.85	11.63	10.89	15.13	12.73	16.94	21.00
Electrical system repair	32.64	22.73	19.20	33.46	34.65	34.70	38.57	45.14
Motor repair, replacement	66.67	23.52	41.32	68.57	72.99	61.57	75.73	111.61
Auto repair service policy	5.37	1.60	1.56	4.21	4.64	7.91	4.29	12.54

	complete income reporters	under $10,000	$10,000– 19,999	$20,000– 29,999	$30,000– 39,999	$40,000– 49,999	$50,000– 69,999	$70,000 or more
Vehicle insurance	$798.29	$298.04	$475.04	$695.43	$825.16	$927.36	$1,051.59	$1,270.85
Vehicle rental, leases, licenses, other charges	**549.91**	**175.36**	**206.08**	**309.32**	**424.37**	**521.09**	**664.44**	**1,332.69**
Leased and rented vehicles	377.99	100.06	115.14	181.13	277.48	331.13	452.80	1,007.24
Rented vehicles	46.43	19.13	18.31	29.19	34.85	52.87	46.53	109.71
Auto rental	7.66	4.77	1.96	8.99	6.85	8.70	6.82	14.68
Auto rental on trips	29.80	11.18	10.57	16.80	21.58	30.65	29.02	76.56
Truck rental	3.20	0.39	3.49	0.79	2.83	2.46	1.68	8.45
Truck rental on trips	5.55	2.79	2.29	2.48	3.59	10.60	7.89	9.99
Leased vehicles	331.56	80.93	96.83	151.94	242.62	278.25	406.27	897.52
Car lease payments	158.12	32.64	50.15	91.14	110.64	131.49	213.65	402.92
Cash down payment (car lease)	13.73	10.39	3.25	6.16	10.45	12.34	10.44	37.08
Termination fee (car lease)	2.20	0.90	0.67	6.77	4.79	0.11	–	2.05
Truck lease payments	147.37	37.01	38.03	47.86	107.49	110.02	174.08	430.09
Cash down payment (truck lease)	8.75	–	4.52	–	8.36	17.86	6.14	23.40
Termination fee (truck lease)	1.40	–	0.21	–	0.89	6.44	1.96	1.99
State and local registration	91.96	36.80	55.18	74.93	82.94	106.01	120.63	156.51
Driver's license	7.21	3.97	4.68	7.18	6.43	7.81	9.00	10.78
Vehicle inspection	10.13	3.35	6.87	8.47	10.81	12.34	12.38	16.13
Parking fees	31.07	20.34	10.61	16.11	21.83	33.66	34.97	71.29
Parking fees in home city, excluding residence	26.57	18.17	9.16	13.70	19.34	27.80	29.11	61.05
Parking fees on trips	4.50	2.17	1.45	2.41	2.50	5.85	5.86	10.24
Tolls	13.12	3.20	1.23	6.37	5.56	11.71	11.99	40.06
Tolls on trips	3.79	1.70	1.57	2.32	3.28	3.81	5.06	7.89
Towing charges	5.12	2.54	4.36	4.28	6.71	5.34	5.80	6.71
Automobile service clubs	9.52	3.42	6.44	8.54	9.34	9.28	11.80	16.08
PUBLIC TRANSPORTATION	**441.25**	**194.20**	**228.88**	**300.18**	**360.02**	**366.21**	**489.18**	**977.89**
Airline fares	272.77	124.65	126.46	189.00	188.30	213.79	314.40	632.12
Intercity bus fares	17.63	8.89	14.57	16.90	14.06	13.68	16.40	32.30
Intracity mass transit fares	50.97	37.73	35.01	42.10	39.14	46.41	47.88	94.19
Local transportation on trips	10.78	5.19	4.99	9.68	8.77	6.49	12.59	23.09
Taxi fares and limousine service on trips	6.33	3.04	2.94	5.69	5.15	3.81	7.39	13.56
Taxi fares and limousine service	14.06	5.18	18.37	9.91	26.05	17.95	4.73	15.86
Intercity train fares	21.20	6.72	15.24	9.76	19.64	17.47	22.77	47.63
Ship fares	45.52	2.25	9.62	15.61	56.91	45.94	61.31	114.63
School bus	1.99	0.56	1.68	1.54	1.99	0.66	1.70	4.51

Note: (–) means sample is too small to make a reliable estimate.
Source: Bureau of Labor Statistics, unpublished tables from the 2000 Consumer Expenditure Survey; calculations by New Strategist

Table 11.7 Transportation: Indexed spending by income, 2000

(indexed average annual spending of consumer units (CU) on transportation, by before-tax income of consumer unit, 2000; complete income reporters only; index definition: an index of 100 is the average for all consumer units; an index of 132 means that spending by consumer units in that group is 32 percent above the average for all consumer units; an index of 68 indicates spending that is 32 percent below the average for all consumer units)

	complete income reporters	under $10,000	$10,000–19,999	$20,000–29,999	$30,000–39,999	$40,000–49,999	$50,000–69,999	$70,000 or more
Average spending of CU, total	$40,238	$16,456	$22,620	$29,852	$35,609	$42,323	$49,245	$75,964
Average spending of CU, index	100	41	56	74	88	105	122	189
Transportation, spending index	100	36	59	76	97	115	128	177
VEHICLE PURCHASES	**100**	**32**	**63**	**73**	**98**	**123**	**127**	**174**
Cars and trucks, new	**100**	**21**	**41**	**72**	**90**	**118**	**123**	**213**
New cars	100	21	46	85	109	108	135	183
New trucks	100	22	34	55	65	131	107	254
Cars and trucks, used	**100**	**42**	**85**	**75**	**107**	**128**	**128**	**136**
Used cars	100	51	93	97	99	119	136	108
Used trucks	100	29	73	44	118	139	117	176
Other vehicles	**100**	**4**	**18**	**48**	**3**	**124**	**211**	**252**
New motorcycles	100	–	–	–	–	69	317	261
Used motorcycles	100	11	16	123	7	246	212	127
GASOLINE AND MOTOR OIL	**100**	**45**	**63**	**83**	**102**	**113**	**131**	**157**
Gasoline	100	44	64	84	102	113	132	155
Diesel fuel	100	28	99	56	100	93	136	162
Gasoline on trips	100	60	52	71	101	112	121	175
Motor oil	100	54	60	101	126	119	138	117
Motor oil on trips	100	60	52	72	102	112	121	176
OTHER VEHICLE EXPENSES	**100**	**36**	**53**	**77**	**95**	**111**	**129**	**184**
Vehicle finance charges	**100**	**21**	**40**	**74**	**101**	**122**	**161**	**176**
Automobile finance charges	100	21	46	87	111	128	153	157
Truck finance charges	100	23	31	62	93	124	167	193
Motorcycle and plane finance charges	100	1	25	34	16	71	238	259
Other vehicle finance charges	100	16	49	58	74	62	175	220
Maintenance and repairs	**100**	**44**	**63**	**84**	**96**	**113**	**117**	**169**
Coolant, additives, brake and transmission fluids	100	43	64	104	92	119	105	164
Tires	100	46	57	82	96	124	120	170
Parts, equipment, and accessories	100	41	69	102	113	133	140	115
Vehicle audio equipment	100	5	–	–	157	–	1	395
Vehicle products	100	15	32	103	88	157	251	77
Miscellaneous auto repair, servicing	100	14	42	78	68	249	70	186
Body work and painting	100	76	70	60	71	128	85	191
Clutch, transmission repair	100	35	70	75	80	129	136	165
Drive shaft and rear-end repair	100	47	59	106	106	109	146	130
Brake work	100	49	57	86	87	101	117	182
Repair to steering or front-end	100	48	80	98	112	74	119	148
Repair to engine cooling system	100	61	71	70	82	108	108	179
Motor tune-up	100	46	69	70	93	83	115	192
Lube, oil change, and oil filters	100	44	63	81	91	109	128	170
Front-end alignment, wheel balance, rotation	100	60	70	94	79	53	132	174
Shock absorber replacement	100	24	63	105	52	142	106	189
Gas tank repair, replacement	100	19	65	63	256	78	77	136
Tire repair and other repair work	100	28	63	74	121	65	114	200
Vehicle air conditioning repair	100	40	82	80	88	103	109	175
Exhaust system repair	100	69	81	76	106	89	118	147
Electrical system repair	100	70	59	103	106	106	118	138
Motor repair, replacement	100	35	62	103	109	92	114	167
Auto repair service policy	100	30	29	78	86	147	80	234

	complete income reporters	under $10,000	$10,000–19,999	$20,000–29,999	$30,000–39,999	$40,000–49,999	$50,000–69,999	$70,000 or more
Vehicle insurance	**100**	**37**	**60**	**87**	**103**	**116**	**132**	**159**
Vehicle rental, leases, licenses, other charges	**100**	**32**	**37**	**56**	**77**	**95**	**121**	**242**
Leased and rented vehicles	100	26	30	48	73	88	120	266
Rented vehicles	100	41	39	63	75	114	100	236
Auto rental	100	62	26	117	89	114	89	192
Auto rental on trips	100	38	35	56	72	103	97	257
Truck rental	100	12	109	25	88	77	53	264
Truck rental on trips	100	50	41	45	65	191	142	180
Leased vehicles	100	24	29	46	73	84	123	271
Car lease payments	100	21	32	58	70	83	135	255
Cash down payment (car lease)	100	76	24	45	76	90	76	270
Termination fee (car lease)	100	41	31	308	218	5	–	93
Truck lease payments	100	25	26	32	73	75	118	292
Cash down payment (truck lease)	100	–	52	–	96	204	70	267
Termination fee (truck lease)	100	–	15	–	64	460	140	142
State and local registration	100	40	60	81	90	115	131	170
Driver's license	100	55	65	100	89	108	125	150
Vehicle inspection	100	33	68	84	107	122	122	159
Parking fees	100	65	34	52	70	108	113	229
Parking fees in home city, excluding residence	100	68	34	52	73	105	110	230
Parking fees on trips	100	48	32	54	56	130	130	228
Tolls	100	24	9	49	42	89	91	305
Tolls on trips	100	45	41	61	87	101	134	208
Towing charges	100	50	85	84	131	104	113	131
Automobile service clubs	100	36	68	90	98	97	124	169
PUBLIC TRANSPORTATION	**100**	**44**	**52**	**68**	**82**	**83**	**111**	**222**
Airline fares	100	46	46	69	69	78	115	232
Intercity bus fares	100	50	83	96	80	78	93	183
Intracity mass transit fares	100	74	69	83	77	91	94	185
Local transportation on trips	100	48	46	90	81	60	117	214
Taxi fares and limousine service on trips	100	48	46	90	81	60	117	214
Taxi fares and limousine service	100	37	131	70	185	128	34	113
Intercity train fares	100	32	72	46	93	82	107	225
Ship fares	100	5	21	34	125	101	135	252
School bus	100	28	84	77	100	33	85	227

Note: (–) means sample is too small to make a reliable estimate.
Source: Calculations by New Strategist based on the 2000 Consumer Expenditure Survey

Table 11.8 Transportation: Indexed per capita spending by income, 2000

(indexed average annual per capita spending of consumer units (CU) on transportation, by before-tax income of consumer unit, 2000; complete income reporters only; index definition: an index of 100 is the average for all consumer units; an index of 132 means that spending by consumer units in that group is 32 percent above the average for all consumer units; an index of 68 indicates spending that is 32 percent below the average for all consumer units)

	complete income reporters	under $10,000	$10,000–19,999	$20,000–29,999	$30,000–39,999	$40,000–49,999	$50,000–69,999	$70,000 or more
Per capita spending of CU, total	$16,095	$9,492	$10,819	$12,438	$14,244	$16,278	$16,981	$23,739
Per capita spending of CU, index	100	59	67	77	88	101	106	147
Transportation, per capita spending index	100	52	71	79	97	111	110	138
VEHICLE PURCHASES	100	46	76	77	98	118	110	136
Cars and trucks, new	100	31	49	75	90	113	106	166
New cars	100	30	55	89	109	104	116	143
New trucks	100	32	41	57	65	126	92	199
Cars and trucks, used	100	60	101	78	107	123	111	106
Used cars	100	73	112	101	99	115	117	84
Used trucks	100	42	87	46	118	134	101	137
Other vehicles	100	6	21	50	3	119	182	197
New motorcycles	100	–	–	–	–	66	274	204
Used motorcycles	100	16	19	128	7	236	183	99
GASOLINE AND MOTOR OIL	100	65	75	86	102	108	113	122
Gasoline	100	64	76	87	102	109	114	121
Diesel fuel	100	41	119	59	100	90	117	127
Gasoline on trips	100	86	62	74	101	108	104	137
Motor oil	100	77	72	105	126	114	119	91
Motor oil on trips	100	86	62	75	102	108	104	138
OTHER VEHICLE EXPENSES	100	51	63	80	95	107	111	144
Vehicle finance charges	100	31	48	77	101	117	139	138
Automobile finance charges	100	30	55	90	111	124	132	123
Truck finance charges	100	33	37	65	93	119	144	150
Motorcycle and plane finance charges	100	1	30	35	16	69	205	202
Other vehicle finance charges	100	22	59	61	74	59	151	172
Maintenance and repairs	100	64	75	88	96	109	101	132
Coolant, additives, brake and transmission fluids	100	62	76	108	92	114	91	128
Tires	100	66	68	85	96	119	104	132
Parts, equipment, and accessories	100	59	83	106	113	128	120	90
Vehicle audio equipment	100	8	–	–	157	–	1	309
Vehicle products	100	21	38	107	88	151	216	61
Miscellaneous auto repair, servicing	100	19	50	81	68	240	60	146
Body work and painting	100	109	84	63	71	123	74	149
Clutch, transmission repair	100	50	84	78	80	124	117	129
Drive shaft and rear-end repair	100	67	71	110	106	105	126	102
Brake work	100	71	68	90	87	97	101	142
Repair to steering or front-end	100	69	96	102	112	71	103	116
Repair to engine cooling system	100	88	85	73	82	104	93	140
Motor tune-up	100	67	83	73	93	80	100	150
Lube, oil change, and oil filters	100	64	75	85	91	105	110	133
Front-end alignment, wheel balance, rotation	100	86	84	97	79	51	114	136
Shock absorber replacement	100	35	75	110	52	137	91	148
Gas tank repair, replacement	100	27	78	65	256	75	66	106
Tire repair and other repair work	100	40	76	77	121	63	98	156
Vehicle air conditioning repair	100	57	98	83	88	99	94	137
Exhaust system repair	100	99	97	79	106	86	102	115
Electrical system repair	100	100	70	107	106	102	102	108
Motor repair, replacement	100	51	74	107	109	89	98	131
Auto repair service policy	100	43	35	82	86	142	69	182

	complete income reporters	under $10,000	$10,000– 19,999	$20,000– 29,999	$30,000– 39,999	$40,000– 49,999	$50,000– 69,999	$70,000 or more
Vehicle insurance	**100**	**54**	**71**	**91**	**103**	**112**	**114**	**124**
Vehicle rental, leases, licenses, other charges	**100**	**46**	**45**	**59**	**77**	**91**	**104**	**189**
Leased and rented vehicles	100	38	36	50	73	84	103	208
Rented vehicles	100	59	47	65	75	109	86	185
Auto rental	100	90	31	122	89	109	77	150
Auto rental on trips	100	54	42	59	72	99	84	201
Truck rental	100	18	130	26	88	74	45	206
Truck rental on trips	100	72	49	47	65	184	123	141
Leased vehicles	100	35	35	48	73	81	106	211
Car lease payments	100	30	38	60	70	80	116	199
Cash down payment (car lease)	100	109	28	47	76	86	66	211
Termination fee (car lease)	100	59	37	321	218	5	–	73
Truck lease payments	100	36	31	34	73	72	102	228
Cash down payment (truck lease)	100	–	62	–	96	196	60	209
Termination fee (truck lease)	100	–	18	–	64	442	121	111
State and local registration	100	58	72	85	90	111	113	133
Driver's license	100	79	78	104	89	104	108	117
Vehicle inspection	100	48	81	87	107	117	105	124
Parking fees	100	94	41	54	70	104	97	179
Parking fees in home city, excluding residence	100	99	41	54	73	101	94	180
Parking fees on trips	100	69	38	56	56	125	112	178
Tolls	100	35	11	51	42	86	79	239
Tolls on trips	100	65	49	64	87	97	115	163
Towing charges	100	72	102	87	131	100	98	102
Automobile service clubs	100	52	81	93	98	94	107	132
PUBLIC TRANSPORTATION	**100**	**63**	**62**	**71**	**82**	**80**	**96**	**173**
Airline fares	100	66	55	72	69	75	99	181
Intercity bus fares	100	73	99	100	80	75	80	143
Intracity mass transit fares	100	107	82	86	77	88	81	144
Local transportation on trips	100	69	55	94	81	58	101	167
Taxi fares and limousine service on trips	100	69	55	94	81	58	101	167
Taxi fares and limousine service	100	53	156	73	185	123	29	88
Intercity train fares	100	46	86	48	93	79	93	176
Ship fares	100	7	25	36	125	97	116	197
School bus	100	40	101	81	100	32	74	177

Note: Per capita indexes account for household size and show how much each person in a particular household demographic segment spends relative to a person in the average household. (–) means sample is too small to make a reliable estimate.
Source: Calculations by New Strategist based on the 2000 Consumer Expenditure Survey

Table 11.9 Transportation: Total spending by income, 2000

(total annual spending on transportation, by before-tax income group of consumer units (CU), 2000; complete income reporters only; numbers in thousands)

	complete income reporters	under $10,000	$10,000– 19,999	$20,000– 29,999	$30,000– 39,999	$40,000– 49,999	$50,000– 69,999	$70,000 or more
Number of consumer units	81,454	10,810	14,714	12,039	9,477	7,653	11,337	15,424
Total spending of all CUs	$3,277,581,892	$177,886,368	$332,833,656	$359,383,292	$337,468,767	$323,898,149	$558,294,760	$1,171,666,422
Transportation, total spending	616,403,960	29,489,033	66,055,659	69,166,342	69,212,426	66,698,191	109,465,537	206,152,403
VEHICLE PURCHASES	**$282,285,353**	**$11,895,688**	**$32,358,158**	**$30,642,024**	**$32,031,786**	**$32,606,448**	**$49,969,982**	**$92,781,992**
Cars and trucks, new	**131,276,968**	**3,728,981**	**9,732,727**	**14,061,672**	**13,767,712**	**14,513,149**	**22,512,108**	**52,960,463**
New cars	76,239,315	2,127,603	6,357,373	9,616,272	9,630,622	7,732,515	14,304,913	26,470,052
New trucks	55,037,653	1,601,450	3,375,354	4,445,401	4,137,090	6,780,635	8,207,194	26,490,412
Cars and trucks, used	**146,946,274**	**8,142,895**	**22,493,537**	**16,290,332**	**18,250,617**	**17,619,119**	**26,266,469**	**37,883,658**
Used cars	85,767,804	5,753,854	14,455,802	12,275,446	9,861,008	9,623,112	16,268,708	17,530,147
Used trucks	61,178,470	2,389,041	8,037,802	4,014,766	8,389,609	7,996,007	9,997,647	20,353,356
Other vehicles	**4,062,926**	**23,848**	**131,828**	**290,020**	**13,457**	**474,256**	**1,191,405**	**1,937,871**
New motorcycles	1,628,265	–	–	–	–	105,152	719,219	804,053
Used motorcycles	1,599,757	23,848	47,097	290,020	13,457	369,028	472,186	384,366
GASOLINE AND MOTOR OIL	**107,184,504**	**6,458,581**	**12,200,957**	**13,097,348**	**12,702,686**	**11,354,144**	**19,605,414**	**31,765,265**
Gasoline	96,985,649	5,706,582	11,139,289	12,008,180	11,479,869	10,295,428	17,843,758	28,512,652
Diesel fuel	1,141,171	43,078	204,529	95,228	132,109	99,872	215,743	351,050
Gasoline on trips	8,095,713	639,696	753,475	854,167	952,344	852,238	1,363,501	2,680,383
Motor oil	879,703	62,731	96,066	131,225	128,792	97,958	168,468	194,188
Motor oil on trips	81,454	6,459	7,597	8,668	9,667	8,571	13,718	27,146
OTHER VEHICLE EXPENSES	**190,993,339**	**9,035,412**	**18,128,782**	**21,813,223**	**21,066,139**	**19,935,070**	**34,344,308**	**66,522,170**
Vehicle finance charges	**27,465,474**	**774,947**	**1,987,172**	**3,018,418**	**3,220,379**	**3,146,761**	**6,144,654**	**9,173,270**
Automobile finance charges	14,113,535	393,402	1,176,274	1,811,388	1,825,555	1,703,634	3,007,819	4,195,791
Truck finance charges	11,452,432	345,006	647,342	1,048,356	1,240,445	1,332,081	2,663,288	4,175,894
Motorcycle and plane finance charges	136,843	144	6,129	6,862	2,559	9,184	45,235	67,094
Other vehicle finance charges	1,762,665	36,359	157,574	151,812	151,916	101,861	428,312	734,491
Maintenance and repairs	**53,710,768**	**3,143,119**	**6,119,616**	**6,698,620**	**6,003,869**	**5,703,322**	**8,745,022**	**17,191,899**
Coolant, additives, brake, transmission fluids	388,536	22,118	44,895	59,713	41,509	43,316	56,798	120,307
Tires	7,525,535	455,558	771,682	912,315	836,630	875,197	1,258,294	2,415,707
Parts, equipment, and accessories	4,347,200	237,842	543,766	656,246	572,032	543,057	845,513	949,039
Vehicle audio equipment	281,831	1,959	–	–	51,460	–	567	211,000
Vehicle products	343,736	6,734	19,989	52,370	35,349	50,816	119,945	50,436
Miscellaneous auto repair, servicing	2,542,994	45,600	193,686	291,344	202,239	595,480	246,013	897,368
Body work and painting	2,196,814	220,771	277,829	195,634	182,053	264,641	261,318	794,490
Clutch, transmission repair	3,646,696	167,617	463,468	402,464	341,456	441,195	687,929	1,142,456
Drive shaft and rear-end repair	309,525	19,161	33,140	48,517	38,192	31,607	62,807	76,349
Brake work	4,613,555	302,735	473,518	587,262	468,922	438,746	751,870	1,590,831
Repair to steering or front-end	1,548,441	98,736	224,235	223,925	202,618	107,065	256,783	435,265
Repair to engine cooling system	1,776,512	143,925	228,453	183,474	170,302	180,840	266,079	603,541
Motor tune-up	3,702,084	227,638	461,524	385,128	400,119	290,125	594,852	1,342,968
Lube, oil change, and oil filters	5,009,421	293,790	567,087	603,034	528,722	514,435	891,202	1,611,500
Front-end alignment, wheel balance, rotation	967,674	76,487	122,896	133,753	89,463	47,831	177,991	319,123
Shock absorber replacement	342,107	10,878	38,866	53,333	20,755	45,688	50,336	122,621
Gas tank repair, replacement	314,412	7,762	36,830	29,134	93,633	22,959	33,671	80,822
Tire repair and other repair work	2,481,903	91,881	284,640	272,563	349,796	152,677	392,827	937,779
Vehicle air conditioning repair	1,677,952	88,203	248,492	198,282	171,344	162,932	253,722	555,418
Exhaust system repair	1,165,607	106,450	171,056	131,105	143,387	97,423	192,049	323,904
Electrical system repair	2,658,659	245,669	282,573	402,825	328,378	265,559	437,268	696,239
Motor repair, replacement	5,430,538	254,245	607,998	825,514	691,726	471,195	858,551	1,721,473
Auto repair service policy	437,408	17,255	23,010	50,684	43,973	60,535	48,636	193,417

	complete income reporters	under $10,000	$10,000– 19,999	$20,000– 29,999	$30,000– 39,999	$40,000– 49,999	$50,000– 69,999	$70,000 or more
Vehicle insurance	$65,023,914	$3,221,805	$6,989,788	$8,372,282	$7,820,041	$7,097,086	$11,921,876	$19,601,590
Vehicle rental, leases, licenses, other charges	**44,792,369**	**1,895,613**	**3,032,273**	**3,723,903**	**4,021,754**	**3,987,902**	**7,532,756**	**20,555,411**
Leased and rented vehicles	30,788,797	1,081,607	1,694,184	2,180,624	2,629,678	2,534,138	5,133,394	15,535,670
Rented vehicles	3,781,909	206,776	269,395	351,418	330,273	404,614	527,511	1,692,167
Auto rental	623,938	51,605	28,858	108,231	64,917	66,581	77,318	226,424
Auto rental on trips	2,427,329	120,802	155,573	202,255	204,514	234,564	329,000	1,180,861
Truck rental	260,653	4,238	51,333	9,511	26,820	18,826	19,046	130,333
Truck rental on trips	452,070	30,130	33,711	29,857	34,022	81,122	89,449	154,086
Leased vehicles	27,006,888	874,832	1,424,709	1,829,206	2,299,310	2,129,447	4,605,883	13,843,348
Car lease payments	12,879,506	352,792	737,873	1,097,234	1,048,535	1,006,293	2,422,150	6,214,638
Cash down payment (car lease)	1,118,363	112,270	47,842	74,160	99,035	94,438	118,358	571,922
Termination fee (car lease)	179,199	9,684	9,882	81,504	45,395	842	–	31,619
Truck lease payments	12,003,876	400,086	559,574	576,187	1,018,683	841,983	1,973,545	6,633,708
Cash down payment (truck lease)	712,723	–	66,466	–	79,228	136,683	69,609	360,922
Termination fee (truck lease)	114,036	–	3,071	–	8,435	49,285	22,221	30,694
State and local registration	7,490,510	397,771	811,981	902,082	786,022	811,295	1,367,582	2,414,010
Driver's license	587,283	42,902	68,819	86,440	60,937	59,770	102,033	166,271
Vehicle inspection	825,129	36,222	101,017	101,970	102,446	94,438	140,352	248,789
Parking fees	2,530,776	219,829	156,148	193,948	206,883	257,600	396,455	1,099,577
Parking fees in home city, excl. residence	2,164,233	196,434	134,778	164,934	183,285	212,753	330,020	941,635
Parking fees on trips	366,543	23,431	21,290	29,014	23,693	44,770	66,435	157,942
Tolls	1,068,676	34,593	18,033	76,688	52,692	89,617	135,931	617,885
Tolls on trips	308,711	18,335	23,084	27,930	31,085	29,158	57,365	121,695
Towing charges	417,044	27,500	64,190	51,527	63,591	40,867	65,755	103,495
Automobile service clubs	775,442	36,924	94,736	102,813	88,515	71,020	133,777	248,018
PUBLIC TRANSPORTATION	**35,941,578**	**2,099,352**	**3,367,762**	**3,613,867**	**3,411,910**	**2,802,605**	**5,545,834**	**15,082,975**
Airline fares	22,218,208	1,347,469	1,860,689	2,275,371	1,784,519	1,636,135	3,564,353	9,749,819
Intercity bus fares	1,436,034	96,087	214,358	203,459	133,247	104,693	185,927	498,195
Intracity mass transit fares	4,151,710	407,844	515,200	506,842	370,930	355,176	542,816	1,452,787
Local transportation on trips	878,074	56,078	73,492	116,538	83,113	49,668	142,733	356,140
Taxi fares and limousine service on trips	515,604	32,883	43,194	68,502	48,807	29,158	83,780	209,149
Taxi fares and limousine service	1,145,243	55,971	270,276	119,306	246,876	137,371	53,624	244,625
Intercity train fares	1,726,825	72,646	224,279	117,501	186,128	133,698	258,143	734,645
Ship fares	3,707,786	24,269	141,522	187,929	539,336	351,579	695,071	1,768,053
School bus	162,093	6,034	24,739	18,540	18,859	5,051	19,273	69,562

Note: Numbers may not add to total because of rounding. (–) means sample is too small to make a reliable estimate.
Source: Calculations by New Strategist based on the 2000 Consumer Expenditure Survey

Table 11.10 Transportation: Market shares by income, 2000

(percentage of total annual spending on transportation accounted for by before-tax income group of consumer units, 2000; complete income reporters only)

	complete income reporters	under $10,000	$10,000– 19,999	$20,000– 29,999	$30,000– 39,999	$40,000– 49,999	$50,000– 69,999	$70,000 or more
Share of total consumer units	100.0%	13.3%	18.1%	14.8%	11.6%	9.4%	13.9%	18.9%
Share of total before-tax income	100.0	1.7	5.9	8.1	9.0	9.3	18.3	47.7
Share of total spending	100.0	5.4	10.2	11.0	10.3	9.9	17.0	35.7
Share of transportation spending	100.0	4.8	10.7	11.2	11.2	10.8	17.8	33.4
VEHICLE PURCHASES	100.0%	4.2%	11.5%	10.9%	11.3%	11.6%	17.7%	32.9%
Cars and trucks, new	100.0	2.8	7.4	10.7	10.5	11.1	17.1	40.3
New cars	100.0	2.8	8.3	12.6	12.6	10.1	18.8	34.7
New trucks	100.0	2.9	6.1	8.1	7.5	12.3	14.9	48.1
Cars and trucks, used	100.0	5.5	15.3	11.1	12.4	12.0	17.9	25.8
Used cars	100.0	6.7	16.9	14.3	11.5	11.2	19.0	20.4
Used trucks	100.0	3.9	13.1	6.6	13.7	13.1	16.3	33.3
Other vehicles	100.0	0.6	3.2	7.1	0.3	11.7	29.3	47.7
New motorcycles	100.0	–	–	–	–	6.5	44.2	49.4
Used motorcycles	100.0	1.5	2.9	18.1	0.8	23.1	29.5	24.0
GASOLINE AND MOTOR OIL	100.0	6.0	11.4	12.2	11.9	10.6	18.3	29.6
Gasoline	100.0	5.9	11.5	12.4	11.8	10.6	18.4	29.4
Diesel fuel	100.0	3.8	17.9	8.3	11.6	8.8	18.9	30.8
Gasoline on trips	100.0	7.9	9.3	10.6	11.8	10.5	16.8	33.1
Motor oil	100.0	7.1	10.9	14.9	14.6	11.1	19.2	22.1
Motor oil on trips	100.0	7.9	9.3	10.6	11.9	10.5	16.8	33.3
OTHER VEHICLE EXPENSES	100.0	4.7	9.5	11.4	11.0	10.4	18.0	34.8
Vehicle finance charges	100.0	2.8	7.2	11.0	11.7	11.5	22.4	33.4
Automobile finance charges	100.0	2.8	8.3	12.8	12.9	12.1	21.3	29.7
Truck finance charges	100.0	3.0	5.7	9.2	10.8	11.6	23.3	36.5
Motorcycle and plane finance charges	100.0	0.1	4.5	5.0	1.9	6.7	33.1	49.0
Other vehicle finance charges	100.0	2.1	8.9	8.6	8.6	5.8	24.3	41.7
Maintenance and repairs	100.0	5.9	11.4	12.5	11.2	10.6	16.3	32.0
Coolant, additives, brake and transmission fluids	100.0	5.7	11.6	15.4	10.7	11.1	14.6	31.0
Tires	100.0	6.1	10.3	12.1	11.1	11.6	16.7	32.1
Parts, equipment, and accessories	100.0	5.5	12.5	15.1	13.2	12.5	19.4	21.8
Vehicle audio equipment	100.0	0.7	–	–	18.3	–	0.2	74.9
Vehicle products	100.0	2.0	5.8	15.2	10.3	14.8	34.9	14.7
Miscellaneous auto repair, servicing	100.0	1.8	7.6	11.5	8.0	23.4	9.7	35.3
Body work and painting	100.0	10.0	12.6	8.9	8.3	12.0	11.9	36.2
Clutch, transmission repair	100.0	4.6	12.7	11.0	9.4	12.1	18.9	31.3
Drive shaft and rear-end repair	100.0	6.2	10.7	15.7	12.3	10.2	20.3	24.7
Brake work	100.0	6.6	10.3	12.7	10.2	9.5	16.3	34.5
Repair to steering or front-end	100.0	6.4	14.5	14.5	13.1	6.9	16.6	28.1
Repair to engine cooling system	100.0	8.1	12.9	10.3	9.6	10.2	15.0	34.0
Motor tune-up	100.0	6.1	12.5	10.4	10.8	7.8	16.1	36.3
Lube, oil change, and oil filters	100.0	5.9	11.3	12.0	10.6	10.3	17.8	32.2
Front-end alignment, wheel balance, rotation	100.0	7.9	12.7	13.8	9.2	4.9	18.4	33.0
Shock absorber replacement	100.0	3.2	11.4	15.6	6.1	13.4	14.7	35.8
Gas tank repair, replacement	100.0	2.5	11.7	9.3	29.8	7.3	10.7	25.7
Tire repair and other repair work	100.0	3.7	11.5	11.0	14.1	6.2	15.8	37.8
Vehicle air conditioning repair	100.0	5.3	14.8	11.8	10.2	9.7	15.1	33.1
Exhaust system repair	100.0	9.1	14.7	11.2	12.3	8.4	16.5	27.8
Electrical system repair	100.0	9.2	10.6	15.2	12.4	10.0	16.4	26.2
Motor repair, replacement	100.0	4.7	11.2	15.2	12.7	8.7	15.8	31.7
Auto repair service policy	100.0	3.9	5.3	11.6	10.1	13.8	11.1	44.2

	complete income reporters	under $10,000	$10,000– 19,999	$20,000– 29,999	$30,000– 39,999	$40,000– 49,999	$50,000– 69,999	$70,000 or more
Vehicle insurance	100.0%	5.0%	10.7%	12.9%	12.0%	10.9%	18.3%	30.1%
Vehicle rental, leases, licenses, other charges	**100.0**	**4.2**	**6.8**	**8.3**	**9.0**	**8.9**	**16.8**	**45.9**
Leased and rented vehicles	100.0	3.5	5.5	7.1	8.5	8.2	16.7	50.5
Rented vehicles	100.0	5.5	7.1	9.3	8.7	10.7	13.9	44.7
Auto rental	100.0	8.3	4.6	17.3	10.4	10.7	12.4	36.3
Auto rental on trips	100.0	5.0	6.4	8.3	8.4	9.7	13.6	48.6
Truck rental	100.0	1.6	19.7	3.6	10.3	7.2	7.3	50.0
Truck rental on trips	100.0	6.7	7.5	6.6	7.5	17.9	19.8	34.1
Leased vehicles	100.0	3.2	5.3	6.8	8.5	7.9	17.1	51.3
Car lease payments	100.0	2.7	5.7	8.5	8.1	7.8	18.8	48.3
Cash down payment (car lease)	100.0	10.0	4.3	6.6	8.9	8.4	10.6	51.1
Termination fee (car lease)	100.0	5.4	5.5	45.5	25.3	0.5	–	17.6
Truck lease payments	100.0	3.3	4.7	4.8	8.5	7.0	16.4	55.3
Cash down payment (truck lease)	100.0	–	9.3	–	11.1	19.2	9.8	50.6
Termination fee (truck lease)	100.0	–	2.7	–	7.4	43.2	19.5	26.9
State and local registration	100.0	5.3	10.8	12.0	10.5	10.8	18.3	32.2
Driver's license	100.0	7.3	11.7	14.7	10.4	10.2	17.4	28.3
Vehicle inspection	100.0	4.4	12.2	12.4	12.4	11.4	17.0	30.2
Parking fees	100.0	8.7	6.2	7.7	8.2	10.2	15.7	43.4
Parking fees in home city, excluding residence	100.0	9.1	6.2	7.6	8.5	9.8	15.2	43.5
Parking fees on trips	100.0	6.4	5.8	7.9	6.5	12.2	18.1	43.1
Tolls	100.0	3.2	1.7	7.2	4.9	8.4	12.7	57.8
Tolls on trips	100.0	5.9	7.5	9.0	10.1	9.4	18.6	39.4
Towing charges	100.0	6.6	15.4	12.4	15.2	9.8	15.8	24.8
Automobile service clubs	100.0	4.8	12.2	13.3	11.4	9.2	17.3	32.0
PUBLIC TRANSPORTATION	**100.0**	**5.8**	**9.4**	**10.1**	**9.5**	**7.8**	**15.4**	**42.0**
Airline fares	100.0	6.1	8.4	10.2	8.0	7.4	16.0	43.9
Intercity bus fares	100.0	6.7	14.9	14.2	9.3	7.3	12.9	34.7
Intracity mass transit fares	100.0	9.8	12.4	12.2	8.9	8.6	13.1	35.0
Local transportation on trips	100.0	6.4	8.4	13.3	9.5	5.7	16.3	40.6
Taxi fares and limousine service on trips	100.0	6.4	8.4	13.3	9.5	5.7	16.2	40.6
Taxi fares and limousine service	100.0	4.9	23.6	10.4	21.6	12.0	4.7	21.4
Intercity train fares	100.0	4.2	13.0	6.8	10.8	7.7	14.9	42.5
Ship fares	100.0	0.7	3.8	5.1	14.5	9.5	18.7	47.7
School bus	100.0	3.7	15.3	11.4	11.6	3.1	11.9	42.9

Note: Numbers may not add to total because of rounding. (–) means sample is too small to make a reliable estimate.
Source: Calculations by New Strategist based on the 2000 Consumer Expenditure Survey

Table 11.11 Transportation: Average spending by household type, 2000

(average annual spending of consumer units (CU) on transportation, by type of consumer unit, 2000)

	total married couples	married couples, no children	married couples with children				single parent, at least one child <18	single person
			total	oldest child under 6	oldest child 6 to 17	oldest child 18 or older		
Number of consumer units (in thousands, add 000)	56,287	22,805	28,777	5,291	15,396	8,090	6,132	32,323
Average number of persons per CU	3.2	2.0	3.9	3.5	4.1	3.8	2.9	1.0
Average before-tax income of CU	$60,588.00	$53,232.00	$66,913.00	$62,928.00	$69,472.00	$64,725.00	$25,095.00	$24,977.00
Average spending of CU, total	48,619.37	42,195.54	53,585.53	50,755.90	54,170.40	54,550.20	28,923.25	23,059.00
Transportation, average spending	9,910.28	8,309.50	11,087.65	10,744.86	10,644.12	12,158.39	5,016.65	3,732.46
VEHICLE PURCHASES	$4,709.30	$3,824.49	$5,364.74	$5,594.20	$5,101.55	$5,715.57	$2,338.37	$1,456.32
Cars and trucks, new	2,277.01	2,113.34	2,477.58	2,640.29	2,378.91	2,558.96	524.24	796.68
New cars	1,235.78	1,250.55	1,248.64	1,209.45	1,111.98	1,534.39	294.23	524.57
New trucks	1,041.23	862.79	1,228.94	1,430.84	1,266.93	1,024.57	230.01	272.11
Cars and trucks, used	2,379.41	1,685.15	2,816.71	2,816.41	2,658.07	3,118.82	1,810.24	628.03
Used cars	1,211.40	849.40	1,401.09	1,167.29	1,268.13	1,807.07	1,552.89	465.73
Used trucks	1,168.02	835.75	1,415.61	1,649.13	1,389.94	1,311.75	257.35	162.30
Other vehicles	52.88	26.00	70.45	137.49	64.58	37.79	3.89	31.61
New motorcycles	22.99	10.34	30.64	11.48	40.45	24.50	3.89	12.97
Used motorcycles	16.57	12.02	16.64	–	24.13	13.28	–	16.02
GASOLINE AND MOTOR OIL	1,696.87	1,411.10	1,879.42	1,593.72	1,865.80	2,092.19	893.51	681.92
Gasoline	1,539.86	1,241.49	1,731.10	1,477.20	1,710.80	1,935.80	832.99	616.19
Diesel fuel	19.77	17.44	17.80	6.75	23.66	13.88	6.67	4.42
Gasoline on trips	122.23	139.81	113.81	97.03	114.76	122.99	47.41	56.19
Motor oil	13.77	10.94	15.55	11.76	15.42	18.28	5.96	4.55
Motor oil on trips	1.23	1.41	1.15	0.98	1.16	1.24	0.48	0.57
OTHER VEHICLE EXPENSES	2,983.85	2,492.58	3,352.41	3,150.05	3,191.64	3,793.09	1,517.71	1,272.38
Vehicle finance charges	456.73	350.42	533.95	551.37	516.56	555.64	217.36	129.34
Automobile finance charges	214.37	172.00	239.67	224.32	210.15	305.90	164.16	79.29
Truck finance charges	211.05	135.59	270.37	310.41	278.61	228.52	51.21	41.43
Motorcycle and plane finance charges	1.58	1.81	1.32	0.28	1.63	1.40	–	1.14
Other vehicle finance charges	29.73	41.01	22.59	16.37	26.18	19.82	1.98	7.47
Maintenance and repairs	776.33	672.60	850.60	712.49	827.07	988.44	469.64	395.67
Coolant, additives, brake and transmission fluids	6.02	3.84	7.58	4.90	8.33	7.91	2.55	2.22
Tires	110.16	94.53	121.89	84.58	118.42	152.91	65.00	52.81
Parts, equipment, and accessories	61.87	49.85	70.23	64.51	62.81	88.08	35.45	23.94
Vehicle audio equipment	4.19	0.03	8.13	–	10.95	8.95	–	0.87
Vehicle products	5.23	3.51	3.86	1.81	3.15	7.06	0.79	3.49
Miscellaneous auto repair, servicing	29.36	25.53	33.04	17.04	39.85	31.97	21.91	25.81
Body work and painting	31.51	28.94	35.69	35.19	26.79	52.98	26.87	14.88
Clutch, transmission repair	53.93	41.85	58.53	33.58	62.98	66.37	28.03	25.56
Drive shaft and rear-end repair	4.48	4.15	4.79	3.38	5.69	3.99	2.49	2.66
Brake work	66.95	55.82	76.73	56.48	76.23	90.92	41.88	34.42
Repair to steering or front-end	22.45	19.58	21.77	19.65	23.24	20.37	17.36	10.00
Repair to engine cooling system	26.62	23.14	28.73	19.16	25.31	41.49	14.41	13.56
Motor tune-up	55.19	48.27	62.40	57.96	64.36	61.59	28.27	27.92
Lube, oil change, and oil filters	72.34	69.26	75.03	71.08	73.38	80.73	42.88	41.22
Front-end alignment, wheel balance, rotation	13.56	10.99	15.60	14.52	17.51	12.66	8.47	6.92
Shock absorber replacement	5.27	3.77	6.30	4.11	8.06	4.40	2.61	2.44
Gas tank repair, replacement	4.44	5.38	3.73	4.11	3.91	3.05	0.33	1.88
Tire repair and other repair work	36.10	31.35	41.38	38.41	44.16	38.05	20.56	21.44
Vehicle air conditioning repair	26.87	30.05	25.37	28.28	24.89	24.39	14.96	10.37
Exhaust system repair	15.66	14.95	16.34	15.61	15.48	18.47	8.25	9.89
Electrical system repair	37.23	34.86	38.19	29.52	33.51	52.77	19.46	20.49
Motor repair, replacement	79.68	67.63	85.92	101.72	70.03	105.84	61.62	38.93
Auto repair service policy	7.21	5.31	9.35	6.88	8.02	13.49	5.49	3.96

	total married couples	married couples, no children	married couples with children				single parent, at least one child <18	single person
			total	oldest child under 6	oldest child 6 to 17	oldest child 18 or older		
Vehicle insurance	**$994.13**	**$836.96**	**$1,097.18**	**$957.39**	**$981.65**	**$1,408.49**	**$554.39**	**$436.88**
Vehicle rental, leases, licenses, other charges	**756.65**	**632.60**	**870.68**	**928.79**	**866.36**	**840.52**	**276.33**	**310.49**
Leased and rented vehicles	552.76	437.40	655.00	728.49	653.09	610.57	183.47	209.02
Rented vehicles	59.36	64.53	58.52	54.68	62.66	53.15	24.75	27.96
Auto rental	7.87	8.23	7.09	5.18	9.83	3.13	5.95	6.35
Auto rental on trips	40.73	46.99	38.60	34.36	36.31	45.72	13.92	17.58
Truck rental	4.15	3.41	5.04	4.49	7.50	0.71	2.01	1.99
Truck rental on trips	6.51	5.69	7.76	10.65	8.96	3.58	2.86	1.69
Leased vehicles	493.41	372.86	596.48	673.80	590.43	557.42	158.72	181.06
Car lease payments	233.25	202.66	261.58	261.43	239.42	303.87	75.88	107.27
Cash down payment (car lease)	15.65	16.36	14.20	20.44	12.71	12.96	11.87	10.64
Termination fee (car lease)	1.54	0.76	2.21	1.90	0.53	5.61	1.61	3.15
Truck lease payments	230.30	146.18	301.16	376.51	316.70	222.31	69.35	56.76
Cash down payment (truck lease)	10.71	5.93	14.25	9.33	17.20	11.87	–	2.98
Termination fee (truck lease)	1.96	0.98	3.07	4.20	3.87	0.81	–	0.26
State and local registration	115.58	111.87	119.72	110.40	114.09	136.53	40.61	46.87
Driver's license	8.96	8.34	9.70	8.30	9.32	11.33	3.54	4.01
Vehicle inspection	12.43	11.08	13.52	13.62	12.72	14.97	5.89	5.01
Parking fees	32.48	30.24	36.87	37.53	39.78	30.90	23.49	26.59
Parking fees in home city, excluding residence	27.55	25.10	31.77	31.15	34.35	27.25	20.84	22.94
Parking fees on trips	4.93	5.15	5.11	6.38	5.43	3.65	2.65	3.65
Tolls	14.52	11.58	17.72	18.16	19.02	14.58	7.24	6.86
Tolls on trips	4.48	4.82	4.34	4.18	4.29	4.56	2.43	2.37
Towing charges	5.21	4.05	5.88	2.92	6.97	5.73	6.22	2.74
Automobile service clubs	10.23	13.23	7.93	5.19	7.07	11.36	3.46	7.02
PUBLIC TRANSPORTATION	**520.26**	**581.33**	**491.08**	**406.90**	**485.12**	**557.54**	**267.05**	**321.83**
Airline fares	352.82	385.46	343.92	314.50	333.42	383.14	130.27	203.51
Intercity bus fares	20.60	23.54	18.96	15.04	17.04	25.18	8.20	11.57
Intracity mass transit fares	42.25	31.01	46.72	40.51	47.87	48.59	70.15	36.43
Local transportation on trips	12.80	14.53	12.14	7.65	11.93	15.48	5.07	9.98
Taxi fares and limousine service on trips	7.52	8.53	7.13	4.49	7.01	9.09	2.98	5.86
Taxi fares and limousine service	6.26	5.62	6.82	2.34	10.33	3.14	14.28	12.75
Intercity train fares	28.25	37.48	23.21	10.43	22.22	33.47	9.22	13.17
Ship fares	46.40	73.50	27.64	11.24	28.40	36.92	21.66	28.16
School bus	3.37	1.65	4.53	0.70	6.90	2.52	5.22	0.39

Note: Average spending figures for total consumer units can be found on Average Spending by Age and Average Spending by Region tables. (–) means sample is too small to make a reliable estimate.
Source: Bureau of Labor Statistics, unpublished tables from the 2000 Consumer Expenditure Survey

Table 11.12 Transportation: Indexed spending by household type, 2000

(indexed average annual spending of consumer units (CU) on transportation, by type of consumer unit, 2000; index definition: an index of 100 is the average for all consumer units; an index of 132 means that spending by consumer units in that group is 32 percent above the average for all consumer units; an index of 68 indicates spending that is 32 percent below the average for all consumer units)

	total married couples	married couples, no children	married couples with children				single parent, at least one child <18	single person
			total	oldest child under 6	oldest child 6 to 17	oldest child 18 or older		
Average spending of CU, total	$48,619	$42,196	$53,586	$50,756	$54,170	$54,550	$28,923	$23,059
Average spending of CU, index	128	111	141	133	142	143	76	61
Transportation, spending index	134	112	149	145	144	164	68	50
VEHICLE PURCHASES	**138**	**112**	**157**	**164**	**149**	**167**	**68**	**43**
Cars and trucks, new	**142**	**132**	**154**	**165**	**148**	**159**	**33**	**50**
New cars	135	136	136	132	121	167	32	57
New trucks	151	125	179	208	184	149	33	40
Cars and trucks, used	**134**	**95**	**159**	**159**	**150**	**176**	**102**	**35**
Used cars	120	84	139	115	125	179	154	46
Used trucks	154	110	187	217	183	173	34	21
Other vehicles	**122**	**60**	**162**	**316**	**149**	**87**	**9**	**73**
New motorcycles	125	56	166	62	219	133	21	70
Used motorcycles	95	69	96	–	139	76	–	92
GASOLINE AND MOTOR OIL	**131**	**109**	**146**	**123**	**144**	**162**	**69**	**53**
Gasoline	131	106	147	126	146	165	71	52
Diesel fuel	152	134	137	52	182	107	51	34
Gasoline on trips	133	152	124	106	125	134	52	61
Motor oil	137	109	155	117	153	182	59	45
Motor oil on trips	132	152	124	105	125	133	52	61
OTHER VEHICLE EXPENSES	**131**	**109**	**147**	**138**	**140**	**166**	**67**	**56**
Vehicle finance charges	**139**	**107**	**163**	**168**	**157**	**169**	**66**	**39**
Automobile finance charges	127	102	142	133	124	181	97	47
Truck finance charges	152	98	195	224	201	165	37	30
Motorcycle and plane finance charges	100	115	84	18	103	89	–	72
Other vehicle finance charges	158	218	120	87	139	105	11	40
Maintenance and repairs	**124**	**108**	**136**	**114**	**133**	**158**	**75**	**63**
Coolant, additives, brake and transmission fluids	135	86	170	110	186	177	57	50
Tires	126	108	140	97	136	175	75	61
Parts, equipment, and accessories	128	103	145	133	130	182	73	49
Vehicle audio equipment	174	1	337	–	454	371	–	36
Vehicle products	128	86	94	44	77	172	19	85
Miscellaneous auto repair, servicing	110	95	124	64	149	120	82	97
Body work and painting	120	110	135	134	102	201	102	56
Clutch, transmission repair	127	98	137	79	148	156	66	60
Drive shaft and rear-end repair	122	113	131	92	155	109	68	73
Brake work	124	103	142	105	141	168	77	64
Repair to steering or front-end	125	109	121	109	129	113	96	55
Repair to engine cooling system	130	113	140	93	123	202	70	66
Motor tune-up	124	109	141	131	145	139	64	63
Lube, oil change, and oil filters	123	118	128	121	125	137	73	70
Front-end alignment, wheel balance, rotation	126	102	145	135	162	117	78	64
Shock absorber replacement	124	89	148	97	190	104	61	57
Gas tank repair, replacement	125	152	105	116	110	86	9	53
Tire repair and other repair work	121	105	139	129	148	128	69	72
Vehicle air conditioning repair	136	152	128	143	126	123	76	52
Exhaust system repair	117	112	122	117	116	138	62	74
Electrical system repair	123	115	126	97	111	174	64	68
Motor repair, replacement	124	105	133	158	109	164	96	60
Auto repair service policy	126	93	164	120	140	236	96	69

	total married couples	married couples, no children	married couples with children			single parent, at least one child <18	single person
			total	oldest child under 6	oldest child 6 to 17	oldest child 18 or older		
Vehicle insurance	**128**	**108**	**141**	**123**	**126**	**181**	**71**	**56**
Vehicle rental, leases, licenses, other charges	**137**	**115**	**158**	**169**	**157**	**153**	**50**	**56**
Leased and rented vehicles	141	111	167	185	166	155	47	53
Rented vehicles	132	144	130	122	139	118	55	62
Auto rental	109	114	98	72	136	43	83	88
Auto rental on trips	138	159	130	116	123	154	47	59
Truck rental	129	106	157	140	234	22	63	62
Truck rental on trips	138	121	165	226	190	76	61	36
Leased vehicles	142	107	171	194	170	160	46	52
Car lease payments	133	116	150	150	137	174	43	61
Cash down payment (car lease)	112	117	102	146	91	93	85	76
Termination fee (car lease)	85	42	122	105	29	310	89	174
Truck lease payments	155	98	203	254	213	150	47	38
Cash down payment (truck lease)	139	77	185	121	223	154	–	39
Termination fee (truck lease)	177	88	277	378	349	73	–	23
State and local registration	136	131	141	130	134	160	48	55
Driver's license	131	122	142	121	136	165	52	59
Vehicle inspection	132	118	144	145	135	159	63	53
Parking fees	111	103	125	128	135	105	80	91
Parking fees in home city, excluding residence	109	99	125	123	136	108	82	91
Parking fees on trips	122	127	126	158	134	90	65	90
Tolls	133	106	163	167	174	134	66	63
Tolls on trips	128	137	124	119	122	130	69	68
Towing charges	111	87	126	62	149	122	133	59
Automobile service clubs	123	158	95	62	85	136	41	84
PUBLIC TRANSPORTATION	**122**	**136**	**115**	**95**	**114**	**131**	**63**	**75**
Airline fares	129	141	126	115	122	140	48	74
Intercity bus fares	128	146	118	93	106	156	51	72
Intracity mass transit fares	89	65	99	85	101	102	148	77
Local transportation on trips	120	136	114	72	112	145	48	94
Taxi fares and limousine service on trips	120	136	114	72	112	145	48	94
Taxi fares and limousine service	52	46	56	19	85	26	118	105
Intercity train fares	134	177	110	49	105	158	44	62
Ship fares	127	201	76	31	78	101	59	77
School bus	149	73	200	31	305	112	231	17

Note: Spending index for total consumer units is 100. (–) means sample is too small to make a reliable estimate.
Source: Calculations by New Strategist based on the 2000 Consumer Expenditure Survey

Table 11.13 Transportation: Indexed per capita spending by household type, 2000

(indexed average annual per capita spending of consumer units (CU) on transportation, by type of consumer unit, 2000; index definition: an index of 100 is the average for all consumer units; an index of 132 means that spending by consumer units in that group is 32 percent above the average for all consumer units; an index of 68 indicates spending that is 32 percent below the average for all consumer units)

	total married couples	married couples, no children	married couples with children				single parent, at least one child <18	single person
			total	oldest child under 6	oldest child 6 to 17	oldest child 18 or older		
Per capita spending of CU, total	$15,194	$21,098	$13,740	$14,502	$13,212	$14,355	$9,974	$23,059
Per capita spending of CU, index	100	139	90	95	87	94	66	152
Transportation, per capita spending index	104	140	96	103	88	108	58	126
VEHICLE PURCHASES	**108**	**140**	**101**	**117**	**91**	**110**	**59**	**107**
Cars and trucks, new	**111**	**165**	**99**	**118**	**90**	**105**	**28**	**124**
New cars	105	170	87	94	74	110	28	143
New trucks	118	157	115	149	112	98	29	99
Cars and trucks, used	**105**	**119**	**102**	**114**	**92**	**116**	**88**	**89**
Used cars	94	105	89	82	76	118	132	115
Used trucks	120	138	120	155	112	114	29	53
Other vehicles	**95**	**75**	**104**	**226**	**91**	**57**	**8**	**182**
New motorcycles	97	70	106	44	134	87	18	176
Used motorcycles	74	86	61	–	85	50	–	230
GASOLINE AND MOTOR OIL	**103**	**137**	**93**	**88**	**88**	**107**	**60**	**132**
Gasoline	102	132	94	90	89	108	61	131
Diesel fuel	119	168	88	37	111	70	44	85
Gasoline on trips	104	190	79	76	76	88	45	153
Motor oil	107	136	99	84	94	120	51	113
Motor oil on trips	103	190	79	75	76	88	44	153
OTHER VEHICLE EXPENSES	**102**	**137**	**94**	**99**	**85**	**109**	**57**	**139**
Vehicle finance charges	**109**	**133**	**104**	**120**	**96**	**111**	**57**	**99**
Automobile finance charges	99	127	91	95	76	119	84	117
Truck finance charges	119	122	125	160	123	108	32	75
Motorcycle and plane finance charges	78	143	54	13	63	58	–	180
Other vehicle finance charges	124	273	77	62	85	69	9	99
Maintenance and repairs	**97**	**135**	**87**	**82**	**81**	**104**	**65**	**159**
Coolant, additives, brake and transmission fluids	105	107	109	78	114	116	49	124
Tires	99	135	90	69	83	115	64	151
Parts, equipment, and accessories	100	129	93	95	79	120	63	124
Vehicle audio equipment	136	2	216	–	277	244	–	90
Vehicle products	100	107	60	32	47	113	17	213
Miscellaneous auto repair, servicing	86	119	79	46	91	79	71	241
Body work and painting	93	137	87	95	62	132	88	141
Clutch, transmission repair	99	123	88	56	90	102	57	150
Drive shaft and rear-end repair	96	142	84	66	95	72	59	182
Brake work	97	129	91	75	86	111	67	159
Repair to steering or front-end	97	136	77	78	79	74	83	139
Repair to engine cooling system	101	141	90	67	75	133	60	165
Motor tune-up	97	136	90	93	88	91	55	157
Lube, oil change, and oil filters	96	147	82	86	76	90	63	175
Front-end alignment, wheel balance, rotation	98	127	93	96	99	77	68	160
Shock absorber replacement	97	111	95	69	116	68	53	144
Gas tank repair, replacement	98	189	67	83	67	57	8	132
Tire repair and other repair work	95	132	89	92	91	84	60	180
Vehicle air conditioning repair	106	190	82	102	77	81	65	131
Exhaust system repair	92	140	79	84	71	91	53	185
Electrical system repair	96	144	81	70	67	115	55	169
Motor repair, replacement	97	131	85	113	66	108	82	151
Auto repair service policy	99	116	105	86	86	155	83	173

	total married couples	married couples, no children	married couples with children				single parent, at least one child <18	single person
			total	oldest child under 6	oldest child 6 to 17	oldest child 18 or older		
Vehicle insurance	**100**	**134**	**90**	**88**	**77**	**119**	**61**	**140**
Vehicle rental, leases, licenses, other charges	**107**	**143**	**101**	**120**	**96**	**100**	**43**	**141**
Leased and rented vehicles	110	139	107	132	101	102	40	133
Rented vehicles	103	179	83	87	85	78	47	156
Auto rental	85	143	63	51	83	29	71	220
Auto rental on trips	107	198	84	83	75	102	41	148
Truck rental	101	133	101	100	142	15	54	155
Truck rental on trips	108	151	106	162	116	50	52	90
Leased vehicles	111	134	110	138	103	105	39	130
Car lease payments	104	145	96	107	83	114	37	153
Cash down payment (car lease)	87	146	65	104	55	61	73	190
Termination fee (car lease)	66	52	78	75	18	204	77	435
Truck lease payments	121	123	130	181	130	99	40	96
Cash down payment (truck lease)	108	96	118	86	136	101	–	97
Termination fee (truck lease)	138	110	177	270	213	48	–	59
State and local registration	106	164	90	93	82	105	41	138
Driver's license	102	152	91	87	83	109	45	146
Vehicle inspection	103	147	92	103	82	105	54	133
Parking fees	86	129	80	91	83	69	69	226
Parking fees in home city, excluding residence	85	124	80	88	83	71	71	226
Parking fees on trips	95	159	81	113	82	59	56	225
Tolls	104	133	104	119	106	88	57	157
Tolls on trips	100	172	79	85	75	85	60	169
Towing charges	87	108	81	45	91	81	115	146
Automobile service clubs	96	198	61	44	52	90	36	210
PUBLIC TRANSPORTATION	**95**	**170**	**74**	**68**	**69**	**86**	**54**	**189**
Airline fares	101	176	80	82	74	92	41	186
Intercity bus fares	100	183	75	67	65	103	44	180
Intracity mass transit fares	70	82	63	61	62	67	128	192
Local transportation on trips	94	170	73	51	68	96	41	234
Taxi fares and limousine service on trips	94	170	73	51	68	96	41	234
Taxi fares and limousine service	40	58	36	14	52	17	101	262
Intercity train fares	104	222	70	35	64	104	38	156
Ship fares	99	251	48	22	47	66	51	192
School bus	116	91	128	22	186	73	199	43

Note: Per capita indexes account for household size and show how much each person in a particular household demographic segment spends relative to a person in the average household. Spending index for total consumer units is 100. (–) means sample is too small to make a reliable estimate.
Source: Calculations by New Strategist based on the 2000 Consumer Expenditure Survey

Table 11.14 Transportation: Total spending by household type, 2000

(total annual spending on transportation, by consumer unit (CU) type, 2000; numbers in thousands)

	total married couples	married couples, no children	married couples with children				single parent, at least one child <18	single person
			total	oldest child under 6	oldest child 6 to 17	oldest child 18 or older		
Number of consumer units	56,287	22,805	28,777	5,291	15,396	8,090	6,132	32,323
Total spending of all CUs	$2,736,638,479	$962,269,290	$1,542,030,797	$268,549,467	$834,007,478	$441,311,118	$177,357,369	$745,336,057
Transportation, total spending	557,819,930	189,498,148	319,069,304	56,851,054	163,876,872	98,361,375	30,762,098	120,644,305
VEHICLE PURCHASES	**$265,072,369**	**$87,217,494**	**$154,381,123**	**$29,598,912**	**$78,543,464**	**$46,238,961**	**$14,338,885**	**$47,072,631**
Cars and trucks, new	**128,166,062**	**48,194,719**	**71,297,320**	**13,969,774**	**36,625,698**	**20,701,986**	**3,214,640**	**25,751,088**
New cars	69,558,349	28,518,793	35,932,113	6,399,200	17,120,044	12,413,215	1,804,218	16,955,676
New trucks	58,607,713	19,675,926	35,365,206	7,570,574	19,505,654	8,288,771	1,410,421	8,795,412
Cars and trucks, used	**133,929,851**	**38,429,846**	**81,056,464**	**14,901,625**	**40,923,646**	**25,231,254**	**11,100,392**	**20,299,814**
Used cars	68,186,072	19,370,567	40,319,167	6,176,131	19,524,129	14,619,196	9,522,321	15,053,791
Used trucks	65,744,342	19,059,279	40,737,009	8,725,547	21,399,516	10,612,058	1,578,070	5,246,023
Other vehicles	**2,976,457**	**592,930**	**2,027,340**	**727,460**	**994,274**	**305,721**	**23,853**	**1,021,730**
New motorcycles	1,294,038	235,804	881,727	60,741	622,768	198,205	23,853	419,229
Used motorcycles	932,676	274,116	478,849	–	371,505	107,435	–	517,814
GASOLINE AND MOTOR OIL	**95,511,722**	**32,180,136**	**54,084,069**	**8,432,373**	**28,725,857**	**16,925,817**	**5,479,003**	**22,041,700**
Gasoline	86,674,100	28,312,179	49,815,865	7,815,865	26,339,477	15,660,622	5,107,895	19,917,109
Diesel fuel	1,112,794	397,719	512,231	35,714	364,269	112,289	40,900	142,868
Gasoline on trips	6,879,960	3,188,367	3,275,110	513,386	1,766,845	994,989	290,718	1,816,229
Motor oil	775,072	249,487	447,482	62,222	237,406	147,885	36,547	147,070
Motor oil on trips	69,233	32,155	33,094	5,185	17,859	10,032	2,943	18,424
OTHER VEHICLE EXPENSES	**167,951,965**	**56,843,287**	**96,472,303**	**16,666,915**	**49,138,489**	**30,686,098**	**9,306,598**	**41,127,139**
Vehicle finance charges	**25,707,962**	**7,991,328**	**15,365,479**	**2,917,299**	**7,952,958**	**4,495,128**	**1,332,852**	**4,180,657**
Automobile finance charges	12,066,244	3,922,460	6,896,984	1,186,877	3,235,469	2,474,731	1,006,629	2,562,891
Truck finance charges	11,879,371	3,092,130	7,780,437	1,642,379	4,289,480	1,848,727	314,020	1,339,142
Motorcycle and plane finance charges	88,933	41,277	37,986	1,481	25,095	11,326	–	36,848
Other vehicle finance charges	1,673,413	935,233	650,072	86,614	403,067	160,344	12,141	241,453
Maintenance and repairs	**43,697,287**	**15,338,643**	**24,477,716**	**3,769,785**	**12,733,570**	**7,996,480**	**2,879,832**	**12,789,241**
Coolant, additives, brake, transmission fluids	338,848	87,571	218,130	25,926	128,249	63,992	15,637	71,757
Tires	6,200,576	2,155,757	3,507,629	447,513	1,823,194	1,237,042	398,580	1,706,978
Parts, equipment, and accessories	3,482,477	1,136,829	2,021,009	341,322	967,023	712,567	217,379	773,813
Vehicle audio equipment	235,843	684	233,957	–	168,586	72,406	–	28,121
Vehicle products	294,381	80,046	111,079	9,577	48,497	57,115	4,844	112,807
Miscellaneous auto repair, servicing	1,652,586	582,212	950,792	90,159	613,531	258,637	134,352	834,257
Body work and painting	1,773,603	659,977	1,027,051	186,190	412,459	428,608	164,767	480,966
Clutch, transmission repair	3,035,558	954,389	1,684,318	177,672	969,640	536,933	171,880	826,176
Drive shaft and rear-end repair	252,166	94,641	137,842	17,884	87,603	32,279	15,269	85,979
Brake work	3,768,415	1,272,975	2,208,059	298,836	1,173,637	735,543	256,808	1,112,558
Repair to steering or front-end	1,263,643	446,522	626,475	103,968	357,803	164,793	106,452	323,230
Repair to engine cooling system	1,498,360	527,708	826,763	101,376	389,673	335,654	88,362	438,300
Motor tune-up	3,106,480	1,100,797	1,795,685	306,666	990,887	498,263	173,352	902,458
Lube, oil change, and oil filters	4,071,802	1,579,474	2,159,138	376,084	1,129,758	653,106	262,940	1,332,354
Front-end alignment, wheel balance, rotation	763,252	250,627	448,921	76,825	269,584	102,419	51,938	223,675
Shock absorber replacement	296,632	85,975	181,295	21,746	124,092	35,596	16,005	78,868
Gas tank repair, replacement	249,914	122,691	107,338	21,746	60,198	24,675	2,024	60,767
Tire repair and other repair work	2,031,961	714,937	1,190,792	203,227	679,887	307,825	126,074	693,005
Vehicle air conditioning repair	1,512,432	685,290	730,072	149,629	383,206	197,315	91,735	335,190
Exhaust system repair	881,454	340,935	470,216	82,593	238,330	149,422	50,589	319,674
Electrical system repair	2,095,565	794,982	1,098,994	156,190	515,920	426,909	119,329	662,298
Motor repair, replacement	4,484,948	1,542,302	2,472,520	538,201	1,078,182	856,246	377,854	1,258,334
Auto repair service policy	405,829	121,095	269,065	36,402	123,476	109,134	33,665	127,999

	total married couples	married couples, no children	married couples with children				single parent, at least one child <18	single person
			total	oldest child under 6	oldest child 6 to 17	oldest child 18 or older		
Vehicle insurance	$55,956,595	$19,086,873	$31,573,549	$5,065,550	$15,113,483	$11,394,684	$3,399,519	$14,121,272
Vehicle rental, leases, licenses, other charges	**42,589,559**	**14,426,443**	**25,055,558**	**4,914,228**	**13,338,479**	**6,799,807**	**1,694,456**	**10,035,968**
Leased and rented vehicles	31,113,202	9,974,907	18,848,935	3,854,441	10,054,974	4,939,511	1,125,038	6,756,153
Rented vehicles	3,341,196	1,471,607	1,684,030	289,312	964,713	429,984	151,767	903,751
Auto rental	442,979	187,685	204,029	27,407	151,343	25,322	36,485	205,251
Auto rental on trips	2,292,570	1,071,607	1,110,792	181,799	559,029	369,875	85,357	568,238
Truck rental	233,591	77,765	145,036	23,757	115,470	5,744	12,325	64,323
Truck rental on trips	366,428	129,760	223,310	56,349	137,948	28,962	17,538	54,626
Leased vehicles	27,772,569	8,503,072	17,164,905	3,565,076	9,090,260	4,509,528	973,271	5,852,402
Car lease payments	13,128,943	4,621,661	7,527,488	1,383,226	3,686,110	2,458,308	465,296	3,467,288
Cash down payment (car lease)	880,892	373,090	408,633	108,148	195,683	104,846	72,787	343,917
Termination fee (car lease)	86,682	17,332	63,597	10,053	8,160	45,385	9,873	101,817
Truck lease payments	12,962,896	3,333,635	8,666,481	1,992,114	4,875,913	1,798,488	425,254	1,834,653
Cash down payment (truck lease)	602,834	135,234	410,072	49,365	264,811	96,028	–	96,323
Termination fee (truck lease)	110,323	22,349	88,345	22,222	59,583	6,553	–	8,404
State and local registration	6,505,651	2,551,195	3,445,182	584,126	1,756,530	1,104,528	249,021	1,514,979
Driver's license	504,332	190,194	279,137	43,915	143,491	91,660	21,707	129,615
Vehicle inspection	699,647	252,679	389,065	72,063	195,837	121,107	36,117	161,938
Parking fees	1,828,202	689,623	1,061,008	198,571	612,453	249,981	144,041	859,469
Parking fees in home city, excluding residence	1,550,707	572,406	914,245	164,815	528,853	220,453	127,791	741,490
Parking fees on trips	277,495	117,446	147,050	33,757	83,600	29,529	16,250	117,979
Tolls	817,287	264,082	509,928	96,085	292,832	117,952	44,396	221,736
Tolls on trips	252,166	109,920	124,892	22,116	66,049	36,890	14,901	76,606
Towing charges	293,255	92,360	169,209	15,450	107,310	46,356	38,141	88,565
Automobile service clubs	575,816	301,710	228,202	27,460	108,850	91,902	21,217	226,907
PUBLIC TRANSPORTATION	**29,283,875**	**13,257,231**	**14,131,809**	**2,152,908**	**7,468,908**	**4,510,499**	**1,637,551**	**10,402,511**
Airline fares	19,859,179	8,790,415	9,896,986	1,664,020	5,133,334	3,099,603	798,816	6,578,054
Intercity bus fares	1,159,512	536,830	545,612	79,577	262,348	203,706	50,282	373,977
Intracity mass transit fares	2,378,126	707,183	1,344,461	214,338	737,007	393,093	430,160	1,177,527
Local transportation on trips	720,474	331,357	349,353	40,476	183,674	125,233	31,089	322,584
Taxi fares and limousine service on trips	423,278	194,527	205,180	23,757	107,926	73,538	18,273	189,413
Taxi fares and limousine service	352,357	128,164	196,259	12,381	159,041	25,403	87,565	412,118
Intercity train fares	1,590,108	854,731	667,914	55,185	342,099	270,772	56,537	425,694
Ship fares	2,611,717	1,676,168	795,396	59,471	437,246	298,683	132,819	910,216
School bus	189,687	37,628	130,360	3,704	106,232	20,387	32,009	12,606

Note: Total spending figures for total consumer units can be found on Total Spending by Age and Total Spending by Region tables. Spending by type of consumer unit will not add to total because not all types of consumer units are shown. (–) means sample is too small to make a reliable estimate.
Source: Calculations by New Strategist based on the 2000 Consumer Expenditure Survey

Table 11.15 Transportation: Market shares by household type, 2000

(percentage of total annual spending on transportation accounted for by types of consumer units, 2000)

	total married couples	married couples, no children	married couples with children				single parent, at least one child <18	single person
			total	oldest child under 6	oldest child 6 to 17	oldest child 18 or older		
Share of total consumer units	51.5%	20.9%	26.3%	4.8%	14.1%	7.4%	5.6%	29.6%
Share of total before-tax income	69.8	24.9	39.4	6.8	21.9	10.7	3.2	16.5
Share of total spending	65.8	23.1	37.1	6.5	20.0	10.6	4.3	17.9
Share of transportation spending	68.8	23.4	39.3	7.0	20.2	12.1	3.8	14.9
VEHICLE PURCHASES	**70.9%**	**23.3%**	**41.3%**	**7.9%**	**21.0%**	**12.4%**	**3.8%**	**12.6%**
Cars and trucks, new	73.0	27.5	40.6	8.0	20.9	11.8	1.8	14.7
New cars	69.4	28.4	35.8	6.4	17.1	12.4	1.8	16.9
New trucks	77.9	26.2	47.0	10.1	25.9	11.0	1.9	11.7
Cars and trucks, used	**69.2**	**19.9**	**41.9**	**7.7**	**21.1**	**13.0**	**5.7**	**10.5**
Used cars	61.7	17.5	36.5	5.6	17.7	13.2	8.6	13.6
Used trucks	79.2	23.0	49.1	10.5	25.8	12.8	1.9	6.3
Other vehicles	**62.6**	**12.5**	**42.7**	**15.3**	**20.9**	**6.4**	**0.5**	**21.5**
New motorcycles	64.1	11.7	43.7	3.0	30.9	9.8	1.2	20.8
Used motorcycles	49.1	14.4	25.2	–	19.5	5.7	–	27.2
GASOLINE AND MOTOR OIL	**67.6**	**22.8**	**38.3**	**6.0**	**20.3**	**12.0**	**3.9**	**15.6**
Gasoline	67.4	22.0	38.7	6.1	20.5	12.2	4.0	15.5
Diesel fuel	78.4	28.0	36.1	2.5	25.7	7.9	2.9	10.1
Gasoline on trips	68.5	31.8	32.6	5.1	17.6	9.9	2.9	18.1
Motor oil	70.5	22.7	40.7	5.7	21.6	13.5	3.3	13.4
Motor oil on trips	68.1	31.6	32.5	5.1	17.6	9.9	2.9	18.1
OTHER VEHICLE EXPENSES	**67.3**	**22.8**	**38.7**	**6.7**	**19.7**	**12.3**	**3.7**	**16.5**
Vehicle finance charges	**71.6**	**22.3**	**42.8**	**8.1**	**22.2**	**12.5**	**3.7**	**11.6**
Automobile finance charges	65.2	21.2	37.3	6.4	17.5	13.4	5.4	13.8
Truck finance charges	78.4	20.4	51.3	10.8	28.3	12.2	2.1	8.8
Motorcycle and plane finance charges	51.5	23.9	22.0	0.9	14.5	6.6	–	21.3
Other vehicle finance charges	81.4	45.5	31.6	4.2	19.6	7.8	0.6	11.7
Maintenance and repairs	**64.1**	**22.5**	**35.9**	**5.5**	**18.7**	**11.7**	**4.2**	**18.7**
Coolant, additives, brake and transmission fluids	69.3	17.9	44.6	5.3	26.2	13.1	3.2	14.7
Tires	65.0	22.6	36.8	4.7	19.1	13.0	4.2	17.9
Parts, equipment, and accessories	65.7	21.4	38.1	6.4	18.2	13.4	4.1	14.6
Vehicle audio equipment	89.5	0.3	88.8	–	64.0	27.5	–	10.7
Vehicle products	65.7	17.9	24.8	2.1	10.8	12.7	1.1	25.2
Miscellaneous auto repair, servicing	56.5	19.9	32.5	3.1	21.0	8.8	4.6	28.5
Body work and painting	61.5	22.9	35.6	6.5	14.3	14.9	5.7	16.7
Clutch, transmission repair	65.1	20.5	36.1	3.8	20.8	11.5	3.7	17.7
Drive shaft and rear-end repair	63.0	23.6	34.4	4.5	21.9	8.1	3.8	21.5
Brake work	63.8	21.5	37.4	5.1	19.9	12.4	4.3	18.8
Repair to steering or front-end	64.1	22.7	31.8	5.3	18.2	8.4	5.4	16.4
Repair to engine cooling system	66.7	23.5	36.8	4.5	17.3	14.9	3.9	19.5
Motor tune-up	64.0	22.7	37.0	6.3	20.4	10.3	3.6	18.6
Lube, oil change, and oil filters	63.4	24.6	33.6	5.9	17.6	10.2	4.1	20.7
Front-end alignment, wheel balance, rotation	64.7	21.2	38.0	6.5	22.8	8.7	4.4	19.0
Shock absorber replacement	63.8	18.5	39.0	4.7	26.7	7.7	3.4	17.0
Gas tank repair, replacement	64.4	31.6	27.6	5.6	15.5	6.4	0.5	15.7
Tire repair and other repair work	62.5	22.0	36.6	6.2	20.9	9.5	3.9	21.3
Vehicle air conditioning repair	69.8	31.6	33.7	6.9	17.7	9.1	4.2	15.5
Exhaust system repair	60.4	23.4	32.2	5.7	16.3	10.2	3.5	21.9
Electrical system repair	63.2	24.0	33.2	4.7	15.6	12.9	3.6	20.0
Motor repair, replacement	63.6	21.9	35.1	7.6	15.3	12.1	5.4	17.8
Auto repair service policy	65.0	19.4	43.1	5.8	19.8	17.5	5.4	20.5

	total married couples	married couples, no children	married couples with children				single parent, at least one child <18	single person
			total	oldest child under 6	oldest child 6 to 17	oldest child 18 or older		
Vehicle insurance	**65.8%**	**22.4%**	**37.1%**	**6.0%**	**17.8%**	**13.4%**	**4.0%**	**16.6%**
Vehicle rental, leases, licenses, other charges	**70.7**	**23.9**	**41.6**	**8.2**	**22.1**	**11.3**	**2.8**	**16.6**
Leased and rented vehicles	72.4	23.2	43.9	9.0	23.4	11.5	2.6	15.7
Rented vehicles	68.0	29.9	34.3	5.9	19.6	8.7	3.1	18.4
Auto rental	56.2	23.8	25.9	3.5	19.2	3.2	4.6	26.0
Auto rental on trips	70.8	33.1	34.3	5.6	17.3	11.4	2.6	17.5
Truck rental	66.5	22.2	41.3	6.8	32.9	1.6	3.5	18.3
Truck rental on trips	71.1	25.2	43.4	10.9	26.8	5.6	3.4	10.6
Leased vehicles	73.0	22.3	45.1	9.4	23.9	11.9	2.6	15.4
Car lease payments	68.7	24.2	39.4	7.2	19.3	12.9	2.4	18.1
Cash down payment (car lease)	57.6	24.4	26.7	7.1	12.8	6.9	4.8	22.5
Termination fee (car lease)	43.8	8.8	32.1	5.1	4.1	22.9	5.0	51.4
Truck lease payments	79.8	20.5	53.4	12.3	30.0	11.1	2.6	11.3
Cash down payment (truck lease)	71.4	16.0	48.6	5.8	31.4	11.4	–	11.4
Termination fee (truck lease)	90.9	18.4	72.8	18.3	49.1	5.4	–	6.9
State and local registration	69.8	27.4	37.0	6.3	18.9	11.9	2.7	16.3
Driver's license	67.3	25.4	37.3	5.9	19.2	12.2	2.9	17.3
Vehicle inspection	68.0	24.6	37.8	7.0	19.0	11.8	3.5	15.7
Parking fees	56.9	21.5	33.0	6.2	19.1	7.8	4.5	26.7
Parking fees in home city, excluding residence	56.0	20.7	33.0	5.9	19.1	8.0	4.6	26.8
Parking fees on trips	62.6	26.5	33.2	7.6	18.9	6.7	3.7	26.6
Tolls	68.6	22.2	42.8	8.1	24.6	9.9	3.7	18.6
Tolls on trips	65.7	28.6	32.5	5.8	17.2	9.6	3.9	20.0
Towing charges	57.3	18.0	33.1	3.0	21.0	9.1	7.5	17.3
Automobile service clubs	63.1	33.0	25.0	3.0	11.9	10.1	2.3	24.8
PUBLIC TRANSPORTATION	**62.8**	**28.4**	**30.3**	**4.6**	**16.0**	**9.7**	**3.5**	**22.3**
Airline fares	66.3	29.3	33.0	5.6	17.1	10.3	2.7	21.9
Intercity bus fares	65.9	30.5	31.0	4.5	14.9	11.6	2.9	21.2
Intracity mass transit fares	45.9	13.6	25.9	4.1	14.2	7.6	8.3	22.7
Local transportation on trips	61.8	28.4	30.0	3.5	15.8	10.7	2.7	27.7
Taxi fares and limousine service on trips	61.8	28.4	30.0	3.5	15.8	10.7	2.7	27.7
Taxi fares and limousine service	26.5	9.6	14.8	0.9	12.0	1.9	6.6	31.0
Intercity train fares	68.8	37.0	28.9	2.4	14.8	11.7	2.4	18.4
Ship fares	65.3	41.9	19.9	1.5	10.9	7.5	3.3	22.8
School bus	76.7	15.2	52.7	1.5	43.0	8.2	13.0	5.1

Note: Market share for total consumer units is 100.0%. Market shares by type of consumer unit will not add to total because not all types of consumer units are shown. (–) means sample is too small to make a reliable estimate.
Source: Calculations by New Strategist based on the 2000 Consumer Expenditure Survey

Table 11.16 Transportation: Average spending by race and Hispanic origin, 2000

(average annual spending by consumer units (CU) on transportation, by race and Hispanic origin of consumer unit reference person, 2000)

	total consumer units	race black	race white and other	Hispanic origin Hispanic	Hispanic origin non-Hispanic
Number of consumer units					
(in thousands, add 000)	109,367	13,230	96,137	9,473	99,894
Average number of persons per CU	2.5	2.7	2.5	3.4	2.4
Average before-tax income of CU	$44,649.00	$32,657.00	$46,260.00	$34,891.00	$45,669.00
Average spending of CU, total	38,044.67	28,152.24	39,406.20	32,734.95	38,548.91
Transportation, average spending	7,417.36	5,214.38	7,720.53	6,719.21	7,483.58
VEHICLE PURCHASES	$3,418.27	$2,284.95	$3,574.23	$3,145.94	$3,444.09
Cars and trucks, new	1,604.95	869.07	1,706.22	1,079.37	1,654.79
New cars	917.02	567.27	965.15	563.93	950.50
New trucks	687.94	301.80	741.08	515.44	704.29
Cars and trucks, used	1,769.85	1,413.57	1,818.88	2,057.51	1,742.57
Used cars	1,011.25	1,013.36	1,010.96	1,212.48	992.17
Used trucks	758.60	400.21	807.92	845.04	750.40
Other vehicles	43.46	2.31	49.13	9.05	46.73
New motorcycles	18.45	–	20.99	6.70	19.57
Used motorcycles	17.38	2.31	19.46	2.35	18.81
GASOLINE AND MOTOR OIL	1,291.25	955.84	1,337.41	1,243.72	1,295.75
Gasoline	1,175.50	897.82	1,213.71	1,164.76	1,176.52
Diesel fuel	12.98	13.28	12.94	4.91	13.74
Gasoline on trips	91.79	38.04	99.19	60.79	94.73
Motor oil	10.05	6.31	10.57	12.65	9.81
Motor oil on trips	0.93	0.38	1.00	0.61	0.96
OTHER VEHICLE EXPENSES	2,281.28	1,705.16	2,360.57	1,944.50	2,313.20
Vehicle finance charges	328.24	289.52	333.57	274.20	333.36
Automobile finance charges	169.25	189.95	166.40	146.90	171.37
Truck finance charges	138.62	98.59	144.13	125.96	139.82
Motorcycle and plane finance charges	1.58	0.12	1.78	0.05	1.72
Other vehicle finance charges	18.79	0.86	21.26	1.29	20.45
Maintenance and repairs	623.76	451.66	647.44	545.61	631.14
Coolant, additives, brake and transmission fluids	4.47	3.96	4.54	4.31	4.48
Tires	87.23	63.23	90.53	73.90	88.49
Parts, equipment, and accessories	48.46	24.93	51.70	59.02	47.46
Vehicle audio equipment	2.41	–	2.75	4.91	2.18
Vehicle products	4.10	3.22	4.22	2.00	4.29
Miscellaneous auto repair, servicing	26.74	15.22	28.32	14.05	27.92
Body work and painting	26.35	13.79	28.08	17.57	27.18
Clutch, transmission repair	42.61	38.62	43.15	42.08	42.66
Drive shaft and rear-end repair	3.66	2.00	3.88	4.52	3.57
Brake work	54.04	47.13	55.00	34.68	55.88
Repair to steering or front-end	18.02	11.61	18.90	21.43	17.70
Repair to engine cooling system	20.55	16.53	21.11	17.31	20.86
Motor tune-up	44.41	35.34	45.66	43.51	44.49
Lube, oil change, and oil filters	58.75	37.90	61.62	50.28	59.55
Front-end alignment, wheel balance, rotation	10.79	8.50	11.10	8.38	11.01
Shock absorber replacement	4.25	2.84	4.44	4.21	4.25
Gas tank repair, replacement	3.55	5.24	3.32	3.58	3.55
Tire repair and other repair work	29.75	23.06	30.67	20.77	30.60
Vehicle air conditioning repair	19.80	12.02	20.87	15.44	20.21
Exhaust system repair	13.34	6.98	14.21	9.53	13.70
Electrical system repair	30.31	20.42	31.68	29.05	30.43
Motor repair, replacement	64.46	57.50	65.42	62.78	64.62
Auto repair service policy	5.71	1.62	6.27	2.29	6.03

	total consumer units	race		Hispanic origin	
		black	white and other	Hispanic	non-Hispanic
Vehicle insurance	$778.13	$633.75	$798.00	$696.31	$785.89
Vehicle rental, leases, licenses, other charges	551.15	330.23	581.56	428.38	562.80
Leased and rented vehicles	392.88	244.12	413.36	297.17	401.96
Rented vehicles	44.95	26.45	47.50	36.49	45.75
Auto rental	7.21	8.67	7.01	3.04	7.60
Auto rental on trips	29.62	13.91	31.78	21.36	30.40
Truck rental	3.21	1.98	3.38	5.32	3.01
Truck rental on trips	4.71	1.90	5.10	6.40	4.55
Leased vehicles	347.93	217.66	365.86	260.68	356.20
Car lease payments	174.84	100.42	185.08	106.77	181.29
Cash down payment (car lease)	13.99	7.22	14.93	16.87	13.72
Termination fee (car lease)	1.81	10.34	0.64	–	1.98
Truck lease payments	148.45	97.15	155.51	124.37	150.74
Cash down payment (truck lease)	7.72	2.53	8.44	9.13	7.59
Termination fee (truck lease)	1.11	–	1.26	3.55	0.88
State and local registration	85.19	42.78	91.03	70.98	86.54
Driver's license	6.85	4.19	7.22	6.13	6.92
Vehicle inspection	9.41	6.39	9.83	11.37	9.23
Parking fees	29.38	18.37	30.90	18.37	30.42
Parking fees in home city, excluding residence	25.33	16.95	26.49	15.46	26.27
Parking fees on trips	4.05	1.42	4.41	2.91	4.16
Tolls	10.90	3.83	11.87	15.45	10.48
Tolls on trips	3.51	2.07	3.71	1.62	3.69
Towing charges	4.68	4.39	4.72	4.01	4.74
Automobile service clubs	8.35	4.09	8.93	3.28	8.83
PUBLIC TRANSPORTATION	426.56	268.43	448.33	385.05	430.53
Airline fares	274.02	108.47	296.81	204.02	280.66
Intercity bus fares	16.10	12.75	16.56	15.16	16.19
Intracity mass transit fares	47.41	97.18	40.56	93.42	43.04
Local transportation on trips	10.66	4.89	11.46	5.97	11.11
Taxi fares and limousine service on trips	6.26	2.87	6.73	3.50	6.52
Taxi fares and limousine service	12.15	19.52	11.13	27.23	10.75
Intercity train fares	21.12	8.79	22.82	10.34	22.15
Ship fares	36.58	11.12	40.08	18.57	38.29
School bus	2.26	2.84	2.18	6.84	1.83

Note: Other races include Asians, Native Americans, and Pacific Islanders. (–) means sample is too small to make a reliable estimate.
Source: Bureau of Labor Statistics, unpublished tables from the 2000 Consumer Expenditure Survey

Table 11.17 Transportation: Indexed spending by race and Hispanic origin, 2000

(indexed average annual spending of consumer units (CU) on transportation, by race and Hispanic origin of consumer unit reference person, 2000; index definition: an index of 100 is the average for all consumer units; an index of 132 means that spending by consumer units in that group is 32 percent above the average for all consumer units; an index of 68 indicates spending that is 32 percent below the average for all consumer units)

	total consumer units	race		Hispanic origin	
		black	white and other	Hispanic	non-Hispanic
Average spending of CU, total	$38,045	$28,152	$39,406	$32,735	$38,549
Average spending of CU, index	100	74	104	86	101
Transportation, spending index	100	70	104	91	101
VEHICLE PURCHASES	100	67	105	92	101
Cars and trucks, new	100	54	106	67	103
New cars	100	62	105	61	104
New trucks	100	44	108	75	102
Cars and trucks, used	100	80	103	116	98
Used cars	100	100	100	120	98
Used trucks	100	53	107	111	99
Other vehicles	100	5	113	21	108
New motorcycles	100	–	114	36	106
Used motorcycles	100	13	112	14	108
GASOLINE AND MOTOR OIL	100	74	104	96	100
Gasoline	100	76	103	99	100
Diesel fuel	100	102	100	38	106
Gasoline on trips	100	41	108	66	103
Motor oil	100	63	105	126	98
Motor oil on trips	100	41	108	66	103
OTHER VEHICLE EXPENSES	100	75	103	85	101
Vehicle finance charges	100	88	102	84	102
Automobile finance charges	100	112	98	87	101
Truck finance charges	100	71	104	91	101
Motorcycle and plane finance charges	100	8	113	3	109
Other vehicle finance charges	100	5	113	7	109
Maintenance and repairs	100	72	104	87	101
Coolant, additives, brake and transmission fluids	100	89	102	96	100
Tires	100	72	104	85	101
Parts, equipment, and accessories	100	51	107	122	98
Vehicle audio equipment	100	–	114	204	90
Vehicle products	100	79	103	49	105
Miscellaneous auto repair, servicing	100	57	106	53	104
Body work and painting	100	52	107	67	103
Clutch, transmission repair	100	91	101	99	100
Drive shaft and rear-end repair	100	55	106	123	98
Brake work	100	87	102	64	103
Repair to steering or front-end	100	64	105	119	98
Repair to engine cooling system	100	80	103	84	102
Motor tune-up	100	80	103	98	100
Lube, oil change, and oil filters	100	65	105	86	101
Front-end alignment, wheel balance, rotation	100	79	103	78	102
Shock absorber replacement	100	67	104	99	100
Gas tank repair, replacement	100	148	94	101	100
Tire repair and other repair work	100	78	103	70	103
Vehicle air conditioning repair	100	61	105	78	102
Exhaust system repair	100	52	107	71	103
Electrical system repair	100	67	105	96	100
Motor repair, replacement	100	89	101	97	100
Auto repair service policy	100	28	110	40	106

	total consumer units	race		Hispanic origin	
		black	white and other	Hispanic	non-Hispanic
Vehicle insurance	**100**	**81**	**103**	**89**	**101**
Vehicle rental, leases, licenses, other charges	**100**	**60**	**106**	**78**	**102**
Leased and rented vehicles	100	62	105	76	102
Rented vehicles	100	59	106	81	102
Auto rental	100	120	97	42	105
Auto rental on trips	100	47	107	72	103
Truck rental	100	62	105	166	94
Truck rental on trips	100	40	108	136	97
Leased vehicles	100	63	105	75	102
Car lease payments	100	57	106	61	104
Cash down payment (car lease)	100	52	107	121	98
Termination fee (car lease)	100	571	35	–	109
Truck lease payments	100	65	105	84	102
Cash down payment (truck lease)	100	33	109	118	98
Termination fee (truck lease)	100	–	114	320	79
State and local registration	100	50	107	83	102
Driver's license	100	61	105	89	101
Vehicle inspection	100	68	104	121	98
Parking fees	100	63	105	63	104
Parking fees in home city, excluding residence	100	67	105	61	104
Parking fees on trips	100	35	109	72	103
Tolls	100	35	109	142	96
Tolls on trips	100	59	106	46	105
Towing charges	100	94	101	86	101
Automobile service clubs	100	49	107	39	106
PUBLIC TRANSPORTATION	**100**	**63**	**105**	**90**	**101**
Airline fares	100	40	108	74	102
Intercity bus fares	100	79	103	94	101
Intracity mass transit fares	100	205	86	197	91
Local transportation on trips	100	46	108	56	104
Taxi fares and limousine service on trips	100	46	108	56	104
Taxi fares and limousine service	100	161	92	224	88
Intercity train fares	100	42	108	49	105
Ship fares	100	30	110	51	105
School bus	100	126	96	303	81

Note: Other races include Asians, Native Americans, and Pacific Islanders. (–) means sample is too small to make a reliable estimate.
Source: Calculations by New Strategist based on the 2000 Consumer Expenditure Survey

Table 11.18 Transportation: Indexed per capita spending by race and Hispanic origin, 2000

(indexed average annual per capita spending of consumer units (CU) on transportation, by race and Hispanic origin of consumer unit reference person, 2000; index definition: an index of 100 is the average for all consumer units; an index of 132 means that spending by consumer units in that group is 32 percent above the average for all consumer units; an index of 68 indicates spending that is 32 percent below the average for all consumer units)

	total consumer units	race		Hispanic origin	
		black	white and other	Hispanic	non-Hispanic
Per capita spending of CU, total	$15,218	$10,427	$15,762	$9,628	$16,062
Per capita spending of CU, index	100	69	104	63	106
Transportation, per capita spending index	100	65	104	67	105
VEHICLE PURCHASES	**100**	**62**	**105**	**68**	**105**
Cars and trucks, new	**100**	**50**	**106**	**49**	**107**
New cars	100	57	105	45	108
New trucks	100	41	108	55	107
Cars and trucks, used	**100**	**74**	**103**	**85**	**103**
Used cars	100	93	100	88	102
Used trucks	100	49	107	82	103
Other vehicles	**100**	**5**	**113**	**15**	**112**
New motorcycles	100	–	114	27	110
Used motorcycles	100	12	112	10	113
GASOLINE AND MOTOR OIL	**100**	**69**	**104**	**71**	**105**
Gasoline	100	71	103	73	104
Diesel fuel	100	95	100	28	110
Gasoline on trips	100	38	108	49	108
Motor oil	100	58	105	93	102
Motor oil on trips	100	38	108	48	108
OTHER VEHICLE EXPENSES	**100**	**69**	**103**	**63**	**106**
Vehicle finance charges	**100**	**82**	**102**	**61**	**106**
Automobile finance charges	100	104	98	64	105
Truck finance charges	100	66	104	67	105
Motorcycle and plane finance charges	100	7	113	2	113
Other vehicle finance charges	100	4	113	5	113
Maintenance and repairs	**100**	**67**	**104**	**64**	**105**
Coolant, additives, brake and transmission fluids	100	82	102	71	104
Tires	100	67	104	62	106
Parts, equipment, and accessories	100	48	107	90	102
Vehicle audio equipment	100	–	114	150	94
Vehicle products	100	73	103	36	109
Miscellaneous auto repair, servicing	100	53	106	39	109
Body work and painting	100	48	107	49	107
Clutch, transmission repair	100	84	101	73	104
Drive shaft and rear-end repair	100	51	106	91	102
Brake work	100	81	102	47	108
Repair to steering or front-end	100	60	105	87	102
Repair to engine cooling system	100	74	103	62	106
Motor tune-up	100	74	103	72	104
Lube, oil change, and oil filters	100	60	105	63	106
Front-end alignment, wheel balance, rotation	100	73	103	57	106
Shock absorber replacement	100	62	104	73	104
Gas tank repair, replacement	100	137	94	74	104
Tire repair and other repair work	100	72	103	51	107
Vehicle air conditioning repair	100	56	105	57	106
Exhaust system repair	100	48	107	53	107
Electrical system repair	100	62	105	70	105
Motor repair, replacement	100	83	101	72	104
Auto repair service policy	100	26	110	29	110

	total consumer units	race		Hispanic origin	
		black	white and other	Hispanic	non-Hispanic
Vehicle insurance	**100**	**75**	**103**	**66**	**105**
Vehicle rental, leases, licenses, other charges	**100**	**55**	**106**	**57**	**106**
Leased and rented vehicles	100	58	105	56	107
Rented vehicles	100	54	106	60	106
Auto rental	100	111	97	31	110
Auto rental on trips	100	43	107	53	107
Truck rental	100	57	105	122	98
Truck rental on trips	100	37	108	100	101
Leased vehicles	100	58	105	55	107
Car lease payments	100	53	106	45	108
Cash down payment (car lease)	100	48	107	89	102
Termination fee (car lease)	100	529	35	–	114
Truck lease payments	100	61	105	62	106
Cash down payment (truck lease)	100	30	109	87	102
Termination fee (truck lease)	100	–	114	235	83
State and local registration	100	46	107	61	106
Driver's license	100	57	105	66	105
Vehicle inspection	100	63	104	89	102
Parking fees	100	58	105	46	108
Parking fees in home city, excluding residence	100	62	105	45	108
Parking fees on trips	100	32	109	53	107
Tolls	100	33	109	104	100
Tolls on trips	100	55	106	34	110
Towing charges	100	87	101	63	106
Automobile service clubs	100	45	107	29	110
PUBLIC TRANSPORTATION	**100**	**58**	**105**	**66**	**105**
Airline fares	100	37	108	55	107
Intercity bus fares	100	73	103	69	105
Intracity mass transit fares	100	190	86	145	95
Local transportation on trips	100	42	108	41	109
Taxi fares and limousine service on trips	100	42	108	41	108
Taxi fares and limousine service	100	149	92	165	92
Intercity train fares	100	39	108	36	109
Ship fares	100	28	110	37	109
School bus	100	116	96	223	84

Note: Per capita indexes account for household size and show how much each person in a particular household demographic segment spends relative to a person in the average household. Other races include Asians, Native Americans, and Pacific Islanders. (–) means sample is too small to make a reliable estimate.
Source: Calculations by New Strategist based on the 2000 Consumer Expenditure Survey

Table 11.19 Transportation: Total spending by race and Hispanic origin, 2000

(total annual spending on transportation, by consumer unit race and Hispanic origin groups, 2000; numbers in thousands)

	total consumer units	race		Hispanic origin	
		black	white and other	Hispanic	non-Hispanic
Number of consumer units	109,367	13,230	96,137	9,473	99,894
Total spending of all consumer units	$4,160,831,424	$372,454,135	$3,788,393,849	$310,098,181	$3,850,804,816
Transportation, total spending	811,214,411	68,986,247	742,228,593	63,651,076	747,564,741
VEHICLE PURCHASES	**$373,845,935**	**$30,229,889**	**$343,615,750**	**$29,801,490**	**$344,043,926**
Cars and trucks, new	**175,528,567**	**11,497,796**	**164,030,872**	**10,224,872**	**165,303,592**
New cars	100,291,726	7,504,982	92,786,626	5,342,109	94,949,247
New trucks	75,237,934	3,992,814	71,245,208	4,882,763	70,354,345
Cars and trucks, used	**193,563,185**	**18,701,531**	**174,861,667**	**19,490,792**	**174,072,288**
Used cars	110,597,379	13,406,753	97,190,662	11,485,823	99,111,830
Used trucks	82,965,806	5,294,778	77,671,005	8,005,064	74,960,458
Other vehicles	**4,753,090**	**30,561**	**4,723,211**	**85,731**	**4,668,047**
New motorcycles	2,017,821	–	2,017,916	63,469	1,954,926
Used motorcycles	1,900,798	30,561	1,870,826	22,262	1,879,006
GASOLINE AND MOTOR OIL	**141,220,139**	**12,645,763**	**128,574,585**	**11,781,760**	**129,437,651**
Gasoline	128,560,909	11,878,159	116,682,438	11,033,771	117,527,289
Diesel fuel	1,419,584	175,694	1,244,013	46,512	1,372,544
Gasoline on trips	10,038,797	503,269	9,535,829	575,864	9,462,959
Motor oil	1,099,138	83,481	1,016,168	119,833	979,960
Motor oil on trips	101,711	5,027	96,137	5,779	95,898
OTHER VEHICLE EXPENSES	**249,496,750**	**22,559,267**	**226,938,118**	**18,420,249**	**231,074,801**
Vehicle finance charges	**35,898,624**	**3,830,350**	**32,068,419**	**2,597,497**	**33,300,664**
Automobile finance charges	18,510,365	2,513,039	15,997,197	1,391,584	17,118,835
Truck finance charges	15,160,454	1,304,346	13,856,226	1,193,219	13,967,179
Motorcycle and plane finance charges	172,800	1,588	171,124	474	171,818
Other vehicle finance charges	2,055,006	11,378	2,043,873	12,220	2,042,832
Maintenance and repairs	**68,218,760**	**5,975,462**	**62,242,939**	**5,168,564**	**63,047,099**
Coolant, additives, brake and transmission fluids	488,870	52,391	436,462	40,829	447,525
Tires	9,540,083	836,533	8,703,283	700,055	8,839,620
Parts, equipment, and accessories	5,299,925	329,824	4,970,283	559,096	4,740,969
Vehicle audio equipment	263,574	–	264,377	46,512	217,769
Vehicle products	448,405	42,601	405,698	18,946	428,545
Miscellaneous auto repair, servicing	2,924,474	201,361	2,722,600	133,096	2,789,040
Body work and painting	2,881,820	182,442	2,699,527	166,441	2,715,119
Clutch, transmission repair	4,660,128	510,943	4,148,312	398,624	4,261,478
Drive shaft and rear-end repair	400,283	26,460	373,012	42,818	356,622
Brake work	5,910,193	623,530	5,287,535	328,524	5,582,077
Repair to steering or front-end	1,970,793	153,600	1,816,989	203,006	1,768,124
Repair to engine cooling system	2,247,492	218,692	2,029,452	163,978	2,083,789
Motor tune-up	4,856,988	467,548	4,389,615	412,170	4,444,284
Lube, oil change, and oil filters	6,425,311	501,417	5,923,962	476,302	5,948,688
Front-end alignment, wheel balance, rotation	1,180,070	112,455	1,067,121	79,384	1,099,833
Shock absorber replacement	464,810	37,573	426,848	39,881	424,550
Gas tank repair, replacement	388,253	69,325	319,175	33,913	354,624
Tire repair and other repair work	3,253,668	305,084	2,948,522	196,754	3,056,756
Vehicle air conditioning repair	2,165,467	159,025	2,006,379	146,263	2,018,858
Exhaust system repair	1,458,956	92,345	1,366,107	90,278	1,368,548
Electrical system repair	3,314,914	270,157	3,045,620	275,191	3,039,774
Motor repair, replacement	7,049,797	760,725	6,289,283	594,715	6,455,150
Auto repair service policy	624,486	21,433	602,779	21,693	602,361

	total consumer units	race		Hispanic origin	
		black	*white and other*	*Hispanic*	*non-Hispanic*
Vehicle insurance	**$85,101,744**	**$8,384,513**	**$76,717,326**	**$6,596,145**	**$78,505,696**
Vehicle rental, leases, licenses, other charges	**60,277,622**	**4,368,943**	**55,909,434**	**4,058,044**	**56,220,343**
Leased and rented vehicles	42,968,107	3,229,708	39,739,190	2,815,091	40,153,392
Rented vehicles	4,916,047	349,934	4,566,508	345,670	4,570,151
Auto rental	788,536	114,704	673,920	28,798	759,194
Auto rental on trips	3,239,451	184,029	3,055,234	202,343	3,036,778
Truck rental	351,068	26,195	324,943	50,396	300,681
Truck rental on trips	515,119	25,137	490,299	60,627	454,518
Leased vehicles	38,052,060	2,879,642	35,172,683	2,469,422	35,582,243
Car lease payments	19,121,726	1,328,557	17,793,036	1,011,432	18,109,783
Cash down payment (car lease)	1,530,044	95,521	1,435,325	159,810	1,370,546
Termination fee (car lease)	197,954	136,798	61,528	–	197,790
Truck lease payments	16,235,531	1,285,295	14,950,265	1,178,157	15,058,022
Cash down payment (truck lease)	844,313	33,472	811,396	86,488	758,195
Termination fee (truck lease)	121,397	–	121,133	33,629	87,907
State and local registration	9,316,975	565,979	8,751,351	672,394	8,644,827
Driver's license	749,164	55,434	694,109	58,069	691,266
Vehicle inspection	1,029,143	84,540	945,027	107,708	922,022
Parking fees	3,213,202	243,035	2,970,633	174,019	3,038,775
Parking fees in home city, excluding residence	2,770,266	224,249	2,546,669	146,453	2,624,215
Parking fees on trips	442,936	18,787	423,964	27,566	415,559
Tolls	1,192,100	50,671	1,141,146	146,358	1,046,889
Tolls on trips	383,878	27,386	356,668	15,346	368,609
Towing charges	511,838	58,080	453,767	37,987	473,498
Automobile service clubs	913,214	54,111	858,503	31,071	882,064
PUBLIC TRANSPORTATION	**46,651,588**	**3,551,329**	**43,101,101**	**3,647,579**	**43,007,364**
Airline fares	29,968,745	1,435,058	28,534,423	1,932,681	28,036,250
Intercity bus fares	1,760,809	168,683	1,592,029	143,611	1,617,284
Intracity mass transit fares	5,185,089	1,285,691	3,899,317	884,968	4,299,438
Local transportation on trips	1,165,852	64,695	1,101,730	56,554	1,109,822
Taxi fares and limousine service on trips	684,637	37,970	647,002	33,156	651,309
Taxi fares and limousine service	1,328,809	258,250	1,070,005	257,950	1,073,861
Intercity train fares	2,309,831	116,292	2,193,846	97,951	2,212,652
Ship fares	4,000,645	147,118	3,853,171	175,914	3,824,941
School bus	247,169	37,573	209,579	64,795	182,806

Note: Other races include Asians, Native Americans, and Pacific Islanders. Numbers may not add to total because of rounding. (–) means sample is too small to make a reliable estimate.
Source: Calculations by New Strategist based on the 2000 Consumer Expenditure Survey

Table 11.20 Transportation: Market shares by race and Hispanic origin, 2000

(percentage of total annual spending on transportation accounted for by consumer unit race and Hispanic origin groups, 2000)

	total consumer units	race		Hispanic origin	
		black	white and other	Hispanic	non-Hispanic
Share of total consumer units	100.0%	12.1%	87.9%	8.7%	91.3%
Share of total before-tax income	100.0	8.8	91.1	6.8	93.4
Share of total spending	100.0	9.0	91.0	7.5	92.5
Share of transportation spending	100.0	8.5	91.5	7.8	92.2
VEHICLE PURCHASES	100.0%	8.1%	91.9%	8.0%	92.0%
Cars and trucks, new	100.0	6.6	93.4	5.8	94.2
New cars	100.0	7.5	92.5	5.3	94.7
New trucks	100.0	5.3	94.7	6.5	93.5
Cars and trucks, used	100.0	9.7	90.3	10.1	89.9
Used cars	100.0	12.1	87.9	10.4	89.6
Used trucks	100.0	6.4	93.6	9.6	90.4
Other vehicles	100.0	0.6	99.4	1.8	98.2
New motorcycles	100.0	–	100.0	3.1	96.9
Used motorcycles	100.0	1.6	98.4	1.2	98.9
GASOLINE AND MOTOR OIL	100.0	9.0	91.0	8.3	91.7
Gasoline	100.0	9.2	90.8	8.6	91.4
Diesel fuel	100.0	12.4	87.6	3.3	96.7
Gasoline on trips	100.0	5.0	95.0	5.7	94.3
Motor oil	100.0	7.6	92.5	10.9	89.2
Motor oil on trips	100.0	4.9	94.5	5.7	94.3
OTHER VEHICLE EXPENSES	100.0	9.0	91.0	7.4	92.6
Vehicle finance charges	100.0	10.7	89.3	7.2	92.8
Automobile finance charges	100.0	13.6	86.4	7.5	92.5
Truck finance charges	100.0	8.6	91.4	7.9	92.1
Motorcycle and plane finance charges	100.0	0.9	99.0	0.3	99.4
Other vehicle finance charges	100.0	0.6	99.5	0.6	99.4
Maintenance and repairs	100.0	8.8	91.2	7.6	92.4
Coolant, additives, brake and transmission fluids	100.0	10.7	89.3	8.4	91.5
Tires	100.0	8.8	91.2	7.3	92.7
Parts, equipment, and accessories	100.0	6.2	93.8	10.5	89.5
Vehicle audio equipment	100.0	–	100.0	17.6	82.6
Vehicle products	100.0	9.5	90.5	4.2	95.6
Miscellaneous auto repair, servicing	100.0	6.9	93.1	4.6	95.4
Body work and painting	100.0	6.3	93.7	5.8	94.2
Clutch, transmission repair	100.0	11.0	89.0	8.6	91.4
Drive shaft and rear-end repair	100.0	6.6	93.2	10.7	89.1
Brake work	100.0	10.6	89.5	5.6	94.4
Repair to steering or front-end	100.0	7.8	92.2	10.3	89.7
Repair to engine cooling system	100.0	9.7	90.3	7.3	92.7
Motor tune-up	100.0	9.6	90.4	8.5	91.5
Lube, oil change, and oil filters	100.0	7.8	92.2	7.4	92.6
Front-end alignment, wheel balance, rotation	100.0	9.5	90.4	6.7	93.2
Shock absorber replacement	100.0	8.1	91.8	8.6	91.3
Gas tank repair, replacement	100.0	17.9	82.2	8.7	91.3
Tire repair and other repair work	100.0	9.4	90.6	6.0	93.9
Vehicle air conditioning repair	100.0	7.3	92.7	6.8	93.2
Exhaust system repair	100.0	6.3	93.6	6.2	93.8
Electrical system repair	100.0	8.1	91.9	8.3	91.7
Motor repair, replacement	100.0	10.8	89.2	8.4	91.6
Auto repair service policy	100.0	3.4	96.5	3.5	96.5

	total consumer units	race		Hispanic origin	
		black	white and other	Hispanic	non-Hispanic
Vehicle insurance	**100.0%**	**9.9%**	**90.1%**	**7.8%**	**92.2%**
Vehicle rental, leases, licenses, other charges	**100.0**	**7.2**	**92.8**	**6.7**	**93.3**
Leased and rented vehicles	100.0	7.5	92.5	6.6	93.4
Rented vehicles	100.0	7.1	92.9	7.0	93.0
Auto rental	100.0	14.5	85.5	3.7	96.3
Auto rental on trips	100.0	5.7	94.3	6.2	93.7
Truck rental	100.0	7.5	92.6	14.4	85.6
Truck rental on trips	100.0	4.9	95.2	11.8	88.2
Leased vehicles	100.0	7.6	92.4	6.5	93.5
Car lease payments	100.0	6.9	93.1	5.3	94.7
Cash down payment (car lease)	100.0	6.2	93.8	10.4	89.6
Termination fee (car lease)	100.0	69.1	31.1	–	99.9
Truck lease payments	100.0	7.9	92.1	7.3	92.7
Cash down payment (truck lease)	100.0	4.0	96.1	10.2	89.8
Termination fee (truck lease)	100.0	–	99.8	27.7	72.4
State and local registration	100.0	6.1	93.9	7.2	92.8
Driver's license	100.0	7.4	92.7	7.8	92.3
Vehicle inspection	100.0	8.2	91.8	10.5	89.6
Parking fees	100.0	7.6	92.5	5.4	94.6
Parking fees in home city, excluding residence	100.0	8.1	91.9	5.3	94.7
Parking fees on trips	100.0	4.2	95.7	6.2	93.8
Tolls	100.0	4.3	95.7	12.3	87.8
Tolls on trips	100.0	7.1	92.9	4.0	96.0
Towing charges	100.0	11.3	88.7	7.4	92.5
Automobile service clubs	100.0	5.9	94.0	3.4	96.6
PUBLIC TRANSPORTATION	**100.0**	**7.6**	**92.4**	**7.8**	**92.2**
Airline fares	100.0	4.8	95.2	6.4	93.6
Intercity bus fares	100.0	9.6	90.4	8.2	91.8
Intracity mass transit fares	100.0	24.8	75.2	17.1	82.9
Local transportation on trips	100.0	5.5	94.5	4.9	95.2
Taxi fares and limousine service on trips	100.0	5.5	94.5	4.8	95.1
Taxi fares and limousine service	100.0	19.4	80.5	19.4	80.8
Intercity train fares	100.0	5.0	95.0	4.2	95.8
Ship fares	100.0	3.7	96.3	4.4	95.6
School bus	100.0	15.2	84.8	26.2	74.0

Note: Other races include Asians, Native Americans, and Pacific Islanders. Numbers may not add to total because of rounding. (–) means sample is too small to make a reliable estimate.
Source: Calculations by New Strategist based on the 2000 Consumer Expenditure Survey

Table 11.21 Transportation: Average spending by region, 2000

(average annual spending of consumer units (CU) on transportation, by region in which consumer unit lives, 2000)

	total consumer units	Northeast	Midwest	South	West
Number of consumer units					
(in thousands, add 000)	109,367	20,994	25,717	38,245	24,410
Average number of persons per CU	2.5	2.5	2.5	2.5	2.6
Average before-tax income of CU	$44,649.00	$47,439.00	$44,377.00	$41,984.00	$46,670.00
Average spending of CU, total	38,044.67	38,901.91	39,212.70	34,707.07	41,328.19
Transportation, average spending	7,417.36	6,663.66	7,840.65	7,210.71	7,943.04
VEHICLE PURCHASES	**$3,418.27**	**$2,718.98**	**$3,758.55**	**$3,565.56**	**$3,430.43**
Cars and trucks, new	**1,604.95**	**1,455.95**	**1,540.39**	**1,631.68**	**1,759.26**
New cars	917.02	963.83	1,025.78	772.80	988.12
New trucks	687.94	492.12	514.61	858.87	771.13
Cars and trucks, used	**1,769.85**	**1,246.50**	**2,132.02**	**1,909.45**	**1,619.68**
Used cars	1,011.25	760.48	1,195.22	1,089.00	911.29
Used trucks	758.60	486.01	936.81	820.45	708.39
Other vehicles	**43.46**	**16.53**	**86.13**	**24.43**	**51.49**
New motorcycles	18.45	10.15	34.11	7.68	25.97
Used motorcycles	17.38	6.38	26.09	16.75	18.66
GASOLINE AND MOTOR OIL	**1,291.25**	**1,093.52**	**1,352.13**	**1,289.53**	**1,399.86**
Gasoline	1,175.50	1,019.60	1,218.11	1,182.47	1,253.78
Diesel fuel	12.98	4.98	12.75	14.54	17.65
Gasoline on trips	91.79	62.09	108.41	80.93	116.84
Motor oil	10.05	6.22	11.77	10.77	10.41
Motor oil on trips	0.93	0.63	1.10	0.82	1.18
OTHER VEHICLE EXPENSES	**2,281.28**	**2,251.46**	**2,327.14**	**2,072.81**	**2,585.90**
Vehicle finance charges	**328.24**	**227.84**	**353.18**	**365.94**	**329.23**
Automobile finance charges	169.25	145.81	173.57	182.92	163.43
Truck finance charges	138.62	73.61	159.37	162.12	135.86
Motorcycle and plane finance charges	1.58	0.63	2.05	1.55	1.94
Other vehicle finance charges	18.79	7.79	18.20	19.36	28.00
Maintenance and repairs	**623.76**	**570.46**	**609.67**	**583.54**	**748.96**
Coolant, additives, brake and transmission fluids	4.47	2.71	5.58	5.11	3.81
Tires	87.23	77.61	80.88	91.54	95.42
Parts, equipment, and accessories	48.46	38.11	48.86	48.08	57.54
Vehicle audio equipment	2.41	0.26	0.06	3.41	5.30
Vehicle products	4.10	2.44	7.80	3.56	2.57
Miscellaneous auto repair, servicing	26.74	15.72	28.75	17.14	50.37
Body work and painting	26.35	28.77	28.00	23.48	27.02
Clutch, transmission repair	42.61	27.82	43.78	44.74	50.75
Drive shaft and rear-end repair	3.66	3.26	4.09	2.96	4.64
Brake work	54.04	70.82	49.21	41.85	63.82
Repair to steering or front-end	18.02	21.11	17.89	15.27	19.81
Repair to engine cooling system	20.55	19.35	19.79	18.39	25.78
Motor tune-up	44.41	52.05	31.76	36.90	62.91
Lube, oil change, and oil filters	58.75	50.34	67.08	54.54	63.80
Front-end alignment, wheel balance, rotation	10.79	14.15	11.87	8.50	10.34
Shock absorber replacement	4.25	4.54	6.51	2.41	4.48
Gas tank repair, replacement	3.55	1.63	4.29	3.87	4.01
Tire repair and other repair work	29.75	28.83	27.21	28.09	35.82
Vehicle air conditioning repair	19.80	12.70	13.85	27.68	19.82
Exhaust system repair	13.34	18.26	14.91	9.11	14.07
Electrical system repair	30.31	26.47	30.76	29.96	33.71
Motor repair, replacement	64.46	49.71	60.29	61.72	85.84
Auto repair service policy	5.71	3.79	6.45	5.23	7.32

	total consumer units	Northeast	Midwest	South	West
Vehicle insurance	**$778.13**	**$807.58**	**$749.77**	**$747.23**	**$831.12**
Vehicle rental, leases, licenses, other charges	**551.15**	**645.58**	**614.52**	**376.10**	**676.59**
Leased and rented vehicles	392.88	488.13	440.28	265.74	460.23
Rented vehicles	44.95	48.46	41.95	36.52	58.31
Auto rental	7.21	7.75	5.67	5.77	10.61
Auto rental on trips	29.62	35.26	28.07	22.87	36.96
Truck rental	3.21	2.53	2.74	2.17	5.93
Truck rental on trips	4.71	2.80	5.37	5.65	4.19
Leased vehicles	347.93	439.68	398.34	229.22	401.91
Car lease payments	174.84	266.73	192.89	107.05	183.00
Cash down payment (car lease)	13.99	30.51	6.46	7.47	17.95
Termination fee (car lease)	1.81	0.88	2.76	2.75	0.14
Truck lease payments	148.45	135.29	188.92	103.33	187.84
Cash down payment (truck lease)	7.72	5.16	6.30	8.04	10.93
Termination fee (truck lease)	1.11	1.11	1.00	0.58	2.05
State and local registration	85.19	39.55	110.63	60.32	136.63
Driver's license	6.85	7.50	7.68	5.77	7.12
Vehicle inspection	9.41	16.47	3.74	6.54	13.83
Parking fees	29.38	41.24	30.93	19.57	32.92
Parking fees in home city, excluding residence	25.33	36.58	27.01	16.16	28.26
Parking fees on trips	4.05	4.66	3.92	3.41	4.66
Tolls	10.90	29.90	4.47	6.76	6.95
Tolls on trips	3.51	8.48	3.15	2.24	1.60
Towing charges	4.68	3.06	5.04	4.08	6.62
Automobile service clubs	8.35	11.23	8.59	5.10	10.71
PUBLIC TRANSPORTATION	**426.56**	**599.71**	**402.84**	**282.81**	**526.84**
Airline fares	274.02	307.70	274.88	195.72	366.84
Intercity bus fares	16.10	18.10	17.89	11.63	19.48
Intracity mass transit fares	47.41	138.03	25.80	16.52	40.62
Local transportation on trips	10.66	13.40	12.55	6.53	12.80
Taxi fares and limousine service on trips	6.26	7.87	7.37	3.83	7.52
Taxi fares and limousine service	12.15	35.25	2.91	7.32	8.53
Intercity train fares	21.12	31.53	22.69	13.19	22.95
Ship fares	36.58	46.23	38.49	23.55	46.68
School bus	2.26	1.60	0.25	4.51	1.43

Source: Bureau of Labor Statistics, unpublished tables from the 2000 Consumer Expenditure Survey

Table 11.22 Transportation: Indexed spending by region, 2000

(indexed average annual spending of consumer units (CU) on transportation, by region in which consumer unit lives, 2000; index definition: an index of 100 is the average for all consumer units; an index of 132 means that spending by consumer units in that group is 32 percent above the average for all consumer units; an index of 68 indicates spending that is 32 percent below the average for all consumer units)

	total consumer units	Northeast	Midwest	South	West
Average spending of CU, total	$38,045	$38,902	$39,213	$34,707	$41,328
Average spending of CU, index	100	102	103	91	109
Transportation, spending index	100	90	106	97	107
VEHICLE PURCHASES	100	80	110	104	100
Cars and trucks, new	100	91	96	102	110
New cars	100	105	112	84	108
New trucks	100	72	75	125	112
Cars and trucks, used	100	70	120	108	92
Used cars	100	75	118	108	90
Used trucks	100	64	123	108	93
Other vehicles	100	38	198	56	118
New motorcycles	100	55	185	42	141
Used motorcycles	100	37	150	96	107
GASOLINE AND MOTOR OIL	100	85	105	100	108
Gasoline	100	87	104	101	107
Diesel fuel	100	38	98	112	136
Gasoline on trips	100	68	118	88	127
Motor oil	100	62	117	107	104
Motor oil on trips	100	68	118	88	127
OTHER VEHICLE EXPENSES	100	99	102	91	113
Vehicle finance charges	100	69	108	111	100
Automobile finance charges	100	86	103	108	97
Truck finance charges	100	53	115	117	98
Motorcycle and plane finance charges	100	40	130	98	123
Other vehicle finance charges	100	41	97	103	149
Maintenance and repairs	100	91	98	94	120
Coolant, additives, brake and transmission fluids	100	61	125	114	85
Tires	100	89	93	105	109
Parts, equipment, and accessories	100	79	101	99	119
Vehicle audio equipment	100	11	2	141	220
Vehicle products	100	60	190	87	63
Miscellaneous auto repair, servicing	100	59	108	64	188
Body work and painting	100	109	106	89	103
Clutch, transmission repair	100	65	103	105	119
Drive shaft and rear-end repair	100	89	112	81	127
Brake work	100	131	91	77	118
Repair to steering or front-end	100	117	99	85	110
Repair to engine cooling system	100	94	96	89	125
Motor tune-up	100	117	72	83	142
Lube, oil change, and oil filters	100	86	114	93	109
Front-end alignment, wheel balance, rotation	100	131	110	79	96
Shock absorber replacement	100	107	153	57	105
Gas tank repair, replacement	100	46	121	109	113
Tire repair and other repair work	100	97	91	94	120
Vehicle air conditioning repair	100	64	70	140	100
Exhaust system repair	100	137	112	68	105
Electrical system repair	100	87	101	99	111
Motor repair, replacement	100	77	94	96	133
Auto repair service policy	100	66	113	92	128

	total consumer units	Northeast	Midwest	South	West
Vehicle insurance	**100**	**104**	**96**	**96**	**107**
Vehicle rental, leases, licenses, other charges	**100**	**117**	**111**	**68**	**123**
Leased and rented vehicles	100	124	112	68	117
Rented vehicles	100	108	93	81	130
Auto rental	100	107	79	80	147
Auto rental on trips	100	119	95	77	125
Truck rental	100	79	85	68	185
Truck rental on trips	100	59	114	120	89
Leased vehicles	100	126	114	66	116
Car lease payments	100	153	110	61	105
Cash down payment (car lease)	100	218	46	53	128
Termination fee (car lease)	100	49	152	152	8
Truck lease payments	100	91	127	70	127
Cash down payment (truck lease)	100	67	82	104	142
Termination fee (truck lease)	100	100	90	52	185
State and local registration	100	46	130	71	160
Driver's license	100	109	112	84	104
Vehicle inspection	100	175	40	70	147
Parking fees	100	140	105	67	112
Parking fees in home city, excluding residence	100	144	107	64	112
Parking fees on trips	100	115	97	84	115
Tolls	100	274	41	62	64
Tolls on trips	100	242	90	64	46
Towing charges	100	65	108	87	141
Automobile service clubs	100	134	103	61	128
PUBLIC TRANSPORTATION	**100**	**141**	**94**	**66**	**124**
Airline fares	100	112	100	71	134
Intercity bus fares	100	112	111	72	121
Intracity mass transit fares	100	291	54	35	86
Local transportation on trips	100	126	118	61	120
Taxi fares and limousine service on trips	100	126	118	61	120
Taxi fares and limousine service	100	290	24	60	70
Intercity train fares	100	149	107	62	109
Ship fares	100	126	105	64	128
School bus	100	71	11	200	63

Source: Calculations by New Strategist based on the 2000 Consumer Expenditure Survey

Table 11.23 Transportation: Indexed per capita spending by region, 2000

(indexed average annual per capita spending of consumer units (CU) on transportation, by region in which consumer unit lives, 2000; index definition: an index of 100 is the average for all consumer units; an index of 132 means that spending by consumer units in that group is 32 percent above the average for all consumer units; an index of 68 indicates spending that is 32 percent below the average for all consumer units)

	total consumer units	Northeast	Midwest	South	West
Per capita spending of CU, total	$15,218	$15,561	$15,685	$13,883	$15,895
Per capita spending of CU, index	100	102	103	91	104
Transportation, per capita spending index	100	90	106	97	103
VEHICLE PURCHASES	100	80	110	104	96
Cars and trucks, new	100	91	96	102	105
New cars	100	105	112	84	104
New trucks	100	72	75	125	108
Cars and trucks, used	100	70	120	108	88
Used cars	100	75	118	108	87
Used trucks	100	64	123	108	90
Other vehicles	100	38	198	56	114
New motorcycles	100	55	185	42	135
Used motorcycles	100	37	150	96	103
GASOLINE AND MOTOR OIL	100	85	105	100	104
Gasoline	100	87	104	101	103
Diesel fuel	100	38	98	112	131
Gasoline on trips	100	68	118	88	122
Motor oil	100	62	117	107	100
Motor oil on trips	100	68	118	88	122
OTHER VEHICLE EXPENSES	100	99	102	91	109
Vehicle finance charges	100	69	108	111	96
Automobile finance charges	100	86	103	108	93
Truck finance charges	100	53	115	117	94
Motorcycle and plane finance charges	100	40	130	98	118
Other vehicle finance charges	100	41	97	103	143
Maintenance and repairs	100	91	98	94	115
Coolant, additives, brake and transmission fluids	100	61	125	114	82
Tires	100	89	93	105	105
Parts, equipment, and accessories	100	79	101	99	114
Vehicle audio equipment	100	11	2	141	211
Vehicle products	100	60	190	87	60
Miscellaneous auto repair, servicing	100	59	108	64	181
Body work and painting	100	109	106	89	99
Clutch, transmission repair	100	65	103	105	115
Drive shaft and rear-end repair	100	89	112	81	122
Brake work	100	131	91	77	114
Repair to steering or front-end	100	117	99	85	106
Repair to engine cooling system	100	94	96	89	121
Motor tune-up	100	117	72	83	136
Lube, oil change, and oil filters	100	86	114	93	104
Front-end alignment, wheel balance, rotation	100	131	110	79	92
Shock absorber replacement	100	107	153	57	101
Gas tank repair, replacement	100	46	121	109	109
Tire repair and other repair work	100	97	91	94	116
Vehicle air conditioning repair	100	64	70	140	96
Exhaust system repair	100	137	112	68	101
Electrical system repair	100	87	101	99	107
Motor repair, replacement	100	77	94	96	128
Auto repair service policy	100	66	113	92	123

	total consumer units	Northeast	Midwest	South	West
Vehicle insurance	**100**	**104**	**96**	**96**	**103**
Vehicle rental, leases, licenses, other charges	**100**	**117**	**111**	**68**	**118**
Leased and rented vehicles	100	124	112	68	113
Rented vehicles	100	108	93	81	125
Auto rental	100	107	79	80	141
Auto rental on trips	100	119	95	77	120
Truck rental	100	79	85	68	178
Truck rental on trips	100	59	114	120	86
Leased vehicles	100	126	114	66	111
Car lease payments	100	153	110	61	101
Cash down payment (car lease)	100	218	46	53	123
Termination fee (car lease)	100	49	152	152	7
Truck lease payments	100	91	127	70	122
Cash down payment (truck lease)	100	67	82	104	136
Termination fee (truck lease)	100	100	90	52	178
State and local registration	100	46	130	71	154
Driver's license	100	109	112	84	100
Vehicle inspection	100	175	40	70	141
Parking fees	100	140	105	67	108
Parking fees in home city, excluding residence	100	144	107	64	107
Parking fees on trips	100	115	97	84	111
Tolls	100	274	41	62	61
Tolls on trips	100	242	90	64	44
Towing charges	100	65	108	87	136
Automobile service clubs	100	134	103	61	123
PUBLIC TRANSPORTATION	**100**	**141**	**94**	**66**	**119**
Airline fares	100	112	100	71	129
Intercity bus fares	100	112	111	72	116
Intracity mass transit fares	100	291	54	35	82
Local transportation on trips	100	126	118	61	115
Taxi fares and limousine service on trips	100	126	118	61	116
Taxi fares and limousine service	100	290	24	60	68
Intercity train fares	100	149	107	62	104
Ship fares	100	126	105	64	123
School bus	100	71	11	200	61

Note: Per capita indexes account for household size and show how much each person in a particular household demographic segment spends relative to a person in the average household.
Source: Calculations by New Strategist based on the 2000 Consumer Expenditure Survey

Table 11.24 Transportation: Total spending by region, 2000

(total annual spending on transportation, by region in which consumer units live, 2000; numbers in thousands)

	total consumer units	Northeast	Midwest	South	West
Number of consumer units	109,367	20,994	25,717	38,245	24,410
Total spending of all consumer units	$4,160,831,424	$816,706,699	$1,008,433,006	$1,327,371,892	$1,008,821,118
Transportation, total spending	811,214,411	139,896,878	201,637,996	275,773,604	193,889,606
VEHICLE PURCHASES	**$373,845,935**	**$57,082,266**	**$96,658,630**	**$136,364,842**	**$83,736,796**
Cars and trucks, new	**175,528,567**	**30,566,214**	**39,614,210**	**62,403,602**	**42,943,537**
New cars	100,291,726	20,234,647	26,379,984	29,555,736	24,120,009
New trucks	75,237,934	10,331,567	13,234,225	32,847,483	18,823,283
Cars and trucks, used	**193,563,185**	**26,169,021**	**54,829,158**	**73,026,915**	**39,536,389**
Used cars	110,597,379	15,965,517	30,737,473	41,648,805	22,244,589
Used trucks	82,965,806	10,203,294	24,091,943	31,378,110	17,291,800
Other vehicles	**4,753,090**	**347,031**	**2,215,005**	**934,325**	**1,256,871**
New motorcycles	2,017,821	213,089	877,207	293,722	633,928
Used motorcycles	1,900,798	133,942	670,957	640,604	455,491
GASOLINE AND MOTOR OIL	**141,220,139**	**22,957,359**	**34,772,727**	**49,318,075**	**34,170,583**
Gasoline	128,560,909	21,405,482	31,326,135	45,223,565	30,604,770
Diesel fuel	1,419,584	104,550	327,892	556,082	430,837
Gasoline on trips	10,038,797	1,303,517	2,787,980	3,095,168	2,852,064
Motor oil	1,099,138	130,583	302,689	411,899	254,108
Motor oil on trips	101,711	13,226	28,289	31,361	28,804
OTHER VEHICLE EXPENSES	**249,496,750**	**47,267,151**	**59,847,059**	**79,274,618**	**63,121,819**
Vehicle finance charges	**35,898,624**	**4,783,273**	**9,082,730**	**13,995,375**	**8,036,504**
Automobile finance charges	18,510,365	3,061,135	4,463,700	6,995,775	3,989,326
Truck finance charges	15,160,454	1,545,368	4,098,518	6,200,279	3,316,343
Motorcycle and plane finance charges	172,800	13,226	52,720	59,280	47,355
Other vehicle finance charges	2,055,006	163,543	468,049	740,423	683,480
Maintenance and repairs	**68,218,760**	**11,976,237**	**15,678,883**	**22,317,487**	**18,282,114**
Coolant, additives, brake and transmission fluids	488,870	56,894	143,501	195,432	93,002
Tires	9,540,083	1,629,344	2,079,991	3,500,947	2,329,202
Parts, equipment, and accessories	5,299,925	800,081	1,256,533	1,838,820	1,404,551
Vehicle audio equipment	263,574	5,458	1,543	130,415	129,373
Vehicle products	448,405	51,225	200,593	136,152	62,734
Miscellaneous auto repair, servicing	2,924,474	330,026	739,364	655,519	1,229,532
Body work and painting	2,881,820	603,997	720,076	897,993	659,558
Clutch, transmission repair	4,660,128	584,053	1,125,890	1,711,081	1,238,808
Drive shaft and rear-end repair	400,283	68,440	105,183	113,205	113,262
Brake work	5,910,193	1,486,795	1,265,534	1,600,553	1,557,846
Repair to steering or front-end	1,970,793	443,183	460,077	584,001	483,562
Repair to engine cooling system	2,247,492	406,234	508,939	703,326	629,290
Motor tune-up	4,856,988	1,092,738	816,772	1,411,241	1,535,633
Lube, oil change, and oil filters	6,425,311	1,056,838	1,725,096	2,085,882	1,557,358
Front-end alignment, wheel balance, rotation	1,180,070	297,065	305,261	325,083	252,399
Shock absorber replacement	464,810	95,313	167,418	92,170	109,357
Gas tank repair, replacement	388,253	34,220	110,326	148,008	97,884
Tire repair and other repair work	3,253,668	605,257	699,760	1,074,302	874,366
Vehicle air conditioning repair	2,165,467	266,624	356,180	1,058,622	483,806
Exhaust system repair	1,458,956	383,350	383,440	348,412	343,449
Electrical system repair	3,314,914	555,711	791,055	1,145,820	822,861
Motor repair, replacement	7,049,797	1,043,612	1,550,478	2,360,481	2,095,354
Auto repair service policy	624,486	79,567	165,875	200,021	178,681

	total consumer units	Northeast	Midwest	South	West
Vehicle insurance	**$85,101,744**	**$16,954,335**	**$19,281,835**	**$28,577,811**	**$20,287,639**
Vehicle rental, leases, licenses, other charges	**60,277,622**	**13,553,307**	**15,803,611**	**14,383,945**	**16,515,562**
Leased and rented vehicles	42,968,107	10,247,801	11,322,681	10,163,226	11,234,214
Rented vehicles	4,916,047	1,017,369	1,078,828	1,396,707	1,423,347
Auto rental	788,536	162,704	145,815	220,674	258,990
Auto rental on trips	3,239,451	740,248	721,876	874,663	902,194
Truck rental	351,068	53,115	70,465	82,992	144,751
Truck rental on trips	515,119	58,783	138,100	216,084	102,278
Leased vehicles	38,052,060	9,230,642	10,244,110	8,766,519	9,810,623
Car lease payments	19,121,726	5,599,730	4,960,552	4,094,127	4,467,030
Cash down payment (car lease)	1,530,044	640,527	166,132	285,690	438,160
Termination fee (car lease)	197,954	18,475	70,979	105,174	3,417
Truck lease payments	16,235,531	2,840,278	4,858,456	3,951,856	4,585,174
Cash down payment (truck lease)	844,313	108,329	162,017	307,490	266,801
Termination fee (truck lease)	121,397	23,303	25,717	22,182	50,041
State and local registration	9,316,975	830,313	2,845,072	2,306,938	3,335,138
Driver's license	749,164	157,455	197,507	220,674	173,799
Vehicle inspection	1,029,143	345,771	96,182	250,122	337,590
Parking fees	3,213,202	865,793	795,427	748,455	803,577
Parking fees in home city, excluding residence	2,770,266	767,961	694,616	618,039	689,827
Parking fees on trips	442,936	97,832	100,811	130,415	113,751
Tolls	1,192,100	627,721	114,955	258,536	169,650
Tolls on trips	383,878	178,029	81,009	85,669	39,056
Towing charges	511,838	64,242	129,614	156,040	161,594
Automobile service clubs	913,214	235,763	220,909	195,050	261,431
PUBLIC TRANSPORTATION	**46,651,588**	**12,590,312**	**10,359,836**	**10,816,068**	**12,860,164**
Airline fares	29,968,745	6,459,854	7,069,089	7,485,311	8,954,564
Intercity bus fares	1,760,809	379,991	460,077	444,789	475,507
Intracity mass transit fares	5,185,089	2,897,802	663,499	631,807	991,534
Local transportation on trips	1,165,852	281,320	322,748	249,740	312,448
Taxi fares and limousine service on trips	684,637	165,223	189,534	146,478	183,563
Taxi fares and limousine service	1,328,809	740,039	74,836	279,953	208,217
Intercity train fares	2,309,831	661,941	583,519	504,452	560,210
Ship fares	4,000,645	970,553	989,847	900,670	1,139,459
School bus	247,169	33,590	6,429	172,485	34,906

Note: Numbers may not add to total because of rounding.
Source: Calculations by New Strategist based on the 2000 Consumer Expenditure Survey

Table 11.25 Transportation: Market shares by region, 2000

(percentage of total annual spending on transportation accounted for by consumer units by region, 2000)

	total consumer units	Northeast	Midwest	South	West
Share of total consumer units	100.0%	19.2%	23.5%	35.0%	22.3%
Share of total before-tax income	100.0	20.4	23.4	32.9	23.3
Share of total spending	100.0	19.6	24.2	31.9	24.2
Share of transportation spending	100.0	17.2	24.9	34.0	23.9
VEHICLE PURCHASES	100.0%	15.3%	25.9%	36.5%	22.4%
Cars and trucks, new	100.0	17.4	22.6	35.6	24.5
New cars	100.0	20.2	26.3	29.5	24.0
New trucks	100.0	13.7	17.6	43.7	25.0
Cars and trucks, used	100.0	13.5	28.3	37.7	20.4
Used cars	100.0	14.4	27.8	37.7	20.1
Used trucks	100.0	12.3	29.0	37.8	20.8
Other vehicles	100.0	7.3	46.6	19.7	26.4
New motorcycles	100.0	10.6	43.5	14.6	31.4
Used motorcycles	100.0	7.0	35.3	33.7	24.0
GASOLINE AND MOTOR OIL	100.0	16.3	24.6	34.9	24.2
Gasoline	100.0	16.7	24.4	35.2	23.8
Diesel fuel	100.0	7.4	23.1	39.2	30.3
Gasoline on trips	100.0	13.0	27.8	30.8	28.4
Motor oil	100.0	11.9	27.5	37.5	23.1
Motor oil on trips	100.0	13.0	27.8	30.8	28.3
OTHER VEHICLE EXPENSES	100.0	18.9	24.0	31.8	25.3
Vehicle finance charges	100.0	13.3	25.3	39.0	22.4
Automobile finance charges	100.0	16.5	24.1	37.8	21.6
Truck finance charges	100.0	10.2	27.0	40.9	21.9
Motorcycle and plane finance charges	100.0	7.7	30.5	34.3	27.4
Other vehicle finance charges	100.0	8.0	22.8	36.0	33.3
Maintenance and repairs	100.0	17.6	23.0	32.7	26.8
Coolant, additives, brake and transmission fluids	100.0	11.6	29.4	40.0	19.0
Tires	100.0	17.1	21.8	36.7	24.4
Parts, equipment, and accessories	100.0	15.1	23.7	34.7	26.5
Vehicle audio equipment	100.0	2.1	0.6	49.5	49.1
Vehicle products	100.0	11.4	44.7	30.4	14.0
Miscellaneous auto repair, servicing	100.0	11.3	25.3	22.4	42.0
Body work and painting	100.0	21.0	25.0	31.2	22.9
Clutch, transmission repair	100.0	12.5	24.2	36.7	26.6
Drive shaft and rear-end repair	100.0	17.1	26.3	28.3	28.3
Brake work	100.0	25.2	21.4	27.1	26.4
Repair to steering or front-end	100.0	22.5	23.3	29.6	24.5
Repair to engine cooling system	100.0	18.1	22.6	31.3	28.0
Motor tune-up	100.0	22.5	16.8	29.1	31.6
Lube, oil change, and oil filters	100.0	16.4	26.8	32.5	24.2
Front-end alignment, wheel balance, rotation	100.0	25.2	25.9	27.5	21.4
Shock absorber replacement	100.0	20.5	36.0	19.8	23.5
Gas tank repair, replacement	100.0	8.8	28.4	38.1	25.2
Tire repair and other repair work	100.0	18.6	21.5	33.0	26.9
Vehicle air conditioning repair	100.0	12.3	16.4	48.9	22.3
Exhaust system repair	100.0	26.3	26.3	23.9	23.5
Electrical system repair	100.0	16.8	23.9	34.6	24.8
Motor repair, replacement	100.0	14.8	22.0	33.5	29.7
Auto repair service policy	100.0	12.7	26.6	32.0	28.6

	total consumer units	Northeast	Midwest	South	West
Vehicle insurance	100.0%	19.9%	22.7%	33.6%	23.8%
Vehicle rental, leases, licenses, other charges	**100.0**	**22.5**	**26.2**	**23.9**	**27.4**
Leased and rented vehicles	100.0	23.8	26.4	23.7	26.1
Rented vehicles	100.0	20.7	21.9	28.4	29.0
Auto rental	100.0	20.6	18.5	28.0	32.8
Auto rental on trips	100.0	22.9	22.3	27.0	27.9
Truck rental	100.0	15.1	20.1	23.6	41.2
Truck rental on trips	100.0	11.4	26.8	41.9	19.9
Leased vehicles	100.0	24.3	26.9	23.0	25.8
Car lease payments	100.0	29.3	25.9	21.4	23.4
Cash down payment (car lease)	100.0	41.9	10.9	18.7	28.6
Termination fee (car lease)	100.0	9.3	35.9	53.1	1.7
Truck lease payments	100.0	17.5	29.9	24.3	28.2
Cash down payment (truck lease)	100.0	12.8	19.2	36.4	31.6
Termination fee (truck lease)	100.0	19.2	21.2	18.3	41.2
State and local registration	100.0	8.9	30.5	24.8	35.8
Driver's license	100.0	21.0	26.4	29.5	23.2
Vehicle inspection	100.0	33.6	9.3	24.3	32.8
Parking fees	100.0	26.9	24.8	23.3	25.0
Parking fees in home city, excluding residence	100.0	27.7	25.1	22.3	24.9
Parking fees on trips	100.0	22.1	22.8	29.4	25.7
Tolls	100.0	52.7	9.6	21.7	14.2
Tolls on trips	100.0	46.4	21.1	22.3	10.2
Towing charges	100.0	12.6	25.3	30.5	31.6
Automobile service clubs	100.0	25.8	24.2	21.4	28.6
PUBLIC TRANSPORTATION	**100.0**	**27.0**	**22.2**	**23.2**	**27.6**
Airline fares	100.0	21.6	23.6	25.0	29.9
Intercity bus fares	100.0	21.6	26.1	25.3	27.0
Intracity mass transit fares	100.0	55.9	12.8	12.2	19.1
Local transportation on trips	100.0	24.1	27.7	21.4	26.8
Taxi fares and limousine service on trips	100.0	24.1	27.7	21.4	26.8
Taxi fares and limousine service	100.0	55.7	5.6	21.1	15.7
Intercity train fares	100.0	28.7	25.3	21.8	24.3
Ship fares	100.0	24.3	24.7	22.5	28.5
School bus	100.0	13.6	2.6	69.8	14.1

Note: Numbers may not add to total because of rounding.
Source: Calculations by New Strategist based on the 2000 Consumer Expenditure Survey

Appendix A

About the Consumer Expenditure Survey

History

The Consumer Expenditure Survey (CEX) is an ongoing study of the day-to-day spending of American households. In taking the survey, government interviewers collect spending data on products and services as well as the amount and sources of household income, changes in saving and debt, and demographic and economic characteristics of household members. Data collection for the CEX is done by the Bureau of the Census, under contract with the Bureau of Labor Statistics. The BLS is responsible for analysis and release of the survey data.

Since the late 19th century, the federal government has conducted expenditure surveys about every ten years. Although the results have been used for a variety of purposes, their primary application is to track consumer prices. Beginning in 1980, the CEX became a continuous survey with annual release of data, with a lag time of about two years between data collection and release. The survey is used to update prices for the market basket of products and services used in calculating the Consumer Price Index.

Description of the Consumer Expenditure Survey

The CEX is two surveys: an interview survey and a diary survey. In the interview portion of the survey, respondents are asked each quarter for five consecutive quarters to report their expenditures for the previous three months. The purchase of big-ticket items such as houses, cars, and major appliances, or recurring expenses such as insurance premiums, utility payments, and rent are recorded by the interview survey. About 95 percent of all expenditures are covered by the interview component.

Expenditures on small, frequently purchased items are recorded during a two-week period by the diary survey. These detailed records include expenses for food and beverages purchased in grocery stores and at restaurants, as well as other items such as tobacco, housekeeping supplies, nonprescription drugs, and personal care products and services. The diary survey is intended to capture expenditures that respondents are likely to forget or recall incorrectly over longer periods of time.

The average spending figures shown in this book are the integrated data from both the diary and interview components of the survey. Integrated data provide a more complete accounting of consumer expenditures than either component of the survey is designed to do alone.

Data collection and processing

Two separate, nationally representative samples are used for the interview and diary surveys. For the interview survey, about 7,500 consumer units are interviewed on a rotating panel basis each quarter for five consecutive quarters. Another 7,500 consumer units keep weekly diaries of spending for two consecutive weeks. Data collection is carried out in 105 areas of the country.

The data are reviewed, audited, and cleaned by the BLS, and then weighted to reflect the number and characteristics of all U.S. consumer units. As with any sample survey, the CEX is subject to two major types of error. Nonsampling error occurs when respondents misinterpret questions or interviewers are inconsistent in the way they ask questions or record answers. Respondents may forget items, recall expenses incorrectly, or deliberately give wrong answers. A respondent may remember how much he or she spent at the grocery store but forget the items picked up at a local convenience store. Most surveys of alcohol consumption or spending on alcohol suffer from this type of underreporting, for example. Nonsampling error can also be caused by mistakes during the various stages of data processing and refinement.

Sampling error occurs when a sample does not accurately represent the population it is supposed to represent. This kind of error is present in every sample-based survey and is minimized by using a proper sampling procedure. As previously mentioned, standard error tables that document the extent of sampling error in the CEX are available from the BLS.

Although the CEX is the best source of information about the spending behavior of American households, it should be treated with caution because of the above problems. Comparisons with consumption data from other sources show that CEX data tend to underestimate expenditures except for rent, fuel, telephone service, furniture, transportation, and personal care services. Despite these problems, the data reveal important spending patterns by demographic segment that can be used to better understand consumer behavior.

The definition of consumer units

The CEX uses consumer units as its sampling unit instead of households, which are the sampling units used by the Census Bureau. The term "household" is used interchangeably with the term "consumer unit" in this book for convenience, although they are not exactly the same. Some households contain more than one consumer unit.

Consumer units are defined by the BLS as either: 1) members of a household who are related by blood, marriage, adoption, or other legal arrangements; 2) a person living alone or sharing a household with others or living as a roomer in a private home or lodging house or in permanent living quarters in a hotel or motel, but who is financially independent; or 3) two persons or more living together who pool their income to make joint expenditure decisions. The BLS defines financial independence in terms of "the three major expenses categories: housing, food, and other living expenses. To be considered financially independent, at least two of the three major expense categories have to be provided by the respondent."

The Census Bureau uses households as its sampling unit in the decennial census and in the monthly Current Population Survey. The Census Bureau's household "consists of all persons who occupy a housing unit. A house, an apartment or other groups of rooms, or a single room is regarded as a housing unit when it is occupied or intended for occupancy as separate living quarters; that is, when the occupants do not live and eat with any other persons in the structure and there is direct access from the outside or through a common hall."

The definition goes on to specify that "a household includes the related family members and all the unrelated persons, if any, such as lodgers, foster children, wards, or employees who share the housing unit. A person living alone in a housing unit or a group of unrelated persons sharing a housing unit as partners is also counted as a household. The count of households excludes group quarters."

Because there can be more than one consumer unit in a household, consumer units outnumber households by several million. Most of the excess consumer units are headed by young adults, under age 25.

For More Information

If you want to know more about the Consumer Expenditure Survey, contact the CEX specialists at the Bureau of Labor Statistics at (202) 691-6900, or visit the Consumer Expenditure Survey home page at http://www.bls.gov/cex/. The CEX web site includes news releases, technical documentation, and current and historical CEX data. The average spending figures for the more than 300 individual products and services analyzed in *Household Spending* are available only in printed reports or PDF files from the BLS by special request.

Appendix B

Reduction of Mortgage Principle

The spending statistics reported by the Consumer Expenditure Survey do not include the amount households spend to reduce their mortgage principle. Since the survey treats home equity as an asset, principle reduction is regarded as asset accumulation rather than an expenditure.

The following table gives the average annual reduction of mortgage principle for the five major demographic variables shown in the book: age of reference person, average before-tax income of consumer unit, type of consumer unit, and race and Hispanic origin of reference person, and region. Adding these amounts to expenditures for the category "owned dwellings" gives a more complete picture of the amount of money people spend on housing.

Average Annual Reduction of Mortgage Principle

(average annual reduction in mortgage principle for owned homes, by age of consumer unit (cu) reference person, average before-tax income of consumer unit, type of consumer unit, race and Hispanic origin of consumer unit reference person, and region in which consumer unit lives, 2000)

	total consumer units	under 25	25 to 34	35 to 44	45 to 54	55 to 64	65 to 74	75 or older
Age of reference person	$892.22	$130.40	$667.68	$1,295.78	$1,356.13	$1,055.83	$555.96	$167.47

	complete income reporters	under $10,000	$10,000– $19,999	$20,000– $29,999	$30,000– $39,999	$40,000– $49,999	$50,000– $69,999	$70,000 or more
Before-tax income of consumer unit	$861.96	$166.51	$270.59	$406.01	$620.25	$889.13	$1,177.52	$2,172.51

	total married couples	married couples, no children	married couples with children			single parent with child under 18	single person
			total	oldest child under age 6	oldest child 6 to 17	oldest child 18 or older		
Type of consumer unit	$1,331.17	$1,018.88	$1,574.51	$1,241.96	$1,705.08	$1,543.50	$465.99	$377.74

	total consumer units	race		Hispanic origin	
		white and other	black	Hispanic	non-Hispanic
Race/Hispanic origin of reference person	$892.22	$941.14	$536.71	$496.78	$929.72

	total consumer units	Northeast	Midwest	South	West
Region in which consumer unit lives	$89.2.22	$908.65	$849.90	$773.47	$1,108.71

Source: Bureau of Labor Statistics, 2000 Consumer Expenditue Survey

Appendix C

Percent Reporting Expenditure and Amount Spent, Average Quarter 2000

(percent of consumer units reporting expenditure and amount spent by purchasers during an average quarter, 2000)

	percent reporting expenditure during quarter	average amount spent per quarter
FOOD	**99.61%**	**$1,296.16**
Food at home	**98.91**	**945.78**
Grocery stores	98.52	626.78
Convenience stores	24.95	232.39
Food prepared by cu on trips	13.59	73.47
Food away from home	**82.25**	**432.38**
Meals at restaurants, carryouts, and other	78.52	329.84
Board (including at school)	1.69	577.37
Catered affairs	1.37	985.77
Food on trips	27.49	196.49
School lunches	10.08	144.99
Meals as pay	1.80	263.47
ALCOHOLIC BEVERAGES	**41.49**	**177.76**
At home	**33.01**	**120.77**
Beer and wine	31.76	101.98
Other alcoholic beverages	9.50	78.71
Away from home	**27.34**	**123.95**
Alcoholic beverages at restaurants, taverns	21.28	119.02
Alcoholic beverages purchased on trips	12.52	68.37
HOUSING	**99.61**	**2,884.92**
Shelter	**97.55**	**1,823.23**
OWNED DWELLINGS	65.76	1,749.67
Mortgage interest and charges	39.35	1,676.50
Mortgage interest	37.00	1,662.49
Interest paid, home equity loan	4.28	573.71
Interest paid, home equity line of credit	2.82	707.09
Prepayment penalty charge	0.03	283.33
Property taxes	64.57	440.82
Maintenance, repairs, insurance, other expenses	35.91	574.32
Homeowners and related insurance	24.27	241.90
Ground rent	1.45	666.72
Maintenance and repair services	12.67	866.06
Painting and papering	1.56	800.16
Plumbing and water heating	3.62	287.43
Heat, air conditioning, electrical work	4.48	441.91
Roofing and gutters	1.01	1,863.12
Other repair and maintenance services	4.29	920.69
Repair/replacement of hard surface flooring	0.54	1,556.02
Repair of built-in appliances	0.37	88.51

(continued)

(continued from previous page)

	percent reporting expenditure during quarter	average amount spent per quarter
Maintenance and repair materials	6.49%	$300.77
Paints, wallpaper and supplies	2.69	148.98
Tools/equipment for painting, wallpapering	2.69	15.99
Plumbing supplies and equipment	0.98	156.38
Electrical supplies, heating/cooling equipment	0.46	236.41
Hard surface flooring, repair and replacement	0.41	425.61
Roofing and gutters	0.33	485.61
Plaster, paneling, siding, windows, doors, screens, awnings	0.94	322.87
Patio, walk, fence, driveway, masonry, brick, stucco work	0.39	38.46
Landscape maintenance	0.46	158.70
Miscellaneous supplies and equipment	1.61	322.98
Insulation, other maintenance/repair	1.33	252.82
Finish basement, remodel rooms, build patios, walks, etc.	0.32	574.22
Property management and security	3.56	217.63
Property management	3.24	165.82
Management and upkeep services for security	1.31	181.30
Parking	1.28	67.38
RENTED DWELLINGS	**32.64**	**1,557.99**
Rent	32.16	1,537.10
Rent as pay	0.68	1,075.00
Maintenance, insurance, and other expenses	3.44	200.15
Tenant's insurance	2.20	100.68
Maintenance and repair services	0.50	556.50
Repair or maintenance services	0.45	554.44
Repair and replacement of hard surface flooring	0.03	900.00
Repair of built-in appliances	0.02	87.50
Maintenance and repair materials	0.93	202.96
Paint, wallpaper, and supplies	0.41	93.90
Painting and wallpapering	0.41	10.37
Plastering, paneling, roofing, gutters, etc.	0.09	133.33
Patio, walk, fence, driveway, masonry, brick, stucco work	0.02	37.50
Plumbing supplies and equipment	0.12	81.25
Electrical supplies, heating and cooling equipment	0.05	125.00
Miscellaneous supplies and equipment	0.25	360.00
Insulation, other maintenance and repair	0.19	121.05
Materials for additions, finishing basements, remodeling rooms	0.07	953.57
Hard surface flooring	0.06	204.17
Landscape maintenance	0.07	214.29
OTHER LODGING	**20.98**	**569.40**
Owned vacation homes	5.02	736.60
Mortgage interest and charges	1.38	1,153.08
Mortgage interest	1.29	1,185.85
Interest paid, home equity loan	0.08	421.88
Interest paid, home equity line of credit	0.04	693.75
Property taxes	4.31	301.45
Maintenance, insurance and other expenses	1.80	448.47
Homeowners and related insurance	1.00	268.50
Ground rent	0.09	825.00
Maintenance and repair services	0.65	521.54

(continued)

(continued from previous page)

	percent reporting expenditure during quarter	average amount spent per quarter
Maintenance and repair materials	0.04%	$300.00
Property management and security	0.50	194.50
Property management	0.46	139.13
Management and upkeep services for security	0.26	127.88
Parking	0.21	77.38
Housing while attending school	1.31	1,494.47
Lodging on out-of-town trips	16.53	380.55
Utilities, Fuels, Public Services	**97.28**	**639.62**
Natural gas	50.17	153.15
Electricity	90.51	251.75
Fuel oil and other fuels	9.22	262.85
Fuel oil	4.04	340.84
Coal	0.06	241.67
Bottled gas	4.81	183.26
Wood and other fuels	0.88	171.02
Telephone services	94.83	231.14
Telephone services in home city, excl. mobile car phones	94.40	200.55
Telephone services for mobile car phones	20.86	143.20
Water and other public services	59.11	125.37
Water and sewerage maintenance	52.40	101.49
Trash and garbage collection	36.96	55.29
Septic tank cleaning	0.29	168.97
Household Services	**49.79**	**337.74**
PERSONAL SERVICES	**9.19**	**887.38**
Babysitting and child care in your own home	2.11	381.64
Babysitting and child care in someone else's home	1.55	525.65
Care for elderly, invalids, handicapped, etc.	0.49	2,570.41
Adult day care centers	0.07	928.57
Day care centers, nursery and preschools	6.20	840.40
OTHER HOUSEHOLD SERVICES	**46.10**	**187.88**
Housekeeping services	6.41	343.80
Gardening, lawn care service	12.58	155.52
Water softening service	1.01	76.98
Nonclothing laundry and dry cleaning, sent out	0.96	38.54
Nonclothing laundry and dry cleaning, coin-operated	5.63	20.60
Termite/pest control services	1.81	132.18
Home security system service fee	4.68	99.73
Other home services	2.39	149.37
Termite/pest control products	0.36	34.03
Moving, storage, and freight express	2.50	324.30
Appliance repair, including service center	2.70	116.48
Reupholstering and furniture repair	0.69	335.51
Repairs/rentals of lawn/garden equipment, hand/power tools, etc.	1.10	112.73
Appliance rental	0.40	235.62
Rental of office equipment for nonbusiness use	0.15	88.33
Repair of computer systems for nonbusiness use	0.48	143.23
Computer information services	25.51	60.13
Rental and installation of dishwashers, range hoods, and garbage disposals	0.02	187.50

(continued)

(continued from previous page)

	percent reporting expenditure during quarter	average amount spent per quarter
Household furnishings and equipment	**53.75%**	**$566.92**
HOUSEHOLD TEXTILES	**17.75**	**114.01**
Bathroom linens	6.05	42.19
Bedroom linens	9.01	95.06
Kitchen and dining room linens	1.97	29.82
Curtains and draperies	2.32	226.94
Slipcovers and decorative pillows	0.84	54.76
Sewing materials for household items	3.71	65.70
Other linens	0.73	52.40
FURNITURE	**11.64**	**838.98**
Mattress and springs	2.25	587.67
Other bedroom furniture	2.49	693.88
Sofas	2.24	994.98
Living room chairs	2.21	495.93
Living room tables	1.61	266.93
Kitchen and dining room furniture	1.77	656.21
Infants' furniture	0.76	204.61
Outdoor furniture	1.71	221.64
Wall units, cabinets, and other furniture	2.94	430.36
FLOOR COVERINGS	**3.03**	**366.17**
Wall-to-wall carpeting (renter)	0.07	492.86
Wall-to-wall carpeting, replacement (owner)	0.46	1,509.78
Floor coverings, nonpermanent	2.55	149.22
MAJOR APPLIANCES	**7.74**	**541.38**
Dishwashers (built-in), garbage disposals, range hoods (renter)	0.10	217.50
Dishwashers (built-in), garbage disposals, range hoods (owner)	0.88	400.57
Refrigerators and freezers (renter)	0.40	459.38
Refrigerators and freezers (owner)	1.41	786.17
Washing machines (renter)	0.35	342.14
Washing machines (owner)	0.93	498.12
Clothes dryers (renter)	0.29	289.66
Clothes dryers (owner)	0.75	400.67
Cooking stoves, ovens (renter)	0.19	368.42
Cooking stoves, ovens (owner)	0.96	623.70
Microwave ovens (renter)	0.50	119.00
Mocrowave ovens (owner)	0.93	197.85
Portable dishwasher (renter)	0.01	400.00
Portable dishwasher (owner)	0.04	475.00
Window air conditioners (renter)	0.17	272.06
Window air conditioners (owner)	0.37	325.68
Electric floor cleaning equipment	1.56	214.74
Sewing machines	0.26	459.62
SMALL APPLIANCES AND MISCELLANEOUS HOUSEWARES	**15.94**	**83.91**
Housewares	9.35	82.86
Plastic dinnerware	1.30	27.88
China and other dinnerware	2.79	84.32
Flatware	1.56	57.85
Glassware	2.55	49.22
Silver serving pieces	0.10	90.00

(continued)

(continued from previous page)

	percent reporting expenditure during quarter	average amount spent per quarter
Other serving pieces	0.84%	$42.56
Nonelectric cookware	3.35	72.46
Small appliances	8.56	65.74
Small electric kitchen appliances	7.22	59.00
Portable heating and cooling equipment	1.67	81.89
MISCELLANEOUS HOUSEHOLD EQUIPMENT	**38.95**	**309.20**
Window coverings	1.53	212.75
Infants' equipment	0.70	96.07
Outdoor equipment	0.80	151.88
Clocks	1.42	59.15
Lamps and lighting fixtures	2.80	96.43
Other household decorative items	9.39	151.57
Telephones and accessories	5.21	78.21
Lawn and garden equipment	3.03	386.30
Power tools	2.07	162.44
Small miscellaneous furnishings	1.39	245.86
Hand tools	2.55	71.18
Indoor plants and fresh flowers	18.39	77.50
Closet and storage items	1.67	57.63
Rental of furniture	0.33	236.36
Luggage	2.01	103.48
Computers and computer hardware, nonbusiness use	4.73	992.76
Computer software and accessories, nonbusiness use	4.23	103.37
Telephone answering devices	0.87	56.61
Calculators	1.02	40.20
Business equipment for home use	0.40	114.38
Smoke alarms (owner)	0.39	35.90
Smoke alarms (renter)	0.09	44.44
Other household appliances (owner)	1.02	186.03
Other household appliances (renter)	0.38	80.26
APPAREL AND SERVICES	**80.03**	**420.66**
Men and boys	**40.54**	**221.96**
MEN'S APPAREL	**33.86**	**201.43**
Suits	2.42	343.29
Sportcoats and tailored jackets	1.73	163.44
Coats and jackets	5.36	127.99
Underwear	9.30	27.82
Hosiery	9.96	17.65
Nightwear	2.01	41.54
Accessories	6.37	38.19
Sweaters and vests	4.72	84.53
Active sportswear	4.13	59.62
Shirts	18.15	77.08
Pants	18.60	88.01
Shorts and shorts sets	5.95	56.89
Uniforms	1.23	112.20
Costumes	0.94	107.98
BOYS' (AGED 2 TO 15) APPAREL	**13.05**	**166.86**
Coats and jackets	2.52	77.78
Sweaters	1.47	60.54
Shirts	6.85	65.33

(continued)

(continued from previous page)

	percent reporting expenditure during quarter	average amount spent per quarter
Underwear	4.13%	$27.18
Nightwear	1.30	46.15
Hosiery	4.21	15.20
Accessories	1.65	24.09
Suits, sportcoats, and vests	1.10	82.73
Pants	6.87	85.12
Shorts and shorts sets	3.72	60.15
Uniforms	2.07	44.20
Active sportswear	0.92	103.53
Costumes	1.38	60.33
Women and girls	**50.87**	**258.05**
WOMEN'S APPAREL	**46.02**	**234.35**
Coats and jackets	6.90	120.87
Dresses	12.92	123.96
Sportcoats and tailored jackets	1.84	113.18
Sweaters and vests	10.32	81.86
Shirts, blouses, and tops	22.67	68.77
Skirts	7.10	58.49
Pants	20.34	81.88
Shorts and shorts sets	8.15	53.87
Active sportswear	5.60	53.97
Nightwear	7.67	42.60
Undergarments	14.55	41.79
Hosiery	16.97	22.29
Suits	4.43	190.74
Accessories	9.10	41.15
Uniforms	2.10	103.45
Costumes	1.40	118.39
GIRLS' (AGED 2 TO 15) APPAREL	**13.28**	**176.34**
Coats and jackets	2.53	68.68
Dresses and suits	3.86	69.17
Shirts, blouses, and sweaters	7.38	75.88
Skirts and pants	6.78	80.20
Shorts and shorts sets	3.69	56.57
Active sportswear	2.11	46.21
Underwear and nightwear	5.22	35.44
Hosiery	4.21	16.63
Accessories	1.94	21.39
Uniforms	0.95	102.63
Costumes	1.38	70.11
Children under age 2	**14.22**	**122.52**
Coats, jackets, and snowsuits	1.98	34.09
Outerwear including dresses	8.59	66.85
Underwear	8.35	100.84
Nightwear and loungewear	3.59	27.79
Accessories	4.69	33.90
Footwear	**32.48**	**100.75**
Men's	12.13	90.56
Boys'	6.32	64.75
Women's	18.67	76.50
Girls'	6.16	54.63

(continued)

(continued from previous page)

	percent reporting expenditure during quarter	average amount spent per quarter
Other apparel products and services	**48.16%**	**$135.51**
Material for making clothes	1.68	47.32
Sewing patterns and notions	2.04	17.16
Watches	4.91	115.22
Jewelry	8.43	318.27
Shoe repair and other shoe services	1.50	30.50
Coin-operated apparel laundry and dry cleaning	16.78	56.51
Apparel alteration, repair, and tailoring services	3.30	43.18
Clothing rental	0.63	133.73
Watch and jewelry repair	3.34	35.48
Professional laundry, dry cleaning	25.07	72.20
Clothing storage	0.10	137.50
TRANSPORTATION	**93.74**	**1,968.15**
Vehicle purchases	**6.56**	**13,026.94**
CARS AND TRUCKS, NEW	1.79	22,415.50
New cars	1.10	20,841.36
New trucks	0.70	24,569.29
CARS AND TRUCKS, USED	4.65	9,515.32
Used cars	3.10	8,155.24
Used trucks	1.65	11,493.94
OTHER VEHICLES	0.17	6,391.18
New motorcycles	0.05	9,225.00
Used motorcycles	0.12	3,620.83
Gasoline and motor oil	**88.56**	**364.51**
Gasoline	87.50	335.86
Diesel fuel	1.11	292.34
Gasoline on out-of-town trips	24.86	92.31
Motor oil	13.75	18.27
Motor oil on out-of-town trips	24.86	0.94
Other vehicle expenses	**80.47**	**697.89**
VEHICLE FINANCE CHARGES	31.20	263.01
Automobile finance charges	20.10	210.51
Truck finance charges	13.55	255.76
Motorcycle and plane finance charges	0.38	103.95
Other vehicle finance charges	1.32	355.87
MAINTENANCE AND REPAIRS	54.47	275.26
Coolant, additives, brake, transmission fluids	8.22	13.59
Tires	9.19	237.30
Parts, equipment, and accessories	11.75	103.11
Vehicle audio equipment	0.12	241.67
Body work and painting	1.44	457.47
Clutch, transmission repair	1.95	546.28
Drive shaft and rear-end repair	0.34	269.12
Brake work	5.56	242.99
Repair to steering or front-end	1.48	304.39
Repair to engine cooling system	2.48	207.16
Motor tune-up	5.75	193.09
Lube, oil change, and oil filters	33.02	44.48
Front-end alignment, wheel balance, rotation	2.50	107.90
Shock absorber replacement	0.45	236.11
Repair tires and other repair work	6.18	120.35

(continued)

(continued from previous page)

	percent reporting expenditure during quarter	average amount spent per quarter
Exhaust system repair	1.83%	$182.24
Electrical system repair	3.55	213.45
Motor repair, replacement	3.26	494.33
Auto repair service policy	0.49	291.33
Vehicle accessories, including labor	0.97	185.82
Vehicle audio equipment, including labor	0.44	250.57
Vehicle air conditioning repair	1.49	332.21
VEHICLE INSURANCE	**50.49**	**385.29**
VEHICLE RENTAL, LEASES, LICENSES, OTHER CHARGES	**42.37**	**318.77**
Leased and rented vehicles	9.73	1,009.46
Rented vehicles	3.80	295.72
Auto rental	0.76	237.17
Auto rental, out-of-town trips	2.71	273.25
Truck rental	0.22	364.77
Truck rental, out-of-town trips	0.30	392.50
Leased vehicles	6.42	1,354.87
Car lease payments	3.74	1,168.72
Cash downpayment (car lease)	0.17	2,057.35
Termination fee (car lease)	0.04	1,131.25
Truck lease payments	3.12	1,189.50
Cash downpayment (truck lease)	0.12	1,608.33
Termination fee (truck lease)	0.04	693.75
State and local registration	18.21	116.95
Driver's license	6.18	27.71
Vehicle inspection	7.19	32.72
Parking fees	12.51	58.71
Parking fees in home city, excluding residence	10.05	63.01
Parking fees, out-of-town trips	3.51	28.85
Tolls on out-of-town trips	7.60	11.55
Towing charges	1.47	79.59
Automobile service clubs	3.33	62.69
Public transportation	**19.88**	**533.06**
Airline fares	11.07	618.83
Intercity bus fares	5.15	78.16
Intracity mass transit fares	7.97	148.71
Local transportation on out-of-town trips	5.86	45.48
Taxi fares and limousine service on trips	5.86	26.71
Taxi fares and limousine service	2.81	84.25
Intercity train fares	4.66	113.30
Ship fares	3.50	261.29
School bus	0.23	245.65
HEALTH CARE	**79.62**	**606.88**
Health insurance	**62.77**	**391.37**
COMMERCIAL HEALTH INSURANCE	**13.11**	**370.69**
Traditional fee for service health plan (not BCBS)	5.46	352.88
Preferred provider health plan (not BCBS)	7.82	375.06
BLUE CROSS, BLUE SHIELD	**14.87**	**390.89**
Traditional fee for service health plan	3.09	403.64
Preferred provider health plan	4.00	380.88
Health maintenance organization	5.08	360.14

(continued)

(continued from previous page)

	percent reporting expenditure during quarter	average amount spent per quarter
Commercial Medicare supplement	2.58%	$424.13
Other BCBS health insurance	0.67	175.75
HEALTH MAINTENANCE PLANS (HMOS)	**19.90**	**320.11**
MEDICARE PAYMENTS	**23.30**	**176.01**
COMMERCIAL MEDICARE SUPPLEMENTS/ OTHER HEALTH INSURANCE	**12.32**	**277.82**
Commercial Medicare supplement (not BCBS)	5.86	376.37
Other health insurance (not BCBS)	6.94	175.40
Medical Services	**44.08**	**321.71**
Physician's services	29.21	115.04
Dental services	16.48	334.94
Eye care services	6.88	127.36
Service by professionals other than physician	4.37	210.93
Lab tests, x-rays	4.18	120.33
Hospital room	1.79	502.09
Hospital services other than room	3.52	292.12
Care in convalescent or nursing home	0.26	3,110.58
Other medical services	1.09	242.20
Prescription drugs	47.39	160.99
Medical supplies	**9.86**	**197.11**
Eyeglasses and contact lenses	8.05	181.46
Hearing aids	0.68	433.09
Medical equipment for general use	0.70	72.86
Supportive/convalescent medical equipment	0.73	108.90
Rental of medical equipment	0.26	81.73
Rental of supportive, convalescent medical equipment	0.44	82.95
ENTERTAINMENT	**89.08**	**495.68**
Fees and admissions	**50.54**	**254.67**
Recreation expenses, out of town trips	10.37	61.45
Social, recreation, civic club membership	12.04	203.86
Fees for participant sports	12.28	145.54
Participant sports, out-of-town trips	5.77	151.86
Movie, theater, opera, ballet	32.71	68.14
Movie, other admissions, out-of-town trips	11.64	96.52
Admission to sports events	7.88	112.09
Admission to sports events, out-of-town trips	11.64	32.17
Fees for recreational lessons	7.20	259.51
Other entertainment services, out-of-town trips	10.37	61.45
Television, radios, sound equipment	**81.03**	**189.74**
TELEVISIONS	**72.09**	**157.28**
Community antenna or cable TV	66.51	120.73
Black and white TV	0.13	148.08
Color TV, console	0.85	887.94
Color TV, portable, table model	2.77	310.02
VCRs and video disc players	2.72	218.75
Video cassettes, tapes, and discs	12.88	40.37
Video game hardware and software	4.79	97.70
Repair of TV, radio, and sound equipment	0.74	109.12
Rental of televisions	0.06	204.17
RADIOS AND SOUND EQUIPMENT	**43.28**	**93.25**
Radios	1.34	91.23

(continued)

(continued from previous page)

	percent reporting expenditure during quarter	average amount spent per quarter
Tape recorders and players	0.43%	$80.23
Sound components and component systems	2.08	278.37
Compact disc, tape, record, video mail order clubs	3.75	56.80
Records, CDs, audio tapes, needles	19.29	51.14
Rental of VCR, radio, sound equipment	0.08	168.75
Musical instruments and accessories	1.79	442.74
Rental and repair of musical instruments	0.36	93.06
Rental of video cassettes, tapes, discs, films	31.82	32.65
Sound equipment accessories	0.85	181.47
Satellite dishes	0.31	217.74
Pets, toys, playground equipment	**40.34**	**185.45**
PETS	**29.40**	**148.78**
Pet purchase, supplies, and medicines	24.70	90.70
Pet services	4.73	102.33
Veterinary services	9.06	182.12
TOYS, GAMES, HOBBIES, AND TRICYCLES	**17.91**	**168.84**
PLAYGROUND EQUIPMENT	**0.44**	**188.64**
Other entertainment supplies, equipment, services	**37.15**	**226.88**
UNMOTORED RECREATIONAL VEHICLES	**0.21**	**5,721.43**
Boat without motor and boat trailers	0.11	3,606.82
Trailer and other attachable campers	0.10	8,047.50
MOTORIZED RECREATIONAL VEHICLES	**0.24**	**8,537.50**
Motorized camper	0.02	26,700.00
Other vehicle	0.11	4,940.91
Motor boats	0.11	8,834.09
RENTAL OF RECREATIONAL VEHICLES	**0.29**	**240.52**
Rental of noncamper trailer	0.01	300.00
Boat and trailer rental, out-of-town trips	0.08	184.38
Rental of camper on out-of-town trips	0.01	1,525.00
Rental of other vehicles, out-of-town trips	0.16	218.75
Rental of boat	0.01	75.00
Rental of other RVs	0.01	75.00
OUTBOARD MOTORS	**0.07**	**1,278.57**
DOCKING AND LANDING FEES	**0.53**	**385.38**
SPORTS, RECREATION, EXERCISE EQUIPMENT	**11.52**	**215.08**
Athletic gear, game tables, exercise equipment	5.81	160.67
Bicycles	1.58	185.60
Camping equipment	0.88	132.95
Hunting and fishing equipment	2.20	170.68
Winter sports equipment	0.51	286.27
Water sports equipment	0.59	349.15
Other sports equipment	1.98	179.92
Rental and repair of miscellaneous sports equipment	0.36	140.28
PHOTOGRAPHIC EQUIPMENT AND SUPPLIES	**31.92**	**73.21**
Film	24.20	22.11
Film processing	23.26	33.78
Repair and rental of photographic equipment	0.08	84.38
Photographic equipment	2.06	245.27
Photographer fees	3.56	141.64

(continued)

(continued from previous page)

	percent reporting expenditure during quarter	average amount spent per quarter
PERSONAL CARE PRODUCTS AND SERVICES	**74.69%**	**$104.81**
Wigs and hairpieces	0.56	52.23
Electric personal care appliances	2.80	41.43
Personal care services	74.12	103.65
READING	**57.54**	**63.58**
Newspaper subscriptions	27.45	43.20
Newspaper, nonsubscriptions	18.57	16.51
Magazine subscriptions	10.86	43.97
Magazines, nonsubscriptions	13.26	17.91
Books purchased through book clubs	3.69	54.40
Books not purchased through book clubs	21.83	56.71
Encyclopedia and other reference book sets	0.11	115.91
EDUCATION	**15.54**	**937.58**
College tuition	4.85	1,872.63
Elementary/high school tuition	2.24	1,131.92
Other schools tuition	1.06	575.94
Other school expenses including rentals	3.70	162.16
Books, supplies for college	4.51	291.91
Books, supplies for elementary, high school	4.21	82.66
Books, supplies for day care, nursery school	0.81	95.37
TOBACCO PRODUCTS, SMOKING SUPPLIES	**26.44**	**299.19**
Cigarettes	24.01	306.02
Other tobacco products	3.68	152.99
FINANCIAL PRODUCTS AND SERVICES		
Miscellaneous financial products and services	**39.17**	**448.56**
Legal fees	3.14	827.71
Funeral expenses	1.97	897.08
Safe deposit box rental	3.62	31.63
Checking accounts, other bank service charges	17.48	28.45
Cemetery lots, vaults, and maintenance fees	0.90	374.17
Accounting fees	6.18	223.22
Finance charges, except mortgage and vehicles	8.79	720.62
Occupational expenses	4.50	534.67
Expenses for other properties	5.60	355.94
Interest paid, home equity line of credit (other property)	0.02	1,225.00
Credit card memberships	1.73	68.06
Cash contributions	**11.20**	**2,661.70**
Cash contributions to non-household members,	1.29	5,737.79
Gifts of cash, stocks, bonds to non-household members	3.16	2,116.14
Contributions to charities	5.72	611.32
Contributions to religious organizations	6.83	1,631.15
Contributions to educational organizations	1.15	433.91
Political contributions	0.75	221.67
Other contributions	0.68	617.65
Personal insurance and pensions	**72.52**	**1,160.00**
Life and other personal insurance	37.66	264.61
Life, endowment, annuity, other personal insurance	36.97	262.35
Other nonhealth insurance	1.81	146.96
Pensions and Social Security	60.63	1,223.12
Deductions for government retirement	2.75	639.27

(continued)

(continued from previous page)

	percent reporting expenditure during quarter	average amount spent per quarter
Deductions for railroad retirement	0.08%	$1,028.12
Deductions for private pensions	9.36	968.59
Nonpayroll deposit to retirement plans	9.52	1,023.24
Deductions for Social Security	59.98	892.13
PERSONAL TAXES	**62.81**	**1,240.83**
Federal income taxes	58.13	1,036.18
State and local income taxes	41.60	337.62
Other taxes	14.56	251.24
GIFTS	**36.23**	**517.83**
Food	1.28	720.12
Housing	16.67	288.26
Household textiles	2.39	68.72
Appliances and miscellaneous housewares	2.84	122.27
Major appliances	0.48	255.73
Small appliances and miscellaneous housewares	2.50	89.80
Miscellaneous household equipment	8.38	116.89
Other housing	6.56	505.26
Apparel and services	19.36	184.01
Males aged two or older	5.75	153.96
Females aged two or older	7.10	165.28
Children under age two	9.56	84.36
Other apparel products and services	4.77	146.17
Jewelry and watches	2.58	196.51
All other apparel products and services	2.44	77.97
Transportation	4.92	345.83
Health care	1.42	615.67
Entertainment	11.88	171.17
Toys, games, hobbies, and tricycles	5.94	124.49
Other entertainment	7.16	180.73
Education	2.62	1,389.22
All other gifts	4.86	251.49

Source: Calculations by New Strategist based on the 2000 Consumer Expenditure Survey

Appendix D

Spending by Product and Service, 2000

(average annual spending of consumer units on products and services, ranked by amount spent, 2000)

Mortgage interest	$2,460.48
Federal income tax	2,409.33
Social Security	2,140.41
Rent	1,977.33
Gasoline and motor oil	1,291.25
Property taxes	1,138.55
Cars, used	1,011.25
Health insurance	982.65
Cars, new	917.02
Electricity	911.44
Insurance, vehicle	778.13
Trucks, used	758.60
Telephone service in home city, excluding mobile phone	757.26
Trucks, new	687.94
Vehicle maintenance and repairs	623.76
Apparel, women's	607.11
State and local income tax	561.80
Dinner at full-service restaurants	487.70
Contributions to religious organizations	445.63
Maintenance and repair services, owned homes	438.92
Retirement accounts, nonpayroll deposits	389.65
Insurance, life and other personal except health	387.97
Lunch at fast-food restaurants and take-outs	368.00
Tuition, college	363.29
Pensions, deductions for private	362.64
Apparel, men's	344.29
Finance charges, vehicle	328.24
Cable TV or community antenna	321.18
Natural gas	307.35
Personal care services	307.31
Drugs, prescription	305.17
Contributions of cash to nonhousehold members including students, ali	296.07
Apparel, children's	295.77
Cigarettes	293.90
Airline fares	274.02
Gifts of cash, stocks, bonds to nonhousehold members	267.48
Food on trips	256.00
Finance charges, except mortgage and vehicle	253.37
Lodging on trips	251.62
Beef	238.19
Insurance, homeowners	234.84
Dental services	220.79
Food on trips	216.06
Water and sewerage maintenance	212.72
Day care centers, nursery schools, preschools	208.42
Lunch at full-service restaurants	208.12
Dinner at fast-food restaurants and take-outs	206.92

(continued)

(continued from previous page)

Computers and computer hardware for nonbusiness use	$187.83
Home equity loan, line of credit interest	177.98
Decorative items for the home	177.30
Car lease payments	174.84
Pork	166.94
Medicare payments	164.04
Fruit, fresh	163.17
Vegetables, fresh	158.72
Snacks and nonalcoholic beverages at fast-food restaurants and take-out	158.55
Shoes, women's	155.95
Truck lease payments	148.45
Vacation homes, owned	147.91
Recreation expenses on trips	145.95
Poultry	145.16
Contributions to charities	139.87
Physician's services	134.41
Carbonated drinks	134.38
Toys, games, hobbies, and tricycles	120.96
Cosmetics, perfume, and bath products	119.91
Milk, fresh	119.61
Telephone service for mobile phone	119.49
Shoes, men's	117.55
Beer and ale at home	112.01
Fish and seafood	110.14
Jewelry	107.32
Legal fees	103.96
Tuition, elementary and high school	101.42
Social, recreation, and civic club memberships	98.18
Occupational expenses, union and professional dues	96.24
Cheese	95.96
Movie, theater, opera, and ballet tickets	89.16
Sofas	89.15
Housekeeping services	88.15
Cereal, ready-to-eat and cooked	86.88
Pet food	85.97
Vehicle registration, state and local	85.19
Bread	84.04
Trash collection	81.74
Lunch at employer or school cafeterias	80.26
Wine at home	80.04
Breakfast at full-service restaurants	79.64
Housing while attending school	78.31
Gardening and lawn care service	78.26
Maintenance and repair materials, owned homes	78.08
Breakfast at fast food restaurants and take-outs	77.12
Hospital services, including room	77.08
Candy and chewing gum	76.30
Fees for recreational lessons	74.74
Laundry and dry cleaning of apparel, professional	72.40
Potato chips and other snacks	71.67
Fees for participant sports	71.49
Funeral expenses	70.69
Deductions for government retirement	70.32
Soaps and detergents	69.27

(continued)

(continued from previous page)

Cleansing and toilet tissues, paper towels, and napkins	$68.45
Lunch meats (cold cuts)	67.99
Lawn and garden supplies	66.97
Veterinary services	66.00
Television sets	65.31
Drugs, nonprescription	65.09
Whiskey and other alcohol (except beer and wine) at restaurants, bars	64.92
Stationery, stationery supplies, and giftwrap	63.65
Beer and ale at restaurants, bars	62.46
Computer information services	61.36
Postage	60.60
Athletic gear, game tables, and exercise equipment	58.64
School lunches	58.46
Eyeglasses and contact lenses	58.43
Plants and fresh flowers, indoor	57.01
Ice cream and related products	56.56
Fruit juice, canned and bottled	56.21
Accounting fees	55.18
Fuel oil	55.08
Catered affairs	54.02
Mattresses and springs	52.89
Books and supplies, college	52.66
Refrigerators and freezers	51.69
Hair care products	51.46
Wall units, cabinets, and miscellaneous furniture	50.61
Care for elderly, invalids, handicapped, etc.	50.38
Books, except book clubs	49.52
Cookies	47.71
Newspaper subscriptions	47.43
Food from vending machines, mobile vendors	47.41
Mass transit, intracity fares	47.41
Lawn and garden equipment	46.82
Kitchen and dining room furniture	46.46
Vitamins, nonprescription	46.19
Bedroom linens	44.52
Living room chairs	43.84
Coffee	41.85
Miscellaneous fees, gambling losses	41.60
Videotape, disc, film rental	41.56
CDs, audio tapes, records	39.46
Board (including at school)	39.03
Motorboats	38.87
Ground rent	38.67
Biscuits and rolls	38.53
Cakes and cupcakes	38.42
Pet purchase, supplies, and medicine	38.10
Laundry and dry cleaning of apparel, coin-operated	37.93
Vegetables, canned	37.42
Shoes, boys'	37.26
Sauces and gravies	37.23
Health care services from nonphysician, professional	36.87
Car rental	36.83
Ship fares	36.58
Canned and packaged soups	35.54

(continued)

(continued from previous page)

Admission to sports events	$35.33
Bottled/tank gas for heating/cooking	35.26
Eye care services	35.05
Whiskey and other alcohol (except beer and wine) at home	34.59
Eggs	34.46
Alcoholic beverages on trips	34.24
Babysitting and child care, other home	32.59
Moving, storage, and freight express	32.43
Care in convalescent or nursing home	32.35
Shoes, girls'	32.33
Baby food	32.26
Babysitting and child care, own home	32.21
Trailer and other attachable campers	32.19
Musical instruments and accessories	31.70
Film processing	31.43
Deodorants, feminine hygiene, miscellaneous products	29.21
Telephones and accessories	29.19
Wall-to-wall carpeting	29.16
Pasta and cornmeal	28.64
Frozen meals	28.50
Salad dressings	27.18
Cooking stoves and ovens	26.75
Frozen vegetables	26.42
Electric floor-cleaning equipment	25.98
Hunting and fishing equipment	25.85
Oral hygiene products	25.78
Parking fees in home city, excluding residence	25.33
Frozen and refrigerated bakery products	24.53
VCRs and video disc players	23.80
Fresh fruit juice	23.44
Fats and oils	23.35
Crackers	23.32
Washing machines	23.32
Sound components and component systems	23.16
Sweetrolls, coffee cakes, doughnuts	22.68
Watches	22.63
Tobacco products, except cigarettes	22.52
Property management, owned homes	21.49
Film	21.40
Motorized campers	21.35
Power tools	21.32
Train fares, intercity	21.12
Curtains and draperies	21.06
Topicals and dressings	20.99
Nuts	20.83
Video cassettes, tapes, and discs	20.80
Salt, spices, and other seasonings	20.65
Photographic equipment	20.21
Photographer fees	20.17
Snacks at full-service restaurants	20.15
Lab tests, X-rays	20.12
Contributions to educational organizations	19.96
Tableware, nonelectric kitchenware	19.90
Bank service charges	19.89

(continued)

(continued from previous page)

Jams and preserves	$19.86
Rice	19.55
Fruit-flavored drinks, noncarbonated	19.42
Pet services	19.36
Magazine subscriptions	19.10
Video game hardware and software	18.72
Home security system service fee	18.67
Salads, prepared	18.55
Motorcycles, new	18.45
Outdoor equipment	18.39
Wine at restaurants and bars	17.79
Bathroom linens	17.55
Computer software and accessories, nonbusiness use	17.49
Motorcycles, used	17.38
Living room tables	17.19
Kitchen appliances, small electric	17.04
Camping equipment	17.02
Butter	17.00
Baking needs	16.96
Sugar	16.80
Cookware, nonelectric	16.67
Bus fares, intercity	16.10
Boats without motors and boat trailers	15.87
Tea	15.68
Canned fruits	15.48
Clothes dryers	15.38
Room-size rugs and other floor coverings, nonpermanent	15.22
Outdoor furniture	15.16
Dishwashers	14.97
Books and supplies, elementary and high school	13.92
Clocks	13.91
Office furniture for home use	13.67
Cemetery lots, vaults, and maintenance fees	13.47
Flour mixes, prepared	13.35
Pies, tarts, and turnovers	13.28
Shaving products	13.19
Window coverings	13.02
Appliance repair, including service center	12.58
Newspapers, nonsubscription	12.26
Taxi fares and limousine service	12.15
Peanut butter	11.81
Hearing aids	11.78
Bicycles	11.73
Repair of miscellaneous household equipment and furnishings	11.73
Cream	11.61
Margarine	11.61
China and other dinnerware	11.43
Maintenance and repair services, rented homes	11.13
Tolls	10.90
Lamps and lighting fixtures	10.80
Fruit juice, frozen	10.74
Local transportation on trips	10.66
Snacks at employer and school cafeterias	10.49
Radios	10.44

(continued)

(continued from previous page)

Laundry and cleaning equipment	$10.08
Dried vegetables	10.05
Olives, pickles, and relishes	9.77
Sewing materials for household items	9.75
Microwave ovens	9.74
Lamb and organ meats	9.71
Vegetable juices	9.59
Termite/pest control services	9.57
Magazines, nonsubscription	9.50
Management and upkeep services for security, owned homes	9.50
Vehicle inspection	9.41
Kitchen and dining room linens	9.31
Prepared desserts	9.31
Reupholstering and furniture repair	9.26
Nondairy cream and imitation milk	9.15
Electric personal care appliances	8.99
Tenant's insurance	8.86
Compact disc, tape, record, and video mail order clubs	8.52
Automobile service clubs	8.35
Luggage	8.32
Water sports equipment	8.24
Docking and landing fees	8.17
Books purchased through book clubs	8.03
Closet and storage items	8.03
Glassware	8.02
Infants' equipment	8.01
Flour	7.98
Truck rental	7.92
Maintenance and repair materials, rented homes	7.55
Hand tools	7.26
Driver's license fee	6.85
Window air conditioners	6.67
Contributions to political organizations	6.65
Hair accessories	6.59
Taxi fares and limousine service on trips	6.26
Infants' furniture	6.22
Laundry and dry cleaning, nonapparel	6.12
Wood and other fuels	6.02
Winter sports equipment	5.84
Pinball, electronic video games	5.80
Apparel repair and tailoring	5.70
Dried fruits	5.50
Portable heating and cooling equipment	5.47
Medical equipment	5.22
Repairs/rental of lawn/garden equipment, hand/power tools, etc.	4.96
Sewing machines	4.78
Material for making clothes	4.75
Watch and jewelry repair	4.74
Credit card memberships	4.71
Sewing patterns and notions	4.69
Towing charges	4.68
Safe deposit box rental	4.58
Bread and cracker products	4.41
Tape recorders and players	4.39

(continued)

(continued from previous page)

Artificial sweeteners	$4.19
Parking fees on trips	4.05
Sound equipment accessories	4.04
Appliance rental	3.77
Breakfast at employer or school cafeterias	3.62
Frozen fruits	3.62
Flatware	3.61
Outboard motors	3.58
Tolls on trips	3.51
Parking, at owned homes	3.45
Clothing rental	3.37
Playground equipment	3.32
Pensions, deductions for railroad retirement	3.29
Repair of TV, radio, and sound equipment	3.23
Furniture rental	3.12
Water softening service	3.11
Books and supplies, day care and nursery school	3.09
Rental of recreational vehicles	2.79
Repair of computer systems for nonbusiness use	2.75
Slipcovers and decorative pillows	2.75
Satellite dishes	2.70
Adult day care centers	2.60
Dinner at employer or school cafeterias	2.35
Silver serving pieces	2.35
Rental of medical equipment	2.31
School bus	2.26
Mutton, goat, and game	2.16
Smoking accessories	2.03
Rental and repair of miscellaneous sports equipment	2.02
Souvenirs	2.00
Telephone answering devices	1.97
Septic tank cleaning	1.96
Business equipment for home use	1.83
Shoe repair and other shoe services	1.83
Calculators	1.64
Plastic dinnerware	1.45
Delivery services	1.41
Rental and repair of musical instruments	1.34
Fireworks	1.18
Wigs and hairpieces	1.17
Visual goods	1.09
Portable dishwasher	0.92
Smoke alarms	0.72
Repair of medical equipment	0.61
Coal	0.58
Clothing storage	0.55
Rental of VCR, radio, and sound equipment	0.54
Rental of office equipment for nonbusiness use	0.53
Encyclopedia and other reference book sets	0.51
Rental of television sets	0.49
Termite/pest control products	0.49
Nonalcoholic beer	0.27
Repair and rental of photographic equipment	0.27

Note: Ranking does not show gift spending, which is included in each product and service category.
Source: Calculations by New Strategist based on the 2000 Consumer Expenditure Survey

Glossary

age The age of the reference person, also called the householder or head of household.

alcoholic beverages Includes beer and ale, wine, whiskey, gin, vodka, rum, and other alcoholic beverages.

apparel, accessories, and related services Includes the following:

• *men's and boys' apparel* Includes coats, jackets, sweaters, vests, sport coats, tailored jackets, slacks, shorts and short sets, sportswear, shirts, underwear, nightwear, hosiery, uniforms, and other accessories.

• *women's and girls' apparel* Includes coats, jackets, furs, sport coats, tailored jackets, sweaters, vests, blouses, shirts, dresses, dungarees, culottes, slacks, shorts, sportswear, underwear, nightwear, uniforms, hosiery, and other accessories.

• *infants' apparel* Includes coats, jackets, snowsuits, underwear, diapers, dresses, crawlers, sleeping garments, hosiery, footwear, and other accessories for children.

• *footwear* Includes articles such as shoes, slippers, boots, and other similar items. It excludes footwear for babies and footwear used for sports such as bowling or golf shoes.

•*other apparel products and services* Includes material for making clothes, shoe repair, alterations and sewing patterns and notions, clothing rental, clothing storage, dry cleaning, sent-out laundry, watches, jewelry, and repairs to watches and jewelry.

average spending The average amount spent per household. The Bureau of Labor Statistics calculates the average for all households in a segment, not just for those who purchased an item. For items purchased by most households, such as bread, average spending figures are an accurate account of actual spending. For products and services purchased by few households during a year's time, such as cars, the average amount spent is much less than what purchasers spend. See Appendix A for the percentage of consumer units reporting an expenditure and the average amount spent by purchasers.

baby boom People born from 1946 through 1964, aged 36 to 54 in 2000.

baby bust People born from 1965 through 1976, aged 24 to 35 in 2000. Also known as Generation X.

cash transfers and contributions Includes cash contributed to persons or organizations outside the consumer unit including alimony and child support payments, care of students away from home, and contributions to religious, educational, charitable, or political organizations.

complete income reporters Respondents who provided values for major sources of income, such as wages and salaries, self-employment income, and Social Security income. Even complete income reporters may not have given a full accounting of all income from all sources.

consumer unit Defined as follows:

• All members of a household who are related by blood, marriage, adoption, or other legal arrangements.

• A person living alone or sharing a household with others or living as a roomer in a private home or lodging house or in permanent living quarters in a hotel or motel, but who is financially independent.

• Two persons or more living together who pool their income to make joint expenditure decisions. Financial independence is determined by the three major expense categories: housing, food, and other living expenses. To be considered financially independent, at least two of the three major expense categories have to be provided by the respondent. For convenience, called households in the text of this book.

consumer unit, composition of The classification of interview households by type according to: (1) relationship of other household members to the reference person; (2) age of the children to the reference person; and (3) combination of relationship to the reference person and age of the children. Stepchildren and adopted children are included with the reference person's own children.

earner A consumer unit member aged 14 or older who worked at least one week during the 12 months prior to the interview date.

education Includes tuition, fees, books, supplies, and equipment for public and private nursery schools, elementary and high schools, colleges and universities, and other schools.

education of reference person The number of years of formal education of the reference person based on the highest grade completed. If the respondent was enrolled at the time of interview, the grade being attended is the one recorded. Those not reporting their education are classified under no school or not reported.

entertainment Includes the following:

• *fees and admissions* Includes fees for participant sports; admissions to sporting events, movies, concerts, plays; health, swimming, tennis, and country club memberships, and other social recreational and fraternal organizations; recreational lessons or instructions; and recreational expenses on trips.

• *television, radio, and sound equipment* Includes television sets, video recorders, video cassettes, tapes, discs, disc players, video game hardware, video game cartridges, cable TV, radios, phonographs, tape recorders and players, sound components, records and tapes, and records and tapes through record clubs, musical instruments, and rental and repair of TV and sound equipment.

• *pets, toys, hobbies, and playground equipment* Includes pet food, pet services, veterinary expenses, toys, games, hobbies, and playground equipment.

• *other entertainment equipment and services* Includes indoor exercise equipment, athletic shoes, bicycles, trailers, campers, camping equipment, rental of cameras and trailers, hunting and fishing equipment, sports equipment, winter sports equipment, water sports equipment, boats, boat motors and boat trailers, rental of boat, landing and docking fees, rental and repair of sports equipment, photographic equipment, film and film processing, photographer fees, repair and rental of photo equipment, fireworks, pinball and electronic video games.

expenditure The transaction cost including excise and sales taxes of goods and services acquired during the survey period. The full cost of each purchase is recorded even though full payment may not have been made at the date of purchase. Expenditure estimates include gifts. Excluded from expenditures are purchases or portions of purchases directly assignable to business purposes and periodic credit or installment payments on goods and services already acquired.

federal income tax Includes federal income tax withheld in the survey year to pay for income earned in survey year plus additional tax paid in survey year to cover any underpayment or under withholding of tax in the year prior to the survey.

financial products and services Includes union dues, professional dues and fees, other occupational expenses, funerals, cemetery lots, and unclassified fees and personal services.

food Includes the following:

• *food at home* Refers to the total expenditures for food at grocery stores or other food stores during the interview period. It is calculated by multiplying the number of visits to a grocery or other food store by the average amount spent per visit. It excludes the purchase of nonfood items.

• *food away from home* Includes all meals (breakfast, lunch, brunch, and dinner) at restaurants, carryouts, and vending machines, including tips, plus meals as pay, special catered affairs such as weddings, bar mitzvahs, and confirmations, and meals away from home on trips.

generation X People born from 1965 through 1976, aged 24 to 35 in 2000. Also known as the baby bust.

gifts of goods and services Includes gift expenditures for people outside of the consumer unit. The amount spent on gifts is also included in individual product and service categories.

health care Includes the following:

• *health insurance* Includes health maintenance plans (HMOs), Blue Cross/Blue Shield, commercial health insurance, Medicare, Medicare supplemental insurance, and other health insurance.

• *medical services* Includes hospital room and services, physicians' services, services of a practitioner other than a physician, eye and dental care, lab tests, X-rays, nursing, therapy services, care in convalescent or nursing home, and other medical care.

• *drugs* Includes prescription and non-prescription drugs, internal and respiratory over-the-counter drugs.

• *medical supplies* Includes eyeglasses and contact lenses, topicals and dressings, antiseptics, bandages, cotton, first aid kits, contraceptives; medical equipment for general use such as syringes, ice bags, thermometers, vaporizers, heating pads; supportive or convalescent medical equipment such as hearing aids, braces, canes, crutches, and walkers.

Hispanic origin The self-identified Hispanic origin of the consumer unit reference person. All consumer units are included in one of two Hispanic origin groups based on the reference person's Hispanic origin: Hispanic or non-Hispanic. Hispanics may be of any race.

household According to the Census Bureau, all the people who occupy a household. A group of unrelated people who share a housing unit as roommates or unmarried partners is also counted as a household. Households do not include group quarters such as college dormitories, prisons, or nurs-

ing homes. A household may contain more than one consumer unit. The terms "household" and "consumer unit" are used interchangeably in this book.

household furnishings and equipment Includes the following:

• *household textiles* Includes bathroom, kitchen, dining room, and other linens, curtains and drapes, slipcovers and decorative pillows, and sewing materials.

• *furniture* Includes living room, dining room, kitchen, bedroom, nursery, porch, lawn, and other outdoor furniture.

• *carpet, rugs, and other floor coverings* Includes installation and replacement of wall-to-wall carpets, room-size rugs, and other soft floor coverings.

• *major appliances* Includes refrigerators, freezers, dishwashers, stoves, ovens, garbage disposals, vacuum cleaners, microwaves, air-conditioners, sewing machines, washing machines and dryers, and floor cleaning equipment.

• *small appliances and miscellaneous housewares* Includes small electrical kitchen appliances, portable heating and cooling equipment, china and other dinnerware, flatware, glassware, silver and other serving pieces, nonelectric cookware, and plastic dinnerware. Excludes personal care appliances.

• *miscellaneous household equipment* Includes typewriters, luggage, lamps and other light fixtures, window coverings, clocks, lawn mowers and gardening equipment, other hand and power tools, telephone answering devices, telephone accessories, computers and computer hardware for home use, calculators, office equipment for home use, floral arrangements and house plants, rental of furniture, closet and storage items, household decorative items, infants' equipment, outdoor equipment, smoke alarms, other household appliances and small miscellaneous furnishing.

household services Includes the following:

• *personal services* Includes baby sitting, day care, and care of elderly and handicapped persons.

• *other household services* Includes housekeeping services, gardening and lawn care services, coin-operated laundry and dry-cleaning of household textiles, termite and pest control products, moving, storage, and freight expenses, repair of household appliances and other household equipment, reupholstering and furniture repair, rental and repair of lawn and gardening tools, and rental of other household equipment.

• *housekeeping supplies* Includes soaps, detergents, other laundry cleaning products, cleansing and toilet tissue, paper towels, napkins, and miscellaneous household products; lawn and garden supplies, postage, stationery, stationery supplies, and gift wrap.

housing tenure "Owner" includes households living in their own homes, cooperatives, condominiums, or townhouses. "Renter" includes households paying rent as well as families living rent free in lieu of wages.

income before taxes The total money earnings and selected money receipts accruing to a consumer unit during the 12 months prior to the interview date. Income includes the following components:

• *wages and salaries* Includes total money earnings for all members of the consumer unit aged 14 or older from all jobs, including civilian wages and salaries, Armed Forces pay and allowances, piece-rate payments, commissions, tips, National Guard or Reserve pay (received for training periods), and cash bonuses before deductions for taxes, pensions, union dues, etc.

• *self-employment income* Includes net business and farm income, which consists of net income (gross receipts minus operating expenses) from a profession or unincorporated business or from the operation of a farm by an owner, tenant, or sharecropper. If the business or farm is a partnership, only an appropriate share of net income is recorded. Losses are also recorded.

• *Social Security, private and government retirement* Includes the following: payments by the federal government made under retirement, survivor, and disability insurance programs to retired persons, dependents of deceased insured workers, or to disabled workers; and private pensions or retirement benefits received by retired persons or their survivors, either directly or through an insurance company.

• *interest, dividends, rental income, and other property income* Includes interest income on savings or bonds; payments made by a corporation to its stockholders, periodic receipts from estates or trust funds; net income or loss from the rental of property, real estate, or farms, and net income or loss from roomers or boarders.

• *unemployment and workers' compensation and veterans' benefits* Includes income from unemployment compensation and workers' compensation, and veterans' payments including educational benefits, but excluding military retirement.

• *public assistance, supplemental security income, and food stamps* Includes public assistance or welfare, including money received from job training grants; supplemental security income paid by federal, state, and local welfare agencies to low-income persons who are aged 65 or older, blind, or disabled; and the value of food stamps obtained.

• *regular contributions for support* Includes alimony and child support as well as any regular contributions from persons outside the consumer unit.

• *other income* Includes money income from care of foster children, cash scholarships, fellowships, or stipends not based on working; and meals and rent as pay.

indexed spending The indexed spending figures compare the spending of each demographic segment with that of the average household. To compute an index, the amount spent on an item by a demographic segment is divided by the amount spent on the item by the average household. That figure is then multiplied by 100. An index of 100 is the average for all households. An index of 132 means average spending by households in a segment is 32 percent above average (100 plus 32). An index of 75 means average spending by households in a segment is 25 percent below average (100 minus 25). Indexed spending figures identify the consumer units that spend the most on a product or service.

life and other personal insurance Includes premiums from whole life and term insurance; endowments; income and other life insurance; mortgage guarantee insurance; mortgage life insurance; premiums for personal life liability, accident and disability; and other non-health insurance other than homes and vehicles.

market share The market share is the percentage of total household spending on an item that is accounted for by a demographic segment. Market shares are calculated by dividing a demographic segment's total spending on an item by the total spending of all households on the item. Total spending on an item for all households is calculated by multiplying average spending by the total number of households (109,367,000 in 2000). Total spending on an item for each demographic segment is calculated by multiplying the segment's average spending by the number of households in the segment. Market shares reveal the demographic segments that account for the largest share of spending on a product or service.

metropolitan statistical area (MSA) As defined by the Office of Management and Budget, a large population nucleus, together with adjacent communities which have a high degree of economic and social integration with the nucleus.

millennial generation People born from 1977 though 1994, and aged 6 through 23 in 2000.

occupation The occupation in which the reference person received the most earnings during the survey period. The occupational categories follow those of the Census of Population. Categories shown in the tables include the following:

• *self-employed* Includes all occupational categories; the reference person is self-employed in own business, professional practice, or farm.

• *wage and salary earners, managers and professionals* Includes executives, administrators, managers, and professional specialties such as architects, engineers, natural and social scientists, lawyers, teachers, writers, health diagnosis and treatment workers, entertainers, and athletes.

• *wage and salary earners, technical, sales, and clerical workers* Includes technicians and related support workers; sales representatives, sales workers, cashiers, and sales-related occupations; and administrative support, including clerical.

• *retired* People who did not work either full- or part-time during the survey period.

personal care Includes products for the hair, oral hygiene products, shaving needs, cosmetics and bath products, suntan lotions and hand creams, electric personal care appliances, incontinence products, other personal care products, personal care services such as hair care services (haircuts, bleaching, tinting, coloring, conditioning treatments, permanents, press, and curls), styling and other services for wigs and hairpieces, body massages or slenderizing treatments, facials, manicures, pedicures, shaves, electrolysis.

race The self-identified race of the consumer unit reference person. All consumer units are included in one of two racial groups based on the reference person's race: black or "white and other." The "other" group includes American Indians, Alaskan natives, Asians, and Pacific Islanders. Hispanics may be of any race.

reading Includes subscriptions for newspapers, magazines, and books through book clubs; purchase of single-copy newspapers and magazines, books, and encyclopedias and other reference books.

reference person The first member mentioned by the respondent when asked to "Start with the name of the person or one of the persons who owns or rents the home." It is with respect to this person that the relationship of other consumer unit members is determined. Also called the householder or head of household.

region Consumer units are classified according to their address at the time of their participation in the survey. The four major census regions of the United States are the following state groupings:

• *Northeast* Connecticut, Maine, Massachusetts, New Hampshire, New Jersey, New York, Pennsylvania, Rhode Island, and Vermont.

• *Midwest* Illinois, Indiana, Iowa, Kansas, Michigan, Minnesota, Missouri, Nebraska, North Dakota, Ohio, South Dakota, and Wisconsin.

• *South* Alabama, Arkansas, Delaware, District of Columbia, Florida, Georgia, Kentucky, Louisiana, Maryland, Mississippi, North Carolina, Oklahoma, South Carolina, Tennessee, Texas, Virginia, and West Virginia.

• *West* Alaska, Arizona, California, Colorado, Hawaii, Idaho, Montana, Nevada, New Mexico, Oregon, Utah, Washington, and Wyoming.

retirement, pensions, and Social Security Includes all Social Security contributions paid by employees; employees' contributions to railroad retirement, government retirement and private pensions programs; retirement programs for self-employed.

shelter Includes the following:

• *owned dwellings* Includes interest on mortgages, property taxes and insurance, refinancing and prepayment charges, ground rent, expenses for property management/security, homeowners' insurance, fire insurance and extended coverage, landscaping expenses for repairs and maintenance contracted out (including periodic maintenance and service contracts), and expenses of materials for owner-performed repairs and maintenance for dwellings used or maintained by the consumer unit, but not dwellings maintained for business or rent.

• *rented dwellings* Includes rent paid for dwellings, rent received as pay, parking fees, maintenance, and other expenses.

• *other lodging* Includes all expenses for vacation homes, school, college, hotels, motels, cottages, trailer camps, and other lodging while out of town.

• *utilities, fuels, and public services* Includes natural gas, electricity, fuel oil, coal, bottled gas, wood, and other fuels; telephone charges; water, garbage and trash collection, sewerage maintenance, septic tank cleaning, and other public services.

size of consumer unit The number of people whose usual place of residence at the time of the interview is in the consumer unit.

state and local income taxes Includes State and local income taxes withheld in the survey year to pay for income earned in survey year plus additional taxes paid in the survey year to cover any underpayment or under withholding of taxes in the year prior to the survey.

tobacco and smoking supplies Includes cigarettes, cigars, snuff, loose smoking tobacco, chewing tobacco, and smoking accessories such as cigarette or cigar holders, pipes, flints, lighters, pipe cleaners, and other smoking products and accessories.

transportation Includes the following:

• *vehicle purchases (net outlay)* Includes the net outlay (purchase price minus trade-in value) on new and used domestic and imported cars and trucks and other vehicles, including motorcycles and private planes.

• *gasoline and motor oil* Includes gasoline, diesel fuel, and motor oil.

• *other vehicle expenses* Includes vehicle finance charges, maintenance and repairs, vehicle insurance, and vehicle rental licenses and other charges.

• *vehicle finance charges* Includes the dollar amount of interest paid for a loan contracted for the purchase of vehicles described above.

• *maintenance and repairs* Includes tires, batteries, tubes, lubrication, filters, coolant, additives, brake and transmission fluids, oil change, brake adjustment and repair, front-end alignment, wheel balancing, steering repair, shock absorber replacement, clutch and transmission repair, electri-

cal system repair, repair to cooling system, drive train repair, drive shaft and rear-end repair, tire repair, other maintenance and services, and auto repair policies.

• *vehicle insurance* Includes the premium paid for insuring cars, trucks, and other vehicles.

• *vehicle rental, licenses, and other charges* Includes leased and rented cars, trucks, motorcycles, and aircraft, inspection fees, state and local registration, drivers' license fees, parking fees, towing charges, and tolls on trips.

• *public transportation* Includes fares for mass transit, buses, trains, airlines, taxis, private school buses, and fares paid on trips for trains, boats, taxis, buses, and trains.

Index

bus fares, intercity, 680–729
business equipment and office furniture for home use, 502–576
butter, 298–397

cabinets, 502–576
cable TV and community antenna, 220–269
    gifts of, 400–474
cafeterias, meals from, 298–397
calculators, 502–576
campers, motorized, 220–269
camping equipment, 220–269
candy, 298–397
    gifts of, 400–474
carbonated drinks, 298–397
care for elderly, invalids, handicapped, 502–576
    gifts of, 400–474
carpeting, wall-to-wall, 502–576
cars
    gifts of, 400–474
    lease payments, 680–729
    new, 2–165, 680–729
    rental, 680–729
    used, 2–165, 680–729
catered affairs, 298–397
    gifts of, 400–474
CD, tape, record, video mail order clubs, 220–269
CDs, 220–269
cemetery lots, vaults, maintenance fees, 273–296
    gifts of, 400–474
cereal, 2–165, 298–397
chairs, living room, 502–576
charitable contributions, 273–296
checking accounts, 273–296
cheese, 298–397
chewing gum, 298–397
    gifts of, 400–474
chicken. *See* Poultry.
child care. *See* Babysitting; and Day care centers, nursery schools, and preschools.
child support, 273–296
china and other dinnerware, 502–576
cigarettes, 654–678
cleaning services. *See* Housekeeping services.
cleaning supplies. See Laundry and cleaning supplies
cleansing and toilet tissues, 502–576
clocks, 502–576
closet and storage items, 502–576
clothes dryers, 502–576
clothing rental, 168–217
clothing storage, 168–217

clubs
    automobile service, 680–729
    book, 654–678
    CD, tape, record, video, 220–269
    social, recreation, and civic, 220–269
coats and jackets, 168–217
    gifts of, 400–474
coffee, 298–397
coffee cakes, 298–397
colas, 298–397
cold cuts, 298–397
college
    books and supplies, 654–678
    books and supplies, gifts of, 400–474
    tuition, 654–678
    tuition, gifts of, 400–474
compact discs, 220–269
computer
    hardware for nonbusiness use, 502–576
    hardware for nonbusiness use, gifts of, 400–474
    information services, 502–576
    repair of systems for nonbusiness use, 502–576
    software for nonbusiness use, 502–576
condiments, 298–397
contact lenses. *See* Eyeglasses and contact lenses.
contributions, cash, 2–165, 273–296
    to charities, 273–296
    to educational organizations, 273–296
    to non-household members, 273–296
    to political organizations, 273–296
    to religious organizations, 273–296
convalescent or nursing home care, 476–500
    gifts of, 400–474
cookies, 298–397
cooking stoves, 502–576
cookware, nonelectric, 502–576
    gifts of, 400–474
cornmeal, 298–397
cosmetics, 654–678
    gifts of, 400–474
costumes, 168–217
crackers, 298–397
cream
    fresh, 2–165, 298–397
    nondairy, 298–397
credit card memberships, 273–296
cupcakes, 298–397
curtains, 502–576

dairy products, 2–165, 298–397
day care, adult, 502–576

motels. *See* Lodging on trips.
motor boats, 220–269
motor oil, 2–165, 680–729
 on trips, 680–729
motorcycles, 680–729
motors, outboard, 220–269
movie tickets, 220–269
 gifts of, 400–474
 on trips, 220–269
musical instruments and accessories, 220–269
 gifts of, 400–474
 rental and repair of, 220–269
mutton, 298–397

napkins, 502–576
natural gas, 578–652
 gifts of, renter, 400–474
newspapers
 nonsubscription, 654–678
 subscription, 654–678
nightwear, 168–217
nonalcoholic beverages, 2–165, 298–397
nondairy cream and imitation milk, 298–397
nonphysician health care professional services, 476–500
nursery schools, books and supplies, 654–678. *See also* Day
 care centers, nursery schools and preschools.
nursing home or convalescent care, 476–500
 gifts of, 400–474
nuts, 298–397

occupational expenses, 273–296
oil
 cooking, 2–165, 298–397
 fuel, 2–165, 578–652
 motor, 2–165, 680–729
olives, 298–397
opera tickets, 220–269
oral hygiene products, 654–678
orange juice, 298–397
oranges, 298–397
outboard motors, 220–269
outdoor equipment, 502–576
 gifts of, 400–474
outdoor furniture, 502–576
ovens
 cooking, 502–576
 microwave, 502–576

painting, of housing, 578–652
pants, 168–217
 gifts of, 400–474
paper towels, 502–576

parking
 fees and tolls on trips, 680–729
 fees in home city, 680–729
pasta, 298–397
pay
 meals as, 298–397
 rent as, 578–652
peanut butter, 298–397
pensions, 2–165, 273–296
perfume, 654–678
 gifts of, 400–474
personal care, 2–165, 654–678
 appliances, 654–678
 products and services, gifts of, 2–165, 400–474
pest control/termites, 502–576
pet food, 220–269
pet purchase, supplies, medicines, 220–269
pet services, 220–269
pets, 2–165, 220–269
photographer's fees, 220–269
photographic equipment, 220–269
physician's services, 476–500
 gifts of, 400–474
pickles, 298–397
pies, tarts, turnovers, 298–397
pillows, decorative, 502–576
pinball and electronic video games, 220–269
plants and fresh flowers, indoor, 502–576
 gifts of, 400–474
playground equipment, 2–165, 220–269
plumbing, 578–652
political contributions, 273–296
pork, 2–165, 298–397
 chops, 298–397
 except bacon, frankfurters, ham, pork chops, sausage, 298–397
postage, 2–165, 502–576
 gifts of, 400–474
potato chips, 298–397
potatoes, 298–397
poultry, 2–165, 298–397
power tools, 502–576
private school. *See* Tuition.
professional dues, 273–296
property
 management, 578–652
 security, 578–652
 taxes, 2–165, 578–652
public
 services, 2–165, 578–652
 transportation, 2–165, 680–729